DOMESDAY PEOPLE

A Prosopography of Persons Occurring
in English Documents 1066–1166

I. Domesday Book

This is the first of two volumes offering for the first time an authoritative and complete prosopography of post-Conquest England, 1066–1166. Based on extensive and wide-ranging research, the two volumes contain over eight thousand entries on persons occurring in the principal English administrative sources for the post-Conquest period – Domesday Book, the Pipe Rolls, and *Cartae Baronum*. Continental origin is a major focus of the entries, as well as the discussion of family and descent of fees which characterise the whole work. An introduction discusses Domesday prospography; appendices give the Latin texts of the Northamptonshire and Lindsey surveys.

Dr K.S.B. KEATS-ROHAN is Director of the Linacre Unit for Prosopographical Research and Fellow of the European Humanities Research Centre, University of Oxford.

*For Brien fitzCount, Ansfrid fitz Ruald, and
the people and town of Wallingford*

DOMESDAY PEOPLE

A Prosopography of Persons Occurring
in English Documents 1066–1166

I. Domesday Book

K. S. B. Keats-Rohan

THE BOYDELL PRESS

First published 1999
The Boydell Press, Woodbridge

ISBN 0 85115 722 X

The Boydell Press is an imprint of Boydell & Brewer Ltd
PO Box 9, Woodbridge, Suffolk IP12 3DF, UK
and of Boydell & Brewer Inc.
PO Box 41026, Rochester, NY 14604–4126, USA

A catalogue record of this publication is available
from the British Library

Library of Congress Catalog Card Number: 98–47670

This publication is printed on acid-free paper

Printed in Great Britain by
St Edmundsbury Press Ltd, Bury St Edmunds, Suffolk

CONTENTS

ILLUSTRATIONS

MAP: The *départements* of modern France, with a rough guide to their
medieval regional counterparts

ACKNOWLEDGEMENTS

This book arises out of the Continental Origins of English Landholders 1066–1166 project, funded by the Leverhulme Trust from 1992–96. I am grateful also to the Aurelius Charitable Trust and the Marc Fitch Fund for smaller grants made in 1997. Although this is very much the work of one person, thanks are inevitably due to a number of scholars from whose conversation, correspondence or other assistance I have profited, of whom only a few can be mentioned: David Bates, Judith A. Green, Hubert Guillotel, Michael C. E. Jones, Gwenaël Le Duc, David Roffe, David Thornton, Ann Williams. Special thanks to the staff of Duke Humphrey's Library in Oxford and Susan Burdell, Modern History Faculty Librarian and her staff, to fellow members of the Société d'Histoire et d'Archéologie de Bretagne and the Society of Genealogists, who have posed questions over the years to which I provided unsatisfactory answers at the time but which were valuable spurs to further research, and to the Conféderation Internationale de Généalogie et d'Héraldique for honouring me with the award of the Prix Brant IV de Koskull 1998 for this work. My greatest debts are to my long-suffering family. My scientist husband Dr John Lloyd has patiently endured the role of sounding-board and put up with years of unsatisfactory standards of cuisine; my young son Anthony has provided hour after hour of loving companionship as I worked.

   I have always said that when completed this work should be dedicated to those but for whom it would never have been begun, namely Brien fitzCount, the Breton lord of Wallingford from c.1113 to 1148, and his steward Ansfrid fitz Ruald. The first time I saw Wallingford I fell in love. A week later I went to live there. Thanks to Brien and Ansfrid I had discovered prosopography by the time I had to leave three years later. Not only that, I had gained a husband who shares my love for Wallingford. With a special thank you to the members of The Wallingford Historical and Archaeological Society for their enthusiasm for my early studies of Wallingford, this work is further dedicated to the people and town of Wallingford.

INTRODUCTION

PREFATORY REMARKS:
NATION, REGION AND MOBILITY

'Ego Rogerius, ex Northmannis Northmannus' is the celebrated opening of a charter for the abbey of Troarn in which the founder, Roger de Montgomery, proclaimed himself a Norman descended from Normans.[1] Consciousness of national origin was expressed in charters of a similar date in the eleventh century by the Bretons Rivallon of Dol, *genere Britannicus*, and Haimo de Sougeal, *patria Brito*.[2] Only slightly later, a wider interest in the question of national origin was displayed by the Anglo-French chronicler of Normandy, Orderic Vitalis, whose most interesting example concerns the Giroie family. The Giroies, vassals of the independent lords of Bellême, acquired land in Normandy before 1029. Orderic wrote of them: 'De Geroi Ernaldi Grossi de Corte Sedaldi Abonii Britonis filii filio cuius progenies Vticensibus multa beneficia contulit, libet hic posteris breuiter intimare quis qualisue fuerit. Hic ex magna nobilitate Francorum et Britonum processit, miraque probitate et audacia temporibus Hugonis Magni et Rotberti regum Francorum nobiliter uiguit. Hildiardi uero sorori eius nuptæ multos filios pepereunt, qui succedenti tempore in Gallia et Anglia atque Apulia hostibus in armis magno terrori fuerunt.'[3] The Norman chroniclers have taught us to believe in a Norman sense of national pride. Their capacity for travel – to Byzantium, Apulia, Spain, England, the Holy Land – is as legendary as their acquisitiveness.[4] But the Normans of the eleventh century merely manifested an extreme form of certain key characteristics of medieval knightly society in general: an attention to the question of origin and nation – because these were linked to family and patrimony – and considerable mobility. Mobility was part and parcel of the military life to which they were dedicated. Diplomacy, pilgrimage and the search for self-advancement were some of the spurs to mobility among these men, each of whom was part of a group and was acting in the service of a superior. A solid moral and spiritual core underpinned the individual's

---

1 R. N. Sauvage, *L'abbaye de Saint-Martin de Troarn* (Caen, 1911), Preuves iii, p. 352.
2 H. Morice, *Histoire ecclésiastique et civile de Bretagne*, Preuves, i (Paris, 1742), 411, 426.
3 *The Ecclesiastical History of Orderic Vitalis*, ed. and trs. Marjorie Chibnall (Oxford, 1969–81), ii, 22: 'Now I must briefly tell who and what manner of man was this Giroie, son of Arnold the Fat of Courceraut, son of Abbo the Breton, whose descendants were such generous benefactors of St. Évroul. He was a member of one of the best families in France and Brittany, and led a life of great courage and distinction whilst Hugh the Great and Robert were kings of the Franks. His sister Hildiard became the mother of three sons and eleven daughters; they made good marriages and bore many sons who were destined to become the scourge of their enemies in Gaul, England, and Apulia.'
4 Cf., on the 'aristocratic diaspora', R. Bartlett, *The Making of Europe. Conquest, Colonization and Cultural Change 950–1350* (London, 1993).

3

experience of the groups to which he belonged by birth and profession, as becomes manifest in the crusading movement and the cult of chivalry.

In the early twelfth century the Breton Maino de Saint-Aubin-d'Aubigné gave a charter for Mont-Saint-Michel in which he stated that the assent of his eldest son Ralph to his grant would have to wait upon the latter's return from Normandy.[5] The absence far from home of key players in such transactions can be paralleled in many other documents, but this one has a special interest for students of English history. The nature of Ralph's business was not specified, nor was reference made to another of Maino's sons, William, who may also have been in Normandy. Some years after 1107 this William acquired a Norman wife who was to bring him a substantial fortune in Lincolnshire in the England of Henry I. He attested the king's charters as William de Albini *Brito*, to distinguish him from the king's Norman butler, also a William de Albini. Understanding medieval feudal society requires that we share its appreciation of nation and ancestry as self-defining characteristics that in no way compromised the individual's ability to travel, both from choice and necessity, beyond established national boundaries. William de Albini *Brito*'s name deliberately identified him as a Breton for a good practical reason, but territorial appellations, such as *pictaviensis*, were routinely used instead of more conventional toponymic or patronymic surnames. Often, as will be shown below, such appellations had memorial functions relating to distant ancestors and bore no relation to the actual birthplaces and homes of their bearers.

*

But if mobility and freedom of movement were central to the experience of eleventh-century military society, these were inappropriate to the administrative practices of the time. Anyone beginning work on English history after 1066 will soon notice an emphasis upon region in the primary sources. Domesday Book is set out according to the counties surveyed, though many of the tenants-in-chief whose holdings it records held land in more than one county.[6] The same county basis was employed in the Pipe Rolls, and the surviving *Cartae* returns of 1166 were arranged under county heading in the Red Book of the Exchequer.[7] Monastic cartularies and chronicles are usually also heavily regional in scope and emphasis. Inevitably, and not unreasonably, the same principles apply in much of the secondary literature. We have the county by county and manor by manor accounts of the indispensable *Victoria County History* and a large corpus of county record or historical societies.[8] Sooner rather than later, however, the remit

---

5 Bibliothèque de la ville d'Avranches, ms. 210. fol. 78.
6 Reference to the editions of Domesday Book is given in note 12 below.
7 Pipe Roll Society Publications, in progress; Hubert Hall, ed., *The Red Book of the Exchequer*, 3 vols (Rolls series, London, 1896), i, 186–445.
8 The *Victoria County History*, established in 1899 and still in progress, has been published by OUP for the Institute of Historical Research since 1933. The work of the county record societies, of which the most recent is the Suffolk Record Society, published by Boydell and Brewer, is invaluable. One of the most justly celebrated contributions is formed by Farrer and Clay's monumental *Early Yorkshire Charters*, vols 1–2 (Edinburgh, 1914–16), vols 3–12 published by the Yorkshire Record Society (rec. ser.

of these organizations means that the primary emphasis upon region is replaced by a narrower focus upon locality. Pursuing problems across county boundaries is not encouraged, and hence many are left unsolved. Such an approach inhibits more general assessments of larger questions related to power, social change, etc., thereby opening up information gaps that still need to be bridged.

Because the primary sources are set out according to county, they are repetitious in terms of the persons recorded, who may have held land in more than one county and/or from more than one tenant-in-chief. Such repetition can pass unnoticed because the same names could take several different forms within the same source, and from source to source. The problem is compounded in the Pipe Rolls and the *Cartae baronum* because the names of persons are rarely specifically associated with manors. In Domesday Book, which is tenant/manor specific, the principal problem is that a high proportion of the name-forms were simple forenames. Clearly, all these administrative sources will be of most value to the modern reader if the identities of the persons recorded could be securely established. Attempts to provide these have not been lacking; indeed, they are so numerous that it is difficult for the novice to know where to begin. To begin is immediately to confront the importance of the descent of fees, and hence of family. Here works such as Sanders' *Baronies*, Farrer's *Honors and Knights' Fees* and the incomparable *Complete Peerage* are ready to assist – provided that the family in which one is interested meets the criteria for discussion in such works.[9] Ultimately, English manorial, honorial and genealogical history after 1066 is rooted in the conquest of England by William of Normandy and the land settlement achieved by 1086. Only by determining the identities of the persons concealed in a repetitious mass of names in the text of Domesday Book can one hope to understand what happened next, or who was who in subsequent records such as the Pipe Rolls. In 1086, when Domesday took its county form, English regionalism was at most twenty years old, and in many cases rather less, as far as its new continental landholders were concerned. Vastly more significant was their continental place of origin, which is all the more important to determine because of the undoubted subsequent importance of the locality of their landholdings in England.[10] Again, historians have not neglected this point, but the seminal work,

---

ext. ser. 1935–65). The contents of the various transactions of county societies are, by contrast, often disappointing.

9 I. J. Sanders, *English Baronies. A Study of Their Origin and Descent 1086–1327* (Oxford, 1960); W. Farrer, *Honors and Knights' Fees*, 3 vols (Manchester, 1923–5); *The Complete Peerage*, new edn by V. Gibbs, H. A. Doubleday, H. H. White and Lord Howard of Walden, 13 vols (London 1910–1959). Ecclesiastical society has not been neglected. We have now Diana Greenway's revised edition (still in progress) of John Le Neve's *Fasti Ecclesiæ Anglicanæ*, published by the Institute of Historical Research since 1968, as well as D. Knowles and C. N. L. Brooke, *Heads of Religious Houses* (Cambridge, 1976), and the British Academy's *English Episcopal Acta* series (published by OUP since 1980), in which the editors are making efforts to identify the bishops' households.

10 The point is magisterially demonstrated in R. Bearman, 'Baldwin de Redvers: some aspects of a baronial career in the reign of King Stephen', *Anglo-Norman Studies* 18 (1996), 19–46.

Lewis Loyd's impeccably researched, posthumously published, *Origins of Some Anglo-Norman Families*, is very incomplete.[11]

Manorial and genealogical post-Conquest history is long overdue for an attempt at synthesis. The current, highly productive, renewal of interest in Domesday Book has made the need to establish systematically and on a solid documentary basis the continental origins of all post-Conquest English land-holders more and more acute.[12] Existing English tenurial practices undoubtedly underlay the creation of the new tenancies-in-chiefs, the future baronies; Domesday Book may well have described the earliest system of 'honours and knights' fees', but for such knowledge to be fruitful it is essential that we know everything we can about the people who turned abstract tenurial principles into the reality of castellanies, honours etc. with all they imply vis-à-vis the exercise of royal power and government.[13] Robert of Mortain, the king's half-brother, had no natural affinities with any place in England. Count of Mortain in western Normandy, he had massive holdings all over England, including the militarily important Rape of Pevensey in Sussex, but his holdings in Suffolk and Cornwall came to him as the result of the withdrawal from England in 1069 of Count Brien (see below).[14] Assessing the Mortain lands in England – where he apparently spent very little time – needs to start with Robert's relationship to the king, and then focus upon his Norman holdings and tenants and their relationship with the Bretons.[15] The

---

[11] L. C. Loyd, *The Origins of Some Anglo-Norman Families*, Harleian Society Publications vol. 103 (Leeds, 1951). A full and exhaustive survey of the question vindicates the majority of Loyd's conclusions. Loyd's interest in origins and genealogy had many precursors, and many have shared the interest in more recent times. No more than a fraction of the literature can be cited here. The real value of all this labour for historical understanding must await the results of the synthesis proposed below.

[12] For the purposes of this Introduction the existence of Domesday is assumed as a fact requiring little explanation. It is of course a complex fact requiring a great deal of explanation. A major new study of Domesday Book is currently being written by Dr David Roffe, hence there is no need here for anything more than an outline bibliography of the subject, which will be found in the notes to chapter 1 below. The standard editions of the text are *Domesday Book, seu Liber Censualis Willelmi Primi Regis Angliae*, ed. Abraham Farley, 2 vols, Record Commission (London, 1783); *Domesday Book, seu Liber Censualis Willelmi Primi Regis Angliae, Additamenta [Exon Domesday]*, Record Commission (London, 1816); *Great Domesday: facsimile*, ed. R. W. H. Erskine, Alecto Historical Editions (London, 1986). The Philimore edition of Domesday Book, General Editor John Morris (40 vols, Chichester 1974–86), provides a facsimile of the Farley folio edition. The translations of this edition are of limited worth, but the reference system used throughout is much the best way of referring to the Domesday text and is normally preferred in the notes to this Introduction.

[13] D. Roffe, 'The Making of Domesday Book Reconsidered', *Haskins Society Journal* 6 (Woodbridge, 1995), 153–166; idem, 'From Thegnage to Barony', *Anglo-Norman Studies* 12 (1990), 157–176; idem, 'Brought to Book', forthcoming; J. C. Holt, '1086', in *Domesday Studies*, ed. J. C. Holt (Woodbridge, 1987).

[14] K. S. B. Keats-Rohan, 'Le rôle des Bretons dans la politique de colonisation normande de l'Angleterre', *Mémoires de la Société d'Histoire et d'Archéologie de Bretagne* 74 (1996), 185–7.

[15] See B. Golding, 'Robert of Mortain', *Anglo-Norman Studies* 13 (1991), 144: 'He may have been amongst the greatest magnates of England, but he was a Norman not an Anglo-Norman.'

foundation of Count Alan's (brother of Brien) honour of Richmond lay in the events of 1069-70 in the North.[16] Alan was the king's second cousin and a count in Brittany, facts of far greater relevance for understanding who his tenants were, his relationship with them, and the relationship of his successors with the English king than that that his favoured holdings lay in Yorkshire and Lincolnshire. These should be statements of the obvious. Peter de Valognes, to take a more subtle example, is assumed to have married Albreda sister of Eudo dapifer, on the grounds of his charter for Binham priory in Essex that described Albreda as sister of a Eudo married to a Rohais.[17] Eudo dapifer, married to Rohais de Clare, and a neighbour of Peter in Essex, appears to fit the bill perfectly.[18] Yet the charter was, remarkably, attested by Roger de Saint-Sauveur, member of the family of the vicomtes of the Cotentin. According to Wace, Nigel II of the Cotentin was at Hastings, but it cannot be shown with certainty that any member of his family held land in England thereafter, though many of his tenants, including Peter, did.[19] Roger's great-uncle was the vicomte Eudo, husband of a Rohais, who died c.1103, when he was succeeded by Roger's brother Nigel, grandson of Nigel II of the Cotentin.[20] It is highly likely that the context of Peter's marriage was west Norman and not East Anglian. Contrary examples, based upon marriages to English heiresses, or the meteoric but essentially local rise of men like Robert d'Oilly and Geoffrey de Mandeville, do not alter the fact that the destiny of post-Conquest landholders in England was determined by their continental region of origin, because that determined their tenurial and familial links, and hence, in the most fundamental sense, *who they were*. This is no less obvious and true for the lesser, and less well-known, tenants-in-chief and their tenants than for the dominant figures who were, for the most part, kinsmen of the king.

*

Some years ago I challenged the notion of a 'Norman Conquest' because I felt then, and still do, that historians had dozed too long over the fundamentally important issues raised by the composition of William's army, both in terms of

16 Keats-Rohan, 'Le rôle des Bretons', 185ff; Dom A. Wilmart, 'Alain le Roux et Alain le Noir', *Annales de Bretagne* 38 (1929), 576–595, P. Jeulin, 'Aperçus sur le comté de Richmond en Angleterre . . . 1066/71–1398', *Annales de Bretagne* 42 (1935), 265–302.
17 *Monasticon Anglicanum*, ed. W. Dugdale, new edn, 6 vols (1817–30), iii, 345–6. The fact that the property of Eudo dapifer's brother Adam in Hertfordshire passed to the Valognes family is adduced as proof of this affiliation, but the argument falls down when one realises that Peter de Valognes acquired a great many Hertfordshire manors after 1086, mostly previously held by persons to whom he cannot have been related; cf. *VCH Herts* iii, 26, 37, 86–7. Little enough of Eudo's own property passed to his surving heirs, his daughter Margaret de Mandeville and sister Muriel's son Walcher.
18 Farrer, *HKF* iii, 393.
19 *Roman du Rou de Wace*, ed. A. Holden, Société des Anciens Textes Français, 3 vols, Paris, 1970–73, lines 8353–62, 8493. Robert of Mortain had a tenant in Suffolk named Eudo fitz Nigel; it is possible that he was the vicomte Eudo fitz Nigel, great-uncle of Roger de Saint-Sauveur.
20 L. Delisle, *Histoire du château et des sires de Saint-Sauveur-le-Vicomte, suivi de pièces justificatives* (Valognes, 1867), 27–31.

individual identities and of region of origin.[21] Of course, the conquest was primarily and predominantly Norman in leadership, motivation and execution and the participation of auxiliary troops from non-Norman nations does not fundamentally alter that fact. The problem with the usual construct of the Norman Conquest is that it introduces an artificial process of dislocation into Norman, and, indeed, to English, history, with serious consequences for the way that the historical evidence can be used and applied. The most significant casualty of the process is Domesday Book, which is at least as informative about Norman society as it is about English society and probably more so. The cohesiveness of the Normans of 1066 was a fairly recent creation of the first fully effective Norman ruler of the eleventh century, whilst the Normanness – *normanitas* – of the Normans was a national Myth still in the process of confection by their literary spokesmen, the chroniclers. Ralph Davis described the Norman Myth twenty years ago, pointing out that 'the Normans' were created from a small group of male warriors from Scandinavia who, given the basis of what became the region of Normandy in 911, intermarried with the local Frankish population and rapidly assimilated Frankish culture. Although most of their tenth-century history is still obscure, we have early eleventh-century evidence indicating that the Norman rulers were then deliberately distancing themselves from their Scandinavian 'homelands', were deliberating seeking external alliances or raising mercenaries from other nations, and that migration to Normandy was proving attractive to men even from regions traditionally hostile to Normandy, such as Anjou. Around the same time the ancestors of what would rapidly be established as Normandy's aristocratic families come clearly into view.[22] It is doubtless safe to assume that the tenth-century ancestors of these men displayed the same loyalty to the ruler as had ensured their own advancement, but the point cannot be demonstrated from the exiguous documentary evidence of the period. The far greater documentary survival of the eleventh century, combined with a vigorous historiographical tradition developing in the middle of the century, permits a fairly clear picture of what happened in that century, which can be briefly summarized. A crisis in ducal power from c.1027 to 1047, the result of a rapid succession of new rulers, power struggles and a minority, was brought to an end after the youthful William II of Normandy crushed a western alliance at the end of a short civil war. Within six years William had made a significant marriage to the daughter of the count of Flanders, and one of his most trusted followers, Roger II de Montgomery, had married the heiress of the seigneurie of Bellême in a move which annexed an important independent border lordship to Normandy; within sixteen years, William annexed the ancient heartland of Neustria, the county of Maine, to Normandy. Three years after that, William led his army to victory at Hastings. Most of the men most prominent in his service after 1040, and in subsequent historical accounts, were associated with eastern Normandy, in the vicinity of the ducal

---

[21] K. S. B. Keats-Rohan, 'William the Conqueror and the Breton contingent in the non-Norman Conquest 1066–1087', *Anglo-Norman Studies* (*Proceedings of the Battle Conference*) xiii (1991), 157–72.

[22] R. H. C. Davis, *The Normans and Their Myth* (London, 1976). The outlines of Norman history were established by David Bates, *Normandy Before 1066* (London, 1982). See also Jean Renaud, *Les Vikings et la Normandie* (Rennes, 1989); E. Searle, *Predatory Kinship and the Creation of Norman Power 840–1066* (Berkeley, 1988).

capital at Rouen. Yet it was upon the west that much of the ducal attention was focussed from early in the eleventh century, as is most significantly manifested by a widescale urbanization of the west – with 'new towns' being created at Caen, Falaise, Alençon, Valognes and Cherbourg, leading fairly rapidly to the creation of a second ducal centre of Caen by 1066.[23]

There is here a whole series of highly significant events emerging from a great increase in the production and survival of documents (principally charters), as well as a subsequent attempt to have certain key phenomena interpreted by professional historiographers. Deriving the maximum information from the charter sources and the maximum understanding from the often intellectualizing and very misleading interpretations of the historiographers requires a full-scale prosopographical survey of eleventh-century Normandy. Such a prosopography would offer the only real hope we have of filling many of the gaps in our current understanding of the tenth century. The value of prosopography is that it produces a mass of information about the individuals and groups that constituted a society (and created and acted upon the institutions that must be considered in relation to them, and not the other way about, as is too often the case), leads to a much clearer understanding of the documents they produced, and induces the researcher to penetrate further and further into unknown archive territory in the search for more texts.[24] With such a prosopography currently beyond reach, Domesday Book comes into its own as the golden opportunity for the professional prosopographer and serious student of Norman history.

Who exactly fought at Hastings has been a matter of abiding interest to a wide range of people for centuries.[25] For the most part, the identity of the participants will remain forever unknown, beyond the trifling figure of less than 40 names yielded from contemporary or near-contemporary sources. Asking the question is nonetheless important, for several reasons: the chroniclers' insistence upon wide-ranging recruitment of auxiliary troops, the clear importance of ducal kin and certain others in Norman government and policy-making, the general eleventh-century context of migrationary movements. Understanding the great age of Norman migration is central to understanding the Norman Myth: what was the basis of the undoubted cohesion of the Normans of the Norman Conquest? What were the forces of inclusion and exclusion at work in Norman military society and how did they wórk? These are just some of the questions raised by the Norman aspect of the problem. From the English side the questions may be put more straightforwardly. The newcomers clearly for the most part displaced the native Old English aristocracy and established themselves in heritable lordships. English genealogical and manorial history starts with the Norman Conquest – or rather, with the settlement as it was recorded in Domesday Book from

---

23 Bates, *Normandy*, 130, who lists Dieppe as the sole example of a 'new town or greatly enlarged community' in the east.
24 The value of such enquiries, and the whys and hows of prosopography, were brilliantly described in K. F. Werner, 'L'apport de la prosopographie à l'histoire des élites', in *Family Trees and the Roots of Politics: British and French prosopography from the tenth to the twelfth centuries*, ed. K. S. B. Keats-Rohan (Woodbridge, 1997).
25 There is an admirable survey of the question in Anthony J. Camp, *My Ancestors Came With the Conqueror. Those who did and some of those who probably did not* (Oxford, 1988; corrected rpt, 1990).

material relating to 1086, twenty years and one generation after the great battle. The individual identity of the newcomers is crucially important to determine in view of the way the society of the time was structured, around family and tenurial ties and obligations. Who was who and how he fitted in was fundamentally important then and must be so now.

Although we cannot make progress on who exactly fought at Hastings the question of the likely general composition of the army remains centrally important to the related question of who settled in England during the reign of William the Conqueror, 1066-1087. Domesday Book suffers numerous defects as evidence for the general question of who settled in the Conqueror's England: it was compiled twenty years after Hastings, it is incomplete as a list of persons holdings fees and is even incomplete in terms of the surnames of those it does record. On the other hand, the time lag is a major strength. It provides an overview of a fairly long and eventful period, starting well before 1066. From the post-Conquest perspective, it shows redistributions of land associated with the Fenland and Northern revolts of 1068-71 and the revolt of the earls in 1075, and the beginnings of settlement with several cases of inheritance by one settler from another. All such cases are very informative about the broader questions relating to 1066.

The value of Domesday Book as evidence both to the identity of the settlers and of the likely composition of the army of 1066 is very firmly focussed upon Domesday Book itself, so a host of important secondary questions immediately arise. What is Domesday Book? Why are persons other than the 200-odd tenants-in-chief and the king mentioned in it at all? How can we determine who was mentioned in it, given that much of it is a repetitious mass of common personal names undistinguished by any form of surname? Pushing past the difficulties to achieve a prosopography of Domesday Book – determing exactly who was who and how many of them there were – will be directly relevant to the antecedent questions of who was/might have been at Hastings, where did he come from and why?

One has to start by elaborating the means by which the questions relating to 1066 can be investigated in terms of those relating to the purposes of Domesday Book, and to the Domesday text. There are several aspects to this. In the first place there is the evidence of the Domesday text itself, which will identify one person with another or distinguish them. Secondly, there is the existence of complementary sources produced in conjunction with the Domesday text, including satellite texts such as Exon Domesday. Thirdly, there is the evidence relating to tenurial structures, both continental and English. As has been abundantly demonstrated time and again, the tenants-in-chief replicated in England the honorial structures of their homelands. Normally, the identity of a tenant will depend upon the identity of his tenant-in-chief. Fourthly, there is the onomastic evidence. Fifthly, one can use later evidence for the descent of fees in conjunction with the Domesday text in order to isolate, and often to identify, individuals.

*

All of these elements have been used in existing studies of Domesday prosopography and will come as no surprise. They are equally valid for both the English and the non-English tenants. English tenants are fully represented in the Prosopography below but, because what follows here is the first fully researched prosopography of the non-English part of the Domesday data, presentation of some of the issues raised will be presented more fully in Chapter 1, followed in turn by a presentation and analysis of Domesday and other contemporary evidence relating to an awareness of region of origin (Chapter 2). The importance of the tenant-in-chief as the focus of his own tenants has often been emphasized, but the tenants-in-chief themselves often need to be considered as interdependent groups rather than just as individuals. Especially important for the non-Norman groups, this point will be discussed in relation to the settlement of Bretons (Chapter 3). With special attention to the non-Norman continental groups having been paid in Chapters 2 and 3, the Conclusion will look in particular at the Normans within the general context of continental origins. Finally, because of the importance of the early post-Domesday surveys in establishing Domesday prosopography, Latin transcripts of two such surveys, the Lindsey and Northants surveys, appear as appendices. The prosopography is heavily dependent upon these texts, which are cited with reference to the transcripts. A brief guide precedes the prosopography itself and a bibliography/list of abbreviations is placed at the end of the book.

Chapter 1

DOMESDAY BOOK AND DOMESDAY PROSOPOGRAPHY

There can be no medievalist of any origin, language or interest who has not at least heard the name of Domesday Book, one of the most remarkable of the innumerable achievements of our medieval ancestors.[1] It used to be said that it came into being as the result of a crisis which, in 1085, saw England threatened by another invasion, this time from Denmark. The king decided that in order to meet such a threat (which in fact never materialized) he needed at his disposal all possible information on what the country he had conquered was worth to him, in terms of taxes and of fighting men. In fact the Danish threat was only one element in the making of a survey which recorded the very considerable changes that had taken place over nearly twenty years from October 1066.[2] What precisely the Book is about, or how it came into being, has been a matter of fierce debate for the past hundred years.[3] Older views that it was either a 'geld book' or a 'feodary' have been challenged by Holt's view that it went beyond both these concepts in being the product of a bargain struck between the king and his men at the Christmas council of 1085, by which the 'barons' agreed to the survey on the understanding that it would recognise their rights to their holdings at that time, for which, in turn, they would perform all necessary feudal dues and obligations to the king.[4]

---

[1] The precursors of Domesday Book are discussed in S. P. J. Harvey, 'Domesday Book and its predecessors', *EHR* 86 (1971), 753–73; J. Percival, 'The precursors of Domesday: Roman and Carolingian land registers', in P. Sawyer ed., *Domesday Book: a Reassessment* (London, 1985), 5–27; H. Loyn, 'The Beyond of Domesday Book', in J. C. Holt, ed., *Domesday Studies* (Woodbridge, 1987), 1–14, R. H. C. Davis, 'Domesday Book: Continental parallels', ibid., 15–40.

[2] The natures of these changes is still a matter of debate; see esp. D. Roffe, 'From Thegnage to Barony: Sake and Soke, Title, and Tenants-in-Chief', *Anglo-Norman Studies* 12 (1989), 157–76. Other references are given in note 12 below.

[3] The questions are rehearsed in F. W. Maitland, *Domesday Book and Beyond*, reissue with introduction by E. Miller (London, 1960); V. H. Galbraith, *Domesday Book. Its Place in Administrative History* (Oxford, 1973); D. C. Douglas, 'Odo, Lanfranc and the Domesday Survey', in *Historical Essays in Honour of James Tait*, ed. J. Edwards, V. Galbraith and E. Jacob (Manchester, 1933), 47–57; E. Miller, 'The Ely land pleas in the reign of William I', *English Historical Review* 62 (1947), 438–56; J. C. Holt, '1086', in *Domesday Studies*, ed. J. C. Holt (Woodbridge, 1987); S. P. J. Harvey, 'Recent Domesday Studies', *EHR* 105 (1980), 121–33; idem, 'Taxation and the ploughland in Domesday Book', in Sawyer, ed., *Domesday reassessment*, 86–103; idem, 'Domesday Book and Anglo-Norman governance', *TRHS*, 5th ser., 25 (1975), 175–93; P. R. Hyams, ' "No Register of Title": the Domesday Inquest and Land Adjudication', *Anglo-Norman Studies* 9 (1986), 127–41; P. Wormald, 'Domesday Lawsuits: a Provisional List and Preliminary Comment', in *England in the Eleventh Century*, ed. C. Hicks (Harlaxton Medieval Studies vol. 2, Stamford, 1992), 61–102. See also David Bates, *A Bibliography of Domesday Book* (Woodbridge, 1985).

[4] Holt, '1086'.

Recent clarification of the procedural questions by Dr David Roffe, however, suggests that Domesday Book is the result of a five-stage inquiry underpinned by two broad themes.[5] One was a survey of the royal lands and revenues, the other, still linked to the question of royal revenue, was a seigneurial document concerned with tenure, as distinct from title to land. Roffe's emphasis on tenure is central to his argument, which puts royal concerns in place of the seigneurial approach favoured by Holt. Appended to the various Domesday counties one often finds a list of claims to the lands recorded in it, many of which were still being pursued after the work was completed.[6] It is notable that all the land claimed by the king was assigned to him in Domesday, whereas the majority of claims of tenants-in-chief accepted by the jurors on the inquiry were nevertheless assigned in the main text to those against whom the claim was made, because they had tenure of them. The underlying axiom was that tenure established by the payment of the tax resulted in a *de facto* title to the land held. Land could be and was usurped by taking over the payment of the tax due on it. Nonetheless, the 'feudal' functions of Domesday Book arose *post factum*. Because the information of the Survey was recast in a seigneurial form which records the earliest grants of knights's fees, Domesday Book came to be regarded by the king's tenants as an authority in the matter of title to land, but for the compilers of Domesday Book 'tenure was the prime concern', not title, which is why so many unresolved claims were recorded.[7]

Setting the controversies aside and trying to put a complex matter simply, we can say that the Domesday Survey divided the country into seven groups of counties known as circuits, and commissioners were sent out to hear the evidence of inquests composed of both *franci* et *anglici*.[8] The detailed information so acquired, which must have been backed up by existing written accounts and certainly generated several more, was summarized in abbreviated form in what is

---

5   D. Roffe, 'The Making of Domesday Book Reconsidered', *Haskins Society Journal* 6 (Woodbridge, 1995), 153–166. I am acutely aware that I am treading on eggshells in this chapter. Shortly before this book went to press, I was privileged to read Dr Roffe's magisterial and as yet unpublished book, *The Domesday Inquest and Domesday Book*, which will change the face of Domesday studies for ever.

6   M. K. Lawson, 'The collection of Danegeld and Heregeld in the reigns of Æthelred II and Cnut', *EHR* 99 (1984), 721–38; cf. Wormald 'Domesday Lawsuits', 75; Roffe, 'The making of Domesday', 159.

7   Roffe, 'The making of Domesday Book', 157–8: '. . . any inquest to do with land could hardly avoid questions of title, and once voices were raised something had to be done to mollify them. However, Great Domesday Book was compiled without very much reference to title; it was tenure that was the prime concern. Those cases that are found in Great Domesday Book are mostly postscriptural appendices, and little attempt was made to correct the entries to which they referred' (p. 165).

8   The internal order of the circuits postulated by C. Stephenson, 'Notes on the composition and interpretation of Domesday Book', *Speculum* 22 (1947), 1–15, is still debated in its detail; cf. A. R. Rumble, 'The palaeography of the Domesday Manuscripts', in Sawyer, ed., *Domesday Reassessment*, 28–49. On the jurors see V. H. Galbraith, *The Making of Domesday Book* (Oxford, 1961), 67–86; R. Welldon Finn, *The Domesday Inquest* (London, 1961), 97–109; R. Fleming, 'Oral Testimony and the Domesday Inquest', *Anglo-Norman Studies* 17 (1994), 101–122; C. P. Lewis, 'The Domesday Jurors', *Haskins Society Journal* 5 (1993), 17–44.

known as Great Domesday Book after the death of William the Conqueror in 1087, in the first part of William II's reign.[9] Domesday Book had achieved its final form, in which the country was shown as consisting of fiefs held by the king or by his tenants-in-chief, men directly answerable to him for their fiefs and the knight-service owed upon them. The tenants of the tenants-in-chief were also recorded, along with a record of who had held the land at the death of Edward the Confessor in 1066, the worth of the holdings then and in 1086, together with its taxable value, and details of the manor's worth in terms of villagers and other inhabitants, livestock, mills and churches. The existence of Little Domesday Book is one of the great 'what-might-have-beens' of history. The information gathered in respect of Circuit 7, containing Essex, Suffolk and Norfolk, one of the earliest English regions to be settled, was set out in the same format as Great Domesday Book, but was not abbreviated to the same extent as Circuits 1–6. Consequently it preserves valuable information about the colonizers that was deliberately omitted in Great Domesday Book. Domesday Book, which still exists as two Books and not one, is capable of being all things to all men – it has been mined extensively by economic historians, and those interested in early Norman feudalism. Consulting Domesday is *de rigeur* for anyone concerning himself with manorial history, or the niceties of genealogical reconstruction. Using it as a record of the state of infeodation achieved by 1086, or as evidence as to Who was Who in the Conqueror's England, requires a full-scale prosopographical investigation of its contents.

It has been calculated that the whole of Domesday Book contains some 45,000 personal names. An obvious corollary of the fact that many tenants-in-chief held land in more than one county is that these 45,000 names do not conceal 45,000 different persons. How many different persons were actually included in Domesday Book is only one of the questions a prosopography of the Book might hope to answer. A prosopography of Domesday Book that identifies, in terms of their families and their continental origins, the non-native landholders named therein, must start by ascertaining their surnames. A surname in this context is any handle that distinguishes one *Radulfus* or *Willelmus* from any other. One always hopes for a toponym, normally the best means of identifying both place of origin and family, but patronymics or soubriquets are also useful. Soubriquets are preferable to patronymics, except where patronymics are hereditary, because they often remain in a family, which can then be localised by the study of continental records. The bulk of the land described in Domesday Book was demesne land held by the king and his tenants-in-chief. Of their tenants, some three-quarters occur only under their forename. If one discounts the demesne tenancies of the churches – as distinct from bishops or abbots – the tenancies of Englishmen and those of the king some 19,500 names remain. 41% per cent, or just over 8000, of these are the forename alone of a tenant. Of course, it is often possible to identify one *Radulfus* or *Willelmus* with another, or to distinguish them, from the Domesday text itself.[10] Analysis of the text is a crucial part of the identification of the

---

9 As shown by C. P. Lewis, 'The earldom of Surrey and the date of Domesday Book', *Historical Research* 63 (1990), 329–36; D. Bates, 'Two Ramsey writs and the Domesday Survey', ibid., 337–39.

10 E.g. *DB Northamptonshire* 18.30–41, where 11 manors are identified by the use of

people named therein. But to discover the identities and origins of Domesday people, and also the true number of the different persons named in Domesday, it is usually necessary to look outside Domesday Book for the surnames lacking in the text.

Of considerable help from the outset is the abundantly well-documented fact that the majority of tenants in England after 1066 held land from those English tenants-in-chief who were also their seigneurs on the Continent.[11] If one can identify the origins of a tenant-in-chief, as one can in about two thirds of cases, one can hope also to identify the origins of his tenants. Much of the work of Lewis Loyd on the 'Origins of Some Anglo-Norman Families' was predicated upon this phenomenon. This key feature of tenurial society, the so-called 'honorial baronage', is crucial to establishing the real historical identity of the persons identified in Domesday, because it enables us to move beyond a mere surname to location in time, place and family, and hence to place a person accurately within the social and political framework of his time. Even so, one cannot simply assume that a tenant shared an origin with his tenant-in-chief. There are plenty of examples of tenants holding from men other than those who might be seen as their natural lords. The reasons why such men held of what we might term 'alien lords' vary from a holding at the command of the king, to the holding from an alien tenant-in-chief of a part of a manor of which another part was held from the 'natural lord'.[12] It is also true that some tenants-in-chief held land as tenants of other tenants-in-chief, and that some tenants had more than one tenant-in-chief.[13] Multiple lordship is found also in the Continental evidence, but in Domesday

---

idem as being held by the same *Radulfus*, and idem 18.42–66, where the tenant is the same *Willelmus*; *DB Sussex* 10.78, distinguishing *Radulfus* and *alter Radulfus*. The Philimore edition of Domesday Book is used throughout this chapter for precision of reference.

[11] This phenomenon was early established in Domesday studies and is confirmed by work on later documents such as the *Cartae baronum*; see, for example, the various papers of J. H. Round, such as 'The counts of Boulogne as English lords', *Studies in Peerage and Family History* (London, 1901); K. Thompson, 'The Norman aristocracy before 1066: the example of the Montgomerys', *Historical Research* 60 (1987), 251–263; J. F. A. Mason, 'The officers and clerks of the Norman earls of Shropshire', *Transactions of the Shropshire Archaeological Society*, 56 (1957–60); B. Golding, 'Robert of Mortain'; R. Mortimer, 'The beginnings of the honour of Clare', *Anglo-Norman Studies* 3 (1980), 119–41; R. Bearman, 'Baldwin de Redvers', *Anglo-Norman Studies* 18 (1996).

[12] E.g. in Lincolnshire Glai, a man of the Breton Alfred of Lincoln, held parts of the manor of Thistleton from both Alfred and Godfrey of Cambrai (*DB Lincolnshire*, 27.48, 51.10). Even more strikingly, Alfred de *Canci*, or of Laughton, a man of Guy de Craon, held parts of the manors of Scawby and Sturton from Kolswein, Osbern of Arques, Odo *balistarius* (whose heiress he married) and Durand Malet, but not from Guy (ibid., 26.17, 41.1, 44.2, 48.2). Marriage was another reason for apparently 'alien' lordships; a good example is provided by Hugh de Hosdeng, tenant and brother-in-law of Roger Bigod (*Comp. Peer.* ix, pp. 578–9 note c).

[13] E.g. Picot the Sheriff, *DB Cambridgeshire* 36, held land of Count Alan, ibid. 14.39; 41; 58. Harduin *de Scalariis*, ibid. 26, was a tenant of Count Alan at ibid. 14.22. Tenant-sharing between Archbishop Lanfranc and Odo of Bayeux was discussed in D. C. Douglas, ed., *Domesday Monachorum of Christ Church, Canterbury* (1944).

Book it is probably closely related to the phenomenon of 'alien lordship', which, in turn, is probably related to the trouble the Normans took not to disrupt the boundaries of Anglo-Saxon lands and jurisdictions. This very concern with English lordships is central to the identification of Domesday tenants, most of whom were given the lands of one or more English *antecessor*. Sometimes the usefulness of the *antecessor* as a guide to the identity of his Domesday successor is mitigated by the fact that he bore a name too common to permit useful distinctions between him and his homonyms, or because the tenants of the relevant Englishman were named instead of him.[14]

The identities of Domesday people can often be discovered by using material contemporary or nearly contemporary with the text. Many of the missing surnames can be supplied from the several preliminary Domesday inquiries still extant, such as the *Inquisitio comitatus Cantabrigiensis*, the *Inquisitio Eliensis* and Exon Domesday.[15] Further information is provided by royal and private charters, the various surveys of Henry I's reign, data in later charters, and the lists of the knights of each tenant-in-chief contained in the *Cartae baronum* of 1166. A valuable but regrettably limited source is the work of that friend of the prosopographer, Orderic Vitalis. Placing the Domesday entries beside the corresponding satellite entries will normally yield (despite some orthographic variants) a satisfying sense that the process is yielding valid identifications. There is, in fact, little choice but to accept that this is so, but in a reassuring majority of cases there is further evidence to confirm such 'inferential' identifications. Usually it will be the case that the satellite material has to be rearranged in order to match the corresponding Domesday entry. There is no one reason for this, but the re-ordering may be of possible significance for identifications. In the case of Exon Domesday it seems that a basically hundredal organization, containing within it the clues to the identities of the tenants named in individual manors, gave way to the 'feudal' structure of Domesday Book in which these identifications were only occasionally preserved by the use of *ipse*. For example, if Exon is consulted according to its hundredal order, it becomes clear that a tenant, such as *Ricardus filius Turulf* in Cornwall,[16] is named in full in his first appearance in a hundred, after which he becomes simply *Ricardus*. He will be re-identified when he first appears in another hundred, and so on. Sometimes these repetitions of *Ricardus* are recorded in Domesday as *Ricardus ipse*, or *ipse*; where this is not so, Exon's peculiarity is of great help in establishing identification, and provides crucial

---

14 Some of the men listed as holders TRE will have been tenants of a principal predecessor or predecessors; the primary predecessor was the *antecessor* from whom a tenant-in-chief derived title, usually by virtue of his sokeright TRE. On this question see Peter Sawyer, '1066–1086: A Tenurial Revolution?', in *Domesday Book: A Reassessment*, ed. P. Sawyer (London, 1985), 71–85; R. Fleming, 'Domesday Book and the Tenurial Revolution', *Anglo-Norman Studies*, 9 (1986), 87–102; and especially, D. Roffe, 'From Thegnage to Barony', 157–76. On identifying Englishmen see C. P. Lewis, 'Joining the Dots: a methodology for identifying the English in Domesday Book', in K. S. B. Keats-Rohan, ed., *Family Trees and the Roots of Politics*, 69–88.

15 On the satellites see H. B. Clarke, 'The Domesday satellites', in Sawyer, *Domesday Reassessment*, 50–70.

16 *DB Cornwall* 1.1, 2.8, 4.16, 5.3.

evidence in the case of *Turstinus vicecomes*, Robert of Mortain's sheriff in Cornwall.[17]

In the majority of cases where a distinguishing surname can be found, the information comes from contemporary or near contemporary English sources, normally the Domesday satellites. Royal confirmations for both English and Norman churches and individual grants to churches are also valuable in establishing surnames.[18] Norman sources are particularly useful for identifying persons with rare personal names. One notable example is provided by Rogo fitz Nigel, a tenant of Baldwin of Exeter who held land in the Cotentin from the lords of Saint-Sauveur.[19] Another of Baldwin's tenants was Cadio, presumably the Cadiou brother of Rogo who occurs in Pipe Roll 31 Henry I.[20] In a number of cases there is simply no information about surnames, and the best one can do with these is to try to distinguish one person from another. In such cases the marked tendency throughout the settlement for tenants to be closely associated in England, as on the continent, with individual tenants-in-chief is a useful guide to the difference between one *Willelmus*, *Rogerius* or *Walterius* and another. There are several examples of men with uncommon names occurring in manors scattered throughout Domesday Book. They often turn out to be clerks, such as Judicael presbyter, who can be identified with a royal priest at Cherbourg.[21]

One of the numerous problems in achieving a continental prosopography for Domesday Book lies in understanding the name behind the often curious, and very varied, forms found throughout the text. Despite the variety, the general rule is that Domesday orthography strove for as accurate a representation as possible for its subject matter.[22] There are very few indisputable cases of cacography in Domesday names, which is all the more remarkable since no one person involved

---

[17] *DB Cornwall* 1.1, 6.1, 5.4.

[18] For example, a list of grants to Jumièges (D. Bates, *Regesta Regis Willelmi Primi*, no. 164) permits us to identify two of Richard de Clare's tenants as Payn de Capellis and Germund de Villare.

[19] In the Cartulary of Saint-Sauveur-le-Vicomte (BN lat. 17137, fol. 19), Rogo camerarius attested a grant by Nigel vicomte. In the portions printed by Delisle, *Saint-Sauveur, Pièces justificatives*, Rogo occurs as the grantor of land in Omonville under vicomte Eudo (no. 45), and in 1081 the same vicomte granted land at Heauville, cant. Les Pieux, Manche, which 'miles quidam Rogos' holds of the inheritance of his wife Roges (i.e. Rohais) [ibid. no. 44). This Rogo was followed by William fitz Rogo, uncle of Simon fitz Rogo and William Monk, son of Richard de Ansgerivilla (Paris, BN lat. 17137, fols 39v–40, 89v, 239, the latter being a grant of Simon fitz Rogo attested by Robert Arundel; cf. the Arundels of Somerset). William and Simon fitz Rogo were benefactors of Montacute priory (Somerset Rec. Soc. vol. 8, nos. 11, 138, 140, 156–7).

[20] *Pipe Roll 31 Henry I*, 156, where the first letter of [C]adiou's name is lost.

[21] *Recueil des actes des ducs de Normandie de 911 à 1066*, ed. M. Fauroux (Caen, 1961), no. 224; *DB Norfolk* 44, *DB Bedfordshire* 55.4.

[22] The very important question of Domesday orthographies has been discussed in various places, including J. Dodgson, 'Some Domesday Personal Names, mainly Post-Conquest', *Nomina* ix (1985), 41–51; idem, 'Domesday Book: Place-Names and Personal Names', in Holt, *Domesday Studies*, 79–99; C. Clark, 'Domesday Book – A Great Red Herring: Thoughts on Some Late Eleventh-Century Orthographies', in *England in the Eleventh Century: Proceedings of the 1990 Harlaxton Symposium*, ed. C. Hicks, Harlaxton Medieval Studies 2 (Stamford, 1992), 317–31.

in the process of achieving the Domesday text can have understood more than a fraction of the onomastic issues with which he was faced. Such understanding can normally only come from a deep, geographically and chronologically broad acquaintance with the names found in continental records, whether personal or place-names. The deleterious effects of letting loose the experts in linguistic onomastics on historical documents, with the Domesday text as the most high-profile casualty, has been demonstrated in masterly fashion by Chris Lewis, so little more needs to be said here.[23] Lewis dealt primarily with the tendency of the so-called expert to convert an Englishman into an Old High German, but one must beware of the sort of onomastic misunderstanding that assumes, for example that the name Hervey is Breton and that therefore so are the bearers of the name.[24] The name found as *Herueius* and *Urvoius* in different contexts at this time could have either a Germanic or a Breton origin. Since *Herueius* is normally the preferred form in documents produced outside Brittany, a good deal more information than the name is required for identifying the origin of its bearer. This problem has other manifestations; for instance, the realization by Horace Round that Robert fitz Wimarc's name was a matronym was fatally complicated by his insistence that it was the Breton personal name Wimarca. Historians since have been divided as to whether or not to regard Robert as part Breton. It seems highly unlikely. Both the *Vita Ædwardi Regis* and William of Poitiers claim some importance for Robert, who according to the former was steward of the royal palace and a kinsman of King Edward, and to the latter was a rich and powerful man, of impeccable lineage, and a relative of Edward's kinsman William the Conqueror. His lineage linked him to the Norman ducal house (hence his relationship to both Edward and William) and he was identified through his mother.[25] His mother was surely therefore a high-born Norman. The point is underlined by William of Poitiers's statement: *Diues quidam . . . natione Normannus, Rodbertus filius Guimarae nobilis mulieris*. It is not unlikely that Robert is identifiable from charters of the abbey of Montivilliers, near Le Havre, Seine-Maritime, which had a strong connexion with Norman ducal women. One of them features the nun Vuimardis/ Wimardis widow of Ansfrid the steward, who gave Ectot to the house c.1046–66, attested by a Robert. She was doubtless the mother at whose request her son Robert de Moyaux (Calvados, cant. Lisieux-1) later gave to the house land that Ansfrid had held in the forest of Rouvray.[26] Robert de Moyaux is otherwise known only as the father of a woman who became a nun of Saint-Léger de Préaux in the later eleventh century.[27]

---

23 C. P. Lewis, 'Joining the Dots', in *Family Trees*, 69–88.
24 Cf. the false statement by J. H. Round: 'The name of Hervey is distinctively Breton', in *VCH Essex* i, 350. One must commend Round's readiness to discover non-Normans, even though he based most such identifications on false premises.
25 J. H. Round, *Feudal England* (London, rpt 1964), pp. 256–7; *Vita Ædwardi Regis*, ed. F. Barlow, 2nd edn (Oxford, 1992), pp. 118–19 and n. 305; *Guillaume de Poitiers, Histoire de Guillaume le Conquérant*, éd. R. Foreville (Paris, 1952), p. 170.
26 J.-M. Bouvris, 'La renaissance de l'abbaye de Montivilliers et son dévelopement jusqu'à la fin du XIe siècle', in *L'Abbaye de Montivilliers à travers les âges. Actes du colloque organisé à Montivilliers le 8 mars 1986; Recueil de l'Association des Amis du Vieux Havre*, no. 48 (Le Havre, 1988), App. nos. 4 and 21.
27 Arturo du Monstier, *Neustria Pia* (Rouen, 1663), p. 524, par. XII.

On the other hand, the names of Alan and Brien are indisputably Breton in origin, but both, especially the former, were well-established in eleventh-century Normandy. They evidence what I think of as 'ultimate ancestry' in preserving the memory of a perhaps distant ancestor, who might have been a migrant or someone already settled in a region subsequently assimilated by the Norsemen (see Chapter 2). Onomastic evidence relating to ancestry has to be contrasted with charter evidence that clearly localizes on the continent a person found within a few years as an English landholder. In this case the evidence relates to what I call the proximate continental origin of the person in question, the assumption being that his likely primary region of origin will be within the same general area of his documentary occurrences. The existence side by side of these types of evidence is part of the promise that expert prosopographical study of eleventh-century Normandy holds out for understanding what happened in the tenth century.

There is another aspect to the problem of name-forms and identification, this time one that puts the cart before the horse. There are several examples of identities foisted upon Domesday names by grim determination alone. One concerns Ralph, a son of Herluin de Conteville by his second marriage to Fredesend. Ralph was half-brother to Odo of Bayeux and Robert of Mortain, facts of some significance for finding Ralph in England, where such a relationship would not have gone unremarked. Odo in particular was not a man to miss an opportunity to promote his own.[28] The search for Ralph has the backing of Orderic Vitalis, who stated that the sons of Herluin, including Ralph, were given extensive lands in England.[29] If that is true, he certainly did not keep them. Domesday prosopography has to be examined on its owns terms and in its own context. There is not the slightest trace of Ralph son of Herluin de Conteville as the evidence stands, though Domesday evidences both a Ralph fitz Herluin and a Ralph de Conteville. Orderic also stated that Geoffrey count of Mortagne was given extensive lands in England: these too were wholly mythical by 1086, if they were ever granted.[30] In this case there is a particular candidate involved, but sometimes this problem is manifested as the desire to find someone with the right name to provide an explanation for an apparent puzzle. Such cases often concern the numerous instances of mediatization or alienation of fiefs which occurred under William II and Henry I or other types of unusual descent of fees.[31] In most cases these involved

---

[28] See D. Bates, 'Odo of Bayeux', *Speculum* 50 (1975); idem, 'Le patronage clérical et intellectuel de l'évêque Odon de Bayeux 1049/50–1097', in *Chapitres et Cathédrales en Normandie, Annales de Normandie, série des Congrès des Sociétés Historiques et Archéologiques de Normandie*, vol. 2 (1997). Bates proposed the identification of Odo's brother with English tenants in suitably cautious fashion in 'Notes sur l'aristocratie normande. ii. Herluin de Conteville et sa famille', *Annales de Normandie* 23 (1973).

[29] Ord. Vit. iv, 98.

[30] Ord. Vit. ii, 266.

[31] On the various aspects of the tenurial changes in Henry's reign see C. W. Hollister, 'The Anglo-Norman civil war of 1101', *EHR* 88 (1973), 315–33; J. C. Holt, 'Politics and Property in Medieval England', *Past and Present* 57 (1972); R. W. Southern, 'The place of Henry I in English history', in *Medieval Humanism* (Oxford, 1970), 206–33; C. W. Hollister and J. W. Baldwin, 'The rise of administrative kingship: Henry I and Philip Augustus', *Amer. Hist. Rev.* 83 (1978), 867–905, repr. *Monarchy, Magnates,*

tenants-in-chief whose male heirs did not succeed to tenancies-in-chief but to mesne tenancies under newly appointed tenants-in-chief. Thus Robert Gernon's Hertfordshire tenant William has been identified as the father of his successor as tenant-in-chief, William de Montfichet, and Ralph, a tenant of Walter de Douai, as forebear of the Ralph Lovel who held one of the two halves into which Walter's fief had been divided by 1135.[32] Whilst such identifications cannot always be ruled out completely, it can at least be observed that there is no unambiguous evidence that any change of tenancy-in-chief after 1086 involved a tenant of the Domesday tenant-in-chief for any reason other than marriage to the latter's heiress. The only example of any proximate connexion between the first tenant-in-chief and his successor concerns the Beaufour barony of Hockering, where Ralph's widow Agnes de Tosny provided the link as wife of his first successor, Hubert de Ryes, and mother of the second, Henry de Ryes.[33]

Using place-names studies is far less problematic for documentary historians and is crucial in prosopography, where the identification of Latin toponyms must be linked at all times to the onomastic evidence. It is not enough to stick a pin in a list of likely-looking modern place-names when trying to identify a medieval toponym – as most of those who have commented on Domesday toponyms have seemed to do. One example concerns Rainald and Hugh de *Valle Torta*, tenants of Robert of Mortain, who have passed into all accounts as of Vautortes, in Maine, though there was no family surnamed *de Valle Torta* at this date in Maine. Exon Domesday, which supplies the surname of these men, also occasionally writes it as de *Torta Valle*.[34] In fact, the pancarte of the abbey of Grestain, founded by Herluin, father of Robert de Mortain, shows beyond all doubt that the family were from a Torteval, identified as Torteval-Quesnay in Calvados, cant. Caumont-l'Eventé, by Véronique Gazeau.[35]

A more subtle example concerns the still surviving de Vere family, who were earls of Oxford for several centuries. They are universally accepted as Norman by English-speaking historians, despite a welter of circumstantial evidence clearly indicating their origin in the Nantais in Brittany. Their Nantais origin is attested by the first documentary appearance of an Alberic de Vere in a charter of Conan II of Brittany given in the early 1050s.[36] In England from the Conquest

---

223–46; W. Kapelle, *The Norman Conquest of the North* (London, 1979), esp. 228–9, and the review of this by C. W. Hollister and R. Fleming in *Speculum* 56 (1981).

32 Miss Fry, *TEAS* v, 181, identified him with the William de Montfichet who, with Roesia his wife and William their son, gave land at Letchworth and Wallington to St Albans 'in the time of Henry I' (confirmed late in his reign by Henry II, *Mon. Ang.* ii, 229). The argument as it stands is merely inferential, and while possibly correct, the evidence is inconclusive. For Ralph, see *Comp. Peer.* viii, 200.

33 *Monasticon Anglicanum* iii, 290.

34 Exon, fol. 218a, *DB Devon* 15.44; Exon, fols 271a, 273b, 278a, 466a, *DB Somerset* 19.28; 43; 67, 45.13; Exon, fols 201a, *DB Cornwall* 2.14, 5.2. Exon's careful distinction of Geoffrey *de Valle* (fols 422a, 423b, 433a) from the men surnamed *de Valle torta* is normally ignored by modern historians.

35 D. Bates and V. Gazeau, 'L'abbaye de Grestain et la famille d'Herluin de Conteville', *Annales de Normandie* 40 (1990), 9–10.

36 Alberic's family probably came from Vair in Ancenis, in the Nantais; he occurs amongst a group of men from the Nantais in a charter given by Conan II c.1050 (discussed by H. Guillotel, 'La place de Châteaubriant dans l'essor des châtellenies

onward, the first English Alberic was a tenant of the powerful Breton tenant-in-chief Count Alan Rufus, and was among a handful of Alan's Bretons who were also tenant-in-chief of their own fees. Alberic is assumed to have originated at Ver, Manche, arr. Coutances, cant. Gavray, because he held land in 1086 of the bishop of Coutances (*DB* i, fol. 220c). Loyd acknowledged that no later evidence established any connexion between Alberic's family and Ver in the Cotentin.[37] Alberic's wife occurs in her own right in Domesday Book (i, fols 24a, 101a); she very probably was from a Cotentin family. There is a real possibility that other de Ver families in England could have originated in the Cotentin,[38] but the mass of evidence indicating Alberic's Breton origins is overwhelming. Much of it was rehearsed by W. R. Powell, though he ultimately rejected it.[39] One of the most striking features of the evidence is that Alberic II founded the priory of Hatfield Broadoak as a cell of Saint-Melaine de Rennes, one of the most important Breton abbeys.[40] The choice is remarkable, since Saint-Melaine was not a recognized pilgrimage centre, nor was it the house most closely connected to Count Alan's family, which favoured Saint-Georges de Rennes. Research has shown that though a cult of Saint Melaine existed outside Brittany, it never reached the Cotentin peninsula, though it is found elsewhere in Normandy.[41]

Continental onomastic evidence can – indeed, must – be combined with an analysis of the circumstances of the English settlement to achieve further clarification of Domesday prosopography. Eustache of Huntingdon provides a case in point. Documents from the dioceses of Cambrai and Beauvais indicate that he can safely be identified with Wace's Eustace of Abbeville, *dépt.* Somme, which straddled the counties of Eu and Ponthieu.[42] Eustace also held land of Countess Judith, whose mother was a former countess of Ponthieu. His own tenants included Ingelrann of Eu, and Alfred de Grandcourt.[43] By far the most interesting

---

bretonnes (xi–xii siècles)', *MSHAB*, 66 (1989), 21, and K. S. B. Keats-Rohan, 'Le problème de la suzeraineté et la lutte pour le pouvoir: la rivalité bretonne et l'état anglo-normand 1066–1154', *MSHAB*, 68 (1991), 63–9.

37 Loyd, *Origins*, 110.

38 Cf. William de Ver, *DB* i, fol. 127c. On the several different Ver families in England see *Comp. Peer.* x, App. J.

39 W. R. Powell, 'The Essex Fees of the Honour of Richmond', *Transactions of the Essex Archaeological Society*, Third Series I, part 3 (1964), 179–189.

40 J. L. Fisher, *Cartularium Prioratus de Colne*, Essex Archaeological Society Occasional Publications I, 1946; F. Jouön des Longrais, 'Les moines de l'abbaye Saint-Melaine de Rennes en Angleterre. Les chartes du prieuré d'Hatfield Regis', *Recueil de travaux offert à M. Clovis Brunel*, v. ii (Paris, 1955).

41 J. Fournée, 'Le culte populaire des saints bretons en Normandie', *Questions d'histoire de Bretagne, Actes du 107 Congrès national des sociétés savantes, section de philologie et d'histoire jusqu'à 1610*, 2 vols (Brest, 1982), ii, 311. Note the escheat to the king in the early thirteenth century of land formerly held by one Walter de Ver, a Breton (*Britonis*), in Suffolk, where Alberic's family held land (*Book of Fees*, 390).

42 *Roman du Rou de Wace*, ed. A. Holden, Société des anciens textes français, 3 vols, (Paris, 1970–73).

43 *DB Northants* 55.3–4, 56.46, *DB Huntingdonshire* 20.4. Ingelran of Eu was brother of Ramsey Abbey's tenant Guy of Eu and was also a tenant of the count of Eu in Sussex; *DB Huntingdonshire* 19.19, *Chart. Chichester*, no. 945, pp. 299–302, here p. 301, *DB Cambridgeshire* 7.2. *Chronicon Abbatiæ Rameseiensis*, ed. W. Dunn Macray (Rolls

example is provided by the Breton settlement, achieved in a series of stages of which the earliest was the grant of a large part of Cambridgeshire to Count Alan (see Chapter 3). He and his men dominated the *Inquisitio Eliensis* and the *Inquisitio Comitatus Cantabrigiensis*, and figure largely in early documents from Cambridgeshire and its hinterland. Analysis of this settlement enables one to posit likely identifications for the long-disputed origins of several of the count's more important tenants. Harduin *de Scalariis*, for example, fits into a group of men surrounding the count who came from the region of Fougères in north-east Brittany.[44] A man named Hamo *de Valenis* came from a Valaines in the county of Rennes, and had nothing to do with Valognes in the Cotentin to which English historians sometimes assign him, despite the careful orthography of Domesday which distinguished his toponym from that of the powerful sheriff of Essex, Peter de *Valognis*.[45] One can also rescue from apparent linguistic obscurity another tenant, who bore the name Halenalt, a hypocoristic form of the name Alan.[46] This information can be usefully applied to the hitherto hopelessly obscure case of Henry I's new man Halenald de Bidun, who was a Breton Alan from Bidon, near Dol, the place from which almost all of Henry's Bretons came.[47] It is an analysis of the Breton settlement that most clearly shows that, despite the efforts of Dr Elisabeth van Houts, Wace's twelfth-century *Roman de Rou* can not be taken at face value as evidence either of the Conqueror's companions in 1066 or of Domesday prosopography, but it does have a valuable role to play in the clarification of Domesday prosopography, as the case of Eustace of Huntingdon shows.[48]

In the Domesday prosopography which follows hereafter some 19,500 records of continental names, excluding the king, have been analysed as 2,468 different people. These people include about 200 tenants-in-chief, and about 600 Englishmen. The work has gone as far as it usefully can for now, with most of the few Domesday persons not present being English. Several specialists have announced an interest in a prosopography of the Domesday English and I am content to leave the work to them.[49] Even if one were to include all the native English and

---

Series, London, 1886), 215, 252, and 262–3, referring to Guy of Eu (Wido de Auco) and his sons Gilbert and John; this Guy seems to have been the same as Guy *dapifer* of Bishop Herbert Losinga of Norwich, a former abbot of Ramsey (1087–91), whose attestation of a confirmation of Henry I followed that of Ingelrann de Ou, ibid., 215.

[44] Cf. the hamlet of Les Echelles, in Saint-Germain-en-Coglès, arr. Fougères, cant. Saint-Brice-en-Coglès (*LINSEE*, Nomenclature des Hameaux, Lieux-Dits, Ecarts: Ille-et-Vilaine). For the Breton settlement in general see below, and more fully in Keats-Rohan, 'Le rôle des Bretons'.

[45] Compare *DB Suffolk* 3.15; 87, Hamo *de Vellenis/Valenis*, ibid., 37, Petrus *de Valonis*.

[46] *DB Suffolk* 3.56; 62, *Halanalt* (altered from *Halant*), *Harlenat*. Following E. Förstemann, *Altdeutsches Namenbuch*, vol. I (2nd edn, Bonn, 1900), 773, this name was translated as Erland in the Phillimore Domesday; on this sort of inappropriate onomastic application see Lewis, 'Joining the Dots', cited above.

[47] In fact, either Bidon or La Ville-Bidon, both near Dol, Ille-et-Vilaine. The genealogy of this family was not well served by J. H. Round, who conflated Halenald I and his son Halenald II in the introduction to *Rotuli de Dominabus*, xli–ii.

[48] E. M. C. van Houts, 'Wace as Historian', in Keats-Rohan, ed., *Family Trees*.

[49] See the splendid study by Ann Williams, *The English and the Norman Conquest* (Woodbridge, 1995).

other landholders named in Domesday Book, and the non-Englishmen named outside the Book in contemporary records, the total of known landholders in the Conqueror's England would still be less than 3,000. These figures can be seen as either surprisingly high – given the scale of repetition for names such as those of Earl Roger de Montgomery or William de Warenne – or surprisingly small, even allowing for the fact that a small number of tenants held land of more than one tenant-in-chief. They are certainly rather smaller than the true total of people of continental origin holding tenancies of land in England in 1086. Many of the charters from which we can identify Domesday tenants record the names of several other tenants and sub-tenants of particular tenants-in-chief whose tenancies are ignored by Domesday Book. In the case of tenants, rather than sub-tenants, the fees will have been recorded in Domesday as held by the tenant-in-chief himself. Some of their lands may have been infeodated only after 1086, but this is probably not true of a majority of such cases.[50] Unfortunately, such evidence is itself patchy, being confined to only a handful of tenants-in-chief, often the more prominent among them, such as William of Warenne and Robert of Mortain, or relating to areas such as Essex and Norfolk where the evidence of the Domesday text is especially strong.[51] It is therefore impossible to formulate a means for calculating what the true number of tenants may have been in 1086. Another problem is that Domesday will often give a tenant as an anonymous *miles* or even *milites*. Many of them can be identified in those parts of the text for which satellite material survives. The majority turn out to be continental landholders who are named in other parts of the Domesday text.

It seems to be the case that the Domesday record as it stands was primarily interested in a level of landownership immediately below the king. The record is divided into chapters headed by the king, the tenants-in-chief, or a miscellaneous collection of kingsmen, often described as servants, thegns, and almsmen. These chapter-headers comprise about a fifth of the 2,477 individuals I have isolated. The greater the importance of the tenant-in-chief, the greater the likelihood that information about his tenants and their tenancies will be forthcoming. Information about sub-tenancies, the tenants of the tenants, which is abundant in contemporary charter material, is extremely rare in Domesday Book. For the greater tenants-in-chief, such as Count Alan and William of Warenne, the average number of different tenants recorded is around 40. Some very important tenants-in-chief who were granted sway over large regions or whole counties, such as Robert of Mortain and Roger of Montgomery, had something like 88 and 120 tenants respectively.[52] These figures are unusual because both Robert and Roger had different groups of tenants on separate parts of their huge holdings. Tenants-in-chief further down the scale, but still wealthy men, such as Ralph and Robert

---

50 On this problem see C. P. Lewis, 'The Domesday Jurors', *Haskins Society Journal* 5 (1993), 17–44.

51 Cf. D. C. Douglas, *The Feudal Book of Bury St Edmunds*, lxvii–lxxxi. Many of these charters are still buried in poor editions in *Monasticon Anglicanum*, e.g. ii, 288–9, iii, 345–6, iv, 148, and (especially problematic) 197–8.

52 Cf. the studies listed in n. 9 above; for ecclesiastical tenants-in-chief, Douglas, *Feudal Book* and *Dom. Mon.*; A. Williams, 'The knights of Shaftesbury Abbey', *Anglo-Norman Studies* 8 (1986); E. King, *Peterborough Abbey, 1066–1310* (Cambridge, 1973).

de Tosny, Ernulf de Hesdin and even Geoffrey de Mandeville, managed to get no more than between 8 and 15 of their men into Domesday Book, though charter evidence shows that several more went unrecorded in each case.

This is not to deny the value of Domesday Book as a witness to the post-Conquest tenurial revolution, but there is little doubt that the makers of Domesday were much less interested in tenancy and sub-tenancy *per se* than we would like them to have been. It certainly seems to be an unreliable guide as to how far the process of infeudation by the tenants-in-chief had gone by 1086. The conclusions of an important study of the Domesday jurors by Chris Lewis were that: 'The jurors are a warning that certain types of landowner are likely to be unrecorded: specifically life-tenants of ecclesiastical manors who were not (or not yet) breaking the terms of their tenure and claiming as their own; tenants of undertenants; and Englishmen with tenures on terms other than military service. There is no evidence that Domesday set out to record such tenure. When the Inquest asked of each manor "Who holds it now?", it expected straightforward answers: either the tenant-in-chief held it in demesne or he had subinfeudated it . . . all lower levels of tenure mattered not one bit to the commissioners.'[53] Since contemporary external evidence indicates that Domesday gives a false picture of the general level of infeudation, we need to discover why anyone below the level of tenant-in-chief or king's man was mentioned in Domesday Book at all, before we can safely use the text as evidence for the pattern and progress of infeudation by 1086. To a considerable extent, the issue is clarified by the suggestions of David Roffe and others about the nature and purpose of the work. The subtenants could be ignored because the question being investigated was who had tenure by virtue of payment of tax. On the face of it, the real question is why were the tenants mentioned at all, since assigning sole responsibility for the tax-yield on individual fiefs to the tenants-in-chief would have considerably simplified the exercise, which could have made a simple note of the fact of infeudation without taking the trouble to identify the tenant. The answer appears to concern the feudal structure of the fiefs themselves. If, as David Roffe has suggested, the tenants named in Domesday held the jurisdiction of their lands, and hence had rights of inheritance as well as tenure, then they became directly responsible for the tax due on their manors.[54] Such tenure entailed concrete obligations to the king as well as to the tenant-in-chief. Only important tenants would have been permitted to establish tenure by the payment of tax. The tenant-in-chief's personal responsibility for the tax due on demesne manors meant that he could use them as resources for the support of family members, or close personal servants, and be protected from tenurial claims by their tenants, who, for the same reason, did not need to be recorded in Domesday Book.

Since only the more important of the tenants of the tenant-in-chief acquired holdings that justified an entry in Domesday Book, we can speculate as to their relationship to their lords, using the tenant-in-chiefs' own direct relationship with the king as a guide. Domesday occasionally identifies the tenants as the *dapifer, camerarius, capellanus*, etc. of a tenant-in-chief. Contemporary documents supply the information in numerous other cases which allow us to identify some

53 C. P. Lewis, 'The Domesday Jurors', 33.
54 Roffe, 'Thegnage to barony'.

of the officials of other honours.[55] It is possible that the tenants of Domesday were, for the most part, men in constant attendance on their lords as office holders of the honour, to which they doubtless owed knight-service. This would accord well with the importance of the individual tenants required by the fiscal/jurisdictional argument, and also with the context of the Salisbury Oath, which underlay the Domesday Survey.[56]

A question requiring further study is the position of women, especially continental women, in Domesday Book.[57] There are few of them, but their occurrence is striking. Some, like the wife of Hugh fitz Grip, were widows in control of important fiefs; others, like the wives of Richard de Clare and Hugh de Grandmesnil, were women whose husbands were living and who had land entered in their own names as tenants-in-chief in Domesday Book.[58] Others were widows living on dower lands. The best-known example is Esilia, widow of William Malet and a major tenant of her son Robert in Suffolk.[59] A lesser known and very interesting example, of a female tenant whose tenement existed in 1086 but was herself not recorded in Domesday Book, is provided by the mother of William of Eu, who in 1084 held 7.5 of 12 hides entered in the Dorset Domesday as being in the lordship of her son.[60] This lady was Beatrice, countess of Eu, whose husband was alive and well and running the county of Eu in Normandy in 1086 and for some years thereafter. Robert of Eu had been granted land in Sussex around 1068 and had administered these estates until about 1080. Thereafter his son and heir William, who held land in eleven other counties in his own right, took over the administration of the Sussex lands. Analysis of the Sussex tenants shows that they were distinct from William's personal tenants elsewhere and had clearly been enfeoffed by Count Robert. Even if Beatrice was in fact dead in 1086, the fact remains that the only English property she can be shown to have held was held from her son William and not from Robert. Was she estranged from her husband? Did she use the revenues of the manor to finance visits to her son in England? Does the relative rarity of female tenure make this tenure seem more remarkable than it really is? We do not know. Although it is possible that Beatrice

---

[55] See J. F. A. Mason, 'Barons and their Officials in the Later Eleventh Century', *Anglo-Norman Studies* 13 (1991), 243–262; cf. J. H. Round, 'The Origin of Belvoir Castle', *EHR* 22 (1907), 508–10.

[56] On these questions, and their relationship to the Salisbury Oath, see D. Roffe, 'From thegnage to barony', and idem, 'Brought to Book: . . .', forthcoming; Holt, '1086'; cf. Mortimer, 'Clare'.

[57] Preliminary studies, such as C. Clark, 'Women's names in post-Conquest England: observations and speculations', *Speculum* 53 (1978), 223–51 and P. Stafford, 'Women in Domesday', *Reading Medieval Studies* 15 (1989), 75–94, are available, but the subject of tenure by women needs further investigation.

[58] *DB Dorset* 55, wife of Hugh fitz Grip; *DB Bedfordshire* 54, *DB Hertfordshire* 43, Adeliz de Grandmesnil; *DB Hertfordshire* 42, Rohais de Clare.

[59] *DB Suffolk* 6.8; 11; 156; 161; 176; 191; 193–5; 199–201; 209; 216; 229–30; 232; 251; 253; 271; 311.

[60] *DB Dorset* 34.11. [*Libri Censualis Vocati Domesday Book, Additamenta ex Codic. Antiquiss.*, vol. 3, Record Commission edition of Domesday Book (London, 1816). Printed in *VCH Dorset* iii, p. 138, by R. B. Pugh, who made the 'natural assumption' that Beatrice had died between 1084, the date of the Geld Rolls, and 1085–6, the date of Domesday (ibid., 120).

died between 1084 and 1086, her failure to appear in Domesday is much more likely to be explained in terms of Domesday's habitual failure to record tenants in demesne manors. Interestingly, the Geld Rolls provide the sole evidence for Beatrice having lived as long as 1084; her only dateable appearances in her husband's charters belong to the period around his foundation of the abbey of Tréport in 1050. In the part of Tréport's pancarte which relates to the time of Count Robert all the early grants were authorised by Robert, his countess and their sons. The later grants were authorised by Robert, his sons and his barons.[61] Whether or not this was significant, or merely due to the scribe who wrote the pancarte, is impossible to say since the originals do not survive. A fuller text of the pancarte is found in a late copy, Paris, Bibliothèque Nationale, ms. nov. acq. lat. 249, fol. 46v, which states that Beatrice was (by a previous marriage) the mother of Roger fitz Turold of Verly, a benefactor of the abbey who died on the voyage to England in 1066, according to a charter for Sainte-Trinité de Rouen.[62] He is thought to have been the father of Turold de Verly, a Domesday tenant of Roger de Montgomery in Shropshire.

The information concerning Beatrice's English tenure comes from a Domesday satellite and is a particularly interesting example of a Domesday failure to record a tenant in a demesne manor. Possibly the holding of Inga sister of Ralph Bainard in his demesne manor of Dunmow, evidenced as well-established by 1104, some time after Ralph's death, was treated in the same way.[63] Daughters also occur in Domesday, some of them married to tenants of their fathers, such as Agnes daughter of Alfred of Marlborough, wife of Turstin the Fleming, but there are other examples unattached to husbands, such as the daughter of Roger de Raimes, who was possibly the same person as his tenant *Guibergis*, and the *nepta* of Geoffrey of Coutances, possibly the same woman as the unnamed wife of his sub-tenant Ingelbald.[64] There is even a case, identified by D. C. Douglas, of a husband and wife holding separate tenures of a single tenant-in-chief. Others are mere names, such as the Matilda who occurs in the Boulogne holding, or the mysterious Iseldis who apparently held a single manor in-chief in Dorset.[65]

Domesday Book mentions marriage several times. To the several examples already mentioned we can add those of Ralph de Limésy, who was given property by the queen at the time of his marriage, and of Walter, the son-in-law and tenant

---

[61] *Cartulaire de l'abbaye de Saint-Michel-du-Tréport*, ed. Laffleur de Kermaingant (Paris, 1880), nos. 1 and 2.

[62] *Chartularium Monasterii Sanctae Trinitiatis de Monte Rothomagi*, ed. by A. Deville as an Appendix to B. Guérard, *Cartulaire de Saint-Bertin* (Paris, 1841), p. 453.

[63] *Monasticon Anglicanum* vi pt 1, p. 147; BL MS Harley 662, fol. 6r.

[64] *DB Herefordshire* 19.6.10 (Marlborough); *DB Devon* 3.86–9 (Coutances); *DB Suffolk* 38.9; 11, *DB Essex* 39.1 (Raimes).

[65] *DB Dorset* 55a (Iseldis), *DB Somerset* 17.8 (Matilda). Geoffrey Talbot and his wife Agnes held separate tenements of Hugh de Gurnay, *DB Essex*, discussed by Douglas in *Dom. Mon.* Agnes's had previously been held by an Osbern, which might indicate some relationship between Agnes and Osbern. Her parentage is obscure, though one possibility is that she was the daughter of Helto of Swanscombe, whose fief was given to Geoffrey Talbot after 1086; it eventually passed to the heirs of Geoffrey and Agnes' daughter, wife of Hugh de Lacy (d.c.1114).

of Gilbert fitz Turold.[66] Other examples of marriage survive only in the Domesday Satellites. One example occurs in Wiltshire where Gunter was a tenant of Humphrey de Insula. The Tax Return for Highworth Hundred (fol. 3a) records that the manor was given by a certain Turold in marriage to his *nepta*, who was presumably Gunter's wife.[67] Marriages between the newcomers and the English had occurred by 1086 and a few of them are hinted at in Domesday's account of a man's *antecessores*; Robert d'Oilly's possession of his father-in-law Wigod of Wallingford's lands, for instance, occurs as his wife's holding – *feudo suæ feminæ*.[68] The details mostly have to be garnered from non-Domesday sources. The first marriage of Walter de Douai to an Englishwoman who brought him the manor of Uffculme is known from the Glastonbury cartulary; in Domesday Book this woman, Edeva, occurs as his English *antecessor* in Uffculme.[69] The phenomenon of marriage to English women, discussed some years ago by Eleanor Searle, seems never to have involved the most prominent tenant-in-chiefs among the Normans.[70] Such men came from and normally still held important Norman lordships and the context of their marriage policies at this date was still firmly Norman. One must beware of the current tendency to exaggerate the amount of inter-marriage at this date, when it was still very rare. Apart from Robert d'Oilly, only two tenants-in-chief (Walter of Douai and Geoffrey de la Guerche) married Englishwomen; neither was a Norman. Whether or not the relatively lower social status of those Normans acquiring English wives is evidence of negative Norman attitudes to inter-marriage with the English is an interesting question requiring more research and analysis. What is clear, however, is that the evidence is dominated by examples of male settlers marrying English heiresses. As far as I know, no one has ever discussed an example of a prominent Norman – apart from the king – providing a relative as bride for an Englishman, yet there are perhaps two examples of such marriages.

An English Alfred occurs in Domesday Norfolk where he held the manor of Attleborough in chief. The service of 2 knights from the fee of Alfred de Athleburgo was granted to William de Albini pincerna by Henry I.[71] William de Albini was the founder of Wymondham priory in Norfolk, to which Yseldis granddaughter of Alfred was an early benefactor, granting land in Besthorpe and Attleborough.[72] Another early benefactor, also of land in Besthorpe, whose charters were attested by clerks from Athelburgh, was Adam son of Alfred, who was a grandson of Peter de Valognes and nephew of Roger de Valognes.[73] It seems certain, therefore, that the Englishman Alfred of Attleborough married a daughter of Peter de Valognes, sheriff of Essex, by whom he had issue Adam and

---

[66] *DB Worcestershire* 20.6.

[67] *DB Wiltshire* 27.6.

[68] *DB Bucks* 19.1. The same entry makes reference to a man of Toki, who was Wigod's son.

[69] *The Great Chartulary of Glastonbury*, ed. Dom A. Watkin, Somerset Record Society vols 59, 63–4 (1944, 1948, 1949–50), i., no. 172, pp. 126–8.

[70] Eleanor Searle, 'Women and the legitimisation of succession at the Norman Conquest', *Anglo-Norman Studies* 3 (1981), 159–70.

[71] *RBE*, 398.

[72] BL Cotton Titus C viii, fol. 23.

[73] Ibid., fols 22, 24.

Roger. He may have been the Alfred *vicecomes* who was co- or under-sheriff of Essex with Hugh de Bucland between c.1101 and 1112, and was a benefactor of Colne priory.

The second example is much more speculative, but perhaps even more interesting. Some time between 1100 and 1107 Roger Bigod and his wife Adelisa (de Tosny) gave a charter for Rochester priory, attested by their sons and daughters William, Humphrey, Gunnora and Matilda.[74] The charter contains a highly unusual *pro anima* clause for Norman the sheriff, who was their Domesday *antecessor* in the manors granted and Roger's predecessor as sheriff in the pre-Conquest period. The normal explanation for this *pro anima* clause would be a relationship between Roger's family and Norman, who is usually assumed to have been an Englishman. There is possibly some evidence for such a relationship.

In the mid-twelfth century Roger fitz Richard of Warkworth was described by his brother-in-law William de Vere as *nepos* of Roger Bigod's son Hugh and as having had an uncle Thomas de Candelent. Roger's ancestry was discussed by Charles Clay, who suggested we read 'Candelent' as Canteloup, the name of a family later found in the area.[75] However, 'Candelent' is the Latin form found in Domesday for the manor of Candlet in Suffolk, which the Englishman Norman the Sheriff held of Roger Bigod in 1086.[76] Could it be that a family link had been forged between the Bigods and the issue of Norman? The link is unlikely to have involved a daughter of Roger, but it may have involved a sister (his sister Matilda was married to his Domesday tenant Hugh de Hosdenc) or a niece. This case has none of the certainty of the Valognes/Attleborough example, but it is just one more glimpse of how much a full analysis of post-Conquest society is waiting to tell us.

---

[74] BL Cotton Domitian A x, fol. 201v–2r.

[75] C. Clay, 'The ancestry of the early lords of Warkworth', *Archaeolgia Aeliana*, 4th ser. 32 (1954), 65–71.

[76] *DB Suffolk* 7.95.

Chapter 2

PROVENANCE AND THE PAST:
TERRITORIAL DESCRIPTORS
AND DOMESDAY PROSOPOGRAPHY

The diversity of Continental origins amongst those responsible for the 'Norman Conquest' of England in 1066 was first noted by the chroniclers of the event. According to William of Poitiers the battle of Hastings was a multi-national affair involving the men of Maine, the French, the Bretons and the men of Aquitaine, as well as the Normans.[1] The passage in question describes a particular manoeuvre and does not in itself exclude the additions to the list found in Orderic Vitalis, who mentioned also the Burgundians and men from north of the Alps.[2] William of Poitiers had stated that Normans, Flemings, French and Bretons had gathered at Saint-Valéry-sur-Somme, in Picardy, for the crossing to England.[3] Accounts of the battle of Hastings make no specific mention of men from Flanders, though William of Poitiers's short list of Hastings warriors begins with the name of Eustace, count of Boulogne, in neighbouring Picardy. In addition to six Normans, it includes also the names of Aimery, vicomte de Thouars in Poitou, and Geoffrey, son of Rotroc count of Perche.[4] The chroniclers are concerned, apparently, with auxiliary troops, composed of the well-born and led by nobles, rather than with mercenaries of the 'cannon-fodder' type. It seems that the battle was fought by a central core of Normans, led by William, with a group of Bretons on the left wing, probably led by Count Alan, and on the right wing an assemblage of auxiliary troops from Maine, Aquitaine and elsewhere, part or all of which was commanded by Eustace count of Boulogne. According to William of Poitiers, the non-Norman auxiliaries of William's victorious army were paid off and returned home shortly after the battle.[5] Men from Anjou, Brittany and Maine

---

[1] *Guillaume de Poitiers, Histoire de Guillaume le Conquérant*, ed. R. Foreville (Paris, 1952) [hereafter, William of Poitiers], p. 192. An earlier version of this chapter was read to a seminar at the Institut historique allemand in Paris on 9 November 1996 at the kind invitation of Professor Werner Paravicini.

[2] Ord. Vit., ii, 144.

[3] William of Poitiers, p. 195: *exercitum e Normannis et Flandrensibus ac Francis et Britonibus aggregavit.*

[4] William of Poitiers, pp. 194–6.

[5] In his account of the battle William of Poitiers distinguishes between the main Norman army and auxiliary troops, led by such men as Amaury of Thouars and Geoffrey of Perche (pp. 194–208). Both these men certainly returned home, probably taking all or most of their men with them. William later refers to men who choose to return home being well-rewarded for their pains by the Conqueror (p. 244). Some instances referred to Normans such as Humphrey de Tilleul, who returned home in 1068; Orderic Vitalis recorded his return suggesting that it meant renouncing any land that had been acquired in England (Ord. Vit., iii, 220). I am grateful to Marjorie Chibnall for observations made in correspondence on the auxiliary troops. Her new edition of William of Poitiers is scheduled for publication in 1999 in the *Oxford Medieval Texts* series.

were still serving in January 1070, complaining bitterly and asking to be discharged, according to Orderic Vitalis.[6] The multi-national lists of William of Poitiers and Orderic Vitalis are for the most part readily comprehensible. William of Normandy, son-in-law of Baldwin count of Flanders, had conquered Maine in 1063, and his family's links with Aquitaine went back to the early tenth century; a more recent alliance linked him to the Burgundian counts of Nevers. Eustace of Boulogne certainly had his own agenda, as the former husband of a sister of Edward the Confessor, but that union had linked him to William's family because Edward's mother was William's great-aunt Emma of Normandy.[7] A young Norman who fought the first engagement of his career at Hastings became count of the French county of Meulan before 1086.[8]

Some twenty years after Hastings the fate of English landholdings was recorded in Domesday Book. Several of the new, foreign, owners of English land bore surnames such as *pictavensis, burgundiensis* and *cenomannensis*. The appearance in Domesday Book or its satellites of such terms, and the more common *brito* and *flandrensis*, is undoubtedly significant and requires investigation within the context of a full prosopographical study of Domesday, and hence ultimately of the whole Conquest phenomenon. Some figures will help to put these descriptors in perspective. In a sample of 2,172 identifiable persons occurring as landholders in Domesday Book, 629 can be known only by a forename, 186 by a patronym, 27 by other relationship terms, such as *frater*, and 515 use a toponymic surname (of which less than twenty relate to English places and were borne by non-Englishmen). 30 persons are identified by Domesday or its satellites with a territorial descriptor, and a further six are distinguished from the English as *francigena* (Arthur and Tual) or *francus* (Gerald, Odo, Godbold, John). Domesday Book is not about who fought at Hastings, so the occurrence in its folia of these surnames is likely to reveal preoccupations distinct from those of the chroniclers of Hastings. Even so, such territorial descriptors should first be considered in terms of the battle formations at Hastings. Orderic mentions Burgundians, and the Bretons were prominent in William of Poitier's account. As for the Flemings, it is often stated that the the right wing, commanded by Count Eustace, was a Franco-Flemish group, or a group of foreign mercenaries that included Flemings. These are statements for which direct evidence in the various contemporary or near contemporary sources for Hastings is wholly wanting.[9] What the sources do show is the participation of Picards from the county of Ponthieu, such as Hugh of Ponthieu, and the county of Boulogne, in the person of

---

6 Ord. Vit., ii, 234.
7 See H. Tanner, 'The expansion of the power and influence of the counts of Boulogne under Eustace II', *Anglo-Norman Studies* 14 (1992), 251–286. Eustace's brother Lambert count of Lens (k. 1054) was the second husband of William's sister Adelaide.
8 William of Poitiers, p. 192.
9 See the items collected in Stephen Morillo, ed., *The Battle of Hastings* (Woodbridge, 1996), including his Introduction, p. xxii. His own reservations and those of others on Flemish participation are recorded by C. M. Gillmor, 'Naval logistics of the cross-Channel operation, 1066', ibid. pp. 127–8, who cites the grant of a *fief-rente* by William I to Baldwin V of Flanders in 1066 as indirect evidence of the hiring of mercenaries. I have had not yet had time to read the recently published account by Jim Bradbury, *The Battle of Hastings* (Sutton, 1998).

Count Eustace.[10] Eustace was the independent ruler of Boulogne, but he was also count of Thérouanne and of Lens in Artois, a region subject to the count of Flanders since the ninth century.[11] The later evidence of Lambert of Ardres, which detailed several persons who went to England in 1066, is also concerned with men subject to Eustace; if these were Artesians (as was Arnulf of Ardres) rather than Picards, then they were nominally subject to the count of Flanders and were described as Flemings.[12] Picardy consisted of twelve counties during the Carolingian period, but its structures had badly decayed since then.[13] Control of the several regions, including Vermandois, Boulogne and Ponthieu, was disputed at various times between rulers of Normandy, Flanders and France. Some of the 'French' – *franci* – referred to by the chroniclers may have included Picards, men such as Arnulf de Hesdin and his brother Ilbod, and Rainer de Brimeux.[14] Of the Flemings from the county of Flanders proper there is no hint before the brief career of Gerbod the Fleming of Saint-Bertin de Saint-Omer in Artois, which seems to have spanned from 1068 – the year the queen, Matilda of Flanders, first came to England – to 1070 at the longest, and the appearance of Gilbert de Ghent at York in 1069.[15] Modern historians normally fail to distinguish the separate regions of Flanders, Artois and Picardy, but did contemporaries? What does *flandrensis* or any other territorial descriptor mean in a Domesday-style context? Does it relate to continental place of origin, or does it preserve a memory of something more remote?

The text of Domesday Book is a much abbreviated summary of more expansive information, with the surnames of the tenants being the commonest casualty of the abbreviation process. Here territorial descriptors relate almost exclusively to tenants-in-chief, such as Maino *Brito*, Walter *Flandrensis*, Albert *Lotharingensis* and (possibly) Hervey *Bituricensis*. As to their tenants, the Domesday satellites yield a William *pictavensis*, a Guy *angevinus*, a Walter *burgundiensis* and

---

10 William of Poitiers, p. 202, shows Eustace commanding 50 knights. For the men of Ponthieu, *Carmen de Hastingae Proelio*, ed. C. Morton and H. Muntz (Oxford, 1972), *passim*.

11 See Tanner, 'The counts of Boulogne', 251, 262–69, esp. 269 and n. 39.

12 Lambert of Ardres, *Historia comitum Ghisnensium*, in *MGH SS* xxiv, pp. 550–642, and ed. De Godefroy de Menilglaize (Paris, 1855).

13 Robert Fossier, *La terre et les hommes en Picardie jusqu'à la fin du XIIIe siècle* (Amiens, 1987).

14 Arnulf, *DB Wiltshire* 25, *DB Gloucestershire* 60, etc.; Ilbod, *DB Oxfordshire* 48; *DB Lincolnshire* 30; Rainer de Brimeux, *DB Lincolnshire* 40; all three came from the modern *département* of Pas-de-Calais.

15 On Gerbod see Christopher Lewis, 'The formation of the honour of Chester, 1066–1100', in *The Earldom of Chester and its Charters. A Tribute to Geoffrey Barraclough*, ed. A. T. Thacker (Chester, 1991), 38–9. Gerbod's family held property south of Ghent in Flanders, and were advocates of Saint-Bertin at Saint-Omer in Artois. He attested Baldwin V of Flanders's foundation charter for Saint Winnoc in 1067, with Eustace de Boulogne (Miraeus et Foppens, *Opera diplomatica et historica*, 4 vols (Louvain, 1743), i, 511–12). For Gilbert's capture at York, see Symeon of Durham, *Opera Omnia*, ed. T. Arnold (Rolls Series, London 1882–5), ii, 188. Of course, although the 1066 expedition was not formally supported by Baldwin of Flanders, some of his vassals could have joined it, under the leadership of Eustace of Boulogne. There is no formal proof either way.

a Walter *cenomannensis*, to name but a few. In the cases of *pictavensis, burgundiensis* and *angevinus*, we can point to contemporary or near-contemporary Norman evidence of families using territorial descriptors as surnames. Such surnames probably indicate immigration to Normandy from these regions at an earlier period. Exchange of personnel between Normandy and Poitou is evidenced for the tenth century, and we know that the Taisson family came to Normandy from Anjou (via the Chartrain) in the early eleventh century. There was a link between the Norman dukes and the Burgundian counts of Nevers shortly before the mid-eleventh century, following the marriage of Adela of Normandy and Renaud, count of Nevers.

The case of the label *cenomannensis* requires caution. The label *cenomannensis* often became the surname Mansel, and that is also found in Normandy around this time. Some interrelationship between Norman and Manceau families in 1066 is not unlikely. The daughter of a Roger de Tosny was married to Guy de Laval in the early eleventh century, so that persons surnamed Mansel occurring some decades later among tenants of the de Tosny family could well have had ancestors who were natives of Maine.[16] Could this be true of Exon Domesday's Walter *cenomannensis*, tenant of Gilbert son of Turold?[17] Perhaps. Persons from Maine, the county conquered by the Normans in 1063 which provided auxiliary troops in 1066, are well-evidenced as English landholders from very early in the reign of William II onwards. There is, however, no indisputable documentary evidence of any landholding by a Manceau layman in England before 1087. The toponym of Turgis *de Meduana*, which does not occur in Domesday Book but can be supplied from the records of Saint Alban's abbey, can refer to Mayenne in the county of Maine, or to Maine itself.[18] Turgis is so unlikely a name for a native Manceau, especially one whose sole overlord in England was Eudo dapifer of Ryes, Calvados, that a Manceau option is easily discounted in favour of Meuvaines in the canton of Ryes. The Almodus who was a tenant of William bishop of Durham in Lincolnshire in 1086 was doubtless the man who surfaced only once thereafter, c.1112, as an archdeacon apparently holding Thorney abbey in custody.[19] He is interesting as a possible example of an ecclesiastic from Maine, where Bishop William had enjoyed two important appointments in the abbeys of Saint-Calais and Saint-Victor. At any rate, the name Almodus was shared by an abbot of

---

16 The Richard Mansel who was a benefactor of the Tosny abbey of Conches in 1080 appears to have been the father of a Richard, benefactor of Savigny, who was certainly a Manceau landholder, *Gall. Christ.* xi Inst. 128; Arch. dépt. de la Mayenne H 33, pp. 115–116. A Mansel family held of the Tosny family at Bailleul-la-Campagne, Eure (L. Musset, 'Les Tosny', *Francia* v (1977), p. 77).

17 *DB Somerset* 42.2–3, identified by the Exon Tax Return for Chewton Hundred, fol. 446a.

18 *Monasticon Anglicanum*, ii, 180, confirmation of grants by Robert and William sons of Turgis de Meduana of land held by Turgis in *DB Essex* 25.2–3. William de Meduana attested a confirmation charter for Walden by King Stephen, BL MS Harley 369, fol. 30r.

19 *DB Lincolnshire* 3.35; 37. Writ of Henry I printed in F. M. Stenton, ed., *Facsimiles of Early Charters in Northamptonshire Collections* (Northants Record Society, 1930), p. 15 (cf. *RRAN* ii, 1033).

Mont-Saint-Michel (subsequently removed to Cerisy by William the Conqueror) who was reputedly of Manceau origin.[20]

Although we should probably interpret appellations such as *pictavensis* and *burgundiensis* as referring to migrant ancestors of men who in 1086 were Normans, this will not normally be true of the descriptors *brito* and *flandrensis*. These cases will be discussed fully below, but we can note that even here there are several possible exceptions. These include three men surnamed *brito* who held land of Abbot Baldwin of Bury St Edmunds. As a native of the Chartrain Baldwin might have recruited men from the numerous families there who descended from Breton ancestors, sometimes going back as far as the tenth century, though it is quite possible that these three, Fulcher, and the brothers Hubert and Rainald, really were Bretons.[21] Bury is in Suffolk, which had a high concentration of Breton settlers by 1086, and there had been a major Breton settlement there since about 1030. A Breton group at Bury might help to clarify the mysterious origins of a man probably related to one of Bury's tenants, but not one of them. This was Hervé *Bituricensis*, who makes best sense if understood within a Breton context, but whose name is an adjectival form of a toponym referring to Berry or to Bourges.[22] The circumstances of the English settlement, when analyzed as a whole, would seem to exclude the very possibility that any settler could have come from Berry. The appellation *bituricensis* was attached to a natural son of Alan III of Brittany.[23] More significantly, perhaps, it occurs in the name of one Rainald *bituricensis* who was alive in the early twelfth century. In an act of his relating to Saint-Vincent du Mans, he is found granting land at Noyen near Le Mans, attesting by his uncle Hugh de Merderel, a native of the same region.[24] Clearly, the appellation *bituricensis* is not necessarily best translated 'de Bourges'.

The surname of the chaplain Albert, *lotharingensis*, poses no difficulties. He

---

20 Dom J. Laporte, 'L'abbaye aux Xe et XIe siècles', *Millénaire monastique du Mont-Saint-Michel*, i, 72–4; idem, 'Les séries abbatiale et priorale du Mont', ibid. 273.

21 *DB Suffolk* 14.68, the brothers Hubert and Rainald Brito, ibid. 14.22, identified from the *Feudal Book of Abbot Baldwin*, in D. C. Douglas, *Feudal Documents of the Abbey of Bury St Edmunds* (Oxford, 1921), pp. 21–2. Ivo and Halderic, both identified as *carnotensis*, attested Baldwin's charters (ibid., charter nos. 100, 106). Baldwin's origins in the Chartrain (and hence also of his brother Frodo) are revealed in *Memorials of St Edmund's Abbey*, ed. T. Arnold, 2 vols, Rolls Series (1890), i, pp. 56 and 344.

22 *DB Suffolk* 67; he was perhaps related to *Petrus clericus*, a tenant of Bury (ibid. 14.13), who should probably be identified with the *Petrus bituricensis* who attested two charters of Abbot Baldwin (*Feudal Book of Bury St Edmunds*, ed. D. C. Douglas, pp. 108–9, nos. 105–6). If Hervey was a relative of Peter then a circuitous route for a connexion with Berry becomes possible through the priory of La Chapelle-Aude, where Abbot Baldwin's abbey of Saint-Denis had a cell. The toponym of his tenant Peter de Paludel (*DB Suffolk* 67.18) could be interpreted in either a Breton (La Palvelle, arr. Saint-James, Manche) or a Berry (Palluau-sur-Indre, Indre) context. The form *Arce[m]bald* of the name of another tenant is distinctive of the Berry region, but cannot be accepted as a reliable variant of the more familiar Erchembald, ibid., 67.21.

23 See K. S. B. Keats-Rohan, 'William I and the Breton contingent in the non-Norman conquest 1060–1087', *Anglo-Norman Studies* 13 (1991), p. 171 and note 71.

24 *Cartulaire de Saint-Vincent au Mans*, ed. Menjot d'Elbenne (Mamers, 1886–1913), no. 395.

was one of several clerics from the diocese of Liège recruited into the English church by Edward the Confessor, who apparently prized the quality of their education.[25] This Albert seems to have left descendants, since his land was afterwards held by a family surnamed *Lohareng*, the Lorrainer.[26] The same surname was used by the descendants of a non-Norman Domesday tenant, Otbert, tenant of William of Picquigny.[27] The descendants of Amalfrid, tenant of Eustace de Boulogne and of the Norman Ralph Baynard, were surnamed *Loholt*.[28] In two early twelfth-century entries in the cartulary of the West Norman abbey of Montebourg, we find Geoffrey *Lohenrenc* and his son William, and Nigel *Lohout* de Flamville.[29] These instances may partly reflect the pre-Conquest interchanges between England, which had numerous Norman, Breton and Lorrainer settlers, and Normandy, where Englishmen are occasionally found.

The territorial appellation *teutonicus* does not appear in Domesday Book, but it might have done. Among the tenants of Hugh of Avranches, earl of Chester, named in Domesday was one Baldric.[30] In England he was known as Baldric of Lindsey, from the part of Lincolnshire where he held land, but at home in the Norman Vexin he was known as Baldric de Bocquencé. He is abundantly, if confusingly, evidenced as a descendant of a certain Baldric *teutonicus* who, according to Orderic Vitalis, went to Normandy in the early eleventh century and took service as archer with Richard II (d.1027).[31] Several other of Baldric the German's descendants also figure in Domesday, including Richard de Courcy and Hugh fitz Grip's widow, Hadvise de Bacqueville.[32] The phenomenon of transregional migration in the Middle Ages has been noted often enough for such a migration not to cause undue surprise, but the general phenomenon still needs far greater investigation. The Norman appetite for migration was itself considerable,

---

[25] Simon Keynes, 'Giso, bishop of Wells', *Anglo-Norman Studies* xix (1997), 205–213. I am unconvinced by the common assumption, on account of his Germanic name, that Regenbald 'the Chancellor' was a Lotharingian. Cf. reference to the house of Raimbald at Caen in an act of c.1030 (Fauroux, 70).

[26] *DB Berkshire* 56, *DB Bedfordsire* 49, *DB Herefordshire* 18; Bedfordshire Record Society 10, p. 264, n. 102. Cf. also Gerard *lotaringus*, a tenant of Count Alan in Cambridgeshire, *DB Cambridgeshire* 14.18–19, identified from *Inquisitio Comitatus Cantabrigiensis*, ed. N. Hamilton (1876), p. 38.

[27] *DB Buckinghamshire* 17.3–4; *Cartulary of Missenden Abbey*, ed. J. G. Jenkins, part I (Buckinghamshire Record Society, 1938), app. C.

[28] *DB Essex* 20.62, 33.10; 18; *VCH Essex* i, 525n.

[29] Paris BN lat. 10087, pp. 103, 154, nos. 265, 491.

[30] *DB Lincolnshire* 13.22; 31; 39, *DB Cheshire* 15.

[31] Ord. Vit. ii, 82. See Judith Green, 'The lords of the Norman Vexin', in John Gillingham and J. C. Holt, ed., *War and Government in the Middle Ages: Essays in Honour of J. O. Prestwich* (Woodbridge, 1984), 46–62.

[32] *DB Oxfordshire* 32, *DB Dorset* 55; Hadvise is identified as the wife of Hugh fitz Grip by her charter for the abbey of Montivilliers, edited in J.-M. Bouvris, 'La renaissance de l'abbaye de Montivilliers et son dévelopement jusqu'à la fin du XIe siècle', in *L'Abbaye de Montivilliers à travers les âges. Actes du colloque organisé à Montivilliers le 8 mars 1986; Recueil de l'Association des Amis du Vieux Havre*, no. 48 (Le Havre, 1988), App. no. 29 (1066–76), 82–3, 'Ego Hadvidis filia Nicolai de Baschelvilla, uxor Hugonis de Varhan . . . annuente magno rege Guillelmo, coram baronibus suis, videlicet . . . et Gaufrido Martello, fratre supradicti Hugonis . . .'.

as eleventh-century movements to Italy, Spain and the Holy Land show. Links between the Normans and the Germans could have arisen from a number of political circumstances throughout the tenth and eleventh centuries, one of them being the marriage in 1036 of Emma of Normandy's daughter Gunhild to Henry III. Orderic Vitalis's mention of *Cisalpini* fighting in the campaign of 1066 must certainly be taken to refer to subjects of the German king and Roman Emperor. A more general background to links between Germany and Normandy was possibly provided by my recent analysis of Dudo of Saint-Quentin's *De moribus*, in which I suggested that the origin of Rollo's wife Poppa should be sought among the German Popponides, and, specifically, that we see her as a grand-daughter of Henry of Thuringia, marquis of Neustria at his death in 878 and ancestor, through his daughter, of the Ottonians.[33]

German-Norman links are perhaps less surprising than the recruitment of Angevins to Normandy in the early eleventh century. Norman-Angevin relations had rarely been good and by the middle of the century they would be extremely bad. One certain example is the Taisson family, of which an early member, Ralph I Taisson, named his father as *Radulfus andegavensis* in his foundation-charter for Fontenay. His son Ralph II married a kinswoman of the Conqueror, Matilda niece of Odo of Bayeux.[34] Another family which sought to integrate itself in Norman society in the early eleventh century was the Fitz Geroie family. Its background is still not well understood, but seems to have combined Breton, Angevin and Manceau elements. Clients of both the seigneur of Mayenne and the Bellême in the mid-eleventh century, their rise and fall in Normandy encompassed only a few decades.[35] Alienating both the seigneurs of Bellême and the Norman duke, the reason for their problems could have been their complex Angevin-Manceau connexions at a time when these regions were in conflict with Normandy. Although Robert fitz Erneis Taisson died at Hastings, the Taisson family make no certain appearance in Domesday Book, but they held English land shortly after 1086.[36] The fitz Giroies made a notional appearance with their kinsman Hugh de Grandmesnil, and at least one of their tenants, William Gulafre, can be found in the Suffolk portion of Domesday Book as a tenant of Robert Malet.[37] But the one man surnamed *angevinus* or *andegavensis* in Domesday Book was a certain Guy, who held land of Eustace de Boulogne in eastern England.[38] It appears from Domesday that Guy had an *avunculus* (maternal uncle) called Osmond, which has led to the very reasonable assumption that

33 K. S. B. Keats-Rohan, 'Poppa "of Bayeux" and her family', *The American Genealogist* 72 (1997), 187–204, also translated as 'Poppa "de Bayeux" et sa famille', forthcoming in *Onomastique et Parenté* II, ed. C. Settipani and K. S. B. Keats-Rohan.

34 L. Musset, 'Actes inédits du XIe siècle. IV Deux nouvelles chartes normandes de l'abbaye de Bourgueil. V. Autour des origines de Saint-Étienne de Fontenay', *Bulletin de la Sociéte des antiquaires de Normandie* 57 (1961–2), 5–41.

35 J.-M. Maillefer, 'Une famille aristocratique aux confins de la Normandie: Les Géré au XIe siècle', *Cahiers des Annales de Normandie* 17 (1985), 175–206.

36 J.-M. Bouvris, *Annales de Normandie* 41 (1991). Ralph Taisson occurs several times in *Pipe Roll 31 Henry I*, 11, 30, 34, 89, 121, 155; the brothers Philip and William Taisson occur ibid., 154.

37 *DB Suffolk* 6.10–11; 14; 25; 65–66; 138–141; 206; 271; 293.

38 *DB Essex* 1.3, 20.30–31; 72–3, *DB Norfolk* 1.1, 5.1, 8.31.

Osmond was either English or Norman, and hence that Guy was a tenant imposed upon Eustace by the king.[39] Nevertheless, such is not necessarily the case, since an Osinmundus, *nepos* of Conon, is found among the witnesses to a charter for La Chapelle given by Eustace II in 1100.[40] Eustace's brother Godfrey was duke of Lorraine, a region that had produced a countess of Anjou in the early eleventh century, and which could well have thereby attracted a handful of Angevin migrants, one of whom subsequently went to England.

Walter *burgundiensis* was a tenant of Gotshelm de Claville in Devon.[41] Gotshelm and his brother Walter could have originated at a Claville in either the département of Seine-Maritime or that of Calvados. The former possibility is perhaps the more likely, but the latter might well be suggested by the fact that later evidence locates a Bourguignon family in the diocese of Saint-Lô in the Cotentin, at Le Mesnil-Guénelon. The family occurs in the cartulary of Montebourg at the end of a century wherein the abbey's benefactors had been the de Reviers family and the successors and tenants of the Nigels of the Cotentin.[42] A Burgundian connexion with this region in the mid-eleventh century concerned the usurpation of L'Isle-Marie, in the canton of Saint-Mère-Eglise, from Nigel of the Cotentin by Guy the Burgundian, son of the count of Nevers.[43] William *Pictaviensis*, a Devonshire tenant of Ralph de Pomerai, is doubtless to be identified with the man of that name who was *fidejussor* for grants to Saint-Etienne de Caen made by Serlo de Lingrèves in the 1080s.[44] The sort of circumstance that gave the younger Roger de Montgomery the appellation *pictaviensis* as the result of his marriage to Almodis of La Marche does not seem to apply to this William le Poitevin, nor to the Roger le Poitevin who can be identified in the Yorkshire Domesday.[45] These men seem to have been naturalized Normans whose soubriquets might well conceal ultimate Poitevin ancestry. The marriage of William Longsword's sister to William of Aquitaine is well-known, as is the subsequent recruitment of monks from Poitou to assist with the reform of the abbey of Jumièges in Normandy. Poitevin monks were sent to Normandy, and may well have been accompanied by laymen who settled there.[46] It is conceivable that such a scenario might account for the appearance in the early eleventh century of two powerful families, the Gifards and their vassals the Malets, whose surname

39 J. H. Round, 'The manor of Colne Engaine', *Transaction of the Essex Archaeological Society*, n.s. 8 (1903), 187–91; for Osmund consult references in the previous note.

40 Miraeus et Foppens, ed., *Opera diplomatica et historica*, 4 vols (Louvain and Brussels, 1723–48), ii, pp. 1311–12, no. clxxii.

41 *DB Devon* 25.(1); 3–4, identified by Exon, fol. 388a–b.

42 Paris BN lat. 10087, pp. 110–11, nos. 290–1.

43 *Les actes de Guillaume le Conquérant et de la Reine Mathilde pour les abbayes caennaises*, ed. L. Musset (Caen, 1967), pp. 128–9, no. 21.

44 *DB Devon* 34.27–8, identified by Exon, fol. 339a; Musset, *Actes caennaises*, 76, 121, nos. 7 and 18. A Hugh *Pictavensis* held of Henry de Pomeroy in 1166 (*Red Book of the Exchequer*, ed. H. Hall, 3 vols (Rolls Series, 1896, p. 260).

45 *DB Yorkshire* 9W99, identified by his donations to St Clement's, York (*VCH Yorks* ii, 165). A tenant of Ilbert de Lacy, a Robert *Pictavensis* held 3 knights' fees of Henry de Lacy in 1166 (*RBE* 422).

46 *The Gesta Normannorum Ducum of William of Jumièges, Orderic Vitalis, and Robert of Torigny*, ed. E. M. C. van Houts (2 vols, Oxford 1992–5), i, 80, 86; cf. Fauroux, *Recueil*, no. 14 *bis*.

possibly means 'malletier', 'the messenger'. The surnames Giffard and Malet are both found in Poitou, and indeed elsewhere. The Giffards became especially well-integrated into Norman society through their marriage into the family of the Osberns of Bolbec, kinsmen of the duchess Gunnor. The second Walter Giffard was subsequently described, apparently, by the chronicler Geoffrey Gaimar as 'Walter the Poitevin of Barbastro', a reference to the 'crusade' against the Moors of Barbastro in 1064 in which Normans are known to have taken part.[47] The description of him as 'the Poitevin' remains mysterious.

The significance of territorial descriptors for those who bore them has now been lost but must then have been very real. They bear evidence to facts that were studiously preserved in the active memory of what in many cases was, or became, a hereditary surname. Whether they refer to a migrant ancestor, or to the more transient connexion of a Norman ancestor with another region, is usually impossible to establish. Sometimes, as with *lotharingensis*, the descriptor may refer to the provenance of its bearer; in other cases, such as those of William *Pictavensis*, the reference is probably to the remoter past and has no relevance to the bearer's provenance. One might distinguish such territorial labels as literal and literary descriptors. It is normally assumed that *brito* and *flandrensis* are literal descriptors, and that in view of the prominent role played by Bretons and Flemings (*sic*) at Hastings their frequent occurrence among Domesday landholders is unsurprising. Of the two, the Bretons are the larger group, as remains true if one includes also those who are identified other than by territorial descriptors. This really is unsurprising, in view of the well-attested Breton involvement at Hastings, the importance then and later of their leaders, William's kinsmen Counts Alan and Brien, and the strong continental links between Bretons and leading Normans such as Robert de Mortain, Hugh d'Avranches and Odo de Bayeux. In the case of *brito* the relationship of descriptor to provenance is generally well supported by distinctive onomastic patterns, and by a wealth of continental documentary evidence. The importance of this group has long been acknowledged, and I have myself recently published a full account of the Breton role in the colonization of England.[48]

The Flemings, by contrast, have been the victims of misunderstandings, false assumptions and simple neglect.[49] Misidentification of the French toponyms of post-Conquest England is common, and often arises out of English unfamiliarity with continental documents, but anyone can be mislead by apparent equivalence.

---

[47] Geoffrey Gaimar, *The Anglo-Norman Metrical Chronicle of Geoffrey Gaimar*, ed. T. Wright, Caxton Soc., 9 (1850), lines 6077–6110.

[48] K. S. B. Keats-Rohan, 'Les Bretons et la politique de la colonisation d'Angleterre (c.1042–1135)', *Mémoires de la Société d'Histoire et d'Archéologie de Bretagne* 73 (1996), 181–215, where full references to the primary and secondary sources will be found. A shorter version follows the present chapter below.

[49] R. H. George, 'The contributions of Flanders to the Conquest of England 1065–1086', *Revue belge de Philologie et d'Histoire* 5 (1926), 81–99, and Johan Verberckmoes, 'Flemish Tenants-in-Chief in Domesday England', idem (1988), 725–756 are the only items available on this question, and both represent a missed opportunity to determine what was meant by *flandrensis* in any context connected with the conquest and colonization of England. Both unquestioningly accept that the presence of *flandrenses* in Domesday Book means that they were present on Hastings' field.

Félix Brassart, for example, wrote a fine history of Douai a century ago in which he identified Walter castellan of Douai with the Domesday tenant-in-chief Walter de Douai, also known as Walscin and as Walter *Flandrensis*.[50] Nevertheless, his companion volume of *preuves* shows beyond all doubt that the Domesday Walter cannot be identified with the castellan. The castellan was driven out of office in the late 1080s, had no issue by his wife Ermengarde and eventually became a monk of Saint-Eloi in the early twelfth century.[51] The English Walter, by contrast, was twice married, firstly to an Englishwoman, and had at least two sons.[52] Brassart's *preuves* and the various chronicles of the Cambrésis leave no doubt that Walter formed part of an extended *parentèle* of the region, traceable from the tenth century onward, which included both Walter the castellan and our Walter of Douai, but they were certainly distinct.

Detailed comparisons of the onomastic evidence of individual Domesday fiefs – i.e. a tenant-in-chief and his tenants – with similar onomastic patterns occurring in Continental families can prove very fruitful. Walter of Douai and a group of persons described in Domesday Book as *flandrensis* – Walter, Walter brother of Seiher, Hugh, and Winemar – provide a good example. Onomastic evidence from the continent, contained in both charters and chronicles, from the diocese of Cambrai clearly indicates that these men originated in the county of Lens in Artois. Domesday's Walter of Douai probably was related to the castellan Walter, though distinct from another relative, Walter de Douai, ancestor of the seigneurs of Montigny-en-Ostrevant. The castellan Walter of Douai, son of Hugh d'Oisi of Douai, was the grandson and heir of Walter castellan of Cambrai (d.1045). This Walter was the son of Walter of Lens, castellan of Cambrai (d.1011); Walter of Lens, who also had a son called Seiher, was the brother of Seiher of Lens and the son of another Walter.[53] There were numerous connexions between these tenants-in-chief – the first three of whom were probably closely related – who held land from each other and from Countess Judith.[54] Countess

50 F. Brassart, *Histoire du château et de la châtellenie de Douai depuis le Xe siècle jusqu'en 1798*, 3 vols (1877–87), i, pp. 49ff, esp. 88–90.

51 Brassart, *Douai*, ii, nos. xii, xxiv.

52 *The Great Chartulary of Glastonbury*, ed. Dom A. Watkin, Somerset Record Society vols 59, 63–4 (1944, 1948, 1949–50), i, no. 172, pp. 126–8, which refers to Walter's English wife Eadgythe widow of Hemming and is attested by his wife Emma. Two other charters refer to Walter's son Geoffrey de Douai and his son Robert, the son of Emma (*Two Chartularies of the Priory of St Peter at Bath*, ed. W. Hunt, Som. Rec. Soc. 7 (1893), nos. 35–6, pp. 38–40).

53 *Chronicon cameracense et atrebatense, sive historia utriusque ecclesiæ . . . conscripta a Balderico Noviomensi*, PL cxlix, cols 119–122, and idem, *Ex historia Cameracensi*, cols 182–194.

54 *DB Bedfordshire* 32, 33, 34, 36, 37, *DB Northamptonshire* 39, 40, 48, 49, 56.54–7. Farrer plausibly suggested that Walter brother of Seiher was uncle to Walter (*HKF* i, 60), who in turn is likely to have been the brother of Hugh. Cf. Brassart, *Douai*, ii, no. xii, given by Walter castellan of Douai in 1076 and mentioning a Walter de Douai son of Ursion (seigneur of Montigny-en-Ostrevant), Sohier de Lohes, two men named Ulric – the name of the Domesday Walter of Douai's steward (*Chart. Glastonbury* i, 228) – and the brother of one of them, Dodin, homonym of a tenant of Countess Judith (*DB Northants.* 56.52). *Cartulaire-Chronique du prieuré de Saint-Georges de Hesdin*, ed. R. Fossier (Paris, 1988), no. 50 (calendared in RRAN i 360), was attested by

Judith, niece of William the Conqueror and of Eustace de Boulogne, was the daughter of Lambert count of Lens.[55] Drogo de La Beuvrière was from Artois, while Sigar and Gunfrid de Chocques were Artesians whose families counted among the *optimates et principes* close to the counts of Flanders.[56] From regions fairly recently annexed to the county of Flanders came Walter de Douai and Guy de Raimbeaucourt (arr. Douai, Nord); Godfrey de Cambrai came from the county of Hainault, which though a separate county was closely associated with Flanders. The sole certain Fleming of the core county of Flanders represented among the landholders of 1086 was Gilbert de Ghent, a kinsman of Queen Matilda and son-in-law of the Norman Hugh de Montfort.[57] At that date the Artesian Fleming Frederick, brother of Gerbod the Fleming, was dead and Gerbod himself had long since returned home; Humphrey de Saint-Bertin of Saint-Omer, who must have been associated with these two, had forfeit his land by 1086, when it was held by William de Warenne and Drogo de La Beuvrière.[58] As with Gerbod, Gilbert's earliest certain appearance in England does not predate the arrival of Matilda of Flanders in 1068. The evidence is a lot less conclusive than for *brito*, but it seems that when Domesday uses *flandrensis* as a literal descriptor it refers to Artesian Flemings. It never certainly applies to Flemish Flemings, or to Picards, a group possibly covered by the term *franci* in the chronicles.[59] This analysis clearly indicates the importance of Eustace de Boulogne as an ally of William of Normandy in 1066. It was he who brought to the battle a contingent of Picards and of Flemings from his own county of Lens in Artois. If any noble subjects of Flemish Flanders fought at the battle (with Gilbert de Gand and Gerbod being the most likely candidates), they did so under Eustace's command. Although Eustace and William quarrelled soon after Hastings and were not reconciled before 1074 at the earliest, the Artesian Flemings and Picards made an unmistakeable impression on the settlement recorded in Domesday Book.[60] Countess Judith, niece to

Wenemar of Lens, as was *Actes des comtes de Flandre (1071–1128)*, ed. F. Vercauteren (Brussels, 1938), no. 18 (1094–5), no. 23 (1093) being attested by Walter de Lens; *Chartes et documents de l'abbaye de Saint-Pierre de Mont-Blandin à Gand*, ed. A. van Lokeren (Gand, 1868), nos. 132–3 (1056) were attested by Robert and Wenemar de Lens.

55 Another of her tenants was Fulcher *parisiacensis*, DB *Bedfordshire* 53.17–18, *Northamptonshire* 56.40. He was possibly a cleric associated with Judith's paternal uncle Godfrey de Boulogne, bishop of Paris 1061–1095.

56 Cf. Ernest Warlop, *The Flemish Nobility Before 1300*, 4 vols (Kortrijk, 1975), ii, 389. Sigar is well-evidenced in contemporary documents, often occurring with his brother Arnulf (Miræus and Foppens, i, 515; Vercauteren, *Actes . . . de Flandre*, no. 70). His relationship to Gunfrid is unclear, but was probably through marriage. Drogo's principal holdings appear in DB *Yorkshire* 15. The descent of the Chocques, or Chokes, fief yields some peculiarly interesting questions; see under Gunfrid de Cioches in the prosopography below.

57 On Gilbert see Warlop, *Flemish Nobility*, iii, pp. 587–93; R. Sherman, 'The Continental Origins of the Ghent family of Lincolnshire', *Nottingham Medieval Studies* 22 (1978), 23–35.

58 Cf. Lewis, above note 14; DB *Norfolk* 8 passim, DB *Suffolk* 26.4, 9 and 48.1.

59 Cf. Renée Doehaerd, '*Flandrenses* dans la *Passio Karoli* de Galbert de Bruges (1127)', *Revue Belge de Philologie et d'Histoire* 71 (1993), 841–9.

60 Cf. Tanner, 'Boulogne', 275.

both the king and to Eustace, doubtless played a significant role in this process. It certainly seems to be the case that the Artesian/Picard settlement was more cohesive and close-knit than either the Bretons or the much larger group of Normans.[61]

In general, it seems that the use of a literary descriptor is an invitation to consider the personal history of its bearer. There are insuperable difficulties in trying to establish what lies behind such labels. In the two eleventh-century examples where we have information that an ancestor was an immigrant – Ralph Taisson *angevinus* and Baldric *teutonicus* – there is no subsequent attempt to memorialize the fact in the names of their descendants. The rapid and highly successful integration of these men and their descendants into Norman society may be sufficient explanation for this. In cases where the labels did become hereditary it may be that an attempt was being made to distinguish between the bearer's provenance and the region from which his ancestors came. This idea can be tested by examining other types of hereditary naming patterns.

A good example is provided by Juhel of Totnes. Established in the important English borough of Totnes in Devon by 1069 at the latest, he was exiled shortly after 1087, with the accession of William II, and his fief was forfeited.[62] By 1113 at the latest he was back and was granted by Henry I a new fief at Barnstaple in Devon, which had been forfeited in 1095 by Robert de Mowbray, nephew and heir of the 1086 holder Geoffrey bishop of Coutances. Juhel had previously founded a priory at Totnes and his foundation charter revealed that the name of his father had been Alfred.[63] Round was the first to notice the significance of this naming pattern, reinforced by the name Alfred being given to Juhel's son Alfred.[64] As he correctly pointed out, the names clearly indicate a Breton origin for the family. But what does origin mean in this context? Juhel's ancestors were obviously Breton, but does this have to mean that he himself came to England from Brittany? Breton names were not uncommon in Normandy during the eleventh century, reflecting in part the earlier occupation of much of western Normandy by the Bretons. More recent migration doubtless occurred throughout the eleventh century, some of it connected with the marriage of Richard II and Judith of Rennes.[65] At a time of conflict between the Breton Alan III and Robert

---

61 Domesday Book quite probably preserves important information about this group which can be used to investigate problems relating to their continental holdings. For a probable example see in the prosopography under Gunfrid de Cioches (Chocques), who probably occurs in Artesian documents as Gunfrid de Houdain.

62 *DB Devon* 17. An account of Judhael's career and a detailed examination of his Domesday estates are found in J. B. Williams, 'Judhael of Totnes: the life and times of a post-Conquest baron', *Anglo-Norman Studies* 16 (1994), 271–289. In all documents apart from Domesday, Judhael's name is written as Juhel. The forms *Juhael* and *Juthael* occur in the Breton Vannetais; I am grateful to M. Gwenaël Le Duc for this information.

63 A facsimile of the foundation charter was published in vol. 2 of H. R. Watkin, *The History of Totnes Priory and Medieval Town* (Torquay, 1917).

64 See J. H. Round, *Feudal England* (1895, rept London, 1964), 255–6.

65 There are two possible indications of this. One is the occurence in a mid eleventh-century charter for Saint-Georges de Boscherville (Fauroux, no. 197) of a Hoel, Ingulf father of Hoel, Alfred presbyter and Alan son of Norman Peignart. Another is the occurrence of men named Brien, Clodoan, Cadiou and Hervé (of which the last three

of Normandy in 1029, a certain Alfred the Giant was found fighting the Bretons with Niel I, vicomte of the Cotentin.[66] Whether Alfred was a Breton quisling, or a Normanized Breton migrant, we cannot say. But Orderic Vitalis subsequently alleged that Juhel son of Alfred the Giant was one of the companions of Robert Curthose in his rebellion against the Conqueror in 1079. We also know from Orderic that after his defeat, Robert and his companions travelled northwards, in the direction of Flanders.[67] We know from a monastic source that Juhel of Totnes made what, outside of the clue provided by Orderic, would seem a most surprising marriage, to the sister of Germond of Picquigny, whose Picard fief lay on the route Robert Curthose took after Gerberoy in 1079.[68] Despite certain difficulties, it is possible, even likely, therefore, that Juhel of Totnes was Orderic's Juhel son of Alfred the Giant of Lièvres, Calvados, cant. Surrain.[69] Furthermore, one of Judhael's most important tenants was a man named Nigel, whose own sons were named Alfred and Juhel.[70] The Nigels of the Cotentin were disgraced by their part in the revolt of the west in 1047, and had spent some decades in eclipse. There is no certain evidence that a member of the seigneurial family was holding land in Domesday England, but unambiguous evidence that some of their tenants were. These men, most notably Rogo *camerarius* of Niel III, are found holding land in the south-west of England of Baldwin de Meulles, sheriff of Devon, and Robert of Mortain. Several Devonshire fiefs were granted to Richard de Réviers, a descendant of Nigel I of the Cotentin, by Henry I in the early twelfth century. A close friend of his son and successor was Alfred son of Judhael of Totnes.[71] Juhel of Totnes cannot be accepted as a Breton pure and simple, any more than we can fail to acknowledge his Breton ancestry. The later receives some confirmation from the fact of the relationship between Alfred the Giant's family and the de Milly family, evidenced by documents of the abbeys of Caen.[72] Rivallon de Milly, a tenant of the count of Mortain who had probably married Alfred's daughter, was a benefactor of the Breton abbey of Redon in the mid-eleventh century.[73]

The repeated use of ancestral names in Juhel's family may have had significance beyond what was customary in name-giving. It could be the first-name equivalent of the same sort of memorial tradition involved in the use of literary territorial descriptors. Such memorial traditions were not inward-looking.

---

may have Germanic origins) among the Domesday tenants of Robert de Tosny of Stafford (*DB Staffordshire* 11.9–10; 15–16; 46; 57–61; 64; 66).

[66] Fauroux, *Recueil*, nos. 33, 69, 99, 195; William of Jumièges, ed. van Houts, ii, 58–9.

[67] Ord. Vit., iii, 100–102.

[68] *Hermani monachi De Miraculis S. Mariae Laudunensis de gestis venerabilis Bartholomei episcopi et S. Norberti Libri Tres*, in *PL*, clvi, cols 983–4.

[69] Fauroux, *Recueil*, 195.

[70] *DB Devon* 17.4–5; 10; 82; *Mon. Ang.* v, 197–8, attested by Alfred fitz Nigel (facsimile in H. R. Watkin, *The History of Totnes Priory and Medieval Town* (Torquay, 1917), vol. 2); *Charters of the Redvers Family and the Earldom of Devon 1090–1217*, ed. R. Bearman, Devon and Cornwall Record Society n.s. 37 (Exeter, 1994), pp. 76–8, Juhel fitz Nigel.

[71] *Gesta Stephani*, ed. K. R. Potter (Oxford, 1976), 36.

[72] *Actes caennnaises*, pp. 86, 131.

[73] *Cartulaire de l'abbaye de Redon*, ed. Aurélien de Courson (Paris, 1863), no. 326.

Documents from eleventh-century Normandy show clearly the extent to which both 'Frankish' and 'Breton' personal names were a normal part of Norman onomastic, attesting both to the process of assimilation between Normans, Franks and Bretons in an earlier period, and the continuing vigour of migration to Normandy, certainly on the part of the Bretons.[74] Doubtless this is true also of the literary territorial descriptor. The information of Orderic Vitalis's *Ecclesiastical History*, and the evidence of Domesday territorial appellations, combines to reinforce the impression that Norman society had proved attractive to numerous migrants from diverse regions over the period of nearly two centuries in which it had existed. Nonetheless, Scandinavian names remained common in Norman families, and Orderic sketched the Norman character in a way that leaves no doubt that they had developed a very distinct notion of their identity, something confirmed by their history. Even so, the degree to which the evidence suggests that their society was much penetrated by inter-regional migration can only reinforce one's suspicions at the emergence of documents and chronicles, in the late eleventh and twelfth centuries, which lay strident and unconvincing emphasis upon the Normanness, the 'Danishness' of several prominent Norman families.[75] The Domesday landholders were overwhelmingly Norman, but the late eleventh-century Norman society they represent was itself multi-national in character. The discovery of migration to Normandy after 911 is not new – what is important is the revelation that the Normans themselves chose to attest to the phenomenon in administrative writing such as the Domesday satellites, at the very time when their self-awareness as a nation becomes prominent in their historical writing. The whole phenomenon becomes more striking still when the results from Domesday Book are contrasted with the much larger-scale migration to England of non-Norman nationals during the century that followed. Fresh Norman migration to England was negligible by comparison.

---

[74] Cf. Fauroux, *Recueil*, nos. 35, 197, 218 (Alan), 94 (Alberic, father of Osmund), 193 (Lambert, father of Torstin), for just a few of many examples. Such examples should invite caution in assessing onomastic patterns. Cf. the case of Robert fitz Wimarc, discussed above p. 19.

[75] See, for example, R. H. C. Davis, *The Normans and Their Myth* (London, 1976); G. A. Loud, 'The "Gens Normannorum" – Myth or Reality?', *Anglo-Norman Studies* 4 (1981), 104–116; C. Potts, '*Atque unum ex diversis gentibus populum effecit*: Historical Tradition and the Norman Identity', *Anglo-Norman Studies* 18 (1996), 139–177; D. Bates, 'Normandy and England after 1066', *EHR* 104 (1989), 853–61; G. A. Loud, 'How "Norman" was the Norman Conquest of Sicily?', *Nottingham Medieval Studies* 25 (1981); K. S. B. Keats-Rohan, 'William I and the Breton contingent in the non-Norman conquest 1060–1087', *Anglo-Norman Studies* 13 (1991), 157–82; A. V. Murray, 'How Norman was the Principality of Antioch?', in K. S. B. Keats-Rohan, ed., *Family Trees and the Roots of Politics: The Prosopography of Britain and France from the Tenth to the Twelfth Century* (Woodbridge, 1997).

Chapter 3

THE BRETONS AND THE NORMAN CONQUEST

The migration of noble Bretons to England cannot be documented before the eleventh century.[1] The story starts, as is well known, with *Radulfus Anglicus* – Ralph the Englishmen – who was the first known lord of Gaël in the county of Rennes. He is interesting for several reasons. He occurs in a Breton document of c.1031 as *Radulfus Anglicus*, during the reign of the Danish Cnut's son Hardecanute in England.[2] His cognomen *Anglicus* means that he was part English by birth. The *Anglo-Saxon Chronicle* says as much, and we know from Domesday Book of other members of his family bearing English names such as Godwin and Ailsi.[3] Perhaps his unknown father had gone first to Normandy with Judith of Rennes, who married Richard II of Normandy, and then a few years later to England with Richard's sister Emma, wife of Aethelred II and then of Cnut. Although before 1042 Ralph the Englishman was still associated with Brittany, thereafter the evidence concerning him shows him to have been an influential figure in the circle of Emma's son King Edward the Confessor, for whom he acted as *staller* or constable.[4] The land that Ralph held was located in eastern England, in the counties of Essex, Suffolk, and Norfolk, as well as Lincolnshire.[5]

---

[1] A longer version of this chapter was published as K. S. B. Keats-Rohan, 'Le rôle des Bretons dans la politique de colonisation normande de l'Angleterre', *Mémoires de la Sociéte d'Histoire et d'Archéologie de Bretagne* 74 (1996). See also M. Jones, 'Notes sur quelques familles bretonnes en Angleterre, après la conquête normande', *MSHAB* 58 (1981), 73–97; H. Guillotel, 'Une famille bretonne aux services du Conquérant: les Baderon', in *Droit privé et institutions régionales: Etudes historiques offertes à Jean Yver* (1976), 361–6. See also the monumental studies of *The Honour of Richmond* by Charles Clay in vols 4 and 5 of *Early Yorkshire Charters* (Yorshire Record Society, 1936–8); W. R. Powell, 'The Essex Fees of the Honour of Richmond', *Transactions of the Essex Archaeological Society*, Third Series I, part 3 (1964), 179–189, G. Minois, 'Les possessions bretonnes dans le comté d'Essex du XIe au XVe siècle', *Annales de Bretagne* 85 (1978), 525–542.

[2] Dom. H. Morice, *Mémoire pour servir de preuves à l'histoire ecclésiastique et civile de Bretagne*, vol. i (Paris, 1742), col. 371, charter of Alan III for Saint-Georges de Rennes, attested by his mother (d.1034). Ralph I and II de Gaël were known as *Anglicus* in Breton charters until at least 1075.

[3] *The Anglo-Saxon Chronicle: a revised edition*, ed. D. Whitelock, D. C. Douglas, S. L. Tucker (London, 1961), *sub anno* 1075. *Domesday Book* i, fols 127b, 131a, 262a, *Goduinus auunculus Radulfi comitis*, 322a, 324a, 350b *Alsio nepoti comitis Radulfi*. Cf. Ann Williams, *The English and the Norman Conquest* (Woodbridge, 1995), 61–2.

[4] K. Mack, 'The stallers: administrative innovation in the reign of Edward the Confessor', *Journal of Medieval History* 12 (1986), 123–134. Ralph attested four of Edward the Confessor's charters, P. H. Sawyer, *Anglo-Saxon Charters: an annotated list and bibliography* (Royal Historical Society, London, 1968), nos. 1028, 1031, 1033, 1034.

[5] The lands of Ralph I and/or Ralph II occur in *Domesday Book*, i, fols 121b, 337b, 347b, 348b, ii, fols 119a–135a, 144a, 147a, 148a, 149a, 157a–158b, 177a, 194a (*In Eccles tenebat Radulfus comes tempore regis Edwardi .iiii. carucatas, postea tenuit*

44

This was the region controlled in 1066, when Harold son of Godwin became king, by Harold's brother Gyrth. Ralph supported William when he invaded in October of that year, and was rewarded by the grant of the earldom of East Anglia. Within a short time, probably by 1069, he was succeeded by his son Ralph of Gaël.[6] This second Ralph married a Breton and had probably lived in Brittany until 1066. In that year he joined the Norman expedition, in the company of Nigel of the Cotentin, who had been an exile in Brittany for some time between 1047 and 1050.[7] Within a few years of his father's death, in 1075, Ralph of Gaël quarrelled with the king and went into revolt. An earlier revolt in the north of England had been savagely repressed by the Conqueror in 1070. So serious had the situation been that it entailed a radical change of policy by the Normans. William had previously sought to emphasize the legitimacy of his rule, which in reality was based upon nothing more than the right of conquest, by pre-serving Old English institutions such as the earldoms which grouped several shires, or counties, under one man. Now he broke up the earldoms and reduced them to single-county units. This meant that Ralph of Gaël now found his earldom reduced from the whole of East Anglia to the single county of Norfolk. Eventually he joined his grievances with those of two other dispossessed earls, Wal-theof and his own brother-in-law the Norman Roger of Hereford.[8] The revolt was swiftly defeated, and the destruction of Ralph and his English family rapidly fol-lowed. He himself escaped to Brittany, which he was later to leave again with his son to meet his death in the Holy Land during the First Crusade.[9] Many of his

---

Radulfus comes filius eius), 202b, 217b, 218b, 229b, 265a, 293a, 297b, 347, 347b, 348b, 409b, 410a, 431a, 446a–b, 448b.

6   *Domesday* ii, 410a, *Radulfus stalra in uadimonio de uice comite Toli, ut hundreto audiuit dire sed non uidit breues neque liberatorem, et tenebat die qua rex Edwardus fuit mortuus, et postea Radulfus filius eius.*

7   Suggested by Wace, *Roman du Rou de Wace*, ed. A. Holden, Société des anciens textes français, 3 vols (Paris, 1970–73), lines 8493–4, *Joste la compaigne Neel chevalcha Roal de Gael.* Wace speaks of Ralph de Gaël, which is always used in English docu-ments to describe the younger Ralph and not his father the Staller. Ralph son of Ralph *Englesi* attested a charter with Count Eudo of Brittany c.1050 (*Cartulaire de l'abbaye de Saint-Aubin d'Angers*, ed. B. de Broussillon (Angers, 1896), Doc. hist. sur l'Anjou, vols 1–3, ii, no. 677). Ralph II had a brother Harduin (*Domesday* i, fols 291b, 338a, *Harduinus frater Radulfi comitis*). Their father was a benefactor of Saint-Riquier (Hariulf, *Chronicon Centulense, Chronique de l'Abbaye de Saint-Riquier*, ed. F. Lot, 240–1), and of St Benet of Holme (Norfolk) (*Domesday* ii, fols 157b, 244a). Cf. *Com-plete Peerage* ix, 568ff, H. Guillotel, 'Montfort-Gaël', forthcoming.

8   C. P. Lewis, 'The early earls of Anglo-Norman England', *Anglo-Norman Studies* 13 (1991), 207–224.

9   'Archbishop Lanfranc, who was entrusted with the governance of England in the king's absence, saw Roger as a youth led astray by the counsel of "evil men". There is no doubt whom the archbishop had in mind. In a letter to the king in Normandy, he annon-ces that he is proceeding against "Ralph the Traitor" and his army of "oath-breakers" and a subsequent missive refers to the "Breton dung" of which the kingdom has been purged.' Williams, *The English*, 60–61. *The Letters of Lanfranc, Archbishop of Canter-bury*, ed. H. Clover and M. Gibson (Oxford, 1979), pp. 33, 34, 35. With Ralph fell his uncle Godwin and and his brother Harduin, *Domesday* ii, fols 131, 262, 90–90b, 223v, 224, 225–225v, 245, 291v, 353–353v, 338, 382v–383, 389.

men, the tenants who held land from him in England, were executed or, if they were lucky, suffered forfeiture and exile. We know little of the individual fates of his men, but the pages relating to East Anglia in Domesday Book are littered with their names. They included Eudo fitz Clamarhoc, who was associated with Conan II of Brittany and Ralph the Large of Gahard in Brittany c.1050.[10] A Wihenoc, also dead in 1086, is probably to be identified with Eudo's companion in Brittany, Wihenoc son of Goranton of Vitré.[11] Others were Walter of Dol, and Lisoius of Moutiers-en-la-Guerche, whose previous contribution to the repression of the revolt in the north was singled out for commendation by the chronicler Orderic Vitalis.[12]

It is certain that at least one of Ralph of Gaël's men had not joined his revolt, and consequently lived to profit from his loyalty. This was the man known as Alfred of Lincoln, who in 1086 claimed land from Count Alan that he himself had held in the time of Earl Ralph.[13] Such a formula is unique in Domesday Book and must mean that Alfred had been Ralph's man. The reason for Alfred's decision not to join Ralph in 1075 was perhaps connected to his marriage with one of the daughters of William Malet, who died fighting the rebel Englishman Hereward the Wake in 1071.[14] William was, like Ralph the Englishman, part English by birth. He held lands in Lincolnshire that had been held by his family before 1066. After the battle of Hastings, at which he played an important part, he was rewarded with the grant of extensive lands centred upon Suffolk. His career was

---

10 *Domesday* i, fols 111a, 138b, 235b, 279a; A. de La Borderie, *Recueil des actes des ducs et princes de Bretagne (XIe, XIe, XIIIe siècles)*, extrait du Bulletin de la Société historique et archéologique d'Ille-et-Vilaine (Rennes, 1888), 31–2, no. xii. Note also the death or forfeiture before 1085 of Ewen le Breton, who had been a tenant of Earl William of Hereford and probably thereafter of William's son Earl Roger, co-rebel of Ralph de Gaël (*Domesday* i, fols 184c–d, *Hanc terram tenuit Ewen brito de Willelmo comite*).

11 *Domesday* ii, fols 116b, 161b, 230a, 231a, 231b, 232a, 234b, 275a, 276a. Cf. M. Brand'Honneur, 'Les Goranton-Hervé de Vitré', *MSHAB* lxx (1993).

12 Walter of Dol, *Domesday* ii, 151a–b, 299b, 321b, 322a, 371a, 377a, 407b, Lisoius, ibid. fols 239b, 240a, 279b, 403a; cf. also Judicael falconer of Earl Ralph II, ibid. fol. 125b (*Iudikello. . .quia erat ancipitrarius comitis [Radulfi]*), Hervé and Bodin de Ver (fol. 242a), of whom Hervé appears to have still held a house in Norfolk in 1086 (fol. 117a), and William son of Gorhan (fol. 441a), all of whose land was held in 1086 by Hervé *Bituricensis*, as appears from a suit brought by Ely abbey shortly before 1075, printed in *Inquisitio Comitatus Cantabrigiensis*, ed. N. Hamilton (1876), 193. On Lisois see Ord. Vit. ii, 230.

13 *Domesday* i, fol. 377d: *Vnam carucatam terrae in Quedhaueringe clamat Aluredus de Lincolia super Alainum comitem. Homines de Hoilant concordant eidem Alueredo, quia et antecessoris sui fuit, et ipse saisitus inde fuit tempore Radulfi comitis.* Alfred held an important tenancy-in-chief in Lincolnshire (ibid. fols 357d–358d). His most important tenant was another Breton, Glai, ancestor of the de Rothwell family; another tenant was Jocelyn son of Lambert, himself a Lincolnshire tenant in chief and father of Gilbert, founder of the order of Sempringham (ibid. fol. 359a–c).

14 The relationship between Alfred and the Malets emerges from data too complex to be rehearsed here. I have published a full study of the difficult but important problems involved in 'Domesday Book and the Malets: patrimony and private histories of public lives', *Nottingham Medieval Studies* 41 (1997), 13–53.

blighted by his failure to defend York against the Danes in 1069, but he remained a loyal servant of King William. Neither his son Robert Malet nor his son-in-law Alfred of Lincoln benefitted much from the redistribution of Ralph of Gaël's lands, but in 1086 Alfred of Lincoln was a wealthy man whose family was to rise steadily during the following decades. There are tantalizing indications in unreliable sources that Ralph of Gaël's father was distantly related to the rebel English noble Hereward the Wake. Most of Hereward's lands in Lincolnshire were given to Oger the Breton, who probably married Hereward's daughter, as David Roffe has shown.[15] This lady subsequently married a Norman, Hugh de Envermeu, predecessor of the later Wake lords of the barony of Bourne.

At least one other man of Breton origin held land in England, in Cambridgeshire, before 1066, and that was an obscure figure called Judicael the Huntsman.[16] Many more arrived in 1066 and thereafter. Count Alan the Red owed his honorific comital title to his birth as one of the elder sons of Count Eudo, brother of Alan III of Brittany.[17] A second cousin of William of Normandy, he entered the latter's service shortly before 1066, acquiring small properties in Rouen and elsewhere.[18] There is no doubt that Alan – and probably also his younger brother Brien – fought at Hastings or that Alan, the most senior of the Bretons to go to England that year, led the Breton contingent that played an important role in the battle. The earliest grant to Alan of land in the newly conquered country undoubtedly lay in Cambridgeshire, where he was the dominant tenant-in-chief long before 1086.[19] Significant tenancies-in-chief were also held there by his men Aubrey de Ver, a Breton, and Harduin de *Scalariis*, whose place of origin cannot be identified with certainty. Harduin's Breton origins are indirectly evidenced by the name of his relative Brien de Scalariis, a tenant of Count Alan in Cambridgeshire whose son Everard was a tenant of Aubri de Ver.[20] Harduin's tenant in Cambridgeshire Ralph de *Felgeres* might have originated in Fougères, though he was distinct from Ralph seigneur of Fougères, a landholder in Buckinghamshire, Devon, Suffolk and Norfolk.[21] Harduin may have been named from the hamlet of Les Echelles, in Saint-Germain-en-Coglès, arr. Fougères, cant. Saint-Brice-en-Coglès. Other tenants were Robert of Moutiers-en-la-Guerche and Hervé de Ispania, who was perhaps named from a fief in Champeaux, near

15 D. Roffe, 'Hereward "the Wake" and the barony of Bourne: a reassessment of a Fenland legend', *Lincolnshire History and Archaeology* 29 (1994), 7–10.

16 *Domesday* i, fols 189a, 193a; all the land of *Judichel venatoris Edwardi regis* was held by Robert, count of Mortain in 1086.

17 Cf. Dom A. Wilmart, 'Alain le Roux et Alain le Noir', *Annales de Bretagne* 38 (1929), 576–595; P. Jeulin, 'Aperçus sur le comté de Richmond en Angleterre . . . 1066/71–1398', *Annales de Bretagne* 42 (1935), 265–302.

18 D. Bates, *Normandy Before 1066* (London/New York, 1982), 83.

19 *Domesday* i, fols 193d–195b. Here his Breton tenants were Brien and Harduin de *Scalariis*, Ralph *Brito*, Wigan de *Mara* (perhaps from Dol; cf. Morice, *Preuves* i, 463), Enisant Musard, Geoffrey (de Burgh), Odo *camerarius*, Wihomarch *dapifer*, Rainald *Brito* and his brother Hubert.

20 *Domesday* i, fol. 194c; *Inquisitio Comitatus Cantabrigiensis*, 28–9; *Domesday* i, fol. 199c.

21 *Inquisitio Comit. Cant.*, 99; William de *Felgeres* of Buckinghamshire, *Domesday* i, 151a, was probably a Norman.

Rennes. Alan also acquired land in Norfolk and Suffolk, where the dominant landholders before 1075 were the part-English Ralph the Constable and his son Ralph of Gaël. By the time of Domesday Book Count Alan and his men had acquired the bulk of Ralph's lands, but the lands formerly held by Alan's brother Brien were then in the hands of the king's half-brother Robert of Mortain.[22]

Brien's story is rather mysterious, but there is no reason to believe that he was associated in the revolt of 1075. He was active in the south-west, at Exeter, fending off a raid by the sons of the former king Harold Godwinsson in 1069.[23] He does not afterwards appear in English documents and we may conclude, with André Wilmart, that he was injured at that time and retired to Brittany to live on for many years as an invalid.[24] Brien was later alleged by his nephew Alan earl of Richmond to have been earl of Cornwall, but there is no direct evidence to support this view. As predecessor of Robert of Mortain, who held almost the whole of Cornwall in 1086, this might be a natural interpretation of Brien's role in Cornwall by his nephew, but there is no firm evidence that Brien had held land there.[25] On the other hand, the occurrence of a handful of men holding only a few manors in Cornwall and nowhere else of Robert of Mortain may suggest that they were enfeoffed by Robert's predecessor, who was probably Count Brien.[26]

Alan's family certainly did not need their descendants to embellish their ancestors' past. Already a rich man by 1070, Alan was to profit enormously from the suppression of the northern revolts in 1070. The county of Yorkshire was divided into four castellanies, entrusted to four of the most reliable warriors in the Conqueror's service. One of them was Count Alan, whose family were ever afterwards associated with, and indeed named from, the *caput* of their new honour at Richmond, in the north of the county.[27] By 1086 Alan had few rivals for dominance in a north-east orientated region of England extending from north

---

22 *Domesday* ii, fols 143a–151a, 292b–298a, where his tenants were Phanceon (some of whose land had been held previously by Walter fitz Bloc), Ribald, Enisan Musard, Wihomarch, Geoffrey (de Burgh), Wigan de *Mara*, Hervé (ancestor of the de Sutton family), Mainard, Halenald (i.e. Alan), Haimo de *Valenis* (perhaps Valaine, or Saint-Christophe-de-Valaines, Ille-et-Vilaine), Ermengot (Ermeniot), and Norman. Norman's manor (fol. 294b) had once been held by Earl Ralph, so Norman may have been the Norman Brito of the *Inquisitio Eliensis* (194, note 21) Alan was also a major land-holder in Lincolnshire, ibid., i, fols 347a–348b, where his tenants were Robert de Moutiers, Landri, ancester of the important Landri family, Picot de Lacelles, Wimund, Eudo, ancestor of the de Mumby family, Stephen, Geoffrey Tornai and Cadiou. Many of the manors listed in these folia had been held by Earl Ralph.

23 Orderic Vitalis, ii, 224, 228.

24 Wilmart, 'Alain le Roux', note 18, 583.

25 No surviving evidence directly associates Count Brien with Cornwall, apart from his nephew's statement that he granted land *pro redempcione anime comitis Brienti auunculi mei de cuius hereditate terram Cornubiae possideo* (*The Cartulary of St Michael's Mount*, ed. P. L. Hull, Devon and Cornwall Record Society, new series v (Exeter, 1962), 6, no. 5). It is clear from Exon Domesday that the man called Brien recorded as a tenant of the count of Mortain in Cornwall by Domesday Book was active at the time the latter was compiled in 1086.

26 *Domesday* i, fols 124a–b (Brien), 125a (Wihumarc), 125a–b (Blohin or Bloicus Brito).

27 Ibid. fols 309a–313b. His Breton tenants here were Enisan Musard, Bodin (Alan's half-brother), Hervé, Landri, Wihomarch (his steward), Odo (his chamberlain), Ribald

Yorkshire almost to London.[28] Alan was a frequent companion of the king on his itineraries, being found in his company in Normandy and Maine as well as England.[29] He unhesitatingly transferred the loyalty he had shown William I to the latter's successor William II in 1087, and played an important part in the subsequent trial of the rebel bishop of Durham, William of Saint Calais, in 1088.[30] He died in 1093 on the morrow of a rather interesting, but impenetrably obscure adventure. We know from letters of Archbishop Anselm that Alan had a sexual relationship with Gunhilda, daughter of King Harold, in the months before his death, probably in August of 1093.[31] Because Gunhilda had taken refuge at the abbey of Wilton Anselm viewed her unflinchingly as a nun, although she seems not to have shared this view. She intended to marry Alan, who apparently died before they were legally united. Probably the intended union was underpinned by important political calculations. At any rate we know from Anselm's second letter that after Alan the Red's death Gunhilda formed a sexual union with Alan's brother and successor Alan the Black. Anselm makes it clear that in this case also marriage was intended. Interestingly, he expresses no concern whatever about the fact that Gunhilda's partners were brothers. The second Alan may have sought to continue the policy by himself marrying his brother's fiancée. The circumstances of these unions cannot now be recovered, but may have had to do with William II's difficulties with King Malcolm of Scotland. According to Anselm's biographer, Eadmer, Malcolm viewed Alan the Red more favourably than he did William II. The king was viewed as a possible spouse for Malcolm's daughter Edith – subsequently the wife of his brother Henry I – according to contemporary sources. Such a union would have linked the blood of the Old English royal house to that of the new Norman kings. But Eadmer alleged that Malcolm intended her for Alan the Red.[32] Given that William's suit was of a woman related to the Old

(another half-brother), Geoffrey (ancestor of the de Burgh family), Robert de Moutiers, and one *Doneuuald*, perhaps the Breton name Donoald.

28 Apart from Cambridgeshire, Suffolk, Norfolk, Lincolnshire, Yorkshire and Dorset (see notes 20, 22, 27, 54), Alan held land in Essex, Hampshire, Hertfordshire, Northamptonshire, and Nottinghamshire (*Domesday* ii, fols 35a–b, i, fols 44b, 136d–137b, 224b, 282c). His tenants in Essex and Hertfordshire were Alberic de Ver, Harduin de *Scalariis*, Hervé d'Espinay.

29 *RRAN* i, nos. 90, 96, 105, 111, 114, 121, 125, 133, 135, 143, 149, 150, 182, 206, 220, 226, 227, 228, 233, 234, 301, 320, 325, 328, 432, 454, 455.

30 Symeon of Durham, *Symonis Monachi Opera Omnia*, ed. T. Arnold (Rolls Series, London, 1885), vol. i, 170–195.

31 F. S. Schmitt, ed., *Sancti Anselmi Opera Omnia* (Edinburgh, 1949), nos. 168–9. These letters help to fix the date of Alan Rufus's death, discussed in K. S. B. Keats-Rohan, 'The Bretons and Normans of England 1066–1154', *Nottingham Medieval Studies* 36 (1992), 77. Ian W. Walker, *Harold The Last Anglo-Saxon King* (1998), 128–9, has suggested that Alan's union with Gunhilda was intended to confirm him in possession of the lands of his principal English predecessor, *Edeua pulcra*, whom he identifes with Harold's first wife Edith Swan-neck. The suggestion is unconvincing because Alan had held the lands in question from very early on in the Conquest settlement; there is no evidence of any threat to his tenure of them at this time.

32 The question was discussed with great sensitivity by R. W. Southern, *Saint Anselm: A Portrait in a Landscape* (Cambridge, 1990), 260–264, who believes Malcolm's project of marrying his daughter to Count Alan posed a considerable threat to his enemy

English royal line represented by Edward the Confessor, the union at that time of Count Alan and a daughter of King Harold is striking, because it destroyed Malcolm's plan to marry his very high-born daughter to a mere vassal of the English king. By entering a union with the daughter of a king officially stigmatized as a usurper since c.1070, Alan the Red was underlining his loyalty to William II.[33] In fact, he and his brother need not have gone to so much trouble. The king was not the marrying kind, and was still unmarried at the time of his death in 1100. There is no other indication that either brother married – they certainly left no known descendants. But they had a strong sense of family nonetheless. At least three of their bastard brothers held lands from Alan the Red in 1086. All three – two of whom had the same mother – founded important baronial families in England.[34] It was later recorded that Alan gave the manor of Sibton in Suffolk to his wetnurse Orwen, subsequently the wife of his man Mainard, who was almost certainly Mainard former chamberlain to Ralph of Gaël.[35]

The bulk of Ralph's forfeited lands in East Anglia was given to Count Alan, lord of Richmond in Yorkshire, or to his men. Count Alan was one of the wealthiest, most privileged and most trusted of the new English tenants-in-chief. In common with four other members of a select group of the wealthiest men he had

William II, on account of Alan's power in a region (Yorkshire) close to Scotland. William's rejection of the girl, upon seeing her wearing a veil in the monastery of Wilton, led to an immediate breach with Malcolm, who angrily removed her from the abbey and took her back to Scotland, saying that he had intended her as the wife of Count Alan, rather than as a nun. We can well believe that Malcolm was angered by William's rejection of his daughter, and the political alliance that would have attended their marriage. Nevertheless, apart from this incident we have no idea why William and Malcolm quarrelled in 1093, and no reason whatever to believe Count Alan to have been part of the problem. Malcolm's reactions at Wilton were later recounted by his daughter to Anselm at a time when she was trying to prove she had never been a nun so that she could marry William's brother Henry. Her account stresses Malcolm's anger upon seeing her veil, which he tore from her head and destroyed, *contestans se comiti Alano me potius in uxorem, quam in contubernium sanctimonialium praedestinasse* (reported in Eadmer, *Historia Novorum in Anglia*, ed. M. Rule (Rolls Series, London, 1884), 121ff). Since Edith was removed from Wilton in August 1093, probably after the death of Alan the Red on 4 August, Malcolm's remark is more likely to have been a jibe at the liaison between Alan and Gunhilda, who had also once worn the veil at Wilton, than a serious statement of his intentions for his daughter. The question was also discussed in Eleanor Searle, 'Women and the legitimisation of succession at the Norman Conquest', *Anglo-Norman Studies* 3 (1981), who sees Alan and Malcolm as allies against William II.

[33] For the development of the ideology of Harold as a usurper and oath-breaker see Lewis, 'The early earls', note 8, and M. Chibnall, *Anglo-Norman England 1066–1166* (Oxford, 1986), 20–21.

[34] Ribald, Bodin and Bardulf, *Domesday* i, fols 309a–312b, ii, fols 144a–149b. See Clay, *Early Yorkshire Charters*, vol. 5, 196–201, 297–306, 316–20. Clay notes that Bodin and Bardulf were apparently sons of the same mother.

[35] P. Brown, ed., *Sibton Abbey Cartularies III* (Suffolk Records Society 9, Woodbridge, 1987), 34, no. 516. This *narratio* tells how Mainard, the count's chamberlain, requested Orwen's hand with her manor of Sibton for his long service. He held the manor in Domesday Book (ii, fol. 293a, *Mainardus*); cf. *Inquisitio Eliensis*, 194, *Mainardus miles Radulfi comitis tenet terra unius carrucae in Campesore de dominio.*

enfeoffed a large number of men in his new lands, the vast majority of whom were Bretons. A few of these were also tenants-in-chief in their own right. In the areas where his lands lay one finds other Breton tenants-in-chief whose lands were not specifically associated in any way with Alan's. This may indicate that they had been recruited by the Normans independently of Count Alan, or that, like Alfred of Lincoln, they were former men of Ralph of Gaël. The latter group may have included Oger the Breton and almost certainly included Tihel of Héllean, a Breton landholder in Suffolk and Norfolk.[36] It perhaps also included Guy de Craon, who on later evidence for the names of his descendants we can identify with Guy son of Robert de Vitré and Bertha de Craon.[37] One of those who acquired lands forfeited in 1075, Guy married a Norman, Isabella daughter of Hugh fitz Baldric, who lost his lands for failing to support William II in 1087.[38] His descendants established the barony of Freiston in Lincolnshire, and from an early date were closely associated with the tenants of Alfred of Lincoln and his Malet relatives.

There is very little direct evidence as to which Bretons fought at Hastings in 1066, though accounts of the battle make it clear that they were numerous. The relatively abundant evidence on the career of Alan the Red puts his participation beyond reasonable doubt. It is confirmed by the evidence of Wace's *Roman de Rou* on the Conqueror's companions. Although Wace actually spoke of Alan

---

36 *Domesday* i, fols 364c–d, 228a, 293d (*Ogerus filius Vngemar, Ogerii Britonis*); ibid. ii, fols 81b–82a, 24a, 261b, 143b, 427b–428a, 373b (*Tihelli Brittonis, Tihellus de Herion, Tihellus de Helion*); cf. *Domesday* i, fol. 117a *uxor Hervei de Helion*. J. H. Round, 'Helion of Helion's Bumpstead', *Transactions of the Essex Archaeological Society*, identified Tihel's toponym with La Croix-Helléan, arr. Pontivy, cant. Josselin, Morbihan. Cf. also (1) Eudo fils de Spirewic, a Domesday tenant-in-chief in Lincolnshire, Norfolk and Suffolk, whose descendants held the honour of Tattershall (Lincs.) (*Domesday* i, fols 359d–360a, ii, fols 245b–246b, 434a–435a); his tenants were Berold, Geoffroi, Rivold, Morvan, Guillaume, Jarnagot; (2) Hervé *Bituricensis*, possibly a Breton though his toponym usually means de Berry (ibid. ii, fols 440b–444a); his tenants were Euen, Rainald, and Peter de *Paludel*, or *Palwelle* (cf. La Vielle-Paluelle, arr. Saint-James, Manche). I am suggesting here that several Bretons came to England under the aegis of Ralph II de Gaël. They held lands directly from the king, so in refusing to support Raoul in 1075 they were acknowledging a higher duty than any owed to Ralph.

37 Morice, *Preuves*, i, 413. Cf. *Domesday* i, fol. 377d: *Wido de Credone tenet in Draitone iiii bovatas terre et in Bichere hundred x bovatas de terre Adestan Godranesune. Hoc calumniatur comes Alanus et Alger homo eius dedit vadimonium baronibus regis ad confirmandum per judicium aut per bellum quod ipse Adestan de his xiiii bovatis saisitus non fuit tempore regis Edwardi. Econtra homo Widonis Alestan de Frantone dedit suum vadimonium ad convincendum quod inde saisitus erat cum saca et soca et Wido inde fuit saisitus ex tempore Radulfi stalre usque nunc et modo tenet*, especially interesting for its specific location of Guy's tenure in the time of Ralph the Staller, father of Ralph de Gaël, i.e. 1066–1069. Guy is a good example of a younger son who made his fortune in England. His elder brother André was later to acquire land in Cornwall upon his marriage to a daughter of Robert of Mortain.

38 *Domesday* i, fols 356c, 48b. The Thorney abbey *Liber Vita* (BL Additional MS 40,000, fol. 3r) provides the name of Guy's wife. His tenant Waldin was probably Waldin Brito, also a tenant-in-chief in Lincolnshire (*Domesday* i, fol. 365b–c).

Fergant, he clearly meant Alan the Red.[39] A long neglected source, Wace was recently re-examined by Elisabeth van Houts, who showed that his evidence must be taken seriously.[40] Nonetheless, Wace's text is of limited use in understanding Breton participation in the conquest. Wace counted the seigneurs of Dinan, Vitré and Fougères among the Conqueror's companions in 1066.[41] Although it was later alleged that the Dinan family acquired land in Devonshire from the Conqueror, it is more likely that the first grant to them occurred after 1100.[42] Robert de Vitré might have fought at Hastings, but he did not settle in England. His son André de Vitré, son-in-law of Robert count of Mortain, held land from Robert in Cornwall in 1086.[43] It is unlikely that André visited England, though his younger son Gervaise later settled on these Cornish lands.[44] The identity of the seigneur of Fougères is a more delicate question, especially since Wace clearly considered him to be a figure of some importance. It seems unlikely to have been Ralph I, since he was still an adolescent in 1066. His father Main, who died shortly before 1066, was associated with the Normans as early as 1050, though no Breton or English evidence associates him with England. Possibly it was Main's bastard brother Alfred who fought at Hastings. By 1086 Ralph of Fougères was married to Avice de Clare, daughter of another of the king's kinsmen, Richard, son of Count Gilbert de Brionne, and granddaughter of yet another, Walter Giffard.[45] Despite their associations with Normans and their possession of lands in England, there is no evidence that any seigneur of Fougères set foot in England until 1124, when Ralph's son Main II went there on a tour of inspection. Unfortunately he soon afterwards died there, at Winchester where the king had recently made new grants to his family, and was buried in the church of

[39] Wace, *Roman de Rou*, line 8689, *Alains Fergant, quens de Bretaigne*, lines 8695–9 *Bien se combat Alains Ferganz, chevalier fu proz e vaillanz, les Bretons vait od sei menant, des Engleis fait damage grant.* Cf. Gaimar, *Lestorie des Engles*, lines 5315–5334, *Li cuens Alains de Bretaine/ Bien ferit od sa cumpaigne;/ Cil i ferit cume barum./ Mult le firent bien Bretun;/ Od le rei vint en ceste terre/ Pur lui aider de sa guerre . . . Le rei servit mult e amat;/ Et il tres bien lui gueredonat:/ Richemunt li donat en Nort,/ bon chaster e bel e fort;/ En plusurs lius en Engleterre/ Li reis li donat de sa terre./ Lunges la tint, e puis finit,/ A Saint Edmund fud enfuit.*

[40] E. van Houts, 'Wace as historian', in Keats-Rohan, ed., *Family Trees and the Roots of Politics*.

[41] Wace, *Roman*, lines 8363–4, *Grant proés en out cil de Felgieres, qui de Bretaigne out genz mult fieres*, line 6370, *et li sire i vint de Dinan*, line 8575, *Cil de Vitrié e d'Urinié*.

[42] M. Jones, *La famille de Dinan en Angleterre au Moyen Age* (Dinan, 1987); K. S. B. Keats-Rohan, 'Wigan the Marshal and other Bretons in Orderic Vitalis's *Ecclesiastical History*', *Journal of Medieval Studies* 29 (1994), 33, 36–7.

[43] *Domesday* i, fol. 125a. The marriage of André de Vitré and a daughter of Robert of Mortain was noted by Robert of Torigny in his *Chronicle*, ed. R. Howlett, *Chronicles of the Reigns of Stephen, Henri II and Richard I* (4 vols, Rolls Series, London, 1889), iv, 200.

[44] His sons Robert and Gervaise occur in *Pipe Roll 31 Henry I*, 159, 161.

[45] E. M. C. van Houts, ed., *The Gesta Normannorum Ducum of Guillaume of Jumièges, Orderic Vitalis, and Robert of Torigny* (2 vols, Oxford, 1993–5), ii, 270, where Robert of Torigny names their sons as Fransualo, Henry and Robert Gifard.

Saint Swithun.[46] This was an intended voyage that had perforce turned into a migration.

There were perhaps four principal elements that forged the shape of the Breton fiefs by 1086: the recruitment of further Bretons after 1066, the withdrawal of Count Brien in or after 1069, the revolt of the North in 1070, and the revolt of Ralph of Gaël in 1075. Between about 1075 and 1086 there emerges a group of Bretons for whom there is no previous English documentation and no reference in the *Roman de Rou*. One was Geoffrey de La Guerche, a tenant-in-chief, predominantly in the Midland counties of Leicestershire and Warwickshire.[47] There seems no reason to suppose he was at Hastings: certainly there is no subsequent evidence attaching Geoffrey to Count Alan's lordship, although one of Alan's tenants, Robert de Moutiers-en-la-Guerche, came from the same region as Geoffrey.[48] Many of the newcomers granted land by William the Conqueror sought to legitimize their hold on their new possessions by marrying representatives of the English families to whom they had previously belonged. Geoffrey de La Guerche did this in marrying Ælfgifu daughter of his predecessor Leofric.[49] Such a move indicates the firm intention to settle in England, but Geoffrey is one of the rare examples of men who eventually decided to give up their English lands and return home. At any rate, he left England in the company of King William II in 1093 and never returned.[50] His lands were redistributed among the Norman favourites of William I and his brother Henry I. These new masters were associated with the descendants of another, minor, Breton tenant-in-chief, Maino the Breton, who held lands centred upon Buckinghamshire.[51]

---

[46] *Rouleau Mortuaire du B. Vital abbé de Savigni*, edn phototypique par L. Delisle (Paris, 1909), titre no. 182, St Peter and St Swithun, Winchester: *Orate et pro speciali fundatore ecclesie nostre. domino Fransgwalone. et domino Gileberto Ricardi filio, avunculi eius* (brother of Avice de Bienfaite).

[47] *Domesday* i, fols 227c, 235c–235d, 291a, 326a, 369b–369c. Since Geoffrey's land in Warwickshire and Leicestershire had previously been held by a single predecessor they are likely to have been granted during the earliest years of the Conquest, perhaps by 1069. See R. Fleming, *Kings and Lords in Conquest England* (Cambridge, 1991), 139, 152, 176.

[48] Robert was perhaps a brother of Lisoius. He held land from Alan in Lincolnshire and Nottinghamshire (*Domesday* i, fols 347a, 282c). For an unknown reason Robert's fee was held after 1086 by Alan's half-brother Ribald (*Early Yorkshire Charters* ii, 158) but was subsequently restored by Alan III the Black to Robert's grandson Robert, son of Geoffroi (*Early Yorkshire Charters* iv, 27–28, no. 26). Robert's origins were given as Moutiers, near La Guerche, by A. S. Ellis in *Yorkshire Archaeological Journal* 5 (1877–8), 323.

[49] Ælfgifu was the daughter of Geoffrey's English predecessor Leofwin of Newnham; she occurs in a grant he made to Saint-Nicholas d'Angers of land in Warwickshire, *Monasticon Anglicanum*, vi (2), 996.

[50] It seems likely that Geoffrey was the son of Sylvester de La Guerche. William and Geoffrey sons of Sylvester occur in a Breton document given after 1093 and attested by a Hervé son of Geoffrey (Morice, *Preuves*, col. 529). Hervé and Stephen de La Guerche made a grant to Marmoutier's priory at Béré for their brother Warin, a monk (Arch. dépt. d'Ille-et-Vilaine IF 330, Béré no. 9). See J.-C. Meuret, 'Familles seigneuriales au confins Anjou-Bretagne', *MSHAB*, 70 (1993), 94.

[51] *Domesday* i, fols 151d–152b. There is no firm indication as to Maino's origin. He was

The short-lived Midland sphere of influence of Geoffrey de La Guerche can appear to form a sort of wedge between the Breton settlement in the north and east so clearly dominated by Count Alan, and the Breton settlements of the south and west. It is possible, though the evidence is exiguous, that the south-west was the centre of an important lordship held by Alan's brother Brien. Count Alan himself held insignificant territories in the south-west.[52] Possibly at some time before 1069 to 1070 the brothers each held land in the western and eastern extremities of England, with Alan's influence preponderant in the east and Brien's in the west. Had Brien's lands in the west not been regranted some time after 1069 to Robert of Mortain, the sharp division seen in Domesday Book between the lands of Count Alan, in the north and east, and those of lesser Bretons, in the south and west, might never have come into being.[53]

In Norfolk and Suffolk the lands forfeited by Walter of Dol in 1075 were regranted to Hugh of Avranches, earl of Chester.[54] This immensely powerful and aristocratic Norman was one of the great marcher lords given responsibility on the dangerous Welsh Marches. As heir to the Norman *vicomté* of Avranches he had extensive contacts with the Bretons of north-east Brittany, especially the men of the seigneurs of Dol-Combour.[55] It is certainly striking that after the revolt of 1075, which brought down Roger of Hereford as well as Ralph of Gaël, the castelry of Monmouth was given to the Breton Wihenoc of Laboussac near Dol. Despite its relatively lowly social status, this appointment made Wihenoc's

identified as Maino Brito from Ercé-en-Lamée (Ille-et-Vilaine) by C. Bouvet, 'A propos des premiers seigneurs de Châteaubriant aux Xe et XIIe siècles', *Bulletin de la sociétée archéologique et historique de Nantes et de Loire-Atlantique* 122 (1986), 77–105. Maino was allied by a second or third marriage with the king's kinsman William de Warenne, *Rotuli de Dominabus*, ed. J. H. Round (Pipe Roll Society, London 1913), 38–9.

[52] Alan had a single manor in Dorset (*Domesday* i, fol. 79a). He probably held it by grant from Queen Matilda, who had held the land of Britric son of Algar, Alan's English predecessor, before her death.

[53] Although there is no direct evidence in Domesday Book that Brien had held the land in Cornwall held by Robert of Mortain in 1086, it does record that part of Robert's small properties in Suffolk had been previously held by Brien, *Domesday* ii, fol. 291a.

[54] *Domesday* ii, 152a–b, 299b, 322a, 377a, 407b. The re-grant of land held by former men of Ralph of Gaël had an effect on honorial geography in Norfolk and Suffolk: see C. P. Lewis, 'The formation of the Honor of Chester 1066–1100', *Journal of the Chester Archaeological Society* 71 (1991), 51.

[55] On Hugh see Keats-Rohan, 'The prosopography of post-Conquest England: four case studies', *Medieval Prosopography* 14.1 (1993), 23–30; L. Musset, 'Actes Inédits du XIe Siècle, I: Les plus anciennes Chartes du Prieuré de Saint-Gabriel (Calvados),' *Bulletin de la Société des Antiquaires de Normandie* 52 (1952–54), 124–29; L. Musset, 'Les origines et le patrimoine de l'abbaye de Saint-Sever', in *La Normandie bénédictine au temps du Guillaume le Conquérant*, ed. J. Daoust (Lille, 1967), pp. 357–367. The unfavourable portrait of this great and able man given by Orderic Vitalis, ii, 260–262, should be compared with the more positive picture of Geffrei Gaimar's *Lestorie des Engles*, op. cit. note 15, lines 5860–74, 6015–6043. Hugh's chaplain Odo son of Ernulf of Dol became a monk of Saint-Evroul (Orderic, iii, 118, 226). The Buckinghamshire tenant-in-chief Jocelyn Brito was Hugh's tenant in the manor of Slapton, Northamptonshire (*Domesday* i, fol. 224d).

family the most senior of the Breton families to be resident in the English south-west by 1086.

By 1086 Wihenoc and his brother Baderon were monks of Saint-Florent-de-Saumur at Monmouth, their position and lands as castellans of Monmouth then being held by Baderon's son William.[56] The importance of their castelry, in the hostile Welsh marches, was considerable. Like Alan the Red's installation at Richmond in Yorkshire, it indicates the level of trust which the Conqueror could place in his Breton allies. Such appointments otherwise went only to the very greatest of the Norman barons, such as Robert of Mortain, Hugh of Avranches, Roger of Montgomery and William of Warenne, all of them, like Alan, related to the king. Wihenoc and Baderon were vassals of the seigneurs of Dol-Combour in north-east Brittany, a region early exposed to links with the Normans, especially those in the diocese of Avranches, in the region of Mont-Saint-Michel.[57] Their former lord, Rivallon of Dol, had been an ally of William in his abortive campaign against Conan II of Brittany in 1064.[58] Men from these regions, as well as the Norman dioceses of Coutances and Bayeux, dominated the settlement of south-west England. Several of Robert of Mortain's tenants had been recruited from north-east Brittany; they included his son-in-law André de Vitré, a Brien, a Wihomarc and an Alfred the Breton, and perhaps also his extremely wealthy butler, another Alfred. Among the tenants-in-chief in 1086 were Theobald fitz Berner, who attested charters of Main I of Fougères in the 1040s and 1050s, and Main's son Ralph I of Fougères.[59] The seigneur of Fougères was the most senior though not the most wealthy of south-western Breton tenants-in-chief, but he was an absent landlord. Robert of Mortain, the dominant landholder in the south-west, may have been regarded by the south-western Bretons as their overall

---

56 J. G. Evans, ed., *The Text of the Book of Llan Dâv reproduced from the Gwysaney Manuscript* (Old Welsh Texts iv, Oxford, 1893, reprinted Aberystwyth, 1980), 277–8, relates that Monmouth castle was built in the early Norman period and half of it given to three Normans. After the revolt of Earl Roger in 1075, the castle was given to Wihenoc. Wihenoc built Monmouth priory as a cell of Saint-Florent-de-Saumur sometime afterward and became a monk there. The castle then passed to Ranulf de Colville, a Norman, before going to William son of Wihenoc's brother Baderon by 1086. Cf. Guillotel, 'Les Baderon' (note 1 above). English historians have supposed that Bretons were appointed in this region because the Breton language bore some similarity to Welsh. However, there is no evidence to suggest that men from north-east Brittany spoke Breton at this date.

57 *Domesday* i, fol. 180d, where William holds the castle and Saint-Florent-de-Saumur holds the castle church; William's other holdings occur on fols 179d, 185c–d, 167a. His tenants were Solomon, Geoffrey and Gerard.

58 William de Poitiers, *Gesta Guillelmi*, 106–112. Often seen by English and Norman historians as a defeat for Conan, this campaign was in fact a victory for Conan, as revealed in a fresh examination of the campaign in Keats-Rohan, 'The Breton Contingent in the non-Norman Conquest', 163–167.

59 *Domesday* i, fols 115b–d. Cf. Fauroux, *Recueil*, nos. 157, 160–162. Ralph de Fougères held a few manors in Devon, Surrey, Buckinghamshire, Norfolk and Suffolk in 1086 (*Domesday* i, fols 113d, 36c, 151c, ii, fols 432b, 263a); he founded a priory at Ipplepen, Devon, for Saint-Pierre-de-Rillé (G. Oliver, *Monasticon Diocesis Exoniensis*, Exeter/London 1886, 300). He always occurs as *de Felgeres*, instead of *de Filgeriis* as is normal in Breton documents.

leader. Even so, like the seigneurs of Fougères and Vitré, Robert was mostly an absent landlord. His constant attendance upon the king and the wide extent of his lands must have meant that he rarely stayed long in any one place.

Examining the post-Conquest settlement of England from the perspective of Domesday Book enables us to make some sharp distinctions. A Breton noble had settled in England long before 1066. He supported the Norman invasion of that year and saw his wealth and power increase as a result. Succeeded within a few years by his son, this original Breton settlement was soon destroyed by the consequences of a failed rebellion. A tiny number of men associated with this lordship had not joined the revolt and maintained their place, sometimes enhancing it, in the new order. The most senior of the Bretons to arrive in 1066 was Count Alan the Red, who was a blood relation of William of Normandy. His status probably meant that he was the overall leader of the Breton contingent, which fought as one at Hastings. The subsequent grant of land to individual Bretons indicates clear divisions between them. The land of Count Alan and the men associated with him was concentrated in the north and east of England, though they held isolated manors in more southerly and westerly areas. There was a thin band of midland and south midland Breton tenancies-in-chief, apparently dominated by Geoffrey de La Guerche. Finally, there was a third group concentrated in the south and west, of whom the most senior resident Breton in 1086 was William fitz Baderon of Laboussac. The divisions between these groups are, for all the odd exceptions, so marked as to require some attempt at explanation. Probably the midland and south-western groups were composed of men who came to England after 1066, but before 1075. This would account for the relatively small size of their holdings. The location of their holdings would have been partly conditioned by availability, and probably also by the location of the holdings of Robert of Mortain and Hugh of Avranches, who doubtless helped to recruit many of the newcomers. Robert's possible role in recruiting additional Bretons to England should not be under-estimated. The failure of the seigneur of Fougères to set foot in England, at least after the initial conquest, is perhaps explained by the dominance of Robert of Mortain in the areas where the Fougères fiefs lay. Some of Ralph de Fougères's Breton lands were subject to the Norman count of Mortain and there was considerable interaction between his tenants and those of Mortain.[60] The lands lay in a region which the Bretons thought of as Breton, but which the Normans had mastered since at least 1030. Residual bad feeling in the area was eventually overcome by the diplomatic brilliance displayed by Robert after his apppointment as count of Mortain c.1050. There may have been some hostility between the northern and southern groups of English Bretons, perhaps related to the Norman invasion of Brittany in 1064. They were never well integrated before 1154, and in 1138 they each declared for rival candidates in the English civil war that began in that year. Nonetheless, each of the groups of Bretons who settled in England after 1066 remained conspicuously loyal to the English king until 1138.

The period 1066 to 1086 is the most important to understand if we are to

---

[60] Cf. *Documents inédits sur l'histoire de Bretagne. Chartes du prieuré de la saint-Trinité Fougères*, ed. A. de La Borderie and Delabigne Villeneuve, *Bullétin archéologique de l'association bretonne* (1851), 191–2, 195–6. Fauroux, *Recueil*, nos. 160–162.

identify the Continental places of origin of English landholders after 1066. Three quarters of those named in Domesday Book in 1086 left descendants traceable in 1166. Of the 25% who did not, some died without heirs and some suffered forfeiture for failing to support either William II or Henry I at their accessions. A tiny minority simply returned home. With the exception of Geoffrey de La Guerche, the Breton settlements endured, surviving each change of ruler with their loyalty to the English crown intact. There is little doubt that loyalty to the Crown was easier for the Breton tenants-in-chief, because if they still retained land abroad it was in Brittany and not in Normandy, which was separated from the English crown between 1087 and 1106. Norman political problems were no concern of the Bretons, who could continue to profit in England from their unflinching loyalty to the English kings. Many of the Bretons who settled in England seem not to have maintained enduring links with their families in Brittany, a fact that would also increase their need to remain loyal to the English king. André de Vitré, an important lord in eastern Brittany, probably never set foot in Cornwall, but his younger son Gervaise took over the lands and lived in England. For all that Breton settlers were vastly outnumbered by Normans, they played important parts in the new order by reason of the dominance in potential trouble-spots such as the North of England and the Welsh Marches. William II appears not to have brought new Bretons to England, but the prominence of the northern Bretons, led successively by the three brothers Alan the Red, Alan the Black and Stephen, was especially marked in this reign, dominated as it was by fighting relating to Wales, Scotland and Maine. Many of William II's recruits came from the county of Maine, conquered by the Normans in 1063 and still in the feeble hands of Robert Curthose till 1095.[61]

When William the Conqueror died he left Normandy to his eldest surviving son and designated heir Robert Curthose, who had several times manifested his unsuitability as a ruler. England was left to his younger son William II. The Conqueror's intentions have been much disputed, but whether or not he was distinguishing between inherited and acquired lands, or simply recording his lack of confidence in Robert, no one can have doubted that sooner or later the brothers would fight each other for the whole of their father's possessions. The question soured the accession of William II and would do so again in 1100 when he was succeeded by the youngest brother Henry. After the Conqueror's death Henry had been count of the Cotentin under Robert Curthose. By 1091 he was the quarry of both his brothers, who besieged him at Mont-Saint-Michel. Allowed to leave unharmed, he entered Brittany via Dol, where he acquired numerous Breton friends.[62] Subsequently entering the service of his brother William, with whom he united in enmity against Robert, he was able to seize the throne after William's death in an accident in August 1100. Immediately faced by a revolt in favour of Robert, he nevertheless had established control by 1102, when he exiled some of the most powerful men in the kingdom. Henry preferred diplomacy to the heavier-handed tactics of forfeiture or war, but in the bellicose

---

61 Men such as Patrick de Sourches, Gilbert *Cenomannis*, and Hamelin and Winebald de Ballon; cf. J. H. Round, 'The family of Ballon', *Studies in Peerage and Family History* (London, 1901), 189–98.

62 Orderic Vitalis, iv, 118–20, 148, 164, 220–226, 250.

William of Mortain, to whom he offered his wife's sister in marriage, his diplomacy met a brick wall. Together with Robert Curthose, William engaged the king at Tinchebrai. Both were captured and spent the rest of their long lives in prison. The vast estates of William in England were now divided up into a series of small baronies, each of them headed by a prominent tenant of the former honour. Clearly, William had not had the support of these men. New tenants were settled on these and other lands forfeited by the rebels of 1102 and 1106. It was noted long ago by J. H. Round that a strikingly high proportion of these so-called 'new men', were either from Brittany or from the Cotentin peninsula.[63] Clearly, the friendships made by Henry between 1087 and 1094 primarily account for this particularity, but it also owed something to the links established between Bretons and Normans during the time of Robert of Mortain. The men of the region remained loyal to Henry against their lord William of Mortain, and they would remain loyal to Henry in the teeth of their hatred for William's eventual successor, Henry's nephew Stephen of Blois.

Taking service with the English king in the period c.1042 to 1135 could be a highly profitable affair for a Breton prepared to play by the rules. If like Ralph of Gaël one choose to gain much and to hold out for more, the loss of everything was the surest and swiftest consequence. It was a useful way to settle younger sons, as the lords of Vitré and Dinan found. It could provide extra revenues in the case of absent landlords like the lords of Fougères. It brought enormous wealth and power to the lords of Richmond, and it radically enhanced the position of lesser men such as William fitz Baderon of Monmouth and Alan fitz Flaad of Dol. Accepting lands in England was not equivalent to self-imposed exile, as the example of the absent landlords and the mainly Breton career of Stephen of Richmond show. One could accept lands and then later renounce them and return home, like Count Brien and Geoffrey de La Guerche. All that was demanded in return was unflinching loyalty to the Crown. For a Breton, free of the unattractive complications of divided allegiance frequently faced by Normans in this period, the conditions of service with the Norman kings of England from 1066 to 1135 were as close to ideal as was possible in the mediaeval world. Considerable numbers of them choose to profit from the opportunities.

---

[63] J. H. Round, *Studies in Peerage and Family History* (London, 1901), 124–5.

CONCLUDING REMARKS:
THE CONTINENTAL ORIGINS OF
DOMESDAY BOOK LANDHOLDERS

Determining a place of origin for each of the landholders occurring in Domesday Book is a complex process which requires a firm focus on the onomastics of both personal and place names. Success is by no means guaranteed, even if one can surmount the initial hurdles provided by missing surnames and unlocalizable tenants-in-chief. Even if one can localize a particular tenant-in-chief, or even if the onomastic evidence is free of the complication of ultimate ancestry outside Normandy, there may remain problems such as the common place-name which cannot be identified with precision within a given area. The difficulties notwithstanding, the value for understanding the composition of 'Norman' society in 1086 of putting a concern with region or nation of origin at the centre of an inquiry into Domesday prosopography has been demonstrated in Chapter 2 above, whilst the prosopography given at length below will confirm that value for the understanding of the English settlement and subsequent English tenurial history.

It is not possible in this Introduction to answer fully any of the questions I have posed as relative to Domesday prospography, or to attempt much in the way of analysis of the results I have obtained. Nevertheless, the results of the first full-scale inquiry into the continental origins of post-Conquest English landholders deserve some attention. Those relating specifically to the Normans will be given separate treatment below. Before venturing some summary statistics for continental origins, an important preliminary point needs to be made. No absolute certainty is claimed for any of the results summarized in the Domesday Prosopography. Indeed, the entire programme of research is based upon the idea of uncertainty, expressed as degrees of probability. The most frequently used words in the prosopography are probably, perhaps and possibly.

Tables 1 and 2 summarize the results of the search for 'surnames' and for continental origins. The native English and Welsh are included in both sets of figures. In 1086 2,468 persons or ecclesiastical communities have been identified as landholders in England. Of this total, 361 are ecclesiastics and 99 are women, 76 of them laywomen; 599 are English and 4 Welsh. Among the 361 ecclesiastics are 135 ecclesiastical communities, 87 of which were founded in pre-Conquest England. On the question of 'surnames', one can add to the figures already cited above (Chapter 2) from a smaller sample of 2,172 identifiable persons occurring as landholders in Domesday Book. Of these 629 can be known only by a forename, 186 by a patronym, 27 by other relationship terms, such as *frater*, and 515 use a toponymic surname (of which less than twenty relate to English places and were borne by non-Englishmen). Forty-six were known by household occupational descriptors such as *camerarius, dapifer, pincerna* or *dispensator*, and 252 bore ecclesiastical titles such as *presbiter, episcopus*.

Introduction

Table 1: Analysis of 2,468 persons by region of origin and estate (1086)

361	ecclesiastics (14.7%)
76	laywomen (3.1%)
599	English (24.3%)
4	Welsh
1552	Normans (62.9% of total, 83.2% of 1865 non-natives)
110	Bretons (4.46% of total, 5.9% of 1865 non-natives)
56	Flemings (2.27% of total, 3.0% of 1865 non-natives)
51	Picards (2.07% of total, 2.7% of 1865 non-natives)

Broadly speaking, the settlement achieved by 1086 shows three principal non-English groups identified in the full group of 2476 persons. By far the largest was composed of 1552 Normans. The second group was composed of the Bretons, who number 110 of the total of 1865 non-English persons identified as holding in 1086. The different strands of this settlement were discussed in Chapter 3. The third group falls into two parts, with 56 Flemings, of whom 55 were from Artois, and 51 Picards (discussed in Chapter 2). These figures would be slightly higher if one included persons who held land before but not in 1086.

Table 2: Analysis of 2,172 persons by 'surname' (1086)

629	forename only (28.9%)
186	patronym (8.6%)
27	other relationship terms, e.g. *frater*
515	toponym (23.7%)
30	territorial descriptor, e.g. *brito* (1.3%)
46	occupational descriptors, e.g. *camerarius* (2.1%)
252	ecclesiastical titles, e.g. *presbiter* (11.6%)

These figures can be compared with those yielded by the still incomplete prosopography down to 1166. Of a current total of 9,348 persons, 7,382 are laymen and 653 laywomen; there are 1,235 male ecclesiastics and 77 female ecclesiastics (of whom the majority are actually communities of nuns rather than individuals). Analysis by name confirms the trend towards toponymic surnames, with 4,065 toponyms, 998 patronyms and 69 other relationship terms; 805 persons have no recoverable surname (the majority of them are persons occurring in Domesday Book) and 399 have no forename (the majority of these are churches rather than persons).

Because most of the persons involved in the complete prosopography will be descendants of the people found in Domesday Book we should expect the figures by origin (Table 4) to mirror those already given for Domesday (Table 1). Of 893 non-Normans (a figure confirming the predominance of the Normans amongst the settlers) there are 543 Bretons, 171 Flemings and 123 Picards. In the Domesday table (Table 1), the Bretons account for 5.9% of the newcomers and the Flemings and Picards for 5.7%. By 1166 the Bretons account for 7.43% of the available figures and the Flemings and Picards for only 4%. Clearly, although the

Breton settlement increases in line with expectation (and the known further recruitment under Henry I), the Flemish/Picard settlement atrophied, despite known recruitment by Henry I.

Table 3: Analysis of 9,348 persons by estate (1066–1166)

7382   laymen (78.97%)
 653   laywomen (6.99%)
1235   male ecclesiastics (13.2%)
  77   female ecclesiastics (0.8%)

Table 4: Analysis of 7,285 persons by ancestors' region of origin (1066–1166)

5238   Normans (71.9%)
 543   Bretons (7.43%)
 294   Flemings and Picards (4%)

Table 5: Analysis of 9348 persons by 'surname' (1066–1166)

 805   forename only (8.6%)
 998   patronym (10.67%)
  69   other relationship term (0.7%)
4065   toponym (43.48%)
 177   household descriptors (1.89%)
 551   ecclesiastical titles (5.89%)

Table 6 represents the provenances in each of the five modern *départements* of Normandy of those persons identified as Normans for whom provenance can be stated with the greatest degree of probability.

Table 6a: Sample of Norman provenance by modern département

Calvados	100 (32%)
Eure	61 (19.9%)
Manche	31 (9.56%)
Orne	29 (9.26%)
Seine-Maritime	92 (29.4%)
Total	313

*

The full list of persons summarized in Table 6a is given below in Table 6b. The results are sufficiently striking to warrant a recapitulation and reformulation of some of the earlier themes of this introduction.

The Normans were the descendants of Vikings who had been granted the territories that were to comprise Normandy between 911 and 924. Their rulers survived as territorial princes despite initial hostility from the Franks, most potently expressed in the assassination of William Longsword on the orders of the count of Flanders in 942. During the tenth century the Normans consolidated the work of accommodation and assimilation they must have begun around 911. Research over the last thirty years has shown that a heavy initial Scandinavian colonization was achieved in tandem with an almost complete survival of Carolingian administrative and jurisdictional forms under the centralizing control of the ruler.[1] The result was an exceptionally stable society, contrasting markedly with the instability of neighbouring regions. Early intermarriage with the local Frankish population was a necessity for a colonization consisting predominantly of men. By c.1000 the Normans were French-speaking Christians who had adopted the language and religion of their maternal ascendants, and they frequently bore Frankish names. In the far west, in the Cotentin peninsula, an important pre-911 colony of Bretons was assimilated in the same way, a process that continued throughout the eleventh century with the arrival of fresh Breton migrants.

The territorial principalities were based on often very ancient units with strong regional characteristics. They were not, however, entirely static or self-contained. Border regions, which could be the subject of fierce competition between neighbouring princes, were particularly important as the points of maximum social and cultural interchange between different regional groups. The still unpublished cartulary of the abbey of Mont-Saint-Michel provides priceless insights into these phenomena in north-west France, and it also strongly indicates that the very dark tenth-century histories of Normandy, Brittany and Maine were heavily interdependent.[2] The same is true even if we turn to Normandy's problems with its more easterly neighbours of Chartres and Meulan in the late tenth and early eleventh centuries; the relations between Brittany, Maine and Normandy are central there too.

The internal stability of the principalities depended upon the effective exercise of power by the princes, which was normally most severely compromised during a princely minority. The proliferation of castle-based territorial lordships within the principalities during the tenth and eleventh centuries produced jurisdictions in direct competition with that of the prince, whose authority was seriously undermined when he was too weak to control the process. The phenomenon can be observed in a certain amount of detail for much of the rest of France, but is still little understood. Great turbulence in Brittany throughout the tenth century, and in Maine from about 980 onward, helped to determine which families were successful in achieving coherent and enduring lordships. In Normandy the process was probably connected with assimilation of the native Frankish aristocracy by intermarriage. Such alliances conveyed inheritance rights which helped to shape

---

[1] For much of what follows, see the references cited in the preface, note 21, above.

[2] Cf. K. S. B. Keats-Rohan, 'Ivo fitz Fulcoin, the counts of Maine, the lords of Bellême and the foundation of L'Abbayette', *Journal of Medieval History* 20 (1994), 3–25; idem, 'Un vassal sans histoire? Hugh II of Maine and the origins of Angevin overlordship in Maine', in idem ed., *Family Trees and the Roots of Politics* (Woodbridge, 1997). I am preparing an edition of the Mont-Saint-Michel cartulary (Bib. Avranches MS 210) for publication in France in 1999.

the new Norman lordships. Conversely, the new Norman rulers could effectively disinherit Frankish families by not forming alliances with them.

There can be little doubt that the seigneurs who emerged all over France in the eleventh century were normally the descendants of tenth century nobles and were not in any sense a new aristocracy. Biological continuity is a central feature of medieval society because it was dominated by the family and the family's inherited landed wealth, or patrimony. The landholding class was the bulwark of an economic system dominated by the possession of land, and it also held the key to political development since its co-operation was crucial to the prince, upon whom, in turn, depended its continued possession of its inheritance. The internal dynamics of this class changed over time. Of special significance was the fact that the extended kin-group structures of ninth-century families had given way by the late-eleventh century to a much more restricted idea of family that concentrated rights of inheritance in the hands of very few of its members. Increasingly the right of inheritance came to focus upon the eldest son. This narrowing of inheritance possibilities effectively dispossessed some family members and has been thought to have lain behind the phenomenon of what Robert Bartlett called 'the aristocratic diaspora' of the eleventh and later centuries.[3] We still lack the detailed genealogical knowledge crucial to an understanding of north-west French aristocratic society.

Bartlett's 'aristocratic diaspora' was dominated in the eleventh century by Normans. More than one expansionary pressure was involved. These may have included a system of selection for the duke's favour in the matter of fresh enfeoffments of land, which meant that some people had to seek land outside Normandy. For landholders in the relatively infertile west of Normandy, limited prospects of expansion within Normandy led to the same result. A key role in aristocratic expansion was played by the relative strength of princely rule, which was extremely weak in Normandy between c.1020 and 1050. The re-establishment of princely authority involved quelling internal rebellion. The result was a significant re-ordering of lordships, and the establishment of an aristocratic clique closely bound by ties of blood and loyalty to the duke. The energies of this group were then turned outwards against external enemies in an aggressive expansionary movement which considerably extended the southern and eastern borders of Normandy. Certain families established in these border regions fell victim to the great expansionary movement now being led from the centre, by comparison with which the earlier migrationary movement, for all that it led to the conquest of Sicily, seems insignificant.

The existence within Normandy of a system of social integration and exclusion, related in part to a still incomplete territorial integration of west and east Normandy, is a well-established phenomenon for the eleventh century. In that period there was a marked dependence by the duke upon his close relatives, and a marked emphasis on placing, or acquiring by marriage, reliable relatives in key positions in the west. From 1000 onward the activities of both the Norman ruler and of his chief followers, the Norman aristocrats, become much better evidenced in surviving documents. Charters from the abbey of Fécamp, established

---

[3] R. Bartlett, *The Making of Europe. Conquest, Colonization and Cultural Change 950–1350* (London, 1993).

on Norman ducal demesne lands in eastern Normandy, show the duke establishing there the followers most closely bound to him.[4] Many of them had real or alleged biological relationships with him, and they and their descendants formed the recognizable aristocracy that dominated late eleventh-century Norman and English history.[5] As such they formed a powerful, 'inclusive', inner clique within Norman society that contrasted strongly with a quasi-autonomous, 'exclusive' and rebellious group settled mainly in western Normandy, which had initially been colonized by Normans distinct from those in eastern Normandy. This lack of integration within Normandy itself seems to have been a major preoccupation of the Norman rulers from the late tenth century onward. Apparently resolved by William the Conqueror by 1086, when there were as many west Norman landholders in England as East Norman, this question of east-west integration in Normandy is of crucial importance in understanding Norman history, as Searle's work highlighted, and demands further serious study. The point that has not been properly investigated is that west Normandy (the Cotentin peninsula) had historical links with Normandy's western and southern neighbours, Brittany and Maine, which it preserved, and often favoured, well into the eleventh century, and even beyond.

The eleventh-century Norman ruler's highly successful dependence upon his kin contrasts markedly with what was happening in other principalities. Most princes tended to inter-marry with other princes, and their seigneurs with each other. In Normandy the effect of this stratification of alliances was greatly lessened by the promotion of the ruler's natural issue to key positions and their inter-marriage with other seigneurial families. Only in Maine can a similar situation be found. Ruled from 900 by counts of Carolingian descents, sections of a native aristocracy can be traced in the county from the late ninth century down to the twelfth. The counts made extra-regional princely marriage-alliances, both for themselves and their issue. Between c.992 and 1015, the count established a number of key castellanies in strategic locations in which he placed a group of his relatives, many of whom were the immigrationary products of the tenth-century extra-regional alliances. The most important of the new seigneuries was located at Mayenne, the site of a Carolingian palace and hence the centre of an ancient and prestigious jurisdiction. It also highlighted an important feature of Manceau history, the west-east division of the county by the river Mayenne. Eleventh-century Maine is notable for the emergence of a highly stratified aristocracy outstandingly loyal to its count, who was often a minor. The chief destabilizing factor was the designs of the princes of Anjou and Normandy upon the county. The conflicts intensified in the 1050s and resulted in the conquest of the county by the Normans in 1063.[6]

By the 1060s emigration from Normandy noticeably starts to involve those

---

4 J. Le Maho, 'L'apparition des seigneuries châtelaines dans le Grand-Caux à l'époque ducale', *Archéologie Médiévale* vi (1976).

5 G. H. White, 'The sisters and nieces of Gunnor, Duchess of Normandy', *The Genealogist*, n.s. 37 (1921); Searle, *Predatory Kinship*, passim; E. van Houts, 'Robert of Torigny as Genealogist', in *Studies in Medieval History Presented to R. Allen Brown*, ed. C. Harper-Bill et al. (Woodbridge, 1989); K. S. B. Keats-Rohan, 'Aspects of Robert of Torigny's Genealogies Revisited', *Nottingham Med. Stud.* 37 (1993), 21–7.

6 Cf. K. S. B. Keats-Rohan, 'Politique et parentèle: les comtes, vicomtes et évêques du

who had incurred the duke's disfavour. This phenomenon is related to the establishment by then of the duke's strong central authority and that of a tightly-controlled and land-hungry clique around him. The increased prestige of the duke by 1060 – the result of 15 years of military victories over internal and external enemies – and the increasing pressure on his landed resources came together in the most spectacular of the Norman expansions, the conquest of England in 1066. The conquest made the Norman duke a king, and greatly enriched him, his closest followers, and a motley collection of other landholders from Brittany and Flanders who had not previously been his subjects. The conquest of England, unlike those of Maine, southern Italy or the Holy Land, was to have a profound impact upon Normandy and upon Norman relations with their continental neighbours, especially the king of France. Norman aristocrats, the leading landholders, became the heads of sometimes very considerable cross-Channel holdings and were not content to accept the decision, taken in 1087, to separate England and Normandy. Their increased wealth and power was a threat to the English kings William I and Henry I, who both sought to curb their power. Under Henry I in particular this involved whole-scale confiscation of some aristocratic holdings, and their regrant to newcomers, noticeably involving men from west Normandy, Brittany and Maine. This phenomenon of the rise of 'new men raised from the dust' was described by the chronicler Orderic Vitalis who noted with disapproval a break with the traditional Norman reliance upon aristocratic kin.[7]

The views of the Norman chroniclers, especially Orderic Vitalis, are crucial to an attempt to understand the inner workings of Norman society. To some extent one has to consider chronicles as the 'sociological' product of a 'sociologist', in that they were always highly personal products and that many of them were written by monks, who held firm views about the right ordering of society, imbued with their faith and often fashioned by their study of the Latin Classics. The one chronicle devoted to tenth-century Normandy is Dudo of St Quentin's *De moribus*, a notoriously propagandizing product of the early eleventh century, which is only just beginning to be understood.[8] After 1050 the Normans embarked upon a golden age of chronicle writing, for which the mainspring was their own achievements. The chronicles of William of Poitiers, William of Jumièges and Orderic Vitalis are all immensely valuable, but all are propagandizing and undoubtedly biased. Orderic stands out among Norman chroniclers for the length of his work, the wealth of its detail, and the fact that for the most part he lived through the period he describes and was intimately acquainted with many of those about whom he wrote. Yet it has been claimed that Orderic was the most 'sociological' of all the Norman chroniclers in fashioning a view of the Normans and their society to which historians have been enslaved ever since.[9] This 'Norman Myth' was the Normans' view of their own irresistible cohesiveness, which put them apart from their contemporaries as invincible warriors in pursuit of clear military objectives and the fulfillment of their quintessential

Mans c.950–1050', *Francia* 26.1, 13–31; D. Pichot, *Le Bas-Maine du Xe au XIIIe siècle: étude d'une société* (Laval, 1995), 131–57.

7 Ord. Vit. vi, 16–7.

8 Dudo of Saint Quentin, *De Moribus et Actis primorum Normanniae Ducum*, ed. J. Lair (Caen, 1865).

9 See references in Chap. 2, note 74 above.

'Normanness'. Ironically, Orderic Vitalis was still putting the final touches to his portrait of a sort of Norman 'master race' in 1135, when the death of Henry I brought to an end the male line of a magnificent series of rulers going back to 911. Orderic was part of a late eleventh- twelfth-century tendency to lay strident and unconvincing emphasis upon the purity of the Norman aristocracy's blood-stock by firmly linking it to Scandinavian ancestry, yet he himself revealed that the ancestor of a large group of families prominent in central Normandy in the mid-eleventh century was a migrant from Germany who arrived shortly before 1027.[10] Other, charter, evidence shows Angevins being settled in Normandy in the mid-eleventh century, and the involvement, and probable settlement there of Poitevins and Burgundians in the tenth and eleventh centuries, not to mention the numerous Bretons who penetrated and formed part of Norman society from its inception. Intermarriage between noble Normans and Manceaux was occurring at least as far back as 997. Much of the evidence for a considerable level of migration to Normandy is preserved in the territorial appellations attaching to Normans recorded in Domesday Book. The names of these men preserved the memory of a past which had no current relevance; they were Normans and they saw themselves, and were seen, as such. Acceptance of Orderic's 'Norman Myth' involves studying Norman society as a closed ethnic phenomenon, whereas it may be best investigated as a cultural phenomenon attesting to the vigour and vitality of a society defined by its adherence and loyalty to its ruler. Disloyalty to the ruler meant exclusion from the magic circle of those who held land and wielded power. Sometimes this exclusion was founded in the accident of geographical location at a time before west and east Normandy were fully integrated. It is possible to read the eleventh-century chroniclers William of Jumièges and Poitiers as the statement of the loyal Normans who formed the closed inner aristocracy of Norman society. The 'Norman Myth' was extremely real, but somewhat different in its reality to the view of it given by Orderic.

*

Table 6b: Sample of Norman provenances by modern département

Calvados

abbatia de Cadomo, Caen
abbatia de Troarn, Troarn
abbatia Sancti Severi, Saint-Sever,
Adam filius Huberti, Ryes, arr. Bayeux
Adelina de Grandmesnil, Grandmesnil, arr. Lisieux
Adelold camerarius, Bayeux
Ansfrid de Valbadon, Vaubadon, arr. Bayeux
Ansketil de Grai, Graye-sur-Mer, arr. Caen
Ansketil de Herolfville, Hérouville-Saint-Clair, arr. Caen
Ansketil de Ros, Rots, arr. Caen
Ascelina Tailebois, Cristot, arr. Caen
Baldwin de Moles, Meulles, arr. Lisieux

[10] Ord. Vit. ii, 82.

Beatrix de Pomerai, La Pommeraye, arr. Falaise
Bigot de Loges, Les Loges, arr. Vire
Boselin de Dives, Dives-sur-Mer, arr. Pont-l'Evêque
Erneis de Buron, Buron, arr. Bayeux
Eudo dapifer Ryes, arr. Bayeux
Fulbert de Doura, Douvres-la-Délivrande, arr. Caen
Gaufrid Marescal, Venoix, arr. Caen
Gaufrid de Ros, Rots, arr. Caen
Gilbert de Salnerville, Sannerville, arr. Caen
Herbert de Furcis, Fourches, arr. Falaise
Herve de Campellis al. Legatus, Campeaux, arr. Vire
Hubert de Curcun, Notre-Dame-de-Courson, arr. Lisieux
Hubert de Montcanisy, Mont-Canisy, cant. Douvres-la-Délivrande, arr. Caen
Hubert de Port, Port-en-Bessin, arr. Bayeux
Hugo Maminot, Crévecoeur, arr. Lisieux
Hugo de Berneres, Bernières, arr. Caen
Hugo de Braibof, Bréboeuf, arr. Caen
Hugo de Corbon, Corbon, arr. Pont-l'Evêque
Hugo de Grandmesnil, Grandmesnil, arr. Lisieux
Hugo de Hotot, Hotot or Hottot
Hugo de Lacy, Lassy, arr. Vire
Hugo de Montgomery, Montgomery, arr. Lisieux
Hugo de Port, Port-en-Bessin, arr. Bayeux
Hugo de Valletorta, Torteval-Quesnay
Humfrid de Cuelai, Cully-le-Patry, arr. Falaise
Ilbert de Lacy Lassy, arr. Vire
Ivo Taillebois, Cristot, arr. Caen
Morin de Cadomo, Caen
Nigel de Burci, Burcy, cant. Vassy
Odo de Berneres, Bernières, arr. Caen
Odo episcopus Baiocensis, Bayeux
Osbern de Broilg, Brouay, arr. Caen
Radulf Paganel, Les Moutiers-Hubert, arr. Lisieux
Radulf de Buron, Buron, arr. Bayeux
Radulf de Montpincon, Montpinçon, arr. Lisieux
Radulf de Pomerai, La Pommeraye, arr. Caen
Radulf de Savenai, Savenay, arr. Vire
Radulf de Tilio, Tilly-sur-Seulles, arr. Caen
Rainald de Valletorta, Torteval-Quesnay
Rainfrid de Bretteville, Bretteville
Ranulf de Columbels, Colombières, arr. Bayeux
Ranulf de Maisnilwarin, Pont-Farcy
Ranulf de Valbadon, Vaubadon, arr. Bayeux
Ricardus de Clare, Orbec, arr. Lisieux
Ricardus de Curcy, Courcy, arr. Falaise
Ricardus de Praeres, Presles, arr. Vire
Ricardus de Redvers, Reviers, arr. Caen
Ricardus de Sackville, Sauqueville-en-Bessin, arr. Caen
Ricardus de Solariis, Soliers

Ricardus filius Turoldi, Damblainville
Robert de Bruis, Brix, arr. Valognes
Robert de Glanville, Glanville
Robert de Heriz, Hérils, comm. Maisons
Robert de Jorz, Jort
Robert de Nuers, Noyers, arr. Caen
Robert de Oilly, Ouilly-le-Basset, arr. Falaise
Robert de Raineville, Reineville, arr. Vire
Robert de Ruellant, Tilleul-en-Auge, arr. Lisieux
Robert de Somerville, Sommervieu, arr. Bayeux
Robert de Tham, Taon, arr. Caen
Roger Bigod, Savenay, arr. Vire
Roger Pictaviensis, Montgomery, arr. Lisieux
Roger comes, Montgomery, arr. Lisieux
Roger de Abernon, Abenon, arr. Lisieux
Roger de Buron, Buron, arr. Bayeux
Roger de Caisneto, Quesnay-Guesnon
Roger de Cucellis, Courseulles-sur-Mer, arr. Caen
Roger de Lacy, Lassy, arr. Vire
Roger de Molis, Meulles, arr. Lisieux
Roger de Oilly, Ouilly-le-Basset
Serlo de Burci, Burcy, cant. Vassy
Serlo de Ros, Rots, arr. Caen
Turgis de Meduana, Meuvaines, arr. Bayeux
Turstin de Giron, Gueron, arr. Bayeux
Walter de Cadomo, Caen
Walter de Cambremer, Cambremer, arr. Caen
Walter de Lacy, Lassy, arr. Vire
Wido de Oilli, Ouilly-le-Basset
Willelm Bertram, Briquebec
Willelm Pantulf, Noron, arr. Falaise
Willelm de Cahaignes, Cahagnes, arr. Vire
Willelm de Cairon, Cairon, arr. Caen
Willelm de Castellon, Castillon, arr. Bayeux
Willelm de Dives, Dives-sur-Mer, arr. Pont-l'Evêque
Willelm de Faleisia, Falaise
Willelm de Locels, Loucelles, arr. Caen
Wimund de Taissel, Tessel, arr. Caen
filius Willelmi de Taon, Thaon, arr. Caen
   Total: 100

Eure

abbatia de Bec, Bec
abbatia de Cormelies, Cormeilles
abbatia de Cruce, La Croix-Saint-Leuffroi
abbatia de Greistan, Grestain
abbatia de Lira, Lyre
abbatia de Pratellis, Préaux
abbatia sancti Petri de Diua, Saint-Pierre-sur-Dive

ecclesia Lisiacensis, Lisieux
Acard de Ivry, Ivry-la-Bataille, arr. Evreux
Alfred de Ispania, Epaignes, arr. Pont-Audemer
Ansfrid de Cormeilles, Cormeilles, arr. Pont-Audemer
Arnald de Nazanda, Nassandres, arr. Bernay
Berengar de Todeni, Tosny, arr. Louviers
Drogo de Andelei, Les Andelys
Durand de Gloucestre, Pîtres
Esilia Malet, Tillières-sur-Aure
Gilbert de Venables, Venables
Gilbert episcopus Ebroicensis, Evreux
Gilbert episcopus Lexoviensis, Lisieux
Goscelin de Cormeilles, Cormeilles, arr. Pont-Audemer
Henricus de Ferrariis, Ferrières-Saint-Hilaire
Herbrand de Ponte Audemer, Pont-Audemer
Hugo de Ispania, Epaignes, arr. Pont-Audemer
Hugo de Ivry, Ivry-la-Bataille, arr. Evreux
Hugo de Manneville, Manneville-sur-Risle
Hugo de Montfort, Montfort-sur-Risle
Ivo de Tigerville, Thierceville, arr. les Andelys
Milo Crispin, Tillières-sur-Avre
Odard de Vernon, Vernon, arr. Evreux
Picot de Percy, Percy-en-Auge, arr. Lisieux
Radulf de Bachepuis, Bacquepuits, arr. Evreux
Radulf de Bernai, Bernay
Radulf de Curbespina, Courbépine, arr. Bernay
Radulf de Tosny, Tosny, arr. Louviers
Ricardus de Vernon, Vernon
Ricardus filius Rainfridi, Bournainville
Richer de Andelei, Les Andelys
Robert comes de Mellent, Beaumont-le-Roger
Robert de Sancto Quintino, Saint-Quentin-des-Isles
Robert de Tosny de Belvoir, Tosny, arr. Louviers
Robert de Tosny de Stafford, Tosny, arr. Louviers
Roger de Bascherville, Bacqueville
Roger de Bellomonte, Beaumont-le-Roger
Roger de Boscnorman, Le Bois-Norman-près-Lyre
Roger de Candos, Candos, arr. Pont-Audemer
Roger de Ebroicis, Evreux
Roger de Ivry, Ivry-la-Bataille, arr. Evreux
Roger de Livet, Livet-en-Ouche, arr. Bernay
Roger de Luxonio, Lisieux
Roger de Mucegros, Mussegros, arr. Les Andelys
Roger de Orbec, Orbec, arr. Lisieux
Roger de Sancto Germano, Saint-Germain-la-Campagne
Turold de Verly, Vesly, arr. Les Andelys
Walter de Gloecestria, Pîtres
Walter de Herbercurt, Hébécourt
Walter de Ispania, Epaignes, arr. Pont-Audemer

Willelm Gulafre, La Goulafrière
Willelm de Ebroicis, Evreux
Willelm de Percy, Percy-en-Auge, arr. Lisieux
Willelm de Schohies, Ecouis, arr. Les Andelys
Willelm filius Osbern, Breteuil
    Total: 61

Manche

abbatia de Monteburg, Montebourg
abbatia Mons Sancti Michaelis, Mont-Saint-Michel
Ansketil de Caesarisburgi, Cherbourg
Corbin de Agnellis, Agneaux
Drogo de Cartrai, Carteret, arr. Valognes
Gaufrid de Trailly, Trelly, arr. Coutances
Haimo de Maci, Macey, arr. Avranches
Hugo comes, Avranches
Hugo de Verly, Vesly, arr. Coutances
Humfrid de Ansleville, Anneville-en-Saire
Humfrid de Bohun, Saint-Georges-le-Bohon, arr. Saint-Lô
Humfrid de Cartrai, Carteret, arr. Valognes
Johannes nepos Waleranni, Veim
Malger de Cartrai Carteret, arr. Valognes
Nigel de Albini, Saint-Martin-d'Aubigny
Nigel de Wast, Le Vast, arr. Cherbourg
Petrus de Valoniis, Valognes
Radulf Baard, Cotentin
Ranulf Peverel, Vengeons, arr. Mortain
Ricardus de Surdeval, Sourdeval, arr. Mortain
Robert Murdac, La Meurdraquière
Robert comes de Moritonio, Mortain
Robert de Bellomonte, Beaumont-le-Hague
Roger de Margella, Margueray, arr. Saint-Lô
Rogo filius Nigelli, Omonville, arr. Cherbourg
Walter de Omonville, Omonville, arr. Coutances
Willelm de Ansleville, Hémevez, arr. Valognes
Willelm de Lestre, Lestre, arr. Valognes
Willelm de Moion, Moyon, arr. Saint-Lô
Willelm filius Wimund, Avranches
    Total: 31

Orne

abbatia de Almenesche, Almenesches
abbatia de Fontaneto, Fontenay-le-Marmion
abbatia de Sais, Sées
Baldric de Lindeseia, Bocquencé
Bernard de Alencun, Alençon
David de Argentan, Argentan
Gerard de Tournai, Tournay-sur-Dive, arr. Argentan
Gilbert de Sancto Audoeno, Saint-Ouen, arr. Argentan

70

Hugo Burdet, Rabodanges
Morin de Sancto Andree, Saint-André-de-Briouze
Norman Venator, Macé
Picot de Sai, Sai
Radulf Basset, Montreuil-au-Houlme
Radulf Chesneduit, Chésneduit
Radulf de Buceio, Boucé
Radulf de Roillei, Rouellé
Rainald de Balliol, Bailleul-en-Gouffern
Ricardus Basset, Montreuil-au-Houlme
Ricardus de Mainilhermer, Le Ménil-Hermei
Ricardus de Montgarolt, Montgaroult
Robert de Braose, Briouze, arr. Argentan
Robert de Montbegon, Mont-Bougon
Robert de Pontchardon, Pontchardon
Robert filius Theobald, Avoine
Roger de Montbegon, Mont-Bougon, arr. Argentan
Turstin de Fontanis, Fontaines-les-Basset
Willelm de Braose, Briouze, arr. Argentan
Willelm de Poillgi, Saint-Léger-sur-Sarthe
uxor Roberti Burdet, Rabodanges
   Total: 29

Seine-Maritime
abbatia de Fiscanno, Fécamp
abbatia de Ultresport, Tréport
abbatia Gemeticensis, Jumièges
abbatia sancte Marie Villarensis, Montivilliers
abbatia sancti Audoeni, Saint-Ouen de Rouen
abbatia sancti Petri
abbatia sancti Victoris, Saint-Victor-en-Caux
abbatia sancti Wandregisil, Saint-Wandrille
ecclesia sancte marie Rotomag', Rouen
Arnald de Busli, Bully, arr. Neufchâtel
Berengar Giffard, Longueville/Scie, arr. Dieppe
Bernard de Sancto Audoeno, Saint-Ouen, arr. Dieppe
Durand Malet, Graville-Sainte-Honorine, arr. Le Havre
Gaufrid Martel, Bacqueville-en-Caux, arr. Dieppe
Gaufrid Talbot, Sainte-Croix-sur-Buchy
Gaufrid de Blanca, Blanques
Gaufrid de Floc, Flocques, arr. Dieppe
Gaufrid de Mandeville, Manneville, arr. Dieppe
Germund de Sancto Audoeno, Saint-Ouen, arr. Dieppe
Gerold de Normanville, Normanville, arr. Neufchâtel
Gilbert de Blosseville, Blosseville, arr. Yvetot
Godefrid de Petraponte, Pierrepont, arr. Neufchâtel
Hugo de Bolebec, Bolbec, arr. Le Havre
Hugo de Gurnai, Gournai-en-Bray, arr. Neufchâtel
Hugo de Wancy, Wanchy-Capeval, arr. Neufchâtel

Ingelran de Auco, Eu, arr. Dieppe
Lambert de Buelles, Bouelles, arr. Neufchâtel
Lambert de Roseto, Rosay, arr. Dieppe
Milo de Belefosse, Allouville-Bellefosse
Nigel de Munneville, Monville, arr. Rouen
Oilard de Balliol, Bailleul-Neuville
Osbern Giffard, Longueville/Scie, arr. Dieppe
Osbern de Novomercato, Neufmarché, arr. Neufchâtel
Osbern de Wancy, Wanchy-Capeval, arr. Neufchâtel
Osbern filius Goisfridi, Bailleul-Neuville, arr. Neufchâtel
Radulf de Bans, Baons-le-Comte
Radulf de Caisneto, Le Quesnay, arr. Neufchâtel
Radulf de Hairon, Héron, cant. Darnetal
Radulf de Langetot, Lanquetot, arr. Le Havre
Radulf de Limesi, Limésy, arr. Rouen
Radulf de Mortemer, Mortemer, arr. Neufchâtel
Radulf de Novo Mercato, Neufmarché, arr. Neufchâtel
Rainald de Petrapont, Pierrepont, arr. Neufchâtel
Rainer de Grandcurt, Grandcourt, arr. Neufchâtel
Ranulf de Sancto Walerico, Saint-Valery-en-Caux, arr. Yvetot
Ricardus Gernet, Maupertuis
Ricardus Talebot, Cleuville
Ricardus de Guerres, Gueures, arr. Dieppe
Robert Malet, Graville-Sainte-Honorine
Robert comes de Ou, Eu, arr. Dieppe
Robert de Claville, Clasville
Robert de Criol, Criel-sur-Mer, arr. Dieppe
Robert de Dun, Le Bourg-Dun, arr. Dieppe
Robert de Pavilly, Pavilly, arr. Rouen
Robert de Petraponte, Pierrepont, arr. Neufchâtel
Robert de Sancto Leodegar, Saint-Léger-aux-Bois
Robert dispensator, Abbetot, arr. Le Havre
Robert filius Geroldi, Roumare, arr. Rouen
Roger de Boscroard, Bosc-le-Hard, arr. Dieppe
Roger de Bully, Bully, arr. Neufchâtel
Roger de Luvetot, Louvetot, arr. Yvetot
Roger de Raimes, Rames, arr. Le Havre
Roger de Sumeri, Sommery, arr. Neufchâtel
Rohais Giffard, Longueville/Scie, arr. Dieppe
Saswalo de Bouvilla, Beuzeville, arr. Dieppe
Turold de Chevrercurt, Quiévrecourt, arr. Neufchâtel
Turstin filius Rolf, Le Bec-aux-Cauchois
Urso de Abitot, Abbetot, arr. Le Havre
Walchelin de Roseto, Rosay, arr. Dieppe
Walter Giffard, Longueville/Scie, arr. Dieppe
Walter de Aincurt, Ancourt, arr. Dieppe
Walter de Appeville, Appeville-le-Petit, arr. Dieppe
Walter de Bec, Le Bec-aux-Cauchois
Walter de Belmes, Beaumais, arr. Dieppe

Walter de Grandcurt, Grandcourt, arr. Neufchâtel
Walter de Mandeville, Manneville, arr. Dieppe
Walter de Mucedent, Muchedent, arr. Dieppe
Walter de Ricarville, Ricarville, arr. Dieppe
Walter filius Grip, Bacqueville-en-Caux, arr. Dieppe
Wido de Auco, Eu, arr. Dieppe
Willelm Belet, Goderville
Willelm de Arcis, Arques-la-Bataille, arr.Dieppe
Willelm de Boscroard, Bosc-le-Hard, arr. Dieppe
Willelm de Cailly, Cailly, arr. Rouen
Willelm de Fiscanno, Fécamp
Willelm de Gemmetico, Jumièges
Willelm de Malleville, Emmaleville, arr. Le Havre
Willelm de Ou, Eu, arr. Dieppe
Willelm de Sancto Leger, Saint-Léger-aux-Bois
Willelm de Septmuels, de Sept-Meules, arr. Dieppe
Willelm de Warenne, Varenne, arr. Dieppe
Willelm de Watteville, Vatteville-la-Rue
    Total: 92

The totals for these tables produce a striking accord with the political structures of later eleventh-century Normandy, as would be further emphasized by
adding in all the provenances judged to be of a lesser degree of probability.
Recruitment is seen to be fairly even throughout western and eastern Normandy,
with perhaps a slight balance in favour of the west. There is a remarkable concentration of men from the environs of Caen, the ducal centre in the west that was a
deliberate creation of the eleventh-century Norman rulers. The other 'new or
greatly extended' towns of Falaise, Alençon, Valognes, Cherbourg and, in particular, Dieppe, are also well represented.[11] The list for Orne is important in that
those listed were for the most part men of Roger de Montgomery, who had
brought most of the region into Normandy with his marriage to Mabel de
Bellême.[12] The eleventh-century duke's well-documented reliance upon his kin is
evident in these lists. Equally evident is the eleventh-century dukes' determination fully to fuse the western and eastern halves of Normandy, and to extend their
boundaries southwards. The settlement recorded in Domesday Book twenty years
after Hastings is probably a fairly accurate representation of the origins of the
warriors of Hastings, even though the personnel of the two events was not and
cannot have been exactly the same. The most significant example of the difference between the two is provided by Roger de Montgomery, who is known to
have been left to govern Normandy with Matilda in 1066, yet was one of the
wealthiest men in England in 1086. Again, Miles Crispin, tenant-in-chief of the

---

[11] Cf. Preface, note 22, above.
[12] J. H. F. Mason, 'The officers and clerks of the Norman earls of Shropshire', *Transactions of the Shropshire Archaeological Society* 56 (1957–60), 244–57; K. Thompson,
'The Norman aristocracy before 1066: the Example of the Montgomerys', *Historical
Research* 40 (1987), 251–63.

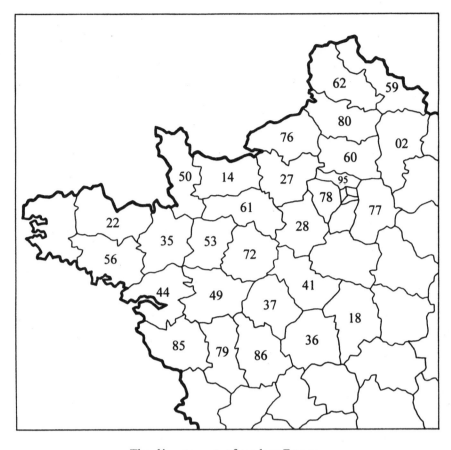

The *départements* of modern France,
with a rough guide to their medieval regional counterparts

02 Aisne (Champagne)
14 Calvados (Normandy)
18 Cher (Berry)
22 Côte-d'Amor (Brittany)
27 Eure (Normandy)
28 Eure-et-Loir (county of Chartres)
35 Ille-et-Vilaine (Brittany)
36 Indre (Berry)
37 Indre-et-Loire (Touraine)
41 Loir-et-Cher (county of Blois)
44 Loire-Atlantique (Brittany)
49 Maine-et-Loire (Anjou)
50 Manche (Normandy)
53 Mayenne (Maine)
56 Morbihan (Brittany)

59 Nord (Artois, Flanders)
60 Oise (France, Chartres)
61 Orne (Normandy)
62 Pas-de-Calais (parts of Picardy, Artois)
72 Sarthe (Maine)
76 Seine-Maritime (Normandy)
77 Seine-et-Marne (France)
78 Yvelines (France)
79 Deux-Sèvres (Poitou in Aquitaine)
80 Somme (Picardy)
85 Vendée (Poitou in Aquitaine)
86 Vienne (Poitou in Aquitaine)
95 Val-d'Oise (France)

extensive honour of Wallingford in 1086, is unlikely to have come to England before c.1080.

As far as the Normans are concerned, the settlement of England, as probably also the initial conquest, was a faithful reflection of the preoccupations of the eleventh-century dukes in whose service the 'Norman Myth' was forged as the cohesive force that made the Norman Conquest possible. Study of the Normans involved in the Conquest and the settlement offers a great deal of information about the process of assimilation by the original Norse settlers of Normandy, subsequent migration to Normandy, and the forces of social inclusion or exclusion at work there. For the Bretons, Artesians and Picards, the Conquest was an opportunity. Far less so for the Normans in general and the socially excluded in particular: for them, to put the matter very crudely, it was another exercise in élitism by an élite.

Domesday prosopography is an extraordinarily rich source of information of many different kinds. It is a history of the conquest and settlement of England. Among other things, it can offer insights into the relations between the Normans and the English in matters such as tenancies and marriage links. Although Domesday prosopography suggests that the Normans still held the English at arms' length in 1086, analysis of all the relevant data will overwhelmingly yield the conclusion that the Norman settlement was firmly rooted in pre-existing English tenurial structures, where a newcomer would receive the benefice of one or more English *antecessores*. Even though enfeoffments made later in the settlement process may have moved further and further from this model, nonetheless the settlement was no free-for-all, any more than the Conquest itself was for the benefit of landless younger sons, as used to be thought. Who can say what Harold II might have achieved, but certainly the conquest of the most sophisticated state of its time by the most ruthlessly efficient entrepreneurs of the time ensured the future of England as the home of innovation in the science of government. A prerequisite of the rapid rise, after 1100, of the administrative bureaucracy created from the military class by Henry I and Roger of Salisbury was the creation, during the tenth and eleventh centuries, of Normandy's 'aristocracy' from a group of men in ducal service who were often kinsmen or affines of the dukes they served. Traditions of military and administrative service to central authorities were not unique to Normandy, but Normandy was unique in using them to create a powerfully cohesive élite capable of achieving whatever it wanted. These traditions and the aristocracy they created are very evident in the study of Domesday Book landholders. In many respects Domesday prosopography is the history in microcosm of Normandy and the Normans.

Appendix I

THE LINDSEY SURVEY

The Lindsey Survey (1115–1118) . . . is the earliest of three similar records compiled during the reign of Henry I. The larger portion of a survey of Leicestershire, made between 1125 and 1130, was printed by Dr Round in *Feudal England*. A Survey of Northamptonshire, of approximately the same date, was translated and compared with Domesday by Dr Round in Volume I of the Victoria History of that County. The Lindsey Survey, unlike the other two, is preserved in a contemporary text. It has long been known. It was first printed by Thomas Hearne in his edition of the Black Book of the Exchequer. In 1883, Mr Chester Waters translated it, apparently from Hearne's text. . . . In 1884 Mr Greenstreet published it in facsimile, with an index, but without any identification of places. Its date was first precisely determined by Dr Round, who also was the first to indicate its great value to the student of danegeld and its assessment.

– F. M. Stenton, Introduction to C. W. Foster and T. Longley, *The Lincolnshire Domesday and the Lindsey Survey* (Lincoln Record Society vol. 19, 1924), which contained a translation of the survey. The notes to the Foster and Longley translation, by far the most commonly used version of the text, contain a full account of the manuscript text, preserved in BL Cotton Claudius C v, which contains both additions by the original scribe and by a much later commentator. Because of the prosopographical importance of this survey, a full Latin text is given below, which combines reference to the manuscript with references to the Foster/Longley translation. The manuscript presentation is in some respects idiosyncratic, as the transcript below will show.

Where place or person name material has been expanded, the expansions appear between square brackets. For other types of text square brackets indicate material that was added by a later scribe. The majority of the very late additions have been omitted, but they were all transcribed in the Foster/Longley notes. On folio 1 it indicates material in a damaged part of the manuscript that Longley was able to read but is no longer visible. Material in italics represents additions by the original scribe, who wrote most of it suprascript without a firm pointer to exactly where it was intended to be read. One significant departure from the Foster/Longley text concerns the name they printed and indexed as Bernard son of Adam. The manuscript unmistakably reads Richard son of Adam.

BL Cotton Claudius C v, The Lindsey Survey

Folio 1 IN WEST TRIDING
[1]. IN MANELI Wap[entac] hab[entur] . . .

1. Comes Ricardus habet xxxiiii c'. et ii b'. et dim' b'. in Halton [et socha].
2. Walterus de Gant in Wintringham xi c., quas Robert Marmion tenet. Et In Risebi ii c'. et ii b'. Et In Santuna i b., quas Walterus de Sancto Paulo tenet.

3. Rogerus Marmion In Wintringeham i c'.
4. Rad[ulf] Painellus In Bertuna xi c'. et v b'. Et In Cheistorp iii b'. Et In Rochesbi v c'. Et In Scallebi iii c'. et vi b'. et dim' Et In Wintringt[on] iii b'.
5. Rannulfus Mischinus v c'. Et In Redburna i c'. et dim'. Et In Hibaldestoua i c'. Et In Rainelestorp dim' c'. Et Saierus habet iii b'. de feudo eius.
6. Abbas de Burc In Alchebarua i c'. Et In Walecota vi c'. et vi b'. Et In Massingeham iiii c'. et vi b'. et dim' Et In Holm iii c'. Et In Ragheniltorp i c'. et i b'. Et In Malmetuna ii c'. Et In Hibaldestoua i c'. et ii b'. Et In Risabi iii b'. Et In Nordmanabi . . . Et In Aschebi iii b'. et dim' quas tenet. . .ri. . .N. . .

Folio 2
7. Gaufridus filius Pagani Inter Massingham [et] Walecota et [Ris]abi v [c' et ..] b'. .
8. Sancta Maria Linco[lniensis] i c'. et ii b'.
(p. 238) 9. Stephanus de Albamara. In Tedolfbi i c'. Et In Normanebi ix c.
10. Dunelmensis episcopus In Steintuna iii b'.
11. Episcopus Linc[olniensis] In Massingham i c'. et 7 b'.
12. Robertus de Haia In Scallebi i c'.
13. In Aplebi Rex ix c'. et ii b'. Et In Santuna i c'. et de hoc sunt in dominio Helle ii c'. et vi b'. In Witena xii c'. *Robertus de Fereris.*
14. Normannus de Areceio In Valecot' i c'. et ii b'. Et In Flichesburc et Cunigesbi xii c'. Et In Wintringtuna ii [c'.]. Et In Cuningesbi et C[rochesbi i c'. et i] b'. et dim' b'. Et In Rochesbi iiii b'. Et In hundr[edum] de Tedolfbi iiii b'. Et In Risabi i b'. Et In Walecota i b'. litigationis. *Ricardus filius Adam.*
15. Aluredus de Lachtuna In Hibaldastowa ii b'.
16. Abbas de Eboraco In Edoluestorp i c'. Et In Wintringtuna i c'. et iii b'.
17. Gillbertus filius Gocelini In Botlesforda et Asebi i c'. et iiii b'. Et In Scallbi ii c'. et bou'. Et In Wadingham v b'. Et In Redburna vii c'. Summa xi c'. et iii b'.
18. Willelmus de Arcis de Scallabi ii c'. et i b'. Et In Redburna iii b'. Et In Hibaldestowa et Gamel[torp].

Folio 3
19. Willelmus Mischin In Scallabi i c'. quam Aluredus de Lactuna tenet Et In Cheistorp iii b'.
20. Comes Stefanus de Moreton In Wadingham i c'. et iii b'. quas Roger de Montebegon tenet.
21. Hugo de Vallo In Steintuna vi b'. et dim' b'.
22. Helpo balistarius In Redburna iii b'. Et In Steintuna dim' b'.
23. Alanus de Credon In Santuna vii b'., quas Aluredus de Lactuna tenet.

(p. 239)
[2]. IN ASLOCAHOU Wapentac Habentur vii hundr' et dim'.
1. Radulfus Paganells In Glenteworda v b'.
2. Rannulfus Meschinus In Nordmanabi v c'. Et In Glentheim iii c'. *Reinfrei tenet* Et In Ounebi v b'. *Gillbert de Calz* Et In Bliburc iiii b'. et dim' bou'.
3. Gillebertus de Calz. Et In Wadingheheim iiii b'. ipse Gillebertus.
4. Steffanus de Albamara In Helmeswella i c'. et ii b'. Et In Glenteworda i c'. et iii b'. Et In Hacatorn vi b'. et dim' b'., quas Anscetillus de Scuris tenet.
5. Rannulfus episcopus In Bliburc vii b'.

6. Robertus episcopus Linc[olniensis] In Nordtuna vi c'. et In Glemtheim et Casnabi vii c'. et vi bou'. Et de istis tenet Martellus de Taneio ii c'. et iiii b'. Et In Ounabi iii c'. et ib' Et In Ingheham *Simon.* [Folio 4] vi b'. Et In Cotes iiii b'. *Simon.*

7. Nigellus de Albeneio In Bliburc ii c'. et iiii b'. et quartam partem unius bouete.

8. Willelmus filius Rastoldi i c'. et i b'. de rege.

9. Gillebertus filius Gocelini In Bliburc vii b'. Et In Harpeswella ii c'. et iiii b'. Et In Glenteworda v b'. Et In Ingeham i c'. et iiii b'. Et In Cotis v b'. Et In Hachetorna iiii c'. et i b'. Et In Ounebi i c'. et v b., quod Robert de Haia tenet. Summa - x c'. et ii b'.

10. Willelmus Meschinus in Camringham i c'., quam Robertus de Haia tenet de illo.

11. Robertus de Haia in Cotis. Et In Camringham iiii c'. Et In Spridlinctuna ii c'. et ii b'. Et In Figlingaham vi c'. et vi b'. Et In Ingeham vi b'. Et in eadem villa iiii b'. de Radulfo de Criol Et In Hacatorna iii (p. 240) b'. Et In Ounabia i c'. et v b'. Et In Haneworda iiii b'.

12. Simon filius Willelmi In Hachethorna i c'. et iiii b'.

13. Hugo de Laval. In Cotis iiii b'. et dim' Et In Hacatorna vi b'. et dim' Et In Frisabi iii c'. et iiii b'. et dim' et quinta parte unius b'. Et In Ounebi ii b'. et dim. b'. Et In Saxsebi dim' b'. Et In Nordmanabi i c. quas Paganus tenet. et Gosfridus frater eius. Et In Ingheham i c.

14. Anfridus de Canceio In Wilgatuna iii c'. et v b'. et dim' b. quas Willelmus de Bussa tenet.

15. Abbas Sancti Nicholai ii c'. et ii b'. et dim'.

16. Archiepiscopus de Eboraco In Harpeswella v. b'. et dim' Et In Hachetorna i c'. et iiii b'. quas Gregorius tenet. In eadem villa i c'. et vii b'. et dim' quas Hugo tenet.

Folio 5

17. Hugo filius Eudonis In Saxsabi ii c'. et v b'. .

18. Comes Stefanus Britannie In Spritlingtuna ii c'. et iii b'. et tertiam partem unius bou. Et In Halmeswella iiii b'.

19. Manaset Arsic In Ounabi ii b'. Et In Glentheim x b'. Et In Gleintaworda vii b., et Walterus filius Willelmi tenet.

20. Helpo Balistarius In Snitrebi x b'. Et In Figlingheim ii b'. et dim' et ferding unius b'.

21. Comes de Moreton In Figlingheim ii c'. et iii b'. et quintam partem unius bouete, quas Rannulf Bilion tenet. Et In Ingheham vi bou'. Et In Haneworda ii b., quas Renaldus Purcellus tenet, et Godefridus.

22. Radulfus de Criol In Ingeham iiii bouetas.

[3]. IN LAGOLFRIS Wup[entac] Habentur xii hundr-.

1. Canonici Sancte Marie habent in Wellatuna. Et In Risun. Et In Wllingheim (p. 241) xiiii c'. et ii b'. *et de istis tenet ecclesia iiii b'. et Robert de Haia ii b'.*

2. Episcopus Linc[olniensis] In Netelham xii c'. Et In Dunham v c'. et iii b'. Et In Carletuna vii c'. Et In Scotstorna ii b'. *Gillebertus de Noua uilla.* Et In Refham iiii b'. quas Gillebertus de Noua uilla tenet.

3. Alanus de Perceio in Saxlabi ii c'. et i b' et tertiam partem unius b'.

4. Robertus de Haia In Scotstorna v c'. Et In Faldinguorda ii c'. et iiii b'. Et In

Risun iii c'. Et In Refham vi b'. Et In Barlinga ii c'. et v b'. Et In Torp i c'. Et In Englabi ii c'. et v b'. et [Folio 6] tertiam partem unius bouete Et In Frisatorp vii b., quas Willelmus filius Anschetilli tenet Et In Brotolbi ii c'. et ii b'.

5. Willelmus Meschinus in Faldinguorda ii c'. et iiii b., quas Radulf Malet tenet.

6. Sancta Maria in Frisetorp ii c'. et i b'. quas Nigel tenuit.

7. Willelmus Turniant. In Faldinguorda i c'.

8. Robertus de Insula In Esatorp ii c., quas Buselinus tenet. Et In Carletuna vi c., quas Alanus de Twit tenet. Et In Burtuna i c'., quam Ricardus de Munte Pinchun tenet.

9. Alfreit de Canceio In Duneham ii c'. et v b'. quas Radulfus canonicus frater Osberti vicecomitis tenet.

10. Ran[ulf] Dunelmensis episcopus In Snarteforde iii c'. quas Goslinus dapifer tenet.

11. Hugo de Vallo In Duneham ii c'. Et In Scotstorne vii b'.

12. Radulfus Paganellus In Duneham ii c'., quas Goslinus dapifer tenet.

13. Normannus de Araceio In Holm i c'. et i b'.

14. Abbas de Burc In Scotstorne et Sutbroc iiii c'. et iiii b'. Et In Fischertune iii c'. Et In Refham iiii c'. et vi b'.

15. Rogerus Marmion In Wllingeheim i c'. et vi b'.

16. Wigotus Lincolie in Broxholm iiii c'. Et In Englebi iii c'. et v b'. et tertiam partem unius bouete.

(p. 242) 17. Manasiet Arsic in Saxlebi i c'. et iiii b., quas Turstinus de Renni tenet.

18. Rodbertus filius regis in Esttorp vi b., quas Hundefot Robertus tenet de Willelmo Turniant.

19. Walterus de Ganto In Burtuna v c'. Et In Scantuna vi c'. Et Turuluestorp ii c'. et vii b'. [Folio 7] Et Astorp iii c'. et ii b., quas Walterus filius Ragemer tenet. Et In Netelham ii b'., quas Rodbertus de Haia tenet Et In B[arlinga] iii b'. quas Rodbertus de Haia tenet. Et In Risun ii c'. *Robertus tenet* Et In Brotulebi i c'. et vi b'. *Robertus de Haia tenet*. Et In Carletune vi b'., quas Fulco Albus tenet.

20. Willelmus de Rollos in Burtuna iii c'., quas Sortebrand filius Vlf tenet.

21. Hugo de Luuetot in Gretwella iii c'.

22. Rogerius de Ganto iiii c'., quas Fulco Albus tenet et Rogerus Macherellus.

23. Roger de Valoniis ii c'., quas Harcherus tenet in Burtuna.

---

[4]. IN CORINGEHAM Wap[entac] Habentur v hundred-.

1. Nigellus de Albaneio habet in Gleinesburc viii c'. Et In Ioltorp i c'. Et In Sumerdebi iiii b'.

2. Comes Stephanus Britannie In Le et Sumerdebi et Iopheim v c., quas Gosfridus filius Treatune [tenet].

3. Robertus de Insula in Coringheham ii c'., quas Ricardus de Monte Pinchun tenet.

4. Episcopus Linc[olniensis] In Greingheham i c'., quam Ricard filius Malger tenet.

5. Ran[ulf] Dunelmensis episcopus In Cletham vi b'.

6. Hugo de Vallo In Torp vi b'. Et In Cletham vi b'. .

7. Alanus de Credun In Blituna i c'. et vi b'. Et In Lactuna iii c'. et ii b'. Et In Scottuna iiii b'.

(p. 243) Folio 8

8. Comes de Moreton In Lactuna ii c'. et vi b'. Et In Torp Et In Tuneoc et Tunstal vi c'. Et In Scottuna iiii b'. Et In Iolthorp iiii b'. Et In Blituna ii b'. quas omnes tenet Roger de Monte.

9. Abbas de Burc In Scottune vi c'. Et In Scotra viii c'. Et In Saltorp iii c'. Et In Ioltorp iiii b'. *Herbertus.* Et In Torp i c. *R. de Villa.* Et In Cletham i c'. Herbertus.

10. Radulfus Mischinus In Dunestal ii c'. Et In Scottuna ii c'., Wido de Vernus [*corr. ex.* Vermis].

11. Gaufridus filius Pagani In Greingheham i c.

[5]. IN HAXEHOLM habentur iiii h'. In uno quoque xii c'. terre Et Nigel de Albeneio tenet eas in dominio.

[6]. IN WELLE Wap[entac] habentur vii hundr'. In uno quoque xii carucate terre.

1. Rodbertus Episcopus Linc[olniensis] habet in hundr' de Neotuna xii c'. Et In hundr' de Stowa et Brantuna x c'. Et In Normannebi et Chezbi viii c'. et iiii b'. Et In hundr' de Vppetune viii c'. et v b'. Et In Martuna iiii c'. Et In Fentuna ii c'. que geldunt a Strettuna. Et Hugo canonicus vi b'. Et de baronibus regis tenet episcopus in Stowa i c'. de Gill[leberto] filio Gocelini Et In Wiflingeheim iii b'. des Brituns. In Viflingeheim eadem villa ii b'. de Hugone de Valo Et de Waltero de Ganto ii b'. in dominio.

[Folio 9] 2. Hugo de Vallo in Strettuna viii c'. Et In Viflingheheim et Stowa iii c'. et iiii b., quas Hamelinus et Rodbertus de Haia tenent, sed Hugo de Luuetot tenet ii b'. inde.

3. Gilebertus filius Gocelini In Viflingheheim vi c'.

4. Rodbertus de Haia In Chetlesbi iii c'.

(p. 244) 5. Rodbertus de Insula In Branzbi ii c'., Ric[ardus] de Monte Pinceoni tenet.

6 . Comes Stefanus Britannie In Burtuna iiii c'. et tertiam partem unius bouete. Et In Martuna vi b'. quas Haco filius Elurici tenet Et In Vptuna i c'. et vi b'. et duas partes unius b'. Et In Wiflingham et Stowa iii c'. et iiii b'. quas uxor Hugonis tenet.

7. Comes de Moreton In Vptuna i c'. et v b'. quas Paganus de Vilers tenet.

8. Odo Sancte Crucis viii c'. inter crementum et carucat' terre.

9. Stefanus Britannie v c'. et ii b'. inter incrementum et terram

10. Columbanus iii c'. et iiii b'. inter inplementum et terram.

11. Ranerus de Euermou vi carucat'.

IN NORTRIDING

[7]. IN WALESCROFT Wap[entac] habentur viii hundr' et In uno quoque xii car'.

1. Stefanus comes de Albamara In Torgimebi i c'. et vii b'. Et In Steintuna vi b'. *Herbertus tenet Sancti Quintini Et In Clachesbi vi b'.*

2. Episcopus Linc[olniensis] In Torgimbi v b'. *Gerardus de Belesbi* Et In Ouresbi ii c'. Et In Chimerebi ii c'. Et In Clachesbi i b.

3. Normannus de Areceio In Torgrimbi i c'. et vi b'. Et In Crochesbi iii b'. Et In Ouresbi ii b'. dim' [Folio 10] et ferding Et In Nordmanabi ii b'. Et In Clachesbi i b'.

4. Rannulfus Meschinus In Torgimbi vi b'. Et In Crochesbi v b'. Et In Wifling-

ham ii b'. Et In Houtuna i c'. Et In Nordmanabi et Clachesbi iii c'. Et In Ouresbi i c'. Et In Toresweia ii b'. Et In Nordmanabi iii b'. quas Alanus tenet.

(p. 245) 5. Robertus de Insula In Torgrimbi i c'. Et In Crochesbi i c'. Et In Binnabroc v c'. et vii b'. Et In Iraforda iii c'. et v b'. et dim' b'.

6. Et Willelmus Turniant i c'. in Binnabroc'

7. Willelmus Meschinus In Crochesbi i c'. quam Willelmus nepos Osberti vicecomitis tenet Et In Media Rasa iii b'. quas Rad[ulfus] Malet tenet Et In Lindwda iiii b'. Et In Nordmanabi v b'. Et In Media Rasa i b'. et tertiam partem unius bouete quas Walter Malet tenet.

8. Alanus de Credun i c'. et dim' b'. Et In Ireforde ii b'. quas Aluredus de Lactuna tenet.

9. Abbas de Eboraco In Osoluabi iiii b'. Et In Osgotabi iiii b'.

10. Willelmus Torniant In Newetuna iii b'.

11. Rad[ulfus] de Criol In Steint' v et dim' b'. Et In Wiflingham i b'. Et In Ottebi i c'. Et In Newetuna iii b'. , quas Robertus de Haia tenet.

12. Alanus de Perci In Steintuna iiii b'. et dim' Et In Wiflingham ii b'. et dim'. Et In Ouresbi vi b'. et dim' b'. Et tertiam partem unius bou'. Et In Torntuna i c'. et iiii b'.

13. Rad[ulfus] Painellus In Teflesbi i c'. et vi b'. Et In Wiflingham i c'. Et In Rasa vii c'. et ii b'. et duas partes unius bouete Et In alia Rasa i c'. et vi b'. Et In Osgotebi i b'. Et In Osoluebi dim' b'. ultra bec' .

14. Et Gillebertus filius Gocelini In Teflesbi i c'. *Et In Wiflingeham i c.* et iiii b'. et dim' Et In Nordmanabi i c'. et i b'. Et In [Folio 11] Blesebi iii c'. Et In Osgotebi i b'. Et In Media Rasa iii b'. quas Robertus de Haia tenet.

15. Comes de Moretonia In Teflesbi i c'. et iiii b'. Et In Cheleseia et Torntuna iiii c'. et iiii b'. Et In Houtuna i c'. Et In Walesbi ii c'. Et In Parua Rasa i c'. et i b'. et omnes tenet Roger de Montebegun Et In Osgotabi iii b'. Et In Sixla ii c'. et iii b'. Et In Ouresbi i c'. et iiii b'. quas monaci de Wighala tenent.

(p. 246) 16. Alanus Linc[olniensis] In Lindwda i c'. et iiii b'. Et In Toreweia *in dominio* v c'. et vi b'. Et In Parua Rasa, *dominio* iiii b'. et dim' et tertiam partem unius bou'. Et In Media Rasa *dominio* ii. b'. et dim' et tertiam partem unius b'.

17. Comes de Mellent In Steintuna i c'.

18. Comes Odo In Newetuna i c'. et iii b'. Et In Osgotabi v b'. Et In Risabi i c'.

19. Comes Britannie In Teflesbi iiii b'.

20. Manaset Arsic In Toft i c'. et vi b'. et tertiam partem unius b'. Et In Ouresbi ii c'. et vi b'. et omnes tenet Walterus filius Willelmi Et In Media Rasa ii c'. et ii b'. quas Gillebertus de Noua Villa tenet.

21. Anfridus de Canceio In Walesbi ii c'.

22. Hugo de Laval In Newetuna vi b'. quas Ricard filius Loswardi tenet.

[8]. IN HAWARDESHOU Wap[entac] habentur vii hundr' et dim' hundr' et in uno quoque xii c'. terre.

1. Comes Britannie In Waltham vi c'. Et In Bernetebi vi c'. Et In Belesbi iiii c'. et iiii bou'. Et In Hadecliua iiii c'. Et In Gunresbi ii c'. Et In Rauendala iii c'. Et In Brigesla i c'. et iiii b'. Et In Aschebi vi b'. Et In

Wada i c'. et iii b'. Et In Aluoldebi i c'. et i b'. Et In [Folio 12] Fembi iii c'. Et In Besabi iii c'. Et In Catebi iii c'. *Walter* Et In Hawardabi ii c'. et ii b'. Et In Newetuna iii c' et iiii b'.

Et In Greinesbi iii c'. *Wimund* Et In Newetuna ii b'. [iii h'. et vi c'. et ii b'. in dominio comitis] Et In Suinahopa *Anfridus* ii c'. et ii b'. et dim' b'.

2. Picotus de Laceles in Fuglestowa ii c'. et ii b'.

(p. 247) 3. Walbert iiii b'. *Rann[ulfus] episcopus* Et In Newetuna Et In Aluoldabi i b'. quam tenet Rogerus de Laci.

4. Comes Ricardus in Fuglestoua vi b'.

5. Ranulf Mischinus In Caburna iiii c'. et iii b'. quas Hugo tenet.

6. Willelmus Mischinus In Rodewella i c'. et vii b'. Et In Caburna i b'. Et In Cucuwalt ii b'. et tertiam partem unius bou'.

7. Radulfus Paganellus ii b'. quas Goslinus tenet [in Rodwella].

8. Alanus de Perci In Caburna i c'. Et In Cucuwald ii b'. quas Robertus de Araceia tenet.

9. Alanus Linc[olniensis] In Rodewella et Caburna v c'. et i b'.

10. Archiepiscopus de Eboraco in Cucuwald i c., *Alanus de Muntcell'*.

11. Episcopus Linc[olniensis] In Belesbi i c'. Et In Rauendala ii b'.

12. Anfridus de Canci In Suinopa ii c'. et iiii b'. et dim' de rege Et In eadem villa ii c'. et ii. b'. et dim' de comite Britannie.

Folio 13.

13. Alanus de Credon In Rauendala i c' et ii b'. Et In Aschebi i c'. et i b'. Et In Brighesla Et In Wada v b'. et dim' b'. et Walterus filius Aluredi tenet omnes istas.

14. Hugo de Laval. In Rauendala i c'. et ii b'. Et In Ascbi i c'. et i b'. Et In Brighela vi b'. Et In Vada v b'. et dim' b'. Et In Toresbi iiii c'. et iii b'.

15. Willelmus filius Haconis In Cucualt vii b'. et dim' *de rege* de Ran[nulfo] Mischini et de Alano de Perci et comite de Moreton.

16. Manasiet Arsic In Rodewella et in Nordcotis iii b'. quas Gillebertus de Noua Villa tenet. *Et Ricardus filius Roolf et Jordanus canonicus tenet i b'. de istis.*

17. Rogerus Marmion In Fuglestoua i c'. et vi b'. quas Picotus tenet.

(p. 248) 18. Ranulf Dunelmensis episcopus ii c'. et vii b'. quas Pinceon dapifer tenet de illo.

19. Carbonellus iiii b'. In Belesbi.

[9]. IN BREDELAI Wap[entac] habentur iii hundr' et dim' et iii b'. et In uno quoque xii čarucat' terre.

1. Hamon dapifer habet xiiii c'. et iiii b'. [In Leyseby et socha -*add.*].

2. Stephanus de Albemara v c'. et iii b'. In Viflesbi iiii c'. Et In Sut Cotun vii b'. et dim' Et In Bredelai dim' b'. Et In Grimesbi ii b'. Et In Hol i b'.

3. Ranulf Mischinus In Tatenai. Et Humberstein Et In Tirnesco et Vada xv c'. et iii b'. [scilicet] in Humberstein xii c'. in dominio Et In Tirnesco i c'. Et In Wada i c'. Et In Alsebi iii b'. Videlicet xii c'. sunt [Folio 14] in dominio. Et Heinfred in Irebi i c.

4. Hugo de Vallo In Cle et Tirnesco i c'. et iiii b'., quas Willelmus filius Haconis tenet.

5. Rex In Grimesbi Et In Sualwa ii c'. et v b'. [computatus infra xiii c'. et iii b'. de Hamone dapifero supra -*add.*]

6. Comes Ric[ardus] In Irebi i c'. et iiii b'. quas Willelmus conestabularius tenet.

7. Comes Britannie In Alesbi ii c'. et iiii b'. Et In Sualwa i c'. et vi b'. .

8. Normannus de Araceio In Cotun iiii b'.

9. Archiepiscopus de Eboraco In Heghelinga et Cle v b'. *Radulfus tenet* iiii Et In Sualwa vi b'. quas Ric[ardus] de Verli tenet.

10. Manasiet Arsic In Heghelinga et Cle i c'. et iiii b'. et dim' quas Gislebertus de Noua Villa tenet Et Osbertus tenet de illis.

11. Alanus Perci quartam partem unius b'.

12. Rodbertus episcopus Linc[olniensis] in Hol' ii b'.

13. Willelmus Mischinus In Cotis Et Irebi iiii c'. et vii b'. In Irebi iiii b'. Et In Cotis i c'. et iii b'.

(p. 249)

14. Radulfus de Criol In Houtuna vii b'.

15. Gosfridus filius Pagani in Sualwa i c'. et ii b'. quas Wimundus tenet.

16. Alanus Linc[olniensis] In Heghelinga et in Sualwa iii c'. et i b'. duas partes unius bouete

17. Ran[ulf] episcopus in Alesbi vi b'.

Folio 15

[10]. IN LUDEBURC Wap[entac] habentur iii hundr' In uno quoque xii carucat' terre.

1. Robertus de Insula In Ludeburc viii c'. Et In Fotrebi iiii c'. et iiii b'. quas Walterus tenet.

2. Robertus episcopus Linc[olniensis] In Wihum ii c'. Et In Ormesbi ii c'. et ii b'.

3. Stefanus de Albamara In Ormesbi iiii c'. et iiii b'.

4. Ran[ulf] Mischinus In Ormesbi ii c'. et ii b'. Et In Parva Grimesbia i c'. et iii b'. Et In Wihum ii c'.

5. Ranulf Dunelmensis episcopus In Fotrebi vii b'.

6. Monaci in Coueham iii c'. Et In Ludena i c'.

7. Alanus de Perci in Caletorp i c'. Et In Grimesbi i c'. et iiii b'. Et In Fotrebi iiii b'. Et In Coueham ii c'.

[11] IN IERBURC Wap[entac] habentur xiiii hundr' In uno quoque xii c'. terre.

1. Stefanus de Albemara xxv c'. et v b'. In Barwa xi c'. Et In Torentuna viii c'. Et In Cotun i c'. Et In Chiluingheholm i c'. Et In Linberga i c'. Et In Golsa ii c'. et iiii b'. Et In Chirnigtuna vi b'. Et In Chetlebi iii b'. et tertiam partem unius bouete.

2. Ranulf Mischinus In Haltun iii c'. et iiii b'. Et In Lopingheham vi b'. Et In Parva Linberga i c'. Et In Chelebi (p. 250) ii b'. Et In Haburc iii b'. Et In Broclesbi iii b' Et In Chelebi ii b'. *Gislebertus de Chaz* Et In Haburc iii b'. Et In Neosum v b'. Et In Brochesbi iii b'.

Folio 16.

3. Radulfus de Criol In Magna Linberga ii c'.

4. Walterus de Ganto In Bartuna et Ferebi et pendiciis xvii c'. Et In Horchestou iiii c'. quas Alanus de Perci tenet.

5. Gosfridus Murdac In Torp et Bechebi i c'. et vi b'.

6. Alanus de Perci In Horchestou iiii c'. Et In Immingeham et Torentuna v c'. Et In Sumerdebi ii c'. et iiii b'. Et In Ounebi ii c'. et iii b'. Et In Haburc i c'. Et In Wituna i b'. et dim' Et In Brunum iiii b'. Et In Seurebi quartam partem unius bouet' Et In Cadenai quartam partem unius b'. Et In Grossebi quartam partem unius bouet'.

7. Rodbertus de Chalz et Gosfridus Halselinus In Wragebi iiii c'. et v b'. et tertiam partem unius b'.

8. Normannus de Araceio In Stalinburc ii c'. et ii b'. Et In Immigheham iiii b'. Et In Lopingheham iiii b'. Et In Chiluingheholm iiii c'. et iii b'. Et In Wttuna vi b'. et dim' Et In Vlesbi vi b'. Et In Parva Linberga iiii b'. Et In Broclesbi ii b'. Et In Chelebi v b'. et tertiam partem unius bouete Et In Haburc iiii b'.

9. Rodbertus Episcopus Linc[olniensis] In Golsa et Wttuna iii c'. Et In Elesham ii c'. et ii b'. Et In Wlfriohebi i c'. et dim' Et In Bechebi i c'. *Gil[lebertus] de Nova Villa tenet.* Et In Chelebi v b'. *ipse Gisl[ebertus]* Et In Vlesbi iiii b'. *ipse Gisl[ebertus]* Et In Stalinburc ii b'. quas Gisl[ebertus] tenet.

10. Rodbertus nepos episcopi In Linberga iii c'. Et In Bondebi vii c'. Et In Stalinburc i c.

11. Hugo de Vallo In Helesham i c'., quam Ric[ardus] filius Osberti vicecomitis tenet.

12. Comes Britannie In Cadenai i c'. et iiii b'. Et In Nordchelesia i c'. Et In Cherlingtuna iiii b'. Et In Seurebi iii b'. Et In Chiluingheholm ii c'. et ii b'.

(p. 251) 13. Comes de Mellent iii c'. et iiii b'. In Crosthestuna et Cherligtuna et Wlfrechebi.

14. Comes Odo In Aldolbi i c'. et ii b'. Et In Grossebi ii c'.

Folio 17

15. Gosfridus filius Pagani In Golsa i c'. et ii b'. Et In Meltuna iii c' Et In Chelebi iii b'. et tertiam partem unius bouete Et In Vttuna vii b'. Et In Brunum ii b'. Et In Haburc ii b'. Et In Broclosbi iii b' Et In Ribi i c'. et iiii b'. Et In Vlesbi iiii c'. et iii b'. Et In Ribi iiii c'. et dim' de comite Ricardo.

16. Rodbertus de Haia In Vlesbi iiii b'. et Rodbertus Greslet v b'. in Neteltuna de rege.

17. Comes Ric[ardus] In Bernetebi vi c'. Et In Wlfrichesbi ii c'. Et In Bechebi i c'. et i b'. Et In Sumerdebi iiii b'. Et In Bertuna ii b'. Et In Haburc i b'. et dim' b'. Et In Ribi iiii c'. et dim' quas Gosfridus filius Pagani tenet Et In Chiluingheholm iii c'. et iiii b'. quas Reinarus de Sali tenuit.

18. Radulfus de Mortuo mari ii c'. In Wittuna.

19. [Ranulf Dunelmensis episcopus In Broclosbi i c'. – *add.*]

20. Manasiet Arsic In Chelebi iiii b'. et dim' Et In Stalinburc iiii b'. Et In Neteltuna i c'. et ii b'. quas Gillebertus de Nouauilla tenet et Ricardus filius Mobs.

21. Archiepiscopus In Stalinburc vi bouet'. Et In Chelebi iiii b'. et dim'.

22. Comes de Moreton In Neteltuna v b'. , Et In Elesham i c'. et ii b'. Et In Clifsebi iiii b'. Et In Husum iiii b'. Et istas omnes tenet Rogerius de Monbegon. Et In Crochestuna vi b'. quas Hugo de Crochestuna tenet.

23. Willelmus de Veceio In Bondebi iiii b'.

24. Willelmus Mischinus In Neteltuna v b'. Et In Vicheim i c'. et ii b'. Et In Huneduna i c'. Et In Safrebi ii c'. et iii b'.

25. Gislebertus Ticio ii c'. et vi b'. In Ferebi et dim' b'., et Nigellus de Albaneio tenet.

26. Alanus Linc[olniensis] In Golsa i c'. et ii b'. Et In Barua i c'. Et In Neosum v b'. Et In Broclesbi i b'. Et In Haburc ii b'.

27. Ricardus Linc[olniensis] filius Osberti vicecomitis in Elesham iii b'.

28. Willelmus Torniant In Neteltuna v b'. Et In Grossebi iii b'.

Folio 18
[12]. IN BOLINBROC Wap[entac] habentur viii hundr'
1. Ran[nulfus] Mischinus habet lx et xix carucat' terre et vi b'.
2. Ranulf episcopus v c'. et ii b'.
3. Rodbertus canonicus de Greinvilla iii c'.
4. Walterus de Ganto iii c'. quas Wigotus tenet.
5. Hugo filius Eudonis iii c'. inter Endrebi et Cal et Oustcal'.
6. Ketelbernus i c'. et vii b'. in Cal'.
7. Comes Britannie in Torp iii b'. quas Eudo de Monbi tenet.

[13]. IN CHEIRETRE Wap[entac] habentur vi hundr'
1. Ran[ulf] Mischinus habet xlvii c'. et iii b'.
2. Radulfus Tasson vi c'.
3. Comes Ricard ii c'. quas Ric[ardus] tenet de Heninghebi.
4. Rodbertus de Haia i c'., quam Ernis tenet. Et In Mintingis v b'. quas Terricus tenuit.
5. Radulfus Paganel In Strettuna et Randebi et Steintuna v c'. et duas partes unius bovete.
6. Rodbertus episcopus Linc[olniensis] In Randebi et Steintuna vi c'.
7. Normannus de Araceio In Calchewella i c'. et iiii b'.
(p. 253) 8. Alanus Linc[olniensis] vi b'. Gisl[ebertus] filius G[ocelini] et Gerardus In Sticheswald.
9. Hugo filius Eudonis v bouet'. in Strettuna.

Folio 19
IN SUTTRIDING
[14]. IN CALNODESHOU Wap[entac] habentur x hundr'

1. Gislebertus filius Gocelini ii c'. In Welletuna quas Ricardus Linc[olniensis] tenet Et In Freschena iiii bouet'.
2. Hugo de Vallo iiii c'. et vi b'. Et de archiepiscopo de Rigesbi ii b'.
3. Comes Britannie iii c'. In Burc'
4. Hugo filius Pinceonis iiii b'. In Freschena.
5. Rogerius de Ganto In Croft ii c'. et iiii b'.
6. Walterus de Ganto xlviii c'. et *iiii b'. et sunt in Welletuna et Hugo Pilatus tenet eas* et de istis omnibus tenet Wigatus iiii b'. Et de his tenet Rogerius de Ganto vi c'. et iiii b'. et Hugo filius Eudonis i c'.
7. Comes Ricardus In Sutrebi ii c'. et iiii b'. Et In Brincla ii c'. Et In Calesbi ii c'. et iiii b'. Et In Freschena et Weinflet viii c'. et vi b'. *Et In Dalbi et Forthintuna xi c., Et In Aschebi v c'. Et In Breitoft et Irebi xi c'.* Suma iii hundr' et vi c'. et vi b'.
8. Ketelbernus i c'.
9. Ranulf Dunelmensis episcopus iiii c'. et iii b'. Et Pinceon tenet.
10. Hugo filius Randulfi vii c'. et ii. b'. et dimid'.
11. Rodbertus de Haia iiii b'. quas Terricus tenuit.
12. Hugo filius Eudonis iiii c'. et v b'. et i c'. de fedio Walteri de Ganto quam Hurueius tenet.
13. Ranulf Mischinus in Waletuna ii c'.

(p. 254) Folio 20

[15]. IN CALSWAT Wapentac habentur x hundr' in uno quoque xii c'. terre.

1. Comes Ricardus In hundr' de Suabi xii c'. Et In hundr' de Lecheburna x c'. Et In Tedolftorp x c'. et vi b'. Et In hundr' de Hotoft viii c'. Et In hundr' de Calesbi vi carucat'. Et In hundr' de Widerna et de Stein i c'. et iiii b'. Et In Drebi iiii b'. Suma iiii hundr' et x c'.

2. Walterus de Ganto xviii c'. et iiii b'. Et de istis tenent filii Ragemeri xiiii c.

3. Alanus de Credon x c'.

4. Comes de Moreton ii c'.

5. Archiepiscopus de Eboraco In Rigesbi iii c'. et vi b'.

6. Comes Britannie in Rigesbi ii c'. et ii b'. quas Ric[ardus] filius Losward tenet Et In Mumbi et pendiciis ix c'. quas Eudo tenet.

7. Ketelbernus de Cal' ii c'. et iiii b'. In Suttuna et Marchebi et Dedloncstorp Et In Hotoft iiii b'.

8. Manasiet Arsic iii c'. quas Wimundus de Abi tenet.

9. Ran[ulf] Mischinus In Humbi ii c., quas Walterus filius Rogeri tenet.

10. Ran[ulf] episcopus i c'. et iiii b'. In Burnetorp quas Willelmus filius Anschetilli tenuit Et In Vlesbi ii b'. quas Pinceon.

11. Hugo filius Eudonis In Aghetorp vi b'.

12. Gislebertus filius Gocelini In Marchebi iiii b'. Et In Maltebi iiii b'. Walterus filius Rag[emer] tenet.

Folio 21

13. Randulfus de Criol In Maltorp et Cumberworda et Suttuna Et In Vlsebi i c'. et vi b'. et dim' b'.

14. Rodbertus de Brus In Alworda iiii b'.

15. Alanus Linc[olniensis] in Hotoft v b'. Ansch[etil] tenet.

16. Hugo filius Randulf i c'. et ii b'.

17. Ricardus Linc[olniensis] filius Osberti vicecomitis ii b'. quas Rad[ulfus] de Chalchesbi tenet.

(p. 255)

[16] IN WRAGHEHOU Wap[entac] habentur ix hundr' in uno quoque xii carucate terre.

1. Comes Ricardus In Steintuna [iusta Langwat] iiii c'. quas filii Rocelini tenent Et In Neobole ii c'. et ii b'. quas Hugo tenet Et In Bolingintuna vi b'. quas Rodbertus filius Hunfridi tenuit Et In Langhetuna iii b'. quas Simon tenet.

2. Ranulf episcopus In Bulingtuna i c'. quam Willelmus filius Ansch[etil] tenuit. Et In Biscopetorp iii c'. Et *in Langetuna* ii b'. quas Pinceon tenet. In Chesfremund iii c'. Et In Ludesfort v c'. et i b'. Et In Apeleia ii c'. *emina* Et In Steinfelda iii c'. *ei tuna.*

3. Alanus de Perci In Ludeforda. Et pendiciis xiii c'. et i b'. Et In Vichenbi iii c'., quas Ric[ardus] tenet Et In Westletebi i c'. et i b'. Et In Becheringa i b'. et dim' Et In Snelleslund *ii b'.* [et] Reresbi *ii b'.* terre Et In Oteun i c'. et ii b'.

4. Archiepiscopus de Eboraco In Benigworda ii c'. et iiii b'. quas Ricardus Linc[olniensis] tenet Et In Pantuna et Barcworda ii c'. et vi b'. quas Gislebertus Ticio tenuit. Et In Lissigtuna et pendiciis vii c'. quas Herbertus filius Albri tenet Et In Wllingheham ii c'. et i b'. et dimid' quas Ric[ardus] de Verli tenet. Et In Grisebi. Et Burc ii c'. et ii b'. quas Ricardus de Verli tenet. Et In Heintuna i c'. et

87

iiii b'. quas ipse Ricardus de Verli tenet. Et In Barcworda vi b'., quas idem Richard de Verli tenet.

Folio 22

5. Comes de Moreton In Heintuna iii c'., quas Albertus tenet.

6. Gosfridus filius Pagani In Wragebi vi c'. Et In Fulnetebi et Randa vi c'. (p. 256) Et In Hattuna v c'. Et In Langhetuna i b'. Et In Pantuna ii c'. Et In Barcworda ii c'. et ii b'. Et In Becheringa iiii b'. Et In Houtuna i c'. Et In Chinetorp ii b'. Et In Burc vi b'. Et In Tirigtuna vii b'., quas Ricardus Linc[olniensis] tenet Et In Herduic v b'. et dim' b'. Et In Tirigtuna altero ii c'. et ii b'.

7. Walterus de Ganto In Bardanai ii c'. Et In Suderei ii b'. Et In Osgotebi ii c'.

8. Rodbertus Greslet i c'. et iiii b'. et dim'. In Caldecota de rege.

9. Rogerius Marmion inter Leghetuna *i c'. et iiii b'.* et Buteita et Ansgotebi ii b'.

10. Ran[ulf] Mischinus In Beniguorda iii c'. et iiii b'. Et In Strutebi ii b'. Et In Buligtuna v b'. Et In Chintorp tertiam partem unius carucat' terre Et In Ludeford iiii b'. et dim' quas monaci de Spaldingis tenent Et In Westletebi vi b'.

11. Gislebertus filius Gocelini In Houtuna i c'. Et In Becheringa dim' b'. Et In Snelleslund i c'. Et In Reresbi i c'. et Sunetorp ii c'. Et In Blesebi ii c'.

12. Normannus de Araceio In Becheringa ii b'.

13. Rodbertus episcopus Linc[olniensis] In Vichinghebi i c'. Et In Snelleslund ii b'. Et In Reresbi i b'. Et In Sunetorp i c'. Et In Langhetuna et Wraghebi i c'. et ii b'. quas Simon filius Willelmi tenet.

14. Radulfus Paganellus Inter Heintuna et Barcworda et Strubi et Suderebi ii c'. et v b'.

15. Manasiet Arsic In Wllingheheim vi b'. et dim' b'. quas Walterus filius Walteri tenet et Willelmus filius Hac[onis].

Folio 23

16. Radulfus de Criol In Wllingheheim i c'. Et In Strubi [*corr. ex* Sutrebi] ii b'. Et In Chintorp tertiam partem unius carucat' terre. Et quartam partem unius b'. Et In Barcworda et Heintuna i c'. Et In Ludeford dim' b'. et v b'. in Sixla.

(p. 257) 17. Alfreit de Canci In Blesebi v b'. et tertiam partem unius b'. quas tenet Wilgrip sed ille iacent ad gel' de Nortriding.

18. Rex In Sotebi iiii c'.

19. Alanus Linc[olniensis] In Tiringtuna ii c'. et iiii b'. quas Gocelinus tenet.

20. Sancta Maria In Suderei ii b'.

21. Ansgot de Burewella In Ludeford iii b'. quas uxor eius tenet.

22. Hugo filius Eudonis In Langhetuna ii b'. Rodbertus de Haia tenet.

23. Hugo de Vallo i c'. in Sixla.

[17]. IN HILLA Wap[entac] habentur vi hundr' in uno quoque xii c'. terre.

1. Comes Ricardus In hundred' de Langhetuna xii c'. Et In hundred' de Hamringheheim xi c'. et iiii b'. Et In Hagwordingheheim iii c'. Et In Salmonebi i c'. Et In Brinche ii c'. Et In Ormeresbi iii c'. Et In Chetlesbi iii c'. et iiii b'. Et In Valmeresgara i c'. Et In Tedforda vi b'. Et In Fuledebi ii c'. Et In Oxecum i c'. et vi b'. et de istis tenet Wigotus x b'. in Wincebi. Summa iii hundr' et v c'. et iiii b'.

Folio 24

2. Archiepiscopus de Eboraco in Tedforda Et In Ormesbi iii c'. et vii b'. Et In Wlfrichesbi ii c'. et ii b'. quas archidiaconus tenet.

3. Normannus de Araceio In Ormesbi iii c'. et vii b'.

4. Comes Britannie In Agwordingheheim iiii b'. quas Wigotus tenet.

5. Ranulf episcopus In Fuletebi et Oxcum iiii c'. et vi b'. quas Pinceon tenet.

6. Ansgotus de Borewella In Walmeresgara ii c.

7. Walterus de Ganto In Wincebi i c'. et ii b'. , quas Wigot tenet Et In Hagwordingheheim iiii b'.

8. Alanus de Perci In Wlfrichebi vi b'.

9. Gislebertus filius Gocelini In Ascbi i c'. et i b'. Et Sumerdebi ii c'. Et In Tedforda (p. 258) xv b'. Et In Hamrigheheim iiii b'. Et In Endrebi vi b'.

10. Stephanus de Albemara In Hagwordingheheim i c'. Et In Ascbi iiii c'. Et In Endrebi iiii b'.

[18]. IN LUDESC Wap[entac] habentur x hundr' In uno quoque xii c'.

1. Comes Britannie In Gertuna iii c'. Et In Welletune iiii c'. Et In Mannebi iii c'. Et In Grimolbi iii c'. et i b'. Et In Salfletebi iii c'. Et In Schitebroc iii c'. Et In Sumercotis iii c'. Et In [Folio 25] Ghermudtorp ii c'. Et In Ierburc ii c'. et v b'. et tertiam partem unius b'. Et In Alvingheheim i c'. et ii b'. et tertiam partem unius b'. Et In Welletune i c'. quam Alanus filius Landri tenuit.

2. Comes Ricard In Tadewella et socha xx c'. et v b'. et dimid' et de istis tenet Wigot In Maltebi x b'. et Ingelram in Tadewella et Haligtune v b'.

3. Ansgotus de Borewella ii c'. *In Burewella* Et In Haghetorp ii c'. Et In Munchetune i c'. et iiii b'. Et In Carletune iiii c'. Et In Wicheim *uxor* i c'. Et In Welletuna iiii b'. Et In Sumercotis i b'.

4. Alanus de Perci In Ristuna et Carletuna ii c'. et iiii b'. quas Ricardus Linc[olniensis] tenet Et In Helchingtuna viii c'. Et In Ludena iiii b'. (5.) Et monaci de Couenam in Ludena i c'.

6. Ranulf episcopus In Cledingtuna et Cheilestorp ii c'. Et In Welletuna ii b'. Et In Scitebroc ii b'. Et In Salfletebi ii b'. Et In Coringtuna dim' b'.

7. Alanus Linc[olniensis] In Catebi i c'. *dominio* Et In Wicheim v b'. et dim' Et In Chelestuna (p. 259) ii c'. et vi b'. et dim' *dominio* Et In Stiuetuna ii c'. *dominio* Et In Cocrigtuna iiii b' *dominio*. Et In Grimolbi vii b'. Ansch[etil] de Egheling.

8. Gosfridus filius Pagani In Grimchiltorp et Catebi i c'. et iiii b'. *quas Radulfus Malet tenet* Et In Welletuna vi b'.

9. Willelmus Mischinus In Vitcala ii b'. *quas Willelmus filius Albrede* tenet. Et In Salfletebi et Scitebroc ii b'. *quas ipse Willelmus tenet.* Et In Catebi i b'. et dim' *Radulfus Malet tenet.*

10. Ran[ulf] Mischinus In Helchingtuna iiii c'. Et Walterus de Beningheborda tenet iii c'. et Alanus Olliet i c'.

11. Episcopus Linc[olniensis] In Luda xii c'. Et In Parua Wicheheim ii b'. et ipse tenet de Comite Ricardo iiii b'.

12. Hugo de Vallo In Vitcala iii c'. et vii b'. et dim' b'. Et In Cocringtuna iii c'. et duas partes unius b'. Et In [Folio 26] Aluingheheim iii b'. et dim' b'. Et In Sumercotis i b'. et dim' b'. Et In Salfletebi iii b'.

13. Radulfus de Criol In Alvingheheim ii b'. et dim' b'. Et In Cocringtuna i c'. et vi b'. Et In Sumercota i b'. Et In Safledebi i b'. et dim' Et In Chedingtuna iiii b'. Et In Wicheheim i c'. Et In Vitcala i c'. et vii b'. et tertiam partem unius bouet'.

14. Rogerus Marmion In Tadewella i c'. quam Turoldus de Bolebec tenet.

15. Rodbertus de Haia In Carletuna et Sumercotis vi b'. Ansgotus tenet.

16 . Radulfus Paganellus In Sumercotis ii. b'. et dim' b'. Et In Welletuna iiii b'.

litigationis Et In Sumercotis duas partes unius b'. Et In Scitebroc dimid' b'. litigationis.

[19]. IN HORNECASTRA Wap[entac] habentur hundr' vi et vi c'. In uno quoque xii c'.
1. Comes Ricard in Scriflebi et Conighesbi v b'.
(p. 260) 2. Rogerus Marmion Inter Scriflebi et Torentuna et Ructuna et Dalbi et Wilghebi et Coningesbi et Holteim xvii c'. et ii b'. Ipse Roger tenet inde ix c'. et vi b'. *in dominio* et Vluietus tenet inde iii c'. et iiii b'. Et Turoldus et Alsie ii c'.
3. Episcopus Dunelmensis Inter Chirchebi et Torp et Martuna et Wispigtuna ix c'. et vi b'.
4. Walterus de Ganto Inter Baburc et Hedlingtuna et Ascbi i c'. et dim' et Timlebi xxiv c.

Folio 27
5. Ranulf Mischinus i c'. et iiii b'. quas Radulfus de Stichesweld tenet In Edlingtuna.
6. Rodbertus de Brus iiii b'. In Aschebi.
7. Stephanus de Albamara Inter Timlebi et Langhetuna et Coninghesbi v c'. et vi b'. Et ii b'. quas Willelmus de Alost inde tenet. Et Osbertus de Hawordingheham tenet ii b'. in Coninghesbi.
8. Alanus Linc[olniensis] Inter Langhetuna et Timlebi et Bochelanda ii c'. quas Alanus cognatus Alani tenet.
9. Radulfus Paganellus In Chirchebi i c'. et ii b'. quas Alli tenet.
10. Hugo filius Eudonis Inter Tatesala et Tumbi et Martuna et Strettuna et Wispingtuna et Wadigworda xv c'. et iiii b'.

Index

Appendix II

THE NORTHAMPTONSHIRE SURVEY

This 'Hydarium' of Northamptonshire is found in a Peterborough Cartulary
(Cott. MS Ves. E 22, fo. 94 *et seq.*). It is drawn up Hundred by Hundred,
like the surveys of Leicestershire and of Lindsey, and is, therefore, probably connected with the assessment of Danegeld. Although it is of special
value for reconstituting the Domesday Vills, the assessment it records so
often varies from that which is found in Domesday that we cannot institute
a close comparison. The introduction of a 'parva virgata' further compli-
cates the reckoning. That the original document was written on a roll is
shown by the use of the phrase 'per alium rotulum'. The statement on fol.
97b that there ought, at one place, to be half a hide more 'per rotulos Wyn-
cestr[ie]', would seem to refer to Domesday; but on the next page we read:

> In Pytesle Abbas de Burgo v hid. [et] dim. set tamen in Rotulis Wyn-
> cestr[ie] vi hid. et iii. parvas virgatas.

Since Domesday records this holding as 'v hid. et una virgata terræ', the
reference (if the text of the survey is right) must clearly be to some other
record preserved in the national treasury.

So wrote J. H. Round in his introduction to 'The Northamptonshire Survey' in
Feudal England, to which he appended 'about a fifth of the Survey as a specimen
of the whole'. He subsequently wrote in greater detail on the survey in *VCH
Northamptonshire*, i, pp. 357–89, where he printed a translation of the whole
survey. He showed that the survey as it survives is based upon a document produced in the time of Henry I, probably shortly before the death of Eudo dapifer in
1120, when some of the Domesday tenants were still alive. At some point at least
a generation later, in the time of Henry II, several of the entries were updated.
Although this composite structure makes the survey difficult to use, it is a valuable source for the identification of tenants and the descent of fees. The document has never been published in its entirety in Latin. A transcript of the
manuscript is given below.

BL Cotton Vespasian E xxii

[fol. 94r] Hydarium de comitatu Norhampton

Hokeslawe
Twywelle. Albr[icus] camerar[ius] ii hidas de feudo Abbatis de Thorneya. Ibidem
de feudo Comitis David. Ibidem de feudo Abbatis Burgi i magnam uirgatam.
In Slipton i hidam et unam uirgatam de feudo Willelmi de Corcy. Ibidem Ricar-
dus filius Hugonis ii partes unius hidae de feudo Burgi. Ibidem Rogerus nepos
Abbatis tertiam partem unius hidae de eodem feudo.
In Suburc ii hidas dim'. de feudo Westmonaster'.

In Lofwyc Th[omas] i hidam et unam uirgatam de feudo de Deneford. Ibidem Radulfus Fleming i uirgatam dim'. de feudo Comitis David. Ibidem Wydo frater eius i magnam uirgatam de feudo de Thorneya.

In Drayton Albricus camerarius dimidiam hidam de feudo Regis.

In Yslep idem Albricus de feudo Regis. Ibidem iiii sokemanni Regis i hidam de feudo Westmonaster'.

In Audewyncle Abbas de Burgo iiii hidas dimidiam quas Ascelinus de Wateruille tenet. Ibidem Galfridus de Glynton i magnam uirgatam de feudo Glovernie pertinens ad Barton. Ibidem Ricardus filius Wydonis iii hidas dim'. uirg'. minus de feudo Regine.

Item in Benifeld Willelmus de Lisurs iii magnas uirg'. de feudo Regis.

In Bernewell' Robertus de Ferar[iis] vi hid'. et i magnam uirgatam de feudo Regis. Ibidem Reginaldus le Moyne vi hid'. de feudo de Rammeseye.

In Lilleford Willelmus Olyfart v hid'. de feudo Regis Scotie.

Nauesford

In Tytheni's Robertus de Ferar[riis] x hid'. Ibidem Ascelinus de Wateruill' iii hid'. et i uirgat'. et tres partes dim'. hid'. de Burgo.

In Thrapston Radulfus filius Oger ii hid'. et i uirg'. de feudo de Brunne. Ibidem Robertus filius Edeline i hid et i uirg'. de feudo de Clare.

In Torpe et Achirche Ascelinus de Wateruill' vi hid'. dim.. de feudo Burgi.

In Clopton Walterus i hid'. et i uirgat'. de feudo Regis. Ibidem iii hid'. dim'. de feudo Burgi. Ibidem Ascelinus dim'. hid'. de feudo Burgi.

Wadenhowe Albricus de Ver ii hid'. et i uirgat'. de feudo Regis David. Ibidem Wymunt de Stok' i uirg'. de feudo Burgi. Ibidem Rogerus Infans ii paruas uirgat'. de eodem feudo. Ibidem Wiuienus de Chirchefelde dim'. hid'. de eodem feudo. Ibidem Galfridus de Gonthorp ii hid'. de eodem feudo. In Catteworthe i hid'. dim'. de feudo Burgi.

Pokebroc

In Pokebroc Robertus de Cauz i hid'. et i uirgat'. de feudo Regis. Ibidem Walterus de Clopton ii hid et dim'. de feudo Burgi. Ibidem Rogerus Marmium i hid'. et i uirgat'. de eodem feudo.

In Armeston de Burgelay ii hid'. dim'. de eodem feudo. Ibidem Turkil i hid de eodem feudo. Ibidem Wydo Maufee i hid'. de eodem feudo. Ibidem Galfridus de Gunthorp ii partes dim'. hid'. de eodem feudo. Ibidem Tedrik' iii partes [fol. 94v] de dim'. hid'. de eodem feodo.

In Pappele i hid'.

In Lillington i hid'.

In Hennington Berengerus le Moyne ii hid'. dim'. de feodo de Rammeseye. Ibidem Ricardus filius Gilberti i hid'. et i uirgat.. et dim'. de feodo Burgi. Ibidem Wydo Maufe dim'. hid'. et dim'. uirgat'. de eodem feodo. Ibidem Reginaldus le Moyne dim'.. hid'. et dim'. uirg'. de eodem feodo.

In Kynesthorp Walterus de Lodington i hid'. et i uirg'. de feodo Burgi. Ibidem Willelmus de Chirchetot dim'. hid'. de feodo Regis.

In Therninge Rogerus Marmioun iii paruas uirgatas de feodo Burgi.

In Ayston Abbas de Burgo iiii hid'. in dominico. Ibidem Papilun dim'. hid'. de eodem feodo. Ibidem Leuenoth dim'. hid'. de eodem feodo.

In Vndele Abbas in dominico vi hid'. Ibidem Vivien i paruam uirgatam.

Duo hundred de Naso

In Stinton Willelmus de Lisurs ii hid'.

In Bernak Fulco Paynel iii hid'.

In Wirthorpe Abbas Croylaund ii hid'. Ibidem de feudo Eudonis Dapiferi i uirg'.

In Eston Simon i hid'. dim'.

In Peychirch'. In Etton'. In Northburg' dim'. uirg.

In dominico Abbatis de Burgo Sancti Petri lxx hid'. et iii uirg'. et dim'.

Hundred de Sutton'

In eadem uilla Dominus Rex habet in dominico iiii hid'. In eadem uilla Willelmus de Quency i hid'. dim'. et paruam uirgat'. terre de Comitatu Leycestrie. Ibidem. Alfredus viii paruas uirgatas de Gilberto de Pinkeny. Ibidem Paganus i hid'. et i paruam uirgatam de feudo Comitis Leycestrie; Robertus filius Osberti tenuit.

In Euenle i hid'. et i paruam uirg'. de feodo Comitis Leycestrie.

In Preston' dim'. hid'. de feodo Comitis Leycestrie.

In Crouelton iiii paruas uirg'. de feudo Comitits Leycestrie. Ibidem Seuarus i hid'. et ii partes uirg'. de feodo Leycestrie. Ibidem Brien filius Comitis i hid'. dim'. et ii paruas uirg'. de feodo de Walingford.

In Neubottle Regis de Reynes vi hid'. et i paruam uirg'. de feodo Comitis Leycestrie; Willelmus de Lepyn tenuit. In Furthingho iiii hid'. de feodo Comitis Leycestrie.

In Cherlington Maynardus i hid'. dim'. et i paruam uirg'. Ibidem Simon Chendut i hid'. dim'. de feodo de Berkamstede et i paruam uirg'. Ibidem Odo dapifer viii paruas uirg'. de feodo de Colescestra.

In Gremesbir Aunsel de Chokes ii hid'. et iiii paruas uirgatas scilicet quarta pars ii hid'.

In Middleton Willelmus Mechin i hid'. et dim'. et i paruam uirgat'. de feodo Willelmi de Curcy.

In alia Middleton Simon Chendut ii hid'. de feodo de Berkamstede.

In Thayniford Mainfenn de Walrentone i hid'. Ibidem Robertus Basset i hid'. de feodo de Walingford.

In Ayno Willelmus de Mandeuille iii hid'.

In Middelton monachi de sancti Eueraldi ii hid'.

In Walton i hid'. cum ii uirg'. in Sutton quas Suonild tenuit.

In Gildeby i hid'. et vii paruas uirg'. de feodo de Mortal'. [*sic*]

[fol. 95r]Hundred de Albodestowe

In Chacombe iiii hid'. de feodo Episcopi Lincoln'.

In Euenl' ii hid'. et i paruam uirg'. minus quas Alouf de Merke tenuit.

In Thorpe ii hid'.

In Stanes Gilbertus de Pinkeny ii hid'.

In Colewych Willelmus ii hid'. et iiii paruas uirg'. Ibidem Otuer i hid'.

In Stotebyr' ii hid'. quas monachi Norh[antone] tenent.

In Rodestone ii hid'. de feodo Comitis Cestrie.

In Wytefeld Gilbertus de Monte ii hid'. et ii uirg'. in dominico.

In Merston Radulfus Murdac iiii hid'. de feodo Comitis Leycestrie.

In Siresham Thomas Sorel i hid'. dim'. Ibidem Comes Leycestrie. i paruam uirg'. Ibidem Gilo dim'. hid'. Ibidem Willelmus filius Alu[red]i iii paruas uirg'.

In Helmenden' Willelmus de Torewell' iiii hid'. de feodo Comitis Leycestrie.
In Chelverdescote dim'. hid'. Idem Comes Leycestrie.
In Brackele et Hausho. Idem Comes vii hid'. dim.

Hundred de Wardon
In Wardon Ricardus Foliot ii hid'. dim'. et i magnam uirgatam, scilicet quarta pars i militis de feodo Regis in capite.
In Eston' et Apeltreya Willelmus de Bolonia vii hid'. de feodo Comitis de Mandeuille.
In Bottolendon Fulco Paynel ii hid'. una ex illis de feodo Cestrie. Ibidem. Willelmus Meschin i hid'. Ibidem i hid'. de feodo Episcopi Lincoln.
In Byfeld viii hid'. de feodo comitis Leycestrie.
In Grapesford que pertinet ad Byfeld i hid'. et ii paruas uirg'.
In Hinton de feodo comitis Willelmus [sic] ii hid'. quas Robertus tenet.
In Farendon. Simon Chendut i hid'. dim'. et i paruam uirgatam de feodo de Berchamstede. Ibidem. Comes Leycestrie iiii paruas uirgatas.
In Hochecote. Rogerus Murdac ii hid'. de feodo Regis Dauid.
In Wodeford. Comes Leycestrie ii hid'. quas Osemundus tenet.
In Byfeld. Rogerus de Reymes ii hid'.
In Aydona. Ricardus filius Wale ii hid'. de feodo Leycestrie.
In Gretteworth. Radulfus de Kaynes ii hid'. de feodo suo.
In Solegraue iiii hid'. de feodo Gilonis fratris Haschuull'.

Graueshende Falewesle
In Falewesle habet dominus Rex ii hid'.
In Chelurdescote ii hid'. de feodo comitis Leycestrie.
In Fardingstone iii hid'. et i paru'. uirg'. Ibidem Heruicus Belet viii paruas uirgatas quas Willelmus de Strafford tenet.
In Wedon' monachi de Becco iiii hid'. de feodo comitis Leycestrie.
In Charwelton ii hid'. et iiii paruas uirg'. de feodo de Berkamstede. Ibidem Abbas de Thorneya iiii paruas uirgatas antiquo scripto dim'. hid'. Ibidem. Hugo de Chahain dim'. hid'. de feodo comitis Leycestrie. Ibidem. iiii paruas uirgatas de feodo Ade de Napton. Ibidem comes Leycestrie iiii paruas uirgatas.
In Catesby iiii hid'. de feodo Willelmi Peuerel.
In Eliden iiii hid'. de feodo de Berkamstede.
In Preston iii hid'. ii paru'. uirg'. minus de feodo Simonis de Wahill. [fol. 95v] Ibidem Ricardus filius Willelmi i hid'. ii paruas uirgatas.
In Lichebarue iiii hid'. de feodo Hugo Pol'.
In Euerdon monachi de Bernay ii hid'. dim'. et ii paruas uirgatas. Ibidem Hugo uicecomes viii paruas uirgatas quas monachi de Dauentre tenent. Ibidem Radulfus de Waundeuille iiii paruas uirgatas. Ibidem Walterus iiii paruas uirgatas.
In Snokescombe iiii paruas uirgatas de feodo comitis Leycestrie.
In Stowe. Johannes de Armenteres iiii hid'. de feodo Gilberti de Gaunt.

Hundredum de Aylwoldesle
In Baddeby et Newenham Abbas de Euesham iiii hid'.
In Norton ii hid'. dim'. et ii paruas uirgatas de feodo de Warewyk.
In Thorp Stephanus de Turs dim'. hid'. Ibidem Willelmus de Nouo Foro iiii paruas uirgatas.

In Beruby ii hid'. de feodo Willelmi Peuerel.

In Gildesboru. Episcopus Lincoln' in dominico ii hid'.

In Stau[er]ton Willelmus de Nouo Foro i hid'. de feodo comitis Leycestrie. Ibidem Stephanus de Welton iii hid'. de feodo Rogeri de Moubray.

In Branndeston Willelmus Trussebot iii hid'. et vi paruas uirg'. de feodo Pagani Peuerel. Ibidem comes Leycestrie iiii paruas uirg'.

In Dauentre Walterus filius Roberti viii hid'. de feodo Regis Scotie.

In Welton Willelmus ii hid'. dim'. et ii paruas uirg'. de feodo comitis Leycestrie. Ibidem Hugo uicecomes v paruas uirgatas dim'. de feodo de Berkamstede. monachi de Dauentre tenent. Ibidem. Ricardus Maulore ii paruas uirgatas.

In Esseby iiii hid'. de feodo comitis Leycestrie.

In Dodeford Radulfus de Chanes iii. hid'.

In Chelredescote Galfridus de Toreuill' i hid'. et ii paruas uirgatas de feodo comitis Leycestrie.

Hundredum de Norton

In Esseby Stephanus ii hid'. et viii paruas uirgatas de feodo Hugonis de Lega.

In Mortona Henricus de Pinkeny i hid'. et dim.

In Wedona Idem Henricus ii hid'. et viii paruas uirg'.

In Plomton Willelmus filius Roberti i hid'. dim'. de feodo Wahill.

In Slapton iiii hid'. de feodo comitis Leycestrie.

In Braddene Paganus i hid'. iiii paruas uirgatas. Ibidem Vitalis Engayne. i hid'. iiii paru'. uirg'. Ibidem Radulfus de Waundeville i hid'. ii paruas uirg.

In parua Blacoluesle Normannus de Sancto Patricio ii hid'. de feodo Peuerel. Item pertinet ad hidagium de Horton. i hid'. et vii paruas uirgatas et dim'.

In alia Blacoluesle. Idem dim'. hid'. Ibidem Rogerus Golofre iii hid'. dim'. et dim'. paru'. uirg'. Ibidem Willelmus de Plumton ii hid'. ii paruas uirg'. Ibidem. Gilbertus i hid'. dim'. et i paruam uirgatam de feodo de Berkamstede. Item in Selueston. Otuerus dim'. hid'. de feodo comitis Willelmi. Ibidem Willelmus de Caynes i hid'. de feodo de Morton'. Ibidem Henricus de Pinkeny dim'. hid'.

In Maydeford Paganus ii hid'. ii paruas uirg'.

In Sewewell' Radulfus i hid'. ii paruas uirg'.

In Pateshill iiii paruas uirgatas.

In Norton et in soca vii hid'. et i magnam uirgatam.

In Atteneston [fol. 96r] Galfridus de Turuill iii paruas uirg'. Ibidem monachi de Becco viii paruas uirg'.

Hundredum de Toucestre

In Gauton Adnotus de Bettune iiii hid'.

In Pateshill Simon de Wahill vii hid'. Ibidem Willelmus de Hocton viii paruas uirg'. Ibidem comes Mauricius de feodo de Botebot ii paruas uirg'.

In Foxleya Simon de Wahilll iiii paruas uirg'. Ibidem Comes Maur' iiii paruas uirg'. de feodo de Berkamstede. Ibidem monachi de Norhantone vi paruas uirg'.

In Hinton Elias ii hid'. de feodo comitis Willelmi.

In Wappenham Henricus de Pinkeny ii hid'. de feodo.

In Eueleia iiii hid'.

In Grimescote Aunsel ii hid'. et iiii paruas uirg'. de feodo Rogeri de Moubray. Ibidem monachi de Donestabel ii hid'. de feodo de Wahille.

In Potton Iohannes de Dauentre i hid'. dim'. et paruam uirgatam. In Tiffeld Wil-

102

lelmus de Pery i hid'. dim'. i paruam uirgatam de feodo comitis Hugonis. Ibidem Walterus de Fortho. i hid'. dim'. et ii paruas uirg'. Ibidem Willelmus de Gaynes vii paruas uirg'.

In Wytlebyr' Ricardus vi paruas uirgatas de feodo de Selueston.

In Touecestre comes de Arundel vii hid'. iii paruas uirg'. Ibidem Wybertus ad ecclesiam vi paruas uirg'. de feodo sancti Wandragesill.

In Graftone abbas de Grestenge iiii hid.

Hundredum de Cleyle

In Stoke et in Aldrinton vii hid'. ii paruas uirg'.

In Bassenham i hid'.

In Wyca Mainfeni ii hid'. de feodo de Wolfrington.

In Pyria Robertus de Ferrar' iii hid'. ii paruas uirgatas de feodo comitis de Ferrar.

In Westpyria iii hid'. dim'. et quinta pars dimid'. hid'. de feodo Willelmi Peuerel.

In Forhoue Walterus ii hid'. de feodo Ricardi filii Willelmi. Ibidem. Willelmus Gernet vii paruas uirgatas de feodo de Berkamstede. Ibidem. comes Leyestrie iii paruas uirgatas.

In Couesgraue Robertus Ryuel viii paruas uirgatas. Ibidem Willelmus le Brun vi paruas uirgatas. Ibidem Ad[am] ix paruas uirgatas.

In Pyria heredes de Salfleto i hid'. quinta pars i hid'. de feodo Regis Dauid.

In Pokesl' Robertus Ryuel vi paruas uirgatas de feodo comitis Leycestrie. Ibidem iiii paruas uirgatas de feodo Regis Dauid.

In Esteneston Ricardus de Le Estre i hid'. dim'. et i paruam uirgatam de feodo de Berkamstede. Ibidem Godefridus et Aldredus viii paruas uirgatas de feodo Willelmi Mauduit.

In Someshale Michael Mauncel vi paruas uirgatas de feodo Willelmi Peuerel de Hecham.

In Wakefeld iiii paruas uirgatas de feodo Regis.

In Hertwell. Nicholas. Hugo. Ad[am]. Rad[ulfus]. iiii hid'. dim'. et paruam uirgatam scilicet quinta pars dim'. hid'. de feodo Walkelin Mamyot.

In Esse. Robertus filius Anketilli i hid'. et ii paruas uirg'. de feodo Willelmi Mauduit.

Adhydam Willelmi Ruffi iiii paruas uirg'.

[fol. 96v] Hundredum de Wymeresle

In Middelton Robertus de Causho et Galfridus v hid'. et i uirgata, scilicet quarta pars i hid'.

In Trop Ascelinus de Chokes ii hid'. dim'. et quarta pars i hid'. Ibidem Hospital' Norhantone dim'. hid'. et quarta pars i hid'.

In Wotton ii hid'. et ii partes dim'. hid'. Ibidem Michael .ii hid'. et terciam partem dim'. hid'.

In Hardingestorn vii hid'. de feodo Regis Dauid.

In Blechesworthe et in Cortenhale. Peuerel vii hid'. et iiii paruas uirgat'. de incremento.

In Quenton quas Gilbertus tenuit.

In Quenton Dauid et Ph[illipus]. i hid'. dim'. et quartam partem i hid'.

In Preston Walterus filius Wyuenni. i hid'. et i uirg'. de feodo Regis Dauid. Ibidem de feodo de Olneya dim'. hid'. In Alecote Rex Dauid terciam partem i hid'.

In Pidenton i hid'. dim'. et i uirg'.

In Houcton Robertus de Pauely i hid'. dim'. uirg'. magna et ii uirg'. de feodo Peuerel. Ibidem R[icardus] [*sic*] Dauid quattuor paruas uirgatas quas Osebertus tenuit. Ibidem Simon i hid'. et i uirg'.

In alia Houcton et in Bramfeld iii hid'. dim'. quas Willelmus de Houcton tenuit.

In Horton Alouf de Merk. ii hid'. et i paruam uirgatam de Wahill. Ibidem de feodo Regis Scoc[ie] iii paru'. uirg'. Ibidem Turgis de Quenton vi paru'. uirg'. de eodem feodo. Ibidem Walterus filius Wyuenii vi paru'. uirg'. de feodo de Olneya.

In Hakelington Nortgold i hid'. Ibidem Turgis de Quenton dim'. hid'. Ibidem monachi de Norhantone i hid'. Ibidem Willelmus de Lisurs dim'. hid'. de feodo de Olneya. Ibidem Walterus filius Wyuenii viii paru'. uirg'. de eodem feodo.

In Cugeho Willelmus i hid'. dim'. i uirg'.

In Whiston Willelmus i hid'. dim'. de feodo Abbatis de Rammes'. Ibidem Rex Dauid i uirgatam magnam. In Dodington idem Rex i hid'. Ibidem Walterus filius Wyuenii. vi paruas uirgatas de feodo de Rammeseya. Ibidem Willelmus de Wytendon x paru'. uirg'. de abbate de Rammeseye.

In Esseby et Chadeston. Willelmus filius Clarenbaldi iii hid'. dim'.

In Gerdele et Grendone vii hid'. et i uirgata minus de feodo Regis Dauid.

Hundredum et dimidium de Hecham

In Eston et Strixton. Michael de Hampslepe iii hid'. dim'. et uirg'. magnam. Ibidem Paganus i uirgatam magnam.

In Bosesete. Rex Dauid ii hid'.

In Neweton. Alnochus de Bidun ii hid'. dim'. minus.

In Wolaston v hid'. dim'. uirg'. de feodo de Chokes. Ibidem Corbelinus ii hid'. dim'. uirg'. minus de feodo Regis Dauid.

In Haregraue Radulfus de Foleuille iii paru'. uirg'. Ibidem Ricardus et Rogerus de Costentyn iii paruas uirgatas. Ibidem Haroldus dim'. hid'.

In Scanewigge. Ascelinus i hid'. et i uirg'. et dim'. de feodo Burgi.

In Yrencestre Nicholas le Sauvage dim'. hid'. de feodo de Wahill.

In Cotes Gilbertus filius Ricardi i hid'. dim'. et i paruam uirgatam de feodo de Deneford.

In alia Cotes Frumboldus de Deneford dim'. hid'. de eodem feodo.

In Cotes [fol. 97r] Iohannes Bidoun i hid'. dim'. et i uirg'. et dim'.

In Ringstede Gilbertus filius Ricardi iiii paru'. uirg'. de feodo de Deneford.

In Raundes. Ibidem. Gilbertus iiii paru'. uirg'. de eodem feodo. Ibidem. Robertus filius Regis de feodo Glouernie. ii hid'. dim'.

In Knoston. Frumboldus i hid'. dim'. et i magnam uirgatam.

In dominico Willelmi Peuerel xxxiii hid'. dim'. et dim'. uirg'.

In Boseyate iii paru'. uirg'. de feodo Willelmi Peuerel.

Hundredum de Neubotlegraue

In Daylington iii hid'. de feodo Abbatis de Burg.

In Duston iiii hid'. de feodo Willelmi Peuerel,

In Vpton. Dominus Rex ii hid'. dim'.

In Horepol iiii hid'. de feodo de Beuuer. Petrus i hid'. dim'. Item aliud de feodo Peuerel.

In Kyselingbyr iii hid'. dim'. de feodo de Gilberti de Gaunt. Ibidem. Comes Ley[cestrie] dim'. hid.

In Buckebrok' iiii hid'. de feodo de Morent'.

In Heyford iiii hid'.

In Clachetorp et in parua Heyford iiii hid'.

In Flora Otuer iiii paru'. uirg'. de feodo comitis Galfridi. Ibidem. Aunsel de Chokes i hid'. et uirgatam antiquo. Ibidem Radulfus filius Sewani de feodo Peuerel dim'. hid'. Ibidem Hugo de Chaneys. i hid'. iiii paru'. uirg'. de feodo de Kaynes.

In Brockehole et in Musecote. Radulfus de Gaynes. i hid'. de feodo de Gaynes. Ibidem Geruasius Samson. i hid'. de feodo War'.

In Neubottle et in Brynton vi hid'.

In Whelton i hid'. de feodo R[ogeri] de Moubray.

In Rauenestorp et in Cheta iiii hid'. de feodo Peuerel.

In Haldeneby iii hid'. de feodo comitis Leycestrie.

In Haddon. Idem comes iiii hid'.

In Brampton. Idem comes iiii hid'.

In Herleston iii hid'.

In Holtrop i hid'. et i paru'. uirg'. de feodo de Berkamstede.

Hundredum de Gildesboru

In Gildesboru Willelmus filius Aldred iii magn'. uirg'. dim'. de feodo Peuerel. Ibidem. Presbiter i paru'. uirg'. de feodo comitis Leycestrie.

In Holewelle Episcopus Lincol' i hid'. et tercia pars i hid'. Robertus de Dyua tenet. Ibidem Comes Leycestrie iii paruas uirg'. Ibidem de feodo Peuerel v paruas uirg'.

In Hortoft Colemannus dim'. hid'. de feodo Peuerel. Ibidem. Comes Leycestrie ii hid'. et i magnam uirgatam. In Cotesbrok Robertus Boteuileyn ii hid'. de feodo de Wahill.

In Creton Aunsel de Chokes. i hid'.

In alia Creton Herbertus dim'. hid'. de feodo Radulfi de Gaynes.

In Westhaddon Hugo uicecomes ii hid'. i magn'. uirg'. Ibidem. Peuerel. i mag'. uirg'. et dim'. Ibidem Aunsel de Chokes i magn'. uirg'. Ibidem Comes Leycestrie dim'. hid'. Ibidem Nigellus de Albeny. dim'. hid'. de feodo Rogeri de Moubray.

In Watford iiii hid'. de feodo Baldewini filii Gilberti.

In Buckeby Serles de Quency ii hid'. dim'. et i magn'. uirgat'. de feodo Aunsel de Chokes. Ibidem Willelmus filius Alfridi dim'. hid'. de feodo Montis Acuti. Ibidem Comes Leycestrie iii magn'. uirg'.

In Creke [fol. 97v] Rogerus de Camuill iii hid'. dim'. et i magna uirg'. de feodo Rogeri de Mounbray.

In Lilleburn' et Cotes Comes Leycestrie iiii hid'. Ibidem. Willelmus Alfridi filius i magnam uirgatam.

In Stanford Abbas de Seleby ii hid'.

In Welleford Willelmus de Wyuill iiii hid'. et i magn'. uirg'. de feodo Rogeri de Mouubray de Gildecote. Ibidem Ad[am] i hid'. dim'. de feodo Baldewyni filii Gilberti.

In Geluertoft ii hid'. et iii pars i hid'. de feodo comitis Leyc'. Ibidem. Rad[ulfus] filius Osmundi dim'. hid'. de feodo Willelmi filii Alur[edi].

In Eltesdon' Hugo uicecomes i hid'. dim'. monachi de Pippewell tenent. Ibidem.

Hug' i magnam uirgatam de feodo Westmonaster[io]. Ibidem Hugo de Kaynes iiii paruas uirg'. Ibidem. Nigellus de Aubeny ii paru'. uirg'. de feodo de Welleford.

In Esseby ii hid'. dim'. de feodo de Couentre. Ibidem Henricus de Mundeuill' i magn'. uirg'. de feodo Peuerel. Ibidem Hugo de Kaynes iii mag. uirg'. Ibidem Robertus dim'. hid'. de feodo de Welleford.

In Wynelwyk iii hid'. et i mag'. uirg'. de feodo de Couentre. Ibidem Robertus Alegod viiii paruas uirg'. de feodo Peuerel. In Nauesbya vii hid'. de feodo Willelmi Peuerel.

In Turleby i hid'. dim'. de feodo comitis Leycestrie. Ibidem Robertus filius Alegod. i hid'. de feodo Peuerel. Item ibidem dim'. hid'. per rotulos Wyncestrie.

In Cotes Robertus Halegod iiii uirgat'. dim.

Hundredum de Mallest'

In Houton de feodo Sancti Edmundi i hid'. Ibidem Rocnuis[?] i hid'. iii uirg'. de feodo de Berkamstede. Ibidem. i hid'. et i uirg'. de feodo Regis Dauid.

In Langeport Simon Malesoures. iiii hid'. de feodo de Wahill. Ibidem de sokagio Sancti Edmundi dim'. hid'.

In Scaldewell Albrem de Ver iii magn'. uirg'. de feodo Oxonie. Ibidem de feodo Sancti Edmundi i hid'. dim'. et i magn'. uirg'. Ibidem Rex Dauid ii hid'. dim'. et i uirg'.

In Walde Comes Albemar' iiii hid'. et iiii uirg'. de feodo Oxonie.

In Faxtone ii hid'. dim'. de feodo de Baillol.

In Waldegraue Henricus iii hid'. dim'. et i magnam uirgatam de feodo Regis Dauid. Ibidem Henricus de Gray iii uirg'. de sokagio de Foxton'. Ibidem Comes Leycestrie dim'. hid'.

In Brikelesworth Simon filius Simonis viii hid'. dim'. de feodo de Corcy. Ibidem Alfredus i hid'. et i uirg'. de feodo de Salesbyrs.

In Thorp iuxta Norhantone v hid'. i uirg'. minus.

In Multon de sokagio de Torp i hid'. dim'. et bou'. Et in Weston i hid.

Hundredum de Speleho.

In Abendon Unfridus de Bassingburne iiii hid'.

In Weston Ricardus iiii hid'.

In parua Billingge iiii hid'.

In magna Billingge iiii hid'.

In Oueston Gilbertus de Milers iiii hid'.

In Multon ii hid'. et iiii paruas uirg'. de feodo Ricardi de Engayne. Ibidem Wydo de Baillol i hid'. dim'. et i paruam uirg'. de feodo [fol. 98r] de Foxton. Ibidem Ricardus de le Pek iiii hid'. de feodo Regis Dauid.

In Boketon iii hid'. et iii paru'. uirg'. de feodo monachorum Sancti Wandragesile.

In Pitteford Henricus Malesures et Philippus iii hid'. dim'. de feodo de Wahill. Ibidem Comes Leycestrie vi paruas uirg'.

In Sprotton' ix paru'. uirg'. de feodo Regis Dauid. Ibidem. de feodo Ricardi Basset iii paru'. uirg'. Ibidem. Comes Leycestrie ii hid'. dim'. et i magnam uirgatam.

Hundredum de Anfordesho

In Wenbugburg de Croylaunde v hid'. dim'. Ibidem Nicholas de Cogeho iii magn. uirg'. de feodo Regis Dauid. Ibidem Comes Leycestrie i hid'.

106

In Herdwyk ix paruas uirg'. de feodo Regis Dauid.
In Eketon iiii hid'. de feodo comitis de Ferrar'. Willelmus de Mungomery tenent
[*sic*].
In Siwell' monachorum Norh[antone]. Et sanctimoniales de Annestowe. iiii hid'.
In Holecote Ad[am] ii hid'. dim'. et i paruam uirg'. de feodo Willelmi de Curcy.
Ibidem i hid'. et iiii paru'. uirg'. de feodo Regis Dauid.
In Esseby iii hid'. de feodo Regis Dauid.
In Wyleby iiii hid'. de feodo Regis Dauid.
In Dodington iiii hid'. de feodo Regis Dauid.
In Barton iiii hid'. de feodo Regis Dauid.

Hundredum de Orlingberge
In Orlingberg' Fucherus Malesoures i hid'. de feodo de Wahill. Ibidem i hid'.
dim'. de feodo Willelmi de Curcy. In Wymale i hid'. dim'. et i uirg'. de feodo de
Wahill.
In Bateshasel Malesoures dim'. hid'. de feodo de Wahill.
In Hysham. Henricus de Ysham ii hid'. et tercia pars i hid'. de feodo de Daun-
deuille. Ibidem. Thom[as] Pyel i hid'. dim'. ii par'. uirg'. dim'. de feodo de
Rameshe. Ibidem Galfridus vi paruas uirgat'. de feodo de Huntingdon.
In Cranesle Hugo Kyde i hid'. dim'. et i bouatam dim'. de feodo de Chokes.
Ibidem Radulfus Meschin v paruas uirg'. de feodo de Geytington. Ibidem Iohan-
nes le Bauld. i mag'. uirg'. Ibidem Foliot ii hid'. dim'. et i paru'. uirg'. de feodo
de Huntingdon.
In Pytesle. Abbas de Burgo v hid'. dim'. set tamen in Rotuli Wincestre vi hid'. et
iii paruas uirg'. Ibidem Ricardus Engayne iii hid'. i uirg'. Ibidem Willelmus filius
Gery dim'. hid'. de feodo Morton'.
In Harudon Reygold i hid'. de feodo Willelmi de Curcy. Ibidem Galfridus ii hid'.
et i bouatam minus de feodo de Huntingdon. Ibidem Nicholas de Cugeho i hid'.
de feodo Regis.
In Haniton dim'. hid'. de feodo comitis Leycestrie. Ibidem i hid'. dim'. de feodo
Regis Dauid.

Hundredum de Stotfolde
In Maydewell Alanus iiii hid'. ii paru'. uirg'. de feodo de Wolrington. Ibidem
Robace ii hid'. de feodo de Rannulfi de Bayouse.
In Keylmers. Idem dim'. hid'. de feodo Sancti Edmundi. Ibidem de feodo de Not-
ingham i hid'. dim'. et dim'. uirg'. Ibidem de socagio de Geytington dim'. hid'.
et i paruam uirg'. Ibidem Eudo filius Harschul i hid'. [fol. 98v] et i paruam uirg'.
de sokagio de Rowell. Ibidem. Ad[am] v paruas uirg'. de feodo Regis Dauid.
In Haselbech episcopus Salesbir' ii hid'. de feodo de Berkamstede. Ibidem
Comes Leycestrie i hid'. de feodo Mor'.
In Clipston Willelmus Peuerel iii hid'. dim'. et i paruam uirg'. de feodo Peuerel.
Ibidem Ad[am] dim'. hid'. et iii paruas uirg'. de feodo Regis Dauid. Ibidem de
socagio de Geytington v paruas uirg'. Ibidem. Maur[icius] x paruas uirg'. de
feodo Sancti Edmundi. Ibidem. de socagio de Rowell i paruam uirg.
In Soleby v hid'. et i uirg'. de feodo Westmon'.
In Sibtoft ii hid'. dim'. et ii partes i uirgate de feodo de seriantye Regis.
In Oxendon i hid'. et i uirg'. de socagio de Rowell. Ibidem. i hid'. de feodo Regis
Dauid.

In parua Oxendon Robertus filius Hugonis i hid'. et iii partes i uirg'. de feodo de Berkamstede. Ibidem. de socagio de Geytington. ii paruas uirg'. Ibidem. Turberd i paru'. uirg'.

In Farendon i hid'. et quarta partes i uirg'. de feodo de Huntingdon. Ibidem. Robertus filius Hugonis iii uirgatas et iii partes i paru'. uirg'. de feodo Sancti Edmundi. Ibidem Willelmus Meschin i paru'. uirg'. de socagio de Geytington.

In Boudon Robertus filius Hugonis ii hid'. et i uirg'. et terciam partem i uirgat'. de feodo de Berkamstede. Ibidem. Rex Dauid i hid'. et terciam partem i uirg'. et terciam partem de tercia parte i uirgat'.

In Thorp Comes Leycestrie iiii magn. uirgat'. et terciam partem i uirgat'.

In Merston. Idem Comes i hid'. dim'. et ii partes i uirgat'. quam Osbertus Trussel tenet.

Hundredum de Rowell

In Hechingtone Willelmus filius Aluid vi hid'.

In Braybrok ii hid'. de socagio de Hechington. Ibidem Wydo Cocus i hid'. Ibidem. Peuerel iii partem i hid'. Ibidem. Iuo ii hid'. cum implemento de ii uirg'. de terra Peuerel et cum dim'. uirg'. de feodo Sancti Edmundi.

In Aringworthe Robertus filius Hugonis et Willelmus filius Albeni ii hid'. et ii partes i hid'. de feodo de Berkamstede. Ibidem Petrus i uirgat'.

In Rowell et in Ouerton et in Lodington. Eudo de Haschull ix hid'. et i paru'. uirg'.

In Lodington Willelmus Constabul[arius] iii uirg'. quas Robertus Le Baud tenet.

In Deseburg Norman et Reg[inaldus] Race ii hid'. et ii partes i hid'. In Pippewell Robertus filius Hugonis dim'. hid'. et terciam partem i hid'. Ibidem. Willelmus de Aubeny dim'. hid'. per alium rotulum. i hid'. et iii partes i hid'. In Riston. Andr[eas] ii hid'. dim'. et terciam partem i hid'. de feodo Regis Dauid. Ibidem. Robertus Basset i hid'. dim'. et i paruas uirg'. de feodo Willelmi de Aubeny. Ibidem. Vitalis Engayne ii partes i hid'. quas Vitalis Louet tenuit. Ibidem. Siricius Bucar' sextam partem i hid'. Ibidem. de socagio de Geytington i paruam uirg'. et dim'. Rogerus de Cranesle tenuit.

In Bereford i hid'. de socagio de Geytington.

In Olendon de eodem socagio dim'. hid'. Ibidem Siricius Bucar' dim'. hid'. dim'. uirg'. de feodo Willelmi Alur[edi]. Ibidem. [fol. 99r] Radulfus Normann' dim'. hid'. dim'. uirg'. de socagio de Rowell.

In Thorp Fucherus Malesoures i hid'. et terciam partem i hid'. de feodo Willelmi Auenel.

In alia Thorp Hervicus Belet ii partes i hid'.

In Drayton i hid'. et dim'. uirg'. de feodo de Rowell. Ibidem. Corbet. dim'. hid'. et iii partes i uirg'. de feodo Regis Dauid. Ibidem. Willelmus Durdent i mag. uirg'. de feodo Menfelyn de Wolfrington.

Hundredum de Stokes

In Wilberdeston et in Stokes Willelmus Daubeny viii hid'. et i uirg'.

In Carleton de socagio Regis dim'. hid'. et i paruam uirg'. dim'. Ibidem. Willelmus Daubeny dim'. hid'. et i paru'. uirgat'. et dim'. Ibidem. Robertus filius Hugonis iii mag. uirg'. et i paruam uirg'. et dim'.

In Brampton de socagio Regis i hid'. Ibidem Basset ii hid'. Ibidem. Radulfus filius Eldewyn iiii hid'. ii paruas uirg'. minus.

In Dingele Alur[edu]s ii hid'. et i uirg'. Ibidem Ricardus Basset i hid'. dim'. et i magn'. uirg'. in dominico suo.

In Sutton et Weston' Ricardus Basset vi hid'.

In Assele Radulfus de Beufo ii hid'. et ii paru'. uirg'. de feodo de Beuu'. Ibidem. Ricardus Basset iiii paru'. uirg'. quas Wydo de Wateruill tenuit. Ibidem Willelmus Daubeny vii paru'. uirg'. Ibidem Rogerus de Sprotton i hid'. de feodo Regis Dauid. Ibidem Berengarius i hid'. i paru'. uirg'. minus quam Wydo de Wateruill tenet de Radulfo de Beufo.

In Cotingham Abbas de Burgo viii hid'.

In Banefeld i hid'. de feodo.

In Rokingham i hid'. de feodo.

Hundredum de Coreby

In Wakerle ii hid'. dim'. de feodo Eudonis filii Huberti.

In Haringworthe v hid'. de feodo Regis Dauid.

In Laxinton et in Hynewyke. Vitalis Engayne. i hid'. dim'. Ibidem. Robertus filius Hugonis i mag'. uirg'.

In Blatherwyk Robertus filius Hugonis et Ricardus Dengayne ii hid'.

In Bolewyk ii hid'.

In Henewyk Vitalis Louet dim'. hid'.

In Deen Radulfus filius Nigelli ii hid'. dim'. de feodo Westmon'

In Neweton et in Acle ii hid'. dim'. de feodo Regis Dauid. Ibidem. Willelmus de Houton' i hid'. dim'. et i magn'. uirg'. de feodo Regis Dauid.

In parua Acle Willelmus filiius Alur[edi] iii uirg'. de feodo Montis Acuti.

In Geytington Dominus Rex i hid'. et i magn'. uirg'. Ibidem. i hid'. et i mag'. uirg'. de feodo Sancti Edmundi.

In Wycle ii hid'. dim'. de feodo comitis de Warenn' de Morteyn.

In Boketon i dim'. [*sic*] de feodo Sancti Edmundi.

In Kirkeby i uirg'. de feodo Hunfredi de Bassingburn.

In Stauerne i uirg'. dim'. de socagio de Bristok.

In Coreby et in Gretton et in Brixstoke x hid'.

Hundredum de Wylebrok

In Lodington Radulfus filius Willelmi ii hid'. dim'. de feodo Burgi. Ibidem Abbas de Ramesh' dim'. hid'.

In Aylington de socagio Burgi i hid'. dim'. Ibidem. [fol. 99v] Willelmus filius Ketelbern dim'. hid'. de feodo de Rameseye.

In Wermington Abbas Burgi i hid'.

In Elmenton Abbas de Croylaund i hid'.

In Tanesouere Hacuil de Sancto Jacobo v hid'. et terciam partem i hid'. Ibidem Salomon ii partes i hid'. de feodo comitis de Warewyk.

In Sothewyk cum Iarewell Willelmus de Lisurs i hid'.

In Fodrengeye vi hid'. de feodo Regis Dauid.

In Cotherstoke Ricardus filius Hugonis i hid'. dim'. de feodo Burgi. Ibidem. Rogerus Infans i hid'. dim'. de eodem feodo.

In Neweton Robertus de Cerneya iii hid'. de feodo Marmiun.

In Eston Simon de Lindon ii hid'.

In Weston Willelmus filius Herewyn ii hid'.

In Nassington vi hid'.

In Glapthorn Galfridus de Normanuill i hid'. dim'. Ibidem. Ridel et Hugo dim'. hid'. et i uirgat'. Ibidem Fulco de Lisurs iii partes i hid'.
In Apethorp ii hid'.
In Clyua i hid'. dim'. et dim'. uirgat'.
In Dodington i hid'.

Hundredum de Suthnaueslunt
Irtlingburg v hid'. dim'. et i paruam uirgat'. de feodo Burgi. Ibidem. Reginaldus de la Bataille iii hid'. dim'. de eodem feodo. Ibidem. Simon Basset i hid'. Auenel de feodo Burgi.
In Adington Ricardus filius Hugonis iii hid'. dim'. de feodo Burgo. Ibidem Willelmus frater Wydonis dim'. uirg'. de feodo de Croylaund. Ibidem Willelmus de Huntingdon. i hid'. et i uirg'. dim'. de feodo de Gloucestr'.
In Wodeford viii hid'. dim'. uirg'. de feodo Burgi. Ibidem Wydo Treylli. i hid'. dim'. de feodo Burgo. Ibidem Reginaldus de la Bataille dim'. uirgat'. Ibidem Willelmus de Houton dim'. hid'.
In alia Adington Albr[icus] camerarius ii hid'. de feodo Regis. Ibidem i hid'. de feodo abbatis [*sic*]. Ibidem. Willelmus filius Wydonis ii hid'. de feodo Abbatis de Croylaund.
In Thingdene de dominico Regis x hid.

Northnaueslunt
In Craneford Bertr[am] de Wedon ii hid'. et i uirgat'. dim'. de feodo Burgi. Ibidem Galfridus camerarius i hid'. de feodo Glouernie. Ibidem Ricardus filius Wydonis. i hid'. de feodo Burgi. Ibidem Mauricius Daundelyn ii hid'. dim'. de feodo Burgi. Ibidem Radulfus filius Rogerii v hid'. de Simon filius Petri.
In Barton Galfridus camerarius v hid'. de feodo Gloucestrie. In Werketon iiii hid'. de feodo Sancti Edmundi.
In Keteringe x hid'. de feodo Burgi
In Grafton' Ricardus de Humaz iiii hid'.
In Burtone Ricardus filius Wydonis viii hid'. dim'. Ibidem. Willelmus de Houton i hid'. dim'.

Index

Alfredus   100, 106
Alnochus de Bidun   104
Alouf de Merk   104
Alouf de Merke   100
Alur[edu]s   109
Andr[eas]   108
Apeltreya   101
Apethorp   110
Aringworthe   108
Armeston   99
Ascelinus   99, 104
Ascelinus de Chokes   103
Ascelinus de Wateruill'   99
Ascelinus de Wateruille   99
Assele   109
Atteneston   102
Audewyncle   99
Auenel   110
Aunsel   102
Aunsel de Chokes   100, 105
Aydona   101
Aylington   109
Ayno   100
Ayston   99

Baddeby   101
Baillol   106
Baldewini filii Gilberti   105
Baldewyni filii Gilberti   105
Banefeld   109
Barton   99, 107, 110
Bassenham   103
Basset   106, 108, 110
Bateshasel   107
Benifeld   99
Berchamstede   101
Bereford   108
Berengarius   109
Berengerus le Moyne   99
Berkamstede   100–103, 105–108
Bernak   100
Bernewell'   99
Bertr[am] de Wedon   110
Beruby   102
Beuuer   104
Billingge   106
Blacoluesle   102
Blatherwyk   109
Blechesworthe   103
Boketon   106, 109
Bolewyk   109
Bosesete   104
Boseyate   104

Botebot   102
Bottolendon   101
Boudon   108
Brackele   101
Braddene   102
Bramfeld   104
Brampton   105, 108
Branndeston   102
Braybrok   108
Brien filius Comitis   100
Brikelesworth   106
Bristok   109
Brixstoke   109
Brockehole   105
Brunne   99
Brynton   105
Buckebrok'   105
Buckeby   105
Burgelay   99
Byfeld   101

Carleton   108
Catesby   101
Catteworthe   99
Cestrie.   100–101
Chacombe   100
Chadeston   104
Charwelton   101
Chelredescote   102
Chelurdescote   101
Chelverdescote   101
Cherlington   100
Cheta   105
Chokes   100, 103–105, 107
Clachetorp   105
Clare   99, 104
Clipston   107
Clopton   99
Clyua   110
Colemannus   105
Colescestra   100
Colewych   100
Comes Albemar'   106
comes de Arundel   103
Comes Leycestrie   100–101, 105–108
comes Mauricius   102
Comitis Cestrie   100
Comitis David   98–99
comitis de Ferrar   103, 107
Comitis de Mandeuille   101
comitis de Warenn' de Morteyn   109
comitis de Warewyk   109
comitis Galfridi   105

DOMESDAY PEOPLE: PROSOPOGRAPHY

PRINCIPLES OF THE PROSOPOGRAPHY

The underlying intention of this work is to provide a prosopographical key to the rich collection of administrative documents produced in the period 1066 to 1166, which England is so uniquely privileged to have produced and preserved. The basis of the Prosopography is therefore these administrative texts, viz, Domesday Book, the Pipe Rolls, the *Cartae Baronum*, as well as Surveys such as the Lindsey Survey and Northants Survey, which is edited here for the first time. A number of charter collections illustrating the material held in the base texts have been used in an integrated database system to produce the Prosopography printed below. Each item in the Prosopography is followed by a list of these 'foundation' references – that is, to the base adminstrative texts and to the selected charter collections. In the Bibliography the 'foundation' texts are marked with an asterisk. The origin of the prosopography in a computer database is evident in the list of references following each entry, which appear in an entirely random order. There are a few references to the Pipe Roll of 31 Henry I, with a page reference in the form: 158–cn, which combines the page number with a county-code. A full list of the county abbreviations will be given in volume II. The bulk of the references for the Prosopography of Domesday Book are from Domesday Book itself. References in the form: i (or ii), fol. 000, are to the two-volume folio-edition of Abraham Farley (1783). Reference to this edition is unavoidably imprecise. Several references to the same folio may be given, but each will relate to a separate occurrence of the subject in the Domesday text.

The entries of the Domesday Book prosopography are listed according to Forename, with the Forename appearing in the form in which it is dominant in Domesday Book, as listed in *Domesday Names: An Index of Personal and Place Names in Domesday Book*, compiled by K. S. B. Keats-Rohan and David E. Thornton (Woodbridge, 1997). The bulk of the Prosopography is a list of persons in first-name order. Persons for whom a 'surname' has been identified are listed first, followed by persons of the same forename who have no 'surname'. The remainder (pp. 503–45) is a list of persons or institutions who lack a forename. In the case of abbeys, priories and cathedral churches some standardization has been enforced, so that all abbeys will be found in this second list under *abbatia . . .*, and all priories and cathedral churches under *ecclesia*, rather than by saint's name or other Domesday forms. The Forename will be an essential guide to the Domesday person in whom one is interested, because here the surnames missing in Domesday Book have been attached to their subjects. In the case of common names there are no shortcuts to finding the person in whom one is interested. It may be necessary to skim most or all of the entries for *Willelm*, for example, in order to find the one required. One should look in both lists for uncommon names such as *Tosard* or composites such as *nepos episcopi*. Persons who have no forename but who are described by their relationship to a person with a forename will be found in the main list according to the relationship term; thus *uxor Radulfi Capellani* will precede *uxor Roberti Burdet* in the list of persons with forenames beginning with *u*.

Each entry seeks to give information about tenancies in 1086, probable or possible continental origin of the non-English persons, family and the descent of fees. The reader should pay careful attention to the distinction between material offered for comparative purposes and material offered as directly concerning the subject of the entry. Reference will always be made to standard works such as Loyd, *Origins*, Sanders, *Baronies*, *Complete Peerage*, etc., wherever relevant. References are not usually given to statements relating to heirs, because these will be the subjects of fully-referenced entries in Volume II of this work. Where '(q.v.)' follows a name it means that there is an entry on that person, either here on in volume II, and it usually means that important supplementary information will be found there. Reference to charter collections is made according to charter numbers; to all other sources, reference is by page, unless stated otherwise; references in the form 35/100 are to charter number then page number. A list of the printed sources and abbreviations used is given below, usually by place; e.g. one should look under 'Caen' for the full reference to Musset, *Actes caen*. References to material in manuscript collections are always given in full. Every effort has been made to include reference to modern or recent monographs, but no attempt has been made to include an exhaustive survey of the literature. Naturally, I have made extensive use of my own relevant publications, which are listed separately in the Bibliography.

Much of this work has been done using a computer database system that I designed to cope with the problems of uncertainty. Most of the careful checks and balances built into that have inevitably been lost here. These checks included a probability code against Domesday references and the suggested identifications with a given person. Here the references are presented in an absolute form which the user should assess for himself. Another problem is that in a well-controlled computer system one can justifiably abandon the impossible search for a fully defensible, standarized way of naming individuals, for whom there may be as many modern forms of his name as there are mediaeval ones. In the one-dimensional format of a book the variety will simply look like inconsistency. I plead guilty before the accusation is made.

It cannot be too strongly emphasized that the prosopography offers information for further consideration, predicated upon the notion of probability, not of certainty. The prosopography is intended as a guide for the researcher, who must explore the information he is given and form his own conclusions. Historical data are by their very nature incomplete and hence their interpretation is contentious. No one, author or reader, can claim anything written here as absolute fact.

The bulk of the references in the prosopography of Domesday Book below are from Domesday Book itself. Unless otherwise stated, all references are to the two-volume folio-edition of Abraham Farley (1783).

Abel Monachus Cantuariensis
Occurs in Domesday Book. Monk of Canterbury according to the Domesday Monachorum.

i, fol. 004d

Abraham Presbiter
Occurs Domesday Gloucestershire. He was archdeacon of Gwent according to J. E. Lloyd, History of Wales (2nd edn 1912) ii, 367.

i, fol. 162a

Acard De Iuri
Norman, Domesday tenant of Hugh de Beauchamp in Bedfordshire; named from Ivry-la-Bataille, Eure, arr. Evreux, cant. Saint-André.

i, fol. 213a

Acard Presbiter
Tenant of Roger de Montgomery in Domesday Sussex.

i, fol. 25c; i, fol. 25a

Acard []
Domesday tenant of William de Picquigny. Possibly the same as Acard de Ivry (q.v.).

i, fol. 177b; i, fol. 177b; i, fol. 148d

Adam Filius Durandi Malis Operibus
Norman, son of Durand Malzor, occurs Domesday Essex.

ii, fol. 094a; ii, fol. 094a; ii, fol. 094a

Adam Filius Huberti
Son of Hubert de Ria, from Ryes, arr. Bayeux, Calvados; a major tenant of Odo bishop of Bayeux in Domesday Book. Brother of an important Norman Domesday tenant-in-chief, Eudo dapifer (q.v.), Humphrey, Robert bishop of Sées, and Muriel wife of Osbern, and perhaps of Ralph fitz Hubert (q.v.). Benefactor of Rochester Cathedral (Mon. Ang. i, 169), he died in 1098, when his heir was his brother Eudo.

i, fol. 134d; i, fol. 134b; i, fol. 134b; i, fol. 134c; i, fol. 007a; i, fol. 134b; i, fol. 010c; i, fol. 008c; i, fol. 010b; i, fol. 011a; i, fol. 012b; i, fol. 134c; i, fol. 156b; i, fol. 156c; i, fol. 156c; i, fol. 156a; i, fol. 156b; i, fol. 156b; i, fol. 155d; i, fol. 220b; i, fol. 156b; i, fol. 008a; i, fol. 008c; i, fol. 009c; i, fol. 009d; i, fol. 31c; i, fol. 31d; i, fol. 008a; i, fol. 008a; i, fol. 008a; i, fol. 008a; i, fol. 008a; i, fol. 006a; i, fol. 014c; Ballard, Inquisition of St Augustine's (1920), fols 20r–23v; i, fol. 006d; i, fol. 008a; i, fol. 006c; i, fol. 134b; i, fol. 134b; i, fol. 008d; i, fol. 009a; i, fol. 009a; i, fol. 009a; i, fol. 010a; i, fol. 010a

Adam Filius Roberti Filii Willelmi
Norman, occurs as a tenant of Odo of Bayeux in Domesday Kent.

i, fol. 008a

Adam []
Tenant of Bishop Remigius of Lincoln in Domesday Lincolnshire.

i, fol. 344c

Adelais Comitissa De Albamarla
Sister or half-sister of William the Conqueror, daughter of Robert I duke of Normandy and an unknown mother. She was married first to Engueran count of Ponthieu, secondly to Lambert count of Lens, by whom she was the mother of Countess Judith (q.v.), and thirdly to Eudes de Champagne, created count of Aumale by William I, by whom she was mother of Stephen count of Aumale. The length of her marital career has led to the occasional suggestion that it was her daughter Adelaide of Ponthieu who married Eudes de Champagne, but that was shown to be an error by Stapleton, Rot. Scacc. Norm., ii, p. xxxi note.

ii, fol. 430b; ii, fol. 091b; ii, fol. 431a; ii, fol. 431a; ii, fol. 431a; ii, fol. 431a; ii, fol. 091b; ii, fol. 431a; ii, fol. 431a; ii, fol. 431a; ii, fol. 430b; ii, fol. 430b; ii, fol. 430b; ii, fol. 430b; ii, fol. 431a; ii, fol. 431a; ii, fol. 091b; ii, fol. 430b

Adelelm De Burgate
Domesday tenant of Aubrey de Vere; he and his descendants were named from one of their holdings. The dominant tenant of Alberic in Suffolk, he may have been his steward. He made a grant to Colne priory, a cell of Abingdon abbey, for his burial, with the assent of Tihel and William (Chron. Abing. ii, 60), of whom the latter was probably his son. His successor by c.1150 was his grandson William fitz William (Colne ch. no. 87), who held two fees of de Vere in 1166.

ii, fol. 077a; ii, fol. 077b; Fisher, Cartularium Prioratus de Colne (Earles C.), No. 87; Fisher, Cartularium Prioratus de Colne (Earles C.), No. 9; Fisher, Cartularium Prioratus de Colne (Earles C.), No. 1; Fisher, Cartularium Prioratus de Colne (Earles C.), No. 2; ii, fol. 419a; ii, fol. 419a; ii, fol. 419a; ii, fol. 419a; ii, fol. 419a; ii, fol. 419a; ii, fol. 419a; ii, fol. 419a; ii, fol. 419a; ii, fol. 419a; ii, fol. 419a

Adelelm De Kingestuna
In 1086 Adelelm held land in Kingston Bagpuize from William fitz Ansculf of Picquigny and Ralph de Bachepuiz held there of Henry de Ferrers. In the Abingdon Chronicle (ii, 30, 120–1) Ralph de Bachepuiz and Adelelm de Kingeston appear together.

i, fol. 61a

Adelelm []
Domesday tenant of Drogo de La Beuvrière in Yorkshire and Leicestershire.

i, fol. 236a; i, fol. 324b

Adelina Joculatrix
Occurs Domesday Hampshire. Whether her soubriquet refers to an ocupation as a jester is doubtful. She was possibly the wife of a jester, or of one who bore the soubriquet joculator.

i, fol. 38d

Adeliz Uxor Hugonis De Grentemaisnil
Daughter of Ivo count of Beaumont-sur-Oise. She married Hugh de Grandmesnil (q.v.) before 1066, when he participated in the conquest of England. Reputedly beautiful, Hugh had to return to Normandy shortly after the conquest to check on

her activities (Ord. Vit. iv, 230) Adeliza's English dower lands were recorded separately from Hugh's in 1086. They included manors in Bedfordshire which Hugh had acquired by exchange with Ralph Taillebois. Her large family is detailed under Hugh of Grandmesnil (q.v.). She died on 11 July 1091 (ibid. 338).

i, fol. 236d; i, fol. 217d; i, fol. 217d; i, fol. 217d; i, fol. 142d; i, fol. 244c; i, fol. 217d; i, fol. 142d; i, fol. 244c; i, fol. 236d

Adelo []
Domesday tenant of Bury St Edmunds. In 1182 his land appears in the Kalendar of Abbot Samson (pp. 16, 64–5, 67–9) as mostly in the hands of Geoffrey Pecche and, in the case of Newton, in those of Rohais de Crammaville.

ii, fol. 362b; Douglas, Feudal Book of Bury St Edmunds (1932), pp. 3–21; ii, fol. 367b; ii, fol. 360a; ii, fol. 360a

Adelold Camerarius
Chamberlain of Odo bishop of Bayeux, occurs Domesday Kent. He occurs as a despoiler of Sainte-Trinité de Caen under Robert Curthose, taking land at Englesqueville-la-Percée and Grandchamp-les-Bains, Calvados (Walmsley, pp. 126, 127). He occurs in a Bayeux charter of 1087–96, CDF, 1436. The three-knight fee of 'Aeloudi Camerarii' is mentioned in the Bayeux Inquest (RBE, 645).

i, fol. 007d; i, fol. 009d; i, fol. 011d; i, fol. 011b; i, fol. 007d

Adelold []
Englishman, canon of Dover in 1086.

Ballard, Inquisition of St Augustine's (1920), fols 24r–28r; i, fol. 001d

Adelolf De Merc
Important Domesday tenant of Eustache II of Boulogne, son of Otbert, also a tenant of Eustache (Round, 'Counts of Boulogne as English lords', in idem, Peerage and Family History). Fleming from Merck-Saint-Liévin, Pas-de-Calais, arr. Saint-Omer, cant. Fauquembergues, in Artois. Eustache de Merc attested a charter of Eustache III in 1119 (Cart. S. John Colchester, pp. 47–8), and Ingelran occurs on the 1129/30 Pipe Roll.

ii, fol. 031b; ii, fol. 029a; ii, fol. 028b; ii, fol. 028a; ii, fol. 027b; ii, fol. 034a; ii, fol. 027b; ii, fol. 028b; Northants Survey, fols 96r–99v; Northants Survey, fols 94r–95v; ii, fol. 032a; ii, fol. 032a; ii, fol. 033a; ii, fol. 033a; ii, fol. 033a

Adelulf []
Domesday tenant of Harduin de Scalariis. Geoffrey fitz Swein, a tenant in 1166 of Harduin's descendants Henry and Stephen de Scalariis, gave a charter for St Neots in which he specified that land he was granting at Croxton that had been held by Elwoldus Flammang, grandfather (auus) of his wife Hadewis (BL Cotton Faust. A iv, fol. 90r).

i, fol. 198b; i, fol. 199a

Ældeva []
Occurs Domesday Berkshire.

i, fol. 63d

Ælmer Presbiter
Occurs Domesday Berkshire.

i, fol. 56c; i, fol. 56c

Ælueue De Londonia
Englishwoman, wife of Wateman of London, occurs Domesday Middlesex.
i, fol. 130d

Agemund []
Occurs Domesday Hampshire.
i, fol. 45a; i, fol. 50a; i, fol. 50b; i, fol. 50b; i, fol. 50c

Agnes Filia Aluredi De Merleberge
Daughter of Alfred of Marlborough, she occurs in Domesday Book as her father's tenant. She had been wife of Turstin Fleming of Wigmore, a rebel who had fallen with his lord Roger, earl of Hereford, in 1075. He was possibly recorded as a tenant of Alfred in 1086, though it is unclear that he was actually still alive.
i, fol. 186a; i, fol. 186b

Agnes Uxor Gaufridi Talebot
Wife of Geoffrey I Talbot (q.v.), whose widow she was in 1129/30. Geoffrey was a tenant of Hugh de Gournay in Essex in 1086, where Agnes also occurs, holding a manor previously held by one Osbern.
ii, fol. 089b; Pipe Roll 31 Henry I, 067–kn

Ailmar Filius Goduini
Occurs Domesday Norfolk.
ii, fol. 272b; ii, fol. 272b; ii, fol. 272b; ii, fol. 272b; ii, fol. 273a; ii, fol. 273a; ii, fol. 272b

Ailmar Prepositus Ricardi
Provost of Richard de Clare.
ii, fol. 103a

Ailuard Filius Belli
Englishman, occurs Domesday Suffolk as a tenant of Richard de Clare.
ii, fol. 391a

Ailuuin Filius Brictmar
English tenant of the bishop of London in Domesday Middlesex.
i, fol. 127c

Ailwin Filius Cheping
Occurs Domesday Berkshire.
i, fol. 63c

Aitard De Vals
Norman, major tenant of Roger Bigod in 1086. Thetford charters of c.1107–10 mention the grants of Aitard and Robert de Vallibus, and were attested by Robert and Aitard de Vallibus. Aitard was perhaps the younger brother of Robert, who was the more prominent tenant of Bigod in 1086. The successors to the Vallibus holdings in 1166 were William fitz Robert de Vaux and Robert de Vaux, holding thirty and five fees respectively. William was certainly the heir of the Domesday Robert; perhaps Robert was Aitard's descendant and heir. Some of his holdings appear to have passed to the Ho (from Howe) family, tenants of the earl sof Arundel; Farrer, HKF iii, 137.
ii, fol. 277b; ii, fol. 184a; ii, fol. 188b; ii, fol. 188b; ii, fol. 125a; ii, fol. 124b; ii,

fol. 124b; ii, fol. 124b; ii, fol. 124b; Dugdale, Monasticon Anglicanum, IV, pp. 148–49, No. II; Dugdale, Monasticon Anglicanum, IV, pp. 148–49, No. II; ii, fol. 124a; ii, fol. 124a; ii, fol. 175b; ii, fol. 175a; ii, fol. 175b; ii, fol. 175a; ii, fol. 175a; ii, fol. 175a; ii, fol. 180a; ii, fol. 180b; ii, fol. 180a; ii, fol. 186a; ii, fol. 186a; ii, fol. 331a; ii, fol. 331a; ii, fol. 331a; ii, fol. 331a

Aitard Presbiter

Norman, occurs Domesday Nottinghamshire.

i, fol. 280a

Aiulf Camerarius

Domesday tenant-in-chief in the south west. Sheriff of Dorset from c.1086 to the early years of Henry I's reign, sheriff of Wiltshire 1086 probably until 1091, and sheriff of Somerset from 1091; cf. Green, Sheriffs, 37, 85, 73. Brother of Humphrey camerarius (VCH Somerset i, 416). He was dead by c.1121, as revealed by Henry I's confirmation charter for Shaftesbury Abbey, to which Aiulf had made a grant for the soul of his wife. (RRAN ii, 346–7).

i, fol. 120c; i, fol. 78b; i, fol. 78d; i, fol. 84c; i, fol. 83a; i, fol. 83a; i, fol. 83a; i, fol. 83a; i, fol. 82d; i, fol. 83a; i, fol. 52a; i, fol. 83a; i, fol. 83a; i, fol. 82d; i, fol. 83a; i, fol. 83a; i, fol. 83a; i, fol. 82d; i, fol. 83a; i, fol. 82d; i, fol. 82d; Pipe Roll 31 Henry I, 014–ds; Dugdale, Monasticon Anglicanum, II, pp. 482–83, No. XIII; i, fol. 82d; i, fol. 109a; i, fol. 116b; i, fol. 63a; i, fol. 73a; i, fol. 73b; Dugdale, Monasticon Anglicanum, II, p. 267, No. X

Akile Sufreint

Occurs Domesday Suffolk.

ii, fol. 334b

Alan Comes

Alan Rufus (fl. 1050–93), second of at least seven legitimate sons of Count Eudo, regent of Brittany from 1040 to 1047, and Agnes alias Orguen his Angevin wife (Cartulaire de Saint-Aubin d'Angers, ii, no. 677; cf. Abbot Stephen of St Mary's, York, in his chronicle, BL Add. 38816, fol. 32r: 'Erat eo tempore quidam comes nomine Alanus nobiliorum Britonum prosapia exortus, Eudonis uidelicet, nobilis comitis Britannie filius, cum essem in seculo familiariter mihi in amicitiis coniunctus, qui morum probitate ac diuitiis huius seculi ualde pollebat'). Alan was called Rufus to distinguish him from a younger brother, Alan Niger. His father Eudo was a brother of the Breton duke Alan III; their mother was an aunt of William the Conqueror. Eudo's status entitled his legitimate sons to bear the honorific title 'comes'. Alan first occurs with his father and some of his brothers in an Angevin charter given c.1050. He was probably recruited into the service of his second cousin William of Normandy before 1066; in 1066 or 1067 William assented to the gift by Alan to Saint-Ouen de Rouen of the church of Saint-Sauveur without Rouen, and of the nearby church of Sainte-Croix des Pelletiers, which had been his gift to Alan (Bates, 243, Arch. dépt. Seine-Maritime, 14H 18, p. 230). In 1066 a Breton contingent, probably including both Alan and his brother Brien, played an important role at Hastings. The list of Alan's brothers in the Saint-Aubin charter does not include Brien, or either of Alan's brothers and successors Alan Niger and Stephen. Alan was probably therefore older than Brien. Brien was certainly given lands in Suffolk, and probably also in Cornwall. After helping to defeat an attack on Exeter by the sons of Harold II in 1069, Brien apparently returned to Brittany, leaving Alan as indisputably the most senior of the Bretons in

England. Alan's position was further enhanced by the fall of Ralph de Gael in 1075, much of whose forfeited land in East Anglia he acquired. He held a great deal of land in Cambridgeshire, Suffolk and Norfolk, where he and two of his men, Aubrey de Vere and Harduin de Scales, dominated the region covered by the Inquisitio Eliensis and the Inquisitio Comitatus Cantabrigiensis. The earliest grants to Alan, like those to his brother Brien, were probably located in this region. The kernel of the vast honour of Richmond, based upon land in Yorkshire and Lincolnshire, for which Alan and his successors are best known, was granted only after the Revolt of the North in 1070. The grant of the northern lands was a measure of the Conqueror's trust. By 1086 Alan was one of the richest and most powerful men in England. He remained close to William I, accompanying him to Normandy and Maine on several occasions after 1066, and attested many of his charters. His importance is sometimes overlooked because his intense loyalty to William I and subsequently to William II meant that he was usually ignored by chroniclers, though he figures among those mentioned as helping William II keep his throne during 1087–88. He played an important role in the process against William bishop of Durham. At his death in 1093 he was succeeded by his brother Alan Niger, of whom there is no trace in English documents before this date. Alan Niger died in 1098 and was succeeded by another brother, Stephen, who had also succeeded to their father's Breton lands. The obit dates for Alans Rufus and Niger have caused much confusion, but can be established by reconciling references in documents of St Mary's Abbey, York, with a letter written by Anselm archbishop of Canterbury. The letter reveals that both Alans had a physical liason with Gunhilda, daughter of the former king Harold II, then living in retirement at Wilton Abbey. Because Anselm regarded Gunhilda as a nun, we cannot know whether she was legally married to either brother, though clearly she willingly entered each relationship. Eadmer (Hist. Nov., 121–6) later alleged that Edith-Matilda, wife of Henry I, had been intended by her father Malcolm of Scotland as the wife of Alan Rufus. No recognized wife, nor any children, is known for either Alan, though the tenants of both in England included three of their illegitimate brothers, Ribald, Bodin and Bardulf, and their wet-nurse Orwen. Founder of St Mary's, York (based upon an earlier refoundation of St Olave) and of a priory at Swavesy, Cambs., a cell of SS Serge and Bacchus, Angers, and a benefactor of St Edmund's at Bury, Alan was buried at Bury St Edmund's, though he was later translated to St Mary's, York, at the request of St Mary's monks. K.S.B. Keats-Rohan, 'Le rôle des Bretons dans la politique de la colonisation normande', MSHAB, lxxiv, 1996, 187ff.

Lincolnshire Claims (Domesday Book), fols 375d–376a; Lincolnshire Claims (Domesday Book), fols 375a–d; Clay, Early Yorkshire Charters (1935), IV, No. 2; Douglas, Feudal Documents from Bury St Edmunds, No. 169; ii, fol. 254a; i, fol. 201d; ii, fol. 148a; ii, fol. 146b; ii, fol. 146b; ii, fol. 290b; ii, fol. 146a; ii, fol. 297b; ii, fol. 297a; ii, fol. 297a; ii, fol. 297a; ii, fol. 297a; ii, fol. 297a; ii, fol. 150b; ii, fol. 150a; ii, fol. 115a; ii, fol. 297a; ii, fol. 146b; ii, fol. 147a; ii, fol. 146b; ii, fol. 146b; ii, fol. 146b; ii, fol. 110b; ii, fol. 145b; ii, fol. 147a; ii, fol. 145b; ii, fol. 145b; ii, fol. 292b; ii, fol. 293b; ii, fol. 293b; ii, fol. 293a; ii, fol. 293b; ii, fol. 293b; ii, fol. 293b; ii, fol. 293b; ii, fol. 293b; ii, fol. 293b; ii, fol. 293b; ii, fol. 297a; ii, fol. 293a; ii, fol. 297a; ii, fol. 296b; ii, fol. 297b; ii, fol. 298a; ii, fol. 298a; ii, fol. 298a; ii, fol. 298a; ii, fol. 298a; ii, fol. 297b; ii, fol. 296b; ii, fol. 297b; ii, fol. 297b; ii, fol. 297b; ii, fol. 145b; ii, fol. 293a; ii, fol. 151a; ii, fol. 177a; ii, fol. 145b; ii, fol. 150b; ii, fol. 151a; ii, fol. 150b; ii, fol. 150b; ii, fol. 150b; ii, fol. 150b; ii, fol. 150b; ii, fol. 150b; ii, fol.

145b; ii, fol. 150b; ii, fol. 150a; ii, fol. 151a; ii, fol. 151a; ii, fol. 151a; ii, fol.
150b; ii, fol. 150b; ii, fol. 150b; ii, fol. 151a; ii, fol. 147b; ii, fol. 147b; ii, fol.
147a; ii, fol. 148b; ii, fol. 149b; ii, fol. 150a; ii, fol. 150b; ii, fol. 145b; ii, fol.
293b; ii, fol. 146b; ii, fol. 149a; ii, fol. 150a; ii, fol. 145a; ii, fol. 147a; ii, fol.
145a; ii, fol. 145a; ii, fol. 145a; ii, fol. 145a; ii, fol. 151a; ii, fol. 145a; ii, fol.
150b; ii, fol. 145a; ii, fol. 144b; ii, fol. 144b; ii, fol. 144b; ii, fol. 137b; ii, fol.
144a; ii, fol. 144b; ii, fol. 145a; ii, fol. 150b; ii, fol. 144a; ii, fol. 150b; ii, fol.
150b; ii, fol. 150b; ii, fol. 145b; ii, fol. 294b; ii, fol. 294a; i, fol. 79a; ii, fol. 035b;
i, fol. 44b; i, fol. 132a; i, fol. 44b; ii, fol. 035b; ii, fol. 148a; i, fol. 44b; ii, fol.
294a; i, fol. 194d; ii, fol. 294b; i, fol. 193d; ii, fol. 294a; ii, fol. 294a; ii, fol. 294a;
ii, fol. 294a; ii, fol. 294b; ii, fol. 294a; ii, fol. 294b; ii, fol. 294a; ii, fol. 294a; ii,
fol. 294a; ii, fol. 294a; ii, fol. 294a; ii, fol. 293a; ii, fol. 294a; i, fol. 195d; i, fol.
137a; i, fol. 137b; i, fol. 137a; i, fol. 137a; i, fol. 199d; i, fol. 193d; i, fol. 193d; i,
fol. 189a; i, fol. 189a; i, fol. 189a; i, fol. 194d; ii, fol. 004a; i, fol. 142a; ii, fol.
294a; i, fol. 195d; i, fol. 195a; i, fol. 195a; i, fol. 194d; i, fol. 193d; i, fol. 194c; i,
fol. 194c; i, fol. 194b; i, fol. 194a; i, fol. 194a; i, fol. 194a; i, fol. 194a; i, fol.
193d; i, fol. 195d; ii, fol. 292b; ii, fol. 293a; ii, fol. 294a; ii, fol. 293a; ii, fol.
293a; ii, fol. 293a; ii, fol. 296b; ii, fol. 293a; ii, fol. 293a; ii, fol. 293a; ii, fol.
293a; ii, fol. 292b; ii, fol. 293b; ii, fol. 292b; ii, fol. 293a; ii, fol. 292b; ii, fol.
292b; ii, fol. 292b; ii, fol. 292b; ii, fol. 293a; ii, fol. 293b; ii, fol. 293b; ii, fol.
293b; ii, fol. 293b; ii, fol. 293b; ii, fol. 293b; ii, fol. 293b; ii, fol. 150a; ii, fol.
292b; ii, fol. 293b; ii, fol. 294a; ii, fol. 294a; ii, fol. 296a; ii, fol. 296b; ii, fol.
292b; ii, fol. 296b; ii, fol. 296b; ii, fol. 296b; ii, fol. 296b; ii, fol. 296b; ii, fol.
296a; ii, fol. 293a; ii, fol. 296a; ii, fol. 294a; ii, fol. 296a; ii, fol. 296a; ii, fol.
295a; ii, fol. 295a; ii, fol. 295a; ii, fol. 295a; ii, fol. 295a; ii, fol. 295a; ii, fol.
295a; ii, fol. 294b; ii, fol. 296a; ii, fol. 293a; ii, fol. 293a; ii, fol. 294b; i, fol.
312d; i, fol. 310b; i, fol. 309a; i, fol. 313b; i, fol. 313a; i, fol. 313b; i, fol. 313a; i,
fol. 313a; i, fol. 312d; i, fol. 312d; i, fol. 312d; i, fol. 313b; i, fol. 312d; i, fol.
313a; i, fol. 311b; i, fol. 313a; i, fol. 313a; i, fol. 313a; i, fol. 313a; i, fol. 313b; i,
fol. 313a; i, fol. 312b; i, fol. 313a; i, fol. 313a; i, fol. 309a; i, fol. 313b; i, fol.
312d; i, fol. 309a; i, fol. 309a; i, fol. 309a; i, fol. 309a; i, fol. 309b; i, fol. 309a; i,
fol. 309d; i, fol. 309a; ii, fol. 149b; i, fol. 310b; ii, fol. 150a; i, fol. 313a; i, fol.
309a; i, fol. 313b; i, fol. 309a; i, fol. 309a; i, fol. 309a; i, fol. 309a; i, fol. 309a; i,
fol. 309a; i, fol. 311b; i, fol. 309a; i, fol. 313a; i, fol. 312b; i, fol. 313b; i, fol.
313b; i, fol. 309a; i, fol. 311c; i, fol. 312a; i, fol. 313a; i, fol. 311b; i, fol. 312a; i,
fol. 311c; i, fol. 312a; i, fol. 312a; i, fol. 311d; i, fol. 311d; i, fol. 311d; i, fol.
313b; i, fol. 311c; i, fol. 312a; i, fol. 312a; i, fol. 298c; i, fol. 298c; i, fol. 298c; i,
fol. 310b; i, fol. 282c; i, fol. 298b; i, fol. 282c; i, fol. 282c; Lincolnshire Claims
(Domesday Book), fol. 377d; Lincolnshire Claims (Domesday Book), fols
376d–377c; Dugdale, *Monasticon Anglicanum*, III, pp. 548–50, No. V; i, fol.
311d; i, fol. 311a; i, fol. 313b; i, fol. 313b; i, fol. 313b; i, fol. 313a; i, fol. 311a; i,
fol. 311c; i, fol. 312c; i, fol. 310a; i, fol. 311b; i, fol. 310b; i, fol. 312a; i, fol.
311c; i, fol. 312b; i, fol. 310d; i, fol. 310c; i, fol. 310c; i, fol. 310c; i, fol. 310c; i,
fol. 310c; i, fol. 310b; i, fol. 311a; i, fol. 312a; i, fol. 312b; i, fol. 312b; i, fol.
312b; i, fol. 311a; i, fol. 348d; i, fol. 347d; i, fol. 348c; i, fol. 347d; i, fol. 347d; i,
fol. 347d; i, fol. 347d; i, fol. 347c; i, fol. 347c; i, fol. 347c; i, fol. 348d; i, fol.
348c; i, fol. 347d; i, fol. 309d; i, fol. 348d; i, fol. 309a; i, fol. 348c; i, fol. 348c; i,
fol. 348c; i, fol. 348b; i, fol. 348c; i, fol. 347c; i, fol. 348c; i, fol. 348c; i, fol.
348c; i, fol. 347d; ii, fol. 148b; ii, fol. 147a; ii, fol. 149b; ii, fol. 149a; ii, fol.
149a; ii, fol. 149a; ii, fol. 149a; ii, fol. 149a; ii, fol. 148b; ii, fol. 150a; i, fol. 347d;
ii, fol. 148a; i, fol. 348b; ii, fol. 148b; i, fol. 347d; i, fol. 347c; i, fol. 348b; i, fol.
348b; i, fol. 348b; i, fol. 348b; i, fol. 348a; i, fol. 348a; i, fol. 348a; i, fol. 348b; i,
fol. 347d; ii, fol. 148b; i, fol. 347b; i, fol. 347b; i, fol. 347b; i, fol. 347b; i, fol.
347b; i, fol. 347a; i, fol. 347a; i, fol. 347a; i, fol. 347a; i, fol. 347a; i, fol. 348c; i,

fol. 347a; i, fol. 348d; i, fol. 347a; i, fol. 309c; i, fol. 309b; i, fol. 309a; i, fol. 309a; i, fol. 309c; i, fol. 309a; i, fol. 309a; i, fol. 309a; i, fol. 309a; i, fol. 309a; i, fol. 309a; i, fol. 309a; i, fol. 347a; i, fol. 348b; i, fol. 348b; i, fol. 348b; i, fol. 348b; i, fol. 347b; i, fol. 348b; i, fol. 348c; i, fol. 347a; i, fol. 347c; i, fol. 347a; i, fol. 347b; i, fol. 347c; i, fol. 347c; i, fol. 347c; i, fol. 347b; i, fol. 347a; i, fol. 348b; i, fol. 347b; i, fol. 347c; i, fol. 347c; i, fol. 347c; i, fol. 347c; Dugdale, Monasticon Anglicanum, III, pp. 548–50, No. V; Gibbs, Early Charters of St Paul's, No. 9; Dugdale, Monasticon Anglicanum, III, p. 547, No. III; Lincolnshire Claims (Domesday Book), fols 375d–376a; Lincolnshire Claims (Domesday Book), fols 375d–376a; Lincolnshire Claims (Domesday Book), fols 375a–d; Clay, Early Yorkshire Charters (1935), IV, No. 101; Clay, Early Yorkshire Charters (1949), VIII, No. 5; Lincolnshire Claims (Domesday Book), fols 375d–376a; i, fol. 298b; i, fol. 224b; i, fol. 282c; ii, fol. 144a; i, fol. 347a; i, fol. 44b; ii, fol. 035a; i, fol. 136d; i, fol. 309a; ii, fol. 292b; Douglas, Feudal Documents from Bury St Edmunds, No. 169; Clay, Early Yorkshire Charters (1935), IV, No. 21; Dugdale, Monasticon Anglicanum, III, pp. 544–46, No. I; Clay, Early Yorkshire Charters (1935), IV, No. 33; Douglas, Feudal Documents from Bury St Edmunds, No. 173; Clay, Early Yorkshire Charters (1935), IV, No. 1

Alan Dapifer Judite Comitisse
Dapifer of Countess Judith and her tenant in 1086. Early benefactor of St Neots as lord of Weald in Eynesbury. His successors were a family named Le Noreis, or Noreis (BL Cotton Faust. A. iv, fols 66v–67r).

i, fol. 207a; Dugdale, Monasticon Anglicanum, III, p. 474, No. XVI; i, fol. 206d; i, fol. 229a; i, fol. 229a

Alan De Bureuuelle
Domesday tenant of Count Alan at Burwell in Cambridgeshire, and a Domesday juror in Staploe. His position in the list of jurors identifies him as an Englishman, though his personal name is Breton. Possibly he was a relic of the pre-Conquest Breton settlement associated with Ralph the Staller.

i, fol. 195c; Hamilton, Inquisitio Eliensis (1876), pp. 97–100; Hamilton, Inquisitio Comitatus Cantabrigiensis, pp. 1–93

Alan []
Domesday tenant of Robert of Mortain in Buckinghamshire; probably the same Alan as held from him in Sussex. His successor in 1166 was Stephen fitz Adam de Weltun (Whilton), who also succeeded to the fees held in 1086 by Osbert of Walter Flandrensis; Farrer, HKF i, 88–9. Since two of Robert's tenants (Richard fitz Turold and Hamelin of Cornwall) occurs in charters of Saint-Evroul relating to Damblainville it might be that this Alan was the Alan de Ducey, Manche, who occurs in another of them (Ord. Vit. ed. Le Prévost v, 187–8) with his wife Gaelun and issue Robert and Albreda; his grant was conceded by his superior Richard fitz Turold.

i, fol. 22d; i, fol. 22a; i, fol. 21c; i, fol. 20c; i, fol. 146b; i, fol. 146b; i, fol. 223b; i, fol. 223b; i, fol. 223b; i, fol. 223b; i, fol. 223b

Alberic Camerarius Regine
Norman, occurs in Domesday Book. To be distinguished from Aubrey de Vere, a chamberlain to Henry I (cf. Comp. Peer. x, App. J, 110). This Aubrey is probably to be identified with the Albericus camerarius regine who gave land at Le Tourp to the abbey of Montebourg. The grant was confirmed in 1107 by Henry I; in a copy of the charter in the cartulary of the piory of Loders (Dorset) the witnesses include

Alberici camerarius and Rasci filii Alberici (Redvers ch. no. 5, Chanteux no. 4, 14–20).

i, fol. 67c; Bearman, Charters of the Redvers Family (1994), No. 5; Bearman, Charters of the Redvers Family (1994), No. 5; i, fol. 74d; i, fol. 74d; i, fol. 63d

Alberic Comes

Named from Coucy-le-Château-Auffrique, Aisne, the inheritance of his wife Ada, daughter of Létard de Marle. Son of a French count, Ivo de Beaumont-sur-Oise, Val-d'Oise. Held land in England after the Conquest, but returned home under suspicion of incompetence in the early 1070s; Symeon of Durham, Historia Regum Anglorum, in Opera, ii, 199, 'Quo in rebus difficilibus parum valente patriamque reverso' (of little use in difficult affairs, he returned to his homeland). He met his death at his castle of Coucy c.1079, after falling victim to a plot orchestrated by his wife Ada and her lover and subsequent second husband Engeran. According to the Vita Sancti Arnulfi (AASS Aug. 11, p. 240), he had been alerted to the plot by his sister Ermengarde, but had trusted his wife instead. See D. Barthémy, Les Deux Ages de la seigneurie banale, Coucy (xie–xiiie siècle), Paris, 1984. At the time of the Domesday Survey most of the land he had held was still in the king's hands; though it is entered there in his name, the text normally states that he had held it, and not that he still held it.

i, fol. 157c; i, fol. 239c; i, fol. 231c; i, fol. 224b; i, fol. 329d; i, fol. 329d; i, fol. 329d

Alberic De Ver

The first Aubrey de Vere was a Domesday tenant of the powerful Breton tenant-in-chief Count Alan Rufus, and was among a handful of Alan's Bretons who were also tenant-in-chief of their own fees. Aubrey's family probably came from Vair in Ancenis, in the Nantais; he occurs amongst a group of men from the Nantais in a charter given by Conan II c.1050 (discussed by H. Guillotel, 'La place de Châteaubriant dans l'essor des châtellenies bretonnes (xi–xii siècles)', MSHAB, 66 (1989), 21, and K. S. B. Keats-Rohan, 'Le problème de la suzeraineté et la lutte pour le pouvoir: la rivalité bretonne et l'état anglo-normand 1066–1154', MSHAB, 68 (1991), 63–9). He is usually assumed to have originated at Ver, (Manche, arr. Coutances, cant. Gavray) because he held land in 1086 of the Bishop of Coutances (Domesday i, fol. 220c), Loyd, Origins, 110. Loyd acknowledged that no later evidence established any connexion between Aubrey's family and Ver in the Cotentin. His wife occurs in her own right in Domesday Book (i, fols 24a, 101a); she very probably was from a Cotentin family. There is a real possibility that other de Ver families in England could have originated in the Cotentin (cf. William de Ver, Domesday i, fol. 127c), but the mass of evidence indicating Aubrey's Breton origins is overwhelming. Much of it was rehearsed by W. R. Powell, 'The Essex Fees of the Honour of Richmond', TEAS, 3rd Ser. I, pt 3 (1964), 179–89, though he ultimately rejected it. One of the most striking features of the evidence is that Aubrey II founded the priory of Hatfield Broadoak, as a cell of Saint-Melaine de Rennes, one of the most important Breton abbeys (J. L. Fisher, Cartularium Prioratus de Colne, Essex Archaeological Society Occasional Publications I, 1946, F. Jouön des Longrais, 'Les moines de l'abbaye Saint-Melaine de Rennes en Angleterre. Les chartes du prieuré d'Hatfield Regis', Recueil de travaux offert à M. Clovis Brunel, t. ii, Paris, 1955) Research has shown that though a cult of Saint Melaine existed outside Brittany, it never reached the Cotentin peninsula, though it is found elsewhere in Normandy (J. Fournée, 'Le culte populaire des saints bretons en Normandie', Questions d'histoire de Bretagne, Actes du 107 Congrès national des sociétés savantes, section de philologie et d'histoire jusqu'à 1610 (2 t., Brest 1982), ii, 311. Note the escheat to the king in the early thirteenth century of land formerly held by one Walter de Ver, a Breton (Britonis), in Suffolk, where Aubrey's family held land (Fees, op. cit., note 61, 390). Of little note in England before 1100, he was possibly more often in Brittany; it was doubtless he who attested a charter of Count Alan's brother Count Geoffrey Boterel as Alberic Aper (Anciens Evêchés iv, 304, cited in Comp. Peer. x, 193ff). Active in Berkshire in the early years of Henry I's reign, he was either or possibly both a justiciar or sheriff (RRAN ii, 576, 695; Chron. Abing. ii, 57–62, 90–1 He died c.1112 and was buried at Colne priory, a cell of Abingdon, which he and his wife Beatrice founded after the death of their son Geoffrey. Father of Alberic II, Geoffrey, William, Robert and Roger; possibly also of a daughter who was mother of Richard de Camville (Comp. Peer. x, app. J, pp. 112–13 note j). K. S. B. Keats-Rohan, 'Le rôle des Bretons dans la politique de la colonisation normande', MSHAB, lxxiv, 1996, 186.

Northants Survey, fols 94r–95v; i, fol. 49c; Northants Survey, fols 96r–99v; Douglas, Feudal Documents from Bury St Edmunds, No. 21; ii, fol. 418b; ii, fol. 418a; ii, fol. 419a; ii, fol. 419a; ii, fol. 449a; ii, fol. 419a; ii, fol. 418b; ii, fol. 418a; i, fol. 130d; ii, fol. 035b; ii, fol. 418b; ii, fol. 107a; ii, fol. 101a; i, fol. 208a; i, fol. 208a; i, fol. 204d; ii, fol. 101a; i, fol. 207a; ii, fol. 418a; ii, fol. 287b; Fisher, Cartularium Prioratus de Colne (Earles C.), No. 1; Chibnall, English Lands of Abbey of Bec (1951), No. XXV; Fisher, Cartularium Prioratus de Colne (Earles C.), No. 13; Fisher, Cartularium Prioratus de Colne (Earles C.), No. 9; Gibbs, Early Charters of St Pauls (1939), No. 46; Hart, Cartularium Monasterii de Rameseia, No. CLXXIV; i, fol. 190a; ii, fol. 076a; ii, fol. 077a; ii, fol. 077a; ii, fol. 077b; Fisher, Cartularium Prioratus de Colne (Earles C.), No. 2; Regesta regum Anglo-Normannorum III, No. 14; Fisher, Cartularium Prioratus de Colne (Earles C.), No. 4; Fisher, Cartularium Prioratus de Colne (Earles C.), No. 3; ii, fol. 077b; Fisher, Cartularium Prioratus de Colne (Earles C.), No. 11; ii, fol. 076b; ii, fol. 076a; i, fol. 199c; i, fol. 199c; i, fol. 199c; i, fol. 199c; Fisher, Cartularium Prioratus de Colne (Earles C.), No. 9; ii, fol. 076a; Fisher, Cartularium Prioratus de Colne (Earles C.), No. 34; i, fol. 199d; ii, fol. 035a; i, fol. 220c; i, fol. 220c; Dugdale, Monasticon Anglicanum, II, p. 603, No. XXVII

Alberic []

Domesday tenant of Baldwin the Sheriff. An Alberic brother of Wiger and nephew of Wiger of Sainte-Mère-Eglise (Manche) occur in a grant to Sainte-Trinité de Caen a. 1082 (Walmsley, Cart. Cust. ii, 120 no. 9); Wiger was the name of an illegitimate son of Baldwin.

i, fol. 115d; i, fol. 106b; i, fol. 106b; i, fol. 106b

Alberic []

Domesday tenant of Geoffrey de la Guerche. Attested his foundation charter for Monks Kirby in 1077.

i, fol. 235d; Mon. Ang. vi, 996

Albert Crematus

Norman, Domesday tenant of Roger of Poitou. He appears to have acquired the holding at Manchester, formerly of one Nigel, that formed the centre of his barony during the reign of William II (Sanders, 130). Alive in 1094, his son Robert had succeeded him by 1115/18. His daughter Emma married Orm son of Ailward

(Fees, 136; Tait, Medieval Manchester and the Beginnings of Lancashire, Manchester, 1904 (rept. Llanerch, 1991) 127ff).

i, fol. 259b; ii, fol. 243b; i, fol. 324d; ii, fol. 347a; i, fol. 255b; i, fol. 254b; i, fol. 255b; i, fol. 255b; i, fol. 255b; i, fol. 352a; ii, fol. 243b; Lindsey Survey, BL ms Cotton Claudius C v, fols 19–27; ii, fol. 347b; i, fol. 270a; i, fol. 270a; i, fol. 270a; ii, fol. 351b; ii, fol. 351b; ii, fol. 351b; ii, fol. 351b; ii, fol. 351b; ii, fol. 351b; ii, fol. 351b

Albert De Sancto Dionisio
Attests two charters of Abbot Albold of Bury St Edmunds. His name indicates that he was associated with Saint-Denis, the Parisian monastery from which Albold's predecessor had come. He may have been the Albert who was Abbot Baldwin's tenant in Domesday Book. The Domesday Albert's land was held by William fitz Robert of Abbot Samson in 1182 (Kalendar, 27 and note).

Douglas, Feudal Book of Bury St Edmunds (1932), pp. 3–21; ii, fol. 020a; ii, fol. 357b; Douglas, Feudal Documents from Bury St Edmunds, No. 108; Douglas, Feudal Documents from Bury St Edmunds, No. 109

Albert Homo Abbatis
A Domesday juror, identified as non-English, in Papworth Hundred, Cambridgeshire, where IE described him as a man of the abbot of Ramsey; can be associated with the unnamed 'francigenus' who was the abbot's tenant in the Hundred. Possibly the same as the Albert francigenus (q.v.) who occurs at Grimston, Norfolk, in the early twelfth century.

i, fol. 192c; Hamilton, Inquisitio Eliensis (1876), pp. 97–100

Albert Lotharingensis
One of several clerics recruited from Lorraine to the England of Edward the Confessor. He served both Edward and his successor William I as chaplain. Occurs as a tenant-in-chief in Domesday Book as Albert the clerk, chaplain or the Lorrainer. He also held tenancies of other tenants-in-chief, including Walter fitz Other. He probably left descendants since all four of his Bedfordshire manors, which passed to the barony of Beauchamp, were later held by persons surnamed Lohareng or Loring (Lorrainer) (cf. Beds. Rec. Soc. 10, p. 264, n. 102); he was represented in the Beauchamp honour in 1166 by Roger, John and Geoffrey Loereng. He died between 1087 and 1096, during which period William II confirmed three churches he had held in Rutland to Westminster abbey (Westminster Ch., 55).

i, fol. 70c; i, fol. 336d; i, fol. 63a; i, fol. 014c; i, fol. 014c; i, fol. 014c; i, fol. 36d; i, fol. 56d; i, fol. 294a; i, fol. 238b; i, fol. 294a; i, fol. 294a; i, fol. 294a; i, fol. 186a; i, fol. 186a; i, fol. 216d; i, fol. 216d; i, fol. 216d; i, fol. 216d; i, fol. 216d

Albold Cocus
Occurs Domesday Hampshire.

i, fol. 38a

Albold Presbiter
Occurs Domesday Suffolk as a tenant of Bury St Edmunds. Father of William fitz Albold (q.v.), who occurs in Bury charters of the early twelfth century, and grandfather of Robert Noel, tenant of the mid-twelfth century (Kalendar of Abbot Samson, pp. 116–17).

ii, fol. 358a; Douglas, Feudal Documents from Bury St Edmunds, No. 25; ii, fol.

360b; Douglas, Feudal Documents from Bury St Edmunds, No. 170; Douglas, Feudal Documents from Bury St Edmunds, No. 104

Alcher []
Domesday tenant of Roger de Montgomery; ancestor of the Alcher or FitzAer family (Eyton, Shrops, ix). The one occurrence, in Sussex, of an Alberic may refer to the same man; manuscript copies of a charter of Roger de Montgomery confuse the name of a certain Fulcone fratre Alcherii and Fulcoio fratre Alberi (CDF, 656); possibly brother of Fulk of Le Pin, whom Orderic names as one of Roger's tenants (Ord. Vit. iii, 140).

> i, fol. 24c; i, fol. 259d; i, fol. 254b; i, fol. 24b; i, fol. 255b; i, fol. 255b; Rees, Cartulary of Shrewsbury Abbey (1975), No. 35

Alcher []
Domesday tenant of Henry de Ferrers.

> i, fol. 248c; ii, fol. 053b; i, fol. 275a; i, fol. 274c; i, fol. 274c; i, fol. 274c; i, fol. 274c; i, fol. 275a

Aldelin []
Domesday tenant of William de Warenne in Lincolnshire. The holding was part of the fees held c.1147/53 by Helias, brother of Fulk de Boseville; see Farrer, HKF iii, 416.

> i, fol. 351d

Alden Presbiter
Englishman, occurs Domesday Lincolnshire.

> i, fol. 371a

Alden []
English thegn in Domesday Nottinghamshire; ancestor of the Cromwell family. See R. Thoroton, The Antiquities of Nottinghamshire, ed and enlarged by J. Thoresby, 3 vols (London, 1797), i, 77.

> i, fol. 292c; i, fol. 292c; i, fol. 292c; i, fol. 292c; i, fol. 282d; i, fol. 292d; i, fol. 293b; i, fol. 293b; i, fol. 293a; i, fol. 293a; i, fol. 293a; i, fol. 292c

Aldene []
Englishman holding land at Tewin, Hertfordshire, which the king had given to him and his mother in memory of his son Richard, killed in the New Forest in 1081. Cf. Eddeue, to whom Queen Matilda made a similar gift; Williams, The English, 79–80.

> i, fol. 141b

Aldi Femina
Englishwoman. Occurs Domesday Surrey.

> i, fol. 30d

Aldit []
Englishwoman, held Wells in Norfolk of the king in 1086.

> ii, fol. 271a; ii, fol. 271a

Aldred Frater Odonis
Englishman, brother of Odo, occurs Domesday. At the time of the Winchester survey, c.1110, some his holdings were then in the hands of Herbert de St Quintin.

According to Round (VCH Somerset i, 417, VCH Hampshire i, 427) he was the Ealdred who occurs in Domesday Devon and Somerset, where he was probably the Aldred *forestarius* of the Tax Return for Exminster Hundred. He married an embroidress employed by Queen Matilda. Cf. Williams, The English, 116.

i, fol. 73d; i, fol. 73d; i, fol. 73d; i, fol. 118b; i, fol. 118b; i, fol. 118b; i, fol. 48d; i, fol. 50d; i, fol. 43c,d; i, fol. 40b; i, fol. 99b; i, fol. 99b; i, fol. 29c; i, fol. 73d; i, fol. 73d

Alestan Anglicus
Occurs Domesday Norfolk as a tenant of Roger Bigod.

ii, fol. 178a; ii, fol. 146a

Alfgar Presbiter
Occurs Domesday Essex.

ii, fol. 104b

Alfhila []
Englishwoman, occurs Domesday Devon.

i, fol. 118c

Alfildis []
Occurs Domesday Wiltshire.

i, fol. 74b

Alfred []
The knight Alfred who was a tenant of William de Warenne at Benfield in Sussex in 1086 was probably the Alfred de la Buera, knight of Ralph de Warenne, William's father, who was a benefactor, with his wife Adheliza, of Sainte-Trinité de Rouen; he attested a charter of Ralph de Warenne given on the eve of the Norman sailing for England in 1066 (Guérard, Cart., pp. 439, 451–2).

i, fol. 27d

Alfric Filius Everwacre
Occurs Domesday Somerset; his patronym is given in Exon. Everwacre minister witnessed a grant to Abbot Wulfwold of Bath made in 1061 by Edward the Confessor (Sawyer, Anglo-Saxon Charters, 1034).

i, fol. 90d; i, fol. 90d

Alfrid []
Domesday tenant of Geoffrey de la Guerche. Attested,before 1093, a charter of Geoffrey de la Guerche for Monks Kirby (Mon. Ang. vi, 996).

i, fol. 227c; i, fol. 235d

Alfsi []
Englishman, Domesday tenant of Henry de Ferrers, benefactor of Tutbury.

i, fol. 275b

Algar Presbiter
Occurs Domesday Devon.

i, fol. 104b

Algar []

English tenant of Robert of Mortain in Cornwall, 1086.

i, fol. 124c; i, fol. 124c; i, fol. 124c; i, fol. 124c; i, fol. 124c; i, fol. 124c

Algar []

Englishman, tenant in 1086 of Guy de Craon at Casthorpe, Lincolnshire. Hugh son of Algar, his son or grandson, held the fee c.1141–66.

i, fol. 368a

Almar De Berlea

Occurs Domesday Essex.

ii, fol. 101b

Almar De Brunna

Aelmer of Bourn, an English thegn of King Edward who continued to hold much of his lands under Count Alan. Also occurs as Almær cild, a juror in Longstowe Hundred, Cambridgeshire. Probably the same as Aelmer son of Colswein. Colswein also continued to hold land under Count Alan; both had previously held of Alan's predecessor Edeva the Fair. See Williams, The English, 88–9.

i, fol. 194d; i, fol. 195d; i, fol. 195d; i, fol. 194b; Hamilton, Inquisitio Eliensis (1876), pp. 97–100; i, fol. 194b; i, fol. 195a; i, fol. 195a; i, fol. 195a; i, fol. 195a; Hamilton, Inquisitio Eliensis (1876), pp. 97–100; Hamilton, Inquisitio Comitatus Cantabrigiensis, pp. 1–93

Almar De Odona

English tenant of Robert of Mortain in Domesday Buckinghamshire. Said to have been ancestor of the de Wedon family of Buckinghamshire (Luffield Chh. pt ii, pp. xlvii–l).

i, fol. 146b; i, fol. 146a; i, fol. 150b; i, fol. 146b; i, fol. 150c

Almar Prepositus Regis

Occurs Domesday Suffolk

ii, fol. 352a

Almar []

English tenant of Robert of Mortain in Cornwall, 1086.

i, fol. 124d

Almar []

English freeman, occurs Domesday Norfolk

ii, fol. 272b; ii, fol. 272b; ii, fol. 272b; ii, fol. 272a; ii, fol. 272a; ii, fol. 272a; ii, fol. 272a; ii, fol. 272a; ii, fol. 272a; ii, fol. 272b; ii, fol. 272b; ii, fol. 272b

Almarus []

Englishman, Domesday tenant of Thorkil of Warwick in Warwickshire. Probably uncle of Thorkil; perhaps father or grandfather of Ketilbiorn of Longdon and Thorkil who attest charters of Siward and Hugh of Arden in the twelfth century; see Williams, 'Vice-comital family', pp. 286–7.

i, fol. 241a; i, fol. 241a; i, fol. 241a; i, fol. 241c; i, fol. 241c

Almodus Archidiaconus

In a writ of c.1112/13, Henry I commanded Almod the archdeacon to restore the manor of Sawbridge, Warwickshire, to the abbey of Thorney, stocked as he had received it. The writ was printed in Early Northamptonshire Charters, p. 15 [cf. RRAN ii, 1033], by Loyd and Stenton, who suggested that Almod had been appointed caretaker of Thorney Abbey following the death of Abbot Gunter in 1112. Almod archdeacon is not otherwise known, but he can plausibly be identified with the sole other person of the name to occur in English documents, the Almodus who was a tenant of Bishop William of Durham in 1086. William had previously been abbot of Saint-Calais in Maine, a region associated with Abbot Almodus of Mont-Saint-Michel, subsequently abbot of Cérisy in Normandy, c.1047, and Abbot Almodus of Redon in Brittany c.1080. A William son of Almod occurs in a charter of Edgar of Scotland to Bishop William and the monks of Durham dated 29 August 1095 (RRAN i, 363, possibly spurious).

> i, fol. 341a; i, fol. 341b

Alnod Cilt
Occurs Domesday Kent.

> Ballard, Inquisition of St Augustine's (1920), fols 24r–28r; Ballard, Inquisition of St Augustine's (1920), fols 20r–23v; i, fol. 001a

Alnod De Braio
Occurs Domesday Devon. Named from Bray in the Tax Return for South Molton Hundred.

> i, fol. 118b

Alnod Monachus
Occurs Domesday Somerset.

> i, fol. 90b

Alnod Presbiter
Occurs Domesday Hampshire.

> i, fol. 44b

Alnod []
English tenant of Robert of Mortain in Cornwall.

> i, fol. 124c; i, fol. 124c

Alnod []
English tenant of Robert of Mortain in Domesday Cornwall.

> i, fol. 124c; i, fol. 124c; i, fol. 124c

Alnulf Presbiter
Occurs Domesday Suffolk.

> ii, fol. 290a

Alred []
Englishman, canon of Dover in 1086; his father had held his prebend before him.

> i, fol. 001c

Alric Archidiaconus
Archdeacon of Worcester diocese. First occurs as tenant of bishop of Worcester in Domesday Worcs. Presumed dead or resigned by February 1114; see FEA ii, 104.

> Darlington, Cartulary of Worcester: Reg. I (1962–3), No. 259; Darlington, Cartulary of Worcester: Reg. I (1962–3), No. 148; Darlington, Cartulary of Worcester: Reg. I (1962–3), No. 52; i, fol. 173a; Darlington, Cartulary of

Worcester: Reg. I (1962–3), No. 3; Darlington, Cartulary of Worcester: Reg. I (1962–3), No. 4; i, fol. 173c; i, fol. 173a

Alric Cocus
Englishman, occurs Domesday Buckinghamshire holding the manor of Steeple Claydon which had previously belonged to Queen Edith; he had probably served her as cook. See Williams, The English, 99.

i, fol. 153a; i, fol. 153a

Alric Wintremelc
Occurs Domesday Bedfordshire.

i, fol. 218d; i, fol. 218d

Alric []
English tenant of Robert of Mortain in Cornwall, 1086.

i, fol. 124c; i, fol. 124c

Alric []
Englishman, Domesday tenant of Roger de Curcella in Somerset.

i, fol. 94a; i, fol. 94a; i, fol. 94a

Alric []
Englishman, held land under Ilbert de Lacy in Domesday Yorkshire. He was succeeded by his son Swein (q.v.), also a Lacy tenant in Domesday. See Hugh Thomas, 'A Yorkshire thegn and his descendants after the Conquest', Medieval Prosopography 8.1 (1987), 1–22.

i, fol. 317a; i, fol. 316b; i, fol. 316d; i, fol. 316d; i, fol. 317a; i, fol. 317d; i, fol. 316c; i, fol. 330c; i, fol. 316c; i, fol. 316c; i, fol. 316d; i, fol. 316d; i, fol. 317c

Alsi Berchenistr-
Englishman. Occurs in Domesday Hampshire, secondly as burchenistr. (misprinted by Farley), representing the English word 'burcniht', meaning 'chamberlain'. Cf. Williams, The English, 116.

i, fol. 50d; i, fol. 50b

Alsi De Ferendone
English thegn, named from Farringdon, Berkshire, where his son Alfwy occurs at Wallingford. He occurs in Domesday Book principally as the predecessor of Geoffrey de Mandeville, but also continued to hold land himself. See Williams, The English, 118–19.

i, fol. 57d; i, fol. 154d; i, fol. 154d; i, fol. 63c; i, fol. 63c; i, fol. 170c; i, fol. 164b; i, fol. 165d; i, fol. 170c; i, fol. 160d

Alsi Filius Brixi
Occurs Domesday Hampshire.

i, fol. 53d; i, fol. 43a,b; i, fol. 49d; i, fol. 49d; i, fol. 50a

Alsi Presbiter
Occurs Domesday Hampshire.

i, fol. 44b

Alsi []
Englishman holding in 1086 land he had held before 1066.

i, fol. 58a

Alsi []
English tenant of Robert of Mortain, 1086, in Cornwall. Perhaps the same as Ailsi [Æthelsige], father of Bernard the Scribe, Nicholas and Jordan, whose grandson Peter of Cornwall (son of Jordan) described Ailsi as a master-builder in the employ of the canons of Launceston. Cf. Williams, The English, 122–3.

i, fol. 124d

Alsi []
Occurs in Domesday Buckinghamshire. Son-in-law of Wulfward White, according to Domesday; cf. VCH i, 216.

i, fol. 153a; i, fol. 153a; i, fol. 153a; i, fol. 153a

Alsi []
English thegn who still held a single manor in Domesday Warwickshire; presumed kinsman of Thorkil of Warwick. See Williams, 'Vicecomital family', and idem, English, p. 104.

i, fol. 244c

Alueua Comitissa
Englishwoman, wife of Earl Algar of Mercia, occurs Domesday Leicestershire.

i, fol. 231d

Alueua []
Englishwoman, occurs Domesday Devon.

i, fol. 118c

Alueua []
Englishwoman, occurs Domesday Essex.

ii, fol. 106a; ii, fol. 106a

Aluid Anglica
Englishwoman, Domesday tenant of Swein of Essex.

ii, fol. 045b

Aluiet Presbiter
Occurs Domesday Somerset.

i, fol. 91c

Aluiet Presbyter
Occurs Domesday Cambridgeshire.

i, fol. 191c

Alured []
Tenant at Hawton, Nottinghamshire, of both Ralph fitz Hubert and Ralph de Limesi in 1086. His connexion, if any, with a family named from Hawton evidenced from c.1212 is unknown; cf. Cart. Thurgarton, p. 187.

i, fol. 289d

Aluredus Brito
Domesday tenant-in-chief in Devon and tenant of Robert of Mortain. Bretons associated with Robert are likely to have originated in the region of Louvigné, in the seigneurie of Fougères (Ille-et-Vilaine), which was partly in the jurisdiction of the count of Mortain. Overlordship of his fief was granted to Richard de Redvers

as part of the honour of Plympton before 1107. He may have been the lineal
ancestor of the Alfred fitz Ivo whose mother held Alfred Brito's demesne manors
of Ugborough, Blaxton and Tamerton Foliot of the honour of Plympton (Redvers
Charters, App. 23, pp. 167–8).

> i, fol. 114d; i, fol. 116a; i, fol. 115d; i, fol. 116a; i, fol. 116a; i, fol. 116a; i, fol.
> 116a; i, fol. 107b; i, fol. 116a; i, fol. 116b; i, fol. 116b; i, fol. 116b; i, fol. 116b; i,
> fol. 116b; i, fol. 116a; i, fol. 105c; i, fol. 105c

Aluredus De Athelburcho

English landholder, occurs Domesday Norfolk. The service of 2 knights from his
fief was granted to William de Albini pincerna by Henry I (RBE, 398). Other
Domesday references to Alfred anglicus are probably to the same person. William
de Albini was the founder of Wymondham priory in Norfolk, to which Yseldis
granddaughter of Alfred was an early benefactor, granting land in Besthorpe and
Attleborough (BL Cotton Titus C viii, fol. 23). Another early benefactor, also of
land in Besthorpe, whose charters were attested by clerks from Attleborough, was
Adam son of Alfred, who was a grandson of Peter de Valognes and brother of
Roger (ibid., fols 22, 24). It appears that the English Alfred of Attleborough
married a daughter of Peter de Valognes, sheriff of Essex, by whom he had issue
Adam and Roger. He may have been the Alfred vicecomes who was co- or
under-sheriff of Essex with Hugh de Bucland between c.1101 and 1112, and was a
benefactor of Colne priory.

> ii, fol. 270b; ii, fol. 270b; ii, fol. 271a; ii, fol. 270b; ii, fol. 178b; Red Book of the
> Exchequer, ed. Hall (1897), pp. 397–99; Fisher, Cartularium Prioratus de Colne
> (Earles C.), No. 9; Fisher, Cartularium Prioratus de Colne (Earles C.), No. 2

Aluredus De Baiunvilla

Attested a sale by Roger Arundel (q.v.) to Abbot William of Caen (Act. caen., p.
108). Alfred does not occur as a Domesday tenant of Roger Arundel, but he held
the manor of Ash Priors from him according to the Tax Return for Kingsbury West.
The manor was claimed as a usurpation of land of the church of Wells in
Domesday, which does not mention Alfred either under the lands of Wells of in
Roger's own fee, where the tenant is given as Givold. This name occurs only once,
and may be a mistake. At any rate in 1166 Osbert de Baiunvilla held one fee de
vetere of Roger's heir Gerbert de Percy (RBE, 217). From Banville, Calvados.

> i, fol. 94d

Aluredus De Canci

Domesday tenant of Guy de Craon in Lincolnshire; probably a Breton, perhaps
from Chancé, Ille-et-Vilaine, arr. Rennes, comm. cant. Bais. Identified from the
occurrence of Alfred of Laughton (named from one of the manors he held of the
fees of Craon) and Alfred of Canci in the Lindsey Survey, who was probably son of
the Domesday Alfred. He held land from several other Lincolnshire
tenants-in-chief, including Odo arbalistarius of Skirpenbeck, whose heiress he
married (Sanders, 78), as appears from the Lindsey Survey of c.1115/18, which
mentions Alfred de Canci, Alfred of Laughton and Walter and Ansfrid de Canceio,
sons of Alfred. Tenure in the fief of Odo Balistarius shows that the Domesday
Alfred's wife had died by 1115/18 when their sons were already in possession of
their inheritance from her. Since both Walter son of Alfred and Alfred of Laughton
were Lindsey tenants of Alan de Craon, and Alfred de Canci was also a landholder
in the fief of Odo Balistarius, it would appear that both Alfred and his wife were

dead in 1115/18 and that their three sons Alfred, Walter and Ansfrid, were their coheirs and successors at that date. Cf. K. S. B. Keats-Rohan, 'Domesday Book and the Malets', Nottingham Medieval Studies xli (1997), 26, 30.

i, fol. 365d; i, fol. 367b; i, fol. 367b; i, fol. 281d; Dugdale, Monasticon Anglicanum, III, pp. 548–50, No. V; i, fol. 357a; i, fol. 357a; i, fol. 364b; i, fol. 364b; i, fol. 365a; i, fol. 365a; i, fol. 367b; i, fol. 367b; i, fol. 367b; i, fol. 367b

Aluredus De Combia

Attested a confirmation charter for Eye Priory by Beatrice Malet, sister of Robert, and wife of William of Arques. William's two Domesday tenants called Alfred in Folkstone, Kent, are likely to have been the same person and probably the same as Alfred de Combia. The second of the Domesday Alfreds is called 'dapifer', steward, and hence was an important person, yet his holding is of much less worth that that of the undistinguished Alfred.

i, fol. 009c; i, fol. 009c; Brown, Eye Priory Cartulary (1992–94), No. 2

Aluredus De Grandcurt

Domesday tenant of Eustache of Huntingdon, whose subsequently held his land of Peterborough Abbey under Roger of Lovetot. The identification is provided by the Estate Book of his descendant Richard de Hotot, discussed in King, Peterborough Abbey, 47ff. Named either from Grandcourt, Somme, cant. Albert, or Grandcourt, Seine-Maritime, cant. Londinières. An Alfred de Grantcort, patris Roberti, was an early benefactor of the abbey of Tréport (BN lat. nov. acq. 249, fol. 26v). He was followed by his son Walter de Grandcourt (q.v.), whose descendants were surnamed de Clopton.

i, fol. 228b; i, fol. 228b; i, fol. 206b

Aluredus De Ispania

Domesday tenant in chief. Norman from Epaignes, Eure, arr. Pont-Audemer, cant. Cormeilles (Loyd, 51–2). Son of Goscelin, and like his father benefactor of Préaux under Roger of Bellomonte (Arch. dép. Eure H 711 fol. 102r–v). At his father's death he was unmarried, but had more than one brother. Two of them were probably the Walter and Hugh de Ispania who occur on his Domesday fief. A royal confirmation of his grant of land in Dorset to Saint-Etienne de Caen was attested by his brother Goscelin and the latter's son of the same name (Bates no. 55) At his death he apparently left a daughter and heiress, Isabel, wife of Robert de Candos (d.1120). Sanders, 67.

i, fol. 87c; i, fol. 90a; i, fol. 77c; i, fol. 186b; i, fol. 186b; i, fol. 86b; i, fol. 64d; i, fol. 97b; i, fol. 115d; i, fol. 115d; i, fol. 115d; i, fol. 97c; i, fol. 97a; i, fol. 97a; i, fol. 97b; i, fol. 73a; i, fol. 97b; i, fol. 97a; i, fol. 97a; i, fol. 186b; i, fol. 162b; i, fol. 162b; i, fol. 82c

Aluredus De Lincole

One of two Bretons established independently of Count Alan and his brother Brien who are revealed by the Lincolnshire Claims in Domesday Book as originally tenants of the de Gael earls of Norfolk. As such, Alfred would have been a native of the county of Rennes, and probably from the seigneurie of Montfort-Gaël. J. H. Round (Feudal England, 254–5) was the first to identify him as a Breton, even though his name Alfred of Lincoln could just as easily identify him as English. But Round discussed him in the context of a Joel of Lincoln who became a monk of Ramsey before 1066 and was almost certainly an Englishman entirely unrelated to

Alfred. Alfred's name indicates that he was active in local government in Lincolnshire and he frequently appears in Lincolnshire documents. A later document relating his successor Alan of Lincoln to the Malet family makes sense is we understand Alfred to have married a daughter of William Malet, sister of the wife of Turold the Sheriff of Lincolnshire. They were probably the parents of two sons, Alan of Lincoln who inherited Alfred's Lincolnshire holdings before 1100, and Alfred, perhaps the elder son and probably the Alfred who held an important fee in the Lincoln fief in Domesday Book as Alfred nepos Turoldi, a formula which is best understood to relate Alfred and Turold in the legal sense by which each held property conveyed by the marriage of William Malet's daughters. The second Alfred retained the name of Lincoln though he did not continue to hold property there after his marriage to the wife of Hugh fitz Grip, which had occurred by 1093 at the latest. K. S. B. Keats-Rohan, 'Domesday Book and the Malets', Nottingham Medieval Studies xli (1997), 27–32.

Lincolnshire Claims (Domesday Book), fols 375a–d; Lincolnshire Claims (Domesday Book), fols 375d–376a; Lincolnshire Claims (Domesday Book), fols 375a–d; i, fol. 336d; i, fol. 358b; i, fol. 357d; i, fol. 358a; i, fol. 358a; i, fol. 358a; i, fol. 358b; i, fol. 358a; i, fol. 358a; i, fol. 358a; i, fol. 358b; i, fol. 357d; i, fol. 358b; i, fol. 357d; i, fol. 358a; i, fol. 358d; i, fol. 357d; i, fol. 357d; i, fol. 293c; i, fol. 293d; i, fol. 358c; i, fol. 358b; i, fol. 358c; Lincolnshire Claims (Domesday Book), fols 375a–d; i, fol. 358b; i, fol. 358b; i, fol. 358b; i, fol. 358a; i, fol. 358b; i, fol. 357d; i, fol. 358c; i, fol. 358c; i, fol. 358c; i, fol. 358d; i, fol. 358a; i, fol. 358b; i, fol. 358a; i, fol. 357d; i, fol. 357d; i, fol. 357d; i, fol. 358d; i, fol. 358b; i, fol. 357d; i, fol. 357d; Bearman, Charters of the Redvers Family (1994), No. 5; i, fol. 215c; i, fol. 215c; Lincolnshire Claims (Domesday Book), fols 376d–377c; Lincolnshire Claims (Domesday Book), fols 375a–d; Lincolnshire Claims (Domesday Book), fol. 377d; i, fol. 215c; i, fol. 215d

Aluredus De Merleberge

Domesday tenant-in-chief from a Norman family established in the south-west before 1066. Domesday Hereford shows that he was nephew of the pre-Conquest Norman Osbern Pentecost and that he had a daughter and heiress Agnes married to Turstin Flandrensis of Wigmore. In 1122 Henry I confirmed ro Bec, inter alia, the tenure of Ralph Pentecost at 'Renelmivilla', Lamberville (Seine-Maritime) and Fumichon (Calvados) (RRAN ii, no 1290, Chanteux no. 171 p. 597). Much of Alfred's holding passed by 1100 to Harold of Ewyas. Harold was a minor in 1086 and Alfred was probably then acting as guardian. It has been said that Alfred's daughter Agnes, a widow in 1086, married secondly Harold of Ewyas Harold, but there is no direct evidence for the suggestion.

i, fol. 91c; i, fol. 91c; i, fol. 172b; i, fol. 173a; i, fol. 87b; i, fol. 175b; i, fol. 70c; i, fol. 47d; i, fol. 70b; i, fol. 70c; i, fol. 70c; i, fol. 70c; i, fol. 186a; i, fol. 70b; i, fol. 181a; i, fol. 70b; i, fol. 70b; i, fol. 186a; i, fol. 181a; i, fol. 180a; i, fol. 186a; i, fol. 186a; i, fol. 186a; i, fol. 186a; i, fol. 186a; i, fol. 97a; i, fol. 186a; i, fol. 91c; i, fol. 91c

Aluredus De Tame

Englishman, named from Thame, Oxfordshire. Occurs Domesday Buckinghamshire.

i, fol. 155c; i, fol. 152c

Aluredus Nepos Turoldi

Alfred II of Lincoln, who acquired the fief of the wife of Hugh fitz Grip centred on Wareham, Dorset, by marriage, whether with her or her daughter and heiress. Father of Robert and Samson de Lincoln, and a daughter who married William fitz Walter of Haselbury. Active as lord of Wareham from c.1087 until c.1129, when his son and successor Robert of Lincoln was active; justiciar in Dorset in 1106 (RRAN ii, 754). He was probably the son of Alfred I de Lincoln, a Domesday tenant-in-chief in Lincolnshire and elsewhere, and brother of Alfred's Lincolnshire successor Alan of Lincoln (q.v.), and possibly occurs in Domesday Lincolnshire as Alfred nepos Turoldi; see K. S. B. Keats-Rohan, 'Domesday Book and the Malets', Nottingham Medieval Studies xli (1997), 27–32.

> Dugdale, Monasticon Anglicanum, III, p. 216, No. V; Dugdale, Monasticon Anglicanum, III, p. 217, No. VII; Finberg, Early Tavistock Charters: ERH, 62, No. II; Finberg, Early Tavistock Charters: ERH, 62, No. IV; Pipe Roll 8 Henry II, 24–sm; Pipe Roll 31 Henry I, 016–ds; Pipe Roll 2 Henry II, 32–sm; Pipe Roll 2 Henry II, 33a–ds; Pipe Roll 2 Henry II, 33b–ds; Pipe Roll 31 Henry I, 015–ds; Dugdale, Monasticon Anglicanum, II, p. 482, No. IX; i, fol. 336c; Red Book of the Exchequer, ed. Hall (1897), pp. 222–24; i, fol. 336c

Aluredus Nepos Wigot

Occurs in Domesday Book. Nephew of Wigod of Wallingford, predecessor of Miles Crispin. His holdings in chief in Oxfordshire had previously been held by Wulfræd, perhaps his father (Williams, Introduction to Gloucestershire Domesday, 39; idem, English, 100ff). Possibly ancestor of Wigod, prior then abbot of Oseney (q.v.), who is likely to have been a relative of Oseney's founder Robert II d'Oilly who was a descendant of Wigod of Wallingford. A Roger fitz Aluredi attested the grant by Wigod's successor Brien fitz Count of the church of Hillingdon to Evesham (BL Cotton Vesp E xxiv, fol. 17r).

> i, fol. 63d; i, fol. 155d; i, fol. 159c; i, fol. 159d; i, fol. 129a; i, fol. 61d; i, fol. 160a; i, fol. 160a; i, fol. 160a

Aluredus Pincerna

Alfred the Butler, by far the wealthiest of the count's Domesday tenants, must be distinguished from a knight called Alfred who held from the count of Eu and from Battle Abbey, and also from an Alfred who held a single manor from William of Warenne. Most of his holdings lay in the south-west, notably near Montacute in Somerset. His grandson Richard fitz William returned a Carta as a Dorset tenant-in-chief in 1166, and held 15 knights' fees on the former Mortain fee in Sussex, held then by Richer de L'Aigle. The complex connexions between the Domesday fees of Alfred, Ralph 'of Dene' and Ansfrid require explanation, but the best that L. Salzman, 'Some Sussex Domesday tenants, II', Sussex Archaeological Collections 58, 171–81 could do was to suggest that a son of the Domesday Ralph married the daughter and heiress of the Domesday Ansfrid. Amongst other holdings in Domesday, Alfred held land in Claverham, Ralph held Dean and Chiddingly, and Ansfrid Waldron and Chalvington. By the 1140s, William Malfet (q.v.) and his wife Basilia, daughter of Robert pincerna de Dene and his wife Seburgis, disposed of land in Claverham and Chiddingly (Chart. Lewes, 117). Robert pincerna and his wife Sibyl gave land in Waldron and Chalvington for the souls of their ancestors – i.e. Ralph's ascendants and those from whom Sibyl had inherited the property she brought to the marriage (ibid., 131–2, granting, apart from Ansfrid's manors, land in Vluehola and la Hamoda, which were also the subject of a grant by Richard pincerna [fitz William fitz Alfred], confirmed by Richer de L'Aigle, ibid., 159). Almost all of Ansfrid's lands passed to the de Dene family, six of whose Domesday manors – Chiddingly, Jervington, Ratton, Cholston, Preston and Brambletye – passed to the eldest son, William, of Alfred and then to his heirs; some of them were the subject of a grant by Alfred himself (Chart. Lewes, 75, Brambletye and Preston). These details permit some simple inferences. The heiress of the Domesday Ralph was the wife of Alfred pincerna, whose eldest son William inherited the bulk of the lands held by his father Alfred in Domesday Book, together with six of the manors acquired through his mother; the bulk of the maternal inheritance went to Robert pincerna, whose brother Ralph 'of Dene' also had some rights therein. A Ralph of Dene appears on Pipe Roll 31 Henry I, 71, rendering 100 gold marks for a plea between him and Hugh de Warelvilla (then the sheriff of the county). Whether he was the Domesday Ralph, his son of the same name, or the son of Alfred, is impossible to say (the chronology of these families is particularly difficult to establish because the Lewes charters have not yet been accurately dated). Robert pincerna's brother Ralph of Dene is evidenced as uncle of Robert's son Ralph in the latter's charter for Bayham Abbey, (Mon. Ang. vi, 911). Alfred had another son, Richard, who occurs in PR 31 Henry I in Northamptonshire. Given that Alfred's sons William and Richard, and his grand-daughter, the wife of William Malfet, all appear in the 1129/30 Pipe Roll, it is possible that Ralph of Dene was the first of Alfred's sons to inherit the bulk of his wife's inheritance, which subsequently passed, for lack of direct heirs, to his brother Robert pincerna. A Lewes charter of Richard fitz William fitz Alfred was apparently attested by his 'patruus' Simon, which ought to refer to his paternal uncle Simon (Chart. Lewes, 74–5). It seems unlikely, however, that we have here yet another son of Alfred, rather than reference to a brother of Richard's mother (i.e. avunculus). The repeated association in the witness lists of their respective charters for Lewes between members of the Dene and Etchingham families possibly indicates a marriage between William fitz Alfred and a sister of Simon fitz Drogo. Links with the Domesday properties of Ranulf, and with the properties and descendants of William de Keynes (Chahaignes) are also noticeable. Sibyl-Seburgis, wife of Robert and mother of Basilia Malfet, was one and the same, and the heiress of the Domesday Ansfrid. She was regarded as two separate women by Salzman. A late Lewes charter shows the involvement of a later William Malfet with the advowson of Waldron, Chart. Lewes, 133–4. It was as Sibyl that the grant of land from the fee of Ansfrid was made to Lewes; later Robert's son Ralph de Dene confirmed grants to Lewes for the soul of his mother Seburgis and his sister Heldehard, whereas in an accord with Prior Hugh of Lewes Robert pincerna occurs with his wife Sibil, and Ralph of Dene and William Malfet his heirs; Seburg is mentioned in the same accord in connexion with William Malfet, who elsewhere named his wife's mother as Sibil. Alfred pincerna, his wife and sons, were listed as early benefactors of St Albans, to which they gave tithes of Crundel, Yorkshre (Cotton Nero D vii, fol. 9); in the necrology of Belvoir priory, a cell of St Albans, Alfred pincerna and Emma his wife occur for 19 January (BL Add. 4936, fol. 17r). A daughter was a nun of Shaftesbury. Alfred was still living c.1103–6 (Sanders, 34).

i, fol. 146c; i, fol. 146c; i, fol. 105b; i, fol. 93a; i, fol. 104c; i, fol. 78c; i, fol. 79d; i, fol. 80a; i, fol. 92d; i, fol. 92d; i, fol. 92c; i, fol. 92c; i, fol. 92c; i, fol. 92c; i, fol.

92c; i, fol. 92c; i, fol. 92c; i, fol. 92c; i, fol. 22b; i, fol. 93a; i, fol. 282d; i, fol. 93a; i, fol. 282d; i, fol. 104d; i, fol. 226b; i, fol. 20c; i, fol. 308c; i, fol. 308c; i, fol. 308c

Aluredus Presbiter
Occurs Domesday Hampshire.

i, fol. 49b; i, fol. 49b; i, fol. 49b; i, fol. 49b

Aluredus []
Domesday tenant of Swein of Essex. His fees were held by Guy II of Rochford at his death c.1185 (Rot. de Dom., 74–7). Guy I of Rochford held three fees of Walter Giffard in 1166.

ii, fol. 047a; ii, fol. 101a; ii, fol. 044b; ii, fol. 101a

Aluredus []
Tenant of Ilbert de Lacy in Domesday Yorkshire. Possibly ancestor of the family of Hay of Aughton. Roger son of Alfred occurs in 1166 (VCH Yorks ii, 164).

i, fol. 315d

Aluredus []
Occurs Domesday Cambridgeshire as a tenant of Harduin de Scalariis. His successor in 1166 was probably Lucas de Mordune who held one third of a fee from Hugh de Scalariis.

i, fol. 198b; i, fol. 200c; i, fol. 198b

Aluredus []
Domesday tenant of the count of Eu in Sussex.

i, fol. 18a

Aluretus Prepositus Ricardi
Alfred provost of Richard de Clare occurs one in Domesday Essex. Possibly this was the first Alfred de Benevilla, brother of William, who occurs in several charters of the de Clare family (cf. Cart. Colchester, p. 141). An Alfred de Benniville (q.v.) occurs in 1129 and also in 1151; the form of Alfred's toponym is not convincingly matched in Normandy; perhaps named from Bénerville-sur-Mer, Calvados.

ii, fol. 103a

Aluric Busch
Englishman. Occurs Domesday Hertfordshire as a tenant of Geoffrey de Bec.

i, fol. 140b

Aluric De Alreforda
Occurs Domesday Essex.

ii, fol. 101b

Aluric De Cainesham
Identified by Tax Return, Keynsham Hundred.

i, fol. 87b

Aluric De Melchesam
Englishman, named from Melksham, occurs Domesday Wiltshire.

i, fol. 73d

Aluric De Stawe
Englishman, occurs Domesday Somerset and Exon.
i, fol. 89c

Aluric De Taceham
English, named from Thatcham in Berkshire. Mentioned in Domesday Book as the only one to have seen the king's writ in respect of a former holding of Godric the Sheriff, alleging that the king gave it to Godric's wife because she kennelled his dogs.
i, fol. 57d

Aluric Filius Rolf
Occurs Domesday. Burgess of Ipswich.
ii, fol. 446a; ii, fol. 446b; ii, fol. 446b

Aluric Frater Edmer
Somerset, identified in Exon.
i, fol. 87c

Aluric Parvus
Occurs Domesday Hampshire and in the south-west.
i, fol. 73d; i, fol. 87a; i, fol. 73d; i, fol. 73d; i, fol. 73d; i, fol. 51c; i, fol. 50d

Aluric Prepositus
English provost; occurs Domesday Suffolk.
ii, fol. 287b

Aluric Presbiter
English priest, occurs Domesday Suffolk as a tenant of Count Alan. Perhaps the same as Aluric presbiter, father of Osward de Thurston (q.v.) to whom Abbot Leofstan of Bury gave the land and church of Thurston (Bury, Feudal Docs, 98).
i, fol. 41b; i, fol. 41b; ii, fol. 295b; ii, fol. 295b; ii, fol. 295b; ii, fol. 295a; ii, fol. 295b; ii, fol. 105b; ii, fol. 446b;

Aluric Presbiter
Occurs Domesday Bedfordshire.
i, fol. 213b

Aluric Venator
Occurs Domesday Dorset. The identifications are suggested by the Tax Returns.
i, fol. 84c; i, fol. 84c; i, fol. 84d; i, fol. 84d; i, fol. 84d; i, fol. 84d

Aluric Wanz
Occurs Domesday Suffolk.
ii, fol. 287a; ii, fol. 287b; ii, fol. 287b; ii, fol. 287b; ii, fol. 287a; ii, fol. 287a; ii, fol. 287a; ii, fol. 287a

Aluric []
Occurs Domesday Hampshire.
i, fol. 51d; i, fol. 51d; i, fol. 51d; i, fol. 51d

Aluric []
English thegn, perhaps uncle of Thorkil of Warwick and brother of Æthelwine (Williams, 'Vicecomital family', 291–2). Tenant of Robert of Stafford in 1086.

i, fol. 242d; i, fol. 250d; i, fol. 244c; i, fol. 242c; i, fol. 242d

Aluricus Chacepul
Occurs Domesday Middlesex.

i, fol. 127c

Aluuard Collinc
Englishman, occurs Domesday Dorset.

i, fol. 73c; i, fol. 73c; i, fol. 73c; i, fol. 84b

Aluuard Crocco
Occurs Domesday Somerset and Exon.

i, fol. 89b

Aluuard De Merdelai
King's thegn and Domesday juror in Broadwater Hundred, Hertfordshire. He was succeeded by Leofstan, brother of his co-tenant Derman in Watton. See Lewis, 'Jurors', 41; VCH Herts iii, 159.

i, fol. 142b; i, fol. 142c; Hamilton, Inquisitio Eliensis (1876), pp. 97–100; i, fol. 137d

Aluuard Mert
Occurs Domesday Devon.

i, fol. 118b; i, fol. 118b

Aluuard Presbiter
Occurs Domesday Wiltshire.

i, fol. 65c; i, fol. 68c

Aluuard []
Englishman, Domesday tenant of Robert of Mortain in Devon and (probably) Cornwall. His successors were a family named de Lega (from Northleigh) who held under the barony of Odcombe; cf. Fees, 793. Ralph de Lega held one fee of Odcombe in 1166.

i, fol. 104d; i, fol. 104d; i, fol. 124c; i, fol. 124c; i, fol. 104c; i, fol. 105b; i, fol. 105c

Aluuardus Anglicus
Occurs Domesday Wiltshire.

i, fol. 66a

Aluuardus Clericus
Occurs Domesday Sussex as a tenant of the bishop of Chichester.

i, fol. 16d

Aluui Ceuresbert
Occurs Domesday Berkshire.

i, fol. 63d

Aluui Frater Brictrici
Englishman, occurs Domesday Wiltshire.
  i, fol. 73c; i, fol. 73c

Aluui Presbiter
Priest of the church of Sutton, according to the Abingdon Chronicle (ii, 27–9, a chirograph attested by his nepos Siward).
  i, fol. 59a

Aluui []
The form Alueius is given in the Tax Return for Fremington Hundred. The Domesday and Exon form Aluui suggests an Englishman Alwi, but Theobald fitz Berner, the tenant-in-chief, was probably a Breton or anyway influential in Brittany, where the name Alueius was not uncommon; cf. Morice, Preuves I, 381, 487. All of Alueius's manors descended in the de Wolrington family.
  i, fol. 116c; i, fol. 116d

Aluuin Coc Bedellus
Englishman, a royal beadle still holding land in Domesday Cambridgeshire.
  i, fol. 190a

Aluuin Dodesone
Occurs Domesday Hertfordshire.
  i, fol. 142b

Aluuin Filius Eduui Cilt
Englishman, Domesday tenant of Roger de Lacy in Herefordshire, where he held some of the lands held previously by his father Edwi Cilt.
  i, fol. 184a; i, fol. 185a

Aluuin Homo Comitis De Ou
Occurs Domesday Sussex.
  i, fol. 19b

Aluuin Prefectus Regis
Englishman, royal provost, occurs Domesday Bedfordshire.
  i, fol. 218c; i, fol. 218c; i, fol. 218c; i, fol. 218c; i, fol. 218c; i, fol. 218c; i, fol. 218c

Aluuin Presbiter
Occurs Domesday Bedfordshire.
  i, fol. 218d

Aluuin []
Englishman, Domesday tenant of the count of Meulan and Thorkil of Warwick in Warwickshire.
  i, fol. 241b; i, fol. 241c; i, fol. 241d

Aluuin []
Occurs Domesday Warwickshire holding land at Compton Scorpion.
  i, fol. 242d

Aluuold []
English Domesday tenant of Theobald fitz Berner in Devon
   i, fol. 115d; i, fol. 115d

Alward Filius Elmundi
Englishman, occurs Domesday Shropshire as a tenant of Earl Roger. His holdings
had been held previously by his father Almund, who is mentioned as holding with
his son in Amaston. See Williams, The English, 90.
   i, fol. 259c; i, fol. 259c; i, fol. 259c; i, fol. 259c; i, fol. 259c

Alward Prepositus
Occurs Domesday Dorset.
   i, fol. 84d

Alward Tainus
Occurs Domesday Somerset.
   i, fol. 87c; i, fol. 87c; i, fol. 87c; i, fol. 87a

Alwardus Aurifaber
Occurs Domesday Berkshire as a king's servant. A William son of Alward
accounted for his father's land and office in Berkshire in 1129/30.
   i, fol. 63c

Alwart []
Occurs Domesday Suffolk. Man of Edric of Laxfield who continued to hold under
Robert Malet.
   ii, fol. 321a

Alwi Filius Saulf
Occurs Domesday Hampshire.
   i, fol. 50a

Alwi Filius Turber
Occurs Domesday Hampshire.
   i, fol. 50b; i, fol. 50b; i, fol. 50b; i, fol. 73d; i, fol. 50a

Alwi Vicecqmes
Englishman, occurs Domesday Oxfordshire.
   i, fol. 160d

Alwin Filius Vluiet
Occurs Domesday Hampshire.
   i, fol. 50d

Alwin Presbiter
Occurs Domesday Wiltshire.
   i, fol. 73d

Alwin Wit
Occurs Domesday Hampshire.
   i, fol. 50c

Alwin []
Englishman, canon of Dover from c.1066 mentioned in Domesday Book.
> Ballard, Inquisition of St Augustine's (1920), fols 24r–28r; i, fol. 001c

Alwold Camerarius
Occurs Domesday Berkshire.
> i, fol. 63d

Alwy Filius Alsi De Ferendone
Son of Alfsi of Faringdon, Berkshire. He held a house in Domesday Wallingford, which was still held in the late twelfth century by his grandson Robert of Astrop. Cf. VCH Oxfordshire i 388.
> i, fol. 161b; i, fol. 161a; i, fol. 56b

Amalger []
Occurs in Domesday and elsewhere as a man of the abbot of St Albans.
> i, fol. 136a; Dugdale, Monasticon Anglicanum, III, pp. 288–89, No. I

Amalric De Dreuues
Amaury of Dreux (Eure-et-Loir), Domesday tenant in Wiltshire.The Amalric who was a Domesday tenant of Miles Crispin and Henry de Ferrers is probably to be identified with the king's man Amaury de Dreux. His holdings of Miles's honour of Wallingford increased when he acquired the lands of William fitz Turold, or of Suleham, probably by marriage. He was dead by c.1130, when his sons Ralph and Robert had divided his lands.
> i, fol. 275d; i, fol. 275d; i, fol. 159c; i, fol. 73c

Ambrosius []
Domesday tenant of William Peverel. Succeeded in the early twelfth century by two sisters (perhaps his daughters), Emma wife of Ivo de Heriz and Ivicia wife of Robert fitz Amaury; HKF i, 154–5; Foulds, Thurgarton, Intro. pp. cxlvii–viii; Abbreviatio Placitorum, 79b–80.
> i, fol. 226b; i, fol. 226a; i, fol. 287d; i, fol. 287c; i, fol. 212c; i, fol. 148b

Amelfrid []
See VCH Essex i, 525n. The Amalfrid who held of Eustache de Boulogne and of Ralph Bainard in Domesday was succeeded by the Lohold family, perhaps indicating an ultimate ancestry in Lorraine.
> ii, fol. 032a; ii, fol. 071a; ii, fol. 69b

Amerland []
Norman, Domesday tenant of Rainald de Balliol. Occurs in a charter of Saint-Martin de Sées (Arch. dépt. Orne H 938, no. cx, fols 50–1), and probably also in Cart. Saint-Vincent du Mans, no. 667. In Liber Winton 532/2b there is reference to Rogerus filius Armerlanc. Cf. Vitalis filius Amerland.
> i, fol. 250c

Amund []
Tenant of Humphrey the Chamberlain in Suffolk. The personal name may represent Haimo. Cf. Haimo or Amund, tenant of Robert of Mortain in the south-west.
> ii, fol. 433a; ii, fol. 433a; ii, fol. 433b; ii, fol. 433b; ii, fol. 433b; ii, fol. 433b; ii, fol. 433a

Andreas De Vitriaco
Breton, son of Robert I seigneur of Vitré, dépt. Ille-et-Vilaine and Bertha de Craon. Married Agnes daughter of Robert count of Mortain shortly before the Domesday survey. Occurs in Domesday Cornwall as the count's tenant. He was succeeded in Brittany by his eldest son Robert II, who occurs on the Pipe Roll of 1129/30 with his brother Gervaise. Father also of Elias and Marquise, wife successively of Theobald de Matefelon, Hugh de Craon and Payn de Vaiges. Cf. M. Brand'Honneur, 'Les Goranton-Hervé de Vitré', MSHAB lxx (1993); Keats-Rohan, 'Le rôle des Bretons dans la politique de la colonisation normande', MSHAB, lxxiv, 1996, 192.

   i, fol. 120a; i, fol. 125a; i, fol. 125a

Anschetil Filius Uspaci
Domesday tenant of Odo of Bayeux in Kent. The Domesday and Domesday Monachorum forms indicate that Ansketil's father was called Ospac/Unspac, A much less convincing patronymic attached to one Ansketil filius Urf/Urphuth occurs in Actes caen. nos. 8 and 11 relating to churchs and tithes he had held in Caen which were exchanged with Queen Matilda with the mediation of Odo of Bayeux.

   ii, fol. 279b

Anschetil Presbyter
Occurs Domesday Bedfordshire.

   i, fol. 213c

Anschetill Capellanus Rogeri Bigod
Norman, occurs as a Domesday tenant of Roger Bigot, whose chaplain he was. His lands were granted to Roger's foundation at Thetford.

   ii, fol. 332a; Regesta Regum Anglo Normannorum II, App. no. cxxvii ; ii, fol. 334b

Anschetill De Grai
Norman, probably from Graye-sur-Mer, Calvados, cant. Ryes, occurs as a royal servant and as a man of the bishop of London in Domesday Book. Probably father of Richard de Graye, whose son became a monk of Eynsham c.1109 (Cart. no. 7). Richard de'Graye occurs from c.1106 in charters of Sainte-Trinité de Caen (Walmsley, pp. 119–20).

   ii, fol. 009a; ii, fol. 024b; ii, fol. 011b; i, fol. 161a; i, fol. 161b; i, fol. 161b; i, fol. 161a; i, fol. 161b; i, fol. 161b; i, fol. 161b; i, fol. 156c; ii, fol. 090a

Anschetill De Herolfville
Norman, from Hérouville-Saint-Clair, Calvados, arr. Caen, Domesday juror in Whittlesford Hundred, Cambridgeshire. He was possibly the tenant named Ansquetil of Picot of Cambridge in Armingford hundred. A charter given by Robert Curthose, between 1087 and 1094, for Sainte-Trinité de Caen was attested by Rainald son of Ansquetil de Herovilla and Odo his brother (Walmsley, pp. 123–4).

   i, fol. 200c; Hamilton, Inquisitio Eliensis (1876), pp. 97–100; Hamilton, Inquisitio Comitatus Cantabrigiensis, pp. 1–93

Anschetill De Rei

The Ansquetil de Rei who accounted in Sussex in 1129/30 is perhaps to be be identified with a Domesday tenant of the count of Eu. In early charters of Tréport there are frequent references to Anscher [Ansger or Aucher] de Riu (Rieux, Seine-Maritime), his son Hugh and grandson Anscher (Cart. Tréport, nos. 1–2).

i, fol. 20b; i, fol. 20b; i, fol. 18b; Pipe Roll 31 Henry I, 071–ss; Pipe Roll 31 Henry I, 070–ss

Anschetill De Tadmartune

Occurs in the list of Abingdon knights (Chron. Abing. ii, 5) as holding land at Chesterton in Oxfordshire. In the Domesday Survey he was the unnamed knight holding at Tadmarton, which he and his son Robert subsequently exhanged for Chesterton in 1105 (ibid. 136–8).

Stevenson, Chronicon Monasterii de Abingdon (1858) vol. II, pp. 4–6; i, fol. 156d

Anschetill Prepositus

Probably Norman provost of the bishop of Thetford; occurs Domesday Norfolk.

ii, fol. 198a

Anschetill []

Domesday tenant of Robert Gernon in Essex and Hertfordshire. By 1166 his fees were held by William de Montfichet of the barony of Montfichet as 'the fee of Geoffrey de Westmole'. Geoffrey of Westmill was presumably a successor of Ansquetil, the tenant in 1086.

ii, fol. 067a; ii, fol. 064b; ii, fol. 063b; i, fol. 138a

Anschetill []

Domesday tenant of Roger de Rames. Probably represented in 1166 by Ansquetil de Mecinge, named from his manor of Messing, Essex.

ii, fol. 083a; ii, fol. 422b

Anschil De Sevecurda

According to the Abingdon Chronicle, Ansketil incurred the wrath of William II and was incarcerated in conditions of some rigour, of which he died after a few days. His property was given to the king's dispencer Turstin, and was held by the latter's son Hugh in the time of Abbot Faritius (1100–13) [Chron. Abing. ii 36–7]. Now homeless, his widow Ansfrida became the mistress of Henry I before his accession in 1100 (Chron. Abing. ii, 122–3) and had by him a son Richard. Henry had her restored to her dowerlands at Bayworth, part of the abbey's manor of Sunningwell. Her son by Ansketil, William, subsequently reacquired half his father's holdings, at Seacourt and Marcham, by marrying Simon despencer's sister, who was niece to Abbot Rainald (ibid., 36–7).

i, fol. 59b; i, fol. 58d; i, fol. 58c; i, fol. 58d; Stevenson, Chronicon Monasterii de Abingdon (1858) vol. II, pp. 4–6

Anschitil De Furnellis

Norman, tenant of Count Alan in 1086; ancestor of the Furneaux family, tenants of the honour of Richmond (EYC v, pp. 179–81). Probably named from either Fourneaux-le-Val, Calvados, arr. Caen, comm. cant. Falaise, or Fourneaux, Manche, arr. Saint-Lô, comm. cant. Tessy-sur-Vire. The Furneaux fee of the honour of Richmond owed the service of eight knights, rendering castle-guard in

October and November. His successor by 1129 was Robert de Furnellis, probaby his son.

> i, fol. 310a; ii, fol. 147b; i, fol. 193d; ii, fol. 149b; Clay, Early Yorkshire Charters (1935), IV, No. 4; Clay, Early Yorkshire Charters (1936), V, No. 282; Clay, Early Yorkshire Charters (1935), IV, No. 1

Anschitil Filius Ameline

Occurs Domesday Dorset as Ansketil son of Amelina; identified as de Caesarisburgo (Cherbourg, Manche) in the Tax Return for Hasler Hundred, fol. 22b. An Ansketil was 'custos' of the chapel of Notre-Dame in the castle of Cherbourg in 1063–8 (Fauroux, 224).

> i, fol. 83b

Anschitil Filius Osmundi

Norman, occurs Domesday Hampshire.

> i, fol. 52a; i, fol. 49c; i, fol. 49c; i, fol. 49c; i, fol. 49c

Anschitil Marescal Abbatis

A Domesday tenant of Abbot Scolland of St Augustine's, Canterbury; occurs in the Excerpta as the abbot's marshall.

> i, fol. 012b; Ballard, Inquisition of St Augustine's (1920), fols 20r–23v

Anschitil Parcher

Norman, occurs Domesday Somerset. Identified by Exon Domesday and the Tax Returns.

> i, fol. 93b; i, fol. 93c; i, fol. 93c; i, fol. 93c; i, fol. 93c; i, fol. 93c; i, fol. 93c; i, fol. 93c; i, fol. 93c; i, fol. 98d; i, fol. 98d; i, fol. 98d

Anschitil []

Occurs in Domesday Lincolnshire as a tenant of Colswein and of Jocelyn fitz Lambert. By 1115/18, the date of the Lindsey Survey, he had been succeeded by his son William.

> i, fol. 359a; i, fol. 356d; i, fol. 359a

Anschitil []

Domesday tenant of Roger Pictaviensis in Lincolnshire. His successors by the date of the Lindsey Survey, 1115/18, were Ranulf Bilion and Hugh of Claxton.

> i, fol. 352c; i, fol. 352c

Anschitil []

Tenant of Roger de Courseulles in Domesday Somerset.

> i, fol. 93b; i, fol. 93c

Anschitil []

Domesday tenant of William Cheever de Pomeroy in Devon.

> i, fol. 110b; i, fol. 110b; i, fol. 110b

Anschitil []

Domesday tenant of Hugh de Port in Hampshire.

> i, fol. 45c,d; i, fol. 45a

Anschitill De Ros

Norman, from Rots, Calvados, arr. Caen, cant. Tilly-sur-Seulles (Loyd, 86), archdeacon of Rochester from c.1086–1107, Domesday tenant of Odo of Bayeux.

See FEA ii, 81.

i, fol. 007a; i, fol. 133b; i, fol. 007a; i, fol. 133b; i, fol. 133b; i, fol. 133b; i, fol. 007c; i, fol. 003c; Ballard, Inquisition of St Augustine's (1920), fols 24r–28r; i, fol. 001d; i, fol. 001d; i, fol. 001d; Douglas, ed., Domesday Monachorum (1944), p. 105; i, fol. 006d; i, fol. 008c; i, fol. 011d; i, fol. 006b; i, fol. 006b; i, fol. 136d; i, fol. 006d; i, fol. 006c; i, fol. 006c; i, fol. 006c; i, fol. 31c; i, fol. 003c; i, fol. 003b; i, fol. 005c

Anschitill De Sancto Medardo
Norman, Domesday tenant of Peterborough Abbey, identified from later documents such as the Descriptio Militum and the Northants Survey. See Hugh Candidus, 162. He was succeeded before c.1116 by his son Richard (father of Geoffrey), who had died by 1129. A St Médard family occur c.1107 in the Cartulary of Préaux (Arch. dépt. Eure H 711, nos. 308, 310), with Geoffrey de Saint-Médard, his son Joscelyn and the latter's nepos Durand; named from Saint-Mards-de-Blacarville, Eure, cant. Pont-Audemer. Richard de St Medard attested a grant of the wife of Berengar, whose lord was Roger de Beaumont, to Saint-Martin-du-Bois c.1060 (Fauroux, 218).

i, fol. 221c; i, fol. 345c; King, Peterborough Descriptio Militum (1969), pp. 97–101

Ansegis []
Occurs Domesday Warwickshire.

i, fol. 243d; i, fol. 244d

Ansel []
Anselm, Domesday tenant of Hugh de Bolebec at Wavendon, Buckinghamshire.

i, fol. 151a

Anselm De Trondeston
Tenant of Bury St Edmund in 1086. Described in the Feudal Book as a man of Frodo, brother of Abbot Baldwin, from whom he held Thrandeston. Father of Anselm.

ii, fol. 371a; Douglas, Feudal Documents from Bury St Edmunds, No. 174; Douglas, Feudal Book of Bury St Edmunds (1932), pp. 3–21

Ansered De Walterville
Norman, Domesday tenant of Peterborough, ancestor of the Watervilles of Overton Waterville, one of two Walterville families to descend from Peterborough tenants. Probably father of the William fitz Ansered who occurs in Huntingdonshire on the 1129/30 Pipe Roll (p. 48).

i, fol. 155c; i, fol. 205b; i, fol. 205b

Ansered []
Domesday tenant of St Augustine's, Canterbury.

Ballard, Inquisition of St Augustine's (1920), fols 20r–23v; i, fol. 012b; i, fol. 012b

Ansfrid Canonicus
Canon of St Pauls, Bedford in 1086.

i, fol. 211a

Ansfrid De Cormelies
Norman follower of William fitz Osbern, from Cormeilles, Eure, arr. Pont-Audemer. Tenant-in-chief in Domesday Gloucestershire where his wife, a niece of Walter de Lacy, is also mentioned (DB Glocs 16.13). His successor was probably Walter de Cormeilles, who was associated with the bishop of Lisieux in 1095 (Sanders, 86).

i, fol. 184c; i, fol. 183a; i, fol. 170a; i, fol. 170a; i, fol. 169d; i, fol. 169d; i, fol. 169d; i, fol. 169d; i, fol. 170a; i, fol. 169d; i, fol. 170a; i, fol. 169d; i, fol. 169d; i, fol. 169d; i, fol. 170a; i, fol. 170a; i, fol. 169d; i, fol. 169d; i, fol. 164b; i, fol. 186b; i, fol. 179c; i, fol. 186b; i, fol. 186b; i, fol. 186c; i, fol. 186b

Ansfrid De Valbadon
Norman, from Vaubadon, Calvados, arr. Bayeux, cant. Balleroy (Loyd, 108), occurs Domesday Northamptonshire. Cf. Ranulf de Vaubadon, who occurs in Domesday Kent, and Osmund de Vaubadon, mentioned in Huntingdonshire.

i, fol. 219a

Ansfrid Masculus Clericus
Norman, Domesday tenant of Odo de Bayeux in Kent; identified as Masculus the clerk in Excerpta.

Ballard, Inquisition of St Augustine's (1920), fols 20r–23v; i, fol. 010c; i, fol. 012c; i, fol. 009d; i, fol. 011b; i, fol. 011b; i, fol. 010b; i, fol. 010b; i, fol. 010b; i, fol. 010b; i, fol. 010b; i, fol. 010a; i, fol. 011a; i, fol. 011a; i, fol. 012d; i, fol. 012d; Ballard, Inquisition of St Augustine's (1920), fols 24r–28r; Ballard, Inquisition of St Augustine's (1920), fols 20r–23v

Ansfrid []
Domesday tenant of Robert of Mortain in Sussex. His heir by c.1100 appears to have been Seburgis or Sibil, wife of Robert pincerna, who was almost certainly the son of Alfred pincerna and the heiress of Ralph de Dene of Westdean. See under Alfred pincerna.

i, fol. 22a; i, fol. 22a; i, fol. 21b; i, fol. 22c; i, fol. 22b; i, fol. 22b; i, fol. 22d; i, fol. 22d; i, fol. 20c; i, fol. 22a; i, fol. 22a; i, fol. 22c; i, fol. 22c; i, fol. 22c

Ansfrid []
Norman, tenant of Gilbert de Bretteville and William d'Eu in Domesday Wiltshire and Dorset. The links of both with the region of Saint-Pierre-sur-Dives might suggest an identification with the Ansfrid who gave land at Corbeaumont, Eure, to Saint-Léger de Préaux before he went to England, after the death of his brother of Roscelin fitz Turolf who had given land at Le Réel; the grant was confirmed c.1077–81 (Neustria Pia, 520–4).

i, fol. 82a; i, fol. 80d; i, fol. 71c; i, fol. 71c; i, fol. 71c; i, fol. 71d; i, fol. 71c

Ansfrid []
Norman, tenant of the bishop of Chichester in Domesday Sussex. He was the ancestor of a family named from his manor at Ferring. His successor Ansfrid de Ferring occurs in the Carta of the bishop of Chichester in 1166 (RBE 199). Cf. Ansfrid tenant of William de Picquigny in DB Surrey 21.3 at Wandsworth, a fee held in 1200 by Theobald de Feringes (Curia Regis Roll i, 230).

i, fol. 16d; i, fol. 28a; i, fol. 17a

Ansfrid []
Norman, Domesday tenant of Geoffrey de Bec in Hertfordshire. Cf. VCH Herts iv, 32.

i, fol. 140b; i, fol. 140b

Ansfrid []
Norman, tenant of Hugh de Montfort in Domesday Kent.

i, fol. 013c

Ansfrid []
Norman, tenant of Walter de Claville in Domesday Devon.

i, fol. 112c

Ansfrid []
Norman, Domesday tenant of Robert de Buci and William fitz Nigel.

i, fol. 266b; i, fol. 234c; i, fol. 234c

Ansger Brito
Breton tenant of Robert of Mortain in Devon and Somerset. Also called Ansgar de Senardi ponte in Exon Tax Returns, and Ansger of Montacute, the name of Robert's castle in Somerset. He and his son and heir Walter were early benefactors of Bermondsey Abbey. Ansger was apparently dead by 1100 and his son Walter disappears after 1108. The line continued until his heirs were bought out of their barony of Odcombe by William Briewer c.1199. The Hervé fitz Ansger who occurs in Domesday may have been another of Ansger's sons. Possibly from Cogles in the Breton seigneurie of Fougères. In 1050 Ansger and his sons Corbin, Ranulf and Herve were associated with a grant at Saint-Brice-en-Cogles to Saint-Florent de Saumur (Arch. dépt. Maine-et-Loire H 3713, fol. lx verso).

i, fol. 92b; i, fol. 92c; i, fol. 92b; i, fol. 93a; i, fol. 93a; i, fol. 92d; i, fol. 93a; i, fol. 79c; i, fol. 86d; i, fol. 79b; i, fol. 79d; i, fol. 91d; i, fol. 91d; i, fol. 79b; Excerpta a Chronicis de Bermondsey, Dugdale, Monasticon, IV, pp. 95–97; i, fol. 116b; i, fol. 116b; i, fol. 116b; i, fol. 116b; i, fol. 116b; i, fol. 116b; i, fol. 116b; i, fol. 116b; i, fol. 99b; i, fol. 104c; i, fol. 104c; i, fol. 104c; i, fol. 104d; i, fol. 116c

Ansger Capellanus
Royal chaplain. Occurs Domesday Northamptonshire.

i, fol. 222d; i, fol. 219a; i, fol. 222d

Ansger Cocus
Occurs as a king's servant in Domesday Book.

ii, fol. 097a; ii, fol. 097a; ii, fol. 097a; i, fol. 87a; i, fol. 73c; i, fol. 98c

Ansger Fouuer
Royal servant. Occurs Domesday Somerset.

i, fol. 97c; i, fol. 106d; i, fol. 98c; i, fol. 98c; i, fol. 98c; i, fol. 98c

Ansger Serviens Regis
Tenant in Devon of the king and the sheriff; distinct from Ansger Brito, but probably the same as either Ansger Focarius or Ansger Cocus.

i, fol. 117d

Ansger []
Domesday tenant of Baldwin the Sheriff. Probably the same person as Ansgar

serviens regis (Anser Focarius?), but distinct from Ansgar Brito of Montacute.

i, fol. 108b; i, fol. 108a; i, fol. 108a; i, fol. 108a; i, fol. 107a; i, fol. 107a; i, fol. 106d; i, fol. 107a; i, fol. 107a

Ansger []
Tenant of Hugh fitz Baldric in Domesday Nottinghamshire.

i, fol. 291c; i, fol. 291c

Ansgot De Burewelle
Apparently a Norman, held land at Burwell, Lincolnshire, in 1086. Subsequently went on pilgrimage to Santiago, establishing monks at Burwell, subject to La Sauve-Majeure at Bordeaux, on his return, c.1110. His initial grant, made at La Sauve-Majeure, had the assent of his wife Eda and was attested by his steward Robert and cook Alwin, and by Hugh de Neubele, Osbert de Ormesvi and Robert fitz Gilbert (CDF, 1239). Another grant to the same house from Ansgod's fief was made by Hugh fitz Osbert and his mother Aeliz (ibid., 1240); quite possibly Aeliz was Ansgod's daughter and Hugh was Hugh de Neubele (probably son of Osbern fitz Tezzo, q.v.). Still holding in 1115/18 at the Lindsey Survey, when his wife was twice named as his tenant. He appears to have lost his land thereafter, with it being regranted first to Humphrey de Albini and then to Robert de Haia (CDF, 1241–2).

Lindsey Survey, BL ms Cotton Claudius C v, fols 19–27; i, fol. 366c; i, fol. 366c; i, fol. 366c; i, fol. 366c; i, fol. 366c; Lindsey Survey, BL ms Cotton Claudius C v, fols 19–27; Lindsey Survey, BL ms Cotton Claudius C v, fols 19–27

Ansgot De Rouecestre
Domesday tenant of Odo of Bayeux in Kent. Probably the same person as Ansgod de Ros (Rots, Calvados), who held one manor of him in Buckinghamshire.

i, fol. 31d; i, fol. 31c; i, fol. 004b; i, fol. 006c; i, fol. 002c; i, fol. 31d; i, fol. 144d; i, fol. 007a; i, fol. 209c; i, fol. 008c; i, fol. 007d; i, fol. 006a; i, fol. 008c; i, fol. 009a; i, fol. 007d; i, fol. 209c

Ansgot Homo Willelmi Comitis
Norman, follower of William fitz Osbern de Breteuil, occurs in Domesday Worcestershire and Herefordshire.

i, fol. 173b; i, fol. 180d; i, fol. 180d

Ansgot Interpres
Occurs Domesday Surrey.

i, fol. 31b; i, fol. 36d

Ansgot Presbiter
Priest, occurs Domesday Warwickshire as a tenant of Geoffrey de La Guerche.

i, fol. 243d

Ansgot Rufus
Norman, Domesday tenant of Ilbert de Lacy at Hampole, identified by a grant to St Clement's, York (EYC iii, 1492).

i, fol. 316a

Ansgot []
The Ansgots who occur in Domesday Sussex as tenants of Robert of Mortain and Roger de Montgomery were probably the same.

i, fol. 65c; i, fol. 22b; i, fol. 22b; i, fol. 21a; i, fol. 20c

Ansgot []
Englishman, occurs Domesday Devonshire, where he still holds part of his former holding.

i, fol. 118b; i, fol. 118b; i, fol. 118b

Arcenbald []
Archembald. Domesday tenant of Hervey Bituricensis.

ii, fol. 443a; ii, fol. 443a

Arnald []
Domesday tenant of Roger Pictaviensis in Suffolk. Cf. Roger filius Ernald.

ii, fol. 347a; i, fol. 25d; ii, fol. 347a

Arnold []
Norman, knight of the archbishop of Canterbury in 1086 and 1093–6. His fee was at Knell in Wingham, Kent (Du Boulay, Lordship of Canterbury, 384–5).

Douglas, ed., Domesday Monachorum (1944), p. 105; i, fol. 003d

Arnulf []
Norman, Domesday tenant of the count of Meulan and Thorkil of Warwick in Warwickshire.

i, fol. 240a; i, fol. 240a

Artor Presbiter
Englishman, occurs Domesday Yorkshire.

i, fol. 330c; i, fol. 330c; i, fol. 330c

Artur Francigenus
Occurs Domesday Worcestershire. Perhaps father of Nigel (q.v.). He was possibly the sheriff Arthur who attested Roger de Montgomery's foundation of the church of Quatford in 1086 (Eyton, Shrops i, 112). Mason suggested that he was under-sheriff of Shropshire (Mason, Clerks, 247).

i, fol. 174d

Artur []
Domesday tenant of Eudo Dapifer. Cf. HKF iii, 275–6.

ii, fol. 104b; ii, fol. 050b; ii, fol. 050b

Ascelin []
Domesday tenant of Swein of Essex; perhaps the same as a tenant of Roger Bigod and early benefactor of Thetford priory.

Regesta Regum Anglo Normannorum II, App. no. cxxvii ; ii, fol. 189b; ii, fol. 045a; ii, fol. 045a; ii, fol. 045a

Aschil Presbiter
Englishman, occurs Domesday Lincolnshire.

i, fol. 367d

Asford []
Englishman, Domesday tenant of Peterborough in Lincolnshire. He was the Asfrothr to whom Abbot Turold granted the lands held previously by Hereward the Wake from the abbey. Cf. Round, Feudal England, 132–3. Occus as a tenant of the Abbey c.1100–16 in the Descriptio Militum. Hugh Candidus, p. 167, identified

some of his land thus: Et præterea dictus Baldewinus [Wake] tenet feodum unius militis in Wytham et Bergham de terra Affordi.

> King, Peterborough Descriptio Militum (1969), pp. 97–101; Lincolnshire Claims (Domesday Book), fols 376d–377c; i, fol. 346b; i, fol. 346b; Lincolnshire Claims (Domesday Book), fols 376b–c; i, fol. 346b; i, fol. 346b; i, fol. 346b; i, fol. 346b; i, fol. 346b

Auesgot []
Occurs Domesday Cambridgeshire as a tenant of Robert Fafiton.

> i, fol. 202a

Augustine []
Domesday tenant of Earl Roger in Sussex.

> i, fol. 25d

Azelin De Heginton
Domesday tenant of Geoffrey Alselin, benefactor of Tutbury.

> i, fol. 276d; i, fol. 276d; Dugdale, Monasticon Anglicanum, III, pp. 392–93, No. II

Azelin De Walterville
Norman, Domesday tenant of Peterborough Abbey at Marholm. Occurs in royal writs between 1095–7 and 1107–14, presumably in his capacity as steward of Peterborough abbey. He married Muriel, by whom he had issue four sons, Hugh, Geoffrey, Ralph and William (Lib. Vit. Thorney, Add. 40, 000, fol. 10v). Hugh had succeeded him by 1129/30.

> Northants Survey, fols 96r–99v; i, fol. 222a; i, fol. 221d; King, Peterborough Descriptio Militum (1969), pp. 97–101; Northants Survey, fols 94r–95v

Azelin []
Domesday tenant of Roger de Montgomery in Staffordshire.

> i, fol. 260c; i, fol. 248b; i, fol. 248b; i, fol. 248b; i, fol. 248b

Azelin []
Royal servant, occurs in the south-west in 1086. All the references to Azelin and Schelin (for Ascelin) in Somerset are doubtless to the same man, a west Norman holding tenancies from the bishop of Coutances, Roger de Courseulles, Roger Arundel and the abbey of Glastonbury.

> i, fol. 88c; i, fol. 89a; i, fol. 88a; i, fol. 88a; i, fol. 88a; i, fol. 88b; i, fol. 88d; i, fol. 88d; i, fol. 89a; i, fol. 89a; i, fol. 88b; i, fol. 90c; i, fol. 89a; i, fol. 90c; i, fol. 94d; i, fol. 99b; i, fol. 83b; i, fol. 165a

Azelin []
Domesday tenant of Waleran Venator. A Robert fitz Asselin was a tenant of Walter II Waleran in 1166.

> i, fol. 82b; i, fol. 72a; i, fol. 72a

Azelina Uxor Radulfi Tailgebosc
Wife of Ralph Taillebois, a widow by 1086.

> i, fol. 218a; i, fol. 218a; i, fol. 218a; i, fol. 218a; i, fol. 153a; i, fol. 153a

Azo Bigod
Norman, Domesday tenant of Rainald de Balliol under Roger de Montgomery in Shropshire, identified by his grant to Shrewsbury abbey. Possibly the same man

was also a Montgomery tenant in Sussex. Perhaps related to Robert Bigot, son of Norman, lord of Pirou and Cerisy in the Cotentin, benefactor in the 1090s of Sées (Arch. dépt. de l'Orne, H938, fols 62b–63, no. cxxxix).

> i, fol. 25b; i, fol. 24a; i, fol. 255b; i, fol. 255a; i, fol. 254c; i, fol. 254b; i, fol. 254c; Rees, Cartulary of Shrewsbury Abbey (1975), No. 35

Azo Presbiter
Occurs Domesday Nottinghamshire on the fee of Roger de Busli.

> i, fol. 285b

Azo []
Peterborough tenant in Northamptonshire in 1086.

> i, fol. 222a; i, fol. 222a

Azor De Lesneis
Englishman recorded in Domesday as having held sake and soke in Sutton and Aylesford Lathes in Kent before 1066.

> Ballard, Inquisition of St Augustine's (1920), fols 24r–28r; i, fol. 001a; Ballard, Inquisition of St Augustine's (1920), fols 24r–28r

Azor Dispensator
Englishman, Azor dispenser of Edward the Confessor, occurs Domesday Berkshire. Cf. Keynes, 'Regenbald the Chancellor', ANS x, p. 207.

> i, fol. 62b

Bagot []
Domesday tenant of Robert de Tosny of Stafford. His descendants were surnamed Bagot, the first of them being his son and successor, c.1130, Hervé. See Wrottesley, History of the Bagot Family, Hist. Coll. Staffs. n.s. xi (1908). A Hugh Bagot attested a charter of William de Tracy (d. c.1172), lord of Bradninch, Devon, given at the castle of Vire, Calvados (BL Cotton Vit. D ix, fol. 57r).

> i, fol. 249b; Pipe Roll 31 Henry I, 074–st; Pipe Roll 31 Henry I, 074–st

Baldric De Lindeseia
Norman, Baudri de Bocquencé, known as de Bosco or, from his English holdings, de Lindsey; son of Baldric Teutonicus (Ord. Vit. ii, 82). Domesday tenant of Earl Hugh of Chester. He was a benefactor of Saint-Evroult, to which he gave land at Farforth and Oxcomb. The grant confirmed by Ranulf I of Chester c.1121–9 in a charter witnessed by Baldric's son Richard. Richard occurs in the Lindsey Survey, 1115/18, holding his father's land at Hemingby. Baldric's wife Billihild was a benefactress of Saint-Evroult, to which she made a grant attested by her sons Robert and Baldric; the grant falls in the period 1091–1126 at the time Billihild was a widow and her son Robert was lord of Bocquencé (Ord. Vit., ed. Le Prévost, v. 184, no. 111). Her grant to St Werburg's, Chester, given before the death of Earl Hugh in 1102, suggests that Baldric died c.1091–1101. See J. Green, 'Lords of the Norman Vexin', in War and Government . . . Essays in honour of J. O. Prestwich, ed. J. Gillingham and J. Holt (Woodbridge, 1984).

> i, fol. 266d; i, fol. 349d; i, fol. 349c; i, fol. 349c; i, fol. 343c; Barraclough, Charters of AN Earls of Chester (1988), No. 11

Baldric []
Domesday tenant of Robert de Tosny of Belvoir.

i, fol. 234a; i, fol. 138a; i, fol. 215b

Baldric []
Norman, Domesday tenant of Jocelyn fitz Lambert in Lincolnshire.

i, fol. 359c; i, fol. 359b; i, fol. 359b

Balduin Abbas De Sancto Edmundo
Native of the Chartrain, monk of Saint-Denis, Paris, prior of St Denis's cell at Leberawe in Alsace, came to England in 1065 and became 'medicus' to Edward the Confessor, prior of Deerhurst and then abbot of Bury St Edmunds (Memorials of St Edmunds Abbey, ed. T. Arnold, RS, 1890, pp. 56 and 344). He died on 4 January 1098. See D. C. Douglas, Introd. to Feudal Documents of Bury St Edmunds; cf. Heads, 32. A. Gransden, 'Baldwin, abbot of Bury St Edmunds', Anglo-Norman Studies 4 (1982).

i, fol. 166b; Douglas, Feudal Documents from Bury St Edmunds, No. 16; Douglas, Feudal Documents from Bury St Edmunds, No. 42; Douglas, Feudal Documents from Bury St Edmunds, No. 32; Douglas, Feudal Documents from Bury St Edmunds, No. 26; Douglas, Feudal Documents from Bury St Edmunds, No. 123; Douglas, Feudal Book of Bury St Edmunds (1932), pp. 3–21; Hamilton, Inquisitio Eliensis (1876), pp. 192–95; i, fol. 166b; i, fol. 166b; Douglas, Feudal Documents from Bury St Edmunds, No. 106; Douglas, Feudal Documents from Bury St Edmunds, No. 70; Douglas, Feudal Documents from Bury St Edmunds, No. 104; Douglas, Feudal Documents from Bury St Edmunds, No. 13; Regesta regum Anglo-Normannorum III, No. 760; ii, fol. 210b; ii, fol. 210a; ii, fol. 210a; ii, fol. 210a; ii, fol. 210a; ii, fol. 210a; i, fol. 192b; ii, fol. 210b; i, fol. 192b; ii, fol. 210b; ii, fol. 210b; ii, fol. 210b; ii, fol. 210b; ii, fol. 211a; ii, fol. 211a; ii, fol. 211a; ii, fol. 211a; ii, fol. 211a; ii, fol. 210b; ii, fol. 209a; ii, fol. 209a; ii, fol. 209a; ii, fol. 209a; ii, fol. 209a; ii, fol. 209a; ii, fol. 209a; ii, fol. 210a; ii, fol. 209a; ii, fol. 209a; ii, fol. 209b; ii, fol. 209a; ii, fol. 209b; ii, fol. 210a; ii, fol. 211b; ii, fol. 211a; ii, fol. 209a; ii, fol. 209a; i, fol. 192b

Balduin Filius Herluin
Domesday tenant of the Picard William de Picquigny in Buckinghamshire. He was Baldwin fitz Herluin (DB Bucks 4.31), whose pre-Conquest holdings were divided between Hugh de Grandmesnil and William de Picquigny before 1086. His father Herluin was mentioned in Hemming's Cartulary of Worcester (ed. Hearne, 267) as having been in the service of Bishop Beorhtheah, whom he accompanied when the bishop conducted Cnut's daughter Gunnild to her wedding with the son of Conrad III. The bishop gave him the manor of Leopard, which Baldwin held of Hugh de Grandmesnil in 1086. Baldwin was steward to Bishop Ealdred of Worcester (Williams, Introd. to Gloucestershire Domesday, 25). In 1166 his fees were held by Bernard de Frankeleges (q.v.).

i, fol. 172b; i, fol. 174a; i, fol. 177b; i, fol. 149a; i, fol. 149a; i, fol. 177b; i, fol. 250a; i, fol. 250a; i, fol. 148d; i, fol. 36a; i, fol. 36a

Balduin Flandrensis
Fleming, held a small Domesday tenancy-in-chief, which formed part of the barony of Bourn, Lincolnshire, by the early twelfth century. Possibly the same Baldwin was a tenant of Drogo de La Beuvrière in Yorkshire. There are no discoverable indications that any descendants of his continued to hold his fees.

Lincolnshire Claims (Domesday Book), fols 376d–377c; i, fol. 325a; i, fol. 324c; i, fol. 324b; i, fol. 219a; i, fol. 370a; i, fol. 370a; i, fol. 370a; i, fol. 370a; i, fol. 370a; i, fol. 364b; i, fol. 364a; i, fol. 370a; i, fol. 324a; i, fol. 324a

Balduin Serviens Regis
Frenchman, probably a Fleming, who occurs as a king's servant in Domesday Hertfordshire. Possibly the same as the Baldwin Cocus, or cum Barba, who was a Domesday juror in Flendish Hundred, Cambridgeshire.

> i, fol. 133d; i, fol. 142a; Hamilton, Inquisitio Eliensis (1876), pp. 97–100; Hamilton, Inquisitio Comitatus Cantabrigiensis, pp. 1–93; i, fol. 142b

Balduin Vicecomes
Baldwin de Meulles (Eure), son of Gilbert count of Brionne and brother of Richard de Clare (q.v.). Lord of an extensive fief centred upon Okehampton in Domesday Devon (Sanders, 69), of which he was sheriff between c.1070 and 1086. His sons succeeded him as sheriff, and even his daughters had residual rights in the shrievalty, but the failure of his sons to produce heirs meant that the real power in Devon passed from his family to that of Richard I de Redvers (q.v.). He appears to have been twice married. His first wife (named Albreda in Mon. Ang. v, 269, 377) was daughter of the Conqueror's aunt ('amita', i.e. sister of his mother Herlève), according to Orderic Vitalis (iv, 208). Domesday names his second wife Emma; she was perhaps from west Normandy, where Baldwin acquired land at Le Bosc-Baudouin. One of his daughters [Matilda] was married to William fitz Wimund of Avranches (q.v.), who was his tenant in 1086; she married secondly Ranulf Avenel (d. c.1128); another daughter Adelicia 'uicecomitissa' appears to have briefly succeeded her three elder brothers as Baldwin's heir before dying without issue in 1142. Baldwin died in 1095 (idem ii, 214, iv, 212), leaving three legitimate sons, Robert (certainly son of Baldwin's first wife, Ord. iv, 208ff), William and Richard, and an illegitimate son Wiger, who was a monk of Bec from c.1093 until c.1133 (idem 212 and note). Comp. Peer. iii, 308–9, 317. Robert inherited Norman lands at Le Sap and Meulles; William inherited the English lands and office of sheriff.

> i, fol. 102a; i, fol. 88d; i, fol. 102a; i, fol. 93a; Dugdale, Monasticon Anglicanum, III, p. 499, No. I; i, fol. 100a; i, fol. 106c; i, fol. 107a; i, fol. 106d; i, fol. 107a; i, fol. 107c; i, fol. 107c; i, fol. 108b; i, fol. 107c; i, fol. 105d; i, fol. 108a; i, fol. 108b; i, fol. 108a; i, fol. 107a; i, fol. 107c; i, fol. 108a; i, fol. 93a; i, fol. 105d; i, fol. 105d; i, fol. 81a/b; i, fol. 105d; i, fol. 105d; i, fol. 106a; i, fol. 106a; i, fol. 105d; i, fol. 106a; i, fol. 106b; Dugdale, Monasticon Anglicanum, III, p. 377, No. I

Balduin []
Tenant of Gotshelm de Claville in Domesday Devonshire; his fee was later held by the Toussaint family. Cf. Baldwin de 'Warten beige' who attested a charter of William I for Giso bishop of Wells at Whitsun 1068 in one of the earliest charters to be attested by the newly arrived queen, Matilda of Flanders. Baldwin de Wartenbeige might be identifiable as the father of Walcher of Wartenbeke (fl. 1088), now Belgium, prov. Hainaut, arr. Mouscron, also known as Walcher of Comines, of which Wartenbeke was a seigneurie. These were closely related to the seigneurs of Comines, in whose family Baldwin was a Leitname (see Warlop, vol. 3, p. 736). Both Gotshelm and Walter de Claville held lands formerly held by Beorhtric son of Ælfgar, the principal English 'antecessor' of Queen Matilda.

> i, fol. 113a; i, fol. 113a

Balduin []

Apparently an Englishman, canon of Dover in 1086 whose prebend had previously been held by his brother Edwin.

Ballard, Inquisition of St Augustine's (1920), fols 24r–28r; i, fol. 001d

Baret []

Domesday tenant of Ilbert de Lacy in Yorkshire, made grants to St Clement's chapel in the castle of Pontefract, EYC iii, no. 1492. His successor in 1166 was Humphrey of Roall.

i, fol. 331c; Dugdale, Monasticon Anglicanum, III, pp. 548–50, No. V; i, fol. 316c; i, fol. 316c; i, fol. 316c

Basuin []

Norman, occurs Domesday Lincolnshire as a tenant of Robert de Tosny of Stafford. His successor by 1166 was Osbert Baswin de Torp, who held three fees of Robert II of Stafford.

i, fol. 368c; i, fol. 368c; i, fol. 368c

Beatrix De Pomerai

Sister, according to Exon Domesday, of Ralph de Pomeray and William Cheever, Domesday tenants-in-chief in Devonshire, of whom she was tenant. A Beatrice de La Pommeraye was a nun of Caen before c.1135 (Charters and Custumals 2, p. 132).

i, fol. 95d; i, fol. 114c; i, fol. 110d; i, fol. 111a

Beluard De Caruen

Belward of Caerwent in Wales.

i, fol. 162b

Benedict Abbas De Salebi

Benedict, a monk of Auxerre, was said to have come to England intending to build a monastery, bringing the finger of St German as a relic for the church. He was living in England in 1069, when he came to the attention of William I, who founded the abbey at Selby in Yorkshire (Mon. Ang. iii, 499). He resigned as abbot in 1096/7, when he retired to Rochester, being succeeded at Selby by Hugh de Lacy. See Heads, 69.

i, fol. 235b; i, fol. 235b; i, fol. 226d; i, fol. 235b; i, fol. 219a; i, fol. 302c; i, fol. 369c; Dugdale, Monasticon Anglicanum, III, p. 499, No. II; Greenway, Charters of the Honour of Mowbray (1972), No. 1; Dugdale, Monasticon Anglicanum, III, p. 499, No. III

Benzelin Archidiaconus

Occurs in Domesday Somerset as a tenant of the bishop of Wells; described as archdeacon in Exon. Archdeacon of Wells under Bishop Giso, he continued in office under Bishop John until c.1100 (EEA x, pp. xxxix–xl).

i, fol. 89c; i, fol. 160b; i, fol. 70a; i, fol. 160b

Berard []

Tenant of Abbot Baldwin of Bury St Edmunds in 1086. He was perhaps the same as the Berard who held Banham from Roger Bigod; the latter holding apparently occus in the grants of the tithes of Ranulf and of Albreda in Banham to Thetford priory c.1107 (RRAN ii, p. 338). For his possible English descendants see Farrer HKF iii, 359–60.

ii, fol. 202a; ii, fol. 189b; ii, fol. 358a; ii, fol. 178b; Douglas, Feudal Book of Bury St Edmunds (1932), pp. 3–21; ii, fol. 359a; ii, fol. 369a; ii, fol. 369a; ii, fol. 362b; ii, fol. 368b; ii, fol. 426a

Berdic Joculator Regis
Royal jester holding three Welsh villages in 1086.

i, fol. 162a

Berengar []
A subtle series of links between people and places where a Berengar of Domesday East Anglia is concerned strongly suggests that all references are to the same person, who is quite possibly Berengar of Le Sap (Orne), who occurs as a benefactor in Roger Bigod's foundation charter for Thetford Priory. His Bury fee was held in 1166 by William de Houe (RBE, 393).

Douglas, Feudal Book of Bury St Edmunds (1932), pp. 3–21; ii, fol. 211b; ii, fol. 70a; ii, fol. 210a; ii, fol. 210a; Dugdale, Monasticon Anglicanum, IV, pp. 148–49, No. II; ii, fol. 103b; ii, fol. 449a; ii, fol. 360b; ii, fol. 360b

Berenger De Todeni
Son of Robert de Tosny de Belvoir, of whom he was a major tenant in 1086 and a tenant-in-chief in his own right. Named after his father's brother Berengar Spina, all three occur in a Marmoutier charter of 1063, when Berengar, probably then still an adolescent, authorised an agreement made by his father (Fauroux, 157). His wife's name was Albreda. After his death his fief passed to Robert de Insula, husband of an Albreda, who is normally assumed to have been his widow but who was in fact his sister. That his successor was not his remarried widow is shown by an entry in the necrology of Belvoir priory, where the anniversaries of Berengar and his 'Albreda uxor eius, deo sancta', i.e. Albreda became a nun, were kept on 29 June (BL Add. 4936, fol. 27, and by the fact that Albreda de Tosny/Insula's land was inherited by Hugh Bigod, son of Berengar's sister Adelisa. One of Hugh's charters (Kirkstall, pp. 188–9) referred to Albreda as his aunt 'amite mee', i.e. she was his mother's sister. Berengar's heir was his eldest sister Albreda, homonym of his wife. Berengar was dead by the time of the Lindsey Survey, c.1115–18, when Robert de Insula held his lands.

i, fol. 352d; i, fol. 353a; i, fol. 353a; i, fol. 353a; i, fol. 353a; i, fol. 353a; i, fol. 352d; i, fol. 352d; i, fol. 353b; i, fol. 352d; Dugdale, Monasticon Anglicanum, III, pp. 288–89, No. I; Dugdale, Monasticon Anglicanum, III, p. 217, No. VII; Clay, Early Yorkshire Charters (1952), IX, No. 133; Dugdale, Monasticon Anglicanum, III, pp. 550–51, No. VII; Dugdale, Monasticon Anglicanum, III, p. 216, No. V; Dugdale, Monasticon Anglicanum, III, pp. 548–50, No. V; i, fol. 159b; i, fol. 154a; i, fol. 298b; i, fol. 291c; i, fol. 337a; Lincolnshire Claims (Domesday Book), fols 375d–376a; i, fol. 361c; i, fol. 314b; i, fol. 314c; i, fol. 314b; i, fol. 314a; i, fol. 314b; i, fol. 314c; i, fol. 314b; i, fol. 314b; i, fol. 314b; i, fol. 314b; i, fol. 314b; i, fol. 314b; i, fol. 314b; i, fol. 314b; i, fol. 314b; i, fol. 314c; i, fol. 314b; i, fol. 314b; i, fol. 314c; i, fol. 314c; i, fol. 314b; Dugdale, Monasticon Anglicanum, III, pp. 548–50, No. V; i, fol. 314c; i, fol. 314c; i, fol. 314c; i, fol. 314c; i, fol. 314c; i, fol. 314c; i, fol. 314c; i, fol. 314b; i, fol. 314c; i, fol. 314c; i, fol. 314c; i, fol. 314c; i, fol. 314c; i, fol. 314c; i, fol. 314c; i, fol. 314c; i, fol. 314c; i, fol. 353c; Dugdale, Monasticon Anglicanum, III, p. 547, No. III; i, fol. 353c; i, fol. 314a; i, fol. 291c; i, fol. 159b; i, fol. 314a; i, fol. 314a

Berenger Giffard
Norman, one of the Giffards of Bolbec and Longueville, Seine-Maritime,

Domesday landholder in Wiltshire and Dorset. Ancestor of the Giffards of Fonthill. Gerold fitz Robert Giffard was his successor in 1166.

i, fol. 72b; i, fol. 82c; i, fol. 72d; i, fol. 72d

Bereuuold []
Occurs Domesday Lincolnshire as a tenant of Gilbert de Gand.

i, fol. 361c; i, fol. 355a; i, fol. 355a

Bernard Barb
Norman, occurs in Domesday Leominster. Possibly the Bernard who was a tenant of Durand of Gloucester, and/or the Bernard holding of Ansfrid de Cormeilles and William d'Ecouis.

i, fol. 180b; i, fol. 186c; i, fol. 186c; i, fol. 186c; i, fol. 186c; i, fol. 180a

Bernard Camerarius
Occurs Domesday Hampshire.

i, fol. 51c

Bernard De Alencun
Hervé Bituricensis's Domesday tenant Bernard de Alencun was doubtless the same person as Robert Malet's tenant Bernard Lundonie: 'Londonia' was the name of a prévôté at Alençon (Orne). Bernard Londons attested a charter given by tenants of the founder of La Ferté Bernard c.1050–61, attested also by Walter Rufus of Bellême (Cart. Marmoutier Dunois, 106–7). The Montgomery-Bellême family, of which Robert Malet's successor as lord of Eye, Roger of Poitou, was a member, were lords of Alençon. Richard and Stephan de Alençon were tenants of Eye under King Stephan (Eye Cart., 15, 24. Herbert of Alençon was a tenant of the honour of Eye c.1200 (RBE, 403).

ii, fol. 442a; ii, fol. 443b; ii, fol. 442b; ii, fol. 442b; ii, fol. 443b; ii, fol. 442b; ii, fol. 442b; ii, fol. 314b

Bernard De Sancto Audoeno
Norman, from Saint-Ouen-sous-Bailli, Seine-Maritime, arr. Dieppe, cant. Envermeu (Loyd, 91). Domesday tenant of William d'Arques in Folkestone, Kent.

ii, fol. 431b; i, fol. 009c

Bernard Panceuolt
Norman, Domesday tenant of William of Eu and Turstin fitz Rolf. In 1166 Humphrey and Eustache Pancevolt occur. A Pancevolt family were associated with Thérouldeville, Seine-Maritime, cant. Valmont in the twelfth century (Le Maho, p. 16; Delisle, Rec. Henri II, ii, 347–9).

i, fol. 71d; i, fol. 80c; i, fol. 169c; i, fol. 163c; i, fol. 163d; i, fol. 97c; i, fol. 97d; i, fol. 71d; i, fol. 80c; i, fol. 52a; i, fol. 51c; i, fol. 72d; i, fol. 47d; i, fol. 47d; i, fol. 47d; i, fol. 47d; i, fol. 47d; i, fol. 47d

Bernard Presbiter
Priest, tenant of Robert of Mortain in Domesday Cornwall. A Bernard was also named in the count's manor of Pevensey, Sussex.

i, fol. 79a; i, fol. 20c; i, fol. 125a

Bernard Sine Napa
Domesday tenant of Baldwin of Exeter in Devon; his byname is supplied from Exon. By 1166 Robert fitz Bernard held for 2.5 fees the Domesday holding of

Bernard Sine Napa (the Napeless). They thereafter passed to Richard Cadiho, who had sold them to divers tenants by 1219 (Trans. Devon Assoc., 44 (1912), p. 326).

i, fol. 106c; i, fol. 106b; i, fol. 107d; i, fol. 107d; i, fol. 107d

Bernard []
Domesday tenant of Eustache de Boulogne. By the early twelfth century the family of Baldwin hereditary constable of Boulogne was a Boulogne tenant in England, holding land recorded in demesne in Domesday (cf. Round, Peerage, 152). A charter given by Eustache and his wife Ida in 1070 (Miraeus et Foppens i, 159–61) was witnessed by Bernard the constable (of Lens in Artois) and his brother Robert. Bernard son of Eustache's Domesday tenant Rumold (q.v.) occurs in 1129 (BM Add. ch. 28344).

ii, fol. 055b; ii, fol. 029a; ii, fol. 033a; ii, fol. 029a; ii, fol. 027b

Bernard []
Domesday tenant of Hugh de Beauchamp and Hugh's probable mother-in-law Azelina wife of Ralph Taillebois.

i, fol. 218a; i, fol. 213d

Bernard []
Domesday tenant of Alfred of Lincoln. Possibly the same as Bernard grandfather of Robert Rabaz (q.v.).

i, fol. 357d; i, fol. 357d; i, fol. 358d

Bernard []
Norman, Domesday tenant of William of Écouis in Herefordshire; possibly the same as the tenant of Durand of Gloucester in Herefordshire (see Bernard Barb) and/or the tenant of Ansfrid de Cormeilles in Gloucestershire. Bernard Cocus and his brother Ralph occurs in charters associated with William d'Écouis for Sainte-Trinité de Rouen (Cart. p. 465).

i, fol. 185c; i, fol. 185c; i, fol. 180b; i, fol. 180b

Bernard []
Norman, Domesday tenant of Ralph Bainard.

ii, fol. 071b; ii, fol. 69b; ii, fol. 070b; ii, fol. 070b

Bernard []
Norman, Domesday tenant of Ansfrid de Cormeilles in two Gloucestershire manors, whereof his son William made grants to Eynsham abbey before 1109 (Cart. Eynsham i, p. 37 and n.).

i, fol. 169d; i, fol. 169d

Bernard []
Norman, tenant of Theobald fitz Berner in Domesday Devon.

i, fol. 115c; i, fol. 115c

Bernard []
Domesday tenant of Roger Bigod in Suffolk. He possibly occurs in William Bigod's Thetford charter of c.1107 as Bernard de Berneham; cf. Gilbert fitz Bernard whose grant of tithes of Waverton were confirmed c.1160.

ii, fol. 341b; Dugdale, Monasticon Anglicanum, IV, pp. 148–49, No. II

Bernardus Accipitrarius
Occurs Domesday Berkshire. Perhaps succeeded by Ared Falconer, who occurs in 1110 (RRAN ii, 956, 961).

i, fol. 63b

Berner Arbalistarius
Norman landholder in Domesday Norfolk.

ii, fol. 214b; ii, fol. 267b; ii, fol. 268a; ii, fol. 267b; ii, fol. 267b; ii, fol. 267b; ii, fol. 267b; ii, fol. 267b; ii, fol. 267b; ii, fol. 268a; ii, fol. 110a; ii, fol. 268a; ii, fol. 268a; ii, fol. 268b; ii, fol. 268b; ii, fol. 268b; ii, fol. 268a; ii, fol. 268a; ii, fol. 382a; ii, fol. 382a; ii, fol. 382b

Berner Nepos Roberti De Perone
Berner nephew of Robert de Péronne (Somme) occurs only once in Domesday Book, as thegn holding of the Bishop of Bayeux's holding; he is found as Robert's heir in the same manor (Appleford) in the Abingdon Chronicle (ii, 21–22). References in Domesday to the abbey's tenant Berner and in the Chronicle to its tenant Berner miles are likely to concern the same person (ibid., 4, 60, 138, 160, 161, 168, 210). Berner miles had a son Hugh (ibid., 168). His holding was subsequently absorbed into the Visdeloup fee (HKF, i, 54).

i, fol. 59a; i, fol. 58d; Stevenson, Chronicon Monasterii de Abingdon (1858) vol. II, pp. 4–6; i, fol. 58d; i, fol. 58d; i, fol. 63d

Berner []
Tenant of Robert of Mortain in Cornwall in 1086.

i, fol. 120d; i, fol. 121b; i, fol. 123d; i, fol. 123d; i, fol. 123d; i, fol. 123d; i, fol. 123d; i, fol. 123d; i, fol. 123d; i, fol. 123d; i, fol. 123d; i, fol. 123d

Berner []
Norman, Domesday under-tenant of Roger de Montgomery, tenant of Roger de Lacy in Herefordshire and in Shropshire, where he was also tenant of William Pantulf. His successors of the Higford family, surnamed from one of his manors, were tenants of the FitzAlans after 1102.

i, fol. 257c; i, fol. 162a; i, fol. 256c; i, fol. 256c; i, fol. 257c; i, fol. 184b; i, fol. 184b

Berner []
Domesday tenant of Maino Brito in Domesday Buckinghamshire. His successor in 1166 was William fitz Geoffrey (Luffield cart. p. lvii, where Berner is confused with Bernard, another of Maino's tenants).

i, fol. 152a; i, fol. 228a

Bernulf []
Domesday tenant of Count Alan in Yorkshire.

Dugdale, Monasticon Anglicanum, III, pp. 548–50, No. V; i, fol. 312a; i, fol. 311b; i, fol. 311b; i, fol. 311c; i, fol. 312b

Bernulf []
Domesday tenant of William I de Percy (posssibly the same as Bernulf, tenant of Count Alan) Father of Gamel, who attested a charter of William II de Percy c.1150.

i, fol. 322a; i, fol. 322a

Berold []
Domesday tenant of the wife of Hugh fitz Grip.

i, fol. 83d

Bertram De Verdun
Norman, from Verdun, a fief in par. Vessey, Manche, cant. Pontorson (Loyd, 109); occurs in Domesday Buckinghamshire. He was a minister in Yorkshire under William II, c.1099–1100. He gave the church of Bosworth, Leicestershire, to St Mary's, York. Cf. Mon. Ang. i, 241; EYC i, 274 and note 11. His heir was his son Norman.

i, fol. 94a; i, fol. 93d; i, fol. 151c; Dugdale, Monasticon Anglicanum, III, pp. 548–50, No. V; i, fol. 151c

Bertram []
Norman, Domesday tenant of Hugh de Montfort in Kent. Succeeded by a son Nigel, who was a benefactor of Monks Horton priory.

i, fol. 013a

Beruold []
Domesday tenant of Eudo fitz Spirewic. His successor in 1166 was Herbert of Massingham.

ii, fol. 245b

Bigot De Loges
Norman, from Les Loges, Calvados, arr. Vire, cant. Aunay-sur-Odon, a Domesday tenant of Earl Hugh of Chester. Distinct from Roger Bigod, lord of Les Loges and Savenay, he may nevertheless have belonged to Roger's family (see commentary for Roger). His sons Hugh and Robert attested Chester charters from the 1120s. HKF ii, 238–9.

Barraclough, Charters of AN Earls of Chester (1988), No. 28; Barraclough, Charters of AN Earls of Chester (1988), No. 3; i, fol. 268a; i, fol. 266d; i, fol. 266d; i, fol. 266d; i, fol. 266d; i, fol. 266d; i, fol. 266d; i, fol. 266d; i, fol. 266d; i, fol. 266d; i, fol. 266d; i, fol. 266d; i, fol. 266d; i, fol. 266d; Barraclough, Charters of AN Earls of Chester (1988), No. 28; Barraclough, Charters of AN Earls of Chester (1988), No. 3; ii, fol. 299a; ii, fol. 299a; ii, fol. 299a; Barraclough, Charters of AN Earls of Chester (1988), No. 28

Blechu []
Occurs in Domesday Cornwall as tenant of Robert of Mortain.

i, fol. 120a; Hull, Cartulary of Launceston Priory (1987), No. 17

Blize []
Man, or monk, or Archbishop Lanfranc.

i, fol. 005a

Blohin Brito
Breton tenant of Robert of Mortain in Domesday Cornwall.

i, fol. 125a; i, fol. 125a; i, fol. 125a; i, fol. 125b; i, fol. 125a

Bodin []
Half-brother of Count Alan Rufus, full brother of Bardulf, and natural son of Eudo brother of Alan III of Brittany. He was described as brother of Bardulf in a charter of Odo camerarius (EYC v, no. 279). He gave his land to Bardulf when, together

with Ribald, another of Count Eudo's sons, he became a monk of St Mary's, York. See EYC v, p. 199.

    i, fol. 310b; i, fol. 310b; i, fol. 310b; i, fol. 309b; i, fol. 309b; i, fol. 310a; i, fol. 310a; i, fol. 310a; i, fol. 310b; i, fol. 312c; i, fol. 309c; i, fol. 310b; i, fol. 310b; i, fol. 310b; i, fol. 311a; i, fol. 311a; i, fol. 310d; i, fol. 310b; i, fol. 311a; i, fol. 311a; i, fol. 311b; i, fol. 311b; i, fol. 312b; Clay, Early Yorkshire Charters (1936), V, No. 282; Clay, Early Yorkshire Charters (1936), V, No. 279

Boia Presbiter
English cleric, occurs Domesday Cornwall. Identified as a clerk of Bodmin in the Exon Tax Returns (fol. 507a).

    i, fol. 120b

Bolle Presbiter
English priest, occurs Domesday in south-west England.

    i, fol. 84a; i, fol. 78c; i, fol. 79a; i, fol. 79a; i, fol. 79a; i, fol. 79a; i, fol. 84a

Bordin []
Domesday tenant of Hermer de Ferrers. The name became a patronymic (cf. RBE, 417). As a personal name it is found in the cartulary of Saint-Quentin de Beauvais (BN lat. n.a. 1921, 48v–9r, 21r).

    ii, fol. 274b; ii, fol. 274b; ii, fol. 274b; ii, fol. 274a; ii, fol. 207b; ii, fol. 206a

Borel []
Domesday tenant of Edward of Salisbury in Wiltshire. His successor in 1166 was Roger Burel, who held two and a half fees of Earl Patrick.

    i, fol. 69d; i, fol. 69d

Boret Presbiter
Englishman. Occurs Domesday Huntingdonshire. Apparently father of Autin of Huntingdon and grandfather of Baldwin and Burred (q.v.), who occur in Ramsey charters of the twelfth century.

    i, fol. 206a

Boselin De Diua
Norman, from Dives-sur-Mer, Calvados, arr. Pont-l'Evêque, cant. Dozulé (Loyd, 37). Occurs in Domesday as a tenant of the count of Mortain in Sussex. and Northamptonshire. He also had a house in London (RRAN i, 166, ap. xx, H. Round, EHR 32, 352). He occurs with his brother Hugh in an exchange of land at Moult with Saint-Etienne de Caen c.1080–7 (Actes caen. no. 28). Both his wife and his son William are mentioned in Domesday. The principal heir of the family's holding in Sussex and Northamptonshire seems to have been William son of Hugh (dead in 1130). See Douglas, Dom. Mon. 37–8. Cf. Herman Boselin, who occurs on the 1129/30 Pipe Roll in London.

    i, fol. 20c; i, fol. 175b; Douglas, ed., Domesday Monachorum (1944), p. 105

Boteric []
Occurs Domesday Norfolk as a tenant of Rainald fitz Ivo. Abbot Gilbert of Caen purchased land from Buteric, attested by Anschitillus vinitor and his sons, and Sasfrid; Sasfrid was perhaps the provost who attested a sale by Berengar de Ingouville, Calvados, cant. Bourgébus, comm. Moult (Actes caen. no. 14, p. 110, 108).

    ii, fol. 232b; ii, fol. 232b; ii, fol. 233b

Botild []

Englishwoman, tenant of the bishop of Lincolnshire in Domesday Nottinghamshire. Perhaps mother of Robert fitz Botild (q.v.), who attested Rufford charters c.1150.

i, fol. 283d

Botilt []

Englishwoman, occurs Domesday Suffolk. Probably the Botild mentioned as a tenant, with her sons, of St Edmund's at Rushbrook, the location of her Domesday holding.

Douglas, Feudal Book of Bury St Edmunds (1932), pp. 22–37; ii, fol. 448b

Bretel De Sancto Claro

Norman, Domesday tenant of Robert de Mortain. Occurs as de Sancto Claro in the Tax Returns and in Mortain charters up to 1102. After 1106 his holdings became a tenancy-in-chief known as the barony of Stoke Trister (Sanders, 84) His successor was probably the William de Saint-Clair who occurs in the Pipe Roll for 1129/30 (cf. Sanders, 84). Walter de Ashley held in 1172.

i, fol. 86c; i, fol. 93a; i, fol. 92d; i, fol. 92d; i, fol. 92d; i, fol. 92d; i, fol. 92c; i, fol. 92a; i, fol. 92a; i, fol. 92a; i, fol. 79c; i, fol. 79c; i, fol. 79b; i, fol. 86b; i, fol. 105c; i, fol. 79b; i, fol. 79d; i, fol. 98c; i, fol. 80a; i, fol. 80a; i, fol. 79d; i, fol. 79d; i, fol. 92a; i, fol. 104d; i, fol. 104d

Brictric []

Tenant of Robert of Mortain in Domesday Cornwall. Possibly the same as Brictric uncle of Bernard the Scribe (q.v.) whose land was given to Wigan father of Ruald in the early twelfth century. Cf. Williams, The English, 122–3.

i, fol. 120a; i, fol. 120a; i, fol. 124d; i, fol. 124d; i, fol. 124d; i, fol. 124d; i, fol. 124d

Brictuin Prepositus

Englishman, occurs Domesday Dorset.

i, fol. 84b; i, fol. 84a; i, fol. 84b; i, fol. 84b; i, fol. 84c; i, fol. 84c; i, fol. 84c; i, fol. 84c; i, fol. 84c; i, fol. 84c

Brictuin []

Tenant of Cerne Abbey before and after 1066.

i, fol. 77d

Brien De Scalariis

The Brien who occurs in Domesday Book holding a single Cambridgeshire manor of Count Alan is probably the same person as the Brien who occurs as a juror in Chilford Hundred and as father of Evrard de Scalariis, a juror in Cheveley Hundred; he was probably a brother, or other kinsman, of the much wealthier Harduin de Scalariis. The Breton name Brien was a characteristic name of the branch of the de Scalariis family that descended from him. Apparently founder of a junior line of de Scalariis, descendants of his grandson Geoffrey fitz Everard, who occurs from the early twelfth century.

i, fol. 194a; Hamilton, Inquisitio Comitatus Cantabrigiensis, pp. 1–93

Brien []

Domesday tenant of William de Warenne. Succeeded by, and possibly ancestor of, the Gargate family; Reginald Gargate occurs in PR 31 Henry I, 5; Roger Gargate was a benefactor of Missenden Abbey c.1160. A Hugh Gargatus occurs in the Cartulary of Préaux (Arch. dépt. Eure 711, 322) in the early twelfth century.

i, fol. 157d; i, fol. 148b

Briend []
Tenant of Robert of Mortain in Cornwall, occurs in the Terre Occupate of Cornwall (471/507b and 471/508) as usurper of the lands of St Petroc. His lands were among those granted to William Boterel by Henry I after 1106.

i, fol. 124a; i, fol. 124a; i, fol. 124a; i, fol. 124a

Briend []
Domesday tenant of Robert de Tosny of Stafford. Father of Ralph, who attested a charter of Nicholas of Stafford (fl.c.1088–c.1138) (Hist. Coll. Staff. ii, 195). His grandson Robert fitz Ralph took the name de Standon from one of his Staffordshire holdings.

i, fol. 368d; i, fol. 368d; i, fol. 249d; i, fol. 248d; i, fol. 242c; i, fol. 248d; i, fol. 248d

Brisard []
Occurs Domesday Lincolnshire as a tenant of Earl Hugh of Chester.

i, fol. 349c; Barraclough, Charters of AN Earls of Chester (1988), No. 1

Bristeua []
Englishwoman, occurs Domesday Oxfordshire.

i, fol. 155c; i, fol. 155a

Bristoard Presbiter
Occurs Domesday Wiltshire.

i, fol. 65c

Bristuard Presbiter
English priest, occurs Domesday Dorset.

i, fol. 79a; i, fol. 79a

Brodo []
Englishman, occurs Domesday Bedfordshire.

i, fol. 218a

Bruman Sochmannus
Occurs Domesday Cambridgeshire.

i, fol. 189c

Brungar Anglicus
Occurs Domesday Somerset.

i, fol. 88b

Bruning []
Englishman, Domesday tenant of Thorkil of Warwick in Warwickshire.

i, fol. 241a

Buered []
Domesday tenant of Robert de Tosny of Stafford. His lands were held in 1166 by Geoffrey of Coppenhall. Ulger of Coppenhall occurs c.1140 (Hist. Coll. Staffs., i, 181, 240–3).

i, fol. 249c; i, fol. 249c

Burcard []
Domesday tenant of Abbot Baldwin of Bury. Perhaps brother of Peter (q.v.).

ii, fol. 366a; ii, fol. 367a; ii, fol. 366a; Douglas, Feudal Book of Bury St Edmunds (1932), pp. 3–21; ii, fol. 117a

Burnard []
Domesday tenant of William of Eu. Ancestor of the Burnard family of Arlesey, on whom see Fowler, Cart. Old Wardon, note 273, pp. 342–6. Charters of his twelfth-century descendants for St Neots priory show that he was one of the two knights holding from William at Edworth (BL Cotton Faust. A iv, fol. 57). Roger Burnard occurs in PR 31 Henry I, 103.

i, fol. 51b; i, fol. 212a; i, fol. 212a

Buterus []
Domesday tenant of Geoffrey de la Guerche in Leicestershire. Attested a charter of Geoffrey giving land in Warwickshire to Saint-Nicholas d'Angers (Mon. Ang. vi, p. 996) before 1093.

i, fol. 235d; i, fol. 235d

Cadio []
Occurs in PR 31 Henry I with his brother Rogo fitz Nigel (q.v.), an important tenant in Domesday Devon of Baldwin the Sheriff from whom Cadio held one manor. The family were tenants of the Norman seigneurs of Saint-Sauveur-le-Vicomte in the Cotentin. Ancestor of the Cadiou or Cadiho family, his successor in 1166 was Ralph fitz Cadio, probably his son.

i, fol. 106a; Pipe Roll 31 Henry I, 156–dv

Cadio []
Domesday tenant of Robert de Tosny of Stafford. Henry II confirmed the grants of Brien son of Cadio to Kenilworth priory (Mon. Ang. vi, 232). Cadio's heir in 1166 was Robert fitz Payn (Hist. Coll. Staffs. i pt i, 173).

i, fol. 158a; i, fol. 248d; i, fol. 248d; i, fol. 248d

Cadiou []
Breton tenant of Count Alan in Domesday Lincolnshire. Quite possibly he was father of Droard fitz Cade, who gave land in Wood Ditton, Cambridgeshire, to Thetford priory (Mon. Ang. v, 142), for the souls of himself, Wimarca his wife, and of Count Stephen (of Brittany) and Earl William de Warenne. The charter was confirmed by his lord Baldwin de Say and Wimarc his wife, possibly the parent's of Droard's wife. The elder Wimarc was possibly a daughter of Wigan de Mara, who held Wood Ditton under Count Alan in 1086. This striking grant shows that Droard held land of both the honors of Richmond and Warenne. Thetford was a Cluniac house, like the Warenne foundation at Lewes. An early benefactor of Lewes was Gladiou joculator, a tenant of Warenne in Essex in 1086. Possibly Alan's Cadio and William de Warenne's Gladiou were one and the same.

i, fol. 347d

Canevaz Mascerel
Norman, Domesday tenant of Richard de Clare in Essex. Occurs in Domesday as Canevaz and Mascerel, and in Stoke-by-Clare charters as Canevaz Mascerel. His descendants Robert and Robert's son Henry, were surnamed Canevaz.

Harper-Bill & Mortimer, Stoke by Clare Cartulary, No. 137; Harper-Bill & Mortimer, Stoke by Clare Cartulary, No. 70; Harper-Bill & Mortimer, Stoke by Clare Cartulary, No. 136; Harper-Bill & Mortimer, Stoke by Clare Cartulary, No. 137; ii, fol. 039b; ii, fol. 102a

Carbonel []
Norman, occurs holding a single manor in Herefordshire in 1086. His name may be a personal name, though it was more commonly used as a byname. Le Melletier identifies him as Hugh Carbonel of Canisy, Manche.

i, fol. 187c

Caurinc []
Domesday tenant of Ralph de Bellofago.

ii, fol. 226a

Chemarhuec []
Breton tenant of Hascoit Musard, occurs Domesday Berkshire.

i, fol. 61d

Chenret []
Occurs Domesday Cambridgeshire.

i, fol. 120a

Chetel Friedai
Englishman, occurs Domesday Norfolk.

ii, fol. 135b; ii, fol. 273b

Chetel Venator
Occurs Domesday Surrey.

i, fol. 36d

Chetelbern []
English thegn, occurs Domesday Lincolnshire.

Lincolnshire Claims (Domesday Book), fols 375a–d; Lincolnshire Claims (Domesday Book), fols 375a–d; i, fol. 370d; i, fol. 370d; i, fol. 370d; i, fol. 370d; i, fol. 370d; i, fol. 370d; i, fol. 370d; i, fol. 370d; i, fol. 370d; i, fol. 336b; Lincolnshire Claims (Domesday Book), fols 375a–d; Lincolnshire Claims (Domesday Book), fols 375a–d; Lindsey Survey, BL ms Cotton Claudius C v, fols 19–27; Lindsey Survey, BL ms Cotton Claudius C v, fols 9–18

Clarebald []
Domesday tenant of Robert de Tosny of Belvoir. Possibly the man who was remembered on 27 October in the necrology of Belvoir priory (BL Add. 4936, fol. 36r).

i, fol. 234a

Clarenbald []
Domesday tenant of Swein of Essex.

ii, fol. 046a

Claron []
Domesday tenant of Roger de Bully, who afterwards attested Roger's foundation charter for Blyth priory. Possibly Claron or Clarembald de Lisores (cf. Ord. Vit. v, 254; RRAN i, 440). His son Ernald attested a Blyth charter for Ralph de

Chevercourt. He may occur in an entry in the Thorney Liber Vitae (BL Add. 40,000, fol. 3r): Clarun. Alburh uxor eius.

Timson, Blyth Priory Cartulary (1973), No. 325; i, fol. 285a; i, fol. 284d

Clibert []
Occurs Domesday Yorkshire

i, fol. 330d; i, fol. 331a; i, fol. 331a; i, fol. 331b

Clodoan []
Domesday tenant of Robert de Tosny of Stafford. The form Glodoan of his name is a cacography for a well-attested Breton name Clodoan (derived from 'clot-', 'glory, renown', and two diminutive suffixes, 'o' and 'an'); Clodouan episcopi telonarius occurs thrice c.1074–6 in Cartulaire de l'Abbaye de Sainte-Croix de Quimperlé (2nd edn L. Maître and Paul de Berthou, Rennes-Paris, 1904), pp. 225–6.

i, fol. 249c; i, fol. 249b

Cola Anglicus
Englishman, occurs Domesday Berkshire. Perhaps the same as the Cola who occurs in Derbyshire as a manor of Henry de Ferrers.

i, fol. 274d; i, fol. 63d; i, fol. 63c; i, fol. 62b; i, fol. 274a

Cola Venator
Englishman, Cola the Huntsman, son of Uluiet (Wulfgeat) the Huntsman; occurs Domesday as a king's thegn. Cf. Williams, The English, 116.

i, fol. 50b; i, fol. 50b; i, fol. 50d

Colebern Presbiter
Occurs Domesday Norfolk.

ii, fol. 263b; ii, fol. 263b

Colegrim []
Englishman, Domesday tenant-in-chief in Lincolnshire, where he also had tenancies from Count Alan and Robert of Stafford at Skinnard. Occurs as Colgrim of Grantham in a Ramsey charter concerned with his brother Leofwine (Cart. Ramsey i, p. 131). He was succeeded by his son Osbert, who held 4 knights' fees of the honour of Richmond in the early twelfth century, and then, before 1130, by Osbert's son Alexander. Ancestor of the family of Ingoldsby. Cf. EYC v, 256–7.

i, fol. 348a; i, fol. 345d; i, fol. 371a; i, fol. 337d

Colgrim Anglicus
Occurs Domesday Somerset as tenant of Bath.

i, fol. 89d

Colne []
Englishman, occurs Domesday Derbyshire. Perhaps father of Edric son of Colne (q.v.).

i, fol. 272c; i, fol. 272c; i, fol. 272c; i, fol. 272c

Colo []
Englishman who held one manor under Robert of Mortain that he had held before 1066. Probably the Cola mentioned elsewhere in Cornwall as no longer holding his former lands. Perhaps the Cola Rigensona named as one of the eight burgesses of

Launceston Priory (Cart. Launceston, 3).

i, fol. 124d

Colsuain Lincolniensis

Englishman, Domesday tenant-in-chief in Lincolnshire. His substantial holdings in 1086 were principally a grant to him by William I, of whom he may have been an official, perhaps town-reeve of Lincoln (Williams, The English, 107). A handful of his holdings were attributed to the earlier possession of his nephew Cola. He was succeeded by 1101 by his son Picot (cf. RRAN ii, 531), who in turn was succeeded early in Henry I's reign by his daughter Muriel, wife of Robert de la Haye. Muriel is often stated to be Colswein's daughter, but her son Richard called Picot son of Colswein his grandfather in a charter of a register of Spalding Priory, BL Add. 35296, fol. 413. Robert de la Haye occurs with his wife Muriel in 1126 in Gallia Christiana xi, Inst. 234.

i, fol. 357b; i, fol. 356d; i, fol. 364a; i, fol. 360d; i, fol. 360d; i, fol. 357c; i, fol. 357c; i, fol. 357c; i, fol. 357c; i, fol. 357c; i, fol. 357b; i, fol. 357b; i, fol. 357a; i, fol. 356d; i, fol. 357b; i, fol. 354c; i, fol. 357b; i, fol. 357b; i, fol. 357a; i, fol. 357a; i, fol. 357c; i, fol. 340c; i, fol. 340c; i, fol. 341a; i, fol. 345d; i, fol. 342a; i, fol. 349c; i, fol. 357c; i, fol. 357a; Lincolnshire Claims (Domesday Book), fols 376b–c; Lincolnshire Claims (Domesday Book), fols 375d–376a; Lincolnshire Claims (Domesday Book), fols 375a–d; Lincolnshire Claims (Domesday Book), fols 376d–377c; i, fol. 357a; i, fol. 356d; i, fol. 357b; i, fol. 357a; i, fol. 356d; i, fol. 356d; i, fol. 356d; i, fol. 356d; i, fol. 356d; i, fol. 356d; i, fol. 356d; i, fol. 356d; i, fol. 356d; i, fol. 356d; i, fol. 357a; i, fol. 357a; i, fol. 356d; Lincolnshire Claims (Domesday Book), fols 376b–c; Lincolnshire Claims (Domesday Book), fols 376d–377c; i, fol. 336c; Lincolnshire Claims (Domesday Book), fols 376d–377c; i, fol. 340c; i, fol. 356d; i, fol. 359a; i, fol. 359a

Colsuain []

Tenant of Geoffrey of Coutances in Domesday Somerset.

i, fol. 112d; i, fol. 88c; i, fol. 88c

Colsuen []

An Englishman who continued to hold his land, previously held under Edeva the Fair, under Count Alan. Father of Aelmer son of Colsuan, who was probably the same as Aelmer of Bourn (q.v.). He and his son were jurors for the Domesday Inquest (IE 98; ICC 51; Lewis, 'Jurors', 42). According to VCH Cambs. i, 355, he was the same person as Colswein of Lincoln, but this is unlikely. See Williams, The English, 88–9.

Hamilton, Inquisitio Comitatus Cantabrigiensis, pp. 1–93; Hamilton, Inquisitio Eliensis (1876), pp. 97–100; i, fol. 194c; i, fol. 194c; i, fol. 194c

Coluin Prepositus

English reeve, occurs Domesday Devon; probably the same man was also a tenant of Baldwin the Sheriff and others. He had administered the property of Queen Edith in Exeter up to and probably beyond her death in 1075; thereafter he worked for William I.

i, fol. 106c; i, fol. 106a; i, fol. 116c; i, fol. 100a; i, fol. 118a; i, fol. 118a; i, fol. 118a; i, fol. 118a; i, fol. 118a; i, fol. 118a; i, fol. 118a; i, fol. 118a

Columbanus Abbas De Egnesham
Norman, occurs in Domesday Book as Colomban the Monk. He became the first abbot of the restored abbey of Eynsham in 1091. The date of his death, and the length of his rule, are unknown, but his successor died in 1128. See Heads, 49.

i, fol. 155b; i, fol. 155b; i, fol. 155b

Conan []
Occurs Domesday Oxfordshire. Possibly Conan, brother of Waleran fitz Ranulf the Moneyer of Caen (Comp. Peer. xii, 272), who had an allod at Amblie. His daughter occurs in charters of Caen c.1080–2 (Actes caen., pp. 55, 83, 94).

i, fol. 155b

Concubina Nigelli Albiniensis
Unnamed concubine of Nigel de Albini of Cainhoe, occurring in Domesday Book.

i, fol. 214b

Conded []
Englishman, occurs Domesday Lincolnshire, where he was a tenant of Colswein.

i, fol. 357a; i, fol. 357b; i, fol. 357b

Constantinus []
Occurs Domesday Gloucestershire as a tenant of the bishop of Worcester. Cf. Hugh and William fitz Constantine.

i, fol. 164d

Corbelin De Petehorda
Undertenant of Earl Roger de Montgomery in Sussex, tenant of Robert fitz Theobald, whose last act for Saint-Martin de Sées he witnessed in 1087, as Corbelin de Petehorda (Petworth, Sussex) (CDF, 655). He had two sons, Richard, called the Constable, and Robert, who occur in a charter of Roger de Montgomery given to Saint-Martin after 1087 (ibid., no. 656).

i, fol. 36d; i, fol. 23d; i, fol. 32d; i, fol. 24a

Corbelin []
Domesday tenant of Countess Judith in Northamptonshire. Occurs also under her successor David of Scotland in the Northants Survey.

Northants Survey, fols 96r–99v; i, fol. 229a

Corbin De Agnellis
Tenant of Odo of Bayeux, from Agneaux, Manche. A charter dated 30 November 1074 shows that Odo of Bayeux bought land from Herbert de Agnellis, with the assent of Ralph of Conches (de Tosny) and William I; it was attested by Herbert and his son Corbin (RRAN i, 75). A Corbin de Agnellis held two fees in the Bayeux Inquest, c.1133 (RBE, 645). Herbert de Agnellis held land at Loucelles, Putot and Saint-Croix-Grand-Tonne in the Bessin (Fauroux, 214).

i, fol. 238d; i, fol. 007d

Cristina []
Englishwoman, sister of Edgar Ætheling and grand-daughter of Edmund Ironside. Occurs in Domesday Oxfordshire and Warwickshire in 1086. She was soon afterwards a nun at Romsey (Flor. of Worcester), though by 1093 she had charge of her niece Edith, subsequently, wife of Henry I. at Wilton abbey (Eadmer, Hist.

Nov., 121–6).

> i, fol. 160b; i, fol. 238a; i, fol. 244b; i, fol. 244b; i, fol. 244b; i, fol. 160b; i, fol. 244b

Croc Venator

Norman, Domesday tenant-in-chief. See Chron. Abing. ii, 83 for a writ addressed to him by Henry I. William of Normandy confirmed to Saint-Martin-du-Bosc, c.1059/66, the grants of Robert and Croc, sons of Roger, in the diocese of Lisieux (Fauroux, 218).

> i, fol. 74d; i, fol. 67b; i, fol. 74c; i, fol. 49a; i, fol. 49a; i, fol. 49a

Culling Burgensis

Occurs Domesday Suffolk.

> ii, fol. 290a

Dauid De Argentomo

Norman, from Argentan, dépt. Orne. Likely to be the same person as David latimer, or Interpreter, who was a tenant of William de Braose in Dorset. His successor and probable son Rainald was himself succeeded by his son John in his office of cup-bearer by 1129/30 (Round, King's Serjeants, 265).

> i, fol. 266a; i, fol. 229b; i, fol. 229b; i, fol. 82a; ii, fol. 031a; i, fol. 229b; i, fol. 202a; i, fol. 202a; i, fol. 216d; i, fol. 216d; i, fol. 83b

Demiblanc []

Dimidius blancus, presumably not an Englishman since his name survived in charters of Colne priory as Myblanc. Domesday tenant of Alberic I de Vere. Nothing else is known of him.

> ii, fol. 077a; ii, fol. 078a; ii, fol. 106a; Fisher, Cartularium Prioratus de Colne (Earles C.), No. 1; Fisher, Cartularium Prioratus de Colne (Earles C.), No. 2

Derinc []

Englishman, occurs Domesday Lincolnshire.

> i, fol. 347d; i, fol. 356a; i, fol. 356a

Derman Londoniensis

Englishman, occurs Domesday Essex, also a knight of the archbishop of Canterbury in 1093–6. An important figure in post-Conquest London. Father of Theoderic. See Douglas, Dom. Mon., 62–3.

> ii, fol. 105a; Douglas, ed., Domesday Monachorum (1944), p. 105; i, fol. 130d

Derman []

English thegn, occurs Domesday Hertfordshire. His heir was his brother Lefstan, who was grandfather of Henry fitz Ailwin, first mayor of London; VCH Herts iii, 159. His land was eventually given to Eudo Dapifer, and then to Haimo de Saint-Clair (ibid., 152).

> i, fol. 154b; i, fol. 142b; i, fol. 142b; i, fol. 142b; i, fol. 142b; i, fol. 142b

Dodeman []

Tenant of several tenants-in-chief of the south-west, natives of western Normandy as he probably was. His name is a Scandinavian word meaning 'outlaw'. His 1166 successor in the Mohun barony of Dunster was William of Ellesworth.

> i, fol. 96b; i, fol. 91a; i, fol. 93a; i, fol. 79b; i, fol. 79c; i, fol. 92b; i, fol. 79c; i, fol. 79d; i, fol. 79c; i, fol. 96b; i, fol. 94c; i, fol. 96a; i, fol. 81c/d; i, fol. 96a; i, fol. 96a; i, fol. 96a

Dodin []
Domesday tenant of Alfred of Lincoln.

 i, fol. 358c; i, fol. 358c; i, fol. 358d

Dodin []
Domesday tenant of Countess Judith and others in Northamptonshire. The widow of Walter Dodin (q.v.), presumably this man's son, is mentioned on the 1129/30 Pipe Roll. His holdings descended in the Butevilain family, of whom Robert occurs in the Northants Survey. See Farrer, HKF i, 80.

 i, fol. 219a; i, fol. 219a; i, fol. 226d; i, fol. 227d; i, fol. 229a; i, fol. 229b; i, fol. 226c; i, fol. 226c; i, fol. 226c

Dodo Monachus
Englishman who, as Dodo monachus (the Monk) was recorded in Domesday Dorset as a landholder in or before 1066. Possibly the Dodo who still held some land as a king's thegn.

 i, fol. 84c; i, fol. 84b; i, fol. 84b

Dodo []
English tenant of Robert of Mortain in Domesday Cornwall.

 i, fol. 120a; i, fol. 124d

Dolfin []
Englishman, occurs Domesday Yorkshire as a king's thegn.

 i, fol. 331d; i, fol. 331d; i, fol. 331d

Domnic []
Domesday tenant of Eudo dapifer.

 i, fol. 212c

Domnus []
Englishman, occurs Domesday Devon.

 i, fol. 101d; i, fol. 105d; i, fol. 118b; i, fol. 118b; i, fol. 99a

Donecan []
Tenant of Robert de Mortain in Domesday Somerset, when his daughter was a nun of Shaftesbury. Possibly the same as Donecan de Airel (Manche, near Cerisy-la-Fôret), who made a death-bed grant to Saint-Etienne de Caen shortly before the death of William the Conqueror. It was taken to Abbot Gilbert by his men Torchetillus presbyter, Guillelmus dapifer and Serlo filius Bernardi molendinarii (Actes caen., 32, p. 132). A grant to the abbey by Wimund fitz Donecan (Donedecani) was confirmed by Henry I between 1129 and 1131 (Chanteux, no. 79, pp. 268–9). A William fitz Turstin, who was known as Donecan, attested a grant of Robert Bertram to Saint-Ouen de Rouen before 1066 (Fauroux, 205).

 i, fol. 93a; Regesta regum Anglo-Normannorum III, No. 818; Pipe Roll 31 Henry I, 019b–w1

Doneuuald []
Occurs in Domesday Yorkshire as a tenant of Count Alan. He was an early benefactor of St Mary's, York. His name is perhaps Breton Donoald. Gamel son of Douenald and Jernegan his son witnessed the settlement made by Robert de Brus on his daughter Agatha on her marriage to Ralph fitz Ribald some time between

178

1145 and 1160; EYC v, pp. 311–12.

i, fol. 312a; Dugdale, Monasticon Anglicanum, III, pp. 548–50, No. V

Dons []
Englishman, occurs Domesday Gloucestershire.

i, fol. 170c

Douenold []
Occurs Domesday Hampshire, Isle of Wight.

i, fol. 53c

Drogo De Andeleia
Occurs Domesday Berkshire as a tenant of Robert d'Oilly, and probably also in Cheshire as a tenant of Earl Hugh, whose son Richard confirmed Drogo's grants to Abingdon. Norman from Les Andelys, Eure, identifiable from Chron. Abingdon ii, 67–70. Probably brother of Richer (q.v.). Becoming ill towards the end of his life, before 13 May 1106, he took the habit at Abingdon, to which he gave a hide of land at Weston on the Green, Oxfordshire. Earl Richard of Chester acquitted Roger fitz Ralph, husband of Drogo's daughter, from the service due on the hide (Chron. Abing. ii, 67, 69). Cf. Farrer, HKF ii, 244.

i, fol. 62d; i, fol. 158b; i, fol. 158b; i, fol. 157b; i, fol. 264c; i, fol. 264c; i, fol. 264c; i, fol. 264b; i, fol. 264b; i, fol. 60b; i, fol. 56c; i, fol. 56c; Barraclough, Charters of AN Earls of Chester (1988), No. 6

Drogo De Beuraria
Fleming, from La Beuvrière, Pas-de-Calais, arr. and cant. Béthune, in Artois; occurs as a Domesday tenant-in-chief in Lincolnshire and Yorkshire, though he had forfeited his lands c. August 1086 (B. English, Lords of Holderness, 6–8). Also a tenant of Ralph and Geoffrey Alselin, in places where he also held land in chief. According to Chron. Melsa, he married a kinswoman of William I, but later killed her and was forced to flee abroad. His lands were regranted to Adelaide of Aumale, the king's sister, and her husband Eudo of Champagne.

i, fol. 304b; ii, fol. 158b; i, fol. 369d; Lincolnshire Claims (Domesday Book), fols 376d–377c; Lincolnshire Claims (Domesday Book), fols 375d–376a; Lincolnshire Claims (Domesday Book), fols 376d–377c; Lincolnshire Claims (Domesday Book), fols 376b–c; i, fol. 340b; ii, fol. 172a; ii, fol. 247b; ii, fol. 247a; ii, fol. 247b; ii, fol. 247a; ii, fol. 247b; ii, fol. 247b; ii, fol. 247a; ii, fol. 247b; ii, fol. 247a; i, fol. 228a; i, fol. 228a; i, fol. 360b; i, fol. 323c; i, fol. 323c; i, fol. 323c; i, fol. 323c; i, fol. 323c; i, fol. 323c; i, fol. 324a; i, fol. 323c; i, fol. 324a; i, fol. 360b; i, fol. 324a; i, fol. 323c; i, fol. 360b; i, fol. 323c; i, fol. 360b; i, fol. 323c; i, fol. 360b; i, fol. 360b; i, fol. 360b; i, fol. 323d; i, fol. 360b; i, fol. 324a; i, fol. 360c; i, fol. 360c; i, fol. 360c; i, fol. 360b; i, fol. 323d; i, fol. 324a; i, fol. 324a; i, fol. 324a; i, fol. 324a; i, fol. 323d; i, fol. 324a; i, fol. 323c; i, fol. 323d; i, fol. 323d; i, fol. 323d; i, fol. 324a; i, fol. 323d; i, fol. 324a; i, fol. 323d; i, fol. 323d; i, fol. 323d; i, fol. 324a; i, fol. 324a; i, fol. 324a; i, fol. 324a; i, fol. 360d; i, fol. 324a; i, fol. 360c; i, fol. 324a; i, fol. 324a; i, fol. 323d; i, fol. 323d; i, fol. 323d; i, fol. 324a; i, fol. 325a; i, fol. 323c; i, fol. 323c; i, fol. 323c; i, fol. 323c; i, fol. 323c; i, fol. 360d; i, fol. 323c; i, fol. 360d; i, fol. 324c; i, fol. 324a; i, fol. 323d; i, fol. 325a; i, fol. 323c; i, fol. 324d; i, fol. 324c; i, fol. 324b; i, fol. 324b; i, fol. 324b; i, fol. 324b; i, fol. 324b; i, fol. 324b; i, fol. 324b; i, fol. 325a; Lincolnshire Claims (Domesday Book), fols 376d–377c; Lincolnshire Claims (Domesday Book), fols 375d–376a; i, fol. 323c; i, fol. 323c; i, fol. 360d; i, fol. 360d; i, fol. 360b; i, fol. 323c; i, fol. 323d; i, fol. 323c; i, fol. 323c; i, fol. 323c; i, fol. 323c; i, fol. 323c; i, fol. 323c; i, fol. 323c; i, fol. 323c; i, fol. 323c; i, fol. 323c; i, fol. 323c; i, fol. 323c; i, fol. 324a; i, fol. 323c; i, fol. 323c; i, fol. 323c; i, fol. 323c; i, fol. 323c; i, fol. 323c; i, fol. 323c; i, fol. 236a; i, fol. 360b; i, fol. 323c; ii, fol. 115b; ii, fol. 432a; i, fol. 323d; i, fol. 323d; ii, fol. 202a; i, fol. 323d; i, fol. 323d; i, fol. 323d; i, fol. 323d; i, fol. 323d; i, fol. 369d

Drogo De Cartrai

Norman, from Carteret, Manche, arr. Valognes, cant. Barneville, major tenant of Geoffrey bishop of Coutances in Domesday Devon; he is identified as de Cartrai and as son of Mauger (Malger de Cartrai) in Exon. Another kinsman, his probable brother Humphrey de Cartrai, also occurs in south-west England in Domesday. He was perhaps father of Rainald de Carteret, who was father of Philip de Carteret (CDF, 725–6), Drogo's successor in 1166, holding 14 fees of the honour of Barnstaple. Cf. Loyd, 25.

i, fol. 102a; i, fol. 103a; i, fol. 103a; i, fol. 103b; i, fol. 103b; i, fol. 103b; i, fol. 103b; i, fol. 103a; i, fol. 103b; i, fol. 103a; i, fol. 103b; i, fol. 103b; i, fol. 103a; i, fol. 103a; i, fol. 103a; i, fol. 103a; i, fol. 103a; i, fol. 103a; i, fol. 103a; i, fol. 103a; i, fol. 103b; i, fol. 103b; i, fol. 103a; i, fol. 102d; i, fol. 102d; i, fol. 103a; i, fol. 103a; i, fol. 103a; i, fol. 103a; i, fol. 102d; i, fol. 102b; i, fol. 102d; i, fol. 102c; i, fol. 102d; i, fol. 102d; i, fol. 102d; i, fol. 102d; i, fol. 102d; i, fol. 102d; i, fol. 102d; i, fol. 102d; i, fol. 102d; i, fol. 103a; i, fol. 102c; i, fol. 102c; i, fol. 102c; i, fol. 103b; i, fol. 102d; i, fol. 102d; i, fol. 102d; i, fol. 102b; i, fol. 102c; i, fol. 102d; i, fol. 102c; i, fol. 102b; i, fol. 102c; i, fol. 102c; i, fol. 102c; i, fol. 102c; i, fol. 102c; i, fol. 102c; i, fol. 102c; i, fol. 102b; i, fol. 102c; i, fol. 102c; i, fol. 102c; i, fol. 102c; i, fol. 102d; i, fol. 102b; i, fol. 102d; i, fol. 102b; i, fol. 102b; i, fol. 102b; i, fol. 102b; i, fol. 102b; i, fol. 102b; i, fol. 102b; i, fol. 102d; i, fol. 102b; i, fol. 102d; i, fol. 102c; i, fol. 88a; i, fol. 88a; i, fol. 87d

Drogo De Montagud

Norman, tenant of Robert de Mortain at the Domesday Survey. One of his daughters became a nun of Shaftesbury. His heir was his son Richard (d. 1161/6); Comp. Peer. s.v. Montagu. His toponym came to be associated with the Mortain castle and barony at Montacute in Somerset, but possibly originally referred to a Norman Montaigu; Le Melletier suggests Montaigu-les-Bois, Manche, cant. Gavray.

i, fol. 104d; i, fol. 92ab; i, fol. 80a; i, fol. 79b; i, fol. 91d; i, fol. 92a; i, fol. 92a; i, fol. 92b; i, fol. 92b; i, fol. 104d; i, fol. 104a; i, fol. 105c; i, fol. 105a; i, fol. 92d; i, fol. 92d; i, fol. 92d; i, fol. 92d; i, fol. 93a; i, fol. 93a; i, fol. 93a; i, fol. 99b; Dugdale, Monasticon Anglicanum, II, pp. 482–83, No. XIII; Regesta regum Anglo-Normannorum III, No. 818

Drogo Filius Ponz

Norman, brother of Walter fitz Pons, a tenant-in-chief in Domesday Gloucestershire and a tenant of the Tosnys. Both he and his brother Walter were succeeded in the early twelfth century by their nephew Richard fitz Pons. They probably originated, like Durand of Gloucester, from the Tosny fief in central Normandy, dépt. Eure, though nothing is known for certain of their background. The name Pontius is found in a Norman document of the early eleventh century. It is also found in the mid-eleventh century in the Angevin family of Taisson, then settled in Normandy. There is no evidence of any relationship between the two families, notwithstanding speculation based upon an Englishman occurring in

Domesday Gloucestershire (see Moore, Philimore edn, notes). In 1071 a William filius Poinz attested a cyrograph between Saint-Wandrille and Ralph fitz Ansered relating to the pays de Talou (Saint-Wandrille, 43).

i, fol. 186d; i, fol. 183b; i, fol. 182d; i, fol. 165a; i, fol. 168b; i, fol. 186c; i, fol. 168d; i, fol. 177a; i, fol. 186c; i, fol. 186c; i, fol. 186c; i, fol. 186c; i, fol. 168d; i, fol. 177a; i, fol. 168d; i, fol. 73a; i, fol. 177a; i, fol. 177a; i, fol. 174d; i, fol. 180b; i, fol. 180b; i, fol. 180b

Drogo []
Norman tenant of William Peverel of Nottingham in Derbyshire. He was succeeded by Helgot, sheriff of Nottinghamshire c.1108, but evidence lacks as to any affiliation. Cf. HKF iii, 188. A Helgot son of Drogo was an early post-Conquest benefactor of St Albans (BL Cotton Nero D vii fol. 118v).

i, fol. 276b; i, fol. 226a; i, fol. 148b

Drogo []
Domesday tenant of William fitz Ansculf de Picquigny.

i, fol. 243a; i, fol. 250b; i, fol. 250a; i, fol. 250a

Drogo []
Norman, Domesday tenant of Robert de Tosny of Stafford. Matheus de Witheleia, named from one of Drogo's holdings, may have been his successor by the early twelfth century; he attested Nicholas fitz Robert of Stafford's charter for Kenilworth (Hist. Coll. Staffs. ii, 181–2).

i, fol. 249d; i, fol. 242d

Durand Canonicus Sancti Pauli
Domesday canon of St Paul's. Prebendary of Twyford by 1102, perhaps also magister scholarum. Last occurs 1111/12. He died before January 1127. See FEA i, 25, 80.

i, fol. 127d; Gibbs, Early Charters of St Pauls (1939), No. 273

Durand Carpentarius
Occurs Domesday Dorset, where he held land of the wife of Hugh fitz Grip and the king.

i, fol. 84a; i, fol. 85a; i, fol. 85a

Durand Clericus
Domesday, clerk of Bury St Edmunds and tenant of Robert Malet. Probably an Englishman.

ii, fol. 316a; ii, fol. 365a; ii, fol. 369b; Douglas, Feudal Book of Bury St Edmunds (1932), pp. 22–37; Douglas, Feudal Book of Bury St Edmunds (1932), pp. 3–21

Durand De Glouuecestre
Norman, from Pîtres, Eure, cant. Pont-de-l'Arche, in the fief of the Tosny family. Tenant-in-chief and sheriff in Domesday Gloucestershire. His brother Roger had been sheriff before him. He was probably dead by 1095, when his nephew Walter fitz Roger was sheriff.

i, fol. 164d; i, fol. 65d; i, fol. 166a; i, fol. 165a; i, fol. 71b; i, fol. 40d; i, fol. 47c; i, fol. 52a; i, fol. 70c; i, fol. 186c; i, fol. 71c; i, fol. 71c; i, fol. 71c; i, fol. 47d; i, fol. 40a; i, fol. 40a; i, fol. 168d; i, fol. 162a; i, fol. 162a; i, fol. 162b; i, fol. 165a; i, fol. 168d; i, fol. 168d; i, fol. 168d; i, fol. 164d; i, fol. 168d

Durand Malet
Tenant-in-chief in Domesday Lincolnshire. Probably a son of William Malet (d. 1071). Ancestor of the Malets of Linwood and Rothwell, his successors c.1115/18 were Ralph and Walter Malet, probably his sons. See K. S. B. Keats-Rohan, 'Domesday Book and the Malets', Nottingham Medieval Studies xli (1997), 13–51.

> i, fol. 36c; i, fol. 291d; i, fol. 365b; i, fol. 365a; i, fol. 365a; i, fol. 365a; i, fol. 291d; i, fol. 365b; i, fol. 365a; i, fol. 365a; i, fol. 365a; i, fol. 365a; i, fol. 365a; i, fol. 365a; i, fol. 365a; i, fol. 365b; i, fol. 365b; i, fol. 365a; i, fol. 365b; i, fol. 365b; i, fol. 365b; i, fol. 365b; i, fol. 236a; i, fol. 236a; i, fol. 236a; Lincolnshire Claims (Domesday Book), fols 375d–376a; i, fol. 365a; ii, fol. 315b; i, fol. 365a; i, fol. 236a; i, fol. 291d

Durand Prepositus
Occurs Domesday Northamptonshire.

> i, fol. 219a

Durand Tonsor
Norman, occurs Domesday Hampshire.

> i, fol. 49b; i, fol. 49b

Durand []
Occurs Domesday Norfolk as tenant of Roger Bigod.

> ii, fol. 189b; ii, fol. 189b; ii, fol. 189b

Durand []
Domesday tenant of William de Moyon. Probably the same as Durand, dapifer of William de Moyon in 1090 (Cart. Bath). He may have been the father of Durand de Moion

> i, fol. 96a; i, fol. 96a; i, fol. 96a; i, fol. 95d; Hunt, Bath Chartulary, Som. Rec. Soc. 7 (1893), No. 34

Durand []
Important Domesday tenant of Harduin de Scalariis. Possibly his holding was represented in 1166 by the five fees held by William fitz Roger of Stephen de Scalariis.

> i, fol. 198a; i, fol. 198a; i, fol. 198a; i, fol. 198d; i, fol. 198d; i, fol. 198c; i, fol. 198a

Durand []
Occurs Domesday Sussex and Northamptonshire as a tenant of Robert of Mortain.

> i, fol. 224a; i, fol. 20d; i, fol. 17c; i, fol. 21c

Durand []
Norman, Domesday tenant of Roger de Montgomery.

> i, fol. 73b; i, fol. 51b; i, fol. 51b; i, fol. 24b

Durand []
Domesday tenant of Hugh de Montfort.

> Ballard, Inquisition of St Augustine's (1920), fols 24r–28r; i, fol. 001a; Hamilton, Inquisitio Eliensis (1876), pp. 192–95

Ebrard []
Norman, Domesday tenant of William de Percy. Ancestor of a family surnamed

from his manor of Leathley. All his manors in Yorkshire passed to his son Hugh. His Lincolnshire manors were held in the mid twelfth century by Robert fitz Robert of Thweng, whose background is otherwise unknown, but who is not unlikely to have been a descendant of Evrard. In 1129 a Robert fitz Payn accounted in Yorkshire for the land of Everard his uncle (avunculi).

> i, fol. 322b; i, fol. 321d; i, fol. 322a; Clay, Early Yorkshire Charters (1955), XI, No. 2; i, fol. 354b; i, fol. 354b; i, fol. 301c; Clay, Early Yorkshire Charters (1955), XI, No. 123

Ebrard []
Occurs Domesday Wiltshire.

> i, fol. 66a; i, fol. 67b

Eddeua []
Englishwoman holding land at farm in Edmondsham, Dorset, of Humphrey the chamberlain. According to the Geld Rolls (VCH Dorset iii, 47) she was a widow whose lands had been freed of geld by Queen Matilda in memory of her son Richard, killed in the New Forest in 1081. Cf. Williams, The English, 79–80.

> i, fol. 83a

Eddeue []
Englishwoman who held the large manor of Chaddesley Corbett, Worcestershire, in 1086. She was perhaps a kinswoman of the earls of Mercia (A. Williams, 'An introduction to the Worcestershire Domesday', 30–1).

> i, fol. 178a

Eddeva Uxor Uluuardi
Englishwoman. Occurs Domesday Buckinghamshire holding from the bishop of Coutances. Described as wife of Wulfward, she is also mentioned as having held land in or before 1066. Her husband Wulfweard White, dead in 1086, had been a wealthy man, with over 150 hides of land in eleven shires (Williams, The English, 99–100). The couple had no sons, but their daughter was given in marriage by Queen Edith to Alsige.

> i, fol. 145b

Eddid []
Englishwoman. Occurs Berkshire Domesday.

> i, fol. 63d

Eddida Monialis
English nun, occurs Domesday Somerset.

> i, fol. 91c

Edelo []
Domesday tenant of Robert de Tosny of Stafford, presumably father of Robert son of Ehelen or Aelem who attested a Kenilworth charter of Nicholas of Stafford c.1122/9 (BL Harley 3650, fol. 14v). Cf. Hist. Coll. Staffs. i pt i, 174–5.

> i, fol. 249a; i, fol. 368d; i, fol. 368c; i, fol. 368c; i, fol. 368c

Edeua Uxor Eduuardi Filii Suani
English widow who held her husband's land at Chafford, Essex, and land in alms in Middlesex, in 1086. According to F.N. Craig, 'Descent from a Domesday goldsmith', The American Genealogist 65.1 (1990), 24ff, she was secondly the

(second) wife of Otto I the Goldsmith.

i, fol. 098b; ii, fol. 098b

Edgar Adeling

Edgar the Atheling, son of Edward the Exile (d. 1057) son of Edmund II Ironside, and great-nephew of Edward the Confessor. Aged about 14 in 1065–6, he was too young to be chosen as Edward's successor in January 1066, though the Anglo-Saxon Chronicle says that he was chosen king by Archbishop Aldred, the citizens of London and earls Edwin and Morcar after the battle of Hastings in October. He submitted to William of Normandy, who was crowned king in December. Between 1066 and 1086 he lived in Scotland, of which his sister Margaret was queen, in England and Normandy. In 1086 he went to Apulia with 200 knights, but soon returned to England. He seems to have had a usually good relationship with William, for whom he probably fought in the 1095 campaign against Robert de Mowbray in Northumberland. In 1097 he commanded an English army that deposed Donald of Scotland and put Edgar's own nephew on the Scottish throne as an English vassal. He participated in the First Crusade, notably as the leading figure of a fleet which took a force of English and north European crusaders to Syria in 1098. According to William of Malmesbury, Historia Regum he was living out his old age in peaceful retirement in England during the reign of Henry I, perhaps dying c.1120/5. N. Hooper, 'Edgar ætheling, Anglo-Saxon prince, rebel and crusader', Anglo-Saxon England 14 (1985).

i, fol. 142a

Edgar Presbiter

English priest, occurs Domesday Wiltshire.

i, fol. 74a

Edmer Frater Aluric

Somerset, occurs with his brother; identified in Exon.

i, fol. 87c

Edmund Filius Aiulf

Occurs Domesday Wiltshire.

i, fol. 74a; i, fol. 74a; i, fol. 74a; i, fol. 74a; i, fol. 74a

Edmund Filius Algot

Englishman, occurs in Domesday Essex, and in Middlesex as a tenant of Odo of Bayeux. Possibly Edmund, prebendary of Chiswick c.1103–5, and therefore perhaps brother of Ralph son of Algod, prebendary of Rugmere (q.v.), who occurs in the Durham Liber Vitae (Surtees Soc. 136, 1923, fol. 42) with his mother Leouerun, brother Edmund and wife Mahald: see FEA i, 41, 74.

ii, fol. 093b; i, fol. 127c; ii, fol. 093b; ii, fol. 093b

Edmund Filius Pagani

English thegn, occurs Domesday Hampshire and Somerset. He held Dunham, Norfolk, in chief, his tenant there being his sister's husband, Rainald the priest.

i, fol. 51d; i, fol. 50d; ii, fol. 264a; ii, fol. 264a; i, fol. 98d; i, fol. 98d; i, fol. 98d; i, fol. 50d; i, fol. 50a; i, fol. 50a

Ednod []
English tenant of Robert of Mortain in Cornwall, 1086.

   i, fol. 124c

Edred Presbiter
Occurs Domesday Berkshire.

   i, fol. 57a

Edric Accipitrarius
English falconer. Occurs Domesday Norfolk.

   ii, fol. 272a; ii, fol. 272a

Edric De Lexefeld
Edric of Laxfield, predecessor of Robert Malet and his father William in much of their fief in Norfolk and Suffolk. An important thegn who had survived, probably somewhat reduced in wealth, a period of disgrace under Edward the Confessor. Domesday (DB Wilts. 67.53) also refers to him as Edric Cecus (the Blind). See Douglas, Feudal Documents, pp. xc–xcii and no. 168.

   Douglas, Feudal Documents from Bury St Edmunds, No. 168; i, fol. 74a; Regesta regum Anglo-Normannorum III, No. 288; Douglas, Feudal Book of Bury St Edmunds (1932), pp. 3–21

Edric Filius Aluric
Englishman, occurs Domesday.

   i, fol. 252d; i, fol. 252d

Edric Filius Chetel
Englishman, occurs Domesday Gloucestershire.

   Regesta regum Anglo-Normannorum III, No. 389; Round, Ancient Charters (1888), No. 10; i, fol. 170c; Regesta regum Anglo-Normannorum III, No. 389; i, fol. 170c

Edric Filius Coln
Englishman, occurs Domesday Derbyshire. Probably son of the Colne who also occurs.

   i, fol. 280b

Edric Prepositus
Edric prepositus is identified as such by the Tax Return for Hasler Hundred.

   i, fol. 84c; i, fol. 84c; i, fol. 84c; i, fol. 84c; i, fol. 84c; i, fol. 84c; i, fol. 84c

Edric []
Englishman, held land in Devon before and after 1066; holding of Geoffrey bishop of Coutances in 1086.

   i, fol. 103b

Eduard Presbiter
Occurs Domesday Essex.

   ii, fol. 105a

Edui Prepositus Regis
Royal provost; occurs Domesday Norfolk.

   ii, fol. 146a

Eduin Canonicus

Occurs Domesday Kent.

Ballard, Inquisition of St Augustine's (1920), fols 24r–28r; i, fol. 001d; i, fol. 001d

Eduin De Buterleio

Occurs Domesday Devon; named in the Tax Returns from Butterleigh, where he had held land before 1066. A Brian de Buterleia, wife Alice and son Richard occurs as a benefactor of St Nicholas, Exeter, temp. Bishop Bartholomew of Exeter, 1161–84 (BL Cotton Vit. D ix, fol. 36v).

i, fol. 118c; i, fol. 118c

Eduin Presbiter

Englishman, occurs Domesday Essex. Possibly to be identified with the Domesday juror in Flendish Hundred, Cambridgeshire.

Hamilton, Inquisitio Comitatus Cantabrigiensis, pp. 1–93; Hamilton, Inquisitio Eliensis (1876), pp. 97–100; ii, fol. 104a

Eduin Venator

English huntsman, occurs Domesday Dorset. Probably the same man held two hides in Kingsclere Hundred, Hampshire, later known as Edmundsthorpe Banham. The manor took its name from Edwin's son Edmund. Edwin, his wife Odelina and their sons Edmund, Eadulf and Ælfwine were commemorated in the Liber Vitae of Hyde Abbey. Cf. Williams, The English, 116.

i, fol. 84b; i, fol. 84b; i, fol. 84c; i, fol. 84c; i, fol. 50c

Eduin []

Occurs Domesday Cheshire.

i, fol. 264b; i, fol. 264b; i, fol. 264c; i, fol. 264c; i, fol. 264c

Eduin []

Englishman, occurs Domesday Cheshire.

i, fol. 264b; i, fol. 264b; i, fol. 264b; i, fol. 264c; i, fol. 264c; i, fol. 264c

Eduuard Cilt

Englishman, occurs Domesday Lincolnshire.

i, fol. 340a

Eduuard De Periton

Englishman, a tenant of the king at Great Offley in Domesday Hertfordshire, named from Pirton. He was probably the unnamed English knight who is entered as holding land in Pirton.

i, fol. 132d; i, fol. 138b

Eduuard Filius Edrici

Englishman, occurs Domesday Devon.

i, fol. 100c

Eduuard Saresberiensis

The richest English tenant-in-chief in Domesday Book, the bulk of his lands lying in Wiltshire. A definitive account of Edward and his family was published in Williams, The English, 106–7. She shows that Edward was a prominent thegn under Edward the Confessor, probably to be identified with Edward dives (the

Rich) who had associations with the north. The bulk of his lands came to him through Wulfwynn of Cresswell, probably his mother. Sheriff of Wiltshire between 1070 and 1087. He was dead by 1120 at the latest, when his eldest son Walter controlled his lands. He was apparently father, by a second wife Matilda, of Edward of Salisbury the younger, who inherited none of his father's lands but held some in Nottinghamshire and Derbyshire of the fee of Ralph fitz Hubert, probably his grandfather. He also had a daughter Matilda, wife of Humphrey de Bohun of Trowbridge.

i, fol. 164b; i, fol. 66d; i, fol. 66d; i, fol. 66c; i, fol. 87b; i, fol. 68b; Douglas, Feudal Documents from Bury St Edmunds, No. 18; Dugdale, Monasticon Anglicanum, III, p. 499, No. I; Douglas, Feudal Documents from Bury St Edmunds, No. 13; Douglas, Feudal Documents from Bury St Edmunds, No. 15; Round, Leicestershire Survey, Round, Feudal England, pp. 161–65; i, fol. 139b; i, fol. 139b; i, fol. 160a; i, fol. 130c; Hart, Cartularium Monasterii de Rameseia, No. CLXXV; i, fol. 46c; i, fol. 69b; i, fol. 80c; i, fol. 69b; i, fol. 69d; i, fol. 69b; i, fol. 69d; i, fol. 69d; i, fol. 80c; i, fol. 69c; i, fol. 69c; i, fol. 69c; i, fol. 69c; i, fol. 36b; i, fol. 69c; i, fol. 69b; i, fol. 69b; i, fol. 69b; i, fol. 69b; i, fol. 69c; i, fol. 150c; i, fol. 46c; i, fol. 150c; i, fol. 69b; i, fol. 98b; i, fol. 98b; i, fol. 98b; i, fol. 160a; i, fol. 74c; i, fol. 67c; i, fol. 43c; i, fol. 154a; i, fol. 74b; i, fol. 64c; i, fol. 64c; i, fol. 64c; i, fol. 64c; i, fol. 64c; Clay, Early Yorkshire Charters (1949), VIII, No. 4; i, fol. 139b; Dugdale, Monasticon Anglicanum, IV, p. 13, No. IV

Edward Venator
Occurs Domesday Dorset.

i, fol. 84d

Edwin Presbiter
Occurs Domesday Hampshire.

i, fol. 49d

Einbold []
Domesday tenant of Ralph Baynard.

ii, fol. 249b; ii, fol. 253a; ii, fol. 249a

Eldild []
English widow, Domesday Wiltshire.

i, fol. 74b

Eldit []
Englishwoman. Occurs in Berkshire Domesday.

i, fol. 63d

Eldred []
Englishman, Domesday tenant of William de Percy in Yorkshire.

Clay, Early Yorkshire Charters (1955), XI, No. 1; i, fol. 322a; i, fol. 322a

Elfin De Breleford
Englishman, Domesday tenant of Henry de Ferrers; named from Brailsford, Derbyshire. He and his son Nicholas were benefactors of Tutbury.

i, fol. 274d; i, fol. 275b; i, fol. 275b; i, fol. 275a; i, fol. 275a; Dugdale, Monasticon Anglicanum, III, pp. 392–93, No. II

Elfric Miles
English knight of the bishop of Salisbury, Dorset Domesday.
i, fol. 77b

Elinant Vicecomes
Norman tenant of Richard de Clare in Domesday Suffolk. Described as vicecomes in Cart. Stoke-by-Clare no 137, temp. Gilbert fitz Richard de Clare. Father of Geoffrey and Adam, who occur in Stoke charters of the early twelfth century.
ii, fol. 392b; ii, fol. 039a; Harper-Bill & Mortimer, Stoke by Clare Cartulary, No. 137; Harper-Bill & Mortimer, Stoke by Clare Cartulary, No. 137; Harper-Bill & Mortimer, Stoke by Clare Cartulary, No. 137; Harper-Bill & Mortimer, Stoke by Clare Cartulary, No. 37; Harper-Bill & Mortimer, Stoke by Clare Cartulary, No. 70; Harper-Bill & Mortimer, Stoke by Clare Cartulary, No. 136

Elmund Pater Alward
Almund, an Englishman, and his son Alweard occurs in Domesday Shropshire as tenants of Earl Roger. The bulk of their pre-Conquest holdings there and in Staffordshire had been given to Rainald de Balliol. See Williams, The English, 90.
i, fol. 259c

Eluui Haussona
Occurs Domesday Somerset; his patronym is supplied by Exon.
i, fol. 89c

Elward Filius Reinbaldi
Occurs Domesday Gloucestershire. Son of Rainbald the Chancellor (q.v.)
i, fol. 170c

Engelbric Canonicus Sancti Pauli
Domesday canon of St Paul's. Benefactor of St Martin le Grand in London before May 1068, he was king's chaplain and first dean of St Martin le Grand. See FEA i, 89.
i, fol. 127c

Engeler []
Domesday tenant of Arnald de Hesdin in Somerset. Probably the same as Ingelerus who attested Arnald's grant of land in England to Saint-George-de-Hesdin (Cart., no. 52).
i, fol. 98b

Engeler []
Norman, Domesday tenant of Earl Roger in Sussex. Has been anachronistically identified as Ingelger de Bohun. His real identity is unknown.
i, fol. 16b; i, fol. 24a

Engenulf []
Norman, Domesday tenant of Waleran Venator in Wiltshire.
i, fol. 72a; i, fol. 72b; i, fol. 72b

Enisan Musard
An important Breton tenant of Count Alan, especially in Yorkshire. The bulk of his holdings were known shortly after his death, before 1130, as the Constable's fee, half of which, with the office of constable, being thereafter held by Roald son of

Harscoit, Constable of Richmond, and his descendants, and the other half by Richard I de Rullos and his descendants. Roald's wife Garsiena was probably the senior Musard heiress, the most likely relationship being that she was eldest daughter of his eldest son; Emma, wife of Richard de Rullos, was perhaps her sister. Alexander Musard, a contemporary of Roald and his son, probably descended from a younger son, or even a daughter, of Enisan. Musard is a byname meaning stupid or lazy in Latin. The importance of Enisan's holdings of Count Alan perhaps indicates that he should be identified with Enisan de Pleveno (Pléven, dépt. Côtes-d'Amor), husband of an illegitimate half-sister of the count, whose tenants included three natural half-brothers and his wet-nurse (Morice, Preuves I, 458, a note added to the foundation charter of Saint-Martin de Lamballe, given by Alan's brother Geoffrey Boterel I, reads: 'Brien videlicet comes Anglice terre et Alainus Rufus eius scilicet successor, alter Alainus qui et Niger dicatur – hic etiam tertius successit in regno – et quidem qui sororem eius bastardam uxorem duxerat, Enisandus de Pleveno.').

i, fol. 309c; i, fol. 309c; i, fol. 309c; i, fol. 309c; i, fol. 309c; i, fol. 309c; i, fol. 309c; i, fol. 309c; i, fol. 309c; i, fol. 309d; i, fol. 309b; i, fol. 309b; i, fol. 311b; i, fol. 310d; i, fol. 310d; i, fol. 309b; i, fol. 312d; i, fol. 309c; i, fol. 311d; i, fol. 311d; i, fol. 309d; i, fol. 311a; i, fol. 195b; ii, fol. 145b; Clay, Early Yorkshire Charters (1935), IV, No. 47; Clay, Early Yorkshire Charters (1936), V, No. 185; Clay, Early Yorkshire Charters (1936), V, No. 218; Dugdale, Monasticon Anglicanum, III, pp. 548–50, No. V; Clay, Early Yorkshire Charters (1935), IV, No. 2

Enselm []
Anselm, Domesday tenant of Count Eustache.

ii, fol. 033b

Erchenbald Flandrensis
Occurs Domesday Devonshire as a tenant of Robert of Mortain; identified as flandrensis in Exon. Had been succeeded by 1129/30 by a son Stephen.

i, fol. 105b; i, fol. 105a; i, fol. 104c; i, fol. 105b; i, fol. 124a; i, fol. 124a; i, fol. 124a; i, fol. 105a; i, fol. 105a

Erchenger Pistor
Norman, occurs Domesday. He, his wife Hugelina, their son Roland and their daughter were benefactors of St Albans, to which they gave tithes at Comberton and Toft in Cambridgeshire (BL Cotton Nero D vii, fol. 98v).

Hamilton, Inquisitio Eliensis (1876), pp. 192–95; i, fol. 189a; i, fol. 202c; i, fol. 202c

Erchenger Presbiter
Occurs Domesday Somerset. Identified as a priest in Exon.

i, fol. 91c

Erchenold []
Occurs Domesday Lincolnshire as a tenant of Bishop Remigius.

i, fol. 344c; i, fol. 344b; i, fol. 344b

Erenburgis []
In Domesday Wiltshire an Erenburgis was recorded as holding land of Waleran Venator that has been held TRE by one Norman. The name probably represents the

feminine Germanic personal name Eremburg.

i, fol. 72a

Erfast []

A leading tenant of Nigel de Albini of Cainhoe, 1086, probably from west Normandy. An Arfast son-in-law of Milo mariscalcus occurs in Actes caen. no. 6 (1082–6). His son Nigel fitz Erfast (q.v.) occurs from c.1110.

i, fol. 214d; i, fol. 214b; i, fol. 214a; i, fol. 214d; i, fol. 211c

Ermenald []

Domesday tenant of Tavistock Abbey in Devon and Cornwall. He appears to have the lineal ancestor of a family surnamed de Alneto, his successor in 1129 being Richard fitz Herbert de Alneto. Finberg, Tavistock Abbey, 13–14.

i, fol. 103c; i, fol. 121c; i, fol. 121c; i, fol. 121b; i, fol. 121b; i, fol. 121b; i, fol. 121c

Ermenfrid de Warwic

Domesday tenant of the count of Meulan and Thorkil of Warwick in Warwickshire. Attested a charter of Geoffrey de La Guerche for Monks Kirby priory, before 1093, as 'Hermenfredus de Warwic' (Mon. Ang. vi, 996).

i, fol. 239a; i, fol. 241a; i, fol. 241c; i, fol. 241c; i, fol. 241d; i, fol. 241d; i, fol. 244c; i, fol. 329b; i, fol. 241a

Ermenfrid []

Domesday tenant of Osbern de Arches in Yorkshire. His land was granted by Osbern to St Mary's, York, shortly before his death c.1115; see EYC i, no. 527 and n. pp. 408–9. Ermenfrid left a son William, father of Bertram of Stiveton, who attested a charter of William of Arches, ibid., no. 534, and n. pp. 413–14.

i, fol. 329b; i, fol. 329b

Ermeniot []

Domesday tenant of Count Alan in Suffolk. His Breton name occurs among the men of Main II, father of Ralph I of Fougères, c. 1050 with Hervey fitz Ermeniot and his sons Pinel and Guy (Arch. dépt. Ille-et-Vilaine, IF 543, Saint-Sauveur-des-Landes, nos. iii, vi). A later Ermengot de Capelwenham gave land in Wenham to St John's, Colchester (Cart, p. 287).

ii, fol. 295a

Ernald De Nazanda

Identified as de Nazanda (Nassandres, Eure, arr. Bernay, cant. Beaumont-le-Roger, in the continental possessions of the de Clare family, Loyd, 71) by charters of Stoke-by-Clare. The toponym was not used by his descendants.

ii, fol. 101b; ii, fol. 101b; ii, fol. 039a; ii, fol. 039a; ii, fol. 039b; Harper-Bill & Mortimer, Stoke by Clare Cartulary, No. 136; Harper-Bill & Mortimer, Stoke by Clare Cartulary, No. 37; Harper-Bill & Mortimer, Stoke by Clare Cartulary, No. 137; Harper-Bill & Mortimer, Stoke by Clare Cartulary, No. 136; Harper-Bill & Mortimer, Stoke by Clare Cartulary, No. 70

Ernald De Ponteio

Tenant of Walter de Douai in Domesday Devon, identified from the Exon Tax Return, which gives him an undertenant Heibod; the toponym perhaps refers to Le Pontoit, Nord, arr. Valenciennes.

i, fol. 111d

Ernald []
Norman, Domesday tenant of Hugh de Grandmesnil.

i, fol. 217d; i, fol. 233a; i, fol. 232c; i, fol. 232c; i, fol. 232c; i, fol. 233a; i, fol. 233a

Ernald []
Norman, Domesday tenant of Robert de Tosny in Staffordshire. Ancestor of the de Walton family. Succeeded by his son Enisan, and then by Enisan's son Arnald (fl. 1129/30). Cf. VCH Staffs v, 4.

i, fol. 248d; i, fol. 176c

Erneis De Burun
Norman, from Buron, Calvados, arr. Falaise, cant. Bretteville-sur-Laize, comm. Fresnay-le-Vieux. Tenant-in-chief in Domesday Yorkshire and Lincolnshire, also a tenant of Odo of Bayeux. He was last mentioned in 1088. He succeeded Hugh fitz Baldric as sheriff of York, according to Hist. Selby. His son Hugh occurs in a charter of 1089–93 for St Mary's, York. By 1115–18 the Buron fief of Hunsingore was held by Geoffrey fitz Payn. His family certainly survived, for a Robert de Buron and his nephew Erneis were benefactors of St Mary's c.1121–30 (EYC x, 1).

i, fol. 342b; i, fol. 349b; i, fol. 362b; Regesta regum Anglo-Normannorum III, No. 179; Regesta regum Anglo-Normannorum III, No. 180; Clay, Early Yorkshire Charters (1955), X, No. 3; Clay, Early Yorkshire Charters (1955), X, No. 3; i, fol. 362c; i, fol. 362c; i, fol. 362c; i, fol. 362c; i, fol. 362c; i, fol. 362b; i, fol. 362c; i, fol. 362c; i, fol. 362c; i, fol. 362c; i, fol. 362c; i, fol. 362b; i, fol. 362c; i, fol. 362c; i, fol. 362c; i, fol. 362b; i, fol. 362b; i, fol. 362b; i, fol. 362b; i, fol. 362c; i, fol. 362c; Lincolnshire Claims (Domesday Book), fols 375a–d; Lincolnshire Claims (Domesday Book), fols 376b–c; i, fol. 298b; i, fol. 328c; i, fol. 328d; i, fol. 328d; i, fol. 328d; i, fol. 328c; i, fol. 328d; i, fol. 328d; i, fol. 328d; i, fol. 328d; i, fol. 328d; i, fol. 328d; i, fol. 328c; i, fol. 328d; i, fol. 328c; i, fol. 328c; i, fol. 328c; i, fol. 328c; i, fol. 328c; i, fol. 328c; i, fol. 328c; i, fol. 328c; i, fol. 328c; i, fol. 328c; i, fol. 328c; i, fol. 328c; i, fol. 328d; i, fol. 328d; i, fol. 328c; Clay, Early Yorkshire Charters (1935), IV, No. 101

Erneis []
Domesday tenant of Giso bishop of Wells.

i, fol. 90d; i, fol. 89b; i, fol. 94b; i, fol. 89c

Erneis []
Norman, Domesday tenant of Hugh de Grandmesnil.

i, fol. 232d; i, fol. 232c

Ernucion []
Montgomery tenant in Shropshire and Sussex. Perhaps the same as Ernucio Balbet, who gave land at Trans and Courtemer (Orne) to Saint-Martin de Sées (Arch. Orne H938, 2r–v), that latter grant being conceded by his brothers Hugh and Warin. It was confirmed by Robert of Bellême, attested by Robert fitz Theobald, another Sussex tenant of Montgomery.

i, fol. 259b; i, fol. 25b; i, fol. 24c; i, fol. 59d

Ernui []
English thegn in pre-Conquest Shropshire who continued to hold land there in

1086 from Roger and Robert fitz Corbet (cf. Williams, The English, 89–90).

    i, fol. 255c; i, fol. 255d; i, fol. 256a

Ernuin Presbiter

English priest who in 1086 continued to hold extensive estates north of the Ribble attributed to Roger Pictaviensis in Domesday Book.

    i, fol. 352b; i, fol. 352a; i, fol. 330c; i, fol. 332b; i, fol. 331a; i, fol. 331a; i, fol. 331a; i, fol. 330c; i, fol. 286c; i, fol. 293a; i, fol. 336a; i, fol. 330d; i, fol. 342a; i, fol. 371a; i, fol. 337d; i, fol. 336b; Lincolnshire Claims (Domesday Book), fols 375d–376a; i, fol. 210b; i, fol. 211a; i, fol. 211a

Ernulf De Arda

Seneschal and later Domesday tenant of Eustache II of Boulogne, from Ardres, Pas-de-Calais. Son of Arnold I d'Ardres and Mathilde de Marquise, grandson of Elbod de Bergues and Adele de Selnesse (Lambert of Ardres; see Warlop, ii, 416 note 122). Lambert of Ardres described his early career as a rapacious and ruthless official of Count Eustache in Artois. By 1086 he had acquired land in the Boulogne fee in England. He married Gertrude of Alost (portrayed by Lambert as an aristocratic virago), by whom he had a large family of four sons and three daughters. He accompanied his wife's relatives on the First Crusade, surviving to die at an advanced age in 1138. He was succeeded in turn by his sons Arnold (murdered by one of his vassals) and Baldwin (father of the chronicler Lambert, who records his death on the Second Crusade), but none of his sons left issue and his eventual heir was the son of his daughter Adelina and Arnold de Mercq. By 1166 their heir was their daughter Christiana, wife of Baldwin count of Guines. Between 1136 and February 1148 the grant of Arnald's Lincolnshire manor of Stevington to Harrold priory by Baldwin de Ardres was confirmed by Bishop Alexander (EEA i, no. 36).

    i, fol. 196a; i, fol. 196a; i, fol. 211b; i, fol. 211b; i, fol. 211b; i, fol. 211b; i, fol. 211b

Ernulf De Bully

Norman, Domesday tenant of his brother Roger de Bully. Attested his brother's foundation charter for Blythe priory (no. 325). Probably father of Jordan de Bully (ibid., no. 331; cf. Introd., pp. xxiv ff).

    i, fol. 286a; Timson, Blyth Priory Cartulary (1973), No. 325

Ernulf De Hesding

From Hesdin, Pas-de-Calais, arr. Montreuil, cant. Hesdin (Loyd, 51), Domesday tenant-in-chief. Apparently a brother or brother-in-law of Wacelin, provost of Beaurain, arr. Montreuil, cant. Campagne-lès-Hesdin, under Walter Tirel of Poix (q.v.) (Fossier, Picardie, p. 240, and idem Cart. de Hesdin). By his wife Emmelina he had issue two sons William and Arnald, and two daughters and eventual coheiresses Matilda, wife first of a William and then of Patrick de Caorces, and Avelina, wife first of Alan fitz Flaad and then of Robert fiz Walter. Possibly father also of Reiner de Hesdin, father of William, who assisted William sheriff of Kent in an inquest of 1127 (Stenton, English Justice, Appendix, no. i, pp. 116–22). One of his kinswomen became a nun of Shaftesbury. His monastic benefactors were extensive and eclectic, and included his local house of Saint-Georges-de-Hesdin, of which the charters frequently refer to his nephew Robert Fretel and his descendants. One of the charters (Cart. Hesdin, no. 52) was a grant by Arnald of land at Norton in England which refers to his chaplain Theodard and was attested by his dapifer Arnulf. He was accused of complicity in the conspiracy led by Robert de Mowbray in 1093, but cleared himself in a judicial duel. He soon afterwards left England on the First Crusade, where he died at Antioch.

i, fol. 249b; Dugdale, Monasticon Anglicanum, II, pp. 482–83, No. XIII; i, fol. 71d; Edwards, Chronicon de Hida, London (1866), pp.301–2; Regesta regum Anglo-Normannorum III, No. 345; i, fol. 66a; i, fol. 70b; Chibnall, English Lands of Abbey of Bec (1951), No. XV; i, fol. 009a; i, fol. 70a; i, fol. 70b; i, fol. 70b; i, fol. 70b; i, fol. 70b; i, fol. 212b; i, fol. 212b; i, fol. 70a; i, fol. 006b; i, fol. 006c; i, fol. 80c; i, fol. 46c; i, fol. 80c; i, fol. 80c; i, fol. 145a; i, fol. 009a; i, fol. 143a; i, fol. 144d; i, fol. 129d; i, fol. 70a; i, fol. 69d; i, fol. 67c; i, fol. 98b; i, fol. 160a; i, fol. 249b; i, fol. 154a; i, fol. 70a; i, fol. 70a; i, fol. 169b; i, fol. 62d; i, fol. 169a; i, fol. 169b; i, fol. 169b; i, fol. 169a; i, fol. 169a; i, fol. 205d; i, fol. 46c; i, fol. 160a; i, fol. 212a; i, fol. 98b; i, fol. 169a; Regesta regum Anglo-Normannorum III, No. 818

Ernulf Silvaticus
Domesday tenant of Baldwin abbot of Bury St Edmunds and one of the knights of the abbey (Douglas, Feudal Book, intro., pp. lxxxiv–v); his byname is provided by the Feudal Book. His successor in 1166 was Hugh de Eleigh.

ii, fol. 363a; ii, fol. 360a; ii, fol. 359b; ii, fol. 359b; Douglas, Feudal Documents from Bury St Edmunds, No. 170

Ernulf []
Domesday tenant of Ilbert de Lacy of Pontefract and benefactor of St Clement at Pontefract (EYC iii, 1492).

i, fol. 316b; i, fol. 316b; i, fol. 316b; i, fol. 316b

Esber Biga
Englishman, occurs Domesday Kent.

i, fol. 001a; Ballard, Inquisition of St Augustine's (1920), fols 20r–23v; Ballard, Inquisition of St Augustine's (1920), fols 20r–23v; Ballard, Inquisition of St Augustine's (1920), fols 24r–28r

Esilia Mater Rotberti Malet
Daughter of Gilbert I Crispin de Tillières and Gunnor d'Aunou. She married William Malet of Graville-Sainte-Honorine, a vassal of the Giffards of Longueville who had landed interests in England in 1066. Mother of a large family, she was briefly imprisoned with the youngest of her children and her husband by the Danes at York in 1069. Her husband died c.1071, leaving her as a wealthy widow disposing of considerable property in dower in Suffolk, where she was recorded as a tenant of her son Robert in Domesday Book. K. S. B. Keats-Rohan, 'Domesday Book and the Malets', Nottingham Medieval Studies xli (1997), 13–51.

Brown, Eye Priory Cartulary (1992–94), No. 1; ii, fol. 310b; ii, fol. 320b; ii, fol. 320b; ii, fol. 417b; ii, fol. 155a; ii, fol. 310b; ii, fol. 322b; ii, fol. 323b; ii, fol. 323b; ii, fol. 323b; ii, fol. 320a; ii, fol. 322a; ii, fol. 320b; ii, fol. 322a; ii, fol. 320b; ii, fol. 318b; ii, fol. 320b; ii, fol. 326a; ii, fol. 322a; ii, fol. 326a; ii, fol. 305a; ii, fol. 325a; ii, fol. 329a; ii, fol. 317b; ii, fol. 317b; ii, fol. 322a; ii, fol. 304b; ii, fol. 320b; ii, fol. 305a; ii, fol. 305b; ii, fol. 322a; ii, fol. 322a; ii, fol. 322a; ii, fol. 322a; ii, fol. 322a; ii, fol. 324b

Estrild Monialis

English nun, occurs Domesday Middlesex.

i, fol. 130c

Eudo Dapifer

Norman, son of Hubert de Ryes, Calvados, arr. Bayeux (Loyd, 40). Dapifer to William I and II and Henry I, he held land of the honour of Préaux in Normandy. In 1086 he held a major tenancy-in-chief in ten counties. Some of his land had earlier been held by the Breton Lisoius de Moutiers, who forfeited his holdings in 1075. In 1086 one of his tenants was Osbert, husband of his sister Muriel. Soon afterwards he acquired the land previously held by his brother Adam, a tenant of Odo of Bayeux. He also took over the tenancy of other fiefs, those of Roger and William de Auberville in Hertfordshire, and of Sasselin in Essex. In 1096–7 he refounded the abbey of St John the Baptist at Colchester. He married Rohais, daughter of Richard de Clare, by whom he had issue a daughter Margaret, wife first of William I de Mandeville and secondly of Otuer fitz Count. He died early in 1120 at his castle of Préaux and was buried at Colchester abbey on 28 February. His honour was then taken over by Henry I and its partial dismemberment quickly followed. See Farrer, HKF iii, 164–8.

ii, fol. 019a; Regesta regum Anglo-Normannorum III, No. 58; ii, fol. 240b; ii, fol. 279b; i, fol. 139b; i, fol. 197d; i, fol. 139a; i, fol. 197d; i, fol. 139a; i, fol. 210d; ii, fol. 240b; ii, fol. 240a; ii, fol. 050a; ii, fol. 240b; ii, fol. 050a; ii, fol. 239b; ii, fol. 402b; ii, fol. 240b; ii, fol. 240b; ii, fol. 403a; ii, fol. 403b; ii, fol. 403a; ii, fol. 403a; ii, fol. 403a; ii, fol. 403a; ii, fol. 402b; ii, fol. 239b; i, fol. 212b; ii, fol. 018b; i, fol. 56d; i, fol. 139a; ii, fol. 049a; i, fol. 212b; i, fol. 132a; ii, fol. 018b; i, fol. 212b; i, fol. 61c; i, fol. 212b; i, fol. 212b; ii, fol. 240a; ii, fol. 006b; ii, fol. 107b; ii, fol. 051b; ii, fol. 051b; ii, fol. 055a; ii, fol. 049b; ii, fol. 049b; i, fol. 215a; ii, fol. 051a; ii, fol. 106a; ii, fol. 050b; ii, fol. 050b; i, fol. 212b; King, Peterborough Descriptio Militum (1969), pp. 97–101; i, fol. 336d; ii, fol. 240a; ii, fol. 240a; i, fol. 205d; i, fol. 205d; ii, fol. 404b; ii, fol. 240a; Dugdale, Monasticon Anglicanum, II, p. 267, No. XI; Dugdale, Monasticon Anglicanum, II, p. 267, No. X; King, Peterborough Descriptio Militum (1969), pp. 97–101; Northants Survey, fols 94r–95v; i, fol. 43c,d; Dugdale, Monasticon Anglicanum, III, pp. 299–300, No. I; Pipe Roll 31 Henry I, 103–bd; Pipe Roll 31 Henry I, 066–kn; Northants Survey, fols 94r–95v; Pipe Roll 31 Henry I, 138a–e; Red Book of the Exchequer, ed. Hall (1897), pp. 354–56; Pipe Roll 31 Henry I, 138b–e; Regesta regum Anglo-Normannorum III, No. 275; Pipe Roll 31 Henry I, 060–e; Pipe Roll 31 Henry I, 139–e; Tremlett and Blakiston, Stogursey Charters (1949), No. 1; ii, fol. 049a; ii, fol. 402b; ii, fol. 239b; Dugdale, Monasticon Anglicanum, III, p. 216, No. IV; Gibbs, Early Charters of St Pauls (1939), No. 16; Gibbs, Early Charters of St Pauls (1939), No. 11; Gibbs, Early Charters of St Pauls (1939), No. 32; Dugdale, Monasticon Anglicanum, III, p. 217, No. VI; Hart, Cartularium Monasterii de Rameseia, No. CLII; Dugdale, Monasticon Anglicanum, II, p. 18, No. IX; Gibbs, Early Charters of St Pauls (1939), No. 24; Hart, Cartularium Monasterii de Rameseia, No. CLI; Douglas, Feudal Documents from Bury St Edmunds, No. 19; Dugdale, Monasticon Anglicanum, IV, p. 148, No. I; Clay, Early Yorkshire Charters (1939), VI, No. 2; Mason, Beauchamp Cartulary Charters (1980), No. 159; Fisher, Cartularium Prioratus de Colne (Earles C.), No. 3; Gibbs, Early Charters of St Pauls (1939), No. 29; Clay, Early Yorkshire Charters (1939), VI, No. 4; Northants Survey, fols 96r–99v; i, fol. 47b; i, fol. 212b; i, fol. 227a; i, fol. 205d; i, fol. 139a; i, fol. 47b; i, fol. 227a; i, fol. 215b

Eudo De Mumbi
Breton tenant of Count Alan in 1086; named from his manor of Mumby, Lincolnshire, in the Lindsey Survey of 1115/18. Alan fitz Eudo of Mumby occurs from 1129/30. EYC v, 279–81.

> i, fol. 347d; i, fol. 347d; Lindsey Survey, BL ms Cotton Claudius C v, fols 19–27; i, fol. 340d; i, fol. 348c; i, fol. 348c; i, fol. 348d; i, fol. 348d; i, fol. 348d; i, fol. 348d; Lindsey Survey, BL ms Cotton Claudius C v, fols 9–18

Eudo Filius Nigelli
Norman, tenant of Robert of Mortain in Domesday Suffolk.

> ii, fol. 292a; ii, fol. 292a; ii, fol. 292a; ii, fol. 292a; ii, fol. 292a; ii, fol. 292a

Eudo Filius Spireuuic
Breton tenant-in-chief in Domesday Suffolk and Lincolnshire, ancestor of the Tattershalls of Tattershall, Lincolnshire, of whom a full account appears in Comp. Peer. xii.1, pp. 645–53. His patronymic is Breton Spirewic He was probably a man of Ralph I de Montfort-Gaël (Ille-et-Vilaine), whose son Ralph II forfeited his holdings in 1075. By the early twelfth century his honour held fees castle-guard at Richmond, one being at Horningtoft, Norfolk. His son Hugh had succeeded by 1118. Sanders, 88; EYC v, 337–8; Lord Curzon and H. A. Tipping, Tattershall Castle; W. H. B., 'The Kirkstead chartulary: De Tateshale', Genealogist n.s. 18 (1902), 89–92.

> i, fol. 340d; i, fol. 343a; i, fol. 359d; i, fol. 359d; ii, fol. 434a; ii, fol. 245b; Lincolnshire Claims (Domesday Book), fols 375a–d; i, fol. 359d; Lincolnshire Claims (Domesday Book), fols 375d–376a; i, fol. 359d; i, fol. 360a; i, fol. 360a; i, fol. 360a; i, fol. 360a; i, fol. 360a; i, fol. 360a; i, fol. 360a; i, fol. 360a; i, fol. 359d; i, fol. 360a; i, fol. 359d; i, fol. 360a; i, fol. 359d; i, fol. 360a; i, fol. 359d; i, fol. 359d; i, fol. 360a; i, fol. 359d; i, fol. 360a; i, fol. 359d; i, fol. 359d; i, fol. 359d; i, fol. 360a; i, fol. 360a; i, fol. 359d; i, fol. 359d; i, fol. 359d; i, fol. 360a; i, fol. 360a; i, fol. 360a; Hamilton, Inquisitio Eliensis (1876), pp. 192–95; ii, fol. 245b; ii, fol. 434b; ii, fol. 434b; ii, fol. 434b; ii, fol. 434b; ii, fol. 434a; ii, fol. 246b; ii, fol. 246a; ii, fol. 246b; ii, fol. 246b; ii, fol. 246b; ii, fol. 246a; ii, fol. 246a; ii, fol. 246a; ii, fol. 246a; ii, fol. 246b; ii, fol. 246a

Eudo []
Domesday tenant of Hascoit Musard in Buckinghamshire

> i, fol. 152c

Euen []
Domesday tenant of Herve Bituricensis in Suffolk. His personal name is Breton. His successor in 1166 was Vivien de Scorneie (Thorney).

> ii, fol. 440b

Euerard Filius Brientii De Scalariis
Brien de Scalariis was, like his relative Harduin, a tenant of Count Alan in 1086 and his son Everard was tenant of another of the count's Bretons, Aubrey de Vere. Scalariis is probably to be identified as the hamlet of Les Echelles in Saint-Germain-en-Coglès (Ille-et-Vilaine). Harduin de Scalariis (q.v.) held the manor of Burwell, Cambridgeshire, under Count Alan in Domesday. Subsequent charters of the abbey of Ramsey relate to Burwell, with Everard's son Geoffrey (de Scalariis) being among the witnesses. It might be true that Everard fitz Brien should be identified with the Everard presbiter de Burewell who gave the church of

Burwell to Ramsey some time in the early twelfth century [cf. IE and Ramsey charters].

> i, fol. 199c; i, fol. 199c; Hamilton, Inquisitio Comitatus Cantabrigiensis, pp. 1–93; Hamilton, Inquisitio Eliensis (1876), pp. 97–100

Euerwin Burgensis
Occurs Domesday Norfolk.

> ii, fol. 117a

Eurard []
Domesday tenant of Geoffrey de Mandeville.

> ii, fol. 063a; ii, fol. 063a

Eurold []
Occurs in Domesday Lincolnshire as a tenant of Jocelyn fitz Lambert. A Eurold attested a charter of Sainte-Trinité de Rouen (Cart., p. 478) concerning Odo Alcepied of Longueville (sur-Scie, Seine-Maritime); a subsequent charter referred to the land at Bili (Billy, Calvados, cant. Bourguébus) once held by Eurold, father of Isembert the monk, from the donor Richard de Portmort.

> i, fol. 359c; i, fol. 359c

Eustachius Clericus
Occurs Domesday Sussex as a tenant of William of Eu. One of the canons of St Mary's Hastings (Suss. Rec. Soc. xliv, 299–302).

> i, fol. 19b

Eustachius Comes
Eustache II count of Boulogne, son of Eustache I (d.1046) and Matilda de Louvain, major landholder in Domesday Book, which also records his second wife Ida of Lorraine; his first wife was Goda sister of Edward the Confessor, an alliance that had originated in the mutual desire of Eustache and Edward to find ways of checking the power of Flanders. Brother of Godfrey bishop of Paris (d. 1095), and Lambert count of Lens (d. 1054), hence also uncle to the Conqueror's niece Countess Judith. In 1066 he was independent ruler of Boulogne, but also a vassal of the count of Flanders as count of Lens and the Ternois. He played a significant role at the battle of Hastings, according to William of Poitiers and the Carmen, but because he quarrelled with the king soon afterwards the Norman accounts are biased against him; his importance was nonetheless clear from the wealth attributed to him in Domesday Book. Eustache was back on the continent by Easter 1067, and in the autumn of that year he led an attack on Dover. At Christmas of that year he was declared forfeit. In 1071 he supported Arnulf III and Richilde of Hainault aginst the usurper Robert the Frisian. His continuing hostility to Robert thereafter led eventually to a reconciliation with William I, c.1074. In 1086 Eustache was the tenth richest landholder recorded in Domesday Book. He died in 1087, leaving issue by his wife Ida Eustache III, Godfrey de Bouillon, duke of Lower Lorraine and Baldwin, later Baldwin I, king of Jerusalem. He also had a daughter [was this the Matilda who was his tenant in Dorset?] married to Conan, count of Montaigu. Father also of a natural son Geoffrey, recorded in Domesday Book. See H. Tanner, 'The Expansion of the Power and Influence of the Counts of Bouologne under Eustache II', Anglo-Norman Studies xiv, 251 ff.

> ii, fol. 022a; ii, fol. 002b; ii, fol. 005a; ii, fol. 005a; ii, fol. 006b; ii, fol. 006b; ii,

fol. 032b; ii, fol. 027a; ii, fol. 031a; i, fol. 137b; ii, fol. 030a; ii, fol. 009a; ii, fol. 030a; ii, fol. 106b; ii, fol. 032a; i, fol. 44c; ii, fol. 034a; ii, fol. 026a; i, fol. 44c; ii, fol. 029b; ii, fol. 103b; ii, fol. 030a; ii, fol. 026b; i, fol. 196a; i, fol. 137b; i, fol. 137b; i, fol. 137b; i, fol. 137b; i, fol. 014a; i, fol. 014a; ii, fol. 026b; ii, fol. 029b; ii, fol. 029b; ii, fol. 027a; ii, fol. 027a; ii, fol. 026b; ii, fol. 027b; ii, fol. 026a; ii, fol. 027b; ii, fol. 028a; ii, fol. 028a; ii, fol. 028b; ii, fol. 028b; ii, fol. 027b; ii, fol. 151b; ii, fol. 303b; ii, fol. 303a; ii, fol. 303a; ii, fol. 303b; ii, fol. 303b; ii, fol. 030a; ii, fol. 151b; ii, fol. 151b; ii, fol. 151b; ii, fol. 151b; ii, fol. 151b; ii, fol. 151b; ii, fol. 151b; ii, fol. 151b; ii, fol. 151a; ii, fol. 032b; ii, fol. 055b; ii, fol. 032b; ii, fol. 151b; ii, fol. 034a; i, fol. 91c; ii, fol. 032b; ii, fol. 032b; ii, fol. 033a; ii, fol. 034a; ii, fol. 034a; ii, fol. 032a; ii, fol. 303a; i, fol. 34b; i, fol. 34b; ii, fol. 034a; Gervers, Cartulary of Knights St John Essex (1982), No. 215; Hamilton, Inquisitio Eliensis (1876), pp. 192–95; ii, fol. 278b; i, fol. 137b; i, fol. 157c; i, fol. 91c; i, fol. 205b; ii, fol. 026a; i, fol. 211b; i, fol. 44c; ii, fol. 151a; ii, fol. 303a; ii, fol. 020b

Eustachius De Huntendon

Sheriff of Huntingdonshire 1080–86. Tenant of Countess Judith, whose mother had first married Engueran II count of Ponthieu. Although Eustache's precise family origins cannot be identified, onomastic evidence surrounding him and his tenants is sufficient to identify him with the Eustache d'Abbeville named by Wace as one of the Conqueror's companions in 1066. Abbeville (dépt. Somme) was in the county of Ponthieu and close to the county of Eu. One of Eustache's tenants was Ingelran d'Eu, also a tenant of Ramsey Abbey, another was Oilard lardarius. The brothers Roger and Rorgo were Ramsey tenants in 1114 (cf. also Freville). Rorgo d'Abbeville and his brothers Simon and Oilard occur as benefactors of the abbey of Bertaucourt in the late eleventh century (BN Coll. Picardie 93, 359, 367). His fief appears to have escheated after his death c.1100. In the Descriptio Militum of Peterborough, dated c.1100–16, Eustache de Winwick occurs, which must refer to Eustache the Sheriff who held the manor in 1086. The entry is anachronistic, since Eustache's fees had already been reallocated, his successor for many of them, Roger de Luvetot, occurring in the same document.

i, fol. 208b; i, fol. 228b; i, fol. 221d; i, fol. 208b; i, fol. 206d; i, fol. 208a; i, fol. 204c; i, fol. 208b; i, fol. 208b; i, fol. 204c; i, fol. 204b; i, fol. 204a; i, fol. 203a; i, fol. 228d; i, fol. 226a; i, fol. 222a; i, fol. 222a; i, fol. 221d; i, fol. 203a; i, fol. 206d; i, fol. 227d; i, fol. 203d; i, fol. 205c; i, fol. 205c; i, fol. 228b; i, fol. 202a; i, fol. 336d; King, Peterborough Descriptio Militum (1969), pp. 97–101; i, fol. 206c; i, fol. 206a; i, fol. 206b; i, fol. 206b; i, fol. 206c; i, fol. 206c; i, fol. 206c; i, fol. 206c; i, fol. 206c; i, fol. 206a; i, fol. 206c; i, fol. 208b; i, fol. 206a

Eustachius []

Norman, Domesday tenant of William de Warenne in Sussex. Benefactor of Lewes Priory. Perhaps Eustache de Torcy, brother of Ricoard. CDF, 116, 1085, for Fécamp was attested by 'Ricuardus de Torce et Eustachius frater eius'.

Clay, Early Yorkshire Charters (1949), VIII, No. 5; i, fol. 26c

Faderlin []

Domesday tenant of Hugh de Port in Hampshire. Son-in-law of the king's servant William Belet, father of Ruald (q.v.). His name is a hypocoristic of the Scandinavian name Fader. There is no suggestion in Domesday, or in the Winton Domesday which mentions his son Ruald, that Faderlin had held land in England before 1066, so he was perhaps a Norman originating in the region of

Port-en-Bessin (Calvados).

> i, fol. 46c; i, fol. 45b; i, fol. 45c; i, fol. 45b; i, fol. 48d

Farman []

Occurs Domesday Kent. Ancestor of the Fareman family of Wrotham; cf. du Boulay, Lordship, 68, 93, 151 note, 154, 265, 391.

> i, fol. 003b

Fastrad []

Tenant of Bishop Giso of Wells and probably a fellow Lorrainer. His son Adelard occurs among the 'milites et ministri' of Giso's successor Bishop John (EEA, Bath/Wells, no. 3).

> i, fol. 89b; i, fol. 89b; i, fol. 89c; i, fol. 89c

Femina Asgari []

Widow. Occurs Domesday.

> i, fol. 132c

Femina Saulf []

Occurs Domesday Hampshire.

> i, fol. 51c

Fenchel Filius Godwin

Englishman, occurs Domesday Lincolnshire and in the Claims, with his three brothers; an antecessor of Eudo fitz Spirewic.

> i, fol. 341b; Lincolnshire Claims (Domesday Book), fols 375a–d; Lincolnshire Claims (Domesday Book), fols 375d–376a

Filia Radulfi Tailgebosc

Daughter and heiress of Ralph Taillebois, wife of Hugh de Beauchamp of Bedford.

> i, fol. 142d; i, fol. 142d

Filia Rogeri De Ramis

Daughter of Roger de Raimes, mentioned as his tenant in Domesday Book. Possibly the same as Roger's tenant Wiberga.

> ii, fol. 082b; ii, fol. 422b; ii, fol. 422b

Filii Arfasti Episcopi

Sons of Bishop Arfast (q.v.) of Thetford.

> ii, fol. 118b

Filii Godrici Malf

The sons of Godric Malf are mentioned in the New Forest section of the Hampshire Domesday.

> i, fol. 51d; i, fol. 51d; i, fol. 50c; i, fol. 51d; i, fol. 51d

Filii Lant []

The five sons of Lant and their mother, occur in Domesday Bedfordshire.

> i, fol. 218d

Filii Osfort []

The four unnamed sons of Osfert occur in Domesday Norfolk.

> ii, fol. 186b

Filius Willelmi De Taon

Norman, son of William de Thaon, Calvados, arr. Caen, cant. Creully (Loyd, 100); Domesday tenant in Kent of Odo de Bayeux; Thaon was part of the fee of Marmion under the bishops of Bayeux. Perhaps the same as Robert de Tham, a tenant of the bishop in Buckinghamshire.

i, fol. 010d; i, fol. 008c

Firmatus []

Domesday tenant of Aubrey de Vere. Occurs as a juror (Firmin) in Chilford Hundred, Cambridgeshire, perhaps also (as Farman), in Staine Hundred. The name is found in Breton, Angevin and Norman documents of the eleventh century, including the Nantais; Morice, Preuves, I, 443–4.

ii, fol. 418b; i, fol. 199d; i, fol. 199d; Hamilton, Inquisitio Comitatus Cantabrigiensis, pp. 1–93

Forne Sigulf

Englishman, son of Sigulfr, occurs Domesday Yorkshire. Benefactor of St Mary's, York. During the 1120s he was a minister of Henry I in Northumberland. His daughter Edith became the king's mistress, and had by him a son Robert fitz Roy; she later married Robert II d'Oilly. Forne was dead by 1129, when his heir was his son Ivo. He was the ancestor of the Greystoke family, named from the barony in Cumberland that he was given by Henry I. Cf. EYC ii, 505ff; Sanders, 50.

i, fol. 330d; Regesta regum Anglo-Normannorum III, No. 119; Dugdale, Monasticon Anglicanum, III, pp. 548–50, No. V

Franco De Falconberg

From Fauquembergues, Pas-de-Calais, identified in Chron. Melsa, Domesday tenant of Drogo de la Beuvrière. Probably father of Robert and William de Falconburg who occur in the early twelfth century. Cf. English, Lords of Holderness.

i, fol. 324c; i, fol. 324d; i, fol. 325a; i, fol. 325a; i, fol. 113b; ii, fol. 432a; ii, fol. 172b

Frater Reinbaldi []

Occurs Domesday Gloucestershire. Brother of Rainbald the Chancellor.

i, fol. 165c

Frauuin []

Occurs Domesday Wiltshire. Possibly the same person as Frawin, Mortain tenant in Cornwall.

i, fol. 74c

Frauuin []

Tenant of Robert of Mortain in Cornwall. He is perhaps the same person as the Frawin de Cornualia who occurs in PR 31 Henry I (160) rendering over £50 for an old debt and 300 gold marks to recover his land.

i, fol. 125a; Pipe Roll 31 Henry I, 160–cn

Fredgis []

Occurs Domesday.

i, fol. 370c; i, fol. 282c; i, fol. 288a; i, fol. 288a

Frodo Frater Abbatis

Brother of Abbot Baldwin of Bury St Edmunds (q.v.), who was a native of the Chartrain. His sons Alan, Gilbert and Hugh attest Bury charters of the early twelfth century.

ii, fol. 363b; ii, fol. 210b; ii, fol. 360a; ii, fol. 366b; ii, fol. 359b; ii, fol. 210b; ii, fol. 368a; ii, fol. 211b; ii, fol. 211b; ii, fol. 359a; ii, fol. 211b; ii, fol. 384b; ii, fol. 281b; ii, fol. 355a; ii, fol. 396a; ii, fol. 355a; ii, fol. 355a; ii, fol. 355a; ii, fol. 355a; ii, fol. 355b; ii, fol. 103b; ii, fol. 092a; ii, fol. 355b; ii, fol. 354b; Douglas, Feudal Book of Bury St Edmunds (1932), pp. 22–37; Douglas, Feudal Documents from Bury St Edmunds, No. 105; Hamilton, Inquisitio Eliensis (1876), pp. 192–95; Douglas, Feudal Book of Bury St Edmunds (1932), pp. 3–21; ii, fol. 354b; ii, fol. 212b; ii, fol. 212a; ii, fol. 212b; ii, fol. 363b; ii, fol. 363b

Frumold []

Domesday tenant of Drogo de la Beuvrière.

i, fol. 324d

Fulbert De Douura

Norman, Domesday tenant in Kent of Odo de Bayeux. Probably named from Douvres-la-Délivrande, arr. Caen, Calvados. He was dead probably by 1127, and certainly by 1129/30, when William fitz Richard accounted in Cornwall to have Fulbert's widow and her dower. His son Hugh (d. 1171/2) succeeded him in the barony of Chilham (Sanders, 111).

i, fol. 009d; i, fol. 212a; ii, fol. 206b; ii, fol. 207b; i, fol. 010a; i, fol. 013d; i, fol. 010c; i, fol. 010c

Fulbert Sacerdos Hermeri

Norman, priest of Hermer de Ferrières and his tenant in 1086.

ii, fol. 207b; ii, fol. 206b; ii, fol. 117a

Fulcher Arbalistarius

Occurs Domesday Devon holding from the king; identified as arbalistarius in Exon. His fief was subsequently absorbed into the honour of Plympton.

i, fol. 117c; i, fol. 117c; i, fol. 117c; i, fol. 117c; i, fol. 117c; i, fol. 117c

Fulcher Brito

Domesday tenant of Abbot Baldwn of Bury St Edmunds. Surnamed Brito in the Feudal Book.

ii, fol. 211b; ii, fol. 209b; ii, fol. 359a; Douglas, Feudal Book of Bury St Edmunds (1932), pp. 3–21

Fulcher De Mayneris

Domesday tenant of Abbot Baldwin of Bury and one of the knights of the abbey (Douglas, Feudal Book, intro. pp. lxxxiv–v), identified from the Feudal Book of Bury. Succeeded by a son Gilbert. Perhaps named from Mesnières-en-Bray, Seine-Maritime, cant. Neufchâtel; in 1107 Walter Tirel de Maisneriis confirmed the grant of his man Ramelin de Mesnil of land in Sept-Meules to the abbey of Tréport (Cart., p. 25); see Loyd, 63. Succeeded by a son Gilbert by the early twelfth century. In 1182 Gilbert fitz Ralph held Fulcher's land for three fees from Abbot Samson (Kalendar, 27 and note).

ii, fol. 211a; ii, fol. 211a; ii, fol. 367b; ii, fol. 366b; ii, fol. 366b; ii, fol. 365b; ii, fol. 365b; ii, fol. 357b; Douglas, Feudal Documents from Bury St Edmunds, No. 170

Fulcher Mala Opa

Tenant of Walter Flandrensis, Robert of Mortain and the Countess Judith in Domesday Northamptonshire. Either an Artesian Fleming or a Norman. He was succeeded by his son Simon, who occurs on the 1129/30 Pipe Roll. Possibly father of Gerard of Withmale and Alfred of Orlingbury, who also appear on the Pipe Roll. Cf. HKF i, 78–80, ii, 341.

> i, fol. 228d; i, fol. 217c; i, fol. 293c; Northants Survey, fols 96r–99v; i, fol. 224a; i, fol. 224a; i, fol. 224a; i, fol. 226c; i, fol. 226c; i, fol. 226c

Fulcher Parisiacensis

Domesday tenant of Countess Judith in Northamptonshire. His byname refers to Paris in France; it possibly relates to an ecclesiastical training rather than a national origin.

> i, fol. 217c; i, fol. 214c; i, fol. 214c; i, fol. 211c

Fulcher []

Norman, Domesday tenant of Roger de Montgomery in Shropshire.

> i, fol. 259b; i, fol. 254b; i, fol. 254c

Fulco De Baiunvilla

Norman, Domesday tenant of Earl Hugh of Chester. Possibly named from Banville, Calvados, cant. Ryes. Cf. HKF ii, 26.

> i, fol. 264c; Barraclough, Charters of AN Earls of Chester (1988), No. 3; Barraclough, Charters of AN Earls of Chester (1988), No. 28

Fulco De Lisoriis

Norman, from either Lisores, Calvados, cant. Livarot, or Lisors, Eure, cant. Lyons. Domesday tenant of Robert of Bully. Identified from Rufford Charters and the Blyth Cartulary (see ibid., p. xxxvi, and EYC iii, 199). By his wife Albereda he had a son Robert.

> i, fol. 319d; i, fol. 278b; i, fol. 284d; i, fol. 284d; i, fol. 285b; i, fol. 285c; i, fol. 285d; i, fol. 286d; i, fol. 278b; i, fol. 319d; i, fol. 319d; i, fol. 320a; i, fol. 286d; i, fol. 285c; Timson, Blyth Priory Cartulary (1973), No. 342; Timson, Blyth Priory Cartulary (1973), No. 325

Fulco Filius Rainfrid

Norman, Domesday tenant of Osbern of Arques in Lincolnshire, and of William de Percy, of whom he was steward, in Yorkshire (VCH Yorks ii, 182). His father Rainfrid became a monk of Evesham and then first prior of Whitby on its refoundation by William de Percy (Mon. Ang. i, 417). In addition to his Yorkshire holdings, he was given a fee at Elkington and Cawthorpe in Lincolnshire by Alan I de Percy. Benefactor of Whitby and St Mary's, York, c.1110–18. Father of Robert (who succeeded him before 1135), William, Gilbert and Hugh. See EYC xi, 92ff.

> i, fol. 329a; i, fol. 323a; i, fol. 321d; i, fol. 354b; i, fol. 354a; i, fol. 354a; Clay, Early Yorkshire Charters (1955), XI, No. 4; Clay, Early Yorkshire Charters (1955), XI, No. 2; Clay, Early Yorkshire Charters (1955), XI, No. 1; Clay, Early Yorkshire Charters (1955), XI, No. 93; i, fol. 329c; i, fol. 329c; i, fol. 329c; i, fol. 329c; i, fol. 329c

Fulco []
Domesday tenant of Alfred Brito in Devon. Possibly the same as Fulk tenant of Judhael of Totnes.

i, fol. 115d

Fulco []
Domesday tenant of Judhael of Totnes. Possibly the same person as Fulk tenant of Alfred Brito.

i, fol. 109b; i, fol. 109b; i, fol. 109b; i, fol. 109b

Fulco []
Domesday tenant of Roger d'Ivry, sworn brother of Robert d'Oilly.

i, fol. 151d; i, fol. 151d

Fulco []
Norman, Domesday tenant of the count of Meulan in Warwickshire. Quite possibly identifiable with the Fulk husband of Hubelina, whose daughter Mazelina was the wife of Samson de Morfarville (q.v.). Some of his holdings were later held by the Butlers of Oversley.

i, fol. 240b; i, fol. 240b; i, fol. 240b

Fulco []
Norman, Domesday tenant of William d'Auberville in Suffolk.

ii, fol. 405a; ii, fol. 405b; ii, fol. 405a

Fulco []
Tenant of Gosbert de Beauvais in Wallington, Hertfordshire, in 1086. Possibly ancestor of the family surnamed from Wallington who occur in the twelfth century (VCH Herts iii, 285).

i, fol. 140d

Fulco []
Norman, tenant in Domesday Shropshire of Roger de Montgomery and Picot de Say. Domesday carefully distinguishes the name of Fulk (Fulco) and another man, Fulcoius (q.v.), though these names are used interchangeably in other documents, so Fulk is to be distinguished from the Fulcoius who was tenant of Rainald de Balliol, Roger's sheriff. Orderic Vitalis names Fulk of Le Pin as one of Roger's tenants (Ord. Vit. iii, 140). As a tenant of the barony of Clun, which survived the disgrace of the Montgomerys in 1102, he may be identifiable with the sheriff Fulk who was described as a 'baron of the county' in the time of Henry I and who has been erroneously identified with Fulcoius (q.v.; Green, Sheriffs, 72).

i, fol. 258c; i, fol. 258c; i, fol. 258b; i, fol. 255a; Dugdale, Monasticon Anglicanum, III, p. 448, No. III

Fulcran []
Domesday tenant of Geoffrey bishop of Coutances in Somerset.

i, fol. 88a; i, fol. 88c; i, fol. 88b; i, fol. 88b; i, fol. 88b; i, fol. 89a

Fulcred De Pesenhale
Domesday tenant of Robert Malet. His origins are obscure, but he was doubtless a Norman either from the Pays de Caux or from the region of Caen. He was a benefactor of Eye Priory, and attested its foundation charter (Cart. no. 1). He was succeeded before 1138 (idem, no. 15) by his son William. Father also of Matilda,

wife of Walter and grandmother of Nicholas of Felsham (Cart. Blythborough, pp. 13, 122).

ii, fol. 327a; ii, fol. 313b; ii, fol. 311a; ii, fol. 313b; Brown, Eye Priory Cartulary (1992–94), No. 1; ii, fol. 313a; ii, fol. 312b

Fulcred []
Occurs Domesday Dorset. Possibly the same person as Fulcred tenant of Geoffrey of Coutances.

i, fol. 83b; i, fol. 83b

Fulcuin []
Domesday tenant of Walter de Douai.

i, fol. 95b

Fulcuius []
Domesday tenant of Count Alan in Cambridgeshire.

i, fol. 194b; i, fol. 194d; i, fol. 194d

Fulcuius []
Norman, tenant in Domesday Shropshire of Rainald de Balliol, sheriff of Roger de Montgomery. Mason, 'Officers and clerks', 247, suggested he was possibly under-sheriff to Rainald, but named him Fulk, which led Green (Sheriffs, 72) to identify him with a sheriff Fulk, described as 'baron of the county', who occurs well into the reign of Henry I. The latter identification is difficult to accept, less because of a perfectly possible confusion of the names Fulco and Fulcoius than because of this man's close involvement with a regime discredited and destroyed in 1102. Perhaps the Fulcoius brother of Alcher/Alberic who attested a charter for Saint-Martin de Sées (Arch. dépt. Orne H 938, 121 cclvii; cf. CDF nos. 656–7, where Round printed the name as Fulk, but recorded the reading of H 938 as Fulcoio). See also under 'Fulco' and 'Alcher'.

i, fol. 259b; i, fol. 259b

Furic []
Englishman, occurs Domesday Suffolk.

ii, fol. 295b; ii, fol. 295b

Game []
Occurs Domesday Yorskhire.

i, fol. 331b; i, fol. 331a; i, fol. 330d; i, fol. 331a; i, fol. 331a

Gamel []
Englishman, a king's thegn occurring in Domesday Staffordshire. Liulf of Audley (one of Gamel's Domesday holdings) accounted a large sum for Gamel's death in 1129/30 (PR 31 Henry I, p. 75).

Pipe Roll 31 Henry I, 075–st; i, fol. 250d; i, fol. 250d; i, fol. 250d

Gamel []
Englishman, tenant at Elland and elsewhere of Ilbert de Lacy in Domesday Yorkshire. Apparently succeeded by his son Leysingr, father of Hugh and Henry de Elland (M. L. Faull and S. A. Moorhouse, West Yorkshire: An Archaeolgical Survey to A.D. 1500 (Wakefield, 1981), p. 243.

i, fol. 316c; i, fol. 315c; i, fol. 316c; i, fol. 316d; i, fol. 316d; i, fol. 317a; i, fol. 317c; i, fol. 317d; i, fol. 331a

Gamel []

Englishman, Domesday tenant of Erneis de Buron, from whom he continued to hold Arkendale. Possibly also a tenant in Lincolnshire. Cf. VCH Yorks ii, 180.

i, fol. 328c; i, fol. 328c

Gamelin []

Tenant of Norman d'Arcy in Domesday Lincolnshire.

i, fol. 361d; i, fol. 361c

Garin Cocus

Occurs Domesday Norfolk holding under Robert Malet.

ii, fol. 156a

Garin []

Domesday tenant of Alberic I de Vere. His son Adam was a benefactor of Colne priory before c.1135.

ii, fol. 076b

Garin []

Norman, Domesday tenant of Ranulf Peverel.

ii, fol. 416b; ii, fol. 072b; ii, fol. 254b; ii, fol. 254a; ii, fol. 254b; ii, fol. 254a; ii, fol. 254a; ii, fol. 254b; ii, fol. 254b

Garmund []

Domesday tenant of William de Moion in Somerset; perhaps the same person as Wimund, William's brother, named in a charter in the Bath Cartulary (p. 38). Warmund (of Portmort) was a tenant in south-west England in 1086, but there was no apparent later connection between his descendants and those of William de Moion.

i, fol. 95c

Garner []

Tenant of Richard de Clare, Domesday Suffolk. His successors by 1166 were the Beaucoudray (Manche, cant. Percy) family.

ii, fol. 038b; ii, fol. 103a

Garner []

Norman, Domesday tenant of Hervey Bituricensis in Suffolk.

ii, fol. 441b; ii, fol. 441a; ii, fol. 441a; ii, fol. 441a

Garner []

Norman, Domesday tenant of Swein of Essex.

ii, fol. 046b; ii, fol. 046a; ii, fol. 044a

Gaufrid De Babingele

Domesday tenant, probably Breton, of Eudo fitz Spirewic. He should probably be identified with the Geoffrey of Babingley who attested a charter of Roger de Valognes for Binham priory in the early twelfth century.

ii, fol. 245b; ii, fol. 245b; Dugdale, Monasticon Anglicanum, III, p. 346, No. II; ii, fol. 434b; ii, fol. 434b

Gerard De Turnai

Norman, from Tournay-sur-Dive, Orne, arr. Argentan, cant. Trun (Loyd, 104), Domesday tenant of Earl Roger in Shropshire. His fees escheated after the death without issue of his daughter Sibil, wife of Haimo Peverel. He was probably dead by the early reign of William II, when his son-in-law takes his place in charters of the earls of Shropshire.

> Rees, Cartulary of Shrewsbury Abbey (1975), No. 35; Rees, Cartulary of Shrewsbury Abbey (1975), No. 24; Rees, Cartulary of Shrewsbury Abbey (1975), No. 19; Pipe Roll 9 Henry II, 03–sp; Pipe Roll 2 Henry II, 44–sp; Pipe Roll 3 Henry II, 089–sp; i, fol. 258d; i, fol. 258d; i, fol. 259a; i, fol. 259a; i, fol. 259a; i, fol. 258d; i, fol. 258d; i, fol. 259a; i, fol. 258d; i, fol. 258d; i, fol. 259a; i, fol. 258d; i, fol. 258d

Gerard Vigil
Occurs Domesday Essex.

> ii, fol. 117a

Gerbod De Friston
Norman, Domesday tenant of Ilbert de Lacy in Yorkshire. Benefactor of St Clement's, Pontefract and perhaps also of Nostell priory. Named from his holding at Walter Fryston. His fees were held in 1166 by William de Friston.

> i, fol. 324c; i, fol. 317b; i, fol. 316b; i, fol. 316b

German []
Occurs Domesday Hampshire in the fief of the monks of Winchester. In 1129/30 Peter chamberlain of the bishop of Winchester accounted for the service of Walchelin fitz German (PR 31 Henry I, 39).

> i, fol. 45a; i, fol. 41b; i, fol. 41b

Germund De Sancto Audoeno
Norman, from Saint-Ouen, Seine-Maritime, arr. Dieppe, cant. Longueville, Domesday tenant of Geoffrey de Mandeville. The Carta of Geoffrey de Mandeville earl of Essex refers to feodum Germundi de Sancto Audoeno, who is identifiable with the Domesday tenant from an early grant to St Albans Abbey by which Germundus de Sancto Audoeno et Cana uxor eius gave tithes in Bolituna, Estawicewurtha, Eastona (BL Cotton Nero D vii, fol. 97r). Germund de Sancto Audoeno occurs as a juror for Broadwater Hundred, Herts, in Inquisitio Eliensis. In 1166 the fee was held by Walter de Cantilupe and Robert Chevacheshulle.

> ii, fol. 062b; i, fol. 149d; i, fol. 139c; i, fol. 139c; i, fol. 139d; Red Book of the Exchequer, ed. Hall (1897), pp. 345–47; Hamilton, Inquisitio Eliensis (1876), pp. 97–100

Germund De Villare
Norman, Domesday tenant of Richard de Clare, father of Swain and Ralph presbyter (Cart. Stoke-by-Clare, nos. 70, 137). He is doubtless to be identified with the Germund de Villare who attested a charter of Hugh Broc for Jumièges in 1088, when Hugh granted the church of Toppesfield which he held of Richard de Clare (CDF, 152). Villare is probably either Villers-en-Ouche, Orne, or Villers-Canivet, Calvados.

> i, fol. 211c; ii, fol. 039b; ii, fol. 102a; Harper-Bill & Mortimer, Stoke by Clare Cartulary, No. 70; ii, fol. 393b; ii, fol. 393b

Gerneber []
Englishman, occurs in Domesday Yorkshire on the Lacy fee.

> i, fol. 317d; i, fol. 316d; i, fol. 316d

Gernio []
Occurs as a king's servant in Domesday Oxfordshire.

i, fol. 160d; i, fol. 154a

Gerold Abbas De Tewkesbiri
Gerald of Avranches, clerk of Earl Hugh of Chester. Monk of Winchester cathedral. Abbot of Cranborne from 1086 until 1102, he transferred the abbey to Tewkesbury that year. He continued as abbot of Tewkesbury until his death on 21 November 1109 or 1110. See Heads, 73. Cf. Ord. Vit. iii, 216, 226ff, who describes the career of the worthy Gerald in Hugh's household, where his preaching encouraged five knights to leave the earl's service to become monks of Saint-Évroul. He had intended to follow them, but illness obliged him to stay in England, where he became a monk of Winchester. Chibnall cites a manuscript history of Tewkesbury Abbey (BM Add. ms. 36985 fol. 1v) as stating that Gerald was the son of a moderately wealthy Norman, Rainald de Breone, who joined Hugh's household in England shortly after 1066. Hugh then had him ordained as his chaplain by Bishop Wulfstan of Worcester.

i, fol. 67c; Dugdale, Monasticon Anglicanum, II, p. 267, No. XI

Gerold []
Norman, under-tenant of Wadard, occurs Domesday Warwickshire.

i, fol. 238d; i, fol. 238d

Gerold []
Domesday tenant of Robert, count of Mortain in Sussex. Perhaps father of Robert fitz Gerold, who attests charters of William, count of Mortain (CDF, 1202, 1205 and note). Probably the same man occurs as Gerard in Dorset.

i, fol. 21d; i, fol. 79d; i, fol. 20c

Gilo Frater Ansculf
Gilo brother of Ansculf, from Picquigny, Somme, arr. Amiens (Loyd, 78), uncle of William, also a Domesday tenant-in-chief. His fief was later known as the barony of Weedon Pinkeny, Northamptonshire (Sanders, 94). He was succeeded c.1100 by his son Gilo II, father of Ralph (q.v.) and Robert, founder of the family of Pinkeny of Moreton Pinkeny. His heir in 1130 was his grandson Ralph fitz Gilo (d. 1158). Comp. Peer. x, 521ff.

Northants Survey, fols 94r–95v; i, fol. 227b; i, fol. 227b; i, fol. 227a; i, fol. 227a; i, fol. 61d; i, fol. 61d; i, fol. 61d; i, fol. 219a; i, fol. 152c; i, fol. 159d; i, fol. 227a; i, fol. 152c; Northants Survey, fols 94r–95v

Girald De Normanville
Norman, from Normanville, Seine-Maritime, arr. Neufchâtel, cant. Argueil, comm. Mesnil-Lieubray (Loyd, 73), Domesday tenant of the count of Eu in Sussex. Identified by CDF 134/39. In 1129/30 he, or his son of the same name, accounted in Leicestershire for half the land of his (maternal) uncle (avunculus) Norman; the other moiety was accounted for by Geoffrey de Clinton, on behalf of Richard de Martinwast, another nephew (PR 31 Henry 1, 83, 86).

i, fol. 18a; i, fol. 18b; i, fol. 18a; Pipe Roll 31 Henry I, 086–1c

Girald De Wilton
Occurs Domesday Wiltshire, priest of Wilton who had held before 1066 and held in 1086 as the king's almsman. Perhaps the same Gerald was a co-tenant with Hugh

of Humphrey de Lisle. The Gerard who held of the nuns of Wilton was probably the same person.

> i, fol. 70d; i, fol. 68a; i, fol. 117a; i, fol. 68c; i, fol. 65b

Girald []
Norman, Domesday tenant of Roger de Lacy.

> i, fol. 184a; i, fol. 184a; i, fol. 184b; i, fol. 168a; i, fol. 184b

Girard Camerarius
Norman, occurs Domesday Gloucestershire.

> i, fol. 163d; i, fol. 163c; i, fol. 162b; i, fol. 162b; i, fol. 166b; i, fol. 166b; i, fol. 163d; i, fol. 163d; i, fol. 166b; i, fol. 166b; i, fol. 166b

Girard Dapifer
Dapifer of Walter de Douai as appears in the Bath Cartulary (p. 39, bis) in a document belonging to the date of Walter's death c.1107. In the 1090s Uluric (q.v.) was dapifer. The Bath document was also attested by a Girardus capellanus.

> i, fol. 91d; i, fol. 95a; i, fol. 111d; i, fol. 111d; i, fol. 111d; Hunt, Bath Chartulary, Som. Rec. Soc. 7 (1893), No. 35

Girard Fossarius
Royal servant, occurs Domesday Somerset; identified as 'fossarius' (ditcher) in Exon.

> i, fol. 98d; i, fol. 93d; i, fol. 90b; i, fol. 90b

Girard Lotaringus
Domesday tenant of Count Alan in Cambridgeshire. His byname, provided in the Inquisitio Comitatus Cantabrigiensis, identifies him as a Lorrainer.

> i, fol. 194a; i, fol. 194a; i, fol. 194a; Hamilton, Inquisitio Comitatus Cantabrigiensis, pp. 1–93; Hamilton, Inquisitio Eliensis (1876), pp. 97–100

Girard []
Held two manors in chief in Devon in Tiverton Hundred; the holdings of a Gerard in Tiverton Hundred of Ralph Paynel were probably of the same man.

> i, fol. 113d; i, fol. 113d; i, fol. 117a; i, fol. 117a

Girard []
Domesday tenant of Robert fitz Corbucion in Essex. Possibly the same as Gerard de Seuci who was mentioned as a benefactor of Thetford by William Bigod (d.1120), brother-in-law of Robert's successor William de Albini pincerna (Mon. Ang. iv, 149).

> ii, fol. 425b; ii, fol. 085a; ii, fol. 086a; ii, fol. 085b

Girard []
Norman, Domesday tenant of Hugh fitz Baldric in Yorkshire.

> i, fol. 327c; i, fol. 327c; i, fol. 327c; i, fol. 327c; i, fol. 327c; i, fol. 327b

Girard []
Norman, Domesday tenant of Robert de Bucy.

> i, fol. 234c; i, fol. 234c; i, fol. 234c; i, fol. 234c; i, fol. 234c

Girard []
Domesday tenant of Gilo de Picquigny in Berkshire. Perhaps ancestor of Ivo de Boveneio (q.v.).

> i, fol. 152c

Girard []
Domesday tenant of Maino Brito of Wolverton.

i, fol. 152a

Girard []
Domesday tenant of Walter fitz Other at Pepperharrow, Surrey. The fee was sold to Ranulf de Broc (q.v.) in the time of Henry I.

i, fol. 36a

Girbert []
Held a small fief in Domesday Leicestershire.

i, fol. 236a; i, fol. 236a; i, fol. 236a

Girold Capellanus
Occurs Domesday Devon. A Gerald capellanus attested a confirmation of William II for the church of Bath in 1091 (RRAN i, 315).

i, fol. 117a; i, fol. 117a

Girold Mareschal
Norman, occurs Domesday Suffolk. Possibly the same man occurs as a tenant of Roger de Raimes in Suffolk and, in Essex, of Swein of Essex. William I granted the land held by Girald mariscalcus in the territory of Caen to Saint-Etienne de Caen (Actes caen. no. 6, p. 69), c.1080–2. Warin fitz Gerold attested a charter of Robert fitz Swein of Essex c.1114/30 (Mon. Ang. v, 22). There is good reason to suppose that the Gerold who held of Swein in the later barony of Rayleigh was the ancestor of the East Anglian fitzGerolds of the twelfth century, starting with the relative rarity of the names Warin and Gerold. Henry fitzGerold (q.v.), steward to Geoffrey III de Mandeville c.1150, was brother and heir of Warin (d. 1158), chamberlain to Henry II in 1154. Both were probably sons of the Robert fitz Gerold whose service of ten knights's fees was given to Geoffrey II de Mandeville when he was created earl in 1141 (RRAN iii, 274–6). Warin fitz Gerold (son of Henry) held half a fee of the Honour of Rayleigh in 1211 (RBE 595).

ii, fol. 083a; ii, fol. 423b; ii, fol. 423b; ii, fol. 083a; ii, fol. 423a; ii, fol. 397b; ii, fol. 044b; ii, fol. 438b; ii, fol. 438b

Girui De Loges
He and his wife Gunnhildr were benefactors of Gloucester Abbey temp. William II (Hist. Glocs. i, 80–1); Gervi's wife held one manor from the king in-chief in Gloucestershire in 1086. Gervi held a manor in Gloucs. from Turstin fitz Rolf. The presumed background as a man of William fitz Osbern suggests that his toponym relates to Les Loges, Seine-Maritime, cant. Etretot.

i, fol. 39a; i, fol. 169c; i, fol. 243d; Regesta regum Anglo-Normannorum III, No. 345

Gislebert Arbalistarius
Norman landholder in Domesday Norfolk and Suffolk.

ii, fol. 268b; ii, fol. 269a; ii, fol. 268b; ii, fol. 268b; ii, fol. 268b; ii, fol. 268b; ii, fol. 269a; ii, fol. 269a; ii, fol. 117a; ii, fol. 444a; ii, fol. 444b; ii, fol. 444b; ii, fol. 444b; ii, fol. 444b; ii, fol. 444b; ii, fol. 444b; ii, fol. 444b; ii, fol. 444b; ii, fol. 444a

Gislebert Basset

Norman, from Ouilly-le-Basset, Orne, Domesday tenant of Robert I d'Oilly in Oxfordshire. One of his sons, Robert, became a monk of Abingdon (Chron. Abing. ii, 145). It was probably he who occurs in the Pipe Roll of 1129.

Pipe Roll 31 Henry I, 004–ox; i, fol. 158b; i, fol. 158b; i, fol. 158c; i, fol. 158c

Gislebert Blund

Norman, Domesday tenant of Robert Malet. Perhaps a brother of Robert Blund (q.v.), whose heir was a son Gilbert; he witnessed William de Rolvilla's charter for Eye (Cart. no. 136). A William Blund occurs in DB Lincs, 49; in the Lindsey Survey his fief was held by William son of Albreda from William Meschin (p. 259). Possibly, like Malet, a native of the Pays-de-Caux. A charter for Saint-Wandrille (ed. Lot, no. 23, p. 68, 1038–48) involved three men from Bennetot (Fauville-en-Caux, Seine-Maritime), viz. Roger Fiquet, Ragenfred Blundus and Ragenfred Calvus.

ii, fol. 311a; ii, fol. 325a; Douglas, Feudal Documents from Bury St Edmunds, No. 107; ii, fol. 316a; ii, fol. 314a; ii, fol. 312a; ii, fol. 312a; ii, fol. 312a; ii, fol. 312a; ii, fol. 312a; ii, fol. 312a; ii, fol. 305b; ii, fol. 305b; ii, fol. 305b

Gislebert Cocus

Occurs Domesday Northamptonshire.

i, fol. 229b; i, fol. 229b; i, fol. 229b; i, fol. 229b; i, fol. 229b

Gislebert Cum Barba

Occurs Domesday Cambridgeshire.

i, fol. 196d

Gislebert De Aquila

Domesday tenant-in-chief in Surrey, son of Richer son of Ingenulf (d. 1085), and Judith, sister of Earl Hugh. From L'Aigle, Orne, arr. Mortagne-sur-Huine (Loyd, 52). Ingenulf fell at the battle of Hastings (Ord. Vit. ii, 176). He married Juliana, daughter of Geoffrey II count of Perche, by whom he four sons, Richer, Geoffrey, Gilbert, and Ingenulf, two of whom drowned in the White Ship in 1120. Served Henry I as a military commander, being granted the honour of Pevensey in Sussex forfeited by William of Mortain in 1106. he died in 1106, when his heir in Normandy 'was his eldest son Richer, subsequently also his heir in England. K.Thompson, 'The lords of Laigle', Anglo-Norman Studies xviii (1996).

i, fol. 36b; Dugdale, Monasticon Anglicanum, III, pp. 377–78, No. III; Gibbs, Early Charters of St Pauls (1939), No. 28; Dugdale, Monasticon Anglicanum, II, p. 267, No. XII; ii, fol. 263a; ii, fol. 263a

Gislebert De Bactune

Norman, Domesday tenant of Roger de Lacy in Herefordshire; probably the Gilbert of Bacton mentioned in Herefordshire Domesday (PR Soc.) rather than Gilbert de Esketot.

i, fol. 184b; i, fol. 184b

Gislebert De Blosseville

Tenant of the Countess Judith; from Blosseville, Seine-Maritime, cant. Saint-Valery-en-Caux. Presumably father of William I de Blosseville, who attested a charter for St Andrews, Northampton in 1113. Cf. HKF ii, 327ff.

i, fol. 217b; i, fol. 152d

Gislebert De Breteuile

Norman, occurs Domesday Hampshire. Sheriff of Berkshire c.1090/4 (RRAN i, 359). In Oxfordshire he held land in the fief formerly of William fitz Osbern, which has led to the assumption that his origin was in the honour of Breteuil. However, other tenants of the fief included Ansquetil de Graye and Robert d'Oilly, who were not men of Breteuil, so the assumption is false. He could have been named for any of numerous Brettevilles in Normandy.

i, fol. 71b; i, fol. 52a; i, fol. 62a; i, fol. 43c; i, fol. 48a; i, fol. 48a; i, fol. 48a; i, fol. 161a; i, fol. 71c; i, fol. 71c; i, fol. 71b; i, fol. 71b; i, fol. 71b; i, fol. 161a; i, fol. 48a; i, fol. 48a

Gislebert De Clive

Domesday tenant of Robert of Mortain in Wiltshire, surnamed de Clive from the manor of Clyffe Pippard in the Tax Returns.

i, fol. 68d; i, fol. 68d; i, fol. 68d

Gislebert De Colauilla

Norman, Domesday tenant of Robert Malet in the honour of Eye, from Colleville, Seine-Maritime, arr. Yvetot, cant. Valmont (Loyd, 30).

ii, fol. 306b; ii, fol. 326b; ii, fol. 326a; ii, fol. 324a; ii, fol. 315b; ii, fol. 319a; ii, fol. 327a; ii, fol. 326b; ii, fol. 327a; ii, fol. 327a

Gislebert De Culumbers

The Domesday tenant of Uffington, Berkshire, of Abingdon Abbey is probably to be identified with the Gilbert de Colombariis who occurs in the Abingdon knight list (Chron. Abin. ii 5). The toponym could refer to Colombières, Calvados, arr. Bayeux, cant. Trévières, or Colombiers-sur-Seulles, Calvados, cant. Ryes.

i, fol. 59b; Stevenson, Chronicon Monasterii de Abingdon (1858) vol. II, pp. 4–6

Gislebert De Esketot

Norman, from Ectot, Calvados, arr. Caen, cant. Villers-Bocage, comm. Epinay-sur-Odon (Loyd, 39), Domesday tenant of Roger de Lacy in Gloucestershire. Identified from his gift to St Peter's, Gloucester, in 1100 (Hist. S. Petri i, 73), which mentioned his son Robert. Richard de Esketot held three fees of the honour of Lacy in 1166.

i, fol. 184c; i, fol. 180b; i, fol. 167d

Gislebert De Gand

Gilbert I de Gand, from Ghent in Flanders. The most nobly born of the English Flemings, he was distantly related to the queen. (Sherman, 'Origins of the Ghent family', Nottingham Med. Studies 22 (1978).) Son of Ralph, lord of Alost, near Ghent, and Gisla. Married Alice, daughter of Hugh de Montfort. Refounded the monastery of Bardney in Lincolnshire as a cell of Sainte-Foi de Conques. Father of Emma, wife of Alan de Percy, a daughter who married Ivo de Grandmesnil and possibly another daughter who married a Baldwin, Gilbert (d.v.p.), Robert, chancellor 1153–4 and his heir Walter, by whom he was succeeded c.1095.

i, fol. 360d; Lincolnshire Claims (Domesday Book), fols 376d–377c; Lincolnshire Claims (Domesday Book), fols 376b–c; Lincolnshire Claims (Domesday Book), fols 376d–377c; Lincolnshire Claims (Domesday Book), fols 375d–376a; Lincolnshire Claims (Domesday Book), fols 375a–d; i, fol. 355b; i, fol. 290c; i, fol. 290c; i, fol. 290c; i, fol. 290c; i, fol. 290c; i, fol. 290c; i, fol. 356a; i, fol. 290c; i, fol. 356a; i, fol. 290d; i, fol. 290d; i, fol. 290c; i, fol.

290d; i, fol. 290d; i, fol. 290c; i, fol. 290c; i, fol. 354c; i, fol. 354d; i, fol. 354d; i, fol. 354c; i, fol. 354c; i, fol. 354c; i, fol. 355c; i, fol. 354c; i, fol. 355c; i, fol. 354c; i, fol. 354d; i, fol. 354d; i, fol. 290d; i, fol. 356a; i, fol. 355d; i, fol. 356c; i, fol. 354c; i, fol. 326b; i, fol. 356a; i, fol. 356a; i, fol. 356a; i, fol. 356a; i, fol. 149d; i, fol. 326b; i, fol. 356a; i, fol. 326b; i, fol. 326b; i, fol. 326b; i, fol. 326b; i, fol. 197c; i, fol. 56b; i, fol. 197c; i, fol. 215b; i, fol. 326b; i, fol. 355d; i, fol. 355d; i, fol. 354d; i, fol. 355d; i, fol. 355d; i, fol. 355d; i, fol. 356a; i, fol. 356a; i, fol. 356a; i, fol. 355c; i, fol. 355c; i, fol. 355c; i, fol. 355c; i, fol. 355c; i, fol. 356a; i, fol. 356a; i, fol. 356a; i, fol. 355d; i, fol. 355b; i, fol. 355b; i, fol. 355b; i, fol. 355b; i, fol. 355d; i, fol. 355b; i, fol. 355c; i, fol. 354d; i, fol. 355a; i, fol. 354d; i, fol. 354d; i, fol. 355a; i, fol. 355b; i, fol. 355a; i, fol. 355b; i, fol. 355a; i, fol. 355a; i, fol. 355a; i, fol. 355a; i, fol. 355a; i, fol. 355a; i, fol. 355a; i, fol. 355a; i, fol. 355a; i, fol. 355a; i, fol. 355a; i, fol. 355c; Lincolnshire Claims (Domesday Book), fols 376b–c; i, fol. 355a; i, fol. 354c; i, fol. 354c; i, fol. 355b; i, fol. 354c; i, fol. 354d; i, fol. 227c; i, fol. 355b; i, fol. 227c; i, fol. 354d; i, fol. 203a; i, fol. 207a; i, fol. 336a; i, fol. 342a; i, fol. 353b; i, fol. 355b; i, fol. 276d; i, fol. 354c; i, fol. 355a; i, fol. 355b; i, fol. 355b; i, fol. 355b; i, fol. 354d; i, fol. 355a; i, fol. 355b; i, fol. 227c; i, fol. 354c; i, fol. 355c; i, fol. 207a; i, fol. 290c; i, fol. 243d; i, fol. 159d; i, fol. 215b; i, fol. 236a; i, fol. 326b; i, fol. 149d; i, fol. 354c; i, fol. 227c; Dugdale, Monasticon Anglicanum, III, p. 547, No. III; Lincolnshire Claims (Domesday Book), fols 375a–d; Lincolnshire Claims (Domesday Book), fols 376d–377c; i, fol. 238a; Lincolnshire Claims (Domesday Book), fols 376b–c; Dugdale, Monasticon Anglicanum, III, pp. 548–50, No. V; Regesta regum Anglo-Normannorum III, No. 124

Gislebert De Noua Uilla

Norman, Domesday tenant of Peterborough Abbey, still holding c.1116. Hugh Candidus, p. 167: Hæres Galfridi de Nevile tenet in Lincolnescire, scilicet in Waletone juxta Folkingham, et Yoltorpe, duas carrucatas terræ, et inde facit plenum servitium unius militis. The Domesday Gilbert was probably the Gilbert who held fees of the bishop of Lincoln in 1115/18 in Scothern and Reepham, which had been held by a Ranulf in 1086. Possibly named from Néville, Seine-Maritime, arr. Yvetot, cant. Saint-Valery; see Loyd, 72–3, Comp. Peer. ix, 491ff.

i, fol. 345d; King, Peterborough Descriptio Militum (1969), pp. 97–101; Lindsey Survey, BL ms Cotton Claudius C v, fols 1–9; Lindsey Survey, BL ms Cotton Claudius C v, fols 9–18; Lindsey Survey, BL ms Cotton Claudius C v, fols 9–18

Gislebert De Salneruilla

Norman, from Sannerville, Calvados, arr. Caen, cant. Troarn, Domesday tenant of Roger Corbet under Earl Roger in Shropshire. He is identified from his grant to Shrewsbury abbey.

i, fol. 255d; Rees, Cartulary of Shrewsbury Abbey (1975), No. 35

Gislebert De Sancto Audoeno

Norman, Domesday tenant of William de Braose in Sussex. Probably the same as Gilbert de Saint-Ouen (sur-Maire, Orne, arr. Argentan, cant. Ecouché), who attests Braose charters; cf. VCH Sussex i, 378–9; CDF, nos. 1110, 1112, 1118. A Ralph de Saint-Ouen was a Braose tenant in Sussex in 1153 (Salter, Oxon chh., no. 9).

i, fol. 28a; i, fol. 28b; i, fol. 28b;

Gislebert De Venables

Norman, Domesday tenant of Earl Hugh. From Venables, Eure, cant. Gaillon. A Malger de Venables attested a confirmation for Saint-Ouen de Rouen by Roger de Clères c.1050/66 (Fauroux, 191). A second Gilbert attested a charter of Warin de Vernon c.1170 (Chester Charters, 160).

> i, fol. 268a; i, fol. 268a; Barraclough, Charters of AN Earls of Chester (1988), No. 3; Barraclough, Charters of AN Earls of Chester (1988), No. 28; Barraclough, Charters of AN Earls of Chester (1988), No. 28; Barraclough, Charters of AN Earls of Chester (1988), No. 3; i, fol. 267a; i, fol. 267a; i, fol. 267a; i, fol. 267a; i, fol. 267a; i, fol. 267a; i, fol. 267a; i, fol. 267a; i, fol. 267a; i, fol. 267a; i, fol. 267a; i, fol. 267a; i, fol. 267b; i, fol. 267a; i, fol. 267a; i, fol. 267a; i, fol. 267a; i, fol. 267b; Barraclough, Charters of AN Earls of Chester (1988), No. 3

Gislebert De Wissand

Domesday tenant of Robert Malet; from Wissant, Pas-de-Calais. Godbert de Witsand attested Robert Malet's foundation charter for Eye (Cart. no. 1). In 1166 Manasser de Wissant held half a fee from William of Avranches, descendant and heir of William of Arques, Robert Malet's brother-in-law, as lord of Folkstone (RBE 192).

> ii, fol. 316b; ii, fol. 306b; ii, fol. 327a; ii, fol. 327a; ii, fol. 327a; ii, fol. 326b; ii, fol. 324a

Gislebert Episcopus Ebroicensis

Son of William fitz Osbern de Breteuil and Alice de Tosny. He became a archdeacon and a canon of Lisieux cathedral, in which capacity he acted for William I on a mission to Pope Alexander II in 1066. He became bishop of Evreux in 1071, and embarked on a long and distinguished career. He consecrated William Bonne-Ame archbishop of Rouen in 1079, and gave the funeral oration for William the Conqueror in 1087. He attended the council of Clermont in 1095 and subsequently took the cross with Robert Curthose duke of Normandy; going to Sicily in the company of Odo fo Bayeux, he conducted Odo's funeral at Palermo in February 1097. He died on 29 August 1112 and was buried in his cathedral. See Bouet/Dosdat, 'Les évêques normands de 985 à 1150', in Les évêques normands du xie siècle, ed. Pierre Bouet and François Neveux (Université Caen, 1995) p. 19.

> ii, fol. 388b; ii, fol. 388b; ii, fol. 388b; ii, fol. 388b

Gislebert Episcopus Lexoviensis

Gilbert Maminot, bishop of Lisieux, 1077–1101, ancestor of the Maminots of West Greenwich, Kent. According to Orderic Vitalis (iii, 18–22) he was the son of a valiant knight, Robert de Courbépine (Eure, arr. Bernay), and was the king's physician and chaplain at the time of his appointment to the see of Lisieux. 'A most skilled physician, he was nevertheless unable to cure himself of his failings as a bishop. . . . Casual and negligent in his worship, he was a tireless devotee of hunting and hawking' (idem, 20–21) A man of great learning, he gathered a number of distinguished priests around him and 'Through his inspired teaching they became learned in arithmetic and astronomy, the many branches of natural sciences and other profound subjects' (idem, 20–23). For all his faults as a priest 'he too great pains to seek out the truth, never hesitating to defend the right with courage, and give justice freely to all who sought it. He dealt mercifully with those wrongdoers who humble confessed their guilt, and gave sound advice for amendment of life to all who were truly penitent.' (idem, 20–1). It was Gilbert who ordained Orderic sub-deacon (idem, vi, 554–5). Gilbert was a participant at the Council of Rouen in 1096 (idem, v, 22–5). He was involved in a dispute lasting ten years with Orderic's monastery of Saint-Evroult. The monks wanted him to bless their abbot, but he refused to do so without a charter by which the abbot promised him canonical obedience. Eventually, in 1091, after the election of Abbot Roger, Gilbert was ordered by the king (William II) to bless the abbot and accept the abbey's customs as they were (idem, v, 260–3). Soon after, Gilbert was one of three bishops involved in the dedication of the abbey church of Saint-Evroult (idem, 264–5). He died in August 1101 (idem, 320).

i, fol. 156d; i, fol. 145d; i, fol. 134d; i, fol. 166d; i, fol. 006d; i, fol. 144a; i, fol. 77c; i, fol. 156d; i, fol. 156d; i, fol. 77c; i, fol. 77c; i, fol. 66b; i, fol. 127c; i, fol. 145a; i, fol. 77c; i, fol. 144b; i, fol. 31d; i, fol. 32b; i, fol. 30b; i, fol. 31c; i, fol. 75d; i, fol. 56d; i, fol. 298b; i, fol. 007a; i, fol. 007a; i, fol. 144d

Gislebert Fauvel
Norman, Domesday tenant of Peterborough Abbey, still holding c.1116. Hugh Candidus, p. 57 (Stapleton, 172 note): wrote of his fees: Primus Gilbertus Fauvel. Hugh Fauvel tenet in Norhamtonscire in Walcote et Suthorpe et pertinentiis suis unam hidam et unam virgatam et dimidiam. In Lincolnescire unam carrucatam in Hilbaldestowe, et inde facit plenum servitium duorum militum.

i, fol. 346a; King, Peterborough Descriptio Militum (1969), pp. 97–101

Gislebert Filius Dame
Norman, Domesday tenant of Ilbert de Lacy in Yorkshire, identified from his grants to St Clement's chapel in the castle of Pontefract, EYC iii, no. 1492. Ancestor of the Stapleton family, he was succeeded by his son Hugh, who occurs c.1120. Cf. Holmes, 'Wapentake of Osgoldcross', Yorks. Arch. Journ. 13, pp. 116–18.

i, fol. 316a; i, fol. 315b

Gislebert Filius Garini
Norman, occurs Domesday Essex.

ii, fol. 004a

Gislebert Filius Goze
Norman, tenant of William de Warenne in Sussex; his patronym is supplied from his benefaction to Lewes Priory.

i, fol. 26b; Clay, Early Yorkshire Charters (1949), VIII, No. 16

Gislebert Filius Salomonis
Norman, minor tenant-in-chief in Domesday Bedfordshire and neighbouring counties. His successor by 1130 was Robert of Meppershal. Cf. Farrer, HKF ii, 380.

i, fol. 217b; i, fol. 216d; ii, fol. 097a; i, fol. 142a; ii, fol. 021b; i, fol. 142a; i, fol. 215b; i, fol. 216d; ii, fol. 097a; i, fol. 216d

Gislebert Filius Turoldi
Norman, Domesday tenant-in-chief. Probably to be identified with Gilbert sheriff of Herefordshire, cf. C. Lewis, Anglo-Norman Studies 7 (1985), 207. Presumably brother of Ilbert fitz Turold (q.v.), sheriff in 1086. He was a landholder in Warwickshire, where he appears to have been identified in a list of barons holding

in the borough as Gilbert Budi, which has been taken to indicate an origin at La Bouille, Seine-Maritime, cant. Grande-Couronne. This identification is certainly incorrect, since La Bouille derives from Latin 'bauucula', derived from 'baua' (mud). He is more likely to have been the Gilbert fitz Turold whose fief at Pont-Erchenfray (Notre-Dame-du-Hamel, Eure) was confirmed to Saint-Evroul by Henry I in 1113 (Ord. Vit. ed. Le Prévost v, 196–9). Gilbert fitz Turold witnessed a charter for Saint-Evroul given by Ralph de Tosny c.1066–72 (Ord. Vit. iii, 126). The byname of his Somerset tenant Walter Cenomannensis (Mansel) further indicates a connexion with the Tosnys.

i, fol. 183b; i, fol. 174c; i, fol. 238a; ii, fol. 093a; i, fol. 98b; i, fol. 243d; i, fol. 186d; i, fol. 168c; i, fol. 176d; Mason, Westminster Abbey Charters (1988), No. 488; Darlington, Cartulary of Worcester: Reg. I (1962–3), No. 21; i, fol. 174d; i, fol. 164d; i, fol. 187a; i, fol. 168c; i, fol. 176d; i, fol. 173c; ii, fol. 093a; i, fol. 166b; i, fol. 168c; i, fol. 168c; i, fol. 187a; i, fol. 175a; i, fol. 87a; i, fol. 187a; i, fol. 187a; i, fol. 187a; i, fol. 186d; i, fol. 186d; i, fol. 181a; i, fol. 175a; i, fol. 187a; i, fol. 183b

Gislebert Frater Roberti Clerici
Occurs Domesday Hampshire as a tenant of the bishop of Winchester.

i, fol. 40b

Gislebert Gibart
Norman, Domesday tenant of Glastonbury Abbey, identified in the Tax Return for Selkley Hundred. He occurs in Winton Domesday (p. 44 no. 63). The fee of Robert Gibart is mentioned in Hist. S. Petri Glocs. ii, 230.

i, fol. 66c

Gislebert Latimer
Domesday tenant of Garsington, Oxfordshire, of Abingdon Abbey. The holding was identified in Chron. Abing. ii 5, milites tenentes, as that of Gilbert the marshal, a probably anachronistic reference to the son of John fitz Gilbert Marshal. Elsewhere, the Abingdon Chronicle identifies Gilbert as Latemer, id est Interpres. He died before 1100, leaving three daughters, married to Ralph Percehaie, Picot and William (ibid., 34–5). William was William de Botendone, who married Gilbert's daughter Agnes; their daughter Adeliz, wife of Robert and mother of Hugh, inherited land in Garsingdon (ibid., 176).

i, fol. 156d; Stevenson, Chronicon Monasterii de Abingdon (1858) vol. II, pp. 4–6

Gislebert Presbiter
Scattered references to a priest Gilbert in Domesday Essex, Surrey and Huntingdonshire are possibly to the same person.

ii, fol. 098a; i, fol. 206d; i, fol. 206d; i, fol. 32b; ii, fol. 098a

Gislebert Presbiter
Gilbert, a Domesday tenant of Roger de Bully, is perhaps to be identified with the priest of that name who attested Roger's foundation charter for Blyth prioy.

i, fol. 285b; Timson, Blyth Priory Cartulary (1973), No. 325

Gislebert Tison
Norman, Domesday tenant-in-chief in Yorkshire. He was dead by 1129/30, when he had been succeeded by his son Adam. At that time his fief had become a mesne

tenancy of the honour of Mowbray. EYC xii, pp. vi; EYC ix, 3–5.

i, fol. 339c; Lindsey Survey, BL ms Cotton Claudius C v, fols 9–18; Lindsey Survey, BL ms Cotton Claudius C v, fols 19–27; Dugdale, Monasticon Anglicanum, III, p. 500, No. VI; i, fol. 326c; i, fol. 326d; i, fol. 326d; i, fol. 327a; i, fol. 327a; i, fol. 327a; i, fol. 327a; i, fol. 326d; i, fol. 326d; i, fol. 326d; i, fol. 326d; i, fol. 326c; i, fol. 327a; i, fol. 326c; i, fol. 326c; i, fol. 326c; i, fol. 326c; i, fol. 326c; i, fol. 326c; i, fol. 326c; i, fol. 326c; i, fol. 326c; i, fol. 326c; i, fol. 291a; i, fol. 291a; i, fol. 291a; i, fol. 291a; i, fol. 291a; i, fol. 326d; i, fol. 291a; i, fol. 326d; i, fol. 327a; i, fol. 326d; i, fol. 327a; i, fol. 326d; i, fol. 327a; i, fol. 327a; i, fol. 326d; i, fol. 327a; i, fol. 327a; i, fol. 291a; i, fol. 291a; i, fol. 326c; i, fol. 354b; Clay, Early Yorkshire Charters (1955), XII, No. 77; Dugdale, Monasticon Anglicanum, III, p. 500, No. VII; Dugdale, Monasticon Anglicanum, III, pp. 548–50, No. V; Clay, Early Yorkshire Charters (1955), XII, No. 15

Gislebert Vicecomes
Domesday tenant of Robert of Mortain in Sussex; presumably sheriff of Pevensey Rape under him.

i, fol. 21d; i, fol. 20d; i, fol. 21a; i, fol. 21a; i, fol. 22d; i, fol. 20c; i, fol. 20c

Gislebert []
Domesday tenant of Abingdon Abbey; cf. list of Abingdon knights, Chron. Abing. ii 5.

Stevenson, Chronicon Monasterii de Abingdon (1858) vol. II, pp. 4–6; i, fol. 59a; i, fol. 59c; i, fol. 59c

Gislebert []
Norman, Domesday tenant of the count of Meulan and Thorkil of Warwick in Warwickshire.

i, fol. 241b; i, fol. 241b; i, fol. 240d; i, fol. 240c; i, fol. 240c; i, fol. 240c; i, fol. 240b; i, fol. 240c

Gislebert []
Norman, Domesday tenant of Robert de Tosny of Stafford. Father of Ilbert fitz Gilbert alias Ilbert of Tene, Robert and William (Salt. Soc. ii pt 1, 217). Ilbert succeeded him before 1129/30.

i, fol. 249c; i, fol. 248d; i, fol. 248d; i, fol. 248d; i, fol. 248d

Gislebert []
A Gilbert held a group of manors in Domesday Suffolk which were afterwards held by the Bigods of the honour of Eye, possibly by grant of King Stephen (Eye Cart ii, p. 73)

ii, fol. 308b; ii, fol. 306b; ii, fol. 307a; ii, fol. 307a; ii, fol. 307a; ii, fol. 307a; ii, fol. 307a; ii, fol. 307a; ii, fol. 307a

Gislebert []
Occurs Domesday Kent as a tenant of St Augustine's.

Ballard, Inquisition of St Augustine's (1920), fols 24r–28r; i, fol. 012c

Gislebert []
Domesday tenant of William fitz Ansculf de Picquigny in Staffordshire. In 1166 his successor Ralph de Euenefeld held two fees of Gervaise Paynel.

i, fol. 249d; i, fol. 249d; i, fol. 249d

Giso Episcopus Wellensis

Giso, a Lorrainer recruited by Edward the Confessor, bishop of Wells from 1060 until his death in 1088. See S. Keynes, 'Giso, Bishop of Wells', Anglo-Norman Studies 19 (1997).

i, fol. 89b; i, fol. 86b; i, fol. 87a; i, fol. 89b; i, fol. 89b; i, fol. 89b; i, fol. 89b; i, fol. 89b; i, fol. 89b; i, fol. 89b; i, fol. 89c; i, fol. 89c; i, fol. 89c; i, fol. 89c; i, fol. 89c; i, fol. 89c; i, fol. 89c; i, fol. 89b; i, fol. 89b

Giuold []

Occurs Domesday Somerset as tenant of William de Moion. Cf. Alfred de Baionvilla.

i, fol. 94d

Gladiou Joculator

Tenant of William de Warenne in Domesday Essex, surnamed joculator in the Lewes Cart. He should perhaps be identified with Cadio (q.v.), a Domesday tenant of Count Alan in Lincolnshire.

ii, fol. 037a

Gleu []

Important Breton tenant of Alfred de Lincoln; perhaps his dapifer and relative; ancestor of the de Rothwell family of Lincolnshire. Father of Alan and Robert (Danelaw Ch. 309).

i, fol. 366b; i, fol. 358c; i, fol. 358c; i, fol. 357d; i, fol. 357d; i, fol. 215c

Goda []

Englishwoman, occurs Domesday Colchester

ii, fol. 105a; ii, fol. 105b; ii, fol. 104b; ii, fol. 105b; ii, fol. 104b; ii, fol. 106a; ii, fol. 105a

Godebold Arbalistarius

Norman, or perhaps Picard, he held land of the king Domesday Devon and Somerset; identified as arbalistarius in the Exon Tax Returns, fol. 502a. Possibly occurs also as a king's thegn in Berkshire. Cf. Godbald whose grant of land at Bosville, Seine-Maritime, cant. Cany-Barville, held of William de Grainville-la-Teinturière, was confirmed to Jumièges c.1060/66 (Fauroux, 220).

i, fol. 63d; i, fol. 98b; i, fol. 61a; i, fol. 98b; i, fol. 117b; i, fol. 117b; i, fol. 117b; i, fol. 117b; i, fol. 117b; i, fol. 117b; i, fol. 117b; i, fol. 117b; i, fol. 117a; i, fol. 117a; i, fol. 117a; i, fol. 117a; i, fol. 117b; i, fol. 117b

Godebold Francus

Norman, tenant of Swein of Essex. According to the foundation charter of Horkesley priory, given by his son Robert Godbald, his wife was named Raginild (Mon. Ang. v, 156), by whom he had issue Robert, Richard and Havisa, possibly the wife of an Osbert fitz Hugh. Described as a 'baron' of Robert fitz Swein when he attended the funeral of Swein of Essex at Westminster (C. Hart, Early Essex Charters, Leicester Univ. Press, 1971, no. 99).

ii, fol. 046a; ii, fol. 047a; ii, fol. 047a; ii, fol. 043b; Dugdale, Monasticon Anglicanum, IV, pp. 156–57, No. I

Godebold Presbiter

Norman, identified by Orderic Vitalis, ii 62, as one of three principal clerks to Roger de Montgomery (Mason, Officers and Clerks, TSAS lvi, 1960, 245–7). He was tenant and sub-tenant (under Helgot) of Roger in Domesday Shrosphire.

i, fol. 253a; i, fol. 259c; i, fol. 253a; i, fol. 253a; Rees, Cartulary of Shrewsbury Abbey (1975), No. 35; i, fol. 258c; i, fol. 253a; Rees, Cartulary of Shrewsbury Abbey (1975), No. 35

Godefrid Arbalistarius
Man of Archbishop Lanfranc, identified from Dom. Mon. Cf. du Boulay, Lordship, 96, 384, 387.

i, fol. 003d

Godefrid Camerarius
Occurs Domesday Devon as tenant of Baldwin of Exeter. Identified as chamberlain in Exon. Cf. Mason, 'Barons and officials', ANS 13 (1991), p. 247.

i, fol. 106c; i, fol. 106c

Godefrid Clericus
Occurs Domesday Sussex as a tenant of Robert of Mortain. Attested William of Mortain's confirmation charter for Lewes priory before 1106 (Lewes cart., p. 75).

i, fol. 22a; i, fol. 20c; i, fol. 22a; i, fol. 21a

Godefrid Dapifer
Occurs Domesday Kent, dapifer of Archbishop Lanfranc, also known as Godfrid of Malling. In Domesday Book he held Thanington. The occurrence of a Godfrey of Thanington in the Milites archiepiscopi of 1093 seems likely , but not certainly, to refer to another person (cf. Douglas, Dom. Mon., 50). Succeeded by the de Lenham family, named after another of Godfrid's Domesday manors. G. Ward, 'Godfrey of Malling', Sussex Notes and Queries 5 (1934–5), 3–6.

Ballard, Inquisition of St Augustine's (1920), fols 20r–23v; i, fol. 16c; i, fol. 004d; i, fol. 003c; Ballard, Inquisition of St Augustine's (1920), fols 20r–23v; i, fol. 004c; i, fol. 004c; Douglas, ed., Domesday Monachorum (1944), p. 105; Douglas, ed., Domesday Monachorum (1944), p. 105; i, fol. 003d

Godefrid De Cambrai
Fleming, from Cambrai, dépt. Nord. His minor tenancy-in-chief in Lincolnshire was added to the barony of Bourne within a few years of 1086. Mentioned, as a tenant of Peterborough, by Hugh Candidus (Chron. 61).

i, fol. 346b; i, fol. 346b; i, fol. 366b; i, fol. 235d; i, fol. 366b; i, fol. 366b; i, fol. 366b; i, fol. 366b; i, fol. 366b; i, fol. 366b; i, fol. 366b; i, fol. 235d; i, fol. 366b

Godefrid De Ciuesfeld
Domesday tenant of Peter de Valognes, and juror in Broadwater Hundred, Hertfordshire. Cf. Lewis, 'Jurors', 35; VCH Herts iii, 87.

i, fol. 141a; i, fol. 141a; Hamilton, Inquisitio Eliensis (1876), pp. 97–100

Godefrid De Petraponte
Domesday tenant of William de Warenne in Sussex. From Pierrepont, Seine-Maritime, arr. Neufchâtel, cant. Londinières (Loyd, 78). Robert de Petroponte and his brother Godfrey were early benefactors of the abbey of Tréport, to which they gave the tithe of Cuverville(sur-Yère), held from Oilard (ibid., note 5). His heir by the early twelfth century was his son William. Benefactor of Lewes priory, he attested a Lewes charter with his son-in-law Nigel.

i, fol. 27b; i, fol. 26b; i, fol. 26c; i, fol. 26c; Clay, Early Yorkshire Charters

(1949), VIII, No. 12; Clay, Early Yorkshire Charters (1949), VIII, No. 13; Round, Ancient Charters (1888), No. 5; Clay, Early Yorkshire Charters (1949), VIII, No. 5; ii, fol. 400a; ii, fol. 399b; ii, fol. 399b; i, fol. 26d; i, fol. 26d

Godefrid Scutularius

Occurs as a king's servant in Domesday Dorset holding land his father had held before 1066. He was possibly an Englishman, since the only other Godfrey in Dorset was one of three knights (milites) holding from the Bishop of Salisbury and the two others were certainly English.

i, fol. 77b; i, fol. 77b; i, fol. 85a

Godefrid []

Norman, Domesday tenant of William de Percy in Yorkshire.

i, fol. 321d; i, fol. 321d; i, fol. 322a; i, fol. 322b; i, fol. 322b

Godefrid []

Domesday tenant of Edward of Salisbury.

i, fol. 69d; i, fol. 69b

Godefrid []

Domesday tenant of Roger d'Ivry in Oxfordshire.

i, fol. 210b; i, fol. 210b; i, fol. 61b; i, fol. 151d; i, fol. 158d; i, fol. 158d; i, fol. 158d

Godefrid []

Domesday tenant of Urse de Abitot.

i, fol. 173c; i, fol. 172d; i, fol. 173c

Godefrid []

Domesday tenant of Swein of Essex.

ii, fol. 045b

Godescal []

Occurs Domesday Wiltshire. His son Osmund was mentioned in a charter of Henry I restoring to Shaftesbury abbey lands usurped from it by laymen (RRAN ii, 1347 and app. clv).

i, fol. 83b; i, fol. 90a; i, fol. 72a; i, fol. 73b; i, fol. 73b

Godeua Comitissa

Englishwoman, wife of earl Leofric of Mercia and grandmother of Earl Edwin. She died before 1086, when her name was entered into Domesday Book in respect of lands not yet regranted.

i, fol. 231d; i, fol. 239c

Godeua Uxor Britrici

Englishwoman, whose identity as wife or widow of Beorhtric emerges from a collation Domesday with Exon and the Tax Returns. Her manors were later given to Ruald fitz Wigan and Guy de Brion.

i, fol. 118c; i, fol. 118c

Godinc []

English tenant of Count Alan. Occurs Domesday Suffolk.

ii, fol. 295b; ii, fol. 295b

Godmund Filius Seric
Englisman, occurs Domesday Herefordshire, often holding or associated with land previouly held by his father Saeric. He held several manors under Roger de Lacy, and may have been the ancestor of the Sarnesfield family; see Wightman, Lacy Family, 158 (who may well be right, but his view that an English toponym is evidence of English ancestry is wholly erroneous).

i, fol. 184d; i, fol. 184d; i, fol. 180a; i, fol. 180b

Godmund Frater Turchil
Englishman, Domesday tenant of his brother Thorkil of Warwick at Great Packington in Warwickshire, and also of William fitz Ansculf de Picquigny. Ancestor of the Le Notte family. In 1210 Henry Le Notte claimed lands at Bushbury and Penn in Staffordshire in right of his great-grandmother Ailleva [Æthelgifu] daughter of Guthmund (Curia Regis Rolls vi, 72). See A. Williams, 'A vice-comital family in pre-Conquest Warwickshire', Anglo-Norman Studies xi, 288.

i, fol. 241a

Godmund []
Englishman, held land in Dorset before and after 1066.

i, fol. 243a; i, fol. 84a

Godric Canonicus Sancti Martini
Canon of Dover in 1086.

i, fol. 002b

Godric Carlesone
Occurs Domesday Kent.

i, fol. 001a; Ballard, Inquisition of St Augustine's (1920), fols 24r–28r

Godric Cratel
Occurs Domesday Buckinghamshire.

i, fol. 153b

Godric Dapifer
Englishman, occurs in Domesday Norfolk and Suffolk in charge of certain king's lands; former steward to the disgraced earl of Norfolk, Ralph de Gael, many of whose former holdings were then in Godric's custody. He was probably related to the earl, a Breton with an English mother. Father by his wife Ingreda of a son Ralph, as appears from charters of St Benet's, Holme, which show that Ralph had a brother Eudo and a nephew Lisewy. Ingreda was perhaps the daughter of the Edwin – husband of an Ingreda – whose land Godric held in 1086. Godwin's predecessor Edwin belonged to a wealthy pre-Conquest family whose estates can be traced from the surviving wills of Edwin, his sister-in-law Wulfgyth and her son Ketel (see EHD ii, pp. 903–8). He appears to have died by c.1114. Cf. Williams, The English, 108–9.

ii, fol. 214b; ii, fol. 166a; ii, fol. 162a; ii, fol. 137a; ii, fol. 199a; ii, fol. 145a; ii, fol. 110b; ii, fol. 204a; ii, fol. 283b; ii, fol. 203a; ii, fol. 286a; ii, fol. 203a; ii, fol. 204a; ii, fol. 204a; ii, fol. 203a; ii, fol. 286b; ii, fol. 277b; ii, fol. 204a; ii, fol. 286b; ii, fol. 286a; ii, fol. 215a; ii, fol. 204b; ii, fol. 286a; ii, fol. 203b; ii, fol. 204a; ii, fol. 286a; ii, fol. 204a; ii, fol. 285a; ii, fol. 182a; ii, fol. 286a; ii, fol. 203b; ii, fol. 355b; ii, fol. 204a; ii, fol. 202a; ii, fol. 286b; ii, fol. 205a; ii, fol.

203b; ii, fol. 204b; ii, fol. 286a; ii, fol. 204b; ii, fol. 204a; ii, fol. 285a; ii, fol. 204b; ii, fol. 285a; ii, fol. 203b; ii, fol. 285a; ii, fol. 285a; ii, fol. 203a; ii, fol. 285a; ii, fol. 285a; ii, fol. 204b; ii, fol. 285a; Douglas, Social Structure of Med. E. Anglia (1927), No. 44; ii, fol. 133a; ii, fol. 204b; ii, fol. 356a; ii, fol. 286a; ii, fol. 203a; ii, fol. 204a; ii, fol. 285a; ii, fol. 203a; ii, fol. 205a; ii, fol. 285a; ii, fol. 285a; ii, fol. 205a; ii, fol. 205a; ii, fol. 285a; ii, fol. 204b; ii, fol. 285a; ii, fol. 356a; ii, fol. 205a; ii, fol. 205b; ii, fol. 203a; ii, fol. 285b; ii, fol. 205a; ii, fol. 205a; ii, fol. 203a; ii, fol. 285b; ii, fol. 331b; ii, fol. 203a; ii, fol. 285b; ii, fol. 205b; ii, fol. 205b; ii, fol. 356a; ii, fol. 285b; ii, fol. 205b; ii, fol. 205a; ii, fol. 007a; i, fol. 309a; Hamilton, Inquisitio Eliensis (1876), pp. 192–95; ii, fol. 285a; ii, fol. 202b; ii, fol. 355b; Clay, Early Yorkshire Charters (1935), IV, No. 2; ii, fol. 285b; ii, fol. 285b; ii, fol. 205b; ii, fol. 285b; ii, fol. 203a; ii, fol. 285b; ii, fol. 356a; ii, fol. 203b; Dugdale, Monasticon Anglicanum, III, p. 87, No. IX; ii, fol. 285b; ii, fol. 286a; ii, fol. 203a; ii, fol. 285b; ii, fol. 285b; ii, fol. 176a; ii, fol. 203a; ii, fol. 285b; ii, fol. 203a; ii, fol. 286a; ii, fol. 203a; ii, fol. 205b; ii, fol. 203a; ii, fol. 356a; ii, fol. 286a; ii, fol. 283b; ii, fol. 285a; ii, fol. 203b; ii, fol. 356a; ii, fol. 203a; ii, fol. 286a; ii, fol. 286a; ii, fol. 286a; ii, fol. 286a; ii, fol. 203b; ii, fol. 203b; ii, fol. 356a; ii, fol. 203b; ii, fol. 202b; ii, fol. 203b; ii, fol. 204a; ii, fol. 355b; ii, fol. 202a; Douglas, Feudal Documents from Bury St Edmunds, No. 12; Douglas, Feudal Documents from Bury St Edmunds, No. 14; ii, fol. 130b; ii, fol. 130a; ii, fol. 131a; ii, fol. 132b; ii, fol. 133b; ii, fol. 132a; ii, fol. 133b; ii, fol. 133b; ii, fol. 130b; ii, fol. 133a; ii, fol. 131b; ii, fol. 133a; ii, fol. 133a; ii, fol. 132a; ii, fol. 131a; ii, fol. 131a; ii, fol. 131a; ii, fol. 131a; ii, fol. 131b; ii, fol. 131a; ii, fol. 133a; ii, fol. 131b; ii, fol. 131b; ii, fol. 131b; ii, fol. 131b; ii, fol. 131b; ii, fol. 131a; ii, fol. 129b; ii, fol. 130b; ii, fol. 130a; ii, fol. 130a; ii, fol. 129b; ii, fol. 130a; ii, fol. 129b; ii, fol. 129b; ii, fol. 129b; ii, fol. 128a; ii, fol. 130b; ii, fol. 130b; ii, fol. 129b; ii, fol. 130b; ii, fol. 134a; ii, fol. 130b; ii, fol. 132a; ii, fol. 133a; ii, fol. 132b; ii, fol. 132a; ii, fol. 132b; ii, fol. 132b; ii, fol. 129b; ii, fol. 132b; ii, fol. 133a; ii, fol. 132a; ii, fol. 132a; ii, fol. 132a; ii, fol. 132a; ii, fol. 132a; ii, fol. 132b; ii, fol. 130a; ii, fol. 132b; ii, fol. 120b; ii, fol. 119a; ii, fol. 128a; ii, fol. 119a; ii, fol. 120a; ii, fol. 120a; ii, fol. 120a; ii, fol. 120a; ii, fol. 120b; ii, fol. 122b; ii, fol. 120b; ii, fol. 119a; ii, fol. 124a; ii, fol. 119a; ii, fol. 123a; ii, fol. 122b; ii, fol. 120b; ii, fol. 122b; ii, fol. 122b; ii, fol. 122b; ii, fol. 133b; ii, fol. 122b; ii, fol. 120b; ii, fol. 128b; ii, fol. 128a; ii, fol. 134a; ii, fol. 128a; ii, fol. 128a; ii, fol. 128a; ii, fol. 129a; ii, fol. 129a; ii, fol. 128a; ii, fol. 119a; ii, fol. 128b; ii, fol. 124a; ii, fol. 128b; ii, fol. 128b; ii, fol. 128b; ii, fol. 128b; ii, fol. 128b; ii, fol. 128b; ii, fol. 129a; ii, fol. 129a; ii, fol. 129a; ii, fol. 119a; ii, fol. 128a; ii, fol. 122a; ii, fol. 121b; ii, fol. 122b; ii, fol. 121b; ii, fol. 121b; ii, fol. 122b; ii, fol. 121b; ii, fol. 122b; ii, fol. 121b; ii, fol. 122b; ii, fol. 122a; ii, fol. 121a; ii, fol. 122a; ii, fol. 122a; ii, fol. 122a; ii, fol. 122a; ii, fol. 122a; ii, fol. 122a; ii, fol. 122a; ii, fol. 122b; ii, fol. 121b; ii, fol. 121b; ii, fol. 123b; ii, fol. 123a; ii, fol. 123a; ii, fol. 122b; ii, fol. 123a; ii, fol. 123a; ii, fol. 123a; ii, fol. 123a; ii, fol. 123b; ii, fol. 121b; ii, fol. 123b; ii, fol. 121a; ii, fol. 123b; ii, fol. 123b; ii, fol. 123b; ii, fol. 123b; ii, fol. 123a; ii, fol. 121b; ii, fol. 121a; ii, fol. 121a; ii, fol. 121a; ii, fol. 121a; ii, fol. 123b; ii, fol. 126a; ii, fol. 127a; ii, fol. 125b; ii, fol. 126a; ii, fol. 126a; ii, fol. 126a; ii, fol. 127a; ii, fol. 126a; ii, fol. 125b; ii, fol. 126a; ii, fol. 125b; ii, fol. 126b; ii, fol. 126b; ii, fol. 126b; ii, fol. 126b; ii, fol. 126b; ii, fol. 126b; ii, fol. 126b; ii, fol. 128a; ii, fol. 134b; ii, fol. 127b; ii, fol. 125a; ii, fol. 135a; ii, fol. 134a; ii, fol. 134a; ii, fol. 134a; ii, fol. 134a; ii, fol. 134b; ii, fol. 134b; ii, fol. 134b; ii, fol. 134b; ii, fol. 125b; ii, fol. 135a; ii, fol. 127a; ii, fol. 135a; ii, fol. 135a; ii, fol. 135b; ii, fol. 135b; ii, fol. 135b; ii, fol. 135b; ii, fol. 134b; ii, fol. 130a; ii, fol. 126a; ii, fol. 124a; ii, fol. 135a; ii, fol. 127a; ii, fol. 133b; ii, fol. 129a; ii, fol. 129a; ii, fol. 129a; ii, fol. 129a; ii, fol.

129a; ii, fol. 129a; ii, fol. 129a; ii, fol. 129a; ii, fol. 129b; ii, fol. 129a; ii, fol. 129b; ii, fol. 129b; ii, fol. 129b; ii, fol. 129b; ii, fol. 130a; ii, fol. 129b; ii, fol. 127b; ii, fol. 127b; ii, fol. 127b; ii, fol. 129a; ii, fol. 124b; ii, fol. 126a; ii, fol. 124b; ii, fol. 124a; ii, fol. 124a; ii, fol. 124a; ii, fol. 124a; ii, fol. 124a; ii, fol. 124a; ii, fol. 127a; ii, fol. 124a; ii, fol. 127a; ii, fol. 125a; ii, fol. 124b; ii, fol. 124b; ii, fol. 124b; ii, fol. 125a; ii, fol. 125a; ii, fol. 125a; ii, fol. 125a; ii, fol. 125a; ii, fol. 124b; ii, fol. 124a; ii, fol. 147a; ii, fol. 147b

Godric De Belesbi
Accounted 5 marks of the pleas of Richard Basset and William de Albini Brito in Lincolnshire in 1130. 20 s. of his amercement was pardoned by the king's writ out of regard for Count Stephen of Brittany (Farrer, HKF, ii, 167). Possibly the same as Godric, a king's thegn who occurs in Beelsby in Domesday Lincolnshire, where he had succeeded his father Agemund.

Pipe Roll 31 Henry I, 116b–ln; Pipe Roll 31 Henry I, 116a–ln; i, fol. 371b

Godric De Burnes
Occurs Domesday Kent.

i, fol. 001a; Ballard, Inquisition of St Augustine's (1920), fols 24r–28r

Godric De Calodelie
Englishman, occurs Domesday Devon; named from Calverleigh in the Tax Return.

i, fol. 118b; i, fol. 118b

Godric De Hecham
Englishman, occurs Domesday Norfolk; named from Echam.

ii, fol. 272b

Godric Latimarius
English translator, as appears from Excerpta; occurs Domesday Kent.

i, fol. 001d

Godric Presbyter
Occurs Domesday Dorset. Identified as priest in the Tax Return for Bere/Barrow Hundred.

i, fol. 84c

Godric Tainus
Englishman, occurs Domesday Herefordshire.

i, fol. 186a

Godric Teignus
Occurs Domesday Buckinghamshire.

i, fol. 145d

Godric Venator
Occurs Domesday Dorset and Wiltshire.

i, fol. 84a; i, fol. 74a; i, fol. 74a

Godric []
Englishman, Domesday tenant of the count of Meulan and Thorkil of Warwick in Warwickshire.

i, fol. 241b; i, fol. 240c; i, fol. 240c; i, fol. 240c

Goduin Bedell
Englishman, occurs Domesday Bedfordshire.
  i, fol. 153b

Goduin Burgensis
Occurs Domesday Bedfordshire.
  i, fol. 218b; i, fol. 30b

Goduin Clecus
Occurs Domesday Wiltshire.
  i, fol. 74a

Goduin Cudhen
Occurs Domesday Essex.
  ii, fol. 017b; ii, fol. 099a; ii, fol. 099a

Goduin De Cicemetona
English thegn, occurs Domesday Devon; named from Chittlehampton in the Tax Return.
  i, fol. 118a; i, fol. 118a; i, fol. 118a; i, fol. 118a; i, fol. 118a; i, fol. 118a; i, fol. 118a; i, fol. 118a; i, fol. 118a

Goduin De Horemera
Englishman, occurs Domesday Hertfordshire; named from Hormead as a juror for Broadwater Hundred.
  Hamilton, Inquisitio Eliensis (1876), pp. 97–100; i, fol. 142a; i, fol. 142a

Goduin De Stantone
Englishman, occurs Domesday Gloucestershire.
  i, fol. 164b

Goduin Diaconus
Englishman, occurs Domesday Essex.
  ii, fol. 098b

Goduin Haldein
Englishman holding land in Domesday Norfolk. He left descendants surnamed Haldein or Haltein.
  ii, fol. 271a; ii, fol. 271b; ii, fol. 271b; ii, fol. 271b; ii, fol. 271b; ii, fol. 271b; ii, fol. 271a; ii, fol. 138a

Goduin Prepositus
Occurs Domesday Dorset.
  i, fol. 84b

Goduin Presbiter
Englishman, occurs Domesday Devon; identified as a priest in Exon.
  i, fol. 104c

Goduin Presbiter
Occurs Domesday Buckinghamshire.
  i, fol. 153a

Goduin Presbiter
Occurs Domesday Somerset; identified as a priest in Exon.
i, fol. 90d

Goduin Presbiter
English tenant of William Peverel of Nottingham in 1086. Some of the land he had held before 1066 was in Peverel's demesne in 1086. His holdings descended in the Stredlegh family (named from Strelley), of whom Walter, second husband of Isilia, occurs temp. Henry I. See HKF i, 178.
i, fol. 288a; i, fol. 287c

Goduin Presbiter
Englishman, occurs Domesday Northamptonshire.
i, fol. 222d; i, fol. 222d; i, fol. 222d; i, fol. 219a

Goduin Venator
Occurs Domesday Dorset.
i, fol. 84b; i, fol. 84b

Goduin []
English tenant of Robert of Mortain in Domesday Cornwall.
i, fol. 124d

Goduin []
English tenant of Guy de Craon in 1086.
i, fol. 367c; i, fol. 368b; i, fol. 368b

Goduinus Accipitrarius
Occurs Domesday Hampshire.
i, fol. 50d

Goduinus Anglicus
Occurs in Domesday Essex as a tenant of Robert fitz Roscelin.
ii, fol. 097a

Goduui Anglicus
Occurs Domesday Bedfordshire as a tenant of Eustache of Boulogne.
i, fol. 211b

Goduuidere De Bedeford
Occurs Domesday Bedfordshire.
i, fol. 218d

Goduuin Uuachefet
Occurs Domesday Essex with his unnamed sons.
ii, fol. 104b

Goduuin []
Englishman, occurs Domesday Norfolk as tenant of Roger Bigod.
ii, fol. 186a; ii, fol. 186a; ii, fol. 186a; ii, fol. 186a; ii, fol. 186a; ii, fol. 186b; ii, fol. 186b; ii, fol. 186b; ii, fol. 186b; ii, fol. 186a

Godwin Burgensis
Occurs Domesday Norfolk.
ii, fol. 117a

Godwin Filius Tuka

Englishman, occurs Domesday Suffolk.

ii, fol. 335b

Goisbert De Beluaco

From Beauvais, Oise, an area under the king of France where several Norman border families, including the de Gurnai, held land. His fief seems to have escheated by the early twelfth century and was given to Rainald d'Argentan (VCH Herts iii, 86–7, 182–3).

Hamilton, Inquisitio Eliensis (1876), pp. 97–100; i, fol. 140d; i, fol. 140d; i, fol. 140d

Goisbert []

Domesday tenant of Theobald fitz Berner in Devon. His successor in 1166 was Joel de Hole (South Hole), who held four fees of the honour of Great Torrington.

i, fol. 115c; i, fol. 115b; i, fol. 115b; i, fol. 115b

Goisbert []

Domesday tenant of Robert de Tosny of Stafford in Oxfordshire.

i, fol. 158a; i, fol. 158a; i, fol. 158a

Goisfrid Alselin

Norman. Major tenant-in-chief in the Midland counties in Domesday Book. He appears originally to have been established with a brother and co-parcener (cf. Walter and Gotshelm of Claville, and Ralph and William Capra de Pomeroy), but by 1086 the brother had been succeeded by his son Ralph de Calz. The two holdings descended separately, with Geoffrey's share going to his son Ralph Halselinus, and Ralph de Calz's to Robert de Calz. Geoffrey was dead by 1129 when both his and his nephew's heirs appear on the Pipe Roll. His surname may be a patronymic. He was possibly related to the Halselin or Hanselin who was a knight of William de Braose (Briouze, Orne) in Sussex. A west Norman origin is probable for this family. The fee of Peter Alselin at Feugerolles was mentioned in a confirmation for the abbey of Mont-Morel by Bishop Alexander of Coutances. Ralph de Calz is very likely to have been named from La Chaux, Orne, not far from Briouze.

i, fol. 276d; i, fol. 369c; i, fol. 370a; i, fol. 289b; i, fol. 370a; i, fol. 289b; i, fol. 369c; i, fol. 370a; i, fol. 369c; i, fol. 280a; i, fol. 369d; i, fol. 369d; i, fol. 369d; i, fol. 369d; i, fol. 369d; i, fol. 369d; i, fol. 275c; i, fol. 369c; i, fol. 276d; i, fol. 276d; i, fol. 276d; i, fol. 276d; i, fol. 276d; i, fol. 276d; i, fol. 370a; i, fol. 276d; i, fol. 289b; i, fol. 274c; i, fol. 369d; i, fol. 369d; i, fol. 289b; i, fol. 289b; i, fol. 227b; i, fol. 227b; i, fol. 280b; i, fol. 276d; i, fol. 289b; i, fol. 289b; i, fol. 326a; i, fol. 289b; i, fol. 369d; i, fol. 289b; i, fol. 289b; i, fol. 289b; i, fol. 289b; i, fol. 289b; i, fol. 289b; i, fol. 289c; i, fol. 336a; i, fol. 289b; i, fol. 336b; i, fol. 289b; i, fol. 326a; i, fol. 326a; i, fol. 326a; i, fol. 289b; i, fol. 326a; i, fol. 289b; i, fol. 326a; i, fol. 289b; i, fol. 289c; i, fol. 289c; i, fol. 289b; i, fol. 289c; i, fol. 289b; i, fol. 219a; i, fol. 369d; i, fol. 369d; i, fol. 235c; i, fol. 227b; i, fol. 326a; i, fol. 289b; Dugdale, Monasticon Anglicanum, III, pp. 392–93, No. II; Lindsey Survey, BL ms Cotton Claudius C v, fols 9–18; Lindsey Survey, BL ms Cotton Claudius C v, fols 9–18

Goisfrid Bainard

A major tenant of Ralph Bainard in 1086, he was presumably Ralph's son and successor of the same name (Sanders, 129). Ralph died around the time of Domesday Book. Between 1077 and 1081 William I confirmed to the Abbey of Saint-Leger de Préaux the grant of the church of Les Rostes by a Godefridus who is thought to have been the Goisfrid Bainard who attested the pancarte of Préaux (Neustria Pia 520f) with Adeliza his wife and William filius Bainardi. Rostes in now a hamlet of the commune of Saint-Leger-des-Rôtes, Eure (V. Gazeau, Annales de Normandie 22, 1988). He subsequently acquired land in Yorkshire of which he was sheriff c.1089–95. According to the Anglo-Saxon Chronicle (E, 1095), he accused William count of Eu of treachery to the king and then overcame him in combat, upon which William was so severely punished that he died of his injuries. Geoffrey was succeeded by his son William, disgraced in 1110, who was probably the William nepos Radulfi of Domesday Book. He was an early benefactor of Little Dunmow priory, making grants for the souls of his parents and uncle (auunculus), and the salvation of Henry I and his wife, his own wife, brother and children (meis liberis), attested by A. his wife and R. his son (BL Harley 662, fol. 6r).

ii, fol. 248b; ii, fol. 248a; ii, fol. 253a; ii, fol. 251b; ii, fol. 250a; ii, fol. 250a; ii, fol. 248b; ii, fol. 248a; ii, fol. 248b; ii, fol. 248b; ii, fol. 248b; ii, fol. 248b; ii, fol. 248b; ii, fol. 248a; ii, fol. 249a; ii, fol. 68b; ii, fol. 095a; ii, fol. 247b; Dugdale, Monasticon Anglicanum, III, pp. 548–50, No. V; ii, fol. 248a; Dugdale, Monasticon Anglicanum, IV, p. 14, No. VI; Clay, Early Yorkshire Charters (1935), IV, No. 2

Goisfrid Camerarius

Probably father of Geoffrey I de Clinton and ancestor of the de Clinton family; from Saint-Pierre-de-Semilly, Manche, arr. Saint-Lô, cant. Saint-Clair (Loyd, 30). See J.H. Round in Ancestor, xi, 156. Occurs in Domesday as chamberlain to the king's daughter Matilda. Founder of the Holy Trinity Priory, Wallingford, a cell of St Albans.

i, fol. 49b; i, fol. 39b; i, fol. 49b

Goisfrid Clericus De Blanca

Norman, from Blanques, Seine-Maritime, comm. cant. Fauville, par. Alvimare, held one of the prebends of Hastings c.1086 as a tenant of the count of Eu (Sussex Rec. Soc. xliv, p. 299). Cf. M. Gardiner, 'Some lost Anglo-Saxon charters and the endowment of Hastings College', Sussex Arch. Coll. 127 (1989), 46.

i, fol. 18b

Goisfrid De Bec

Norman, Domesday tenant-in-chief in Hertfordshire. A Geoffrey Delbec attested a charter of Richard count of Evreux, among others, for Sainte-Trinité de Rouen (Guérard, Cart. pp. 433, 439–40). His fief seems to have escheated soon after 1100. Parts were subsequently granted at different times to Ralph Pincerna (VCH Herts iv, 32), de Clare and Malet of Graville (VCH Herts iii, 37).

i, fol. 133a; i, fol. 140c; i, fol. 136a; i, fol. 136a; i, fol. 140b; i, fol. 140b; i, fol. 140c; i, fol. 135d; i, fol. 132d; i, fol. 140b; i, fol. 132a; Douglas, Feudal Documents from Bury St Edmunds, No. 170; i, fol. 140a

Goisfrid De Burgh

Probably a Breton, a Domesday tenant of Count Alan who took his name from Burrough Green. His successor by the early twelfth century was Thomas de Burgh, father of Philip, fl. 1150/8; EYC v, nos. 256–8; cf. Yorks. Arch. Journ. 30.

i, fol. 195c; ii, fol. 149a; i, fol. 311d; i, fol. 311b; i, fol. 311b; i, fol. 310d; i, fol. 195c; i, fol. 195b; i, fol. 195d

Goisfrid De Floc

Norman, from Flocques, Seine-Maritime, arr. Dieppe, cant. Eu (Loyd, 43), Domesday tenant of the count of Eu in Sussex. One of the canons established at St Mary's, Hastings, by Count Robert, in which post he succeeded his brother Hugh, who must have died before the Domesday Survey (Suss.Rec. Soc. xliv, 299–302, record and confirmation by Count Henry of Eu). Geoffrey can be identified partly through an association with Walter fitz Lambert, who endowed Hugh and Geoffrey's prebend.

i, fol. 20b; i, fol. 19d

Goisfrid De La Wirce

Breton, from La Guerche, dépt. Ille-et-Vilaine, tenant-in-chief in several Midland counties in 1086. Younger son of Sylvester, bishop of Rennes, and brother of William, seigneur de La Guerche; see J.-P. Brunterc'h, 'Puissance temporelle et pouvoir diocésain des evêques de Nantes entre 936 et 1049'. Mém. Soc. d'Histoire et d'Archéologie de Bretagne, lxi (1984), and J.-C. Meuret, 'Familles seigneuriales aux confins Anjou-Bretagne', ibid., lxx (1993), 91ff, He had married Alfgytha, daughter of his English 'antecessor' Leofric of Nuneham (Mon. Ang. vi. (2), 996. There is no trace of him after 1093 in English or Breton documents, though a Hervey son of Geoffrey attests charters of La Guerche in 1115 and 1127. This Hervé was perhaps the same as Hervé brother of Stephen, and of Warin, a monk of Marmoutier at Béré (Arch. dépt. Ille-et-Vilaine IF 3330, Béré no. 9). Geoffrey's English fief was regranted to Nigel de Albini of Mowbray by Henry I. Keats-Rohan, 'Le rôle des Bretons dans la politique de la colonisation normande', MSHAB, lxxiv, 1996, 192–3.

Regesta regum Anglo-Normannorum III, No. 817; Dugdale, Monasticon Anglicanum, III, p. 499, No. I; Dugdale, Monasticon Anglicanum, III, p. 499, No. I; Greenway, Charters of the Honour of Mowbray (1972), No. 1; Dugdale, Monasticon Anglicanum, III, p. 499, No. III; Dugdale, Monasticon Anglicanum, III, pp. 548–50, No. V; i, fol. 326a; Lincolnshire Claims (Domesday Book), fols 376b–c; i, fol. 227c; i, fol. 369c; i, fol. 369c; i, fol. 369c; i, fol. 369c; i, fol. 369c; i, fol. 369c; i, fol. 369c; i, fol. 369c; i, fol. 227c; i, fol. 369c; i, fol. 369c; i, fol. 369b; i, fol. 369c; i, fol. 369c; i, fol. 369c; i, fol. 369b; i, fol. 369b; i, fol. 369b; i, fol. 369b; i, fol. 369b; i, fol. 369b; i, fol. 230a; i, fol. 369b; i, fol. 243c; i, fol. 369b; i, fol. 369b; i, fol. 369b; i, fol. 369c; i, fol. 369b; i, fol. 235c; i, fol. 227c; i, fol. 243c; i, fol. 369b; i, fol. 227c; i, fol. 235c; i, fol. 239c; i, fol. 243c; i, fol. 235c; i, fol. 230a; i, fol. 243c; i, fol. 243c; i, fol. 219a; i, fol. 235c; i, fol. 235d; i, fol. 235c; i, fol. 235c; i, fol. 239c; i, fol. 235c; i, fol. 235d; i, fol. 235c; i, fol. 235c; i, fol. 235c; i, fol. 239c; i, fol. 235d; i, fol. 239c; i, fol. 235c; i, fol. 239c; i, fol. 239c; i, fol. 238a; i, fol. 243c; i, fol. 235c; i, fol. 326a; i, fol. 235c; i, fol. 291a; i, fol. 227c; i, fol. 243c; i, fol. 369b; Greenway, Charters of the Honour of Mowbray (1972), No. 191; Greenway, Charters of the Honour of Mowbray (1972), No. 13; Greenway, Charters of the Honour of Mowbray (1972), No. 192

Goisfrid De Magnavilla

Norman, from Manneville, Seine-Maritime, arr. Dieppe, cant. Bacqueville, now in the combined commune of Le Thil-Manneville (Loyd, 57). Important Domesday tenant-in-chief, with lands concentrated in the south-east. Castellan of the Tower of London. Twice married, to Athelais (Adelais/isa?) and Lescelina, he had several sons, of whom Walter was one of his tenants in 1086; he and Lescelina founded Hurley as a cell of Westminster c.1085. At the same date his daughter Beatrice was the wife of Geoffrey, natural son of Eustache count of Boulogne. He supported the candidature of Robert Curthose as king on the death of William I, but thereafter accepted William II. His eldest son William succeeded him, probably shortly before 1100. See K.S.B. Keats-Rohan, Medieval Prosopography 14.1 (1992), 8ff.

i, fol. 135b; Regesta regum Anglo-Normannorum III, No. 275; ii, fol. 100a; ii, fol. 100b; ii, fol. 100b; ii, fol. 100b; ii, fol. 100b; ii, fol. 100b; ii, fol. 072b; ii, fol. 061a; ii, fol. 012b; ii, fol. 016b; ii, fol. 062a; ii, fol. 060a; ii, fol. 091a; ii, fol. 060a; ii, fol. 057b; ii, fol. 058a; ii, fol. 059a; ii, fol. 060a; ii, fol. 062a; ii, fol. 057b; Regesta regum Anglo-Normannorum III, I, Appendix, no. XXV; Mason, Westminster Abbey Charters (1988), No. 436; Gibbs, Early Charters of St Pauls (1939), No. 14; Gibbs, Early Charters of St Pauls (1939), No. 9; ii, fol. 411b; ii, fol. 411a; ii, fol. 411a; ii, fol. 106b; ii, fol. 413a; ii, fol. 413a; ii, fol. 413a; ii, fol. 412b; ii, fol. 412b; ii, fol. 412b; ii, fol. 412a; ii, fol. 412b; ii, fol. 412a; ii, fol. 413a; ii, fol. 411b; ii, fol. 413a; ii, fol. 412a; ii, fol. 412a; ii, fol. 412a; ii, fol. 412a; ii, fol. 412a; ii, fol. 411b; ii, fol. 411b; ii, fol. 411b; ii, fol. 411b; ii, fol. 411b; ii, fol. 413a; ii, fol. 412a; ii, fol. 413a; ii, fol. 412b; ii, fol. 412b; ii, fol. 413a; ii, fol. 413a; ii, fol. 413a; ii, fol. 411a; ii, fol. 413a; ii, fol. 411a; Gibbs, Early Charters of St Pauls (1939), No. 4; Excerpta a Chronicis de Bermondsey, Dugdale, Monasticon, IV, pp 95–97; Mason, Westminster Abbey Charters (1988), No. 462; Regesta regum Anglo-Normannorum III, No. 274; Regesta regum Anglo-Normannorum III, No. 274; i, fol. 135b; i, fol. 132a; i, fol. 238a; Dugdale, Monasticon Anglicanum, II, p. 267, No. XII; Regesta regum Anglo-Normannorum III, No. 276; i, fol. 162a; i, fol. 62a; i, fol. 243c; i, fol. 159d; i, fol. 227b; i, fol. 62a; i, fol. 135c; i, fol. 62a; i, fol. 36b; i, fol. 36b; i, fol. 36b; i, fol. 140a; i, fol. 139c; i, fol. 139c; i, fol. 151c; i, fol. 139d; i, fol. 62a; i, fol. 243c; i, fol. 227b; i, fol. 149c; i, fol. 139b; i, fol. 129d; i, fol. 129d; i, fol. 129d; i, fol. 127b; i, fol. 129c; i, fol. 129d; i, fol. 149d; i, fol. 149c; i, fol. 149c; i, fol. 197b; i, fol. 149c; i, fol. 159d

Goisfrid De Ria

Domesday tenant of Roger Pictaviensis. Probably to be identified with Geoffrey de Ria, (probably named from Ri, Orne, cant. Putanges-Pont-Ecrepin), who was an early benefactor of Roger's priory at Lancaster, a cell of Sées. See K. Thompsom, 'Monasteries and settlement in Norman Lancashire: unpublished charters of Roger the Poitevin', Trans. Hist. Soc. of Lancs. and Cheshire 140 (1990).

i, fol. 248b; i, fol. 269d; i, fol. 269d; i, fol. 270a

Goisfrid De Ros

Norman from Rots, Calvados, arr. Caen, cant. Tilly-sur-Seulles (Loyd, 86). Domesday tenant of Odo of Bayeux in Kent, probably a relative of Ansquetil (q.v.). His successor by 1129 was Geoffrey II de Ros (Sanders, 105).

i, fol. 003b; i, fol. 014c; i, fol. 006a; i, fol. 008b; i, fol. 006d; Douglas, ed., Domesday Monachorum (1944), p. 105

Goisfrid De Sartes

Domesday tenant of earl Hugh of Chester. Possibly named from Lessard-et-le-Chêne, Calvados, cant. Livarot.

i, fol. 266b; Barraclough, Charters of AN Earls of Chester (1988), No. 3

Goisfrid De Trailgy

Norman, from Trelly, Manche, arr. Coutances, cant. Montmartin-sur-Mer, Domesday tenant of Hugh de Beauchamp in Bedfordshire. He married Albreda, daughter of William Espec of Old Wardon, Bedfordshire, sister and coheiress of Walter Espec. They had four sons, Geoffrey II, William, Gilbert and Nicholas. Benefactor of Thorney Abbey, of which he and his wife became confratres before 1112. They attested the foundation charter of Kirkham priory c.1122. Both probably died soon thereafter. Geoffrey II had succeeded by 1129/30. Sanders, 52–3, 133–4; W. Farrer, 'The Honour of Old Wardon', Bedfordshire Historical Rec. Soc. xi (1927); J. Moore, 'Prosopographical Problems of English libri vitae', in Keats-Rohan ed., Family Trees, 182ff.

i, fol. 103c; i, fol. 210a; Dugdale, Monasticon Anglicanum, II, p. 601, No. XIII; i, fol. 210a

Goisfrid De Valle

Norman, occurs in Domesday Devon as a tenant of Robert of Mortain, and in Somerset as a tenant of Roger de Courseulles. Surnamed de Valle in Exon, perhaps from Vaux-sur-Seulles, Calvados. The grant to the abbey of Troarn by Robert de Valle was confirmed c.1150 by John de Suligny and his wife, successors of Roger de Courseulles and his son (Arch. Calvados, H 7863).

i, fol. 120d; i, fol. 94b; i, fol. 94b; i, fol. 94a; i, fol. 94a; i, fol. 94b; i, fol. 93d; i, fol. 93b; i, fol. 93b; i, fol. 93b; i, fol. 93b; i, fol. 100d

Goisfrid Episcopus Constantiensis

Geofrey de Molbrai, bishop of Coutances, Manche, from 1049 until 1093, apparently named from Montbrai, Manche, arr. Saint-Lô. According to Orderic Vitalis (ii, 266), Robert de Mowbray, earl of Northumberland, was his nephew; he was probaby therefore a brother of the Roger de Mowbray mentioned as a prominent layman by Orderic (iv, 278); according to the De Statu, a source produced at Coutances in the early twelfth century, he had a brother Malger, and was a relative of Nigel de Saint-Sauveur, vicomte of the Cotentin (Gall. Christ. xi, Inst., cols 218–19, 222). Malger bought the bishopric for his brother, leading to an accusation of simony against Geoffrey at the Council of Reims in 1049. In the end, Pope Leo IX accepted the validity of Geoffrey's consecration. He fought at the battle of Hastings, and thereafter acquired extensive estates in England, especially in the south and west. He pursued a cross-Channel career, which saw him effective in English administration whilst rebuilding both his cathedral and the organisation of his Norman see. His health began to fail in 1091, and worsened during 1092, noticeably in September when he conducted the funeral of his kinsman Nigel de Saint-Sauveur. After his death at Coutances on 2 February 1093, his English fief passed to his nephew Robert, who soon lost it for treason against William II. See J. Le Patourel, 'Geoffrey of Montbray, Bishop of Coutances, 1049–1093', EHR 59 (1944).

Dugdale, Monasticon Anglicanum, III, pp. 544–46, No. I; i, fol. 343d; i, fol. 100b; i, fol. 87d; i, fol. 204a; i, fol. 238d; i, fol. 220c; i, fol. 145b; i, fol. 231b; i, fol. 209d; i, fol. 165a; Darlington, Cartulary of Worcester: Reg. I (1962–3), No. 2; King, Peterborough Descriptio Militum (1969), pp. 97–101; i, fol. 100b; Regesta regum Anglo-Normannorum III, No. 261; i, fol. 52a; i, fol. 163b; i, fol. 225d; i, fol. 225d; i, fol. 225d; i, fol. 203a; i, fol. 229b; i, fol. 66c; i, fol. 343d; i, fol. 343d; i, fol. 87d; i, fol. 88b; i, fol. 86c; i, fol. 88c; i, fol. 88c; i, fol. 88c; i, fol.

87b; i, fol. 87d; i, fol. 88a; i, fol. 88c; i, fol. 87d; i, fol. 89a; i, fol. 87d; i, fol. 88c; i, fol. 102b; i, fol. 91a; i, fol. 91a; i, fol. 91a; i, fol. 91a; i, fol. 90a; i, fol. 89a; i, fol. 66d; i, fol. 88c; i, fol. 215c; i, fol. 88d; i, fol. 88d; i, fol. 88d; i, fol. 66b; i, fol. 89a; i, fol. 88c; i, fol. 88c; i, fol. 66b; i, fol. 219a; i, fol. 210a; i, fol. 102b; i, fol. 102a; i, fol. 145d; i, fol. 143a; i, fol. 98b; i, fol. 210a; i, fol. 154a; i, fol. 238a; i, fol. 226d; i, fol. 220c; i, fol. 162b; i, fol. 220c; i, fol. 220c; i, fol. 145b; i, fol. 102c; i, fol. 145b; i, fol. 145c; i, fol. 145c; i, fol. 210a; i, fol. 103a; i, fol. 209d; i, fol. 102b; i, fol. 102b; i, fol. 209d; i, fol. 102a; i, fol. 210b; i, fol. 145b; i, fol. 145c; i, fol. 209d; i, fol. 102a; i, fol. 58c; Hamilton, Inquisitio Eliensis (1876), pp. 192–95

Goisfrid Filius Eustachii Comitis
Occurs Domesday. Natural son of Eustache count of Boulogne who married Beatrice, daughter of Geoffrey de Mandeville before 1086. His grandson Faramus (occ. 1129) became lord of Tingry in the Boulonnais, which passed in the 1180s to his daughter's husband Ingelran de Fiennes. Cf. J.H. Round, in Genealogist, n.s. xii, 145–51.

ii, fol. 027b; i, fol. 36b; Regesta regum Anglo-Normannorum III, I, Appendix, no. XXV

Goisfrid Filius Haimonis
Norman, important tenant of Richard de Clare in 1086. He was succeeded by his son Baldwin, who was steward to Gilbert I de Clare.

Harper-Bill & Mortimer, Stoke by Clare Cartulary, No. 70; Harper-Bill & Mortimer, Stoke by Clare Cartulary, No. 136; Harper-Bill & Mortimer, Stoke by Clare Cartulary, No. 37; Harper-Bill & Mortimer, Stoke by Clare Cartulary, No. 136; Harper-Bill & Mortimer, Stoke by Clare Cartulary, No. 137; Harper-Bill & Mortimer, Stoke by Clare Cartulary, No. 70; Harper-Bill & Mortimer, Stoke by Clare Cartulary, No. 137; Harper-Bill & Mortimer, Stoke by Clare Cartulary, No. 136; ii, fol. 396b; ii, fol. 393b; ii, fol. 393b; ii, fol. 393b; ii, fol. 393b

Goisfrid Filius Malae Terrae
Geoffrey son of Roger Malaterra, occurs Domesday Kent. In 1166 a second Geoffrey held one fee of the barony of Ros (Rots). The Pipe Roll of 1129/30 refers to the daughter of Herbert Maleterre.

i, fol. 009c; Ballard, Inquisition of St Augustine's (1920), fols 20r–23v

Goisfrid Filius Modberti
Occurs Domesday Kent.

Ballard, Inquisition of St Augustine's (1920), fols 24r–28r; i, fol. 001a

Goisfrid Filius Urselli
Geoffrey son of Ursel attested William of Percy's foundation charter for Whitby (Mon. Ang. i, 411–12). He is perhaps to be identified with William's Domesday tenant Goisfrid in Yorkshire, and, in turn, with Geoffrey de Airel, ancestor of the Dairel family who inherited this Geoffrey's interests in Warter, and also those held of de Percy in 1086 by William de Coleville. Cf. EYC xi, 186–8. Around 1100 a Geoffrey fitz Ursell attested a charter for Castle Acre by Rainer de Grandcourt (Seine-Maritime) (Mon. Ang. iii, 50), and soon afterward a Geoffrey fitz Ursell and his wife Adelyz occurs in a number of Eye charters (Cart. Eye, nos. 1, 145–6).

i, fol. 322c; i, fol. 322c; i, fol. 322c; Clay, Early Yorkshire Charters (1955), XI, No. 1

Goisfrid Homo Ivonis

Norman, Domesday tenant of Ivo Taillebois in Lincolnshire. His fees seem to have passed to Gilbert de Calz and Alan Olliet by 1115/18. Cf. Farrer, HKF ii, 179.

i, fol. 351c; i, fol. 351c; i, fol. 350a; i, fol. 350a

Goisfrid Malloret

Norman, occurs Domesday Dorset as a tenant of William de Mohun. His surname is supplied by Exon Domesday.

i, fol. 82a

Goisfrid Malreward

Occurs Domesday Somerset as a tenant of Geoffrey de Coutances; identified from Exon Domesday. Land at Langrune-sur-Mer, Calvados, arr. Caen, cant. Douvres-la-Délivrande, was given by Roger Malreguart to the priory of Saint-Martin-du-Bosc and confirmed by William of Normandy before 1066 (Fauroux, 218).

i, fol. 88d

Goisfrid Marescal

Norman, son and heir of Milo de Venoix, Calvados, arr. Caen, and Lescelina (Loyd, 109; Actes caen., nos. 2 and 8, pp. 55, 84). He succeeded his father at Venoix and in the office of marshal in or before 1070. He was probably the father of his successor Robert de Venoix, who succeeded him before 1129/30. See Comp. Peer. xi, App. E, p. 123.

i, fol. 74c; i, fol. 49a; i, fol. 49b; i, fol. 49b; i, fol. 49b

Goisfrid Martel

Norman, from Bacqueville-en-Caux, Seine-Maritime, arr. Dieppe. Domesday tenant of Geoffrey de Mandeville. He was brother of Hugh fitz Grip, a former sheriff of Dorset whose widow was an important tenant-in-chief in Dorset in 1086 (see under uxor Hugonis filii Grip). Benefactor of Bermondsey. He was dead by 1129/30, when his son William, by his wife Albreda, occurs. See Loyd, 60.

ii, fol. 060a; Excerpta a Chronicis de Bermondsey, Dugdale, Monasticon, IV, pp 95–97; ii, fol. 057b; ii, fol. 061b; ii, fol. 061a; ii, fol. 061a; i, fol. 137d; ii, fol. 062a; Regesta regum Anglo-Normannorum III, No. 1009

Goisfrid Nepos Abbatis

Norman, nephew of Turold abbot of Peterborough, of whom he was a tenant in 1086, identified by the Descriptio Militum (c.1113–16). See King, Peterborough Abbey 1080–1310 (Cambridge, 1973), 41–2. He was succeeded by his son Geoffrey of Gunthorpe, who occurs on the Pipe Roll of 1129 (p.85).

i, fol. 221c; King, Peterborough Descriptio Militum (1969), pp. 97–101

Goisfrid Orlateile

Norman, occurs Domesday Gloucestershire.

i, fol. 36b; i, fol. 168c; i, fol. 168c

Goisfrid Ridel

Mentioned in Domesday Norfolk as having accompanied Roger Bigod's brother William back from Apulia (DB Norfolk 9.88), he was probably the Geoffrey who held Duckmanton in Derbyshire from Hubert fitz Ralph (Foulds, Thurgarton, clxxxii–xxxi). A servant of Henry I, he married Geva, a natural daughter of Hugh earl of Chester and was given with her part of the escheated lands of Robert de Buci. His daughter and heiress Matilda, wife of Richard Basset, succeeded him at his death in the White Ship disaster of 1120 (Sanders, 49). He was probably father of two younger daughters, Mabel, wife first of Richard de St Medard, by whom she was mother of Hugh Ridel, and a daughter who married William Blund (Foedera i, 42). Possibly not of Norman ancestry; a Geoffrey Ridel son of Geoffrey Ridel a monk, was a benefactor to the abbey of Molesmes (Cart., no. 197), c.1076/85, granting land at Saint-Loup-sur-la-Renne), and a Geoffrey Ridel attested a charter of Geoffrey count of Perche of c.1080 (Cart. Nogent-le-Rotrou, from Recueil. Cluny iv, 698, no. 3536). Geoffrey's brother Matthew, a monk of Mont St Michel, was enthroned as abbot of Peterborough on 21 October 1102, but died at Gloucester on 21 October 1103 (Heads, 60).

i, fol. 277a; Stenton, English Feudalism, App., No. 4; Stenton, English Feudalism, App., No. 4; Hart, Cartularium Monasterii de Rameseia, No. CLXVIII; Regesta regum Anglo-Normannorum III, No. 44; Regesta regum Anglo-Normannorum III, No. 43; Barraclough, Charters of AN Earls of Chester (1988), No. 40

Goisfrid Runeville

Domesday tenant of Geoffrey de Bec in Hertfordshire. His surname is probably a toponym, though one that is difficult to identify on account of what is very probably its corrupt Latin form; the only possibly identification seems to be Ranville, Calvados, cant. Troarn.

i, fol. 140d; i, fol. 140d

Goisfrid Talebot

Domesday tenant of Hugh de Gournai in Essex. According to Le Maho (p. 37) the Talbots were an important family of the Petit-Caux (Seine-Maritime, Normandy). Clients of the sires of Gournay-en-Bray, their original patrimony was at Sainte-Croix-sur Buchy, north-east of Rouen. They subsequently held a castral seigneurie at Cleuville (cant. Cany-Barville, Seine-Maritime), known as the 'fief-franc Talbot) under the Giffards. This Geoffrey was probably the same Geoffrey Talbot who became a tenant of Gundulf of Rochester after 1086, was established in Rochester castle by 1100–3 and was dead in 1129–30 (PR 31 Henry I, 67), when his widow Agnes owed 2 gold marks to have her dower rights. His heir was a son Geoffrey Talbot II, who accounted for his father's lands in 1129. Geoffrey's Kent fief, based upon Swanscombe in Kent, had been held by in 1086 by Helto dapifer, a man of Odo of Bayeux. His wife Agnes (who used erroneously to be identified as a de Lacy, see Comp. Peer. ix, 424) was possibly a daughter of Helto. Geoffrey and Agnes had a daughter Sybil, who attested her parents' grant to Colchester (Cart. i, 142). Since Agnes was not a de Lacy, but Cecilia, a coheiress of Sibil, wife of Payn fitz John, who was a grand-daughter of Hugh de Lacy (Wightman, 175), was sometimes surnamed Talbot, and Geoffrey II Talbot was described as a cognatus of Gilbert de Lacy, there was clearly a link between the Talbots and the Lacys. In all likelihood, Adeline or Adelisa, wife of Hugh de Lacy (d.a.1115), was the daughter of Geoffrey and Agnes. Cf. Douglas, Dom. Mon., 49.

ii, fol. 089b; Douglas, ed., Domesday Monachorum (1944), p. 105; ii, fol. 089b

Goisfrid Tournai

Domesday tenant of Count Alan in Lincolnshire.

i, fol. 348d

Goisfrid Vicecomes

Norman, under-tenant of Roger de Montgomery in Domesday Shropshire; early benefactor of Shrewsbury Abbey, where his son Achard later became a monk (Cart. no. 371). Apparently the same as Godefrid vicecomes, sheriff of Roger's son Roger Pictaviensis in Lancashire after 1086 and witness to Roger's charter for his priory at Lancaster; see K. Thompson, 'Monasteries and settlement in Norman Lancashire: unpublished charters of Roger the Poitevin', Trans. Hist. Soc. of Lancs. and Cheshire 140 (1990). Perhaps ancestor of William de Hedlega (Hadley) and his sons (q.v.).

   i, fol. 352a; i, fol. 260b; Rees, Cartulary of Shrewsbury Abbey (1975), No. 35; i, fol. 254d

Goisfrid []

Norman, Domesday tenant of Robert de Tosny of Stafford. He was succeeded by a son William de Wastineis, whose name perhaps identifies Geoffrey as a member of the Wastinel family which held of the honour of Tosny at Veauville-les-Baons, Seine-Maritime, cant. Yerville, and Acquigny, Eure, cant. Louviers (Musset, Les Tosny, Francia v, 76).

   i, fol. 368c; i, fol. 368c; i, fol. 368c; i, fol. 249a; i, fol. 368c; i, fol. 368c

Goisfrid []

Norman, Domesday tenant of the abbey of Peterborough. Succeeded by William of Burghley (q.v.). See Hugh Candidus, 165.

   i, fol. 221c

Goisfrid []

Norman, Domesday tenant of Miles Crispin. His lands were afterwards held by the de Mara family, who were probably his descendants. The grant of land at Beuville, Eure, now Saint-Thurien, cant. Quillebeuf-sur-Seine, by Geoffrey de Lamara to Saint-Martin-du-Bosc was confirmed before 1066 by William of Normandy (Fauroux, 218).

   i, fol. 150b; i, fol. 159d; i, fol. 159c

Goisfrid []

Norman, Domesday tenant of Hugh fitz Baldric.

   i, fol. 328b; i, fol. 328b; i, fol. 328b; i, fol. 328b; i, fol. 328b; i, fol. 328b

Goisfrid []

Tenant of Walchelin bishop of Winchester in Domesday Hampshire.

   i, fol. 41b; i, fol. 40c; i, fol. 40c; i, fol. 40b; i, fol. 40a

Goisfrid []

Tenant of the fitz Azor brothers in Domesday Hampshire.

   i, fol. 53c; i, fol. 53c; i, fol. 53d

Goisfrid []

Domesday tenant of Norman d'Arci.

   i, fol. 361c; i, fol. 361c; i, fol. 361c

Goisfrid []

Domesday tenant of Roger de Bully. Perhaps the same as Roger's steward who attested the Blyth foundation charter as Godefridus dapifer.

i, fol. 286d; i, fol. 284c; i, fol. 285a; i, fol. 285a; i, fol. 286c; i, fol. 286d

Goisfrid []
Domesday tenant of Gilbert de Gand in Lincolnshire. The same Geoffrey was probably also the tenant of Drogo de La Beuvrière, since that Geoffrey's fees were held in 1115/18 by William de Alost (q.v.). Alost is Aalst in Flanders, and was the original home of the Gand family.

i, fol. 360c; i, fol. 360c; i, fol. 360c; i, fol. 360c; i, fol. 227c; i, fol. 355a; i, fol. 355d; i, fol. 355d; i, fol. 293d

Goisfrid []
Domesday tenant of the abbey of Tavistock. Probably represented in 1166 by Reginald of Liddaton.

i, fol. 103d; i, fol. 103c; i, fol. 103c; i, fol. 103c

Goislan De Amundeville
Norman, Domesday tenant of the bishops of Lincoln and Durham in Lincolnshire. Probably father of Jocelyn de Amundeville, who was steward to the bishop in 1129/30, according to Clay, EYC xi, 172ff. Clay was certainly wrong to identify the Jocelyn of 1086 with the Ivelin de Amundeville who attested a Fécamp charter of c.1085 (RRAN i, 207). Ivelin was father of Gilbert, who occurs in a Fécamp charter of 1106 concerned with his father's mill at Argentan (Arch. dépt. Calvados H4368). This misidentification destroys the basis of Loyd's identification of his toponym with Mondeville, Calvados, arr. Caen. Much more likely is the alternative he proposed, Émondeville, Seine-Maritime, arr. Yvetot, which accords well with Jocelyn's dependence upon Bishop Remigius (Loyd, 4 and note 1). A much less likely possibility is Émondeville, Manche, cant. Montebourg, though a later Jocelyn [Goelleni] de Amundeville, vavassor, held a fee of the honour of Bretteville, Manche, in the Cotentin, from Mont-Saint-Michel in 1172 (Torigny, ed. Delisle, ii, 300). On the family see C. Clay in Lincolnshire Architectural and Archaeolgical Society Reports and Papers, vol. 3 pt. 1, (1948), 109–36.

i, fol. 345a; i, fol. 344b; i, fol. 344b; i, fol. 341a; i, fol. 344c; i, fol. 344b

Goismer []
Domesday tenant of Richard de Clare. Father of Auger, Guncelin, Humphrey and Herluin, ancestor, through Humphrey, of the de Camoys family.

Harper-Bill & Mortimer, Stoke by Clare Cartulary, No. 136; Harper-Bill & Mortimer, Stoke by Clare Cartulary, No. 22; Harper-Bill & Mortimer, Stoke by Clare Cartulary, No. 70; ii, fol. 101b; ii, fol. 039a

Golde Mater Ulurici
Englishwoman, occurs Domesday

i, fol. 207c

Gollan []
Englishman, occurs Domesday Cambridgeshire.

i, fol. 194c

Golstan Socmannus Regis Willelmi
Occurs Domesday Essex.

ii, fol. 003a

Gonduin Camerarius

Occurs Domesday Suffolk. Perhaps the same as Gundwin Granetarius of Wiltshire.

ii, fol. 097b; ii, fol. 097b; ii, fol. 436b; ii, fol. 436b

Gosbert []

Tenant of Roger the Poitevin in Domesday Suffolk.

ii, fol. 352b; ii, fol. 352b; ii, fol. 352a; ii, fol. 352b

Goscelin De Hollesleia

Norman, Domesday tenant of Robert Malet and early benefactor of the priory of Eye. The tithe he gave to Eye was afterwards referred to as the tithe of Rocelin of Linstead or Huntingfield. Rocelin's son William occurs in 1155 (Mon. Ang. v, 58), and his grandson William fitz William in 1220. Whether Rocelin was the same person as Jocelin, or his son, remains undetermined (Sibton Cart. ii, 143). Cf. Brown, Eye Cart. Introd. p. 72.

ii, fol. 305b; Brown, Eye Priory Cartulary (1992–94), No. 1; Brown, Eye Priory Cartulary (1992–94), No. 55; Brown, Eye Priory Cartulary (1992–94), No. 3; Brown, Eye Priory Cartulary (1992–94), No. 5

Goscelin Lorimarius

Norman, occurs in Domesday East Anglia, where he was a tenant of Frodo, brother of Abbot Baldwin, of Ely Abbey, and he also held his own fee as Jocelyn Lorimer. Known as Jocelyn of Ely and of Lodden. Between 1114 and 1119 the abbot of Bury made a grant to O. the widow of Jocelyn de Lodden, whose sons Ralph and Gilbert subsequently attest Bury charters. According to the Ramsey Chronicle (249–50), he had a 'nepos' Ralph, brother of Brien. He was perhaps also father of Jocelyn the clerk of Ely, a member of Nigel of Ely's household, remembered by the monks of Ely as the thief of a valuable chalice (Lib. El., pp. 322, 192). His heir by 1202 was Cecilia of Norton, daughter of Christiana of Norton (Feet of Fines Norfolk, Pipe Roll Soc. n.s. 27, no. 381).

ii, fol. 211b; ii, fol. 212b; ii, fol. 370b; Douglas, Feudal Book of Bury St Edmunds (1932), pp. 22–37; Douglas, Feudal Documents from Bury St Edmunds, No. 107; ii, fol. 273a; Douglas, Feudal Book of Bury St Edmunds (1932), pp. 3–21; ii, fol. 094a; ii, fol. 018a; ii, fol. 094a; ii, fol. 002a; ii, fol. 209a; ii, fol. 209b; ii, fol. 209b; Hamilton, Inquisitio Eliensis (1876), pp. 192–95

Goscelm Cocus

Occurs Domesday Dorset.

i, fol. 77c

Goscelm []

Domesday tenant of Theobald fitz Berner. Possibly the same as Goscelin (q.v.).

i, fol. 115c

Gospatric []

Englishman, tenant-in-chief in Domesday Yorkshire. His father Arnketil had been a leading Yorkshire thegn involved in the revolts of 1068 and 1069. He submitted to William at York in 1068, leaving his son Gospatrick as hostage. Gospatrick went on to became the sole thegn to hold at least a part of his father's inheritance in 1086. He was succeeded by his son Uhctred of Allerston, who held most of his father's lands as mesne tenancies rather than in chief. Ancestor of the Mohaut

234

family, descendants of his grandson Simon son of Gospatrick, and also of the Hebden family, descendants of Simon son of Uctred, third son of Gospatric's son Dolfin. VCH Yorks ii, 183–5.

i, fol. 310b; i, fol. 309d; i, fol. 312d; i, fol. 310d; i, fol. 310d; i, fol. 311a; i, fol. 311a; i, fol. 312a; i, fol. 312d; i, fol. 312d; i, fol. 330a; Greenway, Charters of the Honour of Mowbray (1972), No. 392; i, fol. 310a; i, fol. 310d; i, fol. 310d; i, fol. 311a; i, fol. 311b; i, fol. 311d; i, fol. 311d; i, fol. 312a; i, fol. 312c; i, fol. 330a; i, fol. 330a; i, fol. 330a; i, fol. 330a; i, fol. 330a; i, fol. 330a; i, fol. 330a; i, fol. 330a; i, fol. 330a; i, fol. 330a; i, fol. 330a; i, fol. 330a; i, fol. 330a; i, fol. 330a; i, fol. 330a; i, fol. 330b; i, fol. 330a; i, fol. 330b; i, fol. 330a; i, fol. 330a; i, fol. 330b; i, fol. 330a; i, fol. 330b; i, fol. 330b; i, fol. 330b; i, fol. 330b; i, fol. 330b; i, fol. 330b; i, fol. 330b; i, fol. 330b; i, fol. 330b; i, fol. 330b; i, fol. 330a; i, fol. 330b; i, fol. 330b; i, fol. 330b; i, fol. 330b; i, fol. 330b; i, fol. 330b; i, fol. 330a; i, fol. 331d; i, fol. 331d

Got Cill-
Occurs Domesday Colchester.

ii, fol. 105a

Got Flet
Englishman, occurs Domesday Colchester.

ii, fol. 106a

Got Hugo
Occurs Domesday Colchester.

ii, fol. 106a

Gotcelm Canonicus De Execestre
Attached to the end of the fee of Gotshelm de Claville, the holding of this man is easily confused with Gotshelm's. Both Domesday and Exon appear to name him as a Goscelm, but Domesday significantly adds the surname de Execestre and states that he held 'de rege', i.e. in chief. The next two entries are each of individual landholders holding a single manor 'de rege'. It is clear therefore that this person is distinct from Gotshelm of Claville and that the rubric of his chapter has been lost. The Tax Returns for Cliston Hundred calls him Goscelin canonicus, suggesting that, whether a Goscelm or a Goscelin, he was a canon of Exeter.

i, fol. 113a

Gotscelm De Claville
Brother of Walter (q.v.), whose tenancy-in-chief in Devon he shared.

i, fol. 101c; i, fol. 113a; i, fol. 113a; i, fol. 125b; i, fol. 112d; i, fol. 113a; i, fol. 112d; i, fol. 112d; i, fol. 112d; i, fol. 112d; i, fol. 112d; i, fol. 112c; i, fol. 112c; i, fol. 112d; i, fol. 112d; i, fol. 116c

Gozelin Beruin
Occurs Domesday Devon as a tenant of Baldwin the Sheriff. Exon supplies the byname (patronym?).

i, fol. 108a; i, fol. 107c

Gozelin Brito
Breton tenant-in-chief in Domesday Buckinghamshire, also a tenant of Earl Hugh of Chester in Northamptonshire. His heir was a son Hugh, who gave the church of Cublington to Dunstable priory. Hugh married [Isabel], sister of William de

Chesney of Oxon and Bishop Robert of Lincoln, and left an heir Walter de Chesney (Farrer, HKF ii, 216). A passage in the Thorney Liber Vitae (BL Add. 40,000, fol. 3v) lists Goscelinus Brito. Hugo. Adelya. Adid. Ricardus. HKF ii, 216–18.

i, fol. 224d; i, fol. 170b; i, fol. 162b; i, fol. 152b; i, fol. 152b; i, fol. 152b; i, fol. 217a; i, fol. 217a; i, fol. 217a; i, fol. 170b; i, fol. 152b

Gozelin Constabularius
Domesday tenant of William de Warenne in Sussex. Perhaps the same as Jocelyn Trenchefoil, who attests Warenne charters of the early twelfth century and was followed by a second Jocelyn Trenchefoil at a indeterminate date. William Trenchefoil was a knight of Roger fitz Turold [de Vesly, Eure] whose made a grant of land at Sotteville (Seine-Maritime) to Sainte-Trinité de Rouen on the eve of the Hastings expedition. Roger died on the journey, but William Trenchefoil subsequently granted the same with the assent of William I of England (Cart. Sainte-Trinité, p. 453; CDF, 74). Roger was half-brother of William, count of Eu [see under Robert, comes de Ou], who attested a charter by Giles de Merulvilla, granting land at Vesly, with Goscelin Trenchefoil (Hist. Tréport, p. 343).

i, fol. 27c; Clay, Early Yorkshire Charters (1949), VIII, No. 6; Clay, Early Yorkshire Charters (1949), VIII, No. 16

Gozelin De Cormelies
Norman from Cormeilles, Eure, arr. Pont-Audemer (Loyd, 33). Occurs Domesday Hampshire. Probably related to Ansfrid (q.v.).

i, fol. 49b; i, fol. 49b

Gozelin De Rivere
Norman, occurs in Domesday Book as tenant of William d'Eu and Robert fitz Gerold de Roumare. Possibly named from La Rivière-Thibouville, Eure. One of his daughters became a nun of Shaftesbury. Brother of Walter de Rivere, he was guardian for the latter's son Jocelyn in the early twelfth century (Chron. Abing. ii, 23).

i, fol. 97a; i, fol. 86c; i, fol. 61d; i, fol. 61a; Dugdale, Monasticon Anglicanum, II, pp. 482–83, No. XIII; Regesta regum Anglo-Normannorum III, No. 818; i, fol. 73b

Gozelin De Tuschet
Norman, Domesday tenant of Earl Hugh of Chester, identified from a charter of Ranulf II of Chester granting his land in inheritance to his grandson Henry II de Tuschet. See S.P.H. Statham, in Jour. Derbs. Arch. and Nat. Hist. Soc. xiix ns ii pt. ii, and in Genealogist ns 36. HKF ii, 28–32.

i, fol. 263c; i, fol. 349d; i, fol. 273c; i, fol. 267b; i, fol. 267b; i, fol. 267b; Barraclough, Charters of AN Earls of Chester (1988), No. 85; i, fol. 293d

Gozelin Filius Azor
Norman tenant-in-chief in Domesday Hampshire, brother of William, also a tenant-in-chief there. Followers of William fitz Osbern de Breteuil.

i, fol. 53b; i, fol. 53b; i, fol. 53b; i, fol. 53b; i, fol. 53c; i, fol. 53c; i, fol. 53c; i, fol. 53c; i, fol. 53c; i, fol. 52b

Gozelin Filius Lanberti
Tenant-in-chief in Domesday Lincolnshire who held in 1086 lands previously held

by his father Lambert. Probably a Norman. His son Gilbert had succeeded as lord of Redbourne by 1115/18 (Sanders, 74).

i, fol. 350d; i, fol. 350b; i, fol. 344a; Lincolnshire Claims (Domesday Book), fols 376b–c; Lincolnshire Claims (Domesday Book), fols 375d–376a; i, fol. 359a; Lincolnshire Claims (Domesday Book), fols 376b–c; i, fol. 359a; i, fol. 359c; i, fol. 359b; i, fol. 359a; i, fol. 359b; i, fol. 359a; i, fol. 359a; i, fol. 359b; i, fol. 359a; i, fol. 359c; i, fol. 355b; i, fol. 359a; i, fol. 359a; i, fol. 359a; i, fol. 359a; i, fol. 359a; Lincolnshire Claims (Domesday Book), fols 375d–376a; Lincolnshire Claims (Domesday Book), fols 375a–d; i, fol. 359b; i, fol. 359c; i, fol. 359b; i, fol. 359a; i, fol. 359c; i, fol. 359b; i, fol. 359b; i, fol. 359b; i, fol. 359c; i, fol. 359a; i, fol. 359b; i, fol. 359a; i, fol. 359b

Gozelin Homo Comitis Moritoniensis
Norman, Domesday tenant of Robert of Mortain.

i, fol. 21a; i, fol. 21a; i, fol. 21b; ii, fol. 381b

Gozelin Venator
Norman, granted land in Herefordshire by William fitz Osbern.

i, fol. 180c

Gozelin []
Domesday tenant of Theobald fitz Berner. Possibly the same as Baldwin the Sheriff's tenant Gozelin Beruin.

i, fol. 115c

Gozelin []
Domesday tenant of Alfred of Lincoln, still holding in 1115/18. Father of Gilbert de Sempringham, Roger, and a daughter Agnes by an English wife, according to the Vita of his son St Gilbert, where he is described as 'miles strenuus' and 'opulentus' (The Book of St Gilbert, ed. and trans. R. Foreville and G. Keir, Oxford, 1987, p. 10). His heir by 1166 was his daughter Agnes, mother of Roger and Hugh Musteil.

Lindsey Survey, BL ms Cotton Claudius C v, fols 19–27; i, fol. 358d; i, fol. 358d; i, fol. 358d; i, fol. 358c; i, fol. 358a; i, fol. 358a; i, fol. 358a; i, fol. 358a

Gozelin []
Domesday tenant of William Peverel at Watnall, Derbyshire, two-thirds of the tithes of which he gave to Lenton priory at its foundation. The holding passed by 1129 to Ranulf fitz Ingelran, perhaps in marriage with Jocelyn's heiress; HKF i, 151.

Dugdale, Monasticon Anglicanum, IV, pp. 111–12, No. Ia; i, fol. 288a

Gozo []
Domesday tenant of William I de Warenne in Sussex. Described by William II de Warenne as 'nutricius meus' in Lewes cart, p. 14.

i, fol. 26c

Grapinel []
Occurs Domesday Essex as a tenant of Swein of Essex in his demesne manor of Prittlewell. A Robert Grapinel had a quarter fee of the honour of Henry of Essex in 1211 (RBE, 594). Warin Grapinel held one third of a fee in Prittlewell in the time of Henry III (RBE, 739).

ii, fol. 044a

Grento []
Norman, described as 'miles' in Exon Domesday. Tenant of Tavistock Abbey in 1086. Cf. Actes caenn. no. 6, p. 69, the grant to Saint-Etienne de Caen of the land of Grento Haterel by William I, 1080–2.

   i, fol. 103d

Grento []
Occurs once in Domesday Sussex holding 1.5 virgates in Little Horsted of Robert of Mortain. The principal tenant there was one Ranulf [see Ranulf vicecomes], mentioned in a charter for Lewes (Cart. p. 75) by William of Mortain as father of a Hubert (al. Herbert)] who gave land at 'Burgingehest' that Grento held of him. The tithes of William fitz Boselin (de Dives) and Ralph nepos Grentonis in Alfriston were confirmed to Lewes priory by Stephen; cf. L. Salzman, 'Some Sussex Domesday tenants, II', Sussex Archaeological Collections 58, 171–81. Possibly the same as Grento, tenant of Robert's father-in-law Roger de Montgomery.

   i, fol. 255d; i, fol. 22a

Grifin Filius Mariadoc
Gruffydd son of King Maredudd of Deheubarth (d. 1071). Lived in exile on his father's English estates until he was killed, in 1091, by Rhys ap Tewdwr, while trying to recover his Welsh kingdom. Occurs in Domesday Herefordshire. Cf. Robert S. Babcock, 'Rhys ap Tewdwr, king of Deheubarth', Anglo-Norman Studies 16 (1994).

   i, fol. 187c; i, fol. 187c; i, fol. 187c; i, fol. 187c; i, fol. 187c; i, fol. 187c; i, fol. 187c; i, fol. 187c; i, fol. 187a

Grim Prepositus
Englishman, held land of the king in Domesday Essex.

   ii, fol. 098a; ii, fol. 098a; ii, fol. 098a; ii, fol. 004b

Grimbald Aurifaber
Occurs Domesday Wiltshire.

   i, fol. 74a; i, fol. 74a; i, fol. 63b

Grimbald []
Domesday tenant of Countess Judith; ancestor of the Grimbald family. Benefactor of St Andrew's, Northampton; steward to Simon I de Senlis during the 1120s. He left three sons, Robert Grimbald, Hugh and Warner, and a daughter who married Robert de Bagpuiz. Robert appears to have succeeded him in his lands and the office of steward to the earl about 1130/3. Cf. HKF ii, 301ff.

   i, fol. 236c; i, fol. 236c; i, fol. 236d; i, fol. 228c; i, fol. 228c; i, fol. 228c; i, fol. 228c

Grimbold []
Occurs Domesday Essex as tenant of Theoderic Pointel.

   ii, fol. 096b

Gueri Canonicus Sancti Pauli
Domesday canon of St Paul's.

   i, fol. 127d

Guert Homo Alani Comitis
Englishman, occurs Domesday Lincolnshire as a man of Count Alan.

   i, fol. 348d; Lincolnshire Claims (Domesday Book), fol. 377d

Gulbert []
Domesday tenant of William de Warenne in Esssex. A Gulbert son of Ralph de Croix-Mare, Seine-Maritime, cant. Pavilly, attested an act recording sales by Ralph de Warenne (father of William) to Sainte-Trinité de Rouen (Fauroux, 135).

ii, fol. 037a; ii, fol. 037b; ii, fol. 037a

Gulfer []
Domesday tenant of Robert de Tosny of Stafford in Lincolnshire.

i, fol. 368d; i, fol. 368d

Gunduin Granetarius
Occurs Domesday Wiltshire. Perhaps the same as the Gundwin camerarius of Suffolk and Essex.

i, fol. 72d; i, fol. 74d

Gundulf Episcopus Roffensis
Bishop of Rochester 19 March 1077 until his death on 7 March 1108. Monk of Bec and then of Saint-Etienne de Caen; from 1070 until his appointment as bishop in 1077 he was administrative assistant to Archbishop Lanfranc; FEA ii, 75. His Life was written by an anonymous monk of Bec. The Life of Gundulf Bishop of Rochester, ed. R. Thomson, Toronto, 1977; M. Ruud, 'Monks in the World; the case of Gundulf of Rochester', Anglo-Norman Studies 11 (1988); Hirokazu Tsurushima, 'Bishop Gundulf and Rochester Cathedral Priory as an intermediary between English and Normans in Anglo-Norman local society (State, church and society in medieval England, symposium in the Faculty of Education, Kumamoto University, 1992), The Studies in Western History 31 (Fukuoka, Japan, 1993).

Clay, Early Yorkshire Charters (1949), VIII, No. 5; ii, fol. 381a; Dugdale, Monasticon Anglicanum, IV, p. 148, No. I; i, fol. 007c; i, fol. 002c; i, fol. 002c; Regesta regum Anglo-Normannorum III, No. 718; i, fol. 005c; i, fol. 005c; i, fol. 005c; i, fol. 005d; i, fol. 005c; i, fol. 005d; i, fol. 005d; i, fol. 005d; i, fol. 005d; i, fol. 005c; i, fol. 005d; i, fol. 005c; i, fol. 005d; i, fol. 005c; i, fol. 190c; i, fol. 005c; ii, fol. 381a; ii, fol. 381a; Dugdale, Monasticon Anglicanum, III, pp. 544–46, No. I; Douglas, ed., Domesday Monachorum (1944), p. 105; Clay, Early Yorkshire Charters (1949), VIII, No. 6; Dugdale, Monasticon Anglicanum, II, p. 267, No. XI

Gunfrid Archidiaconus
Archdeacon of Norfolk, Domesday tenant of William bishop of Thetford.

ii, fol. 193a; i, fol. 32d; ii, fol. 258b; ii, fol. 193a; ii, fol. 193a; ii, fol. 259a; ii, fol. 259a

Gunfrid De Cioches
Named from Chocques, Pas-de-Calais, in Artois. Domesday tenant-in-chief. There are numerous difficulties presented by the descent of this fief, of which an outline was given in Farrer, HKF i, 20–8. The early descent is separate from that of the fief of Sigar of Chocques, though the two were held by the same person, William de Béthune, by the 1190s. Farrer's assumptions about the relationships between these persons are certainly false, but the true details are very difficult to establish and no completely satisfying answer to the problems emerges. What follows is fairly complex, but the essential proposition is that Gunfrid should be identified with Gunfrid de Houdain, father or grandfather of Anselm de Houdain, his successor by 1129, and that both were known in England as de Chocques from a

lordship in Artois in which they had inherited interests.

In 1129 Anselm de Chokes accounted that his lands might be restored to him. Still holding in 1135 (RBE, 334), he was succeeded thereafter by his son Robert, who returned a carta in 1166. Around 1145 Baldwin castellan of Lens had devised to Robert de Béthune (father of William fl. 1190) the English fief he had inherited as heir of Rainald de Chokes, grandson of Sigar (CDF, 1359). During the 1190s William de Béthune, son of Robert, then holding the fief of Sigar, claimed also the honour of Gunfrid of Chokes alleging that Anselm had been 'auunculus patris meus', i.e. 'uncle of my father' (Curia Regis Roll i, p. 233), a statement which cannot be accommodated within the well-established details of the genealogy of Béthune; that there was some relationship between them nonetheless cannot be doubted.

The Anselm who was Gunfrid's successor in 1129 was probably his son (or perhaps grandson). A charter for St Andrew's Northampton given by Simon de Senlis confirmed a grant by Anselm of Chokes (Cochis) for the souls of his 'antecessores' and was attested by Anselm's brother Humfrid (BL Cotton Vesp. E xvii, fol. 224r, original in BL Cotton Ch. x 14). The cartulary shows beyond doubt that Humfrid was an error (Normanization) for Gunfrid, since a copy of Anselm's charter on the same folium as the confirmation was attested by Gumfrid de Coch'.

In 1120 the lordship of Chocques was divided between Hugh d'Oisy, castellan of Cambrai, Baldwin Rufus, and Anselm de Houdain. Hugh's daughter Clemence took his third of the lordship to William de Béthune upon their marriage in 1129. Baldwin Rufus was probably represented by Baldwin of Lens of c.1145 (either he was the same person or Baldwin of Lens was his descendant); Warlop, iii, 659, has identified him as the brother of William de Béthune. Anselm of Houdain was either father of, or the same as, Anselm, father of Robert and husband of Aigelina de Saint-Pol, whose younger sister Adelaide eventually married Robert de Béthune (son of William and Clemence d'Oisy).

Anselm de Houdain is not unlikely to be the same person as Anselm de Chocques, successor of Gunfrid. The Houdain family of the twelfth century used the name de Chocques (Du Chesne, Béthune, 138). Although Sigar (q.v.) de Chocques and his brother Arnulf are well-evidenced in late-eleventh century charters, there is no reference to a Gunfrid de Chocques. Anselm of Houdain, however, occurs as Anselm de Houdain and as Calvus c.1067 (Miraeus et Foppens, i, 511–13) and 1080, brother of Clarembald, dapifer of the counts of Flanders; Clarembald gave a charter for the souls of Robert II of Flanders, his parents and his brother Anselm in 1102 (Warlop, i, 169). Anselm of Houdain (father of Robert, ut sup.) was steward to Sibil of Anjou, countess of Flanders, in 1148 (ibid. 235). Hugh d'Oisy, one of the three lords of Chocques in 1120, was related to Anselm de Ribemont (Chron. Cambr., col. 184), whose daughter married Walter II Giffard. In 1148 Anselm de Houdain was described as 'consanguineus' of Walter Giffard in a charter of Thierry of Flanders (Mir. et Fopp, ii, 1314). In 1127 Bishop Robert of Arras noted that Evrard the clerk had restored the church of Haut-Bruay, arr. Béthune, to Saint-Pierre d'Abbeville, which had originally been granted by his father Gunfrid de Houdain; one of the witnesses was Oilard decanus de Houdain (Chh. Arras, 45). One can perhaps futher identify Gunfrid de Houdain/Chocques with the Gunfrid castellan of Lens who in 1097 was reprimanded and excommunicated for depredations against the church of Arras, from which he usurped Loos[-en-Gohelle, Pas-de-Calais, arr. Béthune), by Bishop Lambert (Rec.

Hist. Fr., xv, 185). Oilard de Houdain and Anselm his brother attested a charter for Saint-Ghislain in 1126 (Annales de l'abbaye de Saint-Ghislain, Hist. province de Namur vol. viii, p. 350).

These scattered details indicate that the lordship of Chocques was divided into three parts during the later eleventh century. Assuming that at one time the lordship was intact, one could posit a division between three heiresses. One of these will have been the mother of Sigar de Chocques, whose heirs were two daughters; of these the eldest was Hildiard, mother of Rainald de Chocques, but their heir by c.1145 was Baldwin of Lens; this Baldwin was the same as, or the son of, the Baldwin Rufus (de Béthune) who held this third in 1120. The second heiress will have been an ancestor of Hugh d'Oisy of Cambrai, whose daughter took her portion to William de Béthune in 1129. The third heiress was an ancestor of the Anselm de Houdain of 1120, who was father of, or the same as, the Anselm who was Flemish steward in 1148. It seems clear that the Béthune family was keen to acquire the bulk of the lordship of Chocques, both in Artois and in England. All these details combine to confirm the impression that the English Anselm of Chokes (Chocques) should be identified with Anselm de Houdain, and that his father (or possibly grandfather) the Domesday Gunfrid de Chocques should be identified with Gunfrid de Houdain, father on the continental evidence of Oilard decanus, Anselm and Everard clericus; if this Anselm be the same as Gunfrid's successor in 1129, then Gunfrid was father also of a second Gunfrid.

i, fol. 219a; i, fol. 227d; i, fol. 227d; i, fol. 366c; i, fol. 227d; i, fol. 366c; i, fol. 227d; i, fol. 336d; i, fol. 227d; i, fol. 227d; i, fol. 227d; i, fol. 227d; i, fol. 227d; i, fol. 227d; i, fol. 219c; i, fol. 227d; i, fol. 152c; i, fol. 366c; i, fol. 235d; i, fol. 216a; i, fol. 227d; Lincolnshire Claims (Domesday Book), fols 376d–377c

Gunfrid Malduit

Norman, a Domesday tenant in Wiltshire, where he held of the king in chief and from Shaftesbury abbey. His son Walchelin held the Shaftesbury fees c.1130, and Anselin Mauduit in 1166. See A. Williams, 'The knights of Shaftesbury', ANS viii, 216–17.

i, fol. 67d; i, fol. 70c; i, fol. 67a; i, fol. 67c; i, fol. 73a; i, fol. 73a

Gunfrid []

Norman, Domesday tenant of Urse of Abitot.

Round, Fragments from Worcester, Round, Feudal England (1895 : 1946), pp. 146–47; i, fol. 177d; i, fol. 177d

Gunfrid []

Norman, Domesday tenant of Robert de Tosny of Belvoir.

i, fol. 225b; i, fol. 353a; i, fol. 353b

Gunner []

Domesday tenant of Swein of Essex

ii, fol. 048a; ii, fol. 048b

Gunter []

Domesday tenant of Humphrey de Insula in Wilts. in a manor described by the Tax Return for Highworth Hundred (fol. 3a) as having been given by a certain Turold to his 'nepta', presumably Gunter's wife.

i, fol. 70d

Hacon []
Englishman, occurs Domesday Lincolnshire, father of William, occurs Linsdsey Survey, c.1115/18, Ralph and Richard.

i, fol. 352a; i, fol. 362d

Hagebern []
English tenant-in-chief, Domesday Essex.

ii, fol. 006b; ii, fol. 096a; ii, fol. 096a; ii, fol. 096a; ii, fol. 096a

Hagon Prepositus Regis
Englishman, held land of the king as a royal reeve in Domesday Norfolk. His son Ralph's holding was entered after his.

ii, fol. 269b; ii, fol. 270a; ii, fol. 270a; ii, fol. 270a; ii, fol. 270a; ii, fol. 270a; ii, fol. 270a; ii, fol. 270a; ii, fol. 269b; ii, fol. 269b

Haimeric De Arcis
Occurs holding of the king in Domesday Devon. Identified as de Arcis by Exon Domesday. His personal name does not indicate a Norman origin; he was perhaps an Artesian Fleming from Arques, Pas-de-Calais, arr. and cant. Saint-Omer. His fief apparently escheated not long after 1086. His manor of Pultimore passed to the honour of Plympton, and the others to the honour of Great Torrington.

i, fol. 117c; i, fol. 117d; i, fol. 117d; i, fol. 117d; i, fol. 117d

Haimo Dapifer
Norman, son of Haimo Dentatus, lord of Torigny-sur-Vire, Manche, arr. Saint-Lô, a rebel killed in 1047 (Douglas, Dom. Mon., 55–6; Loyd, 50). Haimo the Steward, sheriff of Kent from 1077 until his death c. 1100 when his son Haimo succeeded him as sheriff. Father also of Robert fitz Haimo, who was identified as a grandson of Haimo Dentatus by William of Malmesbury (Gesta Regum, ii 386).

i, fol. 008d; Ballard, Inquisition of St Augustine's (1920), fols 24r–28r; ii, fol. 002a; ii, fol. 056a; ii, fol. 106a; ii, fol. 056a; ii, fol. 055b; ii, fol. 055b; ii, fol. 100b; ii, fol. 100b; Ballard, Inquisition of St Augustine's (1920), fols 20r–23v; ii, fol. 094b; ii, fol. 054b; i, fol. 32d; i, fol. 36c; i, fol. 36c; i, fol. 33a,b; i, fol. 33a,b; i, fol. 33a,b; i, fol. 007a; i, fol. 004b; i, fol. 003d; i, fol. 002d; i, fol. 002a; i, fol. 009c; i, fol. 006d; i, fol. 014b; i, fol. 014b; i, fol. 014b; i, fol. 014b; i, fol. 009c; Douglas, ed., Domesday Monachorum (1944), p. 105; i, fol. 33a,b

Haimo De Maci
Norman, from Macey, Manche, arr. Avranches, cant. Pontorson, a fief of the abbey of Mont-Saint-Michel in the twelfth century (Loyd, 61–2), Domesday tenant of Earl Hugh. His successor in the early twelfth century was Robert, and by 1166, a second Haimo.

i, fol. 68d; i, fol. 69a; i, fol. 69a; i, fol. 268a; i, fol. 268a; i, fol. 268a; i, fol. 264a; i, fol. 263d; i, fol. 266c; i, fol. 266d; i, fol. 266d; i, fol. 266d; i, fol. 266c; i, fol. 266c; i, fol. 266c; Barraclough, Charters of AN Earls of Chester (1988), No. 28; Barraclough, Charters of AN Earls of Chester (1988), No. 28; Barraclough, Charters of AN Earls of Chester (1988), No. 3; Barraclough, Charters of AN Earls of Chester (1988), No. 28; Barraclough, Charters of AN Earls of Chester (1988), No. 3; Barraclough, Charters of AN Earls of Chester (1988), No. 8

Haimo De Valenis
Breton, tenant of Count Alan in 1086. Domesday Book carefully distinguishes the orthography of Hamo's toponym from that of Peter de Valognes. Despite the

subsequent approximation of the orthography of his descendants' name to that of de Valognes, there should be no grounds for confusion between two distinct places. Hamo was an important tenant of Count Alan, and his descendants continued to hold of Alan's successors. His origins must therefore be sought in Brittany. There are two possibilities, Valaine and Saint-Christophe-de-Valains, both dépt. Ille-et-Vilaine. He was succeeded before 1129/30 by his son Theobald; he was father also of Robert, possibly also of Rualon. EYC v, 234–8.

ii, fol. 298a; ii, fol. 297a; ii, fol. 296b; ii, fol. 297a; ii, fol. 296b; ii, fol. 296a; ii, fol. 296a; ii, fol. 293a

Haimo []
Tenant of Robert of Mortain in Domesday Dorset. Grandfather of William fitz John of Weston, who returned a Carta in 1166 (RBE, 219–20).

i, fol. 79b; i, fol. 93a; i, fol. 79c; i, fol. 79b; i, fol. 80a

Haimo []
Domesday tenant of William Capra in Devon.

i, fol. 110c; i, fol. 110d; i, fol. 110c; i, fol. 110c

Hainfrid De Sancto Bertino
Fleming, probably dead by 1086 when he is mentioned in Domesday Book; probably a companion or relative of Gerbod advocate of Saint-Bertin and his brother Frederick, brothers-in-law of William I de Warenne. A Haimfrid was provost of the monastery of Saint-Bertin in 961 (Guérard, Cart., p.154).

ii, fol. 432a

Halanalt []
Domesday tenant of Count Alan in Suffolk. Halanalt's name is a hypocoristic form of the Breton name Alan. Nettlestead was held in the twelfth century by the Boterel family, whose ancestor Alan fitz Aimeric was active in the early twelfth century. Halenad de Nettlestead owed castle-guard at Richmond temp. Henry I (EYC v, 11).

ii, fol. 294b; ii, fol. 295a

Halsard []
Tenant of William de Braose, occurs Domesday Surrey. A William Alsart attested a charter of William II de Braose in 1144 (Oxford Ch., 4). William Hansard held Halsard's Domesday manor of Tadworth, Surrey, in 1242 (Fees, 686).

i, fol. 35d; i, fol. 35d

Hamelin De Cornubie
Sheriff of Cornwall under William of Mortain. As Hamelin of Cornwall (Cornubiæ) he attested a charter of Richard fitz Turold concerning the church of Damblainville (Normandy, Calvados); he may have been identical with the Hamelin fitz William who held the church from Richard fitz Turold, who held it of Alan de Ducey (Ord. Vit. ed. Le Prévost, v, 187–8). Dead by 1129/30 when his widow, sons Baldwin and Robert, and a daughter Emma (wife of Hugh Daniscus), occur on the Pipe Roll.

i, fol. 105a; i, fol. 120a; i, fol. 123a; i, fol. 120d; i, fol. 104c; i, fol. 123a; i, fol. 123a; i, fol. 123a; i, fol. 123a; i, fol. 123a; i, fol. 123a; i, fol. 123b; i, fol. 123b; i, fol. 123b; i, fol. 123b; i, fol. 123b; i, fol. 123b; i, fol. 123b; i, fol. 123b; i, fol. 123b; i, fol. 123b; i, fol. 123b; i, fol. 123b; i, fol. 123b; i, fol. 123b

Hamelin De Petehorda
Undertenant of Earl Roger de Montgomery in Sussex and tenant of Robert fitz Theobald, lord of Petworth, Sussex, whose last act for Saint-Martin de Sées he witnessed in 1087, as Hamelin de Petehorda (Petworth) (CDF, 655).

i, fol. 23d; i, fol. 23d

Hamelin []
Norman, occurs in Domesday Lincolnshire as a tenant of Hugh fitz Baldric. By 1129 he had been succeeded by his son Geoffrey.

i, fol. 356b; i, fol. 356b; i, fol. 298a; i, fol. 356b

Hamelin []
Domesday tenant of Ilbert de Lacy of Pontefract. He was succeeded in the early twelfth century by Robert de Fryston.

i, fol. 316b

Haminc []
English tenant of Robert of Mortain in Domesday Sussex. Ancestor of the Excete/Hecset family, he was succeeded after 1086 by his son Robert. His descendants occur in Cart. Lewes i, pp. 140, 159–60, 171, 176.

i, fol. 21c; i, fol. 21b; i, fol. 20d; i, fol. 21a

Harding De Oxeneford
Englishman, occurs in the Domesday borough of Oxford. Identified in Cart. Eynsham i., p. 37 as Harding de Oxeneford, who went to Jerusalem (probably with the First Crusade) and died there (qui in Ierusalem iuit et ibi mortuus est).

i, fol. 154b

Harding Filius Alnod
Englishman, son of Alnoth or Ednoth the Constable, also called Harding de Meriet in the Tax Return for Crewkerne Hundred, Somerset, from the manor of Merriott, his principal holding in 1086. Although his descendants of the FitzHarding and Meriet families were persons of substance in the twelfth century, Domesday Book reveals that in 1086 Harding had lost most of the lands previousy held by his father, much of which had gone to Hugh of Chester. He was obviously a young man at that date; his second son lived until the 1170s. Father of Nicholas, Robert, a daughter Cecilia (Earldom Glocs. Chh., 28), a daughter who was a nun of Shaftesbury, and probably a son Baldwin (Buckland Cart, Som. Rec. Soc. 25, pp. 184–5). See Williams, The English, 119–20; R. Patterson, 'Robert fitz Harding of Bristol . . .', Haskins Society Journal 1 (1989).

i, fol. 170c; i, fol. 99a; i, fol. 98d; i, fol. 241b; i, fol. 153b; i, fol. 153b; i, fol. 43a; i, fol. 63d; Finberg, Early Tavistock Charters: ERH, 62, No. IV; i, fol. 98d; i, fol. 98d; i, fol. 98d; i, fol. 98d; i, fol. 98d; Dugdale, Monasticon Anglicanum, II, pp. 482–83, No. XIII; Dugdale, Monasticon Anglicanum, II, pp. 482–83, No. XIII; i, fol. 90d; i, fol. 74a; i, fol. 74a; i, fol. 74a

Harduin De Scalariis
Harduin's toponym has caused great confusion for historians, though it can be related to several places all over modern France. He has been seen as a Fleming from Ecalles on the grounds that a certain Baldwin held land of him, but the argument is weak and ignores the several real clues we have as to his origins. Harduin's earliest holdings lay in Cambridgeshire, where he was a major tenant of

the abbey of Ely. He figures largely in the Inquisitiones Eliensis and Comitatus Cantabrigiensis. The most important landholder in the region before 1075, and certainly before 1070, was Count Alan, from whom Harduin held land in addition to his tenancy-in-chief. A Breton origin for Harduin is therefore more likely than not. Harduin's descendants of the de Scalariis family are found in the same region as their relatives of a junior line who descended from Brien de Scalariis, a tenant of Count Alan and doubtless father of Evrard fitz Brien, tenant of another Breton, Aubrey de Vere. The name Brien indisputably indicates Breton ancestry. Harduin's toponym probably indicates that, like several of Count Alan's men, his roots were in the seigneurie of Fougères in north-east Brittany. There is a hamlet of Les Echelles in the commune of Saint-Germain-en-Coglès, Ille-et-Vilaine, arr. Fougères. Two of Harduin's tenants, not named in Domesday Book, at Little Abington (VCH Cambs. viii, s.v.) were Ralph de Felgeres and Robert Brito. The former must be distinguished from Ralph seigneur of Fougères, also a Domesday tenant-in-chief, but may have originated in the same region. Although not associated in Domesday Book with Count Alan's holding in Richmondshire, Harduin early acquired interests there permitting the grant of four carucates to St Mary's, York. At his death, some years after 1086, his lands were divided between his sons Richard and Hugh (Curia Regis Rolls v, 139). He was father also of a son Robert (q.v.), evidenced in Thetford charters of his descendants.

i, fol. 137a; i, fol. 190d; i, fol. 191a; i, fol. 191a; i, fol. 190d; i, fol. 190d; i, fol. 191b; i, fol. 191a; i, fol. 191b; i, fol. 194b; i, fol. 191c; i, fol. 191b; i, fol. 191c; i, fol. 196d; Hamilton, Inquisitio Eliensis (1876), pp. 192–95; i, fol. 190c; Dugdale, Monasticon Anglicanum, II, p. 603, No. XXVII; ii, fol. 003b; i, fol. 141c; i, fol. 199b; i, fol. 193b; i, fol. 198c; i, fol. 198a; i, fol. 198a; i, fol. 141c; i, fol. 199b; i, fol. 142a; i, fol. 199b; i, fol. 199b; i, fol. 141d; i, fol. 198a; i, fol. 198c; i, fol. 199a; i, fol. 142a; i, fol. 199b; i, fol. 132a; i, fol. 198a; i, fol. 199b; i, fol. 198c; i, fol. 198c; i, fol. 197d; i, fol. 197d; i, fol. 199c; i, fol. 198b; i, fol. 198a; i, fol. 199b; i, fol. 198a; i, fol. 198a; i, fol. 197d; i, fol. 197d; i, fol. 141c; Clay, Early Yorkshire Charters (1936), V, No. 352; Dugdale, Monasticon Anglicanum, III, pp. 548–50, No. V

Harduin []
Domesday tenant of William fitz Nigel under earl Hugh in Chester.

i, fol. 266b; i, fol. 266a

Harold De Ewias
Son and heir of Ralph of Dreux, earl of Hereford, and Goda, sister of Edward the Confessor. Minor at the date of Domesday, when his lands were in the custody of Alfred of Marlborough, he took possession of them soon thereafter. Founded the priory of Ewyas Harold in 1100 (Mon. Ang. i 546). He was succeeded by his son Robert sometime after 1100 (Sanders, 85). See D. Bates, 'Lord Sudeley's Ancestors: the family of the counts of Amiens, valois and the Vexin', in The Sudeleys – Lords of Toddington, The Manorial Society of Great Britain (1987); A. Williams, 'The king's nephew: the family, career and connections of Ralph, earl of Hereford', in Studies in Medieval History Presented to R. Allen Brown, ed. C. Harper-Bill et al. (Woodbridge, 1989).

i, fol. 238a; Ellis, 'Landholders of Gloucestershire' (1880), pp. 91–93; i, fol. 244a; i, fol. 169b; i, fol. 177a; i, fol. 244a; i, fol. 244a; i, fol. 169b; i, fol. 177a; i, fol. 169b; Gibbs, Early Charters of St Pauls (1939), No. 198

Hascoit Musard

Breton, Domesday tenant-in-chief. Received a glowing commendation in Liber Eliensis (p. 277), which relates that he became a monk of Ely. They claimed that he had brought with him the manor of Estune (probably Aston Somerville, Gloucestershire), with the assent of his son Robert, but a writ of William II (ibid. 207–8) shows that Harscoit had first granted it to fellow-Breton, Bishop Hervey of Ely, ten years before the bishop was connected with the abbey. His son Robert succeeded him in the early twelfth century (a generation is omitted in Sanders, 83).

> i, fol. 244a; i, fol. 277d; i, fol. 277d; i, fol. 277d; i, fol. 277d; i, fol. 277d; i, fol. 277d; i, fol. 277d; i, fol. 277d; i, fol. 169c; i, fol. 61d; i, fol. 61d; i, fol. 169c; i, fol. 169c; i, fol. 169c; i, fol. 61d; i, fol. 169c; i, fol. 169c; i, fol. 159cd; i, fol. 160ab; i, fol. 159cd; i, fol. 244a; i, fol. 169c; i, fol. 152c; i, fol. 143a

Hato []

Tenant of Count Eustache de Boulogne in Domesday Suffolk. In the early thirteenth century his land was held by Geoffrey de Fercles (Ferques, in the Boulonnais, cant. Marquise, Pas-de-Calais) (Fees 236).

> ii, fol. 303b; ii, fol. 032b

Heldred []

Domesday tenant of Hugh de Port.

> i, fol. 45b; i, fol. 45c

Heldric []

English tenant of Robert of Mortain in Domesday Cornwall.

> i, fol. 125a

Helewis Nepta Eruasti Episcopi

Niece of Bishop Erfast of Thetford (1070–85); his tenant at Witton, Norfolk, in 1086. Cf. Helewisa (Heloise), daughter of Hugh fitz Golde, wife of Ralph fitz Herluin of Hunstanton.

> ii, fol. 200b

Helgot De Castello

Norman tenant of Earl Roger in Domesday Shropshire; ancestor of the Castle Holgate family (Sanders, 28). He was succeeded soon after 1086 by his son Eutrop, and thereafter by a younger son Herbert (Cart. Shrewsbury no. 1). Helgot Dant and his brothers Fulk, William, Robert and Osmund, attested a charter for Saint-Martin de Sées (Arch. dépt. Orne H938, fols 7v–8r); a charter of William d'Echauffour for Sainte-Trinité de Rouen (Cart., p. 442) was attested by Ansfrid fitz Athle [de Montgomery] and Helgo del Maisnil.

> i, fol. 256d; i, fol. 248b; i, fol. 249b; i, fol. 257a; i, fol. 260c; i, fol. 260c; i, fol. 260c; i, fol. 249a; Rees, Cartulary of Shrewsbury Abbey (1975), No. 35; i, fol. 258d; i, fol. 258d; i, fol. 258c; i, fol. 258c; i, fol. 258d; i, fol. 258c; i, fol. 258c; i, fol. 258c; i, fol. 258c; i, fol. 258c; i, fol. 258c; i, fol. 258c; i, fol. 258c; i, fol. 258d; i, fol. 258c

Helgot []

Domesday tenant of Maino Brito. His fees were held in 1166 by Peverel de Beauchamp (Luffield cart., ii, 552).

> i, fol. 152a; i, fol. 152a

Helgot []
Domesday tenant of Robert de Tosny of Stafford. Succeeded by his son Guy, father of Helgot who occurs in 1166, and Philip fitz Elgod, occ. 1166, hereditary forester of Kinver (Hist. Coll. Staffs., ii, 247ff).

i, fol. 249a; i, fol. 249a

Helius []
Tenant of the bishop of Thetford in Domesday Norfolk. His personal name is apparently a cacography for Helias.

ii, fol. 191b; ii, fol. 200a; ii, fol. 200b; ii, fol. 195a; ii, fol. 199b; ii, fol. 199b; ii, fol. 199b

Helto Dapifer
Dapifer of Odo of Bayeux. William I gave to Sainte-Trinité de Caen the service of the holding of Gosfrid fitz Salomon and Helto dapifer in Graye-sur-Mer, Calvados (Actes caen. 22, 1080–85). Helto probably returned to Bayeux with Odo in 1088 (CDF, pp. 530–1), and the fate of his lands is obscure. His principal manor of Swanscombe was held, probably from c. 1090, by Geoffrey I Talbot and his wife Agnes. In 1129 a Helto fitz Richard fitz Malger accounted for his father's lands in Kent (Pipe Roll 31 Henry I, 66). This Helto was the ancestor of the FitzHelto family. Helto is a rare name, so that some relationship between Malger (a tenant of Odo in 1086) or his descendants and Helto is highly likely. Possibly Malger's wife was a daughter of Helto.

i, fol. 006a; i, fol. 009a; i, fol. 008d; i, fol. 144c; i, fol. 144a; i, fol. 144a; i, fol. 144a; i, fol. 144a; i, fol. 144a; i, fol. 002c

Henricus De Ferrariis
Norman, from Ferrières-Saint-Hilaire, Eure, arr. Bernay, cant. Broglie (Loyd, 42), son of Walchelin de Ferrières, who died before 1040 (Ord. Vit., ii, 264). Tenant-in-chief in 1086, especially well endowed in Derbyshire and Nottinghamshire, of which his descendants were earls. The caput of his fief was at Tutbury in Staffordshire, where he and his wife Bertha founded a priory as a cell of Saint-Pierre-sur-Dives sometime between 1087 and Henry's death c.1101, and where Henry was buried. Their foundation charter named three sons, Ingenulf, W[illiam] and Robert. The name of Ingenulf may indicate that Bertha was from the family of L'Aigle. There was also a daughter Amice, wife of Nigel de Albini of Cainhoe. Henry's successor in England was his son Robert. His son Ingenulf, who was always mentioned in the numerous family confirmations for Tutbury and was clearly an important figure in the family, probably succeeded him in Normandy, and was probably the father of Henry II, Henry's grandson and head of the Norman branch c.1130. Sanders, 148; Comp. Peer. iv, 190–203.

i, fol. 273a; i, fol. 57d; i, fol. 151a; Dugdale, Monasticon Anglicanum, III, pp. 391–92, No. I; Dugdale, Monasticon Anglicanum, III, pp. 392–93, No. II; i, fol. 234d; i, fol. 233c; i, fol. 233b; i, fol. 233b; i, fol. 233b; i, fol. 219a; i, fol. 233b; i, fol. 233b; i, fol. 233b; i, fol. 233b; i, fol. 233b; i, fol. 233b; i, fol. 233b; i, fol. 230a; i, fol. 225a; i, fol. 157d; i, fol. 157d; i, fol. 157d; i, fol. 157d; i, fol. 154c; i, fol. 154a; i, fol. 157d; i, fol. 233b; i, fol. 57d; i, fol. 291d; i, fol. 246a; i, fol. 238a; i, fol. 57c; i, fol. 58a; i, fol. 166d; Douglas, Feudal Documents from Bury St Edmunds, No. 14; i, fol. 274a; i, fol. 275a; i, fol. 274c; i, fol. 274a; i, fol. 274a; i, fol. 274b; i, fol. 274a; i, fol. 274d; i, fol. 274a; i, fol. 274a; i, fol. 274a; i, fol. 274b; i, fol. 274a; i, fol. 274a; i, fol. 274b; i, fol. 72b; i, fol. 274a; i, fol. 275d; i, fol. 274d; i, fol. 274b; i, fol. 274d; i, fol. 274b; i, fol. 274d; i, fol. 274c; i, fol. 274b; i, fol. 274c; i, fol. 274b; i, fol. 274d; i, fol. 274d; i, fol. 72b; i, fol. 274b; i, fol. 275c; i, fol. 276a; i, fol. 275b; i, fol. 275b; i, fol. 275b; i, fol. 275b; i, fol. 275b; i, fol. 275b; i, fol. 275c; i, fol. 275b; i, fol. 275c; i, fol. 275c; i, fol. 275c; i, fol. 275c; i, fol. 275c; i, fol. 275c; i, fol. 275c; i, fol. 275a; i, fol. 275b; i, fol. 275d; i, fol. 275c; i, fol. 275d; i, fol. 275b; i, fol. 275d; i, fol. 275d; i, fol. 275d; i, fol. 275c; i, fol. 275d; i, fol. 275d; i, fol. 275d; i, fol. 275a; i, fol. 274a; i, fol. 353c; i, fol. 276a; i, fol. 276a; i, fol. 275d; i, fol. 275d; i, fol. 185b; i, fol. 225a; i, fol. 248c; i, fol. 233b; i, fol. 242b; i, fol. 353c; i, fol. 157d; i, fol. 169a; Hart, Cartularium Monasterii de Rameseia, No. CLI; Dugdale, Monasticon Anglicanum, III, p. 393, No. III; Clay, Early Yorkshire Charters (1949), VIII, No. 5; Dugdale, Monasticon Anglicanum, III, p. 393, No. IV; i, fol. 291d; i, fol. 56b; i, fol. 291d; i, fol. 280b; i, fol. 291d; i, fol. 291d; Dugdale, Monasticon Anglicanum, III, p. 393, No. IV; i, fol. 272d; i, fol. 64d; i, fol. 185b; i, fol. 248c; i, fol. 151a; i, fol. 151a; i, fol. 60c; i, fol. 57c; i, fol. 60c; i, fol. 60c; i, fol. 60d; i, fol. 248c; i, fol. 60c; i, fol. 248c; i, fol. 248c; i, fol. 169a; i, fol. 248c; i, fol. 60d; i, fol. 248c; ii, fol. 057a; ii, fol. 057a; ii, fol. 056b; ii, fol. 056b; ii, fol. 103a; ii, fol. 056b; i, fol. 60d; i, fol. 57d; i, fol. 60d; i, fol. 234d; i, fol. 248b; Dugdale, Monasticon Anglicanum, III, p. 394, No. XI

Henricus De Fifidre

Norman, Domesday tenant of Henry de Ferrers to whom he was perhaps related. Probably to be identified with Henry's dapifer of the name, also known as Henry de Fifhyde. Benefactor of Tutbury.

i, fol. 275a; i, fol. 275a; i, fol. 275a; i, fol. 60c; i, fol. 60d; i, fol. 60d; i, fol. 60b; i, fol. 60d; ii, fol. 057a; Dugdale, Monasticon Anglicanum, III, pp. 392–93, No. II

Henricus Filius Azor

Held a single manor in chief in Domesday Bedfordshire. Possibly a brother of Jocelyn and William fitz Azor.

i, fol. 216c; i, fol. 216c

Henricus Thesaurarius

Apparently one of the foreigners recruited by Edward the Confessor since the Winton Domesday (58) reveals that he had held his land before 1066; it was held by his widow c.1112.

i, fol. 49a; i, fol. 49a; i, fol. 49a; i, fol. 49a; i, fol. 49a

Heppo Balistarius

Norman, tenant-in-chief in Domesday Lincolnshire. His son Jocelyn occurs in the Register of Spalding priory granting land at Surfleet. Shortly afterwards Jocelyn and his wife went on pilgrimage to Jerusalem, from which Jocelyn did not return. By 1133 Jocelyn's widow Matilda had married Hugh fitz Algar. She and Hugh confirmed Jocelyn's grant, attested by their son Herbert (BL Add. 35296, fol. 360). Heppo's fief appears thereafter to have passsed to the Neville and Furnage families (Rot. de Dom. 17). A Heppo, son of Azo and Hermina and brother of Ivo and Richard, a tenant of William, count of Evreux, occurs in a number of Saint-Trinité-de-Rouen charters c.1050/60 (Fauroux, 135, 210, 221.

Lincolnshire Claims (Domesday Book), fols 376d–377c; i, fol. 369a; Lindsey Survey, BL ms Cotton Claudius C v, fols 1–9; i, fol. 369a; i, fol. 369a; i, fol. 369a; i, fol. 369a; i, fol. 369a; i, fol. 369a; i, fol. 369a; i, fol. 369a; i, fol. 369a; i, fol. 369a; i, fol. 369a; i, fol. 369a

Herald []
Occurs Domesday Kent.
> i, fol. 014a; i, fol. 014a

Herbert Camerarius
Domesday tenant-in-chief in Hampshire. He was dead by the time of his appearance in PR 31 Henry I, which (p. 37) reveals that his wife was a sister of Osbert father of Gervaise, that his son and heir was Herbert and that he had a daughter married to Robert de Venoiz, and another daughter (ibid. 125) married to William Croc. Remembered as a predator of the abbey of Abingdon, to which he finally made amends; Chron. Abing. ii, 134 calls him 'regis cubicularius atque thesaurarius'. These offices were held c.1125 by Geoffrey de Clinton, who may have purchased them from Henry I (RRAN ii, 1428); they certainly did not pass to Herbert's son.
> i, fol. 48c; i, fol. 48c; i, fol. 46a; i, fol. 48d; Mason, Westminster Abbey Charters (1988), No. 488; i, fol. 43c,d; i, fol. 45c; i, fol. 48d; i, fol. 48d

Herbert Camerarius Rogeri Bigot
Chamberlain of Roger Bigod, occurs Domesday Norfolk. Possibly Herbert de Cravencum who occurs as an early benefactor of Thetford Priory (Mon. Ang. iv, 148). The toponym may refer to Notre-Dame de Gravenchon, Seine-Maritime, arr. Le Havre, cant. Lillebonne.
> ii, fol. 278b; Dugdale, Monasticon Anglicanum, IV, pp. 150–51, No. VIII; Dugdale, Monasticon Anglicanum, IV, pp. 148–49, No. II; Regesta Regum Anglo Normannorum II, App. no. cxxvii

Herbert De Furcis
Norman, from Furches, Calvados, cant. Morteaux-Couliboeuf, Domesday tenant of Roger de Montgomery and Roger de Lacy. Identified in Shropshire by Eyton, Shropshire v, 44–5. A Herbert de Furchis attested the Holme Lacy charter of 1085. See Wightman, Lacy Family, 154 and n. 4.
> i, fol. 256c; i, fol. 256c; i, fol. 256c; i, fol. 256c; i, fol. 184a; i, fol. 184a; i, fol. 180b

Herbert De Sancto Quintino
Norman, mentioned in an early document of Shaftesbury abbey. In 1166 St Quintin fees were held of the honour of Curry Malet, successors of Roger de Courseulles, who in 1086 had a tenant named Herbert. Perhaps named from Saint-Quentin-sur-le-Homme, Manche, arr. Avranches, cant. Ducey, or Saint-Quentin-les-Chardonnets, Orne, cant. Tinchebray.
> i, fol. 94c; i, fol. 93c; Dugdale, Monasticon Anglicanum, II, pp. 482–83, No. XIII

Herbert II De Sancto Quintino
Norman, probably named from either Saint-Quentin-sur-le-Homme, Manche, arr. Avranches, cant. Ducey, or Saint-Quentin-les-Chardonnets, Orne, cant. Tinchebray. Domesday tenant in Lincolnshire of Odo balistarius and Norman d'Arcy. In the Lindsey Survey of 1115/18 he occurs also as tenant of Stephen count of Aumale. Possibly related to the Herbert de St Quintin who occurs Domesday Somerset and of the Richard de St Quintin who was associated with Robert fitz Haimo in Gloucestershire c.1090. At his death in 1126 he left issue a son Richard and a daughter Alice, wife first of Robert fitz Fulk fitz Rainfrid, Percy steward,

and secondly of Eustache de Merck. His widow was his second wife Agnes daughter of Osbern de Arches (EYC i, no. 541 and note).

> i, fol. 361d; i, fol. 365d; i, fol. 365d; i, fol. 361c; i, fol. 362a; Lindsey Survey, BL ms Cotton Claudius C v, fols 9–18

Herbert Filius Alberici
Domesday tenant of the archbishop of York; identifiable from Lindsey Survey 16.4. Father of Herbert camerarius (regis Scotiae) and William, archbishop of York (q.v.), EYC i, no. 25.

> i, fol. 339d; i, fol. 339c; i, fol. 339c; Lindsey Survey, BL ms Cotton Claudius C v, fols 19–27

Herbert Filius Iuonis
Norman, Domesday tenant in Kent of Odo of Bayeux, associated with his nephew (nepos) Hugh.

> i, fol. 011a; i, fol. 010a; i, fol. 011a; i, fol. 209d; i, fol. 209d; i, fol. 007c; i, fol. 009d; i, fol. 209d

Herbert Filius Remigii
Norman, occurs Domesday Hampshire.

> i, fol. 48d; i, fol. 48d; i, fol. 48d

Herbert Forestarius
Occurs Domesday Hampshire. His son Henry succeeded him by 1129/30.

> i, fol. 66a; i, fol. 39a

Herbert Grammaticus
Norman, one of three principal clerks of Roger de Montgomery named by Orderic Vitalis (ii, 262). Occurs as Roger's tenant in Domesday Shropshire. Archdeacon of Shrewsbury in Chester diocese. Cf. Mason, Officers and Clerks, 253. See EEA xiv, 127.

> i, fol. 255b; i, fol. 258d; Rees, Cartulary of Shrewsbury Abbey (1975), No. 35

Herbert Prefectus Regis
Norman, royal provost; occurs Domesday Bedfordshire.

> i, fol. 218c; i, fol. 218c; i, fol. 218c

Herbert Senescallus
Domesday tenant and seneschal of William de Polli, with whose gift of Devonshire land to Saint-Martin de Sées he was associated (CDF, 656).

> i, fol. 111c

Herbert Serviens Regis
Norman, King's servant, occurs Domesday Leicestershire. Probably the same man as held of Henry de Ferrers in Derbyshire. Ancestor of the FitzHerberts of Twycross, Leicestershire (a Ferrers fee in 1086), and of Norbury, Derbyshire (Nichols, History of Leics., iv, 860). In 1129/30 a Richard fitz Herbert rendered an account in Leicestershire. William fitz Herbert was enfeoffed at Norbury by the prior of Tutbury in 1125 (Cart. Tutbury, no. 88).

> i, fol. 230b; i, fol. 275b; i, fol. 236d; i, fol. 236d; i, fol. 236d; i, fol. 236d

Herbert []
Domesday tenant of William d'Eu.

i, fol. 167a; i, fol. 166d; i, fol. 96c

Herbert []
Domesday tenant of Eustache of Huntingdon.

i, fol. 206b; i, fol. 206b; i, fol. 206a

Herbert []
Domesday tenant of Alfred d'Epaignes in Somerset.

i, fol. 97b; i, fol. 97b; i, fol. 97b

Herbert []
Occurs Domesday Worcestershire as a tenant of Ralph de Tosny and Osbern fitz Richard.

i, fol. 176d; i, fol. 176d; i, fol. 176b; i, fol. 176b

Herbrand De Pont Audemer
Norman, occurs as Herbrand de Pont Audemer, Eure, in the list of Domesday landholders for Hampshire, though his full name was not repeated in his chapter-heading.

i, fol. 53d; i, fol. 49a; i, fol. 175a; i, fol. 177d; i, fol. 49a

Herbrand De Sackville
Norman, tenant of Walter I de Giffard. According to a document of temp. Henry III this Herbrand was father of Jordan, William and Robert de Sauqueville, Seine-Maritime, arr. Dieppe (Loyd, 88 note, citing Round in Peerage and Pedigree i, 287). Round, op. cit. also cited a fourteenth-century text that claimed Herbrand as Walter's steward in Normandy and England; cf. Mason, 'Barons and officials', ANS 13 (1991), p. 255. A charter of Sainte-Trinité de Rouen was attested by Walter Giffard and his dapifer Herbran (Cart., pp. 444–5). Herbrand also had a daughter Avice, wife of Walter d'Auffay, according to Orderic Vitalis, iii, 256. Jordan succeeded him by or during the reign of Henry I (ibid., 258).

i, fol. 147a

Hereberd Fossator
Englishman, occurs Domesday Norwich.

ii, fol. 117a

Hereuuard []
Englishman, Domesday tenant of the count of Meulan and Thorkil of Warwick in Warwickshire.

i, fol. 240a; i, fol. 240c; i, fol. 240c

Herfrid []
Domesday tenant of Odo bishop of Bayeux; perhaps Herfrid of Bavent (Calvados). A Ralph fitz Herfrid gave land in Bavent to Saint-Etienne de Caen (Actes caen. 75, 101, 108). In 1236 the heirs of Haimo de Gatun (Gatton, Surrey) were holding Herfrid's fees of the honour of Peverel of Dover (Fees, 582).

i, fol. 32a; i, fol. 31d; i, fol. 30d; i, fol. 011b; i, fol. 013d; i, fol. 010d; i, fol. 010b

Heringod Homo Archiepiscopi
Man of Archbishop Lanfranc in 1086 and 1093, holding later in Wingham, Kent,

probably at Overland, (Du Boulay, Lordship of Canterbury, 61, 68, 93, 96, 108–10, 117, 374, 383). Identified in Dom. Mon., p. 83. His descendants were surnamed Haringod; Stephen Haringod (q.v.), father of John, occurs c.1155.

i, fol. 003d

Herlebald []
Occurs Domesday Worcestershire.

i, fol. 177c; i, fol. 177c; i, fol. 45a; i, fol. 177c; i, fol. 173d; i, fol. 177d; i, fol. 177c

Herluin Filius Ivonis
Norfolk, tenant of Rainald fitz Ivo, probably his brother. The identification results from the Annexations sections of Norfolk Domesday (DB Norfolk 66.51), where Herluin fitz Ivo is said to have annexed land in a manor held by Rainald. All other references to Herluin are to the tenant of Rainald. His grants to Thetford priory were ascribed to Herluin de Panewrda, named from his manor of Panworth.

Regesta Regum Anglo Normannorum II, App. no. cxxvii; ii, fol. 234a; ii, fol. 232a; ii, fol. 232a; Regesta Regum Anglo Normannorum II, App. no. cxxvii; ii, fol. 234b; ii, fol. 234b

Herluin []
Domesday tenant of Geoffrey of Coutances.

i, fol. 88b; i, fol. 88a; i, fol. 88a; i, fol. 88b

Herman De Dreuues
Occurs Domesday Gloucestershire and elsewhere, from Dreux, Eure-et-Loir. He was perhaps a brother of Almaric de Dreux, who also occurs in Domesday Wiltshire. His representative in 1166 was probably the William de Drocis who held two fees of Robert de Candos.

i, fol. 176c; i, fol. 185a; i, fol. 181a; i, fol. 180d; i, fol. 71c; i, fol. 66a; i, fol. 187a; i, fol. 73b; i, fol. 187a

Herman []
Domesday tenant of Jocelyn fitz Lambert in Lincolnshire.

i, fol. 359b; i, fol. 359c

Hermer De Ferrariis
Norman, who held lands in Domesday Norfolk and Suffolk, later known as the barony of Wormegay Sanders, 101). His origin and family appear distinct from that of Henry de Ferrers (q.v.), but that they were in fact the same (Ferrières-Saint-Hilaire, Eure, arr. Bernay, cant. Broglie) is possibly suggested by the fact that Henry had a Domesday tenant called Polcehart and Hermer's grandson had a tenant William Polcehart. He was succeeded by 1111 by his son Richard (d.a.1130).

ii, fol. 190a; ii, fol. 118a; ii, fol. 205b; ii, fol. 206b; ii, fol. 206a; ii, fol. 207b; ii, fol. 207b; ii, fol. 208a; ii, fol. 205b; ii, fol. 207a; ii, fol. 206a; ii, fol. 206b; ii, fol. 208b; ii, fol. 208a; ii, fol. 206a; ii, fol. 205b; ii, fol. 205b; ii, fol. 207b; ii, fol. 207b; ii, fol. 206a; ii, fol. 207b; ii, fol. 206b; ii, fol. 206b; ii, fol. 207b; ii, fol. 207a; ii, fol. 207a; ii, fol. 206b; ii, fol. 207a; ii, fol. 207a; ii, fol. 206b; ii, fol. 208a; ii, fol. 274a; ii, fol. 274a; ii, fol. 274a; ii, fol. 274a; ii, fol. 274a; ii, fol. 274a; ii, fol. 275a; ii, fol. 275a; ii, fol. 274b; ii, fol. 275a; ii, fol. 275a; ii, fol. 273b; ii, fol. 274b; ii, fol. 274a; ii, fol. 275a; ii, fol. 274b; ii, fol. 274b; ii, fol.

274b; ii, fol. 274b; ii, fol. 274b; ii, fol. 275a; ii, fol. 274b; ii, fol. 274a; ii, fol. 274a; ii, fol. 273b; ii, fol. 274a; ii, fol. 275a; ii, fol. 274a; ii, fol. 274a; ii, fol. 273b; ii, fol. 273b; ii, fol. 274a; ii, fol. 273b; ii, fol. 273b; ii, fol. 274a; ii, fol. 273b; ii, fol. 274a; ii, fol. 273b; ii, fol. 354a; ii, fol. 354a

Hermer []
A knight of Abingdon, who was captured and mutilated by pirates whilst journeying to Normandy on the king's business. No land having yet been assigned to him, the king in his compassion ordered Abbot Adelhelm to see that he was provided for, and hence he was apportioned part of Denchworth (Chron. Abing. ii, 6–7).

i, fol. 59a

Hermer []
Domesday tenant of Walter de Douai and Gotshelm de Claville in Devon. His holdings were afterwards held by persons named from Washbourne.

i, fol. 112d; i, fol. 113a; i, fol. 111d

Hermer []
Norman, Domesday tenant of Ivo Taillebois. Father of Drogo, father of Ralph, who had succeeded his grandfather by 1129. See HKF ii, 92–3.

i, fol. 350a

Hernegrin Monachus
Englishman, occurs Domesday Yorkshire, as a king's thegn. He appears to have become a monk of St Mary's, York, to which he gave most of his land, c.1087. See VCH Yorks ii, 159.

Dugdale, Monasticon Anglicanum, III, p. 547, No. III; Dugdale, Monasticon Anglicanum, III, pp. 548–50, No. V; i, fol. 331a; i, fol. 331a

Hertald Monachus Sancte Trinitatis
Monk of Sainte-Trinité de Rouen.

i, fol. 128d

Herueus Bituricensis
Hervé presents the most difficult and the most interesting questions of any Domesday tenant-in-chief. A tenant-in-chief whose lands were acquired in or shortly after 1075, since most if not all had earlier been held from Ely Abbey by William son of Gorhan, a Breton who fell in the revolt of 1075 (Inquitio Eliensis, 193). Hervé may himself have been a Breton. He had a tenant with the Breton name Euan, and another, Peter de Paludel, whose name could refer to La Palvelle near Saint-James in Normandy. The seigneurs of Saint-James were of a Breton family, one of the few to use the then still rare name Peter. Saint-James is not far from Alençon, whence came Hervé's tenant Bernard. His byname normally means 'from Berry or its capital Bourges', but it is highly unlikely that Hervé came to England from Berry, though his ancestors may have done. Bituricensis was not necessaily a toponym. The various forms of Hervé's name all play on the idea of 'bituricis', from Berry, but might well represent a play on 'bitricus', meaning 'wren'. Short of discovering several lost place-names, some such explanation is required for continental examples of this byname: it had been borne, for example, by Eudo, natural son of Alan III of Brittany (Morice, Preuves I, 401), and by Rainald, son of Hugh de Merderel, a native of Maine (Cart. St Vincent, 395). It was

possible for such a nickname to become a hereditary byname. Hervé held no land of the abbot of Bury St Edmunds, but a certain Peter clericus did. Peter's manors passed to Hervé's heirs of the Pecche family. Though there is no trace of an enfeoffment to Pecche by the abbot, we do know that Hervé's wife and her daughter Isilia Pecche were benefactors of the abbey. In the 1090s Abbot Baldwin's charter were twice attested by Peter Bituricensis. Between 1107 and 1118 Henry I granted to the abbot's demesne the land that had been held by Peter Bituricensis and by Peter clericus Ambianensis. A late ms of Bury (BM Add. 14843, fol. 33v) states that the two Peters were the same man and the demesne manor in question was Hengrave in Suffolk. This suggests that the Domesday Peter clericus and Peter Bituricensis were the same and that Peter was a relative of Hervé, a suspicion reinforced by the unexplained descent of Peter's manors to the heirs of Hervé. As a clerk, Peter's byname could refer to the place where he was trained; as such, it is noteworthy that Baldwin's original abbey of Saint-Denis was well-endowed in Berry, notably at La Chapelle-Aude. If he were a senior relative father or uncle of Hervé, his byname, however acquired, remained with his male heir. Hervé's wife Judith was perhaps a sister or daughter of Robert Malet, since his daughter and heiress Isilia bore the name of Robert's mother and there was a strong Malet connexion with the lands of Hervé's fief. Hervé was probably the father of Hervé who challenged Isilia's son Hamon Pecche's possession of Hervé Bituricensis's lands in 1129. Isilia's marriage occurred after 1107, when her husband William Pecche's first wife was still living. Certain evidence for the name of Hervé's wife survives in the corrupt form Ieuitia in a charter for Bury St Edmunds given by Hamo Pecche. Onomastic evidence shows this form to be a corruption of Judith, comparable with the hypocoristic form Jueta, which is frequently mistranscribed by modern historians as Iveta (cf. Jutta, the German form of the hypocoristic). It could be that Hervé and his wife were the benefactors of New Minster (Hyde) Abbey, Winchester, who occur in the Liber Vitae thus: Vrvog et Iudith coniunx eius necnon patres et matres ipsorum. In the same column of the Liber were written the names of Hervé's Domesday predecessor William son of Gorhan and his (William's) brother Hugh. Vrvog is the Breton form of Hervé's name. The reference to the parents of the Hyde Hervé and Judith is striking, particularly in view of the possible links between our Hervé and Judith with two other Domesday tenants, Peter Bituricensis and Esilia Malet.

ii, fol. 387b; ii, fol. 387b; ii, fol. 388a; ii, fol. 385b; ii, fol. 385b; ii, fol. 440b; ii, fol. 442a; ii, fol. 441b; ii, fol. 442a; ii, fol. 442a; ii, fol. 442a; ii, fol. 441b; ii, fol. 442a; ii, fol. 441b; ii, fol. 442b; ii, fol. 442a; ii, fol. 352a; ii, fol. 441b; ii, fol. 443a; ii, fol. 441b; ii, fol. 441a; ii, fol. 441a; ii, fol. 441a; ii, fol. 440b; ii, fol. 440b; ii, fol. 440b; ii, fol. 441b; ii, fol. 444a; ii, fol. 442b; ii, fol. 444a; ii, fol. 442b; ii, fol. 444a; ii, fol. 443b; ii, fol. 443b; ii, fol. 443a; ii, fol. 443a; ii, fol. 443a; ii, fol. 443a; ii, fol. 443a; ii, fol. 443a; ii, fol. 443b; ii, fol. 444a; ii, fol. 117a; ii, fol. 386b; ii, fol. 387b; ii, fol. 386a; ii, fol. 388b; ii, fol. 384a; ii, fol. 384a; ii, fol. 384a

Herueus De Ispania
Breton, Domesday tenant of Count Alan and probably of Bury St Edmunds (cf. Douglas, Feudal Book, p. cxli, note 5). According to Powell, TEAS, 3rd ser. 1 pt 3, 1964, p. 181 he died before 1093, and was from Epinay, near Rennes. His son William succeeded him. He is possibly to be identified with Hervé de l'Epine (de Spina), first known seigneur of Arbrissel c.1096–1109, who was son of Deusset,

daughter of the Breton Hervé de Martigné, seigneur of Pouancé in Anjou, and his wife Meneczuc. Hervé de l'Epine and his son William both disappear from Breton documents before 1128, when Hervé's nephew Payn was seigneur of Arbrissel. See J.-C. Meuret, 'Familles seigneuriales aux confins Anjou-Bretagne', MSHAB, lxx (1993), 119–26.

ii, fol. 149b; ii, fol. 035a; ii, fol. 035a; ii, fol. 035b; Douglas, Feudal Documents from Bury St Edmunds, No. 169; ii, fol. 035b; ii, fol. 035b; ii, fol. 035b; Douglas, Feudal Book of Bury St Edmunds (1932), pp. 3–21; ii, fol. 358a; Feudal Book, pp. 3–21

Herueus De Salsitona
Occurs as a juror in Whittlesford Hundred, Cambridge, described as of Sawston; to be identified with the tenant of Picot of Cambridge at Trumpington.

i, fol. 200b; Hamilton, Inquisitio Comitatus Cantabrigiensis, pp. 1–93; Hamilton, Inquisitio Eliensis (1876), pp. 97–100

Herueus De Wiltune
Hervey the chamberlain, a royal servant also named of Wilton, occurs Domesday Wiltshire. His land at Netheravon was subsequently exchanged with land at Pevensey by an agreement between Lewes priory and Roger, bishop of Salisbury Cf. VCH Wilts ii, 75, 106.

i, fol. 64c; i, fol. 65b; i, fol. 68b; i, fol. 69b; i, fol. 74c; i, fol. 85a; Regesta regum Anglo-Normannorum III, No. 450; Round, Ancient Charters (1888), No. 31; i, fol. 74c; i, fol. 74c

Herueus Filius Ansgerii
Occurs in a single holding as a tenant of Milton Abbey in Dorset in Domesday Book. Identified as filius Ansgerii in Exon, he was probably a son of Ansger Brito (q.v.), a major tenant of Robert of Mortain whose principal heir was his son Walter.

i, fol. 78b

Herueus Legatus
The descent of Herve's lands in the Haget and Scalebroc families shows that Herve was Herve de Campellis (Campeaux, Calvados, arr. Vire, cant. Le Beny-Bocage). He was an officer in the Domesday Inquest, as indicated by the title 'legatus' which he bears in DB Bucks. His son Robert fitz Hervey was a man of Robert Gernon. Henry I's queen Matilda gave the service he owed Gernon to Abingdon abbey (Chron. Abing. ii, 77). Cf. Loyd, 53, EYC iii, 229. Cf. EYC iii, 1492, grants of Ilbert de Lacy's tenants to St Clement's, Pontefract, named Henry (sic) de Saieo (al. Laceio) as the donor of tithes in Skelbrook.

i, fol. 149a; i, fol. 156c; i, fol. 156a; i, fol. 316a; i, fol. 56d; i, fol. 152c; Dugdale, Monasticon Anglicanum, IV, p. 120, No. I; Dugdale, Monasticon Anglicanum, IV, pp. 120–21, No. II; i, fol. 152c; i, fol. 155d; i, fol. 155d; i, fol. 160c; i, fol. 160c; i, fol. 160c

Herueus []
Domesday tenant of Hugh de Montfort.

i, fol. 014a; i, fol. 013b; ii, fol. 408a; ii, fol. 408b; i, fol. 013c

Herueus []
Domesday tenant of Robert de Tosny of Stafford, ancestor of the de Stretton family. Hervey de Stretton held two fees of Robert II of Stafford in 1166.

i, fol. 242d; i, fol. 249c; i, fol. 249c; i, fol. 249c; i, fol. 249c; i, fol. 249c

Herueus []
Breton, Domesday tenant of Count Alan, ancestor of the Sutton family, named for Sutton on Trent. The family's three fees of the honour of Richmond were held in the early twelfth century by Hervey son of Ricol. Whether this was the same Hervey or his grandson is unknown. Another Hervey was holding by mid-Henry II (Pipe Roll 22 Henry II, 95, 23, etc.), who was father of Richard (d. a.1207), Robert, Roland and Juliana. See Clay, EYC, v, 258–9.

i, fol. 282c; i, fol. 310a; i, fol. 310a; i, fol. 309b; Dugdale, Monasticon Anglicanum, III, pp. 548–50, No. V

Hildebrand Lorimarius
Occurs Domesday Norfolk.

ii, fol. 117a

Homo Willelmi Filii Grosse
Unnamed man of William fitz Grosse.

ii, fol. 098b

Huard De Vernon
Norman, from Vernon, Eure, Domesday tenant of William d'Ecouis and Ralph de Belfago. Perhaps the same as Odard, tenant of Bury St Edmunds in Suffolk. Huard or Odard de Vernon was a benefactor of Bec, to which he gave Le Clos-Blancard in Longueville, near Vernon (Porée, Bec, i, 330–1). Possibly grandson of an earlier Odard, whose son Peter was, with his (Peter's) wife Grisca and brothers Geoffrey, Hugh, Payn and Walter, a benefactor of the abbey of Coulombs in 1052 (BN Coll. Baluze 77, fol. 30v), his father Odard assenting. In 1097 an Odard granted land in his maternal inheritance at Longueville to Jumièges, with the assent of his brother Richard (Arch. dépt. Seine-Maritime 9 h 7, pp. 20–1).

ii, fol. 288b; ii, fol. 367a; ii, fol. 225b; ii, fol. 226a; ii, fol. 223a; ii, fol. 227a; ii, fol. 229a; ii, fol. 229a; ii, fol. 224b; ii, fol. 224b; ii, fol. 353b; ii, fol. 354a; ii, fol. 353b

Hubert Capellanus
Domesday tenant of a single manor in Devon of Walter de Douai, doubtless the Hubert capellanus who attested a Glastonbury document relating to Walter in the 1090s (Cart. Glastonbury i, 128).

i, fol. 95a; i, fol. 112a

Hubert De Curcun
Norman, from Notre-Dame-de-Courson, Calvados, arr. Lisieux, cant. Livarot (Loyd, 37), Domesday tenant of Henry de Ferrers. Succeeded by his son Robert in the time of Abbot Rainald of Abingdon. His grant of tithes to Abingdon at West Lockinge was confirmed after his death by his sons Robert, Hubert and Stephen (Chron. Abing. ii, 32).

Stevenson, Chronicon Monasterii de Abingdon (1858) vol. II, pp. 4–6; i, fol. 248c; i, fol. 58c; i, fol. 60c

Hubert De Montecanisio
A Norman, from Mont-Canisy, Calvados, cant. Douvres-la-Délivrande, comm. Bénouville; important Domesday tenant of Robert Malet and also a minor tenant-in-chief in Suffolk. He gave the manor of Yaxley to Robert's priory of Eye at the time of foundation (Eye Cart., 1), and was also a benefactor of Thetford Priory

(Mon. Ang. iii, 149, 151). In 1115, when his son and successor Hubert began to attest his charters, Hubert was enriched by the grant to him of many of the fees of Godric Dapifer (q.v.). He died as a monk of Abingdon in the time of Abbot Faritius (d. 1117). He and his descendants were benefactors of Abingdon's cell of Colne in Essex, founded in the time of Faritius by Alberic I de Vere (q.v.). Hubert was twice married. His first wife, according to an item in the cartulary of St Benet's, Holme, was an Englishwoman, granddaughter of a certain Aslac, by whom he had issure Hubert, Gilbert and Warin. His second wife was Muriel, daughter of Peter de Valognes, by whom he had three further sons, Roger, Geoffrey and Hugh, whom his mother made a monk of Thetford. Comp. Peer. ix, 411ff.

ii, fol. 306a; ii, fol. 325a; ii, fol. 314a; ii, fol. 320b; ii, fol. 324a; ii, fol. 328a; ii, fol. 324b; i, fol. 20d; ii, fol. 306b; ii, fol. 309a; ii, fol. 309a; ii, fol. 309a; ii, fol. 309b; ii, fol. 154b; ii, fol. 154b; ii, fol. 324b; ii, fol. 326b; ii, fol. 304a; ii, fol. 327b; i, fol. 298b; Dodwell, Charters relating to the Honour of Bacton, No. 5; Regesta Regum Anglo Normannorum II, App. no. cxxvii ; Dugdale, Monasticon Anglicanum, IV, pp. 148–49, No. II; Brown, Eye Priory Cartulary (1992–94), No. 1; Brown, Eye Priory Cartulary (1992–94), No. 14; Brown, Eye Priory Cartulary (1992–94), No. 12; Brown, Eye Priory Cartulary (1992–94), No. 136; Brown, Eye Priory Cartulary (1992–94), No. 26; Brown, Eye Priory Cartulary (1992–94), No. 8; Brown, Eye Priory Cartulary (1992–94), No. 1; ii, fol. 325a; Fisher, Cartularium Prioratus de Colne (Earles C.), No. 64; Dugdale, Monasticon Anglicanum, IV, pp. 150–51, No. VIII; ii, fol. 436a; ii, fol. 319b; Fisher, Cartularium Prioratus de Colne (Earles C.), No. 65; Regesta regum Anglo-Normannorum III, No. 288; Brown, Eye Priory Cartulary (1992–94), No. 166; Brown, Eye Priory Cartulary (1992–94), No. 13; Fisher, Cartularium Prioratus de Colne (Earles C.), No. 14; ii, fol. 088a; ii, fol. 088a; Fisher, Cartularium Prioratus de Colne (Earles C.), No. 69; ii, fol. 309b; ii, fol. 309b; ii, fol. 309b; ii, fol. 309b; ii, fol. 309b

Hubert De Port
Norman, from Port-en-Bessin, Calvados, cant. Ryes (Loyd, 79), likely to have been a brother or other close relative of Hugh de Port, a Domesday tenant-in-chief. Hubert's Domesday holdings were modest. If, as is likely, Adam I de Port (d.1130/3) was his son, then they were later augumented by lands acquired by Adam in Wiltshire, Dorset and Herefordshire during the reign of Henry I. Ancestor of the Ports of Mapledurwell and Kington (Sanders, 57; Comp. Peer. xi, 316–26). Round distinguished between Port of Basing and their undoubted collaterals Port of Mapledurwell in Genealogist vols xvi and xvii.

i, fol. 46c; i, fol. 46c

Hubert De Sancto Claro
Domesday tenant of Robert de Mortain in Somerset, identified in Exon; probably from Saint-Clair-sur-l'Elle, Manche. He attested William de Mortain's notification of grants to Lewes Priory of his father's tenants, including Hubert fitz Ranulf, who was possibly the same person. Cf. Bretel de Sancto Clair, another of the count's tenants.

i, fol. 79c; i, fol. 79c; i, fol. 92a; i, fol. 79c; i, fol. 79c

Hubold []
Domesday tenant of Arnald de Hesdin in Wiltshire.

i, fol. 70b; i, fol. 70b

Hueche []
English tenant of Robert of Mortain in Domesday Cornwall.
i, fol. 125a

Hugo Arbalistarius
Tenant of Robert, count of Eu, in Domesday Sussex.
i, fol. 18c

Hugo Arbalistarius
Domesday tenant of Henry de Ferrers, identified from a grant to Tutbury priory.
i, fol. 274d; Dugdale, Monasticon Anglicanum, III, pp. 392–93, No. II

Hugo Barbatus
Hugo, or Hugolin, Barbatus or Cum Barba, occurs in Domesday Book principally as interpres or latinarius, ie. interpreter. Hugo Interpres is identifiable from his grants to the church of Wells as Hugolin cum Barba (EEA Bath/Wells, no. 3).
i, fol. 89d; i, fol. 49c; i, fol. 87b; Hart, Cartularium Monasterii de Rameseia, No. LVII; i, fol. 99b; i, fol. 99b; i, fol. 99b; i, fol. 50d; i, fol. 50d

Hugo Burdet
Norman, Domesday tenant of Hugh de Grandmesnil and Countess Judith in Leicestershire, son, possibly a younger son, of Robert I Burdet, who was dead in 1086. The Burdets held Rabodanges, cant. Putagnes, Orne, from the Grandmesnil in Normandy, where a senior branch of the family remained. Robert II Burdet (d.1155), a brother or nephew of Hugh, joined the crusade in Spain led by Rotroc count of Mortagne and became prince of Tarragona; see L.J. McCrank, 'Norman Crusaders in the Catalan Reconquest: Robert Burdet and the Principality of Tarragona, 1129–55', Journ. Med. Hist. vii (1981), 67–82; HKF, ii, 329.
i, fol. 232c; i, fol. 232d; i, fol. 236b; i, fol. 236b; i, fol. 236b; i, fol. 236c

Hugo Cementarius
Occurs Domesday Hampshire.
i, fol. 41a

Hugo Clericus
Occurs Domesday Sussex as a tenant of the bishop of Chichester.
i, fol. 16d

Hugo Cocus
Occurs Domesday Berkshire as a tenant of Abingdon Abbey.
i, fol. 58d; i, fol. 58d

Hugo Comes De Cestrie
Hugh of Avranches, earl of Cheste from 1071r, d. 1101. An important figure of great ability, he was the subject of hostile treatment from Orderic Vitalis (ii, 260–2). Son of Richard Goz vicomte of Avranches and a relative, probably half-sister, of William I. This woman was named as Emma daughter of Herleve and Herluin by Dugdale in his Baronage i, 32, but there is no independent evidence as to her name. The likelihood that she was nonetheless a half-sister of William I and sister of Robert of Mortain, is increased by the terms of a letter of Bishop Helinand of Le Mans, referring to a consanguineous marriage projected for the daughter of William of Mortain, discussed in Keats-Rohan, Medieval Prosopography 14.1 (1992), 38–40; for Hugh, ibid., 23–30. By his wife Ermengarde, daughter of Hugh

count of Clermont, he left issue his son Richard. Father of several known bastards, including Robert abbot of Bury and Otuer fitz Count; Geva, wife of Geoffrey Ridel was probably another of them. Sanders, 32, Comp. Peer. iii, 164ff, HKF ii, 1–293.

Lincolnshire Claims (Domesday Book), fols 375d–376a; Barraclough, Charters of AN Earls of Chester (1988), No. 28; Barraclough, Charters of AN Earls of Chester (1988), No. 10; Barraclough, Charters of AN Earls of Chester (1988), No. 3; Barraclough, Charters of AN Earls of Chester (1988), No. 28; Lincolnshire Claims (Domesday Book), fols 375a–d; i, fol. 349a; i, fol. 349a; i, fol. 349b; i, fol. 349a; i, fol. 349a; i, fol. 349a; i, fol. 349a; i, fol. 349a; i, fol. 349a; i, fol. 349a; i, fol. 349a; i, fol. 349a; i, fol. 349a; i, fol. 269a; i, fol. 273c; i, fol. 269a; i, fol. 349a; i, fol. 349a; i, fol. 349b; i, fol. 349a; i, fol. 349a; i, fol. 349a; i, fol. 349b; i, fol. 349b; i, fol. 349a; i, fol. 349c; i, fol. 254b; i, fol. 349b; i, fol. 349b; i, fol. 349a; i, fol. 237a; i, fol. 349a; i, fol. 349a; i, fol. 166c; i, fol. 349a; i, fol. 349b; i, fol. 349b; i, fol. 349a; i, fol. 349c; i, fol. 336b; i, fol. 336a; i, fol. 273c; i, fol. 349a; i, fol. 349b; i, fol. 273c; i, fol. 154a; i, fol. 349a; i, fol. 349a; i, fol. 349a; i, fol. 269a; i, fol. 349c; i, fol. 349b; i, fol. 349a; i, fol. 349c; i, fol. 268a; i, fol. 166c; i, fol. 237a; i, fol. 166c; i, fol. 166c; i, fol. 166c; i, fol. 349a; i, fol. 164d; i, fol. 166c; i, fol. 268b; i, fol. 237a; i, fol. 269a; i, fol. 269a; i, fol. 269a; i, fol. 269a; i, fol. 269a; i, fol. 269a; i, fol. 273c; ii, fol. 301b; ii, fol. 302a; ii, fol. 153a; ii, fol. 300a; ii, fol. 301b; ii, fol. 301b; ii, fol. 299a; ii, fol. 301b; ii, fol. 298b; ii, fol. 300b; ii, fol. 300a; ii, fol. 298b; ii, fol. 298b; ii, fol. 300a; ii, fol. 299a; ii, fol. 299a; i, fol. 237a; ii, fol. 301b; ii, fol. 300a; i, fol. 56c; i, fol. 56b; i, fol. 80b; i, fol. 104c; i, fol. 104c; ii, fol. 298b; i, fol. 104c; ii, fol. 302a; ii, fol. 302a; ii, fol. 302b; ii, fol. 302b; ii, fol. 302b; ii, fol. 302b; ii, fol. 302b; ii, fol. 302a; ii, fol. 302a; i, fol. 104c; i, fol. 237a; ii, fol. 299a; i, fol. 230a; i, fol. 230a; i, fol. 237a; i, fol. 219a; i, fol. 237a; i, fol. 237a; i, fol. 349b; i, fol. 237a; i, fol. 237a; i, fol. 237a; i, fol. 237a; i, fol. 237a; i, fol. 237a; i, fol. 263d; i, fol. 237a; i, fol. 237a; ii, fol. 152b; ii, fol. 299a; ii, fol. 298b; ii, fol. 298b; ii, fol. 298b; ii, fol. 112a; ii, fol. 153a; i, fol. 230a; ii, fol. 152b; i, fol. 349a; ii, fol. 152a; i, fol. 349a; ii, fol. 300a; i, fol. 349a; i, fol. 349a; ii, fol. 300a; i, fol. 349b; ii, fol. 298b; ii, fol. 152b; i, fol. 349c; i, fol. 263c; i, fol. 305a; i, fol. 349d; Pipe Roll 11 Henry II, 007b–nfsf; Pipe Roll 11 Henry II, 007a–nfsf; i, fol. 349d; i, fol. 349d; i, fol. 305a; i, fol. 305a; i, fol. 264a; i, fol. 349c; i, fol. 143a; i, fol. 305a; i, fol. 263d; i, fol. 263d; i, fol. 263d; i, fol. 263d; i, fol. 263d; i, fol. 263d; i, fol. 263d; i, fol. 263d; i, fol. 263d; i, fol. 263d; i, fol. 263c; i, fol. 263d; i, fol. 263c; i, fol. 305a; i, fol. 305a; Barraclough, Charters of AN Earls of Chester (1988), No. 22; Barraclough, Charters of AN Earls of Chester (1988), No. 25; Barraclough, Charters of AN Earls of Chester (1988), No. 27; i, fol. 349a; i, fol. 349d; i, fol. 280b; Pipe Roll 12 Henry II, 019–nfsf; i, fol. 282c; i, fol. 282c; i, fol. 305a; i, fol. 349c; i, fol. 305a; i, fol. 349c; i, fol. 349d; i, fol. 305a; i, fol. 349c; i, fol. 305a; i, fol. 305a; i, fol. 305a; i, fol. 305a; i, fol. 305a; i, fol. 305a; i, fol. 305a; i, fol. 305a; i, fol. 305a; i, fol. 305a; i, fol. 305a; i, fol. 349c; i, fol. 264a; i, fol. 269a; i, fol. 269a; i, fol. 269a; i, fol. 264a; i, fol. 263d; i, fol. 263d; i, fol. 263d; i, fol. 264a; i, fol. 264a; i, fol. 264a; i, fol. 269a; i, fol. 264a; i, fol. 264a; i, fol. 264a; i, fol. 263c; i, fol. 264a; i, fol. 305a; i, fol. 263d; i, fol. 264a; i, fol. 264a; i, fol. 264a; i, fol. 264a; i, fol. 264a; i, fol. 264a; i, fol. 264a; i, fol. 264a; i, fol. 264a; i, fol. 269a; i, fol. 263c; i, fol. 263c; i, fol. 263c; i, fol. 264a; i, fol. 269a; i, fol. 263c; i, fol. 263c; i, fol. 264a; i, fol. 349a; i, fol. 349a; i, fol. 266b; i, fol. 268d; i, fol. 268d; i, fol. 269a; i, fol. 263c; i, fol. 269a; i, fol. 268d; i, fol. 269a; i, fol. 269a; i, fol. 264a; i, fol. 269a; i, fol. 264a; i, fol. 269a; i, fol. 269a; i, fol. 269a; i, fol. 269a; i, fol. 269a; i, fol. 269a; Barraclough, Charters of AN Earls of Chester (1988), No. 12; Ellis, 'Landholders of Gloucestershire' (1880), pp. 91–93; Harper-Bill & Mortimer, Stoke by Clare Cartulary, No. 8; Lincolnshire Claims (Domesday Book), fols

375a–d; Lincolnshire Claims (Domesday Book), fols 375a–d; Barraclough, Some charters of the Earls of Chester, No. 1; Lincolnshire Claims (Domesday Book), fols 375a–d; J. Tait, Foundation Charter of Runcorn Priory, pp. 19–21; i, fol. 269b; Barraclough, Charters of AN Earls of Chester (1988), No. 61; Barraclough, Charters of AN Earls of Chester (1988), No. 29; Lincolnshire Claims (Domesday Book), fols 376d–377c; Barraclough, Charters of AN Earls of Chester (1988), No. 26; i, fol. 305a; i, fol. 91d; i, fol. 146d; i, fol. 237a; i, fol. 349a; i, fol. 239b; i, fol. 166c; i, fol. 157b; ii, fol. 298b; i, fol. 44d; i, fol. 224d; i, fol. 205c; i, fol. 282c; Barraclough, Charters of AN Earls of Chester (1988), No. 13; Barraclough, Charters of AN Earls of Chester (1988), No. 11; Dugdale, Monasticon Anglicanum, IV, pp. 13–14, No. V; Barraclough, Charters of AN Earls of Chester (1988), No. 4; Clay, Early Yorkshire Charters (1949), VIII, No. 5

Hugo Dapifer

Tenant of William fitz Baderon of Monmouth in 1086; doubtless a fellow Breton, probably to be identified with the Hugh dapifer who attested a charter of William and his uncle Wihenoc for St Mary's, Monmouth (CDF, 1133), along with Hugh Rufus and Hugh Bos. Hugh dapifer and his son Rainer attested a charter of 1101/2 for the same house (ibid., 1136).

i, fol. 167a;

Hugo De Avilers

A man named Hugh held a few acres of Robert Malet in Thrandeston in 1086, and a Hugh de Avillers attested the foundation charter of Eye priory sometime before c.1120. Later persons named de Auvillers were tenants of the honour of Eye, and held a serjeanty in Brome and Edwardstone, both of them places associated in 1086 with Robert's tenant Hubert de Montcanisy.

ii, fol. 310a; Regesta regum Anglo-Normannorum III, No. 288; Brown, Eye Priory Cartulary (1992–94), No. 55; Brown, Eye Priory Cartulary (1992–94), No. 5; Brown, Eye Priory Cartulary (1992–94), No. 3

Hugo De Belcamp

Important royal official and major tenant-in-chief in Bedfordshire, of which he was sheriff during William I's reign and early in William II's. He succeeded Ralph Taillebois in the office, having, in all probability, married Ralph's daughter and principal heiress. His fief became the barony of Beauchamp. From Beauchamps, cant. La Haye Pesnel, dépt. Manche, in west Normandy, according to Le Melletier; for other possibilities, Loyd, 20–1, s.v. Broilg. Sanders, 10; G. H. Fowler, 'The Beauchamps, barons of Bedford', in Beds. Hist. Rec. Soc. i, 1–24.

i, fol. 217b; i, fol. 217d; i, fol. 217b; i, fol. 217b; i, fol. 217b; i, fol. 217b; i, fol. 217d; i, fol. 217d; i, fol. 217c; i, fol. 211d; i, fol. 211d; i, fol. 150c; i, fol. 213b; i, fol. 150c; i, fol. 213a; i, fol. 212d; i, fol. 212c; i, fol. 212d; i, fol. 212d; i, fol. 212d; i, fol. 212d; i, fol. 212d; i, fol. 212d; i, fol. 218a; i, fol. 212d; i, fol. 213a; i, fol. 213a; i, fol. 213a; i, fol. 212d; i, fol. 213a; i, fol. 213d; i, fol. 212d; i, fol. 213a; i, fol. 150c; i, fol. 138d; i, fol. 212d; Mason, Westminster Abbey Charters (1988), No. 488; Dugdale, Monasticon Anglicanum, II, p. 602, No. XX; Ransford, Early Charters of Waltham Abbey (1989), No. 13; i, fol. 157d

Hugo De Berneres

Norman, from Bernières-sur-Mer, Calvados, arr. Caen, cant. Douvres (Loyd, 14), occurs Domesday as a tenant of Geoffrey de Mandeville and the abbey of Ely. His successor in 1166 was Ralph de Berneres, father of William.

ii, fol. 019b; i, fol. 199c; i, fol. 127b; ii, fol. 100b; ii, fol. 060b; ii, fol. 060b; ii, fol. 060b

Hugo De Beuerda

Norman, Domesday tenant of Hugh de Montfort. His toponym could refer to several places within a fairly limited area, Le Brévedent, Calvados, near Pont-l'Evêque, Bevredon, near Honfleur, or Saint-Laurent-de-Brèvedent, Seine-Maritime, comm. cant. Harfleur, with the first being the most likely. Around 1147 Hugh's descendant Hugh IV de Montfort made a gift to Bec attested by Philip and Hugh de Bevredan; his wife granted a house at Pont-l'Evêque (CDF, 308). Probably father of Ralph fitz Hugh, who gave tithes of Great Livermere to Thetford priory before 1120 (RRAN ii, p. 339).

ii, fol. 408a; ii, fol. 408a

Hugo De Bolebec

Norman, from Bolbec, Seine-Maritime, arr. Le Havre (Loyd, 17), major tenant of Walter Giffard in 1086. His lands were later known as the barony of Whitchurch, Buckinghamshire. He was succeeded by his son Walter in the early twelfth century. Sanders, 98.

i, fol. 196b; i, fol. 196b; i, fol. 148a; i, fol. 148a; i, fol. 148a; i, fol. 147a; i, fol. 147d; i, fol. 147d; i, fol. 148a; i, fol. 148a; i, fol. 211b; i, fol. 211c; i, fol. 205d; i, fol. 211c; i, fol. 56c; i, fol. 147b; i, fol. 143a; i, fol. 205d; Hamilton, Inquisitio Eliensis (1876), pp. 192–95; i, fol. 150d; i, fol. 157d; i, fol. 150d; i, fol. 150d; i, fol. 150d; i, fol. 150d; i, fol. 150d; i, fol. 150d; i, fol. 150d; i, fol. 150d; i, fol. 147a; i, fol. 147a; i, fol. 56b; i, fol. 56c; i, fol. 157c; i, fol. 157c; i, fol. 157c; i, fol. 157c; i, fol. 157c; i, fol. 157c; i, fol. 157c

Hugo De Bosco Herberti

Domesday tenant of the wife of Hugh fitz Grip in Dorset. His successor by 1129/30 was Tierric (Theoderic) de Bosco Herberti, probably his son. His toponym is difficult to identify; possible is Le Bois-Hébert, Eure, cant. Broglie, or, less likely if the Domesday form of the name is correct, Bois-Hubert, par. comm. Envronville, cant. Fauville-en-Caux.

i, fol. 84a; i, fol. 83b; i, fol. 83b; i, fol. 83c; i, fol. 83c; i, fol. 83d; i, fol. 83d

Hugo De Braiboue

Norman, Domesday tenant of Odo of Bayeux and Ivo Taillebois. Identified in Lincolnshire by his grant to Spalding priory. Father of William, whose son Hugh was a benefactor of Newhouse priory c.1150. Cf. Farrer, HKF ii, 185. Le Melletier identifies his origin as the fief of Brébeuf, which lay between Condé-sur-Vire and Sainte-Suzanne-sur-Vire, Manche, but it could be Bréboeuf, Calvados, arr. Caen, cant. Evrecy, comm. Vacogne; see Loyd, 19–20.

i, fol. 350a; i, fol. 008d; Dugdale, Monasticon Anglicanum, III, p. 217, No. VII; Dugdale, Monasticon Anglicanum, III, p. 216, No. V

Hugo De Caisneto

Hugh son of Ralph de Caisneto (q.v.), occurs in William II de Warenne's confirmation charter for Lewes Priory.

i, fol. 27c; Pipe Roll 31 Henry I, 070–ss

Hugo De Corbun

Norman, from Corbon, Calvados, arr. Pont-l'Evêque, cant. Cambremer,

Domesday tenant of Roger Bigod. Cf. Loyd, 32.

ii, fol. 333a; ii, fol. 176b; ii, fol. 339a; ii, fol. 278a; ii, fol. 335a

Hugo De Dives

Norman, tenant of Robert of Mortain in 1086 in Sussex. See under Boselin de Dives.

i, fol. 22b; i, fol. 20c; i, fol. 21b; i, fol. 20d

Hugo De Dol

Domesday tenant in Devon of William de Falaise. Identified by Exon as de Dol, presumably therefore a Breton from Dol-de-Bretagne, Ille-et-Vilaine. Possibly the same as Hugh Redonensis, since Dol was in the county of Rennes.

i, fol. 111a

Hugo De Essebi

Domesday tenant of Countess Judith in Northamptonshire. The descent of his holdings strongly suggests he should be identified with the Hugo de Essebi, named from Castle Ashby, who attested a charter of Simon I de Senlis for St Andrew's, Northampton. His successor was David de Essebi, who occurs in 1147 as a witness to the foundation of Sawtry abbey. See Farrer, HKF ii, 334.

i, fol. 228d; i, fol. 228d; i, fol. 228d; i, fol. 228d; i, fol. 228d

Hugo De Grentemaisnil

Hugh de Grandmesnil (Calvados, arr. Lisieux, cant. Saint-Pierre-sur-Dives), fl. 1040–94, was the eldest of the three sons of Robert of Grandmesnil and Hawise, daughter of Giroie, lord of Echauffour and Montreuil-l'Argillé (whose relatives were both vassals and rivals of the Bellême family). Hawise was secondly the wife of William, son of Archbishop Robert of Rouen. She eventually became a nun at Montivilliers accompanied by two of her daughters, for whom her son Hugh made provision. When their father died in 1040, Hugh and his brother Robert apparently each inherited part of the family fief. Their youngest brother Arnald and their cousin William de Montreuil went to Apulia as mercenaries c.1050. Hugh and Robert were immortalized by their decision to found a monastery some time around 1050. The site chosen being unsuitable, they followed the advice of their uncle William fitz Giroie and decided to refound the ancient abbey of Saint-Evroul, first compensating the monks of Bec who then owned the ruins. The monk and historian of Saint-Evroult, Orderic Vitalis, tells us of the generous endowment of the abbey by the brothers and their maternal kin. In the same year the younger brother Robert entered the abbey as a monk; he became its abbot in 1059. Falsely accused by Mabel of Bellême, wife of Roger de Montgomery, in the wake of a rebellion by Robert fitz Giroie, Hugh and Robert, among others of their maternal kin, were exiled in 1061. Robert became an abbot in Sicily, but Hugh was recalled in 1064 and subsequently fought with William I at Hastings. The move undoubtedly made his fortune. During William's absence in Normandy in 1067, Hugh was among those left in charge of the vital hinterland of Dover, apparently having special responsability for the region of Winchester. By 1086 he was castellan and sheriff of Leicestershire, where he held sixty-seven manors. He also held extensive property in Nottinghamshire, Hertfordshire, Northamptonshire, Gloucestershire, Warwickshire and Suffolk. Several of his Norman vassals held these lands from him, including Hugh and Robert Burdet, Osbert de Neufmarché and Walter de Beaumais. He returned to Normandy in 1068 to check on the activities of his beautiful French wife Adeliza (d. 11 July 1091), daughter of Ivo count of Beaumont-sur-Oise. Adeliza's English dower lands were recorded separately from Hugh's in 1086. They included manors in Bedfordshire which Hugh had acquired by exchange with Ralph Taillebois. After Ralph's death (before 1086) Hugh disputed Ralph's inheritance with Hugh de Beauchamp, Ralph's son-in-law and principal heir, and the husband of Ralph's niece, Ranulf brother of Ilger. Two of Hugh's sons, Ivo and Aubrey, earned their father's disapproval by joining the revolt of the king's son Robert Curthose in 1078. Hugh was among those who helped to effect a reconciliation between the king and Robert in 1079. Although he supported Curthose against William II in 1087–8, Hugh retained his offices under the new king. He was in Normandy in January 1091, assisting Robert de Courcy, husband of his daughter Rohais, against Robert de Bellême, son of Mabel. This action provoked conflict with Robert Curthose, duke of Normandy, but matters were resolved by the appearance of William II in Normandy. Hugh was in England when he died on 22 February 1098, a few days after becoming a monk of Saint-Evroult, whose habit had previously been sent to him for the purpose. His body was buried at Saint-Evroult, where Orderic Vitalis wrote his epitaph. Hugh and Adeliza had ten children: five daughters, Adelina (married Roger d'Ivry), Rohais (Robert de Courcy), Matilda (Hugh de Montpinçon), Agnes (William de Sai) and Hawise, and five sons, Robert, William, Hugh, Ivo and Aubrey. William (who later settled in Apulia), Ivo and Aubrey were among the 'rope-dancers of Antioch' in 1098. Robert (d.c. 1136) succeeded to Hugh's Norman estates, which he governed as a supporter of Henry I. The English lands went to Ivo, who may previously have acted as his father's steward (dapifer). See Orderic Vitalis, ii, 38, 40, 90, 106, 174, 264; iii, 226, 234–6; iv, 124, 230–36, 336–8; 6, 18, 304. Although his son Ivo lost his English fief to Robert earl of Leicester, Hugh's cross-Channel estates were subsequently reunified when his great-granddaughter Petronilla (CDF 653), daughter of William de Grandmesnil, son of Robert de Grandmesnil and his second wife Emma de Stuteville, married Robert de Beaumont III, earl of Leicester.

Dugdale, Monasticon Anglicanum, II, p. 602, No. XX; Douglas, Feudal Documents from Bury St Edmunds, No. 14; i, fol. 237a; i, fol. 236b; i, fol. 242a; i, fol. 224c; i, fol. 232b; i, fol. 232b; i, fol. 232b; i, fol. 232b; i, fol. 232b; i, fol. 242a; i, fol. 232b; i, fol. 236b; i, fol. 169b; i, fol. 291c; i, fol. 291c; i, fol. 360c; i, fol. 138c; i, fol. 230a; i, fol. 242a; i, fol. 232b; i, fol. 230a; i, fol. 52a; i, fol. 230a; i, fol. 230a; i, fol. 230a; i, fol. 230a; i, fol. 230a; i, fol. 236b; i, fol. 230a; i, fol. 224d; i, fol. 230a; i, fol. 230a; i, fol. 230a; i, fol. 230a; i, fol. 169b; i, fol. 230a; i, fol. 232b; i, fol. 232b; i, fol. 236b; i, fol. 230a; i, fol. 232a; i, fol. 230a; i, fol. 232a; i, fol. 232a; i, fol. 242a; i, fol. 232a; i, fol. 232a; i, fol. 232a; i, fol. 232b; i, fol. 232a; i, fol. 232a; i, fol. 232a; i, fol. 232a; i, fol. 230a; i, fol. 230a; i, fol. 232a; i, fol. 230a; i, fol. 236c; i, fol. 238a; i, fol. 242a; i, fol. 232a; i, fol. 242a; i, fol. 230a; i, fol. 169b; i, fol. 232a; i, fol. 242a; i, fol. 232a; i, fol. 232a; i, fol. 232a; i, fol. 232a; i, fol. 232a; i, fol. 232a; i, fol. 232a; i, fol. 232b; i, fol. 242a; i, fol. 232a; i, fol. 232a; i, fol. 138c; i, fol. 242a; i, fol. 224c; i, fol. 291c; i, fol. 169b; ii, fol. 432a; ii, fol. 432a; i, fol. 215b; i, fol. 134d; i, fol. 173d

Hugo De Gurnai

Norman, from Gournay-en-Bray, Seine-Maritime, arr. Neufchâtel (Loyd, 47), Domesday landholder. His wife was Basilia, daughter of Gerard Fleitei, a prominent and wealthy Norman father also of the wife of Walter Giffard (Robert of Torigny, Interpolations to William of Jumièges, ed. van Houts, ii, 268). His heir was his son Gerard, who died on the First Crusade.

Stenton, English Feudalism, App., No. 28; ii, fol. 089b

Hugo De Hosdenc

Brother-in-law and tenant of Roger Bigod in Domesday Essex and Suffolk (Comp. Peer. ix, 578–9 note c, identifying Roger's brother William with the William Bigurt who attested a charter of 1091 by which Richard brother of Guy de La Roche-Guyon renounced claims upon Saint-Leu-d'Esserent, and with the William Bigot who around the same date granted Fréville (Seine-Maritime, cant. Pavilly) to Saint-Wandrille (Lot, 101). One of the witnesses to the latter was his 'sororius' Hugh de Hosdenc – viz the tenant of Roger Bigod, whose wife Matilda, evidenced in Thetford charters (M.A. v, 148–9), must therefore have been Roger's sister). He and Matilda were benefactors of Thetford priory, their grant being confirmed before 1120 by William Bigod (Mon. Ang. iv, 149). The Domesday orthography of his toponym suggests an origin in a Hodenc in dépt. Oise, or at Hodeng-au-Bois, Seine-Maritime. Persons from one or more of the three possibilities are found, c.1100–1150, in Cart. Saint-Quentin de Beauvais, BN lat. n. a. 1921, fols 45–46v, Robert de Hosdench attests with Walter Giffard, fol. 22, Hugh de Hosden is associated with Ralph Deliés, fol. 106v, Hugh de Hosdenc grants the church of Saint-Pierre at Gerberoy.

Regesta Regum Anglo Normannorum II, App. no. cxxvii ; ii, fol. 341b; ii, fol. 341b; ii, fol. 330b; ii, fol. 337b; ii, fol. 088a; ii, fol. 337a; ii, fol. 405b; ii, fol. 187a; ii, fol. 337a; ii, fol. 337a; Dugdale, Monasticon Anglicanum, IV, pp. 150–51, No. VIII; Dugdale, Monasticon Anglicanum, IV, pp. 148–49, No. II; ii, fol. 190a; ii, fol. 190a; ii, fol. 190a; ii, fol. 190b; ii, fol. 190a

Hugo De Hotot

Norman, Domesday tenant of the Countess Judith. Possibly named from Hotot-en-Auge, Calvados, arr. Pont-L'Evêque, cant. Dozulé, rather than Hottot-les-Bagues, Calvados, cant. Tilly-sur-Seulles. By 1130 his tenures were held by Hugh de Moreville (HKF ii, 356).

i, fol. 367a; i, fol. 217a; i, fol. 293c

Hugo De Ispania

Norman, from Epaignes, Eures, tenant and perhaps brother of Alfred de Ispania (q.v.); surnamed de Ispania in the Tax Return for Cannington Hundred.

i, fol. 97b; i, fol. 97b; i, fol. 97b; i, fol. 97b; i, fol. 97b

Hugo De Iuri

Norman, from Ivry-la-Bataille, dépt. Eure. Occurs in Domesday Book, usually as pincerna. Brother or nephew of Roger d'Ivry, q.v.

i, fol. 190b; i, fol. 157d; i, fol. 157d; i, fol. 224c; i, fol. 83b; i, fol. 224c; i, fol. 216a; i, fol. 216a; i, fol. 216a

Hugo De Laceio

Son of Walter de Lacy and Emma or Emmeline, he was a tenant of his elder brother Roger de Lacy in 1086; from Lassy, arr. Vire, cant. Condé-sur-Noireau, Calvados (Loyd, 53). When Roger was banished in 1096, Hugh took over the Lacy lands in Weobley (Ord. Vit. iv 284), though most of the honour was subsequently restored to the elder line under Gilbert and his son Robert (q.v.). He married Adeline (perhaps daughter of Geoffrey Talbot, q.v.), by whom he left at his death c.1115, a daughter and heiress Sibil, wife of Payn fitz John (d. 1137). See Wightman, Lacy Family, 170–5.

i, fol. 185a; i, fol. 185a; i, fol. 185a; i, fol. 184a; i, fol. 168a; i, fol. 167d; Regesta regum Anglo-Normannorum III, No. 607; Regesta regum Anglo-Normannorum III, No. 312; Ellis, 'Landholders of Gloucestershire' (1880), pp. 91–93; Regesta regum Anglo-Normannorum III, No. 345; Barraclough, Charters of AN Earls of Chester (1988), No. 28; Regesta regum Anglo-Normannorum III, No. 437; Regesta regum Anglo-Normannorum III, No. 398; Barraclough, Charters of AN Earls of Chester (1988), No. 8

Hugo De Manneuile

Domesday tenant of Hugh de Montfort in Kent; named from Manneville-sur-Risle, Eure.

i, fol. 013c

Hugo De Mara

Domesday tenant of Earl Hugh in Cheshire. Perhaps to be identified with Hugh de Mara of Dol, father of a son Wigan, who, in turn is possibly to be identified with the tenant of Count Alan. Hugh occurs in Brittany in the 1080s with his wife Ennokent (Innoguen) and sons Boia, Wigon and Amat (Morice, Preuves I, 463; CDF 1154). Before the earl's death in 1101, Hugh's fief was regranted to Robert fitz Serlo.

Barraclough, Charters of AN Earls of Chester (1988), No. 28; Barraclough, Charters of AN Earls of Chester (1988), No. 3; i, fol. 266c; i, fol. 266c; i, fol. 266c; i, fol. 266c

Hugo De Montefort

Norman, from Montfort-sur-Risle, Eure, arr. Pont-Audemer, cant. Montfort (Loyd, 68), Domesday tenant-in-chief. Shortly after 1066, having acquired land in Kent, he augmented an earlier benefaction to the prior of Saint-Hymer-en-Auge, which he had made for the soul of his father Hugh and of his brothers Ralph and Robert (CDF 357, Bates, 257) He became a monk of Bec c.1088. By his first wife, a daughter of Richard de Beaufour, he left a daughter Alice, wife of Gilbert I de Gand. By his second wife he left two sons, Robert, who succeeded him in Normandy, and Hugh, his successor in England. He probably also had a younger daughter married either to Swein of Essex or to Swein's son Robert fitz Swein, for the latter's son Henry (q.v.), who referred to Hugh as his 'antecessor', inherited Hugh's honour of Haughley (which he forfeited in 1163) before 1154. Sanders, 120; Comp. Peer. x, app. J; the family history was worked out in Douglas, Dom. Mon., 68–70.

i, fol. 009b; ii, fol. 006b; ii, fol. 004b; ii, fol. 406b; ii, fol. 406b; ii, fol. 407b; ii, fol. 407b; ii, fol. 407a; ii, fol. 407a; ii, fol. 407a; ii, fol. 409a; ii, fol. 407a; ii, fol. 406b; ii, fol. 407a; ii, fol. 407b; ii, fol. 407b; ii, fol. 407b; ii, fol. 407b; ii, fol. 406b; ii, fol. 410a; ii, fol. 409b; ii, fol. 409b; ii, fol. 409b; ii, fol. 407b; ii, fol. 409a; ii, fol. 406b; ii, fol. 410a; ii, fol. 406b; ii, fol. 281b; ii, fol. 410a; ii, fol. 410a; ii, fol. 279a; ii, fol. 407a; ii, fol. 408a; ii, fol. 407a; ii, fol. 291a; ii, fol. 053a; ii, fol. 407b; ii, fol. 406a; ii, fol. 406b; ii, fol. 053b; ii, fol. 003a; ii, fol. 406a; ii, fol. 053a; ii, fol. 406a; ii, fol. 053a; ii, fol. 053b; ii, fol. 044b; ii, fol. 053b; ii, fol. 100a; ii, fol. 106b; ii, fol. 100a; ii, fol. 053a; ii, fol. 405b; ii, fol. 409a; ii, fol. 407b; ii, fol. 408b; ii, fol. 408b; ii, fol. 408b; ii, fol. 406a; ii, fol. 408a; ii, fol. 407b; ii, fol. 405b; ii, fol. 408a; ii, fol. 406b; ii, fol. 408a; ii, fol. 409a; ii, fol. 410a; ii, fol. 406a; ii, fol. 406a; ii, fol. 408b; ii, fol. 410a; ii, fol.

409a; ii, fol. 409a; Douglas, Feudal Documents from Bury St Edmunds, No. 10; Dugdale, Monasticon Anglicanum, III, p. 499, No. I; ii, fol. 052b; ii, fol. 405b; i, fol. 011a; i, fol. 013b; i, fol. 013b; i, fol. 013b; i, fol. 013a; i, fol. 013a; i, fol. 013a; i, fol. 011d; i, fol. 011d; i, fol. 013b; i, fol. 011a; i, fol. 010c; i, fol. 010c; i, fol. 011b; i, fol. 013a; i, fol. 011c; i, fol. 013d; i, fol. 013c; i, fol. 013c; i, fol. 013a; i, fol. 013b; i, fol. 013b; i, fol. 013d; i, fol. 013d; i, fol. 013b; i, fol. 013d; ii, fol. 075b; i, fol. 013d; i, fol. 013b; i, fol. 014a; i, fol. 014a; i, fol. 014b; i, fol. 001a; i, fol. 004c; i, fol. 013d; i, fol. 013a; i, fol. 013a; i, fol. 013d; ii, fol. 100a; Douglas, ed., Domesday Monachorum (1944), p. 105; Ballard, Inquisition of St Augustine's (1920), fols 24r–28r; Ballard, Inquisition of St Augustine's (1920), fols 20r–23v; ii, fol. 237b; ii, fol. 237a; ii, fol. 238a; ii, fol. 237b; ii, fol. 237b; ii, fol. 237a; ii, fol. 238a; ii, fol. 237a; ii, fol. 238a; ii, fol. 238b; ii, fol. 237a; ii, fol. 237b; ii, fol. 239a; ii, fol. 239a; ii, fol. 237b; ii, fol. 238a; ii, fol. 237a; ii, fol. 239a; ii, fol. 238b; ii, fol. 238b; ii, fol. 238b; ii, fol. 238b; ii, fol. 237b; ii, fol. 237a

Hugo De Montgumeri

Son of Roger de Montgomery, earl of Shropshire. He was in Normandy at the time of his mother's murder at Bures-sur-Dives, but though he pursued the perpetrators as they fled he was unable to capture them (Ord. Vit. iii, 136). In 1086 he was holding a small fief of the king in Staffordshire. Earl of Shropshire during 1094 to 1098. In 1095 he was among those who supported Curthose against William II but was pardoned after he agreed to pay three thousand pounds (Ord. Vit. iv, 302, 284), he died without issue leaving his elder brother Robert de Bellême as his heir. J. F. A. Mason, 'Roger de Montgomery and his sons', TRHS 5th ser. 13 (1963).

Dugdale, Monasticon Anglicanum, III, pp. 544–46, No. I; Rees, Cartulary of Shrewsbury Abbey (1975), No. 35; i, fol. 248c; i, fol. 248c; Rees, Cartulary of Shrewsbury Abbey (1975), No. 35; Rees, Cartulary of Shrewsbury Abbey (1975), No. 35; i, fol. 246a

Hugo De Port

Norman, from Port-en-Bessin, Calvados, arr. Bayeux, cant. Ryes, Domesday tenant in chief in Hampshire. He occurs in the Liber Vitae of Hyde abbey with his wife Orence. He became a monk of St Peter's, Gloucester shortly before his death in 1096 (Hist.S. Petri. ii, 93), when he was succeeded by his son Henry. Father of a daughter Adelidis who had a house in Winchester c.1107/15, and also of Emma, wife of William I de Percy (Loyd, 79, Sanders, 9, Comp. Peer. xi, 316ff).

i, fol. 38d; i, fol. 46b; i, fol. 40d; i, fol. 46b; i, fol. 46b; i, fol. 006a; i, fol. 45a; i, fol. 45c; i, fol. 007b; i, fol. 43a,b; i, fol. 45a; i, fol. 46b; i, fol. 45a; i, fol. 45b; i, fol. 45a; i, fol. 45a; i, fol. 45a; i, fol. 45b; i, fol. 45b; i, fol. 45b; i, fol. 45b; Ballard, Inquisition of St Augustine's (1920), fols 20r–23v; i, fol. 39a; i, fol. 43c; i, fol. 007b; i, fol. 45d; i, fol. 45d; i, fol. 45d; i, fol. 45d; i, fol. 45d; i, fol. 45d; i, fol. 59d; i, fol. 009b; i, fol. 009b; i, fol. 009b; i, fol. 007d; i, fol. 46b; i, fol. 45c; i, fol. 007b; i, fol. 45d; i, fol. 46b; i, fol. 002d; i, fol. 006a; i, fol. 006a; i, fol. 006a; i, fol. 45d; i, fol. 46a; i, fol. 46b; i, fol. 009b; i, fol. 52a; i, fol. 45b; i, fol. 41c; i, fol. 32a; i, fol. 48c; i, fol. 48a; i, fol. 48a; i, fol. 43b; i, fol. 002c; i, fol. 45c; i, fol. 43b; i, fol. 62d; i, fol. 43c,d; i, fol. 43c,d; i, fol. 43c,d; i, fol. 43c,d; Douglas, ed., Domesday Monachorum (1944), p. 105; i, fol. 32a; i, fol. 43a; i, fol. 45c; i, fol. 45d; i, fol. 219b; i, fol. 219b; i, fol. 219b; i, fol. 219b; i, fol. 219b; i, fol. 219b; i, fol. 219b; i, fol. 219b; i, fol. 219b; i, fol. 219b; i, fol. 010b; i, fol. 219b; i, fol. 199c; i, fol. 199c; i, fol. 83b; i, fol. 010d; i, fol. 010d; i, fol. 010a; i, fol. 006a; i, fol. 44d; ii, fol. 142a; ii, fol. 142a; Regesta regum Anglo-Normannorum III, No. 345; Dugdale, Monasticon Anglicanum, III, p. 499, No. I; i, fol. 011a; i, fol. 011a; i, fol. 011a; i, fol. 011a; i, fol. 39a; i, fol. 39c; i, fol. 47b

Hugo De Sancto Quintino
Norman, probably from Saint-Quentin, Manche, Domesday tenant-in-chief and tenant of Hugh de Port.

ii, fol. 093b; ii, fol. 093a; i, fol. 50d; i, fol. 83a; ii, fol. 093b; i, fol. 83b; ii, fol. 093a; i, fol. 51c; i, fol. 51b; i, fol. 51b; i, fol. 46a; i, fol. 51c; i, fol. 51c; i, fol. 51c

Hugo De Valletorta
Norman, tenant of Robert de Mortain in the south-west; identified as de Valletorta in Exon, he was probably a brother of Rainald de Valletorta (q.v.), from Torteval-Quesnay, Calvados, cant. Caumont-l'Evente. His successor in 1166, Hugh II, held of the honour of Hatch Beauchamp.

i, fol. 99b; i, fol. 105c; i, fol. 92d

Hugo De Verli
Norman, occurs Domesday Essex. He was probably the brother of Robert de Verly (q.v.), from Vesly, Manche. Robert de Verleio, his wife and brother Hugh were among the early benefactors of St Albans (BL Cotton Nero D vii, fol. 118v).The fees of Hugh de Verly were given to William de Albini Pincerna early in the reign of Henry I and were held in 1166 by Roger de Verly.

ii, fol. 063a; Red Book of the Exchequer, ed. Hall (1897), pp. 397–99

Hugo De Villana
Norman, occurs Domesday Somerset, identified as de Villana in Exon. An Ernulf de Villaines attested a Fécamp charter of 1085 for Gulbert de Auffait (RRAN i 207; CDF, 116).

i, fol. 87c

Hugo De Wanci
Norman, from Wanchy-Capeval, cant. Londinières, Seine-Maritime (Loyd, 111), Domesday tenant of William de Warenne in Suffolk and Norfolk. Occurs as a benefactor of Castle Acre priory, a. 1118, with his sons Osbern and Ralph (Mon. Ang. v, 44). Probably father also of Osmodis (q.v.), wife of Philip de Candos, alias de Warenne, of Burnham.

ii, fol. 160a; ii, fol. 164a; ii, fol. 159b; ii, fol. 398b; Dugdale, Monasticon Anglicanum, IV, pp. 49–50, No. II; Dugdale, Monasticon Anglicanum, IV, p. 50, No. III; Dugdale, Monasticon Anglicanum, IV, p. 49, No. I; Dugdale, Monasticon Anglicanum, IV, pp. 49–50, No. II; Clay, Early Yorkshire Charters (1949), VIII, No. 5

Hugo De Widuile
Norman, occurs Domesday Leicestershire and Northamptonshire as a tenant of Hugh de Grandmesnil. Ancestor of the de Wyville or de Widville family, afterwards tenants of the Beaumont earls of Leicester. In 1129/30 Robert de Wiville held his lands. Presumably named from Iville, Eure, arr. Louviers, cant. Le Neubourg. His successors by the early twelfth century were the brothers Ralph and William de Wiville, probably his sons.

i, fol. 219a; i, fol. 230a; i, fol. 232d; i, fol. 232d; i, fol. 233a; i, fol. 233a

Hugo Filius Baldrici
Domesday tenant-in-chief, primarily in Yorkshire and Lincolnshire. His first documentary occurrence was as witness to a charter of Gerold de Roumara for

Saint-Amand de Rouen, c.1067 (CDF 25). He lost his lands after 1086, probably for supporting Robert Curthose against William II at the latter's accession in 1087. A Hugh fitz Baldric attested a charter of Robert Curthose in 1089 (EYC ix, pp. 72–3). An important administrator under William I, he had been sheriff of York in succession to William Malet, holding the office from 1069 until c.1080. Domesday mentions his sons-in-law Walter de Rivere and Guy of Craon. He was a benefactor of the abbey of Préaux (CDF 318), granting lands in his English fief. A benefactor of St Mary, York (Mon. Ang. iii, 550–51), he occurs in the Liber Vitae of Thorney Abbey (BL Add. 40,000, fol. 3r).

Dugdale, Monasticon Anglicanum, III, pp. 548–50, No. V; Dugdale, Monasticon Anglicanum, III, p. 547, No. III; i, fol. 48b; Lincolnshire Claims (Domesday Book), fols 375d–376a; i, fol. 327b; i, fol. 356b; i, fol. 291c; Lincolnshire Claims (Domesday Book), fols 375d–376a; i, fol. 230b; i, fol. 230b; i, fol. 230b; i, fol. 230b; i, fol. 298b; i, fol. 48b; i, fol. 48b; i, fol. 48b; i, fol. 356c; i, fol. 298b; i, fol. 356c; i, fol. 356c; i, fol. 356c; i, fol. 356c; i, fol. 356c; i, fol. 356b; i, fol. 356b; i, fol. 356c; i, fol. 356b; i, fol. 356c; i, fol. 356c; i, fol. 356b; i, fol. 356c; i, fol. 356b; i, fol. 356b; i, fol. 356b; i, fol. 356c; i, fol. 356b; i, fol. 356b; i, fol. 219c; i, fol. 327c; i, fol. 327c; i, fol. 327c; i, fol. 328a; i, fol. 327c; i, fol. 327d; i, fol. 327c; i, fol. 327c; i, fol. 327c; i, fol. 327c; i, fol. 327c; i, fol. 327c; i, fol. 327d; i, fol. 328a; i, fol. 328a; i, fol. 327c; i, fol. 328b; i, fol. 328a; i, fol. 327d; i, fol. 327d; i, fol. 327c; i, fol. 328a; i, fol. 62d; i, fol. 327d; i, fol. 327d; i, fol. 327d; i, fol. 327b; i, fol. 328b; i, fol. 327c; i, fol. 328a; i, fol. 328b; i, fol. 328a; i, fol. 327d; i, fol. 328a; i, fol. 328a; i, fol. 328a; i, fol. 328a; i, fol. 327d; i, fol. 327d; i, fol. 327d; i, fol. 327d; i, fol. 327d; i, fol. 328b; i, fol. 328b; i, fol. 327c; i, fol. 327b; i, fol. 327b; i, fol. 327b; i, fol. 327b; i, fol. 327b; i, fol. 327c; i, fol. 327c; i, fol. 327b; i, fol. 327c; i, fol. 327b; i, fol. 327b; i, fol. 327c; i, fol. 327c; i, fol. 327b; i, fol. 327b; i, fol. 327c; i, fol. 327c; i, fol. 336c; i, fol. 336b; Dugdale, Monasticon Anglicanum, III, pp. 550–51, No. VII; Clay, Early Yorkshire Charters (1952), IX, No. 2; i, fol. 327c; i, fol. 328b; i, fol. 327d; i, fol. 328b; i, fol. 328b; i, fol. 328b; i, fol. 328b; i, fol. 328b; i, fol. 328b; i, fol. 327b; i, fol. 328b; i, fol. 327b; i, fol. 327c; i, fol. 327b; i, fol. 327c; i, fol. 327c; i, fol. 327b; Clay, Early Yorkshire Charters (1952), IX, No. 133; i, fol. 327b; i, fol. 327b; i, fol. 327b; i, fol. 327b; i, fol. 327b; i, fol. 328b; i, fol. 280a

Hugo Filius Constantii

Norman, Domesday tenant of Hugh de Grandmesnil and the count of Meulan at Loxley, Warwickshire, and also of Robert de Tosny in Staffordshire. Probably grandfather of the Robert fitz Odo who held these fees in 1166, and hence likely ancestor of the de Loxley family. He was a benefactor of Saint-Evroul (Ord. Vit. iii, 236). Cf. VCH Staffs, vol. 22.

i, fol. 249a; i, fol. 249a; i, fol. 240d; i, fol. 240d; i, fol. 242b

Hugo Filius Golde

Norman, distinguished by a matronym, Domesday tenant of William de Warenne in Suffolk, Norfolk and Sussex. There are several examples of women called Golda in Caen charters (Actes caen. no. 14, Deville, Analyse, 24). He occurs as a benefactor of Lewes priory, as do his sons Hugh fitz Hugh and Ralph de Plaiz, and his widow Beatrice. Although his son Ralph was the first of the family to be known in contemporary documents as de Plaiz, the reference to a Hugh de Plaiz in a plea of 1194, was quite clearly a reference to Hugh fitz Golde. It shows that he had a daughter, Heloise, married to Ralph fitz Herluin (q.v.), tenant at Hunstanton in

1086. Cf. Farrer, HKF, iii, 334–5. He was probably dead by c.1100 (Lewes Cart i, 62–3).

ii, fol. 168a; ii, fol. 163b; i, fol. 27c; i, fol. 26c; i, fol. 26a; Clay, Early Yorkshire Charters (1949), VIII, No. 5; ii, fol. 398b; ii, fol. 398b; i, fol. 27c; i, fol. 27c

Hugo Filius Gozeri
Norman, held a Buckinghamshire manor as a royal servant in 1086.

i, fol. 153b

Hugo Filius Malgeri
Norman, Domesday tenant of Hugh de Montfort.

ii, fol. 054a; ii, fol. 054a; ii, fol. 054a

Hugo Filius Normanni
Norman, Domesday tenant of Hugh of Chester in Lincolnshire, brother of Ralph, steward to Earl Hugh and his successors Richard and Ranulf I. He died before 1130, when his son William occurs on the Suffolk section of the Pipe Roll. Brother of Ralph, steward of Earl Ranulf I of Chester, whose son Robert de Mohaut was the eventual heir of both brothers. See Farrer, HKF ii, 110–111.

i, fol. 268a; i, fol. 268a; i, fol. 266c; i, fol. 266c; i, fol. 266c; i, fol. 266c; i, fol. 266c; i, fol. 266c; i, fol. 266c; i, fol. 266c; Barraclough, Charters of AN Earls of Chester (1988), No. 6; Barraclough, Charters of AN Earls of Chester (1988), No. 3; Barraclough, Charters of AN Earls of Chester (1988), No. 3; Barraclough, Charters of AN Earls of Chester (1988), No. 28; i, fol. 269b; i, fol. 269b; i, fol. 305a; i, fol. 305a; i, fol. 305a; i, fol. 269b; i, fol. 269b; i, fol. 269b; i, fol. 269b; i, fol. 269b; i, fol. 268d; i, fol. 269b; ii, fol. 298b; ii, fol. 302a; ii, fol. 298b; ii, fol. 301b

Hugo Filius Osberni
Norman, Domesday tenant of Earl Hugh of Chester. A plea of 1194 described him as Hugh Blundus, father of Osbert and Simon (Curia Regis Roll i, 49). His son Osbern attested a charter of earl Richard for St Werburga in 1119. By 1166 his successor was Simon fitz Osbert. See HKF ii, 127–9.

Barraclough, Charters of AN Earls of Chester (1988), No. 13; Barraclough, Charters of AN Earls of Chester (1988), No. 3; Barraclough, Charters of AN Earls of Chester (1988), No. 3; Barraclough, Charters of AN Earls of Chester (1988), No. 8; Barraclough, Charters of AN Earls of Chester (1988), No. 28; Barraclough, Charters of AN Earls of Chester (1988), No. 28; Barraclough, Charters of AN Earls of Chester (1988), No. 28; i, fol. 266c; i, fol. 266d; i, fol. 266c; i, fol. 266d; i, fol. 266c; i, fol. 268d; i, fol. 266d; i, fol. 268d; i, fol. 266c

Hugo Filius Osmundi
Norman, occurs Domesday Hampshire.

i, fol. 49c; i, fol. 51b

Hugo Filius Rannulfi
Norman, Domesday tenant of William de Warenne in Sussex. He was dead by c.1100, when his daughter Fredesend gave land at Plumpton to Lewes priory for his soul (Cart. i, no. 1).

i, fol. 17b; i, fol. 27b

Hugo Filius Turgisi
Norman, tenant of Earl Roger in Domesday Shropshire. His holdings were

regranted to Baldwin de Bollers by Henry I early in the twelfth century.

i, fol. 258d; i, fol. 258d; i, fol. 258d

Hugo Filius Willelmi
Occurs Domesday Kent as a tenant of William d'Arques of Folkestone. perhaps the same person as Hugh de Albertiville (Aubeville), a tenant of the honour who was dead by 1129.

i, fol. 009c

Hugo Flandrensis
Fleming, probably from the Ostrevant (region of Douai, Nord), occurs as a tenant-in-chief in Domesday Bedfordshire. Ancestor of the de la Lega family, named from Thurleigh. He was probably a brother of Walter Flandrensis; see Farrer, HKF i, 69.

i, fol. 215c; i, fol. 215c; i, fol. 215d; i, fol. 216a

Hugo Gosbert
Norman, occurs as a royal servant in Domesday Dorset.

i, fol. 82d; i, fol. 84d; i, fol. 84d; i, fol. 84d; i, fol. 84d

Hugo Grando De Scoca
Norman, occurs Domesday Berkshire and Wiltshire. Possibly same as Hugh Grand of Stoke, ancestor of the Talemasche family of Stoke Talmage.

i, fol. 71d; i, fol. 56c; i, fol. 56b; i, fol. 71d; i, fol. 71d

Hugo Homo W De Scohies
Norman, Domesday tenant of William d'Ecouis in Norfolk A Hugh fitz Ralph and a Hugh son of Roger de Warcliva attested charters of William d'Ecouis for Sainte-Trinité de Rouen (Cart., p. 465).

ii, fol. 117a; ii, fol. 224a; ii, fol. 224a; ii, fol. 225b; ii, fol. 225b; ii, fol. 225b

Hugo Hubald
Norman, occurs Domesday Bedfordshire and Cambridgeshire as a tenant of Osbern fitz Richard and Gilbert fitz Turold. Perhaps to be identified with the Hugh fitz Hubald de Pacy, Eure, who was a benefactor of Saint-Taurin d'Evreux (Gall. Christ. xi, Inst. 138ff).

i, fol. 177a; i, fol. 177a; i, fol. 197c; i, fol. 216c; i, fol. 216c; i, fol. 216c; i, fol. 216c

Hugo Lasne
Norman follower of William fitz Osbern de Breteuil, whose charter for Lyre abbey he attested c.1050 (Fauroux, 120). Occurs among the witnesses to a charter for Saint-Evroul by Fulk de Guernanville, Eure, cant. Breteuil (Ord. Vit. iii, 122). Occurs in Domesday Herefordshire holding a fief later known as the honour of Snodhill. He gave land at Fownhope and elsewhere to Lyre (Mon. Ang. vi, 1093). By the early twelfth century the fief had passed to the Candos family (Sanders, 79).

Ellis, 'Landholders of Gloucestershire' (1880), pp. 91–93; i, fol. 180b; i, fol. 183a; i, fol. 180a; i, fol. 181b; i, fol. 169b; i, fol. 187b; i, fol. 187b; i, fol. 187b; i, fol. 187a; i, fol. 73a; i, fol. 169b; i, fol. 187b; i, fol. 187b; i, fol. 260d; i, fol. 187b; i, fol. 260d; i, fol. 169b; i, fol. 187b; i, fol. 187b; i, fol. 187b; i, fol. 187b; i, fol. 187b; i, fol. 187b; i, fol. 187b; i, fol. 187b; i, fol. 187b; i, fol. 187b; i, fol. 260d; i, fol. 187a; i, fol. 177d; i, fol. 169b

Hugo Maci
Norman, Domesday tenant of Hugh de Port in Hampshire. Possibly from Macey, Manche, arr. Avranches, cant. Pontorson (Loyd, 61–2), as was Haimo, a tenant of Earl Hugh.

i, fol. 44d

Hugo Maltravers
Norman, occurs Domesday Dorset. Apparently ancestor of the Maltravers family, represented in 1129/30 by William, Walter and John, of whom John succeeded to Hugh's Domesday holdings in Dorset and Walter also had interests there.

i, fol. 95c; i, fol. 96a; i, fol. 96b; i, fol. 96c; i, fol. 96c; i, fol. 80d; i, fol. 80d; i, fol. 82a; i, fol. 82a; Bearman, Charters of the Redvers Family (1994), No. 5

Hugo Maminot
Norman, occurs Domesday Gloucestershire. Probably to be identified with Hugh Maminot son of Gilbert Maminot, bishop of Lisieux (q.v.) and a Domesday tenant-in-chief, who was from Courbépine, Eure, arr. Bernay. According to the Exon Tax Returns he was a tenant of Gilbert of Lisieux in Dorset (DB Dorset 6.1). Hugh was lord of an extensive estate centred upon West Greenwich, Kent (Sanders, 97). His wife was a sister of William, Haimo and Payn Peverel of Bourn. At his death, before 1131, he left a son Walchelin I Maminot, and a daughter Emma who married Ralph II de Chesney (Fees, 87).

i, fol. 166d; i, fol. 166d; i, fol. 166d

Hugo Musard
Norman, unrelated to the Bretons Enisan and Harscoit Musard, occurs Domesday. Between 1087 and 1091 Robert Curthose duke of Normandy granted the land of Hugh Mursard at Fécamp to the abbey of Fécamp (Haskins, Norman Institutions, app. E, no. 5).

i, fol. 236d; i, fol. 236d; i, fol. 336d

Hugo Nepos Herberti
Norman, occurs Domesday Kent as a tenant of Odo of Bayeux. Nephew or grandson of another tenant, Herbert fitz Ivo.

i, fol. 001a; ii, fol. 024a; i, fol. 007d; i, fol. 011a; i, fol. 008b; i, fol. 008b; i, fol. 008b; i, fol. 007d; Ballard, Inquisition of St Augustine's (1920), fols 24r–28r; i, fol. 007d; i, fol. 007d; i, fol. 007a; i, fol. 209d; i, fol. 010a; i, fol. 284b; i, fol. 008b

Hugo Petuuolt
Domesday tenant of Harduin de Scalariis in Cambridgeshire; his byname is supplied by IE and ICC. Presumably a Norman, ancestor of Robert Pedfold who occurs in the early twelfth century. Around 1057 Landric Aculeus gave the land of William Pedivolt in Anneville-sur-Seine to Fécamp (Fauroux, 139).

i, fol. 198c; i, fol. 198c; Hamilton, Inquisitio Eliensis (1876), pp. 97–100; Hamilton, Inquisitio Comitatus Cantabrigiensis, pp. 1–93

Hugo Redonensis
Domesday tenant of Baldwin of Exeter in Devon; Exon identifies him as Redonensis, i.e. from Rennes, or the county of Rennes, in north-east Brittany, dépt. Ille-et-Vilaine. Cf. Hugo de Dol, who was possibly the same person.

i, fol. 107c; i, fol. 107c

Hugo Siluestris
King's servant, occurs Domesday Dorset.

i, fol. 83b

Hugo []
Domesday tenant of Roger Arundel; perhaps Hugh de Teuera of the Tax Return for Cannington Hundred.

i, fol. 94c; i, fol. 94c

Hugo []
Norman, Domesday tenant of Peterborough Abbey, succeeded before 1130 by his son Richard of Addington (de Edintune). The fee eventually passed to the Bassingburn family. Cf. King, Peterborough Abbey, 29, note 8 (where the identification of Hugh as de Waterville is unsound).

i, fol. 222a; i, fol. 222a

Hugo []
Domesday tenant of the widow of Hugh fitz Grip in Stafford, Dorset. The heir to his part of a divided manor in 1166 was Jordan de Staffordia (q.v.)

i, fol. 83c

Hugo []
Norman tenant of Ilbert de Lacy of Pontefract in 1086. Whether he was ancestor of his successors of the de Ria (Ryther) family is unknown.

i, fol. 315c

Hugo []
Norman, tenant of Osbern fitz Richard in Domesday Warwickshire.

i, fol. 244a; i, fol. 244a; i, fol. 244a; i, fol. 244a

Hugolin Stirman
Norman ship master, Domesday tenant of the king in Berkshire.

i, fol. 63b; i, fol. 63b; i, fol. 63b

Humfrid Aurei Testiculi
Norman, occurs in Domesday Essex. He attested a confirmation for Saint-Vincent du Mans by Henry I in 1103/6 (RRAN i, 800). Elias aureis testiculis held 10 fees de vetere of Earl William of Gloucester in 1166 (RBE, 288); he was also a tenant of Glastonbury as Elias son of Henry Orescuil (ibid. 223). He is perhaps to be identified with the queen's chamberlain Humphrey (q.v.), brother of Aiulf, a one-time sheriff of Norfolk who was succeeded in Somerset by the Orescuil (later Orcas) family.

ii, fol. 100b

Humfrid De Bohum
Norman, from Saint-Georges-le-Bohon, Manche, arr. Saint-Lô, cant. Carantan (Loyd, 16), occurs holding a single manor in Domesday Book. Before 1067 a Humphrey de Bohun made a grant to Saint-Amand de Rouen for the souls of his three wives (CDF, 90). He was father of several sons, including Robert, who died before 1093, Richard de Meri, who occurs in Domesday Book, Humphrey (d.c. 1129), who married Mabel daughter of Edward of Salisbury, and Ingelger, a monk of Saint-Georges de Bohon (CDF, 1214), and a daughter Adela who occurs on the

1129/30 Pipe Roll as aunt of Humphrey de Bohun. He was also a benefactor of Saint-Léger des Préaux, where two of his daughters were nuns. He was certainly dead by 1093, when his son Richard de Meri was in control of most of the Norman inheritance. Land at Carentan and the English manor went to his younger son Humphrey II. J. Le Melletier, Les seigneurs de Bohun, Coutances 1978.

ii, fol. 262b; ii, fol. 262b; ii, fol. 262b

Humfrid De Cartrai

Norman, from Carteret, Manche, arr. Valognes, cant. Barneville (Loyd, 25), occurs Domesday Devon as H. de Cartrai; his full name is supplied from the Tax Returns. Probably son of Mauger and brother of Drogo.

i, fol. 77b

Humfrid De Cuelai

Norman, from Cully-le-Patry, Calvados, arr. Falaise, cant. Thury-Harcourt (Loyd, 36), Domesday tenant of Roger Bigod in Norfolk.

ii, fol. 179a; ii, fol. 173a

Humfrid Filius Alberici

Norman, tenant of several lords in Domesday East Anglia. His successor by 1129/30 was William de Tresgoz (Troisgots, Manche, arr. Saint-Lô, cant. Tessy-sur-Vire). The relationship between them is unknown. Cf. Salzman, Tresgot, Sussex Arch. Coll. vol. 93, 34–58.

ii, fol. 254a; ii, fol. 075b; ii, fol. 054b; ii, fol. 072a; ii, fol. 053a; ii, fol. 262a; ii, fol. 436a; ii, fol. 262a; ii, fol. 262b; ii, fol. 262b; ii, fol. 436a; ii, fol. 436a; ii, fol. 436a; ii, fol. 436a; ii, fol. 417a; ii, fol. 436a; ii, fol. 436a

Humfrid Filius Roberti

Norman, Domesday tenant of Robert Malet in Suffolk and Norfolk. Benefactor of Eye priory at its foundation (from which some of his Domesday tenancies can be identified). He was father of Adelm of Playford, Fulcher, Miles and Peter. Adelm confirmed his father's grants to Eye soon after 1113.

ii, fol. 154a; ii, fol. 315b; ii, fol. 315b; ii, fol. 329b; ii, fol. 305b; ii, fol. 305b; ii, fol. 305b; Brown, Eye Priory Cartulary (1992–94), No. 55; Brown, Eye Priory Cartulary (1992–94), No. 40; Brown, Eye Priory Cartulary (1992–94), No. 3; Brown, Eye Priory Cartulary (1992–94), No. 5; ii, fol. 318b; ii, fol. 315b; ii, fol. 315a; ii, fol. 315a; ii, fol. 315a; ii, fol. 315a; ii, fol. 315a; ii, fol. 315b; ii, fol. 315a; ii, fol. 315a; ii, fol. 315a; ii, fol. 315a; ii, fol. 315b; ii, fol. 315b; ii, fol. 315b; ii, fol. 315a; ii, fol. 314b; ii, fol. 318b; ii, fol. 318b; ii, fol. 325b; ii, fol. 325b; ii, fol. 325a; ii, fol. 329b; ii, fol. 329b; ii, fol. 329b; ii, fol. 329b; ii, fol. 329b; ii, fol. 329b; ii, fol. 329b; ii, fol. 330a; ii, fol. 329b

Humfrid Filius Roderici

Norman, Domesday tenant of William de Warenne in Suffolk.

ii, fol. 398a; ii, fol. 398a; ii, fol. 381b; Hamilton, Inquisitio Eliensis (1876), pp. 192–95

Humfrid Nepos Ranulfi

Norman, Domesday tenant of Ranulf brother of Ilger. Probably the man described as nepos of Ranulf in DB Norfolk 1.192.

ii, fol. 261a; ii, fol. 260b; ii, fol. 261a; ii, fol. 260b; ii, fol. 260b; ii, fol. 261a; ii, fol. 261a

Humfrid []

Domesday tenant of Peter de Valognes at Walsingham in Norfolk. His land there was given to Binham priory c.1100/07, when he was still tenant. The charter was attested by a Humphrey Comes and a Humphrey Calvus, one of whom was probably this Humphrey.

Dugdale, Monasticon Anglicanum, III, pp. 345–46, No. I; ii, fol. 258a; Dugdale, Monasticon Anglicanum, III, p. 346, No. II

Hunald []

Occurs Domesday Essex.

ii, fol. 096a; ii, fol. 096b

Hunfrid Camerarius

Chamberlain to Queen Matilda, occurring as such in Actes caen. 2, dated 16 June 1066. The same source, no. 8, dated 1082, shows he held land at Bénouville, Calvados. Brother of Aiulf camerarius (q.v.). Possibly sheriff of Norfolk 1087–1100. Part of his holdings lay in Wiltshire. About 1083 he attested a charter of William I granting land at Alton Priors to his cook William Escudet (see William Scutet) as Humfrido camerario dapifero comitis de Pontivi. At this date the count of Ponthieu was Guy, father-in-law of Robert de Bellême. His Leicestershire fief was held at the Leicestershire Survey (1130) by William Camerarius. He was perhaps the same person as Humphrey Aurei Testiculi (q.v.), since the fees of Humphrey Camerarius in Somerset and Gloucestershire passed to the Orescuil (later Orcas) family, presumed descendants of Aurei Testiculi.

i, fol. 163d; i, fol. 163d; i, fol. 163d; i, fol. 163d; i, fol. 163d; i, fol. 52b; i, fol. 90b; i, fol. 163d; i, fol. 99b; i, fol. 98c; i, fol. 170a; i, fol. 49a; i, fol. 236a; ii, fol. 433a; Douglas, Feudal Documents from Bury St Edmunds, No. 17; i, fol. 30c; ii, fol. 433a; ii, fol. 433b; ii, fol. 433a; ii, fol. 433a; i, fol. 63a; i, fol. 83a; i, fol. 99b; i, fol. 83a; i, fol. 99b; ii, fol. 433a; i, fol. 73a; ii, fol. 434a; i, fol. 49a; i, fol. 49a; i, fol. 98c; i, fol. 83a; i, fol. 170a; i, fol. 170a; i, fol. 170a; i, fol. 170a; i, fol. 236a; ii, fol. 434a; i, fol. 230c; ii, fol. 433a; i, fol. 98c; ii, fol. 434a; i, fol. 36c; ii, fol. 433b; ii, fol. 433b; ii, fol. 433a; i, fol. 236a; i, fol. 52a

Hunfrid Cocus

Occurs Domesday Wiltshire.

i, fol. 74c; i, fol. 170a; i, fol. 170a

Hunfrid De Ansleuilla

Norman, Domesday tenant of Eudo dapifer and Guy of Rainbercurt; according to Le Melletier he was named from Anneville-en-Saire, Manche, cant. Barfleur. In 1166 his fees were held by Thomas de Ansleville. As Humphrey of Knebworth (de Knibwurh, de Cnibwrthe), he was an early benefactor of St Albans (BL Cotton Nero D vii, fols 97v, 100r). He was doubtless the Humphrey de Cheneburna who was a Domesday juror in Broadwater Hundred, Cambridgeshire. Ancestor of the Andeville family; Lewis, 'Jurors'; VCH Cambs v, 60, 113, 162, 266; VCH Herts iii, 114.

i, fol. 139b; i, fol. 139a; i, fol. 200a; i, fol. 200a; i, fol. 197d; i, fol. 197d; i, fol. 197d; i, fol. 197d; i, fol. 197c; G. Fowler, Early Cambridgeshire Feodary, EHR (1932), pp. 442–3; G. Fowler, Early Cambridgeshire Feodary, EHR (1932), pp. 442–3; Hamilton, Inquisitio Comitatus Cantabrigiensis, pp. 1–93; i, fol. 132a; Hamilton, Inquisitio Eliensis (1876), pp. 97–100; Hamilton, Inquisitio Eliensis (1876), pp. 97–100

Hunfrid De Buivile
Norman, held land in chief in Domesday Herefordshire. The form 'buie uilla' is found for Biville, Seine-Maritime, cant. Valmont, comm. Ypreville-Biville (Fauroux, 85).

i, fol. 187a; i, fol. 187a; i, fol. 187a

Hunfrid De Costentin
Norman, Domesday tenant of Earl Hugh of Chester. Perhaps the Humphrey de Merestona (Marston, Northants) who granted land in his demesne at Damblainville, Calvados, to Saint-Evroul and was probably a tenant of Robert of Rhuddlan, though he is not named as such in Domesday Book (Ord. Vit. ed. Le Prevost v, 190; cf. ibid. 187). HKF ii, 27.

i, fol. 266b; i, fol. 264c; i, fol. 264c; Barraclough, Charters of AN Earls of Chester (1988), No. 3; Barraclough, Charters of AN Earls of Chester (1988), No. 28

Hunfrid De Insula
His tenancy-in-chief at Castle Combe in Domesday Wiltshire passed soon after 1086 to his daughter Adeline, wife of Rainald I de Dunstanville (Sanders, 28).

i, fol. 71a; i, fol. 70d; i, fol. 71a; i, fol. 70d; i, fol. 71a; i, fol. 71a; i, fol. 71a; i, fol. 71a; i, fol. 71a; i, fol. 71a

Hunfrid De Medehalle
Humphrey of Maidenhill, occurs Domesday Gloucestershire.

i, fol. 162d; i, fol. 170a; i, fol. 170a; i, fol. 170a

Hunfrid De Villy
Norman, Domesday tenant of Ilbert de Lacy in Yorkshire, identified from his grants to St Clement's chapel in the castle of Pontefract, EYC iii no. 1492. Perhaps named from Villy-Bocage, Calvados, arr. Caen, cant. Villiers-Bocage (Loyd, 109). Another Humphrey de Villy – who married his sister Roesia to Hugh fitz Walter – occurs c.1180. Cf. Holmes, 'Wapentake of Osgoldscross', Yorks. Arch. Journ. 12, 73.

i, fol. 317b; i, fol. 316b; i, fol. 315c

Hunfrid Flamme
Occurs Domesday Sussex.

i, fol. 23a

Hunfrid Hasteng
Norman, Domesday tenant of the Breton Harscoit Musard in Warwickshire, ancestor of the Hastang family. He held Chebsey, Staffordshire, from Henry de Ferrers (Hist. Coll. Staffs. i pt. i, 212). Dead by c.1120. Between 1121 and 1127 Henry I confirmed to St Oswald's, Nostell, the grants by vassals of Robert de Lacy and Hugh de Laval, including the gift of Aitrop son of Humphrey Hasteng, his brother Humphrey and the latter's mother Lescelina (EYC iii, 129–33). A subsequent mandate of Henry I reveals another of Humphrey's sons, Salomon the clerk (ibid. p.142). Comp. Peer. vi, 338 ff.

i, fol. 248c; i, fol. 244b; i, fol. 244b; i, fol. 244b

Hunfrid Loripes
Occurs Domesday Kent holding a house in Dover.

Ballard, Inquisition of St Augustine's (1920), fols 24r–28r; i, fol. 001a

Hunfrid Vis De Leuu
Domesday tenant-in-chief in Berkshire, also occurring in Hampshire. Possibly the Humphrey who held land of Milo Crispin, since Walchelin Visdeloup held 1 fee of Wallingford in 1166 (RBE 309). Humphrey had been succeeded by his son Walchelin by 1129/30 (PR 31 Henry I 5). HKF i, 54ff.

i, fol. 71b; i, fol. 71b; i, fol. 159d; i, fol. 63a; i, fol. 63a; i, fol. 63a; i, fol. 63a; i, fol. 56b

Hunfrid []
Tenant of Roger of Montgomery in Domesday Sussex; possibly the father of Walter of Dunstanville, who mentions his parents Humphrey and Rogeria in a charter for La Sauve Majeure, in which he also names his wife's parents as Guy and Agnes (CDF, 1238).

i, fol. 25c

Hunfrid []
Norman, Domesday tenant of Robert of Mortain in Northamptonshire and Buckinghamshire, and possibly also Cornwall.

i, fol. 136c; i, fol. 79c; i, fol. 223c; i, fol. 136d; i, fol. 146d; i, fol. 146d; i, fol. 22b; i, fol. 22d; i, fol. 125a; i, fol. 79b; i, fol. 223b; i, fol. 223b; i, fol. 223b; i, fol. 223b; i, fol. 223b; i, fol. 223a; i, fol. 223a; i, fol. 223b; i, fol. 223b; i, fol. 223b; i, fol. 223a; i, fol. 223b

Hunfrid []
Norman, Domesday tenant of Gilbert Tison and Erneis de Buron in Yorkshire. Early benefactor of St Mary's, York.

Dugdale, Monasticon Anglicanum, III, pp. 548–50, No. V; i, fol. 328d; i, fol. 326d

Hunfrid []
Norman, Domesday tenant of Robert fitz Corbucion. His fees were afterwards held of the honour of Arundel by persons surnamed from his manor of Ingelose, of whom Hervey occurs c.1166; Farrer, HKF iii, 116.

ii, fol. 259b; ii, fol. 260a; ii, fol. 259b; ii, fol. 259a; ii, fol. 259a

Hunger Filius Odini
Son of Odin camerarius (q.v.).

i, fol. 49d; i, fol. 43d; i, fol. 81c/d; i, fol. 85a; i, fol. 85a

Hunnit []
English thegn who continued to hold land in Shropshire, in association with his brother Wulfgeat, after 1066. In 1086 they were tenants of Turold de Verly. His land passed thereafter to another Englishman Thorth, ancestor of the fitzTorets; see Williams, The English, 90.

i, fol. 258a; i, fol. 258a; i, fol. 258a; i, fol. 258a

Iagelin []
Domesday tenant of Theobald fitz Berner and Godbald arbalaster. His personal name is a diminiutive of a Celtic form Jagu, and also occurs as a diminutive of Latin 'Jacob'.

i, fol. 115c; i, fol. 117b

Iarnagot []

Breton, Domesday tenant of Eudo fitz Spirewic in Suffolk. His son Ralph attested charters of the lords of Tattershall in the 1150s. Alberic fitz Gernagot attested a St Benet's, Holme, charter in 1161/2 (Cart., no. 204).

ii, fol. 435a; ii, fol. 434b

Ida Comitissa Boloniensis

Daughter of Godfrey de Bouillon, duke of Lower Lorraine, second wife of Eustache II count of Boulogne (d.1087), mother of Godfrey de Bouillon, hero of the First Crusade and his brothers Baldwin I king of Jerusalem and Eustache III de Boulogne. She was still alive c. 7 June 1106, when Lambert bishop of Arras confirmed the possessions and righs of the collegiate church of Lens at the request of Eustache III of Boulogne, his wife Mary and his mother Ida, described as 'religiose comitissae'. As a widow she lived in retirement near the monastery of La Capelle-Sainte-Marie, which she had founded. In 1130 her granddaughter Matilda countess of Boulogne, wife of Stephen de Blois, took steps towards Ida's eventual canonization by commissioning a Vita from the monks of Vasconvillier (AASS, April 1, 141–44; the process is described in cap. 7 of G. Duby, The Knight, the Lady and the Priest).

Regesta regum Anglo-Normannorum III, No. 76; i, fol. 85a; i, fol. 85a; i, fol. 85a; i, fol. 91d; i, fol. 34b

Ilbert De Laci

Norman, from Lassy, arr. Vire, cant. Condé-sur-Noireau, Calvados (Loyd, 53). Heir of his mother Emma, who was a nun of Saint-Amand de Rouen before 1069 (Cart. Sainte-Trinité de Rouen, pp. 459–60); she was perhaps a daughter of Ilbert marshal (Fauroux, 104) and sister of Ingelran fitz Ilbert (Cart. Sainte-Trinité de Rouen, p. 466). He and his wife Hadruda were benefactors of Sainte-Trinité de Rouen, where their son Hugh was buried (charter printed in Archaelogical Journal iv, p. 249). Tenant-in-chief of a fief based upon Pontefract, Yorkshire in 1086, brother of Walter de Lacy of Weobley (d.1085), probably gained after the lands in Lincolnshire and elsewhere that he held of Odo of Bayeux. He founded the Collegiate Chapel of St Clements in his castle at Pontefract. He died c.1093/5, leaving his successor Robert I de Lacy by his wife Havise (probably the same person as Hadruda above. It has been assumed that he was also father of Hugh, abbot of Selby, but there is no real evidence for this view. His son Robert confirmed a grant of land at Hamilton to Selby made by Ilbert 'pro anima fratris meo Hugonis' (Mon. Ang. iii, pp. 500–1). Since Ilbert is known to have had a son Hugh who died in his father's lifetime it is very difficult to accept this 'pro anima' clause as a reference to a still living son who was a monk of Selby. See Wightman, Lacy Family, 26–45, 48–52, 55–8; Sanders, 138.

Lincolnshire Claims (Domesday Book), fols 375a–d; i, fol. 342d; i, fol. 342b; i, fol. 342a; i, fol. 342b; i, fol. 342b; i, fol. 342b; i, fol. 342b; i, fol. 342b; i, fol. 342a; i, fol. 342c; i, fol. 342d; i, fol. 342d; i, fol. 342d; i, fol. 343a; i, fol. 343b; i, fol. 343b; i, fol. 343c; i, fol. 343c; i, fol. 303c; i, fol. 343a; i, fol. 342a; i, fol. 343a; i, fol. 342c; i, fol. 156c; i, fol. 342b; i, fol. 342a; i, fol. 342a; i, fol. 156c; i, fol. 156c; i, fol. 156a; i, fol. 156a; i, fol. 156a; i, fol. 156a; i, fol. 145a; i, fol. 318a; i, fol. 318a; i, fol. 318a; i, fol. 318a; i, fol. 318a; i, fol. 317d; i, fol. 318a; i, fol. 318a; i, fol. 318a; i, fol. 315c; i, fol. 315c; i, fol. 315c; i, fol. 315c; i, fol. 315c; i, fol. 315c; i, fol. 315c; i, fol. 315a; i, fol. 318a; i, fol. 317d; i, fol. 315a; i, fol.

318a; i, fol. 315a; i, fol. 318a; i, fol. 318a; i, fol. 317d; i, fol. 318a; i, fol. 317d; i, fol. 318b; i, fol. 318a; i, fol. 318b; i, fol. 317b; i, fol. 318a; i, fol. 318a; i, fol. 318a; i, fol. 318a; i, fol. 318a; i, fol. 317d; i, fol. 316b; i, fol. 315b; i, fol. 315a; i, fol. 315b; i, fol. 315b; i, fol. 316c; i, fol. 316c; i, fol. 315b; i, fol. 316c; i, fol. 315a; i, fol. 316c; i, fol. 316d; i, fol. 316d; i, fol. 316d; i, fol. 316a; i, fol. 316a; i, fol. 316b; i, fol. 316a; i, fol. 316c; i, fol. 315d; i, fol. 315a; i, fol. 315a; i, fol. 315a; i, fol. 315a; i, fol. 315d; i, fol. 315d; i, fol. 315b; i, fol. 315d; i, fol. 315d; i, fol. 315a; i, fol. 315c; i, fol. 315c; i, fol. 315b; i, fol. 315b; i, fol. 315b; i, fol. 317b; i, fol. 315a; i, fol. 317b; i, fol. 315a; i, fol. 315d; i, fol. 315a; i, fol. 154c; i, fol. 317b; i, fol. 315d; i, fol. 316a; i, fol. 315a; i, fol. 317a; i, fol. 155d; i, fol. 317b; i, fol. 315a; i, fol. 315a; i, fol. 315a; i, fol. 315a; i, fol. 317c; i, fol. 317c; i, fol. 315a; i, fol. 291b; Dugdale, Monasticon Anglicanum, III, pp. 548–50, No. V; i, fol. 315a; Lincolnshire Claims (Domesday Book), fols 375a–d; i, fol. 291b; i, fol. 317c; i, fol. 353c; i, fol. 291b; i, fol. 291b; i, fol. 291b; i, fol. 291b; i, fol. 291b; i, fol. 291b; i, fol. 364b; i, fol. 353c; i, fol. 291b; i, fol. 318b; i, fol. 317a; i, fol. 315a; i, fol. 318b; i, fol. 317d; i, fol. 56c; i, fol. 317c; i, fol. 318b; i, fol. 315a; i, fol. 318b; i, fol. 318b; i, fol. 318b; i, fol. 317a; i, fol. 317b; i, fol. 317b; i, fol. 318b; i, fol. 317d; i, fol. 317a; i, fol. 318b; i, fol. 317c; i, fol. 317a; i, fol. 317c; i, fol. 317c; i, fol. 317b; i, fol. 317d; i, fol. 317a; i, fol. 317a; i, fol. 317a; i, fol. 317a; i, fol. 317a; i, fol. 317a; i, fol. 317c; i, fol. 315a; i, fol. 353c; i, fol. 291b; Regesta regum Anglo-Normannorum III, No. 817; Dugdale, Monasticon Anglicanum, III, p. 547, No. III; Dugdale, Monasticon Anglicanum, III, p. 499, No. IV; i, fol. 156c; i, fol. 156c; i, fol. 156c; i, fol. 156c; Dugdale, Monasticon Anglicanum, IV, p. 120, No. I; i, fol. 31d; i, fol. 31d; i, fol. 179c

Ilbert De Ramisvilla

Ilbert de Ramisvilla was one of the tenants of Ilbert I de Lacy who made grants to their lord's foundation of St Clement at Pontefract. Domesday make no obvious distinction between Ilbert de Lacy and any tenant of the same name, but it may be that the Ilbert of the second Domesday reference to Campsall was the Ilbert de Ramisvilla who gave land there to St Clement's (EYC ii, 1492). Cf. Robert, another tenant whose land was given to St Clement's by Girald de Rameswilla, named from Reineville, Calvados, arr. Vire, cant. Condé-sur-Noireau, comm. Lassy (Loyd, 84).

i, fol. 315d

Ilbert Filius Turoldi

Norman, occurs Domesday Gloucestershire and Herefordshire. He was probably the Ilbert who was mentioned as sheriff of Hertfordshire in 1086, when a Gilbert who was probably Gilbert fitz Turold (q.v.) was sheriff of Herefordshire. Cf. Green, Sheriffs, 45, 47. These men were possibly brothers, or other close relations. A William and his brother Ilbert also occur in Herefordshire as tenants of Ralph de Tosny. A Northamptonshire charter of the mid twelfth century named Ilbert de Funtainnes as the great-grandfather of Silvester de Bures, who had held a manor of 'Wiche' from a Tosny lord; Fontaines-sous-Jouy was in the Tosny fief. The circumstances suggest that Ilbert de Fontaines should be sought in Domesday Book, where the only Tosny tenant named Ilbert occurs in Herefordshire, though the de Bures's holding was East Anglian. No further advance can be made, but it is at least suggestive that a charter for the abbey of Préaux (Arch. Eure H711 no. 438) given c.1050–60 by Ralph de Warenne and his wife Beatrice, was attested by Hilbert fitz Turold de Fontanis. Ilbert vicecomes and his son Robert were benefactors of the Tosny abbey of Conches in the late eleventh century, granting land at Dinedor (Duura) in Herefordshire (Gall. Christ. xi inst. 128ff); this Ilbert, who was sheriff of Hertfordshire at some time before 1076 (Green, Sheriffs, 47), was Hilbert Hugonis filius who attested a grant to Jumièges by Ralph II de Tosny, as suggested in L. Musset, 'Les Tosny', Francia v (1978), 75.

i, fol. 181b; i, fol. 180a; i, fol. 187a; i, fol. 179c; i, fol. 179d; i, fol. 187a; i, fol. 187a; i, fol. 183b; i, fol. 180b; i, fol. 180c; i, fol. 179c

Ilbert []
Norman, Domesday tenant of Earl Hugh of Chester. Father of Richard I and William de Rullos, his successors by 1129. The origin of Richard and William in Roullours, Calvados, arr. and cant. Vire was established by Clay, EYC v, 95–9.

i, fol. 267c; i, fol. 267c; i, fol. 267c

Ilbert []
Norman, tenant in a single manor of the wife of Hugh fitz Grip in Domesday Dorset.

i, fol. 83d

Ilbod De Hesdin
From Hesdin, Pas-de-Calais, arr. Montreuil, cant. Hesdin (Loyd, 51), he held a small fief in 1086. In the Oxfordshire Domesday's list of landholders he is identified as the brother of Arnulf de Hesdin (q.v.). His fief apparently escheated fairly soon afterwards.

i, fol. 160b; ii, fol. 002a; i, fol. 160b; ii, fol. 095b; ii, fol. 095b; ii, fol. 095b; ii, fol. 096a

Ildebert Turonensis
Occurs Domesday Somerset as a tenant of the bishop of Wells, and perhaps also of Matthew de Mauritanie. Possibly the same as Hildebert steward of John of Tours, bishop of Wells, and almost certainly his brother. He was father of archdeacon John of Wells, fl. 1122–1136 (EEA x, pp. xxxix–xli).

i, fol. 98b; i, fol. 98b; i, fol. 89c; i, fol. 89c

Ilduin []
Domesday tenant of Robert de Tosny in Northamptonshire. Succeeded by his son Ralph by the time of the Northants Survey, c.1127/9; Robert of Brampton held in 1166 of the honour of Belvoir. See Farrer, HKF ii, 393.

i, fol. 234a; i, fol. 225b; i, fol. 225a

Ilger []
Domesday tenant of Robert Gernon. His descendant Christina de Wiham, who held one fee of Gernon's successor William de Montfichet in 1166, took her land to her husband William of Windsor (d.c.1176) (VCH Herts. i, 513; Round, Ancestor 1, pp. 125–6).

ii, fol. 064b; ii, fol. 067a; ii, fol. 065b; ii, fol. 065b

Ilger []
Norman, Domesday tenant of the bishop of Coutances in Gloucestershire and Northamptonshire.

i, fol. 165a; i, fol. 221a

Ingald []
Occurs Domesday Leicestershire.

i, fol. 231b; i, fol. 234c; i, fol. 234b; i, fol. 234b

Ingelbald []
Domesday tenant of Drogo of Carteret and sub-tenant of Geoffrey bishop of Coutances. His wife (q.v.) was a tenant of the bishop and may have been the bishop's niece.

i, fol. 102c

Ingelramn []
Domesday tenant of Arnald de Hesdin in Somerset. Possibly Ingelran nephew of Ingelran count of Hesdin and brother of Walter who attested a grant of English land by Arnald to the priory of Hesdin (Cart. no. 52). An alternative possibility is that he was Ingelran de Beaurain, fl. 1129 (q.v.), who married Arnald's niece Milisend.

i, fol. 98b

Ingelramn []
Norman, occurs Domesday Somerset and Dorset as tenant of Waleran Venator. His successor in 1166 was probably John de Fifhida.

i, fol. 82b

Ingelran De Ou
Domesday tenant of the count of Eu in Sussex and, in Huntingdonshire, of Eustache of Huntingdon and Ramsey Abbey. Henry count of Eu's recital and confirmation of his grandfather Robert's foundation of canons at St Mary's, Hastings, includes reference to the grant of land at Wilting by Ingelran d'Eu (Sussex Rec. Soc. xliv, 299–302), subsequently confirmed by Ingelran's brother Guy. Guy of Eu and Ingelran of Eu both occur in the Ramsey Cartulary, and Guy was one of the abbey's Domesday tenants. Ingelran was probably the Ingelran who was sheriff of the Rape of Hastings in the early twelfth century, attesting two of Count Henry's charters as Ingelran of Hastings. He was apparently succeeded in Huntindonshire, by 1120, by Drogo of Hastings (q.v.), father of Helias and Ralph. The grant of Ingelran de Auco to Huntingdon priory of land at Gidding and Liddington, Hunts., which he held of Eustache of Huntingdon in 1086, was confirmed by Henry I c.1123/35 (Mon. Ang. vi, 79).

i, fol. 206b; i, fol. 204c; i, fol. 206b; i, fol. 18a; i, fol. 17d; i, fol. 18b; i, fol. 18c; i, fol. 18c; i, fol. 18d; Hart, Cartularium Monasterii de Rameseia, No. CLV

Ingelran De Reinbuedcurt
Son of Guy de Raimbeaucourt. Occurs in Domesday Book, but nothing else is known of him.

i, fol. 159d; i, fol. 363d; i, fol. 363d; i, fol. 363d

Ingelran []
Norman, Domesday tenant of Roger de Lacy.

i, fol. 184b; i, fol. 184a

Ingelran []
Norman, occurs in Domesday Shropshire as a tenant of Roger de Mortimer. He was succeeded by the Savage family (Eyton, Shrops, iv, 230, 271).

i, fol. 47a; i, fol. 260b; i, fol. 257a; i, fol. 260b; i, fol. 260b; i, fol. 260c; i, fol. 257a

Ingelran []
Norman, Domesday tenant of Robert de Mortain at Fathingstone, Northamptonshire; perhaps also tenant of Gilo de Picquigny. His successor by the 1160s was Ingelran of Farthingstone (q.v.).

i, fol. 227b; i, fol. 224a

Ingenulf []
Domesday tenant of Robert count of Meulan in Warwickshire, ancestor of the Bourton family.

i, fol. 237b; i, fol. 240a; i, fol. 240b; i, fol. 240a

Ingrann []
Occurs Domesday Nottinghamshire and Derbyshire. Father of Ranulf, who occurs from 1129/30; ancestor of the lords of Alfreton.

i, fol. 278b; i, fol. 278b; i, fol. 285b

Ingulf Monachus
Occurs Domesday Surrey.

i, fol. 34a

Ingulf []
Domesday tenant of William de Scohies.

ii, fol. 223a; ii, fol. 224a; ii, fol. 224a

Isac []
Held lands of the king in East Anglia. A confused entry in the Suffolk Domesday, relating to the lands of Ely Abbey, suggests that Isaac had held some of his land before 1066. A passage in the Norfolk Domesday associates him with 'French' burgesses of Norwich. Several of his holdings had had previous associations with Earl Ralph de Gael, and some of his lands had been the subject of an exchange with Roger Bigod, sheriff of Norfolk and Suffolk in 1086. Isaac appears in Ely's suit of c.1072. Isaac could well have been another of the several examples of Ralph de Gael's Bretons who survived the earl's fall in 1075, perhaps one who had served him in a shrieval or quasi-shrieval capacity. He was succeeded by a son Roland. The carta of Nigel of Ely refers to the holding de vetere of the fee of Rolandi filii Ysaac in Suffolk (RBE, 365). Isaac is probably to be identified with the tenant of Robert Malet in Thornham Parva (Suffolk), who granted land to Eye Priory when he became a monk there in the early twelfth century (Eye Cart. 13; cf. ibid., Introd., ii 52). In 1185 Herbert son of Roland (brother of Lowis Brito, q.v.), then deceased, was recorded as having held Isaac's Domesday holding at Hemingstone by jester serjeanty (Rot. de Dom., 62).

ii, fol. 386b; ii, fol. 352b; ii, fol. 118a; ii, fol. 437a; ii, fol. 264a; Hamilton, Inquisitio Eliensis (1876), pp. 192–95; Brown, Eye Priory Cartulary (1992–94), No. 13; ii, fol. 264a; ii, fol. 264a; ii, fol. 264a; ii, fol. 264a; ii, fol. 264a; ii, fol. 264a; ii, fol. 264a; ii, fol. 438a; ii, fol. 438a; ii, fol. 437b; ii, fol. 437b; ii, fol. 437b; ii, fol. 437b; ii, fol. 438a; ii, fol. 437b; ii, fol. 437b; ii, fol. 437b; ii, fol. 437b

Iseldis []
Occurs once, holding a single manor in chief in Domesday Dorset.

i, fol. 84a

Isembard Artifex

Domesday tenant of Peterborough Abbey; Hugh Candidus, p. 60 (cited Stapleton, 172, note) wrote: Primus Isembard artifex. Martinus de Pappele tenet feodum unius militis in Norhamtonescire, scilicet in Pappele; et inde plenarie respondet.

    i, fol. 221d; i, fol. 140c

Iseuuard []

Domesday tenant of Odo of Bayeux in Oxfordshire. William son of Isward attested a charter of Robert d'Oilly c.1130/5 (Cart. Eynsham i, p. 73).

    i, fol. 155b; i, fol. 155c

Iuichel Presbiter

Held a few manors in Domesday Book. His forename is Breton, but nothing is known of his background. He was probably the Judicael presbyter whom William I appointed as canon of Cherbourg (Fauroux, 224).

    i, fol. 243a; i, fol. 70b; i, fol. 218a; ii, fol. 447a; ii, fol. 438a; ii, fol. 438a; ii, fol. 438a; ii, fol. 438a; ii, fol. 438a; ii, fol. 438b; ii, fol. 263b; ii, fol. 263b; ii, fol. 438a

Iuo De Grandesmesnil

Son of Hugh de Grandmesnil (Calvados, arr. Lisieux, cant. Saint-Pierre-sur-Dives) and Adelisa de Beaumont. Two of his sons died in the White Ship disaster of November 1120 (Ord. Vit. vi, 304). He was possibly the Ivo who was a tenant in 1086 of Hugh de Grandmesnil, whose tenant Ivo was his steward, as suggested in Mason, 'Barons and officials', ANS 13 (1991), p. 256. He was perhaps also tenant of Roger de Montgomery (in Sussex). Ivo and his brother Alberic were among the 'rope-dancers of Antioch' in 1098 (ibid., 18). Their eldest brother Robert (d.c.1136) succeeded to Hugh's Norman estates, which he governed as a supporter of Henry I. The English lands went to Ivo. Shortly after the accession of Henry I in 1100 Ivo was accused of rapine and forced to mortage his land to Robert de Beaumont, count of Meulan, in the hope of buying his favour with the king. The move failed and eventually Ivo was forced into semi-voluntary exile in 1118, the English Grandmesnil estates being absorbed by Robert de Beaumont, who had then been earl of Leicester for about ten years. Ivo had issue at least two sons by his wife, a daughter of Gilbert de Gand, both of whom drowned in the White Ship disaster of November 1120 (ibid., 18, 304, iv, 230–2).

    i, fol. 232c; i, fol. 224c; i, fol. 224c; i, fol. 233a; i, fol. 232c; i, fol. 24c; i, fol. 24a; i, fol. 23a; i, fol. 218a; i, fol. 232d; i, fol. 232d

Iuo De Tigervilla

Norman, Domesday tenant of Robert de Tosny of Belvoir, from Thierceville, Eure, arr. Les Andelys, cant. Gisors. He occurs in the Belvoir foundation charter with his son Berenger (Mon. Ang. ii, 288–9). His other sons Hugh (father of Robert de Ropeslai, q.v.) and Robert were also benefactors of Belvoir. See Loyd, 103. His fees were held in 1166 by Simon de Ropeslai.

    i, fol. 233d; i, fol. 353c; i, fol. 353b; i, fol. 353a; Dugdale, Monasticon Anglicanum, III, pp. 288–89, No. I

Iuo De Verdun

Norman, mentioned as an early benefactor of Thetford in charters of Roger and William Bigod c.1107–10. Possibly the Ivo who held land of Ranulf brother of

Ilger in 1086.

ii, fol. 425a; Dugdale, Monasticon Anglicanum, IV, pp. 148–49, No. II; Dugdale, Monasticon Anglicanum, IV, pp. 148–49, No. II

Iuo Taillebois

Brother of Ralph Taillebois, whom he may have succeeded briefly as sheriff of Bedfordshire after Ralph's death shortly before 1086. From west Normandy, as shows by Ralph's sale of land at Villers to Saint-Eienne de Caen (Actes. caen, p. 106, 127), and by Ivo's gift of the church of Cristot (Calvados, arr. Caen, cant. Tilly-sur-Seulles), attested by his brother Robert (see Loyd, 100). Taillebois is the name of a small hamlet in the commune of Saint-Gervais de Briouze (Calvados). Members of the Taillebois family later held land at Pointel, near Briouze; see J.-M. Bouvris in Revue Avranchin t. lxiv, no. 331, 105 année, June 1987. The William Taillebois who occurs in the Lincolnshire Domesday was doubtless a kinsman, perhaps the son of Thomas Taillebois; Robert and Thomas Taillebois attest Braose charters in the 1080/90s (CDF, 1114, 1119). A notable and ruthless royal official, he was active against both Hereward the Wake and Ralph of Gael in the 1070s. In 1086 Ivo was sheriff of Lincolnshire, where he held a considerable fief as tenant-in-chief. It was formed largely as the result of his marriage to Lucy, daughter and heiress of Turold, sheriff of Lincolnshire c.1066–1083; a grant to Saint-Nicholas d'Angers in 1083 by Ivo and his wife refers to Turold and his wife as deceased. Lucy's marriage portion had come to Turold with the daughter of William Malet, one of Ivo's Domesday predecessors. Ivo died in or shortly after 1093, his fief passing to the heirs of Lucy's third husband, Ranulf I earl of Chester. None of it passed to the heirs of his daughter Beatrice, wife of Ribald brother of Count Alan. The reason is unknown, but does not necessarily mean that Beatrice was illegitimate or not the daughter of Lucy.

i, fol. 345d; i, fol. 337d; i, fol. 359b; i, fol. 346a

Iuo []

Norman, tenant of Robert of Mortain and Walter Giffard in Domesday Buckinghamshire.

i, fol. 147d; i, fol. 146d

Iuo []

Domesday tenant of Gilbert de Ghent in Lincolnshire. Robert de Driby of 1166 was probably his successor.

i, fol. 355c; i, fol. 355a; i, fol. 354d

Johannes Camerarius

Norman, occurs Domesday Gloucestershire.

i, fol. 163d; i, fol. 163d; i, fol. 163d

Johannes Filius Ernuciun

Norman, Domesday tenant of John fitz Waleran de Veim. His successor in 1129 was Hugh fitz Ernucion (PR 31 Henry I, 55), and perhaps also Robert fitz Ernucion (ibid., 148).

ii, fol. 084a

Johannes Filius Waleranni

Norman, son of Waleran fitz Ranulf the moneyer of Veim, Manche, Domesday tenant-in-chief as one of the heirs of his father. He was represented in 1129/30 by his daughter Juliana, wife of William of Hastings (PR 31 Henry I, 58). Comp. Peer. xii, 272.

ii, fol. 084a; ii, fol. 435b; ii, fol. 003a; ii, fol. 084b; ii, fol. 103b; ii, fol. 084b; ii, fol. 435b; ii, fol. 435b; ii, fol. 435b; i, fol. 201d; i, fol. 201d

Johannes Francus
Norman, tenant of Swein of Essex in 1086.

ii, fol. 045b; ii, fol. 044b

Johannes Hostiarius
Norman, an usher in royal service, occurs Domesday Dorset and Somerset. See Round, King's Serjeants, 110.

i, fol. 77d; i, fol. 77d; i, fol. 93c; i, fol. 87c; i, fol. 90c; i, fol. 89b; i, fol. 85a; i, fol. 98c; i, fol. 98c; i, fol. 98c; i, fol. 98c; i, fol. 98c; i, fol. 74c; i, fol. 74c

Johannes Nepos Waleranni
Norman, son of Richard fitz Ranulf the Moneyer of Caen and nephew of Waleran fitz Ranulf; holder of a minor tenancy-in-chief in Domesday East Anglia. His five children, possibly by two wives, achieved some importance during the reign of Henry I, of whom his sons Payn, Eustache and William were prominent servants; his daughters were Alice, abbess of Barking and Agnes, wife of Roger de Valognes. Comp. Peer. xii, 272.

ii, fol. 217a; ii, fol. 094b; ii, fol. 214a; ii, fol. 214a; ii, fol. 214a; ii, fol. 265b; ii, fol. 266a; ii, fol. 266a; ii, fol. 266a; ii, fol. 266a; ii, fol. 266a; ii, fol. 265b; ii, fol. 265b; ii, fol. 265b; ii, fol. 266a; ii, fol. 265b; ii, fol. 372b; Hamilton, Inquisitio Eliensis (1876), pp. 192–95; ii, fol. 094b; ii, fol. 265b

Johannes []
Domesday tenant of Henry de Ferrers. Early benefactor of Tutbury priory.

i, fol. 275b; i, fol. 275b; i, fol. 233c; Dugdale, Monasticon Anglicanum, III, pp. 392–93, No. II

Johannes []
Norman, Domesday tenant of Richard de Clare in Surrey. Possibly father of the William fitz John who held two fees of de Clare in Surrey in 1166.

i, fol. 35a; i, fol. 34d; i, fol. 34d; i, fol. 35b; i, fol. 35b

Johannes []
Norman, Domesday tenant of Eustache of Huntingdon. Probably the same as John tenant of the bishop of Lincoln in Huntingdonshire, and perhaps also of Erneis de Buron in Lincolnshire and Yorkshire. Possibly to be identified with the John whose granddaughter Pampelina, wife of Osbert, was impleaded by the abbot of Peterborough in 1135 (cited in King, Peterborough Abbey, 30). His fees passed to the Longueville family.

i, fol. 362c; i, fol. 227d; i, fol. 206a; i, fol. 203d; i, fol. 203d; i, fol. 206a; i, fol. 328d

Johannes []
Domesday tenant of Osbern de Arcis.

i, fol. 329c

Jouinus []
Jovin, undertenant of Robert of Mortain in 1086, is probably to be identified with

the Jovin Faber the count mentioned in a charter to Launceston priory as one of eight burgesses belonging to the canons. As such, he was an Englishman.

i, fol. 120b; i, fol. 120b; i, fol. 123c; i, fol. 123c; i, fol. 123c; i, fol. 123c; i, fol. 123c; i, fol. 123c; i, fol. 123c; i, fol. 123d; i, fol. 123d; i, fol. 123c; i, fol. 123d; i, fol. 123d; i, fol. 123d; Hull, Cartulary of Launceston Priory (1987), No. 3

Judhel De Totnes

Domesday writes Judhael where every other document concerning this man writes Juhel, but his name remains unmistakeably Breton, an observation confirmed by the fact that his father and son were both named Alfred (Round, Feudal England, 255–6). He appears to have attested a grant of William I, made at Downton, Wiltshire, late in 1082, to Saint-Calais in Maine as 'Ruhalis filii Alvredi (RRAN i, no. 147). The context in which Judhael is found is invariably Norman and in particular west Norman. J.B. Williams, 'Judhael of Totnes: the life and times of a post-Conquest baron', Anglo-Norman Studies 16 (1994), 271–289, has shown that he had held his honour of Totnes since at least 1068, and was still holding it in 1086 according to Domesday. Early in the reign of William II, however, he lost it for unknown reasons which surely involve support for the claims of William's brother Robert Curthose. Orderic Vitalis reported that in 1079 one of the young and reckless companions of Robert Curthose in his war against his father was one Juhel son of Alfred the Giant. After their defeat, Robert and his companions went on to Flanders (Ord. Vit., iii, 100–102). Between 1087 and 1096, when he went on the First Crusade, Robert was duke of Normandy and active there. During the same period we know nothing of Judhael, only that he found favour with Henry I, Robert's rival until 1106, early in the twelfth century. He had certainly been established as lord of the Devonshire honour of Barnstaple by 1113. In 1123, at an advanced age, he retired as a monk to the priory of Saint-Martin-des-Champs he had built at Barnstaple, probably dying shortly thereafter. The identification of Judhael with Orderic's Juhel son of Alfred the Giant is problematic because Judhael was not especially youthful or feckless in 1079, and there is no firm reason to suppose him to have been absent from England between 1079 and 1086. Nevertheless, there are reasons for supposing that Orderic did provide the key to Judhael's origin. The journey of Robert's companions to Flanders very probably passed through or near Picquigny, home of the vicomtes of Amiens. We know from the work of the monk Herman, who records a visit of monks from Laon to Judhael at Barnstaple, that Judhael's wife was the sister of Germond of Picquigny (Hermani monachi De Miraculis S. Mariae Laudunensis de gestis venerabilis Bartholomei episcopi et S. Norberi Libri Tres, in PL, clvi, cols 983–4). Her rapturous welcome of men from her homeland suggests that she had been married from there, and not from the various Picquigny families settled in England. Such a marriage, for a west Norman or Breton, would be difficult to explain without the passage in Orderic. Alfred the Giant was an early benefactor of the abbey of Cerisy (Manche, cant. Cerisy-la-Fôret), of which he became a monk in the mid-eleventh century. His earliest occurrences came in 1028, in a charter of William of Bellême, and in 1029 when he helped Nigel I of the Cotentin to repel Alan III of Brittany's invasion of Normandy (Fauroux, Recueil, nos. 33, 69, 99, 195; William of Jumièges, ed. van Houts, ii, 58–9). He certainly had both sons and daughters, of whom William and Adselina are known, both of them active in the 1080s; another daughter was the mother of William de Milly, and hence probably the wife of

Rivallon de Milly, a Norman with a Breton name who confirmed his tenants' grant to the Breton abbey of Redon, in association with Robert of Mortain, in the mid-eleventh century. Judhael could well have been another of Alfred the Giant's sons. In founding Totnes Priory, a cell of the abbey of SS Serge and Bacchus in Angers, he may have provided the name of another in providing for the soul of his brother Robert. The foundation occurred between 1082 and 1086, and perhaps closer to 1082 since a notable absentee from the witness list is his tenant Nigel. Of Judhael's numerous manors in Devonshire in 1086, ten stand out as the most valuable; 8 of them were held by Judhael and 2 by Nigel, who held several other manors from him. Combined with the fact that Nigel's sons were named Alfred and Juhel, this suggests a strong possibility that Nigel had married a sister of Judhael. Juhel son of Nigel attested Judhael's acts for Barnstaple priory. Both Alfred son of Judhael and Juhel son of Nigel were close to Baldwin I de Redvers, earl of Devon, and head of a network of western Normans in Devon, in the 1130s and 40s; it is not unlikely that Baldwin's wife Adeliza was the sister of Juhel son of Nigel and the niece of Judhael of Totnes (DB Devon 17.4–5; 10; 82; Mon. Ang. v, 197–8, attested by Alfred fitz Nigel (facsimile in Watkin, ii; Redvers Charters pp. 76–8, Juhel fitz Nigel). There is a very strong west Norman 'feel' to Judhael's background and career, but it is difficult to clarify because few of his tenants can be identified – with the exception of the west Norman Ralph de Pomeroy – and because he left no lasting mark on either of his honours. On the other hand, his foundation charter for Totnes priory had numerous witnesses, including two west Normans, Ralph Malbank and Hervey Avenel. The latter does not appear in Domesday Book, but attested William of Mortain's confirmation charter for Montacute priory before 1106. Judhael, or rather Juhel's son Alfred died without issue after his part in the failed campaign of 1139 against King Stephen, when his heir was his sister Aanor, wife of Philip de Braose.

Dugdale, Monasticon Anglicanum, IV, p. 198, No. III; i, fol. 101b; Dugdale, Monasticon Anglicanum, IV, p. 198, No. II; Dugdale, Monasticon Anglicanum, IV, p. 198, No. V; i, fol. 109a; i, fol. 109a; i, fol. 108c; i, fol. 109c; i, fol. 109c; i, fol. 109c; i, fol. 109b; i, fol. 109b; i, fol. 109a; i, fol. 109a; i, fol. 108c; i, fol. 108c; i, fol. 108c; i, fol. 108c; i, fol. 108c; i, fol. 108c; i, fol. 110b; i, fol. 109a; Dugdale, Monasticon Anglicanum, IV, pp. 198–99, No. VI; Dugdale, Monasticon Anglicanum, IV, pp. 197–98, No. I; Dugdale, Monasticon Anglicanum, IV, p. 199, No. VII; Dugdale, Monasticon Anglicanum, IV, pp. 197–98, No. I

Judita Comitissa

Niece of William I, daughter of Lambert, count of Lens and Adelaide. Married c. 1070 to Earl Waltheof, an English nobleman executed for treason in 1076; Judith was one of his accusers (Ord. Vit. ii, 262, 320), but after his death she arranged for him to be honorably buried at Crowland abbey (idem, 322). Her principal heir was her elder daughter Matilda.

i, fol. 206d; Lincolnshire Claims (Domesday Book), fols 376d–377c; Hart, Cartularium Monasterii de Rameseia, No. C; i, fol. 336b; i, fol. 228b; i, fol. 228b; i, fol. 228b; i, fol. 228b; i, fol. 228b; i, fol. 228b; i, fol. 228b; i, fol. 366d; i, fol. 366d; i, fol. 366d; i, fol. 228b; i, fol. 336d; i, fol. 228b; i, fol. 336a; i, fol. 367a; i, fol. 219a; i, fol. 228b; i, fol. 228b; i, fol. 228b; i, fol. 226d; i, fol. 223a; i, fol. 217c; i, fol. 366d; i, fol. 228b; i, fol. 217b; i, fol. 217d; i, fol. 202b; i, fol. 202b; i, fol. 202b; i, fol. 202b; i, fol. 202b; i, fol. 202b; i, fol. 228b; i, fol. 228b; i, fol. 228b; i, fol. 236b; i, fol. 236b; i, fol. 236b; i, fol. 236b; i, fol. 233b; i, fol. 230a; i, fol. 230a; i, fol. 220b; i, fol. 228b; i, fol. 228b; i, fol. 228c; i, fol. 130d; i, fol. 203a; i, fol. 366d; i, fol. 366d; i, fol. 219a; i, fol. 206d; i, fol. 228b; i, fol. 206d; i, fol. 367a; i, fol. 206c; i, fol. 228c; i, fol. 203a; i, fol. 228c; i, fol. 160b; i, fol. 206d; i, fol. 228c; i, fol. 228c; i, fol. 228c; i, fol. 228c; i, fol. 228c; i, fol. 206d; i, fol. 228c; i, fol. 222c; i, fol. 236b; i, fol. 236b; i, fol. 228b; i, fol. 228c; i, fol. 207a; i, fol. 228c; i, fol. 228b; i, fol. 160b; i, fol. 367a; i, fol. 367a; i, fol. 293c; i, fol. 293c; i, fol. 293c; i, fol. 367a; i, fol. 367a; i, fol. 367a; i, fol. 206d; i, fol. 293c; i, fol. 236b; ii, fol. 092a; Hart, Cartularium Monasterii de Rameseia, No. C; i, fol. 228b; i, fol. 160b; i, fol. 152d; i, fol. 217a; i, fol. 366d; ii, fol. 092a; Lincolnshire Claims (Domesday Book), fols 376d–377c; i, fol. 236b

Junain []

Picard or Flemish tenant of Eustache of Boulogne in Domesday Essex. His fees were afterwards held by a family named from Wissant, Pas-de-Calais. His earliest successors seem to have been Serlo de Marceio and his wife Mabilia, early post-Conquest benefactors of St Albans Abbey (BL Cott. Nero D vii, 98r), to which they gave land at Parndon and Fifhide. Mabilia was probably Junain's heiress.

ii, fol. 027a; ii, fol. 031a

Lambert Dapifer

Tenant of Eustache de Boulogne (brother of a Lambert d. 1054) occurs in Domesday Essex. He is probably identical with Lambert dapifer, who occurs in a charter dated 1106 given for St Paul's (no. 198) by Eustache II de Boulogne. Apparently ancestor of a family named from Boreham, of whom Turold (q.v.) was dapifer to William, count of Boulogne. Turold occurs c.1154 with his sons and his brothers Geoffrey, Peverel and Simon.

Gibbs, Early Charters of St Pauls (1939), No. 198; ii, fol. 031a; ii, fol. 031b; ii, fol. 031b; ii, fol. 031b

Lambert De Buelles

Norman, from Bouelles, Seine-Maritime, aar. Neufchâtel. Lambert held Shellow Bowells, Essex, of Geoffrey de Mandeville in Domesday Book. A Lambert de Buelle occurs in the Cartae of 1166; cf. VCH Essex i, 510.

ii, fol. 061a

Lambert De Rosay

Norman, Domesday tenant of William de Warenne. From Rosay, Seine-Maritime, arr. Dieppe, cant. Bellencombre (Loyd, 86). Benefactor of the Warenne priory of Castleacre, Norfolk, his grants being confirmed by his son Walchelin (Mon. Ang. v, 50); the foundation charter mentioned his priest William (ibid.).

ii, fol. 168b; ii, fol. 170a; i, fol. 196c; i, fol. 196c; Dugdale, Monasticon Anglicanum, IV, p. 50, No. III; Dugdale, Monasticon Anglicanum, IV, pp. 49–50, No. II; Dugdale, Monasticon Anglicanum, IV, p. 50, No. III

Lanbert De Watileia

Occurs Domesday Somerset as a tenant of Serlo de Burcy. Named from Whatley in the Tax Returns.

i, fol. 97d; i, fol. 98a

Lanbert Presbiter

Priest, occurs Domesday Wallingford.

i, fol. 56c

Lanbert []

Norman, tenant of the bishop of Salisbury in Domesday Dorset.

i, fol. 77a; i, fol. 77a

Lanbert []

Norman, occurs Domesday Lincolnshire as tenant of Jocelyn fitz Lambert, to whom he was perhaps related. Perhaps the same as Lambert tenant of Odo of Bayeux.

i, fol. 359c; i, fol. 341a

Landric Carpentarius

Occurs Domesday Yorkshire and Lincolnshire. Perhaps the same person as Landric carpentarius, brother of Albert and Gilbert de Gournay(-sur-Aronde, Oise), who occurs in the cartulary of Saint-Quentin de Beauvais (BN lat nov acq 1921, fol. 25v).

i, fol. 331c; i, fol. 331c; i, fol. 298b

Landric De Horneby

Breton tenant of Count Alan in Domesday Yorkshire and Lincolnshire. Attested a charter as Landric de Horneby. Ancestor of the de Welton family, descendants of his son Alan, who is mentioned in the Lindsey Survey of 1115/18. The grant of his sons Ralph and Wigan to St Mary's, York, were confirmed by Henry I before 1132 (RRAN ii, 1752). Hornby was apparently the headquarters of Landric and his descendants, but they did not hold it as an immediate tenure of the honour of Richmond (they held Ainderby Myers in the parish of Hornby); see EYC v, p. 285. K.S.B. Keats-Rohan, 'Le rôle des Bretons dans la politique de la colonisation normande', MSHAB, lxxiv, 1996, 187, with genealogical table on p. 213.

Clay, Early Yorkshire Charters (1935), IV, No. 4; Clay, Early Yorkshire Charters (1936), V, No. 282; i, fol. 347c; i, fol. 348c; i, fol. 347a; i, fol. 310c; i, fol. 312b; i, fol. 310a; i, fol. 310a; Clay, Early Yorkshire Charters (1936), V, No. 138

Landric []

Domesday tenant of Gilo de Picquigny.

i, fol. 61d; i, fol. 227b; i, fol. 227b; i, fol. 227a; i, fol. 227b

Lanfranc Archiepiscopus Cantuariensis

Italian, from Pavia, a wandering scholar in France until c.1042 when he entered the abbey of Bec in Normandy, of which he became prior c.1045. Abbot of Saint-Etienne de Caen in 1063, promoted to archbishop of Canterbury in 1070. Important scholar and able administrator. Died 28 May 1089 (FEA ii, 3). The Letters of Lanfranc, Archbishop of Canterbury, ed. Helen Clover and Margaret Gibson (Oxford, 1979); Margaret Gibson, Lanfranc of Bec (Oxford, 1978).

i, fol. 133b; Dugdale, Monasticon Anglicanum, IV, pp. 12–13, No. II; i, fol. 16b; i, fol. 143d; ii, fol. 372b; i, fol. 155a; i, fol. 155a; Hart, Cartularium Monasterii de Rameseia, No. CXLVIII; Gibbs, Early Charters of St Pauls (1939), No. 16; Dugdale, Monasticon Anglicanum, III, pp. 279–80, No. II; Rees, Cartulary of Shrewsbury Abbey (1975), No. 35; Clay, Early Yorkshire Charters (1949), VIII, No. 3; Gibbs, Early Charters of St Pauls (1939), No. 12; Gibbs, Early Charters of

St Pauls (1939), No. 9; i, fol. 16d; i, fol. 014c; i, fol. 002a; i, fol. 16c; i, fol. 002b; i, fol. 011b; i, fol. 16c; i, fol. 16c; i, fol. 56b; i, fol. 16c; i, fol. 56c; ii, fol. 372b; ii, fol. 372b; i, fol. 143d; i, fol. 143d; i, fol. 012b; i, fol. 127a; i, fol. 127a; ii, fol. 372b; i, fol. 30d; ii, fol. 372b; ii, fol. 372b; i, fol. 143d; i, fol. 16b; i, fol. 16c; i, fol. 31a; i, fol. 16c; i, fol. 30d; i, fol. 30d; i, fol. 30d; ii, fol. 372b; i, fol. 31a; i, fol. 003c; i, fol. 003c; i, fol. 003c; i, fol. 003d; i, fol. 003b; i, fol. 003d; i, fol. 003d; i, fol. 003d; i, fol. 003d; i, fol. 003b; i, fol. 003b; i, fol. 003b; i, fol. 003b; i, fol. 003a; i, fol. 003a; i, fol. 003a; i, fol. 003a; i, fol. 003a; i, fol. 003d; i, fol. 005a; i, fol. 003a; i, fol. 005a; i, fol. 154a; i, fol. 005b; i, fol. 005b; i, fol. 005b; i, fol. 005b; i, fol. 005b; i, fol. 005b; i, fol. 005b; i, fol. 005a; i, fol. 005a; i, fol. 005a; i, fol. 005a; i, fol. 004a; i, fol. 005a; i, fol. 004d; i, fol. 004d; i, fol. 004d; i, fol. 004d; i, fol. 004d; i, fol. 004d; i, fol. 004a; i, fol. 004a; i, fol. 004a; i, fol. 004a; i, fol. 004a; i, fol. 004a; i, fol. 005a; Dugdale, Monasticon Anglicanum, III, pp. 544–46, No. I

Lanzelin De Belvais

Domesday tenant of Countess Judith; ancestor of the Lancelin family. Lancelin de Belvais and his wife were early benefactors of St Albans after 1066 (BL Cotton Nero D vii, fol. 97v). Probably named from Beauvois, Pas-de-Calais, cant. Saint-Pol-sur-Ternois; to be distinguished from a contemporary, Lancelin de Beluaco, a vassal of the French king named from Beauvais, Oise. He was succeeded by his son Robert before 1121/2, when Henry I confirmed the grants of his son Robert fitz Lancelin to the church of St Andrew, Northampton. In 1154/5 Henry II confirmed the grants to Pipewell of Robert Lancelin and his son William. Cf. HKF ii, 353ff.

i, fol. 228d; i, fol. 228d; i, fol. 228d

Laurentius []

Domesday tenant of Robert de Tosny of Stafford. His holdings may later have been held by Geoffrey Martel (Hist. Coll. Staffs. i, 169).

i, fol. 234a; i, fol. 249c; i, fol. 62b

Ledmar De Hamesteda

Occurs Domesday Essex.

ii, fol. 101b

Leduuin Filius Reuene

Englishman, occurs Domesday Lincolnshire.

i, fol. 336a;

Lefstan Presbiter

Occurs Domesday Suffolk.

ii, fol. 290a

Letard []

Domesday tenant of Edward of Salisbury.

i, fol. 69d

Lethelinus []

Domesday tenant of Arnald de Hesdin; his personal name was perhaps Lancelin.

i, fol. 70a

Letmar Prepositus

Occurs Domesday Essex.

ii, fol. 103a

Leuenot []
English tenant of Robert of Mortain in Domesday Cornwall.

i, fol. 120a; i, fol. 124d; i, fol. 124d

Leuric Presbiter
Occurs Domesday Wiltshire.

i, fol. 65b

Leuuard []
Englishman, former tenant of Wigod of Wallingford holding in 1086 from Miles Crispin at 'Langley', Berkshire.

i, fol. 61d

Leuuin De Neuham
English thegn who held land of the king in Domesday Buckinghamshire. His holdings passed to the descendants of Nigel de Berville, who possibly married his daughter (cf. Luffield Chh, pt. 2, pp. lxvii–viii). Benefactor of Abingdon Abbey (Chron. Abing. ii, 12). Possibly he was the same as Leofwine Dodda; see Williams, The English, 117–18 (who, no doubt correctly, detaches this Leofwine from the one-time holder of Newnham Paddox with whom he has sometimes been identified; that Leofwine was predecessor of Geoffrey de la Guerche and was almost certainly dead in 1086).

i, fol. 153a; i, fol. 153a; i, fol. 153a; i, fol. 153a; i, fol. 143a; i, fol. 153a

Leuuin []
Domesday tenant of William de Braose in Sussex. Perhaps the man described as 'armiger' of Ralph de Buceio in a charter of William de Lancinguis for Sele priory in the early twelfth century (CDF, 1132).

i, fol. 28a

Leuuin []
English thegn holding land in Domesday Warwickhsire. Probably a kinsman of Thorkil of Arden. See Williams, 'Vicecomital family', and idem, The English, p. 104.

i, fol. 238c; i, fol. 240a; i, fol. 238d

Leuuinus Chaua
Occurs Domesday Buckinghamshire.

i, fol. 153b

Leuuinus Crist
Occurs Domesday Essex.

ii, fol. 104a

Leuuinus Oavre
King's reeve. Occurs Domesday Buckinghamshire.

i, fol. 153b

Lewin Latinarius
English interpreter, occurs Domesday Herefordshire.

i, fol. 180a; i, fol. 180c

Liboret []
Tenant of Hugh de Beauchamp in Bedfordshire at Cogepol in 1086. The assart of Richard Libor was mentioned in a charter of Old Wardon c.1190 (Cart., no. 292). In 1166 Ralph Wigain, Libor and Ralph fitz Ascelin held half a fee of Simon de Beauchamp. An Odo Libor attested a charter of William de St John for Boxgrove Priory in 1187 (Cart., no. 6); the manse of Warin Liborelli was lost to Mont-Saint-Michel between 1087 and 1131 (Bib. mun., Avranches ms 210, fol. 108v). The personal name is perhaps a diminutive of the Germanic name Liubhart.

i, fol. 214a

Ligulf []
Englishman who kept some of his 1066 holdings under Ilbert de Lacy in Yorkshire.

i, fol. 317d; i, fol. 317d

Loernic []
Tenant of Robert Malet in Domesday Suffolk.

ii, fol. 329a; ii, fol. 329a; ii, fol. 328b; ii, fol. 328b

Lofus Prepositus Regis
Englishman, royal reeve, occurs Domesday Surrey.

i, fol. 31c

Lorchebret []
Occurs Domesday Hampshire.

ii, fol. 106a

Losoard []
Domesday tenant of Odo of Bayeux, subsequently a tenant of the honour of Richmond. By the date of the Lindsey Survey c.1115–18 he had been succeeded by his son Richard, father of Roscelin of Rigsby. Ancestor of the Rolleston or Neville family; see Clay, EYC v, 154–7.

. i, fol. 342d; Lincolnshire Claims (Domesday Book), fols 375d–376a; i, fol. 342a; i, fol. 343a; i, fol. 284b; i, fol. 284b; Lincolnshire Claims (Domesday Book), fols 375a–d; i, fol. 336b; i, fol. 284b

Ludichel []
Judicael, Domesday tenant of Robert de Tosny of Stafford. A Judicael presbyter, chaplain of Nicholas of Stafford after 1138 was perhaps his son. Another may have been the Ralph son of Juhelli who attested a charter for Kenilworth c.1130. See Hist. Coll. Staffs. ii pt. i, pp. 178, 195–7.

i, fol. 242d

Ludo De Utreto
Tenant of Walter de Douai in Domesday Devon and Somerset, also a tenant of Gotshelm de Claville. His toponym is perhaps a poor orthography for Vred (Veretum), near Douai, Nord. Identified by his attestation of a document in Cart. Glastonbury (i, 128). His holdings passed to the Mohun family.

i, fol. 111d; i, fol. 112a; i, fol. 112a; i, fol. 112a; i, fol. 95a; i, fol. 95b; i, fol. 112a; i, fol. 113a; i, fol. 116d; i, fol. 112a; Watkin, Chartulary of Glastonbury 3, SRS 64 (1950), pp. 126–28

Luith Monialis
English nun, occurs Domesday Warwickshire. Her land was afterwards granted to

Kenilworth priory.

> i, fol. 244b; Regesta regum Anglo-Normannorum III, No. 418; i, fol. 238a

Lunen []
Domesday tenant of Count Eustache in Huntingdonshire. His earliest successors in Chesterton and Stibbington were the Merck family (VCH Hunts iii, 218). His holdings were afterwards held for five fees by a family named from Doudeauville, Pas-de-Calais (Round, Boulogne; Fees, 236; Cart. Missenden, 811).

> i, fol. 204d; i, fol. 205b; i, fol. 205b; i, fol. 205b; i, fol. 205b

Macharius []
Domesday tenant of Giso bishop of Wells. Grandfather of Philip fitz William fitz Macus, who occurs as Philip of Wellington in a charter by which Bishop Robert of Bath restored to him the fees his father and grandfather had held of the bishop in Wellington and Chard (EEA x, no. 45, c.1151–58).

> i, fol. 89c

Machus []
Pre- and post-Conquest tenant of St Petroc's, Cornwall.

> i, fol. 121a

Madoc []
Occurs Domesday Shropshire.

> i, fol. 259d; i, fol. 259d

Main De Sancto Claro
The Domesday tenant of Hugh de Montfort in Kent is probably to be identified with the Main de Sancto Claro who attested a charter of Beatrice Malet, wife of William of Arques, Domesday lord of Folkestone in Kent (Eye Cart., no. 2). Fauroux, p. 33, shows that Richard Croc and his wife Benceline left to Préaux land at St-Clair. The identity of the place is obscure but could be either Saint-Clair-d'Arcey, near Bernay, Eure, or Saint-Clair-sur-les-Monts, near Yvetot, Seine-Maritime. His successor may have been the Norman de Assactesford (Ashford) who was an early benefactor of Monk Horton priory (EEA ii, 138).

> i, fol. 013a; Brown, Eye Priory Cartulary (1992–94), No. 2; i, fol. 013a; i, fol. 013a

Mainard Camerarius
Occurs Domesday Norfolk as a man of the abbot of Holm. He was apparently one of several men to survive the disgrace in 1075 of their former lord, the Breton Ralph de Gael. In 1086 he occurs in Domesday as a tenant of Count Alan in Sibton and elsewhere. According to Sibton abbey traditions, he was the count's chamberlain and had married Orwen, a former wet-nurse of the count who had followed him from Brittany after 1066 and been given the manor of Sibton. The couple had two daughters, of whom one, Gemma, was the ancestress of a family surnamed of Sibton.

> ii, fol. 293a; Hamilton, Inquisitio Eliensis (1876), pp. 192–95; Brown, Sibton Abbey Cartularies and Charters (1987), No. 516; ii, fol. 117a; ii, fol. 318a; Brown, Sibton Abbey Cartularies and Charters (1987), No. 516; Brown, Sibton Abbey Cartularies and Charters (1987), No. 516; ii, fol. 117a; Hamilton, Inquisitio Eliensis (1876), pp. 192–95; Dugdale, Monasticon Anglicanum, III, p. 87, No. IX

Mainard []
Domesday tenant of Roger of Poitou in Lincolnshire.

i, fol. 352b; i, fol. 352c; i, fol. 352a

Mainfrid []
Occurs Domesday Somerset and Devon as a tenant of William de Moyon and William Cheever.

i, fol. 110c; i, fol. 95d; i, fol. 96b; i, fol. 96b

Mainfrid []
Occurs Domesday Nottinghamshire as tenant of Ilbert de Lacy.

i, fol. 289d; i, fol. 291b

Maino Brito
A Breton, there is no firm indication as to Maino's origin. He was identified, plausibly enough, with Maino Brito of Rougé from Ercé-en-Lamée (Ille-et-Vilaine) by C. Bouvet, 'A propos des premiers seigneurs de Châteaubriant', Bulletin de la Société archéologique et historique de Nantes et de Loire-Atlantique 122 (1986) 77–105; this argument has in its favour the fact that Maino's son and successor was named Mainfelin, a name found in the Nantais in the eleventh century. He was married more than once, one of his wives probably a relative of William de Warenne (Round, Rot. de Dom. 38–9), another (possibly the same) probably related to William's tenant Brien, since his youngest son Wigan is described as nepos Brientii. A Main Brito attested charters of William I as ruler of Maine between 1063 and 1066, but it is not evident that this was the same as Maino Brito since the acts concern a region of Maine where a family surnamed Brito had been established since the late tenth century and Maino's place in the witness lists indicate he was acting as a Manceau. The Manceau family did not use personal names with a Breton form such as Maino. His son Mainfelin succeeded him as lord of Wolverton by 1129 (Sanders, 100). Cf. pedigree of his descendants in Cart. Luffield ii, p. lxxii.

i, fol. 228a; i, fol. 228a; i, fol. 228a; i, fol. 228a; i, fol. 151d; i, fol. 151d; i, fol. 152b; i, fol. 152a; i, fol. 152a; i, fol. 142a; i, fol. 236a; i, fol. 236a; i, fol. 236a; i, fol. 143a; i, fol. 236a; i, fol. 142a; i, fol. 151d; Regesta Regum Anglo Normannorum II, App. no. cxxvii

Malger De Cartrai
Norman, from Carteret, Manche, arr. Valognes, cant. Barneville (Loyd, 25), Domesday tenant of Robert de Mortain in Devon; probably the father of Drogo son of Malger, also known as Drogo de Cartrai, a major tenant of Geoffrey of Coutances, and of Humphrey de Cartrai. After the fall of William de Mortain in 1106, Mauger's holdings later became the barony of Ashill.

i, fol. 105b; i, fol. 79d; i, fol. 92d; i, fol. 92c; i, fol. 92a; i, fol. 92a; i, fol. 92a; i, fol. 92a; i, fol. 86d; i, fol. 92a; i, fol. 91d; i, fol. 91d; i, fol. 79c; i, fol. 92d; i, fol. 98d

Malger De Rokesle
Norman, Domesday tenant of Odo of Bayeux. He was ancestor of the FitzHelto family of Aldington, Kent. By 1129 he had been succeeded by a grandson, Helto fitz Richard fitz Malger, father of William fitz Helto who gave a mill in Malger's Domesday manor of Farningham to Bermondsey c.1142 (Mon. Ang. v, 96). Malger's son occurs as Richard son of Malger of Roxley (de Rokesle) in Textus

Roffensis p. 182 (Douglas, Dom. Mon., 37). Helto's rare name suggests either that Malger was a relative of Helto dapifer (q.v.), or that his wife was a daughter or sister of Helto.

> i, fol. 004b; i, fol. 006c; Douglas, ed., Domesday Monachorum (1944), p. 105; ii, fol. 024b; ii, fol. 024b; i, fol. 006b; i, fol. 006b; i, fol. 006b

Malger Filius Amici
Domesday tenant of Eustache de Boulogne. In 1100 Count Eustache founded La Chapelle in the Boulonnais and gave it 'terre quam in Anglia Malgherius filius Amici de me tenet in feodo' (Miraeus et Foppens, ii, clxxii, 1311–12).

> ii, fol. 031a

Malger []
Domesday tenant of Gilbert de Gant. He granted his land at Ribton to the priory of Bridlington at the time of its foundation, a. 1114 (Mon. Ang. vi, 284–91). Among the witnesses was Malger de Ergoni, who, with his son Geoffrey, subsequently confirmed the grant, before the death of Walter of Gant (in 1139) (Cart. Bridlington, BL Add. 40008, fol. 21, 35). Malger de Ergoni, i.e. Averham, Yorkshire, was identified as a son of Adam Tison by Clay, EYC xii, 5. The presumption must be that his mother (Adam's wife was called Emma) was the daughter of the Domesday Malger.

> Regesta regum Anglo-Normannorum III, No. 119; i, fol. 277d; i, fol. 277d; i, fol. 277d; i, fol. 277d; i, fol. 277d

Malger []
Norman, Domesday tenant of Remigius of Lincoln. His son Richard held at the time of the Lindsey Survey, c.1115–18. Ancestor of the de Ryes family. See Fees, 194; EYC v, p. 333.

> i, fol. 344c; i, fol. 344c; i, fol. 344b; i, fol. 344c; i, fol. 344b; i, fol. 344b

Malger []
Norman, Domesday tenant of William de Percy. Ancestor of the Vavassour family. Attested Percy charters up to c.1115. See VCH Yorks ii, 170.

> Clay, Early Yorkshire Charters (1955), XI, No. 2; i, fol. 321c; i, fol. 321c; i, fol. 321c; i, fol. 321c; i, fol. 321c; i, fol. 316b

Malger []
Norman, Domesday tenant of Walter de Aincurt. Probably ancestor of Geoffrey de Staunton and Thomas de Rolleston who held four fees of Walter II d'Aincourt in 1166; see Foulds, Thurgarton Cart., pp. xliii, xlvii–viii.

> i, fol. 288c; i, fol. 288c; i, fol. 288c

Malger []
Norman, Domesday tenant of Walchelin bishop of Winchester.

> i, fol. 41b; i, fol. 40c; i, fol. 52c

Malger []
Norman, Domesday tenant of Roger Bigod in Norfolk.

> ii, fol. 189a; ii, fol. 189b

Manasser Arsic
Granted the former holdings of Wadard (q.v.) as the barony of Cogges (Sanders, 36), he occurs in Oxfordshire documents between 1100 and 1110, and in the

Lindsey Survey (1115–18), sometime after which he was succeeded by his son Robert, father of Manasser II (fl. 1160). He is probably to be identified with the Manasser who occurs in the Oxfordshire Domesday; possibly he was Domesday's 'son of Manasser', possibly Manasser Cook, who occurs in Somerset. On 5 July 1110 at Stanford Henry I confirmed to Fécamp the grant of land in England by Manasser Arsic, his wife and son Robert (Chanteux, no. 178). According to Le Maho, the family held the fief of Bléville, in the pays de Caux, of Fécamp during the twelfth century; he suggests they were of English ancestry, part of an Anglo-Saxon colony which settled on the mouth of the Seine in the eleventh and twelfth centuries. Given Manasser's name, the views of G.A. Moriarty, 'The barony of Cogges', Proc. Oxon. Arch. Soc. 74 (1929), 310–12, repeated in Chibnall, 'Fécamp and England', in L'Abbaye benedictine de Fécamp – Ouvrage scientifique du xiiie centenaire 658–1758, t. 1, Fécamp 1959, p. 132, that they originated in the Boulonnais, would seem more convincing; the rulers of Boulogne were associated with England in the mid-eleventh century by the marriage of Eustache II de Boulogne (q.v.) and Goda.

i, fol. 160d; Lindsey Survey, BL ms Cotton Claudius C v, fols 1–9; Lindsey Survey, BL ms Cotton Claudius C v, fols 9–18; Lindsey Survey, BL ms Cotton Claudius C v, fols 1–9; Lindsey Survey, BL ms Cotton Claudius C v, fols 9–18; Lindsey Survey, BL ms Cotton Claudius C v, fols 19–27; Regesta regum Anglo-Normannorum III, No. 152; i, fol. 154a

Manasses Cocus
Occurs Domesday Dorset, where he is identifiable from the Tax Return for Brownshall Hundred. His wife occurs in Domesday Somerset.

i, fol. 77a

Manstan []
Englishman, burgess of Colchester, occurs Domesday.

ii, fol. 105a; ii, fol. 105a

Mansune []
Occurs Domesday Hampshire.

ii, fol. 106a; ii, fol. 106a

Manuuin []
Englishman, burgess of Colchester, occurs Domesday.

ii, fol. 105b; ii, fol. 106a; ii, fol. 105a; ii, fol. 105a; ii, fol. 105a; ii, fol. 105b; ii, fol. 105b; ii, fol. 104b; ii, fol. 104a

Marcherius []
Domesday tenant of Saint Augustine's, Canterbury.

Ballard, Inquisition of St Augustine's (1920), fols 24r–28r; i, fol. 012c

Marcud []
Welshman, Domesday tenant of Earl Hugh of Chester.

i, fol. 269a; i, fol. 269a

Martin []
Minor Domesday tenant-in-chief, in Buckinghamshire and Lincolnshire. A charter in Chron. Ramsey (pp. 253–4), 1120–30, was attested by Martin fitz Ulf of Lincoln.

Lincolnshire Claims (Domesday Book), fols 376d–377c; i, fol. 365b; i, fol. 365b; i, fol. 365b; i, fol. 365b; i, fol. 152c; i, fol. 365b; i, fol. 152c

Mater Roberti De Lacy

Mentioned in Domesday as mother of Roger de Lacy, she was the wife, and after 1085 the widow, of Walter de Lacy of Weobley. Her name is given as Emma and Emmelina in Hist. S. Petri Glocs. i 15, 122, 224, 227, 258, 351.

Regesta regum Anglo-Normannorum III, No. 345; i, fol. 168a; i, fol. 168a

Matfrid []

Domesday juror in Radfield Hundred, Cambridgeshire, recorded as one of two unnamed knights holding in Dullingham of Count Alan. His successor c.1125 was his son Ralph. Lewis, 'Jurors', 37; VCH Cambs vi, 162.

Hamilton, Inquisitio Comitatus Cantabrigiensis, pp. 1–93; i, fol. 195d

Matheus De Mauritania

Norman, his Domesday holdings of the king in Dorset and Berkshire were held as a larder serjeanty (Round, King's Serjeants, 231 ff). In 1129/30 Picard de Domfront accounted for what Robert de Mortagne owed for the land of his uncle Matthew de Mortagne. His successors thereafter were the Monk family, descendants of the Domfronts.

Pipe Roll 31 Henry I, 053–e/ht; i, fol. 170b; i, fol. 73b; i, fol. 63b; i, fol. 98b; i, fol. 82c; i, fol. 82c; i, fol. 170b; ii, fol. 091b; ii, fol. 091b; ii, fol. 091b

Matheus []

Presumably a Norman, Domesday tenant of Colswein of Lincoln. His son Julian attested a charter of Picot son of Colswein dated 1111 (Mon. Ang. iii, 218). Robert son of Julian occurs in 1166.

i, fol. 357c; i, fol. 357a; i, fol. 357a; i, fol. 357a

Matildis Regina

Daughter of Baldwin V of Flanders. Despite papal prohibition, she married William of Normandy in the early 1050s. During the Hastings campaign she remained as regent in Normandy, but joined her husband for her coronation as queen in 1067. Founder of the abbeys of Sainte-Trinité de Caen and Sainte-Marie du Pré at Rouen. She died on 2 November 1083.

Dugdale, Monasticon Anglicanum, III, p. 473, No. XI; Dugdale, Monasticon Anglicanum, III, pp. 330–31, No. III; i, fol. 209b; i, fol. 152c; i, fol. 152d; Hart, Cartularium Monasterii de Rameseia, No. XXXV; Dugdale, Monasticon Anglicanum, IV, p. 14, No. VI; i, fol. 238a; Dugdale, Monasticon Anglicanum, V, p. 175, No. I; Dugdale, Monasticon Anglicanum, III, p. 216, No. V; Dugdale, Monasticon Anglicanum, III, p. 217, No. VII; Dugdale, Monasticon Anglicanum, III, pp. 391–92, No. I; Dugdale, Monasticon Anglicanum, III, p. 346, No. II; Dugdale, Monasticon Anglicanum, III, p. 547, No. III; Dugdale, Monasticon Anglicanum, V, p. 175, No. I; Dugdale, Monasticon Anglicanum, III, pp. 346–47, No. III; Dugdale, Monasticon Anglicanum, IV, pp. 12–13, No. II; Dugdale, Monasticon Anglicanum, III, p. 500, No. VI; Dugdale, Monasticon Anglicanum, III, pp. 345–46, No. I; Dugdale, Monasticon Anglicanum, IV, p. 13, No. IV; Dugdale, Monasticon Anglicanum, IV, pp. 111–12, No. Ia; Dugdale, Monasticon Anglicanum, IV, p. 148, No. I; ii, fol. 117a; Clay, Early Yorkshire Charters (1955), XII, No. 15; Barraclough, Charters of AN Earls of Chester (1988), No. 3; Barraclough, Charters of AN Earls of Chester (1988), No. 28; Rees, Cartulary of Shrewsbury Abbey (1975), No. 35; Clay, Early Yorkshire

Charters (1935), IV, No. 1; Elvey, Luffield Priory Charters (1968–75), No. 1; Clay, Early Yorkshire Charters (1949), VIII, No. 4; i, fol. 152c; Clay, Early Yorkshire Charters (1949), VIII, No. 2; Brown, Eye Priory Cartulary (1992–94), No. 1; Clay, Early Yorkshire Charters (1939), VI, No. 1

Matildis []
Domesday tenant of Eustache de Boulogne in Somerset, probably a kinswoman.

i, fol. 91d

Mauricius Episcopus Londoniensis
Archdeacon of Le Mans and chaplain to William I, nominated bishop of London on 25 December 1085, died in office 25/6 September 1107. See FEA i, 1.

Gibbs, Early Charters of St Pauls (1939), No. 23; Gibbs, Early Charters of St Pauls (1939), No. 5; Clay, Early Yorkshire Charters (1949), VIII, No. 2; Gibbs, Early Charters of St Pauls (1939), No. 14; ii, fol. 012b; ii, fol. 011a; ii, fol. 009a; Gibbs, Early Charters of St Pauls (1939), No. 10; i, fol. 133c; Dugdale, Monasticon Anglicanum, II, p. 18, No. IX; Gibbs, Early Charters of St Pauls (1939), No. 29; Ransford, Early Charters of Waltham Abbey (1989), No. 4; i, fol. 91b; i, fol. 87a; i, fol. 75d; i, fol. 86d; i, fol. 91a; Gibbs, Early Charters of St Pauls (1939), No. 198; Gibbs, Early Charters of St Pauls (1939), No. 18; i, fol. 91b; Gibbs, Early Charters of St Pauls (1939), No, 59; ii, fol. 009a; ii, fol. 009a; ii, fol. 011a; ii, fol. 010a; ii, fol. 010b; ii, fol. 010b; ii, fol. 011a; ii, fol. 011a; ii, fol. 010a; i, fol. 130c; i, fol. 130b; ii, fol. 010b; i, fol. 127c; i, fol. 134a; i, fol. 133c; i, fol. 127b; i, fol. 133c; i, fol. 134a; i, fol. 140a; i, fol. 77c; Gibbs, Early Charters of St Pauls (1939), No. 18; Dugdale, Monasticon Anglicanum, II, p. 267, No. XI; Dugdale, Monasticon Anglicanum, III, pp. 544–46, No. I; Douglas, Feudal Documents from Bury St Edmunds, No. 21; Fisher, Cartularium Prioratus de Colne (Earles C.), No. 11; Gibbs, Early Charters of St Pauls (1939), No. 17; Gibbs, Early Charters of St Pauls (1939), No. 22; Gibbs, Early Charters of St Pauls (1939), No. 15; Fisher, Cartularium Prioratus de Colne (Earles C.), No. 3

Mechenta []
Englishwoman, occurs Domesday Leicestershire.

i, fol. 233c

Meinard Vigil
Occurs Domesday Essex.

ii, fol. 117a

Milo Crispin
From the family of Crispin of Tillières-sur-Avre, Eure, he apparently came to England c.1080. At Easter 1084 he married the daughter and heiress of Robert d'Oilly and his English wife, the daughter of Wigod, acquiring thereby half of the pre-Conquest lordship of Wigod of Wallingford, held as a tenancy-in-chief in 1086. A favourite of Henry I, he died in 1107, leaving a daughter and heiress Matilda, who took the honour of Wallingford to her husband Brien fitzCount c. 1113. Cf. K.S.B. Keats-Rohan, 'The devolution of the honour of Wallingford', Oxoniensia liv, 1988.

i, fol. 56b; i, fol. 56b; i, fol. 56b; i, fol. 56b; i, fol. 56b; i, fol. 56b; i, fol. 56b; i, fol. 154a; i, fol. 71c; i, fol. 61c; i, fol. 212a; i, fol. 212a; i, fol. 217b; i, fol. 159b; i, fol. 61c; i, fol. 36c; i, fol. 71b; i, fol. 71b; i, fol. 71b; i, fol. 71b; i, fol. 74d; i, fol. 56b; i, fol. 159b; i, fol. 162d; i, fol. 169c; i, fol. 159b; i, fol. 159c; i, fol. 159c; i, fol. 159b; i, fol. 159b; i, fol. 159b; i, fol. 159b; i, fol. 159b; i, fol. 159b; i, fol. 169c; i, fol. 159b; Dugdale, Monasticon Anglicanum, III, p. 547, No. III; i, fol. 169c; i, fol. 159b; i, fol. 149d; i, fol. 212a; Tremlett and Blakiston, Stogursey Charters (1949), No. 1; Clay, Early Yorkshire Charters (1949), VIII, No. 4; Dugdale, Monasticon Anglicanum, IV, p. 13, No. IV; i, fol. 150a; i, fol. 150a; i, fol. 150a

Milo De Belefol

From Allouville-Bellefosse, cant. Yvetot, Seine-Maritime, Normandy, Domesday tenant of Roger de Raimes. His son Gerard succeeded, but was dead in 1129/30 when his widow accounted that she and her son William might have their land in peace (PR 31 Henry I, 96). Another son, Robert, attested an Eye charter of the 1120s.

ii, fol. 423b; ii, fol. 422a; ii, fol. 422a; ii, fol. 422a; ii, fol. 422a; ii, fol. 422a; ii, fol. 423a; ii, fol. 423a

Milo Moli

Probably to be distinguished from Miles Crispin, who would otherwise seem most naturally to occur at this point in Domesday, since a de Molay family occurs in the Honour of Wallingford during the twelfth century. Possibly named from Le Molay, Calvados, cant. Balleroy.

i, fol. 56c

Milo Portarius

Royal servant; occurs Domesday Hampshire.

i, fol. 49c; i, fol. 49c

Modbert Filius Lamberti

Norman, tenant of Baldwin of Exeter in Domesday Devon; identifed as son of a Lambert in Exon.

i, fol. 106b; i, fol. 106c; i, fol. 107d; i, fol. 107d; i, fol. 107d; i, fol. 106a

Moduin []

English tenant-in-chief, Domesday Essex. Possibly father of Roger filius Mouuini who occurs in Ramsey documents of the early twelfth century claiming land held by his uncle Turkil in Sawtry, Huntingdonshire. In 1086 Turkil was recorded as an 'antecessor' of Countess Judith in the manor of Sawtry (Chron. Ram., 264–5; Cart. Rams. i, pp. 247–8; DB Hunts 20.2).

ii, fol. 095a; ii, fol. 095b; ii, fol. 095a; ii, fol. 095a; ii, fol. 095b; ii, fol. 095b; ii, fol. 095b; ii, fol. 095b; ii, fol. 095a

Morcar []

Occurs Domesday Buckinghamshire.

i, fol. 145c; i, fol. 152d; i, fol. 152d

Mordephese Libera Femina Algari

Englishwoman, occurs Domesday Norfolk.

ii, fol. 149b

Morel []

Domesday tenant of Bishop William of Thetford. Occurs in an Ely plea of c.1072. Cf. Morel de Merlay. Abbot William's purchase of land on a isle on the Laize from Morel, a man of Robert Marmion, was confirmed c.1080/3 (Actes caen. 14, p. 108) Perhaps father of Hugh Morel, who attested a Norwich charter of c.1121/35 (EEA, vi, 35).

ii, fol. 192b; Hamilton, Inquisitio Eliensis (1876), pp. 192–95

Morin De Cadomo
Norman, from Caen, Calvados, Domesday tenant of Baldwin of Exeter in Devon, identified by the Tax Returns for Colyton and Halberton Hundreds.

i, fol. 108c; i, fol. 108c; i, fol. 108c; i, fol. 117d

Morin De Chitehurst
Norman, occurs Domesday Sussex as a tenant of Robert of Mortain and Roger de Montgomery. The same person perhaps also occurs as Robert's tenant in Cambridgeshire, where his son Roger was a juror in the Domesday inquest. His son Robert gave tithes to Lewes. The one knight fee of Morin de Chitehurst was given to William de Albini pincerna, who subsequently gave much of Morin's holding to Henry I Hose. Farrer, HKF iii, 52, 83.

i, fol. 193b; i, fol. 193b; i, fol. 193d; i, fol. 22d; i, fol. 25b; i, fol. 23d; i, fol. 23a; i, fol. 22b; i, fol. 21b; i, fol. 20d; i, fol. 23b; Red Book of the Exchequer, ed. Hall (1897), pp. 200–02

Morin De Sancto Andree
Morin, Domesday tenant of William of Braose in Sussex, probably the same as Morin of Saint-André-de-Briouze (Orne), who attested Braose charters of the 1090s. Cf. VCH Sussex i, 378–9; CDF nos. 1110, 1112, 1118.

i, fol. 29b; i, fol. 29b; i, fol. 29b

Mortuing []
Englishman, occurs Domesday Bedfordshire.

i, fol. 213d

Moruan []
Breton, Domesday tenant of Eudo fitz Spirewic.

ii, fol. 246a; ii, fol. 246a; ii, fol. 434a

Moruuin []
Englishman, 1066 and 1086 tenant of Ely Abbey in Suffolk.

ii, fol. 384a; ii, fol. 384a

Moyses []
Domesday tenant of Geoffrey bishop of Coutances in Somerset.

i, fol. 88d; i, fol. 88d

Muceull []
Tenant of Picot de Grentebrige. One Osulf Muceolus attested a charter for Preaux concerning the land of Hugh d'Avesnes in the time of Roger de Beaumont; Geoffrey his son occurs at a similiar date (Cart. Preaux, Arch. dépt. Eure 711, nos. 294, 415). A Walter Musuell attested a charter of Count Guy of Ponthieu for Saint-Josse-sur-Mer (BN lat. 11926, fols 118v–119).

i, fol. 201c

Mundret []
Englishman, occurs Domesday Suffolk.

ii, fol. 301a; ii, fol. 301b

Mundret []
Englishman, occurs Domesday Cheshire, of which he had been sheriff. See Mason, 'Officers and Clerks', 246 and n. 17.

i, fol. 264a; i, fol. 264c; i, fol. 267d; i, fol. 253d; i, fol. 263d

Muriel Uxor Rogeri De Busli

Wife of Roger de Bully, given in marriage by Queen Matilda, who endowed her with the manor of Sampford in Devon. It has been suggested that she was the sister of Eudo dapifer, but his sister was married to Osbern in 1086, when Roger was still alive and married to Muriel.

i, fol. 113a; Timson, Blyth Priory Cartulary (1973), No. 325

Nepos Willelmi Filii Azor

Nephew or other kinsman of William fitz Azor, occurs Domesday Hampshire.

i, fol. 53b; i, fol. 53b

Nicolaus Aurifaber

Goldsmith to Earl Hugh of Chester, occurs Domesday Norfolk.

ii, fol. 279a

Nicolaus Balistarius

Norman, occurs Domesday Devon. In the Hist. S. Petri Gloucestriæ i, 74, it was recorded that between 1095 and 1100 the abbot of Gloucester exchanged the manor of Ailstone in Warks, held in 1086 by Nicholas Balistarius, with Plymtree in Devon; subsequently, idem, ii, 125–6, the holder of Ailstone was named as Nicholas de la Pole. The surname also appears as Pulain; cf. Fees, 795, which refers to Nicholas's Domesday manor of Webbery as Wybbebeyre Nicholai Pulain. R. Lennard, Rural England, p. 144, identified this Nicholas with the Nicholas who farmed the Warwickshire land of Countess Godiva for the king in 1086, though Eyton, in Domesday Studies 556n, identified him with the Nicholas who seems to have been sheriff of Staffordshire in 1086. Benefactor of Plympton and Montacute priories (Mon. Exon, 135; Cart. Montacute, 9). A justiciar temp. Henry I, he had a wife Matilda and two sons Robert and Ralph (VCH Warks iii, 111). Benefactor of Plympton priory (Oliver, Mon. Exon, 135) and Montacute (Cart. 9/125). His heir in 1166 was perhaps Maurice de Pola (q.v.), subsequently lord of Poorstock, whose FitzPayne successors held Nicholas's Devonshire holdings in the thirteenth century (Fees, 788).

i, fol. 70c; i, fol. 97a; i, fol. 244b; i, fol. 117c; i, fol. 117b; i, fol. 117b; i, fol. 117b; i, fol. 117c; i, fol. 117b; i, fol. 117c; i, fol. 244b; i, fol. 238a; i, fol. 117c; i, fol. 244b; i, fol. 117c; Regesta regum Anglo-Normannorum III, No. 345

Nicolaus De Kenet

Norman, Domesday tenant of William de Warenne and Alfred of Marlborough. Domesday juror in Staplehoe hundred, Cambridgeshire. Ancestor of the de Kenet family, named from his manor in Cambridgeshire.

i, fol. 196c; ii, fol. 398a; ii, fol. 398a; ii, fol. 398b; i, fol. 70c; Hamilton, Inquisitio Eliensis (1876), pp. 97–100; Hamilton, Inquisitio Comitatus Cantabrigiensis, pp. 1–93

Nicolaus []

Domesday tenant of Abingdon Abbey.

i, fol. 59a

Nicolaus []

Norman, occurs once in the Staffordshire Domesday in a context suggesting he was then sheriff. Distinct from Nicholas of Stafford, son and heir of Robert de

Tosny of Stafford, Burton charters allege that this Nicholas married Eda, sister of Geoffrey Maleterre abbot of Burton, in 1094, by whom he left a daughter and a son, Stephen de Bellocampo. The history of the manor of Cotes, which he obtained through his marriage and which was the subject of a series of royal writs, gives firm grounds for the identification of this Nicholas with the sheriff of Staffordshire who occurs after 1086, early in the reign of Henry I. His successor as sheriff c. 1109 was Robert de Piro.The identification of Nicholas the sheriff with the Nicholas who farmed the land of Godiva in Warwickshire for the king in 1086, made by Eyton in Domesday Studies 556n, is less plausible than Lennard's identification of that Nicholas as Nicholas Arbalisterius (q.v.). See Burton Cartulary, Hist. Coll. Staffs. v pt. 1. The history of Cotes suggests that Nicholas was an ancestor of Stephen de Bellocampo (q.v.), but he cannot have been his father; the relationship was probably through females. Cf. Green, Sheriffs, 75; Comp. Peer. xii(2), App. F.

i, fol. 239c; i, fol. 239c; i, fol. 239c; i, fol. 239c; i, fol. 239c; i, fol. 239c; i, fol. 239c; i, fol. 239c; i, fol. 250c

Nigel De Albingi

Son of William, seigneur of Saint-Martin-d'Aubigny, Manche, arr. Coutances, (Loyd, 7), brother of Abbot Richard of St Albans. Ancestor of the de Albini family of Cainhoe, Bedfordshire (Sanders, 26). Married Amice de Ferrers, by whom he had three sons, Henry, William and Nigel (Mon. Ang. ii, 279, 392–3), and a daughter Adeliza (q.v.)who attested a charter of his son Henry and was probably the wife of Richard fitz Osbert (BL Lansdowne 229, fol. 147r). A concubine of his was mentioned in Domesday Bedfordshire. He was succeeded by Henry shortly before 1100. See L. Loyd, 'The origin of the family of Aubigny of Cainhoe', Bed. Hist. Rec. Soc. xix (1937), 101–9; Comp. Peer. ix, 366–7.

i, fol. 274b; i, fol. 60c; i, fol. 152d; i, fol. 56b; i, fol. 63c; i, fol. 233c; i, fol. 210d; i, fol. 214d; i, fol. 214a; i, fol. 214b; i, fol. 214b; i, fol. 214b; i, fol. 214b; Dugdale, Monasticon Anglicanum, III, p, 279, No. Ib; Dugdale, Monasticon Anglicanum, III, pp. 279–80, No. II; i, fol. 244b; i, fol. 244b; i, fol. 151c; i, fol. 244b; i, fol. 236a; i, fol. 214a; Dugdale, Monasticon Anglicanum, III, pp. 392–93, No. II; i, fol. 214b

Nigel De Bereuile

Norman, from an unidentified Berville in Normandy, occurs in Domesday Buckinghamshire as successor to Leofwin of Nuneham (Courtenay), in whose holdings he was succeeded by the FitzNigel family. It is likely that he married a daughter of Leofwin. His heir c.1138 was Nigel II de Berevile, also known as Nigel de Bechamtone. See Cart. Luffield, pt. 2, pp. lxvii–viii.

i, fol. 151c; i, fol. 151c

Nigel De Burceio

Norman, from Burcy, Calvados, arr. Vire, cant. Vassy, Domesday tenant of Earl Hugh. Possibly succeeded by a second Nigel.

i, fol. 267d; i, fol. 267d; i, fol. 267d; Barraclough, Charters of AN Earls of Chester (1988), No. 28; Barraclough, Charters of AN Earls of Chester (1988), No. 3

Nigel De Gurnai

Norman, tenant of Geoffrey bishop of Coutances in Domesday Somerset. His heir by 1112 was Havise de Gurnai (q.v.), perhaps his daughter, wife of Roger fitz Hamelin de Ballon.

i, fol. 88b; i, fol. 88b; i, fol. 88c; i, fol. 88d; i, fol. 88d; i, fol. 88d; i, fol. 88b; i, fol. 88b

Nigel De Monneuile

Norman, from Monville, Seine-Maritime, arr. Rouen, cant. Clères (Loyd, 69), occurs as knight of the archbishop of Canterbury in Domesday Book and in 1093–6, when he was identified as de Munneville (Monville) in the Milites archiepiscopi. His fee was at Fleet, in the manor of Wingham, Kent (Du Boulay, Lordship of Canterbury, 384). Founder of Folkestone priory, a cell of Lonlay, c.1095, and also a benefactor of Bermondsey (Mon. Ang. iv, 672; v, 96) He married Emma, daughter of another Kentish landholder, William of Arques. His holdings passed after his death c.1103 to his daughter Matilda, wife of Rualon d'Avranches (d.1130–4), as the barony of Folkestone (ib, 674). His widow Emma married secondly Manasser count of Guînes.

Excerpta a Chronicis de Bermondsey, Dugdale, Monasticon, IV, pp 95–97; i, fol. 298a; Douglas, ed., Domesday Monachorum (1944), p. 105

Nigel De Stafford

Norman, Domesday tenant-in-chief and sheriff of Staffordshire. Ancestor of the de Greslai family, named from Greasley, Derbyshire. He was succeeded by his son William. Another son, Nicholas de Greseleia, was a benefactor of Kenilworth c.1122–9, for which his charters name his brother William, wife Margaret and son Simon (BL Harley 3650, fols 30v–31r).

i, fol. 250c; i, fol. 250c; i, fol. 250c; i, fol. 250c; i, fol. 247b; i, fol. 247b; i, fol. 247b; i, fol. 250c; i, fol. 250d; i, fol. 250d; i, fol. 250c; i, fol. 247a; i, fol. 247a; i, fol. 233b; i, fol. 233c; i, fol. 233c; i, fol. 247b; i, fol. 250c; Barraclough, Charters of AN Earls of Chester (1988), No. 7; i, fol. 278a; i, fol. 278a; i, fol. 278a; i, fol. 278a; i, fol. 278a

Nigel De Wast

Norman, from Le Vast, Manche, arr. Cherbourg, cant. Saint-Pierre-Eglise (Loyd, 112) Domesday tenant of Nigel de Albini. Emma wife of Nigel de Wast occurs in the Liber Vitae of Hyde Abbey (Hants. Rec. Soc. 5, 124). Benefactor of St Albans.

i, fol. 214c; i, fol. 214b; i, fol. 214b; i, fol. 214b; Dugdale, Monasticon Anglicanum, III, p. 276, No. I; i, fol. 214c; i, fol. 151c

Nigel De Watacra

Norman, knight of the archbishop of Canterbury in 1086 and 1093–6. His fee lay in the manor of Petham, Kent (Du Boulay, Lordship of Canterbury, 362). Surnamed from Whiteacre, in Waltham, near Petham.

i, fol. 003c; Douglas, ed., Domesday Monachorum (1944), p. 105

Nigel Fossard

A west Norman, one of two principal Domesday tenants of Robert count Mortain in Yorkshire. In 1088 the Fossard lands became a tenancy in chief known as the barony of Mulgrave (Sanders, 66). Nigel was a benefactor of St Mary's, York (Mon. Ang. iii, 551). His charter was attested by Robert Fossard, probably his son and successor of that name, Ansquetil de Bulmer, and Walter Fossard, perhaps another son. He was also father of Gertrude, wife of Robert de Meinil and then of Jordan Paynel. Ansquetil de Bulmer was steward (dapifer) to Robert Fossard c.1126 (RRAN ii, 1627); he is likely to have related to Nigel and his sons. Nigel died c.1120. VCH Yorks ii, 219ff.

> i, fol. 306d; i, fol. 306c; i, fol. 306d; i, fol. 306d; i, fol. 306d; i, fol. 306d; i, fol. 307a; i, fol. 306d; i, fol. 306d; i, fol. 307b; i, fol. 306c; i, fol. 307a; i, fol. 307a; i, fol. 307a; i, fol. 307a; i, fol. 307a; i, fol. 307a; i, fol. 308c; i, fol. 308b; i, fol. 308b; i, fol. 308a; i, fol. 307a; i, fol. 306d; i, fol. 307b; i, fol. 307b; i, fol. 307b; i, fol. 307c; i, fol. 307c; i, fol. 307c; i, fol. 307d; i, fol. 306d; i, fol. 307a; i, fol. 306d; i, fol. 306c; i, fol. 306d; i, fol. 306d; i, fol. 306c; i, fol. 307d; i, fol. 307d; i, fol. 308a; i, fol. 306c; i, fol. 306c; i, fol. 306c; i, fol. 306c; i, fol. 306d; i, fol. 306c; i, fol. 306a; i, fol. 306c; i, fol. 306b; i, fol. 306b; i, fol. 306c; i, fol. 306c; i, fol. 306c; i, fol. 306a; i, fol. 306c; i, fol. 306a; i, fol. 306c; i, fol. 306b; i, fol. 305c; i, fol. 306c; i, fol. 305c; i, fol. 305c; i, fol. 305c; i, fol. 305d; i, fol. 305d; i, fol. 306c; i, fol. 306a; i, fol. 306b; i, fol. 305b; i, fol. 306a; i, fol. 306a; i, fol. 306a; i, fol. 306a; i, fol. 306a; i, fol. 306a; i, fol. 306a; i, fol. 306a; i, fol. 305b; i, fol. 304d; i, fol. 305b; i, fol. 305b; i, fol. 305b; i, fol. 305b; i, fol. 305b; i, fol. 305b; i, fol. 306a; i, fol. 307a; i, fol. 306a; i, fol. 306a; i, fol. 306a; i, fol. 305b; Hart, Cartularium Monasterii de Rameseia, No. XXXV; i, fol. 298a; Dugdale, Monasticon Anglicanum, III, pp. 548–50, No. V; i, fol. 298a

Nigel Medicus

Norman, he held land of the king in Domesday Wiltshire; described as 'presbyter' in the Tax Return for Calne Hundred. He was possibly physician to the king, as his name suggests. Ancestor of the Calne family, named from his holding in Wiltshire. Also a tenant of Roger de Montgomery.

> i, fol. 51a; i, fol. 64d; i, fol. 64d; i, fol. 51b; i, fol. 51b; i, fol. 51b; i, fol. 51a; Ballard, Inquisition of St Augustine's (1920), fols 24r–28r; i, fol. 90d; i, fol. 260d; i, fol. 183a; i, fol. 49b; i, fol. 65b; i, fol. 162d; i, fol. 001d; i, fol. 73b; i, fol. 73b; i, fol. 73b; i, fol. 183a; i, fol. 49b; i, fol. 183a; i, fol. 52a; i, fol. 183a; i, fol. 73b; i, fol. 176a; i, fol. 183a; i, fol. 183a; i, fol. 183a; i, fol. 183a; i, fol. 252d; i, fol. 260d; i, fol. 260d; i, fol. 176a; i, fol. 259a; i, fol. 259a; i, fol. 259a; i, fol. 259a

Nigel []

Tenant of Robert of Mortain in Domesday Cornwall. His holdings passed in the early twelfth century, with those of Brien, to William Boterel.

> i, fol. 123c; i, fol. 123c; i, fol. 123c; i, fol. 123c; i, fol. 123c; i, fol. 123b; i, fol. 123c; i, fol. 123c; i, fol. 123c; i, fol. 123c; i, fol. 123c

Nigel []

Tenant of Judhael of Totnes, possibly his brother-in-law. His son Alfred attested Judhael's charter for Barnstaple (Mon. Ang. v, 197–8), and another son Juhel attested charters of Baldwin I de Redvers (q.v.) in 1146. His successor in 1166 was Richard de Vieuxpont, who had eight fees of the honour of Totnes.

> i, fol. 109d; i, fol. 108c; i, fol. 108c; i, fol. 108c; i, fol. 108c; i, fol. 108c; i, fol. 108c; i, fol. 108c; i, fol. 108c

Nigel []

Domesday tenant of William de Warenne in Sussex; perhaps the son-in-law of Godfrey de Pierrepont. Nigel was succeeded by a son Ralph, from whom descended the de Hangleton family (VCH Sussex vii, 68).

> i, fol. 27c; i, fol. 27c; i, fol. 26b; i, fol. 26d; Clay, Early Yorkshire Charters (1949), VIII, No. 13; Round, Ancient Charters (1888), No. 5

Nigel []

Domesday tenant of Robert Gernon. In 1166 his land at Wivenhoe was held by Richard Bataille.

i, fol. 130b; ii, fol. 67b; ii, fol. 053b; ii, fol. 066a; ii, fol. 066a; ii, fol. 066a

Nigel []

Occurs Domesday Sussex holding land of William [de Ansterville] in the Montgomery Rape of Arundel. Probably distinct from Nigel medicus, a tenant of Earl Roger elsewhere. After the fall of Montgomery in 1102 his Sussex holdings were eventually acquired by the de Sartilly (Manche) family, of whom there is no reason to believe Nigel to have the ancestor (pace Farrer – HKF iii, 60 – et al.). His land at Warningcamp was afterwards held by the Alta Ripa family (HKF iii, 91)

i, fol. 24b; i, fol. 25c; i, fol. 51a; i, fol. 25c; i, fol. 24d; i, fol. 23a; i, fol. 23c

Nigel []

Norman, Domesday tenant of Ivo Taillebois and the bishop of Durham in Lincolnshire. His heir at the time of the Lindsey Survey (1115/18) was Gilbert de Calz, probably from La Chaux, Orne, arr. Alençon, cant. La Ferté-Macé. Gilbert was very probably his son. He is likely to have been father also of a son Nigel de Broclesbi, named from his manor of Brocklesby, who was father of Gilbert (q.v.), an early benefactor of Newhouse, Alan, and Henry, a clerk. Newhouse was founded by Peter of Goxhill (de Gausa), whose 'nepos' Herbert was Herbert de Calz, successor and probable son of Gilbert de Calz. Since the holdings of Peter, another of Ivo Taillebois's tenants in 1086, descended with Nigel's fees, it is possible that Nigel acquired Peter's holding by marriage with the latter's heiress. Cf. HKF ii, 188–90, 206.

i, fol. 340c; i, fol. 341b; i, fol. 340c; i, fol. 340c; i, fol. 350d; i, fol. 341c; i, fol. 350b; i, fol. 350c; i, fol. 350c; Dugdale, Monasticon Anglicanum, III, p. 216, No. V

Nigel []

Norman, Domesday tenant of Tavistock abbey.

i, fol. 103c; i, fol. 103d

Nigel []

Norman, Domesday tenant of Robert fitz Corbucion in Essex and Norfolk.

ii, fol. 085a; ii, fol. 085b; ii, fol. 253b; ii, fol. 259a; ii, fol. 259b; ii, fol. 260a

Nigel []

Norman, Domesday tenant of Miles Crispin.

i, fol. 150b; i, fol. 150b; i, fol. 150c

Nigel []

Domesday tenant of William fitz Stur in Domesday Isle of Wight. Perhaps the seneschal (dapifer) Nigel who attested a charter of William's son Hugh c.1087–1100 (CDF, 1178).

i, fol. 53a

Nigel []

Norman, tenant of William I de Mohun in 1086; his successor in 1166, holding three fees, was Alexander of Bathealton.

i, fol. 96b; i, fol. 96a

Norgiot []
Domesday tenant of Countess Judith and Guy de Raimbeaucourt. Probably the same person occurs in the Northants Survey of c.1127/9. Apparently succeeded by families surnamed 'of Cogenhoe' (de Cugenho) and Noriot; see Farrer, HKF ii, 388–9.

i, fol. 229a; i, fol. 227a; i, fol. 226d; i, fol. 220d; Northants Survey, fols 96r–99v

Noriolt []
Tenant of Ralph Bainard in Domesday Suffolk.

ii, fol. 413b

Norman Crassus
Norman, occurs Domesday Lincolnshire and Yorkshire.

Dugdale, Monasticon Anglicanum, III, p. 216, No. V; i, fol. 362a; Lincolnshire Claims (Domesday Book), fols 376b–c; i, fol. 362a; Lincolnshire Claims (Domesday Book), fols 376b–c; i, fol. 336c; i, fol. 362a; i, fol. 336a

Norman De Adreci
Norman tenant-in-chief in Domesday Lincolnshire; also a tenant there of William de Percy, as the Lindsey Survey shows. Le Melletier suggested an origin Arcie, Manche, hamlet of comm. Saint-Aubin-de-Terregatte cant. Saint-James, but the Percy connection makes Saint-Clair-d'Arcey, Eure, cant. Bernay, more likely. He was still alive at the time of the Lindsey Survey (c.1115–18), and was succeeded by his son Robert thereafter (Sanders, 67). His sons Robert and Herve occur on Pipe Roll 31 Henry I.

i, fol. 353d; i, fol. 353d; i, fol. 353d; Lincolnshire Claims (Domesday Book), fols 375d–376a; Lincolnshire Claims (Domesday Book), fols 375a–d; i, fol. 362a; i, fol. 361d; i, fol. 361d; i, fol. 361d; i, fol. 361d; i, fol. 362a; i, fol. 361d; i, fol. 361d; i, fol. 362a; i, fol. 361c; i, fol. 361d; i, fol. 361c; i, fol. 361d; i, fol. 361d; i, fol. 361d; i, fol. 361c; i, fol. 361d; i, fol. 362a; i, fol. 362a; i, fol. 361d; i, fol. 362a; i, fol. 362a; i, fol. 361d; Lincolnshire Claims (Domesday Book), fols 376b–c; i, fol. 362a; i, fol. 361d; i, fol. 361c; Lindsey Survey, BL ms Cotton Claudius C v, fols 19–27; Lindsey Survey, BL ms Cotton Claudius C v, fols 9–18; Lindsey Survey, BL ms Cotton Claudius C v, fols 1–9; Dugdale, Monasticon Anglicanum, III, pp. 548–50, No. V; Lindsey Survey, BL ms Cotton Claudius C v, fols 9–18; Lindsey Survey, BL ms Cotton Claudius C v, fols 1–9; Lincolnshire Claims (Domesday Book), fols. 375a–d; i, fol. 340c; Dugdale, Monasticon Anglicanum, III, pp. 544–46, No. I; Barraclough, Charters of AN Earls of Chester (1988), No. 28; Barraclough, Charters of AN Earls of Chester (1988), No. 3

Norman De Nosterfeld
Tenant of Alberic de Vere in Domesday Cambridgeshire and juror in Chilford Hundred; Lewis, 'Jurors', 37; VCH Cambs. vi, 52.

i, fol. 199d; i, fol. 199c; Hamilton, Inquisitio Comitatus Cantabrigiensis, pp. 1–93

Norman Filius Siuuard Presbiteri
Englishman, son of Siward the priest, occurs Domesday Lincolnshire. Farrer suggested he was the Norman who granted land in Lincoln to St Mary's, York (EYC i, p. 274 n.7; Mon. Ang. vi, 1272; cf. Lindsey Survey introd. p. xxxii).

Dugdale, Monasticon Anglicanum, III, pp. 548–50, No. V; i, fol. 280b; i, fol. 336b

Norman Porcarius

Norman, occurs Domesday Herefordshire; probably a tenant of William fitz Norman.

i, fol. 101c; i, fol. 179c

Norman Venator

Norman, Domesday tenant of William de Warenne and undertenant of Roger de Montgomery. An early royal confirmation for Saint-Martin de Sées included the land at Macé, Orne, given by Norman Venator on making his son a monk (CDF 657, Bates, 270). Benefactor of Lewes Priory.

i, fol. 26b; i, fol. 259b; i, fol. 259a; i, fol. 259a; i, fol. 259b; i, fol. 259b; i, fol. 259b; i, fol. 18b; Rees, Cartulary of Shrewsbury Abbey (1975), No. 35

Norman Vicecomes

Occurs in Domesday Suffolk, where he had held land before 1066. He was sheriff of Suffolk early in William's reign, c.1066–70. He was succeeded by a son Ralph, who was a benefactor of Thetford priory at its foundation a.1107. It is possible that he was related by marriage to Roger Bigod, his post-Conquest successor as sheriff from whom Norman held land. Roger and his wife Adelisa gave a charter for Rochester priory c.1100–7 (Cotton Domitian A x, fols 201v–2r) containing an unusual 'pro anima' clause for Norman the sheriff, their English predecessor in the manors granted. Roger fitz Richard of Warkworth (q.v.) was described by his brother-in-law William de Vere as 'nepos' of Roger's son Hugh Bigod and as having had an uncle Thomas de Candelent, whose name is a reference to the Suffolk manor of Candlet, held in 1086 by Norman from Roger Bigod.

ii, fol. 356b; ii, fol. 312a; ii, fol. 316b; ii, fol. 316b; ii, fol. 332a; ii, fol. 332a; ii, fol. 338b; ii, fol. 339b; ii, fol. 341a; ii, fol. 340a; ii, fol. 340a; ii, fol. 340a; ii, fol. 340a; ii, fol. 340b; ii, fol. 340b; ii, fol. 340b; ii, fol. 341a; ii, fol. 340a; ii, fol. 341a; ii, fol. 340b; ii, fol. 341a; ii, fol. 340b; ii, fol. 340b; ii, fol. 339b; ii, fol. 340b; ii, fol. 340a; ii, fol. 339b; ii, fol. 331b; ii, fol. 344b; ii, fol. 344a; ii, fol. 344b; ii, fol. 344a; ii, fol. 344b; ii, fol. 344b; ii, fol. 344a; ii, fol. 344b; ii, fol. 344a; ii, fol. 344a; ii, fol. 344a; ii, fol. 344a; ii, fol. 344a; ii, fol. 438a; ii, fol. 327a; ii, fol. 438a

Norman []

A knight, 'miles', who made his son Eudo a monk of Abingdon (Chron. Abing. ii, 169–70) in the time of Abbot Vincent.

i, fol. 61d

Norman []

Bedfordshire tenant of Eudo Dapifer who had held his manor before 1066.

i, fol. 212c

Norman []

Norman, Domesday tenant of Geoffrey Alselin in Leicestershire. Possibly the same Norman also held land of the forfeited tenancy of Aubrey de Coucy. He appears to be identifiable with the Norman who had been succeeded by 1129/30 by two nephews, Gerold de Normanville and Richard de Martinwast (Manche). Richard II de Martinwast was a fee holder de vetere of one of Geoffrey's heirs, Ralph Anselin, in 1166.

i, fol. 234a; i, fol. 231c; Pipe Roll 31 Henry I, 086–lc; Pipe Roll 31 Henry I, 083–nh; i, fol. 231d; i, fol. 231d; i, fol. 231d; i, fol. 235c; i, fol. 235c; i, fol. 235c; i, fol. 235c; i, fol. 235c

Odard Balistarius
Norman, occurs Domesday Surrey.

i, fol. 36d; i, fol. 36d

Odard De Hotot
Norman, Domesday tenant of Robert and Berenger de Tosny of Belvoir. Probably named from Hotot-en-Auge, Calvados, arr. Pont-L'Evêque, cant. Dozulé, rather than Hottot-les-Bagues, Calvados, cant. Tilly-sur-Seulles. In 1129/30 William de Hotot accounted to have right concerning the land of his father from William I de Albini Brito, son-in-law and heir of Robert de Tosny; his father may have been the Hugh de Hotot addressed in a Belvoir charter of Henry I (RRAN ii, 1152). Ralph and his son Roger de Hotot granted land at Bottlesford to Belvoir priory in the later twelfth century (BL Add. 4936, fol. 10).

i, fol. 234a; Dugdale, Monasticon Anglicanum, III, pp. 288–89, No. I

Odard De Nuers
Norman, tenant of Geoffrey I de Mandeville in Hertfordshire; Domesday juror in the Broadwater Hundreds, Hertfordshire. Perhaps from Noyers, Eure, arr. Les Andelys, cant. Gisors. He was perhaps the same as the Hugh who was Mandeville tenant of Barkway, Hertfordshire, in 1086; the manor was held by the Noyers (Noeriis) family in the 1140s. VCH Herts iv, 30, followed by Lewis, 'Jurors', 36, assumes the name of Huard (variant of Odard) was an error for Hugh, but the truth is more likely to be the other way around, or that Hugh was a separate person whose fee was inherited by or given to the Noyers family.

i, fol. 139d; i, fol. 139d; ii, fol. 048a; Hamilton, Inquisitio Eliensis (1876), pp. 97–100

Odard []
Norman, tenant and sub-tenant of Hugh earl of Chester in 1086. Father of Hugh and Gilbert (Runcorn priory Foundation charter), he was succeeded by Hugh, who died c.1129–30.

i, fol. 266b; i, fol. 266b; i, fol. 266b; i, fol. 266b; i, fol. 266b; i, fol. 267d

Odard []
Norman, Domesday tenant of Hugh de Grandmaisnil and the count of Meulan.

i, fol. 232d; i, fol. 233a; i, fol. 240d; i, fol. 232c; i, fol. 232c

Odelin []
Norman, Domesday tenant of Geoffrey bishop of Coutances in Northamptonshire. Succeeded by his son Robert, who occurs in the Northants Survey.

i, fol. 227a; i, fol. 220d

Odelin []
Occurs Domesday Kent as a tenant of St Augustine's.

i, fol. 012c; Ballard, Inquisition of St Augustine's (1920), fols 24r–28r

Odin Camerarius
Odin, or Audoen. occurs Domesday Wiltshire, and in Hampshire as Odin of Windsor. Father of Hunger (q.v.), a king's thegn in Domesday Dorset. Both personal names are old Frankish, being found in the Vexin and the Beauvaisis from the ninth century, as well as in eleventh century Normandy (cf. Fauroux, 95, 186, 193). Possibly an Englishman; so Williams, The English, 80.

i, fol. 74d; i, fol. 74d; i, fol. 41c

Odin []
Occurs Domesday Wales.

> i, fol. 269a; i, fol. 269a; i, fol. 269a; i, fol. 269b; i, fol. 269b

Odo Arbalistarius
Norman, Domesday tenant-in-chief in Lincolnshire. His tenant Alfred was probably his son-in-law Alfred de Canci, whose sons had inherited Odo's lands by c.1115.

> i, fol. 365d; i, fol. 329d; i, fol. 329d; i, fol. 329d; i, fol. 329d; i, fol. 329d; i, fol. 329d; i, fol. 329d; i, fol. 329d; i, fol. 329d; i, fol. 366a; i, fol. 338b; i, fol. 298b; i, fol. 365d; i, fol. 366a; i, fol. 365d; i, fol. 366a; i, fol. 365d; i, fol. 365d; i, fol. 365d; i, fol. 365d; i, fol. 366a; Dugdale, Monasticon Anglicanum, III, p. 547, No. III; Dugdale, Monasticon Anglicanum, III, pp. 548–50, No. V; i, fol. 365d

Odo Camerarius
Chamberlain of Count Alan, occurs Domesday Book. Succeeded before 1130 by his son Robert. EYC v, 167–9.

> i, fol. 310d; i, fol. 310d; i, fol. 310c; i, fol. 310c; i, fol. 310c; i, fol. 194b; i, fol. 194c; i, fol. 194b; i, fol. 195c; i, fol. 195c; Clay, Early Yorkshire Charters (1935), IV, No. 4; Clay, Early Yorkshire Charters (1936), V, No. 279; Clay, Early Yorkshire Charters (1935), IV, No. 2; Clay, Early Yorkshire Charters (1935), IV, No. 1

Odo De Bennigwrde
Norman, Domesday tenant of Ivo Taillebois in Lincolnshire, ancestor of the Benniworth family. He had been succeeded by his son Walter in 1129/30. He may have been the Odo who held part of Croxby under Norman d'Arcy. See Farrer, HKF ii, 178–9.

> i, fol. 350d; i, fol. 361d; i, fol. 350a; i, fol. 350b

Odo De Berneres
Norman, from Bernières, Calvados, cant. Morteaux-Couliboeuf, Domesday tenant of Earl Roger in Shropshire, identified from his grant to Shrewsbury abbey. His holdings were among those granted to the FitzAlans after 1102. His son, Roger fitz Odo de Rusberia, named from Rushbury, held by Odo from Roger de Lacy in 1086, confirmed his father's grant to Shrewsbury c.1155.

> i, fol. 254c; i, fol. 254c; i, fol. 254c; i, fol. 256c; i, fol. 254b; i, fol. 254b; Rees, Cartulary of Shrewsbury Abbey (1975), No. 35; i, fol. 257d; i, fol. 257d; i, fol. 257d; i, fol. 257d

Odo De Furnelt
Norman, Domesday tenant of Roger Arundel in Domesday Somerset; identified from the Tax Returns, fol. 81a. A west Norman, he was probably from Fourneaux, comm. cant. Tessy-sur-Vire in Manche, rather than Fourneaux-le-Val, comm. cant. Falaise, Calvados. Ancestor of the Furnellis or Furneaux family of Devonshire. His successor by 1129/30, was Geoffrey de Furnellis, probably his son.

> i, fol. 94c

Odo De Wincestre
English thegn, brother of Ealdred and possibly son of Eadric, occurs Domesday Hampshire and elsewhere. Cf. Williams, The English, 116.

i, fol. 51c; i, fol. 29c; i, fol. 44c; i, fol. 49d; i, fol. 73c; i, fol. 63c; i, fol. 49b; i, fol. 63c; i, fol. 63c; i, fol. 63c; i, fol. 49d; i, fol. 49d; i, fol. 49d; i, fol. 29c

Odo Episcopus Baiocensis
Son of Herluin de Conteville and Herlève, half-brother of William the Conqueror and full brother of Robert, count of Mortain. Appointed bishop of Bayeux by William in 1049. In 1066 he accompanied his brother's expedition to England and fought at the battle of Hastings. Castellan of Dover and earl of Kent, he acquired great wealth and pretensions. His ambitions on the papacy led to arrest by his brother and the loss of his estates. Temporarily restored by William II, his part in a conspiracy against the king led to his permanent exile and forfeiture in 1088. Important figure in the Normandy of Robert Curthose, he took the Cross in 1095 and set out for the Holy Land with Robert; he died at Palermo in 1096 and was buried there. An effective bishop of his see, he commissioned the Bayeux Tapestry, which still hangs in Odo's cathedral. Father of at least one natural son, John. See D. Bates, 'Odo of Bayeux', Speculum 50 (1975); idem, 'Notes sur l'aristocratie normande. ii. Herluin de Conteville et sa famille', Annales de Normandie 23 (1973); idem 'Le patronage clérical et intellectuel de l'évêque Odon de bayeux 1049/50–1097', in Chapitres et Cathédrales en Normandie, Annales de Normandie, série des Congrès des Sociétés Historiques et Archéolgiques de Normandie, vol. 2 (1997).

Gibbs, Early Charters of St Pauls (1939), No. 19; Dugdale, Monasticon Anglicanum, III, p. 499, No. I; ii, fol. 373a; Dugdale, Monasticon Anglicanum, III, p. 501, No. XIII; Dugdale, Monasticon Anglicanum, III, p. 500, No. V; Clay, Early Yorkshire Charters (1949), VIII, No. 3; Dugdale, Monasticon Anglicanum, III, pp. 544–46, No. I; Pipe Roll 31 Henry I, 063–kn; Regesta regum Anglo-Normannorum III, No. 56; Regesta regum Anglo-Normannorum III, No. 61; Lincolnshire Claims (Domesday Book), fols 375a–d; Round, Fragments from Worcester, Round, Feudal England (1895 : 1946), pp. 146–47; Pipe Roll 5 Henry II, 58–kn; Pipe Roll 31 Henry I, 064–kn; i, fol. 284b; i, fol. 209c; i, fol. 176a; i, fol. 342a; i, fol. 144a; i, fol. 155c; i, fol. 220b; ii, fol. 022b; i, fol. 134b; i, fol. 87d; i, fol. 238d; ii, fol. 142a; Lincolnshire Claims (Domesday Book), fols 375a–d; Ballard, Inquisition of St Augustine's (1920), fols 20r–23v; Dugdale, Monasticon Anglicanum, III, p. 499, No. III; i, fol. 343b; i, fol. 343b; i, fol. 343b; i, fol. 343b; i, fol. 343a; i, fol. 343b; i, fol. 343b; i, fol. 343b; i, fol. 343a; i, fol. 342b; i, fol. 343b; i, fol. 343b; i, fol. 343b; i, fol. 343a; i, fol. 343b; i, fol. 343b; i, fol. 342b; i, fol. 342c; i, fol. 342c; i, fol. 342d; i, fol. 343c; i, fol. 343c; i, fol. 342d; i, fol. 343b; i, fol. 342c; i, fol. 343b; i, fol. 342c; i, fol. 343b; i, fol. 342d; i, fol. 343b; i, fol. 342b; i, fol. 342b; i, fol. 342b; i, fol. 342c; i, fol. 343a; i, fol. 342c; i, fol. 343a; i, fol. 342d; i, fol. 342c; i, fol. 342b; i, fol. 342d; i, fol. 342c; i, fol. 342b; Regesta regum Anglo-Normannorum III, No. 53; Regesta regum Anglo-Normannorum III, No. 52; Regesta regum Anglo-Normannorum III, No. 57; i, fol. 342b; i, fol. 342b; ii, fol. 375a; ii, fol. 373b; ii, fol. 375b; ii, fol. 375b; ii, fol. 375b; ii, fol. 375b; ii, fol. 375b; ii, fol. 374b; ii, fol. 375a; ii, fol. 374b; ii, fol. 375a; ii, fol. 375a; ii, fol. 375a; ii, fol. 375a; ii, fol. 375a; ii, fol. 375a; ii, fol. 375a; ii, fol. 375a; ii, fol. 375b; ii, fol. 023b; i, fol. 31b; ii, fol. 026a; ii, fol. 012a; ii, fol. 023b; ii, fol. 142b; ii, fol. 373b; ii, fol. 025b; ii, fol. 374a; ii, fol. 023b; ii, fol. 375a; ii, fol. 022b; ii, fol. 022b; ii, fol. 373b; i, fol. 134b; ii, fol. 375a; ii, fol. 012a; ii, fol. 374b; ii, fol. 374b; ii, fol. 374b; ii, fol. 025a; ii, fol. 378a; i, fol. 31b; i, fol. 31b; i, fol. 31b; i, fol. 31d; i, fol. 32a; i, fol. 32a; i, fol. 34a; ii, fol. 377a; i, fol. 134c; i, fol. 31b; ii, fol. 142b; i, fol. 34b; i, fol. 68b; i, fol. 145a; i, fol. 144b; i, fol. 209c; ii, fol. 023b; i, fol. 134b; i, fol. 001c; i, fol. 144d; ii, fol.

376a; ii, fol. 376b; ii, fol. 376b; ii, fol. 376b; ii, fol. 376b; ii, fol. 376b; ii, fol. 376a; ii, fol. 376a; i, fol. 31b; ii, fol. 376a; i, fol. 31b; ii, fol. 376a; ii, fol. 376a; ii, fol. 376a; ii, fol. 375b; ii, fol. 450a; i, fol. 87d; i, fol. 30c; i, fol. 31b; i, fol. 31b; ii, fol. 376a; i, fol. 004d; i, fol. 001c; ii, fol. 023b; i, fol. 010d; i, fol. 009d; i, fol. 001c; i, fol. 001c; ii, fol. 378a; i, fol. 007c; i, fol. 010a; i, fol. 007b; i, fol. 002b; ii, fol. 377a; ii, fol. 378a; ii, fol. 142b; ii, fol. 378b; ii, fol. 378a; ii, fol. 378a; ii, fol. 378a; i, fol. 001c; i, fol. 154a; Lincolnshire Claims (Domesday Book), fols 375d–376a; Lincolnshire Claims (Domesday Book), fols 375a–d; i, fol. 155d; i, fol. 155c; i, fol. 155c; i, fol. 155c; i, fol. 010b; i, fol. 156b; ii, fol. 143a; i, fol. 155d; i, fol. 012a; i, fol. 007d; i, fol. 008a; i, fol. 008c; i, fol. 008d; i, fol. 009a; i, fol. 009b; i, fol. 009c; i, fol. 155d; ii, fol. 142a; ii, fol. 142b; ii, fol. 378a; ii, fol. 142b; ii, fol. 143b; ii, fol. 142b; ii, fol. 142b; ii, fol. 378a; ii, fol. 142b; ii, fol. 142b; ii, fol. 142a; ii, fol. 142a; i, fol. 014c; ii, fol. 142b; i, fol. 013d; ii, fol. 143a; ii, fol. 143b; ii, fol. 282a; ii, fol. 143b; ii, fol. 142b; ii, fol. 377a; ii, fol. 378a; ii, fol. 378a; ii, fol. 377a; ii, fol. 143a; i, fol. 001a; ii, fol. 378a; ii, fol. 377b; ii, fol. 142b; ii, fol. 377b; ii, fol. 143a; ii, fol. 377a; ii, fol. 378a; ii, fol. 143a; ii, fol. 143a; ii, fol. 143a; ii, fol. 143a; ii, fol. 143a; ii, fol. 143a; ii, fol. 143a; ii, fol. 377b; i, fol. 008d; Darlington, Cartulary of Worcester: Reg. I (1962–3), No. 23

Odo Filius Edrici

Englishman, occurs Domesday Devon; his patronym is supplied by the Tax Returns. His holdings passed to the de Dune family under the Honour of Plympton (cf. Thorn, notes to DB Devon 52.22–25).

i, fol. 118b; i, fol. 118b; i, fol. 118b; i, fol. 118b

Odo Filius Eurebold

Occurs Domesday Dorset.

i, fol. 83b; i, fol. 83b; i, fol. 83b; i, fol. 83b

Odo Filius Gamelin

Norman, Domesday tenant-in-chief in Devonshire. He married the daughter of a neighbouring tenant-in-chief, Theobald fitz Berner. Early benefactor of St Peter's, Gloucester (Hist. S. Petri Gloc.) His lands became known as the honour or barony of Great Torrington. Two of his daughters became nuns of Shrewsbury. His son and successor was William fitz Odo (Sanders, 48). Gamalin kinsman of Ansger, who gave land at Pressagny-l'Orgueilleux, Eure, is mentioned in a confirmation for the abbeys of Préaux (Bates, 216).

i, fol. 98a; Regesta regum Anglo-Normannorum III, No. 345; i, fol. 116d; i, fol. 116c; i, fol. 116c; i, fol. 116c; i, fol. 116c; i, fol. 116c; i, fol. 116c; i, fol. 116c; i, fol. 116d; i, fol. 116d; i, fol. 116d; i, fol. 116d; i, fol. 116d; i, fol. 116d; i, fol. 116c; Regesta regum Anglo-Normannorum III, No. 818

Odo Flandrensis

Occurs in a single manor in Domesday Somerset as a king's servant.

i, fol. 99b

Odo Francus

Norman, Domesday tenant of Swein of Essex. Perhaps the father of William fitz Odo who attested a charter of Robert fitz Swein (Mon. Ang. v, 22–3); cf. William filius Odonis, another of Swein's tenants, who was either the same as this witness or the father of another, Richard fitz William.

ii, fol. 044b; ii, fol. 046b; ii, fol. 046b; ii, fol. 043b; ii, fol. 018b

Odo []
Tenant of Robert of Mortain in Cornwall, 1086.

i, fol. 121b; i, fol. 121b; i, fol. 124c; i, fol. 124b; i, fol. 124b; i, fol. 124c; i, fol. 124b; i, fol. 124b

Odo []
Tenant of Judhael of Totnes; probably the Odo seneschal who attested a charter of Judhael concerning the priory of Totnes (Mon. Ang. iv, 630). In 1166 his successor William Buzun (q.v.) held seven and a half fees of the honour of Totnes.

i, fol. 109c; i, fol. 109b; i, fol. 109d; i, fol. 109d; i, fol. 109d; i, fol. 109d; i, fol. 109d; i, fol. 109d; i, fol. 109d

Odo []
Norman, Domesday tenant of Roger de Lacy.

i, fol. 184c; i, fol. 184c; i, fol. 184c; i, fol. 184c

Odo []
Domesday tenant of Herve Bituricensis in Domesday Suffolk.

ii, fol. 443a; ii, fol. 443b; ii, fol. 444a; ii, fol. 444a

Odolina []
Occurs Domesday Wiltshire holding 1 hide of the king in Marten. In a confirmation charter for Westminster Abbey [Bates {323}] probably written in the twelfth century but incorporating authentic eleventh-century information, it was recorded that a woman named Eodelina had granted one hide in Marten to the abbey, the grant being confirmed by William I at the request of his wife Matilda (d.1082). Later she became a religious (deo sacrata) at Westminster and gave all her London property to the abbey. Although this grant was not made before William's death in 1087, there is no reason to doubt that it was made subsequently.

i, fol. 74b

Offers []
Englishman who continued to hold his lands in Cornwall under Robert of Mortain.

i, fol. 124b; i, fol. 124b; i, fol. 124b; i, fol. 124b; i, fol. 124b; i, fol. 124b; i, fol. 124b; i, fol. 124b; i, fol. 124b; i, fol. 124b; i, fol. 124b

Offran []
English thegn, occurs Domesday Lincolnshire and in the Claims.

Lincolnshire Claims (Domesday Book), fols 376d–377c; i, fol. 358c; i, fol. 370c

Oger Brito
Breton. Occurs as witness to Count Alan's charter for Swavesey c.1086. Domesday tenant-in-chief in Lincolnshire and elsewhere, who was called Oger filius Vngemar in the Rutland section of Domesday. For his father's name cf. Gingomar father of Haimo de Sougéal, fl. 1060 (Morice, Preuves I, 411). In Lincolnshire he held lands that had been previously held by the celebrated English rebel thegn, Hereward the Wake. He may have married a daughter and heiress of Hereward, subsequently the wife of Hugh of Envermeu (see Roffe, 'Hereward the Wake', Lincs. Hist. & Arch. 29, 1994, 7–10). Father of Ralph and Conan, he was succeeded by his son Ralph c.1130.

Lincolnshire Claims (Domesday Book), fols 376d–377c; i, fol. 228a; i, fol. 227a; i, fol. 362d; i, fol. 228a; i, fol. 364c; i, fol. 364c; i, fol. 364c; i, fol. 364c; i, fol. 364c; i, fol. 364d; i, fol. 364c; i, fol. 364c; i, fol. 364c; i, fol. 364c; i, fol. 364c; i, fol. 364c; i, fol. 364d; i, fol. 364d; i, fol. 364c; i, fol. 364c; i, fol. 364d; i, fol. 364c; i, fol. 364c; i, fol. 364c; i, fol. 364c; i, fol. 364c; i, fol. 364c; i, fol. 364c; i, fol. 236a; i, fol. 364c; i, fol. 236a; Clay, Early Yorkshire Charters (1935), IV, No. 1; i, fol. 293d

Oger De Londonia
Occurs Domesday.

i, fol. 208a

Oger []
Domesday tenant of Waleran Venator.

i, fol. 82c

Ogis []
Domesday tenant of Roger de Courseulles and William de Moyon in Somerset and Dorset. He attested a charter of William de Moyon for Bath in 1090.

Hunt, Bath Chartulary, Som. Rec. Soc. 7 (1893), No. 34; i, fol. 94a; i, fol. 94a; i, fol. 94a; i, fol. 82a; i, fol. 95d

Oidelard Dapifer
Occurs in Domesday Kent as a tenant of Saint Augustine's church. Identified by Excerpta as dapifer. In the Kent section of PR 31 Henry I, 65, Lambert son of Odelard accounted to have the dower of his step-mother after her death.

Ballard, Inquisition of St Augustine's (1920), fols 24r–28r; i, fol. 012c; i, fol. 012c

Oidelard Lardarius
Tenant of Eustache of Huntingdon in Domesday. About 1102 Henry I issued a writ to Roger sheriff of Huntingdon ordering him to reseise Abbot Aldwin of Ramsey of the land that the son of Oidelard holds unjustly (RRAN ii, 582; Chron. Ram., p. 217).

i, fol. 206b; i, fol. 206b; i, fol. 228b; i, fol. 206b

Oidelard []
Important Domesday tenant of Ralph de Mortemer, perhaps his dapifer. He had been succeeded by 1130 by his son Ralph fitz Oilard de Alra (PR 31 Henry I, 123).

i, fol. 260c; i, fol. 159a; i, fol. 183c; i, fol. 51b; i, fol. 47a; i, fol. 47a; i, fol. 72b; i, fol. 62d; i, fol. 62d

Oismelin []
Domesday tenant of Roger de Montgomery in Sussex, including a holding at Merston which he gave to Troarn (CDF, 470). Several persons of this names occur in documents relating to the Montgomerys and their foundations, but this person is most likely to have been Oismelin de Sai (Orne), husband of Avice (Gall. Christ. xi, Inst. 152–3, Saint-Martin de Sées) and brother of Robert Picot de Sai, one of Roger's most important tenants in Shropshire. The rarity of his personal name suggests he should be identified with Oismelin, knight of the archbishop of Canterbury in 1093–6 as in 1086 at Pagham, Sussex (cf. Douglas, Dom. Mon., 37).

i, fol. 16c; i, fol. 47b; i, fol. 25a; i, fol. 25d; Regesta regum Anglo-Normannorum III, No. 902; Douglas, ed., Domesday Monachorum (1944), p. 105

Olbald []
Domesday tenant of Gunfrid de Chocques at Floore, Northamptonshire. His successors before 1166 were the Disel family, perhaps named from Izel-lès-Equerchin, Pas-de-Calais, arr. Arras, cant. Vimy. Gerald son of Walter Disel held one fee of the honour of Chokes in 1166; HKF i, 44–5. Perhaps the same as Wibald (q.v.).

    i, fol. 227d

Oliuer []
A Breton, or possibly a Norman of the Avranchin. Tenant of Theobald fitz Berner in Domesday Devon; also a tenant of half a hide of Baldwin the Sheriff, according to the Tax Return for Colyton Hundred, fol. 69b.

    i, fol. 115d; i, fol. 115c; i, fol. 115c; i, fol. 115c

Ordgar []
Englishman, Domesday tenant of Miles Crispin in Oxfordshire.

    i, fol. 161a; i, fol. 159c; i, fol. 159c

Ordmær De Bellingeham
Englishman, juror in the Domesday Inquest, who had held Badlingham, Cambs., under Edeva the Fair and continued to hold it under Count Alan. Probably the same as Ordmer, Edeva's man, who had lost possession of 4 hides in Wilbraham. Lewis, 'Jurors', 43. He was one of the jurors of a shire-court who were fined for giving a false judgement, c.1077/82, in a case between Bishop Gundulf of Rochester and Picot of Cambridge (see Williams, The English, 87).

    i, fol. 195c; Hamilton, Inquisitio Comitatus Cantabrigiensis, pp. 1–93; Hamilton, Inquisitio Eliensis (1876), pp. 97–100

Ordric Tainus
Occurs Domesday Somerset.

    i, fol. 87a

Ordric []
Englishman, Domesday tenant of the count of Meulan and Thorkil of Warwick in Warwickshire. Probably a kinshman of Thorkil; see Williams, 'Vicecomital family', and idem, The English, p. 104.

    i, fol. 243a; i, fol. 244c; i, fol. 241b; i, fol. 241b; i, fol. 241b

Ordui De Bedeford
Occurs Domesday Bedfordshire.

    i, fol. 210c

Ordulf Tainus
Occurs Domesday Somerset.

    i, fol. 87a

Orduui Burgensis
Occurs Domesday Bedfordshire.

    i, fol. 218b

Orgar []
Occurs Domesday Berkshire.

    i, fol. 56c

Orger Prepositus Abbatis Baldwini

Englishman, reeve of Abbot Baldwin of Bury, occurs Domesday Suffolk.

ii, fol. 371a

Orm De Acoura

Englishman, Domesday tenant of Henry de Ferrers, benefactor of Tutbury. Ancestor of the Okeover family. Around 1121/7 he attested a covenant between Burton abbey and Robert de Ferrers with his son-in-law Andrew (BL Chh., no. 9).

i, fol. 275d; i, fol. 275b; i, fol. 275b; Dugdale, Monasticon Anglicanum, III, pp. 392–93, No. II; Pipe Roll 31 Henry I, 075–st

Ornod []

Ordnoth, an Englishman who had previously held land in Papworth from the Norman Robert fitz Wimarc and held it in 1086 from Eustache the Sheriff by the king's order. Another portion of his landholding there was held in 1086 by Eustache's man Walter de Belmeis.

i, fol. 199d

Osbern Accipitrarius

Occurs Domesday Hampshire.

i, fol. 49c; i, fol. 49c

Osbern Clericus

Occurs Domesday Sussex as a tenant of Osbern bishop of Exeter.

i, fol. 17c

Osbern Clericus Episcopi

Norman, occurs in Domesday Book as a clerk of Bishop Remigius of Lincoln.

i, fol. 344c

Osbern De Arcis

Domesday tenant-in-chief in Lincolnshire and Yorkshire. He was dead by the date of the Lindsey Survey, 1115/18, when his son William had succeeded him. He also left a daughter Agnes, successively the wife of Herbert of St Quintin, Robert de Fauconberg and William Foliot. He was probably the ancestor of several other branches of the Arcis family, and so father also of Peter and Gilbert (fl. 1130). Probably named from Arques-la-Bataille, Seine-Maritime, arr. Dieppe, cant. Offranville, there is no evidence of any relationship between Osbern and William d'Arques, lord of Folkestone.

Dugdale, Monasticon Anglicanum, III, pp. 548–50, No. V; Dugdale, Monasticon Anglicanum, III, p. 547, No. III; i, fol. 329a; i, fol. 298b; Lincolnshire Claims (Domesday Book), fols 376d–377c; i, fol. 329c; i, fol. 329a; i, fol. 329a; i, fol. 329b; i, fol. 329b; i, fol. 329a; i, fol. 329c; i, fol. 329c; i, fol. 329c; i, fol. 329c; i, fol. 329c; i, fol. 329c; i, fol. 329a; i, fol. 329a; i, fol. 329c; i, fol. 329a; i, fol. 329c; i, fol. 364b; i, fol. 329c; i, fol. 329c; i, fol. 329a; i, fol. 364b

Osbern De Novomercato

Domesday tenant of Hugh de Grandmesnil, whose fees were later held by the Neufmarché family, probably his descendants, and originally from Neufmarché, cant. Gournai-en-Brai, Seine-Maritime (cf. Porée, Histoire de l'abbaye du Bec ii, 648). Osbert/n de Novoforo (Neufmarché) attested a charter of Gerard [de Roumare] of August 1067 for Saint-Amand de Rouen (CDF, nos. 87–8). Cf.

Crouch, 'A divided aristocracy?', in Bates and Curry ed. England and Normandy in the Middle Ages (1994), p. 54n.

> i, fol. 232d; i, fol. 232c; i, fol. 242a; i, fol. 224c; i, fol. 224c; i, fol. 224c

Osbern De Ow
Norman, from Eu, Seine-Martime, arr. Dieppe, occurs Domesday Surrey. An Osbern de Aucis occurs in a charter of Richard II of Normand, c.997–1007 (Fauroux, 10). Geoffrey and Ansfrid sons of Osbern vicomte of Eu occur c.1050 (ibid., 119, 123).

> i, fol. 31a; i, fol. 30c

Osbern De Salceid
Norman, occurs in Domesday Devonshire holding several manors in chief which subsequently formed part of the Redvers honour of Plympton. Possibly named from Saussey, Calvados, arr. Caen, cant. Villers-Bocage, comm. Epinay-sur-Odon. His heirs, Richard and Robert de Salcei, attested Redvers charters from c.1130.

> i, fol. 117a; i, fol. 117a; i, fol. 116d; i, fol. 117a; i, fol. 117a; i, fol. 117a; i, fol. 116d

Osbern De Wanceio
Norman, from Wanchy-Capeval, Seine-Maritime, cant. Londinières. Held land in the fief of Richard de Clare in Domesday Suffolk that Richard claimed for the holding of his predecessor Finn. He was perhaps the son of Hugh de Wanchy, a tenant of William de Warenne, who occurs with his father and brother in a Castle Acre deed before 1118 (Mon. Ang. v, 44)

> ii, fol. 394a; ii, fol. 394a; ii, fol. 394a; ii, fol. 394a; ii, fol. 394a

Osbern Episcopus Exoniensis
Osbern fitz Osbern, brother of William fitz Osbern, bishop of Exeter from April 1072 until his death in 1103. See EEA xi, pp. xxxii–iii.

> i, fol. 30a; i, fol. 165a; i, fol. 17b; i, fol. 43a; ii, fol. 201b; i, fol. 155a; i, fol. 164a; ii, fol. 202a; ii, fol. 202a; i, fol. 17c; i, fol. 58c; i, fol. 31b; i, fol. 64d; ii, fol. 202a; i, fol. 65c; ii, fol. 201b; ii, fol. 202a; ii, fol. 202a; i, fol. 162a; i, fol. 162a; ii, fol. 201b; ii, fol. 202a; i, fol. 17b; i, fol. 165a; i, fol. 165a; i, fol. 43a; i, fol. 101d; i, fol. 101d; i, fol. 101d; i, fol. 101d; i, fol. 101d; i, fol. 101d; i, fol. 101d; i, fol. 102a; i, fol. 101d; i, fol. 101d; i, fol. 101d; i, fol. 102a; i, fol. 102a; i, fol. 102a; i, fol. 102a; i, fol. 102a; i, fol. 101d; i, fol. 102a; i, fol. 101d; i, fol. 101d; i, fol. 120c; i, fol. 120c; i, fol. 120c; i, fol. 120c; i, fol. 120c; i, fol. 120d; i, fol. 120c; Dugdale, Monasticon Anglicanum, II, p. 267, No. XI

Osbern Filius Goisfridi
Norman, Domesday tenant of the count of Eu in Sussex. Identifiable as Osbern fitz Geoffrey de Balliol, from Bailleul-Neuville, Seine-Maritime, arr. Neufchâtel, cant. Londinières (cf. Loyd, 11). Probably father of Oilard de Balliol, a Domesday tenant of Richard de Clare.

> i, fol. 18b; i, fol. 18b; i, fol. 18b; i, fol. 20b; i, fol. 19b; i, fol. 19b; i, fol. 19b; i, fol. 19b; i, fol. 19a; i, fol. 19a; i, fol. 19a; i, fol. 19b; i, fol. 19a

Osbern Filius Hugonis
Norman, tenant of the count of Eu in Domesday Sussex; identified as fitz Hugh by the Chronicle of Battle Abbey, 255.

> i, fol. 20a

Osbern Filius Letardi

Norman, occurs Domesday Kent as a tenant of Odo de Bayeux.

i, fol. 011d; i, fol. 011c; i, fol. 004c; i, fol. 011c; i, fol. 012c; i, fol. 011b; i, fol. 011c; i, fol. 009d; i, fol. 009d; i, fol. 011b; Ballard, Inquisition of St Augustine's (1920), fols 24r–28r

Osbern Filius Ricardi Scrob

Norman, Domesday tenant-in-chief, son of Richard Scrob of Richard's Castle, Herefordshire (Sanders, 75). He married Nesta daughter of Gruffyd ap Llywellyn, by whom he had issue his heir Hugh and a daughter, Nesta (or Agnes), wife of Bernard of Neufmarché by 1088, according to Orderic Vitalis (vi, 124). Perhaps father also of Turstin, who attested a charter of Osbern fitz Pons as brother of Hugh fitz Osbern (BL Chh. no. 5).

i, fol. 180a; Darlington, Cartulary of Worcester: Reg. I (1962–3), No. 152; Darlington, Cartulary of Worcester: Reg. I (1962–3), No. 147; Regesta regum Anglo-Normannorum III, No. 964; i, fol. 176c; i, fol. 292a; i, fol. 186d; i, fol. 244a; i, fol. 260a; i, fol. 216c; i, fol. 168c; Regesta regum Anglo-Normannorum III, No. 963; i, fol. 238a; Darlington, Cartulary of Worcester: Reg. I (1962–3), No. 149; Darlington, Cartulary of Worcester: Reg. I (1962–3), No. 154; i, fol. 260a; i, fol. 186d; i, fol. 260a; i, fol. 186d; i, fol. 292a; i, fol. 186d; i, fol. 180b; i, fol. 186d; i, fol. 260a; i, fol. 186d; i, fol. 186d; i, fol. 244a; i, fol. 292a; i, fol. 186d; i, fol. 186d; i, fol. 186d; i, fol. 260a; i, fol. 186d; i, fol. 247d; i, fol. 260a; i, fol. 186d; i, fol. 260a; i, fol. 186d; i, fol. 163a; i, fol. 260a; i, fol. 186d; i, fol. 186d; i, fol. 186d; i, fol. 260a; i, fol. 186d; i, fol. 173c; i, fol. 172d; i, fol. 186d; i, fol. 163a; i, fol. 186d; i, fol. 186d; i, fol. 186d; i, fol. 186d; Darlington, Cartulary of Worcester: Reg. I (1962–3), No. 153; Darlington, Cartulary of Worcester: Reg. I (1962–3), No. 159; i, fol. 176d; i, fol. 176d; i, fol. 176c; i, fol. 176d; i, fol. 176d; i, fol. 176d; i, fol. 176d; i, fol. 176d; i, fol. 176c; Darlington, Cartulary of Worcester: Reg. I (1962–3), No. 148; i, fol. 257d; i, fol. 257d

Osbern Filius Tezzonis

Norman, Domesday tenant of Earl Hugh of Chester. He granted land in Newball, Lincolnshire, to Saint-Evroul. By 1115/18, some of his land in Lincolnshire was held by Hugh de Neubele and some by the sons of Roscelin. Cf. Farrer, HKF ii, 175–6, who suggested that Hugh was Osbert's heir. Hugh de Neubele attested a grant by Ansgot of Burwell of, inter alia, demesne land at Carlton in Burwell to La Sauve-Majeure early in the time of Henry I. A grant of meadowland at Carlton of probably similiar date was given for the same abbey by Hugh fitz Osbert and Aeliz his mother, witnessed by Hugh's brothers Hervey and William (CDF, 1239–40).

i, fol. 268a; i, fol. 349d; i, fol. 349c; i, fol. 349c; Barraclough, Charters of AN Earls of Chester (1988), No. 11; i, fol. 268d; i, fol. 268d; i, fol. 267c; i, fol. 267c; i, fol. 267c; i, fol. 267c; i, fol. 267c; Barraclough, Charters of AN Earls of Chester (1988), No. 1

Osbern Filius Walteri

Norman, husband of Muriel sister of Eudo Dapifer, and father of Walcher. Identified from Hist. Ramsey. 207, 232 Ancestor of the de Leyham family. In 1086 he held manors of Little Barford in Bedfordshire from the king and from Eudo dapifer. Cf. HKF iii, 177ff.

i, fol. 210d; i, fol. 216c; i, fol. 216c

Osbern Giffard

Norman, member of the family of Giffard of Longueville, Seine-Maritime. The abbot of Saint-Etienne de Caen had a plea against Osbern Giffard and his wife Adeguisa (Hadvise) in September 1077 (Deville, Analyse, 20–1). He died before 1096 and left Elias, probably his son, to succeed him at Elston in Orcheston St George, Wiltshire (Sanders, 115–16). There is a genealogy of this family in BM Add. 37124.

> i, fol. 52a; i, fol. 98a; i, fol. 98a; i, fol. 98a; i, fol. 72d; i, fol. 72d; i, fol. 72d; i, fol. 72d; i, fol. 72d; i, fol. 72d; i, fol. 72d; i, fol. 72d; i, fol. 72d; i, fol. 82c; i, fol. 62a; i, fol. 168c; i, fol. 168c; i, fol. 168c; i, fol. 168c; i, fol. 164d; i, fol. 160b; i, fol. 219a; i, fol. 72d; i, fol. 98a; i, fol. 168c; i, fol. 160b; i, fol. 66c; Darlington, Cartulary of Worcester: Reg. I (1962–3), No. 21

Osbern Mascels

Norman, Domesday tenant of Ranulf Peverel in Suffolk. The land and meadow of Osbern Masculus was given to Saint-Etienne de Caen by William I (Actes caen., no. 6, p. 69). A second Osbern Masculus occurs in the 1140s.

> ii, fol. 282a; ii, fol. 417a

Osbern Paisforere

Norman, tenant of Odo of Bayeux in Domesday Kent. He was probably the Osbert who was ancestor of the de Aldeglosa family which held his manor of Aldglose in the twelfth century. The benefice of Hugh Paisfolet at St Marcouf (Manche, cant. Montebourg) in the Cotentin is mentioned c.1082 (Fauroux, 234). Robert Paiseforere de Husseburn is mentioned in the Thorney cartulary (i, fol. 235r); Fulk Paisforirer attested a grant to Bermondsey by William fitz Helto of Aldington, Kent (BL Harley 4757, fol. 13r).

> i, fol. 011b; Stenton, English Feudalism, App., No. 38; i, fol. 004a; i, fol. 009a; i, fol. 009a; i, fol. 010b; i, fol. 010b; i, fol. 011c; i, fol. 011c; i, fol. 009d; i, fol. 010d; i, fol. 010d; Douglas, ed., Domesday Monachorum (1944), p. 105; i, fol. 006b; i, fol. 010d

Osbern Piscator

Occurs Domesday Bedfordshire holding land of the king. The holding was absorbed in the barony of Beauchamp soon after 1086.

> i, fol. 216c; i, fol. 216c; i, fol. 216c; i, fol. 216c

Osbern Presbiter

Occurs Domesday Wiltshire.

> i, fol. 73b; i, fol. 65a; i, fol. 68c

Osbern Presbiter Vicecomes

Norman priest, sheriff of Lincolnshire between 1093 and 1116. Father of Richard, surnamed de Lincoln in the Lindsey Survey, and William Torniant, among others. A manor held by an Osbert of William de Percy in Domesday was held by Richard in the Lindsey Survey; Alan de Percy and Walter de Gant sought to recover land against William Torniant in 1129 (PR 31 Henry I, 25). Cf. W. Farrer, 'The sheriffs of Lincolnshire and Yorkshire, 1066–1130', EHR xxx (1915), 277–85; VCH Lincs. ii, 170.

> i, fol. 353d; i, fol. 340b; i, fol. 354b; i, fol. 354b; i, fol. 340b; i, fol. 366c; i, fol. 366c; i, fol. 339d; i, fol. 366c; i, fol. 366c; Regesta regum Anglo-Normannorum III, No. 817; Clay, Early Yorkshire Charters (1939), VI, No. 2; Clay, Early

Yorkshire Charters (1952), IX, No. 3; Clay, Early Yorkshire Charters (1952), IX, No. 2; Round, Ancient Charters (1888), No. 1; Dugdale, Monasticon Anglicanum, III, p. 218, No. XII

Osbern []
Norman, Domesday tenant of Geoffrey bishop of Coutances.

i, fol. 109a; i, fol. 77b; i, fol. 77b; i, fol. 103b

Osbern []
Tenant of Odo of Bayeux in several Hertfordshire manors. There is no clue as to whether he was one of two Osberns to hold of Odo in Kent (Paisforere and fitz Letard) or a third. The Hertfordshire estates passed intact to Hugh de Port after 1086 and were held from Hugh and his descendants by a family named from Clothall. Robert de Clothalle held in 1166 (VCH Herts iii, 222).

i, fol. 134d; i, fol. 134d; i, fol. 134d; i, fol. 134d; i, fol. 134c; i, fol. 134c; i, fol. 134c; i, fol. 134c; i, fol. 134b

Osbern []
Domesday tenant of Swein of Essex.

ii, fol. 042a; ii, fol. 042a; ii, fol. 047b

Osbern []
Domesday tenant of the abbey of Abingdon at West Hendred also occurs in an early twelfth century survey of the abbey.

i, fol. 60b; Douglas, 'Some early surveys of Abingdon' (1929), EHR, 44 (1929), 623–25

Osbert De Broilg
Norman, from Brouay, Calvados, arr. Caen, cant. Tilly-sur-Seulles; see Loyd, 20. Domesday tenant of Countess Judith and Hugh de Beauchamp in Bedfordshire. The next known holder of his fees, Robert de Broi (d. 1141/60), was probably his grandson. The Osbern who held land at Stapleford, Lincolnshire, from the Countess was perhaps the same man; he seems to have been an ancestor of the Disney (de Isigny) family. Cf. Farrer, HKF i, 310–11.

i, fol. 217c; i, fol. 217b; i, fol. 366d; i, fol. 213c; i, fol. 213b

Osbert []
Domesday tenant of Walter Flandrensis. His holdings passed to the Welton family of Whilton, Northamptonshire, who also succeeded to the Domesday fees held by Alan of the count of Mortain. Farrer, HKF i, 88–9.

i, fol. 215c; i, fol. 215d; i, fol. 215d

Osgar De Bedeford
Occurs Domesday Bedfordshire.

i, fol. 218b

Osiet Prefectus Regis
Royal provost. Occurs Domesday Bedfordshire.

i, fol. 218d; i, fol. 218d

Osmund Benz
Occurs Domesday Derbyshire.

i, fol. 278c

Osmund Canonicus
Canon of St Pauls, Bedford in 1086.

i, fol. 211a

Osmund De Straham
Norman, Domesday juror in the Ely Hundreds, Cambridgeshire; named from Stretham. Probably the Osmund who was a tenant of Picot of Cambridge at Landbeach.

i, fol. 201c; Hamilton, Inquisitio Eliensis (1876), pp. 97–100

Osmund Episcopus Saresberiensis
Nephew of Arestaldus, who was commemorated at Salisbury (Leland, Itin. I, 266). Royal chancellor, bishop of Salisbury from mid-1078 until his death on 3 December 1099. Canonised on 1 January 1457. FEA iv, 1–2.

Gibbs, Early Charters of St Pauls (1939), No. 5; Gibbs, Early Charters of St Pauls (1939), No. 9; Dugdale, Monasticon Anglicanum, IV, p. 13, No. IV; Clay, Early Yorkshire Charters (1949), VIII, No. 4; Regesta regum Anglo-Normannorum III, No. 791; i, fol. 343d; i, fol. 87d; i, fol. 155a; Gibbs, Early Charters of St Pauls (1939), No. 12; Dugdale, Monasticon Anglicanum, II, p. 267, No. X; Mason, Westminster Abbey Charters (1988), No. 462; i, fol. 57d; i, fol. 73c; i, fol. 65c; i, fol. 70a; Lincolnshire Claims (Domesday Book), fols 376d–377c; Regesta regum Anglo-Normannorum III, No. 795; i, fol. 56c; i, fol. 343d; i, fol. 77b; i, fol. 77b; i, fol. 77a; i, fol. 77a; i, fol. 77a; i, fol. 77a; i, fol. 77b; i, fol. 77a; i, fol. 77b; i, fol. 77a; i, fol. 77a; i, fol. 77a; i, fol. 77a; i, fol. 75d; i, fol. 75d; i, fol. 75d; i, fol. 75d; i, fol. 75d; i, fol. 75d; i, fol. 58b; i, fol. 58b; i, fol. 66a; i, fol. 155a; i, fol. 66a; i, fol. 66a; i, fol. 66a; i, fol. 87d; Dugdale, Monasticon Anglicanum, III, pp. 544–46, No. I

Osmund Pistor
Baker, occurs Domesday Dorset. His holdings were a baker serjeanty based at Wool after 1086 (RBE ii, 547).

i, fol. 85a; i, fol. 85a

Osmund []
Domesday tenant of Swein in Dorset. Possibly the same as Osmund the Interpreter (Latimarius) who occurs in a Tax Return, fol. 11b.

i, fol. 73c; i, fol. 84c

Osmund []
Domesday tenant of Gotshelm de Claville in Devon. His fees were held in the early thirteenth century by a family surnamed Lampre (Fees, 780).

i, fol. 112d; i, fol. 112d; i, fol. 112d

Osmund []
Occurs Domesday Sussex as tenant of William de Warenne.

i, fol. 27c

Osmund []
Occurs Domesday Northants as tenant of Odo of Bayeux.

i, fol. 224b; i, fol. 220d

Osmund Nepos Gisonis Episcopi Wellensis
Occurs as a tenant of Giso bishop of Wells in Domesday Somerset; identified as nepos episcopi (nephew or kinsman) in the Tax Returns, fol. 78b.

i, fol. 89a; i, fol. 89c

Osuuard De Trusseberie

Englishman, Domesday tenant of Gilbert fitz Turold at Trewsbury, Gloucestershire. Attested a charter of Osbern fitz Pons temp. Henry I as Osward de Trusseberie (BL Chh., no. 5).

i, fol. 168c

Oswar []

English knight of the bishop of Salisbury, occurs Dorset Domesday.

i, fol. 77b

Oswold Tainus

English thegn, brother of Abbot Wulfwold of Chertsey, occurs as a landholder in Domesday Surrey.

i, fol. 35d; i, fol. 35d; i, fol. 36d; i, fol. 36d; i, fol. 36d; i, fol. 36d

Otbert De Merck

Fleming from Merck-Saint-Liévin, Pas-de-Calais, comm. and cant. Fauquembergues, in Artois, Domesday tenant of William de Picquigny in Northamptonshire, and probably also in Buckinghamshire. According to an item in the Missenden Cartulary, Otbert was succeeded in his Buckinghamshire holdings by Reiner de Lohereng, who held Morton Pinkeny in the time of Henry I. Father of Adelolf de Merck, an important tenant of Eustache de Boulogne in 1086; cf. Round, 'Counts of Boulogne', in Peerage, etc.

i, fol. 227b; i, fol. 226b; i, fol. 149a; i, fol. 148c; i, fol. 148c; i, fol. 226c; i, fol. 226c; i, fol. 226c; i, fol. 226c

Otbert De Surreia

Occurs Domesday Surrey as a tenant of Odo of Bayeux; probably the Otbert de Surreia mentioned as a man of the abbot in a Westminster charter.

i, fol. 30a; i, fol. 31c; Mason, Westminster Abbey Charters (1988), No. 488

Otbold []

Occurs in the south-west in Domesday Book.

i, fol. 77a; i, fol. 77b; i, fol. 66a

Othelin De Hidun

Tenant of Baldwin the Sheriff of Devon, holding inter alia the manor of Clyst Hydon. As Otelin de Hydune he granted the church of Clyst Hydon to St Nicholas' Exeter for his soul and the soul of his brother Geoffrey (Gaufridi) and for the souls of his wife and sons, witnessed by Gozelin and Osbern priests, Radulf nepos Alwredi, Robert de (?) Adeville, Gereus filius Watzon, Robert de Ver (BL Cott. Vit. D ix, fol. 168v); the grant was confirmed by Bishop Osbern (d. 1103) (ibid. fol. 169r).

i, fol. 106b; i, fol. 106c; i, fol. 107d; i, fol. 107d; i, fol. 107a; i, fol. 107c; i, fol. 108c; i, fol. 107d

Otto Aurifaber

Domesday tenant-in-chief, also a tenant of Bury St Edmunds. He married Leofgifu, the widow of a citizen of London, by whom he had issue his son Otto II, who had succeeded him by 1098, and secondly, after 1086, Edeva, widow of Edward fitz Swein. See Douglas, Feud. Docs, pp. cxxxviii–ix; F.N. Craig, 'Descent from a Domesday goldsmith', The American Genealogist 65.1 (1990), 24ff.

ii, fol. 358a; ii, fol. 287a; ii, fol. 286b; ii, fol. 286b; i, fol. 190a; ii, fol. 106b; ii, fol. 098a; ii, fol. 004a; ii, fol. 003b; ii, fol. 098a; Douglas, Feudal Documents from Bury St Edmunds, No. 29; Mason, Westminster Abbey Charters (1988), No. 488

Pagan Dapifer
Major Domesday tenant of Harduin de Scalariis. Identified in IE as Harduin's dapifer, he is likely to have been close to Harduin, perhaps related to him. In 1214 Juliana widow of Robert fitz Payn sought dower in Conington, Cambridgeshire (one of Payn's 1086 holdings) against Geoffrey de Sackville (Curia Regis Roll vii, p. 92).

i, fol. 142a; i, fol. 199a; i, fol. 199a; i, fol. 199a; i, fol. 199a; i, fol. 198a; i, fol. 199a; Hamilton, Inquisitio Eliensis (1876), pp. 97–100; Hamilton, Inquisitio Comitatus Cantabrigiensis, pp. 1–93

Pagan De Capellis
Norman, Domesday tenant of Richard de Clare in Suffolk. His three manors were held by Alberic de Capellis from the early twelfth century onward, thus permitting his identifcation as the Payn de Capellis who attested a charter for Jumièges given in 1079 by a tenant of Richard de Clare (CDF, 152). La Chapelle-Haute-Grue, Calvados, cant. Livarot, is not far from Orbec.

ii, fol. 396b; ii, fol. 396a; ii, fol. 396a

Pagan []
Domesday tenant of Gilbert de Breteville.

i, fol. 62a; i, fol. 62a

Pagan []
Domesday tenant of William fitz Ansculf of Picquigny. In 1166 his Buckinghamshire fees were held by Ralph and Walter Mansel (q.v.).

i, fol. 177b; i, fol. 149a; i, fol. 149a; i, fol. 148d; i, fol. 148d; i, fol. 148d; i, fol. 148c; i, fol. 148c

Pagan []
Domesday tenant of William Peverel of Nottingham in Northamptonshire; father of Robert, an early benefactor of Lenton priory; HKF i, 171.

i, fol. 148b; i, fol. 235b; i, fol. 288a; i, fol. 226a

Pagan []
Domesday tenant of Swein of Essex.

ii, fol. 045a; ii, fol. 042b

Pagan []
Domesday tenant of Roger Bigod.

ii, fol. 183b

Pagan []
Domesday tenant of Roger de Ivry. Probably ancestor of the Westbury family, of whom Adelelm occurs c.1140 and Payn of Westbury (q.v.) c.1160.

i, fol. 151d; i, fol. 159a; i, fol. 161a

Pagen []
Domesday tenant of Earl Hugh of Chester.

i, fol. 265a; i, fol. 266b; i, fol. 266b; i, fol. 266b

Pagen []
Domesday tenant of Earl Roger of Shrewsbury in Sussex.

i, fol. 23a; i, fol. 25c

Petrus Burgensis
Occurs Domesday Hertfordshire.

i, fol. 142b

Petrus Clericus
Cf. Herve Bituricensis, where it is suggested that the Domesday tenant Peter identified in the Feudal Book as Peter clericus was the same person as Peter Bituricensis, also known as 'clericus Ambianensis' (clerk of Amiens).

Douglas, Feudal Documents from Bury St Edmunds, No. 94; Douglas, Feudal Documents from Bury St Edmunds, No. 106; Douglas, Feudal Documents from Bury St Edmunds, No. 105; Douglas, Feudal Documents from Bury St Edmunds, No. 30; ii, fol. 358a; Douglas, Feudal Documents from Bury St Edmunds, No. 34

Petrus Dapifer
Domesday steward of abbot Baldwin of Bury St Edmunds. He was succeeded by his sons Richard (a monk in 1112) and Adam dapifer (fl. 1120–48) (q.v.).

ii, fol. 360a; ii, fol. 363a; ii, fol. 364a; ii, fol. 362a; Douglas, Feudal Book of Bury St Edmunds (1932), pp. 3–21; ii, fol. 117a

Petrus De Paludel
Domesday tenant of Hervé Bituricensis (q.v.). Adam de Palwelle held of Hervé's successors in 1166 (RBE, 366).

ii, fol. 443a; ii, fol. 442b; ii, fol. 442b

Petrus De Valonges
Norman, from Valognes, Manche, tenant-in-chief in Domesday East Anglia. Sheriff of Essex in 1086, a post he probably held both earlier and later (Green, Sheriffs, 39). Founder of Binham priory c.1107, he died soon afterwards, c.1109; he was remembered on 20 March in the Belvoir necrology (Add. 4936, fol. 20r). His wife Albreda was the sister of a Eudo married to a Rohais. It has been assumed that this refers to Eudo dapifer and his wife Rohais de Clare, but it is much more likely to refer to Eudo vicomte de Saint-Sauveur (d. 1103) and his wife (VCH Herts iii, 26; cf. ibid. 37, 86–7). Albreda's brother was mentioned in the Binham foundation charter, which was attested by Roger de Saint-Sauveur, Eudo's nephew and successor. Peter was father of his heir Roger, William, Muriel, secondly the wife of Hubert I de Montcanisy, and a daughter who married an Englishman, Alfred of Athleborough (q.v.).

ii, fol. 170a; ii, fol. 006a; ii, fol. 004b; ii, fol. 366b; ii, fol. 278b; i, fol. 134d; i, fol. 141d; i, fol. 134b; ii, fol. 006a; i, fol. 336b; i, fol. 336a; i, fol. 368d; i, fol. 190a; i, fol. 336b; i, fol. 141a; i, fol. 141b; i, fol. 141a; i, fol. 141b; i, fol. 141b; i, fol. 132a; i, fol. 141b; i, fol. 141b; i, fol. 141a; i, fol. 141a; i, fol. 368d; i, fol. 140d; Douglas, Feudal Documents from Bury St Edmunds, No. 31; Douglas, Feudal Book of Bury St Edmunds (1932), pp. 22–37; ii, fol. 012b; Douglas, Feudal Documents from Bury St Edmunds, No. 9; ii, fol. 194a; ii, fol. 420b; ii, fol. 421a; ii, fol. 421a; ii, fol. 421a; ii, fol. 421a; ii, fol. 421a; ii, fol. 421a; ii, fol. 421a; ii, fol. 421a; ii, fol. 421b; ii, fol. 420b; ii, fol. 421a; ii, fol. 421a; ii, fol. 421a; ii, fol. 420b; ii, fol. 366a; Gibbs, Early Charters of St Pauls (1939), No. 4; Gibbs, Early Charters of

St Pauls (1939), No. 10; Dugdale, Monasticon Anglicanum, III, p. 346, No. II; Douglas, Social Structure of Med. E. Anglia (1927), No. 36; Dugdale, Monasticon Anglicanum, III, pp. 345–46, No. I; Douglas, Feudal Documents from Bury St Edmunds, No. 26; Regesta regum Anglo-Normannorum III, No. 261; Douglas, Social Structure of Med. E. Anglia (1927), No. 35; Red Book of the Exchequer, ed. Hall (1897), pp. 397–99; Dugdale, Monasticon Anglicanum, III, pp. 345–46, No. I; Douglas, Social Structure of Med. E. Anglia (1927), No. 37; Dugdale, Monasticon Anglicanum, III, pp. 346–47, No. III; Dugdale, Monasticon Anglicanum, III, p. 347, No. IV; Dugdale, Monasticon Anglicanum, III, p. 346, No. II; Gibbs, Early Charters of St Pauls (1939), No. 56; Mason, Westminster Abbey Charters (1988), No. 488; ii, fol. 365b; ii, fol. 366a; Dugdale, Monasticon Anglicanum, III, pp. 548–50, No. V; ii, fol. 366a; Hamilton, Inquisitio Eliensis (1876), pp. 192–95; Douglas, Feudal Documents from Bury St Edmunds, No. 168; Gibbs, Early Charters of St Pauls (1939), No. 5; ii, fol. 367b; ii, fol. 367b; ii, fol. 256a; ii, fol. 256b; ii, fol. 256b; ii, fol. 257b; ii, fol. 257b; ii, fol. 257a; ii, fol. 258b; ii, fol. 257a; ii, fol. 286b; ii, fol. 257b; ii, fol. 256a; ii, fol. 257b; ii, fol. 079a; ii, fol. 258a; ii, fol. 258a; ii, fol. 258a; ii, fol. 258b; ii, fol. 278b; ii, fol. 257b; ii, fol. 258a; ii, fol. 079a; ii, fol. 079a; ii, fol. 257b; ii, fol. 078a; ii, fol. 078b; ii, fol. 078b; ii, fol. 257a; ii, fol. 079a; ii, fol. 079a; ii, fol. 078a; ii, fol. 256a; i, fol. 132a; ii, fol. 090b; i, fol. 133b; ii, fol. 001b; i, fol. 135c; ii, fol. 107a; ii, fol. 169a; ii, fol. 169a

Petrus Frater Burchard
Domesday tenant of Bury St Edmunds.

ii, fol. 358b; Douglas, Feudal Book of Bury St Edmunds (1932), pp. 3–21

Petrus []
Norman, Domesday tenant of Ivo Taillebois in Lincolnshire. His holding passed to the heirs of Nigel de Broclesbi (q.v.) of the Calz family (HKF ii, 206).

i, fol. 350d; i, fol. 350b

Petrus []
Norman, Domesday tenant of Robert d'Oilly in Oxfordshire. Probable ancestor of a family named from his holding in Wheatfield; a Peter of Wheatfield attested d'Oilly charters c.1150.

i, fol. 161a; i, fol. 158b; i, fol. 158b

Phanceon []
Breton tenant of Alberic de Vere. The personal name occurs in numerous Breton and Angevin documents; cf. Cart. Redon, no. cccxx (Frossai-le-Migron); Morice, Preuves, I, 510–11. Thought to have been succeeded by two coheirs, of whom one was Matilda, mother of Gelduin (q.v.) and Peter of Nerford, Norfolk (Comp. Peer. ix, 466). His immediate successor was William or Nerford, who occurs in the early twelfth century; William was certainly the father of Gelduin and possibly also of Gelduin's supposed collateral Geoffrey of Narford.

ii, fol. 144a; ii, fol. 146a; ii, fol. 145b; ii, fol. 145b

Picot De Friardel
Norman, from Friardel, Calvados, arr. Lisieux, cant. Orbec (Loyd, 44). Picot de Friadel attested a charter of Gilbert fitz Richard before 1100; he is probably to be identified with Picot, Domesday tenant of Richard de Clare.

i, fol. 35a; i, fol. 35a; i, fol. 35a; Douglas, Feudal Documents from Bury St Edmunds, No. 170; i, fol. 35b; i, fol. 35b

Picot De Grentebrige

Sheriff of Cambridegshire from c.1071 until 1086 and possibly as late as 1100. Most of his holdings lay in Cambridgeshire, where he was also a tenant of the abbey of Ely. No other Picot had influence in the region, which appears to require that we see in Picot the Picot de Bavent mentioned in a writ of Henry I of 1105 (RRAN ii, 685) addressed to the sheriff of Cambs. A Picot de Bavent attested a Bury document of 1112 (FD, 172). The date of Picot's death is unknown, but it occurred a few years after the foundation of St Giles's, Cambrige, by Picot and his second wife Hugolina in 1092, according to the Liber. Bernewelle. Farrer (Feudal Cambs) suggested that the sheriff and Picot de Bavent were the same person, but this identification is untenable. The service of one knight owed by Picot de Bavent (q.v.) was granted to William d'Albini pincerna by Henry I, according to his Carta. Charters of Wymondham priory show that the tenement in question lay at Besthorpe, Norfolk – held by the king in 1086 – and that it descended in a family surnamed de Bavent.

Picot's name is a nickname based on the word 'pic' (pick, pickaxe). It must therefore not be confused, as it frequently has been, with Pirot, the name of a tenant of Eudo Dapifer whose name is a hypocoristic of Peter (Pierrot). Picot and Pirot (q.v.) were different persons, as is abundantly demonstrated by the descent of their lands. Coincidentally, Pirot's name could be represented by the Ralph Pilot who gave land in Bavent to Saint-Etienne de Caen as a tenant of Hubert de Ryes, brother of Eudo Dapifer, but a variant of Ralph's surname, Pitot, could represent Picot.

In 1086 Picot was married to a daughter of Robert Gernon, probably the same woman as his second wife Hugolina. Domesday records that one of his daughters married Ralph de Saint-Germain, one of Picot's tenants, as was Picot's brother Roger. According to a Fine from Richard I's reign (PR Soc. n.s. 24, 225, dated 10 Ric I), Ralph de Saint-Germain's wife was called Agnes and she was the issue of Picot's first wife. The same fines shows that Picot had other daughters, and that the Picot family – represented in the fine by Robert Picot grandson of Henry Picot – were the descendants of Picot's second marriage. His eldest son Robert forfeited his father's honour of Bourn for some revolt in the time of Henry I; by 1122 Payn Peverel was holding Picot's honour of Bourn (Lib. Bern.). Among the fees of the bishopric of Bayeux recorded in the Bayeux Inquest of c.1132 (RBE 646) were those of Gernon, and the three-knight fees of Picot.

i, fol. 190a; i, fol. 191b; i, fol. 190a; i, fol. 190a; i, fol. 190b; i, fol. 190c; i, fol. 195b; i, fol. 194d; i, fol. 194d; i, fol. 201d; i, fol. 200a; i, fol. 201d; ii, fol. 289a; i, fol. 190d; ii, fol. 289a; ii, fol. 289a; ii, fol. 289a; i, fol. 202c; i, fol. 190a; ii, fol. 004a; i, fol. 202b; i, fol. 202b; i, fol. 202b; i, fol. 202b; i, fol. 200b; i, fol. 201b; i, fol. 200c; i, fol. 201c; i, fol. 201c; i, fol. 201a; i, fol. 200d; i, fol. 201a; i, fol. 200c; i, fol. 200c; i, fol. 200c; i, fol. 200b; i, fol. 200b; i, fol. 200b; i, fol. 200b; i, fol. 200b; i, fol. 189a; i, fol. 189a; i, fol. 197a; i, fol. 197a; i, fol. 197a; i, fol. 199d; ii, fol. 003b; i, fol. 190c; Hamilton, Inquisitio Eliensis (1876), pp. 192–95; Hamilton, Inquisitio Comitatus Cantabrigiensis, pp. 1–93; i, fol. 189a; G. Fowler, Early Cambridgeshire Feodary, EHR (1932), pp. 442–3; G. Fowler, Early Cambridgeshire Feodary, EHR (1932), pp. 442–3

Picot De Lascels

Domesday tenant of Count Alan in Lincolnshire and Yorkshire. In the early twelfth century his holdings were reckoned as five knights' fees, owing castle-guard at Richmond in October and November (EYC v, 182–3). Still alive in 1115/18, his son Roger was already active by that time. There are no firm indications as to the identification of his toponym. As a tenant only of Count Alan there must be an assumption that he was a Breton in origin. A possible derivation is Céaux, Manche, cant. Ducey, a place then in Normandy but part of Brittany before c.1009/29; cf. Dauzat/Rostaing,

i, fol. 347b; i, fol. 310d; i, fol. 347b; i, fol. 347b; i, fol. 309d; i, fol. 309d; i, fol. 309d; i, fol. 309d; i, fol. 309d; Lindsey Survey, BL ms Cotton Claudius C v, fols 9–18; Lindsey Survey, BL ms Cotton Claudius C v, fols 9–18; Clay, Early Yorkshire Charters (1936), V, No. 352; Clay, Early Yorkshire Charters (1936), V, No. 279

Picot De Percy

Norman, Domesday tenant of William de Percy, of whom he may have been a relative. He was succeeded c.1114 by Robert, perhaps his son, ancestor of the family of Percy of Bolton Percy (EYC xi, 104). A list of donations to Whitby includes reference to a grant by Robert de Percy, son of Pichot de Percy, of the church of Sutton (Mon. Ang. i, 410–11); Picot held Sutton upon Derwent in 1086.

i, fol. 322c; i, fol. 321c; Clay, Early Yorkshire Charters (1955), XI, No. 98; Clay, Early Yorkshire Charters (1955), XI, No. 2; Clay, Early Yorkshire Charters (1955), XI, No. 4; Clay, Early Yorkshire Charters (1955), XI, No. 97

Picot De Sai

Norman, Robert Picot de Sai, Orne, arr. and cant. Argentan (Loyd, 96). Domesday tenant of Earl Roger in Shropshire. Benefactor of the Montgomery foundation at Saint-Martin-de-Sées, where he occurs with his wife Adeloia (previously the wife of William de Coimes) and sons Robert and Henry, and in association with his brother Payn de Sai and an Oismelin de Sai (Gall. Christ. xi, Inst. 152–3, Arch. dépt. Orne H938, fol. 99). He was succeeded by his son Henry, baron of Clun, before 1121 (Sanders, 112).

i, fol. 252d; i, fol. 255d; i, fol. 25a; Rees, Cartulary of Shrewsbury Abbey (1975), No. 35; i, fol. 258b; i, fol. 258b; i, fol. 258b; i, fol. 258b; i, fol. 258b; i, fol. 258b; i, fol. 258b; i, fol. 258b; i, fol. 258b; i, fol. 258b; i, fol. 258b; i, fol. 258b; i, fol. 258b; i, fol. 258b; i, fol. 258a; i, fol. 258a; i, fol. 258a; i, fol. 258a; i, fol. 258a; i, fol. 258a; i, fol. 258b; i, fol. 258b

Pincun []

Domesday tenant of Alberic de Vere; possibly the same as Phanceon, a Breton tenant of Count Alan, or possibly the same as the man the Abingdon Chronicle, ii, 59, calls Picot, dapifer of Alberic c.1105/11.

ii, fol. 076b

Pirot []

Important tenant of Eudo Dapifer, and of Nigel d'Albini, he clearly originated in western Normandy. His name, a hypocoristic form of Peter (Pierrot), was adopted as a patronymic surname by his descendants. A Ralph Pilot or Pitot sold land in Bavent to Abbot William of Caen before 1083 (Actes caen. no 14, 108) with the assent of his lord Hubert de Ryes, brother of Eudo dapifer. The variants of this name produce a critical difficulty because Pilot is exchangeable with Pirot, but not with Picot, while Pitot is exchangeable with Picot, the difficulty being that a family descended from a Picot de Bavent (who was certainly not the same man as Pirot) occurs from the early twelfth century. His holding at Streatley, Bedfordshire, was described in Domesday as his wife's 'maritagium'. His heir Ralph Pirot occurs c.1120 and Alan Pirot in 1166. See Farrer, HKF iii, 155–7, 217–19.

ii, fol. 403b; ii, fol. 050a; i, fol. 212c; i, fol. 212c; i, fol. 197c; i, fol. 197c; i, fol. 197c; i, fol. 214c; i, fol. 214c; i, fol. 214c

Pleines De Slepe
Tenant of the abbey of Ramsey in 1086, named from his manor of Slepes, now St Ives. He occurs as a benefactor of Ramsey abbey, with his wife Beatrice and two of their sons William and Richard; their daughters were also mentioned.

i, fol. 204c; Hart, Cartularium Monasterii de Rameseia, No. XL

Polcehard []
Tenant of Henry de Ferrers in Domesday Berkshire. Oin Polcehart, probably his son, was pardoned geld in Berkshire in 1129/30. In 1166 William Polcehart held one fee of William de Wormegay, successor to the Domesday fee of Hermer de Ferrers.

i, fol. 60c; i, fol. 63d

Quenild Monialis
English nun. Occurs Domesday Gloucestershire.

i, fol. 170c

Quintin []
Domesday tenant of William de Ecouis and the bishop of Salisbury.

ii, fol. 223b; ii, fol. 225a; i, fol. 66a; i, fol. 66a

R Ouethel
Occurs Domesday Suffolk.

ii, fol. 440a

Rabel Artifex
Norman, occurs Domesday Norfolk. In 1111 the holding of Robert son of Rabel was given by Henry I to Robert fitz Walter (RRAN ii, 987).

ii, fol. 117a; ii, fol. 269b; ii, fol. 269b; ii, fol. 269b; ii, fol. 269b; ii, fol. 269b; ii, fol. 279b; ii, fol. 279b; ii, fol. 279b

Rabel []
Domesday tenant of Robert of Mortain in Cornwall, with a relatively uncommon personal name. Cf. Hubert son of Rabel de Moscuns (Montchamp, Calvados, cant. Le Beny-Bocage) who was a benefactor of Troarn in 1119 (BN lat. 10086, fols 64–5).

i, fol. 125a; i, fol. 125a

Rademer []
Fleming, Domesday tenant of Gilbert de Gand. His grandson William fitz Walter married a sister of Gilbert de Gand, earl of Lincoln. (Rot. de Dom., 9). His sons Walter and Gilbert (q.v.) occur in the Lindsey Survey of 1115/18 and in 1129/30.

i, fol. 355b; i, fol. 355c; i, fol. 355c; i, fol. 354c; i, fol. 354c

Radfred Presbiter
Occurs Domesday Hampshire.

i, fol. 38a

Radfrid []
Occurs Domesday Norfolk; tenant of Bury St Edmunds.

Douglas, Feudal Book of Bury St Edmunds (1932), pp. 3–21; ii, fol. 212a; ii, fol. 215b

Radulf Arbalistarius
Norman landholder in Domesday Norfolk.

ii, fol. 269a; ii, fol. 269a; ii, fol. 269a; ii, fol. 117a; ii, fol. 445a; ii, fol. 445a; ii, fol. 445a; ii, fol. 445a; ii, fol. 445a

Radulf Baiard
Ralph, tenant of the bishop of London at Albury, Hertfordshire, in 1086, was succeeded by the Baard family of whom he was probably the ancestor (cf. VCH Herts iv, 5). The Baards were from the Cotentin, occurring as benefactors of the abbeys of Montebourg and Saint-Sauveur (Delisle, Saint-Sauveur, piece justif. 45/50–55, Arch. Calvados F 5276).

i, fol. 133d; i, fol. 133d; Hamilton, Inquisitio Eliensis (1876), pp. 97–100

Radulf Baignard
Norman tenant-in-chief, from Saint-Leger-des-Rôtes, Eure, sheriff of Essex and London sometime between 1072 and 1080/6, who gave his name to Baynard's Castle. He died close to the date of Domesday Book, when he was lord of Little Dunmow, Essex (Sanders, 129). His principal tenant, Geoffrey Bainard (q.v.), was probably his son and successor of that name. R. Mortimer, 'The Baynards of Baynards Castle', Studies in Medieval History Presented to R. Allen Brown, ed. Harper-Bill et al. (Woodbridge, 1989).

ii, fol. 227b; ii, fol. 109b; ii, fol. 68b; ii, fol. 413b; ii, fol. 275a; ii, fol. 275a; ii, fol. 275a; ii, fol. 275a; ii, fol. 275a; ii, fol. 275b; ii, fol. 275b; ii, fol. 275b; ii, fol. 275b; ii, fol. 275b; ii, fol. 275a; ii, fol. 004b; ii, fol. 013b; ii, fol. 008b; ii, fol. 014b; ii, fol. 414b; ii, fol. 69a; ii, fol. 415b; ii, fol. 69b; ii, fol. 031a; ii, fol. 70a; ii, fol. 071a; ii, fol. 071a; ii, fol. 101a; ii, fol. 101a; ii, fol. 002a; ii, fol. 69b; ii, fol. 414a; ii, fol. 414b; ii, fol. 414a; ii, fol. 69a; ii, fol. 414a; ii, fol. 414a; ii, fol. 414a; ii, fol. 414a; ii, fol. 413b; ii, fol. 413b; ii, fol. 415a; ii, fol. 415b; ii, fol. 415b; ii, fol. 415b; ii, fol. 415b; ii, fol. 413b; ii, fol. 006b; ii, fol. 107a; ii, fol. 247b; ii, fol. 251a; ii, fol. 251a; ii, fol. 251a; ii, fol. 250b; ii, fol. 250b; ii, fol. 250b; ii, fol. 250b; ii, fol. 251a; ii, fol. 251a; ii, fol. 250b; ii, fol. 253a; ii, fol. 251b; ii, fol. 252a; ii, fol. 251a; ii, fol. 252a; ii, fol. 252a; ii, fol. 252a; ii, fol. 252b; ii, fol. 252b; ii, fol. 252b; ii, fol. 251b; ii, fol. 253a; ii, fol. 253a; ii, fol. 253a; ii, fol. 251a; ii, fol. 251a; ii, fol. 251a; ii, fol. 252b; ii, fol. 251a; ii, fol. 253b; ii, fol. 251b; ii, fol. 251b; ii, fol. 251b; ii, fol. 251b; Gibbs, Early Charters of St Pauls (1939), No. 4; Douglas, ed., Domesday Monachorum (1944), p. 105; i, fol. 138c; i, fol. 31d; i, fol. 16b; i, fol. 128b; i, fol. 31a; i, fol. 138b; ii, fol. 248b; i, fol. 132a; ii, fol. 249b; ii, fol. 250b; ii, fol. 250b; ii, fol. 250b; ii, fol. 250a; ii, fol. 250a; ii, fol. 250a; ii, fol. 247b; ii, fol. 249b; ii, fol. 247b; ii, fol. 249b; ii, fol. 249b; ii, fol. 249b; ii, fol. 249b; ii, fol. 249a; ii, fol. 249a; ii, fol. 249a; ii, fol. 249a; ii, fol. 248b; ii, fol. 248a; ii, fol. 249b; ii, fol. 247b

Radulf Basset
Domesday tenant of Robert de Oilli in Buckinghamshire. Ancestor of a prolific family of royal adminstrators. Served as a justiciar under Henry I. Father of Richard, Nicholas, Turstin and Ralph, a clerk. The family originated at Montreuil-au-Houlme, Orne, arr. Argentan, cant. Briouze (Loyd, 12) and gave their name to Ouilly-le-Basset (Calvados). The first to occur was Osmund Basset,

who was a vassal of the fitz Giroie kin of Hugh de Grandmesnil (q.v.); he and his brothers attested a grant by Hugh's mother Hadvise to Montivilliers c.1050; see Orderic Vitalis ii, 30. Ralph's prominence under Henry I was such as to attract the label of 'new man . . . raised from the dust' from Orderic (ibid. vi, 16). Land in the allod of Ralph Basset at Fonatanias Obsimine (perhaps Fontaine-Halbout, Calvados, arr. Falaise, comm. Bretteville-sur-Laize). was confirmed to Saint-Evroul by Henry I in 1113 (Ord. Vit. ed. Le Prévost v, 196–9).

> Dugdale, Monasticon Anglicanum, III, pp. 86–87, No. VIII; Hart, Cartularium Monasterii de Rameseia, No. CLXIV; Round, Ancient Charters (1888), No. 6; Pipe Roll 31 Henry I, 123–bk; Pipe Roll 31 Henry I, 110–ln; Pipe Roll 31 Henry I, 096–sf; Pipe Roll 31 Henry I, 092–nf; Pipe Roll 31 Henry I, 009a–ntdb; Pipe Roll 31 Henry I, 018–wl; Pipe Roll 31 Henry I, 145–lo; Pipe Roll 31 Henry I, 009b–ntdb; Pipe Roll 31 Henry I, 019–wl; Pipe Roll 31 Henry I, 101a–bu; Pipe Roll 31 Henry I, 031–ynb; Pipe Roll 31 Henry I, 124–bk; Pipe Roll 31 Henry I, 049a–sr; Pipe Roll 31 Henry I, 049b–sr; Pipe Roll 31 Henry I, 114–ln; Gibbs, Early Charters of St Pauls (1939), No. 46; Pipe Roll 31 Henry I, 101b–bu; Regesta Regum Anglo Normannorum II, App. no. cxxvii ; i, fol. 149c; Chibnall, English Lands of Abbey of Bec (1951), No. XVII; Hart, Cartularium Monasterii de Rameseia, No. CLXXVIII; Red Book of the Exchequer, ed. Hall (1897), pp. 329–31; Salter, Cartulary of Oseney Abbey (1929–36), No. 1047; i, fol. 137d

Radulf Bloiet
Occurs in Domesday Somerset and Hampshire as a tenant of William of Eu. Benefactor of St Peter's, Gloucester, in the time of William II (Hist. S. Petri i, 110). Probably related to Robert Bloet, bishop of Lincoln from 1094–1123 whose family is discussed by R. Foreville in Studia Anselmiana xli (Rome, 1957), 21 n. The Bloets are strongly evidenced in west Normandy, at Doumesnil, Bricqueville-la-Blouette, Manche, comm. cant. Coutances, and elsewhere (Actes caen. nos. 8, 14; Gall. Christ. xi, Inst. 228, etc.).

> i, fol. 166d; i, fol. 96c; i, fol. 96c; Ellis, 'Landholders of Gloucestershire' (1880), pp. 91–93; i, fol. 47b; Regesta regum Anglo-Normannorum III, No. 345

Radulf Botin
Norman, occurs Domesday Devon as a tenant of William Hostiarius. His surname is supplied by Exon. Ralph Botin and his brother Walter Botin were benefactors of St Nicholas, Exeter, in the twelfth century (BL Cotton Vit. D ix, fol. 44v).

> i, fol. 117d

Radulf Camerarius
Domesday tenant and chamberlain of Archbishop Lanfranc.

> i, fol. 004a; Ballard, Inquisition of St Augustine's (1920), fols 20r–23v; i, fol. 003d; i, fol. 003b

Radulf Canonicus Sancti Martini
Canon of Dover, occurs Domesday Kent.

> i, fol. 001c; Ballard, Inquisition of St Augustine's (1920), fols 24r–28r

Radulf Carnotensis
Occurs Domesday Leicestershire as tenant of lands once held in chief by Aubrey de Coucy. Richard l'Abbe held his fee at Wanlip c.1156; HKF i, 219.

> i, fol. 231d; i, fol. 231d; i, fol. 231d

Radulf Chesneduit

Norman, perhaps named from Chéneduit, near Putanges, Orne, though the name is rarely expressed as a toponym; Chesnedouit was a fief of Briouze. Tenant of Robert de Mortain in 1086 in Bedfordshire. He married Alice, who brought him land at Cheddington, Buckinghamshire. He appears to have died between 1100 and 1116, as suggested by a charter of Henry I confirming an agreement between Simon Chesneduit and the abbot of Thorney (RRAN ii, app. xxxiii). Between 1118 and c.1129 Henry I confirmed to Nostell the grant of Alice widow of Ralph Chesneduit and her sons Simon and Hugh (RRAN ii, 1678, and p. 371, no. ccxlv). His successor Simon was dead by 1129.

  i, fol. 136d; i, fol. 146c; i, fol. 146c; i, fol. 146c; i, fol. 146c; i, fol. 146d; i, fol. 146b; i, fol. 146c; i, fol. 157b; i, fol. 223c; i, fol. 223c; i, fol. 223c; i, fol. 223c; i, fol. 223c; i, fol. 223c; i, fol. 223c; i, fol. 223c; i, fol. 223c; i, fol. 223b; i, fol. 223b; i, fol. 223b

Radulf Cocus

Norman, Domesday tenant, and presumably cook, to Helgot of Castle Holgate in Shropshire.

  i, fol. 259b

Radulf Dapifer

Tenant of the wife of Hugh fitz Griip in Domesday Dorset; identified as steward in Exon.

  i, fol. 83d

Radulf Dapifer

Norman, from Montpinçon, Calvados, arr. Lisieux, cant. Saint-Pierre-sur-Dives (Loyd, 69), occurs Domesday Lincolnshire. Described as 'Radulf de Monte Pincionis, dapifer Guillelmo magni regis Anglorum' by Orderic Vitalis (iii, 164), he occurs in Domesday as Radulfus dapifer. According to Orderic, he was devoted to Saint-Evroul, and endowed the entry there of a worthy clerk, a scholar of Rheims named John. He died on a 13 February between 1080 and 1103 (ibid.). Orderic mentions that two of his sons, Hugh and Ralph, were present with their mother Adelisa at their father's funeral, when they confirmed their father's gifts to Saint-Evroul. Hugh was probably already married to Matilda, daughter of Hugh de Grandmesnil (d.1098) (ibid. 166). His heir in England by the time of the Lindsey Survey, 1115/18, was Richard de Montpincon, presumably another of his sons.

  i, fol. 342a; i, fol. 224b; i, fol. 366c; i, fol. 366c

Radulf De Bachepuis

Norman, occurs in Domesday Book as a tenant of Henry de Ferrers. From Bacquepuits, Eure, arr. and cant. Evreux (Loyd, 10). Both he and his son and successor Henry were dead by 1113, when they had been succeeded by another son, Robert (Chron. Abingdon, ii, 121).

  i, fol. 274c; i, fol. 274c; i, fol. 274c; i, fol. 60b; i, fol. 60c; Dugdale, Monasticon Anglicanum, III, pp. 392–93, No. II

Radulf De Badpalmas

Norman, probably named from Bapeaume-lés-Rouen, Seine-Maritime, occurs Domesday Lincolnshire.

  i, fol. 336b

Radulf De Bans

Norman, tenant in Cambridgeshire of Count Alan, Picot the Sheriff and Guy de Raimbeaucourt; also a Domesday juror in Thriplow Hundred. From Baons-le-Comte, Seine-Maritime. His successor by 1129/30 was William de Bans.

i, fol. 194a; i, fol. 200b; i, fol. 200a; i, fol. 200a; i, fol. 200d; i, fol. 200d; i, fol. 200d; i, fol. 200d; Hamilton, Inquisitio Eliensis (1876), pp. 97–100; G. Fowler, Early Cambridgeshire Feodary, EHR (1932), pp. 442–3; i, fol. 189a; Hamilton, Inquisitio Eliensis (1876), pp. 97–100; Hamilton, Inquisitio Comitatus Cantabrigiensis, pp. 1–93; Hamilton, Inquisitio Comitatus Cantabrigiensis, pp. 1–93

Radulf De Bellofago

Norman, Domesday lord of Hockering, Norfolk. Probably named from Beaufour, Calvados, cant. Cambremer. Probably the same as Ralph de Bellofago sheriff of Norfolk c.1108–1111/1115, possibly of Suffolk c.1091–1102. He is likely to have been a member of a family which produced William, bishop of Thetford in 1086 (q.v.), and the wife of Hugh de Montfort, descended from their ancestor Richard de Beaufour. He married Agnes, daughter of Robert de Tosny of Belvoir and Adelais and had issue a son Richard. He was doubtless also father of a son Ralph. His widow, as Agnes de Bellofago, married secondly Hubert I de Ryes, who took over the tenancy-in-chief of Hockering, despite the fact that Ralph and Agnes had surviving male issue.

ii, fol. 318b; Regesta Regum Anglo Normannorum II, App. no. cxxvii ; ii, fol. 138a; Dugdale, Monasticon Anglicanum, IV, pp. 150–51, No. VIII; Brown, Eye Priory Cartulary (1992–94), No. 9; ii, fol. 279a; ii, fol. 279a; ii, fol. 279a; ii, fol. 354b; ii, fol. 214b; ii, fol. 354b; ii, fol. 354a; ii, fol. 137b; ii, fol. 118a; ii, fol. 354b; ii, fol. 110b; ii, fol. 354a; ii, fol. 229a; ii, fol. 229b; ii, fol. 229b; ii, fol. 229b; ii, fol. 229b; ii, fol. 229b; ii, fol. 229b; ii, fol. 229a; ii, fol. 229a; ii, fol. 229a; ii, fol. 229a; ii, fol. 230a; ii, fol. 230a; ii, fol. 229b; ii, fol. 228a; ii, fol. 227b; ii, fol. 228a; ii, fol. 228a; ii, fol. 228b; ii, fol. 228b; ii, fol. 228a; ii, fol. 229a; ii, fol. 229a; ii, fol. 228a; ii, fol. 228b; ii, fol. 230a; ii, fol. 228b; ii, fol. 228b; ii, fol. 228a; ii, fol. 230a; ii, fol. 226b; ii, fol. 227a; ii, fol. 229a; ii, fol. 225b; ii, fol. 229a; ii, fol. 226a; ii, fol. 226a; ii, fol. 226b; ii, fol. 226a; ii, fol. 226b; ii, fol. 226b; ii, fol. 226a; ii, fol. 227a; ii, fol. 227a; ii, fol. 227a; ii, fol. 227a; Douglas, Social Structure of Med. E. Anglia (1927), No. 35; ii, fol. 226a; ii, fol. 230a; ii, fol. 229b; ii, fol. 230a; ii, fol. 228b; ii, fol. 226a; ii, fol. 228b; ii, fol. 227b; ii, fol. 229b; ii, fol. 230a; ii, fol. 230a; ii, fol. 229a; ii, fol. 230a; ii, fol. 230a; ii, fol. 230a; ii, fol. 229b; ii, fol. 229b; ii, fol. 229b; ii, fol. 229b; ii, fol. 228b; Brown, Eye Priory Cartulary (1992–94), No. 10; ii, fol. 225b; Hart, Cartularium Monasterii de Rameseia, No. LXXXI; ii, fol. 319a; ii, fol. 319a

Radulf De Berchelai

Norman, brother of Roger (q.v.), occurs Domesday Gloucestershire.

i, fol. 168b; i, fol. 168b; i, fol. 168b

Radulf De Bernai

Norman from Bernay, Eure, a tenant of William fitz Osbern and sheriff under him in Herefordshire. Notoriously rapacious as sheriff, he did not survive the fall of William's heir Earl Roger. He was imprisoned and his fees declared forfeit some time before 1086. Cf. C. Lewis in Anglo-Norman Studies vii (1985), 207–8.

i, fol. 180c; i, fol. 179c

Radulf De Brueria
Norman, Domesday tenant of Baldwin of Exeter. His successor in 1166 was
Antony de Brueria, who held five fees of Robert fitz Roy.

i, fol. 108b; i, fol. 106b; i, fol. 106a; i, fol. 108b; i, fol. 106c; i, fol. 106c

Radulf De Buceio
Ralph fitz Landric de Buceio, from Boucé, Orne arr. Argentan (Loyd, 21), tenant
of William de Braose in Sussex; attested Braose charters for Sele Priory, a cell of
Saint-Florent-de Saumur (CDF 1110, 1112). In another such charter (ibid. 1132)
he attested with Leuuinus his 'armiger', perhaps the English tenant of that name
who also occurs on the Braose fief in 1086.

i, fol. 28c; i, fol. 28c; i, fol. 28c; i, fol. 28c; i, fol. 29a

Radulf De Burun
Norman, from Buron, Calvados. Domesday lord of Horsley, Derbyshire.
Apparently dead by 1102. Succeeded by Hugh de Buron, d.1156 (Sanders, 122–3).

i, fol. 277c; i, fol. 277c; i, fol. 277c; i, fol. 280a; i, fol. 290a; i, fol. 290a; i, fol.
290a; i, fol. 290a; i, fol. 290a

Radulf De Caisned
Norman, from Le Quesnay, Seine-Maritime, arr. Neufchâtel, cant. and comm.
Saint-Saëns (Loyd, 27–8), Domesday tenant of William de Warenne and others.
His wife Matilda predeceased him and he made grants for her soul to Lewes priory.
He was succeeded in the early twelfth century by his son William, and eventually
by the issue of his son Ralph; father also of Hugh and Sibil, wife of Robert fitz
Walter de Caen.

i, fol. 26c; ii, fol. 159b; i, fol. 27c; ii, fol. 169b; ii, fol. 169a; ii, fol. 171a; i, fol.
159c; i, fol. 129c; i, fol. 17b; Clay, Early Yorkshire Charters (1949), VIII, No. 5;
Dugdale, Monasticon Anglicanum, IV, p. 14, No. VI; Clay, Early Yorkshire
Charters (1949), VIII, No. 13; Clay, Early Yorkshire Charters (1949), VIII, No.
12; Douglas, Social Structure of Med. E. Anglia (1927), No. 4; ii, fol. 157a; ii,
fol. 157a; ii, fol. 161a; ii, fol. 160b; ii, fol. 160b; ii, fol. 170a; ii, fol. 169b; ii, fol.
169b; i, fol. 27a; i, fol. 27a; i, fol. 27a; i, fol. 27b; i, fol. 27c; i, fol. 27c

Radulf De Contevilla
One of two tenants named Ralph holding of Walter de Douai and the abbot of
Glastonbury in 1086, he is identified by Exon Domesday. Probably from one of
two Contevilles in Pas-de-Calais, Conteville near Saint-Pol-sur-Ternoise, or
Conteville-lès-Boulogne. Winebald of Ballon's grant of Upton to Bermondsey
priory (prob. c.1093–1112) was attested by Ralph de Conteville, his wife Holdiard
and their daughters Matilda and Hawise (BL Harley 4757, fol. 7). Richard de
Conteville was Glastonbury's tenant in 1189 (Feodary, p. 95).

i, fol. 112a; i, fol. 112a; i, fol. 95b; i, fol. 90d; i, fol. 95a; Douglas, Feudal
Documents from Bury St Edmunds, No. 108; Hunt, Bath Chartulary, Som. Rec.
Soc. 7 (1893), No. 35; Watkin, Chartulary of Glastonbury 3, SRS 64 (1950), pp.
126–28; i, fol. 95c; i, fol. 95c

Radulf De Creneburne
Tenant of the abbot of Cranborne in 1086; so named in the Tax Return for
Cranborne Hundred. Probably ancestor of Warin of Cranborne (q.v.) who was
sheriff of Dorset in 1164.

i, fol. 77d; i, fol. 83b

Radulf De Curbespine
Norman, from Courbépine, Eure, arr. Bernay, a tenant of Odo of Bayeux, St Augustine's and Hugh de Montfort in Domesday Kent. Probably a relative of Gilbert Maminot, bishop of Lisieux, who was a son of Robert de Courbépine. His Domesday manors descended in the Maminot family from Hugh Maminot, son of Bishop Gilbert (cf. VCH Herts ii, 27).

i, fol. 134d; i, fol. 008b; i, fol. 008b; Ballard, Inquisition of St Augustine's (1920), fols 24r–28r; i, fol. 012c; i, fol. 011d; ii, fol. 373b; ii, fol. 374a; i, fol. 007c; i, fol. 011b; i, fol. 002a; i, fol. 002a; i, fol. 007c; i, fol. 011d; i, fol. 001a; i, fol. 002b; i, fol. 011d; i, fol. 013b; i, fol. 011c; i, fol. 011b; i, fol. 011a; i, fol. 011a; i, fol. 010d; i, fol. 010d; i, fol. 010d; i, fol. 010c; i, fol. 009d; i, fol. 009d; i, fol. 011d; i, fol. 011c

Radulf De Dene
Norman tenant of Robert de Mortain in Domesday Sussex, known from his tenure at West Dean as Ralph de Dene. A detailed analysis of the descent of his holdings indicates that they passed by marriage (probably with his daughter) to Alfred pincerna (q.v.).

i, fol. 20c; i, fol. 21d; i, fol. 21d; i, fol. 22a; i, fol. 21b; i, fol. 22a; i, fol. 20d; i, fol. 21a; i, fol. 21a; i, fol. 21b; i, fol. 21b; i, fol. 21b; i, fol. 21d; i, fol. 22c; i, fol. 22d; i, fol. 22c

Radulf De Felgeres
Domesday tenant of Harduin de Scalariis and a juror in Cambridgeshire; Lewis, 'Jurors', 38; VCH Cambs ix, 344. Ancestor of a tenant family of the honour of Richmond, to be distinguished from that of the seigneurs of Fougères. Alan de Felgeres held one fee of Hugh de Scalariis in 1166.

i, fol. 199a; Hamilton, Inquisitio Eliensis (1876), pp. 97–100

Radulf De Ferno
Occurs as a knight of Archbishop Lanfranc; probably the Ralph holding at Lavant in Sussex (Du Boulay, Lordship of Canterbury, 352), jointly with William Pollex by 1093–6.

i, fol. 16c; Douglas, ed., Domesday Monachorum (1944), p. 105

Radulf De Filgeriis
Ralph I seigneur de Fougères in Brittany (dépt. Ille-et-Vilaine). Succeeded his father Main II c.1064 as a minor. Before 1086 had married Avice, daughter of Richard de Clare and Rohais Giffard and become a tenant-in-chief in England, which he probably never visited (Keats-Rohan, 'Le rôle des Bretons dans la politique de la colonisation normande', MSHAB, lxxiv, 1996, 192). The identity of his wife was given by Robert of Torigny in his Interpolations to The Gesta Normannorum Ducum of Guillaume of Jumièges (ed. van Houts, ii, 270), where Robert names their sons as Fransualo, Henri and Robert Gifard. The information is confirmed elsewhere, for when Ralph died in 1124 his son Main Fransgualo visited his English property, but died at Winchester and was buried in St Swithin's, after which the following entry was made in the mortuary roll of Abbot Vitalis: Orate et pro speciali fundatore ecclesie nostre. domino Frangswalone. et domino Gileberto Ricardi filio, avunculi eius (brother of Avice de Bienfaite) (Rouleau Mortuaire du B. Vital abbé de Savigni, edn phototypique par L. Delisle Paris (1909), titre no. 182). Ralph was then succeeded as seigneur by his son Henry. The

third son, Robert Giffard, was given the escheated lordship of Weare in Devon by
Henry I before 1129/30.

i, fol. 36c; ii, fol. 263a; i, fol. 151c; i, fol. 151c; i, fol. 63d; ii, fol. 263a; i, fol. 36c;
i, fol. 151c; ii, fol. 263a; ii, fol. 432b; ii, fol. 278a; ii, fol. 432b; ii, fol. 432a; ii,
fol. 432a; i, fol. 113d; i, fol. 113d

Radulf De Greinville

Norman, from Grainville-la-Teinturière, Seine-Maritime, arr. Yvetot, cant. Cany
(Loyd, 47); probably the Ralph who held a single manor in Domesday
Buckinghamshire from Walter Giffard as suggested by Early Bucks. Chh., no. 1.
Before 1087 Ralph de Granvilla attested a charter for Cerisy by Walter Giffard.
Subsequently there were separate English and Norman branches of the family.
suggesting that Ralph was succeeded by two sons. The Norman branch was related
to Walter II Giffard, whose wife Agnes de Ribemont's sister Fredesende was
mother of Eustache fitz Eustache de Greinville; see Le Maho, 45. Gerard de
Greinville was pardoned Danegeld in Buckinghamshire in 1129/30.

i, fol. 147b

Radulf De Hairun

Official and probably tenant of Geoffrey I de Mandeville c.1086. Richard and
Ralph de Hairun were Mandeville tenants in 1166. Named from Le Héron,
Seine-Maritime, cant. Darnétal. Cf. Fauroux, 39.

ii, fol. 058b; Mason, Westminster Abbey Charters (1988), No. 436; Mason,
Westminster Abbey Charters (1988), No. 436; Mason, Westminster Abbey
Charters (1988), No. 462

Radulf De Haluile

Occurs as a king's servant in Domesday Wiltshire. Possibly named from
Hauville-en-Roumois, Eure, cant. Routot.

i, fol. 74c; i, fol. 74c; i, fol. 74c

Radulf De Hastinges

Norman, occurs Domesday Essex; father of Robert who also occurs in Domesday.
Probably named from Hastings, Suffffolk, a fee of Roger de Raimes.

ii, fol. 083b

Radulf De Insula

Norman, occurs Domesday Bedfordshire. William I confirmed to Montivilliers,
before 1073, the gift of Robert de Insula, with his wife and sons Ralph and Robert,
of the tithe of the church of Manneville-ès-Plains, Seine-Maritime, cant.
Saint-Valery-en-Caux, for his daughter Adeleia, a nun (Gall. Christ. xi, App.
329D; Bouvris, Montivilliers, no. 29).

i, fol. 217a; i, fol. 217a; i, fol. 217a; i, fol. 217a; i, fol. 217a

Radulf De Langetot

Norman, from Lanquetot, Seine-Maritime, arr. Le Havre, cant. Bolbec, a follower
and tenant of Walter I Giffard (Loyd, 53). Tenant of Abingdon Abbey in the early
twelfth century, His daughters were Matilda wife of Ranulf fitz Walter and Alice
wife of Roger de Chesny. Matilda occurs as sister of Ranulf de Langetoth in a
confirmation charter for Thetford by Walter Giffard (BL Lansdowne 229, fol.
145v); this was probably the Ralph de Langetot of 1129.

i, fol. 157c; i, fol. 148a; i, fol. 148a; i, fol. 147d; i, fol. 147d; i, fol. 147d; Douglas,

'Some early surveys of Abingdon' (1929), E.H.R., 44 (1929), 623–25; i, fol. 211c; i, fol. 211c; i, fol. 211c; i, fol. 211c; ii, fol. 430a; ii, fol. 430a; ii, fol. 430a

Radulf De Limeseio

Norman from Limésy, Seine-Maritime, arr. Rouen, cant. Pavilly (Loyd, 54). Domesday tenant-in-chief, lord of Cavendish, Suffolk. Founder, c.1093, with his wife A. of Hertford priory, a cell of St Albans. Appears to have died soon after 1093 leaving a son Ralph II, d.c.1129. He was probably the father of Matilda, wife of Nicholas of Stafford (q.v.). A Hugh de Limesi occurs in a charter of c.1070 for Sainte-Trinité de Rouen (Guérard, Cart., p. 439). Sanders, 29.

ii, fol. 090b; ii, fol. 090b; ii, fol. 090b; ii, fol. 002b; ii, fol. 002b; ii, fol. 002b; ii, fol. 090b; ii, fol. 090a; ii, fol. 090a; ii, fol. 090a; Dugdale, Monasticon Anglicanum, III, pp. 299–300, No. I; Dugdale, Monasticon Anglicanum, III, pp. 299–300, No. I; i, fol. 164a; i, fol. 97a; ii, fol. 428b; ii, fol. 428b; ii, fol. 429a; ii, fol. 429a; i, fol. 97a; ii, fol. 429a; ii, fol. 428b; i, fol. 97a; ii, fol. 428b; ii, fol. 428b; ii, fol. 428a; ii, fol. 428a; ii, fol. 429a; i, fol. 91b; i, fol. 140b; i, fol. 39a; i, fol. 113c; i, fol. 113c; i, fol. 140b; i, fol. 113c; ii, fol. 428a; i, fol. 289d; i, fol. 289d; i, fol. 289d; i, fol. 289d; i, fol. 289d; i, fol. 289d; i, fol. 289d; i, fol. 97a; i, fol. 243a; ii, fol. 449a; i, fol. 238a; i, fol. 97a; i, fol. 289d; i, fol. 97a; ii, fol. 429a; ii, fol. 429a; i, fol. 225c; i, fol. 243a; i, fol. 97a; i, fol. 289d; ii, fol. 428a; ii, fol. 245a; ii, fol. 245a; ii, fol. 245a; ii, fol. 245a; i, fol. 138b; i, fol. 138b; i, fol. 138b; i, fol. 138b; i, fol. 138b

Radulf De Marci

Tenant of Haimo Dapifer, a west Norman. There is a Marcy (-les-Grèves) near Avranches, Manche. Apparently the same as the tenant of Count Eustache, from he held land at Higham, Suffolk (DB 05.6). RRAN iii, 234 is a confirmation to St John's Colchester of a grant at land in the same manor by Ida wife of Radulf de Marci. Ralph was possibly from Marcy near Homblières, or Marcy-sous-Marle, both dépt. Aisne, but his connexion with Eustache most likely arose through his wife, who shared the name Ida, not then found in Norman families, with Eustache's wife. A charter for the Hospitallers of c.1200 by Beatrice de Lucy of land in Chrishall, Essex (Cart. St John, no. 217), a manor entered only under Count Eustache's name in Domesday Book, was attested by domino Serlone de Marci and domino Hamone de Marci. An earlier Serlo was probably Ralph's son and successor. Haimo son of Serlo de Marci occurs in PR 31 Henry I, 54. Serlo de Marceio and his wife Mabilia occur among the benefactors of St Albans Abbey (BL Cott. Nero D vii, 98r), to which they gave land at Fifhide and Parndon which had been held in 1086 by Junain from Eustache de Boulogne; Mabel was probably Junain's heiress. Cf. Cart Saint-Sauveur-le-Vicomte, BN lat. 17137, fols 20v–21, Euuina wife of Ralph de Marceio, with Albreda her daughter, grants land held in dower in Bretteville and Guillemaisnil for the souls of her husband and her son Simon, attested by William fitz Robert, Osmund, Robert fitz Haimonis. William de Manneville, brother of Roger de Sottewast, makes a grant for the death of Simon de Marceio in the presence of vicomte Roger (k. 1137) (ibid. fol. 23).

ii, fol. 056a; ii, fol. 054b; ii, fol. 055a; ii, fol. 002b; ii, fol. 303b; ii, fol. 026b; ii, fol. 028a; ii, fol. 032b; ii, fol. 055a; ii, fol. 055a; ii, fol. 055a; ii, fol. 056a; ii, fol. 056a

Radulf De Montgomery

Norman, from Saint-Germain or Sainte-Foy-de-Montgomery, Calvados, arr. Lisieux, cant. Livarot; see Loyd, 68. Domesday tenant of Henry de Ferrers. The family held 4 fees of Earl Ferrers in 1166. Ralph is identified from Curia Regis Rolls, v, 41 and Fees, 993.

i, fol. 225a; i, fol. 275a; i, fol. 275a; i, fol. 275a; i, fol. 275a; i, fol. 275a

Radulf De Mortemer
Son of Roger de Mortemer (q.v.), whom he succeeded shortly before 1086 as lord of Wigmore (Sanders, 98). Cf. Comp. Peer. ix, 266–84. Named from Mortemer, cant. Neufchâtel-en-Bray, Seine-Maritime (Loyd, 70). Ralph became a close associate of William II, with whom he fought in Normandy in 1089–90 against Robert Curthose. In 1104 he supported Henry I against Robert Curthose. He appears to have died soon afterwards at the family's abbey of Saint-Victor-en-Caux. He was twice married, first to Melisende, who was dead by 30 March 1088 (the date of a charter for Jumièges which he attested on behalf of his man Ralph fitz Ansered, Haskins, Norm. Inst. p. 290), and secondly to Mabel. His daughter Havise, wife of Stephen count of Aumale, was the daughter of Melisende, but it unclear which of his wives was the mother of his sons Hugh and Ralph. The relationship of the Mortemers to the Warenne family is established in Keats-Rohan, 'Aspects of Robert of Torigny's Genealogies Revisted', Nottingham Medieva Studies xxxvii (1993).

i, fol. 52a; Lincolnshire Claims (Domesday Book), fols 375d–376a; i, fol. 47a; i, fol. 47a; i, fol. 47a; i, fol. 260c; i, fol. 180a; i, fol. 180a; i, fol. 183c; i, fol. 260b; i, fol. 180b; i, fol. 183c; i, fol. 183c; i, fol. 183c; i, fol. 183c; i, fol. 183c; i, fol. 183c; i, fol. 72b; i, fol. 183c; i, fol. 176c; i, fol. 180b; i, fol. 46d; i, fol. 72b; i, fol. 72b; i, fol. 72b; i, fol. 47a; i, fol. 41a; i, fol. 52a; i, fol. 45d; i, fol. 41c; i, fol. 62c; i, fol. 46d; i, fol. 47a; i, fol. 47a; i, fol. 46d; i, fol. 47a; i, fol. 47a; i, fol. 62c; i, fol. 62d; i, fol. 260a; i, fol. 46d; i, fol. 180a; i, fol. 252a; i, fol. 183d; i, fol. 183d; Lincolnshire Claims (Domesday Book), fols 376b–c; i, fol. 257a; i, fol. 183d; i, fol. 187c; i, fol. 260a; i, fol. 183d; i, fol. 183d; i, fol. 183d; i, fol. 183d; i, fol. 183d; i, fol. 183d; i, fol. 256d; i, fol. 176c; i, fol. 183c; i, fol. 260a; i, fol. 260c; i, fol. 260c; i, fol. 260c; i, fol. 260c; i, fol. 260a; i, fol. 260a; i, fol. 257a; i, fol. 176c; i, fol. 179d; i, fol. 183c; i, fol. 257a; i, fol. 257a; i, fol. 257a; i, fol. 260a; i, fol. 243a; i, fol. 159a; i, fol. 260a; i, fol. 325b; i, fol. 363a; i, fol. 235a; i, fol. 46d; i, fol. 183c; i, fol. 95d; i, fol. 176c; i, fol. 363a; i, fol. 363a; i, fol. 363a; i, fol. 363a; i, fol. 363a; i, fol. 260b; i, fol. 260b; i, fol. 260b; Darlington, Cartulary of Worcester: Reg. I (1962–3), No. 270; Regesta regum Anglo-Normannorum III, No. 964; i, fol. 325b; i, fol. 325b; i, fol. 325b; i, fol. 325c; i, fol. 325b; i, fol. 325b; i, fol. 325b; i, fol. 325b; i, fol. 325b; i, fol. 325b; i, fol. 325c; i, fol. 325b; i, fol. 325c; i, fol. 325b; i, fol. 325b; i, fol. 325b; i, fol. 325b; i, fol. 325b; i, fol. 325b; i, fol. 325c; i, fol. 325b; i, fol. 325b; i, fol. 325b; i, fol. 325b

Radulf De Neuilla
Norman, Domesday tenant of Peterborough. Hugh Candidus, p. 164: Hæres Radulfi de Nevile tenet decem carrucatas terræ in Lincolnescire, scilicet in Scottone, Malmetone. Et in Norhamtonscire unam hydam et dimidiam, scilicet in Holme, Rayniltorp, et inde facit plenum servitium trium militum. Ancestor of the Nevilles of Essex. He is possibly to be identified with the Ralph who held Habrough etc. from Alfred of Lincoln (Comp. Peer. ix, 476). He, or his successor (possibly son) of the same name witnessed the foundation charter of Bridlington priory, given c.1114 by Walter de Gand. Possibly named from Néville, Seine-Maritime, arr. Yvetot, cant. Saint-Valery; see Loyd, 72–3.

i, fol. 357d; i, fol. 357d; i, fol. 358b; i, fol. 346a; i, fol. 346a; Lincolnshire Claims

(Domesday Book), fols 376b–c; King, Peterborough Descriptio Militum (1969), pp. 97–101

Radulf De Nouo Fori

Norman, from Neufmarché, Seine-Maritime, cant. Gournai-en-Bray (cf. Loyd, 72), a Domesday tenant of Roger de Bully. He was succeeded some time after 1086 by his son William, who had died by 1129/30, when his heir was his sister and her husband William of Whatton, as appears from Blyth Priory Charters.

i, fol. 286c; Timson, Blyth Priory Cartulary (1973), No. 325

Radulf De Pomerei

Norman, from La Pommeraye, Calvados, arr. Falaise, cant. Thury-Harcourt (Loyd, 78), Domesday tenant-in-chief in Devonshire. Ralph de Pomeroy occurs in Domesday in lands associated with his brother William Capra and their sister Beatrice, who was their tenant. Also a tenant of Juhel of Totnes, his Totnes fees passed to the Haccomb family, descendants of Stephen (q.v.), before 1166. He apparently died before 1100, and was succeeded first by his son, William, who made a gift to St Peter's, Gloucester, c.1072–1104 and d.s.p. c.1114, and Jocelyn, who died before 1129/30. E. B. Powley, The House of De La Pomeroi (Liverpool, 1944); Sanders, 106.

i, fol. 105c; i, fol. 107c; i, fol. 107d; i, fol. 106d; i, fol. 109b; i, fol. 109a; i, fol. 110d; i, fol. 110c; i, fol. 110d; i, fol. 110c; i, fol. 110b; i, fol. 110c; i, fol. 109a; i, fol. 100b; i, fol. 105d; i, fol. 114d; i, fol. 114d; i, fol. 114d; i, fol. 114d; i, fol. 114a; i, fol. 114a; i, fol. 113d; i, fol. 114c; i, fol. 114b; i, fol. 114c; i, fol. 114c; i, fol. 114c; i, fol. 114b; i, fol. 114a; i, fol. 114c; i, fol. 114a; i, fol. 114b; i, fol. 114b; i, fol. 114d; i, fol. 114b; i, fol. 114c; i, fol. 114b; i, fol. 95d; i, fol. 114a; i, fol. 114a; i, fol. 114a; i, fol. 114a; i, fol. 114a; i, fol. 114a; i, fol. 114a; i, fol. 114a; i, fol. 114c; i, fol. 114a; i, fol. 114b; i, fol. 114a; i, fol. 114b; i, fol. 114d; i, fol. 95d; i, fol. 106c; i, fol. 106c; i, fol. 109a; i, fol. 109a; i, fol. 109a; i, fol. 109a; i, fol. 109a

Radulf De Roilliaco

Norman, named from Rouellé, Orne, arr. and cant. Domfront, in the Passais, tenant of Ralph Paynel in 1086. By 1166 his holdings, save those in Somerset which apparently escheated, had passed to three coheiresses, perhaps his grand-daughters, married to Matthew de Courcy, Robert de Bayeux and William de Plaiz. See EYC vi 134; Loyd, 87.

i, fol. 168b; Clay, Early Yorkshire Charters (1939), VI, No. 2; Clay, Early Yorkshire Charters (1939), VI, No. 12; Clay, Early Yorkshire Charters (1939), VI, No. 4; Clay, Early Yorkshire Charters (1939), VI, No. 4; Clay, Early Yorkshire Charters (1939), VI, No. 2; Clay, Early Yorkshire Charters (1939), VI, No. 86; Clay, Early Yorkshire Charters (1939), VI, No. 1; i, fol. 95d; i, fol. 95d; i, fol. 95d; i, fol. 95d

Radulf De Salceit

Norman, Domesday tenant of Roger de Lacy. Cf. Wightman, Lacy Family, 155 and n. 1. Named from Le Saussey, Calvados, arr. Caen, cant. Villers-Bocage, comm. Epinay-sur-Odon (Loyd, 93). His heir in 1166 was a second Ralph de Salceit.

i, fol. 167d; i, fol. 167d; i, fol. 184c; i, fol. 184b; i, fol. 184b; i, fol. 181b; Ellis, 'Landholders of Gloucestershire' (1880), pp. 91–93

Radulf De Sancto Germano

Norman, son-in-law of Picot the sheriff of Cambridge, whose daughter Agnes he married. He acquired with her land at Milton, Cambridgeshire, later the subject of dispute between Picot's descendants (Feet Fines 10 Ric. I, PR Soc. n.s. 24, 225), which he held from Picot in 1086.

i, fol. 201c

Radulf De Sancto Samsone

Norman, occurs Domesday Kent as a tenant of the canons of St Martin at Dover. Possibly named from Saint-Samson, Calvados, cant. Troarn, or from Saint-Samson-sur-Risle, Eure. The latter, in the region of Conteville, in the lordship of Odo de Bayeux's father, and Montfort-sur-Risle, another Kent landholder, was a fee of the archbishop of Dol mentioned in several early twelfth-century charters from Préaux. In one of them Osbern de St Samson occurs with his wife Havise, sons Ralph and Richard and nephew Amalric (Cart. Préaux, fol. 106v). Roger earl of Warwick (1119–53) later confirmed to Préaux the grant of Ralph de St Samson of land in Warmington, Orlavescote and Soleswella in England (ibid. fol. 48v; CDF 335). An Odo de Saint-Samson was described as 'nepos' of Bishop Odo of Bayeux in Acta Sanctorum, Jul. v, 393.

Ballard, Inquisition of St Augustine's (1920), fols 24r–28r; i, fol. 001c

Radulf De Sancto Wandregisil

Norman, Domesday tenant of Archbishop Lanfranc at Garrington, Kent; identified in Excerpta as Ralph de Saint-Wandrille, probably Saint-Wandrille-Rançon, Seine-Maritime.

i, fol. 012a; Ballard, Inquisition of St Augustine's (1920), fols 20r–23v

Radulf De Sauenie

Norman, from Savenay, Calvados, arr. Vire, cant. Villers-Bocage, comm. Courvaudon, Domesday tenant of Roger Bigod, lord of Savenay (Loyd, 14, 36). Probably father of Fulco Saviniensis, who attested a charter for Thetford of William Bigod.

ii, fol. 373b; ii, fol. 373b; ii, fol. 373b; ii, fol. 373b; ii, fol. 373b; ii, fol. 373b; ii, fol. 417a; ii, fol. 377a; ii, fol. 378b; ii, fol. 375b; ii, fol. 376b; ii, fol. 376b; ii, fol. 376b; ii, fol. 376b; ii, fol. 377a; ii, fol. 377a; ii, fol. 384b; ii, fol. 418a; ii, fol. 417b; ii, fol. 417a; ii, fol. 376b; ii, fol. 375b; Hamilton, Inquisitio Eliensis (1876), pp. 192–95; Hamilton, Inquisitio Eliensis (1876), pp. 192–95; ii, fol. 373b; ii, fol. 374a; ii, fol. 345a; ii, fol. 345a; ii, fol. 345a; ii, fol. 345a; ii, fol. 345a; ii, fol. 345a

Radulf De Stortuna

Domesday tenant of Walter de Douai (Nord), distinct from Ralph de Conteville, with whom he attested a Bath charter for Walter's wife Emmelina. His holdings were a group of manors formerly held by Alwacre, an Englishman who was a tenant of Glastonbury abbey in 1086. He has been identified, surely erroneously, with Walter's coheir Ralph Lovel (q.v.). His successor Robert of Stourton (Wiltshire) held three fees of Henry Lovel in 1166.

i, fol. 95c; i, fol. 95c; i, fol. 95c; i, fol. 72a; Hunt, Bath Chartulary, Som. Rec. Soc. 7 (1893), No. 35

Radulf De Tilio

Norman, probably named from Tilly-sur-Seulles, arr. Caen, Calvados, occurs Domesday Devonshire as a tenant of Tavistock abbey. Identified from Exon.

i, fol. 103c

Radulf De Todeni

Norman, from Tosny, Eure, arr. Louviers, cant. Gaillon (Loyd, 104), said to have fought at Hastings. Son of Roger de Tosny (d.1040), brother of the wife of William fitz Osbern and of Robert de Tosny of Stafford, like him a Domesday tenant-in-chief. He married Isabel, daughter of Simon I de Montfort-l-Amaury, by whom he left issue a son Ralph at his death early in 1102 (Sanders, 117)). Father also of Godehild, wife of Baldwin de Boulogne, later Baldwin I of Jerusalem, whom she acompanied on the First Crusade, dying in the Holy Land in 1097. He died on a 24 March, probably in 1102 and was succeeded by his son Ralph (his eldests son Roger having predeceased him); his widow survived him by several years as a nun of Haute-Bruyère, a cell of Fontevrailt (Ord. Vit. iii, 128). See L. Musset, 'Les Tosny', Francia v (1977), 45–80.

Mason, Beauchamp Cartulary Charters (1980), No. 357; ii, fol. 091a; i, fol. 52a; i, fol. 138a; i, fol. 183b; i, fol. 183b; i, fol. 183c; i, fol. 183c; i, fol. 183b; i, fol. 176a; i, fol. 176a; i, fol. 176a; i, fol. 176b; i, fol. 176b; i, fol. 176b; i, fol. 168b; i, fol. 183b; i, fol. 183b; i, fol. 183b; i, fol. 176b; i, fol. 176a; i, fol. 183b; i, fol. 138a; i, fol. 168b; ii, fol. 136b; ii, fol. 232a; ii, fol. 236a; ii, fol. 236a; ii, fol. 236a; ii, fol. 236a; ii, fol. 245a; ii, fol. 235b; ii, fol. 236a; ii, fol. 236a; ii, fol. 236a; ii, fol. 236a; ii, fol. 235b; ii, fol. 236a; ii, fol. 236b; ii, fol. 235a; ii, fol. 235b; ii, fol. 235a; ii, fol. 235a; ii, fol. 235b; ii, fol. 235b; ii, fol. 235b; ii, fol. 235b; ii, fol. 235a; ii, fol. 236a; ii, fol. 236b; ii, fol. 235a; ii, fol. 236b; ii, fol. 235a; ii, fol. 235b; ii, fol. 235a; ii, fol. 236a; ii, fol. 236b; ii, fol. 236b; ii, fol. 235b; ii, fol. 235a

Radulf De Turlauilla

Domesday tenant of Roger Bigod. Named perhaps from Tourville-en-Auge, Calvados. Apparently succeeded by Robert de Turlaville by 1129.

ii, fol. 340b; ii, fol. 339a; ii, fol. 341b; ii, fol. 341a; ii, fol. 341b; ii, fol. 341b; ii, fol. 173b; ii, fol. 173b; ii, fol. 173b; ii, fol. 173b

Radulf Fatatus

Domesday tenant of Peter de Valognes in Essex and Norfolk. His byname occurs in various forms. In a charter of Saint-Vincent du Mans of c.1068 (Cart., 490), one Fatetus brother of a Reginald fitz Hubert, occurs. Fatatus was probably not a patronymic but a byname from the Latin 'fatare, fatatus', from Fata, goddess of Destiny, meaning 'enchanted'. Its vernacular form might suggest modern French fâcheux, 'troublesome'. Cf. also the occurrence of a Robert Affectatus whose tithe at Bretteville-l'Orguilleuse (Calvados) was given to Grestain before 1082. The manors held by this Ralph were held in 1166 by his daughter Agnes, widow of Fulk of Montpincon, mother of several children including her son and heir Ralph. Agnes gave a number of charters for Binham priory in which she confirmed the grants of her father Ralph Fatatus of land in Parva Ryburgh, made, with the consent of Roger I de Valognes, for the soul of Peter I de Valognes (d.c.1109), at the time Ralph became a monk of the house (BL Cotton Claudius D xiii, fol. 164v). Fulk de Montpincon occurs with Roger son of Peter I de Valognes (Mon. Ang. iii, 346), Ralph of Ruiburc and Ralph and Ranulf 'Faed'. The last two were perhaps sons of Ralph who predeceased him or his nephews. The long suit between Agnes and Adam fitz Alfred (q.v.) concerning Ryburgh suggests that Adam's wife Bertha was also a daughter of Ralph Fatatus.

ii, fol. 257a; ii, fol. 256b; Dodwell, Charters relating to the Honour of Bacton, No. 2; Dugdale, Monasticon Anglicanum, III, pp. 345–46, No. I; Douglas,

Feudal Documents from Bury St Edmunds, No. 168; ii, fol. 257a; ii, fol. 079a; ii, fol. 079a; Regesta regum Anglo-Normannorum III, No. 814

Radulf Filius Algoti
Canon of St Pauls and prebendary of Rugmere c.1104–1132/3), who occurs in the Durham Liber Vitae (Surtees Soc. 136, 1923, fol. 42) with his mother Leouerun, brother Edmund and wife Mahald: see FEA i, 41, 74.

i, fol. 127d; Douglas, Feudal Documents from Bury St Edmunds, No. 133

Radulf Filius Brien
Brother of William fitz Brien and probably the son of 'the wife of Brien', ancestor of the de Bricett family. The name Brien shows that their ultimate origin was Breton. Though they did not necessarily come from Brittany rather than Normandy to England, their tenures of Maurice bishop of London and Ranulf Peverel are compatible with a Breton origin; certainly, the later members of this family are constantly found in association with people bearing Breton names. Ralph and his wife Emma founded the priory of Bricett, Suffolk, c.1115, as a cell of the abbey of Saint-Léonard de Noblac in Limoges, the foundation charter also revealing that the brothers had a sister Christiana. The choice of mother-house is so striking as to suggest that Ralph and his wife had become aquainted with it during a pilgrimage. Ralph also founded a Cluniac priory at Stansgate, Essex, before 1121 (Anc. Chh., no. 8).

ii, fol. 012b; ii, fol. 099b; ii, fol. 012a; ii, fol. 417a; ii, fol. 417a; ii, fol. 009a; ii, fol. 074b; ii, fol. 075a

Radulf Filius Comitis
Norman, held Lambourn, Berkshire, in 1086. There appears to be no earl or count in England or Normandy in 1086 with a known legitimate or illegitimate son named Ralph, with the exception of Robert, count of Eu. His sons Ralph, Robert and William are mentioned in his charters for the abbey of Tréport until about this date, after which only William occurs.

i, fol. 62d

Radulf Filius Goscelin
Domesday tenant of William de Polli, with whose gift of Devonshire land to Saint-Martin de Sées he was associated (CDF 656).

i, fol. 111c; i, fol. 111c; i, fol. 111b; i, fol. 111b

Radulf Filius Gunfridi
Occurs Domesday Sussex as tenant of Robert of Mortain. There were two Ralphs holding of the count of Mortain, of whom the more important was Ralph of Dene; both occurred together in ibid. 10.1. The first single occurrence of a Ralph gives his name in full as Ralph fitz Gunfrid. The tenure, at Easthall, is very obscure after 1086, in contrast to the holdings of Ralph de Dene and his heirs.

i, fol. 22a; i, fol. 20d

Radulf Filius Hagonis
Held three manors of the king in Domesday Norfolk. Son of the royal provost Hagon whose holdings were recorded immediately before his. The combined holding passed to the Warenne family. Between 1138 and 1148 William II de Warenne confirmed to Binham priory the grant of his brother Rainald of rent payable by 'Roger filius Rad. filii Hagne in terre de Geist' (Guist, DB Norfolk 56.2

(BL Cotton Claudius D xiii, fol. 20v).

ii, fol. 270a; ii, fol. 270a; ii, fol. 267a; ii, fol. 270a; ii, fol. 270a

Radulf Filius Herluini

Norman, occurs in Domesday East Anglia holding of the king, of Roger Bigod and of John nepos Waleranni, which tenures might imply a west Norman origin. Probably also the tenant called Ralph who held of Rainald fitz Ivo in two places where Ralph fitz Herluin held land in chief; if so, perhaps he was the son of Herluin fitz Ivo, a tenant of Rainald and perhaps his brother. He was also known as Ralph of Hunstanton. Benefactor of Roger Bigod's priory of Thetford. By his wife Heloise, daughter of Hugh fitz Gold of Barnham, Suffolk, he had issue two sons, Simon fitz Ralph and Rainald le Brun, who both died without issue, and a daughter Matilda, wife of Roland Lestrange (extraneus), whose issue were Ralph's heirs by the time of Henry II. See Farrer HKF iii, 117.

ii, fol. 231b; ii, fol. 231b; ii, fol. 190a; ii, fol. 190a; ii, fol. 183a; ii, fol. 183a; Dugdale, Monasticon Anglicanum, IV, pp. 148–49, No. II; ii, fol. 173b; ii, fol. 178a; ii, fol. 173b; ii, fol. 174a; ii, fol. 173b; ii, fol. 173b; ii, fol. 222a; ii, fol. 173b; ii, fol. 173b; ii, fol. 277b

Radulf Filius Huberti

Norman, Domesday tenant-in-chief, first lord of Crick, Derbyshire (Sanders, 37, whose account omits the next two generations). He was succeeded some time after 1086 by his son Odo fitz Ralph, who is mentioned in the 1129 Pipe Roll. Probably father also of Matilda, second wife of Edward of Salisbury (q.v.).

i, fol. 277b; i, fol. 277b; i, fol. 277a; i, fol. 369a; i, fol. 250c; i, fol. 235a; i, fol. 289c; i, fol. 280a; i, fol. 280b; i, fol. 277c; i, fol. 277c; i, fol. 289c; i, fol. 369a; i, fol. 277c; i, fol. 276a; i, fol. 277c; i, fol. 289c; i, fol. 273b; i, fol. 277b; i, fol. 277b; i, fol. 277a; i, fol. 277a; i, fol. 277a; i, fol. 277b; i, fol. 277b; i, fol. 277b; i, fol. 277b; i, fol. 277a; i, fol. 289c; i, fol. 277b; i, fol. 277b; i, fol. 289c; i, fol. 289c; i, fol. 277b; i, fol. 277b; i, fol. 289d; i, fol. 277b; i, fol. 277b; i, fol. 277b; i, fol. 289c; i, fol. 277b; i, fol. 289c; i, fol. 277b; i, fol. 289d; i, fol. 289d; i, fol. 289d; i, fol. 277c

Radulf Filius Osmundi

Occurs Domesday Huntingdonshire as a tenant of Alberic de Vere; perhaps a son of Osmund de Vaubadon (Calvados, arr. Bayeux, cant. Balleroy), whose son Ranulf was a tenant of Odo of Bayeux, as was Alberic's wife. His heir was Payn of Hemmingford (fl. 1139/66), who held three fees of Alberic III de Vere in 1166.

i, fol. 207b; i, fol. 207a; i, fol. 207a; i, fol. 204d; i, fol. 207b; i, fol. 208a

Radulf Filius Pagani

Norman tenant of William Capra de Pomeroy in 1086, identified by Exon as fitz Payn. Probably brother of Roger fitz Payn, who was a tenant of William's brother Ralph de Pomeroy.

i, fol. 110d

Radulf Filius Ricardi

Occurs Domesday Kent as a tenant of Hugh de Montfort.

i, fol. 013c; i, fol. 013c

Radulf Filius Roberti

Tenant of Odo of Bayeux in Domesday Kent. Between 1080 and 1083 William I confirmed purchases made by the abbots of Caen, including from Ralph fitz Robert; another purchase mentioned in the same confirmation was attested by Ralph son of Robert de Ceusio (Cheux, Calvados, cant. Tilly-sur-Seulle) (Actes caen., no. 14, pp. 107, 110).

i, fol. 011b

Radulf Filius Seifridi
Domesday tenant-in-chief in Berkshire, where his brother Roger and son-in-law Ralph also occur. A near contemporary was Ralph son of Seifrid of Escures (Calvados), abbot of Saint-Evroult and later archbishop of Canterbury. This Ralph is likely to have been a nephew of the other.

i, fol. 62d; i, fol. 41c; i, fol. 41a; i, fol. 56b

Radulf Filius Tedrici
Norman, tenant of William de Braose in Domesday Sussex, benefactor of Battle Abbey (Chron Battle, 88). He attested CDF nos. 1112–1114 for William de Braose between 1080 and c.1093–6.

i, fol. 29a; i, fol. 29a; i, fol. 29a; i, fol. 29a; i, fol. 29a

Radulf Filius Turoldi
Norman tenant of Odo of Bayeux in Domesday Kent; son of Torold of Rochester (q.v.). Attested a charter of Saint-Etienne de Caen before 1083 (Actes caen., no. 11, p. 95).

ii, fol. 025b; ii, fol. 025b; ii, fol. 025b; ii, fol. 025a; ii, fol. 025b; i, fol. 006a; i, fol. 006d; i, fol. 007b; i, fol. 004b; i, fol. 008d; i, fol. 007c; i, fol. 009a; i, fol. 006a; i, fol. 008d; ii, fol. 023a; ii, fol. 025a; ii, fol. 023a; ii, fol. 023a; ii, fol. 022b; ii, fol. 022b; ii, fol. 022b; i, fol. 007b; ii, fol. 024a; i, fol. 007c; i, fol. 007d; ii, fol. 006b; ii, fol. 025a

Radulf Filius Unspac
Occurs Domesday Kent holding Eynsford of the archbishop of Canterbury. By 1129 he had been succeeded by his nephew William I de Ainesforde. Probably dead by 1107, when William de Eynesford attested a charter of Bishop Gundulf (RRAN i, 845). The family is discussed by Douglas, in Domesday Monachorum, 44–6. Cf. Ansketil fitz Uspac, a tenant of Odo of Bayeux in 1086, perhaps a relative.

i, fol. 004b

Radulf Framen
King's servant, occurs Domesday Leicestershire.

i, fol. 236d

Radulf Gener Radulfi
Occurs in Domesday Berkshire as son-in-law of Ralph fitz Seifrid.

i, fol. 62d

Radulf Grossus
Norman, Domesday tenant of Bury St Edmunds in Suffolk, occurring as Radulf Crassus in the Feudal Book. Probably the same person as Radulf Grossus, an early benefactor of the Suffolk priory of Eye.

ii, fol. 362a; ii, fol. 360a; Douglas, Feudal Book of Bury St Edmunds (1932), pp. 3–21; Regesta regum Anglo-Normannorum III, No. 288

Radulf Latimar

Interpreter, occurs Domesday Cambridgeshire.

> i, fol. 191c; ii, fol. 101a

Radulf Malherbe

Early benefactor of William I Peverel of Nottingham's foundation at Lenton. Perhaps the same as his Domesday tenant.

> i, fol. 148b

Radulf Paganel

Norman, from a family associated with Moutiers-Hubert, Calvados, arr. Lisieux, cant. Livarot, and Hambye, Manche, arr. Coutances, cant. Gavray (Loyd, 77), Domesday tenant-in-chief in Yorkshire and elsewhere. He apparently married twice: first a daughter or sister of Ilbert de Lacy of Pontefract, and secondly Matilda, probably daughter and coheir of Richard de Sourdeval, whose Domesday lands passed to Ralph's descendants. He refounded Holy Trinity, York, as a cell of Marmoutier, which he endowed with the assent of his wife Matilda and sons William, Jordan, Helias and Alexander. He and Matilda also had a daughter who married William de Mundeville. He died between 1118 and 1124. See Clay, EYC vi, 1–4.

> Lindsey Survey, BL ms Cotton Claudius C v, fols 9–18; Lindsey Survey, BL ms Cotton Claudius C v, fols 19–27; Clay, Early Yorkshire Charters (1939), VI, No. 3; Barraclough, Charters of AN Earls of Chester (1988), No. 5; Lindsey Survey, BL ms Cotton Claudius C v, fols 1–9; Regesta regum Anglo-Normannorum III, No. 985; Lindsey Survey, BL ms Cotton Claudius C v, fols 1–9; Clay, Early Yorkshire Charters (1939), VI, No. 2; Clay, Early Yorkshire Charters (1939), VI, No. 1; Lindsey Survey, BL ms Cotton Claudius C v, fols 19–27; Clay, Early Yorkshire Charters (1939), VI, No. 4; Lindsey Survey, BL ms Cotton Claudius C v, fols 9–18; Clay, Early Yorkshire Charters (1939), VI, No. 86; i, fol. 325d; i, fol. 325d; i, fol. 325d; i, fol. 325d; i, fol. 325d; i, fol. 326a; i, fol. 362d; i, fol. 325d; i, fol. 326a; i, fol. 325d; i, fol. 325d; i, fol. 326a; i, fol. 325d; i, fol. 325d; i, fol. 325d; i, fol. 325d; i, fol. 325d; i, fol. 362d; i, fol. 325d; i, fol. 363a; i, fol. 325d; i, fol. 113d; i, fol. 113d; i, fol. 113d; i, fol. 113d; i, fol. 113d; i, fol. 113d; i, fol. 325d; i, fol. 362d; Lincolnshire Claims (Domesday Book), fols 376d–377c; i, fol. 336a; i, fol. 336b; i, fol. 363a; i, fol. 362d; Lincolnshire Claims (Domesday Book), fols 376b–c; i, fol. 298b; i, fol. 362d; i, fol. 363a; i, fol. 363a; i, fol. 362d; i, fol. 113d; i, fol. 362d; i, fol. 362d; i, fol. 362d; i, fol. 363a; i, fol. 95d; i, fol. 362d; i, fol. 225c; i, fol. 168b; Dugdale, Monasticon Anglicanum, III, p. 501, No. XV; Lindsey Survey, BL ms Cotton Claudius C v, fols 1–9; Clay, Early Yorkshire Charters (1939), VI, No. 10; Clay, Early Yorkshire Charters (1939), VI, No. 9; Dugdale, Monasticon Anglicanum, III, pp. 548–50, No. V; Lindsey Survey, BL ms Cotton Claudius C v, fols 9–18; Clay, Early Yorkshire Charters (1939), VI, No. 14; Clay, Early Yorkshire Charters (1939), VI, No. 133

Radulf Passelewe

Norman, from the Cotentin. Occurs in Domesday Bedfordshire as tenant of Walter Spec/Espec. Administrative official in East Anglia under William II and Henry I (H.A. Cronne, in Univ. Birmingham Hist. Journ. vi, 1958, 18, pp. 28–9). William de Houghton accounted for his land in 1129/30.

> i, fol. 214d; Dodwell, Charters relating to the Honour of Bacton, No. 5; Douglas, Feudal Documents from Bury St Edmunds, No. 29; Douglas, Feudal Documents

from Bury St Edmunds, No. 32; Douglas, Feudal Documents from Bury St Edmunds, No. 30; Brown, Eye Priory Cartulary (1992–94), No. 10; Pipe Roll 31 Henry I, 090–nfsf; Douglas, Feudal Documents from Bury St Edmunds, No. 33; Douglas, Feudal Documents from Bury St Edmunds, No. 25; Dugdale, Monasticon Anglicanum, IV, pp. 148–49, No. II; Douglas, Social Structure of Med. E. Anglia (1927), No. 35; Hart, Cartularium Monasterii de Rameseia, No. LXXXI

Radulf Percehaie
Norman, occurs Domesday Berkshire. He was son-in-law of Gilbert Latimer, a tenant of Abingdon abbey (Chron. Abing. ii, 34–5, 89). Baldwin de Redvers confirmed to Montebourg the alms that Ranulf Percehaie and Ansquetil his brother had given (BN lat. 10087, p. 216).

i, fol. 56c

Radulf Pincerna
Norman, Domesday tenant of Ilbert de Lacy in Yorkshire. As Ralph pincena he made grants to St Clement's chapel in the castle of Pontefract, EYC iii, no. 1492. In 1166 his manor of Thorpe Aldelin was held by William fitz Aldelin.

i, fol. 316a;

Radulf Pinel
Norman, held land in chief of the king in Domesday Essex and Suffolk. The fee of four knights once of Ralph Pinel was held in 1166 by Geoffrey de Mandeville, earl of Essex (RBE 346). A charter of 1066 for Saint-André d'Avranches was attested by a Ralph Pinel and his two sons Arnulf and Ralph (Fauroux, 229). The byname is common in west Norman cartularies of the late eleventh and twelfth centuries (e.g. Cart Montebourg, BN lat. 10087, no. 506, Cart. Saint-Sauveur-le-Vicomte, fols 74, 78v, Arch. dépt. Calvados H 6682, Saint-André-de-Gouffern, charters of Robert Pinel de Saceio and his son William). Richard Pinel attested charters of Colne priory during the 1130s.

Red Book of the Exchequer, ed. Hall (1897), pp. 345–47; ii, fol. 097a; ii, fol. 097a; ii, fol. 106a; ii, fol. 437a; ii, fol. 437a; ii, fol. 097a; ii, fol. 437a

Radulf Pipin
Norman, occurs Domesday Leicestershire as a tenant of Robert de Bucy.

i, fol. 234c; i, fol. 234c; i, fol. 234c

Radulf Presbiter
Norman cleric; occurs Domesday Somerset as a tenant of the count of Mortain. He has been identified as the count's chancellor, who occurs in charters of Montacute and Launceston priories chaplain and as 'Ranulf cancellarius' (Golding, 'Robert of Mortain, ANS 13 (1991), 138–9).

i, fol. 79b; i, fol. 93a

Radulf Presbiter
A priest holding land of the Breton Count Alan in Domesday Cambridgeshire.

i, fol. 194c

Radulf Presbiter
The Domesday tenant of the count of Eu called Ralph is likely to be identifiable as Ralph Tayard (Taillard), one of the canons of St Mary's Hastings; (Sussex Rec. Soc. xliv, 299–302, record and confirmation by Henry count of Eu). Andrew and

Robert Taillard, sons of Durand Taillard, were Sussex landholders in 1155 (Cartae Antiquae 11–20, no. 563) Robert Tayard attested a Boxgrove charter of c.1167 (Chart. Boxgrove, Sussex Rec. Soc. lix, no. 103). Thomas fitz Roger Teillart de Kylebou (Quilleboeuf-sur-Seine, Eure) occurs in BN lat. 5424, pp. 91–2, in 1130.

i, fol. 18c; i, fol. 18b; i, fol. 17c

Radulf Presbiter

Priest, tenant of Gilbert de Gand in 1086.

i, fol. 356a

Radulf Rufus

Norman, Domesday tenant of the bishop of Coutances in Domesday Somerset. His undistinguished byname, supplied by Exon Domesday, is of limited use in tracing his origins but one may note a Ralph Rufus, 'nepos' of Archbishop Baldric of Dol, who attested Préaux charters of Osbern de St Samson in the early twelfth century (Cart. Préaux, fol. 106r–v).

i, fol. 88d; i, fol. 87d; i, fol. 89a; i, fol. 89a

Radulf Sturmit

Norman, occurs Domesday Norfolk as a tenant of Ralph Bainard. Cf. Richard Sturmit.

ii, fol. 253a; ii, fol. 252b; ii, fol. 252b; ii, fol. 252b

Radulf Tortusmanus

Occurs in Domesday Somerset as a tenant of the Bishop of Wells and of Glastonbury Abbey: his byname is supplied by Exon. In 1166 Robert Pukerel held 1 fee of Glastonbury that had been held by Geoffrey Tortesmains (RBE, 223). The Glastonbury Feodary recorded that Henry Tortemeyns had paid homage to the abbot in 1189.

i, fol. 90d; i, fol. 90a; i, fol. 89c; i, fol. 90c

Radulf Trenchart

Occurs Domesday Somerset as tenant of Turstin fitz Rolf; his byname occurs in Exon and the Tax Returns. A Trenchart attested a charter of Saint-Georges de Boscherville of c.1050–66 (Fauroux, 194). Payn Trenchart, a Redvers tenant, occurs c.1130–43 (PR 31 Henry I, 41; Quarr Abbey ch. 1).

i, fol. 97d

Radulf Venator

Norman, tenant of earl Hugh in Domesday Cheshire.

i, fol. 268d; i, fol. 267b; i, fol. 268d; Barraclough, Charters of AN Earls of Chester (1988), No. 28; Barraclough, Charters of AN Earls of Chester (1988), No. 3

Radulf Viso Lupi

Occurs Domesday Norfolk; cf. Humphrey Visdeloup.

ii, fol. 118a

Radulf Vitalis

Occurs Domesday Devon as a tenant of Odo fitz Gamelin. Surnamed Vitalis in Exon, he was probably son of the Vitalis who had held land before 1066 belonging in 1086 to Odo or to his father-in-law Theobald fitz Berner. His successor in 1166 was Philip of Huish, who held three fees of William of Great Torrington.

i, fol. 116c; i, fol. 116c; i, fol. 116c

Radulf []
Norman, Domesday tenant of Eudo Dapifer in Bedfordshire and Norfolk. He was succeeded by the de Tyvill family, of whom he may have been the ancestor, as suggested in Farrer, HKF iii, 180.

ii, fol. 240a; ii, fol. 239b; i, fol. 212c

Radulf []
Domesday tenant of Judhael of Totnes. To be distinguished from Ralph de Pomerai, another of Judhael's tenants, this Ralph may have been the Ralph Malbanc who attested Judhael's charter for Totnes (Mon. Ang. iv, 630, no. ii).

i, fol. 109c; i, fol. 110a; i, fol. 109c; i, fol. 109b; i, fol. 109b; i, fol. 109c; i, fol. 109c; i, fol. 110b; i, fol. 109c; i, fol. 109c; i, fol. 109c; i, fol. 108c; i, fol. 109b; i, fol. 109b; i, fol. 109c; i, fol. 110a; i, fol. 110a; i, fol. 110a; i, fol. 110a; i, fol. 110a; i, fol. 110a

Radulf []
Domesday tenant of the abbey of Tavistock in Devon; his holdings descended to a family named Cornutus or Cornu, perhaps his descendants.

i, fol. 103d; i, fol. 103c; i, fol. 103c

Radulf []
Occurs Domesday Sussex holding of the Montgomery Rape of Arundel. His holdings were later held by the Sanzaver family, later members of whom were known as de Chesney from a mid-twelfth marriage. This Ralph may well have been the Sanzaver ancestor, but he was distinct from Ralph de Chesney, a tenant in Pevensey Rape. His earliest successor, William fitz Ralph fl. c.1130–58, gave the church of Buddington to Lewes priory; HKF iii, 24.

i, fol. 23c; i, fol. 23a; i, fol. 23d; i, fol. 23c

Radulf []
Norman, occurs Domesday Gloucestershire. His descendants of the de Kerdiff (Cardiff) family were stewards of the earls of Gloucester in the mid-twelfth century.

i, fol. 163c; i, fol. 163c

Radulf []
Norman, Domesday tenant of William of Écouis.

i, fol. 180b

Radulf []
Domesday tenant of the bishop of Lincoln in Leicestershire; possibly the same man was the tenant at Dunsby and Silk Willoughby in Lincolnshire. The latter was succeeded by c.1100 by Osbert I Silvain.

i, fol. 344c; i, fol. 345a; i, fol. 231a; i, fol. 231a; i, fol. 231a; i, fol. 231a; i, fol. 231a; i, fol. 231a; i, fol. 231a

Radulf []
Norman, under-tenant of Earl Roger in Domesday Shropshire; his holdings all passed to the de Costentin family soon after 1086. Probably father of Hugh de Costentin (Eyton, Shrops, i, 133).

i, fol. 256b; i, fol. 255b; i, fol. 255b

Radulf []

Domesday tenant of Countess Judith in Leicestershire. Succeeded by the Folvilles, of whom the earliest may have been the Ralph de Folville who occurs in the Northants Survey. They were perhaps named from Folleville, Eure, cant. Thiberville. HKF ii, 320, 73.

i, fol. 236d; i, fol. 236c; i, fol. 236c

Radulf []

Domesday tenant of Eudo Dapifer at Dunmow, Essex, whose fee had passed to the de Berneres family (from Bernières-sur-Mer, Calvados, arr. Caen, cant. Douvres) by 1166. Farrer, followed by Loyd, falsely derived the de Berneres from Ralph, instead of their true ancestor Hugh de Berneres (HKF iii, 213–14; Loyd, 14); there was possibly a link by marriage.

ii, fol. 050a

Radulf []

Domesday tenant of Swein of Essex. A Jordan fitz Ralph attested a charter of Swein's son Robert (Mon. Ang. v, 22).

ii, fol. 046a

Radulf []

Tenant of Count Alan at Hintlesham, Suffolk, in 1086. In 1126 the land was given to Aubrey de Vere by Alan son of Ralph and his mother Agnes, a grant confirmed by Count Stephen (of Brittany) and Henry I (cf. Comp. Peer. x, 195–9).

ii, fol. 296a

Radulf []

Domesday tenant of Waleran Venator. His successor by 1166 was probably Herbert of Foxcote.

i, fol. 48b; i, fol. 48b

Radulf []

Domesday tenant of Alberic de Vere at Thunderley in Essex. In 1143 the manor was held by Alexander, son of Rivallon and Adelisa, husband of Hawise and benefactor of Hatfield Regis priory (BL Add. ch. 28323).

ii, fol. 076b; ii, fol. 076b; ii, fol. 076b

Radulf []

Norman, tenant of Ilbert de Lacy of Pontefract in 1086. Perhaps the same as Ralph son of Edeline who was a benefactor to Ilbert's priory of St Clement (EYC iii, 1492). Cf. VCH ii, 165.

i, fol. 316b; i, fol. 316b; i, fol. 316b; i, fol. 316b

Radulf []

Tenant of William fitz Ansculf in Domesday Staffordshire. His successor by the early twelfth century, Guy de Offeni, was perhaps his son. Wrottesley suggested Guy – father of William and Ralph – was named from Offignies (dépt. Somme) in Picardy (see Worcs. Cart, PR Soc. p. xxviii).

i, fol. 250b

Radulf Nepos Goisfridi Alselin

Norman, nephew of Geoffrey Alselin (q.v.). The close association between him and his uncle in Domesday Book suggests that by 1086 he had succeeded to his father's share of a fief granted jointly to Geoffrey and his brother, Ralph's father. He was dead by 1129/30, when his son Robert de Calz occurs on the Pipe Roll. His wife had some connexion with Robert Bloet, bishop of Lincoln (RBE, 340). Calz is probably La Chaux, Orne, arr. Alençon, cant. La Ferté-Macé (cf. Dauzat/ Rostaing, s.v. Calm).

i, fol. 370a; i, fol. 369d; i, fol. 219a; i, fol. 369d; i, fol. 336a; i, fol. 369d; i, fol. 369d; i, fol. 369d; i, fol. 369d

Raimar Frater Walteri De Duaco

Brother of Walter de Douai whose name was incorrectly written Rademar in Devon Domesday. Was he Raimar provost of Saint-Amé de Douai in 1076 under Walter I castellan of Douai (Brassart, Preuves no. xii)?

i, fol. 111d; i, fol. 95c; i, fol. 95b; i, fol. 95b; i, fol. 95b; i, fol. 95a; i, fol. 95a; i, fol. 95a; i, fol. 95c; Hunt, Bath Chartulary, Som. Rec. Soc. 7 (1893), No. 35; Hunt, Bath Chartulary, Som. Rec. Soc. 7 (1893), No. 35

Rainald Arcarius

Occurs as a king's servant in Domesday Oxfordshire.

i, fol. 160c; i, fol. 160c

Rainald Balistarius

Norman, occurs Domesday Essex.

ii, fol. 097b; ii, fol. 097b; Hamilton, Inquisitio Eliensis (1876), pp. 192–95

Rainald Brito

Tenant of Bury St Edmunds in 1086 with his brother Hubert Brito. Probably neither left issue, since the land of Rainald and Hubert, probably the two brothers, was regranted to another tenant of the abbey in the early twelfth century. A Rainald Brito attested a charter for Sainte-Trinité de Rouen given by a man of Ralph II de Warenne (father of William, q.v.) (Cart., p. 443).

ii, fol. 445a; ii, fol. 445a; Douglas, Feudal Book of Bury St Edmunds (1932), pp. 22–37

Rainald Canutus

Domesday tenant of Miles Crispin; his surname is provided in the Exon Tax Returns for some Wiltshire Hundreds. Walter Canute held 5 fees of Miles's successors in the honour of Wallingford in 1166 (RBE 309), Richard Canute held 1 fee of Margaret de Bohun in Gloucestershire (ibid. 294). Humphrey Canute was a man of Bishop Gundulf of Rochester (Mon. Ang. i, 169). Richard I (d.1199) confirmed a grant to Saint-Taurin d'Evreux of the tithe of Croise and a church at Pacy (Eure) by a man of Robert Canute (Gall. Christ. xi, Inst. 140).

i, fol. 159d; i, fol. 71b; i, fol. 71b; i, fol. 71b; i, fol. 71b; i, fol. 71b; i, fol. 57c; i, fol. 56c; i, fol. 56b; i, fol. 159c; i, fol. 159c; i, fol. 161b; i, fol. 71b; i, fol. 73b; i, fol. 154d; i, fol. 154d; i, fol. 154d; i, fol. 154d; i, fol. 154d; i, fol. 158c; i, fol. 158c; i, fol. 158d; i, fol. 158d; i, fol. 161b; i, fol. 161b; i, fol. 161b

Rainald Capellanus

Occurs Domesday Gloucestershire, where grant to him for life as a chaplain of Queen Matilda is mentioned.

i, fol. 163d

Rainald Croc
Occurs Domesday Hampshire.

i, fol. 52a; i, fol. 49a

Rainald Dapifer
The Rainald man of Roger Bigod mentioned in Domesday Norfolk was possibly the Rainald dapifer who occurs in William Bigod's confirmation charter for Thetford priory as a benefactor c.1107.

Dugdale, Monasticon Anglicanum, IV, pp. 148–49, No. II; Dugdale, Monasticon Anglicanum, IV, pp. 148–49, No. II; ii, fol. 116b

Rainald De Balgiole
Norman, from Bailleul-en-Gouffern, Orne, cant. Trun (Loyd, 11). Tenant of Earl Roger of in Shropshire. In 1086 he was Roger's sheriff, in succession to Warin the Bald, whose widow Amiera, kinswoman ('nepta', possibly niece) of Earl Roger, he married (Ord. Vit. iii, 140). He seems to have been the guardian of Warin's son Hugh, who held his father's land and office for a short time after 1102. He returned to Normandy upon the fall of the Montgomerys in 1102. He defied Henry I there in 1119, and at some time fought in the Spanish crusades (Ord. Vit. vi, 214–16, 402) He was dead by 1144, when Geoffrey of Anjou confirmed his son Rainald's grant for his soul, his wife's, and that of another son, William (RRAN iii, 407).

i, fol. 253c; i, fol. 239b; i, fol. 25d; i, fol. 24b; i, fol. 254c; i, fol. 24d; i, fol. 268a; i, fol. 253c; i, fol. 253d; i, fol. 248a; i, fol. 248a; i, fol. 248a; i, fol. 259d; i, fol. 254c; Rees, Cartulary of Shrewsbury Abbey (1975), No. 35; i, fol. 267c; i, fol. 267c; i, fol. 250c; Regesta regum Anglo-Normannorum III, No. 407; i, fol. 250c; i, fol. 250c; i, fol. 250c; i, fol. 250c; i, fol. 254d; i, fol. 255a; i, fol. 255a; i, fol. 255b; i, fol. 254d; i, fol. 255a; i, fol. 254d; i, fol. 255a; i, fol. 254d; i, fol. 255a; i, fol. 255a; i, fol. 254d; i, fol. 254d; i, fol. 254b; i, fol. 255b; i, fol. 255b; i, fol. 254b; i, fol. 254c; i, fol. 255a; i, fol. 254d; i, fol. 254d; i, fol. 254d; i, fol. 255a; i, fol. 255a; i, fol. 255a; i, fol. 255a; i, fol. 255a; i, fol. 254d; Rees, Cartulary of Shrewsbury Abbey (1975), No. 35; i, fol. 239b; i, fol. 239b; i, fol. 239b

Rainald De Campania
Domesday tenant of Geoffrey de la Guerche. Raginaldus de Campania attested a charter of Geoffrey for Monks Kirby priory before 1093 (Mon. Ang. vi, 996).

i, fol. 369b

Rainald De Perapund
Norman, Domesday tenant of William bishop of Thetford. Perhaps named from Pierrepont, Calvados, cant. Pont-d'Ouilly.

ii, fol. 200a; ii, fol. 195a; ii, fol. 200a; ii, fol. 196a; ii, fol. 199b; ii, fol. 201b

Rainald De Sancta Elena
Norman, a Domesday tenant and knight of Abingdon abbey named from the parish of St Helen. On 16 January 1112 the abbey of Jumièges made an agreement with Rainald of St Helen concerning land near Argentan, atested by William Picot, Rainald Puniant and Robert fitz Ralph (Ch. Jumièges, liv, 114–15).

i, fol. 59a; i, fol. 59c; i, fol. 58c; i, fol. 58d; i, fol. 59a; i, fol. 58c; i, fol. 58c; Stevenson, Chronicon Monasterii de Abingdon (1858) vol. II, pp. 4–6

Rainald De Valletorta
Norman, from Torteval-Quesnay, Calvados, cant. Caumont-l'Evente, a major tenant of Robert de Mortain in Domesday Cornwall and Devon. His origin is

indicated by grants made to the abbey of Grestain, founded by Herluin de Conteville, father of Robert de Mortain. A Ralph de Torteval was a benefactor of Saint-Evroul de Mortain in 1082. Rainald's predecessor was a Ralph who was presumably dead in 1086, when a Hugh de Valletorte was also the count's tenant. Rainald was an important tenant of the count, with especially large holding in Cornwall. The Exon Tax Returns show that he had at least four subtenants – Odo, Turstin, Letard and Frotmund – who were not mentioned as such in Domesday. After the forfeiture of William de Mortain in 1106, the Valletorte or Vautort family was one of those which thereafter held its fees in chief of the king, as the barony of Trematon (Sanders, 90). This is probably the Rainald de Vautort active until shortly before 1129/30, when Roger I de Vautort, presumably his son, had succeeded.

i, fol. 92b; i, fol. 120d; i, fol. 92c; i, fol. 105c; i, fol. 105d; i, fol. 105b; i, fol. 105b; i, fol. 105b; i, fol. 105b; i, fol. 122b; i, fol. 122a; i, fol. 122a; i, fol. 122a; i, fol. 122a; i, fol. 122a; i, fol. 122a; i, fol. 122a; i, fol. 122a; i, fol. 122a; i, fol. 122b; i, fol. 122a; i, fol. 122a; i, fol. 122a; i, fol. 122b; i, fol. 122b; i, fol. 122a; i, fol. 122b; i, fol. 122b; i, fol. 122a; i, fol. 122b; i, fol. 122a; i, fol. 122b; i, fol. 122b; i, fol. 122b; i, fol. 122b; i, fol. 122a; i, fol. 122a; i, fol. 122b; i, fol. 122a; i, fol. 122b; i, fol. 122b; i, fol. 122a; i, fol. 122b; i, fol. 104d; i, fol. 104d; i, fol. 104d; i, fol. 104d; i, fol. 104d; i, fol. 105a; i, fol. 105a; i, fol. 105b; i, fol. 105b; i, fol. 105b; i, fol. 105b; i, fol. 105c; i, fol. 105c; i, fol. 105c; i, fol. 105c; i, fol. 105c; i, fol. 105c; i, fol. 105c; i, fol. 105d; i, fol. 105d; i, fol. 100d; i, fol. 100d; i, fol. 100d; i, fol. 100d

Rainald Filius Croc
Norman, probably follower of William fitz Osbern de Breteuil, occurs Domesday Hampshire and Isle of Wight. CF. Croc Venator.

i, fol. 49a; i, fol. 52b

Rainald Filius Iuonis
Norman, Domesday tenant-in-chief. His holding was mediatised soon after 1086 and held under Richard de Clare. His tenant Herluin fitz Ivo was probably his brother.

ii, fol. 230a; Douglas, Feudal Documents from Bury St Edmunds, No. 170; ii, fol. 234a; ii, fol. 276a; ii, fol. 232b; ii, fol. 233b; ii, fol. 233b; ii, fol. 233b; ii, fol. 214a; ii, fol. 233b; ii, fol. 110a; ii, fol. 234a; ii, fol. 232b; ii, fol. 234a; ii, fol. 233b; ii, fol. 234b; ii, fol. 234b; ii, fol. 232b; ii, fol. 233b; ii, fol. 230a; ii, fol. 231a; ii, fol. 232b; ii, fol. 276a; ii, fol. 232b; ii, fol. 230b; ii, fol. 230a; ii, fol. 234a; ii, fol. 230b; ii, fol. 234b; ii, fol. 230b; ii, fol. 230b; ii, fol. 230b; ii, fol. 230b; ii, fol. 234a; ii, fol. 161b; ii, fol. 230b; ii, fol. 115a; ii, fol. 230b; ii, fol. 230b; ii, fol. 234b; ii, fol. 231b; ii, fol. 234b; ii, fol. 232a; ii, fol. 232a; ii, fol. 231b; ii, fol. 232b; ii, fol. 231b; ii, fol. 117b; ii, fol. 116b; ii, fol. 230b; ii, fol. 230a; ii, fol. 230b; ii, fol. 116b; ii, fol. 230b; ii, fol. 232b; ii, fol. 230b; ii, fol. 275b; ii, fol. 275b; ii, fol. 275b; ii, fol. 275b; ii, fol. 232a; ii, fol. 233b; ii, fol. 276a; ii, fol. 276a; ii, fol. 231a; ii, fol. 230b; ii, fol. 230b; ii, fol. 231a; ii, fol. 231a; ii, fol. 233b; ii, fol. 231a; ii, fol. 234b; ii, fol. 117a; ii, fol. 232b; Douglas, Feudal Documents from Bury St Edmunds, No. 170

Rainald Presbiter
Occurs Domesday Norfolk. Apparently a priest who married the sister of Edmund fitz Pagan.

ii, fol. 264a

Rainald Wadard

Norman, Domesday tenant of Odo of Bayeux in Oxfordshire. He occurs both as Rainald Wadard and as son of Wadard. Probably son of Odo's famous tenant Wadard, who was represented on the Bayeux tapestry. Wadard lost his land when Odo did, but Rainald's holdings were independent of his putative father's and he appears to have survived to become the ancestor of the Oxfordshire Wadard or Waard family. A confirmation by Richard II of Normandy for Fécamp of August 1024 (Fauroux, 34) includes the grant made by Lora, wife of Rainald called Wadard, viz her rights in Airan (Calvados, cant. Bourguébus).

i, fol. 155d; i, fol. 155d; i, fol. 159a; i, fol. 156d

Rainald []

Domesday tenant of Ruald Adobed in Devon.

i, fol. 115a; i, fol. 115b; i, fol. 115b; i, fol. 115a; i, fol. 115a; i, fol. 115b; i, fol. 115b; i, fol. 115b

Rainald []

Domesday tenant of Colswein of Lincoln.

i, fol. 357b

Rainald []

Domesday tenant of Hervey Bituricensis. His successor in 1166 was probably Fulk de Tisteden, who held one fee of Haimo Pecche at Thistleton.

ii, fol. 441b; ii, fol. 440b; ii, fol. 442b

Rainald []

Tenant of Count Alan and Alberic de Ver in 1086; possibly the same as Rainald Brito or Rainald de Duneham (for Downham?), a juror in Ely Hundred, Cambridgeshire.

i, fol. 194d; i, fol. 199c; Hamilton, Inquisitio Eliensis (1876), pp. 97–100

Rainald []

Norman, Domesday tenant of Geoffrey de Mandeveille at Shelley and probably also at Frinton, since the fees were still held together in the late thirteenth century; cf. Round, VCH Essex i, 508.

ii, fol. 057b; ii, fol. 059b

Rainald []

Domesday tenant of the archbishop of York at Nunwick. His successor in 1166 was Ralph of Nunwick (de Nowewica).

i, fol. 303d

Rainbald Aurifaber

Occurs Domesday Norfolk.

ii, fol. 273a; ii, fol. 273a

Rainbald De Tubbeneia

Domesday tenant of the abbey of Abingdon. Called 'gener' (son-in-law) of Abbot Rainald of Abingdon (1084–1100) in Chron. Abin. ii 37. He quarrelled with the king and was forced to take refuge in Flanders, but a few years later accompanied the count of Flanders to a meeting with the king, who pardoned him and restored his land (ibid., 37–42). The chronicler calls him Rainbald de Tubbeneia when he records that Rainbald's son Adelelm became a monk of Abingdon (ibid., 170). He occurs twice in the abbey's list of knights (ibid., 4–5), a later list showing that the two references were to the same person (ibid., 311).

Stevenson, Chronicon Monasterii de Abingdon (1858) vol. II, pp. 4–6; Stevenson, Chronicon Monasterii de Abingdon (1858) vol. II, pp. 4–6; i, fol. 58d; i, fol. 58d; i, fol. 58d

Rainbald Presbiter

Cleric who found favour with Edward the Confessor in the late 1050s, acting as chancellor in the early 1060s. Clearly one of Edward's foreign favourites, his origins are obscure. There is no reason to view his name as 'German', it was a Germanic name used occasionally by Normans. It is not impossible that he was the same as Rainbald the nephew of Bishop Peter of Chester, who was one of Edward's Norman favourites. Priest of Frome, he was particulary attached to Cirencester. See Simon Keynes, 'Regenbald the Chancellor (sic)', ANS, 185–222. Rainbald's brother and son Alweald, also occur in Domesday Book.

i, fol. 57b; i, fol. 70b; Regesta regum Anglo-Normannorum III, No. 189; i, fol. 160b; i, fol. 91b; i, fol. 166b; i, fol. 162d; i, fol. 86c; i, fol. 160b; i, fol. 63b; i, fol. 63b; i, fol. 68c; i, fol. 68c; i, fol. 56c; i, fol. 79a; i, fol. 65c; i, fol. 65c; i, fol. 56d; i, fol. 166d; i, fol. 166d; i, fol. 166d; i, fol. 166d; i, fol. 86c; i, fol. 146a; i, fol. 166c; i, fol. 146a

Rainer Dapifer

Domesday tenant of Baldwin de Meulles, sheriff of Devon; identified as his steward by Exon. He was succeeded by the Langford family (Mason, 'Barons and officials', ANS 13 (1991), p. 246).

i, fol. 106a; i, fol. 106a; i, fol. 106d; i, fol. 107d; i, fol. 107d; i, fol. 107d; i, fol. 107c; i, fol. 107b; i, fol. 107b

Rainer De Grantcurt

Norman, from Grandcourt, Seine-Maritime, arr. Neufchâtel, cant. Londinières (Loyd, 47). Domesday tenant of William de Warenne in Norfolk. Identified from his grant to Castle Acre priory of land at Tattersett, where his undertenant was Hugh de Picquigny. Occurs in the time of William II de Warenne (d. 1138). Perhaps a younger brother or son of Walter de Grandcourt.

ii, fol. 168b; ii, fol. 170a; Dugdale, Monasticon Anglicanum, IV, p. 51, No. IV; Clay, Early Yorkshire Charters (1949), VIII, No. 24; Dugdale, Monasticon Anglicanum, IV, p. 50, No. III; Dugdale, Monasticon Anglicanum, IV, pp. 49–50, No. II

Rainfrid De Bretteville

Norman, Domesday tenant of Ivo Taillebois. Identified by a grant to Spalding priory. His son Alfred, ancestor of the Glentham family, occurs in 1130 accounting to hold his land in peace. Named from one of several places named Bretteville in Calvados. Cf. HKF ii, 169–70.

i, fol. 350b; Lindsey Survey, BL ms Cotton Claudius C v, fols 1–9

Ranulf []

Domesday tenant of Geoffrey de la Guerche in Nottinghamshire. Attested, before 1093, a charter of Geoffrey de la Guerche for Monks Kirby (Mon. Ang. vi, 996).

i, fol. 291a

Rannulf Clericus Archiepiscopi
Norman, clerk of Archbishop Thomas I of York and his tenant at Lavington, Lincolnshire, in 1086.

    i, fol. 340b

Rannulf De Sancto Walarico
Norman, from Saint-Valery-en-Caux, Seine-Maritime, arr. Yvetot, occurs as a tenant-in-chief in Domesday Lincolnshire. By 1115–18, the date of the Lindsey Survey, his land, including his tenancies of the bishop of Lincoln, were held by Gilbert de Neville. See Loyd, 92.

    i, fol. 344c; i, fol. 344b; i, fol. 344b; Lincolnshire Claims (Domesday Book), fols 376b–c; i, fol. 364d; i, fol. 364d; i, fol. 364d; i, fol. 364d; i, fol. 364d; i, fol. 364d; i, fol. 364d

Rannulf De Strengestan
Norman, Domesday tenant of Alfred de Ispania (Epaignes, Eure). Named in the Tax Returns from Stringston in Cannington Hundred, Somerset. Benefactor of Goldcliff priory in the time of Alfred's successor Isabel de Candos. In 1166 his fee was held by Hugh Fiquet (q.v.) of Alfred's successor Philip de Colombariis. The Fiquet family were benefactors of Préaux in the late eleventh century, associated with Vannecrocq, Eure (CDF 323–4).

    Regesta regum Anglo-Normannorum III, No. 373; i, fol. 97b; i, fol. 97b; i, fol. 97b; Regesta regum Anglo-Normannorum III, No. 373

Rannulf De Valbadon
Norman, from Vaubadon, Calvados, arr. Bayeux, cant. Balleroy, Domesday tenant of Odo of Bayeux in Kent. In 1210–12 Richard de Vabadone was doing castleguard at Dover for the Maminot ward (RBE, 617); see Loyd, 108.

    i, fol. 012c; i, fol. 011d; Ballard, Inquisition of St Augustine's (1920), fols 24r–28r

Rannulf Frater Walteri Abbatis
Norman, Domesday tenant of his brother Abbot Walter of Evesham (1077–1104) in Warwickshire (VCH Warks. i, 282).

    i, fol. 239b

Rannulf Gernon
Norman, brother of Robert Gernon (Chron. Abing. ii 98), a Domesday tenant-in-chief from whom he held a manor in Cambridgeshire. William Gernon and his brother Ralph, probably his sons, occur in the Cambridgeshire section of the Pipe Roll of 31 Henry I (p. 45). He was perhaps also father of Geoffrey Gernon, who occurs c. 1150 and bore the name of one of Robert Gernon's nephews (Chron. Abing., loc. cit.). Cf. VCH Bedfordshire. iv, 149; VCH Essex iv, 262–3; CDF, 292).

    i, fol. 196d

Rannulf Grammaticus
Norman, Domesday tenant of Ilbert de Lacy in Yorkshire, identified from his grants to St Clement's chapel in the castle of Pontefract, EYC iii, no. 1492. Cf. Holmes, 'Wapentake of Osgoldscross', Yorks. Arch. Journ. 13, 108–9.

    i, fol. 316b; i, fol. 315a; i, fol. 315a

Rannulf Vicecomes
Domesday tenant of Robert of Mortain in Sussex. Probably the same person who occurs in two Lewes charters of William of Mortain, once as Ranulf vicecomes and once as father of Herbert, the deed being witnessed by Hubert of St Clair, a Mortain tenant elsewhere (Lewes Cart., pp. 75, 119). Ranulf father of Herbert, certainly the same as the Domesday tenant, is shown by these charters to have died c.1100–3.

 i, fol. 21d; i, fol. 22a; i, fol. 21b; i, fol. 20d; i, fol. 22a

Rannulf Vicecomes De Surreia
Norman, described as 'vicecomes' in Domesday Book. possibly sheriff of Surrey, an office he may also have held during c.1093–1107 (Green, Sheriffs, 78).

 i, fol. 30a; ii, fol. 005a

Rannulf []
Domesday tenant of Robert de Mortain in Hertfordshire, and probably also in Buckinghamshire. The count's tenant Ranulf in Sussex was father of a Herbert. Robert de Haia (La Haye-du-Puits, Manche) was son of Ranulf the seneschal of Robert of Mortain, as appears from his foundation charter for Boxgrove priory in Sussex, a cell of the west Norman abbey of Lessay (Cart. Boxgrove no. 4, p. 16), but there is no reason to identify the seneschal with the Domesday tenant.

 i, fol. 22b; i, fol. 146b; i, fol. 146c; i, fol. 146d; i, fol. 146c; i, fol. 136d; i, fol. 136c; i, fol. 136c

Rannulf []
Tenant of Alfred of Lincoln at Brackenborough in 1086. He was represented in 1166 by Ranulf of Brackenborough. Possibly same as Ranulf, tenant of Guy de Craon, whose Craon fee at Welby passed to a family surnamed de Roches or Rok (Fees, 183).

 i, fol. 367c; i, fol. 367c; i, fol. 358a; i, fol. 358a

Rannulf []
Norman, tenant of Roger de Courseulle in Domesday Somerset.

 i, fol. 93c

Rannulf []
Domesday tenant of William d'Eu in Devon.

 i, fol. 111c; i, fol. 111c

Rannulf []
Norman, tenant of Turstin filtz Rolf in Dorset in 1086.

 i, fol. 80d; i, fol. 80d; i, fol. 80c

Ranulf De Columbels
Norman, Domesday tenant of Odo de Bayeux in Kent. Named from either Colombières, Calvados, arr. Bayeux, cant. Trévières or cant. Ryes (Loyd, 30). His holding passed to a family named de Bermelinges, from West Barming, holding under the Crevequers (HKF iii, 292).

 i, fol. 009b; i, fol. 009b; i, fol. 009b; Ballard, Inquisition of St Augustine's (1920), fols 20r–23v; i, fol. 011d; i, fol. 002a; i, fol. 008d; i, fol. 002a; i, fol. 002a; i, fol. 008c; i, fol. 001a; i, fol. 001a; i, fol. 007b; i, fol. 002b; Ballard, Inquisition of St Augustine's (1920), fols 24r–28r; i, fol. 009b; i, fol. 009d; i, fol. 012c

Ranulf De Maisnilwarin

Norman, from Le Mesnil Guérin, is now Pont-Farcy, comm. cant. Saint-Sever, Calvados, Domesday tenant of Hugh of Avranches, earl of Chester. Ancestor of the Mainwaring family. See Farrer, HKF, ii, 227–9.

i, fol. 60b; i, fol. 268d; i, fol. 268a; i, fol. 268a; i, fol. 268a; i, fol. 264b; i, fol. 264b; ii, fol. 279a; i, fol. 267b; i, fol. 267b; i, fol. 267b; i, fol. 267b; i, fol. 267b; i, fol. 267b; i, fol. 267b; i, fol. 267b; i, fol. 267b; i, fol. 267b; i, fol. 267b; i, fol. 267b; ii, fol. 152b; ii, fol. 152a

Ranulf Episcopus Dunelmensis

Ranulf Flambard. Occurs as a Domesday tenant. From 1092 until 1100 he controlled the abbey of Chertsey (Ann. Winchester, 37; cf. Heads, 38) Became bishop of Durham 29 May, consecrated 5 June 1099. Died in office 5 September 1128. Father by an Englishwoman, Alveva, of, inter alia, Ranulf the archdeacon (q.v.) and Elias prebendary of Sneating (FEA i, 77). See C.N.L. Brooke, 'Married men among the English higher clergy', Cambridge Hist. Journ. 12 (1956) 187–8, R.W. Southern, 'Ranulf Flambard', in Medieval Humanism (Oxford, 1970). H.S. Offler, 'Ranulf Flambard as bishop of Durham 1099–1128', Durham University Journal 64 (1971). J. Prestwich, 'The career of Ranulf Flambard', Anglo-Norman Durham, ed. D. Rollason et al. (1994). FEA ii, 29.

Brown, Eye Priory Cartulary (1992–94), No. 9; Greenway, Charters of the Honour of Mowbray (1972), No. 9; Greenway, Charters of the Honour of Mowbray (1972), No. 7; Dugdale, Monasticon Anglicanum, II, p. 267, No. XI; Greenway, Charters of the Honour of Mowbray (1972), No. 8; Greenway, Charters of the Honour of Mowbray (1972), No. 10; Chibnall, English Lands of Abbey of Bec (1951), No. XXXV; Gibbs, Early Charters of St Pauls (1939), No. 6; Gibbs, Early Charters of St Pauls (1939), No. 20; Greenway, Charters of the Honour of Mowbray (1972), No. 4; Lindsey Survey, BL ms Cotton Claudius C v, fols 1–9; Regesta regum Anglo-Normannorum III, No. 789; Lindsey Survey, BL ms Cotton Claudius C v, fols 19–27; Lindsey Survey, BL ms Cotton Claudius C v, fols 1–9; Lindsey Survey, BL ms Cotton Claudius C v, fols 9–18; Gibbs, Early Charters of St Pauls (1939), No. 17; Bearman, Charters of the Redvers Family (1994), No. 5; Dugdale, Monasticon Anglicanum, II, p. 18, No. IX; Mason, Beauchamp Cartulary Charters (1980), No. 162; Mason, Beauchamp Cartulary Charters (1980), No. 163; Dugdale, Monasticon Anglicanum, III, p. 500, No. X; Gibbs, Early Charters of St Pauls (1939), No. 8; Lindsey Survey, BL ms Cotton Claudius C v, fols 9–18; Lindsey Survey, BL ms Cotton Claudius C v, fols 1–9; Lindsey Survey, BL ms Cotton Claudius C v, fols 19–27; Lindsey Survey, BL ms Cotton Claudius C v, fols 9–18; i, fol. 67a; i, fol. 127b; i, fol. 89d; i, fol. 157a; i, fol. 49b; i, fol. 154a; i, fol. 58b; i, fol. 49b; i, fol. 30d; i, fol. 30d; i, fol. 30d; i, fol. 51b; i, fol. 51b; i, fol. 51b

Ranulf Filius Walteri

Norman, major tenant of Roger Bigod in Domesday Norfolk. Benefactor of the Bigod foundation at Thetford, for which his charters show that he married Matilda de Lanquetot; one of his charters mentions his son Gilbert and Gilbert's wife Richildis; others mention his daughter Agnes, who married Robert de Vaux (Vallibus, q.v.); a charter of Agnes mentions her brother Simon (BL Lansdowne 229, fol. 145v). His grants to Thetford, with the assent of his son Gilbert, were confirmed by Henry I (RRAN ii, 1246 and p. 338).

ii, fol. 338b; ii, fol. 307a; Dugdale, Monasticon Anglicanum, IV, pp. 150–51, No. VIII; Dugdale, Monasticon Anglicanum, IV, pp. 148–49, No. II; ii, fol. 174a; ii, fol. 176b; ii, fol. 176a; ii, fol. 277a; ii, fol. 277a; ii, fol. 188b; ii, fol. 179a; ii, fol. 175a; ii, fol. 180b; ii, fol. 173b; ii, fol. 173b; ii, fol. 173b; ii, fol. 277a; ii, fol. 174a; ii, fol. 178b; Hamilton, Inquisitio Eliensis (1876), pp. 192–95; ii, fol. 333b; ii, fol. 117b; ii, fol. 333a; ii, fol. 343b; Regesta Regum Anglo Normannorum II, App. no. cxxvii ; ii, fol. 185b; ii, fol. 185b; ii, fol. 185b; ii, fol. 185b; ii, fol. 186a; ii, fol. 185b; ii, fol. 185b; ii, fol. 185b; ii, fol. 338b; ii, fol. 338b; ii, fol. 338b; ii, fol. 338b

Ranulf Frater Ilgeri

Norman, Domesday tenant-in-chief in several counties, and tenant of Countess Judith and William of Picquigny in Bedfordshire and Huntingdonshire. Sheriff of Huntingdonshire sometime between 1092 and 1100 (Green, Sheriffs, 48). A Domesday entry reveals that he married a niece of Ralph Taillebois, a pre-Domesday sheriff of Bedfordshire. He died c.1100 when his fief escheated and was broken up, with most being granted to Roger fitz Richard de Clare (VCH Herts iii, 368). His brother Ilger was possibly the Ilger who was tutor to William I's son Robert Curthose (CDF, 1173). Ranulf occurs as one of the despoilers of Sainte-Trinité de Caen (Walmsley, p.126; CDF, 424).

i, fol. 203c; ii, fol. 085b; i, fol. 203c; Hart, Cartularium Monasterii de Rameseia, No. XXXVI; Hart, Cartularium Monasterii de Rameseia, No. XXXVII; ii, fol. 080b; ii, fol. 081a; ii, fol. 260b; ii, fol. 080a; ii, fol. 015b; ii, fol. 080b; ii, fol. 080b; ii, fol. 081a; ii, fol. 261a; ii, fol. 261a; ii, fol. 001b; ii, fol. 260b; ii, fol. 260b; ii, fol. 425a; ii, fol. 423b; ii, fol. 423b; ii, fol. 006b; ii, fol. 080a; ii, fol. 423b; ii, fol. 423b; ii, fol. 424a; ii, fol. 425a; ii, fol. 261a; ii, fol. 425a; ii, fol. 425a; ii, fol. 425a; ii, fol. 080b; i, fol. 203c; i, fol. 207a; i, fol. 207b; i, fol. 203c; i, fol. 203c; i, fol. 203c; i, fol. 203c; i, fol. 215b; i, fol. 215b; i, fol. 130d; i, fol. 138c; i, fol. 217d; i, fol. 201d; Hart, Cartularium Monasterii de Rameseia, No. CLII; Hart, Cartularium Monasterii de Rameseia, No. CLIII; Hart, Cartularium Monasterii de Rameseia, No. CXLIX; i, fol. 207b; ii, fol. 079a; ii, fol. 260b; ii, fol. 423b; i, fol. 138c; i, fol. 215b; Hart, Cartularium Monasterii de Rameseia, No. CL

Ranulf Nepos

Norman, occurs Domesday Suffolk as a tenant of William de Warenne at Middleton. Before 1138 his tithes there had been granted to Lewes priory by William fitz Ranulf, presumably his son. His byname becomes French Le Neveu. He was possibly the same Ranulf as William's tenant in Essex.

ii, fol. 038a; ii, fol. 037b; ii, fol. 037a; ii, fol. 036a; ii, fol. 400a

Ranulf Peuerel

Norman, from Vengeons, Manche, comm. cant. Sourdeval (Cart. Montacute, no. 151). Domesday tenant-in-chief in East Anglia. His wife Athelida was a confrater of St Albans (BL Cotton Nero D vii, fol. 119). (The spurious account of this marriage, with Ranulf's wife converted into an Ingelrica, mistress of William I, as printed in Mon. Ang. iii, is unworthy of repetition.) He died c.1091 and was buried in St Paul's cathedral. His successor was his son William, who was dead by the time of the 1129/30 Pipe Roll. Reference to Math- Peverel on the same roll could be either to a Matthew Peverel (q.v.) active at the time, or to Ranulf's daughter, Matilda (q.v.), then the wife of Robert fitz Martin. Matilda, who was heir of her brother William, had Peverel nephews (Richard, Hugh and Ranulf; (BL Cotton Vit. D ix, fol. 40r), as well as issue of her own. Nevertheless, by 1129/30 Ranulf's Domesday lordship of Hatfield Peverel had been definitively resumed by the crown. The Ranulf de Vengeons who occurs on the 1129 Pipe Roll was probably a relative of this family. There is no formal evidence of any relationship between the various Peverels who occur in England, but it is most likely that they were at least members of the same, essentially West Norman, kin group. Most writers have confused Matilda's husband with the Peverel heir, as in L. C. and L. Hulmet, 'Vengeons', Revue Avranchin 88e Année, t. xlvii, no. 265, 301ff.

i, fol. 255c; i, fol. 255c; Hamilton, Inquisitio Eliensis (1876), pp. 192–95; Gibbs, Early Charters of St Pauls (1939), No. 9; ii, fol. 254a; ii, fol. 254b; ii, fol. 254a; ii, fol. 254b; ii, fol. 254b; ii, fol. 254a; ii, fol. 416b; ii, fol. 417b; ii, fol. 416a; ii, fol. 416a; ii, fol. 417a; ii, fol. 417b; ii, fol. 416a; ii, fol. 418a; ii, fol. 417a; ii, fol. 416a; ii, fol. 416a; ii, fol. 416b; ii, fol. 416b; ii, fol. 416b; ii, fol. 416a; ii, fol. 417b; ii, fol. 416a; ii, fol. 416a; ii, fol. 397b; i, fol. 159a; i, fol. 009a; i, fol. 128b; i, fol. 256d; i, fol. 256d; i, fol. 256d; i, fol. 256d; i, fol. 56b; Gibbs, Early Charters of St Pauls (1939), No. 61; i, fol. 159a; ii, fol. 416a; Gibbs, Early Charters of St Pauls (1939), No. 219; Regesta regum Anglo-Normannorum III, No. 345; ii, fol. 071b; ii, fol. 099b; ii, fol. 393b; ii, fol. 074b; ii, fol. 107a; ii, fol. 074b; ii, fol. 072b; ii, fol. 073a; ii, fol. 031b; ii, fol. 073a; ii, fol. 019a; ii, fol. 073b; ii, fol. 074b; ii, fol. 073b; ii, fol. 099b; ii, fol. 004b; ii, fol. 075b; ii, fol. 075a; ii, fol. 279b; ii, fol. 075a; ii, fol. 073b; ii, fol. 074b; ii, fol. 074b; ii, fol. 074a; ii, fol. 075a; ii, fol. 002a; ii, fol. 018b; ii, fol. 099b

Ranulf []

Domesday tenant of Hervey Bituricensis. Probably represented in 1166 by Osbern de Hasfeld, who held one fee at Ashfield of Hervey's grandson Haimo Pecche.

ii, fol. 441a; ii, fol. 443a; ii, fol. 443a

Rauenot []

Occurs Domesday Essex as a tenant of Ranulf Peverel.

ii, fol. 073a; ii, fol. 075a

Rayner Carpentarius

Occurs Domesday Herefordshire.

i, fol. 187c; i, fol. 187c

Rayner De Brimou

Picard, from Brimeux, Pas-de-Calais, arr. Montreuil. Tenant-in-chief in Domesday Lincolnshire, and tenant of Drogo de La Beuvrière. He may have accompanied Drogo into exile around the time of Domesday Book (English, Holderness, 138).

Lincolnshire Claims (Domesday Book), fols 375a–d; i, fol. 324d; i, fol. 324c; i, fol. 303b; Lincolnshire Claims (Domesday Book), fols 375a–d; i, fol. 364a; i, fol. 364b; i, fol. 364a; i, fol. 364b; i, fol. 364a; i, fol. 364a; i, fol. 364a; i, fol. 364b; i, fol. 364b; i, fol. 364a; i, fol. 364a; i, fol. 364a; i, fol. 364b; i, fol. 364b; i, fol. 364b; i, fol. 364b; i, fol. 364b; i, fol. 364a; i, fol. 364a; i, fol. 364a; Lincolnshire Claims (Domesday Book), fols 375d–376a; i, fol. 364b; i, fol. 364a

Rayner De Tungelande

A Rainer who held land at Thonglands in Tugford from Rainald de Balliol in Domesday Shropshire probably became a tenant of the abbey when Rainald gave it the greater part of Tugford. Land which was leased by Abbot Fulchred to him for life became the subject of a dispute with the abbey after his death, when his son William refused to give it up (Cart. Shrewsbury, no. 1). Robert of Thonglands was a tenant of William fitz Alan in 1166. Rainer may have been the same as the Rainer prepositus whose grant to Shrewsbury abbey was confirmed by Henry II (ibid., p. 42).

i, fol. 254b; Rees, Cartulary of Shrewsbury Abbey (1975), No. 35

Rayner []
Tenant of Jocelyn fitz Lambert in Domesday Lincolnshire. Possibly succeeded by the Osbert son of Adam of Somersby who occurs on Pipe Roll 31 Henry I (p. 112).

i, fol. 359c; i, fol. 359b; i, fol. 359c; i, fol. 359c

Raynouuard []
Tenant of Ralph fitz Hubert in Domesday Derbyshire.

i, fol. 277a; i, fol. 277a; i, fol. 277a

Reinbert Dapifer
Norman, occurs in Domesday Sussex as a major tenant of the count of Eu. Evidenced as dapifer c.1086, and as sheriff of the Rape of Hastings between 1086 and 1106 (VCH Sussex i, 352; RRAN ii, nos. 691, 752). His heir c.1100 was his probable son-in-law Drogo de Pevenesel (VCH Sussex ix, 212). Drogo was dead by 1129, when his son Simon fitz Drogo (q.v.) occurs on the Pipe Roll. Reinbert had 'nepotes' (probably nephews) who occur with Drogo c.1100; one of them, Warmund, was possibly the Wermund de Petra who attested a charter of Henry d'Eu in 1107 (CDF, 233). He was probably a relative of the Alan, son of Reimbert and Albreda), who made a grant to Lewes c.1140 attested by Simon fitz Drogo (Cart. Lewes. i, p. 177).

i, fol. 19d; i, fol. 19d; i, fol. 19d; i, fol. 19d; i, fol. 19c; i, fol. 19c; i, fol. 19c; i, fol. 19c; i, fol. 19c; i, fol. 19c; i, fol. 19c; i, fol. 19c; i, fol. 19c; i, fol. 18c; i, fol. 19d; i, fol. 18b; i, fol. 20a; i, fol. 17d; i, fol. 17d; i, fol. 19c; i, fol. 18a; i, fol. 19d; i, fol. 18c; i, fol. 18c; i, fol. 19b; i, fol. 19b; i, fol. 19b; i, fol. 19b; i, fol. 19b; i, fol. 19b; i, fol. 18a; i, fol. 18d; i, fol. 18d; i, fol. 19d; i, fol. 19d

Remigius Episcopus Lincolniensis
Monk of Fécamp, he accompanied William I on the expedition of 1066. Bishop of Dorchester from c.1067, transferred his see – the largest in the country – to Lincoln in 1072; died 8 May 1092. Apparently a relative of William I; on his life and influential career see D. Bates, Remigius of Lincoln (Lincoln, 1995). FEA iii, 1, EEA i, xxxi–ii.

Dugdale, Monasticon Anglicanum, IV, p. 13, No. IV; i, fol. 336b; Lincolnshire Claims (Domesday Book), fols 376d–377c; i, fol. 340b; Clay, Early Yorkshire Charters (1949), VIII, No. 4; Dugdale, Monasticon Anglicanum, III, p. 499, No. I; i, fol. 210b; i, fol. 344a; i, fol. 283d; i, fol. 155a; i, fol. 221a; Dugdale, Monasticon Anglicanum, III, p. 216, No. V; Dugdale, Monasticon Anglicanum, III, p. 499, No. II; Dugdale, Monasticon Anglicanum, III, p. 216, No. V; i, fol. 341a; i, fol. 366b; Lincolnshire Claims (Domesday Book), fols 376d–377c; Lincolnshire Claims (Domesday Book), fols 375d–376a; Lincolnshire Claims (Domesday Book), fol. 377d; i, fol. 283d; i, fol. 208c; i, fol. 283d; i, fol. 336a; i, fol. 209b; i, fol. 336a; i, fol. 283d; i, fol. 283d; i, fol. 283d; i, fol. 366d; i, fol. 283d; i, fol. 283d; i, fol. 283d; i, fol. 283d; i, fol. 283d; i, fol. 283d; i, fol. 283d; i, fol. 283d; i, fol. 284a; i, fol. 283d; i, fol. 344d; i, fol. 283d; i, fol. 283d; i, fol. 345a; i, fol. 283d; i, fol. 283d; i, fol. 283d; i, fol. 344d; i, fol. 344a; i, fol. 344a; i, fol. 344a; i, fol. 344a; i, fol. 344a; i, fol. 344c; i, fol. 344a; i, fol. 210c; Lincolnshire Claims (Domesday Book), fols 376b–c; i, fol. 210c; i, fol. 56b; i, fol. 56c; i, fol. 143a; i, fol. 209a; i, fol. 344b; i, fol. 344d; i, fol. 345a; i, fol. 283d;

i, fol. 344d; i, fol. 344a; i, fol. 344d; i, fol. 344a; i, fol. 344d; i, fol. 283d; i, fol.
344d; i, fol. 344d; i, fol. 344c; i, fol. 344c; i, fol. 344a; i, fol. 344a; i, fol. 344a; i,
fol. 344a; i, fol. 344d; i, fol. 203d; i, fol. 203d; i, fol. 338c; i, fol. 143d; i, fol.
144a; i, fol. 345a; i, fol. 221a; i, fol. 221a; i, fol. 221a; i, fol. 221a; i, fol. 155b;
Lincolnshire Claims (Domesday Book), fols 375d–376a; i, fol. 337a; i, fol.
230b; i, fol. 155b; i, fol. 155a; i, fol. 155b; i, fol. 155b; i, fol. 155a; i, fol. 231a; i,
fol. 230b; i, fol. 231a; i, fol. 143b; i, fol. 190b; i, fol. 143d; i, fol. 154a; Dugdale,
Monasticon Anglicanum, III, p. 217, No. VII; i, fol. 203d; Dugdale, Monasticon
Anglicanum, III, p. 216, No. IV; Hamilton, Inquisitio Eliensis (1876), pp.
192–95; Hamilton, Inquisitio Eliensis (1876), pp. 192–95

Remir []

Domesday tenant of William of Eu in Sussex. On account of the rarity of his
personal name, Remir is doubtless to be identified with Remir d'Envermeu, son of
Osbern and brother of Geoffrey and Walter (BN lat. 10058, Cart. Saint-Laurent
d'Envermeu, p. 4).

i, fol. 19d; i, fol. 20a

Reneuuald []

Domesday tenant of Walter de Douai.

i, fol. 111d; i, fol. 95a; i, fol. 95a; i, fol. 95b; i, fol. 95b; i, fol. 95b; i, fol. 95b

Restold []

Norman, Domesday tenant of Odo of Bayeux and Archbishop Lanfranc, and a
knight of the archbishop of Canterbury in 1093–6 (Douglas, Dom. Mon., 30).
William son of Restold occurs in the Lindsey Survey (1115/18). A Richilda
daughter of Restolda gave land at Calix, in Caen, to the nuns of Sainte-Trinité
c.1083 (Walmsley, p. 116).

i, fol. 264a; i, fol. 31d; i, fol. 25c; i, fol. 366a; i, fol. 30d; ii, fol. 083b; Douglas,
ed., Domesday Monachorum (1944), p. 105; i, fol. 366a

Ribald Frater Comitis Alani

Natural son of Count Eudo of Brittany and so half-brother of Count Alan, from
whom he held considerable estates in 1086, principally in Yorkshire and
Lincolnshire. He married Beatrice, daughter of Ivo Taillebois, and was ancestor of
the lords of Middleham, Yorks. He was succeeded by his son Ralph c.1121. See
EYC v, 297–306; H. C. Fitz Herbert, 'An original pedigree of Taillebois and
Neville' Genealogist n.s. iii, 31, giving Ribald and Beatrice's issue as Ralph,
Hervey, Rainald and William Taillebois.

i, fol. 312b; i, fol. 311d; i, fol. 311c; i, fol. 311d; i, fol. 312b; Dugdale,
Monasticon Anglicanum, III, pp. 548–50, No. V; i, fol. 311b; i, fol. 311b; i, fol.
313a; i, fol. 313a; i, fol. 311c; Clay, Early Yorkshire Charters (1935), IV, No. 4; ii,
fol. 146b; ii, fol. 144b; ii, fol. 149a; ii, fol. 149a; ii, fol. 145b; Clay, Early
Yorkshire Charters (1936), V, No. 358; Clay, Early Yorkshire Charters (1935), IV,
No. 1; Dugdale, Monasticon Anglicanum, III, pp. 546–47, No. II; Dugdale,
Monasticon Anglicanum, III, p. 553, No. XX; ii, fol. 144b; ii, fol. 144b; ii, fol.
144b; ii, fol. 146a; ii, fol. 146a; ii, fol. 146a; ii, fol. 146a; ii, fol. 146a; ii, fol.
148a; ii, fol. 148a; ii, fol. 148a; ii, fol. 149a; ii, fol. 149a; ii, fol. 149a; ii, fol.
149a; ii, fol. 150a; ii, fol. 150a; ii, fol. 150a

Ricardus Basset

Occurs in Domesady Book; a relative of Ralph Basset (q.v.).

i, fol. 215b

Ricardus Caluus

Domesday tenant of Bury St Edmunds, named in the Feudal Book.

ii, fol. 362b

Ricardus Capellani Comitis

In 1086 the chaplains of Earl Roger of Shrewsbury were mentioned as holding land at Morville, where the church of St Gregory had been given to Shrewsbury Abbey. In a later document of the abbey one of the chaplains was named as Richard de Mainilhermer, who became a monk of the abbey and was buried there. His son Hubert was a layman who sought to retain his father's prebend, prompting the monks to seek the aid of Henry I in resolving the matter (Cart Shrewsbury no. 1). Probably named from Le Ménil-Hermei, Orne, cant. Putanges-Pont-Ecrépin.

i, fol. 253b

Ricardus De Barra

Norman, perhaps named from Barre-en-Ouche, Eure, occurs Domesday Somerset as a tenant of Ralph de Mortemer, identified from Exon. Perhaps the same man held from Ralph elsewhere. His successor in Somerset in 1166 was William Barre.

i, fol. 95d

Ricardus De Curci

Richard de Courcy, Norman from Courcy, Calvados, cant. Saint-Pierre-sur-Dives (Loyd, 36), probably a son of Robert de Courcy; his mother was named Hebrea and his wife, Wandelmode (CDF, 1193). Occurs as a minor Domesday tenant-in-chief. He was succeeded in England by his son William, dapifer of Henry I, and in Normandy by his son Robert. He was one of a few to attest charters for both William II and his brother Robert Curthose in 1087–8. He was named as one of the despoilers of the abbey of Sainte-Trinité-de-Caen after 1087 (Haskins, NI, 63–4). He appears to have died c.1088.

i, fol. 159a; i, fol. 159a; i, fol. 154a; i, fol. 154c; i, fol. 159a; i, fol. 159a

Ricardus De Guerres

Norman, from Gueures, Seine-Maritime, arr. Dieppe, cant. Bacqueville, Domesday tenant of Geoffrey de Mandeville at Little Canfield, Essex, identified from a grant to Lewes priory (CDF 1391). His successor Adelard de Guerres attested for William de Mandeville in the early twelfth century (Mon. Ang. iv, 149). Manasser de Guerres paid relief in 1129. Cf. Loyd, 48–9.

ii, fol. 100a

Ricardus De Maris

Norman, occurs as knight of the archbishop of Canterbury in 1093–6. In 1086 he held of Odo of Bayeux at Ospringe. Perhaps ancestor of the de Marisco or Mares family, or whom John de Marisco held a fee of the archbishopric at East Preston in Aylesford, in the Honour of Talbot (du Boulay, Lordship, 365).

Douglas, ed., Domesday Monachorum (1944), p. 105; i, fol. 010a

Ricardus De Meri

Richard de Meri, son and, after the death of an older brother Robert, Norman heir of Humphrey de Bohun, from Saint-Georges-de-Bohon, Manche, arr. Saint-Lô, cant. Carentan. In 1086 he held a single manor in Somerset as tenant of Alfred d'Epaignes (Eure); his toponym occurs in Exon. Occurs with his father in a charter of c.1080. In 1092 he made an accord with the monks of Saint-Georges-de-Bohun, who took his little son Humphrey to be educated. It was reaffirmed soon after, with Richard's wife Lucy and their issue Robert, Henry, Humphrey and Hadvisa, attested by Richard's father Humphrey (CDF, 1212–14). Richard's daughter Muriel married Savaric fitz Cana (q.v.) of Sussex. Her descendants were eventual heirs of Richard, whose son and successor Ingelran was childless.

i, fol. 97b; i, fol. 97b

Ricardus De Montgarolt

Norman, from Montgaroult, Orne, cant. Ecouché, Domesday tenant of Earl Roger de Montgomery in Shropshire. Benefactor of Saint-Martin de Sées (Arch. dépt. Orne H fols 61/71v, 30/38v), and early benefactor of Shrewsbury abbey.

i, fol. 257a; i, fol. 259d; Rees, Cartulary of Shrewsbury Abbey (1975), No. 35

Ricardus De Neville

Norman, Domesday tenant of Baldwin the Sheriff in Devon, identified in a single manor as de Neville in Exon. Possibly the same man is intended in several other occurrences of Richards on this fief. Probably named from Neuville-sur-Authou, Eure, near Brionne. Baldwin was son of Gilbert, count of Brionne.

i, fol. 106d; i, fol. 108b; i, fol. 106b; i, fol. 106b; i, fol. 106b; i, fol. 106b; i, fol. 106b; i, fol. 106a

Ricardus De Newercha

Norman, occurs Domesday Oxfordshire; surnamed de Newercha in Cart. Eynsham i, 37.

i, fol. 155c

Ricardus De Pesimari

Tenant of Gilbert de Bretteville in 1086. Mentioned in the Abingdon Chronicle as alive in 1105 (ii, 31); also occurs with his son Philip de Pesimari (Peasmore) (ibid., ii, 120.

i, fol. 62a

Ricardus De Praeres

Norman, from Presles, Calvados, Domesday tenant of Earl Hugh of Chester, to whom he was distantly related. See Keats-Rohan, 'Prosopography of post-Conquest England', Medieval Prosopography 14.1 (1992), 23–8. Father of William and Adam. HKF ii, 143–4.

i, fol. 265b; Barraclough, Charters of AN Earls of Chester (1988), No. 28; Barraclough, Charters of AN Earls of Chester (1988), No. 8; Barraclough, Charters of AN Earls of Chester (1988), No. 28

Ricardus De Redvers

Norman, from Reviers, Calvados, arr. Caen, cant. Creully; held a single identifiable manor in Domesday Book, in Dorset. After the accession of Henry I he was given the honour of Plympton, a collection of former Domesday tenancies-in-chief that was to become the earldom of Devon in the time of Richard's son Baldwin (Sanders, 137). Apparently son of Baldwin, a brother of a Richard de Redvers who d. c. 1050; these brothers were the sons of an unknown father, perhaps Hugh de Vernon, and the daughter of Fulk fitz Osmund, whose mother Satselina was a niece of the Norman duchess Gunnor, according to Robert of Torigny (discussed in Keats-Rohan, 'Aspects of Robert of Torigny's genealogies revisited', Nottingham Medieval Studies 37 (1993); R. Bearman, Redvers

Charters, Introduction). By his wife Adleisa, daughter of William I Peverel of Nottingham, he left issue Baldwin, Robert de Sainte-Mère-Eglise, Hugh de Vernon, William de Vernon and Hawise, later wife of William I de Roumare, earl of Lincoln. He died in 1107, when his successor Baldwin was still a minor.

Bearman, Charters of the Redvers Family (1994), No. 37; Regesta regum Anglo-Normannorum III, No. 903; Regesta regum Anglo-Normannorum III, No. 594; Bearman, Charters of the Redvers Family (1994), App. I No. 1; Bearman, Charters of the Redvers Family (1994), No. 3; Bearman, Charters of the Redvers Family (1994), No. 15; Bearman, Charters of the Redvers Family (1994), No. 34; Bearman, Charters of the Redvers Family (1994), No. 33; Bearman, Charters of the Redvers Family (1994), No. 24; Bearman, Charters of the Redvers Family (1994), App. II No. 9; Bearman, Charters of the Redvers Family (1994), No. 5; i, fol. 83b; Bearman, Charters of the Redvers Family (1994), No. 2; Bearman, Charters of the Redvers Family (1994), No. 110; Bearman, Charters of the Redvers Family (1994), No. 1; Dugdale, Monasticon Anglicanum, III, pp. 377–78, No. III; Bearman, Charters of the Redvers Family (1994), App. I No. 3; Bearman, Charters of the Redvers Family (1994), No. 10; Bearman, Charters of the Redvers Family (1994), No. 4; Bearman, Charters of the Redvers Family (1994), App. II No. 10; Bearman, Charters of the Redvers Family (1994), App. II No. 1; Bearman, Charters of the Redvers Family (1994), No. 9; Finberg, Early Tavistock Charters: EHR, 62, No. II; Bearman, Charters of the Redvers Family (1994), No. 19; Bearman, Charters of the Redvers Family (1994), App. I No. 4a; Bearman, Charters of the Redvers Family (1994), App. I No. 4; Bearman, Charters of the Redvers Family (1994), App. II No. 2; Bearman, Charters of the Redvers Family (1994), No. 25; Bearman, Charters of the Redvers Family (1994), No. 27; Bearman, Charters of the Redvers Family (1994), No. 13; Bearman, Charters of the Redvers Family (1994), No. 4

Ricardus De Sachanuilla

Norman, major tenant of Eudo dapifer and others in Domesday East Anglia; named from Sauqueville-en-Besin, Calvados, arr. Caen, cant. Creully (Loyd, 88). He was succeeded by William de Sackville, and then by the latter's nephew Richard de Ansty (q.v.). Cf. HKF iii, 27; J. H. Round, 'The Essex Sackvilles', Archaeological Journal lxic, 218.

ii, fol. 050b; ii, fol. 051a; ii, fol. 049a; ii, fol. 051b; ii, fol. 051a; ii, fol. 051a; ii, fol. 239b; i, fol. 139b; Red Book of the Exchequer, ed. Hall (1897), pp. 363–66; ii, fol. 049b; ii, fol. 049b; ii, fol. 049b; ii, fol. 049b; ii, fol. 049b

Ricardus De Sancto Claro

Norman, occurs Domesday as a tenant of Ralph de Beaufour. He gave land from his Suffolk manor of Wortham to Shaftesbury Abbey with his daughter, a nun. Perhaps named from Saint-Clair-sur-l'Elle, Manche.

ii, fol. 228a; ii, fol. 226b; ii, fol. 226a; Regesta regum Anglo-Normannorum III, No. 818; Dugdale, Monasticon Anglicanum, IV, p. 50, No. III; Dugdale, Monasticon Anglicanum, IV, p. 50, No. III; Dugdale, Monasticon Anglicanum, IV, p. 51, No. VII; ii, fol. 354b; ii, fol. 354b; ii, fol. 354b; ii, fol. 117b; ii, fol. 117a; ii, fol. 227b; ii, fol. 227b; ii, fol. 227b; ii, fol. 229a; ii, fol. 229a; ii, fol. 229b; ii, fol. 229b; ii, fol. 229b; ii, fol. 229b; ii, fol. 229b

Ricardus De Solariis

Norman, occurs as Richard de Solariis in an early Gloucestershire Survey; named from Soliers, Calvados, cant. Bourgébus. He can be identified with the tenant of William de Écouis and Ansfrid of Cormeilles in Herefordshire. A second Richard de Solariis occurs c.1154.

i, fol. 186b; i, fol. 186b; i, fol. 180b; Ellis, 'Landholders of Gloucestershire' (1880), pp. 91–93

Ricardus De Spineto

Norman, whose land at (Little) Snoring, Norfolk, which he held as a tenant of Ralph Fatatus, was given c.1100/07 to Binham priory by Peter I de Valognes. He was probably the same Richard who was Peter's tenant in 1086.

ii, fol. 257b; Dugdale, Monasticon Anglicanum, III, pp. 345–46, No. I; Douglas, Social Structure of Med. E. Anglia (1927), No. 35

Ricardus De Surdeval

Norman, from Sourdeval, Manche, arr. Mortain (Loyd, 99), Domesday tenant of Mortain in Yorkshire. He established one of the prebends of Saint-Evroul de Mortain, granting half the vill of Le Fresne-Poret (RRAN i, 159; Pouëssel, 129–34). See EYC vi, p. 4 note. His land in Yorkshire went to Ralph Paynel, whose second wife Matilda was probably Richard's daughter (Sanders, 55).

i, fol. 307c; i, fol. 307a; i, fol. 307a; i, fol. 307a; i, fol. 307a; i, fol. 307a; i, fol. 307a; i, fol. 307a; i, fol. 307a; i, fol. 308a; i, fol. 308b; i, fol. 307a; i, fol. 306d; i, fol. 307c; i, fol. 306d; i, fol. 307c; i, fol. 307c; i, fol. 308b; i, fol. 308b; i, fol. 308b; i, fol. 308a; i, fol. 308a; i, fol. 308a; i, fol. 308a; i, fol. 308a; i, fol. 308a; i, fol. 308a; i, fol. 308a; i, fol. 308a; i, fol. 308b; i, fol. 305b; i, fol. 308a; i, fol. 307d; i, fol. 307d; i, fol. 307c; i, fol. 305c; i, fol. 305d; i, fol. 305c; i, fol. 305c; i, fol. 306c; i, fol. 305c; i, fol. 308a; i, fol. 305c; i, fol. 308b; i, fol. 305d; i, fol. 305c; i, fol. 306b; i, fol. 305b; i, fol. 308c; i, fol. 308b; i, fol. 308c; i, fol. 305d; i, fol. 308c; i, fol. 305c; i, fol. 308c; Pipe Roll 6 Henry II, 15–y; Pipe Roll 4 Henry II, 148–y; i, fol. 298a; i, fol. 305b

Ricardus De Vernon

Norman, tenant of Earl Hugh in Domesday; possibly named from Vernon, Eure. arr. Evreux., though Vaire-sur-Mer, Calvados is also possible from the form of his toponym. He was succeeded soon after 1086 by his brother Walter, and then by their nephew Walchelin. HKF ii, 232.

ii, fol. 152a; Barraclough, Charters of AN Earls of Chester (1988), No. 28; i, fol. 265a; i, fol. 265a; i, fol. 265a; i, fol. 265a; i, fol. 265a; i, fol. 265a; i, fol. 265a; Barraclough, Charters of AN Earls of Chester (1988), No. 28; i, fol. 265a; i, fol. 265a; i, fol. 265a; i, fol. 265a; Barraclough, Charters of AN Earls of Chester (1988), No. 3; i, fol. 265a; Barraclough, Charters of AN Earls of Chester (1988), No. 3

Ricardus Episcopus Londoniensis

Norman, from Beaumais-sur-Dive, Calvados, arr. Falaise, cant. Morteaux-Couliboeuf (Loyd, 13), tenant of Roger de Montgomery in Domesday Shropshire. He was one of Roger's clerks, and possibly also his steward (see Mason, Officers and Clerks, 253–4). He was later bishop of London, from 24 May 1108 until his death on 16 January 1127. See FEA i, 1.

i, fol. 258c; i, fol. 258c; Gibbs, Early Charters of St Pauls (1939), No. 47; Rees, Cartulary of Shrewsbury Abbey (1975), No. 35; Gibbs, Early Charters of St Pauls (1939), No. 273; Gibbs, Early Charters of St Pauls (1939), No. 95; Gibbs, Early Charters of St Pauls (1939), No. 46; Mason, Beauchamp Cartulary Charters (1980), No. 4; Regesta regum Anglo-Normannorum III, No. 499; Gibbs, Early Charters of St Pauls (1939), No. 28; Ransford, Early Charters of

Waltham Abbey (1989), No. 8; Hart, Cartularium Monasterii de Rameseia, No. CLXVIII; Ransford, Early Charters of Waltham Abbey (1989), No. 10; Gibbs, Early Charters of St Pauls (1939), No. 25; Gibbs, Early Charters of St Pauls (1939), No. 62; Regesta Regum Anglo Normannorum II, App. no. cxxvii; Dugdale, Monasticon Anglicanum, II, p. 267, No. XII; Dugdale, Monasticon Anglicanum, II, p. 18, No. XI; Gibbs, Early Charters of St Pauls (1939), No. 61; Gibbs, Early Charters of St Pauls (1939), No. 63; Dugdale, Monasticon Anglicanum, III, p. 295, No. I; Ransford, Early Charters of Waltham Abbey (1989), No. 15; Gibbs, Early Charters of St Pauls (1939), No. 60; Rees, Cartulary of Shrewsbury Abbey (1975), No. 35

Ricardus Filius Alan

Norman, Domesday tenant of William bishop of Thetford at Hemsby, in West Flegg hundred, and at other places in East Flegg hundred, Norfolk. Attested a charter of Bishop Herbert of c.1107/19 as Richard de Flegg (EEA vi, no. 19). Father of Roger.

ii, fol. 195b; ii, fol. 115b; Dodwell, Charters relating to the Honour of Bacton, No. 5; ii, fol. 197a; ii, fol. 197a

Ricardus Filius Erfasti

Norman tenant-in-chief in Domesday Yorkshire. His land escheated soon after 1086 and was granted to Ralph Paynel. He is perhaps to be identified with Richard son of Herfast, bishop of Elmham/Thetford from 1070–86.

i, fol. 327a; Dugdale, Monasticon Anglicanum, IV, pp. 148–49, No. II; i, fol. 298b; i, fol. 327a; i, fol. 327a; i, fol. 327a; i, fol. 327a; i, fol. 327a; i, fol. 327a

Ricardus Filius Gisleberti Comitis

Norman, son of Gilbert count of Brionne, a kinsman of William the Conqueror, and brother of Baldwin de Meulles, sheriff of Exeter; lord of Orbec, Eure, arr. Lisieux, and Clare, Suffolk (Sanders, 34). He married Rohais, daughter of Walter I Giffard, and had issue by her Roger, Gilbert, Walter, Robert and Richard, a monk of Bec later abbot of Ely, Rohais, wife of Eudo Dapifer and Adelisa, wife of Walter Tirel de Poix, who was one of Richard's tenants in 1086. He had retired from the world to become a monk of Bec at the priory he had established at St Neots by April 1088, when his son Gilbert was active in the region of Rochester defending the interests of William II. He died in May 1089 or 1090 and was buried at St Neot's. See Douglas, Dom. Mon. 40; Comp. Peer. iii, 242. R. Mortimer, 'The beginnings of the Honour of Clare', ANS 3 (1981); idem 'Land and service: the tenants of the Honour of Clare', ANS 8 (1985); J. Ward, 'Fashions in monastic endowments: the foundations of the Clare family 1066–1314', Journal of Ecclesiastical History 32 (1981); idem, 'Royal service and reward:the Clare family and the Crown, 1066–1154', ANS xi (1989).

ii, fol. 050a; ii, fol. 448a; Clay, Early Yorkshire Charters (1949), VIII, No. 4; i, fol. 007d; i, fol. 004d; i, fol. 006d; i, fol. 004d; i, fol. 007b; i, fol. 003b; i, fol. 005c; i, fol. 008c; i, fol. 35b; i, fol. 35b; i, fol. 35b; i, fol. 35c; i, fol. 009a; i, fol. 35c; i, fol. 003a; i, fol. 35c; i, fol. 004b; i, fol. 007a; i, fol. 014b; i, fol. 014b; i, fol. 006a; i, fol. 007d; i, fol. 006a; i, fol. 007c; i, fol. 003b; i, fol. 008d; i, fol. 30d; i, fol. 004b; i, fol. 35a; i, fol. 35c; i, fol. 34c; i, fol. 34c; i, fol. 35d; i, fol. 35c; i, fol. 35d; i, fol. 30b; i, fol. 35c; i, fol. 35a; i, fol. 35b; i, fol. 35d; i, fol. 35d; i, fol. 35c; Dugdale, Monasticon Anglicanum, III, p. 499, No. I; ii, fol. 038b; Dugdale, Monasticon Anglicanum, IV, p. 14, No. VI; Regesta regum Anglo-Normannorum III, No. 345; Gervers, Cartulary of Knights St John, II (1996),

No. 111; i, fol. 216b; ii, fol. 389b; Douglas, Feudal Documents from Bury St Edmunds, No. 9; ii, fol. 003b; Douglas, Feudal Documents from Bury St Edmunds, No. 10; Ballard, Inquisition of St Augustine's (1920), fols 20r–23v; ii, fol. 060a; Chibnall, English Lands of Abbey of Bec (1951), No. XL; ii, fol. 038b; ii, fol. 041a; ii, fol. 041a; ii, fol. 041b; ii, fol. 040a; ii, fol. 040b; ii, fol. 040a; ii, fol. 040a; ii, fol. 038b; ii, fol. 040a; ii, fol. 041a; ii, fol. 040a; ii, fol. 039b; ii, fol. 040a; ii, fol. 040a; ii, fol. 040a; ii, fol. 040a; ii, fol. 040a; ii, fol. 039b; ii, fol. 040a; ii, fol. 040b; ii, fol. 040a; ii, fol. 385a; Chibnall, English Lands of Abbey of Bec (1951), No. XLI; ii, fol. 395a; ii, fol. 394b; ii, fol. 395a; ii, fol. 393a; ii, fol. 394a; ii, fol. 394a; ii, fol. 393b; ii, fol. 393a; ii, fol. 393a; ii, fol. 393a; ii, fol. 396b; ii, fol. 392b; ii, fol. 395a; ii, fol. 397b; ii, fol. 448a; ii, fol. 448a; ii, fol. 448a; ii, fol. 397b; ii, fol. 392b; ii, fol. 390a; ii, fol. 390b; ii, fol. 391b; ii, fol. 390b; ii, fol. 395a; ii, fol. 389b; ii, fol. 389b; ii, fol. 395a; ii, fol. 390a; ii, fol. 395a; i, fol. 130b; ii, fol. 395a; ii, fol. 396b; ii, fol. 392b; ii, fol. 395a; ii, fol. 395a; ii, fol. 395a; ii, fol. 395a; ii, fol. 397a; ii, fol. 389b; ii, fol. 390b; ii, fol. 391b; ii, fol. 391a; ii, fol. 391b; ii, fol. 395a; ii, fol. 391a; ii, fol. 391b; ii, fol. 391a; ii, fol. 391a; ii, fol. 391a; ii, fol. 397a; ii, fol. 392a; ii, fol. 390b; ii, fol. 391a; ii, fol. 390b; ii, fol. 391b; ii, fol. 392a; ii, fol. 392a; ii, fol. 392a; ii, fol. 392a; ii, fol. 392b; ii, fol. 392a; ii, fol. 392b; ii, fol. 392b; ii, fol. 392b; ii, fol. 392b; ii, fol. 390b; ii, fol. 397a; ii, fol. 397b; ii, fol. 397b; ii, fol. 396a; ii, fol. 397b; i, fol. 216b; ii, fol. 391a; ii, fol. 397a; ii, fol. 391b; ii, fol. 397a; ii, fol. 397a; ii, fol. 397a; ii, fol. 397a; ii, fol. 397a; ii, fol. 391b; ii, fol. 397b; ii, fol. 397a; ii, fol. 391b; ii, fol. 392a; ii, fol. 392a; ii, fol. 392a; ii, fol. 392a; ii, fol. 391b; ii, fol. 397b; ii, fol. 397a; ii, fol. 397a; ii, fol. 391b; ii, fol. 102b; ii, fol. 102b; ii, fol. 102b; ii, fol. 102b; ii, fol. 102b; ii, fol. 102b; ii, fol. 102b; ii, fol. 102b; ii, fol. 102b; i, fol. 004b; i, fol. 004b

Ricardus Filius Rainfridi

Norman, Domesday tenant of Miles Crispin. He occurs in a confirmation charter of William I for the abbey of Bec as the donor of a moiety of the church and tithe of Bournainville (Eure), the other moiety being granted by William Crispin the younger (Porée, Histoire du Bec, i, 331, 646). The same charter confirmed the gift of Richard's tenant Erchembald de Faverols. He also gave land in his demesne in three English manors to Bec before c.1086/7 (Salter, EHR 1925, pp. 74–6). He gave 2 hides at Brokestal to Abingdon Abbey on the day he died, a 6 November c.1109–17. The grant was subsequently confirmed at the request of Abbot Faritius (d.1117) by Richard's son Hugh (q.v.), with the assent of his lords Brien fitz Count and Matilda of Wallingford (Chron. Abing. ii, 28, 108–9, 111)

i, fol. 159d; i, fol. 159c; i, fol. 150a; i, fol. 150a; i, fol. 61d; i, fol. 61d

Ricardus Filius Turolf

Domesday tenant of Robert of Mortain in Cornwall and elsewhere. Founder of Tywardreth priory, a cell of SS Serge and Bachus, Angers, and ancestor of the Cardinam family. Probably the same as Richard fitz Turold who held the church of Damblainville (arr. Morteaux-le-Couliboeuf, Calvados, Normandy) from Alan de Ducey (Le Prévost ed. Ord. Vit, v, 187–8). See I.N. Soulsby, 'Richard fitz Turold, lord of Penhallam in Cornwall', Medieval Archaeology 20 (1976). He has been identified with the count's steward (dapifer) Richard; see Mason, 'Barons and officials', ANS 13 (1991), p. 246. He was succeeded by his son William c.1110 (Sanders, 110). The obit of his wife Emma was remembered at Saint-Serge d'Angers on 24 November (Emma soror –, mater Willelmi filii Ricardi Cornubie', Bib. mun. d'Angers ms 837 (753), fol. 58, cited in Barlow,

EEA xi, 140, note p. 128.

> i, fol. 120a; i, fol. 105a; i, fol. 105b; i, fol. 105a; i, fol. 105d; i, fol. 105c; i, fol. 107c; i, fol. 120d; i, fol. 121a; i, fol. 122b; i, fol. 122c; i, fol. 92d; i, fol. 122c; i, fol. 122b; i, fol. 122c; i, fol. 122b; i, fol. 122b; i, fol. 122c; i, fol. 122d; i, fol. 122c; i, fol. 122c; i, fol. 122c; i, fol. 122c; i, fol. 122c; i, fol. 122c; i, fol. 122c; i, fol. 122c; i, fol. 122c; i, fol. 122c; i, fol. 122c; i, fol. 122c; i, fol. 122d; i, fol. 122d; i, fol. 122d; i, fol. 122d; i, fol. 122d; i, fol. 122d; i, fol. 122d; Hull, Cartulary of Launceston Priory (1987), No. 14; i, fol. 113c; i, fol. 113c; i, fol. 113c; i, fol. 113c

Ricardus Filius Willelmi

Norman, tenant of Patricksbourne in Domesday Kent. The manor was afterwards held by the Patrick family of La Lande-Patri, Orne, arr. Domfront, cant. Flers (Loyd, 76). This Richard could have been the son of the William Patrick who occurs c.1082 (Actes caen. 14, p. 107). Cf. Sanders, 135.

> i, fol. 009b

Ricardus Forestarius

Norman, occurs Domesday Staffordshire and Warwickshire. His land and forest office appear to have passed with his daughter to William Croc, father of Walter Croc who accounted for Richard's lands in 1129/30.

> i, fol. 250d; Pipe Roll 31 Henry I, 107–wk; i, fol. 244c; i, fol. 250c; i, fol. 238b; i, fol. 244c; i, fol. 244c; i, fol. 244c; i, fol. 244c; i, fol. 244c; i, fol. 250c; i, fol. 250c; i, fol. 250c; i, fol. 250c; i, fol. 250c

Ricardus Fresle

Occurs Domesday Nottinghamshire. Richard Freslart and Geoffrey his nephew ('nepos') attested a charter of Préaux relating to Hugh Fiquet of Wannescrot, a man of Robert Malet and Hugh de Montfort (cited Le Prévost, Eure, 129–30).

> i, fol. 280a

Ricardus Gernet

Domesday tenant of Geoffrey de Mandeville. Some of the occurrences of a Richard in the Mandeville fief may refer to Geoffrey's son of that name. The Gernet holding was clearly important since Alexander Gernet held 4 fees de vetere of Mandeville in 1166 (RBE, 345). The Gernet family were vassals of the abbey of Fécamp in Normandy (RRAN 423, 1562), from which they held Maupertuis and its dependencies at Gerville and Le Mesnil (Seine-Maritime).

> ii, fol. 058b; ii, fol. 061b; ii, fol. 061b; i, fol. 197b; Hamilton, Inquisitio Eliensis (1876), pp. 97–100; Hamilton, Inquisitio Comitatus Cantabrigiensis, pp. 1–93; ii, fol. 059a; ii, fol. 059a; ii, fol. 058b

Ricardus Guet

Richard Guet, appears in the Castleacre Cartulary as the brother of William I de Warenne's wife, whether Gundreda or an otherwise unknown successor. According to Farrer, HKF, iii, 298–9, he should be identified with William's tenant Richard in Essex. He has been falsely identified with the Goet family of Montmirail-en-Perche, in which the name Richard is not found. He was certainly a Richard Goz, a member of the family of the vicomtes of Avranches, and probably the Richard son of Robert Goiz who was brother of William, a benefactor of Saint-Etienne de Caen (Actes caen. 18, pp. 121–2). The Goz family is discussed in Keats-Rohan, Medieval Prosopography 14.1, 25–30, and Musset, 'Saint-Gabriel' and idem 'Saint-Sever'.

> ii, fol. 037a; ii, fol. 037b; ii, fol. 036a; ii, fol. 036a; ii, fol. 038a; ii, fol. 038a; ii, fol. 038a; Excerpta a Chronicis de Bermondsey, Dugdale, Monasticon, IV, pp. 95–97

Ricardus Houerel

Domesday tenant of Robert Malet, who gave his land in 'Winerdestowe' to his priory of Eye (Cart., no. 1). A Godfrid Huuvel appears in a twelfth century charter for the abbey of Montebourg associated with land at Givernay, cant. Gasny, Eure (BN lat. 10087, 79/185). In 1221 William de Bello Campo gave rent owed by Laurence Hovel to Saint-Amand de Rouen (Arch. dépt. 55 H non coté, carton 6); a Hovel family held land at Saint-Sever and Saint-Martin de Mailloc (Calvados) in the late Middle Ages (Arch. dépt. Calvados F 5280 and 5607).

> ii, fol. 371a; ii, fol. 328a; Douglas, Feudal Book of Bury St Edmunds (1932), pp. 3–21; Regesta regum Anglo-Normannorum III, No. 288; Brown, Eye Priory Cartulary (1992–94), No. 5; Brown, Eye Priory Cartulary (1992–94), No. 55; Brown, Eye Priory Cartulary (1992–94), No. 3; Brown, Eye Priory Cartulary (1992–94), No. 1; ii, fol. 436b; ii, fol. 436a

Ricardus Ingania

Norman, brother of William Ingaine. Both held land in chief in Domesday Northamptonshire that had been associated with a forest serjeanty that had been held before 1066 by Ælfwine Venator, 'the Huntsman'; cf. Round, Feudal England, 130. The forestership was principally associated with Richard's fief, known as that of Engaine of Abington. William's holding, for a hunting serjeanty, was that of Engaine of Pytchley. Richard is evidenced witnessing charters up till c.1110. What follows here is a fresh attempt to explain the obscure descent and tangled pedigree of these fees, rejecting the earlier attempts of Comp. Peer. v, 72/3; Fowler, Cart. Old Wardon, note 71a, pp. 309–15. In 1166 the heir of Richard Engaine was his grandson Fulk de Lisores, whose Carta reveals that Richard was married more than once and that he had given land to the husbands of his two daughters (RBE, 333), one of whom may have been the Hugh de Auco who accounted for the daughter and office of Richard Ingaine in 1129/30. At the same date the heir to the fee of Pytchley, held by William Ingaine in 1086, was Richard II Engaine, fl. 1156–77. This Richard was the son of Vitalis. Fulk de Lisores occurs as both the son of Vitalis Engaine and the son of William de Lisores (Pytchley Book of Fees, p.130; Mon. Ang. ii, 602). The dates and the fact that both references relate to the fee of Engaine of Abington show that the same man is intended. Since Vitalis Engaine, son of the Richard Engaine of 1086, accounted for part of the lands of William de Lisores in 1130 it is most probable that Vitalis was father of Fulk de Lisores by a daughter of William de Lisores. This Vitalis son of Richard was the same Vitalis who controlled the Pytchley fee of his uncle William Ingaine, as indicated by his account in 1129/30 to 'rehave' his land of Laxton (PR 31 Henry I, 82). By a second marriage, to the daughter of Fulk the sheriff, Vitalis was father of Richard II Engaine of Pytchley. Thenceforth the Abington fee descended with Fulk de Lisores and the Pytchley fee with Richard II Engaine. This simple solution was, in fact, provided long ago by Hugh Candidus, p. 61 (Stapleton, 170 note), who wrote: Vitalis fuit pater Fulconis de Lisures, et Ricardi Engayne, qui genuit secundum Ricardum. The occurrence of both a Richard and Vitalis Engaine in the Northants Survey has confused the issue, since much of that document is anachronistic to its central date of c.1127 in referring back to Domesday Book or forward to a point in the 1170s.

i, fol. 229b; Northants Survey, fols 96r–99v; Northants Survey, fols 96r–99v; King, Peterborough Descriptio Militum (1969), pp. 97–101; i, fol. 160c; i, fol. 151d; i, fol. 151d; i, fol. 208b; i, fol. 219a; i, fol. 229b; i, fol. 229b; i, fol. 229b; i, fol. 229b

Ricardus Legatus
Occurs Domesday Gloucestershire.

i, fol. 168c; i, fol. 168c

Ricardus Miles
Norman, Domesday tenant of Hugh fitz Baldric. Richard 'miles' attested a grant by Hugh fitz Baldric for St Mary, York Perhaps the Richard who occurs as uncle of Fulk and Alan sons of Nigel, who occur in a group of entries headed by Hugh fitz Baldric in the Thorney Liber Vitae (BL Add. 40,000, fol. 3r)

i, fol. 291c; Dugdale, Monasticon Anglicanum, III, pp. 550–51, No. VII

Ricardus Pincerna
Domesday tenant and butler of Rainald de Bailleul-en-Gouffern, Orne, cant. Trun, in Shropshire; Mason, 'Barons and officials', ANS 13 (1991), p. 247.

i, fol. 255b; i, fol. 254d; i, fol. 254c; i, fol. 254c; i, fol. 254b; i, fol. 254b; i, fol. 253b

Ricardus Pincerna
Norman, Domesday tenant and butler of Earl Hugh of Chester.

Barraclough, Charters of AN Earls of Chester (1988), No. 26; Barraclough, Charters of AN Earls of Chester (1988), No. 8; i, fol. 265a; i, fol. 265a

Ricardus Presbiter
The priest Richard who attested Roger de Bully's foundation charter for Blyth priory was possibly the same as his Domesday tenant of the name.

i, fol. 285a; Timson, Blyth Priory Cartulary (1973), No. 325

Ricardus Puingiant
Norman, occurs Domesday Wiltshire. An Alan fitz Norman Peignardi attested a grant of Ingelran fitz Ilbert and his wife to Saint-Etienne de Caen c.1079–87 (Actes. caen no. 18, p. 121; see also Fauroux, no. 197). A Roger Puinnant attested an early confirmation foundation charter for Kenilworth priory in the time of Henry I (BL Harley 3650, 135), and a Rainald Puniant occurs on 16 January 1112 in a charter for Jumièges relating to land near Argentan (Ch. Jumièges liv, 114–15).

i, fol. 68a; i, fol. 52a; i, fol. 159a; i, fol. 62c; i, fol. 62b; i, fol. 56d; i, fol. 159a; i, fol. 48a; i, fol. 48a; i, fol. 73b; i, fol. 73b; i, fol. 216b; i, fol. 216b; i, fol. 216b

Ricardus Sturmit
Norman, occurs Domesday Wiltshire as a royal servant. His successor Henry Esturmit accounted for the ministry and land of his father in 1129/30, the ministry possibly being associated with the forest of Marlborough; Adam de Haredena accounted for the farm of the land. His byname is Old French 'estormi', 'stunned, overwhelmed'. During the minority of William I (1037–47) the brothers Gilbert and Turstin made a gift for their sister Bencelina to the abbey of Préaux, associated with Turstin's wife Masciria and sons Sturmid and Roger (Le Prévost, Eure, ii, 495). Henry II confirmed to Lessay the grant of Geoffrey Esturmi at Vesly,

Manche (Delisle, Recueil, ii, p. 302).

> i, fol. 256b; Pipe Roll 31 Henry I, 023a–wl; Pipe Roll 31 Henry I, 023b–wl; i, fol. 48a; i, fol. 74c; i, fol. 73b; i, fol. 41a; i, fol. 32d; i, fol. 74c; i, fol. 67d; i, fol. 74c; i, fol. 74c; i, fol. 48a

Ricardus Talebot

Domesday tenant of Walter Giffard, of whom the family were vassals in Normandy at Cleuville, Seine-Maritime, cant. Cany-Barville (see Gauffrid Talbot). A charter of Abbot Nicholas of Saint-Ouen de Rouen of 1087–92, cited by Le Maho (p. 51), gave to Richard Talbot the domain of Ancouteville in exchange for part of that of Gouy, near Rouen. In 1166 a second Richard Talbot held three fees of the honour of Giffard in Buckinghamshire.

> i, fol. 147b; i, fol. 148a; i, fol. 211c

Ricardus Venator

Norman, occurs Domesday Warwickshire as a king's servant.

> i, fol. 238a; i, fol. 244c; i, fol. 244c

Ricardus []

Domesday tenant of the abbey of Peterborough; succeeded before 1130 by his son Robert.

> i, fol. 222a

Ricardus []

Domesday tenant of William de Braose. A Richard de Molinellis – perhaps named for Moulines, Calvados, cant. Thury-Harcourt – attested a charter of William de Braose for Saint-Florent before 1080 (CDF, 1112).

> i, fol. 28b; i, fol. 82b; i, fol. 82a; i, fol. 82b; i, fol. 47b

Ricardus []

Domesday tenant of Gilbert Tison in Yorkshire.

> i, fol. 326c; i, fol. 326c; i, fol. 326c

Ricardus []

Norman, tenant of Ralph fitz Hubert in Domesday Nottighamshire. His successor and probable descendant in the female line by c.1150 was Ralph I Brito of Annesley (cf. Thurgarton, 1160 and note).

> i, fol. 289d

Ricardus []

Norman, tenant of Roger de Mortemer in Shropshire in 1086. His holdings at Brompton and elsewhere went to the family of Brian of Brompton (q.v.); Eyton, Shrops, iv, 240.

> i, fol. 260b; i, fol. 260b; i, fol. 260c; i, fol. 260c; i, fol. 260c; i, fol. 260c; i, fol. 260b

Richer Clericus De Andeli

King's clerk. Occurs Domesday Hampshire, where he was a tenant of Bishop Walchelin of Winchester. From Les Andelys, Eure; probably brother of Drogo, a tenant of Robert d'Oilly. In 1166 Walter son of Geoffrey des Andelys held 3 fees of the bishop of Winchester.

> Mason, Westminster Abbey Charters (1988), No. 488; i, fol. 40d; i, fol. 40c; i, fol. 41b; i, fol. 65d; i, fol. 91b; i, fol. 65d; i, fol. 41d; i, fol. 41d; i, fol. 41d; i, fol. 52a

Ricoard Archidiaconus
Tenant of William de Warenne in Domesday Sussex. Perhaps to be identified as Ricoard de Torcheio (Torcy, Seine-Maritime, comm. cant. Longueville); cf. Arch. dépt. Orne H 33 charter by William II Warenne attested by Jordan de Blosseville and Richoard de Torcheio. CDF 116, 1085, for Fécamp was attested by Ricuardus de Torce et Eustachius frater eius.

> Clay, Early Yorkshire Charters (1949), VIII, No. 5; i, fol. 26b; Clay, Early Yorkshire Charters (1949), VIII, No. 13; Round, Ancient Charters (1888), No. 5; Clay, Early Yorkshire Charters (1949), VIII, No. 26; i, fol. 26b; Clay, Early Yorkshire Charters (1949), VIII, No. 6

Ricoard []
Tenant of Bury St Edmunds, Domesday Norfolk. Both the Domesday and the Feudal Book orthographies of his name suggest that he was a Ricoard and not a Richard.

> ii, fol. 209a; ii, fol. 212a; Douglas, Feudal Book of Bury St Edmunds (1932), pp. 3–21; ii, fol. 209b; ii, fol. 209b

Riculf []
Tenant of Walter de Claville in Domesday Devon.

> i, fol. 112c; i, fol. 112c; i, fol. 112c

Riculf []
Domesday tenant of Bishop Maurice of London in Hertfordshire, where he was a Domesday juror in Broadwater Hundred.

> i, fol. 011a; i, fol. 134a; Hamilton, Inquisitio Eliensis (1876), pp. 97–100

Rippe []
Domesday tenant of Turstin fitz Rolf in Somerset.

> i, fol. 97c

Riset De Wales
Welshman, ocurs Domesday Herefordshire. Probably to be identified with Rhys ap Tewdwr, ruler of Deheubarth from c.1078. In 1081 he was driven out by Caradoc ap Gruffydd, and took refuge in St David's. He subsequently allied himself with Gruffydd ap Cynan, former ruler of Gwynedd, and rebuilt his former position in Deheubarth, with Norman assistance. By 1093 he was at odds with new Norman regime in Wales, and whilst attacking some Normans building castles in Brycheiniog, he was killed. He married Gwladus, daughter of Rhiwallon ap Cynfyn of Powys, by whom he had issue Gruffydd ap Rhys (d.1137), his successor in Deheubarth (who married Gwenllian, daughter of Rhys's ally Gruffydd ap Cynan), Hywel, and a daughter Nesta who married Gerald of Windsor. Robert S. Babcock, 'Rhys ap Tewdwr, king of Deheubarth', Anglo-Norman Studies 16 (1994).

> i, fol. 179b

Riuold []
Breton tenant of Eudo fitz Spirewic. He holding at Docking in Domesday Norfolk was held by Richer de Doching in 1166.

> ii, fol. 245b; ii, fol. 245b; ii, fol. 246a; ii, fol. 245b

Robert Arbalistarius

Norman, occurs Domesday Norfolk, father of Odo balistarius of Winstead. Actes caen. no. 13, 1079–83 includes a grant by the wife of Robert Balistarius in Sequeville-en-Bessin (Calvados, Normandy). He and his son attested a charter of Abbot Richer of Holme (1101–Jan. 1125), Chh. St Benet's, 118.

ii, fol. 269a; ii, fol. 269a; ii, fol. 118a; ii, fol. 219a

Robert Atillet

Norman, occurs Domesday Devon as a tenant of Roger Arundel. His surname is supplied by Exon Domesday. In 1127 William de Tilly (-sur-Seulles, Calvados), confirmed to Troarn the land of Gerold Atillet (BN lat 10086, fol. 65). His successor by 1166 was Thomas Latille.

i, fol. 82c; i, fol. 82d

Robert Baro

Occurs Domesday Norwich.

ii, fol. 117a

Robert Bastard

Domesday tenant-in-chief in Devon; his fief was incorporated in the honour of Plymton created for Richard I de Redvers by Henry I early in his reign. In 1166 his successors were Robert and William Bastard.

i, fol. 113c; i, fol. 113c; i, fol. 113c; i, fol. 113c; i, fol. 113c; i, fol. 113c; i, fol. 113c; i, fol. 113b

Robert Blund

Domesday tenant-in-chief in Suffolk and Wiltshire; sheriff of Norfolk sometime before 1086 (Green, Sheriffs 60). According to DB Suffolk 66.10, he inherited his fief from his brother Ralph. In DB Wiltshire mention is made of his two sons-in-law William of Audley (Audrieu?) and Robert de Albamara. Succeeded by his son Gilbert, who was holding in the time of Henry I. William son of Gilbert Blunt was holding in 1166. A far-fetched story of visions in Orderic Vitalis (iv, 236–50) concerns a priest Walchelin from the diocese of Lisieux who sees a vision of his brother and former guardian Robert son of Ralph Blond. Robert was possibly related to Gilbert Blund (q.v.), a tenant of Robert Malet. Cf. Douglas, Feudal Bury, pp. xci–ii.

i, fol. 225c; Hamilton, Inquisitio Eliensis (1876), pp. 192–95; ii, fol. 367b; ii, fol. 367b; ii, fol. 367b; ii, fol. 370a; ii, fol. 438b; ii, fol. 199a; ii, fol. 076b; ii, fol. 438b; ii, fol. 439b; ii, fol. 439a; ii, fol. 439a; ii, fol. 439a; ii, fol. 439a; ii, fol. 439b; ii, fol. 439a; ii, fol. 438b; ii, fol. 439b; ii, fol. 438b; ii, fol. 391a; ii, fol. 118a; ii, fol. 103a; ii, fol. 439a

Robert Calvus

Domesday tenant of Harduin de Scalariis.

i, fol. 198d; i, fol. 198d

Robert Clericus

Norman cleric, brother of Gilbert, occurs Domesday Hampshire.

i, fol. 40b

Robert Cocus

Domesday tenant of the count of Eu in Sussex.

i, fol. 18c; i, fol. 013c; i, fol. 18a; i, fol. 18a

Robert Cocus
Norman, tenant of Earl Hugh in Domesday Cheshire.

i, fol. 264d; i, fol. 264d

Robert Comes De Mellent
Son of Roger de Beaumont-le-Roger, Eure, arr. Bernay (Loyd, 13) and Adeline, sister and heir of Hugh count of Meulan; succeeded his mother before 1086 and his father c.1088/93. According to William of Poitiers, his first engagement as a knight was on the field of Hastings, where he performed outstandingly well. Supporter of both William II and Henry I against their brother Robert Curthose, he became earl of Leicester c.1107, augmenting his holdings there with the lands forfeited by Ivo de Grandmesnil. He died in 1118, leaving three sons by his wife Isabel de Vermandois, subsequently the wife of William II de Warenne. His son Robert succeeded him as earl of Leicester and Robert's younger twin Waleran succeeded as count of Meulan. Comp. Peer. vii, 522 ff; Sanders, 61.

Dugdale, Monasticon Anglicanum, IV, pp. 111–12, No. Ia; Chibnall, English Lands of Abbey of Bec (1951), No. XX; i, fol. 240a; i, fol. 231c; i, fol. 224b; i, fol. 240a; i, fol. 238a; i, fol. 231c; i, fol. 239d; i, fol. 240a; i, fol. 239d; i, fol. 239d; i, fol. 239d; i, fol. 239d; i, fol. 224ab; i, fol. 239d; i, fol. 238a; i, fol. 239d; i, fol. 240a; i, fol. 239d; i, fol. 240c; i, fol. 240b; i, fol. 240a; i, fol. 240a; i, fol. 231c; i, fol. 239d; i, fol. 239d; i, fol. 239d; i, fol. 241d; i, fol. 239d; i, fol. 239d; i, fol. 231c; i, fol. 240a; i, fol. 239d; i, fol. 224ab; i, fol. 231c; Lindsey Survey, BL ms Cotton Claudius C v, fols 9–18; Lindsey Survey, BL ms Cotton Claudius C v, fols 9–18; Pipe Roll 31 Henry I, 013a–ds; Dugdale, Monasticon Anglicanum, II, p. 267, No. X; Regesta regum Anglo-Normannorum III, No. 439; Hart, Cartularium Monasterii de Rameseia, No. CLVIII; Hart, Cartularium Monasterii de Rameseia, No. CLXVIII; Gibbs, Early Charters of St Pauls (1939), No. 25; Gibbs, Early Charters of St Pauls (1939), No. 31; Mason, Beauchamp Cartulary Charters (1980), No. 4; Douglas, Feudal Documents from Bury St Edmunds, No. 17; Gibbs, Early Charters of St Pauls (1939), No. 15; Douglas, Feudal Documents from Bury St Edmunds, No. 34; Dugdale, Monasticon Anglicanum, III, p. 86, No. VI; Hart, Cartularium Monasterii de Rameseia, No. CLXII; Mason, Beauchamp Cartulary Charters (1980), No. 5; Regesta regum Anglo-Normannorum III, No. 607; Pipe Roll 31 Henry I, 016–ds; Pipe Roll 31 Henry I, 041–hm; Pipe Roll 31 Henry I, 126–bk; Pipe Roll 31 Henry I, 126–bk; Pipe Roll 31 Henry I, 041–hm; Pipe Roll 31 Henry I, 046–cm; Pipe Roll 31 Henry I, 107–wk; Pipe Roll 31 Henry I, 107–wk; i, fol. 231c; i, fol. 224b; Darlington, Cartulary of Worcester: Reg. I (1962–3), No. 116; Dugdale, Monasticon Anglicanum, V, p. 175, No. I; Chibnall, English Lands of Abbey of Bec (1951), No. XVI; Regesta regum Anglo-Normannorum III, No. 16; Greenway, Charters of the Honour of Mowbray (1972), No. 10; Bearman, Charters of the Redvers Family (1994), No. 5; Regesta regum Anglo-Normannorum III, No. 438; Clay, Early Yorkshire Charters (1952), IX, No. 2; Elvey, Luffield Priory Charters (1968–75), No. 1

Robert Comes De Moritonie
Son of Herluin de Conteville and Herlève, mother of William the Conqueror; full brother of Odo of Bayeux. He was granted the county of Mortain by his brother c.1048. His work in the region was of critical importance in achieving harmony both with west Normans and their eastern counterparts, and between the Normans and the Bretons; his diplomatic successes here were later to provide a model for Henry I (K. S. B. Keats-Rohan, 'Le rôle des Bretons dans la politique de la

colonisation normande', MSHAB, lxxiv, 1996, 195–202). He accompanied his brother on the expedition of 1066 and is one of the few known to have fought at Hastings. He was given one of the important defensive Rapes of Sussex at Pevensey, where he built a castle. He received extensive holdings throughout the country, with a notable predominance in the south-west, where some of his holdings in Cornwall came to him as a result of the withdrawal c.1069/70 of Count Brien of Brittany, brother of Alan Rufus (Keats-Rohan, op. cit., 186–192) He married first Matilda (d.c.1084), daughter of Roger de Montgomery, earl of Shrewsbury, and Mabel de Bellême, by whom he had issue a son William, Emma, wife of William, count of Toulouse, Agnes, wife of André I de Vitré (a tenant of the count in Cornwall), and Denise, wife of Guy II de Laval. By his second wife Almodis he had further issue, though apparently none survived into adulthood. See K.S.B. Keats-Rohan, Medieval Prosopography 14.1 1992, 30–46; B. Golding, 'Robert of Mortain', Anglo-Norman Studies 13 (1991).

i, fol. 307b; i, fol. 305d; i, fol. 306b; i, fol. 306b; i, fol. 307b; i, fol. 305d; i, fol. 307b; i, fol. 305d; i, fol. 307b; i, fol. 305d; i, fol. 305d; i, fol. 305d; i, fol. 305d; i, fol. 305d; i, fol. 305d; i, fol. 307d; i, fol. 306b; i, fol. 307d; i, fol. 306a; i, fol. 307a; i, fol. 307d; i, fol. 306b; i, fol. 305d; i, fol. 306b; i, fol. 305d; i, fol. 306b; i, fol. 307a; i, fol. 306a; i, fol. 306a; i, fol. 306a; i, fol. 305d; i, fol. 305d; i, fol. 306b; i, fol. 282d; Hamilton, Inquisitio Eliensis (1876), pp. 192–95; ii, fol. 281b; ii, fol. 144a; ii, fol. 144a; i, fol. 282d; i, fol. 282d; i, fol. 282d; i, fol. 282d; ii, fol. 291a; ii, fol. 291a; ii, fol. 292a; ii, fol. 291b; ii, fol. 291b; ii, fol. 291b; ii, fol. 291b; ii, fol. 291b; ii, fol. 291b; ii, fol. 291a; ii, fol. 292a; ii, fol. 291a; ii, fol. 291b; ii, fol. 291a; ii, fol. 291a; ii, fol. 291a; ii, fol. 291a; ii, fol. 291a; ii, fol. 291a; ii, fol. 291b; i, fol. 129b; i, fol. 129c; i, fol. 129b; i, fol. 129b; i, fol. 129b; i, fol. 307d; i, fol. 306c; i, fol. 20c; i, fol. 20c; i, fol. 307d; i, fol. 307b; i, fol. 305c; i, fol. 305d; i, fol. 21c; i, fol. 305d; i, fol. 307c; i, fol. 306b; i, fol. 305c; i, fol. 305c; i, fol. 305d; i, fol. 307d; i, fol. 307b; i, fol. 21c; i, fol. 307c; i, fol. 307c; i, fol. 305d; i, fol. 306a; i, fol. 307c; i, fol. 306c; i, fol. 305d; i, fol. 305d; i, fol. 20d; i, fol. 22d; i, fol. 21c; i, fol. 22d; i, fol. 22d; i, fol. 307d; i, fol. 22a; i, fol. 22c; i, fol. 20c; i, fol. 20c; i, fol. 21a; i, fol. 21a; i, fol. 21a; i, fol. 21a; i, fol. 22b; i, fol. 22d; i, fol. 22a; i, fol. 21d; i, fol. 21d; i, fol. 21d; i, fol. 21d; i, fol. 22d; i, fol. 21d; i, fol. 22c; i, fol. 21a; i, fol. 22b; i, fol. 22b; i, fol. 22b; i, fol. 22b; i, fol. 22c; i, fol. 22c; i, fol. 305c; i, fol. 305d; i, fol. 308c; i, fol. 307a; i, fol. 305d; i, fol. 306b; i, fol. 306b; i, fol. 306d; i, fol. 306b; i, fol. 306b; i, fol. 306b; i, fol. 308c; i, fol. 308c; i, fol. 305c; i, fol. 298a; i, fol. 305b; i, fol. 308c; i, fol. 308c; i, fol. 308c; i, fol. 307b; i, fol. 305d; i, fol. 306b; i, fol. 306b; i, fol. 306d; i, fol. 306b; i, fol. 305d; i, fol. 305d; i, fol. 306b; i, fol. 305d; i, fol. 305c; i, fol. 306a; i, fol. 306b; i, fol. 306b; i, fol. 306a; i, fol. 306a; i, fol. 307b; i, fol. 306a; i, fol. 307b; i, fol. 307a; i, fol. 307d; i, fol. 307d; i, fol. 308c; i, fol. 306c; i, fol. 305d; i, fol. 305d; i, fol. 306c; i, fol. 305b; i, fol. 308b; i, fol. 305b; i, fol. 307d; i, fol. 305b; i, fol. 308b; i, fol. 308b; i, fol. 308b; i, fol. 308b; i, fol. 308b; i, fol. 308b; i, fol. 305c; i, fol. 307b; i, fol. 308b; i, fol. 308b; i, fol. 308b; i, fol. 305c; i, fol. 305d; Hull, Cartulary of Launceston Priory (1987), No. 3; i, fol. 30b; i, fol. 86d; i, fol. 68c; i, fol. 219a; i, fol. 223a; i, fol. 87c; i, fol. 223a; i, fol. 223a; i, fol. 223a; i, fol. 26c; i, fol. 223a; i, fol. 17d; i, fol. 223a; i, fol. 223a; i, fol. 223a; i, fol. 224a; i, fol. 224a; i, fol. 223a; i, fol. 223a; i, fol. 223a; i, fol. 223a; i, fol. 223a; i, fol. 52a; i, fol. 78d; i, fol. 32b; i, fol. 121d; i, fol. 121c; i, fol. 121c; i, fol. 121c; i, fol. 121c; i, fol. 146c; i, fol. 84c; i, fol. 121c; i, fol. 104c; i, fol. 120a; i, fol. 121b; i, fol. 100d; i, fol. 100d; i, fol. 101b; i, fol. 121d; i, fol. 121c; i, fol. 189a; i, fol. 121d; i, fol. 120a; i, fol. 79d; i, fol. 121b; i, fol. 121b; i, fol. 121b; i, fol. 121d; i, fol. 121d; i, fol. 121c; i, fol. 121d; i, fol. 121d; i, fol. 121d; i, fol. 121d; i, fol. 121c; i, fol. 121d; i, fol. 105b; i, fol. 121d; i, fol. 121d; i, fol. 34b; i, fol. 91d; i, fol. 79d; i, fol. 146b; i, fol. 146a; i, fol. 79d; i, fol. 79d; i, fol. 79d; i, fol. 121c; i, fol. 79d; i, fol. 34b; i, fol. 34b; i, fol. 93a; i, fol. 93a; i, fol. 93a; i, fol. 92d; i, fol. 92c; i, fol. 92c; i, fol. 92b; i, fol. 94b; i, fol. 79c; i, fol. 154a; i, fol. 44c; i, fol. 79b; i, fol. 79b; i, fol. 79b; i, fol. 80a; i, fol. 79c; i, fol. 146c; i, fol. 79c; i, fol. 34b; i, fol. 79c; i, fol. 79d; i, fol. 120c; i, fol. 79d; i, fol. 79d; i, fol. 79d; i, fol. 79d; i, fol. 135d; i, fol. 105b; i, fol. 80a; i, fol. 114a; i, fol. 121a; i, fol. 121a; i, fol. 121b; i, fol. 121a; i, fol. 105a; i, fol. 121a; i, fol. 105a; i, fol. 104c; i, fol. 121d; i, fol. 121b; i, fol. 121a; i, fol. 115a; i, fol. 121a; i, fol. 104c; i, fol. 68d; i, fol. 68d; i, fol. 104c; i, fol. 104c; i, fol. 104c; i, fol. 121b; i, fol. 91a; i, fol. 121d; i, fol. 104c; i, fol. 121a; i, fol. 136c; i, fol. 91b; i, fol. 91a; i, fol. 91a; i, fol. 91a; i, fol. 91a; i, fol. 90d; i, fol. 121c; i, fol. 120d; i, fol. 121d; i, fol. 120d; i, fol. 136d; i, fol. 121c; i, fol. 136c; i, fol. 91d; i, fol. 136c; i, fol. 121a; i, fol. 282d; i, fol. 16b; Hart, Cartularium Monasterii de Rameseia, No. XXXV; Hart, Cartularium Monasterii de Rameseia, No. CXLVIII; Darlington, Cartulary of Worcester: Reg. I (1962–3), No. 2; Dugdale, Monasticon Anglicanum, III, pp. 288–89, No. I; i, fol. 20c; ii, fol. 143b; ii, fol. 291a; i, fol. 20a; i, fol. 16c; i, fol. 223a; i, fol. 100b; i, fol. 146a; i, fol. 91d; i, fol. 157b; i, fol. 44c; i, fol. 305b; i, fol. 136c; ii, fol. 409a; i, fol. 166c; i, fol. 166c; i, fol. 39c

Robert Comes De Ou
Norman, a relative of William the Conqueror, son of William, count successively of the Hiémois and of Eu (Seine-Maritime, arr. Dieppe). and Lesceline, an heiress in the region of Saint-Pierre-sur-Dives (Eure). One of the few known to have fought at the battle of Hastings, he was soon afterwards given charge of the key strategic area of the Rape of Hastings (J. F. A. Mason, 'The Rapes of Sussex and the Norman Conquest', Sussex Arch. Coll. 102 (1964), 68–94). Active in royal service until c.1080, he seems thereafter to have retired to his lands in Normandy and left the running of his English estates to his son William, who in 1086 held an extensive fief of his own as well as the custody of his father's. Robert died about 1092, when his son William succeeded him as count of Eu. Robert's wife was a certain Beatrice, previously married to Turold de Verly, by whom she had a son Roger, as appears from records of the abbey of Tréport, which Robert founded c.1090 (ms. nov. acq. lat. 249, fol. 46v). They had at least three sons, Ralph, Robert and William, but nothing is known of the first two outside their father's charters for Tréport.

Ballard, Inquisition of St Augustine's (1920), fols 20r–23v; ii, fol. 063a; i, fol. 17d; i, fol. 19a; i, fol. 19a; i, fol. 17d; i, fol. 007d; i, fol. 004b; i, fol. 004a; i, fol. 19b; i, fol. 17d; i, fol. 19a; i, fol. 19a; i, fol. 18c; i, fol. 18a; i, fol. 18b; i, fol. 18b; i, fol. 19d; i, fol. 18b; i, fol. 18a; i, fol. 18c; i, fol. 17d; i, fol. 18c; i, fol. 18b; i, fol. 17d; i, fol. 19a; i, fol. 205c; i, fol. 18d; i, fol. 20b; i, fol. 19d; i, fol. 19a; i, fol. 19a; i, fol. 19a; i, fol. 19b; i, fol. 19a; i, fol. 19a; i, fol. 20a; i, fol. 20a; i, fol. 18d; i, fol. 19a; i, fol. 18d; i, fol. 19a; i, fol. 19b; i, fol. 18d; i, fol. 19d; Douglas, Feudal Documents from Bury St Edmunds, No. 10; Clay, Early Yorkshire Charters (1949), VIII, No. 5; ii, fol. 063a; i, fol. 205c; i, fol. 18a

Robert Corbet
Norman, brother of Roger (q.v.), tenant of Earl Roger in Shropshire, successors of their father Corbet (Ord. Vit. ii, 272). His daughter Sibil, mistress of Henry I and mother of Rainald earl of Cornwall, married Herbert fitz Herbert the chamberlain, and her sister Alice married William I Boterel of Cornwall. L. Musset, 'Administration et justice', Cahiers des annales de Normandie no. 17 (1985), 147, derives the family from the region of Boitron and Essay, near Sées, Orne.

i, fol. 253c; Round, Ancient Charters (1888), No. 26; Rees, Cartulary of Shrewsbury Abbey (1975), No. 35; i, fol. 256a; i, fol. 256a; i, fol. 256a; i, fol. 256a; i, fol. 256a; i, fol. 256a; i, fol. 256a; i, fol. 256a; i, fol. 256a; i, fol. 256a; i, fol. 256a; i, fol. 256a; ii, fol. 250a; Rees, Cartulary of Shrewsbury Abbey (1975), No. 35; Rees, Cartulary of Shrewsbury Abbey (1975), No. 35

Robert De Albamara

Norman, tenant-in-chief in Domesday Devon, ancestor of the Damarrell family. His wife was a daughter of Robert Blund, according to a reference in Exon Domesday. His toponym presumably refers to Aumale, Seine-Maritime, arr. Neufchâtel.

i, fol. 113b; i, fol. 113b; i, fol. 113b; i, fol. 113a; i, fol. 113b; i, fol. 113a; i, fol. 113a; i, fol. 113b; i, fol. 113b; i, fol. 113b; i, fol. 113a; i, fol. 113a; i, fol. 113b; i, fol. 73b

Robert De Aluers

Norman, occurs Domesday Northampton.

i, fol. 219a;

Robert De Anseville

Norman, from Incheville, Seine-Maritime. A cleric who occurs Domesday Sussex as a tenant of the bishop of Chichester, his toponym is provided in a charter preserved in the Chartulary of the High Church of Chichester (Sussex Rec. Soc. xliv, no. 980). Cf. Rainald de Anseville, heir of Wibert, a tenant in 1086 of the count of Eu (VCH Sussex ix, 398; HKF iii, 376), and Hugh de Anseville, a benefactor of the count's abbey at Tréport, where his son Gilbert was a monk (Cart. Tréport, 2).

i, fol. 16d

Robert De Armenteres

Fleming, from Armentières, Nord. Occurs Domesday Berkshire as a tenant of Gilbert de Gand. He attested a charter of Gilbert for Abingdon Abbey in 1086 (Chron. Abing. ii, 12–13). His successor by 1127 was Henry d'Armentières, brother of a Robert. They were probably his sons.

i, fol. 354c; i, fol. 354c; i, fol. 354c; i, fol. 354c; i, fol. 62a; i, fol. 227c; i, fol. 56c; i, fol. 159d; i, fol. 159d

Robert De Barbes

Tenant of Odo of Bayeux in Domesday Kent. Possibly named from Barbières, Calvados, cant. Creully, comm. Thaon.

i, fol. 011b

Robert De Bascherville

Norman, perhaps named from Bacqueville, Eure, Domesday tenant of Roger de Lacy. In 1109, on his return from the First Crusade ('de Jerusalem reversus'), he gave a hide without the walls of Gloucester which became a garden for the monks of St Peter (Hist. S. Petri i, 81). He may have been related to Roger de Bascherville, a tenant of Ralph de Tosny in Gloucestershire.

i, fol. 184b; i, fol. 185a; i, fol. 185a; i, fol. 184d

Robert De Bellomonte

Norman, from comm. cant. Beaumont-le-Hague, Manche, Domesday tenant of Baldwin the Sheriff in Devon; identified in Exon and the Tax Returns. His successor by 1166 was Thomas de Bellomonte. The family occurs in the cartularies of Montebourg and Saint-Sauveur-le-Vicomte.

i, fol. 106d; i, fol. 106d; i, fol. 106d; i, fol. 106d; i, fol. 106d

Robert De Blideburc
Norman, occurs Domesday Suffolk, named from Blythborough.

ii, fol. 415a; ii, fol. 331a; ii, fol. 331a

Robert De Braose
Norman, Domesday tenant of William de Braose in Wiltshire. One of the Tax Return texts (fol. 15a) identifies him as 'de Braose'. He may well have been a brother of William (q.v.), and father of the Payn de Braose who was a contemporary of William's only son Philip.

i, fol. 72a

Robert De Buci
Domesday tenant-in-chief, lord of Great Weldon, Northamptonshire. Probably named from Boucey, Manche, cant. Pontorson, in the vicomté of Avranches. His lands mostly passed with Geva, daughter of Earl Hugh of Chester, to her husband Geoffrey Ridel. After 1122 they were held by Richard Basset, son-in-law of Geva. He was also an undertenant in Leicestershire and Northamptonshire of the Countess Judith. These holdings were given, probably by Simon I de Senlis, to Robert fitz Vitalis, father of Simon de Foxton.

i, fol. 236c; i, fol. 228c; i, fol. 232c; i, fol. 236b; i, fol. 232b; i, fol. 236b; i, fol. 236b; i, fol. 236b; i, fol. 236c; i, fol. 232b; i, fol. 236c; i, fol. 232b; i, fol. 236b; i, fol. 250c; i, fol. 250c; i, fol. 225b; i, fol. 234b; i, fol. 234b; i, fol. 234b; i, fol. 225b; i, fol. 234b; i, fol. 225b; i, fol. 234b; i, fol. 225c; i, fol. 225b; i, fol. 225b; i, fol. 225b; i, fol. 234b; i, fol. 225b; i, fol. 225b; i, fol. 236c; i, fol. 236c; i, fol. 229a; i, fol. 229a

Robert De Clauilla
Domesday tenant of Robert Malet; from Clasville, Seine-Maritime, cant. Cany-Barville (see Le Maho, 43).

ii, fol. 314b; ii, fol. 308a

Robert De Cruel
Norman, named from Criel-sur-Mer, Seine-Maritime, arr. Dieppe, cant. Eu (Loyd, 36), Domesday tenant of the count of Eu in Sussex.

i, fol. 18b; i, fol. 18b

Robert De Curcun
Norman, Domesday tenant of Roger Bigod; perhaps named from Courson, Calvados, cant. Saint-Sever-de-Calvados. His successor William de Curcun held three fees of Hugh Bigod in 1166. Possibly also ancestor of the Osbert fitz William (q.v.) who also held three fees of Bigod in 1166. Osbert's mother's sister was Emma de Curcun (Cart. Blythborough no. 400). Robert's steward Gervi de Monnai [Gyrenner de Mouneyn] is mentioned in Annales of Bury St Edmunds i, 79.

ii, fol. 187a; ii, fol. 331b; ii, fol. 299b; ii, fol. 175b; ii, fol. 175b; ii, fol. 336a; ii, fol. 336a; ii, fol. 181b; ii, fol. 175b; ii, fol. 175b; ii, fol. 331b; ii, fol. 331b; ii, fol. 331a; ii, fol. 331b; ii, fol. 333b; ii, fol. 449a; ii, fol. 449a

Robert De Dun

Norman tenant of Henry de Ferrers in Domesday Derbyshire. As Robert de Dun he gave tithes in Dalbury to Tutbury, Cart. no. 52. Probably from Le Bourg-Dun, Seine-Maritime, arr. Dieppe, cant. Offranville; see Loyd 38.

i, fol. 276a; Red Book of the Exchequer, ed. Hall (1897), pp. 336–40; Dugdale, Monasticon Anglicanum, III, pp. 392–93, No. II

Robert De Gatemore

Norman, Domesday tenant of Roger Arundel. Identified as 'de Gatemore' in Exon, the toponym is unidentified. In 1166 Alfred de Gatimor held fees of Arundel's successor. In 1236 Robert's land was held by Rainald de Albamara or Damarrel.

i, fol. 94d; i, fol. 94d; i, fol. 94c; i, fol. 94c

Robert De Gimiges

Occurs Domesday Lincolnshire as an undertenant of Peterborough, tenant of Godfrey de Cambrai, and as tenant in the Descriptio Militum of c.1100–16. Perhaps named from Gamaches, Somme. Hugh Candidus, p. 58 (Stapleton, 175 note), identifies his successor as an undertenant of Baldwin Wake, remarking: Et Robertus de Gunges de eodem Baldewino in Lincolnescire, scilicet in Careby, Byamel, novem carucatas terræ; et in Norhamtonescire duas partes dimidiæ virgatæ, scilicet in Burgo, pro feodis duorum militum.

i, fol. 346b; Stenton, Documents illustrative of Danelaw (1920), No. 470; King, Peterborough Descriptio Militum (1969), pp. 97–101; i, fol. 366b; i, fol. 366b; i, fol. 366b

Robert De Glanuilla

Norman tenant of Robert Malet in Domesday; probably from Glanville, Calvados, arr. Pont-l'Evéque, cant. Dozulé. See R. Mortimer, 'The family of Ranulf de Glanville', BIHR 54 (1981).

ii, fol. 309a; ii, fol. 314b; ii, fol. 315b; ii, fol. 327a; ii, fol. 319a; ii, fol. 319a; ii, fol. 400b; ii, fol. 400b; ii, fol. 400b; ii, fol. 400b; ii, fol. 309a; ii, fol. 329a; ii, fol. 329a; ii, fol. 317b; ii, fol. 317b; ii, fol. 317b; ii, fol. 317b; ii, fol. 317b; ii, fol. 304a; ii, fol. 304b; ii, fol. 308b; ii, fol. 219b; ii, fol. 308b; ii, fol. 308b

Robert De Harde

Kinght of Archbishop Lanfranc in 1086 and 1093; named for a manor in Kent. Cf. du Boulay, Lordship, 356, 362, 380.

Douglas, ed., Domesday Monachorum (1944), p. 105; i, fol. 003d; i, fol. 004a

Robert De Hastinges

Norman, occurs in Domesday Sussex. Possibly the same as the Robert of Hastings who occurs in Domesday Essex, as does his father Ralph. He occurs in two early precepts of Henry I for Battle Abbey as Robert of Hastings and Robert fitz Ralph (RRAN ii, app. xvi and xxxii). The Sussex Robert was certainly succeeded before 1129 by his son William, then married to Juliana, an Essex heiress, daughter of John fitz Waleran.

i, fol. 17b; ii, fol. 107b

Robert De Heriz

Norman, Domesday tenant of William Peverel and Henry de Ferrers; from Hérils, now in the commune of Maisons, cant. Trévières, Calvados. Benefactor of Lenton priory, founded by William Peverel. Apparently sheriff of Nottinghamshire and

Derbyshire in the period 1110–14, he was dead by 1128. He was succeeded by Ivo de Heriz, probably his son, though at Stapleford he was followed by Geoffrey de Heriz, father of Robert (HKF i, 181). See Foulds, Thurgarton Cart. Introd., p. cxlvii.

> i, fol. 287c; i, fol. 276b; i, fol. 273a; Dugdale, Monasticon Anglicanum, IV, pp. 111–12, No. Ia

Robert De Hinton
Domesday juror in Flendish Hundred, Cambridgeshire, and tenant of Count Alan; Lewis, 'Jurors', 39.

> i, fol. 194c; i, fol. 194d; i, fol. 190b; i, fol. 193d; Hamilton, Inquisitio Comitatus Cantabrigiensis, pp. 1–93

Robert De Jor
Norman, from Jort, Calvados, arr. Saint-Pierre-sur-Dives, occurs as a king's servant in Domesday Leicestershire. In 1166 a second Robert de Jort held one fee de vetere of the honour of Blyth under Nigel de Luvetot (RBE, 373). A Robert fitz Nigel granted the church of Jort with six acres to Saint-Désir de Lisieux, with the assent of his brothers, c.1049–58 (Fauroux, 140).

> Round, Leicestershire Survey, Round, Feudal England, pp. 161–65; i, fol. 236d; i, fol. 236d

Robert De Monte Begonis
Norman, brother of Roger de Montbegon (q.v.), named once in Domesday Book.

> ii, fol. 099a

Robert De Mosters
Breton, from Moutiers-en-La Guerche, dépt. Ille-et-Vilaine (A. S. Ellis, in Yorkshire Archaeological Journal 5, 1877–8, p. 323). Married to Muriel, by whom he had two sons, Lisoius and Geoffrey, as appears from the charters of their grandson Robert II fitz Geoffrey. He may have been brother of Lisoius de Moutiers, the Breton predecessor of Eudo dapifer in a number of East Anglian manors who was disgraced in 1075 (Ord. Vit. ii, 230). For an unknown reason Robert lost control of his fees after 1086, when they were given to Count Alan's half-brother Ribald (EYC ii, 158), but they were later returned to Robert's heirs by Alan III (EYC iv, 27–8, no. 26).

> i, fol. 312d; i, fol. 282c; i, fol. 312d; i, fol. 313a; Clay, Early Yorkshire Charters (1935), IV, No. 26; Clay, Early Yorkshire Charters (1936), V, No. 333; Clay, Early Yorkshire Charters (1936), V, No. 328; i, fol. 282c; Dugdale, Monasticon Anglicanum, III, pp. 548–50, No. V; Clay, Early Yorkshire Charters (1936), V, No. 328; i, fol. 347a; i, fol. 347a; i, fol. 313a; i, fol. 313a; i, fol. 313a; i, fol. 313a; i, fol. 313a; i, fol. 313a

Robert De Nouuers
Norman, from Noyers, Calvados, arr. Caen, cant. Villers-Bocage, Domesday tenant of the bishop of Lisieux in Buckinghamshire, and probably also of Walter Giffard. Cf. Loyd, 74. Succeeded early in the twelfth century by William of Missenden, father of Hugh de Noers fl. 1141.

> i, fol. 148a; i, fol. 145d; i, fol. 145d; i, fol. 145a

Robert De Odburuile
Norman, occurs Domesday Somerset as a king's servant. His successor c.1160 was

a second Robert who was a tenant of Hugh de Courseulles, suggesting an origin at Auberville, Calvados, cant. Dozulé.

i, fol. 90b; i, fol. 98c; i, fol. 98c; i, fol. 98c; i, fol. 98c; i, fol. 98c; i, fol. 86b

Robert De Oilli
Norman, from Ouilly-le-Basset, Calvados. He made his fortune by his prowess during the Hastings campaign. Shortly after, he was given Alditha, daughter of a rich English thegn, Wigod of Wallingford, in marriage, and thereby acquired a significant fief, subsequently augmented by further grants, notably in Oxfordshire and its hinterland. He built, on royal orders, castles at Wallingford and then at Oxford, and was castellan of each and sheriff of Berkshire and Oxfordshire during the Conqueror's reign. He also enjoyed some influence in Warwickshire as lord of Wallingford. At Easter 1084 his daughter and heiress Matilda married Miles Crispin, who then assumed his father-in-law's responsibilities as castellan of Wallingford. Close friend and sworn brother of Roger d'Ivry (q.v.), with whom he founded the canonry of St Georges in the Castle at Oxford (Cart. Oseney iv, 1). He died c.1091/2, and was buried at Abingdon, as was his wife (Chron. Abing. ii, 12–13). He was succeeded in what would later be the Oxfordshire barony of Hook Norton by his brother Nigel d'Oilly (Sanders, 54). The Wallingford lands of his wife were all inherited by their daughter (Keats-Rohan, 'Wallingford', Oxoniensia 1989, 312–15).

i, fol. 238b; i, fol. 158a; i, fol. 59a; i, fol. 157b; i, fol. 156d; i, fol. 157b; i, fol. 161b; i, fol. 144c; i, fol. 57a; i, fol. 57a; i, fol. 222a; i, fol. 144c; i, fol. 156a; i, fol. 156b; i, fol. 156c; i, fol. 158a; i, fol. 158b; i, fol. 156d; i, fol. 158b; i, fol. 160d; i, fol. 158a; i, fol. 158b; i, fol. 160d; i, fol. 158b; i, fol. 158b; i, fol. 158b; i, fol. 154a; i, fol. 158a; i, fol. 56c; i, fol. 62b; i, fol. 57d; i, fol. 155a; i, fol. 225b; i, fol. 168c; i, fol. 215b; i, fol. 149b

Robert De Olecumbe
Domesday tenant of the count of Eu in Sussex. Named from the count's manor of Ulcombe, Kent.

i, fol. 19d

Robert De Pavilly
Norman, from Pavilly, Seine-Maritime, Domesday tenant of William Peverel of Nottingham. Between c.1104 and 1106 he was sheriff of Leicestershire and Northamptonshire.

i, fol. 273d; i, fol. 226b; i, fol. 226a; i, fol. 226a; Northants Survey, fols 96r–99v; Dugdale, Monasticon Anglicanum, IV, pp. 111–12, No. Ia

Robert De Petraponte
Norman, Domesday tenant of William de Warenne in Suffolk and Sussex, brother of Godfrey (q.v.). From Pierrepont, Seine-Maritime, arr. Neufchâtel, cant. Londinières (Loyd, 78).

i, fol. 27a; Clay, Early Yorkshire Charters (1949), VIII, No. 13; Round, Ancient Charters (1888), No. 5; ii, fol. 399a; ii, fol. 399a; ii, fol. 399a; ii, fol. 399a

Robert De Pontcardon
Norman, from Pontchardon, Orne arr. Argentan, cant. Vimoutiers (Loyd, 83), occurs Domesday Devon as a tenant of Baldwin the Sheriff. His successor in 1166 was William de Pontchardon.

i, fol. 106d; i, fol. 107a; i, fol. 106d; i, fol. 100b; i, fol. 138a; i, fol. 106d; i, fol. 106d

Robert De Roelent
Robert of Rhuddlan, son of Humphrey de Tilleul (en-Auge, Calvados, arr. Lisieux, cant. Saint-Pierre-sur-Dives, comm. Saint-Georges-en-Auge, Loyd, 85) and Adelina, daughter of Robert de Grandmesnil (father of Hugh q.v.) and Havise daughter of Giroie (Ord. Vit. iv, 136). His career in England began when he went there as a boy with his father in the time of Edward the Confessor, whom he served as squire and by whom he was knighted (Ord. Vit. iv, 136–8). He returned to his home for a visit, and returned after the battle of Hastings with his kinsman Hugh of Avranches. Subsequently a major tenant of his kinsman, now Earl Hugh of Chester, he was killed in a Welsh campaign subsequent to his return from the siege of Rochester where he had supported the Montgomery rising in favour of Robert Curthose, in July 1093/4 (Chibnall, in Ord. Vit. iv, pp. xxxv–vi) Benefactor of Saint-Evroul, the monastery re-established by his Grandmesnil/Giroie relatives, in association with his brother Roger; his grant was subsequently confirmed by his son William (CDF, 632–3), who later died in the White Ship disaster of November 1120 (Ord. Vit. vi, 304). He occurs several times in the chronicle of Orderic Vitalis (iv, 112, 124, 136–46), who wrote of him: 'He was a strong and agile knight, both eloquent and terrible, open-handed and admirable for his many good qualities . . . This worthy champion remained a friend to the church in the midst of all his knightly duties; he truly loved and honoured clerks and monks, and he gave alms freely to the poor according to his means.'

i, fol. 146d; i, fol. 166c; i, fol. 269b; i, fol. 269b; i, fol. 264d; i, fol. 264d; i, fol. 264d; i, fol. 264d; i, fol. 264d; Barraclough, Charters of AN Earls of Chester (1988), No. 1; i, fol. 269b; i, fol. 268d; i, fol. 269b; i, fol. 268d; i, fol. 268d; i, fol. 269b; i, fol. 269b; i, fol. 269b; i, fol. 269b; i, fol. 269a; i, fol. 269b; i, fol. 269a; i, fol. 269b; i, fol. 269b; i, fol. 269b; i, fol. 269b; i, fol. 269b; i, fol. 269b; i, fol. 269a; i, fol. 269a; i, fol. 269a; i, fol. 269a; i, fol. 269a; i, fol. 269a; i, fol. 269a; i, fol. 269b; i, fol. 269a; i, fol. 269a; i, fol. 269a; i, fol. 269a; i, fol. 269b; i, fol. 269b; i, fol. 269b; i, fol. 269a; i, fol. 269a; i, fol. 269a; i, fol. 269b; i, fol. 269a; i, fol. 269a; i, fol. 269a; i, fol. 269a; i, fol. 269a; i, fol. 269a; i, fol. 269a; i, fol. 269b; i, fol. 269a; i, fol. 269a; Barraclough, Charters of AN Earls of Chester (1988), No. 11; Lindsey Survey, BL ms Cotton Claudius C v, fols 19–27; i, fol. 224d; i, fol. 224d; i, fol. 224d; i, fol. 224d; i, fol. 224d; i, fol. 224d; i, fol. 224d; i, fol. 224d

Robert De Romenel
Landholder in Domesday Kent, named from Romsey; apparently succeeded 1093–6 by Lambert de Romenel (Mil. arch. 105). His holding was by a hawking serjeanty tenure; Round, King's Serjeants, 307–9.

i, fol. 013b; Ballard, Inquisition of St Augustine's (1920), fols 24r–28r; i, fol. 011a; i, fol. 002b; i, fol. 011a; i, fol. 002b; i, fol. 011a; i, fol. 011a; i, fol. 010d; i, fol. 010d; i, fol. 001a; i, fol. 145a; i, fol. 002b; i, fol. 004c; i, fol. 011a

Robert De Sancto Quintino
Norman, probably from Saint-Quentin-des-Isles, Eure, cant. Broglie (Loyd, 92), Domesday tenant of Henry de Ferrers. Identified from Cart. Tutbury, no. 52.

i, fol. 275b; Dugdale, Monasticon Anglicanum, III, pp. 392–93, No. II

Robert De Somerville
Norman, Domesday tenant of Ilbert de Lacy in Yorkshire, identified from his grants to St Clement's chapel in the castle of Pontefract, EYC iii, no. 1492. Named

from Sommervieu, Calvados, arr. Bayeux. A William de Somerville attested a Lacy charter before 1140. Walter de Somerville held one fee of the Lacy honour of Pontefract in 1166. Cf. Kirkstall, pp. 121–2 note.

i, fol. 315b; i, fol. 315b; i, fol. 315b

Robert De Stratford
Norman, Domesday tenant of Swein of Essex, named from his holding at Stratford.

ii, fol. 445b; ii, fol. 445b; ii, fol. 445b; ii, fol. 445b

Robert De Tham
Occurs in Domesday Buckinghamshire as a tenant of Odo de Bayeux. Perhaps the same person as 'the son of William de Thaon' who occurs in Domesday Kent. Alternatively, the same as the Robert who held in Thame of the bishop of Lincoln in Oxfordshire, who, in turn, was probably the same as Robert d'Oilly.

i, fol. 155c; i, fol. 145a

Robert De Todeni De Beluedeir
Norman, from Tosny, Eure, arr. Louviers, cant. Gaillon (Loyd, 104), a relative of Robert of Stafford and Ralph de Tosny, he was from a branch of the Tosnys that held land at Guerny and Vesly, Eure, cant. Gisors. Lord of Belvoir, Lincolnshire, in 1086; founder with his wife Adelais of Belvoir priory, a cell of St Albans. Both were later buried there. In 1086 his principal tenant was his son Berengar, who first occurs in a document recording an agreement with Marmoutier of c.1060, which mentions Robert's brother Berengar Spina and his nephew John de Laval (Fauroux, 211, CDF, 1167, 1171; see Loyd, 74). At his death c.1093 his Norman heir was his son Berengar (q.v.), who was an English tenant-in-chief in his own right, and his English heir was his son William. Both died without issue, as did their youngest brother Geoffrey, leaving Robert's daughters as his eventual heirs in the early twelfth century. The eldest, Albreda (q.v.), first inherited both the portion of the eldest son Berengar and the Belvoir lands of the younger sons, for in 1115/18 her husband Robert de Insula held both lordships. After her death without issue, before 1129, her younger sister Adelisa inherited the English lordship of Belvoir, with the lordship of Berengar de Tosny going to Adelisa's surviving son Hugh Bigod (q.v.) as heir of his aunt Albreda. Probably by 1129 Henry I designated the youngest daughter of Adelisa, Cecilia Bigod, wife of William de Albini Brito (q.v.), as heir to Belvoir; the lordship remained in the Albini Brito family (Sanders, 12). Robert's younger daughter Agnes was wife first of Ralph de Beaufour and secondly of Hubert I de Ryes. The Norman lordship had passed to Berengar's heir Earl Hugh Bigod by 1166. Hugh occurs in a Norman record of 1172 (RBE 642) as holding land of the fee of Conches and Tosny, indicating that Robert's tenure was of his senior Tosny collaterals.

Robert's background has caused some debate over the years. Orderic's Interpolation in William of Jumièges (van Houts 2, 94) says that Roger of Conches fought briefly in Spain c.1035. This may have been a separate incident to the prolonged stay in Spain of a Roger, usually identified as de Tosny, mentioned in the chronicles of Adhemar and Clarius of Sens (Adhemar de Chabannes, Chronique, ed. J. Chavanon (Paris, 1897), pp. 178–9; Clarius de Sens, Annales de Saint-Pierre-le-Vif, ed. Dune, Bibl. historiques de l'Yonne, vol. 2 (1863), 501) as having spent some time in Spain, where he married the daughter of Ramon Berenguer I of Barcelona (then dead) c.1018. In his Ecclesiastical History 2, 68,

Orderic once refers to a Roger 'the Spaniard' and he may do so to distinguish him from the Roger de Tosny, founder of Conches, he mentions elsewhere (ibid., 10, 40, 140). The younger Roger was perhaps the nephew of the elder. To suppose that there were two Rogers resolves a problem unsatisfactorily discussed in L. Musset, 'Aux origines d'une classe dirigeante: les Tosny, grands barons normands du Xe au XIIIe siècle', Francia 5 (1978), 52, M. Aurell, Les noces du comte. Marriage et pouvoir en Catalogne (785–1213), Paris 1995, 56–8, and Keats-Rohan, 'The prosopography of post-Conquest England', 35. The elder Roger was possibly the father of Robert de Tosny, lord of Belvoir in Lincolnshire, father of a Berengar and brother of Berengar Hispina. On this view Roger of Conches is absolved of the charge of bigamy, since Stephanie of Barcelona was alive during the time of Roger's marriage with the French or Norman Godehildis, subsequently the wife of Richard count of Evreux. Both Rogers died around the same time, Roger II c.1040, and Roger I by 1038 when Stephanie married her second husband Garcia of Navarre.

Dugdale, Monasticon Anglicanum, III, pp. 288–89, No. I; Dugdale, Monasticon Anglicanum, III, p. 290, No. VIII; Dugdale, Monasticon Anglicanum, III, p. 499, No. I; ii, fol. 090b; ii, fol. 090b; Lincolnshire Claims (Domesday Book), fols 376d–377c; i, fol. 353a; i, fol. 353b; i, fol. 353a; i, fol. 353a; i, fol. 353b; i, fol. 353b; i, fol. 352d; i, fol. 353a; i, fol. 352d; i, fol. 233d; i, fol. 219a; i, fol. 233d; i, fol. 233d; i, fol. 233d; i, fol. 233d; i, fol. 233d; i, fol. 233d; i, fol. 233d; i, fol. 230c; i, fol. 353b; i, fol. 353c; i, fol. 353a; i, fol. 353b; i, fol. 353b; i, fol. 353b; i, fol. 353b; Lincolnshire Claims (Domesday Book), fols 376d–377c; i, fol. 353c; Lincolnshire Claims (Domesday Book), fols 376b–c; i, fol. 225a; i, fol. 225a; i, fol. 225a; i, fol. 225a; i, fol. 225a; i, fol. 225a; i, fol. 314a; i, fol. 149b; i, fol. 138a; i, fol. 215b; i, fol. 352d; i, fol. 233d; i, fol. 225a; ii, fol. 429b; ii, fol. 429a; ii, fol. 429b; ii, fol. 429b; ii, fol. 429b; ii, fol. 429a; Lincolnshire Claims (Domesday Book), fols 376d–377c; Dugdale, Monasticon Anglicanum, III, p. 290, No. VII

Robert De Todeni De Stafford

Norman, from Tosny, Eure, arr. Louviers, cant. Gaillon (Loyd, 104), son of Roger and brother of Ralph de Tosny (q.v.), known as Robert de Stafford from the county of his principal holdings in 1086 (Sanders, 81). Occurs in 1072 as a benefactor of Evesham, and again in 1088, when he was a monk of the house lying ill there, where he is assumed to have died soon afterwards (Hist. Coll. Staff. ii pt. 1, pp. 178, 182). His second charter directs that he, his wife and son Nicholas should be buried in the house. His son seems to have been buried at Stone priory; the traditions of Stone regarding Robert I are unreliable (Mon. Ang. vi, 231). Cf. L. Musset, Les Tosny', Francia v (1978), 45–80.

Dugdale, Monasticon Anglicanum, II, p. 18, No. X; i, fol. 238a; i, fol. 368d; i, fol. 242c; i, fol. 242c; i, fol. 242c; i, fol. 368c; i, fol. 368d; i, fol. 242c; i, fol. 242c; i, fol. 368c; i, fol. 242c; i, fol. 368d; i, fol. 368c; i, fol. 246a; i, fol. 242c; i, fol. 368c; i, fol. 242c; i, fol. 242c; Lincolnshire Claims (Domesday Book), fols 376d–377c; i, fol. 249a; i, fol. 248d; i, fol. 248d; i, fol. 248d; i, fol. 248d; i, fol. 248d; i, fol. 248d; i, fol. 248d; i, fol. 248d; i, fol. 248d; i, fol. 249b; i, fol. 249c; i, fol. 249b; i, fol. 249a; i, fol. 248d; i, fol. 248d; i, fol. 248d; i, fol. 248d; i, fol. 248d; i, fol. 248d; i, fol. 248d; i, fol. 248d; i, fol. 246a; i, fol. 225b; Lincolnshire Claims (Domesday Book), fols 376d–377c; i, fol. 158a; i, fol. 368c; i, fol. 248d; i, fol. 158a; i, fol. 242c; i, fol. 176c; i, fol. 353a; i, fol. 168b; i, fol. 168b; i, fol. 168b; i, fol. 168b; i, fol. 168b

Robert De Vallibus

Norman, Domesday tenant of Roger Bigod, perhaps a relative of Aitard de Vallibus; possibly named from Vaux-sur-Seulles, Calvados, arr. Bayeux. Founder of Pentney priory, Norfolk, c.1130. He married Agnes (q.v.), daughter of Ranulf fitz Walter, by whom he had three sons, William, Oliver and Henry, according to Pentney tradition (Mon. Ang. vi, 69). He was also father of Ralph, and a daughter Agnes. Robert must have been a young man in 1086. Possibly he had only recently succeeded his father, who is perhaps to be identified with William de Partenai (q.v.), who was probably named from the Vaux manor of Pentney.

ii, fol. 176b; ii, fol. 176b; ii, fol. 336a; ii, fol. 335a; ii, fol. 336a; ii, fol. 335b; ii, fol. 335b; ii, fol. 335b; ii, fol. 335b; ii, fol. 335b; ii, fol. 283a; ii, fol. 312a; ii, fol. 354a; ii, fol. 333a; ii, fol. 333b; ii, fol. 333a; ii, fol. 177a; ii, fol. 177a; ii, fol. 332a; ii, fol. 190b; ii, fol. 173a; ii, fol. 190b; ii, fol. 181a; ii, fol. 181a; ii, fol. 177a; ii, fol. 225b; ii, fol. 087b; ii, fol. 173a; ii, fol. 087b; ii, fol. 212a; ii, fol. 177b; ii, fol. 177b; ii, fol. 177b; ii, fol. 212a; ii, fol. 212a; ii, fol. 173a; ii, fol. 212a; ii, fol. 212a; ii, fol. 173a; ii, fol. 173a; ii, fol. 173a; ii, fol. 173a; ii, fol. 212a; ii, fol. 332b; ii, fol. 332b; ii, fol. 332b; ii, fol. 332b; ii, fol. 332b; ii, fol. 332b; ii, fol. 332b; ii, fol. 332b; Douglas, Feudal Documents from Bury St Edmunds, No. 168; ii, fol. 183a; ii, fol. 183a; Dugdale, Monasticon Anglicanum, IV, pp. 148–49, No. II; Dugdale, Monasticon Anglicanum, IV, pp. 150–51, No. VIII; Regesta Regum Anglo Normannorum II, App. no. cxxvii; Dugdale, Monasticon Anglicanum, IV, pp. 150–51, No. VIII; ii, fol. 190a; Dugdale, Monasticon Anglicanum, IV, pp. 52–53, No. XVI

Robert De Veci

Norman, perhaps named from Vessey, Manche, cant. Pontorson. The bulk of his Domesday tenancy-in-chief was incorporated in the new earldom of Warwickshire by c.1088, when much of it was granted to Robert fitz Ansquetil de Harcourt, a distant kinsman of the Beaumont earl of Warwick.

Lincolnshire Claims (Domesday Book), fols 376d–377c; i, fol. 230a; i, fol. 242d; i, fol. 230a; i, fol. 242d; i, fol. 234a; i, fol. 234a; i, fol. 225b; i, fol. 234a; i, fol. 242d; i, fol. 225b; i, fol. 363b; i, fol. 363b; i, fol. 363b; i, fol. 363b; i, fol. 363b; i, fol. 363b; i, fol. 363b; i, fol. 363b; i, fol. 363b; i, fol. 363b; i, fol. 256d

Robert De Verli

Norman, tenant of Robert Gernon and landholder in Domesday East Anglia. Probably named from Vesly, Manche, arr. Coutances, cant. Lessay; Vesly, Eure is also possible. Robert de Verleio, his wife and brother Hugh were among the early benefactors of St Albans (BL Cotton Nero D vii, fol. 118v).

ii, fol. 066b; ii, fol. 262a; ii, fol. 064b; ii, fol. 065a; ii, fol. 67b; ii, fol. 437a; ii, fol. 68b; ii, fol. 437a; ii, fol. 262a; ii, fol. 262a; ii, fol. 262a; ii, fol. 262a; ii, fol. 262a; ii, fol. 437a; ii, fol. 262a; Dugdale, Monasticon Anglicanum, IV, pp. 49–50, No. II

Robert De Wateuilla

Norman, from Vatteville, Eure, arr. Saint-Pierre-du-Vauray, or Vatteville-la-Rue, Seine-Maritime, comm. arr. La Mailleraye-sur-Seine. Domesday tenant of Richard de Clare. He was probably the son of William de Watteville, a Domesday landholder and tenant of William de Warenne and of the abbey of Chertsey, including in the Surrey manor of Esher. Before 1128 Robert de Watteville gave land at Esher to Chertsey (EEA viii, no. 4). C.1139 his successor William occurs.

This William confirmed his gifts to Bermondsey as William fitz Robert fitz William de Watteville in a charter attested by Henry count of Eu (d. 1140) (BL Harley 4757, fol. 3v).

ii, fol. 039a; ii, fol. 041b; i, fol. 35a; i, fol. 34d; i, fol. 34d; i, fol. 34d; i, fol. 34d; i, fol. 35a; i, fol. 35b; i, fol. 30a; i, fol. 34c

Robert Dispensator
Norman, brother of Urso d'Abbetot, Domesday tenant-in-chief. He was certainly married, though whether it was the gifts of him, as Robert de Abitot, and his wife Lesca, that were confirmed by Stephen (RRAN iii, 749), is uncertain. His heir was his brother Urso.

i, fol. 72a; i, fol. 66b; i, fol. 363c; i, fol. 363c; i, fol. 173a; i, fol. 363c; i, fol. 363c; i, fol. 363c; i, fol. 230a; i, fol. 363c; i, fol. 363c; i, fol. 363c; i, fol. 363c; i, fol. 173a; i, fol. 363c; i, fol. 173a; i, fol. 172d; i, fol. 363c; i, fol. 173d; Mason, Westminster Abbey Charters (1988), No. 488; Darlington, Cartulary of Worcester: Reg. I (1962–3), No. 21; i, fol. 206b; i, fol. 363d; Dugdale, Monasticon Anglicanum, II, p. 267, No. X; i, fol. 174a; i, fol. 363c; Lincolnshire Claims (Domesday Book), fols 375a–d; i, fol. 363c; i, fol. 173c; i, fol. 363d; i, fol. 242d; i, fol. 242d; i, fol. 242d; i, fol. 242d; i, fol. 363c; i, fol. 363c; i, fol. 175b; i, fol. 168b; i, fol. 235a; i, fol. 234d; i, fol. 234d; i, fol. 234d; i, fol. 234d; i, fol. 235a; i, fol. 234d; i, fol. 235a; i, fol. 235a; i, fol. 235a; i, fol. 234d; i, fol. 234d; i, fol. 234d; i, fol. 234d; i, fol. 234d; i, fol. 234d; i, fol. 234d; i, fol. 235a; i, fol. 234d; Regesta regum Anglo-Normannorum III, No. 68; Darlington, Cartulary of Worcester: Reg. I (1962–3), No. 5; Lincolnshire Claims (Domesday Book), fols 375d–376a; i, fol. 242d; i, fol. 234d; i, fol. 363c; i, fol. 168b

Robert Dispensator
The Robert despencer who attested Roger de Bully's foundation charter for Blyth priory was clearly not his famous contemporary of the Abitot family, so was probably Roger's own despencer, and perhaps the Domesday tenant of the name. In 1166 Robert II de Jort held one fee of the honour of Blyth, but the Domesday holdings of Robert I de Jort were in Leicestershire, not in Nottinghamshire where Roger's tenant Robert occurs.

i, fol. 284d; i, fol. 284c; i, fol. 284c; Timson, Blyth Priory Cartulary (1973), No. 325

Robert Episcopus Cestrensis
Son of Rainer, probably from Limésy, Seine-Maritime; probably relative of the tenant-in-chief Ralph de Limesi. Royal clerk, canon of St Paul's by 1085, nominated bishop of Chester 25 December 1085; transferred his see to Coventry in 1102; died in office 1 September 1117. He had at least three children, a daughter Celestria, wife of Noel, a daughter wife of Ralph de Mara, who was given land at Fillongley, Warwickshire, and a son Richard. See EEA 14, pp. xxxii–vi.

Greenway, Charters of the Honour of Mowbray (1972), No. 10; Chibnall, English Lands of Abbey of Bec (1951), No. XXXV; Dugdale, Monasticon Anglicanum, II, p. 267, No. XI; Dugdale, Monasticon Anglicanum, III, pp. 544–46, No. I; Darlington, Cartulary of Worcester: Reg. I (1962–3), No. 267; Darlington, Cartulary of Worcester: Reg. I (1962–3), No. 265; J. Tait, Foundation Charter of Runcorn Priory, pp. 19–21; Dugdale, Monasticon Anglicanum, III, pp. 86–87, No. VIII; i, fol. 252b; i, fol. 247a; i, fol. 238c; i, fol. 135a; Rees, Cartulary of Shrewsbury Abbey (1975), No. 35; Gibbs, Early

Charters of St Pauls (1939), No. 22; i, fol. 247a; i, fol. 247b; i, fol. 247a; i, fol. 247a; i, fol. 247a; i, fol. 247a; i, fol. 247a; i, fol. 247a; i, fol. 247a; i, fol. 247b; i, fol. 247a; i, fol. 252b; i, fol. 247a; i, fol. 247a; i, fol. 247b; i, fol. 247b; i, fol. 247b; i, fol. 247a; i, fol. 252b; i, fol. 247b; i, fol. 263a; i, fol. 247a; i, fol. 247a; i, fol. 247a; i, fol. 135a; i, fol. 135a; i, fol. 135a; i, fol. 263a; i, fol. 247a; i, fol. 273b; i, fol. 247a; i, fol. 273b; i, fol. 273b; i, fol. 273b; i, fol. 252b; i, fol. 252b; i, fol. 238a; i, fol. 247a; i, fol. 247a; i, fol. 247a; i, fol. 247a; i, fol. 246a; i, fol. 252b; i, fol. 273b; i, fol. 247b; i, fol. 252b; i, fol. 135a; i, fol. 252b; i, fol. 264b; i, fol. 264b; i, fol. 247a; i, fol. 263a; i, fol. 238c; i, fol. 263a; i, fol. 247a; i, fol. 263a; i, fol. 263a; i, fol. 243b; i, fol. 238c; i, fol. 238c; i, fol. 264b

Robert Episcopus Herefordensis

Robert Losinga was probably educated in the schools of Liège and remained an active intellectual thereafter. Probably became a clerk of Edward the Confessor c. 1050. A friend of Bishop Wulfstan of Worcester, he was appointed bishop of Hereford in December 1079; He died in office on 26 June 1095. The first dean of Hereford, who occurs in 1085, was Gerard, perhaps the bishop's brother of the same name (EEA vii, pp. xxxiii–iv).

i, fol. 252b; i, fol. 174b; ii, fol. 026a; Hart, Cartularium Monasterii de Rameseia, No. CLXIV; Dugdale, Monasticon Anglicanum, III, p. 216, No. V; i, fol. 255d; i, fol. 181c; i, fol. 182d; i, fol. 155a; i, fol. 252b; i, fol. 173a; i, fol. 174b; i, fol. 174b; i, fol. 173a; i, fol. 165a; i, fol. 165a; i, fol. 154a; ii, fol. 026a; ii, fol. 005a; ii, fol. 005a; Dugdale, Monasticon Anglicanum, III, p. 217, No. VII; Dugdale, Monasticon Anglicanum, III, pp. 544–46, No. I

Robert Fafiton

Norman, son of Fafiton, occurs Domesday Huntingdonshire and as a tenant of Picot of Cambridge. He was succeeded by his son Eustache and then by the latter's son Aubin, who confirmed gifts of his father and grandfather to St Neot's in 1159 (Gorham, St Neot's, no. 467; BL Cotton Faust. A iv, fol. 89v; VCH Cambs. v, s.v. Burnash).

i, fol. 200c; i, fol. 193b; i, fol. 193b; i, fol. 130c; i, fol. 202a; i, fol. 202a; i, fol. 130b; i, fol. 130b; i, fol. 201d; i, fol. 215c; i, fol. 215b; i, fol. 207b; i, fol. 207b; i, fol. 207b

Robert Fardenc

Occurs Suffolk Domesday.

ii, fol. 371a

Robert Filius Corbution

Norman, occurs Domesday Norfolk. Perhaps a brother of William fitz Corbucion (q.v.). His fief was given to William de Albini Pincerna by Henry I early in the twelfth century. It continues to occur in the records as 'terre Corbucon'.

Red Book of the Exchequer, ed. Hall (1897), pp. 397–99; Pipe Roll 3 Henry II, 073–e; ii, fol. 085a; ii, fol. 258b; ii, fol. 425b; ii, fol. 250a; ii, fol. 250a; ii, fol. 249b; ii, fol. 140a; ii, fol. 003a; ii, fol. 259b; ii, fol. 085a; ii, fol. 260a; ii, fol. 253b; ii, fol. 003a; ii, fol. 085a; ii, fol. 258b; ii, fol. 260a; ii, fol. 259b; ii, fol. 260a; ii, fol. 260a; ii, fol. 260a; ii, fol. 259b; ii, fol. 249b; ii, fol. 259a; ii, fol. 259a; ii, fol. 259a; ii, fol. 425b; ii, fol. 425b; ii, fol. 425b

Robert Filius Fulcheredi

Domesday tenant of Robert Malet in Suffolk.

ii, fol. 308b; ii, fol. 308b; ii, fol. 308b; ii, fol. 308b; ii, fol. 308b; ii, fol. 308b; ii, fol. 308a; ii, fol. 308a; ii, fol. 308a

Robert Filius Geroldi

Norman, from Roumare, Seine-Maritime, arr. Rouen, cant. Maromme (Loyd, 87). son of Gerold de Roumare, castellan of Neufmarché, and his wife Albreda (CDF, 87–8). Domesday tenant-in-chief, brother of Roger ancestor of the English Roumare family. Benefactor of Bec, to which he gave land at Cleeve in Somerset on his return from a campaign in Wales, attested by his brother Roger. Robert's heirs were the descendants of his brother Roger (q.v.).

i, fol. 97a; i, fol. 46c; Dugdale, Monasticon Anglicanum, II, p. 267, No. X; i, fol. 80c; Chibnall, English Lands of Abbey of Bec (1951), No. VIII; i, fol. 80c; i, fol. 80c; i, fol. 46c; i, fol. 46d; i, fol. 46d; i, fol. 46d; i, fol. 46c; i, fol. 46d; i, fol. 46d; Chibnall, English Lands of Abbey of Bec (1951), No. XXXVI; i, fol. 97a; i, fol. 62b; i, fol. 62b

Robert Filius Gilbert

Found in the Tax Return of South Petherton Hundred; tenant of William de Moion in 1086.

i, fol. 95c

Robert Filius Goberti

Norman, occurs Domesday Essex, and as a knight of the archbishop of Canterbury in 1093–6, holding at Godinton in Chelsfield, kent (Du Boulay, Lordship of Canterbury, 345–6). He occurs in a writ of 1089–1093 addressed to Robert count of Eu, wrongly assigned to Richard fitz Gilbert in RRAN i, 260, on which see Douglas, Dom. Mon., 37.

ii, fol. 097b; ii, fol. 097b; Douglas, ed., Domesday Monachorum (1944), p. 105

Robert Filius Herberti

Norman, occurs Domesday Somerset as a tenant of Roger de Courseulles; identified from the Tax Returns

i, fol. 94b; i, fol. 94b; i, fol. 94b

Robert Filius Hugonis

Norman, Domesday tenant of Earl Hugh in Cheshire, lord of Malpas. His successors were apparently two daughters, Letitia wife of Richard Patrick and Mabel, wife of William Belward (Ormerod, History of Cheshire i, 688–92, ii 598).

i, fol. 60b; Barraclough, Charters of AN Earls of Chester (1988), No. 3; Barraclough, Charters of AN Earls of Chester (1988), No. 3; i, fol. 264d; i, fol. 264b; i, fol. 264b; i, fol. 264d; i, fol. 264c; i, fol. 264b; i, fol. 264d; i, fol. 264c; i, fol. 264c; i, fol. 264b; i, fol. 264d; i, fol. 264d; i, fol. 264c; i, fol. 264c; i, fol. 264b; i, fol. 264c; i, fol. 264b

Robert Filius Iuonis

Norman tenant of Robert de Mortain in 1086, identified as son of Ivo and as constable of Robert de Mortain. (probably at Montacute, Somerset) by Exon Domesday and the Tax Returns. His lands passed to the Beauchamp family by 1150, and perhaps as early as 1092. Indeed, he may even have been identical with the Robert de Beauchamp of 1092. See Sanders, 51; J. Batten, 'The barony of Beauchamp in Somerset', Proc. Somersetshire. Arch. and Nat. Hist. Soc. xxxvi (1891), 20–59.

i, fol. 79c; i, fol. 92a; i, fol. 92a; i, fol. 92b; i, fol. 92d; i, fol. 92b; i, fol. 93a; i, fol. 79b; i, fol. 79b; i, fol. 91d; i, fol. 79c; i, fol. 79b; i, fol. 79c; i, fol. 80a; i, fol. 79d;

i, fol. 104c; i, fol. 107a; i, fol. 108a; i, fol. 106c; i, fol. 79b; i, fol. 79b; i, fol. 79c; i, fol. 79c

Robert Filius Murdrac

Norman, from La Meurdraquière, Manche, cant. Bréhal (LeMelletier), held a small fief in Domesday Oxfordshire. About May 1081 he attested at Winchester a confirmation by William I for Saint-Evroul (RRAN i 140 , Bates 254; Ord. Vit. iii, 240.He attested a notification of Henry I given on 13 September 1114 (RRAN ii, 1063).

i, fol. 160b; i, fol. 49c; i, fol. 160b

Robert Filius Nigelli

Norman, Domesday tenant of Ranulf brother of Ilger in Bedfordshire.

i, fol. 215b

Robert Filius Radulfi

Norman, occurs Domesday Oxfordshire as a royal servant.

i, fol. 74c; i, fol. 160c; i, fol. 160c

Robert Filius Rolf

Norman, occurs Domesday Wiltshire and Berkshire.

i, fol. 72c; i, fol. 72c; i, fol. 63d

Robert Filius Roscelini

Probably a Picard, he was a major Domesday tenant of Eustache count of Boulogne. He was succeeded by the Triket family, of whom he was probably the ancestor (VCH Herts iv, 20; Mon. Ang. vi, 152). Ralph Triket or Trichet occurs 1129/30.

i, fol. 137b; i, fol. 137b; i, fol. 137b; i, fol. 95d; ii, fol. 097a; ii, fol. 097a; i, fol. 137b; i, fol. 130c; i, fol. 211b

Robert Filius Serlonis

Norman, Domesday tenant of Henry de Ferrers. Identified from the foundation charter of Tutbury, Cart. no. 52.

i, fol. 274d

Robert Filius Tetbaldi

Norman, from Avoine, Orne, cant. Ecouché; cf. the grant to Saint-Martin de Sées by Theobald de Avenia attested by his son Robert (Arch. Orne H 938, fol. 6v); L. Musset, 'Administration et justice', Cahiers des annales de Normandie no. 17 (1985), 147. Major tenant of Roger de Montgomery in Sussex (Ord. Vit. iii, 140). Benefactor, as Robert of Arundel, of Lewes Priory. In his last hours, in 1087, he made a grant of Toddington, near Arundel, to the monks of Saint-Martin de Sées, in association with his son Hugh. His wife Emma was mentioned as predeceased. Following the fall of the Montgomerys in 1102 his fee escheated to the crown. Nothing further is heard of his son Hugh.

i, fol. 24c; i, fol. 24c; i, fol. 24c; i, fol. 24c; i, fol. 24c; i, fol. 24c; i, fol. 24d; i, fol. 24a; i, fol. 23d; i, fol. 24b; i, fol. 24b; i, fol. 23c; i, fol. 23c; i, fol. 23c; i, fol. 23c; i, fol. 23c; i, fol. 23d; i, fol. 23d; i, fol. 23d; i, fol. 23b; i, fol. 24c; i, fol. 24c; Rees, Cartulary of Shrewsbury Abbey (1975), No. 35; i, fol. 256d; i, fol. 23a; i, fol. 23b; i, fol. 23b; i, fol. 256d; Rees, Cartulary of Shrewsbury Abbey (1975), No. 35; i, fol. 23c; i, fol. 23b; i, fol. 23b; i, fol. 23b; i, fol. 23d; i, fol. 23d; i, fol. 24d; i, fol. 24d; i, fol. 24d; i, fol. 25a; i, fol. 25a

Robert Filius Turstini

Norman, occurs Domesday Oxfordshire. A royal dispenser; Round, EHR xxix, 355, idem King's Serjeants, 186ff. His successor was Tustin, dispenser to William II, whose son Hugh was dispenser early in the reign of Henry I. These were probably his son and grandson.

i, fol. 160c; i, fol. 160c

Robert Filius Walchelini

Norman, Domesday tenant of Odo of Bayeux in Oxfordshire. His grant of tithes at Wickham were confirmed to Eynsham Abbey by Henry I on December 25 1109 (Cart. Eynsham i, pp. 36–7).

i, fol. 155c; i, fol. 155c

Robert Filius Walteri

Norman, occurs in Domesday Buckinghamshire as tenant of Robert d'Oilly. Other holdings by a Robert from Robert d'Oilly followed the same descent, being found in the hands of Luvel de Brai (q.v., perhaps named from Bray-la-Campagne, Calvados)) by 1129/30.

i, fol. 145b; i, fol. 158c; i, fol. 149b

Robert Filius Walteri

Occurs Domesday Somerset as tenant of Robert of Mortain, identified in Exon as fitz Walter.

i, fol. 92b

Robert Filius Warini

Norman, Domesday juror in Northstow Hundred, Cambridgeshire; possibly the same as the Robert who held land in that hundred from Picot of Cambridge (Lewis, 'Jurors', 39).

i, fol. 201c; i, fol. 201b; Hamilton, Inquisitio Eliensis (1876), pp. 97–100; Hamilton, Inquisitio Comitatus Cantabrigiensis, pp. 1–93

Robert Filius Watsonis

Knight of Archbishop Lanfranc, from whom he held six fees in 1086 and 1093. His successor by 1171 to a reduced holding was Thomas fitz Thomas fitz Bernard (cf. du Boulay, Canterbury, 99 note 3, 331).

Douglas, ed., Domesday Monachorum (1944), p. 105; i, fol. 005b; i, fol. 004a

Robert Filius Widelin

Norman, Domesday tenant of Henry de Ferrers, identified from early grants to Tutbury priory (no. 52; cf. VCH Derbys i, 292).

i, fol. 233c; i, fol. 233c; i, fol. 233c; i, fol. 233c

Robert Filius Willelmi

Norman, occurs in Domesday Somerset as a tenant of Roger de Courseulles. His patronymic is provided by Exon.

i, fol. 93b; i, fol. 93b

Robert Filius Willelmi

Norman, held land of the king and others in Domesday Nottinghamshire and Derbyshire

i, fol. 282c; i, fol. 292a; i, fol. 278a; i, fol. 292a; i, fol. 292a; i, fol. 282c; i, fol. 292a

Robert Fossard

Son of Nigel Fossard, a Domesday tenant of Mortain in Yorkshire. He succeeded his father as lord of Mulgrave c.1120 (Sanders, 66). He occurs in 1129/30 with his wife Ascelina. He and his wife were benefactors of Nostell (RRAN ii, 1627, where her name is given as Osceria). At his death c.1135 he was succeeded by his son William (d.c.1170).

> Pipe Roll 31 Henry I, 025–ynb; i, fol. 332c; i, fol. 332c; Pipe Roll 31 Henry I, 031–ynb

Robert Frumentinus

Tenant of the wife of Hugh fitz Grip; identified in Exon.

> i, fol. 84a

Robert Gernon

West Norman, tenant-in-chief in several Domesday counties. The Gernon fee at 'Conde' (probably Condé-sur-Noireau, Calvados, arr. Vire) and 'Ivelon' was held of the bishopric of Bayeux (RBE, 646). A Robert Guerno gave land at Montrabot, Manche, cant. Saint-Jean-des-Baisants to Saint-Laurent de Longues (M. Beziers, Mém. dioc. de Bayeux, iii, p. 463). Perhaps this is the Robert Gernon who occurs in Fauroux, nos. 152 and 199, attesting in the latter with William de Vauville; cf. the association, c.1120, of a Ranulf Gernon with the sons of William de Vauville in Cart. Saint-Sauveur, BN lat. 17137, fols 90–1. One of his Domesday tenants was his son-in-law Picot of Cambridge (q.v.). The succession to his fief offers a number of difficulties. Robert gave land in Wiltshire to St Peter's, Gloucester (Cart. S. Petri ii, 164–74), and land in Buckinghamshire that he gave he gave to St Peter's and subsequently to Queen Matilda was given to Abingdon Abbey by Henry I (Chron. Abin. ii, 97–100). Robert apparently visited Abingdon in 1118 (Cart. S. Petri ii, 173–4), but died soon afterwards, since between 1120 and 1123 the overlordship of his fief was held by William de Montfichet, as appears from a writ of Henry I who refers to Robert Gernon as 'antecessor tui' (RRAN ii, 1402). The reason for the mediatisation of the Gernon fief is not known, but Robert certainly left issue. The Abingdon Chronicle shows that Robert had two sons, Alfred and Matthew, a brother Ranulf, and three 'nepotes', Geoffrey, Fulk and Payn (Chron. ii, 98). In 1130 Alfred Gernon occurs on the Pipe Roll clearly holding part of the fief of his father Robert, probably under William de Montfichet. Alfred attested a charter of King Stephen given at Norwich in 1140 (RRAN iii, 399). He perhaps died without issue, though he occurs with his wife Juliana in a Savigny charter (Bib. mun. Flers 23, 701–2), attested by his brother Matthew, in which he granted land in Middlesex, part of Robert's Domesday holding. This undermines the testimony of Bishop Nicholas of Llandaff, who stated c.1160/70, that he had been at Abingdon when Robert visited in 1118, and that when Robert died without an heir, Henry I had given his land to William de Montfichet, father of Gilbert (Cart. S. Petri ii, 174).

> i, fol. 94b; ii, fol. 072b; ii, fol. 002b; ii, fol. 002b; i, fol. 197a; ii, fol. 067a; i, fol. 196d; ii, fol. 279a; ii, fol. 016b; ii, fol. 090b; i, fol. 197a; i, fol. 196d; i, fol. 196d; ii, fol. 010b; i, fol. 130b; i, fol. 185b; i, fol. 185b; i, fol. 149c; i, fol. 149c; i, fol. 137d; i, fol. 185b; Regesta regum Anglo-Normannorum III, No. 345; ii, fol. 420a; ii, fol. 420a; ii, fol. 420a; ii, fol. 420a; ii, fol. 420a; ii, fol. 420b; ii, fol. 420b; ii, fol. 420b; ii, fol. 064a; ii, fol. 066b; ii, fol. 065b; ii, fol. 065a; ii, fol. 065b; ii, fol. 063b; ii, fol. 065b; ii, fol. 065a; ii, fol. 68b; ii, fol. 066b; ii, fol. 064b;

ii, fol. 064a; ii, fol. 67b; ii, fol. 255b; ii, fol. 255a; ii, fol. 255a; ii, fol. 255b; ii, fol. 255b; ii, fol. 063b; ii, fol. 419b; ii, fol. 255a; ii, fol. 007a; ii, fol. 017b

Robert Herecom
Occurs Domesday Somerset as a tenant of Roger de Courseulles. His byname occurs in Exon.

i, fol. 93b

Robert Hostiarius
Occurs Domesday Leicestershire and Cambridgeshire. Son of William. Cf. William Hostiarius. In 1130 his Leicestershire fees were held by Henry Tuschet.

i, fol. 202a; i, fol. 237a; i, fol. 235a; i, fol. 235a

Robert Inuesratus
Norman, Domesday tenant of Robert Gernon. His byname 'lasciuus' means 'playful' in Classical Latin, as does 'inuesratus', deriving from later Latin invitiare, yielding Old French envoise. Ancestor of the Lenveise family. In 1129 Robert de Cairon made a grant to St Neot's of land held by Robert Enveise. A Ralph Lenveiseth attested a charter for Fécamp by William Talbot (Coll. Moreau 341, fol. 27). Robert and Hugh Lenveseiz attested the foundation of Kirkstead abbey in 1131 (Mon. Ang. i, 208–9).

Dugdale, Monasticon Anglicanum, III, p. 473, No. XII; ii, fol. 015a; ii, fol. 066b

Robert Latinarius
English interpereter, occurs Domesday Kent where he held land of Odo de Bayeux. Son of Æthelric the priest of Chatham and Godgifu (Wharton, Anglia Sacra i, 340; Du Boulay, Canterbury, 99). He died c.1100, leaving a wife who became a pensioner of St Andrew's, Rochester, and a daughter married to a priest named Brod; see H.Tsurushima, Anglo-Norman Studies xiv, 329–31. Possibly the same as Robert Leofgeat (Liuegit) who held half a knight's fee of the archbishop in 1093/6; the fees of both Roberts passed to the Crevequer family (du Boulay, Lordship of Canterbury, 387); see Williams, The English, 84 note 63.

i, fol. 008b; i, fol. 012a; i, fol. 011c; i, fol. 008b; i, fol. 008c; i, fol. 007b; i, fol. 007b; i, fol. 006c; i, fol. 008d; Douglas, ed., Domesday Monachorum (1944), p. 105

Robert Lorimarus
Norman, occurs Domesday Norfolk.

ii, fol. 117a

Robert Malet
Son of William Malet (d. c.1071) of Graville-Sainte-Honorine, Seine-Maritime, and Esilia Crispin of Tillières. Succeeded his father in Normandy and a large English fief centred upon Eye, Suffolk, c.1071. Soon after 1087 Eye was controlled by Roger Pictaviensis, but by 1100 Robert was back in England in possession of Eye. He received the king's permission to found a cell of the abbey of Bernay at Eye before 1087, but it is unlikely to have been built before the early year's of Henry I's reign, when Robert was royal chamberlain. His last recorded appearance was in late August-September 1107, when he left for Normandy with the king. There is an exhaustive study of this man in K.S.B. Keats-Rohan, 'Domesday Book and the Malets', Nottingham Medieval Studies xli (1997),

13–51, where it is suggested that Robert was twice married, once to a daughter of Hugh de Montfort, that he was father of William II Malet, who forfeited Eye in 1110, and of Robert Malet (q.v.), ancestor of the Malets of Curry Malet, Somerset, and that he may have died as a monk of Bec after 1107.

Regesta regum Anglo-Normannorum III, No. 288; ii, fol. 103b; Stenton, English Feudalism, App., No. 11; Brown, Eye Priory Cartulary (1992–94), No. 53; Regesta regum Anglo-Normannorum III, No. 713; Douglas, Feudal Documents from Bury St Edmunds, No. 22; Brown, Eye Priory Cartulary (1992–94), No. 5; Brown, Eye Priory Cartulary (1992–94), No. 3; Fisher, Cartularium Prioratus de Colne (Earles C.), No. 3; Douglas, Feudal Documents from Bury St Edmunds, No. 24; Brown, Eye Priory Cartulary (1992–94), No. 326; Douglas, Feudal Documents from Bury St Edmunds, No. 23; Brown, Sibton Abbey Cartularies and Charters (1987), No. 547; Lincolnshire Claims (Domesday Book), fols 376d–377c; ii, fol. 328b; ii, fol. 385a; ii, fol. 329a; ii, fol. 334b; ii, fol. 155b; ii, fol. 384a; i, fol. 320c; ii, fol. 184b; ii, fol. 328b; ii, fol. 155b; i, fol. 320d; i, fol. 320d; i, fol. 320d; i, fol. 320c; i, fol. 320d; i, fol. 320c; i, fol. 320c; i, fol. 320c; i, fol. 320c; i, fol. 320c; i, fol. 320d; ii, fol. 386b; i, fol. 320c; ii, fol. 153b; i, fol. 320c; i, fol. 320c; i, fol. 320c; i, fol. 320c; i, fol. 320c; ii, fol. 154b; ii, fol. 154a; ii, fol. 153b; ii, fol. 153b; ii, fol. 154b; ii, fol. 155a; ii, fol. 311a; ii, fol. 154a; ii, fol. 155b; ii, fol. 155a; ii, fol. 153b; ii, fol. 148b; ii, fol. 385b; ii, fol. 154b; ii, fol. 332a; ii, fol. 449b; ii, fol. 387a; ii, fol. 387a; ii, fol. 387a; ii, fol. 387a; ii, fol. 387a; ii, fol. 388a; ii, fol. 388b; ii, fol. 154a; ii, fol. 443a; i, fol. 320c; ii, fol. 155b; i, fol. 320d; ii, fol. 329a; ii, fol. 154b; ii, fol. 171b; i, fol. 298b; i, fol. 320c; i, fol. 368b; ii, fol. 156a; Lincolnshire Claims (Domesday Book), fols 376d–377c; ii, fol. 304a; ii, fol. 156a; ii, fol. 219b; ii, fol. 148b; Regesta regum Anglo-Normannorum III, No. 634; i, fol. 293d; Brown, Eye Priory Cartulary (1992–94), No. 1; Regesta regum Anglo-Normannorum III, No. 635; Brown, Eye Priory Cartulary (1992–94), No. 166; Brown, Eye Priory Cartulary (1992–94), No. 34; Brown, Eye Priory Cartulary (1992–94), No. 54; ii, fol. 088b; ii, fol. 171b; ii, fol. 156a; ii, fol. 155b; ii, fol. 156a; i, fol. 320d; ii, fol. 133b; i, fol. 320d; i, fol. 320d; i, fol. 320d; i, fol. 320d; i, fol. 320c; i, fol. 320d; i, fol. 320c; i, fol. 320d; i, fol. 320d; ii, fol. 155b; i, fol. 320d; ii, fol. 155b; i, fol. 320d; i, fol. 320d; i, fol. 320d; i, fol. 321a; i, fol. 321a; i, fol. 321a; i, fol. 368b; i, fol. 368b; i, fol. 368b; i, fol. 368b; i, fol. 368b; i, fol. 368b; i, fol. 320d; ii, fol. 400a; Regesta regum Anglo-Normannorum III, No. 288; ii, fol. 309b; ii, fol. 323b; ii, fol. 323b; ii, fol. 323b; ii, fol. 323b; ii, fol. 310b; ii, fol. 323a; ii, fol. 310b; ii, fol. 323b; ii, fol. 326a; ii, fol. 323a; ii, fol. 322b; ii, fol. 322b; ii, fol. 326a; ii, fol. 326a; ii, fol. 310b; ii, fol. 310b; ii, fol. 322a; ii, fol. 307a; ii, fol. 323a; ii, fol. 307b; ii, fol. 307b; ii, fol. 309a; ii, fol. 309b; ii, fol. 309a; ii, fol. 306b; ii, fol. 309a; ii, fol. 309b; ii, fol. 309b; ii, fol. 322b; ii, fol. 309b; ii, fol. 322b; ii, fol. 322b; ii, fol. 322b; ii, fol. 307b; ii, fol. 307b; ii, fol. 322b; ii, fol. 322b; ii, fol. 322b; ii, fol. 323a; ii, fol. 323a; ii, fol. 323b; ii, fol. 323a; ii, fol. 307a; ii, fol. 306b; ii, fol. 318a; ii, fol. 324b; ii, fol. 320b; ii, fol. 319a; ii, fol. 319a; ii, fol. 318b; ii, fol. 319a; ii, fol. 318b; ii, fol. 319a; ii, fol. 318a; ii, fol. 326b; ii, fol. 319a; ii, fol. 320a; ii, fol. 322a; ii, fol. 319a; ii, fol. 319b; ii, fol. 319b; ii, fol. 318b; ii, fol. 320b; ii, fol. 321a; ii, fol. 321a; ii, fol. 326b; ii, fol. 326b; ii, fol. 321a; ii, fol. 321a; ii, fol. 319a; ii, fol. 326b; ii, fol. 320a; ii, fol. 321b; ii, fol. 321b; ii, fol. 321b; ii, fol. 326b; ii, fol. 326b; ii, fol. 321b; ii, fol. 321a; ii, fol. 318b; ii, fol. 321b; ii, fol. 324b; ii, fol. 326b; ii, fol. 325a; ii, fol. 325b; ii, fol. 325b; ii, fol. 325b; ii, fol. 323b; ii, fol. 325b; ii, fol. 321b; ii, fol. 325a; ii, fol. 323b; ii, fol. 325a; ii, fol. 325a; ii, fol. 325a; ii, fol. 325a; ii, fol. 324b; ii, fol. 326a; ii, fol. 325b; ii, fol. 324b; ii, fol. 319b; ii, fol. 319b; ii, fol. 317a; ii, fol. 319b; ii, fol. 309b; ii, fol. 319b; ii, fol. 324a; ii, fol. 326a; ii, fol.

320a; ii, fol. 324b; ii, fol. 324a; ii, fol. 324a; ii, fol. 324b; ii, fol. 324a; ii, fol. 326a; ii, fol. 323b; ii, fol. 323b; ii, fol. 324a; ii, fol. 316a; ii, fol. 314a; ii, fol. 316b; ii, fol. 314a; ii, fol. 310b; ii, fol. 314a; ii, fol. 313b; ii, fol. 314b; ii, fol. 314b; ii, fol. 315b; ii, fol. 311a; ii, fol. 315b; ii, fol. 314a; ii, fol. 316b; ii, fol. 310b; ii, fol. 310b; ii, fol. 311a; ii, fol. 311a; ii, fol. 312a; ii, fol. 313b; ii, fol. 312b; ii, fol. 313b; ii, fol. 312b; ii, fol. 313a; ii, fol. 313a; ii, fol. 315b; ii, fol. 327b; Hamilton, Inquisitio Eliensis (1876), pp. 192–95; i, fol. 291d; i, fol. 291d; ii, fol. 325a; ii, fol. 329a; ii, fol. 329b; ii, fol. 328b; ii, fol. 328b; ii, fol. 328a; ii, fol. 314a; ii, fol. 327b; ii, fol. 314a; ii, fol. 327b; ii, fol. 327b; ii, fol. 327a; ii, fol. 327a; ii, fol. 326b; ii, fol. 328a; i, fol. 36c; ii, fol. 326b; ii, fol. 324b; ii, fol. 314a; ii, fol. 313b; ii, fol. 314a; ii, fol. 327b; ii, fol. 314a; ii, fol. 305a; ii, fol. 310b; ii, fol. 305b; ii, fol. 304a; ii, fol. 306a; ii, fol. 306a; ii, fol. 306b; ii, fol. 306b; ii, fol. 306b; ii, fol. 305a; ii, fol. 305b; ii, fol. 306b; ii, fol. 304a; ii, fol. 304a; ii, fol. 304a; ii, fol. 306b; ii, fol. 310b; ii, fol. 309b; ii, fol. 309b; ii, fol. 310a; ii, fol. 310a; ii, fol. 310a; ii, fol. 310a; ii, fol. 310a; ii, fol. 312b; ii, fol. 317a; ii, fol. 318a; ii, fol. 304b; ii, fol. 317a; ii, fol. 304b; ii, fol. 317b; ii, fol. 317b; ii, fol. 317a; ii, fol. 318a; ii, fol. 318a; ii, fol. 317b; ii, fol. 310b; ii, fol. 321a; ii, fol. 317a; ii, fol. 304b; ii, fol. 306a; ii, fol. 317a; ii, fol. 317a; ii, fol. 316b; ii, fol. 317a; ii, fol. 316b; ii, fol. 317a; ii, fol. 317a; ii, fol. 326b; ii, fol. 317a; ii, fol. 317a; ii, fol. 088a; i, fol. 368b; i, fol. 320c; ii, fol. 153b; ii, fol. 304a; Dugdale, Monasticon Anglicanum, IV, p. 148, No. I; Regesta regum Anglo-Normannorum III, No. 180; Brown, Eye Priory Cartulary (1992–94), No. 44; Brown, Eye Priory Cartulary (1992–94), No. 52; Brown, Eye Priory Cartulary (1992–94), No. 46; Brown, Eye Priory Cartulary (1992–94), No. 8; Douglas, Feudal Documents from Bury St Edmunds, No. 2; Brown, Eye Priory Cartulary (1992–94), No. 9; Brown, Eye Priory Cartulary (1992–94), No. 55; Brown, Eye Priory Cartulary (1992–94), No. 35; Brown, Eye Priory Cartulary (1992–94), No. 33; Brown, Eye Priory Cartulary (1992–94), No. 14; Brown, Eye Priory Cartulary (1992–94), No. 11; Brown, Eye Priory Cartulary (1992–94), No. 10; Brown, Eye Priory Cartulary (1992–94), No. 36; Brown, Eye Priory Cartulary (1992–94), No. 6; Brown, Eye Priory Cartulary (1992–94), No. 2; Dugdale, Monasticon Anglicanum, IV, p. 149, No. III

Robert Marescal

Norman, occurs as a marshal in Domesday Wiltshire. Possibly the father of Gilbert Marshal, father of the celebrated John Marshal whose family fortunes were rooted in Wiltshire (PR 31 Henry I, 18). See Comp. Peer. x, App. G.

i, fol. 73b; i, fol. 73b

Robert Nepos Hugonis

Domesday tenant of the wife of Hugh fitz Grip.

i, fol. 84a

Robert Niger

Occurs Domesday Kent and in the Excerpta for St Augustine's of Canterbury. Cf. Willelm Niger.

Ballard, Inquisition of St Augustine's (1920), fols 24r–28r; i, fol. 001c; i, fol. 001a; i, fol. 001d

Robert Parler

Occurs Domesday Worcestershire as a tenant of Gilbert fitz Turold under the abbot of Westminster. Father or grandfather of Isnard Parler (q.v.), who was succeeded by his descendants the de Offeny family. Isnard was a rare name in Normandy; cf.

Isnard de Saint-Martin-d'Ecublei, Orne (Ord. Vit. vi, 198).

i, fol. 175a

Robert Pincerna

Norman, occurs Domesday Shropshire. Butler to Roger de Montgomery, earl of Shrewsbury. His fief apparently escheated on the fall of the Montgomerys in 1102. Cf. Mason, Officers and Clerks, 249.

i, fol. 255a; i, fol. 253d; i, fol. 256b; i, fol. 256b; i, fol. 256b

Robert Presbiter

One of two priests holding land in Domesday Cambridgeshire of the Breton Count Alan.

i, fol. 194c

Robert Puer

Norman, tenant of the wife of Hugh fitz Grip. He occurs as Robert puer in Exon, and possibly as Robert fitz Ralph in the Exon Tax Returns, fol. 23a.

i, fol. 84a; i, fol. 84a

Robert Pultrel

Norman, Domesday tenant of Robert, count of Meulan, ancestor of a Leicestershire family. Identified by the gifts he made to Saint-Evroul, recorded by Orderic Vitalis (iii, 238). HKF ii, 69–70.

i, fol. 237a; i, fol. 236c; i, fol. 237b

Robert Saluagius

Norman, Domesday tenant of William de Braose in Sussex. His byname was common enough, being associated inter alia with Authieux-sur-Calonne, Calvados, in the later Middle Ages (VCH Sussex i, 379; Arch. dépt Calvados, F5601). William de Braose's grant to Saint-Florent-de Saumur for the soul of Ralph fitz Waldi (CDF, 1112) was conceded first by his man Robert fitz Ivo at Courteilles (Orne), and thereafter by his son Philip de Braose, whose charter was given as he set off for Jerusalem and was attested by Robert Salvagius (Arch. dépt. Maine-et-Loire H3713, fol. 121).

i, fol. 28d; i, fol. 29a; i, fol. 29a; i, fol. 29a; i, fol. 28d; i, fol. 28d; i, fol. 28d; i, fol. 28d; i, fol. 29b; i, fol. 29b

Robert Sanctus Leger

Domesday tenant of the count of Eu; from Saint-Leger-aux-Bois, Seine-Maritime, arr. Neufchâtel, cant. Blangy (Loyd, 90). In 1166 Thomas de St Leger held 4 fees of John, count of Eu.

i, fol. 18b

Robert Trublet

An entry in Domesday Kent refers to one Turbatus, where Excerpta reads Robert Trublet, doubtless intending the same person.

Ballard, Inquisition of St Augustine's (1920), fols 24r–28r; i, fol. 001d

Robert Venator

Norman, Domesday tenant of Henry de Ferrers in Leicestershire; also a tenant in Warwickshire. Benefactor of Tutbury.

i, fol. 233c; i, fol. 242c; i, fol. 242b; Dugdale, Monasticon Anglicanum, III, pp. 392–93, No. II

Robert []
Two manors held in 1086 by Robert from Earl Hugh of Chester descended together to Richard fitz Nigel and his heirs by c.1150. See Farrer, HKF ii, 242.

i, fol. 157b, 237a

Robert []
Tenant of Ralph de Pomeroy in Domesday Devon. His successor in 1166 was Roger de Champeus

i, fol. 114c

Robert []
Domesday tenant of Swein of Essex. Possibly the same as the Robert who held Bromfield of Earl Roger in Domesday Shropshire. The Domesday text notes that the land had been forfeited in 1065 by the royal priest Spirites. It was then lost to the the church of St Mary of Bromfield because Robert fitz Wimarc, father of Swein, gave to his daughter's husband. The church complained, and the king (Edward) had ordered that the property be restored to the church and Robert's son-in-law compensated elsewhere, but he died before this command could be implemented. The text concluded that now Robert holds of Earl Roger. It has been suggested that this is an anachronistic reference to Robert fitz Wimarc himself, who died several years before 1086, or that this Robert may have been fitzWimarc's son-in-law The first possibility is unlikely. This Robert is either the other's son-in-law, as suggested by A. Williams on Robert fitzWimarc, New DNB, or a Robert unconnected with either fitzWimarc or his daughter.

i, fol. 252d; ii, fol. 045a; ii, fol. 045b; ii, fol. 047b

Robert []
Domesday tenant of William de Poilli, possibly the same as his son Robert, or the Robert de Osereto who attested William's second grant of Devonshire land to Saint-Martin de Sées (CDF 657).

i, fol. 111c; i, fol. 111c

Robert []
Domesday tenant or tenants of Arnald de Hesding, who had a nephew Robert Fretel. Arnald's charter granting land in England to Saint-Georges de Hesdin (Cart. Hesdin, 52) was attested by Robertus filius Milonis and Robertus Malcovenant.

i, fol. 70a; i, fol. 70a; i, fol. 70a; i, fol. 70a; i, fol. 70a

Robert []
Domesday tenant of Judhael of Totnes. A Robert Tornator and a Robert son of David occur in Judhael's charter for Totnes (Mon. Ang iv, 630 no. ii, Watkin, Totnes ii, Plate I). The sole manor held by this Robert, Poulston, was held in the early thirteenth century by one Alan Bughedon (Fees 776). A later French copy BN lat. 5445, fol. 269) of Juhel's foundation charter for Totnes claimed Robert fitz David as granter of an otherwise unidentified holding Bocchedona.

i, fol. 109b

Robert []
Domesday tenant of Robert Gernon in Essex; succeeded by the de Plaiz family, VCH Essex i, 520.

ii, fol. 066b

Robert []
Occurs Domesday Gloucestershire. His descendants held Doynton until the thirteenth century. see C. Ross, Cartulary of St Mark's Hospital, Bristol, Bristol Rec. Soc. 21 (1959), pp. 180–1, 183–6, 217–19, 243, 247–87.

i, fol. 165b; i, fol. 165b; i, fol. 165b

Robert []
Norman, Domesday tenant of William bishop of Durham in Yorkshire. Thought to have been ancestor of the de Conyers family, derived from Cornières, Calvados, cant. Caumont in Durham Episcopal Charters, no. 12 note. The first known member of the Conyers family was Roger, occurs c.1128 (EYC ii, 944).

i, fol. 304d; i, fol. 304d; i, fol. 304d; i, fol. 304d; i, fol. 304d; i, fol. 304d

Robert []
Norman, Domesday tenant of Ilbert de Lacy in Yorkshire. His holdings were given to St Clement's chapel in the castle of Pontefract by Girald de Ramesvilla, who was probably either his father or his son EYC iii, no. 1492. Gerald was named from Reineville, Calvados, arr. Vire, cant. Condé-sur-Noireau, comm. Lassy (Loyd, 84). William de Rainville held four fees of the Lacys in 1166.

i, fol. 316a; i, fol. 316a; i, fol. 316a

Robert []
Norman, Domesday tenant of William of Écouis.

i, fol. 180b

Robert []
Domesday tenant of Drogo de Beuvrière.

i, fol. 360b; i, fol. 360b; i, fol. 360b; i, fol. 324c

Robert []
Norman, Domesday tenant of the count of Meulan in Warwickshire and elsewhere. Unlikely to be the same as Robert fitz Erembald, or Robert pincerna, father of Ralph pincerna, ancestor of the Butlers of Oversley. In common with other Meulan tenants, there is no straightforward descent of fees from 1086. Several later Butler holdings were held in 1086 by Fulco (q.v.), including Claybrook, Warwickshire, whereof Robert fitz Erchembald gave tithes to the abbey of Beaumont-le-Roger (Chanteux, no. 84). A Robert fitz Erchembald and his wife Matilda gave half a hide at Condicote, Glocestershire, to St Peter's in 1128 in circumstances suggesting he then had a deceased former wife Agnes (Hist. S. Petri. Glocs. i, 69–70).

i, fol. 168a; i, fol. 240b; i, fol. 240b

Robert []
Domesday tenant of Geoffrey de la Guerche. Attested, before 1093, a charter of Geoffrey de la Guerche for Monks Kirby (Mon. Ang. vi, 996).

i, fol. 235d; i, fol. 235d; i, fol. 369b

Robert []
A tenant of the wife of Hugh fitz Grip in 1086 at Durweston. If the 'Warwann' of Durweston who held two fees of Alfred II of Lincoln in 1166 was Robert's desendant, then he was presumably identical with another of the Roberts holding of the fief in 1086.

i, fol. 83d

Robert []
Norman, tenant of Ralph fitz Hubert in Domesday Derbyshire. His fees were held by the Hathersage family under the Stutevilles in the barony of Crich by the early thirteenth century (cf. Foulds, Thurgarton, p. cxxxviii).

i, fol. 277a; i, fol. 277a; i, fol. 277a; i, fol. 277a; i, fol. 277a; i, fol. 277a

Robert []
Tenant of William fitz Ansculf in Domesday Staffordshire.

i, fol. 148d; i, fol. 249d; i, fol. 249d; i, fol. 250a; i, fol. 250a; i, fol. 250a; i, fol. 250a

Robert []
Domesday tenant of William Capra in Devon. His successor in 1166 was Richard Le Baron (q.v.).

i, fol. 110d; i, fol. 110b

Roderius []
Norman tenant of Maurice bishop of London in Hertfordshire; Domesday juror in Broadwater Hundred.

i, fol. 133c

Roger Aculeus
Domesday tenant of Nicholas arbalistarius in Devon. His Latin byname also occurs as French Aiguillon. Osmund Aculeus, Richard and Roger sold their allod in the territory of Caumont-sur-Dive (Calvados) to Lanfranc, abbot of Caen (Actes caen. 4, 1066–72), to which he gave land; a Landric Aculeus gave to Fécamp the tithe of Anneville-sur-Seine, Seine-Maritime (Fauroux, 139, 1057).

i, fol. 117c; i, fol. 117b; i, fol. 117b

Roger Arundel
West country tenant-in-chief in 1086, from La Brehoulière, Manche, cant. Subligny (A. Dupont, Histoire du département de la Manche, ii, 63). He sold land to Saint-Etienne de Caen to Abbot William (Act. caen. p. 108), attested by Alfred de Baiunvilla (q.v.), Robert filius Mainardi, Goisfrid pratarius. According to the Tax Return for Kingsbury West, 'Alueredus homo Rogeri Arundelli' held Ash Priors from Roger. It was claimed Roger held this land in chief wrongfully, it being a manor of the Bishop of Wells. In his own chapter, Roger's tenant is named as Givold. He may also have held land of William de Moyon and Roger de Courseulles that passed to a younger son (RBE, 226, 227), since by then his fief, the honour of Poorstock (Sanders, 72), was held by Gerbert de Percy with the sister and heir of Roger II Arundel, probably Roger's grandson.

i, fol. 94c; i, fol. 82c; i, fol. 82d; i, fol. 82d; i, fol. 82d; i, fol. 82d; i, fol. 82c; i, fol. 94c; i, fol. 94c; i, fol. 94d; i, fol. 94d; i, fol. 94d; i, fol. 94d; i, fol. 94d; i, fol. 94d; i, fol. 94d; i, fol. 89d; i, fol. 94c

Roger Baolt
Domesday tenant of Roger de Montgomery, Sussex. His surname is provided by a charter recording his grant of land at Arundel to Saint-Martin de Sées (CDF, 660) A Hubert Baolt occurs c.1125 in the Cartulary of Préaux (Arch. dépt. de l'Orne H 711, nos. 310 and 378). Cf. HKF iii, 89–90.

i, fol. 24d; i, fol. 24d

Roger Bigod

Seigneur of Les Loges, Calvados, arr. Vire, cant. Aunay-sur-Odon and Savenay, arr. Vire, cant. Villers-Bocage, comm. Courvaudon (Loyd, 14), under the bishop of Bayeux (Red Book 646). Sheriff of Norfolk for most of William I's reign, and from 1100 until his death in 1107; during the 1070s and 1080s alternated with Robert Malet as sheriff of Suffolk (Green, Sheriffs, 60, 76). Although he is usually credited with two wives, it is fairly clear that he was married only once, to Adelisa (q.v.), daughter and eventual heiress of Robert de Tosny of Belvoir who is traditionally viewed as mother of Hugh, his eventual heir, Cecilia (Adelisa's eventual heir) and (another) Matilda. Their charter for Rochester priory referred to their sons and daughters and was attested by William their son, Humfrid Bigod, Gunnora and Matilda their daughters, which shows that the clerk Humphrey Bigod who occurs until c.1118 was their son (Cotton Domitian A x, fols 201v–2r). This charter tellingly refers to King Henry, making it highly unlikely that Roger acquired a second wife and second family before his death in 1107. [The evidence is very limited, but it may be noted that charters for Thetford – founded by Roger and Adelisa de Tosny – by William and Gunnor Bigod mention their father, mother, brothers and sisters with no reference to stepmother or half-blood; Thetford register, BL Lansdowne 229, fol. 145v–7]. The charter contains an unusual 'pro anima' clause for Norman the sheriff, their English predecessor in the manors granted. Conceivably there was a relationship between Roger's family and Norman by that date, as is suggested by the fact that Roger fitz Richard of Warkworth (q.v.) was described by his brother-in-law William de Vere as 'nepos' of Roger's son Hugh Bigod, and as having had an uncle Thomas de Candelent, whose name is a reference to the Suffolk manor of Candlet, held in 1086 by Norman from Roger Bigod. It is likely that Roger's children were born from the late 1090s onwards, and that the youngest of them were Hugh and Cecilia. The view that all his children were minors at his death in 1107 was expressed in A. Wareham, 'Motives and politics of the Bigod family c.1066–1177', Anglo-Norman Studies 17 (1995).

Roger's brother William is mentioned in Domesday Book; he was probably also a brother of Hugh Bigot, who occurs in DB Suffolk. William occurs in the Cart. Saint-Leu d'Esserent (pp. 5, 6) and, c.1091, gave land at Fréville (Seine-Maritme, arr. Rouen, cant. Pavilly), with the assent of Guy de La Roche-Guyon, to Saint-Wandrille (no. 45). His sister Matilda was married to his tenant Hugh de Hosdenc (q.v.); see Comp. Peer. ix, 576, note c. He was doubtless also related to Earl Hugh of Chester's tenant Bigot of Loges, and to Robert Bigot, son of Norman, lord of Pirou and Cerisy in the Cotentin, benefactor in the 1090s of Sées (Arch. Orne H938, 62b–63, no. cxxxix). This Robert, husband of Emma and father of Richard and Robert, was perhaps the same as the Robert Bigot, kinsman of Richard of Avranches (father of Earl Hugh), mentioned by Ord. Vit. in his interpolations of William of Jumièges (ed. van Houts, ii, 126–7). Roger founded the priory of the BVM at Thetford, 1103–4, in lieu of a projected pilgrimage to Jerusalem (Mon. Ang. iv, 151–3); colonized by monks from the Warenne foundation at Lewes, it was a dependency of Cluny. He died in September 1107 and was buried at Norwich. See Comp. Peer. ix, 575–9; Sanders, 46–7.

Regesta Regum Anglo Normannorum II, App. no. cxxvii ; Ransford, Early Charters of Waltham Abbey (1989), No. 4; Barraclough, Charters of AN Earls of Chester (1988), No. 3; Red Book of the Exchequer, ed. Hall (1897), pp. 397–99;

Dugdale, Monasticon Anglicanum, IV, pp. 13–14, No. V; Dugdale, Monasticon Anglicanum, IV, pp. 150–51, No. VIII; Dugdale, Monasticon Anglicanum, IV, pp. 150–51, No. VIII; Red Book of the Exchequer, ed. Hall (1897), pp. 395–97; ii, fol. 205a; ii, fol. 373a; ii, fol. 118b; ii, fol. 118b; ii, fol. 302b; ii, fol. 312b; ii, fol. 373a; ii, fol. 150b; Hart, Cartularium Monasterii de Rameseia, No. CLXIV; Dugdale, Monasticon Anglicanum, IV, p. 198, No. II; ii, fol. 211a; ii, fol. 210b; ii, fol. 214b; ii, fol. 215b; ii, fol. 215b; ii, fol. 277a; ii, fol. 210a; ii, fol. 278a; ii, fol. 235b; ii, fol. 143a; ii, fol. 109b; ii, fol. 110a; ii, fol. 115a; ii, fol. 116a; ii, fol. 117b; ii, fol. 153a; ii, fol. 137b; ii, fol. 190a; ii, fol. 143b; ii, fol. 143b; ii, fol. 143b; ii, fol. 143b; ii, fol. 143b; ii, fol. 177b; ii, fol. 187a; ii, fol. 118a; ii, fol. 190b; Dugdale, Monasticon Anglicanum, III, pp. 330–31, No. III; Douglas, Feudal Documents from Bury St Edmunds, No. 33; Douglas, Feudal Documents from Bury St Edmunds, No. 32; Douglas, Feudal Documents from Bury St Edmunds, No. 29; Douglas, Feudal Documents from Bury St Edmunds, No. 30; Douglas, Feudal Documents from Bury St Edmunds, No. 25; Douglas, Feudal Documents from Bury St Edmunds, No. 27; Douglas, Feudal Documents from Bury St Edmunds, No. 26; Douglas, Feudal Documents from Bury St Edmunds, No. 21; Douglas, Feudal Documents from Bury St Edmunds, No. 22; Douglas, Feudal Documents from Bury St Edmunds, No. 23; Clay, Early Yorkshire Charters (1952), IX, No. 2; Gibbs, Early Charters of St Pauls (1939), No. 41; Hart, Cartularium Monasterii de Rameseia, No. CLIX; Mason, Beauchamp Cartulary Charters (1980), No. 159; Hart, Cartularium Monasterii de Rameseia, No. LXXXI; Hart, Cartularium Monasterii de Rameseia, No. CXLVIII; ii, fol. 184b; ii, fol. 184b; ii, fol. 184b; ii, fol. 184b; ii, fol. 184b; ii, fol. 184b; ii, fol. 184b; ii, fol. 184b; ii, fol. 184b; ii, fol. 185a; ii, fol. 184a; ii, fol. 185a; ii, fol. 185a; ii, fol. 185a; ii, fol. 185a; ii, fol. 185b; ii, fol. 185b; ii, fol. 185b; ii, fol. 186a; ii, fol. 186b; ii, fol. 186b; ii, fol. 186b; ii, fol. 185a; ii, fol. 183a; ii, fol. 183b; ii, fol. 183b; ii, fol. 183b; ii, fol. 183b; ii, fol. 183b; ii, fol. 183b; ii, fol. 183b; ii, fol. 183b; ii, fol. 184b; ii, fol. 183a; ii, fol. 184a; ii, fol. 183a; ii, fol. 183b; ii, fol. 184a; ii, fol. 187b; ii, fol. 186b; ii, fol. 184a; ii, fol. 184a; ii, fol. 184a; ii, fol. 183a; ii, fol. 184a; ii, fol. 183b; ii, fol. 189a; ii, fol. 188a; ii, fol. 187a; ii, fol. 188b; ii, fol. 188b; ii, fol. 189a; ii, fol. 189a; ii, fol. 189a; ii, fol. 189a; ii, fol. 187a; ii, fol. 189a; ii, fol. 188a; ii, fol. 189a; ii, fol. 189a; ii, fol. 189a; ii, fol. 189a; ii, fol. 189a; ii, fol. 189a; ii, fol. 189b; ii, fol. 189b; ii, fol. 189b; ii, fol. 189b; ii, fol. 189b; ii, fol. 189a; ii, fol. 187b; ii, fol. 187a; ii, fol. 187a; ii, fol. 187a; ii, fol. 187a; ii, fol. 182a; ii, fol. 187b; ii, fol. 182a; ii, fol. 187b; ii, fol. 188a; ii, fol. 187b; ii, fol. 188a; ii, fol. 187b; ii, fol. 187b; ii, fol. 187b; ii, fol. 187b; ii, fol. 187b; ii, fol. 187b; ii, fol. 187b; ii, fol. 188a; ii, fol. 188a; ii, fol. 188a; ii, fol. 188a; ii, fol. 187b; ii, fol. 177b; ii, fol. 179a; ii, fol. 176b; ii, fol. 177a; ii, fol. 177a; ii, fol. 177a; ii, fol. 177a; ii, fol. 177a; ii, fol. 177a; ii, fol. 177b; ii, fol. 176b; ii, fol. 177b; ii, fol. 176a; ii, fol. 177b; ii, fol. 178a; ii, fol. 178a; ii, fol. 178a; ii, fol. 178b; ii, fol. 178b; ii, fol. 178b; ii, fol. 178b; ii, fol. 178b; ii, fol. 178b; ii, fol. 182a; ii, fol. 177b; ii, fol. 175a; Excerpta a Chronicis de Bermondsey, Dugdale, Monasticon, IV, pp. 95–97; Douglas, Feudal Book of Bury St Edmunds (1932), pp. 3–21; ii, fol. 173a; ii, fol. 174a; ii, fol. 174a; ii, fol. 174a; ii, fol. 174a; ii, fol. 174b; ii, fol. 174b; ii, fol. 176b; ii, fol. 174b; ii, fol. 179b; ii, fol. 175a; ii, fol. 175b; ii, fol. 176a; ii, fol. 176a; ii, fol. 176a; ii, fol. 176a; ii, fol. 176a; ii, fol. 176a; ii, fol. 176a; ii, fol. 174b; ii, fol. 181a; ii, fol. 181a; ii, fol. 179a; ii, fol. 181a; ii, fol. 181a; ii, fol. 181a; ii, fol. 181a; ii, fol. 181a; ii, fol. 181a; ii, fol. 181a; ii, fol. 181a; ii, fol. 182a; ii, fol. 181a; ii, fol. 180b; ii, fol. 181a; ii, fol. 181a; ii, fol. 181b; ii, fol. 181b; ii, fol. 182a; ii, fol. 182a; ii, fol. 182a; ii, fol. 189b; ii, fol. 182a; ii, fol. 189b; ii, fol. 182a; ii, fol. 182a; ii, fol. 181a; ii, fol. 179b; ii, fol. 179b; ii, fol. 179b; ii, fol. 179b; ii, fol. 179b; ii, fol. 179b; ii, fol. 179b; ii, fol.

179b; ii, fol. 179b; ii, fol. 179b; ii, fol. 181a; ii, fol. 179b; ii, fol. 180b; ii, fol. 180a; ii, fol. 180a; ii, fol. 180a; ii, fol. 180a; ii, fol. 180a; ii, fol. 180a; ii, fol. 180b; ii, fol. 180b; ii, fol. 180b; ii, fol. 180b; ii, fol. 180b; ii, fol. 180b; ii, fol. 179b; ii, fol. 335a; ii, fol. 299a; ii, fol. 334a; ii, fol. 334a; ii, fol. 334a; ii, fol. 334b; ii, fol. 334b; ii, fol. 334b; ii, fol. 334b; ii, fol. 334a; ii, fol. 335a; ii, fol. 334a; ii, fol. 335a; ii, fol. 335b; ii, fol. 335b; ii, fol. 335b; ii, fol. 336a; ii, fol. 336a; ii, fol. 336a; ii, fol. 337b; ii, fol. 290a; ii, fol. 339a; ii, fol. 335a; ii, fol. 331a; ii, fol. 290a; ii, fol. 290a; ii, fol. 290a; ii, fol. 290b; ii, fol. 189b; ii, fol. 299b; ii, fol. 189b; ii, fol. 330b; ii, fol. 334a; ii, fol. 331a; ii, fol. 339a; ii, fol. 331b; ii, fol. 332a; ii, fol. 333a; ii, fol. 333a; ii, fol. 333a; ii, fol. 333b; ii, fol. 333b; ii, fol. 333b; ii, fol. 334a; ii, fol. 334a; ii, fol. 330b; ii, fol. 378a; ii, fol. 338b; ii, fol. 369b; ii, fol. 369b; ii, fol. 373a; ii, fol. 373a; ii, fol. 374b; ii, fol. 375b; ii, fol. 377a; ii, fol. 345b; ii, fol. 377b; ii, fol. 345b; ii, fol. 378b; ii, fol. 378b; ii, fol. 378b; ii, fol. 385a; ii, fol. 385a; ii, fol. 385a; ii, fol. 385a; ii, fol. 385b; ii, fol. 385b; ii, fol. 448b; ii, fol. 377b; ii, fol. 342a; ii, fol. 339b; ii, fol. 339b; ii, fol. 341a; ii, fol. 341a; ii, fol. 341b; ii, fol. 341b; ii, fol. 341b; ii, fol. 342a; ii, fol. 369b; ii, fol. 342a; ii, fol. 339a; ii, fol. 343b; ii, fol. 343b; ii, fol. 343b; ii, fol. 343b; ii, fol. 343b; ii, fol. 343b; ii, fol. 344a; ii, fol. 344b; ii, fol. 344b; ii, fol. 345a; ii, fol. 345b; ii, fol. 342a; ii, fol. 190a; ii, fol. 278a; ii, fol. 087b; ii, fol. 190a; ii, fol. 190a; ii, fol. 190a; ii, fol. 190a; ii, fol. 190a; ii, fol. 190a; ii, fol. 189b; ii, fol. 299b; ii, fol. 189b; ii, fol. 189b; ii, fol. 189b; ii, fol. 189b; ii, fol. 189b; ii, fol. 330b; Dugdale, Monasticon Anglicanum, II, p. 267, No. XI; ii, fol. 179a; Dugdale, Monasticon Anglicanum, III, p. 216, No. IV; Dugdale, Monasticon Anglicanum, III, p. 330, No. II; ii, fol. 173a; ii, fol. 087b; Dugdale, Monasticon Anglicanum, IV, pp. 148–49, No. II; Dugdale, Monasticon Anglicanum, III, p. 217, No. VI; Douglas, Feudal Documents from Bury St Edmunds, No. 8; Hart, Cartularium Monasterii de Rameseia, No. CLIV; Douglas, Feudal Documents from Bury St Edmunds, No. 12; Hart, Cartularium Monasterii de Rameseia, No. CLVII; Hart, Cartularium Monasterii de Rameseia, No. CLXXIX; ii, fol. 282b; ii, fol. 282b; ii, fol. 282b; ii, fol. 282b; ii, fol. 282b; ii, fol. 282b; ii, fol. 282a; ii, fol. 284a; ii, fol. 282a; ii, fol. 282a; ii, fol. 282a; ii, fol. 282a; ii, fol. 282a; ii, fol. 282b; ii, fol. 282b; Dugdale, Monasticon Anglicanum, IV, p. 149, No. III; ii, fol. 152b; ii, fol. 152b; ii, fol. 152b; ii, fol. 152b; ii, fol. 153a; ii, fol. 374a; ii, fol. 383a; ii, fol. 282a; ii, fol. 374b; ii, fol. 282b; ii, fol. 281b; ii, fol. 281b; ii, fol. 281b; ii, fol. 281b; ii, fol. 282a; ii, fol. 282a; ii, fol. 153a; ii, fol. 284a; ii, fol. 282b; ii, fol. 283b; ii, fol. 282b; ii, fol. 284a; ii, fol. 284a; ii, fol. 284a; ii, fol. 284a; ii, fol. 284a; ii, fol. 284a; ii, fol. 284a; ii, fol. 284a; ii, fol. 284a; ii, fol. 283b; ii, fol. 284a; ii, fol. 284b; ii, fol. 284b; ii, fol. 284b; ii, fol. 284b; ii, fol. 284b; ii, fol. 284b; ii, fol. 284a; ii, fol. 284b; ii, fol. 283b; ii, fol. 284b; ii, fol. 284b; ii, fol. 284b; ii, fol. 284b; ii, fol. 284a; ii, fol. 284a; ii, fol. 284a; ii, fol. 284b; ii, fol. 283a; ii, fol. 283b; ii, fol. 283a; ii, fol. 283b; ii, fol. 283a; ii, fol. 283a; ii, fol. 283a; ii, fol. 283a; ii, fol. 283a; ii, fol. 283a; ii, fol. 283a; ii, fol. 283a; ii, fol. 283a; ii, fol. 283a; ii, fol. 282b; ii, fol. 282b; ii, fol. 283a; ii, fol. 283b; ii, fol. 283b; ii, fol. 283b; ii, fol. 283b; ii, fol. 283b; ii, fol. 283a; ii, fol. 283b; ii, fol. 283a; ii, fol. 283b; ii, fol. 283b; ii, fol. 283b; ii, fol. 283b; ii, fol. 283b; ii, fol. 283b; Dugdale, Monasticon Anglicanum, III, p. 377, No. II; Dugdale, Monasticon Anglicanum, IV, p. 148, No. I; ii, fol. 118b; Hamilton, Inquisitio Eliensis (1876), pp. 192–95; ii, fol. 393a

Roger Brito

Occurs Domesday Somerset as tenant of Athelney Abbey.

i, fol. 91b

Roger Buissel

Domesday tenant in Somerset and Dorset of the wife of Hugh fitz Grip and Roger Arundel. Represented in the mid-twelfth century by Bardulf Bussel of Little Cheselbourne and his brother Gervaise of Watercombe (Cart. Montacute nos. 118, 124, 126), and in 1166 by Samson Roc.

i, fol. 83c; i, fol. 94d

Roger Clericus

Occurs Domesday Sussex as a tenant of Robert of Mortain.

i, fol. 20c; i, fol. 22a; i, fol. 21a; i, fol. 20c; i, fol. 22a; i, fol. 22a

Roger Comes

Son of Roger I of Montgomery, a kinsman, friend and trusted companion of his contemporary William I, whom he supported during his minority. He fought at Domfront in 1048 and about that time made a significant marriage to Mabel daughter of William Talvas de Bellême. Though she had brothers, she became the family's heiress in order to permit a peace between her family and the dukes of Normandy after many years of conflict between them. He supplied ships for the Norman invasion of England in 1066, but did not accompany the expedition, remaining behind to assist the duchess Matilda in ruling Normandy in William's absence. He joined the king in England in 1067 and rapidly began the accumulation of one of the largest estates in Domesday Book, including Chichester Rape in Sussex and the whole county of Shropshire, of which he became earl in 1071. Founder of the abbeys of Saint-Martin de Sées, Almenesches, and Shrewsbury. His first wife was murdered c.1077 (Ord. Vit. iii, 136), and he subsequently married Adelaide du Puiset (ibid., 138), by whom he had a son Everard. Father by Mabel de Bellême of Robert de Bellême, Roger Pictaviensis, Hugh, Arnulf, Philip a clerk, Matilda, wife of Robert de Mortain, Mabel wife of Hugh de Châteauneuf, and Sibil, wife of Robert fitz Haimo. He became a monk of Shrewsbury shortly before his death on 27 July 1094 (Comp. Peer. xi, 687). For the family background see K. Thompson in BIHR 60 (1987); J.F.A. Mason, 'Roger de Montgomery and his sons', TRHS 5th ser. 13 (1963). Named from Saint-Germain-de-Montgomery, Calvados, arr. Lisieux, cant. Livarot; see Loyd, 68.

i, fol. 254a; i, fol. 248a; i, fol. 129a; i, fol. 129a; i, fol. 129a; i, fol. 129a; i, fol. 254a; i, fol. 254a; i, fol. 254a; i, fol. 254a; i, fol. 254a; i, fol. 23a; i, fol. 254a; i, fol. 23b; i, fol. 254a; i, fol. 254a; i, fol. 254a; i, fol. 254a; i, fol. 254a; i, fol. 254a; i, fol. 254a; i, fol. 254a; i, fol. 254a; i, fol. 193b; i, fol. 248c; i, fol. 248b; i, fol. 248b; i, fol. 254a; i, fol. 51a; i, fol. 193c; i, fol. 193c; i, fol. 193c; i, fol. 137b; i, fol. 193b; i, fol. 193b; i, fol. 193b; i, fol. 193b; i, fol. 193c; i, fol. 193c; i, fol. 44c; i, fol. 23a; i, fol. 44d; i, fol. 248b; i, fol. 36c; i, fol. 34b; i, fol. 23a; i, fol. 23a; i, fol. 25b; i, fol. 68d; i, fol. 36c; i, fol. 25d; i, fol. 25b; i, fol. 24c; i, fol. 24a; i, fol. 23d; i, fol. 23d; i, fol. 44d; i, fol. 253c; i, fol. 253d; i, fol. 253d; i, fol. 253d; i, fol. 253b; i, fol. 253d; i, fol. 253b; i, fol. 248a; i, fol. 253d; i, fol. 176a; i, fol. 253d; i, fol. 253c; i, fol. 253c; i, fol. 253c; i, fol. 253c; i, fol. 253b; i, fol. 253b; i, fol. 253d; i, fol. 269b; i, fol. 239b; i, fol. 239b; i, fol. 253d; i, fol. 259d; i, fol. 254a; i, fol. 246a; i, fol. 253d; i, fol. 259d; i, fol. 259d; i, fol. 259d; i, fol. 259d; i, fol. 259d; i, fol. 254a; i, fol. 253b; i, fol. 254a; i, fol. 248a; i, fol. 253d; i, fol. 254a; i, fol. 254a; i, fol. 253d; i, fol. 253b; i, fol. 254a; i, fol. 25d; i, fol. 25b; i, fol. 23b; i, fol. 253a; i, fol. 49a; Regesta regum Anglo-Normannorum III, No. 902; Rees, Cartulary of Shrewsbury Abbey (1975), No. 35; Rees, Cartulary of Shrewsbury Abbey (1975), No. 19; Gibbs, Early Charters of St Pauls (1939), No. 16; Gibbs,

Early Charters of St Pauls (1939), No. 9; Dugdale, Monasticon Anglicanum, IV, p. 113, No. II; Harper-Bill & Mortimer, Stoke by Clare Cartulary, No. 433; Regesta regum Anglo-Normannorum III, No. 181; Clay, Early Yorkshire Charters (1949), VIII, No. 5; i, fol. 253b; i, fol. 166c; i, fol. 239b; i, fol. 248a; i, fol. 44c; i, fol. 23a; i, fol. 137b; i, fol. 176a

Roger Corbet

Norman, brother of Robert, Domesday tenant of Earl Roger in Shropshire in succession to their father Corbet (Ord. Vit. ii, 272). His holdings were afterwards known as the barony of Cause. He was a benefactor of Shrewsbury abbey, as were his son Everard and Simon, according to Henry II's confirmation charter (Cart., no. 36 p. 42). Apparently succeeded c.1121 by a son Robert; see Sanders, 29. According to L. Musset, 'Administration et justice', Cahiers des annales de Normandie no. 17 (1985), 147, the family probably came from the region of Boitron and Essay, near Sées, Orne.

i, fol. 253c; i, fol. 253c; i, fol. 253c; i, fol. 254a; i, fol. 254a; i, fol. 254a; i, fol. 253c; i, fol. 254a; i, fol. 254a; i, fol. 254a; i, fol. 254a; Rees, Cartulary of Shrewsbury Abbey (1975), No. 35; i, fol. 254a; Rees, Cartulary of Shrewsbury Abbey (1975), No. 35; i, fol. 255d; i, fol. 255d; i, fol. 255d; i, fol. 255c; i, fol. 255d; i, fol. 255c; i, fol. 255c; i, fol. 255c; i, fol. 255c; i, fol. 255d; i, fol. 255c; i, fol. 255d; i, fol. 255c; i, fol. 255c; i, fol. 255d; i, fol. 255d; i, fol. 255d; Rees, Cartulary of Shrewsbury Abbey (1975), No. 35; i, fol. 255d

Roger Daniel

Norman cleric, occurs Domesday Sussex as a tenant of William of Eu. A canon of St Mary's Hastings (Sussex Rec. Soc. xliv, 299–302, record and confirmation by Henry count of Eu). The manse once of Roger Daniel was confirmed by Henry II to the church of Sainte-Marie d'Eu (BN lat. 13094, fol. 39v).

i, fol. 20a; i, fol. 18b; i, fol. 18c

Roger De Abernon

Norman, from Abenon, Calvados, arr. Lisieux, cant. Orbec (Loyd, 1), a Domesday tenant of Richard de Clare. He appears to have been dead by c.1100, after which his sons Walter, Ingelran and Jordan occur. C.A.F. Meekings, 'Notes on the Abernon family before 1236', Surrey Archaeolgical Collections 72 (1980).

i, fol. 35c; i, fol. 35a; i, fol. 34c; i, fol. 35b; ii, fol. 395b; ii, fol. 394b; ii, fol. 394b

Roger De Bascheruilla

Norman, occurs Domesday Gloucestershire as a tenant of Ralph de Tosny; probably from Bacqueville, Eure. A Robert de Bascherville was tenant of Roger de Lacy in Gloucestershire. Some of the Gloucestershire manors held by a Roger did not descend in the Bascherville family. Cf. Roger II de Glocestrie.

i, fol. 168b; i, fol. 168b; i, fol. 243a; i, fol. 168b; Round, Ancient Charters (1888), No. 11; Round, Ancient Charters (1888), No. 13; Round, Ancient Charters (1888), No. 6; i, fol. 168b; i, fol. 168b

Roger De Bellomonte

Norman, from Beaumont-le-Roger, dépt. Eure. Son of Humphrey de Vielles and Alberada. He was vicomte of Rouen c.1050. He married Adelina, daughter and heiress of Hugh, count of Meulan. At the time of Domesday Book, in which Roger occurs as a tenant-in-chief, his son Robert had inherited the county of Meulan and occurs in Domesday as count. He founded the monastery at Beaumont-le-Roger in

1088. Around 1094 he became a monk at Saint-Pierre de Préaux, the monastery founded by his parents, dying a few years later. See Ord. Vit. ii, 14, iii, 426. Father also of Henry, earl of Warwick, and Albreda, abbess of Saint-Léger de Préaux.

> i, fol. 144b; i, fol. 134b; i, fol. 144b; i, fol. 144b; i, fol. 144b; i, fol. 144c; i, fol. 144b; i, fol. 144a; i, fol. 144b; i, fol. 144b; Dugdale, Monasticon Anglicanum, V, p. 175, No. I; Elvey, Luffield Priory Charters (1968–75), No. 1; i, fol. 80b; i, fol. 80b; i, fol. 80b; i, fol. 80b; i, fol. 80b; i, fol. 80b; i, fol. 80b; i, fol. 168a

Roger De Berchelai

Norman, occurs in Domesday Gloucestershire, where he was reeve of Berkeley, together with his brother Ralph. He died c.1091–3 as a monk of Gloucester, having restored to the monks the manor of Shotover which he had held unjustly (Chron S. Petri i, 112, 122). He was probably father of Roger II of Berkeley and his brother Eustache of Nympesfield. Green, Government, 234, suggests that the family came from the neighbourhood of Aumale, Seine-Maritime, since Roger I and his wife Rissa made a grant to the canons of Saint-Martin d'Auchy near Aumale (Archaeologia vol. 26, pp. 358–60), and c.1154/60 Roger III secured from Bernard de Saint-Valery freedom of the port of Saint-Valery-sur-Somme. Sanders, 114. Comp. Peer. ii, 123–4.

> i, fol. 165b; i, fol. 163b; i, fol. 163b; i, fol. 163a; Regesta regum Anglo-Normannorum III, No. 345; i, fol. 168a; i, fol. 168a; i, fol. 168a; i, fol. 72c; i, fol. 162a; i, fol. 72c; i, fol. 72c; i, fol. 162b; i, fol. 168a; Dugdale, Monasticon Anglicanum, II, pp. 482–83, No. XIII; Regesta regum Anglo-Normannorum III, No. 818; Regesta regum Anglo-Normannorum III, No. 345; i, fol. 163b; i, fol. 163b; i, fol. 163b; i, fol. 163b; i, fol. 163b; i, fol. 163b

Roger De Boscnorman

Occurs Domesday Northamptonshire. Probably named for Le Bois-Normand-près-Lyre, Eure.

> i, fol. 219a

Roger De Boscroard

Roger de Boscroard, from Bosc-le-Hard, Seine-Maritime, cant. Bellencombre (Loyd, 18), brother of William (q.v.); major tenants of Robert de Tosny of Belvoir.

> ii, fol. 091a; ii, fol. 091a; i, fol. 353a; i, fol. 149b

Roger De Burun

Norman, named from Buron, Calvados, arr. Falaise, cant. Bretteville-sur-Laize, comm. Fresnay-le-Vieux. Domesday tenant of Geoffrey de Bec at Bengeo, and probably elsewhere, in Hertfordshire. His successor, probably his son, c.1120 was Robert de Buron, grandfather of Roger, the tenant in 1206; VCH Herts iii, 417, 426. Occurs as an early benefactor of St Albans, to which he gave a manse 'super ripam Thele' (BL Cotton Nero D vii, 92v–3r).

> i, fol. 140d; i, fol. 140a; i, fol. 140c

Roger De Busli

Norman from Bully, Seine-Maritime, arr. and cant. Neufchâtel (Loyd, 21). Domesday tenant-in-chief whose fief became the honour of Tickhill, Yorkshire, often referred to as the honour of Blyth. He held a manor in Devon given to him by Queen Matilda with his wife, Muriel. After his death his lands were seized by Robert of Bellême, but he lost all his lands in 1102. According to Orderic Vitalis (v, 224–6 and n.), Robert was a kinsman (cognatus) of Roger. The fief remained in royal hands until Stephen granted it to Henry count of Eu, son of William count of Eu and Beatrice, daughter of Roger. His son Roger II was possibly a minor at the date of his death in 1098/9, and though he may briefly have held his father's lands he appears to have left no issue. Benefactor of Sainte-Trinité de Rouen (Cart., p. 444).

i, fol. 237a; Regesta regum Anglo-Normannorum III, No. 109; Timson, Blyth Priory Cartulary (1973), No. 326; Regesta regum Anglo-Normannorum III, No. 178; Regesta regum Anglo-Normannorum III, No. 345; i, fol. 270a; i, fol. 270a; i, fol. 163c; i, fol. 270a; i, fol. 319a; i, fol. 234d; i, fol. 319a; i, fol. 319a; i, fol. 319a; i, fol. 319a; i, fol. 319a; i, fol. 286b; i, fol. 319a; i, fol. 234c; i, fol. 319a; i, fol. 319a; i, fol. 319a; i, fol. 319a; i, fol. 320a; i, fol. 320a; i, fol. 320a; i, fol. 320a; i, fol. 319c; i, fol. 319a; i, fol. 286d; i, fol. 285c; i, fol. 285c; i, fol. 285c; i, fol. 285c; i, fol. 286a; i, fol. 285d; i, fol. 286a; i, fol. 319a; i, fol. 285d; i, fol. 285c; i, fol. 286d; i, fol. 286d; i, fol. 286d; i, fol. 286b; i, fol. 285d; i, fol. 319b; i, fol. 285c; i, fol. 319b; i, fol. 285c; i, fol. 285d; i, fol. 319d; i, fol. 319c; i, fol. 319b; i, fol. 319c; i, fol. 319c; i, fol. 319c; i, fol. 319c; i, fol. 319d; i, fol. 319d; i, fol. 113a; i, fol. 319d; i, fol. 319c; i, fol. 319d; i, fol. 319d; i, fol. 319d; i, fol. 320a; i, fol. 319d; i, fol. 319d; i, fol. 319d; i, fol. 319d; i, fol. 319d; i, fol. 320a; i, fol. 319d; i, fol. 319b; i, fol. 319b; i, fol. 287a; i, fol. 319b; i, fol. 319b; i, fol. 319b; i, fol. 319b; i, fol. 319c; i, fol. 319b; i, fol. 319c; i, fol. 319b; i, fol. 319c; i, fol. 319b; i, fol. 319a; i, fol. 319a; i, fol. 319b; i, fol. 319c; i, fol. 319c; i, fol. 319c; i, fol. 319c; i, fol. 319c; i, fol. 319c; i, fol. 319c; i, fol. 285a; i, fol. 280a; i, fol. 284d; i, fol. 284c; i, fol. 284d; i, fol. 284d; i, fol. 285a; i, fol. 285a; i, fol. 286b; i, fol. 285a; i, fol. 286c; i, fol. 285a; i, fol. 285b; i, fol. 285b; i, fol. 284d; i, fol. 352d; i, fol. 278b; i, fol. 285b; i, fol. 352d; i, fol. 285d; i, fol. 285a; i, fol. 286b; i, fol. 319a; i, fol. 319a; i, fol. 286c; i, fol. 286b; i, fol. 286b; i, fol. 286b; i, fol. 286b; i, fol. 286b; i, fol. 286b; i, fol. 352d; i, fol. 286c; i, fol. 286c; i, fol. 286c; i, fol. 286c; i, fol. 286d; i, fol. 286d; i, fol. 286d; i, fol. 286d; i, fol. 286d; i, fol. 287a; i, fol. 286b; i, fol. 286a; i, fol. 278b; i, fol. 285b; i, fol. 285b; i, fol. 352d; i, fol. 286a; i, fol. 286a; i, fol. 286a; i, fol. 278b; i, fol. 286a; i, fol. 284d; i, fol. 286a; i, fol. 286a; i, fol. 285b; i, fol. 286d; i, fol. 286a; i, fol. 286a; i, fol. 286a; i, fol. 286a; i, fol. 286a; i, fol. 286a; i, fol. 286a; i, fol. 284c; i, fol. 286b; i, fol. 285b; i, fol. 286b; i, fol. 286b; i, fol. 285b; i, fol. 286b; i, fol. 284c; i, fol. 284c; i, fol. 284c; i, fol. 284d; i, fol. 284c; i, fol. 284c; i, fol. 284d; i, fol. 284c; i, fol. 278b; i, fol. 284c; i, fol. 284c; i, fol. 337a; i, fol. 336a; i, fol. 319a; i, fol. 352d; i, fol. 234c; i, fol. 284c; i, fol. 287a; Clay, Early Yorkshire Charters (1949), VIII, No. 5; Timson, Blyth Priory Cartulary (1973), No. 325

Roger De Caisneto

Norman, Domesday tenant of Robert I d'Oilly. He married, c.1085/90, Alice de Langetot, by whom he had issue at least ten children, including Hugh, Robert (bishop of Lincoln), Ralph, William, Roger, Hawise, Beatrice and Isabel. He died before 1130, and was probably dead by 1109. His family was thoroughly discussed in Salter, Eynsham Cart. i, pp. 411ff, but his conclusion that there was an initial relationship between Roger and Ralph de Caisneto of Sussex is untenable. There may have been a later relationship between the two families, but it is very likely that the Oxfordshire Caisneto or Chesney family originated at Quesnay-Guesnon, Calvados, cant. Caumont-l'Evente, near the home of the Oilly family.

i, fol. 158b; i, fol. 158c; Salter, Cartualry of Eynsham, i (1906), no. 124; i, fol. 225b; i, fol. 225b

Roger De Candos

Norman, from Candos, Eure, arr. Pont-Audemer, cant. Montfort-sur-Risle, comm.

Illeville-sur-Montfort (Loyd, 26). Domesday tenant of Hugh de Montfort in Suffolk His son Robert (d.1120) was lord of Caerleon and Snodhill in the early twelfth century, when a Philip de Candos occurs in Suffolk and Norfolk. A late-eleventh or early twelfth century record of the despoliation of estates of Sainte-Trinité de Caen mentioned the tithe of Hénouville, Seine-Maritime, cant. Duclair, usurped by William camerarius son of Roger de Candos (Walmsley, p. 126).

ii, fol. 407a; i, fol. 013b; ii, fol. 406b; Dugdale, Monasticon Anglicanum, III, pp. 447–48, No. II; Regesta regum Anglo-Normannorum III, No. 373; ii, fol. 406a; ii, fol. 406a; ii, fol. 410a; ii, fol. 410a; ii, fol. 406a; ii, fol. 410a; ii, fol. 409b; ii, fol. 409b; ii, fol. 405b; Dugdale, Monasticon Anglicanum, III, p. 448, No. III

Roger De Cilderlaio

Norman, tenant of the bishop of Lincoln in Childerley, Cambridgeshire, in Chesterton Hundred, where he was a Domesday juror. Ancestor of the Childerley family; Lewis, 'Jurors', 39; VCH Cambs ix, 42–3.

i, fol. 190c; Hamilton, Inquisitio Eliensis (1876), pp. 97–100

Roger De Curcellis

Norman, from Courseulles-sur-Mer, Calvados, arr. Caen, cant. Creully (Loyd, 33). Son of William de Courseulles, whom he had succeeded by 1086 as Domesday tenant-in-chief in Somerset, and a tenant of Earl Roger in Shropshire. According to charters for the abbey of Troarn (of which his father was also a benefactor), he had a wife Elisabeth and four sons, Wandrille, Stephen, William and Walchelin (Sauvage, Troarn, Preuves ii, V); possibly also father of Waldric son of Roger de Courseulles. Also a benefactor of Montebourg (BN lat. 10087, pp. 11, 59). He attested charters of Henry I until c.1115. Before 1166, and possibly c.1115, he or his heirs lost their tenancy-in-chief to the Malets, though they continued to hold land in Somerset. Five fees of the bishopric of Bayeux were attributed to a Roger de Corcella in the Bayeux Inquest, c.1132, which was sworn by Wandrille de Corsella, among others (RBE, 645).

i, fol. 90c; i, fol. 90a; i, fol. 90a; i, fol. 90a; i, fol. 90a; i, fol. 90a; i, fol. 90a; i, fol. 88b; i, fol. 90a; i, fol. 90c; i, fol. 90b; i, fol. 90d; i, fol. 90d; i, fol. 90d; i, fol. 90b; i, fol. 90c; i, fol. 90c; i, fol. 114d; i, fol. 88c; i, fol. 88c; i, fol. 91b; i, fol. 91a; i, fol. 91b; i, fol. 96c; i, fol. 93b; Douglas, Feudal Documents from Bury St Edmunds, No. 30; Douglas, Feudal Documents from Bury St Edmunds, No. 29; i, fol. 94a; i, fol. 94c; i, fol. 93d; i, fol. 94b; i, fol. 94b; i, fol. 94a; i, fol. 93d; i, fol. 94a; i, fol. 94a; i, fol. 93d; i, fol. 256b; i, fol. 94a; i, fol. 93d; i, fol. 256b; i, fol. 93d; i, fol. 93b; i, fol. 93b; i, fol. 93b; i, fol. 93b; i, fol. 72c; i, fol. 256b; i, fol. 256b; i, fol. 256b; i, fol. 93b; i, fol. 90b; i, fol. 90b; i, fol. 90b

Roger De Ebrois

Norman, from Evreux, Eure, Domesday tenant of William d'Ecouis in Norfolk.

ii, fol. 222b; ii, fol. 225b; ii, fol. 222b; ii, fol. 222b; ii, fol. 222b

Roger De Iurei

Norman from Ivry-la-Bataille, Eure, arr. Evreux, cant. Saint-André (Loyd, 52). Brother or uncle of Hugh pincerna of Ivry, also a Domesday tenant-in-chief. In Domesday Book his lands often followed those of his close friend and sworn brother Robert I d'Oilly, with whom he was co-founder of St George in the Castle, precursor of Oseney (Cart. iv, 1). His wife Adelina, daughter of Hugh de Grandmesnil, occurs in Domesday Oxfordshire. Her name and that of their daughter Adelisa occurs in Chron. Abingdon ii, 72–4. Adelina's grant of the manor of Rowington, Warwickshire, to Reading Abbey identifies the Domesday tenant of Hugh de Grandmesnil there as Roger d'Ivry. For his identification with Roger pincerna, knight of the archbishop of Canterbury in 1093–6, see Douglas, Dom. Mon., 56). Forgeries in the Oseney Cartulary (iv, 27) suggest that Roger had a son Geoffrey, but there is no evidence that he had any sons at the time of his death. Adelina died at the end of 1110 and was certainly succeeded by her daughter Adelisa, who died c.1133. The fief was subsequently granted to Rainald de Saint-Valèry.

i, fol. 144d; i, fol. 221a; i, fol. 155a; i, fol. 157c; i, fol. 161b; i, fol. 156a; i, fol. 156d; i, fol. 144d; i, fol. 144c; i, fol. 161a; Salter, Cartulary of Oseney Abbey (1929–36), No. 2; i, fol. 158c; i, fol. 242b; i, fol. 151d; Salter, Cartulary of Oseney Abbey (1929–36), No. 1A; i, fol. 164c; i, fol. 168a; i, fol. 168a; i, fol. 168a; i, fol. 168a; i, fol. 62c; i, fol. 62c; i, fol. 62c; i, fol. 62c; i, fol. 62c; i, fol. 168a; i, fol. 154a; i, fol. 143a; i, fol. 158d; i, fol. 158c; i, fol. 159a; i, fol. 238a; i, fol. 161a; i, fol. 158d; i, fol. 158c; i, fol. 156d; i, fol. 155c; i, fol. 242b; i, fol. 158d; i, fol. 205d; i, fol. 168b; i, fol. 224d; i, fol. 224d; Salter, Cartulary of Oseney Abbey (1929–36), No. 18; i, fol. 205d; i, fol. 58b; i, fol. 168d; i, fol. 144d; Douglas, ed., Domesday Monachorum (1944), p. 105; i, fol. 242a; i, fol. 242a

Roger De Laci
Norman, from Lassy, arr. Vire, cant. Condé-sur-Noireau, Calvados (Loyd, 53), son of Walter de Lacy and nephew of Ilbert. He succeeded his father in 1085 and held the lordship of Weobley, in Herefordshire and Gloucestershire, in Domesday Book. He supported Robert Curthose against William II in 1088 and 1094, when he was banished and forfeited his lands to his brother Hugh. Returning to Normandy, he was prominent in the service of Robert Curthose. He died there sometime after Robert's fall in 1106, leaving a son and heir Gilbert (Sanders, 95). See Wightman, Lacy Family, 130–3, 169–74.

i, fol. 183b; i, fol. 248b; Rees, Cartulary of Shrewsbury Abbey (1975), No. 35; i, fol. 166c

Roger De Livet
Norman, from Livet-en-Ouche, Eure, arr. Bernay, cant. Beaumesnil (Loyd, 55). Domesday tenant of Henry de Ferrers in Leicestershire. Benefactor of Tutbury. Robert de Livet occurs temp. Henry I.

i, fol. 274b; i, fol. 275a; i, fol. 274c; i, fol. 274b; i, fol. 233b; i, fol. 233b; i, fol. 233c; Dugdale, Monasticon Anglicanum, III, pp. 392–93, No. II; i, fol. 233c; i, fol. 233c; i, fol. 233c; i, fol. 233c; i, fol. 233c

Roger De Luxonio
Norman, from Lisieux, Eure, occurs Domesday Somerset as tenant of William de Moyon; identified from Exon.

i, fol. 95c

Roger De Margella
Norman, Domesday tenant of Roger Arundel. Exon supplies his toponym which probably refers to Margueray, Manche, arr. Saint-Lô, cant. Percy. His successor in 1166 was William de Margellis.

i, fol. 82c

Roger De Millai

Norman, tenant of Earl Hugh in Domesday Leicestershire. The Domesday form of his toponym suggests an origin in Meslay, Calvados, cant. Thury-Harcourt, rather than Milly, Manche. Cf. William de Milly, whose heirs in 1107 were his sons Alfred and Roger.

i, fol. 237a; i, fol. 264c; Barraclough, Charters of AN Earls of Chester (1988), No. 1; Barraclough, Charters of AN Earls of Chester (1988), No. 10; Barraclough, Charters of AN Earls of Chester (1988), No. 11

Roger De Moles

Norman, from Meulles, Calvados, arr. Lisieux, cant. Orbec (Loyd, 65), Domesday tenant of Baldwin de Meulles, sheriff of Devon. Probably ancestor of the Moels family (Comp. Peer, ix, 1). By 1129/30 he appears to have been succeeded by a second Roger, who occurs in a defective passage in the Pipe Roll which refers to his brothers. His successor in 1166 was Joel de Moels.

i, fol. 106a; i, fol. 106a; i, fol. 106a; i, fol. 106a; i, fol. 108a; i, fol. 106d; i, fol. 106a

Roger De Montbegon

Norman, from Mont Bougon, Orne, arr. Argentan, cant. Exmes, comm. Saint-Pierr-la-Rivière, Domesday tenant of Roger Pictaviensis de Montgomery. Roger of Montbegon gave a charter for Sées (CDF, 663) in which he mentions his brother Robert and his Mancelle wife Cecilia. Roger of Montbegon was possibly the Roger who held land in Lincs from Ivo Taillebois (DB Lincs 14.30; 33; 39. Their son or grandson Ernald de Montbegon occurs in Stephen's reign (holding Sproatley and Newsham, Yorks, of William of Aumâle, VCH Yorks ii, 172). Roger held a sizeable fee from Roger of Poitou, and his descendants were important tenants of the Honour of Lancaster. Roger and his wife had issue a son Roger and a daughter Beatrice, wife of Ansketin de Ros. They were possibly also parents of Ernald (q.v.) and Fulcoius. See K.S.B. Keats-Rohan, 'Roger de Montbegon and his family', Trans. Hist. Soc. Lancs. Cheshire, 144 (1994), 181–5.

i, fol. 352b; i, fol. 352a; i, fol. 325a; i, fol. 269d; i, fol. 269d; i, fol. 352a; i, fol. 352a; Lindsey Survey, BL ms Cotton Claudius C v, fols 9–18; Lindsey Survey, BL ms Cotton Claudius C v, fols 1–9; Regesta regum Anglo-Normannorum III, No. 178; Lindsey Survey, BL ms Cotton Claudius C v, fols 1–9; Pipe Roll 31 Henry I, 116–ln; Lindsey Survey, BL ms Cotton Claudius C v, fols 9–18

Roger De Mucelgros

Norman, from Mussegros, Eure, arr. Les Andelys, cant. Fleury-sur-Andelle, comm. Ecouis (Loyd, 71). Occurs Domesday holding from the king and from Ralph de Tosny. Attested a charter of Ralph de Tosny for Saint-Evroul c.1070 (Ord. Vit. iii, 126). His successor Hervey de Muscegros occurs c.1140/50. Cf. L. Musset, 'Les Tosny', Francia v (1978), 77.

i, fol. 183b; i, fol. 185b; i, fol. 185b; i, fol. 185b

Roger De Oburuilla

Domesday tenant-in-chief in Suffolk, brother of William (q.v.). He appears to have been the eldest son and principal heir of Serius de Auberville (Calvados, arr. Pont-l'Evêque, cant. Dozulé), who occurs in an Ely plea of c.1072. His younger brother William, who was probably his tenant of that name, also held some of their father's land in chief. Both tenancies-in-chief were given to Eudo Dapifer after

1087. Roger's land at Elmsett, Suffolk, passed to Ralph de Amblie some time between 1100 and 1120 (Farrer, HKF iii, 174).

ii, fol. 404a; ii, fol. 404b; ii, fol. 404b; ii, fol. 404b; ii, fol. 404a; ii, fol. 404b; ii, fol. 404b; ii, fol. 382b; ii, fol. 405a; ii, fol. 404a; ii, fol. 404a; ii, fol. 404a; ii, fol. 404a; ii, fol. 404a; ii, fol. 403b; ii, fol. 382b; ii, fol. 404a; ii, fol. 404a; ii, fol. 405a; ii, fol. 405a; ii, fol. 404a; ii, fol. 404a; ii, fol. 404b; ii, fol. 405a; ii, fol. 404b; ii, fol. 403b; ii, fol. 103b; ii, fol. 384a; ii, fol. 383a; ii, fol. 384a; ii, fol. 384a; ii, fol. 281b; ii, fol. 052b; ii, fol. 052a; ii, fol. 052a; ii, fol. 052a; ii, fol. 052a; ii, fol. 052a

Roger De Oilli

Norman, from Ouilly-le-Basset, Calvados. Occurs in Domesday Gloucestershire as a tenant of Osbern fitz Richard. Also a tenant in Oxfordshire of Robert I de Oilly, of whom he may have a nephew, or possibly a brother. He occurs in several acts of Henry I, and is called constabularius in Chron. Abingdon. i, 126. His last certain appearance was on PR 31 Henry I.

i, fol. 158c; Pipe Roll 31 Henry I, 006b–ox; Pipe Roll 31 Henry I, 006a–ox; i, fol. 168c; Hart, Cartularium Monasterii de Rameseia, No. CLV; i, fol. 158c; i, fol. 158c

Roger De Olnei

Occurs as a tenant of Countess Judith in Domesday Buckinghamshire, named from the bishop of Coutances's manor of Olney. Cf. Farrer, HKF i, 400, 408.

i, fol. 152d; i, fol. 152d; i, fol. 152d

Roger De Orbec

Norman, from Orbec, Calvados, arr. Lisieux, Domesday tenant of Richard de Clare in Suffolk. His successor c.1138–49 was Richard de Orbec. Cf. Loyd, 75.

ii, fol. 447b; ii, fol. 393b

Roger De Ostreham

Norman, mentioned under Dover in Domesday Kent; named either from Westerham, a manor of Count Eustache (DB Kent 10.1, or from Ouistreham, Calvados, cant. Douvres.

Ballard, Inquisition of St Augustine's (1920), fols 24r–28r; i, fol. 001a

Roger De Ramis

Norman, from Rames, Seine-Maritime, arr. Le Havre, cant. Saint-Romain-de-Colbosc (Loyd, 84), Domesday tenant-in-chief. He was succeeded at an unknown date by his son William, who had himself been succeeded by his sons Roger II and Robert by 1130 (PR 31 Henry I, 54). Sanders, 139; A.L. Raimes, 'The family of Reynes of Wherstead in Suffolk', Proceedings of the Suffolk Institute of Archaeology xxiii, pt. 2; J.H. Round, Geoffrey de Mandeville, 399–404.

i, fol. 130c; i, fol. 130c; ii, fol. 087b; ii, fol. 006b; ii, fol. 214b; ii, fol. 014b; ii, fol. 421b; ii, fol. 421b; ii, fol. 421b; ii, fol. 421b; ii, fol. 421b; ii, fol. 422a; ii, fol. 083b; ii, fol. 082b; ii, fol. 422b; ii, fol. 263b; ii, fol. 263b; ii, fol. 263b; ii, fol. 083b; ii, fol. 083a; ii, fol. 083b; ii, fol. 083b; ii, fol. 083a; ii, fol. 422b; ii, fol. 083a; ii, fol. 423a; ii, fol. 083b; ii, fol. 083b; ii, fol. 263a; ii, fol. 422b; ii, fol. 394a; ii, fol. 393b; ii, fol. 393b; ii, fol. 374b; ii, fol. 423b; ii, fol. 337b; ii, fol. 449b; ii, fol. 422a; ii, fol. 422b; ii, fol. 422b; ii, fol. 422b; ii, fol. 422b; ii, fol. 422b; ii, fol. 423a; ii, fol. 423a; ii, fol. 423b; ii, fol. 338a; ii, fol. 082b; ii, fol. 421b; ii, fol. 263a; i, fol. 127b

Roger De Roerico
Norman, Domesday tenant of Baldwin of Exeter in Devon, identified from the Tax Return.

i, fol. 108c

Roger De Sancto Germano
Norman, from Saint-Germain-la-Campagne, Eure, arr. Bernay (Loyd, 94), Domesday tenant of Richard de Clare in Suffolk, identified from a grant of land at Bentley made after his death by his widow and son to Stoke priory. William de St German and Emma his mother gave their tithes of Bentley and elsewhere for the soul of Roger their lord, as Walter brother of Roger had once held (Stoke-by-Clare Cart. no. 137).

ii, fol. 040b; ii, fol. 040b; Harper-Bill & Mortimer, Stoke by Clare Cartulary, No. 136; Harper-Bill & Mortimer, Stoke by Clare Cartulary, No. 37; Harper-Bill & Mortimer, Stoke by Clare Cartulary, No. 39; Harper-Bill & Mortimer, Stoke by Clare Cartulary, No. 166; ii, fol. 448a; ii, fol. 392b

Roger De Stantone
Norman, occurs Domesday Somerset; named from Stanton in the Exon Tax Return Keynsham Hundred.

i, fol. 87b

Roger De Sumeri
Named from Sommery, Seine-Maritime, arr. Neufchâtel (cf. Loyd, 63), Domesday tenant of Eustache count of Boulogne in Domesday Cambridgeshire and Essex. His son Roger II occurs 1105–30.

ii, fol. 026b; i, fol. 197a; i, fol. 197b; ii, fol. 034a; ii, fol. 034a; ii, fol. 033b

Roger Deus Salvæt Dominas
Occurs Domesday Essex. Apparently succeeded by William, possibly his son, whose heir c.1131–3 was William de Glanville, to whom Henry I granted in inheritance the serjeanty of his uncle William de Salt les Dames (RRAN ii, 1835). The vernacular toponymic form of William's name, replacing the Latin byname of Roger, occurs in a much later document (Cal. Chart. R. i, 422). Cf. F.N. Craig, 'The Glanvilles and Roger God-Save-The-Ladies', The American Genealogist 71.4 (1996), 200–4.

ii, fol. 021b; ii, fol. 096b; ii, fol. 096b; ii, fol. 096b; ii, fol. 096b

Roger Dispensator
Domesday tenant and dispenser of Geoffrey, bishop of Coutances, identified in Exon.

i, fol. 88c

Roger Filius Ansketil
Norman, Domesday tenant in Kent of Odo of Bayeux. Ansketil of Maltot (Calvados, cant. Evrecy) and his son Roger occur in charters for Saint-Etienne de Caen of the 1080s (Actes caen. 7 and 18).

ii, fol. 006b; i, fol. 011d; i, fol. 010c

Roger Filius Ernaldi
Domesday tenant of Roger Pictaviensis in Suffolk. Ancestor of a line of men called Ernald Ruffus associated with Hasketon to occur in the Eye Cartulary in the

twelfth century and later. No tenant is named in Robert Malet's manor of Hasketon (DB Suffolk 6.118;126), but a Roger fitz Ernald occurs in the part of Hasketon formerly held by William Malet and then given to Roger of Poitou (ibid., 8.8;12). Roger fitz Ernald attested the foundation of Lancaster priory in 1094 with Ernald Barbarota, Roger of Montbegon (CDF, 664–5). His son Ernald fitz Roger, known as Ernald Ruffus, succeeded him by 1125. See Brown, Eye Cart. ii, pp. 78–9.

ii, fol. 347b; ii, fol. 346b; ii, fol. 346b; ii, fol. 346b; ii, fol. 346b; ii, fol. 346b

Roger Filius Pagani

Domesday tenant of Baldwin the Sheriff and Ralph de Pomeroy in Devon; probably brother of Ralph fitz Payn, tenant of William Capra de Pomeroy. Richard fitz Payn held his Pomeroy fees in 1166. Cf. CDF, 1455, a charter of Jocelyn de Pomeroy attested by William fitz Payn and his sons.

i, fol. 114a; i, fol. 108b

Roger Filius Radulfi

Norman, occurs in Domesday Gloucestershire, and in Somerset as a tenant of Geoffrey, bishop of Coutances. It was suggested by A. S. Ellis, 'Manorial history of Clifton', Transactions of Bristol and Gloucestershire Archaeological Society 3 (1878–9), that he was a younger son of Ralph of Berkeley.

i, fol. 88b; i, fol. 170b; i, fol. 170b; i, fol. 170b

Roger Filius Renardi

Norman, Domesday tenant of William de Warenne in Norfolk. His successors in the twelfth century were a series of Roberts de Mortemer-sur-Eaulne, Seine-Maritime (Loyd, 70), the first of whom occurs in the time of William II de Warenne (1088–1138). Roger was probably the ancestor of this family. Cf. Comp. Peer. ix, 243; Farrer, HKF iii, 385.

ii, fol. 162b; ii, fol. 266b; ii, fol. 266b; ii, fol. 266b; ii, fol. 267b; ii, fol. 267b; ii, fol. 267b; ii, fol. 267b; ii, fol. 267a; ii, fol. 267a; ii, fol. 267a; ii, fol. 266b; ii, fol. 266b; ii, fol. 267b; ii, fol. 266b; ii, fol. 266b; ii, fol. 267a; ii, fol. 266b; ii, fol. 267a

Roger Filius Seifridi

Norman, occurs Domesday Berkshire. Brother of Ralph fitz Seifrid. The combined holdings passed to the honour of Wallingford, of which a Geoffrey fitz Seifrid was a tenant in 1166. Cf. Farrer, in Boarstall Cart. app., pp. 318, 322.

i, fol. 62d; i, fol. 62d; i, fol. 56c

Roger Filius Teodrici

Norman, Domeday tenant of Hugh de Beauchamp in Domesday Bedfordshire.

i, fol. 213d

Roger Flandrensis

Domesday tenant of Ruald Adobed in Domesday Devon, identified by Exon.

i, fol. 115a; i, fol. 115a

Roger Flavus

Norman, Domesday tenant of Ralph de Pomeroy. Surnamed Flavus (Blund) in Exon.

i, fol. 114b

Roger Infans

Norman, Domesday tenant of the abbey of Peterborough, identified from the Descriptio Militum. Hugh Candidus, p. 54 (Stapleton, 170 note), wrote: Primus Rogerus Infans. Rogerus de Torpel tenet in Northamptonescire duodecim hydas terræ, scilicet in Torpel. Makeseye, Ufforde, Pilketone, Clapethorn, Cotherstoke, Northburc, Leaulme, Badingtone et Estone et pertinentiis suis, et inde facit servicium sex militum'. He was presumably dead by 1129 when [his sons] Robert and Roger de Torpel occur on the Pipe Roll of 31 Henry I, p. 85. According to a Peterborough manuscript, cited by King, Peterborough Abbey, 27–8, Roger had a daughter who married Richard de Raimbeaucourt; the same item records that his son Robert later suffered from leprosy.

i, fol. 221d; i, fol. 221d; King, Peterborough Descriptio Militum (1969), pp. 97–101; Northants Survey, fols 96r–99v; Northants Survey, fols 94r–95v

Roger Longus Ensis

Norman, Domesday tenant of the bishop of Thetford in Norfolk.

ii, fol. 198a; ii, fol. 198a; ii, fol. 198a

Roger Malfed

Norman, Domesday tenant of Peterbourgh Abbey. Hugh Candidus, p. 59 (Stapleton, 170–1 note), wrote: Primus Rogerus Malfe. Hæres Rogeri Malfe tenet in Norhamptonescire, scilicet in Wodeforde et Kynesthorpe et oertinentiis, quinque hidas et tres virgatas; et inde fait pleum servitium duorum militum.

i, fol. 222a; i, fol. 222a; King, Peterborough Descriptio Militum (1969), pp. 97–101

Roger Marescal

Norman, royal marshal, occurs Domesday Essex.

ii, fol. 094a; ii, fol. 094a; ii, fol. 094a; ii, fol. 094a; ii, fol. 094a

Roger Miles Archiepiscopi

Knight of Archbishop Lanfranc in 1086; probably same as the knight of Odo of Bayeux

i, fol. 005b

Roger Miles Johannis

Domesday knight of John fitz Walerann. Benefactor of Bermondsey Abbey in 1094, to which his grants were confirmed by his daughter Matilda and her husband Hasculf de Tany in 1107 (Mon. Ang. v, 88, 96, 101; Ann. Mon. iii, 428, 430–1).

ii, fol. 082b; ii, fol. 084b; ii, fol. 084b; Excerpta a Chronicis de Bermondsey, Dugdale, Monasticon, IV, pp. 95–97

Roger Minister Petri

Norman, occurs in Domesday Book as an official of Peter de Valognes. Possibly same as the Roger who held at Parndon in Essex under Ranulf frater Ilger and Peter de Valognes.

ii, fol. 080a; ii, fol. 081b; ii, fol. 080a; ii, fol. 078b; Dugdale, Monasticon Anglicanum, III, pp. 345–46, No. I; i, fol. 138d

Roger Pictavensis

Son of Roger de Montgomery and Mabel de Bellême. Granted land that later became the county of Lancashire before 1086, he was not actually in possession of it at the time of the Domesday Survey. K. Thompson, 'Monasteries and settlement in Norman Lancashire: unpublished charters of Roger the Poitevin', Trans. Hist. Soc. of Lancs. and Cheshire 140 (1990). Probably loyal to William II on his accession and a friend, he nonetheless fell with the rest of his family in 1102. He retired to Aquitaine, where by a series of unforeseen deaths his wife had become countess of La Marche. His descendants were heirs of La Marche. C.P. Lewis, 'The King and Eye', EHR 103 (1989), 569–87.

Barraclough, Charters of AN Earls of Chester (1988), No. 88; Barraclough, Charters of AN Earls of Chester (1988), No. 90; Barraclough, Charters of AN Earls of Chester (1988), No. 63; Rees, Cartulary of Shrewsbury Abbey (1975), No. 35; ii, fol. 117a; Tremlett and Blakiston, Stogursey Charters (1949), No. 1; Round, Ancient Charters (1888), No. 39; Pipe Roll 31 Henry I, 027b–ynb; i, fol. 352a; ii, fol. 089a; i, fol. 353d; i, fol. 352a; i, fol. 352a; i, fol. 352a; ii, fol. 089a; ii, fol. 089a; ii, fol. 089a; ii, fol. 065b; i, fol. 352a; ii, fol. 140b; i, fol. 352b; i, fol. 352c; i, fol. 352c; i, fol. 270a; i, fol. 269d; i, fol. 270a; i, fol. 270a; i, fol. 352b; i, fol. 270a; i, fol. 270a; i, fol. 270a; i, fol. 270a; i, fol. 269d; i, fol. 270a; i, fol. 269d; i, fol. 269d; i, fol. 269d; i, fol. 269d; i, fol. 269d; i, fol. 270a; i, fol. 269c; i, fol. 270a; i, fol. 352c; i, fol. 352b; i, fol. 352b; i, fol. 352b; i, fol. 352b; i, fol. 352b; i, fol. 352b; i, fol. 352b; i, fol. 352b; i, fol. 352b; i, fol. 352a; i, fol. 352c; i, fol. 352a; i, fol. 352c; i, fol. 352c; i, fol. 352b; i, fol. 352b; i, fol. 352b; i, fol. 352a; i, fol. 352a; i, fol. 269c; i, fol. 352b; i, fol. 352a; i, fol. 352c; i, fol. 352b; i, fol. 352c; i, fol. 269c; i, fol. 269c; i, fol. 269c; i, fol. 269c; i, fol. 269c; i, fol. 269c; i, fol. 269c; i, fol. 269c; i, fol. 270a; i, fol. 269c; i, fol. 269c; i, fol. 269c; i, fol. 269c; i, fol. 269c; i, fol. 269c; i, fol. 269c; i, fol. 269c; i, fol. 269c; i, fol. 269c; i, fol. 269c; i, fol. 269c; i, fol. 269c; i, fol. 269c; i, fol. 089b; i, fol. 269c; i, fol. 269c; i, fol. 269c; i, fol. 269d; i, fol. 269c; i, fol. 270a; i, fol. 269c; i, fol. 269c; i, fol. 269c; i, fol. 269c; i, fol. 269c; i, fol. 269c; i, fol. 269c; i, fol. 269c; i, fol. 269c; i, fol. 269c; i, fol. 269c; i, fol. 269c; i, fol. 269c; i, fol. 269c; i, fol. 332a; i, fol. 332b; i, fol. 332b; i, fol. 332b; i, fol. 332a; i, fol. 332a; i, fol. 332a; i, fol. 332a; i, fol. 332a; i, fol. 332a; i, fol. 332a; i, fol. 332a; i, fol. 332a; i, fol. 332a; i, fol. 332a; i, fol. 332a; i, fol. 332a; i, fol. 332b; i, fol. 332a; i, fol. 332a; i, fol. 332a; i, fol. 332a; i, fol. 332a; i, fol. 332a; i, fol. 332a; i, fol. 332b; ii, fol. 281b; i, fol. 332b; i, fol. 332b; i, fol. 332b; i, fol. 332b; i, fol. 332b; i, fol. 332b; i, fol. 332b; i, fol. 332b; i, fol. 332a; i, fol. 332b; i, fol. 332a; i, fol. 332b; i, fol. 332b; i, fol. 332b; i, fol. 332a; i, fol. 332b; i, fol. 332b; i, fol. 332b; i, fol. 332b; i, fol. 332b; i, fol. 332b; i, fol. 332b; i, fol. 332b; i, fol. 332b; i, fol. 332b; i, fol. 290b; i, fol. 332a; i, fol. 332a; i, fol. 332a; i, fol. 332a; i, fol. 332a; i, fol. 332a; i, fol. 332a; i, fol. 332a; i, fol. 332a; i, fol. 332a; i, fol. 332a; i, fol. 332a; i, fol. 290b; i, fol. 290b; Pipe Roll 31 Henry I, 027a–ynb; i, fol. 290b; i, fol. 290b; i, fol. 290b; i, fol. 290b; i, fol. 290b; i, fol. 290b; i, fol. 290b; Lincolnshire Claims (Domesday Book), fols 375a–d; i, fol. 332a; ii, fol. 089a; i, fol. 332a; i, fol. 290b; i, fol. 352a; ii, fol. 243a; i, fol. 39c; ii, fol. 346a; ii, fol. 352b; ii, fol. 348b; ii, fol. 348b; ii, fol. 353a; ii, fol. 348a; ii, fol. 348b; ii, fol. 353a; ii, fol. 353a; ii, fol. 350b; ii, fol. 348b; ii, fol. 348b; ii, fol. 353a; ii, fol. 352b; ii, fol. 347b; ii, fol. 347a; ii, fol. 347a; ii, fol. 346b; ii, fol. 350b; ii, fol. 352b; ii, fol. 348a; ii, fol. 349a; ii, fol. 349a; ii, fol. 349a; ii, fol. 348a; ii, fol. 348a; ii, fol. 352b; ii, fol. 350a; ii, fol. 350b; ii, fol. 243b; ii, fol. 349a; ii, fol. 243b; ii, fol. 243a; ii, fol. 106b; ii, fol. 244a; ii, fol. 347a; ii, fol. 244a; ii, fol. 350b; ii, fol. 346a; ii, fol. 353a; ii, fol. 243b; ii, fol. 346a; ii, fol. 243b; ii, fol.

348a; ii, fol. 348a; ii, fol. 244b; ii, fol. 348b; ii, fol. 349a; ii, fol. 353a; ii, fol. 349a; ii, fol. 243b; ii, fol. 348a; ii, fol. 244b; ii, fol. 352b; ii, fol. 352b; ii, fol. 349a; ii, fol. 346a; ii, fol. 244a; ii, fol. 244a; ii, fol. 244a; ii, fol. 352b; ii, fol. 244b; ii, fol. 352a; ii, fol. 349a; ii, fol. 346b; ii, fol. 350a; ii, fol. 351a; ii, fol. 349b; ii, fol. 350b; ii, fol. 352a; ii, fol. 346a; ii, fol. 352b; ii, fol. 346a; ii, fol. 350a; ii, fol. 352b; ii, fol. 348a; ii, fol. 352a; ii, fol. 348a; ii, fol. 352a; ii, fol. 352a; ii, fol. 352a; ii, fol. 352a; ii, fol. 352b; ii, fol. 349b; ii, fol. 346a; ii, fol. 352a; ii, fol. 346b; ii, fol. 350a; ii, fol. 349a; ii, fol. 346b; ii, fol. 352a; ii, fol. 346a; ii, fol. 349b; ii, fol. 350b; ii, fol. 347b; ii, fol. 347b; ii, fol. 350b; ii, fol. 351b; ii, fol. 347b; ii, fol. 350a; ii, fol. 346b; ii, fol. 349b; ii, fol. 347a; ii, fol. 349b; ii, fol. 349b; ii, fol. 350b; ii, fol. 350a; ii, fol. 347a; ii, fol. 350b; ii, fol. 348a; ii, fol. 349b; ii, fol. 348a; ii, fol. 347b; ii, fol. 352b; ii, fol. 347b; ii, fol. 351a; ii, fol. 347b; ii, fol. 347b; ii, fol. 351a; ii, fol. 351a; ii, fol. 351a; ii, fol. 351b; ii, fol. 348a; ii, fol. 347b; ii, fol. 349b; ii, fol. 243a; ii, fol. 346a; Douglas, Feudal Documents from Bury St Edmunds, No. 188; Douglas, Feudal Documents from Bury St Edmunds, No. 69; Regesta regum Anglo-Normannorum III, No. 471; Rees, Cartulary of Shrewsbury Abbey (1975), No. 35; Regesta regum Anglo-Normannorum III, No. 180; Regesta regum Anglo-Normannorum III, No. 768; Regesta regum Anglo-Normannorum III, No. 178

Roger Presbiter
Occurs Domesday Bedfordshire.

i, fol. 213d; i, fol. 214a

Roger Presbiter
Occurs Domesday Berkshire as a tenant of the bishop of Salisbury; perhaps the same as Roger presbiter (q.v.) who occurs in Bedfordshire.

i, fol. 58b

Roger Venator
Norman, brother of Norman Venator (the Hunter), Domesday tenant of Roger de Montgomery in Shropshire. Succeeded in the barony of Pulverbatch by a son Roger (Sanders, 73).

i, fol. 259b; i, fol. 176a; i, fol. 259b; i, fol. 259b; i, fol. 259b; i, fol. 259b; i, fol. 259b; i, fol. 253b; i, fol. 254c

Roger []
Domesday tenant of Geoffrey de la Guerche. Attested his foundation charter for Monks Kirby in 1077.

i, fol. 235d; Mon. Ang. vi, 996

Roger []
Norman, from Louvetot, Seine-Maritime, arr. Yvetot, cant. Caudebec (Loyd, 55–6), occurs Domesday; cf. EY Families, 53–6. Succeeded c.1129 by William de Luvetot.

i, fol. 287a; i, fol. 286d; i, fol. 286d; i, fol. 286c; i, fol. 286c; i, fol. 285d; i, fol. 286a; i, fol. 285c; i, fol. 284c; King, Peterborough Descriptio Militum (1969), pp. 97–101

Roger []
Norman, Domesday tenant of Peterborough. By the early twelfth century his land was held by Torold de Meltone (q.v.).

i, fol. 221c; i, fol. 346a

Roger []
Norman, Domesday tenant of Bishop Remigius of Lincoln.

i, fol. 344b; i, fol. 344b; i, fol. 189a

Roger []
Domesday tenant of Swein of Essex.

ii, fol. 045b; ii, fol. 045b

Roger []
Domesday tenant of Gilbert de Gand.

i, fol. 355b; i, fol. 355b; i, fol. 355c; i, fol. 355b; i, fol. 355d

Roger []
Norman, Domesday tenant of Waleran Venator at Tytheley, Hampshire. The holding performed the serjeanty of looking after hunting hounds. His successor in 1166 was William 'de Luverez' (i.e. of the hounds); Round, King's Serjeants, 294.

i, fol. 48c; i, fol. 48c; i, fol. 48c

Roger []
Domesday tenant of Ivo Taillebois in Lincolnshire.

i, fol. 350d; i, fol. 350c; i, fol. 350c

Roger []
Norman, tenant of Roger Corbet under Earl Roger in Domesday Shropshire. Apparently ancestor of a family named Burnel. Cf. Eyton, Shrops, vi, 121; VCH Shrops viii, 7.

i, fol. 255c

Roger []
Norman tenant of Robert of Mortain in Cornwall.

i, fol. 125b; i, fol. 125b; i, fol. 125b; i, fol. 125b

Roger []
Domesday tenant of Countess Judith at Oakington. Apparently succeeded by the Olifart family, of whom Roger Olifart occurs not long after 1086 attesting a charter for St Andrew's, Northampton, for Simon I de Senlis (Mon. Ang. v, 190). See Farrer, HKF ii, 354.

i, fol. 202c

Roger Frater Picoti De Grentebrige
Norman, brother of Picot the sheriff of Cambridge, identified as his brother's tenant in Inquisitio Eliensis.

i, fol. 201a; i, fol. 201a; i, fol. 201a; i, fol. 201b; i, fol. 201c; i, fol. 201b

Roger Ii De Gloecestria
A Roger held land at Lassington, Gloucestershire, from the archbishop of York in 1086. It is highly likely that he was related to Walter of Gloucester and the latter's uncle Durand. Distinct from Roger brother of Durand of Gloucester, who died shortly before 1086, he was perhaps that Roger's younger son. Soon after, described as Roger of Gloucester, he made a grant to St Peter's Gloucester of land once of Ulketel (his 'antecessor' in Lassington) for the soul of his brother Herbert, and in 1102 he made an exchange of land with the abbot (Hist. S. Petri Glocs. i, 112, 118; cf. ibid. 235–6). The manor of Westmill in Hertfordshire was held in

412

1086 by a Roger, from Ralph de Tosny. Both manors were held in 1166 by Werric de Marinis (probably Marigny, Calvados, arr. Bayeux, cant. Ryes), the former from the archbishop of York. This seems to annul the possibility of an anachronistic reference to Roger in Domesday Gloucestershire. He was possibly also a tenant of Ralph de Tosny in Gloucestershire, most of whose manors were held by a man or men named Roger, who in one case only was certainly Roger de Bascherville.

i, fol. 164d; i, fol. 138b

Roger Ii Pictavensis
Norman, Lacy tenant in Domesday Yorkshire, identified from a grant to St Clement's, York. His successor Robert was active c.1154–75.

i, fol. 317c; Dugdale, Monasticon Anglicanum, IV, p. 120, No. I

Rogo Filius Nigelli
Important tenant of Baldwin the Sheriff in Domesday Devonshire, his name was given incorrectly as Drogo in the Somerset Domesday. Exon Domesday provides his true name and adds interesting further information in naming his as Rogo son of Nigel. Rogo's name is so rare that it can be identified with certainty from Norman records, where he is found as a tenant of the Nigels of Saint-Sauveur in the Cotentin. In the Cartulary of Saint-Sauveur-le-Vicomte (BN lat. 17137, fol. 19, Rogo camerarius attested a grant by Nigel vicomte. In the portions printed by Delisle, Saint-Sauveur, Pièces justificatives, Rogo occurs as the grantor of land in Omonville under vicomte Eudo (no. 45), and in 1081 the same vicomte granted land at Heauville, Manche, cant. Les Pieux, which 'miles quidam Rogos' holds of the inheritance of his wife Roges (i.e. Rohais) [ibid. no. 44]. This Rogo was followed by William fitz Rogo, uncle of Simon fitz Rogo and William Monk, son of Richard de Ansgerivilla (lat. 17137, fols 39v–40, 89v, 239, the latter being a grant of Simon fitz Rogo attested by Robert Arundel; cf. the Arundels of Somerset). William and Simon fitz Rogo were benefactor of Montacute priory (Somerset Rec. Soc. vol 8, nos 11, 138, 140, 156–7). Rogo also appears with his brother [C]adiou in PR 31 Henry I, 156, doubtless the same person as Baldwin's Domesday tenant Cadio.

i, fol. 107a; i, fol. 107a; i, fol. 107b; i, fol. 107c; i, fol. 108b; i, fol. 108c; i, fol. 108b; Pipe Roll 31 Henry I, 156–dv; i, fol. 93a; i, fol. 93a

Rohais Uxor Ricardi Filii Gisleberti
Daughter of Walter I Giffard and his wife, a daughter of Gerard Fleitel. Wife of Richard de Clare, son of Gilbert count of Brionne. Occurs as a landholder in her own right in Domesday Book.

i, fol. 229a; i, fol. 207b; i, fol. 142d; i, fol. 142d; Douglas, Feudal Documents from Bury St Edmunds, No. 170; Dugdale, Monasticon Anglicanum, III, p. 473, No. XI; i, fol. 207b

Rohard []
Domesday tenant of Giso bishop of Wells.

i, fol. 89c; i, fol. 89c

Roland []
Domesday tenant of Eudo Dapifer. Ancestor of the de Lindon family, named from Lyndon in Rutland. In 1129/30 John, son of Odo of Bayeux, had a plea against Simon fitz Rolland of Lindon; see HKF iii, 281 ff.

ii, fol. 239b; i, fol. 227a; i, fol. 227a; i, fol. 212c; i, fol. 25c

Roland []

Domesday tenant of Roger of Montgomery.

i, fol. 23c; i, fol. 25a

Rolf []

Domesday tenant of Walter de Douai.

i, fol. 111d; i, fol. 111d

Rolland Archidiaconus

Occurs Domesday Cornwall. Identified as archdeacon in Exon.

i, fol. 120d

Roric []

Domesday tenant of Bury St Edmunds; identified in Abbot Samson's Kalendar (p. 4 and note) as son of Brictheve. He apparently had four sons, including Fulk son of Reric, William and Simon, whose grandson Gilbert son of Simon the priest son of Simon occurs in Abbot Samson's Kalendar (p.12 and note).

Douglas, Feudal Book of Bury St Edmunds (1932), pp. 3–21; ii, fol. 362b; ii, fol. 365b

Rotbert De Bruis

Norman, from Brix, Manche, arr. Valognes. He was given a large fief in Yorkshire by Henry I in 1106. Between 1120 and 1129 an account of the fief was written into Domesday Book. In 1124 he was given the lordship of Annandale by David of Scotland c.1124. He died in 1142 and was succeeded by his son Adam. He also had a son Robert, as appears from a charter for Saint-Sauveur (BN lat. 17137 no. 158 fols 135v–6). His son Adam (d.1143–4 – his charter for Saint-Sauveur cited above is dated 1144) married Jueta de Archis, by whom he had issue Adam II and William. Sanders, 77; P. King, 'The return of the fee of Robert de Brus in Domesday', Yorkshire Archaeological Journal 60 (1988).

i, fol. 332c; Barraclough, Charters of AN Earls of Chester (1988), No. 5; Pipe Roll 31 Henry I, 028a–ynb; Pipe Roll 31 Henry I, 028b–ynb; Hart, Cartularium Monasterii de Rameseia, No. CLXVII; Pipe Roll 31 Henry I, 029–ynb; i, fol. 333a; i, fol. 333a; i, fol. 333a; i, fol. 333a; i, fol. 333a; i, fol. 332d; i, fol. 332d; i, fol. 332c; i, fol. 332c; i, fol. 333a; i, fol. 332c; i, fol. 333a; i, fol. 332c; i, fol. 332c; i, fol. 332d; i, fol. 332c; i, fol. 332c; i, fol. 332c; i, fol. 332c; i, fol. 332c; i, fol. 332c; i, fol. 332d; i, fol. 332d; i, fol. 332d; i, fol. 332d; i, fol. 332d; i, fol. 332c; i, fol. 332c; i, fol. 332c; i, fol. 332c; i, fol. 332c; i, fol. 332c; i, fol. 332c; i, fol. 332c; i, fol. 332c; i, fol. 332c; i, fol. 332c; i, fol. 332d; i, fol. 332c; i, fol. 332d; i, fol. 332c; i, fol. 332c; i, fol. 332c; i, fol. 332c; i, fol. 332c; i, fol. 332c; i, fol. 332c; i, fol. 332d; i, fol. 332d; i, fol. 332d; i, fol. 332d; i, fol. 332d; i, fol. 332c; i, fol. 332d; i, fol. 332c; i, fol. 332d; i, fol. 332c; i, fol. 332c; i, fol. 332d; i, fol. 332d; i, fol. 332c; i, fol. 332d; i, fol. 332d; i, fol. 332d; i, fol. 332d; i, fol. 332d; i, fol. 332d; i, fol. 332d; i, fol. 332d; i, fol. 332d; i, fol. 332d; i, fol. 332d; i, fol. 333a; i, fol. 332d; i, fol. 332d; i, fol. 332d; i, fol. 333a; i, fol. 332c; i, fol. 333a; i, fol. 332d; i, fol. 332d; i, fol. 332d; i, fol. 332d; i, fol. 332d; i, fol. 332d; i, fol. 332d; i, fol. 332d; i, fol. 332d; i, fol. 332d; i, fol. 332d; Franklin, Cartulary of Daventry Priory (1988), No. 3; Regesta regum Anglo-Normannorum III, No. 985; Regesta regum Anglo-Normannorum III, No. 119; Regesta regum Anglo-Normannorum III, No. 942; Red Book of the Exchequer, ed. Hall (1897), pp. 434–35; Franklin, Cartulary of Daventry Priory (1988), No. 2; Clay, Early Yorkshire Charters (1939), VI, No. 4; Clay, Early Yorkshire

Charters (1939), VI, No. 3; Mason, Beauchamp Cartulary Charters (1980), No. 4; Dugdale, Monasticon Anglicanum, III, pp. 548–50, No. V; Lindsey Survey, BL ms Cotton Claudius C v, fols 19–27; Clay, Early Yorkshire Charters (1955), XI, No. 4

Rotroc []
Occurs Domesday Oxfordshire as a tenant of the bishop of Lisieux. Probably a relative of Geoffrey, count of Mortagne, son of Rotroc de Mortagne, who was among those said to have fought at Hastings in 1066.

i, fol. 156d; i, fol. 156d

Rozelin []
Norman, Domesday tenant of Earl Hugh in Lincolnshire, and probably also of William de Percy in Yorkshire. He successors were the de Normanville family, of whom he was possibly the ancestor; HKF ii, 176. His sons occur in the Lindsey Survey.

i, fol. 321d; i, fol. 321d; i, fol. 321d; i, fol. 321c; i, fol. 349b; Barraclough, Charters of AN Earls of Chester (1988), No. 11

Ruald Adobed
Domesday tenant-in-chief in Devon. Probably a Breton. At the end of his life he became a monk of the priory of St Nicholas, Exeter, to which his grants were confirmed before 1103 (Oliver, Monasticon Exoniensis, 119). He died without direct heirs and his fief was regranted by Henry I to Robert Giffard, son of the Breton Ralph I of Fougères (Radulf de Filgeriis), another Devonshire tenant-in-chief, who held it under the de Redvers honour of Plymton.

i, fol. 115b; i, fol. 115b; i, fol. 115b; i, fol. 115b; i, fol. 115b; i, fol. 115a; i, fol. 115a; i, fol. 115a; i, fol. 115a; i, fol. 115a; i, fol. 115a; i, fol. 115a; i, fol. 114d; i, fol. 114d

Ruald []
The Ruald who occurs as a tenant of Westminster at Lomer, Hampshire, in 1086 was probably the son of Faderlin (q.v.), a tenant of Hugh de Port. He held land in Winchester c. 1110, according to Winton Domesday, 39 (29), 156–7. His successor in 1166 was Henry fitz Ruald of Woodcutt.

i, fol. 43a

Rualon []
Tenant of Nigel de Albini and Hugh de Bellocampo in Domesday Bedfordshire. He may have been a relative of Nigel, since the name occurs in his family; Rivallon son of Roger de Albini occurs in a charter for Cormèry (Cart. 49), dated 1070–1110. Possibly ancestor of Roger and Stephen of Pulloxhill (q.v.) who attest charter of Robert de Albini of Cainhoe c.1140.

i, fol. 214b; i, fol. 213c; i, fol. 213c; i, fol. 215a

Rumold De Cotis
Domesday tenant of Eustache count of Boulogne in Hertfordshire, surnamed from Cotton, Cambs in ICC (VCH Cambs v, 190, 202; Lewis, 'Jurors', 39). Occurs in a charter of Eustache's grandson William c.1129 as having married his sister to Hugh fitz Ulger and dowered her with the consent of his sons Payn and Bernard (BM Add. chs. 28344, 28346). A Hertfordshire plea of 1196 and 1198 involved Robert Rumbold and Richard fitz Peter. Robert claimed hereditary right by

descent from Bernard 'avunculi patris sui' (Curia Regis Roll 7 Richard I, 80, 9 Richard I, 110) in respect of two of the three manors held by Rumold in Domesday Book. In view of the names of Rumold's sons it is clear that Robert was the grandson of Payn fitz Rumold, and that his surname was a patronymic derived from Rumbold. Robert Rumbold son of Adam Rumbold of Cheshull was a benefactor Little Dunmow priory (BL Harley 662, fol. 41r).

   i, fol. 137b; i, fol. 137b; i, fol. 137b; Hamilton, Inquisitio Comitatus
   Cantabrigiensis, pp. 1–93; Hamilton, Inquisitio Eliensis (1876), pp. 97–100

Rumold Presbiter

Occurs Domesday Gloucestershire and Somerset as a tenant of Matthew de Mortagne. Probably to be identified with the priest who held of the king in Wiltshire, where Matthew also held a manor in chief.

   i, fol. 98b; i, fol. 170b; i, fol. 170b; i, fol. 65b

Sagar Sochmannus

Occurs Domesday Cambridgeshire.

   i, fol. 190a

Saieua []

English widow, occurs Domesday Wiltshire.

   i, fol. 74b; i, fol. 73d

Salomon Presbyter

Occurs Domesday Bedfordshire as tenant of Robert d'Oilli.

   i, fol. 215b

Salomon []

Breton, Domesday tenant of William fitz Baderon. He can be identified with Salomon decanus, who held land in Mezvoit in Dol of the seigneurs of Dol-Combour; father by Bilihildis of William decanus, Main, Geoffrey and Euen, cited in La Borderie, Recueil, 1885, no. xviii, 42–3, who says that Salomon and his son were not ecclesiastics but lay officers below the rank of provost. Salomon and William his son attested a charter of Wihenoc and William fitz Baderon for Monmouth priory (CDF, 1133) before 1087.

   i, fol. 185c; i, fol. 185c

Samson Episcopus Wigornensis

Samson, treasurer of Bayeux, chaplain to William I; brother of Thomas I archbishop of York. He rejected an appointment to the see of Le Mans in 1081 (Ord. Vit. ii, 300). Bishop of Worcester from 8 June 1096 until his death on 5 May 1112. FEA ii, 99.

   i, fol. 87d; Salter, Cartulary of Oseney Abbey (1929–36), No. 1A; Regesta
   regum Anglo-Normannorum III, No. 964; Red Book of the Exchequer, ed. Hall
   (1897), pp. 300–01; Regesta regum Anglo-Normannorum III, No. 345;
   Bearman, Charters of the Redvers Family (1994), No. 5; Darlington, Cartulary
   of Worcester: Reg. I (1962–3), No. 260; Round, Ancient Charters (1888), No. 3;
   Darlington, Cartulary of Worcester: Reg. I (1962–3), No. 21; Darlington,
   Cartulary of Worcester: Reg. I (1962–3), No. 265; Darlington, Cartulary of
   Worcester: Reg. I (1962–3), No. 62; Darlington, Cartulary of Worcester: Reg. I
   (1962–3), No. 261; Regesta regum Anglo-Normannorum III, No. 969;
   Darlington, Cartulary of Worcester: Reg. I (1962–3), No. 262; Ellis,

'Landholders of Gloucestershire' (1880), pp. 91–93; Darlington, Cartulary of Worcester: Reg. I (1962–3), No. 259; Darlington, Cartulary of Worcester: Reg. I (1962–3), No. 267; Darlington, Cartulary of Worcester: Reg. I (1962–3), No. 147; Dugdale, Monasticon Anglicanum, II, p. 267, No. XI

Saric Frater Gest
Englishman, occurs Domesday Wiltshire.

i, fol. 74b; i, fol. 74b

Sasfrid []
Domesday tenant of William Peverel of Nottingham. Father of Philip de Essebi, HKF i, 168.

Dugdale, Monasticon Anglicanum, IV, pp. 111–12, No. Ia; i, fol. 287c; i, fol. 226a; i, fol. 288a; i, fol. 235b

Sasfrid []
Domesday tenant of William Pantulf under Earl Roger in Shropshire.

i, fol. 257b; i, fol. 257b

Sasselin []
Domesday tenant-in-chief in East Anglia. After 1086 his land was given to Eudo Dapifer.

ii, fol. 092b; ii, fol. 436b; ii, fol. 092b; ii, fol. 092b; ii, fol. 093a; ii, fol. 092b; ii, fol. 092b; ii, fol. 092b; ii, fol. 092b; ii, fol. 436b; ii, fol. 436b; ii, fol. 437a; ii, fol. 437a

Sasuualo De Botuile
Domesday tenant of Geoffrey de Mandeville and father of William, another of Geoffrey's tenants. His successors in 1166 appear to have been Otuel de Bouville and Saswalo de Oseville. Probably named from Beuzeville, Seine-Maritime, arr. Dieppe, cant. Bellencombre, comm. Beaumont-le-Hareng (cf. Loyd, 19).

i, fol. 62a; i, fol. 62a; Hamilton, Inquisitio Eliensis (1876), pp. 192–95; Hamilton, Inquisitio Eliensis (1876), pp. 192–95; i, fol. 159d; i, fol. 159d

Sasuualo []
Norman, Domesday tenant of Henry de Ferrers. Father of Henry, Fulcher and Hugh, who attested a covenant between Geoffrey abbot of Burton and Robert de Ferrers c.1121–9 (BL Chh., no. 9). Ancestor of the Shirley and Ireton families.

i, fol. 274d; i, fol. 276a; i, fol. 242b; i, fol. 275a; i, fol. 353c; i, fol. 225a; Dugdale, Monasticon Anglicanum, III, pp. 392–93, No. II

Saulf De Oxeneford
Occurs Domesday Wallingford, in Berkshire.

i, fol. 56b

Saulf []
Englishman, occurs in Domesday Devon

i, fol. 118c; i, fol. 118c; i, fol. 118c

Sauuin Presbiter
Occurs Domesday Devon.

i, fol. 104b

Sawold []
Occurs Domesday Oxfordshire.

i, fol. 160d; i, fol. 160d; i, fol. 160d

Scolland []
Domesday tenant of William of Warenne in Sussex. Escollant del Alneito attested a charter of William de Moulins for Saint-Evroul (Ord. Vit, ed. Le Prévost v, 189–90), and Ingulf Escollant attested a charter given by a man of Ralph de Warenne, William's father, for Sainte-Trinité de Rouen (Guérard, Cart., 443).

i, fol. 27d

Segrim []
Englishman, a Domesday burgess of Oxford.

i, fol. 154b; i, fol. 154b

Seifrid Prepositus
Tenant of Picot of Cambridge, identified as reeve of Wetherley Hundred, Cambs, in IE. He gave land in Haslingfield to St Mary's, York, before 1100. Before 1083, a Sasfrid prepositus sold land to Abbot William of Caen; he also stood as warranty for the sale by Lescelina and her son Frederick (Actes caen., 14, pp. 108, 110).

i, fol. 200c; Dugdale, Monasticon Anglicanum, III, pp. 548–50, No. V; i, fol. 200d; Hamilton, Inquisitio Comitatus Cantabrigiensis, pp. 1–93; Hamilton, Inquisitio Eliensis (1876), pp. 97–100

Seman []
Englishman, occurs Domesday Surrey.

i, fol. 35c; i, fol. 36d

Seolf Prepositus Episcopi
Englishman, provost of the bishop of Thetford; occurs Domesday Norfolk.

ii, fol. 198b

Serlo Abbas De Glocestrie
Canon of Avranches cathedral, then monk of Mont-Saint-Michel. Five years later, in 1072, at the suggestion of Osmund, later bishop of Salisbury, he was appointed abbot of Gloucester. He rebuilt the abbey, which was consecrated in 1100, but the church and the city were burnt in 1102. In his declining years he appointed Odo the cellarer his coadjutant. He died in March 1114 aged around 78 years (Cart. S. Petri i, 10–13). Heads, 52.

Regesta regum Anglo-Normannorum III, No. 345; i, fol. 164c; Dugdale, Monasticon Anglicanum, II, p. 267, No. XI; Dugdale, Monasticon Anglicanum, III, pp. 544–46, No. I

Serlo De Burci
Norman, from Burcy, Calvados, arr. Vire, comm. cant. Vassy, Domesday tenant-in-chief in Somerset and tenant of the bishop of Wells. He died around 1086, when his daughter Geva, was wife of William de Falaise (q.v.) and another daughter was a nun of Shaftesbury. His heirs were the FitzMartins, descendants of Geva and her first husband, Martin (cf. Sanders, 15).

i, fol. 90d; i, fol. 90d; i, fol. 90c; i, fol. 90b; i, fol. 89c; i, fol. 90c; i, fol. 66c; i, fol. 77b; i, fol. 97d; i, fol. 82d; i, fol. 98a; i, fol. 98a; i, fol. 97d; i, fol. 98a; i, fol. 86c; i, fol. 97d; i, fol. 82d; i, fol. 97d; i, fol. 98a; Dugdale, Monasticon Anglicanum, II, pp. 482–83, No. XIII; i, fol. 87a; i, fol. 97d

Serlo De Muntalurone
Norman, Domesday tenant of Ranulf Peverel in Essex. A hide of his manor at Pitsea was given by William Peverel to St John's. Colchester, and confirmed in 1119 by Henry I and Serlo's brother Robert de Montalurone (Cart., p. 142).

ii, fol. 073a; ii, fol. 072a; ii, fol. 072a; ii, fol. 071b; ii, fol. 071b; ii, fol. 072a

Serlo De Ros
Norman, from Rots, Calvados, arr. Caen, cant. Tilly-sur-Seulles (Loyd, 86), Domesday tenant in Bedfordshire of Hugh de Beauchamp and William Speke.

i, fol. 213c; i, fol. 213c; i, fol. 214d

Serlo []
Tenant of Haimo dapifer in Essex in 1086. One of two major tenants of Haimo, the other being Ralph de Marcy (q.v.). Round (VCH Essex, i, 500) thought this was Serlo de Marcy and that the two were later represented by men named de Marcy holding three and four fees respectively of Haimo's heirs, the earls of Gloucester.

ii, fol. 056a; ii, fol. 055b; ii, fol. 055a; ii, fol. 055a; ii, fol. 054b

Serlo []
Norman, Domesday tenant of William Peverel of Nottingham. Perhaps Serlo Blund of the Lenton foundation charter. Ancestor of the de Pleselei (Pleasley) family; HKF iii, 173–4.

i, fol. 277a; i, fol. 276b; Dugdale, Monasticon Anglicanum, IV, pp. 111–12, No. Ia

Seuuen Canonicus Sancti Martini
Canon of Dover in 1086.

i, fol. 002b

Sibold De Lufwic
Probably an Artesian Fleming, Domesday tenant of Countess Judith at Lowick, Northamptonshire. Succeeded in the early twelfth century by Ralph Fleming, brother of Guy. As Ralph son of Segbold de Lufwic, Ralph was involved in a dispute with Thorney over land he took whilst seeking fraternity in the time of Abbot Gunter (English Lawsuits, Selden Soc. vol. 107, 1991, nos. 193–4).

i, fol. 228a; i, fol. 228a

Sigar Dapifer
Englishman, juror in the Domesday Inquest (ICC 43), formerly steward to Asgar the Constable (ICC 39), antecessor of Geoffrey de Mandeville. He was a tenant of Geoffrey in 1086. Possibly he acted as Geoffrey's reeve (Williams, The English, 87).

i, fol. 197a; i, fol. 197a; i, fol. 197b; i, fol. 197b; Hamilton, Inquisitio Eliensis (1876), pp. 97–100; Hamilton, Inquisitio Comitatus Cantabrigiensis, pp. 1–93

Sigar De Cioches
Fleming, from Chocques, Pas-de-Calais, in the county of Hainault, held a small tenancy-in-chief in 1086. As Segardi de Joches he attested a charter of Baldwin count of Hainault (later count of Flanders) in 1087 (Miraeus et Foppens i, xxviii 515), together with Arnulf de Joches They had both attested another of the count's charters in 1071 (Brassart, Douai ii, Preuves ix, 13–14). Baldwin's confirmation for the abbey of Crepis in 1091 was attested by Segardi de Cioches et Arnulfi

fratris eius (BN Coll. Moreau 36, 188); both were 'optimates' of the count, for whom they also attested an Anchin charter of 1095/6 (Actes . . . de Flandre, 70). They were doubtless kinsman of Arnulf de Chocques, the priest who was chaplain to the nuns of Sainte-Trinité de Caen and a beneficiary of the will of Odo of Bayeux, later accompanying the First Crusade as chaplain of Robert of Normandy; he was elected patriarch of Jerusalem in 1118; possibly both Arnulfs were the same. See D. C. Douglas, 'Domesday tenant of Hawling', EHR 84 (1965), 28–30, who makes the most valuable comments to ever have been made on the patriarch Arnulf. Sigar was probably the same Sigar whose grant to the abbey of Chocques was confirmed by Milo bishop of Thérouanne in 1147 (Hist. abb. de Chocques, pièces just. vii, 540–42). He was father of Hildiardis, mother of Rainald de Chocques. Rainald granted land at Yanworth to St Peter's, Gloucester, which was confirmed by King Stephen c.1130/9, and by Robert de Béthune, overlord of Chocques. The complexities of the devolution of the Chokes fees were dealt with unsatisfactorily in HKF i, 20ff; for a new attempt to resolve the difficulties see under Gunfrid de Cioches.

> i, fol. 219a; i, fol. 170b; i, fol. 228a; i, fol. 170b; i, fol. 170b; i, fol. 142a; i, fol. 142b; i, fol. 216a; i, fol. 228a; i, fol. 142a; i, fol. 170b; i, fol. 216a

Sigar []
Englishman, canon of Dover in 1086; his father had held his prebend before him.

> i, fol. 001d; Ballard, Inquisition of St Augustine's (1920), fols 24r–28r

Simeon Abbas De Ely
Simeon, brother of Walchelin bishop of Winchester, prior of Winchester. Appointed abbot of Ely in 1082 (Annales de Wintonia, 33); he died on 21 November, probably in 1093. There are problems dating his abbacy, see Heads, 43.

> ii, fol. 424a; ii, fol. 276a; ii, fol. 049a; ii, fol. 118b; ii, fol. 117a; i, fol. 191b; i, fol. 191b; i, fol. 191c; i, fol. 191d; i, fol. 191c; i, fol. 191c; i, fol. 191d; i, fol. 191d; i, fol. 191b; i, fol. 191d; i, fol. 191c; i, fol. 191c; i, fol. 191d; i, fol. 191d; i, fol. 191c; i, fol. 191a; i, fol. 190d; i, fol. 190d; i, fol. 190d; i, fol. 190d; i, fol. 191b; i, fol. 191a; i, fol. 191d; i, fol. 191a; i, fol. 191a; i, fol. 191a; i, fol. 191a; i, fol. 191b; i, fol. 192a; i, fol. 191b; i, fol. 190d; i, fol. 192b; i, fol. 203a; i, fol. 204a; i, fol. 204a; i, fol. 204a; i, fol. 204a; i, fol. 204a; i, fol. 189a; i, fol. 135a; i, fol. 135a; i, fol. 135a; i, fol. 192a; i, fol. 192b; i, fol. 190c; i, fol. 192a; i, fol. 192a; i, fol. 192a; i, fol. 192a; i, fol. 192a; i, fol. 192b; i, fol. 192a; i, fol. 192b; i, fol. 192b; i, fol. 192b; i, fol. 192b; i, fol. 192b; i, fol. 192b; i, fol. 192b; i, fol. 192b; i, fol. 199c; i, fol. 336c; i, fol. 135a

Simon []
Domesday tenant of William de Warenne.

> ii, fol. 161b; ii, fol. 162a; ii, fol. 162a; ii, fol. 169b; ii, fol. 037a; ii, fol. 164a; ii, fol. 164a

Simon []
Tenant of Heppo arbalaster in Domesday Lincolnshire.

> i, fol. 369a; i, fol. 369a

Sinod []
Domesday tenant of the bishop of Salisbury.

> i, fol. 77b; i, fol. 77a; i, fol. 77a

Sired Canonicus Sancti Martini
Canon of St Martin's Dover, occurs in Domesday Book.

    i, fol. 002b; Ballard, Inquisition of St Augustine's (1920), fols 24r–28r

Sired De Cilleham
Englishman, occurs Domesday Dover.

    i, fol. 001c; Ballard, Inquisition of St Augustine's (1920), fols 24r–28r; Ballard, Inquisition of St Augustine's (1920), fols 20r–23v; i, fol. 001a

Sireuuold []
English tenant of Robert of Mortain in Domesday Cornwall.

    i, fol. 124d

Siric Camerarius
Occurs Domesday Hampshire.

    i, fol. 50a

Siric []
Englishman, occurs Domesday Essex.

    ii, fol. 042a; ii, fol. 048a; ii, fol. 047b

Siuuard De Horemeda
Englishman, Domesday juror in Edwinstree Hundred, Hertfordshire; perhaps the same as a tenat of Geoffrey de Mandeville and Harduin de Scalariis (Lewis, 'Jurors', 43).

    i, fol. 141c; i, fol. 139c; Hamilton, Inquisitio Eliensis (1876), pp. 97–100

Siuuard Presbiter
Occurs Domesday Essex.

    ii, fol. 105b

Siuuard Presbiter
Englishman, occurs Domesday Lincolnshire and in the Claims.

    i, fol. 371b; i, fol. 371b; i, fol. 371b; Lincolnshire Claims (Domesday Book), fols 375d–376a

Siuuard Tainus
Occurs Domesday Wiltshire.

    i, fol. 71b

Siward Grossus
Englishman, occurs as a tenant in Earl Roger's Domesday Shropshire. Called Siward Grossus in Shrewsbury Cart. no. 1. Described by Orderic Vitalis as Siward son of Aethelgar, a kinsman (cognatus) of Edward the Confessor. He had built a chapel of St Peter, but was persuaded to cede its site to Earl Roger for the latter's foundation of the monastery of St Peter's, Shrewsbury, in exchange for Cheney Longville (Ord. Vit. ii, 416).

    i, fol. 260a; i, fol. 259c; i, fol. 259c; i, fol. 259d

Siward Venator
Occurs Domesday Hampshire.

    i, fol. 43c,d; i, fol. 160d

Sortebrand Filius Ulf

English thegn, occurs Domesday Lincolnshire. Son of Ulf son of Sortebrand, a pre-Conquest lawman in Lincoln.

i, fol. 348d; i, fol. 370d; i, fol. 370d; i, fol. 370d; i, fol. 370d; Lincolnshire Claims (Domesday Book), fols 376b–c; i, fol. 370d; i, fol. 336b; i, fol. 336a; Lindsey Survey, BL ms Cotton Claudius C v, fols 1–9; Lincolnshire Claims (Domesday Book), fols 376d–377c

Sprot []

Occurs Domesday Hampshire

ii, fol. 104b; ii, fol. 104b; ii, fol. 106a

Stanard Anglicus

English tenant-in-chief in Domesday East Anglia, son of Æthelwy of Thetford who had probably been a sheriff of Norfolk before 1066. Also tenant of various Normans, including Roger Bigod. Perhaps the same as Stanhard of Silverley, a Domesday juror in Cambridgeshire. Richard son of Stanhard (q.v.) and William his son attest Bury charters c.1133/40. Benefactors of Bury St Edmunds included Leofstan dapifer of Abbot Leofstan (d.1065) and his kinsman ('cognatus') Stanardus (Mon. Ang. iii, 140).

ii, fol. 183a; ii, fol. 098b; ii, fol. 104b; ii, fol. 174a; ii, fol. 105b; ii, fol. 445b; ii, fol. 179a; Hamilton, Inquisitio Eliensis (1876), pp. 97–100; Hamilton, Inquisitio Comitatus Cantabrigiensis, pp. 1–93; ii, fol. 445b; ii, fol. 174b; ii, fol. 174b; ii, fol. 174b; ii, fol. 174b; ii, fol. 174b; ii, fol. 174b; ii, fol. 174b; ii, fol. 174b; ii, fol. 174b; ii, fol. 174b; ii, fol. 180a; ii, fol. 180a; ii, fol. 185b; ii, fol. 185b; ii, fol. 185a; ii, fol. 185a; ii, fol. 330b; ii, fol. 330b

Starcolf []

English tenant-in-chief, Domesday Norfolk.

ii, fol. 271b; ii, fol. 271b; ii, fol. 271b

Stefan Capellanus

Occurs Domesday Somerset. Apparently a royal chaplain, he may have been the same person as the Stephanus capellanus who was the predecessor of the chaplain Rainald as holder of land and gardens at Bayeux which William I gave to Jumièges c.1078–83 (RRAN i, 193). Niel presbyter stated c.1054/5, that he and Stephen the chaplain had been in the service of William of Normandy at Mont-Saint-Michel when he, Nigel, decided to become a monk there (Fauroux, 132).

i, fol. 89c; i, fol. 91c

Stefan Carpentarius

Occurs Domesday Wiltshire as a king's servant. Perhaps the same as Stephen fitz Fulcred, who occurs in Worcestershire.

i, fol. 73c; i, fol. 73c

Stefan Filius Fulcheredi

The three references to a Stephen in Domesday Herefordshire, where he was associated with the castelry of Caerleon, are to the same person. His tenancies from Drogo fitz Pons and William d'Ecouis perhaps indicate an origin in the honour of Tosny. He was probably the same person as Stephen fitz Fulcred who occurs in Worcestershire. An Evesham document of c.1078/1108 gave his name as Stephanus filius Wlwi (BL Cotton Vespasian B xxxiv, fol. 11).

i, fol. 180b; i, fol. 185c; i, fol. 187c; i, fol. 173b

Stefan Stirman

Norman, possibly from Barfleur (Manche, near Quettehou) as suggested by Le Melletier. He was a ship-builder. According to Orderic Vitalis (vi, 296) he took William the Conqueror to England in his own ship in 1066. Occurs as a landholder in Domesday Book in 1086. His son Thomas was the ship-wright who built the White Ship, which sank disastrously in 1120 (ibid.).

i, fol. 214b; i, fol. 60d; i, fol. 61a; i, fol. 61a; i, fol. 243d; i, fol. 243d; i, fol. 238d; i, fol. 238d; i, fol. 243d; i, fol. 63c; i, fol. 238a; i, fol. 52a

Stefan []

Domesday tenant of Baldwin the Sheriff, ancestor of the de Haccomb family. William fitz Stephen held one fee of Robert fitz Roy in 1166. Stephen de Haccomb occurs 1242/3 (Fees, 785, 768, 792).

i, fol. 107c; i, fol. 108b; i, fol. 107c

Stefan []

Domesday tenant of Judhael of Totnes. His holdings were subsequently detached from the honour of Totnes and went to the Redvers barony of Plympton.

i, fol. 109d; i, fol. 110b

Stephan Abbas Sancte Marie Eboraci

First abbot of St Mary's, York, from c.1080 until his death on 9 April 1112. Probably a Breton. He claimed the founder Count Alan as a friend in his chronicle of St Mary's origins (BL Add. 38816, fols 32r, 33r, 'cum essem in seculo familiariter mihi in amicitiis coniunctus'). See Heads, 84.

Dugdale, Monasticon Anglicanum, III, pp. 544–46, No. I; Dugdale, Monasticon Anglicanum, II, p. 267, No. XI; i, fol. 305a; i, fol. 314a; i, fol. 314a; i, fol. 314a; i, fol. 314a; i, fol. 314a; i, fol. 305a; Clay, Early Yorkshire Charters (1952), IX, No. 133; Clay, Early Yorkshire Charters (1936), V, No. 358; Dugdale, Monasticon Anglicanum, III, pp. 550–51, No. VII; Dugdale, Monasticon Anglicanum, III, p. 553, No. XX; Clay, Early Yorkshire Charters (1952), IX, No. 1; Clay, Early Yorkshire Charters (1935), IV, No. 2; Dugdale, Monasticon Anglicanum, III, pp. 546–47, No. II; Clay, Early Yorkshire Charters (1935), IV, No. 4

Stigand Episcopus Cicestrensis

Norman, royal chaplain, appointed and consecrated bishop of Selsey in 1070, transferred his see to Chichester in 1075; died 29 August 1087. See FEA v, 1.

i, fol. 16d; i, fol. 16b; i, fol. 16d; i, fol. 16d; i, fol. 16d; i, fol. 17a; i, fol. 17a; i, fol. 16d; i, fol. 17a; i, fol. 17a; i, fol. 17a

Suain Filius Azur

Englishman, occurs Domesday Northamptonshire. His holdings passed to Geoffrey I de Mauquenchy, a monk of Abingdon by 1117.

i, fol. 228a; i, fol. 228a; i, fol. 219a

Suartinc Filius Hardecanuti

Englishman, occurs Domesday Leicestershire.

i, fol. 336a; i, fol. 336a

Suarting []

Occurs in Domesday Buckinghamshire.

i, fol. 149d; i, fol. 153b

Suen De Exssessa

Son of Robert fitz Wimarc (q.v., identified here and in the Introduction as Robert de Moyaux, Calvados, cant. Lisieux-1), whom he succeeded between c.1075 and 1086. He was dead by 1114, when his son Robert had succeeded him (Sanders, 139). His sons Robert and William and his widow made a grant to Westminster abbey for his soul on the day he was buried (C. Hart, Early Essex Charters, Leicester Univ. Press, 1971, no. 99).

i, fol. 84d; i, fol. 84c; ii, fol. 023b; ii, fol. 023b; ii, fol. 004a; Gibbs, Early Charters of St Pauls (1939), No. 20; Dugdale, Monasticon Anglicanum, III, pp. 472–73, No. VII; Gibbs, Early Charters of St Pauls (1939), No. 17; i, fol. 205d; ii, fol. 047a; ii, fol. 046b; ii, fol. 047b; ii, fol. 043a; ii, fol. 046b; ii, fol. 045a; ii, fol. 044b; ii, fol. 044a; ii, fol. 043a; ii, fol. 043a; ii, fol. 043a; ii, fol. 047a; ii, fol. 043a; ii, fol. 043b; ii, fol. 043b; ii, fol. 044a; ii, fol. 043a; ii, fol. 044a; ii, fol. 042a; ii, fol. 401a; ii, fol. 401b; ii, fol. 401b; ii, fol. 402a; ii, fol. 401a; ii, fol. 401a; ii, fol. 402a; ii, fol. 401a; ii, fol. 401a; ii, fol. 402b; ii, fol. 401a; ii, fol. 401b; ii, fol. 402b; ii, fol. 401a; i, fol. 84b; i, fol. 84b; Dugdale, Monasticon Anglicanum, IV, pp. 156–57, No. I; i, fol. 160a; i, fol. 74b

Suen []

Englishman, occurs Domesday Lincolnshire and in the Claims.

i, fol. 358c; i, fol. 370b; i, fol. 370c; Lincolnshire Claims (Domesday Book), fols 376b–c

Suerting []

Englishman, occurs Domesday Buckinghamshire.

i, fol. 153b; i, fol. 150c; i, fol. 150b; i, fol. 153b; i, fol. 149c

Sueting Avus Mathie

English tenant of Abingdon Abbey at Wheatley, Oxon, in 1086. Identified as the grandfather of Matthew [of Wheatley] in the knight list (Chron. Abing. ii, 5).

i, fol. 156d; Stevenson, Chronicon Monasterii de Abingdon (1858) vol. II, pp. 4–6

Suetman Monetarius

English moneyer. Occurs Domesday Oxfordshire.

i, fol. 154b

Suuen Filius Ailric

Son of Ailric. Both he and his father were Domesday tenants of Ilbert de Lacy in Yorkshire. He was later given an extensive estate in Cumberland by Henry I. Father of Adam fitz Swein and Henry. In 1129/30 Hervey de Veceio accounted to have Swein's widow and her dower. See Hugh Thomas, 'A Yorkshire thegn and his descendants after the Conquest', Medieval Prosopography 8.1 (1987), 1–22.

i, fol. 316d; i, fol. 317d; Dugdale, Monasticon Anglicanum, IV, pp. 120–21, No. II; Dugdale, Monasticon Anglicanum, IV, p. 120, No. I; Dugdale, Monasticon Anglicanum, IV, p. 121, No. III; i, fol. 316d; i, fol. 317d

Tascelin Presbiter

Occurs Domesday Essex.

ii, fol. 003b; ii, fol. 010b

Tebald Clericus

Tenant of Abbot Baldwin of Bury St Edmunds, 1086.

ii, fol. 358a; Douglas, Feudal Book of Bury St Edmunds (1932), pp. 3–21; ii, fol. 117a

Tedric Pointel

Norman, Domesday tenant of William de Warenne, he also held land in chief. Possibly from a family evidenced in the county of Evreux (Eure) in the eleventh and early twelfth centuries. William, Richard and Walter Pointel attested a charter of Préaux (Arch. dépt. Eure H 711, no. 410), and a William Pointel was a partisan of Amaury de Montfort in 1118 (Ord. Vit. vi, 205).

i, fol. 211d; ii, fol. 023a; ii, fol. 023a; ii, fol. 023b; ii, fol. 099b; ii, fol. 099b; ii, fol. 099b; ii, fol. 099a; ii, fol. 096b; ii, fol. 071a; ii, fol. 096a; ii, fol. 099b; ii, fol. 002a; ii, fol. 096a; ii, fol. 096a; ii, fol. 69a; ii, fol. 69a

Teoderic []

Occurs in Domesday Wiltshire as a tenant of Malmesbury abbey and Edward of Salisbury.

i, fol. 69c; i, fol. 67b; i, fol. 67b

Teodulf []

Tenant of Roger de Montgomery, earl of Shrewsbury, in 1086. Theodulf cementarius and his son Walter attested a charter of the 1090s for Saint-Martin-de-Sées. In another charter, probably of 1110, a Theodulf was mentioned in a charter of his brother Hugh, a priest, with their mother Legarde (Arch. Orne. H 938, fols 7v–8r, 19).

i, fol. 259b; i, fol. 259b

Tetbald Filius Berneri

Probably to be identified with the Theobald fitz Berner who was attached to William I by 1063, when he attested a series of William's charters for Marmoutiers (Fauroux, Recueil, nos. 157, 160, 161, 162). Two of these charters also involved the Breton seigneur Main of Fougères, whose son Ralph was, like Theobald, a tenant-in-chief in Devon in 1086. Theobald was probably himself a Breton and may have been the man who attested a charter for SS Serge and Bacchus given by Rivallon of Montreuil, a vassal of Robert de Vitré (father of two Domesday landholders) [Morice, Preuves I, 418]; another witness was Wihenoc fitz Caradoc de Laboussac, uncle of another tenant-in-chief, William fitz Baderon. Theobald's heir was a daughter who married Odo fitz Gamelin, their combined fiefs subsequently becoming the honour of Great Torrington (Sanders, 48). He was described as 'socer odonis' (Odo's father-in-law) in the Tax Returns, fol. 497a. K.S.B. Keats-Rohan, 'Le rôle des Bretons dans la politique de la colonisation normande', MSHAB, lxxiv, 1996, 196.

i, fol. 115c; i, fol. 115c; i, fol. 115d; i, fol. 115d; i, fol. 115c; i, fol. 115d; i, fol. 115c; i, fol. 115c; i, fol. 115c; i, fol. 115c; i, fol. 115c; i, fol. 115b; i, fol. 115b; i, fol. 115d

Tetbald Homo Comitisse

Tenant of Countess Judith in 1086. The Theobald (q.v.) who occurs in the Daventry cartulary (nos. 8, 113). as a man of Judith's daughter Matilda I de Senlis c.1140 was perhaps his son.

i, fol. 227d; i, fol. 216a; i, fol. 213c; i, fol. 212b

Tetbald Medicus
Norman, occurs Domesday Wiltshire. Described as 'medicus' in the Tax Return
for Cricklade Hundred.

i, fol. 69d; i, fol. 74c

Tetbald Presbiter
Occurs Domesday Sussex as a tenant of William of Eu.

i, fol. 20a

Tetbald []
Tenant, in Domesday Cambridgeshire and Hertfordshire, of Harduin de Scalariis,
possibly his relative. A Theobald de Scalariis occurs in the time of Harduin's
successor Stephen. Father of a son Fulk who occurs in 1130 and grandfather of
Theobald fitz Fulk, a Scalariis tenant in 1166. Ancestor of the FitzRalph family,
named from Ralph fitz Fulk II fitz Theobald. See Fowler, Cart. Old Wardon, note
79, p. 317.

i, fol. 141c; i, fol. 141c; i, fol. 141c; i, fol. 141c; i, fol. 141d; i, fol. 141d; i, fol.
141d; i, fol. 141d; i, fol. 141d; i, fol. 141d; i, fol. 141d; Hamilton, Inquisitio
Comitatus Cantabrigiensis, pp. 1–93; Hamilton, Inquisitio Eliensis (1876), pp.
97–100

Tetbald []
Occurs in Domesday in holdings associated with Roger Pictaviensis. Perhaps same
as a tenant of Earl Hugh of Chester.

i, fol. 269d; i, fol. 269d; i, fol. 237a

Tetbald []
Domesday tenant of Drogo de La Beuvrière.

i, fol. 324d; i, fol. 360b

Tetbert []
Domesday Knight of William de Braose in Sussex. Subsequently won over by the
reputation for sanctity of Battle Abbey, he became one of its monks (Chron. Battle,
88–90).

i, fol. 28c

Tezelin Coquus
Norman, Domesday tenant of William de Warenne in Sussex, and of Walter fitz
Other in Surrey, where he also held the manor of Addington in chief. His son
William was a benefactor of Lewes in the time of William II de Warenne
(1088–1138). Cf. Round, King's Serjeants, 243; HKF iii, 347.

i, fol. 36a; i, fol. 36d; i, fol. 26d; i, fol. 26d

Tezelin []
Domesday tenant of Hugh of Port in Hampshire; perhaps the same as the Tescelin
holding land under Osbern of Salisbury in Dorset.

i, fol. 77b; i, fol. 45c; i, fol. 45c

Tezelin []
Norman, occurs Domesday Cheshire and Herefordshire.

i, fol. 184d; i, fol. 267d; i, fol. 184c

Theodric []
Named as a Domesday tenant of Peter de Valognes, probably father of William fitz Theoderic who attested the foundation charter of Binham c.1100–07, and of the Hugh fitz Theoderic referred to a charter of Evrard bishop of Norwich concerning Roger de Valognes. Hugh fitz Theoderic is likely to have the father of Peter's grandson William of Bacton (q.v.). The Domesday reference is possibly an anachronism since it is likely that this Theoderic was the same person as the brother of Walter the deacon, a Domesday tenant-in-chief who had succeeded his brother by 1086; alternatively, he may have been the son of that Theoderic.

ii, fol. 257b; ii, fol. 257a; Dodwell, Charters relating to the Honour of Bacton, No. 3

Theodric Aurifaber
Landholder in Domesday Berkshire.

i, fol. 60b; i, fol. 58a; i, fol. 155c; i, fol. 160d; i, fol. 160d; i, fol. 160d; i, fol. 36d; i, fol. 63b; i, fol. 63b; i, fol. 63b; i, fol. 63b; i, fol. 63b

Thochi []
Englishman, held Ludecote jointly with Ralph Cocus from Roger, earl of Shrewsbury in 1086. Early benefactor of Shrewsbury Abbey.

i, fol. 259b; Rees, Cartulary of Shrewsbury Abbey (1975), No. 35

Thomas Archiepiscopus Eboracensis
Son of a priest, and brother of Bishop Samson of Worcester. Known as Thomas of Bayeux; royal chaplain and treasurer of Bayeux cathedral, appointed archbishop of York 24 May 1070 and consecrated on 25 December; died 11 September 1100. See EEA v, pp. xxi–iv.

i, fol. 164c; i, fol. 303a; Pipe Roll 8 Henry II, 03–lcwk; i, fol. 339c

Tigerus []
Norman, Domesday tenant of Robert Malet; apparently left descendants surnamed Tigier. He can probably be identified as Tigier de Ponte Erchenfredi (now Notre-Dame-du-Hamel, Eure), who attested a charter for Saint-Evroul, given by Ralph de Drumare, with Hivelinus his father and Vitalis his man (Ord. Vit., ed. Le Prévost v, 188).

ii, fol. 306a; ii, fol. 315b; ii, fol. 326a

Tihel De Helion
Breton, from Helléan, Morbihan, arr. Pontivy, cant. Josselin, according to a guess by J. H. Round, 'Helion of Helions Bumpstead', TEAS n.x. viii, 187–91. He held land in East Anglia in chief in 1086, possibly indicating an original association with Ralph de Gael, who forfeited his land and earldom of Norfolk in 1075. Such an association would support an origin in Helléan. He also held land of Odo of Bayeux, and was possibly the Cambridgeshire juror described as a reeve of Ely. William de Helion, probably his son, occurs in the time of Henry I. K.S.B. Keats-Rohan, 'Le rôle des Bretons dans la politique de la colonisation normande', MSHAB, lxxiv, 1996, 188.

ii, fol. 023a; ii, fol. 261b; ii, fol. 373a; ii, fol. 081b; ii, fol. 082a; ii, fol. 082a; ii, fol. 082a; ii, fol. 082b; ii, fol. 082b; ii, fol. 082a; ii, fol. 143b; ii, fol. 373b; ii, fol. 427b; ii, fol. 427b; ii, fol. 427b; ii, fol. 024a; Hamilton, Inquisitio Eliensis (1876), pp. 97–100; Hamilton, Inquisitio Eliensis (1876), pp. 97–100; Hamilton, Inquisitio Comitatus Cantabrigiensis, pp. 1–93

Toli []
Englishman, Domesday tenant of Miles Crispin in Oxfordshire.

i, fol. 159d; i, fol. 159c

Torchil De Digesuuelle
Englishman, Domesday juror in Broadwater Hundred, Hertfordshire; tenant of Geoffrey de Mandeville at Digswell, where he had earlier held under Asgar the Staller (Lewis, 'Jurors', 43).

Hamilton, Inquisitio Eliensis (1876), pp. 97–100; i, fol. 139c

Toret De Wrochecestria
Englishman, Domesday tenant under Roger de Montgomery in Shropshire. He also occurs as predecessor in some manors, including Wroxeter, from which he was named in a charter of Henry II for Shrewsbury abbey (Cart., no. 36, p. 42). The lands he had held in 1066 were given to Rainald de Balliol, from whom he held 9 hides of it. By c. 1108 he had acquired the Domesday holding of another English thegn, Hunnit. Presumably ancestor of the fitzTorets. See Williams, The English, 90.

i, fol. 259c; i, fol. 255c; Rees, Cartulary of Shrewsbury Abbey (1975), No. 35; i, fol. 254d; i, fol. 254d

Toui Presbyter
Occurs Domesday Bedfordshire.

i, fol. 209d

Toui []
English tenant-in-chief, Domesday Norfolk.

ii, fol. 264b; ii, fol. 265a; ii, fol. 265a; ii, fol. 265a; ii, fol. 264b; ii, fol. 265a; ii, fol. 265a; ii, fol. 265a; ii, fol. 265a; ii, fol. 265a; ii, fol. 264b; ii, fol. 264b; ii, fol. 264b; ii, fol. 264b; ii, fol. 264b; ii, fol. 265a; ii, fol. 264b

Toui []
Englishman, held part of Ampney in Domesday Gloucestershire. The holding was subsequently given to St Peter's by Winebald de Ballon (Hist. S. Petri. Glocs. i, 61).

i, fol. 169c

Tual Francigenus
Occurs Domesday Cheshire as a tenant of Robert de Rhuddlan. His personal name is Breton. Cf. Tuduald Rufus, who with Hugh Brito and Theobald fitz Berner (q.v.) attested a charter of Main de Fougères with William of Normandy c.1050/64 (Fauroux, 162).

i, fol. 269b

Tuder Walensis
Occurs in Domesday Book as holding a Welsh district from Roger de Montgomery. Probably he was Tudur ap Rhys Sais. Cf. F.C. Suppe, 'Who was Rhys Sais?', Haskins Society Journal 7 (1995).

i, fol. 253c

Turbern []
Englishman, occurs Domesday Yorkshire.

i, fol. 331c; i, fol. 331c; i, fol. 331c

Turbert Filius Chembel
Englishman, occurs on the Pipe Roll 31 Henry I for Wiltshire, excused on account of his poverty monies owed for a treasury plea against him. Perhaps the Turbert who occurs in the Wiltshire Domesday.

i, fol. 74c; Pipe Roll 31 Henry I, 019b–wl; Pipe Roll 31 Henry I, 019a–wl

Turbert []
Englishman, Domesday tenant of Countess Judith.

Northants Survey, fols 96r–99v; i, fol. 221a; i, fol. 228d; i, fol. 145c; i, fol. 217c

Turchetil []
English free man whose lands in Norfolk went to Hermer de Ferrariis (q.v.), from whom he apparently still held the manor of Islington in 1086.

ii, fol. 207a; ii, fol. 207a

Turchil Presbiter
English priest who shared a church with Boret before 1066 and still held from Eustache of Huntingdon in 1086.

i, fol. 206a

Turchill De Warwic
English tenant-in-chief in Domesday Warwickshire and elsewhere. Son of Æthelwine sheriff of Warwick (d. a.1083). Described by the Abingdon Chronicle as 'a great nobleman ... dwelling in the region of Arden' (Chron. Abing. ii, 8), he was exceptionally wealthy for an Englishman of 1086. According to a detailed investigation by A. Williams, 'A vice-comital family in pre-Conquest Warwickshire', Anglo-Norman Studies xi, most of his holding in Domesday Warwickshire was a family inheritance, and many of his English tenants were his relatives. Domesday names two of them, Guthmund and Ketelbern, as his brothers. In the time of William II his tenancy-in-chief was made part of the newly created earldom of Warwick, which was given to Henry, brother of the count of Meulan of 1086, several of whose manors had formerly been held by members of Thorkil's family. Thorkil left issue by two marriages, the second to a woman called Leveruna, mother of his principal heir Siward.

i, fol. 160c; i, fol. 238a; i, fol. 240d; i, fol. 240d; i, fol. 240d; i, fol. 240d; i, fol. 160c; i, fol. 240d; i, fol. 240d; i, fol. 240d

Turchill Prepositus
Occurs Domesday Essex.

ii, fol. 098b; ii, fol. 098b

Turgis Anglicus
Englishman, occurs Domesday Bedfordshire as a tenant of Geoffrey bishop of Coutances.

i, fol. 210b

Turgis De Meduana
Norman from Meuvaines, Calvados, cant. Ryes. Tenant of Eudo Dapifer of Ryes. The toponym is supplied by a list of the benefactors of St Alban's Abbey, who included Robert and William sons of Turgis de Meduana (Mon. Ang. ii, 220).

ii, fol. 049a; ii, fol. 049a

Turgis []
Domesday tenant of Nigel de Albini, Bedfordshire.

i, fol. 214a; i, fol. 214a; i, fol. 214a; i, fol. 214c

Turgis []
Tenant of Judhael of Totnes; probably the Turgis *miles de la Foresta* who attested Judhael's charter for Totnes Priory (Mon. Ang iv, 630, no. ii); possibly the Turgis kinsman of the steward Geoffrey mentioned in another charter (Watkins, Totnes i). The surname de Foresta occurs in the later twelfth century in Devon (cf. Redvers ch., App., pp. 198–9). Hugh de Foresta was a tenant of Totnes at Worthele in Fees, 770.

i, fol. 109c; i, fol. 109c; i, fol. 109d; i, fol. 109c; i, fol. 109c; i, fol. 109d; i, fol. 109b; i, fol. 109a; i, fol. 110a; i, fol. 110a; i, fol. 110a; i, fol. 110a; i, fol. 110a

Turgis []
Domesday tenant of William de Moyon.

i, fol. 96c; i, fol. 95d; i, fol. 96b

Turgis []
Domesday tenant of Peter de Valognes; his holding at Rudham, Norfolk, was granted to Binham before 1107 in a charter which he attested.

ii, fol. 256a; ii, fol. 257b; Dugdale, Monasticon Anglicanum, III, pp. 345–46, No. I; ii, fol. 078a

Turgis []
Englishman recorded in Domesday as having held sake and soke in Sutton and Aylesford Lathes in Kent before 1066.

Ballard, Inquisition of St Augustine's (1920), fols 24r–28r; i, fol. 001a

Turold Abbas De Burg
Turold, monk of Fécamp, abbot of Malmesbury from c.1066/7 until his appointment to Peterborough in 1070. He died in early April 1098. Some Peterborough documents call him 'nepos' of William the Conqueror. Cf. Candidus, 77–86; Heads, 58.

i, fol. 370c; King, Peterborough Descriptio Militum (1969), pp. 97–101; i, fol. 219a; i, fol. 205b; i, fol. 205b; i, fol. 205a; i, fol. 336b; i, fol. 336b; i, fol. 210c; i, fol. 336d; i, fol. 360d; Lincolnshire Claims (Domesday Book), fols 376d–377c; Lincolnshire Claims (Domesday Book), fols 376b–c; i, fol. 336d; i, fol. 345d; i, fol. 345d; Lincolnshire Claims (Domesday Book), fols 376b–c; Douglas, Feudal Documents from Bury St Edmunds, No. 11; i, fol. 203c

Turold De Cheuerchort
Norman, from Quiévrecourt, Seine-Maritime, arr. and cant. Neufchâtel (Loyd, 21), tenant of Roger de Bully. His descendants were afterwards notable in Nottinghamshire, but there is a possible confusion with Turold de Lisores in making identifications from the Domesday text. Probably father of Ralph, a benefactor of Worksop priory (VCH Notts i, 225).

i, fol. 285d; i, fol. 285c; i, fol. 285b; i, fol. 284c; Timson, Blyth Priory Cartulary (1973), No. 325

Turold De Lisoriis
Norman, Domesday tenant of Roger de Bully; brother of Fulk de Lisores, another of Roger's tenants. His holdings are very difficult to distinguish from those of

430

Turold de Chevrecourt. Early in the twelfth century he made a grant to Blyth priory for the soul of his wife Beatrice, with the assent of his son William. Possibly the same as Turold who held at Greetwell, Lincolnshire, from Roger de Bully and who occurs elsewhere in the text as Turold of Greetwell. At the time of the Lindsey Survey the tenement of Roger's tenant Turold at Greetwell was held by Hugh de Luvetot.

i, fol. 352d; i, fol. 285b; i, fol. 336b; Timson, Blyth Priory Cartulary (1973), No. 325; Timson, Blyth Priory Cartulary (1973), No. 341

Turold De Rouecestre
Norman who was steward (dapifer) and tenant of Odo of Bayeux before his death around the time of the Domesday inquest (Cart. Westminster, no. 48); his name is found in Domesday, which recorded the bulk of his holding as having passed to his son Ralph.

ii, fol. 025a; ii, fol. 101b; ii, fol. 017b

Turold De Verly
Norman, from Vesly, Eure, arr. Les Andelys, tenant of Roger de Montgomery in Domesday Shropshire. Identified as Turold de Verleio in Cart. Shrewsbury p. 34. His son and heir Robert was also a benefactor of Shrewsbury. His origins are doubtless to be sought in the family of the Roger fitz Turold who gave land at Vesly to Tréport, at the time of its foundation by Robert count of Eu and his wife Beatrice, c.1050. Beatrice was Roger's mother by a previous marriage (ms. nov. acq. lat. 249, fol. 46v). Roger subsequently set out with William I on his voyage to England in 1066, but died on the journey. This Turold was either his son or another relative.

i, fol. 253a; Rees, Cartulary of Shrewsbury Abbey (1975), No. 35; i, fol. 258a; i, fol. 258a; i, fol. 257d; i, fol. 258a; i, fol. 257d; i, fol. 257d; i, fol. 258a

Turold De Wokendon
A Norman, named from Ockendon, Essex, dapifer of Geoffrey I de Mandeville, of whom he was a Domesday tenant. In 1085, when Geoffrey founded Hurley priory, Turold's son Ralph became an oblate there (Westminster Ch. 462).

i, fol. 139d; i, fol. 139c; ii, fol. 057b; Mason, Westminster Abbey Charters (1988), No. 462; Mason, Westminster Abbey Charters (1988), No. 462

Turold Nepos Wigot
Nephew of Wigod of Wallingford, tenant, as was his son William, of Earl Roger de Montgomery. Much of the land assigned to him in Domesday Book was previously held by Osmund, who was perhaps his father (A. William, The English, 102).

i, fol. 34c; i, fol. 34c; i, fol. 44c; i, fol. 44c; i, fol. 34c; i, fol. 166c; i, fol. 68d; i, fol. 68d

Turold Presbiter
Occurs Domesday Berkshire.

i, fol. 60b

Turold Presbiter
Occurs Domesday Lincolnshire, tenant of Colswein.

i, fol. 356d; i, fol. 352c

Turold []
Domesday tenant of the wife of Hugh fitz Grip. His successor in 1166 was Geoffrey of Warmwell, son of Gunfrid (Cart. Montacute, no. 119).

i, fol. 83d; i, fol. 83d

Turold []
Tenant of Swein of Essex. Succeeded after 1086 by Robert Waste (q.v.) and c.1130 by Gilbert, who referred to Torold and Robert his 'antecessores' in a grant to St Neots (Mon. Ang. iii, 472–3). Turold was still alive when he attended the funeral of Swein of Essex at Westminster, described as a 'baron' of Robert fitz Swein (C. Hart, Early Essex Charters, Leicester Univ. Press, 1971, no. 99). Robert Waste made a grant of land in Turold's manor of Waresley mentioning Gunnor, wife of his lord Robert fitz Swein, his own wife and her father William fitz Gerei (ibid.). The surname is found in eastern Normandy in the twelfth century, e.g. Arch. dépt. Seine-Maritime 8 H 2 Foucarmont; Delisle, Rec. Henri II ii, no. cxxx. William de Rothomag' (Rouen) confirmed the grant that Turold his grandfather had made of land at Waresley (BL Cotton Faust. A iv, fol. 90v). William de Rouen's charter mentions his kinsman (cognatus) William de Falesham, who held of him in Waresley. William fitz Gerei was perhaps the same as Turold's grandson William de Rouen. The Laurence de Rotomag' who accounted in Essex in 1129 was perhaps another of Turold's descendants.

For the possibility that he was brother of William fitz Odo and son of Odo, both tenants of Swein in 1086, see under Robert fitz Godbald (son of another tenant of Swein) and his wife Beatrice.

i, fol. 205d; ii, fol. 042b; ii, fol. 042b

Turold []
Domesday tenant of Ranulf Peverel. His holdings were all held in 1185 by the heirs of Stephen fitz Richard de Bellocampo (q.v).

ii, fol. 417b; ii, fol. 099b; ii, fol. 075b; ii, fol. 075b; ii, fol. 074a; ii, fol. 074a; ii, fol. 074b

Turold []
Domesday tenant of William de Warenne. He was probably the man described as Turold de Guningham who gave the church of Witton (?Wolterton, Cambs.) to Castle Acre priory before 1118. Cf. HKF iii, 437.

ii, fol. 158b; ii, fol. 157b; ii, fol. 158a; ii, fol. 159a; ii, fol. 159a; ii, fol. 158b; ii, fol. 158b; ii, fol. 158b; ii, fol. 158b; ii, fol. 172a; ii, fol. 172a; ii, fol. 172a

Turold []
Domesday tenant of Roger Bigot. Probably the same as Turold dapifer of Robert de Curzon (Ann. Bury S. Edmunds i, 79), who was a major tenant of Roger. Cf. Farrer, HKF iii, 150, for his Bacun successors in one of his holdings.

ii, fol. 178a; ii, fol. 178a; ii, fol. 177b; ii, fol. 175b; ii, fol. 177b; ii, fol. 186b

Turstin Burgensis
Occurs Domesday Norfolk.

ii, fol. 173a

Turstin Camerarius
Norman, Domesday tenant-in-chief in Hampshire and Bedfordshire. Cf. VCH Beds. ii, 83–5.

i, fol. 210a; i, fol. 218a; i, fol. 48a; i, fol. 216c; i, fol. 48a; i, fol. 216d; i, fol. 216c; i, fol. 216c; i, fol. 216d; i, fol. 74d; i, fol. 52a

Turstin De Cormeliis

The Turstin who was a tenant of Ansfrid de Cormeilles in 1086 was perhaps the same as the Turstin de Cormeilles, Eure, who occurs in a document of c.1085/1100 holding burgesses in Gloucester (perhaps as heir of Ansfrid).

i, fol. 169d; Ellis, 'Landholders of Gloucestershire' (1880), pp. 91–93

Turstin De Fontanis

Undertenant in Sussex of Roger de Montgomery and tenant of Robert fitz Theobald, whose last act for Saint-Martin de Sées he witnessed in 1087 as Turstin de Petehorda (Petworth, Sussex) (CDF, 655). Probably named from Fontaines-les-Basset, Orne, cant. Trun. His grant of land at Mundham, Sussex (held by Alcher in Domesday Book) to Troarn was first confirmed by Henry I c.1100–7 (Chanteux, no. 176; RRAN ii, 524). Cf. HKF iii, 17, 90.

i, fol. 23c; Regesta regum Anglo-Normannorum III, No. 902

Turstin De Giron

Norman, from Gueron, Calvados, arr. cant. Bayeux (Loyd, 45), Domesday tenant of Odo of Bayeux in Buckinghamshire and Kent.

i, fol. 144d; i, fol. 010c

Turstin De Wigemore

Described in Domesday Book as Turstin Flandrensis and as Turstin of Wigmore. He appears to have originally settled with William fitz Osbern in Herefordshire, but lost most of his holdings for adherence to William's rebel son Earl Roger in 1075. In 1086 he held only a couple of manors from his wife Agnes's father Alfred of Marlborough.

i, fol. 186b; i, fol. 186a

Turstin Filius Haimfrid

The identification of the Turstin who held land from Shaftesbury Abbey was made by A. Williams, 'Knights of Shaftesbury Abbey', ANS viii, 217–18, 228–9; ancestor of the de Hazeldon family, his father's name also occus as Rainfrid and his mother may have been English. His Shaftesbury holdings were in the hands of his son Roger c.1130.

Dugdale, Monasticon Anglicanum, II, pp. 482–83, No. XIII; i, fol. 67c; i, fol. 67c; i, fol. 67c; Regesta regum Anglo-Normannorum III, No. 818

Turstin Filius Ricardi

Norman, Domesday tenant of Robert Gernon; his patronym is provided by the Inquisitio Comitatus Cantabrigiensis.

i, fol. 196d

Turstin Filius Rolf

Norman, from Le Bec-aux-Cauchois, Seine-Maritime, cant. Valmont, standard bearer of the Normans at the battle of Hastings (Ord. Vit. iii 172–3: 'Turstinus filius Rolonis vexilum Normannorum portavit'; Wace, ll 8697ff: 'E cil qui tient son gonfanon/-Tostein filz Rou le Blanc ont non, Del Bec coste Fescamp fu nez, chevalier proz e renomez-/Tostein le fist hardiement'). A tenant-in-chief in 1086, he lost his fief during the reign of William II. He attested a gift by Walter de Bec to

Saint-Georges de Boscherville c.1060 (Fauroux, 167), and himself made a grant of his part of the church of Crasville, confirmed by Henry I in 1114 (Chanteux, no. 16, 62ff). His fief was given to Winebald de Ballon by Henry I and was held by the latter's grandson Henry de Novomercato. See Round, 'The family of Ballon', in idem, Peerage, 181ff; Sanders, 68.

i, fol. 185c; i, fol. 90b; i, fol. 147b; i, fol. 97c; i, fol. 151b; i, fol. 185d; i, fol. 169c; i, fol. 47d; i, fol. 97c; i, fol. 99b; i, fol. 63a; i, fol. 97c; i, fol. 97d; i, fol. 97c; i, fol. 147a; i, fol. 80c; i, fol. 47d; i, fol. 169d; i, fol. 63a; i, fol. 169c; i, fol. 166b; i, fol. 165a; i, fol. 164d; i, fol. 162b; i, fol. 162b; i, fol. 169c; i, fol. 169d; i, fol. 169d; i, fol. 185d; i, fol. 97c; i, fol. 151b; i, fol. 174c

Turstin Filius Widonis
Norman, landholder in Domesday Suffolk and Norfolk. A major tenant of Roger Bigod, he was probably ancestor of the Crek family, named from his holding at Creake. Granted the tithe of Finningham Suffolk to St Peter's, Gloucester, in the time of abbot Serlo (Cart. i, 79, 351). Possibly son of the Guy (Wido) de Saint-Quentin who gave tithes at Savenay to Cerisy when he became a monk there, before 1082 (Chanteux, no. 44).

ii, fol. 223b; ii, fol. 179a; ii, fol. 179a; ii, fol. 343b; ii, fol. 185a; ii, fol. 343b; ii, fol. 343b; ii, fol. 344a; ii, fol. 183b; ii, fol. 183b; ii, fol. 184a; ii, fol. 184a; ii, fol. 343b

Turstin MacHinator
Norman engineer, occurs Domesday Hampshire.
i, fol. 52a

Turstin Mantel
Norman, minor landholder in Domesday Buckinghamshire and Northamptonshire, where he held land of Walter Giffard, William Peverel and Henry de Ferrers.

i, fol. 226b; i, fol. 226a; i, fol. 151c; i, fol. 151c; i, fol. 151c; i, fol. 151c; Dugdale, Monasticon Anglicanum, IV, pp. 111–12, No. Ia; Dugdale, Monasticon Anglicanum, IV, p. 113, No. II; Regesta regum Anglo-Normannorum III, No. 589

Turstin Paruus
Occurs Domesday Hampshire.
i, fol. 41a

Turstin Presbiter
Priest, occurs Domesday Buckinghamshire as tenant of Miles Crispin.
i, fol. 150b

Turstin Rufus
Occurs Domesday Hampshire.
i, fol. 41a

Turstin Tinel
Norman. He and his wife occurs as Domesday tenants of Odo of Bayeux in Kent. Warengar Tinel attested a grant by Godfrid de Vernon, Eure, and his wife to Sainte-Trinité de Rouen (Arch. dépt. Seine-Maritime 27 H I, fol. 6). Much later a Roger Tinel and his wife Beatrice occur as benefactors of Saint-Nicholas d'Evreux (BN lat. 94, 89/103).

i, fol. 011c; i, fol. 011c; i, fol. 011c; i, fol. 011b

Turstin Uuiscart

Minor tenant in Domesday Essex, who held from the west Norman John fitz Waleran (q.v.). A William Wiscardo attested a Montebourg charter given by Richard de Sauceio, man of Richard de Redvers (BN lat. 10087 202/668); a Godefrid Wiscart and his son Gausfred attested a charter for Troarn c.1079/82 (CDF, 466; Bates, 283). Turstin's land was given by Eudo dapifer to St John's, Colchester, in 1119 (Cart., 1). Baldwin Wiscart was his successor in 1166.

ii, fol. 084a; ii, fol. 106b

Turstin Vicecomes

Domesday tenant in Cornwall under Robert of Mortain. He occurs in Exon Domesday as Turstin vicecomes, indicating that he was the count's sheriff in the county. The office was held by his co-tenant Hamelin in the time of William of Mortain (1094–1106). Father of Baldwin son of Turstin who was mentioned in an early charter of Tywardreth priory (Mon. Exon., 39), as a benefactor in the time of the founder Richard fitz Turold (q.v.) with the assent of his father and his brothers.

i, fol. 125b; i, fol. 91d; i, fol. 92b; i, fol. 120a; i, fol. 120a; i, fol. 120a; i, fol. 120a; i, fol. 122d; i, fol. 122d; i, fol. 123b; i, fol. 86b; i, fol. 87a; i, fol. 122d; i, fol. 122d; i, fol. 122d; i, fol. 122d; i, fol. 123a; i, fol. 123a; i, fol. 122d; i, fol. 123a; i, fol. 123b; i, fol. 123a; i, fol. 123a; i, fol. 123a; i, fol. 123a; i, fol. 122d; i, fol. 122d; i, fol. 122d; i, fol. 123a

Turstin []

Norman, Domesday tenant of Ralph de Mortemer, ancestor of a family named from Lingen in Shropshire. He has been identified with Turstin of Wigmore, alias Turstin Flandrensis, but the identification is difficult to accept (Eyton, Shrops, ix, 343.

i, fol. 260b; i, fol. 260b; i, fol. 256d

Uctebrand []

Englishman, occurs Domesday Derbyshire.

i, fol. 273a; i, fol. 273a

Uctred Filius Ligulf

Eldest of the two sons of Ligulf, adviser to Bishop Walcher of Durham, who married Ealdgyth, maternal aunt of Earl Waltheof (d. 1075). Ligulf was murdered by the bishop's kinsman Gilbert in 1080; both Gilbert and Walcher died soon afterwards in the ensuing feud. The lands of a Ligulf were given to Robert of Mortain and held of him by Richard de Surdeval and Nigel Fossard. At Rudstone Uctred a king's thegn had succeeded a Ligulf, suggesting a link between this holding. See Williams, The English, 67–8.

i, fol. 331a; Dugdale, Monasticon Anglicanum, III, pp. 548–50, No. V

Uctred Filius Ulf

English tenant of Count Alan in Domesday Yorkshire. Succeeded his father Ulfr at Middleton – of which he gave the church to St Mary's, York – and Kneeton. See VCH Yorks ii, 158.

Dugdale, Monasticon Anglicanum, III, pp. 548–50, No. V; i, fol. 309b; i, fol. 309b

Uctred []

Englishman, Domesday tenant of Richard de Sourdeval in Yorkshire. Identified by

Farrer with Uhtred son of Thorketill of Cleveland, a benefactor of Whitby priory. He appears to have been the predecessor, and possibly the ancestor, of the Ivo de Seton who held lands at Cleveland in the time of Henry II (VCH Yorks ii, 154).

i, fol. 305b

Ulbert Frater Ulf
Englishman, occurs Domesday Lincolnshire.

i, fol. 336a

Ulchetel Homo Hermeri
Englishan, occurs in Domesday as man of Hermer de Ferrers.

ii, fol. 270b; ii, fol. 213a

Ulchetel []
Englishman, Domesday tenant of the count of Meulan and Thorkil of Warwick in Warwickshire.

i, fol. 240c

Ulfac []
Englishman, occurs Domesday Staffordshire.

i, fol. 249b; i, fol. 249b

Ulfketel Prepositus Regis
Englishman, royal provost; occurs Domesday Norfolk.

ii, fol. 176b

Ulfstan Episcopus Wigornensis
Wulfstan II, bishop from 29 August 1062 until 20 January 1095. Canonised 14 May 1203. FEA ii, 99. J.W. Lamb, Saint Wulfstan, Prelate and Patriot (London, 1933).

Darlington, Cartulary of Worcester: Reg. I (1962–3), No. 53; Darlington, Cartulary of Worcester: Reg. I (1962–3), No. 62; i, fol. 238c; Darlington, Cartulary of Worcester: Reg. I (1962–3), No. 2; Darlington, Cartulary of Worcester: Reg. I (1962–3), No. 23; i, fol. 173b; i, fol. 173b; i, fol. 173b; i, fol. 173b; i, fol. 173b; i, fol. 173a; i, fol. 172d; i, fol. 173c; i, fol. 173c; i, fol. 173c; i, fol. 182a; i, fol. 173b; i, fol. 164d; i, fol. 165a; i, fol. 164d; Darlington, Cartulary of Worcester: Reg. I (1962–3), No. 5; Regesta regum Anglo-Normannorum III, No. 964; i, fol. 238c; i, fol. 238c; i, fol. 238c; i, fol. 238c; i, fol. 238c; i, fol. 238a; i, fol. 172d; Darlington, Cartulary of Worcester: Reg. I (1962–3), No. 4; Darlington, Cartulary of Worcester: Reg. I (1962–3), No. 3; Darlington, Cartulary of Worcester: Reg. I (1962–3), No. 52; Darlington, Cartulary of Worcester: Reg. I (1962–3), No. 55; Regesta regum Anglo-Normannorum III, No. 345

Ulketel Prepositus Regis
Englishman, royal reeve in Domesday Norfolk.

ii, fol. 177a; ii, fol. 177a; ii, fol. 177a; ii, fol. 177a; ii, fol. 270b; ii, fol. 270b; ii, fol. 270b; ii, fol. 270b; ii, fol. 270b

Ulmar Burgensis
Occurs Domesday Bedfordshire.

i, fol. 218b

Ulmar Prepositus Regis
Englishman, royal reeve, occurs Suffolk.
ii, fol. 448b; ii, fol. 448b

Ulric De Oxeneford
Occurs Domesday Kent as a canon of Dover. His prebend in Cornilo hundred was given to him by Alan, a clerk of Odo, bishop of Bayeux, who had been given it by the bishop.
i, fol. 001c; Ballard, Inquisition of St Augustine's (1920), fols 24r–28r; i, fol. 001d

Ulric Venator
Occurs Domesday Hampshire. His holding was later known as the manor or serjeanty of Tytherley. In 1129/30 William de Pontearch, sheriff of Hampshire, had custody of the land of Walter son of Uluric Venator until his heir could hold the land (PR 31 Henry I 37).
i, fol. 84b; i, fol. 50d

Ulric Waula
Occurs Domesday Wiltshire.
i, fol. 74b

Ulsi Prebendarius Regis
Englishman, royal prebendary, occurs Bedfordshire.
i, fol. 218b

Ulsi []
English tenant of Robert of Mortain in Cornwall, 1086.
i, fol. 124d; i, fol. 124d; i, fol. 124d

Ulstan Eudlac
Englishman, occurs Domesday Colchester.
ii, fol. 104a

Ulstan Filius Uluuin
Englishman, occurs Domesday Kent.
i, fol. 001d

Ulueua Uxor Phin
Englishwoman, occurs Domesday Essex. Wife of Phin the Dane (VCH Essex i, 348–9), whose Essex holdings were held by Richard de Clare in 1086. She was probably the Wulfeva who held in Cambridgeshire of Richard. William II gave her land to Eudo Dapifer in 1099/1100. This was probably connected with Eudo's marriage to a daughter of Richard de Clare, through which he acquired other property once of Phin the dane (Farrer, HKF ii, 220).
ii, fol. 105b; i, fol. 196c; i, fol. 196c; ii, fol. 098a; ii, fol. 098b; ii, fol. 098a

Uluiet Presbiter
English priest, occurs Domesday Lincolnshire.
i, fol. 336a; i, fol. 336b

Uluiet Venator
Occurs Domesday Dorset. Wulfgeat, King Edward's Huntsman, father of Cola the Huntsman. Cf. Williams, The English, 116.
i, fol. 84b; i, fol. 74b; i, fol. 50c

Uluiet []
Tenant of Glastonbury Abbey before and after 1066.
    i, fol. 77c

Uluiet []
Englishman, occurs Domesday Norfolk.
    ii, fol. 135a; ii, fol. 135a

Uluric Dapifer
Domesday tenant of Walter de Douai. His personal name, easily misunderstood as belonging to an English Wulfric, was common in Flemish documents of the period. A charter of Walter I castellan of Douai, continental overlord of the Domesday Walter, given on 14 September 1076 (Brassart, Preuves, no. xii) was attested by Ulric Heirini filius and Ulricus filius Walteri Scabini (cf. Ralph Heirun, tenant in 1166 of Walter's successor Henry Lovel). He was doubtless the same man as the Wluric dapifer who attested a document for Walter in the 1090s (Cart. Glaston. i, 128).
    i, fol. 95b; i, fol. 111d; Watkin, Chartulary of Glastonbury 3, SRS 64 (1950), pp. 126–28

Uluric Tainus
Occurs Domesday Buckinghamshire.
    i, fol. 145d

Uluric Venator
Englishman, occurs Domesday Wiltshire.
    i, fol. 74a; i, fol. 74b; i, fol. 74b; i, fol. 74a; i, fol. 74b; i, fol. 84b; i, fol. 84b; i, fol. 74a; i, fol. 74a; i, fol. 74b

Uluuard Presbiter
Occurs Domesday Sussex.
    i, fol. 18c

Uluuart Presbiter
Occurs Domesday Essex.
    ii, fol. 105a

Uluui Bullokesege
Domesday's Vluui is identifiable as the Englishman Wlfuui Bullokesege from Chron. Abingdon ii, 131–2.
    i, fol. 59a

Uluuin Presbiter
English priest, occurs Domesday Suffolk.
    ii, fol. 431a; ii, fol. 290a

Uluuinus Monitor
English burgess, occurs Domesday Colchester.
    ii, fol. 104b

Ulviet []
Englishman continuing to hold land under Robert of Stafford in 1086.
    i, fol. 249a; i, fol. 249a; i, fol. 249a

Ulward Prebendarius Regis
Occurs Domesday Wiltshire.

i, fol. 74b; i, fol. 74b

Ulwart de Wanforde
English priest, occurs Domesday Suffolk as a tenant of Count Alan. Perhaps the same as Aluric presbyter, father of Oswald de Turston (q.v.) to whom Abbot Leofstan of Bury gave the land and church of Thurston (Bury, Feudal Docs, 98).

ii, fol. 357b, 358b; Feudal Docs. of Bury St Edmunds, 26, 38, 105, 170, 174

Urfer []
Domesday tenant of Robert de Tosny of Stafford. His holdings were held in 1166 by Roger fitz Henry (Hist. Coll. Staffs. i, 171).

i, fol. 242d; i, fol. 248d; i, fol. 249c; i, fol. 249c

Urso De Abitot
Domesday tenant-in-chief, sheriff of Worcestershire from c.1069 until his death in 1108 (Sanders, 75); he apparently inherited the lands and offices in England of his brother Robert the dispencer after 1086. A Norman from Abbetot, Seine-Maritime, arr. Le Havre, cant. Saint-Romain, he was a tenant in Normandy of the chamberains of Tancarville. His son and heir Roger was banished by Henry I in 1114, leaving the daughters of Urse and their husbands Roger Marmion and Walter I de Beauchamp as heirs to his lands. Charters for Saint-Georges- de-Boscherville suggest that he also had a son Robert (see Loyd, 1).

i, fol. 176a; i, fol. 174b; i, fol. 174a; i, fol. 173c; i, fol. 173b; i, fol. 244a; i, fol. 238c; i, fol. 174b; i, fol. 174c; i, fol. 157a; i, fol. 175b; i, fol. 176d; i, fol. 176b; i, fol. 176a; i, fol. 176a; i, fol. 174d; i, fol. 175c; i, fol. 174c; i, fol. 176a; i, fol. 174d; i, fol. 175d; i, fol. 174d; i, fol. 175b; i, fol. 175c; i, fol. 174c; i, fol. 174c; i, fol. 243d; i, fol. 243d; i, fol. 243d; Dugdale, Monasticon Anglicanum, III, p. 447, No. I; Round, Ancient Charters (1888), No. 1; i, fol. 187c; i, fol. 169c; i, fol. 177c; Gibbs, Early Charters of St Pauls (1939), No. 41; Fisher, Cartularium Prioratus de Colne (Earles C.), No. 3; i, fol. 180a; i, fol. 180b; Regesta regum Anglo-Normannorum III, No. 68; i, fol. 177d; Darlington, Cartulary of Worcester: Reg. I (1962–3), No. 260; Hart, Cartularium Monasterii de Rameseia, No. CLX; Hart, Cartularium Monasterii de Rameseia, No. CLIX; Hart, Cartularium Monasterii de Rameseia, No. CLVII; Douglas, Feudal Documents from Bury St Edmunds, No. 27; Darlington, Cartulary of Worcester: Reg. I (1962–3), No. 261; Douglas, Feudal Documents from Bury St Edmunds, No. 28; Hart, Cartularium Monasterii de Rameseia, No. CLXIV; Dugdale, Monasticon Anglicanum, IV, p. 149, No. III; Darlington, Cartulary of Worcester: Reg. I (1962–3), No. 5; Darlington, Cartulary of Worcester: Reg. I (1962–3), No. 338; Darlington, Cartulary of Worcester: Reg. I (1962–3), No. 2; i, fol. 169c; Mason, Westminster Abbey Charters (1988), No. 488; i, fol. 172c; i, fol. 172a; i, fol. 172c; i, fol. 172a; i, fol. 172a; i, fol. 172a; i, fol. 172c; i, fol. 172a; i, fol. 172a; i, fol. 172c; i, fol. 175a; i, fol. 172d; Darlington, Cartulary of Worcester: Reg. I (1962–3), No. 3; i, fol. 175a; i, fol. 172d; i, fol. 175c; i, fol. 172d; i, fol. 175a; i, fol. 175a; i, fol. 175a; i, fol. 174a; i, fol. 172d; i, fol. 172d; i, fol. 172d; i, fol. 172d; i, fol. 175c; i, fol. 173a; i, fol. 173a; i, fol. 173a; i, fol. 173a; i, fol. 173a; i, fol. 173c; i, fol. 173c; i, fol. 175b; i, fol. 175b

Urso De Berseres
Domesday tenant-in-chief of a single manor in Buckinghamshire. The evidence of Pipe Roll Henry I (22, 23, 102) concerning Richard fitz Urse and of the Cartae

baronum (RBE 223, 240) concerning his son Rainald, indicate that this Urso was also the Domesday tenant of Glastonbury and Waleran Venator in Wiltshire, and ancestor of the FitzUrse family. He was perhaps the same as Urso (q.v.) tenant of Arnald de Hesdin. There are three places called Berchères in the Chartrain, dépt. Eure-et-Loir, and one in the dépt. of Seine-et-Marne. An Ursionis quondam domini Berciaci occurs in a thirteenth-century obituary from the abbey of Barbeaux (Obit. Sens, i, 34). More likely perhaps is an origin in Bersée, Nord.

i, fol. 82b; i, fol. 66d; i, fol. 66d; i, fol. 152b; i, fol. 152b

Urso []

Domesday tenant of Arnald de Hesdin, probably to be distinguished from another Urso who was apparently ancestor of the FitzUrse (see Urso de Berseres). An Ursio de Doullens (Somme, arr. Amiens) attested a charter for Saint-Georges-de-Hesdin for Arnald's nephew Robert Fretel (Cart. Chron. no. 54). His successor Henry fitz Urse held one fee of Earl Patrick in 1166.

i, fol. 70b; i, fol. 70b; i, fol. 80c; i, fol. 80c

Uruoius Homo Rafridi

Man of Radfrid, a tenant of Bury St Edmunds in 1086. The Domesday orthography of his name suggests he was Breton. A tenant under William d'Ecouis (Scohies) of land that had been claimed by Earl Ralph de Gael from Radfrid, he was possibly therefore the man named as Hervey de Vere of whom Domesday records a holding of Earl Ralph obtained in similar circumstances.

ii, fol. 221b

Uulric De Branduna

Englishman, occurs Domesday Essex.

ii, fol. 101b

Uxor Alberici De Ver

The probably west Norman wife of Alberic I de Vere occurs in Domesday as a tenant of the bishops of Coutances and Bayeux. She was named Beatrice in Alberic's foundation charter for Colne priory (q.v.).

ii, fol. 024a; ii, fol. 024a; ii, fol. 101a; ii, fol. 101a; Fisher, Cartularium Prioratus de Colne (Earles C.), No. 1; Fisher, Cartularium Prioratus de Colne (Earles C.), No. 9; Fisher, Cartularium Prioratus de Colne (Earles C.), No. 2; Fisher, Cartularium Prioratus de Colne (Earles C.), No. 13

Uxor Aluuii []

Occurs in Domesday Wiltshire.

i, fol. 69b

Uxor Balduini Vicecomitis

Second wife of Baldwin de Meulles, sheriff of Devon (q.v.), who occurs in Domesday Book. Exon Domesday gives her name as Emma. She and her husband gave tithes of the forêt d'Avranchin (near la Chaise-Baudoin, Manche, cant. Brécey) to Saint-Etienne de Caen (Actes caen., 2, p. 55).

i, fol. 107d; i, fol. 107b

Uxor Boselini De Diue

Wife of Boselin de Dives, she held a single manor in Cambridgeshire of the king in 1086.

i, fol. 202c

Uxor Brien []
Mother of Ralph and William sons of Brien (q.v.), presumably a widow at the date of her occurrence in Domesday as a tenant of Maurice, bishop of London.

i, fol. 127b

Uxor Edrici []
Englishwoman. Occurs Domesday Wiltshire as a tenant of Arnald de Hesdin. Her personal name, Estrit, is supplied in the Tax Return, Studfold Hundred. She was widow of Eadric, sheriff of Wiltshire before 1066 (RRAN i, 9). Cf. Williams, The English, 11, 106.

i, fol. 70a; i, fol. 70a

Uxor Fratris Ulurici Venatoris
This lady occurs in Domesday Dorset as the wife of the brother of Uluric (Wulfric), who was probably Uluric Hunter, as indicated by the Tax Return for Charborough Hundred. She may have been the woman named Vlueva (Wulfeva) who occurs in the same Tax Return.

i, fol. 84b

Uxor Geri De Loges
Gunnild, occurs as the wife of Ghervi of Loges in Domesday. Her name is supplied by a grant she made as a widow to St Peter's, Gloucester, in 1090 (Hist. S. Petri, i, 80–1).

i, fol. 170b; i, fol. 170b

Uxor Hervei De Helion
Widow of Hervey de Helion, a Breton, occurs Domesday Devon. Identified as Ima and Emma the widow (vidua) in the Exon Tax Returns, fols 68b–69a. Doubtless mother of Hervey's Helion successors in the region, of whom William de Helion, steward of Baldwin de Redvers, occurs from c.1140.

i, fol. 108b; i, fol. 117a; i, fol. 117a; i, fol. 117a

Uxor Hugonis Filii Grip
Widow of Hugh fitz Grip, sheriff of Dorset, who was dead by 1086. Around 1070 the wife of Hugh fitz Grip occurs in a Montivilliers charter where she is identified as Hawise daughter of Nicholas de Bacqueville: 'Ego Hadvidis filia Nicolai de Baschelvilla, uxor Hugonis de Varhan . . . annuente magno rege Guillelmo, coram baronibus suis, videlicet. . . . et Gaufrido Martello, fratre supradicti Hugonis . . .' (J-M. Bouvris, 'La renaissance de l'abbaye de Montivilliers', App. no. 29 (1066–76), 82–3). This is possibly the same woman. If so she is unlikely to be the woman who took Hugh's lands to Alfred of Lincoln soon after 1086, because he was much younger than Hawise would have been and he had issue by his wife, who was perhaps Hawise's daughter. Another possibilty, less likely, is that Hugh's widow was a woman other than Hawise.

i, fol. 77c; i, fol. 77b; i, fol. 77c; i, fol. 78a; i, fol. 78b; i, fol. 66c; i, fol. 84d; i, fol. 77c; i, fol. 83d; i, fol. 78c; i, fol. 82b; i, fol. 83c; i, fol. 78d; i, fol. 83c; i, fol. 83d; i, fol. 83c; i, fol. 84a; i, fol. 83c; i, fol. 83d; i, fol. 84a; i, fol. 84a; i, fol. 83c; i, fol. 77a; i, fol. 83c

Uxor Ingelbaldi []
Probably the wife of Ingelbald, tenant of Drogo de Carteret and a sub-tenant of Brito Geoffrey of Coutances. She occurs in Devon holding three manors which

descended together with a fourth manor described as being held by 'neptis episcopi', a niece or other female relative of Bishop Geoffrey. It is possible that the wife of Ingelbald and the bishop's niece were one and the same.

i, fol. 103b; i, fol. 103b; i, fol. 103b

Uxor Manasses Coci
Occurs Domesday Somerset.

i, fol. 89b; i, fol. 98d; i, fol. 98d

Uxor Militis Rogeri De Ramis
Unnamed wife of a knight of Roger de Raimes in 1086, probably the same as 'the wife of Henry'. Both holdings lay in Tendring Hundred and were mentioned close together in Domesday. Cf. the woman named Wiberga and an unnamed daughter of Roger who are also mentioned as Roger's tenants.

ii, fol. 083b; ii, fol. 083b

Uxor Quintini []
Occurs Domesday Leicestershire as one of a handful of English almsmen of the king. Presumably a widow.

i, fol. 231b; i, fol. 231b

Uxor Radulfi Capellani
Occurs Domesday Herefordshire.

i, fol. 187c; i, fol. 187c

Uxor Roberti Burdet
Occurs as a tenant of Hugh de Grandmesnil in Domesday Leicestershire, probably holding in dower since her husband Robert was dead in 1086. Mother of Hugh Burdet (q.v.), to whom her land descended.

i, fol. 232c; i, fol. 234c

Uxor Salie []
Tenant of Richard de Clare, occurs Domesday Surrey. Her status, whether as tenant in her own right or as a widow, is uncertain. Cf. Salio presbyter, witness to a charter of Stoke-by-Clare (Cart., 137) in the early twelfth century.

i, fol. 34d; i, fol. 34d; i, fol. 35b

Uxor Siuuardi Presbyteri
Englishwoman, occurs Domesday Lincolnshire.

i, fol. 336b

Uxor Uluuard []
Englishwoman, occurs in Domerset Somerset.

i, fol. 87b

Uxor Wenesii []
Occurs in Domesday Wiltshire.

i, fol. 74b

Uxor Willelmi De Wateuile
The wife of William de Watteville was, like her husband, a tenant of Willliam de Warenne in Domesday Sussex.

i, fol. 27b; i, fol. 27b

Uxoris Rogeri De Iuri
Occurs as the wife of Roger d'Ivry (q.v.) in Domesday Oxfordshire. She was Adelina, a daughter of Hugh de Grandmesnil and Adelicia de Beaumont. Her husband predeceased her and she herself died c.1110/11 (Ord. Vit. ii, 166, Chron. Abing. ii, 72–3). She gave charters for Abingdon Abbey (Chron. Abingdon ii, 72–4, RRAN ii, 973 as a widow. She was also a benefactor of St Peter's, Gloucester (Cart., i, 176, ii, 19; RRAN ii, 684,1006,1041). and of Saint-Evroul (RRAN ii, 1235). She held a small amount of land in her own right in Domesday Book, including at Islip, Oxfordshire, which she gave to the abbey of Bec (Porée, Bec, i, 468, citing BN lat. 12884, fol. 259). Around 1125, when Robert de Courcy gave Bec the manor of Cottisford, Bec renounced its claim on the church and mill of Islip and on the land of Ralph Macer. Ralph Macer was a tenant of Adelina's daughter Adelisa in Rowington, Warwickshire, a manor held in 1086 by Roger d'Ivry from Hugh de Grandmesnil. Adelisa confirmed several of her mother's grants. There is little doubt that she was the sole surviving child and heir of both her parents.

Regesta regum Anglo-Normannorum III, No. 345; i, fol. 160b; i, fol. 160c; i, fol. 160b

Vitalis De Canterbire
Occurs Domesday Kent as a tenant of Archbishop Lanfranc and Odo of Bayeux, ancestor of the de Shofford (in Maidstone) family. Succeed by his son Haimo, father of William, temp. Henry I. On Haimo son of Vitalis of Shofford see W.G. Urry, 'Normans in Canterbury', Ann. de Normandie 1958, 131–2.

i, fol. 007a; Ballard, Inquisition of St Augustine's (1920), fols 24r–28r; Douglas, ed., Domesday Monachorum (1944), p. 105; i, fol. 003c; i, fol. 012d; Ballard, Inquisition of St Augustine's (1920), fols 20r–23v; i, fol. 003d; i, fol. 010a; i, fol. 010a; i, fol. 003d

Vitalis De Colinton
Domesday tenant of Baldwin of Exeter, Odo fitz Gamelin and Roger de Courseulles. Surnamed de Colinton, from Colyton, in Exon, he had held some of the land recorded as his in 1086 in or before 1066.

i, fol. 98a; i, fol. 94c; i, fol. 94b; i, fol. 80b; i, fol. 116d; i, fol. 107d

Vitalis Presbiter
Occurs Domesday Hampshire and perhaps also in Wiltshire. Succeeded by a son Turstin, whose holdings Henry I gave as a prebend to Roger, bishop of Salisbury, c.1107 (Sarum Charters, ii; RRAN ii, 824).

i, fol. 65c; i, fol. 39b

Vitalis []
Occurs in Essex Domesdayas a tenant of Ranulf Peverel.

ii, fol. 074a; ii, fol. 073b; ii, fol. 055b; ii, fol. 039a

Vitalis []
Domesday tenant of Robert de Tosny of Stafford. His son Arnold of Hilderstone was a benefactor of Stone priory in 1136 (VCH Staffs iv, 33).

i, fol. 249a

Vitalis []
Domesday tenant of Guy de Craon in Lincolnshire.

i, fol. 367c; i, fol. 367d; i, fol. 368a

W Hurant
Occurs once as a tenant of Richard de Clare in Domesday Suffolk in Denham. The tithes of Denham were given to Stoke prioy by Richard fitz Hugh (q.v.) before 1117.

ii, fol. 390b

W Peret
Domesday tenant of Richard de Clare in Suffolk.

ii, fol. 396b

Wadard []
Norman, tenant of Odo of Bayeux in Domesday Kent, he was one of the knights represented by name in the Bayeux tapestry (cf. H. Prentout, in Revue historique 176, 1935, pp. 21–3). He shared the forfeiture of Odo of Bayeux, effective at the time he appeared in Domesday Book, though he was probably the father of another of Odo's tenants, Rainald Wadard (q.v.), who retained his holdings. He possibly occurs in the cartulary of Préaux (see Prentout op. cit.), where Wadard and two of his sons, Martin and Simon, attest a grant of the tithes of Marbuef (Eure) c.1078/96. Wadard's Domesday holdings were granted to Manasser Arsic early in the reign of Henry I (Sanders, 36).

i, fol. 155d; i, fol. 156a; i, fol. 342d; i, fol. 343a; i, fol. 343a; i, fol. 343b; i, fol. 343c; i, fol. 342c; i, fol. 342c; i, fol. 155d; i, fol. 156b; i, fol. 156a; i, fol. 156a; i, fol. 156a; i, fol. 156a; i, fol. 156c; i, fol. 156b; i, fol. 155d; i, fol. 156b; i, fol. 156b; i, fol. 156b; i, fol. 156b; i, fol. 32a; i, fol. 001a; i, fol. 012c; i, fol. 007c; i, fol. 002b; i, fol. 156b; i, fol. 002d; Ballard, Inquisition of St Augustine's (1920), fols 24r–28r; i, fol. 77b; i, fol. 77b; i, fol. 66b; i, fol. 342c; i, fol. 238d; i, fol. 238d; i, fol. 342a; i, fol. 342a; i, fol. 342a; i, fol. 342b; i, fol. 012c; i, fol. 006b; i, fol. 006b; i, fol. 010c; i, fol. 010c

Wala Presbiter
Occurs Domesday Norfolk.

ii, fol. 117a; ii, fol. 118a

Walbert []
Occurs in Domesday Lincolnshire and the Lindsey Survey (1115/18) as a tenant of the bishop of Durham. Possibly the same as the Walbert who occurs in Domesday Staffordshire as a tenant of William de Picquigny.

Lindsey Survey, BL ms Cotton Claudius C v, fols 9–18; i, fol. 340c; i, fol. 250a; i, fol. 341b; i, fol. 249b; i, fol. 250a; i, fol. 249d; i, fol. 340c

Walchelin De Rosay
Domesday tenant of William de Warenne. Identified as son of Lambert de Rosay, another of William's tenants, by grants to Castle Acre priory. From Rosay, Seine-Maritime, arr. Dieppe, cant. Bellencombre (Loyd, 86).

ii, fol. 162b; Dugdale, Monasticon Anglicanum, IV, p. 49, No. I; Clay, Early Yorkshire Charters (1949), VIII, No. 22; Dugdale, Monasticon Anglicanum, IV, p. 50, No. III

Walchelin Episcopus Wintonensis
Royal chaplain, canon of Rouen; brother of Simeon abbot of Ely and uncle of
Gerard the chancellor, later archbishop of York (cf. D. Spear, 'The canons of
Rouen in the ducal period', Annales de Normandie, 41, 1991). Bishop from 23
May 1070 until his death on 3 January 1098. EEA viii, pp. xxx–ii.

Dugdale, Monasticon Anglicanum, IV, p. 13, No. IV; Clay, Early Yorkshire
Charters (1949), VIII, No. 4; i, fol. 38c; i, fol. 87c; i, fol. 133b; i, fol. 155a;
Gibbs, Early Charters of St Pauls (1939), No. 13; Gibbs, Early Charters of St
Pauls (1939), No. 15; Hart, Cartularium Monasterii de Rameseia, No. CL;
Regesta regum Anglo-Normannorum III, No. 261; Douglas, Feudal Documents
from Bury St Edmunds, No. 17; Regesta regum Anglo-Normannorum III, I,
Appendix, no. XXV; i, fol. 56b; i, fol. 90d; i, fol. 51a; i, fol. 38b; i, fol. 51a; ii, fol.
107b; Mason, Westminster Abbey Charters (1988), No. 488; i, fol. 51a; i, fol.
87d; i, fol. 154a; i, fol. 58b; i, fol. 58b; i, fol. 52c; i, fol. 58b; i, fol. 58b; i, fol.
155a; i, fol. 155a; i, fol. 65c; i, fol. 65c; i, fol. 65d; i, fol. 65d; i, fol. 65d; i, fol.
65d; i, fol. 65d; i, fol. 65d; i, fol. 65d; i, fol. 31a; i, fol. 65d; i, fol. 87d; i, fol. 87c;
i, fol. 87c; i, fol. 40b; i, fol. 41a; i, fol. 40a; i, fol. 40a; i, fol. 41d; i, fol. 40a; i, fol.
40a; i, fol. 40b; i, fol. 40b; i, fol. 40b; i, fol. 87c; i, fol. 143d; i, fol. 190b; i, fol.
190b; i, fol. 65c; i, fol. 190b; i, fol. 143d; i, fol. 87c; i, fol. 41a; i, fol. 87c; i, fol.
133b; i, fol. 40c; i, fol. 41b; i, fol. 41b; i, fol. 87c; i, fol. 41a; i, fol. 87c; i, fol. 40d;
i, fol. 40c; i, fol. 41d; i, fol. 40c; i, fol. 41c; i, fol. 41a; i, fol. 40c; i, fol. 40d; i, fol.
41d; i, fol. 40c; i, fol. 41d; i, fol. 40d; i, fol. 41d; i, fol. 41d; i, fol. 40c; i, fol. 87c;
i, fol. 87c; i, fol. 87c; i, fol. 87c; i, fol. 87c; i, fol. 41b; i, fol. 40a; i, fol. 41d; i, fol.
87c; i, fol. 87c; i, fol. 41c; i, fol. 87c; i, fol. 40c; i, fol. 87c; i, fol. 41c; i, fol. 41c; i,
fol. 41c; i, fol. 41a; i, fol. 87c; i, fol. 87c; i, fol. 87c; Dugdale, Monasticon
Anglicanum, III, pp. 544–46, No. I; Clay, Early Yorkshire Charters (1949), VIII,
No. 6; Dugdale, Monasticon Anglicanum, III, p. 377, No. II; i, fol. 40a; i, fol.
143d; Dugdale, Monasticon Anglicanum, II, p. 267, No. X

Walchelin []
Norman, Domesday tenant of Walter de Aincourt in Nottinghamshire. Perhaps an
ancestor of the Croc family of Aslacton; cf. Foulds, Thurgarton Cart., p. 214.

i, fol. 288d; i, fol. 288d

Walchelin []
Domesday tenant of the bishop of Coutances. His Northamptonshire holdings
were given to Simon I de Senlis of Northampton. See Farrer, HKF ii, 324.

i, fol. 225b; i, fol. 220c; i, fol. 220c; i, fol. 220c; i, fol. 220c; i, fol. 220c; i, fol.
220c

Walchelin []
Norman, Domesday tenant of Henry de Ferrers. Possibly a relative of Henry,
whose father was named Walchelin. Benefactor of Tutbury. Ancestor of the
Boscherville family; cf. Cart. Tutbury, 125.

Dugdale, Monasticon Anglicanum, III, pp. 392–93, No. II; i, fol. 233b; i, fol.
242b; i, fol. 274d; i, fol. 242b

Walchelin []
Domesday tenant of Earl Roger.

i, fol. 257c; i, fol. 257c

Walchelin Nepos Episcopi
Walchelin, nepos of Bishop Walchelin of Winchester (1070–98), occurs in

Domesday as a tenant of Archbishop Thomas of York.

> i, fol. 340b; i, fol. 340b; i, fol. 340b; i, fol. 340b; i, fol. 230b; i, fol. 230b; i, fol. 230b; i, fol. 230b; i, fol. 340a; i, fol. 340a; i, fol. 303a; i, fol. 164c

Walcher []
Norman, Domesday tenant of Ralph Bainard in Essex.

> ii, fol. 70a; ii, fol. 69a

Waldin Brito
Tenant-in-chief in Domesday Lincolnshire and tenant of another Breton, Guy de Craon.

> i, fol. 367c; Lincolnshire Claims (Domesday Book), fols 376d–377c; i, fol. 365c; i, fol. 365b; i, fol. 365b; i, fol. 365b

Waldin Ingeniator
Tenant-in-chief in Domesday Lincolnshire, where his tenant was William. William was almost certainly the ancestor of the de Kyme family of Sotby, Lincolnshire (Sanders, 79; Farrer, HKF ii, 118–19). In 1115/18, at the Lindsey Survey, Simon fitz William was holding Waldin's manors in chief, suggesting that his father was Waldin's heir, either his son or son-in-law.

> i, fol. 298a; i, fol. 353d; i, fol. 298a; i, fol. 365c; i, fol. 365c; i, fol. 365c; i, fol. 365c; i, fol. 365c; i, fol. 365c; i, fol. 365c

Waldin []
Domesday tenant of Judhael of Totnes. In the thirteenth century his fees were held by the Pipards (Fees, 775, 794).

> i, fol. 110a; i, fol. 108c; i, fol. 110a; i, fol. 109c

Waleran Filius Ranulfi
Waleran son of Ranulf the moneyer, from Vaims, Manche, in west Normandy, father of John fitz Waleran, a Domesday tenant-in-chief in Essex. He granted the church of Westcheap, London, and that of Bures St Mary, Essex, to Sainte-Trinité de Caen (Actes caen. nos. 4–5), before 1077. His son had succeeded by 1086. He is mentioned in the 1129 Pipe Roll as the grandfather of John's daughter Juliana. Comp. Peer. xii, 272.

> Hamilton, Inquisitio Eliensis (1876), pp. 192–95; Pipe Roll 31 Henry I, 058–e; Pipe Roll 31 Henry I, 058–e; ii, fol. 006b

Waleran Venator
Norman, Domesday tenant-in-chief (Sanders, 96). His heir in 1129/30 appears to have been his grandson Waleran fitz William.

> i, fol. 77a; i, fol. 47a; i, fol. 50a; i, fol. 65c; ii, fol. 101b; i, fol. 66d; i, fol. 77c; i, fol. 48b; i, fol. 43c,d; i, fol. 51c; i, fol. 72a; i, fol. 48c; i, fol. 48b; i, fol. 72a; i, fol. 72b; i, fol. 72b; i, fol. 72a; i, fol. 82c; i, fol. 82b

Wallef []
Englishman, Domesday tenant of the count of Meulan in Warwickshire.

> i, fol. 240b; i, fol. 240b; i, fol. 240c

Walo []
Domesday tenant of the count of Eu in Sussex. A confirmation by Henry I for Saint-Martin le Bois of 1107–1110 recorded the grants of the men of Henry count of Eu, including that of Walo de Hairencurt (Héricourt-en-Caux, Seine-Maritime)

in Normandy and in England at Hooe (Chanteux, Rec. Actes. Henri I, no. 9). Although Walo does not occur at Hooe in Domesday, this reference is probably to the same person.

i, fol. 19b; i, fol. 18c

Walo []

Domesday tenant of Jocelyn fitz Lambert in Lincolnshire,

i, fol. 359b; i, fol. 359a

Walter Arbalistarius

Domesday tenant of Robert Malet in Suffolk. Benefactor of Eye Priory (Cart., 1; cf. ibid., 326).

ii, fol. 154a; ii, fol. 324a; ii, fol. 324a; Brown, Eye Priory Cartulary (1992–94), No. 40; Brown, Eye Priory Cartulary (1992–94), No. 55; Brown, Eye Priory Cartulary (1992–94), No. 326; Brown, Eye Priory Cartulary (1992–94), No. 1; ii, fol. 320a; Brown, Eye Priory Cartulary (1992–94), No. 1; i, fol. 169a; i, fol. 162a; i, fol. 169a; i, fol. 169a; i, fol. 169a; i, fol. 169a; i, fol. 162b; ii, fol. 321a; ii, fol. 321a; ii, fol. 321a

Walter Arbalistarius

Domesday tenant of Roger de Limesy in Somerset, described in Exon as arbalistarius; probably not the man of the name who was a tenant of Robert Malet in Suffolk, but perhaps the man who occurs in Ralph's charter for Hertford priory as Walter de Bibbeswrde.

i, fol. 97a; Dugdale, Monasticon Anglicanum, III, pp. 299–300, No. I

Walter Burgundiensis

Tenant of Gotshelm de Claville in Domesday Devon. His surname is given as Borgundiensis (relative to DB 25.1 where he is not named as Gotshelm's tenant) and Borgoin in Exon. A family of this surname occurs at Le Ménil-Guenelon in the Cotentin in the early thirteenth century (BN 10087, 111/291, 110–11/290; BN lat. 5441(2), p. 36).

i, fol. 112d; i, fol. 112d

Walter Canonicus Sancti Pauli

Domesday canon of St Paul's. See FEA i, 89.

i, fol. 128b

Walter Cenomannensis

Occurs Domesday Somerset as a tenant of Gilbert fitz Turold (q.v.), who was probably a man of the Tosnys. His byname, which refers to Maine or its capital Le Mans, is provided by the Tax Return for Chewton Hundred. The Mansel family held of the honour of Tosny at Bailleul-la-Campagne, Eure, cant. Saint-André (Musset, 'Les Tosny', Francia v, p. 77).

i, fol. 98b; i, fol. 98b

Walter Cocus

Occurs in Domesday Essex.

ii, fol. 095a; ii, fol. 095a; ii, fol. 095a

Walter Dapifer

Domesday tenant of Walter de Claville, identified as his steward (dapifer) in Exon.

i, fol. 112b; i, fol. 112b; i, fol. 112b

Walter Dapifer

Tenant of Peter de Valognes; probably the man named Walter dapifer in Peter's foundation charter for Binham.

ii, fol. 079a; Dugdale, Monasticon Anglicanum, III, pp. 345–46, No. I

Walter De Aincurt

Domesday tenant-in-chief, from Ancourt, Seine-Maritime, arr. Dieppe, cant. Offranville, lord of Blankney, Lincolnshire (Loyd, 2; Sanders, 15). He was dead by 1103 and was succeeded by his son Ralph. Another son William died whilst being raised at the court of William I, according to a Lincoln cathedral epitaph which claimed Walter as a kinsman of both the king and Bishop Remigius of Lincoln (Stenton, Eng. Feud. p. 32 note; Bates, Remigius, p. 3). Walter and his descendants are discussed in Foulds, Cart. Thurgarton, pp. xl–cxx.

i, fol. 221a; i, fol. 221a; i, fol. 144a; i, fol. 340a; i, fol. 144a; i, fol. 144a; i, fol. 144a; i, fol. 326b; i, fol. 361a; i, fol. 226b; i, fol. 288c; i, fol. 276c; i, fol. 289a; i, fol. 276c; i, fol. 276c; i, fol. 276c; i, fol. 276c; i, fol. 276c; i, fol. 276c; i, fol. 276c; i, fol. 276c; i, fol. 276c; i, fol. 276c; i, fol. 276c; i, fol. 226b; i, fol. 276c; i, fol. 361a; i, fol. 361a; i, fol. 361a; i, fol. 340a; i, fol. 361a; i, fol. 361a; i, fol. 361b; i, fol. 361b; i, fol. 326b; i, fol. 326b; i, fol. 361b; i, fol. 326b; i, fol. 361b; i, fol. 361b; i, fol. 361b; i, fol. 361a; i, fol. 326b; i, fol. 288c; i, fol. 361b; i, fol. 288c; i, fol. 288d; i, fol. 289a; i, fol. 288c; i, fol. 288c; i, fol. 288c; i, fol. 288c; i, fol. 288c; i, fol. 288d; i, fol. 288d; i, fol. 288d; i, fol. 288c; Lincolnshire Claims (Domesday Book), fols 376d–377c; i, fol. 288c; i, fol. 289a; i, fol. 361b; i, fol. 289a; i, fol. 289a; i, fol. 289a; i, fol. 288d; i, fol. 289a; i, fol. 289a; i, fol. 288d; i, fol. 288d; i, fol. 288d; i, fol. 288d; i, fol. 288d; i, fol. 288d; i, fol. 288d; i, fol. 289a; Clay, Early Yorkshire Charters (1949), VIII, No. 5; Dugdale, Monasticon Anglicanum, III, pp. 548–50, No. V

Walter De Appeuile

Domesday tenant of William of Arques in Kent; named from Appeville-le-Petit, Seine-Maritime, arr. Dieppe, cant. Offranville, comm. Hautot-sur-Mer (Loyd, 5).

i, fol. 009c

Walter De Bec

Norman, from Le Bec-aux-Cauchois, Seine-Maritime, cant. Valmont, a dependency of Angerville-la-Martel, Domesday tenant of Walter Giffard. Occurs as a benefactor of Saint-Georges-de-Boscherville c.1060 (Fauroux, 197). Walter II Giffard and his wife Agnes made a grant to Tréport attested by Robert de Becco and Walter his brother (Hist. Tréport, 236ff). Walter de Bec was pardoned Danegeld in Buckinghamshire in 1129/30; this was probably the son of the Domesday Walter.

i, fol. 147c; Pipe Roll 31 Henry I, 102–bu

Walter De Belmeis

Walter de Beaumais, tenant of Eustache of Huntingdon and hence probably from Beaumais, Seine-Maritime, cant. Duclair. Perhaps the same as the Gauterius de Belmes who gave an acre of land in Montigny, Seine-Maritime, cant. Maromme, to Saint-Georges-de-Boscherville before 1066 (Fauroux, 197, p. 385). In IE, 111, he appears as Walter de Helmes. A second Walter de Belmeis (q.v.) occurs in Huntingdonshire in the 1150s.

i, fol. 199d; i, fol. 199d; Hart, Cartularium Monasterii de Rameseia, No. CXLIX

Walter De Burh
Occurs Domesday Worcestershire.

i, fol. 173d

Walter De Cadomo
Walter fitz Alberic de Cadomo, Norman from Caen (Calvados). Important Domesday tenant of Robert Malet, attested the foundation charter of Eye priory as Walter of Huntingfield. According to a foundation narrative of Sibton Abbey (Cart., no. 470), in 1066 Walter came to England with Robert Malet (Walterus de Cadomo venit [in Angliam] cum Roberto Malet) and afterwards held the barony of Horsford under Robert. Horsford was but a manor held under the honour of Eye by Walter's descendants, but the word reflects the importance of Walter's holdings from Robert. Walter fitz Alberic attested a gift of land to the abbey of Montivilliers made by Robert fitz Theobald of Epouville with the consent of Walter Giffard, c.1065–76 (Bouvris, App. no. 28). Father of three sons, Robert (ancestor of the de Chesny family), Ralph and Roger (ancestor of the Huntingfield family). See C.P. Lewis, 'The King and Eye', EHR, 103 (1989), 577–8; K.S.B. Keats-Rohan, 'Domesday Book and the Malets', Nottingham Medieval Studies xli (1997), 13–51.

ii, fol. 155a; ii, fol. 155a; ii, fol. 155a; ii, fol. 154b; ii, fol. 154b; ii, fol. 154a; i, fol. 196b; ii, fol. 154a; ii, fol. 325b; ii, fol. 325b; ii, fol. 324b; ii, fol. 324b; ii, fol. 317a; ii, fol. 312b; ii, fol. 313a; ii, fol. 312b; ii, fol. 154a; ii, fol. 320a; ii, fol. 304b; ii, fol. 329b; ii, fol. 327b; ii, fol. 313b; ii, fol. 304b; ii, fol. 328a; ii, fol. 394b; ii, fol. 313b; ii, fol. 314a; ii, fol. 318a; ii, fol. 318a; ii, fol. 318a; ii, fol. 318a; Brown, Sibton Abbey Cartularies and Charters (1987), No. 470; ii, fol. 318a; Brown, Sibton Abbey Cartularies and Charters (1987), No. 479; ii, fol. 276b; ii, fol. 304a; ii, fol. 306b; ii, fol. 306b; i, fol. 196b; i, fol. 196b; ii, fol. 306b; ii, fol. 319b; ii, fol. 319a; ii, fol. 327b; ii, fol. 310b; ii, fol. 308a; ii, fol. 308a; ii, fol. 308a; ii, fol. 308a; ii, fol. 308a

Walter De Cambremer
Occurs Domesday Kent, named from Cambremer, Calvados, arr. Caen.

i, fol. 001c; Ballard, Inquisition of St Augustine's (1920), fols 24r–28r

Walter De Clauile
Norman, brother of Gotshelm, tenants-in-chief and co-tenants in Devon in 1086. In 1166 his heir was a second Walter de Claville, brother of Ralph and Gilbert, who held his fees of the honour of Gloucester. His toponym could refer to several different and widely scattered places in Normandy.

i, fol. 108a; i, fol. 112c; i, fol. 112b; i, fol. 112c; i, fol. 112b; i, fol. 112c; i, fol. 112c; i, fol. 112b; i, fol. 112c; i, fol. 112c; i, fol. 112c; i, fol. 112b

Walter De Cleis
Norman, Domesday juror in Northstow and Chilford Hundreds, Cambridgeshire. Possibly the Walter who was a tenant of both Picot of Cambridge and Count Alan in Northstow Hundred (Lewis, 'Jurors', 40). Probably named from Clais, Seine-Maritime, cant. Londinières.

i, fol. 201b; i, fol. 195b; Hamilton, Inquisitio Comitatus Cantabrigiensis, pp. 1–93; Hamilton, Inquisitio Eliensis (1876), pp. 97–100; Hamilton, Inquisitio Comitatus Cantabrigiensis, pp. 1–93

Walter De Duaco

Also known in Domesday or Exon Domesday as Walter Flandrensis and by a hypocoristic form of his name, Walscin, Walter of Douai, Nord, was falsely identified with Walter I castellan of Douai by Felix Brassart, who published the documents that prove the two were different persons (Histoire du château et de la châtellenie de Douai depuis le Xe siècle jusqu'en 1798, 3 vols, 1877–87, i, pp. 49ff., esp. 88–90, ii, nos. xii, xxiv). The castellan was married to Ermentrude but had no heirs, was disgraced in the 1080s and thereafter lived for several years as a monk of Saint-Eloi. England's Walter of Douai was doubtless one of the castellan's men and quite possibly a close relation. The castellan attested charters in the company of Sigar and Arnulf de Cioches, of whom the former was also a Domesday tenant-in-chief. The Domesday Walter married twice, firstly to an English woman, Eadgytha widow of Hemming (Cart. Glastonbury i, 126–8), whose is named in Domesday as Walter's predecessor for the manor of Uffculme, Devon, and secondly to Emma, mother of his sons Geoffrey and Robert. An illness tempted him, on the advice of his brother Raimar, a clerk, to become a monk of Glastonbury; however, his tenants forcibly tore his monk's robes off and dragged him back into the lay estate, fearful that they might never again have such a good lord, even though the monks had got as far as tonsuring him and still had his hair to prove it. He died c.1107 when his fief was divided into the honour of Bampton, which went to his son Robert, and that of Castle Cary, which passed to Ralph Lovel whose relationship to Walter is unknown. Ralph's first certain appearance was in 1122 (RRAN ii, 1342) so it is possible that he was either Walter's grandson, son of Geoffrey, or Geoffrey's son-in-law. Geoffrey survived his father but disappears from documents shortly afterwards.

Brassart's preuves and the various chronicles of the Cambresis leave no doubt that Walter formed part of an extended parentèle of the region, traceable from the tenth century onward, which included both Walter the castellan and our Walter of Douai. He appears to have been one of a group of Flemish Domesday tenants-in-chief, called Walter, Walter brother of Seiher, Hugh, and Winemar. There were numerous connexions between these tenants-in-chief – the first three of whom were probably closely related – who held land from each other and from Countess Judith (DB Bedfordshire 32, 33, 34, 36, 37, DB Northamptonshire 39, 40, 48, 49, 56.54–7). Farrer plausibly suggested that Walter brother of Seiher was uncle to Walter (HKF i, 60), who in turn is likely to have been the brother of Hugh. Cf. Brassart, Douai, ii, no. xii, given by Walter castellan of Douai in 1076 and mentioning a Walter de Douai son of Ursion [not identifiable with our Walter], Sohier de Lohes, two men named Ulric – the name of the Domesday Walter of Douai's steward (Chart. Glastonbury i, 228) – and the brother of one of them, Dodin, homonym of a tenant of Countess Judith (DB Morthants. 56.52). Cart. de Hesdin, no. 50 (calendared in RRAN i, 360), was attested by Wenemar of Lens, as was Actes des comtes de Flandres, no. 18 (1094–5), no. 23 (1093) being attested by Walter de Lens; Cartulaire de Saint-Pierre de Mont-Blandin, nos. 132–3 (1056) were attested by Robert and Wenemar de Lens. Onomastic evidence from the continent, contained in both charters and chronicles, from the diocese of Cambrai clearly indicates that these men originated in the county of Lens, as did Countess Judith who was daughter of Lambert count of Lens. Walter castellan of Douai, son of Hugh d'Oisi of Douai, was the grandson and heir of Walter castellan of Cambrai (d.1045). This Walter was the son of Walter of Lens, castellan of Cambrai (d.1011); Walter of Lens, who had a second son called Walter le Jeune and a son Seiher, was the brother of Seiher of Lens and the son of another Walter (Chronicon cameracense et atrebatense, sive historia utriusque ecclesiæ . . . conscripta a Balderico Noviomensi, PL cxlix, col. 119–122, and idem, Ex historia Cameracensi, col. 182).

i, fol. 90d; i, fol. 90a; i, fol. 90b; i, fol. 90b; ii, fol. 091a; ii, fol. 091a; ii, fol. 091a; i, fol. 93b; i, fol. 111d; i, fol. 98c; i, fol. 111d; i, fol. 112a; i, fol. 112a; i, fol. 111d; i, fol. 111d; i, fol. 006d; i, fol. 95a; i, fol. 95b; i, fol. 95a; i, fol. 111c; i, fol. 95c; i, fol. 111d; i, fol. 95c; i, fol. 95c; i, fol. 95b; i, fol. 95a; i, fol. 95a; i, fol. 95b; i, fol. 36a; i, fol. 95b; Hunt, Bath Chartulary, Som. Rec. Soc. 7 (1893), No. 35; Watkin, Chartulary of Glastonbury 3, SRS 64 (1950), pp. 126–28

Walter De Gloecestria
Walter son of Roger de Pitres, nephew of Durand of Gloucester. Norman from Pitres, Eure, cant. Pont-de-l'Arche. The name of his mother, Adeliza, is supplied in Cart. S. Petri Gloc. i, 81, 125, 188–9, 353; ii, 129. He occurs ibid., i, 123, as donor of Westwood for the soul of his brother Herbert, and confirming a grant of his father Roger at Colne (ibid., ii, 235). At his death in 1129 he left issue by his wife Bertha of Miles of Gloucester (q.v.) and Matilda, wife of Richard fitz Pons (q.v.); Comp. Peer. vi, 451–7.

Walker, Charters of the Earldom of Hereford (1964), No. 11; Walker, Charters of the Earldom of Hereford (1964), No. 69; Clay, Early Yorkshire Charters (1955), X, No. 2; Darlington, Cartulary of Worcester: Reg. I (1962–3), No. 40; Round, Ancient Charters (1888), No. 11; Brown, Eye Priory Cartulary (1992–94), No. 26; Round, Ancient Charters (1888), No. 10; Round, Ancient Charters (1888), No. 3; Rees, Cartulary of Shrewsbury Abbey (1975), No. 35; Pipe Roll 31 Henry I, 107–wk; Regesta regum Anglo-Normannorum III, No. 345; Hart, Cartularium Monasterii de Rameseia, No. CLXXVIII; Round, Ancient Charters (1888), No. 13; Walker, Charters of the Earldom of Hereford (1964), No. 60; Ellis, 'Landholders of Gloucestershire' (1880), pp. 91–93; Dugdale, Monasticon Anglicanum, III, p. 448, No. III; Chibnall, English Lands of Abbey of Bec (1951), No. XVII; i, fol. 169a; i, fol. 48c; i, fol. 164d; i, fol. 48c; i, fol. 169a; i, fol. 169a; Mason, Beauchamp Cartulary Charters (1980), No. 5; Stenton, English Feudalism, App., No. 44; Hart, Cartularium Monasterii de Rameseia, No. CLXVIII; i, fol. 186c; i, fol. 186c; Walker, Charters of the Earldom of Hereford (1964), No. 1; Regesta regum Anglo-Normannorum III, No. 389; Darlington, Cartulary of Worcester: Reg. I (1962–3), No. 40; Darlington, Cartulary of Worcester: Reg. I (1962–3), No. 24; Darlington, Cartulary of Worcester: Reg. I (1962–3), No. 39; Regesta regum Anglo-Normannorum III, No. 345; Ellis, 'Landholders of Gloucestershire' (1880), pp. 91–93; Regesta regum Anglo-Normannorum III, No. 345

Walter De Grandcurt
Norman, from Grandcourt, Seine-Maritime, arr. Neufchâtel, cant. Londinières (Loyd, 47), Domesday tenant of William de Warenne. Benefactor of Lewes priory, his grants were confirmed by William II de Warenne (1088–1138), in whose time Ralph and Reiner de Grandcourt (q.v.) occur. Cf. Farrer, HKF iii, 389; Genealogist n.s. xxi, 20. His land at Burnham Thorpe and Harpley, Norfolk, passed to Philip de Candos (q.v.) by the early twelfth century. According to an inquest of 43 Henry III, Walter died without issue and was succeeded by a brother Hugh, father of Ralph (d.s.p.) and Humphrey (Genealogist xxi, p. 20, citing Curia Regis Roll)

ii, fol. 169a; i, fol. 196c; ii, fol. 161b; Clay, Early Yorkshire Charters (1949),

VIII, No. 12; i, fol. 196b; Dugdale, Monasticon Anglicanum, IV, p. 14, No. VI; Clay, Early Yorkshire Charters (1949), VIII, No. 6; ii, fol. 169a; ii, fol. 169a

Walter De Herbercourt
Domesday tenant of William de Warenne in Norfolk. Walter de Herbercourt, from Hébécourt, cant. Etrepagny, Eure, is identifiable from a charter in the Castle Acre Cartulary (BL 2110, fol. 5v)

ii, fol. 162b; ii, fol. 162b

Walter De Ispania
Brother of Alfred de Ispania (q.v.) according to Exon. A Walter de Hispania attested a charter of Ralph fitz Roger de Conches (Tosny) for Saint-Evroul (Le Prevost, Eure, iii, 283).

i, fol. 97c; i, fol. 97a; i, fol. 97c

Walter De Laceio
Norman from Lassy, arr. Vire, cant. Condé-le-Noireau, Calvados (Loyd, 53), brother of Ilbert de Lacy of Pontefract. First Lacy lord of Weobley, Herefordshire, he died in 1085 (Hist. S. Petri Glocs. i, 73), when he was succeeded by his son Roger. He left by his wife Emma or Emmelina his heir Roger, Hugh, Walter, abbot of Gloucester. See Wightman, Lacy Family, 55–6, 120–9, 168–9; Sanders, 94. For a corrective of Wightman's view that Walter de Lacy was a man of William fitz Osbern of Breteuil, see C. Lewis in Anglo-Norman Studies vii (1985), 203–4.

Walker, Charters of the Earldom of Hereford (1964), No. 18; Regesta regum Anglo-Normannorum III, No. 345; Walker, Charters of the Earldom of Hereford (1964), No. 63; i, fol. 164a; Regesta regum Anglo-Normannorum III, No. 398

Walter De Magnavilla
Son and tenant of Geoffrey de Mandeville in Domesday Essex. He and his wife Gunnild gave their Essex manors of Chatham, Notley, Broomfield and Ridley to St Albans Abbey (Mon. Ang. ii, 220). William, Walter and Richard de Mandeville, sons of Geoffrey, attested his charter for Westminster 1085/6 (Westminster Chh., 462). He was probably succeeded in the early twelfth century by his son William, father of Walter II de Mandeville (q.v.), who occurs c.1160.

ii, fol. 060a; ii, fol. 060a; ii, fol. 058a; ii, fol. 058a; i, fol. 139d; Mason, Westminster Abbey Charters (1988), No. 462; ii, fol. 058b; ii, fol. 058b

Walter De Mucedent
Norman, from Muchedent, Seine-Maritime, arr. Dieppe, cant. Longueville-sur-Scie, tenant in Domesday Middlesex of Walter fitz Other.

i, fol. 130a; i, fol. 130a

Walter De Omonville
Norman, Domesday tenant of Ruald Abobed in Devon; his toponym is supplied by Exon Domesday. He was perhaps named from Omonville-La-Foliot, Manche, arr. Coutances, cant. La Haye-du-Puits, comm. Denneville, since Foliots appear in this part of Devon soon after 1086.

i, fol. 114d; i, fol. 115b; i, fol. 115b; i, fol. 115a; i, fol. 115a

Walter De Portes
The Walter who was tenant of Ralph de Tosny at Almely in Worcestershire in 1086 was probably the same person as the G. de Portes who attested Tosny charters of the 1120s. By 1150 the tenant was named as Richard de Portis in the

Worcestershire Survey. Named from Portes, Eure, cant. Conches, in the Tosny fief.Cf. Musset, 'Les Tosny', Francia v, 76–7.

i, fol. 176b; i, fol. 176b; i, fol. 176b; Mason, Beauchamp Cartulary Charters (1980), No. 358; Mason, Beauchamp Cartulary Charters (1980), No. 356

Walter De Ricarville

Norman, from Ricarville, Seine-Maritime, arr. Dieppe, cant. Envermeu (Loyd, 86). Occurs in Milites archiepiscopi as a man of Archbishop Lanfranc, probably the same as the Walter who held of Lanfranc at Malling in Sussex (Douglas, Dom. Mon, 41–2). Sheriff of Pevensey Rape sometime between 1086 and 1095. Some time before his death in 1095, Robert de Mortain complained that Walter of Ricarville had usurped land in Sussex that he had given to a cell of Mortain at Withyham in Hartfield; in 1086 this was held by a Walter, who was possibly de Ricarville, though could have been another Walter, ancestor of the Folkington family. Another possibility is that the two Walters were the same. In 1166 Robert de Ricarville held 10 fees of the count of Eu. In the twelfth century a Richard de Ricarville attested a Lewes charter concerning Beverington, also held in 1086 by a Walter from the count of Mortain (Chart. Lewes i, 134).

i, fol. 16c; i, fol. 21d; Douglas, ed., Domesday Monachorum (1944), p. 105

Walter De Risboil

Norman, Domesday tenant of Robert Malet in Suffolk. Walter is mentioned twice in Domesday. The form given for his toponym appears to relate to no place in Normandy and is likely to have been a cacography. One of the manors he held was Clakestorp, in Eyke. Land there was given for the founding of Eye by William de Rovilla, who, with his second wife Beatrice, gave his own charter for Eye granting the church of St Botulph, Iken, with land in Great Glemham, part of which was in the fief of Count Alan (Eye Cart., 136). Robert's tenants in Eye and Great Glemham included 'Walter' (DB Suffolk, 6.45; 191). Alan's tenants included W. Bole. Clakestorp seems to have passed to the Montcanisy fee of the honour of Eye (Brown, Eye Cart. ii, pp. 65–6). Rolville is La-Trinité-de Réville, Eure, cant. Broglie, where the Malet's held land from Robert's father's marriage to Esilia Crispin which they gave to Bec; see K. S. B. Keats-Rohan, 'Domesday Book and the Malets', Nottingham Medieval Studies xli (1997), 20–1, elaborating Porée, Histoire de Bec, i, 334 note 4. Also possible is Rebetz, Seine-Maritime, cant. Buchy.

ii, fol. 320a; ii, fol. 306b; ii, fol. 306a; ii, fol. 327a; ii, fol. 327a

Walter De Riuere

Norman, tenant-in-chief in Domeday Hampshire, and a tenant of Abingdon in Berkshire; brother of Jocelyn de Rivere. Possibly named from La Rivière-Thibouville, Eure. Occurs in Domesday Wiltshire as a son-in-law of Hugh fitz Baldric. At his death c.1084–97, in the time of Abbot Rainald of Abingdon, he left a son Walter, a minor in the custody of his uncle Jocelyn (Chron. Abing. ii, 23).

Stevenson, Chronicon Monasterii de Abingdon (1858) vol. II, pp. 4–6; i, fol. 58d; i, fol. 58d; i, fol. 73a

Walter De Sancto Walarico

Picard, son of Bernard, advocate of Saint-Valery-sur-Somme, seigneur of Dommart-en-Ponthieu, a descendant of Richard III of Normandy, according to Orderic Vitalis, who gave Bernard's parents as Gilbert advocate of Saint-Valéry and a daughter of Richard III and Papia 'de Envermeu' (Ord. Vit., iii, 252; v, 34). Father of Bernard, Walter and Guy (BN Coll. Picardie 93, p. 362). With his son Bernard he accompanied Robert duke of Normandy on the First Crusade (ibid., 58). Several kinsmen of his wife Elisabeth, sister of the Frenchman Miles de Montlhéry, were also on the expedition. In 1086 he held a small tenancy-in-chief in England. By 1129/30 he had been succeeded by his grandson Rainald, son of Bernard.

> i, fol. 130b; i, fol. 130a; ii, fol. 432b; ii, fol. 432b; ii, fol. 432b; ii, fol. 432b; ii, fol. 432b; ii, fol. 432b; Ellis, 'Landholders of Gloucestershire' (1880), pp. 91–93

Walter De Vernon

Norman tenant of Earl Hugh in Cheshire, Staffordshire and Oxfordshire. Brother, of Richard de Vernon (q.v.), and uncle of a Walchelin who succeeded him at Ness, Prenton and Ledsham. He occurs in a charter of 1113 (RRAN ii, 1022) and in the 1119 charter for St Werburgh given by Earl Richard, of which the authenticity is not beyond reproach. He was succeeded by a son Richard who was later deprived of the inheritance by Ranulf II (Rob. Torigny Chron. p. 172), though it was later restored, c.1154, to Richard's son Walter. HKF ii, 276.

> i, fol. 263d; i, fol. 157b; i, fol. 151a; Barraclough, Charters of AN Earls of Chester (1988), No. 3; Barraclough, Charters of AN Earls of Chester (1988), No. 28; i, fol. 265b; i, fol. 265b; i, fol. 265b; i, fol. 265b; i, fol. 151a; i, fol. 151a; i, fol. 151a; Barraclough, Charters of AN Earls of Chester (1988), No. 28; Barraclough, Charters of AN Earls of Chester (1988), No. 8; Barraclough, Charters of AN Earls of Chester (1988), No. 141

Walter Diaconus

Domesday tenant-in-chief in Suffolk and Essex. His fief was afterwards known as the barony of Little Easton (Sanders, 130). Domesday records that some of the fief had previously been held by Walter's brother Theoderic; other parts had been given to Walter by Queen Matilda. Father of his successor Robert fitz Walter alias Robert of Windsor (q.v.), Walter Mascerel, Alexander of Wix and Edith, wife first of Ralph, steward of Bury St Edmunds and secondly of Maurice of Windsor. Cf. L. Landon, 'The barony of Little Easton and the family of Hastings', Trans. Essex Arch. Soc. xix; B. Dodwell, 'Charters relating to the Honour of Bacton', in Stenton Miscellany.

> ii, fol. 086a; i, fol. 169a; ii, fol. 426a; ii, fol. 427a; ii, fol. 087a; ii, fol. 086b; ii, fol. 086b; ii, fol. 193a; ii, fol. 086b; ii, fol. 426b; ii, fol. 426a; ii, fol. 426a; ii, fol. 427a; ii, fol. 426b; ii, fol. 086a; ii, fol. 426b; ii, fol. 427b; ii, fol. 426b; ii, fol. 427a; ii, fol. 427a; ii, fol. 427a; ii, fol. 427b; ii, fol. 427b; ii, fol. 427b; ii, fol. 426b; ii, fol. 391a; ii, fol. 193a; ii, fol. 006b; i, fol. 169a; ii, fol. 117b; i, fol. 79a

Walter Filius Ercold

Norman, a tenant of Roger de Lacy in Domesday Gloucestershire. Wightman, Lacy Family, p. 156 n, suggested that he was the Walter who also occurs as a Lacy tenant in Herefordshire. He further suggested that the apparent escheat of this fee suggests that Walter rebelled with his lord in 1094 and shared his forfeiture and banishment.

> i, fol. 185a; i, fol. 184c; i, fol. 185a; i, fol. 184c; i, fol. 180b; i, fol. 168a

Walter Filius Grip

Norman, Domesday tenant of Robert Malet in Suffolk. Brother of Hugh fitz Grip, the sheriff of Dorset who had died by 1086. A charter of Hugh's wife Hadwise for

Montivilliers (Bouvris, app., no. 29, pp. 82–3) was attested by Geoffrey Martel, Hugh's brother and lord of Bacqueville-en-Caux, Seine-Maritime. William Martel, son of Geoffrey Martel another of Robert Malet's Suffolk tenants, confirmed to Eye Priory the grant of land at Fressingfield made by his uncle Walter fitz Grip (Eye Cart., 24).

ii, fol. 329b; Brown, Eye Priory Cartulary (1992–94), No. 1; ii, fol. 329b; ii, fol. 329b; ii, fol. 330a; ii, fol. 330a; Brown, Eye Priory Cartulary (1992–94), No. 24; ii, fol. 316a; ii, fol. 316a; ii, fol. 316a; ii, fol. 316a; ii, fol. 316a; ii, fol. 316a; ii, fol. 329a

Walter Filius Guiberti
Occurs Domesday Essex.

ii, fol. 003b

Walter Filius Ingelberti
Occurs Domesday Kent.

i, fol. 009c

Walter Filius Lanberti
Norman, Domesday tenant of the count of Eu in Sussex. Certainly an ancestor of the Scoteny family of Sussex and Lincolnshire, whether he was himself from Etocquigny, Seine-Maritime, arr. Dieppe, cant. Eu, comm. Saint-Martin-le-Gaillard cannot be established. His successor by c.1107 was Ingelran de Scotney, possibly his brother. Walter fitz Lambert had endowed the prebend of Hugh and Geoffrey de Flocques (Sussex Rec. Soc. xliv, p. 299); subsequently Ingelran de Scoteny gave a dwelling at 'Esteda' for the soul of his brother and himself (ibid. p. 302; CDF, 399). Cf. VCH Sussex ix, 253, 278.

i, fol. 20a; i, fol. 18c; i, fol. 19c; i, fol. 19c; i, fol. 19c; i, fol. 19c; i, fol. 19c; i, fol. 19c; i, fol. 19c; i, fol. 17d; i, fol. 18c; i, fol. 19b; i, fol. 19b; i, fol. 20a; i, fol. 20b

Walter Filius Other
Norman tenant-in-chief, keeper of the forest of Windsor and castellan of Windsor castle; he and heirs were surnamed de Windesore. As forester, he angered the monks of Abingdon by taking four hides in Winkfield to increase the forest of Windsor; he, his wife Beatrice and son William, subsequently restored them to Abbot Faritius (Chron. Abing. ii, 7, 132). His father's name suggests he came from western Normandy; perhaps a brother of Ranulf fitz Other who occurs in acts of Saint-Etienne de Caen (Actes caen., pp. 55, 76, 107, 108). Ancestor of the FitzGerald and Carew families. Cf. Round, 'Origins of the Fitzgeralds', Ancestor i (1902), 119, ii (1902), 91–8, he was father of William of Eton, Robert, Gerald, Rainald steward to Queen Adelisa, Maurice, steward of Bury St Edmunds, and Hugh of Horsley. Hugh augmented his father's grant of tithes in Horsley and Compton, Surrey, to Chertsey abbey in the time of William Giffard bishop of Winchester (Cart. Chertsey, 45, 54). Walter was succeeded by his son William between 1100 and 1116 (Sanders, 116).

i, fol. 151a; i, fol. 48c; i, fol. 56b; i, fol. 48c; i, fol. 56d; i, fol. 48c; i, fol. 130a; i, fol. 43c; i, fol. 36a; i, fol. 36a; i, fol. 151a; i, fol. 36a; i, fol. 151a; i, fol. 151a; i, fol. 30a; i, fol. 61c; i, fol. 61c; i, fol. 61c; i, fol. 61c

Walter Filius Ponz
Norman, brother of Drogo fitz Pons, and like him a tenant-in-chief in Domesday Gloucestershire. Both he and his brother Drogo were succeeded in the early twelfth

century by their nephew Richard fitz Pons.

i, fol. 168d; i, fol. 160a; i, fol. 164c; i, fol. 168d; i, fol. 61b; i, fol. 154c; i, fol. 160a; i, fol. 160a; i, fol. 160a

Walter Filius Radulfi Capellani

Occurs in Domesday Herefordshire in a holding associated with his mother, widow of Ralph the chaplain; obviously, he was a minor in 1086.

i, fol. 187c

Walter Filius Richeri

Norman, occurs as tenant in a single manor of Robert Malet in Suffolk. The Eye foundation charter was attested by Walter of Huntingfield (Walter fitz Aubrey of Caen), Walter de Canovilla and Walter balistarius, of whom the first and last were named as Robert's tenants in Domesday Book. Canouville is near Cany-Barville in the Pays-de-Caux.

ii, fol. 313a

Walter Flandrensis

Domesday tenant-in-chief in Bedfordshire. He was probably related to a number of the other Flemings whose holdings were concentrated on this region, and were also tenants of Judith of Lens (see under Walter de Duaco). He is likely to have been son of Seiher and nephew of Walter brother of Seiher, and probably brother of Hugh Flandrensis, The group probably originated from Artois, a region subject to Flanders that included the county of Lens. His descendants were lords of the honour of Odell. His successor was Simon d. c.1147–51. It has been suggested that his immediate successor was William Flandrensis, who accounted in 1129/30 for the widow of Richard de St Medard (BHRS x, p. 266), but this does not seem particularly likely. See Farrer, HKF i, 61–102.

i, fol. 210d; i, fol. 215c; i, fol. 139a; i, fol. 151b; i, fol. 226c; i, fol. 215c; i, fol. 215d; i, fol. 215d; i, fol. 139a; i, fol. 139a; i, fol. 215d; i, fol. 226d; i, fol. 139a; i, fol. 215d; i, fol. 219a; i, fol. 215c

Walter Frater Seiheri

Occurs Domesday Bedfordshire, where Walter Flandrensis, son of Seiher, presumably his nephew, was also a tenant-in-chief. His holdings descended with the other Walter's honour of Wahull (Odell); HKF i, 61. For his possible background see under Walter de Duaco (Douai).

i, fol. 216a; i, fol. 216a

Walter Gener Gisleberti

Occurs in Domesday Worcestershire as a tenant of his father-in-law Gilbert fitz Turold. Possibly the same as Walter Ponther (q.v.).

i, fol. 177a

Walter Giffard

Norman, from Longueville-sur-Scie, Seine-Maritime, arr. Dieppe (Loyd, 45), Domesday tenant-in-chief. Son of Walter Giffard of Bolbec. Married a daughter of Gerard Fleitel, by whom he had issue Walter II Giffard, William, bishop of Winchester, and Rohais, wife of Richard I de Clare. He died soon after 1086. See Le Maho, 31ff; K.S.B. Keats-Rohan, Medieval Prosopography 14.1 (1992), 12–22.

i, fol. 50a; ii, fol. 115a; i, fol. 205c; i, fol. 95a; i, fol. 211b; i, fol. 147a; i, fol.

157c; i, fol. 57a; i, fol. 56b; i, fol. 56c; i, fol. 147a; i, fol. 147b; i, fol. 147c; i, fol. 56b; i, fol. 147d; i, fol. 196a; i, fol. 71c; i, fol. 147c; i, fol. 60b; i, fol. 60b; i, fol. 59a; i, fol. 147a; i, fol. 157c; i, fol. 147a; i, fol. 60b; ii, fol. 112a; ii, fol. 114a; ii, fol. 426a; ii, fol. 114b; ii, fol. 430a; ii, fol. 430a; ii, fol. 430a; ii, fol. 241b; ii, fol. 241a; i, fol. 154a; ii, fol. 243a; ii, fol. 242a; ii, fol. 242a; ii, fol. 242b; ii, fol. 242b; ii, fol. 242a; ii, fol. 242a; ii, fol. 242a; ii, fol. 242b; ii, fol. 241a; ii, fol. 242a; ii, fol. 241a; ii, fol. 241b; ii, fol. 241b; ii, fol. 241b; ii, fol. 241b; ii, fol. 242b; ii, fol. 241a; ii, fol. 242b; ii, fol. 241a; ii, fol. 242b; ii, fol. 243a; ii, fol. 241b; ii, fol. 242b; ii, fol. 241a; ii, fol. 241a; ii, fol. 242b; ii, fol. 241a; ii, fol. 242b; ii, fol. 243a; ii, fol. 240b; ii, fol. 240b; ii, fol. 241a; ii, fol. 242a; ii, fol. 240b; Clay, Early Yorkshire Charters (1949), VIII, No. 4; Hamilton, Inquisitio Eliensis (1876), pp. 192–95; Clay, Early Yorkshire Charters (1949), VIII, No. 5

Walter Haket
Norman, Domesday tenant of Walter Giffard in Buckinghamshire, from a family which gave its name to La Mesnil-Haquet, now Charlemesnil, Seine-Maritime, cant. Longueville, comm. Manéhouville. Probably the Walter son of Ralph (Rodulf) Haket who attested his father's grant of land in Montivilliers, held of William fitz Godefrid, to Sainte-Trinité de Rouen (Guérard, Cart. pp. 434–5).

i, fol. 148a

Walter Hosed
Norman, occurs Domesday Somerset as a tenant of Giso bishop of Wells, identified as 'hosatus' from the Bath cartulary. Probably brother of William Hosatus. His byname becomes Hose or Hussey. Persons surnamed Hose occur in a charter of Arnulf priest of Neufbourg, Eure, for Préaux (Arch. dépt. Eure H711, fol. 56v, no. 131).

i, fol. 90c; i, fol. 89d; i, fol. 98a; i, fol. 89d; i, fol. 64c

Walter Monachus
Norman, Domesday tenant of Adelisa widow of Ralph Taillebois. A Domesday juror in Armingford Hundred, Cambridgeshire. Ancestor of a prolific family surnamed Monk or Moine (cf. Fowler, Cart. Wardon, note 279, pp. 344–5), of whom Hervey and his son Oliver occur c.1120 in Ramsey charters.

i, fol. 218b; Hamilton, Inquisitio Eliensis (1876), pp. 97–100; i, fol. 206a; i, fol. 218a; i, fol. 202c; Hamilton, Inquisitio Comitatus Cantabrigiensis, pp. 1–93

Walter Pincerna
Norman, Domesday tenant of Baldwin the Sheriff; identified as pincerna (butler) from Exon; cf. Mason, 'Barons and officials', ANS 13 (1991), p. 247.

i, fol. 107d; i, fol. 106b; i, fol. 106c; i, fol. 106c; i, fol. 106c

Walter Pontherius
Domesday tenant of the church of Worcester and Westminster Abbey in Worcestershire, and of St Peter's in Gloucestershire. His byname occurs as 'ponther' and 'puher'; his descendants occur as 'puher'. It has been alleged to refer to an origin in Picardy (Reaney, Dictionary of British Surnames, 2nd edn 1976, p. 278); there is no independent evidence of his origins. His grandson Hugh Puher (q.v.) held twelve fees of the bishop of Worcester in 1166.

i, fol. 172d; i, fol. 172d; Darlington, Cartulary of Worcester: Reg. I (1962–3), No. 214; i, fol. 175a; i, fol. 175a; i, fol. 174d; i, fol. 174c; i, fol. 175c; i, fol. 172d; i, fol. 175a; i, fol. 175a; i, fol. 173c; i, fol. 173c; i, fol. 173c; i, fol. 174a; i, fol.

173d; i, fol. 173c; i, fol. 166b; i, fol. 166b; i, fol. 166b; Regesta regum Anglo-Normannorum III, No. 964

Walter Silvestris
Occurs Domesday Devon as a tenant of Walter de Claville; his byname is supplied by Exon.

i, fol. 112b; i, fol. 112b

Walter Tirel
Domesday tenant of Richard de Clare, whose daughter he had married. Seigneur of Poix in Ponthieu, he was accused of having loosed the fatal arrow that killed William II in 1100 and was obliged to flee from England (Ord. Vit. v, 288–94). His son Hugh subsequently granted land in England for the soul of his mother when she was buried at Conflans. Sometime between 1124 and 1135 his other son, Walter junior, died and was buried at Pontoise; on that occasion the younger Walter's surviving brother Hugh confirmed the gifts to the house of their mother, though their father Walter was still alive (Cart. Pontoise, no. lxxxv, pp. 67–8). Walter, his wife Adelicia and son Hugh were benefactors of Saint-Quentin de Beauvais (BN lat. n.a. 1921, fol. 12v), to which they granted land in England. A separate grant mentions his sons Hugh and Walter and daughter Ada (ibid., fol. 80v). A Salisbury charter of c. 1155, granting the church of Chardstock (Devon), was given by Gilbert/Gerbert de Percy who described Walter Tirel as his 'avus' (Sarum Chh, no. xx). Chardstock was held by Walter and William of the bishop of Salisbury in Domesday Book. Walter eventually went to Jerusalem and died as a penitent (Ord. Vit. v, 294) Cf. Round, Feudal England, 355–362.

i, fol. 77b; i, fol. 87d; i, fol. 87d; ii, fol. 041a

Walter Tonitruus
Domesday tenant of the wife of Hugh fitz Grip, identified in Exon Domesday. A Walter Tonitruus and his son of the same name occur in charters of Vaucelles and of Saint-Lazare de Cambrai between 1138 and 1160 (Arch. dépt. du Nord 19 H 1, fols 11v–12v, 18v–19v; idem, 28 H 96, fols 1v–2r). His successor in 1166 was Alfred Tonarre, who held two fees of Alfred II of Lincoln.

i, fol. 83c; i, fol. 83d; i, fol. 84a; i, fol. 84a

Walter Vinitor
Domesday tenant of William fitz Ansculf de Picquigny.

i, fol. 36a

Walter []
Domesday tenant of Geoffrey de la Guerche in Leicestershire. Two Walters attested, before 1093, a charter of Geoffrey de la Guerche for Monks Kirby (Mon. Ang. vi, 996). One of them was named as 'Walterius de Pallentuna', apparently a reference to Pillerton, Warwickshire, in the Grandmesnil fee.

i, fol. 235d

Walter []
Domesday tenant of Jocelyn fitz Lambert in Lincolnshire.

i, fol. 359c; i, fol. 359c

Walter []
Domesday tenant of Robert de Mortain and William de Warenne in Sussex;

succeeded by the de Folkington family. HKF iii, 353–5.

ii, fol. 036b; i, fol. 146d; i, fol. 20c; i, fol. 22a; i, fol. 21d; i, fol. 21a; i, fol. 26d; i, fol. 224a; i, fol. 224a; i, fol. 20d; i, fol. 20c

Walter []
Domesday tenant of Drogo de la Beuvrière.

i, fol. 324d; i, fol. 324b; i, fol. 324b

Walter []
Norman, Domesday tenant of William de Braose in Domesday Dorset.

i, fol. 82b; i, fol. 82a; i, fol. 82a; i, fol. 82b

Walter []
Norman, Domesday tenant of William I Peverel of Nottingham. By the early twelfth century his fees were held by Norman de St Patrick (Saint-Patrice-de-Claid, Manche, cant. Periers).

i, fol. 226b

Walter []
Domesday tenant of Hugh de Grandmesnil in Leicestershire.

i, fol. 224c; i, fol. 232d; i, fol. 233a; i, fol. 233a; i, fol. 233a

Walter []
Domesday tenant of William fitz Ansculf de Picquigny.

i, fol. 157c; i, fol. 177b; i, fol. 148c; i, fol. 148c

Walter []
Domesday tenant of Swein of Essex. A Raymond son of Walter attested a charter of Robert fitz Swein c.1114/21 (Mon. Ang. v, 22).

ii, fol. 046a; ii, fol. 044b; ii, fol. 043a; ii, fol. 042b; ii, fol. 042a

Walter []
One or more Walters occur in Domesday Shropshire as an under-tenant of Earl Roger under several tenants.

i, fol. 257b; i, fol. 254b; i, fol. 256d; i, fol. 258b; i, fol. 257d

Walter []
Held Lilford of Countess Judith in 1086. His successors were the Olifart family, of whom William Olifart (q.v.) occurs in 1129/30. See Farrer, HKF ii, 354–5.

i, fol. 229a

Warenger []
Domesday tenant of Roger Bigod and Roger de Raimes in Essex and Norfolk, and possibly also of Waleran Venator in Dorset. He (or his successor) may appear in a confirmation for Thetford priory as Warner of Totinton, where he held in 1086 from both Roger Bigod and Roger de Raimes. The passage otherwise relates primarily to tenants of Robert fitz Swein of Essex, whose father had a Domesday tenant Warner, but no land in Totington. In 1166 Warner de Totintune held half a fee of Roger de Raimes and possibly also from Robert de Raimes. The fee held of Waleran Venator was apparently that held in 1166 by Julian of Manston. The personal name is very rare; the only eleventh-century examples discovered concern Warengar Tinel, who attested a charter of Godfrid de Vernonnet for Sainte-Trinité-de-Rouen with Adam de Pressagni-l'Orgueilleux, Eure (Cart., pp.

429–30; Arch. dépt. Seine-Maritime 27 H I, fol. 6, and 'Guarengero de Quercu' who attested a grant of Ralph de Tornaico for Lyre (Arch. dépt. de l'Eure H 438), probably some time c.1071–93.

> ii, fol. 375a; ii, fol. 374b; ii, fol. 294b; ii, fol. 083a; ii, fol. 423a; ii, fol. 189a; ii, fol. 188b; i, fol. 82b; ii, fol. 374a; ii, fol. 337b; ii, fol. 337b; ii, fol. 139b; Regesta Regum Anglo Normannorum II, App. no. cxxvii ; ii, fol. 087b; ii, fol. 087b; ii, fol. 087b; ii, fol. 263a; ii, fol. 263b; ii, fol. 263b; ii, fol. 338a; ii, fol. 338a; ii, fol. 338a; ii, fol. 338a; ii, fol. 338a; ii, fol. 338a; ii, fol. 377b; ii, fol. 377b

Warin Arbalistarius
Occurs Domesday Wiltshire.

> i, fol. 74d

Warin Buissel
Norman, Domesday tenant of Roger Pictaviensis. Brother of Albert. He occurs in the time of William II with his wife Matilda and issue Richard, Walter, Albert, Sibil and Matilda. Benefactor of Penwortham priory (Chetham Soc. 30, 1853, nos. 3–7). See VCH Lancs. i, 335. The Boissel family is evidenced in the Cartulary of Saint-Vincent du Mans (nos. 380, 841). They survived Roger's fall and became tenants of the new Honour of Lancaster; the Yorkshire land held by Warin Boissel, however, was given to Robert Malet by Henry I. Cf. Roger Boissel, tenant of Hadvise de Bacqueville, DB Dorset 55.3, and Odard Boissel, who attested a gift to La-Trinité, Rouen, by Benedict de Verly (Cart., no. xcvi).

> Barraclough, Charters of AN Earls of Chester (1988), No. 91; i, fol. 269d; i, fol. 269d; i, fol. 270a

Warin De Favarcis
Occurs as witness to two deeds of Abingdon Abbey given between 1100 and 1113. He was possibly the same as the abbey's knight-tenant Warin, who occurs in Domesday Book (Chron. Abing. ii, 100, 145, 161).

> Douglas, 'Some early surveys of Abingdon' (1929), EHR, 44 (1929), 623–25; i, fol. 239a; Stevenson, Chronicon Monasterii de Abingdon (1858) vol. II, pp. 4–6; i, fol. 59c; i, fol. 58d

Warin Filius Burnini
Domesday tenant of Earl Hugh of Chester and Robert Malet; other occurrences of a Warin in Robert's fief probably refer to the same man. In a charter for the abbeys of Caen one Burning was described as a parishioner of Caen (Actes caen, no. 17, 18 July 1083). An origin in Caen would accord well with Warin's tenure of both Hugh and Robert.

> ii, fol. 152b; ii, fol. 153a; ii, fol. 327b; ii, fol. 301a; ii, fol. 301a; ii, fol. 300b; ii, fol. 300b; ii, fol. 300b; ii, fol. 300b; ii, fol. 301a; ii, fol. 301a; ii, fol. 301a; ii, fol. 301a; ii, fol. 301a; ii, fol. 301a; ii, fol. 301a; ii, fol. 310a; ii, fol. 310a

Warin Malicorne
Warin Malicorne attested a charter of Robert de Tosny of Stafford in 1088 (Hist. Coll. Staffs. ii, 181–8. He was probably the Warin who occurs as Robert's tenant in Staffordshire and Warwickshire.

> i, fol. 249c; i, fol. 249c

Warin Vicecomes
Warin, Domesday tenant of William de Warenne in Sussex, whom he apparently

served as sheriff of the Rape of Lewes. He attested William II's confirmation charter for Lewes as Warin vicecomes. His son Ralph's grant to Lewes was confirmed by Henry I.

i, fol. 26b; Clay, Early Yorkshire Charters (1949), VIII, No. 6

Warin []
Norman, Domesday tenant of William Cheever de Pomeroy in Domesday Devon.

i, fol. 110d; i, fol. 110d; i, fol. 110c; i, fol. 111a

Warin []
Domesday tenant of Judhael of Totnes; probably the Warin dispencer of Judhael's charter for Totnes Priory (Mon. Ang iv, 630, no. ii).

i, fol. 109a

Warin []
Norman, Domesday tenant of Robert de Bucy.

i, fol. 234b; i, fol. 234c

Warin []
Norman, tenant and under-tenant of Roger de Montgomery. His Shropshire manors, held of William Pantolf, were later held by the Eyton family; Eyton, Shrops, viii, 26, 36; VCH Shrops xi, 139.

i, fol. 24b; i, fol. 25c; i, fol. 24d; i, fol. 24c; i, fol. 25b; i, foi. 24b; i, fol. 257c; i, fol. 257c; i, fol. 257c; i, fol. 17c

Warin []
Domesday tenant of the count of Meulan in Domesday Warwickshire.

i, fol. 242c; i, fol. 241d; i, fol. 240c

Warinbold []
Norman, Domesday tenant of Hermer de Ferrers in Norfolk.

ii, fol. 274b; ii, fol. 207a

Warmund Venator
Norman, tenant of Earl Hugh in Domesday Cheshire.

i, fol. 269b

Warmund []
Norman, tenant of William de Mohun and others in the south-west in 1086. A daughter of his was a nun of Shaftesbury.

Dugdale, Monasticon Anglicanum, II, pp. 482–83, No. XIII; i, fol. 90a; i, fol. 94c; i, fol. 87b; i, fol. 77c; i, fol. 96c; i, fol. 93a

Warner []
Norman, Domesday tenant of William Peverel in Derbyshire and Nottinghamshire. His son Robert, father of William, was an early benefactor of Lenton priory; HKF iii, 148.

i, fol. 276b; i, fol. 287c; i, fol. 287d; i, fol. 276b; i, fol. 276b; i, fol. 276b; i, fol. 276b; i, fol. 276b

Warner []
Domesday tenant of Guy de Craon in Lincolnshire. Probably ancestor of the Pointon or Poynton family. Warner son of Rivallon fitz Froger of Montreuil-sur-Perouse, Ille-et-Vilaine, and his wife Adeluvia was associated in his parents

grant to Saint-Serge, attested by Robert de Vitré [father of Guy de Craon] and Theobald fitz Berner (Morice, Preuves, I, 412).

i, fol. 367c; i, fol. 367b; i, fol. 367b

Wenelinc []
Domesday tenant of Hugh de Beauchamp.

i, fol. 213d

Wenenc Presbiter
Domesday priest of William of Eu in Sussex.

i, fol. 18b; i, fol. 18b; i, fol. 18a; i, fol. 17d; i, fol. 18a; i, fol. 18a; i, fol. 18c; i, fol. 18d; i, fol. 18a

Wenric De Palences
Domesday tenant of Abingdon Abbey, identified as Gueres de Palences who occurs in the abbey's list of knights (Chron. Abing. ii, 5).

i, fol. 156d; i, fol. 156d; i, fol. 59b; Stevenson, Chronicon Monasterii de Abingdon (1858) vol. II, pp. 4–6

Werric []
Domesday tenant of Tihel de Hellean in Suffolk.

ii, fol. 261b; ii, fol. 261b

Wesman []
Occurs in Domesday Surrey and Kent. He holds in Surrey of the fee of Mandeville from Geoffrey of Boulogne, who had married Geoffrey de Mandeville's daughter. A Guesman attested a charter of Saint-Trinité de Rouen (Cart., pp. 434–5) by Ralph Hacket, tenant of William fitz Godfrid of Arques, in the mid eleventh century. Geoffrey son of Wesman and Matilda his wife gave their part of the church of 'Marsei' (Orne) as heirs of Hervé, brother of Fulcher Malherbe, Matilda's father, to Saint-Vigor de Cerisy, attested by Count Robert (of Mortain) and Serlo bishop of Sées (1091–1123) (Chanteux, no. 44, p. 153; BN fr. nov. acq. 21659, p. 8).

i, fol. 009c; i, fol. 36b

Wiard []
Norman, Domesday tenant of Swein of Essex; probably the same as Oilard son of Adelelm who attested a charter of Robert fitz Swein (Mon. Ang. v, 22).

ii, fol. 044b

Wibald []
Domesday tenant of Gunfrid de Chocques at Wingrave and Rowsham, Buckinghamshire. The greater part of these manors were held by the honour of Wallingford. The Chocques portion seems early to have passed to the honour of Weedon Pinkeny; cf. HKF i, 45–6. Wibald was possibly the same as Olbald (q.v.).

i, fol. 152c

Wibert Presbiter
Norman priest, occurs Domesday Berkshire as a tenant of Geoffrey de Mandeville, and in Hampshire as a tenant of Walchelin bishop of Winchester.

i, fol. 40d; i, fol. 57b; i, fol. 62a

Wibert []
Norman, Domesday tenant of the count of Eu in Sussex. Succeeded by his son
William, and then by the latter's heir (probably nephew) Rainald de Anseville (i.e.
Incheville, Seine-Maritime). Rainald was perhaps related to Hugh de Hansevilla,
who attested a charter of Henry count of Eu in 1106 (CDF, 399), and/or to Robert
de Anseville, who was a tenant of the bishop of Chichester in 1086 (DB Sussex
3.3). Wiberts occur several times in charters of Tréport, the abbey founded by the
count of Eu; the most prominent among them was Wibert de Duneio (Cart.
Tréport, no. 1). See VCH Sussex ix, 398; BL Add. ch. 20161; Farrer, HKF ii, 376.

    i, fol. 20b; i, fol. 18a; i, fol. 18a; i, fol. 18c; i, fol. 18d; i, fol. 19a; i, fol. 19a; i, fol.
19a; i, fol. 19a; i, fol. 18a

Wibert []
Norman, knight of the archbishop of Canterbury in 1086 and 1093–6. His fee was
at Knell in Wingham, Kent (Du Boulay, Lordship of Canterbury, 384–5).

    i, fol. 011c; Douglas, ed., Domesday Monachorum (1944), p. 105

Wibert []
Tenant of William fitz Ansculf de Picquigny in 1086.

    i, fol. 177a; i, fol. 149a

Widald []
Domesday tenant of Alan de Craon at Rippingale, Lincolnshire. The fee had
descended to Richard Luvet in 1166.

    i, fol. 367b

Widard []
Norman, occurs in Domesday as tenant of Roger de Lacy and others.

    i, fol. 260c; i, fol. 186c; i, fol. 186c; i, fol. 232d; i, fol. 162a; i, fol. 259d

Wido Angevin
Domesday tenant of Eustache of Boulogne in East Anglia, where mention is made
of his maternal uncle (avunculus) Osmund, who apparently bore a Norman name.
Round suggested that Guy's lands were a grant of the king rather than of Eustache,
but this is not necessarily the case. A grant by Eustache of Boulogne in 1100 to La
Chapelle, relating to England, was attested by Osinmund Extacio, 'nepos' of
Conon (Miraeus et Foppens ii, pp. 1311–12). The lands of Baldwin son of Guy
passed to William fitz Robert, perhaps via the latter's wife Gila (Sibton Cart. i, p.
15). In the early thirteenth century it was recorded that Robert fitz Roger held
seven fees in Thorpe Wydonis Andegavensis of the Honour of Boulogne (Fees,
236). Wydo Andegavensis and his wife were benefactors of St Albans's (BL
Cotton Nero D vii, fol. 97v).

    i, fol. 196a; ii, fol. 151a; ii, fol. 151a; ii, fol. 151a; ii, fol. 109b; ii, fol. 029a; ii,
fol. 029a; ii, fol. 033b; ii, fol. 033b; ii, fol. 161b

Wido De Auco
Domesday tenant of Ramsey Abbey in Cambridgeshire, and subsequently also in
Huntingdonshire. Appears from the Ramsey Chronicle to be the same as Wido de
Auco (Guy of Eu). A charter of Count Henry of Eu relating to his grandfather
Robert's foundation of canons at St Mary's Hastings shows that Robert's
Domesday tenant Ingelran was Ingelran of Eu (q.v.), brother of Guy. Guy was later
steward (dapifer) of Herbert Losinga, bishop of Norwich. He was succeeded by his

sons John, later steward of the bishop of Norwich, and Gilbert, father of Guy the younger, in 1120 (Chron. Ramsey, pp. 229–30).

i, fol. 192c; Dodwell, Charters relating to the Honour of Bacton, No. 1; Hart, Cartularium Monasterii de Rameseia, No. L; Hart, Cartularium Monasterii de Rameseia, No. LXXIV; Douglas, Social Structure of Med. E. Anglia (1927), No. 35; Hart, Cartularium Monasterii de Rameseia, No. XLII; Hart, Cartularium Monasterii de Rameseia, No. CLV; Hamilton, Inquisitio Eliensis (1876), pp. 97–100; Hamilton, Inquisitio Comitatus Cantabrigiensis, pp. 1–93; Red Book of the Exchequer, ed. Hall (1897), pp. 401–02

Wido De Credon

Guy 'of Craon', in Anjou, can be confidently identified with a Breton, younger son of Robert I de Vitré and his Angevin wife Berthe de Craon (Morice, Preuves I, 413). The Lincolnshire Claims of Domesday Book suggest that he was a Breton who had formerly held some of his land under Ralph I de Gael, Earl of East Anglia (d.1069). After 1075 and the revolt and fall of Ralph II de Gael, Guy acquired some of the lands then forfeited by Ralph and his supporters. His tenancy-in-chief lay principally in Lincolnshire and was later known as the barony of Freiston (Sanders, 47). He had married the daughter of another northern tenant-in-chief, Hugh fitz Baldric, by the date of Domesday Book. The Thorney Abbey Liber Vitae (BM Add. 40000, fol. 3r) shows that her name was Isabella. The same source also shows that he had a son Lisoius, an important name in the family of Bertha de Craon (ibid., fol. 3r; Mon. Ang. iv, 125). Active in Lincolnshire in the early 1090s, when he attested grants to Spalding Priory (Mon. Ang. iii, 120), he had been succeeded by his son Alan (q.v.) by 1114. Alan's charters show that Guy was father also of two daughters, Emma, mother of William fitz Roger de Caen of Huntingfield, and Alice. K.S.B. Keats-Rohan, 'Le rôle des Bretons dans la politique de la colonisation normande', MSHAB, lxxiv, 1996, 188–9; idem, 'Le problème de la suzeraineté et la lutte pour le pouvoir: la rivalité bretonne et l'état anglo-normand 1066–1154', MSHAB, 68 (1991), 53–6; E. M. Poynton, 'The fee of Creon', Genealogist n.s. 18, 162–6, 219ff.

i, fol. 281d; i, fol. 48b; i, fol. 367b; i, fol. 367c; i, fol. 368a; i, fol. 368a; i, fol. 368a; i, fol. 368a; i, fol. 368a; i, fol. 368a; i, fol. 368a; i, fol. 368a; i, fol. 367b; i, fol. 367d; i, fol. 367c; i, fol. 367d; i, fol. 367b; i, fol. 367d; i, fol. 368a; i, fol. 368a; i, fol. 368b; i, fol. 368b; i, fol. 367b; i, fol. 368b; i, fol. 368b; i, fol. 367d; i, fol. 367d; Lincolnshire Claims (Domesday Book), fols 376d–377c; i, fol. 368a; i, fol. 367d; i, fol. 367b; i, fol. 367d; i, fol. 367d; i, fol. 367d; i, fol. 367c; i, fol. 367d; i, fol. 367d; i, fol. 367c; i, fol. 368a; i, fol. 367c; i, fol. 367b; i, fol. 368a; i, fol. 367c; i, fol. 367b; Dugdale, Monasticon Anglicanum, III, p. 217, No. VII; Dugdale, Monasticon Anglicanum, III, p. 216, No. V; Lincolnshire Claims (Domesday Book), fol. 377d; i, fol. 235b; Lincolnshire Claims (Domesday Book), fol. 377d; i, fol. 235b; i, fol. 235b; i, fol. 355d; Lincolnshire Claims (Domesday Book), fols 376b–c; Lincolnshire Claims (Domesday Book), fols 376d–377c; i, fol. 340b; i, fol. 356c; i, fol. 356c

Wido De Oilgi

Occurs in Domesday Book. Brother of Robert I and Nigel d'Oilly (RRAN i, 207, 466; Lincs. Reg. Antiq. i, p.13).

i, fol. 160a; i, fol. 160a; Pipe Roll 31 Henry I, 002–ox

Wido De Reinbuecurt

From Raimbeaucourt, Nord, near Douai. His son Ingeran occurs in Domesday

Book, but he was succeeded by another son Richard. His date of death is unknown, but Richard (q.v.) controlled his fief during the 1120s.

i, fol. 201a; Stenton, English Feudalism, App., No. 8; Stenton, English Feudalism, App., No. 8; i, fol. 219a; Hamilton, Inquisitio Eliensis (1876), pp. 192–95; i, fol. 199d; i, fol. 200a; Dugdale, Monasticon Anglicanum, III, p. 499, No. II; Dugdale, Monasticon Anglicanum, III, p. 499, No. I; Regesta regum Anglo-Normannorum III, No. 817; i, fol. 154a; i, fol. 235a; i, fol. 226d; i, fol. 363d; i, fol. 226d; i, fol. 226d; i, fol. 159d; G. Fowler, Early Cambridgeshire Feodary, EHR (1932), pp. 442–3; G. Fowler, Early Cambridgeshire Feodary, EHR (1932), pp. 442–3; G. Fowler, Early Cambridgeshire Feodary, EHR (1932), pp. 442–3; i, fol. 336d; i, fol. 191c; G. Fowler, Early Cambridgeshire Feodary, EHR (1932), pp. 442–3; i, fol. 235a; Lincolnshire Claims (Domesday Book), fols 376d–377c

Wido Presbiter
Norman cleric, tenant of the bishop of Coutances in Domesday Somerset. Perhaps the same as Guy, tenant of Roger Arundel, whose successor in 1166 was probably Thomas de Hasweia (i.e. Halswell)

i, fol. 94d; i, fol. 82d; i, fol. 88c; i, fol. 88c

Wido Presbiter
Priest, Domesday tenant of Geoffrey de Bec in Hertfordshire.

i, fol. 140c; i, fol. 140c

Wido []
Norman, occurs as a tenant of Roger de Montgomery in Domesday Sussex. His holding apparently escheated and is later found as a serjeanty; VCH Sussex iv, 104.

i, fol. 23a

Wielard De Balliol
Norman, from Bailleul-Neuville, Seine-Maritime, arr. Neufchâtel, cant. Londinières (Loyd, 11), Domesday tenant of Richard de Clare and son of Osbern fitz Geoffrey de Bailleul, a tenant of the count of Eu in Sussex. He is identified by his appearance, with his wife Ida, in Stoke-by-Clare ch. no. 137. Possibly still active c.1112, his eventual heir was his grandson Osbern, who died 1162/6 (Cart. Castleacre, ßL Harley 2110, fol. 102).

i, fol. 26c; ii, fol. 397a; ii, fol. 041b; ii, fol. 103a; ii, fol. 039b; ii, fol. 101b; ii, fol. 396b; Harper-Bill & Mortimer, Stoke by Clare Cartulary, No. 137

Wigan De Mara
Breton tenant of Count Alan in 1086. Possibly the same as Wigan son of Hugh de Mara, who held land of the archbishopric of Dol in north-east Brittany. Hugh occurs in Brittany in the 1080s with his wife Ennokent (Innoguen) and sons Boia, Wigon and Amat (Morice, Preuves I, 463). Father of Wigan II de Mara, he was succeeded before 1135 by his eldest son William. See EYC v, 288ff.

i, fol. 195b; Clay, Early Yorkshire Charters (1936), V, No. 351

Wigar De Horeuuella
English juror in Odsey Hundred, Hertfordshire; tenant of Harduin de Scalariis (Lewis, 'Jurors', 44).

i, fol. 141c; i, fol. 141c; Hamilton, Inquisitio Eliensis (1876), pp. 97–100

Wiger De Bennaham

Englishman, holding land of the king at Benham, Berkshire, in 1086. Father of Hugh fitz Wigar of Benham, a benefactor of Abingdon in 1110 (Chron. Abing. ii, 145).

i, fol. 253a

Wigod []

Domesday tenant of Robert of Mortain in Buckinghamshire.

i, fol. 146a

Wihenoc []

Breton, landholder in East Anglia before 1075. His association with Eudo fitz Clamarhoc there may indicate an origin in the Wihenoc-Goranton family of Vitré, Ille-et-Vilaine. See M. Brand'Honneur, 'Les Goranton-Hervé de Vitré', MSHAB lxx (1993), who notes that the Wihenoc fitz Goranton evident in Breton documents from 1040 disappears after 1066, when he is replaced in Breton documents by his brother Hervé.

ii, fol. 190b; Hamilton, Inquisitio Eliensis (1876), pp. 192–95

Wihomarc Dapifer

Breton, Domesday tenant and steward of Count Alan, from whom he held the steward's fee, assessed in the early twelfth century at fifteeen knights. Ancestor of the Thornton family of Thornton Steward. Founder of St Martin's, Richmond, a cell of St Mary's, York. He continued as steward under Alan's successors Alan II and Stephen. He was dead by 1129/30, when his sons Warner and Roger had divided his lands. See EYC v, 17–19.

Clay, Early Yorkshire Charters (1936), V, No. 282; i, fol. 195c; i, fol. 195c; i, fol. 311c; i, fol. 310c; i, fol. 311c; i, fol. 125a; i, fol. 120a; i, fol. 125a; ii, fol. 146b; i, fol. 195d; i, fol. 195d; Clay, Early Yorkshire Charters (1935), IV, No. 4; Clay, Early Yorkshire Charters (1935), IV, No. 1; Dugdale, Monasticon Anglicanum, III, pp. 548–50, No. V; Clay, Early Yorkshire Charters (1936), V, No. 138; ii, fol. 147a; ii, fol. 147a; ii, fol. 147a; ii, fol. 147a; ii, fol. 148a; ii, fol. 148a; ii, fol. 148a; ii, fol. 148a; ii, fol. 148b; ii, fol. 148a; ii, fol. 148b

Wihtmar []

English tenant of Roger Bigod in Domesday Suffolk, from whom he held land he had held in 1066.

ii, fol. 342a; ii, fol. 342a; ii, fol. 342a; ii, fol. 342a; ii, fol. 342a; ii, fol. 342a; ii, fol. 342a; ii, fol. 342a

Wihuenec []

Breton (Wihenoc), Domesday tenant of Alfred Brito in Devon.

i, fol. 115d; i, fol. 116a; i, fol. 116a

Willelm Alis

Tenant-in-chief in Domesday Hampshire. Important follower of William fitz Osbern. According to D. Crouch, The Beaumont Twins, p. 106, he was probably lord of Les Bottereaux in the honour of Breteuil. According to Le Prévost in Cartulaire de Louviers, t. i, he may have been a member of the family of Sacquenville, Eure, arr. Evreux. He gave land at Marnefer (Marnafai), Orne, near La Ferté-Frenel to Saint-Evroul (Ord. Vit. ed. Le Prévost v, 189; Ord. Vit. iii, 122, 130).

i, fol. 48c; i, fol. 48c

Willelm Arcuarius
Norman landholder in Domesday Hampshire.

 i, fol. 48d; i, fol. 48d; i, fol. 48d

Willelm Bainard
The son and heir of Geoffrey Bainard, who succeeded his father Ralph Bainard soon after the date of Domesday Book, was a William Bainard who suffered forfeiture and exile in 1110 for unknown reasons (ASC, 1110; Sanders, 129). The William 'nepos Radulfi' of Domesday Book was probably the same man, grandson of Ralph Bainard. This view is supported by the Cartulary of Dunmow Priory (BM Harley 662) which relates its foundation in 1104 by 'Inga soror Radulfi Bainardi maioris' (fol. 6r) with the assent of her son Ralph Bainard the younger. It also records that her son Geoffrey Bainard, like his mother a tenant of William Bainard, confirmed his mother's grant at the time he became a canon, mentioning his uncle [Ralph Bainard I] and his brother [Ralph II] (ibid., loc. cit.).

 Mason, Westminster Abbey Charters (1988), No. 488; ii, fol. 415a; ii, fol. 415a; ii, fol. 415a; ii, fol. 415a; ii, fol. 415a

Willelm Balt
Occurs Domesday Essex and Hertfordshire as a tenant of Bishop Maurice of London. Succeeded by the Bald or Baud family, probably his descendants, of whom Simon was the fee-holder in 1166. See J. H. Round, 'The Baud Family', TEAS n.s. 10, p. 347.

 i, fol. 133c; i, fol. 133c; i, fol. 133c; ii, fol. 011b; ii, fol. 012a; ii, fol. 011b

Willelm Basset
Domesday tenant of Hugo de Bellocampo in Bedfordshire; probably a close relative of Ralph Basset (q.v.)

 i, fol. 213b

Willelm Belet
Described in Domesday as 'serviens regis'. His family were established on ducal demesne land near Goderville, Seine-Maritime (Le Maho, 'L'apparition des seigneuries châtelains dans le Grand-Caux', Archéologie Médiévale 6 (1976) 10). Presumed ancestor of the English Belets or Bellets, he had a daughter married to a certain Faderlin (q.v.). Cf. CDF, 322.

 i, fol. 80d; i, fol. 80d; i, fol. 84d; i, fol. 80d; i, fol. 48d; i, fol. 48d; i, fol. 75d; i, fol. 85a; i, fol. 85a; i, fol. 56d; i, fol. 85a; Pipe Roll 7 Henry II, 47–ds; i, fol. 85a; i, fol. 84d; i, fol. 80d; i, fol. 80d

Willelm Bertram
Norman, held Polhampton in chief in Domesday Hampshire; occurs c.1110 in the Winchester Survey. His family were lords of Bricquebec, Calvados; descendants of Turstin de Bastembourg and collaterals of Hugh de Montfort (q.v.). William was possibly a younger son of Robert Bertram and Susanna (cf. Fauroux, 205). Cf. G. Saige, Cartulaire de l'abbaye de Fontenay le Marmion, Monaco 1885. He witnessed charters between 1079 and 1089 (RRAN i, 168, 310). William Bertram (d. c.1150). lord of Mitford in the time of Henry I, was perhaps his descendant.

 i, fol. 47b; i, fol. 47b

Willelm Blund
Occurs Domesday Lincolnshire holding a small fief in chief. A William holding

land in the same places from Alfred of Lincoln was perhaps the same person. In the Lindsey Survey, c.1115/18, William son of Albreda held the fief from William Meschin.

> i, fol. 358a; i, fol. 358a; i, fol. 366a; Lincolnshire Claims (Domesday Book), fols 375d–376a; Lincolnshire Claims (Domesday Book), fols 375a–d; i, fol. 366a; i, fol. 366a; i, fol. 366a; i, fol. 366a; i, fol. 366a; i, fol. 366a; i, fol. 366a

Willelm Brant
Occurs Domesday Norfolk as a tenant of William de Warenne.

> ii, fol. 159b

Willelm Brito
Occurs in Domesday as a tenant of Richard de Clare or his wife Rohais, whose daughter Avice had married a Breton, Ralph I de Fougères, by 1086. Although Brito in Domesday normally means Breton, William could have been a Norman; cf. William, surnamed Brito, of Bourgtheroulde-Infreville, dépt. Eure, who made a quitclaim to the abbey of Tréport c.1107 (Hist. abb. Tréport, 347).

> i, fol. 196c; i, fol. 207b

Willelm Buenuasleth
Norman, Domesday tenant-in-chief in Leicestershire, and as a tenant of Geoffrey bishop of Coutances in Buckinghamshire.

> i, fol. 241c; i, fol. 241d; i, fol. 238a; i, fol. 235b; i, fol. 235b; i, fol. 243b; i, fol. 243b; i, fol. 243c

Willelm Caluus
A William Calvus (the Bald), occurs in Domesday Gloucester. A William Calvus de Warcliva, man of William d'Ecouis (de Scohies), his wife Adeline and Benzelin their son, were benefactors of Sainte-Trinité de Rouen (Guérard, Cart. p. 465).

> i, fol. 162a

Willelm Camerarius
Norman, chamberlain to the king and tenant-in-chief in Domesday Bedfordshire, Buckinghamshire and Gloucestershire. A late-eleventh or early twelfth-century record of the despoliation of estates of Sainte-Trinité de Caen mentioned the tithe of Hénouville, Seine-Maritime, cant. Duclair, usurped by William camerarius son of Roger de Candos (Walmsley, p. 126). A confirmation charter for Saint-Etienne de Caen by William I (1066–77) referred to the land of William camerarius at Cully, Calvados. cant. Creully (Actes caen. p. 64). If it was the latter William who attested an act of 1082 for Sainte-Trinité de Caen as son of Ralph (ibid., p. 90), then he was was perhaps the same as William de Tancarville, and therefore not the English William.

> i, fol. 216b; i, fol. 167a; i, fol. 151b; i, fol. 216b; i, fol. 190a; i, fol. 128d; i, fol. 127c; i, fol. 127a; i, fol. 209b; i, fol. 35d; i, fol. 216b; ii, fol. 287a; i, fol. 209c; ii, fol. 015a; i, fol. 167a; ii, fol. 286b; ii, fol. 286b; i, fol. 216b

Willelm Cardon
Domesday tenant of Geoffrey de Mandeville. A Ralph Cardon gave land at Carbec to Grestain before 1082 (Bates/Gazeau, p.18).

> ii, fol. 100b; ii, fol. 062b; ii, fol. 062b; ii, fol. 019b; ii, fol. 033b

Willelm Chieure

Domesday tenant-in-chief, William Capra, or Cheever, brother of Ralph de Pomeroy (q.v.) and Beatrice. His fief, later known as the honour of Bradninch, escheated and was regranted to William de Tracy, a natural son of Henry I. Cf. Sanders, 20; VCH Devon i, 560–604. Sibil daughter of William Capra was the wife of Robert II Burdet de Cullei (now Rabodanges, Orne), whom she accompanied to Tarragone (Ord. Vit. vi, 404; cf. Hugh Burdet).

> i, fol. 82d; i, fol. 124a; i, fol. 113a; i, fol. 103d; i, fol. 100b; i, fol. 110c; i, fol. 110b; i, fol. 110c; i, fol. 110b; i, fol. 110b; i, fol. 110d; i, fol. 110b; i, fol. 110b; i, fol. 110b; i, fol. 110b; i, fol. 110c; i, fol. 110d; i, fol. 110d; i, fol. 110d; i, fol. 110d; i, fol. 110c; i, fol. 110d; i, fol. 110d; i, fol. 110d; i, fol. 110d; i, fol. 110c; i, fol. 110c; i, fol. 110c; i, fol. 110b

Willelm Clericus

Occurs Domesday Sussex as a tenant of the bishop of Chichester.

> i, fol. 17a

Willelm Comes Ebroicensis

Son of Richard count of Evreux and Godehild, he fought at Hastings in 1066 according to William of Poitiers. He succeeded his father as count of Evreux in 1067. In 1086 he held a modest Domesday tenancy-in-chief. Founder of the priory of Noyon-sur-Andelle. His wife Havise was a daughter of the count of Nevers (Ord. Vit. vi, 148). They had no issue and at William's death on 18 April 1118 his heir was his nephew Amaury de Montfort-l'Amaury, son of his sister Agnes. His lively career, including opposition to Robert de Bellême, and the ups and downs of his relations with Henry I (for whom he fought at Tinchebray in 1106), were charted by Orderic Vitalis (vi, 34, 40, 65, 146–8, 180, 188, 204).

> i, fol. 60a; i, fol. 60a; i, fol. 60a; i, fol. 56c; i, fol. 60b; i, fol. 60a; i, fol. 60b; i, fol. 60a; i, fol. 60a; i, fol. 60a; i, fol. 60b; i, fol. 60a; i, fol. 52a; i, fol. 60a; i, fol. 157b; i, fol. 157b; i, fol. 157b; i, fol. 157b; i, fol. 157b; i, fol. 156c; i, fol. 157b; i, fol. 157b; i, fol. 157b; i, fol. 157b; i, fol. 154a; i, fol. 60a; i, fol. 157b

Willelm Corbun

Norman, occurs Domesday Essex as a tenant of Robert Gernon.

> ii, fol. 064b

Willelm Corniol

Norman, occurs Domesday Wiltshire. An earlier William Cornola attested a charter of Hugh bishop of Bayeux for Saint-Amand de Rouen of c.1042–9 (Fauroux, 116).

> i, fol. 74c; i, fol. 73c; i, fol. 74d

Willelm Dapifer Episcopi

Dapifer of Geoffrey, bishop of Coutances, of whom he was a Domesday tenant. Le Patourel (EHR, 1944, p. 154) wondered whether William the steward was the same as William de Merlao (Meslay, Calvados, cant. Thury-Harcourt), who claimed, on Geoffrey's behalf, compensation for 200 animals seized by the bishop of Durham's men (Symeonis Monachi Opera Omnia, i, 190–1). William de Merlay was appointd first lord of Morpeth, Northumberland, by Henry I; he was dead in 1129, leaving a son Ranulf (Sanders, 65, RRAN ii, 1848–9). The family was said to have held Morpeth 'de conquestu' (Fees, 201), and while that is impossible, it might indicate a Domesday ancestor; cf. Mason, 'Barons and officials', ANS 13 (1991), p. 249.

i, fol. 145b; i, fol. 145c; i, fol. 145b; i, fol. 210a; i, fol. 210a

Willelm De Aldrie

Norman, Domesday tenant and steward of his kinsman William of Eu; the Anglo-Saxon Chronicle calls him son of William's mother's sister. Possibly the same as William son-in-law of Robert Blund who was surnamed 'de Aldreleia' in the Tax Return for Rowborough Hundred. Probably named from Audrieu, Calvados, arr. Caen, cant. Tilly-sur-Seulles (Loyd, 3). When William count of Eu was arrested and condemned for treason in 1095, the king ordered the execution by hanging of William of Audrie. Despite provoking an outcry on behalf of a man widely seen as falsely accused, the sentence was duly carried out.

i, fol. 80d; i, fol. 73b; Edwards, Chronicon de Hida, London (1866), pp. 301–2; i, fol. 71c; i, fol. 71d

Willelm De Alno

Norman, occurs Domesday Suffolk as a tenant of Robert Gernon. His successor in 1166 was Richard de Aune. Probably named from Aunay-sur-Odon, Calvados.

ii, fol. 67b; ii, fol. 420b; ii, fol. 420b; ii, fol. 420a; ii, fol. 420a; ii, fol. 419b; ii, fol. 419b; ii, fol. 420a; ii, fol. 419b; ii, fol. 419b

Willelm De Ansleuile

Domesday tenant of Roger de Montgomery in Sussex. Farrer's identification of the Sussex William with Roger's tenant William de Ansleville in Hampshire (HKF iii, 56) was reiterated by Musset, 'Administration et justice', Cah. Ann. Norm. 17 (1985), 147, identifying Ansleville with Hémevez, cant. Montebourg, Manche. William appears to have shared the fall of his Montgomery overlords in 1102, his lands being regranted by Henry I to Robert de La Haye, whose descendants held them as the honour of Halnaker.

i, fol. 23a; i, fol. 23a; i, fol. 23c; i, fol. 44c; i, fol. 24b; i, fol. 24b; i, fol. 25c; i, fol. 25c; i, fol. 25c; i, fol. 25d; i, fol. 25c; i, fol. 25d

Willelm De Arcis

A Norman, from Arques-la-Bataille, Seine-Maritime, arr. Dieppe, cant. Offranville (Loyd, 5), Domesday tenant of Robert Malet and Odo of Bayeux. His wife was Robert's sister Beatrice (Eye Cart., 2), by whom he had two daughters, Emma, his heiress, who took his honour of Folkestone to the issue of her first marriage to Nigel de Munville (q.v.), and Maud, wife of William de Tancarville. Douglas argued strongly for the most obvious origin for this man, as the son of Godfrey vicomte of Arques and a daughter of Jocelyn vicomte of Rouen (Dom. Mon. 43–4). He was rightly sceptical of the view that this William was related to the Osbern de Arcis who was his Domesday contemporary. See T. Stapleton, 'Observations upon the succession to the barony of William of Arques . . .', Arch. Journ. 31 (1886) 216ff. William was named as the lord of Folkestone in 1093, but appears to have been succeeded by his daughter Emma and her husband Nigel de Munville (d.1103) soon afterwards (Sanders, 45).

Regesta regum Anglo-Normannorum III, No. 635; Chibnall, English Lands of Abbey of Bec (1951), No. XXV; Douglas, ed., Domesday Monachorum (1944), p. 105; Regesta regum Anglo-Normannorum III, No. 634; ii, fol. 320a; ii, fol. 431b; ii, fol. 431b; ii, fol. 431b; ii, fol. 431b; ii, fol. 407a; i, fol. 003d; i, fol. 009c

Willelm De Babingleia

Domesday tenant of Peter de Valognes at Babingley, Norfolk. Occurs as William of

Babingley in the foundation charter of Binham, c.1100–07, and as William of Rudham, a manor held in 1086 by Turgis.

ii, fol. 256a; Dugdale, Monasticon Anglicanum, III, pp. 345–46, No. I; Dugdale, Monasticon Anglicanum, III, pp. 345–46, No. I

Willelm De Bosco

Norman, prominent tenant in Domesday East Anglia, chiefly of Roger Bigod and Ranulf brother of Ilger. Possibly named from Le Boscq, Manche, a fee of Mont-Saint-Michel held as of the diocese of Coutances. He was succeeded by c.1107 by Robert de Bosco, probably his son.

ii, fol. 079a; ii, fol. 081a; ii, fol. 081b; i, fol. 138c; ii, fol. 081b; Hamilton, Inquisitio Eliensis (1876), pp. 192–95; ii, fol. 081a; ii, fol. 424a; Dugdale, Monasticon Anglicanum, IV, pp. 148–49, No. II; ii, fol. 425a; ii, fol. 424b; ii, fol. 344a; ii, fol. 424a; ii, fol. 424b; ii, fol. 424b; ii, fol. 424b; ii, fol. 424b; ii, fol. 424b; ii, fol. 424a; ii, fol. 424a; ii, fol. 424a; ii, fol. 342a; ii, fol. 342a

Willelm De Boscroard

Norman, Domesday tenant of Robert de Tosny of Belvoir, of whom his brother Roger was also a tenant. They probably originated from Bosc-le-Hard, Seine-Maritime, cant. Bellencombre (Loyd, 18). William and his wife Adeliza gave their manor of Tallington, Lincolnshire, to St Albans (Mon. Ang. ii, 220; cf. BL Cotton Nero D vii, fol. 92v), a grant confirmed by his son William, other sons, and his 'nepos' Simon. His grandson Ralph occurs c.1124/35. Simon grandson of William occurs c.1160.

i, fol. 353a; Dugdale, Monasticon Anglicanum, III, pp. 288–89, No. I; i, fol. 149b; i, fol. 149b

Willelm De Bouuilla

William de Bouville (Beuzeville, Seine-Maritime), and his father Saswal were both tenants of Geoffrey de Mandeville in 1086. He was dead by 1126 at the latest. In 1129/30 Adam of Dunmow accounted for the farm of the land once of William de Bouville for the past three years.

ii, fol. 059b; ii, fol. 062a; ii, fol. 061b; ii, fol. 061b; ii, fol. 374a; Pipe Roll 31 Henry I, 060–e; Pipe Roll 31 Henry I, 053–e/ht; ii, fol. 412b; ii, fol. 411a; ii, fol. 412b; ii, fol. 411a; ii, fol. 411a; ii, fol. 413a; ii, fol. 412a; ii, fol. 412a

Willelm De Braose

Norman, from Briouze-Saint-Gervais, Orne, arr. Argentan, cant. Briouze, son of Gunnor, a nun of Sainte-Trinité de Caen in the 1080s. By 1072 at the latest he was one of the five castellans holding the militarily important Sussex Rapes. His holding was known by the late twelfth century as the Rape or Honour of Bramber. He also had holdings in the south-west in Dorset, where he had a tenant Robert (q.v.) likely to have been his brother, and in Hampshire. He founded a priory of Saint-Florent de Saumur at Sele in Sussex, some of his grants being the subject of a series of disputes, some of them with his son and heir Philip. He died between 1093 and 1096. His wife's identity is unknown, but she was probably a close relative of the Ralph son of Waldi for whose soul William made a grant to Saint-Florent in the 1080s (CDF, 1112); cf. William Gualdi, who fought the sons of Harold at Exeter with Brien of Brittany in 1069 (Ord. Vit. ii, 224). His issue was an only son Philip, and Agnes, wife of Robert fitz Ansquetil de Harcourt. For Bramber, see Sanders, 108.

i, fol. 28a; i, fol. 78d; i, fol. 47b; i, fol. 65c; i, fol. 28a; i, fol. 28a; i, fol. 28a; i, fol. 28a; i, fol. 28a; i, fol. 28d; i, fol. 28a; i, fol. 28a; i, fol. 28b; i, fol. 27c; i, fol. 28b; i, fol. 28b; i, fol. 61b; i, fol. 26d; i, fol. 24d; i, fol. 16d; i, fol. 16d; i, fol. 28a; Douglas, ed., Domesday Monachorum (1944), p. 105

Willelm De Burnouilla

Norman, perhaps from Bourneville, Eure, arr. Pont-Audemer, major tenant of Roger Bigod in Domesday Suffolk. Benefactor with his wife Aliva of Thetford priory before 1110; his daughter Alicia was also a benefactor. In 1166 his successor another William de Burnoville held three fees of Hugh Bigod.

Hamilton, Inquisitio Eliensis (1876), pp. 192–95; Hamilton, Inquisitio Eliensis (1876), pp. 192–95; ii, fol. 183b; Regesta Regum Anglo Normannorum II, App. no. cxxvii ; Dugdale, Monasticon Anglicanum, IV, pp. 150–51, No. VIII; ii, fol. 337a; ii, fol. 336b; ii, fol. 336b; ii, fol. 336b; ii, fol. 336b; ii, fol. 282a; ii, fol. 336b; ii, fol. 343a; ii, fol. 343a; ii, fol. 343a; ii, fol. 343a; ii, fol. 336a; ii, fol. 336b; ii, fol. 336b; ii, fol. 342a; ii, fol. 342a; Dugdale, Monasticon Anglicanum, IV, pp. 148–49, No. II

Willelm De Bursigni

Domesday tenant of Barking Abbey in Essex. Possibly named from Boursigny, Calvados.

ii, fol. 018b

Willelm De Bussa

Occurs in the Lindsey Survey, 1115/18, holding land of Ansfrid de Canci, who had succeeded to the Domesday tenancy-in-chief of Odo Balistarius. Possibly the same as the William who was Odo's tenant in a different holding in 1086.

i, fol. 365d; Lindsey Survey, BL ms Cotton Claudius C v, fols 1–9

Willelm De Cadomo

Occurs Domesday Suffolk on the Malet fee; cf. Walter de Cadomo.

ii, fol. 310a

Willelm De Cahaingnes

Norman, from Cahagnes, Calvados, arr. Vire, cant. Aunay-sur-Odon (Loyd, 52). Major tenant of Robert of Mortain in several Domesday counties. He was sheriff of Northamptonshire in 1086, and again in the early years of Henry I. His widow Adelicia made a grant for his soul to Lewes priory, with the assent of their son Hugh (Mon. Ang. v, 14). His lands were divided between his three sons, of whom Hugh held the forest of Northamtonshire in 1129/30.

i, fol. 22b; i, fol. 20c; i, fol. 22b; i, fol. 225c; i, fol. 149d; i, fol. 201d; i, fol. 201d; i, fol. 20c; i, fol. 20d; i, fol. 20d; i, fol. 16c; i, fol. 225c; i, fol. 20d; i, fol. 20d; Hart, Cartularium Monasterii de Rameseia, No. CXLVII; Dugdale, Monasticon Anglicanum, IV, p. 14, No. VI; i, fol. 223c; i, fol. 223c; i, fol. 223c; i, fol. 223c; i, fol. 223c; i, fol. 223c; i, fol. 223c; i, fol. 223c; i, fol. 223d; i, fol. 223d; i, fol. 223d; i, fol. 223c; i, fol. 223d; i, fol. 223c; i, fol. 223d; i, fol. 223d; i, fol. 223d; i, fol. 223d; i, fol. 223d; i, fol. 223d; i, fol. 223d; i, fol. 223d; i, fol. 223c; i, fol. 223c; i, fol. 223c; i, fol. 223d; i, fol. 21d; i, fol. 21d; i, fol. 22c; i, fol. 22c; i, fol. 22c; i, fol. 22d; i, fol. 22d

Willelm De Cailly

Norman, from Cailly, Seine-Maritime, arr. Rouen, cant. Clères (Loyd, 22). Domesday juror in Thriplow Hundred, Cambridgeshire. He was a tenant of

William de Warenne at Heacham, Norfolk, as shown in the Lewes Cartulary, but the fee was afterwards detached from the Warenne lands and added to those of Skipton. See EYC vii, 109–10; Farrer, HKF iii, 382–4.

ii, fol. 163a; ii, fol. 164b; ii, fol. 161a; i, fol. 196c; ii, fol. 160a; Clay, Early Yorkshire Charters (1949), VIII, No. 12; Hamilton, Inquisitio Comitatus Cantabrigiensis, pp. 1–93; Dugdale, Monasticon Anglicanum, IV, p. 14, No. VI; Hamilton, Inquisitio Eliensis (1876), pp. 97–100; ii, fol. 167b; ii, fol. 167b

Willelm De Caron
Norman, from Cairon, Calvados arr. Caen, cant. Creully (Loyd, 25), occurs Domesday Bedfordshire as a tenant of Eudo Dapifer. He left two sons, Robert and Ralph, at the time of his death, possibly c.1100. Cf. Farrer, HKF iii, 256.

i, fol. 212b; i, fol. 212c; i, fol. 212c; i, fol. 210c; i, fol. 210b; i, fol. 210b; i, fol. 210b; i, fol. 214d; i, fol. 210c; i, fol. 212b

Willelm De Castellon
Norman, from Castillon, Calvados, arr. Bayeux, cant. Balleroy, tenant of Odo of Bayeux in Domesday Buckingham. Cf. Loyd, 25.

i, fol. 143a

Willelm De Chernet
Norman, occurs as a tenant of the wife of Hugh fitz Grip in Domesday Dorset, and of Hugh de Port in Hampshire. The form of his toponym limits the possibilities to Carnet, Manche, cant. Saint-James. His successor in 1166 was Hugh de Kernet, who held one fee of Alfred II of Lincoln. A William de Kernet, and his wife Odeline, with the consent of Peter de Saint-Hilaire, gave land at Montdaigne to Savigny c.1124–50 (Delisle, Recueil, no. lxxxi). In 1168 William de Cherneto was dapifer of Harscoit de Saint-James (BN lat. 5444.1, pp. 167–8).

i, fol. 46a; i, fol. 44d; i, fol. 83c; i, fol. 83c; i, fol. 44d; i, fol. 44d; i, fol. 50d

Willelm De Coleuile
Norman, Domesday tenant of William de Percy in Yorkshire.

i, fol. 322c; i, fol. 322d; i, fol. 322b

Willelm De Curcellis
Norman, from Courseulles-sur-Mer, Calvados, arr. Caen, cant. Creully (Loyd, 33). Mentioned once in Domesday Somerset and identified in Exon, he is assumed to have been the father of Roger de Courseulles, a considerable landholder in Somerset in 1086. His sister Havise was wife of Hugh de Crasmesnil; all three are mentioned as benefactors of the abbey of Fontenay (RRAN i, 117). He sold land near Evrecy to Saint-Etienne de Caen (Actes caen., 14). The grants of William and his wife Agnes, their son Roger and his wife Elisabeth were confirmed to Troarn, c.1150, by John de Suligny and his wife as of their 'antecessores' (Arch. Calv. H 7863).

i, fol. 92a

Willelm De Dalmari
Occurs Domesday as a royal servant and as a tenant of Hugh fitz Grip's widow in Dorset. In 1166 the latter fees were held by his descendant Almaric de Sturtres (i.e. Sturthill) from Alfred II of Lincoln. William's toponym is difficult to identify, though it can be stated with certainty that it does not relate to Daumeray in Anjou, as is often suggested; much more likely is Amayé-sur-Seulles or

Amayé-sur-Orne, Calvados.

i, fol. 83d; i, fol. 83c; i, fol. 84d; i, fol. 85a; i, fol. 93d; i, fol. 93d

Willelm De Ebroicis

Norman, from Evreux, Eure. Domesday tenant of Roger de Lacy in Gloucestershire. Identified in Wightman, Lacy Family, 144, 154 note 5. He was a benefactor of St Peter's, Gloucester (RRAN ii, p. 410). His wife Heloise granted land to St Peter's that had been given to her by Walter de Lacy in matrimonium, suggesting that she was a daughter or other kinswoman of Walter (Hist. S. Petri i, 88). His successor by 1166 was Walter d'Evreux.

i, fol. 185b; i, fol. 184c; i, fol. 184b; i, fol. 184a; i, fol. 184a; i, fol. 184a; i, fol. 167d; i, fol. 167d; Regesta regum Anglo-Normannorum III, No. 345

Willelm De Eddesham

Norman, occurs Domesday Kent; named for Addisham. Early benefactor of St Albans (BL Cotton Nero D vii, fol. 119). Du Boulay, Canterbury, 64, 96, 333, 366.

Douglas, ed., Domesday Monachorum (1944), p. 105; i, fol. 004c; i, fol. 005a

Willelm De Faleise

Norman, Domesday tenant-in-chief in Somerset, from Falaise, Calvados. It has been suggested, P. Busey, 'William of Falaise', Notes and Queries for Somerset and Dorset vol. 33, Sept. 1992, pt. 236, pp. 146–7, that he was son of William de Moulins, who was son of Walter de Falaise, brother of Herlève, mother of William I and Odo of Bayeux. The grounds are that William's daughter Sibil was later described as 'nepta' (kinswoman) of Henry I, who married her to Baldwin de Bullers. William married Geva, daughter and heiress of Serlo de Burcy, by whom he had issue two daughters, Emma, wife first of William fitz Humphrey and secondly of William de Courcy, and Sibil. Between 1100 and 1107 William and Geva founded the priory of Stogursey as a cell of Lonlay. Sanders, 15; Comp. Peer. viii, 530ff.

i, fol. 96c; i, fol. 82a; i, fol. 111b; i, fol. 111b; i, fol. 111a; i, fol. 111a; i, fol. 111a; i, fol. 111a; i, fol. 111a; i, fol. 111a; i, fol. 82a; i, fol. 82a; i, fol. 95d; i, fol. 96c; i, fol. 95d; i, fol. 95d; i, fol. 96c; i, fol. 111a; Tremlett and Blakiston, Stogursey Charters (1949), No. 8; Tremlett and Blakiston, Stogursey Charters (1949), No. 1; Tremlett and Blakiston, Stogursey Charters (1949), No. 4; Tremlett and Blakiston, Stogursey Charters (1949), No. 5; Tremlett and Blakiston, Stogursey Charters (1949), No. (9)

Willelm De Felgeres

Occurs Domesday Buckinghamshire holding a single manor of the king. Probably a Norman; at any rate unnconnected with the Breton Ralph de Fougères, a tenant-in-chief in Buckinghamshire.

i, fol. 151b; i, fol. 151b

Willelm De Fiscanno

Named from Fécamp, Seine-Maritime, occurs Domesday Hampshire.

Pipe Roll 31 Henry I, 077–gl; Regesta regum Anglo-Normannorum III, No. 67; i, fol. 41b

Willelm De Gemmetico

According to the Abingdon Chronicle (ii, 93, 129), William of Jumièges was given land alienated to him by Abbot Rainald, who, like his predecessor Abbot Adelelm, had been a monk of Jumièges. William restored the land to Abingdon in the time of Abbot Faritius.

i, fol. 58d

Willelm De Lancewrda

Domesday tenant of Robert Gernon in Hertfordshire, called William of Letchworth as a juror for Broadwater Hundred. Miss Fry, TEAS v, 181, identified him with the William de Montfichet who, with Roesia his wife and William their son, gave land at Letchworth and Wallington to St Albans 'in the time of Henry I' (confirmed late in his reign by Henry II, Mon. Ang. ii, 229; cf. VCH Herts iii, 120). The argument as is stands is merely inferential, and while possibly correct, the evidence is inconclusive. A William de Montfichet granted land at Saint-Marcouf to Cerisy between 1082 and 1087. Geoffrey Gaimar alleged that a William de Montifchet was with William II when he met his death in the New Forest in 1100. Although he had two sons of his own, Gernon's tenancy in chief was taken over, c. 1120, by a William de Montfichet, husband of Margaret de Clare, who died soon after 1134 leaving minor sons and a nephew William de Montfichet.

i, fol. 138a; i, fol. 138a; i, fol. 138a; i, fol. 138a; i, fol. 137d; i, fol. 137d; i, fol. 137d; i, fol. 137d; Hamilton, Inquisitio Eliensis (1876), pp. 97–100; i, fol. 137d; i, fol. 137d

Willelm De Lestra

Norman, Domesday tenant of Robert de Mortain, from Lestre, Manche, arr. Valognes, cant. Montebourg (Loyd, 53). Occurs as a witness in a copy of a grant by Robert to the abbey of Marmoutier, followed by 'Ricardus dapifer, eius filius' (CDF, 1203). In the foundation charter of the Abbaye Blanche at Neufbourg by William of Mortain in 1105 (Gall. Christ. xi, Inst. 108–9), Richard de Lestre appears as the donor of land his mother held in Sourdeval. William was father also of Jordan, whose son Richard made a grant for his grandfather's soul to Montacute priory (Cart. Montacute, 136/160–1), and probably also of Roger (q.v.).

i, fol. 79b; i, fol. 93a; i, fol. 105b; i, fol. 79d; i, fol. 79d; i, fol. 92b; Bearman, Charters of the Redvers Family (1994), App. II No. 7; i, fol. 80a; i, fol. 80a; i, fol. 80a; Bearman, Charters of the Redvers Family (1994), No. 5

Willelm De Locels

Norman, from Loucelles, Calvados, arr. Caen, cant. Tilly-sur-Seulles (Loyd, 55), Domesday tenant of Hugh I de Beauchamp. His successor c.1114–30 was Richard de Loucelles.

i, fol. 213b; i, fol. 213b

Willelm De Malleuilla

Norman, from Emalleville, Seine-Maritime, arr. Le Havre, cant. Goderville, comm. Saint-Sauveur-d'Emalleville, Domesday tenant of Robert Malet of Eye, Suffolk. Cf. Loyd, 40.

ii, fol. 306b; ii, fol. 307a; ii, fol. 307a

Willelm De Mara

Norman, occurs Domesday as a tenant of William of Eu and as a Domesday juror in Cheveley Hundred, Cambridgeshire. Turstin de Mara, brother of William, was an early post-Conquest benefactor of St Albans Abbey, to which he granted land in Welwyn, Herts (Mon. Ang. ii, 220), and 'Robertus de Mara, similiter'. Welwyn was one of William's holdings in 1086.

Hamilton, Inquisitio Eliensis (1876), pp. 97–100; Hamilton, Inquisitio Comitatus Cantabrigiensis, pp. 1–93; i, fol. 71d; i, fol. 138d; i, fol. 139a; ii, fol. 373a

Willelm De Moion

Norman from Moyon, Manche, arr. Saint-Lô, cant. Tessy-sur-Vire (Loyd, 66), Domesday tenant-in-chief. Sheriff of Somerset sometime between 1066 and 1083 and possibly from 1083 to 1089. A charter in the Bath Cartulary (no. 34) gives his wife as Adeline, his sons as Geoffrey and Robert and his brothers as Wimund; it was attested by Durand his steward (dapifer), probably his Domesday tenant of that name and another of his brothers. His fief was later known as the barony of Dunster (Sanders, 114). His son William had succeeded him by 1129/30. H. Maxwell-Lyte, A History of Dunster; idem, The Honour of Dunster, Som. Rec. Soc. xxxiii.

i, fol. 95c; i, fol. 82b; i, fol. 82a; i, fol. 87b; i, fol. 81c/d; i, fol. 81c/d; i, fol. 81c/d; i, fol. 81c/d; i, fol. 111d; i, fol. 82a; Hunt, Bath Chartulary, Som. Rec. Soc. 7 (1893), No. 34; i, fol. 96a; i, fol. 96b; i, fol. 95d; i, fol. 96c; i, fol. 96b; i, fol. 96c; i, fol. 96b; i, fol. 95d; i, fol. 96a; i, fol. 95c; i, fol. 95c; i, fol. 95d; i, fol. 96b; i, fol. 95d; i, fol. 95d; i, fol. 95d; i, fol. 95d; i, fol. 95c; i, fol. 96a; i, fol. 96b; i, fol. 96a; i, fol. 95d; i, fol. 86b

Willelm De Monasteriis

Norman tenant of the widow of Hugh fitz Grip in Domesday Dorset; his toponym is supplied by Exon. He had been succeeded by Robert de Monasteriis by 1129, and by William in 1166.

i, fol. 83c; i, fol. 83d; i, fol. 83c; i, fol. 77d

Willelm De Moncellis

Norman, from Monceaux, Calvados, arr. and cant. Bayeux (Loyd, 67), Domesday tenant in Somerset of Geoffrey, bishop of Coutances. His toponym is given in Exon Domesday. His successor in 1166 was William de Muncellis, who held one fee of Oliver de Tracy.

i, fol. 87d; i, fol. 87d; i, fol. 88b; i, fol. 88b; i, fol. 88c; i, fol. 88d; i, fol. 89a; i, fol. 89a

Willelm De Nuers

Norman, perhaps from Noyers, Eure, arr. Les Andelys, cant. Gisors, occurs in Domesday Suffolk and Norfolk as a tenant principally of the bishop of Thetford, William de Beaufour. Possibly he was also a tenant of Robert de Tosny of Belvoir at Hose in Leicestershire, though this does not appear in Domesday; the holding was subsequently granted to Belvoir and confirmed by Henry I (Cal. Chart. Rolls, 1327–41, p. 295; Loyd, 74). Simon de Nuers held one fee of the bishop of Norfolk in 1166.

ii, fol. 195a; ii, fol. 288a; ii, fol. 288a; ii, fol. 288b; ii, fol. 195b; ii, fol. 288b; ii, fol. 288a; ii, fol. 289a; ii, fol. 288b; ii, fol. 288b; ii, fol. 288a; ii, fol. 380b; ii, fol. 380b; ii, fol. 380b; ii, fol. 380b; ii, fol. 288a; ii, fol. 288b; ii, fol. 288a; ii, fol. 289a; ii, fol. 288a; ii, fol. 288a; ii, fol. 288b; ii, fol. 195b; ii, fol. 195b; ii, fol. 289a; ii, fol. 199b; ii, fol. 288a; ii, fol. 194b; ii, fol. 289a; ii, fol. 288a; ii, fol. 198a; ii, fol. 289a; ii, fol. 196b; ii, fol. 288a; ii, fol. 288b; ii, fol. 288b; ii, fol. 194b; ii, fol. 289a; ii, fol. 137a; ii, fol. 141a; ii, fol. 141b; ii, fol. 141a; ii, fol. 141b; ii, fol. 141a; ii, fol. 140a; ii, fol. 141a; ii, fol. 141b; ii, fol. 141b; ii, fol. 138a; ii, fol. 139b; ii, fol. 141b; ii, fol. 141b; ii, fol. 139a; ii, fol. 138a; ii, fol.

139a; ii, fol. 139a; ii, fol. 139a; ii, fol. 139a; ii, fol. 138a; ii, fol. 139b; ii, fol.
138a; ii, fol. 139b; ii, fol. 139b; ii, fol. 139b; ii, fol. 139a; ii, fol. 141b; ii, fol.
139a; ii, fol. 138a; ii, fol. 136a; ii, fol. 141b; ii, fol. 138a; ii, fol. 141b; ii, fol.
135b; ii, fol. 121a; ii, fol. 116b; ii, fol. 136b; ii, fol. 137b; ii, fol. 137a; ii, fol.
135b; ii, fol. 138a; ii, fol. 136a; ii, fol. 137b; ii, fol. 199b; ii, fol. 192b; ii, fol.
192b; ii, fol. 215b; ii, fol. 199a; ii, fol. 138a; ii, fol. 199b; ii, fol. 136a; ii, fol.
200a; ii, fol. 198b; ii, fol. 138a; ii, fol. 137a; ii, fol. 137a; ii, fol. 137a; ii, fol.
137b; ii, fol. 198b; ii, fol. 141a; ii, fol. 141b; ii, fol. 140b; ii, fol. 140a; ii, fol.
140a; ii, fol. 140a; ii, fol. 140b; ii, fol. 138a; ii, fol. 140b; ii, fol. 141a; ii, fol.
135b; ii, fol. 141a; ii, fol. 136a; ii, fol. 141a; ii, fol. 141a; ii, fol. 136b; ii, fol.
136a; ii, fol. 136a; ii, fol. 140b; ii, fol. 137a; ii, fol. 141a; ii, fol. 136b; ii, fol.
136b; ii, fol. 136b; ii, fol. 136b; ii, fol. 137a; ii, fol. 137a; ii, fol. 136a; ii, fol.
140b; ii, fol. 141a; ii, fol. 136b; ii, fol. 117b; i, fol. 189d; ii, fol. 198b; ii, fol.
194a; ii, fol. 198b

Willelm De Odburuile

Norman, occurs Domesday Suffolk where he held land in chief and as a tenant of
his elder brother Roger. Doubtless son of Serius (q.v.), who ocurrs c.1072. From
Auberville, Calvados, arr. Pont-l'Evêque, cant. Dozulé. Possibly father of Richard
fitz William fitz Seiric of the 1129 Pipe Roll (p. 53). His tenancy-in-chief, like his
brother's, was granted to Eudo Dapifer after 1087. A plea of 1286 alleged that
William had issue three sons, of whom the eldest, William, died without issue. The
second, Peter, was ancestor in the maternal line of Richard de la Rokele (fl. 1286);
the third son, Jordan, was father of Matilda, maternal ancestor of Robert de
Willasham (fl. 1286); see Farrer, HKF iii, 246–7.

ii, fol. 404b; ii, fol. 404b; i, fol. 139a; i, fol. 139a; ii, fol. 405a; ii, fol. 405b; ii, fol.
405a; ii, fol. 405b; ii, fol. 405b; ii, fol. 405a

Willelm De Orenge

Domesday tenant of Hugh de Bellocampo in Buckinghamshire. Possibly named
from Origny-le-Butin or Origny-le-Roux, Orne, cant. Bellême. A successor of the
same name occurs in 1166.

i, fol. 150d

Willelm De Ow

William of Eu, son and heir of Robert count of Eu (d. 1092–3) and Beatrice, occurs
as a tenant-in-chief in nine Domesday counties. The holdings of the count of Eu in
Sussex, Huntingdonshire and Essex were still in his father's name in 1086, but
were being administered by William, his father having retired to Normandy by
about 1080. He was twice married, first to Beatrice, sister of Roger de Bully, and
secondly to Helisend, sister of Earl Hugh of Chester. Implicated in the revolt of
1095 against William II, he was denounced and condemned as a traitor. The
severity of his physical punishment led quickly to his death. His cousin and
steward William of Audrie met a more merciful death by hanging at the same time.
His son Henry succeeded him as count; father also of William 'de Grandcourt'
(Ord. Vit. vi, 350), Robert (father of Thomas de Briancon, Mon. Ang. iv, 86; Feet
of Fines, Essex, i, 13) and Albreda. Most of the land he held in Domesday Book
was given to Roger fitz Richard de Clare, becoming the honour of Striguil.

Douglas, ed., Domesday Monachorum (1944), p. 105; Regesta regum
Anglo-Normannorum III, No. 345; Fisher, Cartularium Prioratus de Colne
(Earles C.), No. 65; i, fol. 96c; i, fol. 138d; i, fol. 166d; i, fol. 47b; i, fol. 162b; i,
fol. 96c; i, fol. 67b; i, fol. 96c; i, fol. 48d; i, fol. 71c; i, fol. 138d; i, fol. 96c; i, fol.

80d; i, fol. 96c; i, fol. 100b; i, fol. 138d; i, fol. 80d; i, fol. 138d; i, fol. 80d; i, fol. 80d; i, fol. 71d; i, fol. 47b; i, fol. 96c; i, fol. 164b; i, fol. 166d; i, fol. 162b; i, fol. 166d; i, fol. 162b; i, fol. 166d; i, fol. 61a; i, fol. 166d; i, fol. 211d; i, fol. 166d; i, fol. 212a; i, fol. 166d; i, fol. 167a; i, fol. 167a; i, fol. 47b; i, fol. 47b; i, fol. 162b; Edwards, Chronicon de Hida, London (1866), pp. 301–2; i, fol. 211d

Willelm De Partenai

Occurs Domesday Norfolk in a section relating to usurpations of land. The context suggests that he was associated with Roger Bigod. It is likely that his toponym is an error for Pentenai (Pentney), a manor held by Robert de Vallibus from Roger. Robert was perhaps the son of William, who was not necessarily alive in 1086 (though he may have been the monk William de Vallibus who was mentioned in connexion with the foundation of Thetford priory, Mon. Ang. iv, 152). His own son was named William. Attempts to take the toponym at face value and refer to Parthenay in Brittany (Ille-et-Vilaine), or in Aquitaine (Deux-Sèvres), are thoroughly unconvincing.

ii, fol. 448b; ii, fol. 448b; ii, fol. 448b; ii, fol. 448b; ii, fol. 448b; ii, fol. 278b

Willelm De Perci

Norman, Domesday tenant-in-chief in Yorkshire and elsewhere. His origin is variously given as Percy, Manche, arr. Saint-Lô, or as Percy-en-Auge, Eure, arr. Lisieux, cant. Mézidon (see Comp. Peer, x, 435–44). Despite his close associations with Hugh of Avranches, earl of Chester (of whom he was a tenant), and Hugh de Port (his father-in-law), the latter alternative was demonstrated the correct one in Comp. Peer, x, 435, note b. William and Ernald de Percy were benefactors of Saint-Pierre-sur Dives (near Lisieux) (Chanteux, Rec. Henri I, no. 60), while the Cotentin Percys who occur in Cart. Saint-Sauveur, BN lat. 17137, fols 24v, 192v, 219) show no links with the English family. He was associated with Yorkshire as early as 1070. He fought in the Scottish campaign of 1072. He built a castle at Topcliffe, and refounded Whitby Abbey. His brother Serlo became the second prior at Whitby, and his nephew William the abbot. By his wife Emma de Port he had four sons, his successor Alan, Richard of Dursley, Walter and William. He joined the First Crusade in 1096, becoming lord of part of the Jubal Sumaq in Syria before his death near Jerusalem in 1098. Much information on William is provided by the Whitby Cartulary, in which he was credited with the cognomen Algernuns (Mon. Ang. i, 410–11). For the descent of his barony of Topcliffe, Yorkshire, see Sanders, 148.

i, fol. 305a; Clay, Early Yorkshire Charters (1955), XI, No. 123; i, fol. 353d; i, fol. 46c; i, fol. 321c; i, fol. 304c; i, fol. 304c; Lincolnshire Claims (Domesday Book), fols. 375a–d; Barraclough, Charters of AN Earls of Chester (1988), No. 5; i, fol. 322a; i, fol. 322a; i, fol. 322a; i, fol. 322a; i, fol. 322a; i, fol. 322c; i, fol. 322a; i, fol. 323b; i, fol. 322b; i, fol. 321c; i, fol. 322a; i, fol. 322d; i, fol. 322d; i, fol. 322d; i, fol. 322d; i, fol. 322d; i, fol. 322c; i, fol. 322c; i, fol. 321d; i, fol. 323b; i, fol. 323b; i, fol. 323b; i, fol. 323b; i, fol. 323b; i, fol. 321c; i, fol. 323b; i, fol. 323a; i, fol. 322b; i, fol. 322b; i, fol. 321d; i, fol. 322b; i, fol. 322b; i, fol. 322c; i, fol. 322b; i, fol. 322b; i, fol. 322b; i, fol. 322b; i, fol. 322b; i, fol. 322b; i, fol. 322b; i, fol. 322b; i, fol. 322b; i, fol. 322b; i, fol. 322b; i, fol. 322b; i, fol. 321d; i, fol. 323a; i, fol. 321c; i, fol. 321c; i, fol. 322b; i, fol. 322b; i, fol. 322b; i, fol. 322b; i, fol. 322b; i, fol. 322b; i, fol. 322b; i, fol. 322b; i, fol. 322b; i, fol. 322b; i, fol. 322a; i, fol. 353d; i, fol. 322c; i, fol. 354a; i, fol. 323a; i, fol. 354b; i, fol. 354b; i, fol. 291c; i, fol. 298a; i, fol. 298a; i, fol. 298a; i, fol. 354a; i, fol. 354a; i, fol. 344a;

i, fol. 354a; i, fol. 354a; i, fol. 353d; i, fol. 354a; i, fol. 353d; i, fol. 353d; i, fol.
353d; i, fol. 353d; i, fol. 353d; i, fol. 354a; i, fol. 354a; i, fol. 353d; Lincolnshire
Claims (Domesday Book), fols. 375d–376a; i, fol. 353d; i, fol. 322c; i, fol. 323a;
i, fol. 46c; i, fol. 322d; i, fol. 322d; i, fol. 323a; i, fol. 323a; i, fol. 323a; i, fol.
323a; i, fol. 354a; i, fol. 323a; i, fol. 354a; i, fol. 323a; i, fol. 321c; i, fol. 354b; i,
fol. 323a; i, fol. 321c; Regesta regum Anglo-Normannorum III, No. 942; i, fol.
359b; Dugdale, Monasticon Anglicanum, III, pp. 544–46, No. I; i, fol. 305a;
Lincolnshire Claims (Domesday Book), fols. 375a–d; i, fol. 305a; i, fol. 305a; i,
fol. 305a; i, fol. 305a; i, fol. 305a; i, fol. 305a; i, fol. 305a; i, fol. 305a; i, fol. 305a;
i, fol. 305a

Willelm De Poillgi

His toponym is now Saint-Léger-sur-Sarthe, dépt. Orne, Normandy. William gave
the church of Sanctus Leodegarus de Polleio to Saint-Martin de Sées in 1091,
when his wife occurs as Basilia and his son as Robert; Robert was 'ultramare',
presumably in England, at the time (Cartulary, Arch. dépt. Orne H 938, no. cii, fols
47–48). The grant was confirmed by Earl Roger de Montgomery. Robert son of
William occurs in relation to the grant of Saint-Léger in 1101 (idem, fol. 49, no.
cv). Around 1080 Robert de Polliaco occurs as dapifer of Earl Roger in the region
of Sées (Musset, 'Admin. et justice', Cahiers des Annales de Normandie no17,
1985, 129–148); he may have been the son or the father of William. The family's
close connexion with the Montgomerys perhaps explains why they disappear from
view in England in the early twelfth century, when William's fief was merged with
the Honour of Plympton.

i, fol. 111b; i, fol. 111b; i, fol. 111b; i, fol. 111b; i, fol. 111b; i, fol. 111b; i, fol.
111b; i, fol. 111c; i, fol. 111c; i, fol. 111c; i, fol. 111c; i, fol. 111c; i, fol. 111b

Willelm De Rollestun

Norman, Domesday tenant of Henry de Ferrers. As William of Rollaston he gave
his tithes from his demesne to Tutbury (Cart., 52).

i, fol. 275d

Willelm De Sai

Norman, occurs as W. de Saio in a Gloucester survey of c.1086/1100. He should
doubtless be identified with the William who held manors in Shropshire from
Roger de Lacy that descended in the de Say family of Stokesay. He had been
succeeded by 1100 by Theoderic de Say, possibly his son, to whom further grants
of land were made by the Lacys.

i, fol. 256b; i, fol. 256b; Ellis, 'Landholders of Gloucestershire' (1880), pp.
91–93

Willelm De Sancto Leger

Norman, from Saint-Léger-aux-Bois, Seine-Maritime, arr. Neufchâtel, cant.
Blangy. Domesday tenant of the count of Eu in Sussex, benefactor of Battle Abbey
(Chron., 120). Father of Clarembald (Mon. Ang. iii, 246–7) His successor in 1166
was Thomas de St Leger. Cf. Loyd, 90.

i, fol. 18a; i, fol. 18c

Willelm De Scohies

Norman, from Écouis, Eure, arr. Les Andelys, cant. Fleury-sur-Andelle (Loyd,
39–40), Domesday tenant-in-chief. He gave land at Banham, Norfolk, to St
Mary's, York, and other land in Norfolk to Saint-Etienne de Caen.

Dugdale, Monasticon Anglicanum, III, pp. 548–50, No. V; ii, fol. 088b; i, fol. 185c; ii, fol. 221b; ii, fol. 088b; ii, fol. 213b; ii, fol. 213b; ii, fol. 225a; ii, fol. 222a; ii, fol. 221b; ii, fol. 223b; ii, fol. 215b; ii, fol. 223a; ii, fol. 222a; ii, fol. 222a; ii, fol. 225a; ii, fol. 225a; ii, fol. 223b; ii, fol. 223a; ii, fol. 224b; ii, fol. 223b; i, fol. 82b; i, fol. 82b; ii, fol. 224a; ii, fol. 225a; ii, fol. 225a; ii, fol. 225b; ii, fol. 222a; ii, fol. 224b; ii, fol. 224b; ii, fol. 222a; ii, fol. 222b; ii, fol. 224a; ii, fol. 225a; ii, fol. 223b; ii, fol. 221b; ii, fol. 223b; i, fol. 185c; i, fol. 185c; i, fol. 185c; ii, fol. 225a; i, fol. 185c; ii, fol. 225b; i, fol. 185c; i, fol. 185c; ii, fol. 225a; ii, fol. 222b; ii, fol. 222b; ii, fol. 223a; ii, fol. 224b; ii, fol. 224b; ii, fol. 224b; ii, fol. 223a; ii, fol. 223a; ii, fol. 223a; ii, fol. 224b; i, fol. 185c; ii, fol. 353b; ii, fol. 383a; ii, fol. 354a; ii, fol. 353a; ii, fol. 117a; ii, fol. 384a; ii, fol. 354a; ii, fol. 109b; Dugdale, Monasticon Anglicanum, III, p. 547, No. III

Willelm De Septmuels

Norman, from Sept-Meules, Seine-Maritime, arr. Dieppe, cant. Eu (Loyd, 97), Domesday tenant of Robert count of Eu. A second William occurs as a tenant of the bishop of London in 1166 (RBE, 186). Before 1162 Henry II confirmed to Foucarmont the gifts of Rainald and Roger de Septmeules and Amabilis their mother (CDF, 186).

i, fol. 18b; i, fol. 19d

Willelm De Ver

Held a small fee in Domesday Middlesex. Probably a Norman; certainly unrelated to Alberic de Ver.

i, fol. 127c

Willelm De Verly

Norman, probably named from Vesly, Manche, arr. Coutances, cant. Lessay, Domesday tenant of the archbishop of York. His Lincolnshire holdings are identifiable from the Lindsey Survey of 1115/18, by when he had been succeeded by Richard de Verli. Probably father of Jueta (Judith] de Verly, wife of Ansquetil de Scuris (q.v.).

i, fol. 339d; i, fol. 339d; i, fol. 340a; i, fol. 339c; i, fol. 339c; i, fol. 303d

Willelm De Warenna

Norman, from Varenne, Seine-Martime, cant. Bellencombre (Loyd, 111–12), son of Ralph II de Warenne and Emma. Domesday tenant-in-chief, holding the militarily important rape of Lewes in Sussex, where he founded a Cluniac priory c.1078/82. He supported William II against Odo of Bayeux and Robert of Mortain in the spring of 1088, being created earl of Surrey shortly after 16 April 1088. He was mortally wounded at the siege of Pevensey before the end of May 1088; he died on 24 June 1088, and was buried at Lewes. He was twice married, first to Gundreda, sister of Gerbod the Fleming, earl of Chester, who died in childbirth at Castle Acre on 27 May 1085 and was buried in the chapter-house at Lewes, and secondly to the sister of Richard Guet, probably a member of the Goz family of Avranches. He left issue by Gundreda his successor in England William II, Rainald, who succeeded to his mother's Flemish possessions, and a daughter Edith, first the wife of Gerard de Gournai and secondly of Drogo de Monchy. Comp. Peer. xii.1, 491–512, Sanders, 128, EYC viii, passim. The early genealogy of the family and its relationship to the Mortemers is established in Keats-Rohan, 'Aspects of Robert of Torigny's Genealogies Revisted', Nottingham Medieval Studies xxxvii (1993).

ii, fol. 085b; ii, fol. 085a; ii, fol. 161a; Dugdale, Monasticon Anglicanum, IV, p. 49, No. I; Dugdale, Monasticon Anglicanum, III, pp. 544–46, No. I; Dugdale, Monasticon Anglicanum, IV, p. 14, No. VI; Dugdale, Monasticon Anglicanum, IV, p. 50, No. III; Clay, Early Yorkshire Charters (1949), VIII, No. 10; Clay, Early Yorkshire Charters (1949), VIII, No. 6; ii, fol. 213a; ii, fol. 213a; ii, fol. 084a; ii, fol. 136b; ii, fol. 136a; ii, fol. 213b; ii, fol. 213b; ii, fol. 215b; ii, fol. 212b; ii, fol. 137b; Clay, Early Yorkshire Charters (1949), VIII, No. 4; ii, fol. 019a; ii, fol. 276b; ii, fol. 115a; ii, fol. 110b; i, fol. 47b; ii, fol. 398a; ii, fol. 400b; ii, fol. 400a; ii, fol. 398a; i, fol. 351d; ii, fol. 398a; ii, fol. 399a; i, fol. 205c; i, fol. 148b; i, fol. 157d; i, fol. 321b; i, fol. 211d; i, fol. 351d; i, fol. 26a; i, fol. 26a; i, fol. 26a; i, fol. 26b; i, fol. 26b; i, fol. 56b; i, fol. 257b; i, fol. 26a; i, fol. 157d; Dugdale, Monasticon Anglicanum, IV, p. 13, No. IV; ii, fol. 400a; ii, fol. 277a; ii, fol. 036a; ii, fol. 157a; ii, fol. 109b; Lincolnshire Claims (Domesday Book), fols 376d–377c; Clay, Early Yorkshire Charters (1949), VIII, No. 4; ii, fol. 167a; ii, fol. 161a; ii, fol. 161a; ii, fol. 161a; ii, fol. 167a; ii, fol. 166b; ii, fol. 168a; ii, fol. 168a; ii, fol. 161a; ii, fol. 158b; ii, fol. 161a; ii, fol. 161a; ii, fol. 161b; ii, fol. 161a; ii, fol. 159b; ii, fol. 161a; ii, fol. 159b; ii, fol. 161a; i, fol. 196b; ii, fol. 160a; ii, fol. 158a; ii, fol. 158a; ii, fol. 167a; ii, fol. 170a; ii, fol. 161a; ii, fol. 170b; ii, fol. 169b; ii, fol. 168a; ii, fol. 159a; ii, fol. 168b; ii, fol. 160a; ii, fol. 170a; ii, fol. 170a; ii, fol. 170a; ii, fol. 170a; ii, fol. 170a; ii, fol. 170a; ii, fol. 170b; ii, fol. 167a; ii, fol. 170a; ii, fol. 167a; ii, fol. 168b; ii, fol. 168a; ii, fol. 166b; ii, fol. 166b; ii, fol. 166b; ii, fol. 166b; ii, fol. 166b; ii, fol. 167a; ii, fol. 167a; ii, fol. 167a; ii, fol. 170b; ii, fol. 157a; ii, fol. 159a; ii, fol. 036a; ii, fol. 161b; ii, fol. 161b; ii, fol. 161b; ii, fol. 161b; ii, fol. 161b; ii, fol. 161a; ii, fol. 036a; ii, fol. 157b; ii, fol. 160a; ii, fol. 037b; ii, fol. 038a; ii, fol. 157b; ii, fol. 157b; ii, fol. 158b; ii, fol. 161a; ii, fol. 161a; ii, fol. 157b; ii, fol. 157b; ii, fol. 157a; ii, fol. 158b; ii, fol. 157a; ii, fol. 161a; ii, fol. 157a; ii, fol. 158a; ii, fol. 160b; ii, fol. 160a; ii, fol. 158a; i, fol. 148b; ii, fol. 159b; ii, fol. 160a; ii, fol. 160b; i, fol. 196c; ii, fol. 159b; ii, fol. 160a; ii, fol. 160a; ii, fol. 159b; ii, fol. 160b; ii, fol. 162b; ii, fol. 160a; ii, fol. 159a; ii, fol. 157a; ii, fol. 158b; ii, fol. 159a; ii, fol. 038a; ii, fol. 159a; ii, fol. 158b; ii, fol. 158b; ii, fol. 036b; ii, fol. 169b; ii, fol. 157a; ii, fol. 160b; ii, fol. 171b; i, fol. 321b; ii, fol. 172a; i, fol. 321b; i, fol. 321b; ii, fol. 171a; ii, fol. 171b; ii, fol. 171b; ii, fol. 171b; ii, fol. 215a; ii, fol. 171b; ii, fol. 171b; ii, fol. 171b; ii, fol. 251b; ii, fol. 171a; ii, fol. 169a; ii, fol. 170b; ii, fol. 171b; ii, fol. 162a; ii, fol. 262b; ii, fol. 171a; ii, fol. 172a; i, fol. 321b; ii, fol. 172a; ii, fol. 168a; ii, fol. 171b; ii, fol. 171b; ii, fol. 171a; ii, fol. 170b; ii, fol. 172b; ii, fol. 172a; i, fol. 321a; Clay, Early Yorkshire Charters (1949), VIII, No. 5; Clay, Early Yorkshire Charters (1949), VIII, No. 2; Clay, Early Yorkshire Charters (1949), VIII, No. 3; Hamilton, Inquisitio Eliensis (1876), pp. 192–95; i, fol. 205c; i, fol. 205c; i, fol. 321b; i, fol. 321b; i, fol. 321a; i, fol. 321a; i, fol. 321b; i, fol. 321a; i, fol. 321b; i, fol. 321a; i, fol. 321b; i, fol. 321a; i, fol. 321b; i, fol. 321b; i, fol. 321b; i, fol. 321b; i, fol. 321b; i, fol. 321b; i, fol. 321b; i, fol. 321a; i, fol. 321b; i, fol. 321b; i, fol. 321b; i, fol. 321b; i, fol. 321a; i, fol. 321a; i, fol. 321b; ii, fol. 162b; ii, fol. 163a; ii, fol. 163a; ii, fol. 162b; ii, fol. 163b; ii, fol. 162a; ii, fol. 162b; ii, fol. 163a; ii, fol. 162b; ii, fol. 172a; ii, fol. 162a; ii, fol. 162a; ii, fol. 162a; ii, fol. 162a; ii, fol. 162a; ii, fol. 162b; ii, fol. 168b; ii, fol. 168b; ii, fol. 168b; ii, fol. 168b; ii, fol. 166a; ii, fol. 168b; ii, fol. 163b; ii, fol. 168b; ii, fol. 163a; ii, fol. 168a; ii, fol. 170a; ii, fol. 166a; ii, fol. 163b; ii, fol. 163b; ii, fol. 163a; ii, fol. 163a; ii, fol. 166b; ii, fol. 166a; ii, fol. 164b; ii, fol. 162b; ii, fol. 164b; ii, fol. 165a; ii, fol. 164b; ii, fol. 166b; ii, fol. 165a; ii, fol. 163b; ii, fol. 164b; ii, fol. 166a; ii, fol. 164b; ii, fol. 164a; ii, fol. 164b; ii, fol. 171b; ii, fol. 164a; ii, fol. 166a; ii, fol. 170b; ii, fol. 166a; ii, fol. 166a; ii, fol. 164a; ii, fol. 164a; ii, fol. 164a; ii, fol. 163b; ii, fol. 165a; ii, fol. 166b; ii, fol. 166a; i, fol. 211d; i, fol. 211d; i, fol. 211d; i, fol. 211d; i, fol. 211d; i, fol. 211d;

Dugdale, Monasticon Anglicanum, III, pp. 548–50, No. V; ii, fol. 167b; ii, fol. 015b; i, fol. 22d; ii, fol. 018a; ii, fol. 015b; Dugdale, Monasticon Anglicanum, IV, pp. 12–13, No. II; Clay, Early Yorkshire Charters (1949), VIII, No. 1; ii, fol. 165a; ii, fol. 165a; Clay, Early Yorkshire Charters (1949), VIII, No. 15

Willelm De Wateuilla

Norman, from Vatteville-la-Rue, Seine-Maritime, comm. arr. La Mailleraye-sur-Seine, or Vatteville, Eure, arr. Saint-Pierre-du-Vauray. Domesday tenant of William de Warenne in Sussex and Essex, also a tenant of Chertsey Abbey in Surrey. His Warenne fees appear later to have been granted to Rainald II de Warenne: VCH vii, 80; Farrer, HKF iii, 323–4. William may have been the father of Robert de Watteville, an important tenant of Richard fitz Gilbert de Clare in Surrey in 1086. Between 1107 and 1128 Bishop William of Winchester confirmed to Chertsey abbey a grant made by Robert de Watteville, which included land in Esher (EEA viii, no. 4), where William de Watteville had held land of the abbey in 1086. He and his wife granted land in Croismare to Jumièges, confirmed by William I before 1087 (CDF, 152). It was confirmed later by Eudo fitz Erneis, husband of his great-grandaughter Felicia (BN lat. 5424, pp. 86–7).

ii, fol. 036b; ii, fol. 106b; i, fol. 26d; i, fol. 27c; i, fol. 27b; i, fol. 27a; i, fol. 32c; i, fol. 26c; i, fol. 32c; i, fol. 32d; ii, fol. 435a; ii, fol. 435a; ii, fol. 445a; ii, fol. 435a

Willelm Diaconus

William the deacon also occurs in DB Essex as William 'nepos episcopi'. VCH Essex i, 418 suggests that his uncle was William, bishop of London from 1051 to 1075. A notification of c.1085–7 grants to Bishop Maurice of London the land that William the deacon and Ralph his brother hold of the king (RRAN i, 277).

ii, fol. 094b; ii, fol. 094b; i, fol. 57a; ii, fol. 094b; ii, fol. 106b

Willelm Dispensator

Occurs Domesday Kent as dispenser of Archbishop Lanfranc and in the Milites archiepiscopi (c.1093/6) as William of Wrotham; cf. Du Boulay, Canterbury, 96, 252, 351.

Douglas, ed., Domesday Monachorum (1944), p. 105; i, fol. 003b

Willelm Dur-

Norman, occurs Domesday Wiltshire as a tenant of Alfred of Marlborough. His surname is given in contracted form, which cannot be certainly expanded as Durus or Duredent or some such. Conceivably he was William de Durville, who was named as a tenant of the count of Mortain in the Exon Tax Returns for Somerset. The Durville family were tenants in the twelfth century of land at Compton Durville and Loxton, which descended to the Tresgoz family, heirs of Alfred. Another part of Compton Durville was held in 1086 by Mauger de Carteret, of whom William may have been an undertenant.

i, fol. 70c

Willelm Episcopus De Tetfort

William de Beaufour, royal clerk. Nominated bishop of Thetford 25 December 1085. He died or resigned before 27 January 1091. See FEA ii, 55. Probably brother of Ralph de Beaufour, a tenant-in-chief (EEA vi, p. xxviii). Possibly the clerk William who, with his brother Robert de Belfou, attested an act of Humphrey de Bohun before 1066 (Fauroux, 185; CDF, 90). Robert was perhaps the son of Richard de Beaufour (brother of a Humphrey) who occurs as a nephew of Bishop

John of Avranches in 1066 (Fauroux, 229). Richard's daughter was married to Hugh de Montfort, a Domesday tenant in East Anglia. See also Ralph de Bellofago.

i, fol. 56d; i, fol. 65c; ii, fol. 191a; ii, fol. 379b; ii, fol. 379a; ii, fol. 118b; ii, fol. 125a; ii, fol. 115a; ii, fol. 200a; ii, fol. 201b; ii, fol. 201b; ii, fol. 201a; ii, fol. 201a; ii, fol. 116b; ii, fol. 194a; ii, fol. 201a; ii, fol. 201a; ii, fol. 191b; ii, fol. 116b; ii, fol. 200b; ii, fol. 191a; ii, fol. 191a; ii, fol. 191a; ii, fol. 191b; ii, fol. 191b; ii, fol. 115a; ii, fol. 195b; ii, fol. 200a; ii, fol. 196b; ii, fol. 195b; ii, fol. 195b; ii, fol. 196a; ii, fol. 196a; ii, fol. 201a; ii, fol. 196a; ii, fol. 200b; ii, fol. 196b; ii, fol. 196b; ii, fol. 201a; ii, fol. 200b; ii, fol. 200b; ii, fol. 200b; ii, fol. 200b; ii, fol. 200b; ii, fol. 191a; ii, fol. 195a; ii, fol. 192a; ii, fol. 193b; ii, fol. 191b; ii, fol. 193b; ii, fol. 192a; ii, fol. 192a; ii, fol. 192a; ii, fol. 191b; ii, fol. 192a; ii, fol. 193b; ii, fol. 192a; ii, fol. 192b; ii, fol. 192a; ii, fol. 193a; ii, fol. 192a; ii, fol. 192a; ii, fol. 192b; ii, fol. 194a; ii, fol. 194a; ii, fol. 192a; ii, fol. 193b; ii, fol. 194b; ii, fol. 194a; ii, fol. 115a; ii, fol. 201a; ii, fol. 116b; ii, fol. 118b; ii, fol. 193b; ii, fol. 191a; ii, fol. 193b; ii, fol. 193a; ii, fol. 192b; ii, fol. 192b; ii, fol. 192b; ii, fol. 192b; ii, fol. 193a; ii, fol. 192a; ii, fol. 194a; ii, fol. 192b; ii, fol. 191b; ii, fol. 197a; ii, fol. 198a; ii, fol. 196b; ii, fol. 197b; ii, fol. 197b; ii, fol. 197a; ii, fol. 197b; ii, fol. 197b; ii, fol. 196a; ii, fol. 197b; ii, fol. 197b; ii, fol. 197a; ii, fol. 197a; ii, fol. 197a; ii, fol. 198a; ii, fol. 200b; ii, fol. 200a; ii, fol. 201a; ii, fol. 194b; ii, fol. 196b; ii, fol. 197b; ii, fol. 194b; ii, fol. 197a; ii, fol. 194b; ii, fol. 198b; ii, fol. 195b; ii, fol. 195b; ii, fol. 194b; ii, fol. 195a; ii, fol. 194b; ii, fol. 195a; ii, fol. 195a; ii, fol. 195a; ii, fol. 198b; ii, fol. 198b; ii, fol. 199a; ii, fol. 199a; ii, fol. 199a; ii, fol. 199a; ii, fol. 199a; ii, fol. 198a; ii, fol. 195b; ii, fol. 379b; ii, fol. 379b; ii, fol. 380a; ii, fol. 381a; ii, fol. 381a; ii, fol. 380b; ii, fol. 380b; ii, fol. 380b; ii, fol. 381a; ii, fol. 380b; ii, fol. 380a; ii, fol. 379b; ii, fol. 379a; ii, fol. 379b; ii, fol. 379b; ii, fol. 379b; ii, fol. 379b; ii, fol. 380a; ii, fol. 380a; ii, fol. 379b; ii, fol. 380b; ii, fol. 379b; ii, fol. 379b; ii, fol. 379b; ii, fol. 379b; ii, fol. 379b; ii, fol. 380a; ii, fol. 379a; ii, fol. 379a; ii, fol. 379a; ii, fol. 379b; ii, fol. 380a; ii, fol. 380a; ii, fol. 380a; ii, fol. 380a; ii, fol. 380a; ii, fol. 379a; ii, fol. 379b; ii, fol. 379b; Clay, Early Yorkshire Charters (1949), VIII, No. 5

Willelm Episcopus Dunelmensis

William, monk of Saint-Calais in the county of Maine (dépt. Sarthe), bishop of Durham 9 November 1080 – 2 January 1096 (FEA ii, 29). P. Chaplais, 'William of Saint-Calais and Domesday Book', Domesday Studies, ed. J.C. Holt (Woodbridge, 1987); W. Aird, 'Absent friends: the career of Bishop William of St Calais', Anglo-Norman Durham, ed. D. Rollason et al. (Woodbridge, 1994).

Regesta regum Anglo-Normannorum III, No. 255; Dugdale, Monasticon Anglicanum, III, pp. 544–46, No. I; Gibbs, Early Charters of St Pauls (1939), No. 12; Dugdale, Monasticon Anglicanum, IV, p. 13, No. IV; i, fol. 351b; i, fol. 359d; i, fol. 304c; i, fol. 220b; i, fol. 340c; i, fol. 210c; ii, fol. 015b; Clay, Early Yorkshire Charters (1949), VIII, No. 4; Dugdale, Monasticon Anglicanum, III, p. 216, No. V; Lincolnshire Claims (Domesday Book), fols 376d–377c; Dugdale, Monasticon Anglicanum, III, p. 216, No. IV; Hart, Cartularium Monasterii de Rameseia, No. CXLVII; Gibbs, Early Charters of St Pauls (1939), No. 16; Dugdale, Monasticon Anglicanum, III, p. 217, No. VI; i, fol. 359d; i, fol. 304d; i, fol. 304c; i, fol. 304c; i, fol. 304c; i, fol. 304c; i, fol. 304c; i, fol. 304c; i, fol. 304d; i, fol. 304c; i, fol. 304c; i, fol. 304c; i, fol. 304c; i, fol. 304c; i, fol. 304c; i, fol. 304c; i, fol. 304d; i, fol. 304c; i, fol. 304c; i, fol. 304d; i, fol. 304d; i, fol. 304c; i, fol. 304c; i, fol. 210c; ii, fol. 015b; i, fol. 210c; i, fol. 304d; i, fol. 304c; i, fol. 304c; i, fol. 304c; i, fol. 304c; i, fol. 304c; i, fol. 304c; i, fol. 304c; i, fol. 304c; i, fol. 304d; i, fol. 304c; i, fol. 304c; i, fol. 304c; i, fol. 304c; i, fol. 304c; i, fol. 304c; i, fol. 304c; i, fol. 304c; i, fol. 304c; i, fol. 304c; i, fol. 304c; i, fol. 304c; i, fol. 304d; i, fol. 304c; i, fol. 340d; i, fol. 312d; i, fol. 340d; i, fol. 340d; i, fol. 340d; i, fol. 340d; i, fol. 340d; i, fol. 337d; i, fol. 340d; i, fol. 340d; i, fol. 220b; i, fol. 340d; i, fol. 341b; i, fol. 340d; i, fol. 304c; i, fol. 304c; i, fol. 304c; i, fol. 359d; i, fol. 304c; Lincolnshire Claims (Domesday Book), fols 376d–377c; Lincolnshire Claims (Domesday Book), fols 375a–d; Lincolnshire Claims (Domesday Book), fols 375d–376a; i, fol. 340c; i, fol. 341b; i, fol. 312d; i, fol. 58b; i, fol. 341c; i, fol. 341c; i, fol. 341a; i, fol. 340c; i, fol. 341c; i, fol. 341c; i, fol. 340d; i, fol. 341c; i, fol. 340d; i, fol. 341b; i, fol. 341b; i, fol. 341a; i, fol. 341a; i, fol. 341a; i, fol. 341b; i, fol. 341c; i, fol. 340d; i, fol. 340d; i, fol. 340d; i, fol. 340d; i, fol. 341b; i, fol. 298a; Dugdale, Monasticon Anglicanum, III, pp. 548–50, No. V; Ransford, Early Charters of Waltham Abbey (1989), No. 5

Willelm Filius Ansculf

William fitz Ansculf, a Picard from Picquigny, Somme, arr. Amiens (Loyd, 78), nephew of Gilo (q.v.). His Domesday tenancy-in-chief was later known as the barony of Dudley, Worcestershire (Sanders, 113). His heir was a daughter Beatrice, wife of Fulk Paynel (d.1130–8). J. Blair, 'William fitz Ansculf and the Abinger motte', Archaeological Journal, 138 (1981).

i, fol. 69c; i, fol. 226b; i, fol. 177a; i, fol. 243a; i, fol. 157c; i, fol. 148c; i, fol. 249d; i, fol. 207a; i, fol. 74d; i, fol. 74d; i, fol. 74c; i, fol. 36a; i, fol. 36a; i, fol. 36a; i, fol. 148d; i, fol. 35d; i, fol. 148d; i, fol. 148d; i, fol. 148d; i, fol. 149a; i, fol. 36a; i, fol. 35d; i, fol. 177b; i, fol. 249d; i, fol. 177b; i, fol. 250a; i, fol. 249d; i, fol. 177b; i, fol. 249d; i, fol. 246a; i, fol. 35c; i, fol. 61a; i, fol. 60d; i, fol. 61a

Willelm Filius Azor

Norman tenant-in-chief in Domesday Hampshire, brother of Jocelyn, also a tenant-in-chief there. Followers of William fitz Osbern de Breteuil.

i, fol. 53a; i, fol. 52b; i, fol. 53d; i, fol. 53b; i, fol. 53c; i, fol. 53c; i, fol. 52b; i, fol. 53b; i, fol. 53b; i, fol. 53b; i, fol. 53b; i, fol. 53b; i, fol. 53b; i, fol. 53a; i, fol. 53b; i, fol. 53a; i, fol. 53a; i, fol. 53b; i, fol. 52b

Willelm Filius Baderon

Son of the Breton Baderon of La Boussac (near Dol, dépt. Ille-et-Vilaine), succeeded his father and uncle Wihenoc as castellan of Monmouth before 1086 as a young man (Book of Llan Dâw, pp. 277–8). His charters to his father and uncles's priory of St Mary, Monmouth, a cell of St Florent de Saumur, contain much information about his family and followers (CDF, 1133–1138). He was married to Havise, by whom he had issue Baderon, his successor, Robert Walensis, and two daughters, Jueta [Judith] and Advenia; one of his daughters was the mother of Richard de Cormeilles (ibid., 1139). His brothers Robert and Payn occur in the same charters. He died at an unknown date before 1144. Sanders, 65; H. Guillotel, 'Une famille bretonne au service du Conquérant: les Baderon', Droit privé et institutions régionales: Études historiques offerts à Jean Yver (1976), 361–6.

i, fol. 179d; i, fol. 162a; i, fol. 48c; i, fol. 185c; i, fol. 167a; i, fol. 179d; Ellis, 'Landholders of Gloucestershire' (1880), pp. 91–93; i, fol. 167a; i, fol. 185d; i, fol. 185c; i, fol. 167a; i, fol. 180d; i, fol. 167a; i, fol. 185d; i, fol. 180d; i, fol. 174d; i, fol. 185d; i, fol. 185d; i, fol. 48c; i, fol. 167a; i, fol. 48c; i, fol. 166b; i, fol. 163a; i, fol. 166a; i, fol. 167a; i, fol. 166b; i, fol. 185d; i, fol. 166b; i, fol. 167a; i, fol. 167a; i, fol. 167a; i, fol. 167a; i, fol. 167a; i, fol. 167a; i, fol. 179c

Willelm Filius Bonardi
Domesday tenant of William de Braose in Sussex.

    i, fol. 29a; i, fol. 29b

Willelm Filius Boselin
The Domesday tenant of Robert de Mortain in Sussex. was probably son of Hugh, brother of Boselin de Dives, from Dives-sur-Mer, Calvados, arr. Pont-l'Evêque, cant. Dozulé (Loyd, 37), rather than Boselin's son William, who occurs in Domesday Northamptonshire. He was dead by 1129/30, when his heir was his son Hugh. See Douglas, Dom. Mon., 38–9.

    i, fol. 16b; i, fol. 21d; i, fol. 22a; i, fol. 20c; i, fol. 219a; i, fol. 219a; i, fol. 22b; i, fol. 22b

Willelm Filius Brien
Brother of Ralph fitz Brien (q.v.) and probably son of 'the wife of Brien'. Almost nothing is known of William, who must have predeceased his brother, who was still active c.1115–20, but whose charters do not mention William.

    ii, fol. 011a

Willelm Filius Constantini
Norman, Domesday tenant-in-chief in Essex. His land became part of the Montcanisy fief in the twelfth century, probably as the result of mediatization. In 1166 Ralph fitz Peter fitz Constantine held two fees of the honour of Eudo dapifer from Henry fitz Gerold (VCH Essex iv, 262). Ralph fitz Herfrid and Ralph fitz Constantine sold land at Bavent, Calvados, to Saint-Etienne de Caen, confirmed 1079/83 by Odo of Bayeux (Actes caen. no. 13). Constantine, kinsman of the sons of Humphrey de Bohun (q.v.) attested a grant of Humphrey's recorded in a confirmation charter for Saint-Léger de Préaux (Bates, 216).

    ii, fol. 097a; i, fol. 151b; ii, fol. 097a

Willelm Filius Corbucion
Norman, Domesday tenant-in-chief. About 1050–60 William of Normandy granted jurisdiction over land held in Normandy to the abbey of Saint-Père-de-Chartres in an act attested by Corbutio de Falesia (Falaise, dépt. Calvados); in an act dated 4 August 1060, also for Saint-Père de Chartres William fitz Corbucion occurs as a witness (Fauroux, nos 146–7). A Corbuzzo, father of Maurice, occurs c.1034–68 associated with Gozelin vicomte of Arques, Seine-Maritime; granted land at Gruchet (prob. -le-Valasse, Seine-Maritime, comm. cant. Bolbec) to the abbey of Sainte-Trinité de Rouen (CDF, 76). His successor in 1166 was his grandson Peter Corbucion, al. Peter of Studley.

    i, fol. 243a; i, fol. 177c; Darlington, Cartulary of Worcester: Reg. I (1962–3), No. 5; i, fol. 177c; i, fol. 243b; i, fol. 250b; i, fol. 243b; i, fol. 238a; i, fol. 243b; i, fol. 243b; i, fol. 243b; i, fol. 174d; i, fol. 61b; i, fol. 61b

Willelm Filius Ermenfridi
Occurs Domesday Kent as a man of Archbishop Lanfranc; identified as fitz Ermenfrid in the Domesday Monachorum. Cf. Du Boulay, Canterbury, 355.

    i, fol. 005a

Willelm Filius Gaufridi
Canon of Dover, occurs Domesday Kent.

    Ballard, Inquisition of St Augustine's (1920), fols 24r–28r; i, fol. 001d; Ballard, Inquisition of St Augustine's (1920), fols 24r–28r

Willelm Filius Goisfridi

Occurs Domesday Dover.

i, fol. 001a

Willelm Filius Grosse

Norman, Domesday tenant of Hugh de Montfort.

ii, fol. 098b; ii, fol. 100a; ii, fol. 100a; ii, fol. 052b; Hamilton, Inquisitio Eliensis (1876), pp. 192–95; ii, fol. 019b; ii, fol. 409b; ii, fol. 409b; ii, fol. 002a; i, fol. 013d; Douglas, Feudal Book of Bury St Edmunds (1932), pp. 22–37

Willelm Filius Malger

Occurs as a tenant of William fitz Ansculf de Picquigny in Domesday Northamptonshire.

i, fol. 226b

Willelm Filius Manne

Domesday tenant-in-chief, also a tenant of William de Braose in Sussex. In Hampshire his manor had been held before 1066 by one Aluric. William was said to have received it with his wife. His Buckinghamshire manor had been held before 1066 by 'Aluric camerarius regis Edwardi'. William's wife was perhaps the English heiress of King Edward's chamberlain. By 1148 his Buckinghamshire holding in chief had passed to a family surnamed de Calz. His holding from William de Braose, one of whose charters he attested as 'Willelmus Magni filius' (CDF, 1110), suggests he was from western Normandy. His father's name was Manni; cf. Manni father of Gilbert who occurs c.1050 in a charter for Saint-Georges de Boscherville (Fauroux, 197).

i, fol. 160b; i, fol. 48c; i, fol. 151b; i, fol. 28b; i, fol. 151b; i, fol. 48c; i, fol. 160b

Willelm Filius Nigelli

Norman, tenant of Earl Hugh of Chester, whom he served as constable. Probably the same as the Domesday tenant of Robert of Mortain in Buckinghamshire. William fitz Nigel de Haga (de la Haye, of which there are several in dépt. Manche) attested a pancarte of Saint-Etienne de Caen, 1079–87 (Actes caen., 18). He died before 1130, when his son William (d.s.p. a. 1149) was his heir. He also had two daughters, Matilda wife of Albert Grelley, and his principal heiress Agnes, wife of Eustache fitz John, through whom the constableship passed to her descendants. HKF ii, 64, 193–4, 250 ff. William appears to have been related to Walter de Gand, who described him as 'nepos meus' (VCH Lancashire i, 298).

i, fol. 349b; i, fol. 349b; i, fol. 269d; i, fol. 268a; i, fol. 157b; J. Tait, Foundation Charter of Runcorn Priory, pp. 19–21; Barraclough, Charters of AN Earls of Chester (1988), No. 28; Lindsey Survey, BL ms Cotton Claudius C v, fols 9–18; Barraclough, Charters of AN Earls of Chester (1988), No. 13; Barraclough, Charters of AN Earls of Chester (1988), No. 3; Stenton, English Feudalism, App., No. 4; Barraclough, Charters of AN Earls of Chester (1988), No. 28; Barraclough, Charters of AN Earls of Chester (1988), No. 12; Barraclough, Charters of AN Earls of Chester (1988), No. 8; Barraclough, Charters of AN Earls of Chester (1988), No. 3; Regesta regum Anglo-Normannorum III, No. 119; Barraclough, Charters of AN Earls of Chester (1988), No. 6; Barraclough, Some charters of the Earls of Chester, No. 1; Barraclough, Charters of AN Earls of Chester (1988), No. 3; Barraclough, Charters of AN Earls of Chester (1988), No. 3; Barraclough, Charters of AN Earls of Chester (1988), No. 28; Barraclough, Charters of AN Earls of Chester (1988), No. 28; i, fol. 266b; i, fol.

266a; i, fol. 266a; i, fol. 266a; i, fol. 266a; i, fol. 266b; i, fol. 266b; i, fol. 266b; i, fol. 349b; i, fol. 146b; i, fol. 266b; i, fol. 266a; i, fol. 266a; i, fol. 266b; i, fol. 266a; i, fol. 266a; i, fol. 266a; i, fol. 266a; i, fol. 266a; Regesta regum Anglo-Normannorum III, No. 119; i, fol. 266a; ii, fol. 300b; ii, fol. 300a; ii, fol. 300b

Willelm Filius Normanni

Norman, tenant-in-chief in Herefordshire and Gloucestershire, where he was a forester associated with the forest of Dean. He was succeeded by his son Hugh fitz William, sometimes known as Hugh of Kilpeck, from the family's chief holding. A William fitz Norman occurs in an eleventh-century charter of Sainte-Trinité de Rouen (Guérard, p. 467; Arch. dépt. Seine-Maritime 27 H I p. 38) granting land at Requiercort, doyenné de Baudemont. VCH Herefordshire i, 336; Hereford Domesday, 108–9.

i, fol. 167c; i, fol. 185d; i, fol. 28c; i, fol. 28c; i, fol. 167c; i, fol. 167c; i, fol. 167c; i, fol. 167c; i, fol. 167c; i, fol. 28c; i, fol. 180a; i, fol. 167c; i, fol. 180b; i, fol. 179c; i, fol. 180a; i, fol. 181a; i, fol. 185d; i, fol. 179c; i, fol. 185d; i, fol. 185d; i, fol. 181b; i, fol. 53c

Willelm Filius Odonis

Norman, tenant of Swein of Essex in a single manor in 1086. Possibly the son of Swein's more prominent tenant Odo. A William fitz Odo attested Robert fitz Swein's grant of Prittelwell to Cluny (Mon. Ang. v, 22). It is impossible to know whether the latter was the Domesday tenant of that name, or the son of the Domesday Odo. A Richard son of William also attested the Prittelwell charter, perhaps indicating that both the Domesday tenants had at this date (c.1120?) been succeeded by their sons. It is tempting to identify William fitz Odo with the father of Beatrice (q.v.), wife of Robert, son of Godbold, another of Swein's tenants. The patronym of Beatrice's father has been lost, but he was brother of a Turold (the name of another of Swein's tenants), who provided her dower at her marriage.

Dugdale, Monasticon Anglicanum, IV, pp. 156–57, No. I; ii, fol. 043a

Willelm Filius Ogeri

Norman, Domesday tenant of Odo of Bayeux in Kent. Occurs with Odo in a Bayeux charter of 1087–96, CDF, 1435. Perhaps a brother of Ranulf fitz Oger (or Ulger) who occurs in acts of Saint-Etienne de Caen (Act. caen., pp. 75, 121, 135, 140).

i, fol. 001a; i, fol. 001c; i, fol. 144c; i, fol. 001c; Ballard, Inquisition of St Augustine's (1920), fols 24r–28r; i, fol. 006d; i, fol. 006d

Willelm Filius Osberni

Norman, seigneur of Breteuil and Pacy, Eure, one of the most important of the Conqueror's followers in 1066. His father Osbern was a nephew of Gunnor, wife of Richard I of Normandy, and his mother Emma a descendant of William I Longsword of Normandy; his brother was Osbern bishop of Exeter (d.1103), Founder of the monasteries of Cormeilles and Lyre – where his wife Adelisa, sister of Ralph de Tosny was buried (Ord. Vit. ii, 282 In 1071 he was summoned, as regent of Normandy, by Philip of France to the assistance of Arnald of Flanders; he was accompanied by a small following of only ten knights and was killed at the battle of Cassel and then buried at his monastery of Cormeilles (ibid.). His Norman inheritance at Breteuil and Pacy was inherited by his son William, the younger son Roger taking over the English lands, centred upon Hereford (Ord. Vit. iii, 128). His daughter Emma's marriage to Ralph II de Gael, earl of Norfolk, in 1075, led to the treason and forfeiture of his son Roger. S. F. Hockey, 'William fitz Osbern and the endowment of his abbey of Lyre', Ango-Norman Studies 3 (1981); C. Lewis, 'The Norman settlement of Herefordshire under William I', ANS vii (1985).

> i, fol. 161a; Dugdale, Monasticon Anglicanum, III, p. 377, No. I; Regesta regum Anglo-Normannorum III, No. 437

Willelm Filius Osmundi
Occurs in Domesday Wallingford.

> i, fol. 56c

Willelm Filius Radulfi
Norman, Domesday tenant of Peterbourgh Abbey, still holding c.1116.

> i, fol. 346a; i, fol. 221d; King, Peterborough Descriptio Militum (1969), pp. 97–101

Willelm Filius Rainaldi
Norman, Domesday tenant of William de Warenne in Suffolk and Sussex. Possibly the ancestor of the Poynings family, named from the manor he held in Sussex (cf. Comp. Peer. x, 656; Loyd, 82). His father was probably the Rainald fitz Reiner, alias Rainald de Puninges son of Reiner (Mon. Ang. v, 14) who gaves tithes at Pangdean to Lewes priory, in which case he would probably have succeeded his father close to 1086. His successor Adam I de Poynings occurs from c.1135–47. See Farrer, HKF iii, 327.

> ii, fol. 167b; ii, fol. 399b; ii, fol. 399b; ii, fol. 399b; ii, fol. 399b; ii, fol. 400b; i, fol. 27a; i, fol. 214d; i, fol. 27d; i, fol. 27a; i, fol. 27a; ii, fol. 400a

Willelm Filius Raineuuardi
Occurs as a tenant of Eudo dapifer in Domesday Bedfordshire. Raineguard, parishioner of Bourg l'Abbé, Caen, and his sons Girald and Rannulf occur in Actes caen. 17, p. 119.

> i, fol. 215a

Willelm Filius Rannulfi
Norman, Domesday tenant of William de Braose. Identified by Douglas, Dom. Mon. 50, with William de Ifelde, knight of the archbishop of Canterbury in 1093–6. Walter of Ifield owed half a knight service to the archbishop in 1171 (Du Boulay, Canterbury, 350).

> Douglas, ed., Domesday Monachorum (1944), p. 105; i, fol. 28d; i, fol. 29b; i, fol. 29b; i, fol. 28c; i, fol. 28c; i, fol. 28c

Willelm Filius Ricardi
Occurs Domesday Berkshire

> i, fol. 61b; i, fol. 61b; i, fol. 61b

Willelm Filius Ricardi
Norman, occurs Domesday Gloucestershire in an ambiguous passage that probably should be expanded to indicate him as a brother of Osbern fitz Richard Scrop.

> i, fol. 163a

Willelm Filius Roberti
Norman, Domesday tenant of Roger de Courseulles; possibly the same person was

also a tenant of the bishop of Bayeux in Kent.

i, fol. 93c; i, fol. 94b; i, fol. 94b; i, fol. 93c; i, fol. 008a

Willelm Filius Stur

Norman, tenant-in-chief in Domesday Hampshire and the Isle of Wight, from which his descendants derived the surname de Insula (de Lisle). In the time of William II (1087–1100) his son Hugh de Insula gave to Marmoutier the tithe of the mill of Torlavilla (Tourlaville, Manche); Hugh's brothers Roger and Gervaise assented to the grant, for which Ralph the prior gave Hugh a mule; Hugh in turn gave it to Roger, who was about to go to Rome (CDF, 1178). Estur steward (dapifer) of Humphrey de Bohun attested a charter of the latter recorded in the pancarte of Préaux (Bates, 216). The land of Estur son of Wigot was confirmed to Marmoutier

i, fol. 52d; i, fol. 48d; Bearman, Charters of the Redvers Family (1994), No. 24; Bearman, Charters of the Redvers Family (1994), No. 42; i, fol. 52d; i, fol. 52a; i, fol. 48d; i, fol. 52d; i, fol. 52d; i, fol. 52d; i, fol. 52b; i, fol. 52d; i, fol. 52c; i, fol. 53a; i, fol. 53a; i, fol. 53a; i, fol. 52d; i, fol. 53a; i, fol. 52d; i, fol. 53a; i, fol. 53a; i, fol. 52d

Willelm Filius Tedaldi

Norman, Occurs in Domesday Dover. Probably to be identified with the William fitz Tedbald/ Tedald/Tebald (i.e. Theobald) who frequently attested charters on behalf of Saint-Etienne de Caen. Lanfranc as abbot purchased land from him 'inter duos Uldones', referring to the Odon, a tributary of the Orne river (Actes caen., pp. 74, 76, 108–10, 121; ibid., p. 116, as a former parishioner of Caen).

i, fol. 001a; i, fol. 001d; i, fol. 001a; Ballard, Inquisition of St Augustine's (1920), fols 24r–28r

Willelm Filius Tirri

A William fitz Tirri attested a charter of Hugh fitz Baldric for St Mary's, York, before 1087 (Mon. Ang. iii, 500–1). He is probably to be identified with Hugh's Domesday tenant William, and certainly with the tenant of William de Percy at Wetherby. See EYC ix, no. 133, note p. 220. A William fitz Theoderic confirmed to Sainte-Trinité de Caen land at Billy (Calvados, cant. Bourgébus) in his wife's inheritance (Actes caen., 8/84).

i, fol. 328a; Clay, Early Yorkshire Charters (1952), IX, No. 133; Dugdale, Monasticon Anglicanum, III, pp. 550–51, No. VII; i, fol. 322b

Willelm Filius Turoldi

Englishman, son of Turold nepos of Wigod, pre-Conquest lord of Wallingford; also known as William de Suleham, from his manor in Berkshire. In 1086 he was a tenant of Miles Crispin, then lord of Wallingford, and of Roger de Montgomery. The fees he held of the latter were given to Brien fitz Count, who married the heiress of Wallingford, by Henry I. A confirmation by William I for Bec, given 1081/7, lists the grants of Hugh fitz Miles of the demesne he held of Miles Crispin at Adwell, Chesterton and Henton; the confirmation also mentions Swyncombe, which was held of Miles by the abbey of Bec in 1086. All three manors were held by William in 1086, suggesting that the grant to him of these holdings was fairly recent. William married the sister of John, mother by a previous marriage of Lescelina, an heiress in Chilton, Berks (Chron. Abingdon, ii, 131). He was succeeded by Amaury, probably his son-in-law (or perhaps the husband of

Lescelina), who was dead by c.1130.

> i, fol. 159c; i, fol. 159c; i, fol. 61c; i, fol. 61c; i, fol. 61c; i, fol. 36c; i, fol. 159c; i, fol. 159c

Willelm Filius Widonis
Norman, Domesday tenant-in-chief in Somerset and Gloucestershire.

> i, fol. 167b; i, fol. 95d; i, fol. 95d; i, fol. 167b; i, fol. 167b; i, fol. 72b

Willelm Filius Wimundi
Domesday tenant of Baldwin of Exeter, whose daughter he married. Identified as William fitz Wimund in Exon, he is well evidenced as William fitz Wimund of Avranches. He and his son Robert were benefactors of Mont-Saint-Michel (Bibl. mun. Avranches ms 210, fol. 83r–v). In one item (ibid., 83v), dated 1066 but which, on account of a reference to Bishop Michael of Avranches, must be dated 1069–84, William's wife was named Matilda. He was probably dead by 1130 when his son Robert, married in 1129 to Hadvise daughter of Gelduin de Dol, appears on the Pipe Roll 31 Henry I, p. 155, on account of that marriage.

> i, fol. 106c

Willelm Frater Gundulfi Episcopi Rovecensis
William brother of Bishop Gundulf of Rochester occurs as such in Excerpta, and as William de Detlinge in the Milites archiepiscopi of 1093–6, but was unnamed in Domesday Book. According to the Vita Gundulfi, Gundulf's parents (and hence, presumably, William's), were Hatheguin and Adelesia, natives of the Norman Vexin.

> Douglas, ed., Domesday Monachorum (1944), p. 105; i, fol. 003b

Willelm Folet
Norman, occurs Domesday Kent as a tenant of Archbishop Lanfranc and Hugh de Montfort, and as a knight of the archbishop in 1093. Cf. RRAN i, 458. Fulk Folet held one fee of Daniel de Crevecoeur in 1166. Du Boulay, Canterbury, 41, 373, 378. Hugh's successors Adelina de Montfort and her husbands confirmed to Thetford priory the grant by Turold (Thurald) Folet when he became a monk there (BL Lansdowne 229, fol. 146v).

> i, fol. 004c; Douglas, ed., Domesday Monachorum (1944), p. 105; i, fol. 005b; i, fol. 004c; i, fol. 004c

Willelm Frater Ilberti
Norman, tenant of Roger de Tosny, as was his brother Ilbert.

> i, fol. 183b

Willelm Froissart
Norman tenant of Hugh de Beauchamp in Domesday Bedfordshire. A Humphrey Froissart attested a Préaux charter concerning Epaignes, Eure, in 1158 (Arch. de l'Eure H711, no. 371).

> i, fol. 213b; i, fol. 213b

Willelm Froisselew
Norman, occurs holding a small fief in Domesday Gloucestershire. He occurs as a benefactor of St Peter's, Gloucester in a confirmation of c.1196 (Hist. S. Petri i, 230). Other parts of his holding were given c.1126 by Richard fitz Nigel and his wife Emma, who made two of their sons, William and Turstin, monks of the house

(ibid. 107, 118, 319). Emma was perhaps William's daughter and heiress.

Ellis, 'Landholders of Gloucestershire' (1880), pp. 91–93; i, fol. 167c; i, fol. 167c; i, fol. 167c; i, fol. 167c

Willelm Gros

Norman, tenant of Walter Espec in Domesday Bedfordshire. The land of William Crassus at Villers and La Mare in Caen (Calvados) was given to Sainte-Etienne de Caen 1066/77 (Actes caen. no. 4, pp. 62, 64).

i, fol. 215a

Willelm Guizenbod

References in Domesday Gloucestershire and Wiltshire reveal that a certain Richard had been married by William I to the widow of Ailwin the Sheriff, probably a sheriff of Herefordshire, certainly distinct from the sheriff of warwickshire. Himself dead in 1086, his small fief was held by his son William Guizenbod, whose byname is English meaning 'cursed, or foretold, by a witch' (Williams, Introd. to Gloucestershire Domesday, 35). By 1108 the fief had become part of the earldom of Leicester. About the same time it passed to Roger de Watteville, and thereafter to his heirs of the Bois Arnault family (Hist. MSS. Com., Hastings i, 328). Before 1107 a notification of Robert count of Meulan stated that he had been requested by William Guizenboeht to concede William 's grant to Abingdon (Chron. Abing. ii, 102–3), which William did for himself, his wife and his son. One of the witnesses was William Niger, a man of William Guizenboded.

Ellis, 'Landholders of Gloucestershire' (1880), pp. 91–93; i, fol. 167b; i, fol. 177c; i, fol. 167b; i, fol. 167b; i, fol. 167b; i, fol. 167b; i, fol. 167b; i, fol. 167b; i, fol. 167b; i, fol. 167b; i, fol. 167b; i, fol. 167b

Willelm Gulafra

William Gulafre, Domesday tenant of Robert Malet. Roger Goulafré, lord of Le Mesnil-Bernard, now La Goulafrière, Eure, cant. Broglie, a vasssal of William fitz William Giroie and chamberlain of Arnald d'Echauffour, is mentioned by Orderic Vitalis (ii, 34, 124, 98); a confirmation charter for Saint-Georges de Boscherville mentions the gift of Ralph and Walter, a monk, for the soul of their father Robert Galfre (Fauroux, 197). Roger Gulafre was pardoned Danegeld in Suffolk in 1129 (PR 31 Henry I, 96). Whether Roger was his son or grandson is clear, but he was apparently father of a William, whose grants were confirmed to Eye (Cart., no. 40) In the early thirteenth century Philip Gulafre held four fees of the Honour of Eye (RBE, 411); in 1166 Hugh Gulafre held three fees from the Somerset barony of William de Courcy (ibid. 224).

ii, fol. 155a; ii, fol. 154a; ii, fol. 305a; Brown, Eye Priory Cartulary (1992–94), No. 55; Brown, Eye Priory Cartulary (1992–94), No. 40; Brown, Eye Priory Cartulary (1992–94), No. 1; Brown, Eye Priory Cartulary (1992–94), No. 136; ii, fol. 327b; ii, fol. 310a; ii, fol. 305a; ii, fol. 316b; ii, fol. 305a; ii, fol. 321a; ii, fol. 326a; ii, fol. 305b; ii, fol. 316b; ii, fol. 316b; ii, fol. 310a; ii, fol. 306a; ii, fol. 305b; ii, fol. 316b; Regesta regum Anglo-Normannorum III, No. 288

Willelm Homo Hermeri

Norman, tenant of Hermer de Ferrers in Domesday Norfolk.

ii, fol. 207b; ii, fol. 205b; ii, fol. 117a

Willelm Homo Picoti Vicecomitis

Norman, tenant of Picot of Cambridge at Girton; Domesday juror in Longstow

Hundred, Cambridgeshire.

> Hamilton, Inquisitio Comitatus Cantabrigiensis, pp. 1–93; i, fol. 201b; Hamilton, Inquisitio Eliensis (1876), pp. 97–100

Willelm Hosed

Norman, occurs Domesday Somerset, where the Bath cartulary identifies him as a tenant of Giso bishop of Wells. Probably brother of Walter Hosatus.

> i, fol. 88d; i, fol. 89d; i, fol. 99b

Willelm Hostiarius

Norman, royal usher; occurs Domesday Devonshire.

> i, fol. 103d; i, fol. 292a; i, fol. 292a; i, fol. 292a; i, fol. 117d; i, fol. 117d; i, fol. 117d; i, fol. 117d; i, fol. 117d; i, fol. 117d; i, fol. 117d

Willelm Ingania

Norman, had land in Domesday Northamptonshire and elsewhere by hunter serjeanty; his brother Richard (q.v.) held a forestership in the same area. His holding was afterwards known as the fee of Engaine of Pytchley. He appears to have been succeeded soon after 1086 by his brother Richard. The Pytchely fee had descended to a junior line of Engaine of Abington by 1156. See under 'Ricardus Ingania'.

> i, fol. 216b; i, fol. 229b; i, fol. 225c; i, fol. 207b; i, fol. 207b; i, fol. 206b; i, fol. 219a; i, fol. 225c; i, fol. 225c; i, fol. 229b; i, fol. 229b

Willelm Leuric

An English tenant-in-chief in Gloucestershire and elsewhere in 1086. Most of his holdings had previously been held by Asgot, whom A. Williams, 'A vice-comital family in pre-Conquest Warwickshire', Anglo-Norman Studies xi, 289, identifies as his father Osgod of Hailes, who was 'a leading man of the shire'; see further idem William, Introd. to Gloucestershire Domesday, 24–5.

> i, fol. 167c; i, fol. 160b; ii, fol. 093a; ii, fol. 103a; i, fol. 167c; i, fol. 167c; i, fol. 167c; ii, fol. 093a

Willelm Louet

Norman, Domesday tenant-in-chief; perhaps from the Luvet family which held land at Condé-sur-Risle (Crouch, 'A divided aristocracy?', in Bates and Curry ed. England and Normandy in the Middle Ages (1994), p. 55n). Early benefactor of St Albans, to which he gave Flitwick, Bedfordshire (Mon. Ang. ii, 220).

> i, fol. 242a; i, fol. 232d; i, fol. 140b; i, fol. 140a; i, fol. 226b; i, fol. 216b; i, fol. 61b; i, fol. 61b; i, fol. 216b; i, fol. 61b; i, fol. 56b; i, fol. 216b; i, fol. 235c; i, fol. 235c; i, fol. 235c; i, fol. 235c; i, fol. 235c; i, fol. 226b

Willelm Malbedeng

Norman, Domesday tenant of Earl Hugh of Chester and Roger of Montgomery. His wife was named Adelisa. He had been succeeded by 1130 by his son Hugh (Farrer, HKF ii, 261ff; cf. Hist. Coll. Staffs. n.s. xii, 118ff).

> i, fol. 80a; i, fol. 248b; i, fol. 80b; i, fol. 80a; i, fol. 80a; i, fol. 263c; i, fol. 248b; i, fol. 80a; i, fol. 80b; i, fol. 80b; i, fol. 80b; i, fol. 80b; i, fol. 80b; Barraclough, Charters of AN Earls of Chester (1988), No. 28; Barraclough, Charters of AN Earls of Chester (1988), No. 3; Barraclough, Charters of AN Earls of Chester (1988), No. 28; Barraclough, Charters of AN Earls of Chester (1988), No. 3; Barraclough, Charters of AN Earls of Chester (1988), No. 3; i, fol. 265c; i, fol.

265d; i, fol. 265b; i, fol. 268b; i, fol. 266a; i, fol. 265b; i, fol. 265b; i, fol. 266a; i,
fol. 257c; i, fol. 266a; i, fol. 265d; i, fol. 265b; i, fol. 265b; i, fol. 265b; i, fol.
265b; i, fol. 257c; i, fol. 265d; i, fol. 265c; i, fol. 265b; i, fol. 265b; i, fol. 265d; i,
fol. 265d; i, fol. 265c; i, fol. 265c; i, fol. 265d; i, fol. 265c; i, fol. 265c; i, fol.
265c; i, fol. 265c; i, fol. 265c; i, fol. 265d; i, fol. 257c; i, fol. 265c; i, fol. 257c; i,
fol. 265d; i, fol. 265d; i, fol. 265d; i, fol. 265d; i, fol. 265c; i, fol. 265d; i, fol.
265c; i, fol. 265c; i, fol. 265c; i, fol. 265c; i, fol. 265d; i, fol. 265c; i, fol. 265d; i,
fol. 265c; i, fol. 265d; Barraclough, Charters of AN Earls of Chester (1988), No.
28; Barraclough, Charters of AN Earls of Chester (1988), No. 28; i, fol. 268d

Willelm Maldoit
Norman, from Saint-Martin-du-Bosc, Eure, arr. Les Andelys, cant. and comm.
Etrepagny (Loyd, 62), Domesday tenant-in-chief. By his wife Hadvise he was
father of Robert Mauduit (drowned in 1120), William II Mauduit, chamberlain of
Henry I, Albreda wife of Fulk d'Ouville, and a daughter who married Hugh fitz
John de St Martin. Havise was apparently secondly the wife of William I de
Ainesford (q.v., RRAN ii, p. 340), perhaps as his second wife. R. W. Eyton,
'Pedigree of the baronial house of Mauduit', Herald and Genealogist vii, 385ff.

i, fol. 58d; i, fol. 47c; i, fol. 47c; i, fol. 47c; i, fol. 47c; i, fol. 47c; i, fol. 46c; i, fol.
47c; i, fol. 47c; i, fol. 47c; Mason, Beauchamp Cartulary Charters (1980), No.
159; i, fol. 47c

Willelm Nepos Gaufridi De Magnauilla
'Willelmus de magna villa, nepos Gaufridi', according to ICC, p. 26; nephew or
grandson of his lord Geoffrey de Mandeville. Possibly an error for William son of
Geoffrey (q.v.).

i, fol. 197a

Willelm Nepos Walchelini Episcopi
Norman, nephew of Bishop Walchelin of Winchester. Tenant of Richard de Clare
in Domesday Surrey.

i, fol. 34d

Willelm Niger
Tenant of Baldwin the Sheriff in a group of Devonshire manors lying in Silverton
Hundred. In the first of them William is identified as William Niger in Exon. One
of them was the manor of Aller, and the Tax Return for the Hundred refers to the
holding of William of Aller (de Alre). Cf. William Niger, enfeoffed at Sibton,
Suffolk, by Walter de Caen. In the early twelfth century the monks of
Mont-Saint-Michel complained that Thomas de St John had usurped the manse of
William Niger 'ad nemus Biuie', i.e. Bevais, a now-lost forest in cant. Sartilly,
Manche (Bib. mun. Avranches, ms. 210, fol. 107v).

i, fol. 107b; i, fol. 107b; i, fol. 107b; i, fol. 107b; i, fol. 107b; i, fol. 107b; i, fol.
107b

Willelm Pantulf
Norman, from Noron, Calvados, arr. Falaise (Loyd, 76), Domesday tenant of Earl
Roger in Shropshire. Deprived of his fees by Roger's successor Robert de Bellême,
he was subsequently reinstated by Henry I. He had been suspected of the murder of
Roger's wife Mabel, and had fled, but later cleared himself of the charge (Ord. Vit.
iii, 160–2). According to Orderic Vitalis his mother was named Beatrice and he
had a sister Helwise (Ord. Vit. iii, 154–8; see also ibid., pp. 162–4, iv. 72). By his

wife Lescelina, with whom he founded the priory of Noron, he was father of Philip, Ivo, Arnald and Robert. He was succeeded in 1112 by his son Robert (Sanders, 94).

i, fol. 248b; i, fol. 248b; i, fol. 248b; i, fol. 248b; i, fol. 257b; i, fol. 257c; i, fol. 257c; i, fol. 257c; i, fol. 257c; i, fol. 257b; i, fol. 257c; i, fol. 257b; i, fol. 257c; i, fol. 257c; i, fol. 257c; i, fol. 257b; i, fol. 257b; i, fol. 257b; i, fol. 257b; i, fol. 257b; i, fol. 257b; i, fol. 257b; i, fol. 257b; i, fol. 257b; i, fol. 257c

Willelm Peccatus

Norman, occurs Domesday Suffolk as a tenant of Richard de Clare, Aubrey de Vere and Roger Bigod. He married first an Englishwoman, Alfwen (Chron. Ramesiensis, 228, 233, 271), and secondly Isilia, daughter of Hervé Bituricensis, through whom he acquired the lordship of Great Bealings, Suffolk (Sanders, 48). Father of Haimo, Ralph, Simon and Basilia. For his descendants, Pecche of Bourn, see Comp. Peer. viii, 331 ff.

ii, fol. 175a; ii, fol. 039a; ii, fol. 105b; ii, fol. 396b; ii, fol. 077a; ii, fol. 390b

Willelm Peurel De Nottingeham

Norman, major tenant-in-chief centred upon Nottinghamshire and Derbyshire. There is no direct evidence of any relationship with Ranulf Peverel, also a Domesday tenant-in-chief, but it is highly likely that they were related and possibly quite closely. Both held lordships in west Normandy, Ranulf at Vengeons, Manche, cant. Sourdeval, and William at 'Turgistorp' which he mentioned as 'feudum meum' in a gift to Saint-Sauveur-le-Vicomte (BN lat. 17137, 351/243v); this was probably 'Torgistorp' near Barfleur, Manche, where land was confirmed to the abbey by Henry II (Recueil i, pp. 329, 331, 455–6), rather than Village-Turgis, near Granville, Manche. Founder of the priory of St James at Northampton, and of Lenton priory, Nottinghamshire, a cell of Cluny, his foundation charter mentioned his brother Robert. By his wife Adeline he had issue two sons named William, of whom one predeceased him, and a daughter Adeliz who married Richard I de Redvers. He died on 28 January 1113/14, according to an obituary of St James, Northampton (BL Cotton Tiberius E v, fol. 1v). According to the same obituary his wife predeceased him, but in fact she occurs as the mother of his successor William II Peverel in the 1129/30 Pipe Roll. Cf. Comp. Peer. iv, app. I, 761 ff. On the honour of Peverel see HKF i, 146 ff.

i, fol. 220b; i, fol. 220b; i, fol. 220b; i, fol. 220b; i, fol. 216b; i, fol. 220b; i, fol. 220b; i, fol. 220b

Willelm Pictauiensis

Occurs in Domesday Book as a canon of Dover in 1086. Possibly the historian of the same name, a Norman named from his studies in Poitiers; see R. H. C. Davis, 'William of Poitiers and his history of William the Conqueror', The Writing of History in the Middle Ages; essays Presented to Richard William Southern, ed. R. H. C. Davis and J. M. Wallace-Hadrill (Oxford, 1981), p. 90.

i, fol. 001d; i, fol. 001d; Ballard, Inquisition of St Augustine's (1920), fols 24r–28r

Willelm Pictavensis

Norman, surnamed Poitevin according to Exon, Domesday tenant of Ralph de Pomeroy in Devon. William Pictaviensis and William de Hotot were pledges for Serlo de Lingèvres in a grant to Saint-Etienne de Caen before 1082 (Actes caen.

no. 7, p. 76). In 1166 his successor, another William Pictavensis, held 4 fees of Henry de Pomeroy.

i, fol. 114b; i, fol. 114b; i, fol. 114c; i, fol. 114c; i, fol. 114c

Willelm Pictavensis
Norman, tenant of Ilbert de Lacy in 1086. Identified from his benefaction to Ilbert's priory of St Clement, Pontefract. His descendants retained his byname.

i, fol. 315d; i, fol. 315d

Willelm Portarius
Occurs Domesday Devon. Identified as 'portitor' in Exon and as 'portarius' in the Tax Returns.

i, fol. 117d

Willelm Presbiter
A William was one of three priest to attest Roger de Bully's foundation charter for Blythe priory; possibly the same as a tenant of Roger in 1086.

i, fol. 286c; Timson, Blyth Priory Cartulary (1973), No. 325

Willelm Presbiter
Occurs Domesday Worcestershire as a tenant of Westminster Abbey.

i, fol. 174c

Willelm Presbiter
Priest of Countess Judith, held of her at Mintings in Domesday Lincolnshire.

i, fol. 367a

Willelm Rex
Son of Robert I of Normandy and Herlève. Succeeded his father as a minor in 1035. Married Matilda, daughter of Baldwin V of Flanders c.1051/2. Annexed the county of Maine in 1063 and conquered England in 1066. Ordered the Domesday Survey at Christmas 1085. Died in Normandy on 9 September 1087 and was buried at his foundation of Saint-Etienne de Caen. One of the most discussed figures of the Middle Ages. See, for example, the biographies by David C. Douglas (1964) and David Bates, William the Conqueror (London, 1989).

Dugdale, Monasticon Anglicanum, III, p. 448, No. III; Dugdale, Monasticon Anglicanum, III, pp. 544–46, No. I; Regesta regum Anglo-Normannorum III, No. 99; Regesta regum Anglo-Normannorum III, No. 717; Regesta regum Anglo-Normannorum III, No. 749; Clay, Early Yorkshire Charters (1949), VIII, No. 10; Dugdale, Monasticon Anglicanum, IV, pp. 148–49, No. II; Barraclough, Charters of AN Earls of Chester (1988), No. 3; Barraclough, Charters of AN Earls of Chester (1988), No. 28; Dugdale, Monasticon Anglicanum, III, p. 346, No. II; Dugdale, Monasticon Anglicanum, III, pp. 346–47, No. III; Dugdale, Monasticon Anglicanum, III, pp. 345–46, No. I; Dugdale, Monasticon Anglicanum, III, p. 365, No. II; Regesta regum Anglo-Normannorum III, No. 53; Regesta regum Anglo-Normannorum III, No. 345; Dugdale, Monasticon Anglicanum, IV, p. 148, No. I; i, fol. 38a; Regesta regum Anglo-Normannorum III, No. 487; Regesta regum Anglo-Normannorum III, No. 50; Regesta regum Anglo-Normannorum III, No. 75a; Regesta regum Anglo-Normannorum III, No. 136; Regesta regum Anglo-Normannorum III, No. 154; Regesta regum Anglo-Normannorum III, No. 156; Regesta regum Anglo-Normannorum III, No. 760; Regesta regum Anglo-Normannorum III, No. 942; Regesta regum Anglo-Normannorum III, No. 945; King, Peterborough Descriptio Militum (1969), pp. 97–101; Domesday Book, *passim*

Willelm Scriba
Occurs Domesday Gloucestershire. Named in the Book of Llandaff as one of the barons of William fitz Osbert, earl of Hereford (d.1071).

  i, fol. 162a

Willelm Scutet
Norman tenant of Robert Malet in Domesday Suffolk. A man of the same name was one of the king's cooks (RRAN i, 270). Occurs as a tenant of Romsey abbey in Domesday Wiltshire having restored land to it given as dower for two of his daughters who were nuns there (RRAN ii, 883; EHR vol. 34, no. 173); cf. RRAN ii, 874, re Ernulf Descuit and his daughter, nun of Romsey). A William Escural or Scurel and Geoffrey his brother witnessed a charter for Eye by Ralph Hovel in the late twelfth century (Cart Eye, 139; cf. nos. 241, 427 etc.).

  i, fol. 68b; i, fol. 68b; i, fol. 74c; i, fol. 65c; i, fol. 65b; ii, fol. 310a; ii, fol. 339a; ii, fol. 310a

Willelm Spec
Norman, from a family associated with the de Albinis of the Cotentin (RRAN ii, p. 354, no. clxxvii). Domesday tenant-in-chief in Bedfordshire. Succeeded by his son Walter (Sanders, 52).

  i, fol. 215a; i, fol. 215b; i, fol. 215a; i, fol. 214d; i, fol. 215a; i, fol. 215a; i, fol. 215a; i, fol. 218b; i, fol. 215a

Willelm Taillebois
Norman, occurs Domesday Lincolnshire; presumably a relative of Ivo and Ralph Taillebois. His small fief was later given by Henry I to Robert I de Brus.

  i, fol. 370b; i, fol. 370b; i, fol. 370b

Willelm []
Domesday tenant of Judhael of Totnes. His successor in 1166 was William de Reigny (q.v.).

  i, fol. 110a; i, fol. 110a; i, fol. 109d; i, fol. 110a; i, fol. 109d; i, fol. 109d; i, fol. 109d; i, fol. 109d; i, fol. 109d

Willelm []
One of probably two Williams, tenants of Judhael of Totnes.

  i, fol. 109b; i, fol. 109b; i, fol. 109b; i, fol. 108c; i, fol. 108c

Willelm []
Tenant of Alfred Brito in Domesday Devon. Perhaps the same as one of two Williams holding from Juhel of Totnes.

  i, fol. 116a; i, fol. 116a; i, fol. 116a

Willelm []
Tenant of Waldin Ingeniator in Domesday Lincolnshire. By 1115/18, the date of the Lindsey Survey, Simon fitz William, very likely his son and heir, was holding Waldin's land in chief. This suggests that William was Waldin's heir, perhaps his son or son-in-law. Sanders, 79–80; HKF ii, 118–19.

  i, fol. 365c; i, fol. 365c; i, fol. 365c; i, fol. 365c; i, fol. 365c

Willelm []
Domesday tenant of Robert fitz Hugh at Tilstone Fearnall, which was shortly afterward associated in a gift to St Werburg with Robert de Tremous, brother of

Ranulf, who was possibly named from Les Trois-Monts, Calvados, arr. Caen (Chester Charters, 3, 28).

i, fol. 264c

Willelm []
Domesday tenant of the widow of Hugh fitz Grip in Stafford, Dorset. The heir to his part of a divided manor in 1166 was Terric (Theoderic) de Turberville (q.v.).

i, fol. 83c

Willelm []
Domesday tenant of Urso d'Abetot in Worcestershire; his successor Walter of Doverdale held one fee of William de Beauchamp in 1166.

i, fol. 172b; i, fol. 177d; i, fol. 177c; i, fol. 177c

Willelm []
Domesday tenant of Kolswein of Lincoln.

i, fol. 357b; i, fol. 357c; i, fol. 357c; i, fol. 357c; i, fol. 357c

Willelm []
Domesday tenant of Gilbert de Gand at Lusby, Lincolnshire. His successor by the early twelfth century was Saher de Arcelles (q.v.). A William de Arcele (Aerseele, arr. Thielt, Flanders), attested a charter of Charles the Good count of Flanders in 1120 (Actes Flandre no. 95). At the date of the Lindsey Survey (1115/18) the tenant was Wigod (of Lincoln?].

i, fol. 354d

Willelm []
Domesday tenant of Geoffrey de la Guerche.

i, fol. 235d; i, fol. 235d; i, fol. 235d

Willelm []
Domesday tenant of Ilbert de Lacy of Pontefract. Assumed to have been the ancestor of his sucessors of the de Dai family (VCH Yorks ii, 165).

i, fol. 315b

Wimer Dapifer
Norman, Domesday tenant of William de Warenne, dapifer of William II de Warenne, whose charters he attested as late as c.1130. In a charter for Castle Acre priory Osmund de Stuteville, husband of his great-grand-daughter Isabel, referred to him as 'Wimar seneschal de Gressinghale', Gressinghall being one of the manors he held in 1086. By his wife Gila he left two sons, Roger and Walter. Charters for Castle Acre also give him two 'nepotes', Geoffrey and Sewalo. He ended his life as a monk of Castle Acre. His heir in 1129/30 was his grandson William fitz Roger. Cf. Farrer, HKF iii, 395–6.

ii, fol. 118a; ii, fol. 157b; ii, fol. 168a; ii, fol. 165a; ii, fol. 166a; Dugdale, Monasticon Anglicanum, IV, p. 50, No. III; Dugdale, Monasticon Anglicanum, IV, pp. 49–50, No. II; Clay, Early Yorkshire Charters (1949), VIII, No. 22; Dugdale, Monasticon Anglicanum, IV, p. 49, No. I; ii, fol. 165a; ii, fol. 165a; ii, fol. 165a; ii, fol. 165a; Dugdale, Monasticon Anglicanum, IV, p. 52, No. XIII; ii, fol. 398b

Wimund De Abi
Domesday tenant of Count Alan at Grainsby, Lincolnshire; also a tenant of Roger de Poitou at Swallow. He occurs in the Lindsey Survey, c.1115/18, once as

497

Wimund de Abi. By 1135 he had been succeeded by Eudo of Grainsby, who gave the church of Aby to Greenfield priory. Cf. EYC x, pp. 53–4.

> Lindsey Survey, BL ms Cotton Claudius C v, fols 9–18; i, fol. 352a; i, fol. 347c; i, fol. 347b; i, fol. 347b; i, fol. 137a; i, fol. 137a; Lindsey Survey, BL ms Cotton Claudius C v, fols 19–27

Wimund De Liueland

Norman, knight of the archbishop of Canterbury in 1093–6. Named from Leaveland Court, held in 1086 by Richard the Constable. Possibly the same man as Wimund tenant of the bishop of Bayeux's holding in Domesday Oxfordshire. Cf. Du Boulay, Lordship of Canterbury, 96.

> i, fol. 160a; i, fol. 156c; Douglas, ed., Domesday Monachorum (1944), p. 105

Wimund De Taissel

Norman, from Tessel, Calvados, arr. Caen, cant. Tilly-sur-Seulles, Domesday tenant of Hugh de Beauchamp in Bedfordshire (cf. Loyd, 100).

> i, fol. 209d; i, fol. 213b; i, fol. 213c; i, fol. 213c; i, fol. 213c

Wimund []

Tenant of Ivo Taillebois in Domesday Lincolnshire. His fees were held in 1115/18 by Walter fitz Roger from Ranulf Meschin; HKF ii, 86, 91.

> i, fol. 351d; i, fol. 351d; i, fol. 351b; i, fol. 350a; i, fol. 342c; i, fol. 351a

Wimund []

Norman, Domesday tenant of Ralph Bainard in Essex, possibly also of Haimo dapifer.

> ii, fol. 273b; ii, fol. 056a; ii, fol. 249b

Wimund []

Norman, Domesday tenant of Abingdon abbey.

> i, fol. 59b; i, fol. 59c

Winemar Flandrensis

Fleming, Domesday tenant-in-chief and tenant of Countess Judith. Possibly the same as Winemer of Lens, who attested a charter of Saint-Georges-de-Hesdin c.1087–1111 (Cart. Hesdin, 50), or a member of the castellan family of Lillers in Artois (near Béthune). Sometimes named after Hanslope, his son Michael adopted the style. His other son, Walter, left descendants surnamed of Preston, from Preston Deanery. He died c.1104, when Michael was his principal heir (cf. charter of Matilda II, RRAN ii, app. xlvi). Sanders, 50; Farrer, HKF i, 95ff. Cf. the entry for Walter de Duaco.

> i, fol. 226d; i, fol. 220d; i, fol. 226d; i, fol. 226c; i, fol. 227b; i, fol. 226d; i, fol. 111a; i, fol. 220d; i, fol. 219a; i, fol. 227d; i, fol. 226d; ii, fol. 105a; ii, fol. 277a; i, fol. 229b; i, fol. 229a; i, fol. 152b; i, fol. 152b; i, fol. 229a; i, fol. 229a; i, fol. 229a; i, fol. 229a; i, fol. 229a; i, fol. 229a; i, fol. 229a; i, fol. 229a; i, fol. 229a

Wintrehard []

Norman, Domesday tenant of Walter de Aincurt. He had two sons, Walter and Hugh, of whom Walter had succeeded him by c.1139. His fees were held in 1166 by his grandson Robert fitz Walter. See Foulds, Cart. Thurgarton, no. 172, notes pp.109–10.

> i, fol. 361b

Wizo []
Probably a Fleming, Domesday tenant of Drogo de la Beuvrière.

i, fol. 360c; i, fol. 323d

Wlmar []
Englishman holding of the king in Domesday Suffolk.

ii, fol. 445b; ii, fol. 445b

Wluuard []
English tenant of Robert of Mortain in Domesday Cornwall.

i, fol. 120a; i, fol. 120a; i, fol. 124d

Wluuius Piscator
Englishman, occurs Domesday Oxfordshire.

i, fol. 154b

[] Abbas Cormeliensis
William, monk of Bec under Abbot Herluin, appointed abbot of Cormeilles, Eure, c.1071. He died on a 27 July according to the abbey's necrology; Orderic Vitalis gave the year as 1109, when Archbishop Anselm died (vi, 168).

i, fol. 52a; i, fol. 163a

[] Abbas De Abendone
Rainald was appointed abbot of Abingdon on 19 June 1084, succeeding Abbot Athelelm. He was a former chaplain to William I and a monk of Jumièges at the date of his appointment (Hist. Abingdon, ii, 15–16]. He died in 1097. See Heads, 24.

i, fol. 56b; i, fol. 241d; i, fol. 241d; i, fol. 56c; Barraclough, Charters of AN Earls of Chester (1988), No. 2; Dugdale, Monasticon Anglicanum, III, pp. 544–46, No. I

[] Abbas De Bernai
Osbern, brother of Vitalis, abbot of Westminster and his predecessor as abbot of Bernay, a post he held from 1076 until some time after 1091.

ii, fol. 389a; ii, fol. 389a; ii, fol. 389a; ii, fol. 389a; ii, fol. 389a; ii, fol. 389a; ii, fol. 389a; ii, fol. 389a

[] Abbas De Burtone
Geoffrey de Mala Terra, monk of Winchester, appointed abbot of Burton in 1085. He was expelled in 1094 (Ann. Burton 185, Heads, 31). According to a reconstructed writ in the Burton Cartulary (9–10), Geoffrey was deposed for marrying his sister to Nicholas sheriff of Staffordshire, to whom he gave the manor of Cotes.

i, fol. 280b; i, fol. 273b; i, fol. 273b; i, fol. 273b; i, fol. 273b; i, fol. 273b; i, fol. 273b; i, fol. 273b; i, fol. 273b; i, fol. 273b; i, fol. 273b; i, fol. 273b; i, fol. 273b; i, fol. 273b; i, fol. 273b; i, fol. 273b; i, fol. 273b

[] Abbas De Certesia
Odo, abbot of Chertsey from c.1084 until his resignation in 1092 (Ann. Winchester, 34). He was restored in 1100. The date of his death is unknown; his successor was elected in 1107 (Heads, 38).

Dugdale, Monasticon Anglicanum, II, p. 267, No. XI; i, fol. 32b

[] Abbas De Cluniaco

Hugh, born in 1024, great-nephew of Hugh, bishop of Auxerre. Entered Cluny at the age of 14. Before he was 21 he became prior, and was unanimously elected as abbot on the death of Abbot Odilo on 1 January 1049. Thereafter an adviser to nine popes, he came to exercise a dominating influence in ecclesiastical and political affairs. He took a leading part in the organization of the First Crusade at the Council of Clermont in 1096. He died in 1109 and was canonized by Calixtus II (also a Burgundian) in 1120. A. L'Huillier, Vie de Saint Hugues (Solesmes, 1888); Noreen Hunt, Cluny Under Saint Hugh 1049–1109 (1967).

Dugdale, Monasticon Anglicanum, IV, pp. 12–13, No. II; Clay, Early Yorkshire Charters (1949), VIII, No. 2; i, fol. 196b

[] Abbas De Couentreu

Leofwin II, occurs as abbot in 1075, though the evidence is problematic (Heads, 40).

i, fol. 238a; i, fol. 219a

[] Abbas De Croiland

According to Orderic Vitalis (ii, 344–6), Ingulf was an Englishman by birth and had been a royal clerk; after his return from a pilgrimage to Jerusalem he went to Saint-Wandrille and was received as a monk by Abbot Gerbert, whom he subsequently served as prior. He was appointed abbot of Croyland in 1085/6 by William I, after the deposition of Abbot Wulfketel at Christmas 1085. He died on 16 November 1109. Cf. Heads, 42.

i, fol. 193a; i, fol. 193a; i, fol. 192d; i, fol. 192d; i, fol. 204a; Dugdale, Monasticon Anglicanum, III, pp. 544–46, No. I

[] Abbas De Cruce Sancti Leuffredi

Abbot of La Croix-Saint-Leufroy, dépt Eure, Normandy. The abbot in 1070 and 1079 was Odilo, mentioned by Orderic Vitalis in connexion with one of his monks, Guitmund, who became bishop of Aversa in 1088; Orderic described him as an illiterate who could not see the worth of Guitmund (Ord. Vit. ii, 278–80). Cf. the list in Robert of Torigny, De immutatione, 197.

i, fol. 34a

[] Abbas De Evesham

Walter was appointed abbot of Evesham in 1077. He died on 20 January 1104 (Heads, 47).

i, fol. 174a; i, fol. 174a; i, fol. 219a; Dugdale, Monasticon Anglicanum, II, p. 267, No. XI; Ellis, 'Landholders of Gloucestershire' (1880), pp. 91–93; Dugdale, Monasticon Anglicanum, III, pp. 544–46, No. I

[] Abbas De Fiscanno

William de Rots, Calvados, first dean of Bayeux cathedral, then briefly a monk of Saint-Etienne de Caen. Abbot of Fécamp from 1079 until 1107.

i, fol. 17b; i, fol. 17b; i, fol. 17b; i, fol. 129b

[] Abbas De Gand

Abbot of Saint-Pierre au Mont Blandin, Ghent in 1086.

i, fol. 012d

[] Abbas De Gemmetico

Abbot of Jumièges, Seine-Maritime, Normandy. 'The monk Gontard was transferred from the abbey of St Wandrille by the choice of wise men; and became abbot of Jumièges [in 1078] after the death of Abbot Robert.' (Ord. Vit. ii, 294–5). See Saint-Wandrille, 36.

i, fol. 87b; i, fol. 65b

[] Abbas De Grestain

Abbot of Grestain, Eure, Normandy, founded by Robert of Mortain's father Herluin de Conteville in 1050. Geoffrey, monk of Saint-Serge d'Angers, left his monastery c.1066 to become the first abbot of Grestain, which had been governed until then by Prior Rainald de la Rocque. He died in 1114. Cf. V. Gazeau, 'Quelques exemples de carrières abbatiales en Normandie aux XIe–XII siècles', in K. S. B. Keats-Rohan ed., Family Trees (1997), 318–20.

i, fol. 21c; i, fol. 21c; i, fol. 21c; i, fol. 21c; i, fol. 21c; i, fol. 20d; i, fol. 193b

[] Abbas De Holm

Æfwold, abbot of St Benet's, Holme, Norfolk, from 1064 until his death on 14 November 1089 (Heads, 67).

Dugdale, Monasticon Anglicanum, III, pp. 88–89, No. XXI; ii, fol. 224a; Dugdale, Monasticon Anglicanum, III, p. 89, No. XXII

[] Abbas De Hortune

Osirich occurs as abbot of Horton in 1075. Nothing more is known (Heads, 53).

i, fol. 121b

[] Abbas De Labatailge

Gosbert, first abbot (1076–1095) of William I's foundation of St Martin's, Battle. A monk of Marmoutier, the mother-house of his abbey, he was prepared to quarrel with Marmoutier to preserve the rights of his abbey. His life as abbot and death on 27 July 1095 were recorded in the Chronicle of Battle Abbey, ed. E. Searle, 1980. Cf. Heads, 29.

i, fol. 34a; i, fol. 60a; i, fol. 59d; i, fol. 59d; i, fol. 56b; i, fol. 17d; i, fol. 17d; i, fol. 17d; i, fol. 17d; i, fol. 17d; i, fol. 011d

[] Abbas De Lira

Domesday refers to the abbot of Lyre, Normandy. Little is known of the early abbots. Ernald occurs c.1072 and Hildebert in 1116; cf. Gall. Christ xi, 645–6. Robert of Torigny, De Immutatione, p. 198, appears to say that Ernald and Hildebert were formerly monks of St Evroul.

i, fol. 52b; i, fol. 52a; i, fol. 39c; i, fol. 38d

[] Abbas De Malmesberia

Warin, abbot of Malmesbury from 1070 until his death c.1091 (Heads, 55).

i, fol. 164b; i, fol. 238a

[] Abbas De Ramesie

Ælfsige (Ælsi), monk of Winchester, abbot of St Augustine's, Canterbury, 1061–c.1067. Abbot of Ramsey, Hunts, 1070–87, Chron. Ram., 340. His career offers certain difficulties; see Heads, 35–6, 62, R.W. Southern, Med. and Renaisance Studies 4 (1958), 194ff.

i, fol. 203b; i, fol. 192d; i, fol. 205a; i, fol. 192c; i, fol. 192c; i, fol. 192c; i, fol.

192d; i, fol. 192d; i, fol. 192d; i, fol. 136b; i, fol. 204b; i, fol. 204c; i, fol. 204c; i, fol. 204d; i, fol. 204d; i, fol. 204d; i, fol. 204d; i, fol. 204c; i, fol. 204b; i, fol. 204b; i, fol. 204b; i, fol. 204b; i, fol. 204b; i, fol. 204d; i, fol. 203d; i, fol. 204d; i, fol. 204c; i, fol. 204b; i, fol. 204c; i, fol. 204c; i, fol. 204c; i, fol. 212a; i, fol. 219a; ii, fol. 134a; i, fol. 192c; i, fol. 192c; i, fol. 192c; i, fol. 210d; i, fol. 210d; i, fol. 210d; i, fol. 210d; i, fol. 210d; i, fol. 210d; Hart, Cartularium Monasterii de Rameseia, No. LXXXI; Hart, Cartularium Monasterii de Rameseia, No. CLIX; Hart, Cartularium Monasterii de Rameseia, No. CLXXX

[] Abbas De Sancto Albano
Paul, monk of Saint-Etienne de Caen, nephew of the Italian archbishop Lanfranc. Elected abbot of St Albans in 1077, he died 11 November 1093. Extremely effective abbot of St Albans, one of the greatest of the Old English houses, he assured its future greatness by attracting numerous benefactions from the new non-English landholders (GASA i, 51–66). Cf. Heads, 66.

i, fol. 145d; i, fol. 145d; i, fol. 146a; i, fol. 56c; Dugdale, Monasticon Anglicanum, III, pp. 299–300, No. I; i, fol. 135d; i, fol. 135c; i, fol. 135c; i, fol. 135c; i, fol. 135c; i, fol. 135c; i, fol. 135c; i, fol. 135d; i, fol. 135d; i, fol. 135d; i, fol. 135d; i, fol. 136a; i, fol. 136a; i, fol. 136a; i, fol. 136a; i, fol. 136a; i, fol. 135c; Dugdale, Monasticon Anglicanum, III, pp. 288–89, No. I

[] Abbas De Sancto Ebrulfo
Mainer, son of Gunscelin of Echauffour, monk, prior and abbot (1066–1089) of Saint-Evroult (Normandy, dépt. Orne). Rebuilder of the abbey, it was he who accepted the young Orderic Vitalis, chronicler of the abbey, as an oblate. He and his monks protected William Pantulf when the latter was falsely accused of the murder of Mabel of Bellême in 1077 or 1078. See Orderic Vitalis, ii, 46, 74, etc., and iii, 118–20, etc..

i, fol. 193c; i, fol. 193c

[] Abbas De Superdiua
Fulk of Guernanville (comm. cant. Breteuil, Eure, Normandy), son of Fulk dean of Evreux and Orielde, monk of Saint-Evroult chosen as prior by Abbot Mainard. c.1078 he became abbot of Saint-Pierre-sur-Dives, a Norman abbey founded by Countess Lescelina wife of William of Eu. He took with him four monks of Saint-Evroul, included Bernard Matthew his kinsman (cognatus), according to Orderic Vitalis (ii, 354–6). The severity of his rule earned him many enemies and he was deposed in 1092. He was restored five or seven years later and died as abbot on 3 April 1106 (Ord. Vit., v, 212, vi, 72). As prior of Saint-Evroult he was sent on a private mission to Countess Bertha at Brie and returned with a tooth of Saint-Evroult, obtained through the offices of a friend, the Norman chaplain of the countess (Ord. Vit. iii, 336–7).

i, fol. 59d; i, fol. 59d

[] Abbas De Thorneye
Gunter of Le Mans, royal chaplain and archdeacon of Salisbury, Monk of Saint-Wandrille and Battle. Appointed abbot of Thorney at Christmas 1085, he introduced the customs of Marmoutier (mother-house of Battle) there and completely rebuilt the church. He was briefly guardian of Battle abbey (of which the abbot died in 1102) c.1106, but neglected it to return to his own abbey. A nephew, Ralph, who had accompanied him also soon returned to Thorney. He died on 18 July 1112. See Ord. Vit. vi, 150–4, Chron. Battle Abbey, 116–17, Heads, 72,

FEA iv, 24.

> Dugdale, Monasticon Anglicanum, II, p. 601, No. XIII; i, fol. 205a; i, fol. 205a; i, fol. 205a; i, fol. 205a; i, fol. 205a; i, fol. 205a; i, fol. 205a; i, fol. 205a; i, fol. 192d; i, fol. 211a; Dugdale, Monasticon Anglicanum, II, p. 603, No. XXVII

[] Abbas De Westmonasterio

Gilbert Crispin, son of William I Crispin and Eva de Montfort, monk of Bec. Abbot of Westminster from c.1085 until his death on 6 December 1117. See J. Armitage Robinson, Gilbert Crispin, Abbot of Westminster (Cambridge 1911), Heads, 77.

> Mason, Westminster Abbey Charters (1988), No. 462; Regesta regum Anglo-Normannorum III, No. 926; ii, fol. 106b; i, fol. 35c; i, fol. 211a; i, fol. 135c; i, fol. 135b; i, fol. 135b; i, fol. 135b; i, fol. 135b; i, fol. 135b; i, fol. 135b; i, fol. 135b; i, fol. 17a; i, fol. 43a; i, fol. 145d; i, fol. 145d; i, fol. 128c; i, fol. 128b; i, fol. 128b; i, fol. 128c; i, fol. 128c; i, fol. 128c; i, fol. 128c; i, fol. 128d; i, fol. 128b; Dugdale, Monasticon Anglicanum, III, p. 448, No. III; Lincolnshire Claims (Domesday Book), fols 376d–377c; Dugdale, Monasticon Anglicanum, III, pp. 447–48, No. II; Dugdale, Monasticon Anglicanum, II, p. 18, No. IX; Mason, Westminster Abbey Charters (1988), No. 488; Fisher, Cartularium Prioratus de Colne (Earles C.), No. 3; Dugdale, Monasticon Anglicanum, III, pp. 447–48, No. II; Dugdale, Monasticon Anglicanum, II, p. 267, No. XI; Dugdale, Monasticon Anglicanum, III, pp. 544–46, No. I

[] Abbas De Wintonie

Rivallon, monk, probably a Breton, former prior of Mont-Saint-Michel; abbot of New Minster, Winchester 1072 until his death, possibly 17 January, 1088. Cf. Heads, 80.

> i, fol. 56c; i, fol. 17c; i, fol. 17c

[] Abbas Sancte Trinitatis Rotomag

Walter, abbot of Sainte-Trinité de Rouen. Attended the funeral of William I at Caen, according to Orderic Vitalis (iv, 104).

> i, fol. 128d

[] Abbas Sancti Augustini

Scolland, one of a group of monks of Mont-Saint-Michel promoted to abbacies in England by William I. Abbot of Saint Augustine's, Canterbury, he died a few days before William I in 1087. Cf. Ord. Vit. ii, 248–9; in his edition of Orderic, Le Prévost suggested Scolland came from Pontécoulant (Pons Scollandi) (Calvados); the Cartulary of Mont-Saint-Michel refers to the land of Scolland of Yquelon, Manche (Avranches, Bib. mun. 210 fol. 108r)). The Excerpta Sancti Augustini refer to two of the abbey's men as Acarius and Marcarius. They may be some connexion between them and their abbot since the same three rare names – Scolland, Acarius and Macarius – recur in the family of Bardulf, half-brother of Count Alan.

> Ballard, Inquisition of St Augustine's (1920), fols 20r–23v; i, fol. 001d; i, fol. 010b; i, fol. 012a; i, fol. 002a; i, fol. 012a; i, fol. 012a; i, fol. 012a; i, fol. 012b; i, fol. 012a; i, fol. 012b; i, fol. 012a; i, fol. 007d; i, fol. 006c; i, fol. 002d; i, fol. 012a; i, fol. 012c; i, fol. 012d; i, fol. 012d; i, fol. 012d; i, fol. 012d; i, fol. 012b; i, fol. 012c; i, fol. 012c; i, fol. 012c; i, fol. 012c; i, fol. 012b; i, fol. 012b; i, fol. 012b; i, fol. 012b; i, fol. 012d; Ballard, Inquisition of St Augustine's (1920), fols 24r–28r

[] Abbas Sancti Wandregisili
Girbert, abbot of Saint-Wandrille, 1063–1089.

i, fol. 193a

[] Abbatia Abodesberiensis
Abbotsbury Abbey, Dorset, founded for canons c.1026; changed to Benedictine monastery and church built for monks from Cerne in 1044.

i, fol. 78c; i, fol. 78c; i, fol. 78b; i, fol. 78c; i, fol. 78c; i, fol. 78c; i, fol. 78c; Regesta regum Anglo-Normannorum III, No. 1; Pipe Roll 2 Henry II, 33–ds; Pipe Roll 5 Henry II, 43–ds

[] Abbatia Bucfestrensis
Buckfast Abbey, Devon, founded 1018. Became a daughter-house of Savigny (order of Cîteaux) in 1139.

i, fol. 104a; i, fol. 104a; i, fol. 104a; i, fol. 104a; i, fol. 104a; i, fol. 104a; i, fol. 104a; i, fol. 104a; i, fol. 104a; i, fol. 103d; i, fol. 103d; i, fol. 103d; i, fol. 104a

[] Abbatia Cerneliensis
Cerne Abbey, Dorset, reestablished for Benedictine monks by 987. In 1086 the abbot was William d'Agon, former monk of Mont-Saint-Michel. B.F. Lock, 'The Cartulary of Cerne Abbey', Proc. Dorset Nat. Hist. & Antiq. Field Club, xxviii (1907), 65–95; xxix (1908), 195–223.

i, fol. 78a; i, fol. 77d; i, fol. 78a; i, fol. 78a; i, fol. 78a; i, fol. 78a; i, fol. 77d; i, fol. 78a; i, fol. 78a; i, fol. 78a; i, fol. 77d; i, fol. 78a; i, fol. 77d; i, fol. 78a; i, fol. 78a; i, fol. 78a; Pipe Roll 5 Henry II, 43–ds; Pipe Roll 2 Henry II, 33–ds

[] Abbatia De Abbendone
Abingdon Abbey, Berkshire, founded 675. C.F. Slade and Gabrielle Lambrick, Two cartularies of Abingdon Abbey, Oxford Historical Society N.S. 32–33 (Oxford, 1990–92); Chronicon Monasterii de Abingdon, ed. J. Stevenson, 2 vols, Rolls Series, London, 1858.

i, fol. 59c; i, fol. 59a; i, fol. 59a; i, fol. 59a; i, fol. 59a; i, fol. 59b; i, fol. 58c; i, fol. 59c; i, fol. 59a; i, fol. 59b; i, fol. 59c; i, fol. 59c; i, fol. 59a; i, fol. 58d; i, fol. 58c; i, fol. 58d; i, fol. 59b; i, fol. 58d; i, fol. 59b; i, fol. 58d; i, fol. 59a; i, fol. 59a; i, fol. 59c; i, fol. 59c; i, fol. 59b; i, fol. 156d; i, fol. 156d; i, fol. 154a; i, fol. 156d; Regesta regum Anglo-Normannorum III, No. 7; Red Book of the Exchequer, ed. Hall (1897), pp. 305–06; Fisher, Cartularium Prioratus de Colne (Earles C.), No. 8; Fisher, Cartularium Prioratus de Colne (Earles C.), No. 7; i, fol. 239a; i, fol. 169a; Fisher, Cartularium Prioratus de Colne (Earles C.), No. 1; i, fol. 166a; Regesta regum Anglo-Normannorum III, No. 14; Fisher, Cartularium Prioratus de Colne (Earles C.), No. 4; Douglas, 'Some early surveys of Abingdon' (1929), E.H.R., 44 (1929), 623–25; Regesta regum Anglo-Normannorum III, No. 5; Fisher, Cartularium Prioratus de Colne (Earles C.), No. 14; Fisher, Cartularium Prioratus de Colne (Earles C.), No. 64; Fisher, Cartularium Prioratus de Colne (Earles C.), No. 64; Regesta regum Anglo-Normannorum III, No. 4; Regesta regum Anglo-Normannorum III, No. 11; Fisher, Cartularium Prioratus de Colne (Earles C.), No. 11; Fisher, Cartularium Prioratus de Colne (Earles C.), No. 3; Fisher, Cartularium Prioratus de Colne (Earles C.), No. 9; Pipe Roll 2 Henry II, 35–bk; Pipe Roll 5 Henry II, 37–bkfr; Regesta regum Anglo-Normannorum III, No. 10; Fisher, Cartularium Prioratus de Colne (Earles C.), No. 13; Pipe Roll 5 Henry II, 35–bk; Fisher, Cartularium Prioratus de Colne (Earles C.), No. 2; Fisher, Cartularium Prioratus de Colne (Earles C.), No. 31; Fisher, Cartularium Prioratus de Colne (Earles C.), No. 64; Regesta regum Anglo-Normannorum III,

No. 9; Regesta regum Anglo-Normannorum III, No. 8; i, fol. 156d; i, fol. 166a

[] Abbatia De Almanesches

Abbey of Almenêches (Normandy, Orne) founded by Roger de Montgomery earl of Shrewsbury in lands formerly of his wife Mabel de Bellême's family. Arch. dépt. de l'Orne H 3916–17. L. Musset, 'Les premiers temps de l'abbaye d'Almenèches des origines au XIIe siècle', in L'abbaye d'Almenèches-Argentan et sainte Opportune. Sa vie et son culte, ed. Dom Y. Chaussy (Paris, 1970).

i, fol. 24d; i, fol. 24d; i, fol. 25a

[] Abbatia De Ambresberie

Amesbury Abbey, Wiltshire, founded c.979.

i, fol. 60a; i, fol. 60a; i, fol. 57c; Pipe Roll 4 Henry II, 117a–wl; Pipe Roll 31 Henry I, 022–wl; Pipe Roll 31 Henry I, 126–bk; Pipe Roll 4 Henry II, 117b–wl; Pipe Roll 31 Henry I, 126–bk; i, fol. 68c; i, fol. 68c; i, fol. 68c; i, fol. 68c; i, fol. 68c

[] Abbatia De Athelneye

Athelney Abbey, Somerset, refounded c.960. E. H. Bates, Two Cartularies of the Benedictine Abbeys of Muchelney and Athelney in the County of Somerset (Somerset Record Society, 14, 1899).

i, fol. 91a; i, fol. 78c; i, fol. 91b; i, fol. 91b; i, fol. 91b; i, fol. 91b; i, fol. 91a; Regesta regum Anglo-Normannorum III, No. 28

[] Abbatia De Bec

Abbey of Bec, Eure, Normandy. See André Porée, Histoire de l'abbaye du Bec, (Evreux 1901, rpt. Brussels, 1980); S. Vaughn, The Abbey of Bec and the Anglo-Norman State 1034–1135 (Woodbridge, 1982).

Chibnall, English Lands of Abbey of Bec (1951), No. V; Regesta regum Anglo-Normannorum III, No. 73; Harper-Bill & Mortimer, Stoke by Clare Cartulary, No. 1; Regesta regum Anglo-Normannorum III, No. 74; Regesta regum Anglo-Normannorum III, No. 75a; Regesta regum Anglo-Normannorum III, No. 79; Regesta regum Anglo-Normannorum III, No. 75a; i, fol. 68c; Dugdale, Monasticon Anglicanum, III, p. 473, No. IX; Chibnall, English Lands of Abbey of Bec (1951), No. VIII; Chibnall, English Lands of Abbey of Bec (1951), No. XI; Chibnall, English Lands of Abbey of Bec (1951), No. V; Chibnall, English Lands of Abbey of Bec (1951), No. II; Chibnall, English Lands of Abbey of Bec (1951), No. XXIX; Chibnall, English Lands of Abbey of Bec (1951), No. XV; Chibnall, English Lands of Abbey of Bec (1951), No. I; Regesta regum Anglo-Normannorum III, No. 76; Greenway, Charters of the Honour of Mowbray (1972), No. 11; Chibnall, English Lands of Abbey of Bec (1951), No. XXV; Harper-Bill & Mortimer, Stoke by Clare Cartulary, No. 136; Harper-Bill & Mortimer, Stoke by Clare Cartulary, No. 137; Harper-Bill & Mortimer, Stoke by Clare Cartulary, No. 70; Chibnall, English Lands of Abbey of Bec (1951), No. XIV; Chibnall, English Lands of Abbey of Bec (1951), No. XLVIII; Chibnall, English Lands of Abbey of Bec (1951), No. XXXIX; Chibnall, English Lands of Abbey of Bec (1951), No. XLI; Chibnall, English Lands of Abbey of Bec (1951), No. XXVI; Chibnall, English Lands of Abbey of Bec (1951), No. XLIX; Chibnall, English Lands of Abbey of Bec (1951), No. XL; Chibnall, English Lands of Abbey of Bec (1951), No. XVI; Regesta regum Anglo-Normannorum III, No. 80; Regesta regum Anglo-Normannorum III, No. 74; Chibnall, English Lands of Abbey of Bec (1951), No. VIII; Regesta regum Anglo-Normannorum III, No. 373; Chibnall, English Lands of Abbey of Bec

(1951), No. XLIX; Regesta regum Anglo-Normannorum III, No. 78; Northants Survey, fols 94r–95v; i, fol. 159d; Dugdale, Monasticon Anglicanum, III, p. 473, No. VIII; Chibnall, English Lands of Abbey of Bec (1951), No. XXI; Chibnall, English Lands of Abbey of Bec (1951), No. XI; Pipe Roll 8 Henry II, 13–wl; Pipe Roll 2 Henry II, 34–bk; Pipe Roll 2 Henry II, 17–e; Pipe Roll 8 Henry II, 02a–lcwk; Pipe Roll 2 Henry II, 13–hn; Pipe Roll 12 Henry II, 016–wc; Pipe Roll 2 Henry II, 37–ox; Pipe Roll 2 Henry II, 14b–hn; Pipe Roll 5 Henry II, 18–bubd; Pipe Roll 2 Henry II, 26–ln; Pipe Roll 4 Henry II, 150–ox; Pipe Roll 2 Henry II, 11–sr; Pipe Roll 2 Henry II, 18–e; Pipe Roll 4 Henry II, 159–dv; Pipe Roll 5 Henry II, 56–sr; Pipe Roll 8 Henry II, 47–sr; Pipe Roll 12 Henry II, 001–ln; Pipe Roll 6 Henry II, 18b–wl; Pipe Roll 12 Henry II, 017–nfsf; Pipe Roll 6 Henry II, 18a–wl; Pipe Roll 8 Henry II, 23–sm; Pipe Roll 7 Henry II, 15a–ln; Pipe Roll 6 Henry II, 37–nhbub; Pipe Roll 2 Henry II, 61–ss; Pipe Roll 10 Henry II, 30–bubd; Pipe Roll 10 Henry II, 33–nfsf; Pipe Roll 2 Henry II, 31–sm; Pipe Roll 4 Henry II, 114–mx; Pipe Roll 4 Henry II, 162–sr; Pipe Roll 7 Henry II, 12–bubd; Pipe Roll 2 Henry II, 12a–sr; Pipe Roll 8 Henry II, 66–nfsf; Pipe Roll 8 Henry II, 24–ds; Pipe Roll 2 Henry II, 59b–wl; Pipe Roll 4 Henry II, 117–wl; Pipe Roll 8 Henry II, 05–dv; Pipe Roll 9 Henry II, 21–bubd; Pipe Roll 8 Henry II, 02b–lcwk; Pipe Roll 9 Henry II, 28–nfsf; Pipe Roll 2 Henry II, 55–hm; Pipe Roll 8 Henry II, 67–lo; Pipe Roll 7 Henry II, 15b–ln; Pipe Roll 8 Henry II, 65–nfsf; Pipe Roll 8 Henry II, 62–nfsf; Pipe Roll 8 Henry II, 28–ox; Pipe Roll 8 Henry II, 17–ln; Pipe Roll 2 Henry II, 59a–wl; Pipe Roll 11 Henry II, 025–wy; Pipe Roll 4 Henry II, 122–sm; Pipe Roll 11 Henry II, 034–ln; Pipe Roll 2 Henry II, 38–ox; Pipe Roll 4 Henry II, 133–e; Pipe Roll 6 Henry II, 52a–dv; Pipe Roll 4 Henry II, 141–wy; Pipe Roll 8 Henry II, 49–cmhn; Pipe Roll 8 Henry II, 34–wc; Pipe Roll 6 Henry II, 40–wy; Pipe Roll 6 Henry II, 41–ds; Pipe Roll 4 Henry II, 137–ln; Pipe Roll 6 Henry II, 42–ds; Pipe Roll 2 Henry II, 12b–sr; Pipe Roll 4 Henry II, 185–wk; Pipe Roll 4 Henry II, 124–bk; Pipe Roll 2 Henry II, 23–bubd; Pipe Roll 8 Henry II, 41–bubd; Pipe Roll 2 Henry II, 14a–hn; Pipe Roll 4 Henry II, 142–nh; Pipe Roll 10 Henry II, 22–ln; Pipe Roll 2 Henry II, 33–ds; Pipe Roll 8 Henry II, 44–bk; Pipe Roll 4 Henry II, 182–ss; Pipe Roll 2 Henry II, 25–ln; Pipe Roll 6 Henry II, 20–wl; Pipe Roll 8 Henry II, 31–ss; Pipe Roll 6 Henry II, 58–sm; Pipe Roll 11 Henry II, 003–nfsf; Pipe Roll 2 Henry II, 44–wk; Pipe Roll 6 Henry II, 52b–dv; Regesta regum Anglo-Normannorum III, No. 782; Pipe Roll 31 Henry I, 152–mx; Pipe Roll 31 Henry I, 015–ds; Pipe Roll 31 Henry I, 121–ln; Pipe Roll 31 Henry I, 056–e; Pipe Roll 31 Henry I, 051–sr; Pipe Roll 31 Henry I, 109–ln; Pipe Roll 31 Henry I, 060–e; Pipe Roll 31 Henry I, 070–ss; Pipe Roll 31 Henry I, 072–ss; Pipe Roll 31 Henry I, 095–nf; Pipe Roll 31 Henry I, 104–bd; Pipe Roll 31 Henry I, 022a–wl; Pipe Roll 31 Henry I, 099–sf; Pipe Roll 31 Henry I, 099–sf; Pipe Roll 31 Henry I, 072–ss; Pipe Roll 31 Henry I, 049–hn; Pipe Roll 31 Henry I, 056–e; Pipe Roll 31 Henry I, 022b–wl; Pipe Roll 31 Henry I, 060–e; Pipe Roll 31 Henry I, 095–nf; Pipe Roll 31 Henry I, 070–ss; Pipe Roll 31 Henry I, 005–ox; Pipe Roll 31 Henry I, 049–hn; Pipe Roll 31 Henry I, 121–ln; Pipe Roll 31 Henry I, 051–sr; Pipe Roll 31 Henry I, 104–bd; Pipe Roll 31 Henry I, 135–pe; Pipe Roll 31 Henry I, 109–ln; Chibnall, English Lands of Abbey of Bec (1951), No. XXIV; Regesta regum Anglo-Normannorum III, No. 781; Regesta regum Anglo-Normannorum III, No. 77; Pipe Roll 2 Henry II, 07–nf; Regesta regum Anglo-Normannorum III, No. 75; Chibnall, English Lands of Abbey of Bec (1951), No. XXII; Chibnall, English Lands of Abbey of Bec (1951), No. XXXVI; Chibnall, English Lands of Abbey of Bec (1951), No. L; Pipe Roll 7 Henry II, 44–sr; Chibnall, English Lands of Abbey of Bec (1951), No. LI; Chibnall, English Lands of Abbey of Bec (1951), No. XXIV; i, fol. 34d; i, fol. 34d; Dugdale, Monasticon Anglicanum, III, p. 473, No. XII; Dugdale, Monasticon Anglicanum, III, pp. 472–73, No. VII; Dugdale, Monasticon

Anglicanum, III, p. 473, No. XI; Greenway, Charters of the Honour of Mowbray (1972), No. 3; Greenway, Charters of the Honour of Mowbray (1972), No. 2

[] Abbatia De Berchinges
Barking Abbey, Essex, founded c.666.

i, fol. 34a; i, fol. 34a; i, fol. 211a; Regesta regum Anglo-Normannorum III, No. 34; i, fol. 146a; Regesta regum Anglo-Normannorum III, No. 36; Regesta regum Anglo-Normannorum III, No. 34; Regesta regum Anglo-Normannorum III, No. 32; Regesta regum Anglo-Normannorum III, No. 33; Regesta regum Anglo-Normannorum III, No. 35; Regesta regum Anglo-Normannorum III, No. 38; Regesta regum Anglo-Normannorum III, No. 37; ii, fol. 017b

[] Abbatia De Bertone
Abbey of SS Mary and Modwen, Burton-on-Trent, Staffordshire, founded 1002–4 by Wulfric Spott. G. Wrottesley, 'The Burton Chartulary', William Salt Arch. Soc. Coll. Hist. Staffordshire v, pt. 1 (1894).

i, fol. 246a; i, fol. 239a; i, fol. 247c; i, fol. 247c; i, fol. 247c; i, fol. 247c; i, fol. 247c; i, fol. 247c; i, fol. 247c; Regesta regum Anglo-Normannorum III, No. 136; i, fol. 239a; Barraclough, Charters of AN Earls of Chester (1988), No. 115; i, fol. 247c

[] Abbatia De Burg
Peterborough Abbey, Huntingdonshire, founded 655–6, rebuilt as the abbey of St Peter after a century of dereliction c.966. J.D. Martin, The Cartularies and Registers of Peterborough Abbey (Northants Rec. Soc., 1978); Edmund King, Peterborough Abbey 1086–1310, A study in the land market, Cambridge, 1973; E. King, 'The Peterborough "Descriptio Militum" (Henry I)', EHR 84 (1969), 84–101.

Round, Leicestershire Survey, Round, Feudal England, pp. 161–65; Regesta regum Anglo-Normannorum III, No. 656; i, fol. 231b; i, fol. 231b; Pipe Roll 31 Henry I, 082–nh; Pipe Roll 31 Henry I, 082–nh; i, fol. 221b; i, fol. 221b; i, fol. 221b; i, fol. 221b; i, fol. 221b; i, fol. 221c; i, fol. 221b; i, fol. 221b; i, fol. 221b; i, fol. 221b; i, fol. 221b; i, fol. 221c; i, fol. 221b; i, fol. 221c; i, fol. 221c; i, fol. 221c; i, fol. 221c; i, fol. 221c; Northants Survey, fols 94r–95v; Regesta regum Anglo-Normannorum III, No. 660; Regesta regum Anglo-Normannorum III, No. 657; Regesta regum Anglo-Normannorum III, No. 659; Regesta regum Anglo-Normannorum III, No. 655; Regesta regum Anglo-Normannorum III, No. 658; i, fol. 221c; Pipe Roll 5 Henry II, 17b–nh; Pipe Roll 2 Henry II, 41–nh; Douglas, Feudal Documents from Bury St Edmunds, No. 31; i, fol. 345c; i, fol. 346a; i, fol. 345c; i, fol. 284c; i, fol. 221b; i, fol. 231b; i, fol. 345c; i, fol. 210c; i, fol. 205b; i, fol. 346a; Lincolnshire Claims (Domesday Book), fols 376b–c; Lincolnshire Claims (Domesday Book), fols 376d–377c; i, fol. 346a; i, fol. 345c; i, fol. 345c; i, fol. 345c; i, fol. 345d; i, fol. 345d; i, fol. 345d; i, fol. 346a; i, fol. 345c; i, fol. 346a; i, fol. 346a; i, fol. 345c; i, fol. 345c; i, fol. 284c; i, fol. 284c; i, fol. 346a

[] Abbatia De Cadomo Sancti Stephani
Abbey of Saint-Etienne at Caen, Normandy, dépt. Calvados, founded by William I and Matilda. E. Deville, Analyse d'un ancien cartulaire de l'abbaye de Saint-Etienne de Caen, Evreux, 1905; L. Musset, Les Actes de Guillaume le Conquérant et de la reine Mathilde pour les abbayes caennaises, Caen, 1967.

i, fol. 91b; i, fol. 78c; i, fol. 104b; i, fol. 78c; i, fol. 78c; Pipe Roll 2 Henry II, 34–bk; Pipe Roll 2 Henry II, 33–ds; i, fol. 75b; i, fol. 91b; ii, fol. 022a; ii, fol.

221b; i, fol. 65a; ii, fol. 221b; ii, fol. 221b; ii, fol. 022a

[] Abbatia De Certesy

Chertsey Abbey, Surrey, founded 666; rebuilt after destruction by Danes in 964. Chertsey Cartularies, 3 vols, Surrey Record Society xii, 1915–33.

Pipe Roll 8 Henry II, 47a–sr; i, fol. 59d; i, fol. 32d; i, fol. 32c; i, fol. 32c; i, fol. 32c; i, fol. 32c; i, fol. 32c; i, fol. 32c; i, fol. 32c; i, fol. 32d; i, fol. 32d; i, fol. 32d; i, fol. 32d; i, fol. 33a,b; i, fol. 34a; i, fol. 34a; i, fol. 32d; Regesta regum Anglo-Normannorum III, No. 169; Pipe Roll 31 Henry I, 140–bk; Pipe Roll 8 Henry II, 47b–sr; i, fol. 43c; Pipe Roll 5 Henry II, 56b–sr; Pipe Roll 2 Henry II, 12b–sr; Regesta regum Anglo-Normannorum III, No. 170

[] Abbatia De Cetriz

Abbey of the Blessed Virgin, Chatteris, Cambs, founded by Ednoth bishop of Dorchester, c.1006–16.

Pipe Roll 31 Henry I, 044–cm; Pipe Roll 31 Henry I, 044–cm; ii, fol. 389a; i, fol. 193a; i, fol. 193a; i, fol. 193a; i, fol. 193a; i, fol. 136b; Pipe Roll 31 Henry I, 044–srcmh; pipe, 29, 044–srcmh; i, fol. 193a; ii, fol. 017b; ii, fol. 389a; ii, fol. 018a; i, fol. 52c; ii, fol. 389a; ii, fol. 018a; ii, fol. 017b; ii, fol. 017b; ii, fol. 017b; ii, fol. 018a; ii, fol. 018a; ii, fol. 018a; ii, fol. 018b; ii, fol. 018b; ii, fol. 017b

[] Abbatia De Cirecestre

First founded in the ninth century, there was a poorly endowed secular college at Cirencester, Gloucestershire, in 1086. In 1117 Henry I began to build an Augustinian abbey there, endowing it with the lands once held by Regenbald the Chancellor (q.v.). The first abbot was consecrated in 1131. C.D. Ross, The Cartulary of Cirencester Abbey, Gloucestershire, 2 vols, Oxford, 1964.

Walker, Charters of the Earldom of Hereford (1964), No. 56; i, fol. 166c; Pipe Roll 3 Henry II, 100–gl; Pipe Roll 3 Henry II, 104–nh; Pipe Roll 11 Henry II, 011–gl; Pipe Roll 7 Henry II, 21–gl; Pipe Roll 4 Henry II, 167–gl; Pipe Roll 6 Henry II, 28–gl; Pipe Roll 9 Henry II, 08–gl; Pipe Roll 8 Henry II, 59–gl; Pipe Roll 5 Henry II, 27–gl; Pipe Roll 10 Henry II, 17–gl; Pipe Roll 2 Henry II, 49–gl; i, fol. 166c; Regesta regum Anglo-Normannorum III, No. 189; Regesta regum Anglo-Normannorum III, No. 193; pipe, 29, 079–gl; pipe, 29, 079–gl; Regesta regum Anglo-Normannorum III, No. 192; Regesta regum Anglo-Normannorum III, No. 191; Walker, Charters of the Earldom of Hereford (1964), No. 29; Pipe Roll 12 Henry II, 077–gl; i, fol. 167d

[] Abbatia De Cormelies

Abbey of Cormeilles (Eure), founded by William fitz Osbern c.1060 on his estates near Breteuil; William was buried there after his death in 1071 (Ord. Vit. ii, 12–13). Arch. dépt. Eure II F 148, cartulary of the priory of Wootton.

i, fol. 49b; i, fol. 164b; i, fol. 174b; i, fol. 174b; i, fol. 182d; i, fol. 182d; i, fol. 166a; Pipe Roll 3 Henry II, 093–hf; Pipe Roll 3 Henry II, 107–hm; Pipe Roll 7 Henry II, 21–gl; Pipe Roll 7 Henry II, 19–hf; Pipe Roll 6 Henry II, 29–hf; Pipe Roll 12 Henry II, 083–hf; Pipe Roll 1 Henry II (RBE, ii), 656–wo; Pipe Roll 8 Henry II, 59–gl; Pipe Roll 9 Henry II, 08–gl; Pipe Roll 9 Henry II, 04–wo; Pipe Roll 8 Henry II, 55–wo; Pipe Roll 3 Henry II, 100–gl; Pipe Roll 5 Henry II, 50–hm; Pipe Roll 3 Henry II, 091–wo; Pipe Roll 4 Henry II, 178–hm; Pipe Roll 5 Henry II, 23–wo; Pipe Roll 6 Henry II, 23–wo; Pipe Roll 9 Henry II, 06–hf; Pipe Roll 4 Henry II, 144–hf; Pipe Roll 6 Henry II, 27–gl; Pipe Roll 10 Henry II, 03–wo; Pipe Roll 5 Henry II, 49–hf; Pipe Roll 7 Henry II, 54–wo; Pipe Roll 9 Henry II, 56–hm; Pipe Roll 4 Henry II, 167–gl; Pipe Roll 2 Henry II, 53–hm;

Pipe Roll 4 Henry II, 155–wo; Pipe Roll 2 Henry II, 51–hf; Pipe Roll 10 Henry II, 17–gl; Pipe Roll 10 Henry II, 27–hm; Pipe Roll 2 Henry II, 49–gl; Pipe Roll 5 Henry II, 26–gl; Pipe Roll 6 Henry II, 22–hm; Pipe Roll 8 Henry II, 39–hm; Pipe Roll 10 Henry II, 05–hf; Pipe Roll 11 Henry II, 098–wo; Pipe Roll 11 Henry II, 044–hm; Pipe Roll 11 Henry II, 100–hf; Pipe Roll 7 Henry II, 59–hm; Pipe Roll 11 Henry II, 011–gl; Pipe Roll 12 Henry II, 109–hm; Pipe Roll 2 Henry II, 62–wo; Pipe Roll 12 Henry II, 080–wo; Pipe Roll 8 Henry II, 58–hf; Pipe Roll 12 Henry II, 077–gl; i, fol. 179c; i, fol. 180a; i, fol. 179c; i, fol. 179d; i, fol. 184d; i, fol. 179d; i, fol. 179d; i, fol. 179c; i, fol. 166a; i, fol. 180c; i, fol. 179d

[] Abbatia De Couentreu

Abbey of SS Mary, Peter and Osburg at Coventry; founded by Leofric earl of Mercia and his wife Godiva; received papal confirmation in 1043. Mon. Ang. iii, pp. 183ff.

i, fol. 238d; i, fol. 222c; i, fol. 239a; i, fol. 222c; i, fol. 238d; i, fol. 231b; i, fol. 239a; i, fol. 231b; i, fol. 238d; i, fol. 230a; i, fol. 239a; i, fol. 239a; i, fol. 239a; i, fol. 231b; i, fol. 238d; i, fol. 239a; i, fol. 231b; i, fol. 239a; i, fol. 231b; i, fol. 239a; i, fol. 239a; i, fol. 238d; i, fol. 222c; i, fol. 231b; i, fol. 222c; i, fol. 238d; i, fol. 239a; i, fol. 238d; i, fol. 238d; i, fol. 238d; i, fol. 238d; i, fol. 222c; i, fol. 174b; i, fol. 166a; i, fol. 166a; i, fol. 231b

[] Abbatia De Creneburne

Abbey of SS Mary and Bartholomew, Cranbourne, Dorset, founded c.980 or earlier.

i, fol. 84a; i, fol. 104a; i, fol. 77d; i, fol. 77d; i, fol. 77d; i, fol. 77d; i, fol. 77d; i, fol. 67c

[] Abbatia De Cruiland

Abbey of St Guthlac, who settled at Crowland, Lincolnshire, in 699. Register, Oxford, All Souls College, ms 32.

Round, Leicestershire Survey, Round, Feudal England, pp. 161–65; i, fol. 231b; i, fol. 222c; i, fol. 222c; i, fol. 222c; i, fol. 222c; i, fol. 222c; i, fol. 231b; i, fol. 231b; i, fol. 230a; i, fol. 222c; i, fol. 204a; i, fol. 231b; i, fol. 222c; Dugdale, Monasticon Anglicanum, II, p. 120, No. XX; Regesta regum Anglo-Normannorum III, No. 249; Regesta regum Anglo-Normannorum III, No. 251; Barraclough, Charters of AN Earls of Chester (1988), No. 201; Regesta regum Anglo-Normannorum III, No. 252; Regesta regum Anglo-Normannorum III, No. 250; Round, Fragments from Worcester, Round, Feudal England (1895 : 1946), pp. 146–47; Lincolnshire Claims (Domesday Book), fols 376d–377c; i, fol. 182d; i, fol. 176a; Dugdale, Monasticon Anglicanum, V, p. 125, No. I; i, fol. 346d; Stenton, Documents illustrative of Danelaw (1920), No. 515; Round, Fragments from Worcester, Round, Feudal England (1895: 1946), p. 146; Stenton, Documents illustrative of Danelaw (1920), No. 516; i, fol. 346d; i, fol. 346d; i, fol. 346d; i, fol. 346d; i, fol. 346d; i, fol. 346d; i, fol. 346d; i, fol. 346d

[] Abbatia De Elnestou

Abbey of St Mary and St Helen at Elstow, Bedfordshire, founded by Countess Judith c.1078.

i, fol. 217a; i, fol. 217a; i, fol. 217b; Pipe Roll 31 Henry I, 062–ht; Pipe Roll 31 Henry I, 062–ht

[] Abbatia De Ely

Abbey of St Etheldreda, Ely, Cambs, refounded for Benedictines in 970. Became the cathedral priory of the new see of Ely in 1109. Liber Eliensis, ed. E. O. Blake,

Camden 3rd Series, xcii, 1962. N. Hamilton, Inquisitio Comitatus Cantabrigiensis
Dugdale, Monasticon Anglicanum, IV, pp. 148–49, No. II; i, fol. 204a; i, fol.
191d; Regesta regum Anglo-Normannorum III, No. 35; Regesta regum
Anglo-Normannorum III, No. 36; Hamilton, Inquisitio Eliensis (1876), pp.
192–95; Regesta regum Anglo-Normannorum III, No. 261; Regesta regum
Anglo-Normannorum III, No. 267; ii, fol. 097b; ii, fol. 054a; Regesta regum
Anglo-Normannorum III, No. 268; Regesta regum Anglo-Normannorum III,
No. 262; Regesta regum Anglo-Normannorum III, No. 260; Regesta regum
Anglo-Normannorum III, No. 264; Regesta regum Anglo-Normannorum III,
No. 265; Regesta regum Anglo-Normannorum III, No. 266; Regesta regum
Anglo-Normannorum III, No. 269; ii, fol. 019a; ii, fol. 213a; ii, fol. 213a; ii, fol.
212b; ii, fol. 214b; ii, fol. 214a; ii, fol. 213b; ii, fol. 212b; ii, fol. 212b; ii, fol.
213a; ii, fol. 214a; ii, fol. 214b; ii, fol. 213b; ii, fol. 213a; ii, fol. 213b; ii, fol.
213a; ii, fol. 213a; ii, fol. 215a; ii, fol. 213a; ii, fol. 214a; ii, fol. 213a; ii, fol.
213a; ii, fol. 214a; ii, fol. 213b; ii, fol. 019a; ii, fol. 018b; ii, fol. 215a; ii, fol.
213b; ii, fol. 214a; ii, fol. 214b; ii, fol. 214b; ii, fol. 214b; ii, fol. 214b; ii, fol.
214b; ii, fol. 214b; ii, fol. 215a; ii, fol. 214a; ii, fol. 019a; ii, fol. 019a; ii, fol.
215a; ii, fol. 019b; ii, fol. 215a; ii, fol. 213b; ii, fol. 215a; ii, fol. 250b; ii, fol.
388a; ii, fol. 387b; ii, fol. 384b; ii, fol. 388a; ii, fol. 387b; ii, fol. 387a; ii, fol.
387a; ii, fol. 387b; ii, fol. 387b; ii, fol. 387b; ii, fol. 387b; ii, fol. 387b; ii, fol.
387a; ii, fol. 387a; ii, fol. 387a; ii, fol. 385a; ii, fol. 387b; ii, fol. 388b; ii, fol.
384b; ii, fol. 384b; ii, fol. 388b; ii, fol. 385b; ii, fol. 388a; ii, fol. 388a; ii, fol.
384a; ii, fol. 384b; ii, fol. 382a; ii, fol. 385b; ii, fol. 381b; ii, fol. 385b; ii, fol.
385a; ii, fol. 388a; ii, fol. 382a; ii, fol. 388b; ii, fol. 386a; ii, fol. 382b; ii, fol.
386a; ii, fol. 387a; ii, fol. 382a; ii, fol. 388a; ii, fol. 382a; ii, fol. 388a; ii, fol.
383a; ii, fol. 386b; ii, fol. 387a; ii, fol. 386b; ii, fol. 386b; ii, fol. 386b; ii, fol.
386b; ii, fol. 387b; ii, fol. 386b; ii, fol. 386a; ii, fol. 386b; ii, fol. 386b; ii, fol.
385a; ii, fol. 386b; ii, fol. 386a; ii, fol. 386a; ii, fol. 386a; ii, fol. 386b; ii, fol.
388b; ii, fol. 382a; ii, fol. 387a; ii, fol. 381b; ii, fol. 381b; ii, fol. 382b; ii, fol.
387a; ii, fol. 388b; ii, fol. 381b; ii, fol. 386b; ii, fol. 383a; ii, fol. 383a; ii, fol.
388a; ii, fol. 388a; ii, fol. 388a; ii, fol. 388a; ii, fol. 388b; ii, fol. 384a; ii, fol.
384a; ii, fol. 381b; ii, fol. 382b; ii, fol. 388b; ii, fol. 382b; ii, fol. 384a; ii, fol.
384a; ii, fol. 388b; ii, fol. 388b; ii, fol. 384a; ii, fol. 383a; ii, fol. 383a; ii, fol.
382a; ii, fol. 382a; ii, fol. 384a; ii, fol. 384a; ii, fol. 383a; Dugdale, Monasticon
Anglicanum, III, p. 472, No. III; ii, fol. 018b; ii, fol. 381b

[] Abbatia De Euesham

Evesham Abbey, Worcestershire, founded by St Egwin, bishop of Worcester c.701.
Mon. Ang. ii, 10ff; W. Tindal, Hist. Evesham (Evesham, 1794); Chronicon
Abbatiae de Evesham, ed. W. D. Macray, Rolls Series, London, 1863.

Northants Survey, fols 94r–95v; Barraclough, Charters of AN Earls of Chester
(1988), No. 91; i, fol. 154a; Pipe Roll 6 Henry II, 28–gl; i, fol. 239b; i, fol. 239b;
i, fol. 222d; i, fol. 239b; i, fol. 239b; Red Book of the Exchequer, ed. Hall (1897),
pp. 301–02; Round, Fragments from Worcester, Round, Feudal England (1895 :
1946), pp. 146–47; Pipe Roll 31 Henry I, 109–wk; Pipe Roll 31 Henry I,
109–wk; i, fol. 175d; i, fol. 175d; i, fol. 175d; i, fol. 175d; i, fol. 175d; i, fol.
175c; i, fol. 175c; i, fol. 175c; i, fol. 175d; i, fol. 175d; i, fol. 175d; i, fol. 175d; i,
fol. 175d; i, fol. 175d; i, fol. 175d; i, fol. 175d; i, fol. 175d; i, fol. 175d; i, fol.
175c; i, fol. 175c; i, fol. 175d; i, fol. 176a; i, fol. 175c; i, fol. 239b; i, fol. 222d;
Dugdale, Monasticon Anglicanum, II, p. 18, No. IX; i, fol. 166a; i, fol. 166a; i,
fol. 165d; i, fol. 166a; i, fol. 165d; i, fol. 165d; i, fol. 166a; i, fol. 166a; i, fol.
166a; i, fol. 166a; i, fol. 166a; Dugdale, Monasticon Anglicanum, II, p. 18, No.
X; Dugdale, Monasticon Anglicanum, II, p. 18, No. XI; Pipe Roll 5 Henry II,

25–wo; Pipe Roll 2 Henry II, 63–wo; Barraclough, Charters of AN Earls of Chester (1988), No. 90; i, fol. 165d

[] Abbatia De Fontaneto

Abbey of Saint Etienne de Fontenay, Normandy (Orne), founded by Ralph Taisson c.1070 (Gall. Christ. xi, inst. 63–4). L. Musset, 'Actes inédits du XIIe siècle. IV Deux nouvelles chartes normandes de l'abbaye de Bourgueil. V. Autour des origines de Saint-Étienne de Fontenay', Bulletin de la Sociéte archéologique de Normandie, 57 (1961–2) 5–41.

Regesta regum Anglo-Normannorum III, No. 324; i, fol. 72d; Regesta regum Anglo-Normannorum III, No. 325; Regesta regum Anglo-Normannorum III, No. 326

[] Abbatia De Glastingberie

Glastonbury Abbey, Somerset, foundation traditions date from the sixth century. The Great Chartulary of Glastonbury, ed. Dom Aelred Watkin, Somerset Record Society lix, lxiii–iv, 1947–56.

Pipe Roll 4 Henry II, 121–sm; i, fol. 59c; Red Book of the Exchequer, ed. Hall (1897), pp. 222–24; Pipe Roll 31 Henry I, 156–dv; Pipe Roll 6 Henry II, 58–sm; Pipe Roll 31 Henry I, 068–ss; Pipe Roll 31 Henry I, 068–ss; i, fol. 43c; i, fol. 165b; i, fol. 103c; i, fol. 69d; i, fol. 90a; i, fol. 90a; i, fol. 90c; i, fol. 90c; i, fol. 90b; i, fol. 90d; i, fol. 90a; i, fol. 90a; i, fol. 90b; i, fol. 90b; i, fol. 90d; i, fol. 90d; i, fol. 90c; i, fol. 90c; i, fol. 90c; i, fol. 90d; i, fol. 90d; i, fol. 90b; i, fol. 90b; i, fol. 77c; i, fol. 66c; i, fol. 66c; i, fol. 66d; i, fol. 66c; i, fol. 66c; i, fol. 66d; i, fol. 66d; i, fol. 66d; i, fol. 66d; i, fol. 66d; i, fol. 66c; i, fol. 66d; i, fol. 66c; Regesta regum Anglo-Normannorum III, No. 343; Regesta regum Anglo-Normannorum III, No. 341; Regesta regum Anglo-Normannorum III, No. 342; Pipe Roll 5 Henry II, 22–sm; Pipe Roll 2 Henry II, 32–sm; Pipe Roll 6 Henry II, 58–sm; i, fol. 165b; i, fol. 90a; i, fol. 77c

[] Abbatia De Glouuecestre

St Peter's Abbey, Gloucester, refounded c.1058 on the site of an older monastery of SS Peter and Paul dating from c.681. Historia et cartularium monasterii sancti Petri Gloucestriae, ed. W.H. Hart, 3 vols, Rolls Series, London 1863–7.

Regesta regum Anglo-Normannorum III, No. 362; i, fol. 43b; Regesta regum Anglo-Normannorum III, No. 358; i, fol. 174b; i, fol. 174b; i, fol. 43b; Regesta regum Anglo-Normannorum III, No. 360; Regesta regum Anglo-Normannorum III, No. 357; Walker, Charters of St Peters Abbey, Gloucester, No. 5; Regesta regum Anglo-Normannorum III, No. 352; Regesta regum Anglo-Normannorum III, No. 345; Regesta regum Anglo-Normannorum III, No. 361; Regesta regum Anglo-Normannorum III, No. 365a; Regesta regum Anglo-Normannorum III, No. 362a; Regesta regum Anglo-Normannorum III, No. 353; Barraclough, Charters of AN Earls of Chester (1988), No. 116; Pipe Roll 31 Henry I, 079–gl; Pipe Roll 31 Henry I, 079–gl; Regesta regum Anglo-Normannorum III, No. 347; Regesta regum Anglo-Normannorum III, No. 351; Pipe Roll 6 Henry II, 23–wo; Pipe Roll 11 Henry II, 098–wo; Pipe Roll 12 Henry II, 080–wo; Pipe Roll 9 Henry II, 04–wo; Pipe Roll 10 Henry II, 03–wo; Pipe Roll 7 Henry II, 54–wo; Pipe Roll 8 Henry II, 55–wo; Regesta regum Anglo-Normannorum III, No. 395; Regesta regum Anglo-Normannorum III, No. 349; Regesta regum Anglo-Normannorum III, No. 364; Regesta regum Anglo-Normannorum III, No. 365; Round, Fragments from Worcester, Round, Feudal England (1895: 1946), p. 146; Walker, Charters of St Peters Abbey, Gloucester, No. 6; Regesta regum Anglo-Normannorum III, No. 397; Regesta regum Anglo-Normannorum

511

III, No. 348; Pipe Roll 10 Henry II, 18–gl; i, fol. 182d; i, fol. 182d; i, fol. 182d; i, fol. 165c; i, fol. 182d; Regesta regum Anglo-Normannorum III, No. 346; Regesta regum Anglo-Normannorum III, No. 363b; Regesta regum Anglo-Normannorum III, No. 363; Regesta regum Anglo-Normannorum III, No. 362a; i, fol. 181a; i, fol. 165c; i, fol. 165c; i, fol. 165c; i, fol. 165c; i, fol. 165c; i, fol. 165c; i, fol. 165c; i, fol. 165c; i, fol. 165c; i, fol. 165c; i, fol. 165c; i, fol. 165c; i, fol. 165d; i, fol. 165c; i, fol. 165c; i, fol. 165c; i, fol. 165c

[] Abbatia De Grestain

Abbey of Grestain, (Normandy, Eure) founded in 1050 by Herluin de Conteville, father of Robert count of Mortain and Odo of Bayeux. See D. Bates and V. Gazeau, 'L'abbaye de Grestain et la famille d'Herluin de Conteville', Annales de Normandie 40 (1990)

Northants Survey, fols 94r–95v; i, fol. 43c; i, fol. 222d; i, fol. 222d; i, fol. 222d; i, fol. 222d; i, fol. 222d; i, fol. 222d; i, fol. 92c; i, fol. 43c; i, fol. 222d; i, fol. 146b; i, fol. 146c; i, fol. 68d; ii, fol. 291b; ii, fol. 291b

[] Abbatia De Labatailge

Battle Abbey, Sussex, founded by William the Conqueror in 1067 at the site of the Battle of Hastings. Colonized by monks from Marmoutier, the abbey remained independent of Marmoutier; see Chronicle of Battle Abbey, ed. E. Searle, Oxford, 1980. [Alfred Walter Francis Fuller], Charters of Battle Abbey in the Fuller Collection in the University of London Library (London, 1979).

i, fol. 157a; i, fol. 101b; i, fol. 100d; i, fol. 157a; i, fol. 104b; i, fol. 104a; i, fol. 17d; Regesta regum Anglo-Normannorum III, No. 51; Round, Ancient Charters (1888), No. 15; i, fol. 100b; Pipe Roll 8 Henry II, 44–bk; Dugdale, Monasticon Anglicanum, III, p. 377, No. I; ii, fol. 020b; ii, fol. 020b; ii, fol. 020b

[] Abbatia De Lira

Abbey of Lyre, founded c.1046 by William fitz Osbern (Ord. Vit. ii, 12), whose wife Adeliza was buried there (ibid., 282). Ch. Guéry, Histoire de l'abbaye de Lyre (Evreux, 1917); early grants from English lands occur as confirmations in the Carisbrooke cartulary, BL Egerton 3667, fols 20v, 25, 79v; cf. Mon. Ang. vi, 1041, 1092.There is an eighteenth-century copy of the cartulary at Château de Semilly, Collection du Marquis de Mathan. S.F. Hockey, 'William fitz Osbern and the endowment of his abbey of Lyre', Anglo-Norman Studies 3 (1981).

Regesta regum Anglo-Normannorum III, No. 495; i, fol. 52c; i, fol. 164a; i, fol. 166a; i, fol. 182d; i, fol. 182d; Bearman, Charters of the Redvers Family (1994), App. I No. 4; i, fol. 52b; Pipe Roll 4 Henry II, 155b–wo; Pipe Roll 10 Henry II, 27–hm; Pipe Roll 9 Henry II, 56–hm; Pipe Roll 10 Henry II, 05–hf; Pipe Roll 10 Henry II, 04–wo; Pipe Roll 6 Henry II, 24–wo; Pipe Roll 3 Henry II, 093–hf; Pipe Roll 3 Henry II, 107–hm; Pipe Roll 11 Henry II, 044–hm; Pipe Roll 4 Henry II, 144–hf; Pipe Roll 6 Henry II, 22–hm; Pipe Roll 7 Henry II, 55–wo; Pipe Roll 8 Henry II, 58–hf; Pipe Roll 6 Henry II, 29–hf; Pipe Roll 6 Henry II, 23–wo; Pipe Roll 2 Henry II, 53–hm; Pipe Roll 4 Henry II, 178–hm; Pipe Roll 5 Henry II, 23b–wo; Pipe Roll 9 Henry II, 06–hf; Pipe Roll 11 Henry II, 100–hf; Pipe Roll 9 Henry II, 05–wo; Pipe Roll 5 Henry II, 49–hf; Pipe Roll 8 Henry II, 56–wo; Pipe Roll 7 Henry II, 54–wo; Pipe Roll 8 Henry II, 39–hm; Pipe Roll 12 Henry II, 081–wo; Pipe Roll 5 Henry II, 50–hm; Pipe Roll 9 Henry II, 04–wo; Pipe Roll 2 Henry II, 51–hf; Pipe Roll 12 Henry II, 080–wo; Pipe Roll 12 Henry II, 083–hf; Pipe Roll 7 Henry II, 19–hf; Pipe Roll 8 Henry II, 55–wo; Pipe Roll 7 Henry II, 59–hm; Pipe Roll 10 Henry II, 03–wo; Pipe Roll 11 Henry II, 098–wo; Pipe Roll 12 Henry II, 109–hm; i, fol. 181b; i, fol. 180d; i, fol. 166a

[] Abbatia De Malmesberie
Malmesbury Abbey, Wiltshire, refounded for Benedictine monks c.965. Registrum Malmesburiense, ed. J. S. Brewer and C. T. Martin, 2 vols, Rolls Series, London, 1879–80.

> Jenkins, Cartulary of Missenden Abbey, III (1962), No. 664; i, fol. 239a; Pipe Roll 8 Henry II, 14–wl; i, fol. 165b; i, fol. 239a; i, fol. 67a; i, fol. 67a; i, fol. 67b; i, fol. 67a; i, fol. 67a; i, fol. 67a; i, fol. 67b; i, fol. 67b; i, fol. 67b; i, fol. 66d; i, fol. 67b; Regesta regum Anglo-Normannorum III, No. 574; Pipe Roll 7 Henry II, 09–wl; pipe, 55, 60–wl; Pipe Roll 7 Henry II, 08–wl; Pipe Roll 12 Henry II, 071–wl; Pipe Roll 5 Henry II, 38–wl; Pipe Roll 6 Henry II, 16–wl; Pipe Roll 11 Henry II, 055–wl; Pipe Roll 9 Henry II, 45–wl; Pipe Roll 4 Henry II, 115–wl; Pipe Roll 8 Henry II, 11–wl; Pipe Roll 3 Henry II, 077–wl; Pipe Roll 10 Henry II, 13–wl; i, fol. 165b

[] Abbatia De Micelenie
Abbey of Muchelney, Somerset, refounded 939. E. H. Bates, Two Cartularies of the Benedictine Abbeys of Muchelney and Athelney in the County of Somerset (Somerset Record Society, 14, 1899).

> Red Book of the Exchequer, ed. Hall (1897), p. 224; i, fol. 91a; i, fol. 91a; i, fol. 91a; i, fol. 91a; i, fol. 91a; i, fol. 91a; i, fol. 91a; i, fol. 91a; i, fol. 91a; i, fol. 91a; i, fol. 91a

[] Abbatia De Middeltune
Milton Abbey, Dorset, Benedictine house from 964. Mon. Ang. ii, 348ff.

> Red Book of the Exchequer, ed. Hall (1897), pp. 210–22; i, fol. 43c; i, fol. 78b; i, fol. 78b; i, fol. 78b; i, fol. 78b; i, fol. 78b; i, fol. 78b; i, fol. 78b; i, fol. 78b; i, fol. 78a; i, fol. 78b; i, fol. 78b; i, fol. 78b; i, fol. 78b; i, fol. 78b; Red Book of the Exchequer, ed. Hall (1897), pp. 210–22; Pipe Roll 5 Henry II, 43–ds; pipe, 55, 33–ds

[] Abbatia De Monte Sancti Michaelis
Abbey of Mont-Saint-Michel, dioc. Avranches, Normandy. The twelfth century cartulary ms. Avranches Bib. mun. 210 is being edited by K.S.B. Keats-Rohan for publication in France.

> i, fol. 56d; Regesta regum Anglo-Normannorum III, No. 180; i, fol. 104b; i, fol. 104b; i, fol. 104b; i, fol. 43a; Clay, Early Yorkshire Charters (1935), IV, No. 12; Clay, Early Yorkshire Charters (1935), IV, No. 54; i, fol. 107b; Pipe Roll 6 Henry II, 52–dv; i, fol. 43a; Clay, Early Yorkshire Charters (1935), IV, No. 72; i, fol. 65b

[] Abbatia De Monteburg
Montebourg Abbey, Normandy, dépt. Manche; copy of cartulary in BN lat. 10087.

> Bearman, Charters of the Redvers Family (1994), App. II No. 2; Bearman, Charters of the Redvers Family (1994), No. 37; Bearman, Charters of the Redvers Family (1994), No. 5; Bearman, Charters of the Redvers Family (1994), No. 2; Bearman, Charters of the Redvers Family (1994), App. II No. 5; Bearman, Charters of the Redvers Family (1994), No. 9; Bearman, Charters of the Redvers Family (1994), App. II No. 6; Bearman, Charters of the Redvers Family (1994), No. 38; Bearman, Charters of the Redvers Family (1994), App. II No. 10; Bearman, Charters of the Redvers Family (1994), App. II No. 1; i, fol. 91b; Regesta regum Anglo-Normannorum III, No. 594; Bearman, Charters of the Redvers Family (1994), No. 40; Pipe Roll 8 Henry II, 25–ds; i, fol. 73b; i, fol. 91b; Bearman, Charters of the Redvers Family (1994), No. 23; Bearman, Charters of the Redvers Family (1994), No. 10

[] Abbatia De Persore

Pershore Abbey, Worcestershire, secular nuns and monks were replaced c.970 by Benedictine monks. Mon. Ang. ii, 413ff; PRO, Exch., Augm. Off (Misc. Bks. 61), general cartulary.

Ellis, 'Landholders of Gloucestershire' (1880), pp. 91–93; Round, Fragments from Worcester, Round, Feudal England (1895 : 1946), pp. 146–47; i, fol. 175b; i, fol. 175b; i, fol. 175c; i, fol. 175b; i, fol. 175b; i, fol. 175b; i, fol. 175b; i, fol. 175b

[] Abbatia De Pratellis

Abbey of Saint-Pierre de Préaux (Normandy, Eure), founded c.1035–40 by Humphrey de Vielles, father of Roger de Beaumont (Ord. Vit. ii, 12–13). There is a cartulary in Arch. dépt. de l'Eure, H 711.

i, fol. 60b; i, fol. 157a; i, fol. 157a; Pipe Roll 31 Henry I, 015a–ds; i, fol. 240c

[] Abbatia De Ramesy

Ramsey Abbey, Hunts., founded c.969. Cartularium monasterii de Rameseia. ed. W. H. Hart and P. A. Lyons, 3 vols, Rolls Series, 1884–93; Chronicon abbatiae Rameseiensis, ed. W. D. Macray, Rolls Series, London 1886. J.A. Raftis, The estates of Ramsey Abbey (Toronto, 1957).

Northants Survey, fols 96r–99v; i, fol. 222b; i, fol. 222b; i, fol. 222b; i, fol. 222b; i, fol. 222c; i, fol. 222b; i, fol. 222c; i, fol. 222c; Pipe Roll 7 Henry II, 11–bubd; Hart, Cartularium Monasterii de Rameseia, No. LXX; Hart, Cartularium Monasterii de Rameseia, No. CLVIII; Hart, Cartularium Monasterii de Rameseia, No. CLXIII; Hart, Cartularium Monasterii de Rameseia, No. LXXVIII; Hart, Cartularium Monasterii de Rameseia, No. CLXXI; i, fol. 208c; Hart, Cartularium Monasterii de Rameseia, No. CLXI; Hart, Cartularium Monasterii de Rameseia, No. LXI; Hart, Cartularium Monasterii de Rameseia, No. LXXIII; Hart, Cartularium Monasterii de Rameseia, No. CLXV; Hart, Cartularium Monasterii de Rameseia, No. LIV; Hart, Cartularium Monasterii de Rameseia, No. LXXVI; Hart, Cartularium Monasterii de Rameseia, No. CXCI; Hart, Cartularium Monasterii de Rameseia, No. CLXIV; Hart, Cartularium Monasterii de Rameseia, No. XCVI; Hart, Cartularium Monasterii de Rameseia, No. CLXXXII; Hart, Cartularium Monasterii de Rameseia, No. XCIV; Hart, Cartularium Monasterii de Rameseia, No. XCVII; Hart, Cartularium Monasterii de Rameseia, No. XCIII; Hart, Cartularium Monasterii de Rameseia, No. CXCIII; Hart, Cartularium Monasterii de Rameseia, No. LIX; Hart, Cartularium Monasterii de Rameseia, No. LXX; Hart, Cartularium Monasterii de Rameseia, No. CXCVII; Round, Ancient Charters (1888), No. 14; Hart, Cartularium Monasterii de Rameseia, No. LXXV; Regesta regum Anglo-Normannorum III, No. 669; Regesta regum Anglo-Normannorum III, No. 667; Hart, Cartularium Monasterii de Rameseia, No. XLIX; Hart, Cartularium Monasterii de Rameseia, No. XXXVI; Hart, Cartularium Monasterii de Rameseia, No. XXXV; Pipe Roll 2 Henry II, 14–hn; Pipe Roll 5 Henry II, 55–hn; Hart, Cartularium Monasterii de Rameseia, No. CLXX; Hart, Cartularium Monasterii de Rameseia, No. CXLVII; Hart, Cartularium Monasterii de Rameseia, No. CLVI; ii, fol. 378b; i, fol. 346c; i, fol. 210d; i, fol. 136b; i, fol. 222b; i, fol. 204b; i, fol. 208a; Lincolnshire Claims (Domesday Book), fol. 377d; Lincolnshire Claims (Domesday Book), fols 376d–377c; ii, fol. 215b; ii, fol. 215b; ii, fol. 215a; ii, fol. 215b; ii, fol. 215b; ii, fol. 215b; ii, fol. 215b; ii, fol. 215b; ii, fol. 215b; ii, fol. 215b; i, fol. 346c; i, fol. 346c; i, fol. 346c; i, fol. 346c; i, fol. 346c

[] Abbatia De Romesy

Romsey Abbey, Hants, founded c.907. Some material is found in the fourteenth century cartulary of its former priory at Edington, Wiltshire, in BL Lansdowne 442.

i, fol. 44a; i, fol. 44a; i, fol. 44a; i, fol. 43d; i, fol. 43d; i, fol. 43d; i, fol. 43d; i, fol. 68b; i, fol. 68b; Regesta regum Anglo-Normannorum III, No. 722; Regesta regum Anglo-Normannorum III, No. 724

[] Abbatia De Sais Sancti Martini

Abbey of Saint-Martin de Sées, Normandy, dépt. Orne, founded by Roger de Montgomery (Ord. Vit. ii, 66–8). Cartulary, Sées, Arch. secrètes de l'Evêché, copy in in Arch. dépt. de l'Orne, H938.

i, fol. 24b; Pipe Roll 31 Henry I, 052–e/ht; Pipe Roll 31 Henry I, 052–e/ht; Regesta regum Anglo-Normannorum III, No. 185; Pipe Roll 3 Henry II, 084b–ln; Pipe Roll 3 Henry II, 084a–ln; Regesta regum Anglo-Normannorum III, No. 815; i, fol. 23a; i, fol. 25c; i, fol. 25a

[] Abbatia De Tauestoch

Tavistock Abbey, Devon, founded in the late tenth century by Ealdorman Ordgar. H. P. R. Finberg, 'Some early Tavistock Charters', English Historical Review, 62 (1947), 352–77.

Finberg, Early Tavistock Charters: ERH, 62, No. I; Finberg, Early Tavistock Charters: ERH, 62, No. XI; i, fol. 103c; i, fol. 103c; i, fol. 78c; i, fol. 78c; i, fol. 103c; i, fol. 103d; i, fol. 103d; i, fol. 103d; i, fol. 103c; i, fol. 103d; i, fol. 103d; i, fol. 103c; Finberg, Early Tavistock Charters: ERH, 62, No. XIV; Finberg, Early Tavistock Charters: ERH, 62, No. III; Pipe Roll 2 Henry II, 46–dv; Finberg, Early Tavistock Charters: ERH, 62, No. IV; Finberg, Early Tavistock Charters: ERH, 62, No. II; Finberg, Early Tavistock Charters: ERH, 62, No. VII; Finberg, Early Tavistock Charters: ERH, 62, No. XV; Finberg, Early Tavistock Charters: ERH, 62, No. XXIV; Bearman, Charters of the Redvers Family (1994), No. 12; Bearman, Charters of the Redvers Family (1994), App. II No. 12

[] Abbatia De Toedekesberie

Tewkesbury Abbey, Gloucestershire, founded 715, refounded as a cell of Cranborne; in 1102 the positions were reversed when Cranborne became a cell of Tewkesbury. BL Cotton Cleopatra A vii; Ann. Tewkesbury, in Annales Monastici, ed. H. R. Luard, 5 vols, Rolls Series, London 1864–9, vol. 1.

i, fol. 163c; i, fol. 163c; i, fol. 163c; i, fol. 163c; i, fol. 163c; i, fol. 163c; i, fol. 163c; Regesta regum Anglo-Normannorum III, No. 869; Regesta regum Anglo-Normannorum III, No. 872; Regesta regum Anglo-Normannorum III, No. 871; Pipe Roll 10 Henry II, 04–wo; Pipe Roll 9 Henry II, 05–wo; Pipe Roll 12 Henry II, 081–wo; Pipe Roll 11 Henry II, 099–wo; Regesta regum Anglo-Normannorum III, No. 870

[] Abbatia De Tornyg

Thorney Abbey, Cambridgeshire; founded 972–3. Cartulary (Liber Rubeus) Cambridge University Library ms Add. 3020–1.

Northants Survey, fols 94r–95v; Regesta regum Anglo-Normannorum III, No. 893; i, fol. 222c; Regesta regum Anglo-Normannorum III, No. 889; Northants Survey, fols 94r–95v; Regesta regum Anglo-Normannorum III, No. 884; i, fol. 222c; Dugdale, Monasticon Anglicanum, II, p. 601, No. IX; Dugdale, Monasticon Anglicanum, II, p. 603, No. XXV; Dugdale, Monasticon

Anglicanum, II, p. 602, No. XVII; Dugdale, Monasticon Anglicanum, II, p. 603, No. XXIV; Dugdale, Monasticon Anglicanum, II, pp. 602–03, No. XXI; Regesta regum Anglo-Normannorum III, No. 890; Clay, Early Yorkshire Charters (1952), IX, No. 63; Regesta regum Anglo-Normannorum III, No. 879; Regesta regum Anglo-Normannorum III, No. 891; Regesta regum Anglo-Normannorum III, No. 881; Dugdale, Monasticon Anglicanum, II, p. 601, No. XIII; Dugdale, Monasticon Anglicanum, II, p. 603, No. XXVII; Dugdale, Monasticon Anglicanum, II, p. 602, No. XX; Regesta regum Anglo-Normannorum III, No. 888; Dugdale, Monasticon Anglicanum, II, p. 602, No. XIV; i, fol. 211a; i, fol. 205a; Barraclough, Charters of AN Earls of Chester (1988), No. 58; Dugdale, Monasticon Anglicanum, II, p. 601, No. X; Dugdale, Monasticon Anglicanum, II, p. 603, No. XXIII; Dugdale, Monasticon Anglicanum, II, p. 602, No. XIX

[] Abbatia De Troarz

Abbey of Troarn (Normandy, Calvados), founded by Roger I of Montgomery c.1050 (Ord. Vit. ii, 20–2). See R.N. Sauvage, L'abbaye de Saint-Martin de Troarn, (Caen, 1911); BN lat. 10086.

i, fol. 25d; i, fol. 25d; i, fol. 44d; i, fol. 166c; i, fol. 166c; Barraclough, Charters of AN Earls of Chester (1988), No. 9; Regesta regum Anglo-Normannorum III, No. 902

[] Abbatia De Ultresport

Abbey of Le Tréport (Normandy, Seine-Maritime), founded by Robert count of Eu and his wife Beatrice c.1059. See Cartulaire de l'abbaye de Saint-Michel-du-Tréport, ed. Laffleur de Kermaingant (Paris, 1880).

i, fol. 18b; i, fol. 19d

[] Abbatia De Warwelle

Wherwell Abbey, Hants., founded c.986. BL Egerton 2104, general cartulary.

i, fol. 44a; i, fol. 44a; i, fol. 44a; i, fol. 44a; i, fol. 44a; i, fol. 44a; i, fol. 44a

[] Abbatia De Westmonasterio

Abbey of St Peter, Westminster, Originally founded in the seventh century, the abbey was rebuilt on a grand scale by Edward the Confessor after 1045. J. Armitage Robinson and M. R. James, MSS of Westminster Abbey (Cambridge, 1909).

i, fol. 59d; i, fol. 222b; i, fol. 222b; i, fol. 247c; i, fol. 43c; i, fol. 32b; i, fol. 32b; i, fol. 32b; i, fol. 135b; Pipe Roll 4 Henry II, 161–st; Pipe Roll 4 Henry II, 155–wo; Pipe Roll 4 Henry II, 162–sr; Pipe Roll 5 Henry II, 23–wo; Round, Fragments from Worcester, Round, Feudal England (1895 : 1946), pp. 146–47; i, fol. 67b; i, fol. 175a; i, fol. 174c; i, fol. 166b; i, fol. 174c; i, fol. 174c; i, fol. 174c; i, fol. 166b; i, fol. 174c; i, fol. 174c; i, fol. 166b; i, fol. 166b; i, fol. 174c; i, fol. 166b; i, fol. 174d; i, fol. 174c; i, fol. 174d; i, fol. 174d; i, fol. 174d; i, fol. 174c; Red Book of the Exchequer, ed. Hall (1897), pp. 188–98; Regesta regum Anglo-Normannorum III, No. 931; Regesta regum Anglo-Normannorum III, No. 213; Regesta regum Anglo-Normannorum III, No. 932; Regesta regum Anglo-Normannorum III, No. 929; Regesta regum Anglo-Normannorum III, No. 940; Regesta regum Anglo-Normannorum III, No. 941; Regesta regum Anglo-Normannorum III, No. 939; Pipe Roll 2 Henry II, 63–wo; Pipe Roll 10 Henry II, 03–wo; Pipe Roll 11 Henry II, 098–wo; Pipe Roll 5 Henry II, 56–sr; Pipe Roll 7 Henry II, 54a–wo; Pipe Roll 12 Henry II, 080–wo; Pipe Roll 6 Henry II, 23–wo; Pipe Roll 9 Henry II, 04–wo; Pipe Roll 8 Henry II, 55–wo; Regesta regum Anglo-Normannorum III, No. 933; Pipe Roll 2 Henry II, 12a–sr; Pipe

Roll 2 Henry II, 12b–sr; Regesta regum Anglo-Normannorum III, No. 938; i, fol. 346b; i, fol. 222b; ii, fol. 014a; Regesta regum Anglo-Normannorum III, No. 936; i, fol. 370a; i, fol. 43c; i, fol. 145d; i, fol. 17a; i, fol. 211a; i, fol. 166b; i, fol. 247c; i, fol. 174c; Lincolnshire Claims (Domesday Book), fols 376d–377c; i, fol. 61b; Mason, Westminster Abbey Charters (1988), No. 350; Mason, Westminster Abbey Charters (1988), No. 462; Mason, Westminster Abbey Charters (1988), No. 436; Mason, Westminster Abbey Charters (1988), No. 488; Mason, Westminster Abbey Charters (1988), No. 475; ii, fol. 014b; ii, fol. 014a; ii, fol. 015a; ii, fol. 015a; ii, fol. 015a; ii, fol. 015a; ii, fol. 014b; ii, fol. 015a; ii, fol. 014b; ii, fol. 014a; ii, fol. 014a; ii, fol. 014a; ii, fol. 160a; ii, fol. 100a; i, fol. 32b; i, fol. 346b; i, fol. 346b

[] Abbatia De Wiltune
Wilton Abbey, Wilts., founded 830, refounded 890. Registrum Wiltunense, ed. R. C. Hoare et al. (London, 1827).

Pipe Roll 31 Henry I, 020–wl; i, fol. 52d; crbr, rb, p. 239; i, fol. 79a; i, fol. 79a; i, fol. 68a; i, fol. 68b; i, fol. 68a; i, fol. 68a; i, fol. 68a; i, fol. 67d; i, fol. 68a; i, fol. 68a; i, fol. 68a; i, fol. 68b; i, fol. 68b; i, fol. 68b; i, fol. 68a; i, fol. 67d; i, fol. 68a; i, fol. 67d; i, fol. 67d; i, fol. 68b; i, fol. 68a; Pipe Roll 31 Henry I, 013–dswl; Pipe Roll 2 Henry II, 60–wl; Pipe Roll 7 Henry II, 09–wl; Pipe Roll 5 Henry II, 40b–wl; Pipe Roll 8 Henry II, 14–wl; i, fol. 52d

[] Abbatia De Wincelcumbe
Abbey of Winchcombe, Gloucestershire, refounded for Benedictine monks c.970. D. Royce, Landboc sive Registrum Monasterii Beatiae Mariae Virginis et Sancti Cenhelmi de Winchelcumba, 2 vols (Exeter, 1892–93)

i, fol. 239a; i, fol. 157a; i, fol. 157a; i, fol. 165d; i, fol. 157a; i, fol. 239a; crbr, rb, pp. 287–88; i, fol. 165d; i, fol. 165d; i, fol. 165d; i, fol. 165d; i, fol. 165d; i, fol. 165d; i, fol. 165d; i, fol. 165d; i, fol. 165d; i, fol. 165d; Pipe Roll 4 Henry II, 141–wy; Pipe Roll 5 Henry II, 28–gl; Pipe Roll 2 Henry II, 50–gl

[] Abbatia De Wincestre
Abbey of St Mary and St Edburga at Winchester, Hants, known as Nunnaminster, founded c.900 by King Alfred.

i, fol. 43d; i, fol. 43d; i, fol. 43d; i, fol. 43d; i, fol. 43d; Pipe Roll 31 Henry I, 121–ln; Pipe Roll 31 Henry I, 023–wl; Pipe Roll 31 Henry I, 125–bk; Pipe Roll 31 Henry I, 041–hm; Pipe Roll 31 Henry I, 121–ln; Pipe Roll 31 Henry I, 041–hm; Pipe Roll 31 Henry I, 125–bk; i, fol. 73a; i, fol. 68b; i, fol. 68b; i, fol. 68b; i, fol. 43d

[] Abbatia De Wincestre Sancti Petri
Abbey of St Peter, Winchester, Hants., founded as the New Minster in 901 by Edward the Elder on a site to the north of the Old Minster (Cathedral). The site was inconvenient and was subsequently removed to Hyde in 1110. When the building was rebuilt after destruction in 1141 it became known as Hyde Abbey. E. Edwards, Liber Monasterii de Hyda, Rolls Series, London, 1856; Mon. Ang. ii, 434 ff; BL Cotton Domit. A xix, fols 22–237. Simon Keynes, ed. The Liber Vitae of the New Minster and Hyde Abbey, Winchester, English Manuscripts in Facsimile 26, Copenhagen 1996.

i, fol. 59d; i, fol. 43c,d; i, fol. 43a; i, fol. 43a; i, fol. 43b; i, fol. 43b; i, fol. 43b; i, fol. 43b; i, fol. 43b; i, fol. 43a,b; i, fol. 43a,b; i, fol. 43c,d; i, fol. 43c,d; i, fol. 43a,b; i, fol. 32b; i, fol. 67c; i, fol. 67c; i, fol. 67c; i, fol. 67b; i, fol. 67b; i, fol. 67b; i, fol. 77d; i, fol. 17c; i, fol. 43a

[] Abbatia Fiscanensis

Abbey of Fécamp, Normandy, dépt. Seine-Maritime. L'Abbaye benedictine de Fécamp – Ouvrage scientifique du xiiie centenaire 658–1758, t. 1, Fécamp 1959. Cartulary copies and extracts in Bib. mun. Rouen mss 1207, 1210; Arch. dépt. Seine-Maritime 7 H 9; BN lat. nov. acq. 2412; BN Coll. Baluze, vol. lxxiii, fols 33–52; BN at 17048, pp. 561–74.

    i, fol. 17b; Regesta regum Anglo-Normannorum III, No. 303

[] Abbatia Gemmeticensis

Abbey of Jumièges, Normandy, Seine-Maritime; one of the most important of the Norman abbeys. See Chartes de l'abbaye de Jumièges, ed. J.-J. Vernier, 2 vols, Soc. Hist. Norm., 1916.

    i, fol. 43c; Regesta regum Anglo-Normannorum III, No. 417; i, fol. 43c

[] Abbatia Hortunensis

Horton Abbey, Dorset, refounded for Benedictines c.1050 as a cell of Sherborne Abbey.

    i, fol. 104a; i, fol. 104a; i, fol. 104a; i, fol. 78c; i, fol. 78c; i, fol. 78c; i, fol. 78c; i, fol. 104a

[] Abbatia Majoris Monasterii

Abbey of Marmoutier at Tours in the Loire Valley. One of the oldest and most important of the French abbeys.

    i, fol. 79b; Regesta regum Anglo-Normannorum III, No. 578; Clay, Early Yorkshire Charters (1939), VI, No. 3; Clay, Early Yorkshire Charters (1939), VI, No. 49; Clay, Early Yorkshire Charters (1939), VI, No. 2

[] Abbatia Sancte Marie Villaris

Abbey of Montivilliers, Normandy, dépt Seine-Maritime. Refounded in the early eleventh century by Richard II of Normandy, whose aunt Beatrice was abbess. See L'Abbaye de Montivilliers à travers les âges. Actes du colloque organisé à Montivilliers le 8 mars 1986; Recueil de l'Association des Amis du Vieux Havre, no. 48 (1988), especially, J-M. Bouvris, 'La renaissance de l'abbaye de Montivilliers et son dévelopement jusqu'à la fin du XIe siècle'.

    i, fol. 79a

[] Abbatia Sancte Trinitatis Cadomensis

Abbey of Sainte-Trinité de Caen founded for nuns by William I and his wife Matilda, one of two houses founded in 1059 as expiation for their marriage within the prohibited degrees. L. Musset, Les Actes de Guillaume le Conquérant et de la reine Mathilde pour les abbayes caennaises, Caen, 1967; John Walmsley, ed. Charters and Custumals of the Abbey of Holy Trinity, Caen Part 2 The French Estates (Records of Social and Economic History n.s. 22, Oxford, 1994).

    i, fol. 166c; i, fol. 166c; i, fol. 166c; i, fol. 104b; i, fol. 79a; Regesta regum Anglo-Normannorum III, No. 137; Pipe Roll 8 Henry II, 65–nfsf; ii, fol. 021b; ii, fol. 021b; ii, fol. 021b

[] Abbatia Sancte Wareburg

St Werburgh's Abbey, Cheshire; founded soon after 907 for secular clerks; refounded for Benedictine monks by Hugh earl of Chester 1092–3, provided from Bec by Anselm of Canterbury. Chartulary of Chester Abbey, ed. J. Tait, Chetham Society, n.s., lxxix, lxxxii (1920–3).

i, fol. 263b; i, fol. 263b; i, fol. 263b; i, fol. 263b; i, fol. 263b; i, fol. 263c; i, fol. 263b; i, fol. 263b; i, fol. 263b; i, fol. 263b; i, fol. 263b; i, fol. 263b; i, fol. 263c; i, fol. 263b; i, fol. 263b; i, fol. 263b; i, fol. 264a; Barraclough, Charters of AN Earls of Chester (1988), No. 3; Barraclough, Charters of AN Earls of Chester (1988), No. 13; Barraclough, Charters of AN Earls of Chester (1988), No. 29; Barraclough, Charters of AN Earls of Chester (1988), No. 26; Barraclough, Charters of AN Earls of Chester (1988), No. 21; Barraclough, Charters of AN Earls of Chester (1988), No. 8; Barraclough, Charters of AN Earls of Chester (1988), No. 27; Barraclough, Charters of AN Earls of Chester (1988), No. 25; Barraclough, Charters of AN Earls of Chester (1988), No. 129; Barraclough, Charters of AN Earls of Chester (1988), No. 32; Barraclough, Charters of AN Earls of Chester (1988), No. 23; Barraclough, Charters of AN Earls of Chester (1988), No. 28; Barraclough, Charters of AN Earls of Chester (1988), No. 24

[] Abbatia Sancti Albani

St Albans Abbey, Herts., founded c. 793 and refounded c. 970. Benefactors of the early Norman period are listed in BL Cotton Nero D viii, fols 118ff. Gesta Abbatum Monasterii Sancti Albani a Thoma Walsingham . . . compilata, ed. H. T. Riley, 3 vols, Rolls Ser., London, 1867–9.

i, fol. 59d; Greenway, Charters of the Honour of Mowbray (1972), No. 3; Greenway, Charters of the Honour of Mowbray (1972), No. 2; i, fol. 213a; Dugdale, Monasticon Anglicanum, III, p. 300, No. II; Dugdale, Monasticon Anglicanum, III, p. 295, No. I; Dugdale, Monasticon Anglicanum, III, pp. 299–300, No. I; Dugdale, Monasticon Anglicanum, III, pp. 345–46, No. I; Dugdale, Monasticon Anglicanum, III, pp. 288–89, No. I; Regesta regum Anglo-Normannorum III, No. 743; Regesta regum Anglo-Normannorum III, No. 745; Regesta regum Anglo-Normannorum III, No. 746; Regesta regum Anglo-Normannorum III, No. 740; Regesta regum Anglo-Normannorum III, No. 744; i, fol. 135c; Pipe Roll 5 Henry II, 06–ht; Pipe Roll 2 Henry II, 21–ht; Regesta regum Anglo-Normannorum III, No. 105; Dugdale, Monasticon Anglicanum, III, p. 280, No. IV; Regesta regum Anglo-Normannorum III, No. 742; Regesta regum Anglo-Normannorum III, No. 741; Gibbs, Early Charters of St Pauls (1939), No. 154; i, fol. 145d; Regesta regum Anglo-Normannorum III, No. 973; Dugdale, Monasticon Anglicanum, III, p. 276–77, No. II; Dugdale, Monasticon Anglicanum, III, p. 276, No. I; Dugdale, Monasticon Anglicanum, III, p. 331, No. IV; Barraclough, Charters of AN Earls of Chester (1988), No. 7; Dugdale, Monasticon Anglicanum, III, pp. 345–46, No. I; Dugdale, Monasticon Anglicanum, III, p. 290, No. V; i, fol. 56c

[] Abbatia Sancti Audoeni

Abbey of Saint-Ouen, Rouen. Cartulary Arch. dépt. Seine-Maritime 14 H 18; another, BN lat. 5423; fragment of another, BN lat. 12777, pp. 106–25.

Pipe Roll 2 Henry II, 17–e; Pipe Roll 2 Henry II, 18–e; Pipe Roll 5 Henry II, 05–e; Regesta regum Anglo-Normannorum III, No. 733; ii, fol. 022a; ii, fol. 022a; ii, fol. 022a

[] Abbatia Sancti Benedicti De Holmo

Abbey of Saint Benet of Holme, Norfolk. First founded c.800, refounded as a Benedictine monastery for 26 monks by Cnut in 1019; 12 monks were sent to colonize Bury St Edmunds in 1020. F.M. Stenton, 'St Benet of Holme and the Norman Conquest', EHR 33 (1922); Cartulary of St Benet of Holme, ed. J. R. West, 2 vols, Norwich Record Society ii and iii, 1932.

Regesta regum Anglo-Normannorum III, No. 399; Regesta regum Anglo-Normannorum III, No. 400; Dugdale, Monasticon Anglicanum, III, p. 86, No. VI; Dugdale, Monasticon Anglicanum, III, p. 88, No. XVI; Dugdale, Monasticon Anglicanum, III, p. 86, No. V; Dugdale, Monasticon Anglicanum, III, p. 88, No. XVIII; Dugdale, Monasticon Anglicanum, III, p. 87, No. IX; Dugdale, Monasticon Anglicanum, III, pp. 86–87, No. VIII; Regesta regum Anglo-Normannorum III, No. 402; Pipe Roll 5 Henry II, 12–nfsf; Dugdale, Monasticon Anglicanum, III, p. 88, No. XVII; Douglas, Social Structure of Med. E. Anglia (1927), No. 48; Dugdale, Monasticon Anglicanum, III, p. 88, No. XX; ii, fol. 216a; Dugdale, Monasticon Anglicanum, III, p. 87, No. X; Regesta regum Anglo-Normannorum III, No. 405; ii, fol. 248b; ii, fol. 264b; ii, fol. 378b; ii, fol. 216a; ii, fol. 216a; ii, fol. 216b; ii, fol. 217a; ii, fol. 216a; ii, fol. 216a; ii, fol. 216a; ii, fol. 216a; ii, fol. 216a; ii, fol. 216a; ii, fol. 216a; ii, fol. 216a; ii, fol. 217b; ii, fol. 216a; ii, fol. 217b; ii, fol. 216a; ii, fol. 218a; ii, fol. 216b; ii, fol. 216a; ii, fol. 216a; ii, fol. 217b; ii, fol. 216a; ii, fol. 217a; ii, fol. 216b; ii, fol. 216b; ii, fol. 216b; ii, fol. 216b; ii, fol. 216a; ii, fol. 217a; ii, fol. 221a; ii, fol. 220b; ii, fol. 220b; ii, fol. 221a; ii, fol. 221a; ii, fol. 259b; ii, fol. 221a; ii, fol. 220b; ii, fol. 216b; ii, fol. 217a; ii, fol. 217a; ii, fol. 217a; ii, fol. 217a; ii, fol. 217b; ii, fol. 217a; ii, fol. 217a; ii, fol. 216b; ii, fol. 216b; ii, fol. 217a; ii, fol. 217a; ii, fol. 219b; ii, fol. 217a; ii, fol. 216b; ii, fol. 218a; ii, fol. 217b; ii, fol. 217b; ii, fol. 217b; ii, fol. 217b; ii, fol. 217a; ii, fol. 219b; ii, fol. 218b; ii, fol. 220b; ii, fol. 218b; ii, fol. 218b; ii, fol. 218b; ii, fol. 218b; ii, fol. 218a; ii, fol. 218a; ii, fol. 218a; ii, fol. 218b; ii, fol. 219a; ii, fol. 216b; ii, fol. 219b; ii, fol. 219a; ii, fol. 219b; ii, fol. 219b; ii, fol. 218b; ii, fol. 219b; ii, fol. 220a; ii, fol. 219a; ii, fol. 219a; ii, fol. 219a; ii, fol. 219a; ii, fol. 219a; ii, fol. 219a; ii, fol. 219a; ii, fol. 219b; ii, fol. 220a; ii, fol. 219b; ii, fol. 220a; ii, fol. 216b; ii, fol. 216a; ii, fol. 220a; ii, fol. 220b; ii, fol. 220a; ii, fol. 220b; ii, fol. 220b; ii, fol. 220b; ii, fol. 220a; ii, fol. 220a; ii, fol. 220a; ii, fol. 220a; ii, fol. 219a; ii, fol. 220a; ii, fol. 218b; ii, fol. 218a; ii, fol. 218b; ii, fol. 218b; ii, fol. 217a; ii, fol. 220a; ii, fol. 218a; ii, fol. 218a; ii, fol. 218a; ii, fol. 221a; ii, fol. 220b; ii, fol. 218a; ii, fol. 218a; ii, fol. 218a; ii, fol. 220b; ii, fol. 218b; ii, fol. 219b

[] Abbatia Sancti Dionisii Parisii

Abbey of Saint-Denis in Paris.

i, fol. 174b; i, fol. 157a; i, fol. 166b; i, fol. 166b; i, fol. 166b; i, fol. 166b; i, fol. 166b; i, fol. 166b; i, fol. 166b; i, fol. 166b; i, fol. 166b; i, fol. 166b; i, fol. 166b; i, fol. 166b; Pipe Roll 9 Henry II, 49–ox; Round, Fragments from Worcester, Round, Feudal England (1895: 1946), p. 146; i, fol. 174b; i, fol. 157a; i, fol. 166b

[] Abbatia Sancti Ebrulfi

Abbey of Saint-Evroul, Orne, refounded c.1050 by William and Robert de Grandmesnil; see Orderic Vitalis, ed. Chibnall, vol. ii; and idem, ed. Le Prévost, vol. v, pp. 182ff, Rotulus primus monasterii S. Ebrulfi (saec. xi exeunte).

Round, Ancient Charters (1888), No. 18; Barraclough, Charters of AN Earls of Chester (1988), No. 11; i, fol. 242a; Barraclough, Charters of AN Earls of Chester (1988), No. 10; Greenway, Charters of the Honour of Mowbray (1972), No. 17; i, fol. 248a; i, fol. 248a; i, fol. 166c; Northants Survey, fols 94r–95v; i, fol. 238a; Pipe Roll 8 Henry II, 60–gl; Clay, Early Yorkshire Charters (1949), VIII, No. 26; Regesta regum Anglo-Normannorum III, No. 774; i, fol. 23a; i, fol. 166c; Barraclough, Charters of AN Earls of Chester (1988), No. 1; i, fol. 248a

[] Abbatia Sancti Edmundi

Abbey of Bury St Edmund's, Suffolk, founded for seculars c.633, replaced by 20 monks from St Benet's, Holm, in 1020–2.

Douglas, Feudal Documents from Bury St Edmunds, No. 28; Douglas, Feudal Documents from Bury St Edmunds, No. 53; Douglas, Feudal Documents from Bury St Edmunds, No. 47; Douglas, Feudal Documents from Bury St Edmunds, No. 46; i, fol. 154a; i, fol. 222b; i, fol. 222b; i, fol. 222b; i, fol. 222b; i, fol. 222b; i, fol. 222b; i, fol. 222b; i, fol. 222b; i, fol. 222b; i, fol. 222b; i, fol. 222b; i, fol. 222b; Douglas, Feudal Documents from Bury St Edmunds, No. 82; Douglas, Feudal Documents from Bury St Edmunds, No. 70; Regesta regum Anglo-Normannorum III, No. 755; Douglas, Feudal Documents from Bury St Edmunds, No. 58; Douglas, Feudal Documents from Bury St Edmunds, No. 87; Douglas, Feudal Documents from Bury St Edmunds, No. 194; Douglas, Feudal Documents from Bury St Edmunds, No. 39; Douglas, Feudal Documents from Bury St Edmunds, No. 41; Douglas, Feudal Documents from Bury St Edmunds, No. 48; Regesta regum Anglo-Normannorum III, No. 36; Regesta regum Anglo-Normannorum III, No. 35; Douglas, Feudal Documents from Bury St Edmunds, No. 133; Douglas, Feudal Documents from Bury St Edmunds, No. 133; Douglas, Feudal Documents from Bury St Edmunds, No. 65; Douglas, Feudal Documents from Bury St Edmunds, No. 182; Regesta regum Anglo-Normannorum III, No. 765; Douglas, Feudal Documents from Bury St Edmunds, No. 84; Dodwell, Charters relating to the Honour of Bacton, No. 5; Douglas, Feudal Documents from Bury St Edmunds, No. 102; Douglas, Feudal Documents from Bury St Edmunds, No. 197; Regesta regum Anglo-Normannorum III, No. 762; Douglas, Feudal Documents from Bury St Edmunds, No. 85; Douglas, Feudal Documents from Bury St Edmunds, No. 194; Douglas, Feudal Documents from Bury St Edmunds, No. 66; Douglas, Feudal Documents from Bury St Edmunds, No. 69; Douglas, Feudal Documents from Bury St Edmunds, No. 76; Douglas, Feudal Documents from Bury St Edmunds, No. 213; Douglas, Feudal Documents from Bury St Edmunds, No. 88; Douglas, Feudal Documents from Bury St Edmunds, No. 204; Douglas, Feudal Documents from Bury St Edmunds, No. 72; Douglas, Feudal Documents from Bury St Edmunds, No. 94; Regesta regum Anglo-Normannorum III, No. 758; Regesta regum Anglo-Normannorum III, No. 761; Regesta regum Anglo-Normannorum III, No. 768; Douglas, Feudal Documents from Bury St Edmunds, No. 205; Douglas, Feudal Documents from Bury St Edmunds, No. 71; Douglas, Feudal Documents from Bury St Edmunds, No. 80; Douglas, Feudal Documents from Bury St Edmunds, No. 186; Douglas, Feudal Documents from Bury St Edmunds, No. 177; Dodwell, Charters relating to the Honour of Bacton, No. 6; Pipe Roll 5 Henry II, 11–nfsf; Pipe Roll 2 Henry II, 08–sf; Pipe Roll 9 Henry II, 28–nfsf; Pipe Roll 6 Henry II, 02–nfsf; Pipe Roll 10 Henry II, 33–nfsf; Pipe Roll 12 Henry II, 017–nfsf; Pipe Roll 8 Henry II, 62–nfsf; Pipe Roll 11 Henry II, 003–nfsf; Pipe Roll 5 Henry II, 08–nfsf; Pipe Roll 4 Henry II, 125–nfsf; Regesta regum Anglo-Normannorum III, No. 766; Douglas, Feudal Documents from Bury St Edmunds, No. 60; Douglas, Feudal Documents from Bury St Edmunds, No. 184; Douglas, Feudal Documents from Bury St Edmunds, No. 104; Douglas, Feudal Documents from Bury St Edmunds, No. 191; Douglas, Feudal Documents from Bury St Edmunds, No. 18; Douglas, Feudal Documents from Bury St Edmunds, No. 21; Douglas, Feudal Documents from Bury St Edmunds, No. 3; pipe,Pipe Roll 2 Henry II, 17–e; Regesta regum Anglo-Normannorum III, No. 756; Pipe Roll 2 Henry II, 41–nh; Regesta regum Anglo-Normannorum III, No. 773; Pipe Roll 2 Henry II, 18–e; Regesta regum Anglo-Normannorum III, No. 752; i, fol. 210c; Northants Survey, fols 96r–99v; Red Book of the Exchequer, ed. Hall (1897), pp. 392–94; Pipe Roll 2 Henry II, 07–nf; Pipe Roll 2 Henry II, 10–sf; Pipe Roll 2 Henry II, 09b–sf; Pipe Roll 2 Henry II, 09a–sf; Regesta regum Anglo-Normannorum III, No. 373; ii, fol. 356b; i, fol. 222b; ii, fol. 019b; Regesta regum Anglo-

Normannorum III, No. 769; Regesta regum Anglo-Normannorum III, No. 757; Regesta regum Anglo-Normannorum III, No. 767; Regesta regum Anglo-Normannorum III, No. 770; Red Book of the Exchequer, ed. Hall (1897), pp. 354–56; Pipe Roll 3 Henry II, 107–wi; Douglas, Feudal Book of Bury St Edmunds (1932), pp. 3–21; Douglas, Feudal Documents from Bury St Edmunds, No. 4; ii, fol. 366b; ii, fol. 367a; ii, fol. 366a; ii, fol. 357b; ii, fol. 368a; ii, fol. 366b; ii, fol. 366a; ii, fol. 366a; ii, fol. 365b; ii, fol. 365b; ii, fol. 368b; ii, fol. 365b; ii, fol. 368b; ii, fol. 369a; ii, fol. 369a; ii, fol. 369a; ii, fol. 369a; ii, fol. 369a; ii, fol. 369a; ii, fol. 365b; ii, fol. 357b; ii, fol. 357a; ii, fol. 356b; ii, fol. 359a; ii, fol. 364a; ii, fol. 358b; ii, fol. 368b; ii, fol. 358b; ii, fol. 357b; ii, fol. 358b; ii, fol. 357b; ii, fol. 366b; ii, fol. 358b; ii, fol. 358b; ii, fol. 358a; ii, fol. 362b; ii, fol. 366a; ii, fol. 367a; ii, fol. 367a; ii, fol. 367a; ii, fol. 367a; ii, fol. 367a; ii, fol. 366b; ii, fol. 357b; ii, fol. 364b; ii, fol. 365a; ii, fol. 364b; ii, fol. 365a; ii, fol. 360b; ii, fol. 365a; ii, fol. 364b; ii, fol. 364b; ii, fol. 364b; ii, fol. 360b; ii, fol. 363b; ii, fol. 359a; ii, fol. 364a; ii, fol. 364b; ii, fol. 364a; ii, fol. 364a; ii, fol. 364a; ii, fol. 364a; ii, fol. 019b; ii, fol. 364b; ii, fol. 130a; ii, fol. 371b; ii, fol. 364b; ii, fol. 363b; ii, fol. 368b; ii, fol. 365a; ii, fol. 368b; ii, fol. 368a; ii, fol. 368a; ii, fol. 368a; ii, fol. 365a; ii, fol. 368a; ii, fol. 360a; ii, fol. 360a; ii, fol. 368a; ii, fol. 363b; ii, fol. 359a; ii, fol. 359a; ii, fol. 359b; ii, fol. 359b; ii, fol. 359b; ii, fol. 359b; ii, fol. 360a; ii, fol. 360a; ii, fol. 360a; ii, fol. 360b; ii, fol. 368b; ii, fol. 371b; ii, fol. 371a; ii, fol. 370b; ii, fol. 371a; ii, fol. 371a; ii, fol. 371a; ii, fol. 371b; ii, fol. 371b; ii, fol. 371b; ii, fol. 371b; ii, fol. 371b; ii, fol. 371b; ii, fol. 370b; ii, fol. 371b; ii, fol. 371a; ii, fol. 371b; ii, fol. 371b; ii, fol. 372a; ii, fol. 370b; ii, fol. 371b; ii, fol. 370b; ii, fol. 370b; ii, fol. 370b; ii, fol. 370b; ii, fol. 370b; ii, fol. 370b; ii, fol. 369a; ii, fol. 371a; ii, fol. 371b; ii, fol. 361a; ii, fol. 361a; ii, fol. 361a; ii, fol. 361a; ii, fol. 361a; ii, fol. 363a; ii, fol. 362a; ii, fol. 362a; ii, fol. 362a; ii, fol. 362a; ii, fol. 361b; ii, fol. 363a; ii, fol. 371a; ii, fol. 361b; ii, fol. 371a; ii, fol. 362a; ii, fol. 361b; ii, fol. 361b; ii, fol. 361b; ii, fol. 361b; ii, fol. 361a; ii, fol. 361b; ii, fol. 361a; ii, fol. 361a; ii, fol. 371a; ii, fol. 371a; ii, fol. 371a; ii, fol. 371a; ii, fol. 361a; ii, fol. 357a; ii, fol. 370b; ii, fol. 370a; ii, fol. 369b; ii, fol. 369b; ii, fol. 369b; ii, fol. 370a; ii, fol. 357a; ii, fol. 369a; ii, fol. 369a; ii, fol. 370a; ii, fol. 369b; ii, fol. 370a; ii, fol. 357a; ii, fol. 370a; ii, fol. 357a; ii, fol. 357a; ii, fol. 357a; ii, fol. 356b; ii, fol. 356b; ii, fol. 356b; ii, fol. 356b; ii, fol. 357b; ii, fol. 019b; ii, fol. 356b; ii, fol. 020a; ii, fol. 020a; ii, fol. 020a; ii, fol. 019b; ii, fol. 362b; ii, fol. 370b; ii, fol. 370b; ii, fol. 363b; ii, fol. 362a; ii, fol. 363a; ii, fol. 361a; ii, fol. 361a; ii, fol. 361a; ii, fol. 362b; ii, fol. 363a; ii, fol. 361a; ii, fol. 370a; ii, fol. 362a; ii, fol. 020a; ii, fol. 362b; ii, fol. 362b; ii, fol. 362b; ii, fol. 362b; ii, fol. 362b; ii, fol. 362b; ii, fol. 362a; ii, fol. 371b; ii, fol. 371a; ii, fol. 370a; ii, fol. 371b; ii, fol. 369b; ii, fol. 370a; ii, fol. 370a; ii, fol. 362b

[] Abbatia Sancti Florentii De Salmur
Abbey of Saint-Florent de Saumur, one of the great Benedictine abbeys in the Touraine. CDF, nos. 1109–1156; Liber Niger, BN nov. acq. lat. 1930; Liber Albus, Arch. dépt. Maine-et-Loire H3713.

i, fol. 180d

[] Abbatia Sancti Karileffi
Abbey of Saint-Calais (Sarthe) in the county of Maine. Cartulaire de l'abbaye de Saint-Calais, L. Froger (Mamers etc., 1888, Soc. hist. arch. du Maine).

i, fol. 340d; i, fol. 340d

[] Abbatia Sancti Nicolai Andegauensis
Abbey of Saint-Nicholas at Angers in Anjou. Arch. dépt. de Maine-et-Loire,

Y. Labande-Mailfert, Cartulaire, ms non coté; H397, etc.

Dugdale, Monasticon Anglicanum, III, pp. 215–16, No. II; Dugdale, Monasticon Anglicanum, III, p. 216, No. V; Greenway, Charters of the Honour of Mowbray (1972), No. 13; Regesta regum Anglo-Normannorum III, No. 20; i, fol. 214d

[] Abbatia Sancti Petri Cluniacensis

Abbey near Mâcon in Burgundy founded by William the Pious of Aquitaine in 909. Recueil des chartes de l'abbaye de Cluny, 6 vols, Paris, 1876–93, ed. A. Bernard et A. Bruel.

Dugdale, Monasticon Anglicanum, III, pp. 345–46, No. I; Regesta regum Anglo-Normannorum III, No. 204; Pipe Roll 31 Henry I, 048–hn; Pipe Roll 31 Henry I, 048–hn; Regesta regum Anglo-Normannorum III, No. 206; i, fol. 205d; Pipe Roll 2 Henry II, 34–bk; Pipe Roll 3 Henry II, 080–bk; Pipe Roll 10 Henry II, 42a–bk; Pipe Roll 10 Henry II, 42b–bk; Pipe Roll 7 Henry II, 52–bk; Pipe Roll 4 Henry II, 123–bk; Pipe Roll 11 Henry II, 073–bk; Pipe Roll 4 Henry II, 145–rt; Pipe Roll 12 Henry II, 120–bk; Pipe Roll 9 Henry II, 51–bk; Pipe Roll 5 Henry II, 36–bk; Pipe Roll 8 Henry II, 43–bk; Pipe Roll 6 Henry II, 21–bk; Regesta regum Anglo-Normannorum III, No. 300; Clay, Early Yorkshire Charters (1949), VIII, No. 3

[] Abbatia Sancti Petri Culturae

Abbey of Saint-Pierre-de-la-Couture in Maine. Cartulaire de Saint-Pierre-de-la-Couture, ed. Bénédictines de Solesmes, Le Mans 1881.

i, fol. 147d

[] Abbatia Sancti Petri De Castellion

Abbey of Conches, founded by Roger de Tosny, lord of Conches, before 1040. Copies of cartulary material in Arch. dépt. de l'Eure H262, BN lat. 13816, fols 461–76.

i, fol. 183b

[] Abbatia Sancti Petri De Salopesberie

Abbey of SS Peter and Paul, Shrewsbury, Shropshire, founded in 1083 by Roger de Montgomery, earl of Shrewsbury. Una Rees, The Cartulary of Shrewsbury Abbey, 2 vols (Aberystwyth, 1975).

Barraclough, Charters of AN Earls of Chester (1988), No. 62; i, fol. 253b; i, fol. 253d; i, fol. 253c; i, fol. 253b; i, fol. 254a; i, fol. 253b; i, fol. 254b; Barraclough, Charters of AN Earls of Chester (1988), No. 63; Barraclough, Charters of AN Earls of Chester (1988), No. 64; i, fol. 253b; Rees, Cartulary of Shrewsbury Abbey (1975), No. 28; Rees, Cartulary of Shrewsbury Abbey (1975), No. 24; Rees, Cartulary of Shrewsbury Abbey (1975), No. 19; Rees, Cartulary of Shrewsbury Abbey (1975), No. 25; Pipe Roll 9 Henry II, 03–sp; Pipe Roll 11 Henry II, 090–sp; Pipe Roll 5 Henry II, 62a–sp; Pipe Roll 2 Henry II, 43–sp; Pipe Roll 4 Henry II, 170–sp; Pipe Roll 6 Henry II, 25–sp; Pipe Roll 12 Henry II, 059–sp

[] Abbatia Sancti Petri Super Diuam

Abbey of Saint-Pierre-sur-Dives, refounded c.1040 by Lescelina, wife of William count of Eu.

Regesta regum Anglo-Normannorum III, No. 56; i, fol. 274b; i, fol. 274b; i, fol. 227c

[] Abbatia Sancti Remigii Remis
Cathedral of Saint-Rémi at Reims (Marne).

i, fol. 222d; i, fol. 252b; Regesta regum Anglo-Normannorum III, No. 714; i, fol. 222d; Pipe Roll 31 Henry I, 074–st; Pipe Roll 31 Henry I, 074–st; i, fol. 247c; i, fol. 252b; i, fol. 222d

[] Abbatia Sancti Ricarii
Abbey of Saint-Riquier in Picardie (Somme). Hariulf, Chronicon centulense, ed. F. Lot (Paris, 1894).

ii, fol. 167b

[] Abbatia Sancti Severi
Abbey of Saint-Sever, Normandy (Calvados), founded shortly before 1071 by Hugh vicomte of Avranches, later earl of Chester, who appointed Ascelin (or Anselm), a monk of Jumièges, as first abbot. L. Musset, 'Les origines et le patrimonie de l'abbaye de Saint-Sever', in La Normandie bénédictine au temps du Guillaume le Conquérant, ed. J. Daoust (Lille, 1967).

i, fol. 91d; i, fol. 349d

[] Abbatia Sancti Victoris
Abbey of Saint-Victor-en-Caux (Normandy, Seine-Maritime), founded as a priory by Roger I de Mortemer, raised at his request to the status of abbey in 1074. Recueil des chartes de Saint-Victeur-en-Caux, ed. Ch. de Robillard de Beaurepaire, Mél. soc. hist. Normandie, 5me ser., 1898, 333–453

i, fol. 46d

[] Abbatia Sancti Walerici
Abbey of Saint-Valery-en-Caux, Normandy.

ii, fol. 020b; ii, fol. 020b; ii, fol. 021a; ii, fol. 021a; ii, fol. 021a; ii, fol. 021a; ii, fol. 021a; ii, fol. 021a

[] Abbatia Sancti Wandregisili
Abbey of Saint-Wandrille, Normandy. F. Lot, Études critiques sur l'abbaye de Saint-Wandrille, Paris, 1913.

i, fol. 78c; i, fol. 78c; i, fol. 78c; i, fol. 78c; Regesta regum Anglo-Normannorum III, No. 780; Northants Survey, fols 94r–95v; i, fol. 190c; i, fol. 75a; i, fol. 229a; i, fol. 65a; i, fol. 65c; i, fol. 65c

[] Abbatia Sceptesberiensis
Shaftesbury Abbey, Dorset, founded c. 888. Originally the abbey of St Mary, it was called St Edward's after the body of St Edward, king and martyr, was translated there from Wareham c.982. Cartulary, BL Harley 61; Mon. Ang. iv, 474ff; A. Williams, 'Knights of Shaftesbury Abbey', ANS viii (1986); K. Cooke, 'Donors and daughters: Shaftesbury Abbey's benefactors, endowments and nuns, c.1086–1130', ANS 12 (1990).

i, fol. 17d; Pipe Roll 4 Henry II, 117–wl; Pipe Roll 31 Henry I, 021–wl; Red Book of the Exchequer, ed. Hall (1897), pp. 213–14; i, fol. 78d; i, fol. 78d; i, fol. 78d; i, fol. 78d; i, fol. 78d; i, fol. 67d; i, fol. 78d; i, fol. 78d; i, fol. 78d; i, fol. 78d; i, fol. 67c; i, fol. 78d; i, fol. 78d; i, fol. 67c; i, fol. 67d; i, fol. 67d; i, fol. 67d; i, fol. 78d; i, fol. 78d; i, fol. 98a; i, fol. 91b; Pipe Roll 4 Henry II, 117–wl; Regesta regum Anglo-Normannorum III, No. 818; Pipe Roll 2 Henry II, 33–ds; Pipe Roll 8 Henry II, 14–wl; Dugdale, Monasticon Anglicanum, II, p. 482, No. IX; i, fol. 91b; i, fol. 17d

[] Abbatissa De Ambresberie
Abbess of Amesbury, Wiltshire.
 i, fol. 60a

[] Abbatissa De Berchinges
Ælfgyva, abbess of Barking, Essex, during the reign of William I. She died on an 11 May in an unknown year before 1114. See Heads, 208.
 i, fol. 128d; i, fol. 146a; i, fol. 211a; ii, fol. 107a

[] Abbatissa De Cetriz
Abbess of Chatteris, Cambs.
 i, fol. 136b; i, fol. 193a

[] Abbatissa De Sceptesberie
Eulalia, abbess of Shaftesbury, appointed in 1074 (Ann. Winchester 30). Continued in office until c.1106/7. A kinswoman of Thomas, who had land at Atworth in Bradford-on-Avon from Shaftesbury Abbey, (see A. Williams, 'The knights of Shaftesbury', ANS viii, 220–1). See Heads, 219.
 i, fol. 75a

[] Abbatissa De Waruuella
Abbess of Wherwell. In 1051 the abbess was a sister of Edward the Confessor. A successor, an abbess Matilda, died before 1113. See Heads, 222.
 i, fol. 44a; i, fol. 52a

[] Abbatissa De Wincestre
Alice, abbess of Winchester, 'Nunnaminster', appointed in 1084 (Ann. Winchester 34). Still in office in 1102/3, when she was named Athelits in a letter of St Anselm (no. 276). See Heads, 223.
 i, fol. 43d; i, fol. 59d; i, fol. 48b

[] Accipitrarius
Unnamed falconer, who had held his land before 1066 and was probably therefore an Englishman.
 i, fol. 24b

[] Anglica Mulier
Englishwoman holding of the abbot of Malmesbury in Domesday Wiltshire.
 i, fol. 67a

[] Anglicus
Englishman. Occurs in Domesday Middlesex as a tenant of Walter of St. Valéry described as 'miles probatus'.
 i, fol. 130a

[] Blancard
Norman, Domesday tenant of Roger Pictaviensis. Ancestor of a family surnamed Blanchard, of whom Gilbert Blanchard and his brother Romphar occur in Gilbertine Charters of the time of Henry II (Sixle, nos. 32–3). A Blanchard, in the presence of Ralph bishop of Coutances (1091–1110) quitclaimed his father's grant in the church of Saint-Hilaire de Méautis (Deville, Analyse de Caen, 38). In 1207 a William Blanchard gave a house at Domfront to l'Abbaye Blanche at Mortain (B.

Poulle, Revue Avranchin, Sept. 1989, 107e Année, t. lxviii, no. 340, pp. 253ff).

i, fol. 352c; i, fol. 352b; i, fol. 352b

[] Clericus Hugonis

Norman, occurs as the clerk of Hugh de Grandmesnil who held of him at Willicote, Gloucestershire, in 1086. Hugh de Grandmesnil gave to Saint-Evroul what 'Hugo clericus de Sappo' held of him at Willicote and elsewhere in England (Ord. Vit. iii, 236). This identifies the clerk as Hugh, from Le Sap, Orne, cant. Vimoutiers. He attested the foundation charter of Monks Kirby priory in 1077.

i, fol. 169b; i, fol. 233a; Mon. Ang. vi, 996

[] Ecclesia Baiocensis

Cathedral church of Bayeux. E. Anquetil, Le Livre Rouge de l'évêché de Bayeux, 2 vols, Bayeux, 1908–11; Antiquus cartularius ecclesiae Baiocensis (Livre Noir), ed. V. Bourrienne, 2 vols (Rouen, 1902–3).

Regesta regum Anglo-Normannorum III, No. 58; Regesta regum Anglo-Normannorum III, No. 58; Regesta regum Anglo-Normannorum III, No. 56; i, fol. 31d; i, fol. 31c; i, fol. 31c; i, fol. 31c; Regesta regum Anglo-Normannorum III, No. 61; Regesta regum Anglo-Normannorum III, No. 53; Regesta regum Anglo-Normannorum III, No. 57; Regesta regum Anglo-Normannorum III, No. 59

[] Ecclesia Cantuariensis

Christ Church Cathedral Priory, Canterbury; its clergy were referred to as monks in 832. R.A.L. Smith, Canterbury Cathedral Priory (Cambridge, 1943).

Regesta regum Anglo-Normannorum III, No. 148; Regesta regum Anglo-Normannorum III, No. 149; Regesta regum Anglo-Normannorum III, No. 145; Regesta regum Anglo-Normannorum III, No. 143; Regesta regum Anglo-Normannorum III, No. 51; Stenton, English Feudalism, App., No. 16; Regesta regum Anglo-Normannorum III, No. 142; Regesta regum Anglo-Normannorum III, No. 151; i, fol. 003c; i, fol. 005b; i, fol. 003b; i, fol. 004b; ii, fol. 103a; Regesta regum Anglo-Normannorum III, No. 144; Regesta regum Anglo-Normannorum III, No. 141; Regesta regum Anglo-Normannorum III, No. 146; Pipe Roll 8 Henry II, 42–bubd; Regesta regum Anglo-Normannorum III, No. 147; Regesta regum Anglo-Normannorum III, No. 150; ii, fol. 008a; ii, fol. 008a; ii, fol. 008a; ii, fol. 008a; ii, fol. 008a; ii, fol. 008b; ii, fol. 008b; ii, fol. 008a; ii, fol. 008b

[] Ecclesia Constantiensis

Cathedral church of Coutances, Manche. Cartulaire factice by L. Delisle, BN lat. nov. acq. 1018–19; Livre blanc, Coutances, Archives de l'évêché, copy BN lat. nov. acq. 1364.

i, fol. 79a

[] Ecclesia De Bada

Abbey of St Peter, Bath, Somerset; refounded 963–4. Frances M. R. Ramsey, English Episcopal Acta X: Bath and Wells 1061–1205 (Oxford, 1995); Two Chartularies of the Priory of St Peter at Bath, ed. W. Hunt, Somerset Record Society 7 (London, 1893).

i, fol. 165b; i, fol. 89d; i, fol. 89d; i, fol. 89d; i, fol. 89d; i, fol. 89d; i, fol. 89d; i, fol. 89d; i, fol. 89d; i, fol. 89d; i, fol. 89d; i, fol. 89d; Hunt, Bath Chartulary, Som. Rec. Soc. 7 (1893), No. 34; Hunt, Bath Chartulary, Som. Rec. Soc. 7 (1893), No. 35; Regesta regum Anglo-Normannorum III, No. 49; Hunt, Bath Chartulary, Som. Rec. Soc. 7 (1893), No. 35; Regesta regum Anglo-Normannorum III, No.

47; Clay, Early Yorkshire Charters (1952), IX, No. 166; Clay, Early Yorkshire Charters (1952), IX, No. 165; Regesta regum Anglo-Normannorum III, No. 45; Regesta regum Anglo-Normannorum III, No. 48; Dugdale, Monasticon Anglicanum, II, p. 267, No. XII; Dugdale, Monasticon Anglicanum, II, p. 267, No. X; i, fol. 165b; i, fol. 165b

[] Ecclesia De Bedeforde
The collegiate church of St Paul was established at Bedford after 1066 on the site of a defunct abbey.

i, fol. 217d

[] Ecclesia De Grantham
Paris church of Saint Wulfram of Grantham, Lincolnshire.

i, fol. 343d; i, fol. 343d

[] Ecclesia De Hantone
Secular college of St Peter and St Mary, Wolverhampton, founded possibly in 659. Refounded as a royal chapel in 1203.

i, fol. 247d; i, fol. 247d; i, fol. 247d; i, fol. 247d; i, fol. 247d; i, fol. 247d; i, fol. 247d; i, fol. 247d; i, fol. 247d; i, fol. 247d; i, fol. 247d; i, fol. 247d; i, fol. 247d; i, fol. 247d

[] Ecclesia De Hereford
Cathedral church of Hereford.

i, fol. 165a; i, fol. 181c; i, fol. 182c; i, fol. 182a; i, fol. 182a; i, fol. 182a; i, fol. 181d; i, fol. 182a; i, fol. 181c; i, fol. 182a; i, fol. 182b; i, fol. 181d; i, fol. 181c; i, fol. 181d; i, fol. 181d; i, fol. 182b; i, fol. 181d; i, fol. 182a; i, fol. 182c; i, fol. 182b; i, fol. 181d; i, fol. 182c; i, fol. 182c; i, fol. 182c; i, fol. 182c; i, fol. 182c; i, fol. 182c; i, fol. 182c; i, fol. 181c; i, fol. 181c; i, fol. 182b; i, fol. 182b; i, fol. 182b; i, fol. 181c; i, fol. 182a; i, fol. 182a; i, fol. 182a; i, fol. 182b; i, fol. 182b; i, fol. 182b; i, fol. 182b; i, fol. 182a; i, fol. 181c; i, fol. 181c; i, fol. 182c; i, fol. 181c; i, fol. 181c; i, fol. 181c; i, fol. 181c; i, fol. 181c; Walker, Charters of the Earldom of Hereford (1964), No. 42; i, fol. 184a

[] Ecclesia De Lincolia
Cathedral church of Lincoln. The Registrum Antiquissimum of the Cathedral Church of Lincoln, ed. C. W. Foster and K. Major, 9 vols, Lincoln Record Society, 1931–68.

Pipe Roll 4 Henry II, 143–nh; Pipe Roll 31 Henry I, 109–ln; Pipe Roll 8 Henry II, 27–ox; Pipe Roll 31 Henry I, 109–ln; Pipe Roll 8 Henry II, 09–nh; Pipe Roll 12 Henry II, 117–ox; Pipe Roll 12 Henry II, 005–ln; Pipe Roll 10 Henry II, 08–ox; Pipe Roll 31 Henry I, 121–ln; Pipe Roll 11 Henry II, 095–nh; Pipe Roll 12 Henry II, 005–ln; Pipe Roll 7 Henry II, 26–ox; Pipe Roll 9 Henry II, 66–ln; Pipe Roll 12 Henry II, 064–nh; Pipe Roll 7 Henry II, 34–nh; Pipe Roll 10 Henry II, 63, 23–ln; Pipe Roll 9 Henry II, 42–nh; Pipe Roll 11 Henry II, 068–ox; Pipe Roll 9 Henry II, 48–ox; Pipe Roll 31 Henry I, 121–ln; Pipe Roll 11 Henry II, 039–ln; Pipe Roll 10 Henry II, 63, 32–nh; Pipe Roll 7 Henry II, 15–ln; Pipe Roll 10 Henry II, 63, 22–ln; Pipe Roll 8 Henry II, 17–ln; Pipe Roll 4 Henry II, 136–ln; Pipe Roll 6 Henry II, 44–ln; Pipe Roll 5 Henry II, 34–ox; Pipe Roll 5 Henry II, 17–nh; Pipe Roll 2 Henry II, 28–ln; Pipe Roll 3 Henry II, 085–y; Pipe Roll 4 Henry II, 150–ox; Pipe Roll 6 Henry II, 09–ox; Pipe Roll 5 Henry II, 64–ln; Pipe Roll 2 Henry II, 42–nh; Pipe Roll 6 Henry II, 38–nhbub; Pipe Roll 1 Henry II (RBE, ii), 657–ln; Regesta regum Anglo-Normannorum III, No. 494; Regesta regum Anglo-Normannorum III, No. 472; Regesta regum Anglo-Normannorum

III, No. 479; Regesta regum Anglo-Normannorum III, No. 483; Regesta regum Anglo-Normannorum III, No. 477; Clay, Early Yorkshire Charters (1947), VII, No. 56; Regesta regum Anglo-Normannorum III, No. 485; Regesta regum Anglo-Normannorum III, No. 491; Gibbs, Early Charters of St Pauls (1939), No. 156; Regesta regum Anglo-Normannorum III, No. 489; Regesta regum Anglo-Normannorum III, No. 487; Regesta regum Anglo-Normannorum III, No. 481; Regesta regum Anglo-Normannorum III, No. 486; Regesta regum Anglo-Normannorum III, No. 474; Regesta regum Anglo-Normannorum III, No. 478; Regesta regum Anglo-Normannorum III, No. 473; Regesta regum Anglo-Normannorum III, No. 484; Lincolnshire Claims (Domesday Book), fols 375a–d; Clay, Early Yorkshire Charters (1939), VI, No. 77; Lindsey Survey, BL ms Cotton Claudius C v, fols 19–27; i, fol. 336b; Lindsey Survey, BL ms Cotton Claudius C v, fols 1–9; i, fol. 344a; Clay, Early Yorkshire Charters (1952), IX, No. 2; Lincolnshire Claims (Domesday Book), fols 375d–376a; Regesta regum Anglo-Normannorum III, No. 492; Barraclough, Charters of AN Earls of Chester (1988), No. 52; Barraclough, Charters of AN Earls of Chester (1988), No. 104; Barraclough, Charters of AN Earls of Chester (1988), No. 108

[] Ecclesia De Mellinges

Canons of Malling, Sussex, subject to the archbishop of Canterbury.

Chibnall, English Lands of Abbey of Bec (1951), No. I; i, fol. 16c

[] Ecclesia De Plintone

Collegiate church of Plympton, Devon, established by 909; dissolved and refounded for Augustinian canons in 1121 by William Warelwast bishop of Exeter. Extracts from lost cartulary in Oxford, Bodl. James 23, pp. 151–70; BL Harley 6974, fols 28–30.

i, fol. 100c; Pipe Roll 6 Henry II, 52–dv; Bearman, Charters of the Redvers Family (1994), No. 13; Bearman, Charters of the Redvers Family (1994), No. 45; Bearman, Charters of the Redvers Family (1994), App. II No. 8; Bearman, Charters of the Redvers Family (1994), No. 22

[] Ecclesia De Suauesy

Swavesey Priory, Cambridgeshire, founded by Count Alan Rufus before 1086 as a cell of SS Serge and Bacchus, Angers. There are copies of some thirteenth century material in BL Add. 5849 (Cole mss. vol. xlviii), pp. 36–45.

Clay, Early Yorkshire Charters (1935), IV, No. 1; i, fol. 195b

[] Ecclesia De Wirecestre

Cathedral priory of Worcester diocese, created in 680. Rebuilt by Bishop Wulfstan after 1062, who increased the number of monks from 12 to 50. R. R. Darlington, The Cartulary of Worcester Cathedral Priory (Register I), Pipe Roll Soc., NS 38 (London, 1962–63); Thomas Hearne, Hemingi Chartularium Ecclesiae Wigorniensis, 2 vols (Oxford, 1723).

i, fol. 172c; i, fol. 164d; Darlington, Cartulary of Worcester: Reg. I (1962–3), No. 144; i, fol. 173b; i, fol. 174a; i, fol. 174a; i, fol. 174a; i, fol. 173d

[] Ecclesia Lisiacensis

Cathedral church of Lisieux, Eure, Normandy. R.N. Sauvage, 'Fragment d'un cartulaire de Saint-Pierre-de-Lisieux', Études Lexoviennes 3 (1928), 327–57.

i, fol. 68c

[] Ecclesia Romane
St Peter's, Rome.

i, fol. 91b; i, fol. 91b

[] Ecclesia Sanctae Milburgae
A monastery was founded at Wenlock before 690 on land purchased from Merewald, whose daughter Milberga (grand-daughter of Penda of Mercia) subsequently gave her name to the community. Refounded as a secular college by Leofric of Merica c.1017/35, it was refounded again as a Benedictine monastery subject to the Cluniac house of La Charité-sur-Loire. Eyton, Shrops, iii, 224 ff.

i, fol. 252c; i, fol. 252c; i, fol. 252c; i, fol. 252c; i, fol. 252d; i, fol. 252c; i, fol. 252c; i, fol. 252c; i, fol. 252d; i, fol. 252d; i, fol. 252d; i, fol. 252c; Barraclough, Charters of AN Earls of Chester (1988), No. 109

[] Ecclesia Sancte Berrione
Priory of St Buryan (St Beriana), Cornwall, founded c.930 by King Athelstan for secular canons.

i, fol. 121b

[] Ecclesia Sancte Crucis De Waltham
Church of the Holy Cross at Waltham, Essex, refounded as a collegiate church by Harold Godwineson and dedicated in 1060. After his defeat as king at Hastings, Harold was buried there (Chronicle of Waltham Abbey, introd. by M. Chibnall). Refounded for Augustinian canons by Henry II in 1177, became an abbey in 1184. Rosalind Ransford, The Early Charters of the Augustinian Canons of Waltham Abbey, Essex, 1062–1230 (Woodbridge, 1989).

i, fol. 140b; i, fol. 136c; i, fol. 136c; Ransford, Early Charters of Waltham Abbey (1989), No. 5; Ransford, Early Charters of Waltham Abbey (1989), No. 6; Ransford, Early Charters of Waltham Abbey (1989), No. 22; Pipe Roll 8 Henry II, 72–e/ht; Ransford, Early Charters of Waltham Abbey (1989), No. 10; Pipe Roll 5 Henry II, 18–bubd; Pipe Roll 8 Henry II, 41–bubd; Pipe Roll 8 Henry II, 70–e/ht; Ransford, Early Charters of Waltham Abbey (1989), No. 13; Ransford, Early Charters of Waltham Abbey (1989), No. 17; Regesta regum Anglo-Normannorum III, No. 916; i, fol. 136c; ii, fol. 015b; Ransford, Early Charters of Waltham Abbey (1989), No. 16; Regesta regum Anglo-Normannorum III, No. 917; Ransford, Early Charters of Waltham Abbey (1989), No. 2; Ransford, Early Charters of Waltham Abbey (1989), No. 25; Ransford, Early Charters of Waltham Abbey (1989), No. 22; Ransford, Early Charters of Waltham Abbey (1989), No. 8; Ransford, Early Charters of Waltham Abbey (1989), No. 15; Ransford, Early Charters of Waltham Abbey (1989), No. 18; Ransford, Early Charters of Waltham Abbey (1989), No. 13; Ransford, Early Charters of Waltham Abbey (1989), No. 6; ii, fol. 016a; ii, fol. 016b; ii, fol. 016b; ii, fol. 016a; ii, fol. 016b; ii, fol. 016a; ii, fol. 015b; ii, fol. 016a; ii, fol. 016a; ii, fol. 016a; ii, fol. 016a; ii, fol. 016a

[] Ecclesia Sancte Fridesuide De Oxonie
St Frideswide's, Oxford, rebuilt for secular canons in 1004. Reestablished as an Augustinian priory by Roger bishop of Salisbury between 1111 and 1122, when Wimund became prior of canons from Holy Trinity, London. S. R. Wigram, Cartulary of the Monastery of St Frideswide at Oxford, 2 vols, Oxford Historical Society 28 (1895), 31 (1896).

Regesta regum Anglo-Normannorum III, No. 642; i, fol. 146a; i, fol. 157a;

Regesta regum Anglo-Normannorum III, No. 640; i, fol. 154b; Regesta regum Anglo-Normannorum III, No. 637; Pipe Roll 6 Henry II, 08–ox; Pipe Roll 3 Henry II, 082a–ox; Pipe Roll 5 Henry II, 34–ox; Pipe Roll 9 Henry II, 47–ox; Pipe Roll 7 Henry II, 25–ox; Pipe Roll 10 Henry II, 07–ox; Pipe Roll 4 Henry II, 149–ox; Pipe Roll 8 Henry II, 26b–ox; Pipe Roll 3 Henry II, 082b–ox; Pipe Roll 1 Henry II (RBE, ii), 657–ox; Pipe Roll 2 Henry II, 36–ox; i, fol. 157a; Chibnall, English Lands of Abbey of Bec (1951), No. XXII; Salter, Cartulary of Oseney Abbey (1929–36), No. 508; Regesta regum Anglo-Normannorum III, No. 646; Regesta regum Anglo-Normannorum III, No. 649; Regesta regum Anglo-Normannorum III, No. 645; Regesta regum Anglo-Normannorum III, No. 643; Regesta regum Anglo-Normannorum III, No. 639; Regesta regum Anglo-Normannorum III, No. 644; Regesta regum Anglo-Normannorum III, No. 641; Regesta regum Anglo-Normannorum III, No. 648; Regesta regum Anglo-Normannorum III, No. 638; i, fol. 143d

[] Ecclesia Sancte Juliane
Church of Saint Juliana, Shropshire, first mentioned in Domesday Book, and later a royal free chapel. See T. Arden et al., 'The church and parish of St Juliana in Salop', Trans Shrops. Arch Soc. ser. i, 10 (1887), 157–348.

i, fol. 253a; i, fol. 253a

[] Ecclesia Sancte Mariae De Totnes
Priory of St Mary, Totnes' founded as a cell of Saint-Serge et Saint-Bach at Angers by Juhel of Totnes shortly before 1086, when it is mentioned in Domesday Book. H. R. Watkin, The History of Totnes Priory and Medieval
Town, 2 vols (Torquay, 1917).

i, fol. 109c

[] Ecclesia Sancte Marie
Collegiate church of St Mary founded within the castle of Exeter by Baldwin the Sheriff before 1086.

i, fol. 107b; i, fol. 107b; i, fol. 107b; i, fol. 107b

[] Ecclesia Sancte Marie
Pre-Conquest minster church of St Mary, Bromfield, Shropshire.

i, fol. 252d; i, fol. 252d

[] Ecclesia Sancte Marie
Pre-Conquest church of St Mary, Shrewsbury; VCH Shrops ii, 119–23, Mon. Ang. vi, 1464.

i, fol. 252d; i, fol. 252d; i, fol. 252d; i, fol. 252d

[] Ecclesia Sancte Marie De Lanchei
Church of Lambeth. Assigned in dower to Goda, sister of Edward the Confessor, it returned to the royal demesne after her death without issue. William I subsequently gave it to Rochester priory, which received other property of Goda.

i, fol. 166c; i, fol. 34b

[] Ecclesia Sancte Marie Rotomagensis
Cathedral Church of Rouen, Seine-Maritime.

Regesta regum Anglo-Normannorum III, No. 726; i, fol. 104b; i, fol. 104b; i, fol. 100b

[] Ecclesia Sancte Trinitatis De Thuinam

The collegiate church of Holy Trinity, Twineham, Hants., existed in the time of Edward the Confessor. It was headed before 1099 by Ranulf Flambard, who rebuilt the church. Later known as Christchurch, it was refounded as a priory of Augustinian canons in 1150, with the assent of Baldwin de Redvers, whose family owned the church and manor by grant of Henry I. General cartulary, BL Cotton Tiberius D vi.

> i, fol. 44b; i, fol. 44b; Bearman, Charters of the Redvers Family (1994), No. 49; Bearman, Charters of the Redvers Family (1994), No. 50; Pipe Roll 4 Henry II, 172-hm; i, fol. 44b; Bearman, Charters of the Redvers Family (1994), No. 52; Bearman, Charters of the Redvers Family (1994), No. 11; Bearman, Charters of the Redvers Family (1994), No. 43; Bearman, Charters of the Redvers Family (1994), App. II No. 9; Bearman, Charters of the Redvers Family (1994), No. 53; Bearman, Charters of the Redivers Family (1994), No. 51; Bearman, Charters of the Redivers Family (1994), No. 48

[] Ecclesia Sancti Achebranbi

St Achebran's, Cornwall.

> i, fol. 121b

[] Ecclesia Sancti Almundi

Pre-Conquest church of St Almund, Shropshire. Later became the basis of Lilleshall priory.

> Regesta regum Anglo-Normannorum III, No. 312; i, fol. 253a; i, fol. 253a; i, fol. 253a; i, fol. 253a; i, fol. 253a; i, fol. 253a; i, fol. 253a

[] Ecclesia Sancti Andreae Wellensis

Cathedral church of Wells, Somerset. Frances M. R. Ramsey, English Episcopal Acta X: Bath and Wells 1061–1205 (Oxford, 1995)

> i, fol. 89b; i, fol. 89c; i, fol. 89c; Regesta regum Anglo-Normannorum III, No. 924

[] Ecclesia Sancti Carentoch

St Carentoch's, Cornwall.

> i, fol. 121b

[] Ecclesia Sancti Cedde

Pre-Conquest church of St Chad in Shrewsbury.

> i, fol. 259b; i, fol. 252b; i, fol. 253a; i, fol. 253a; i, fol. 253a; i, fol. 253a; i, fol. 253a; i, fol. 263a

[] Ecclesia Sancti Constantini

Church of St Constantine, Cornwall.

> i, fol. 121b

[] Ecclesia Sancti Cuthberti Dunelmensis

Cathedral church of Durham. established for seculars by Bishop Aldhun when he brought the body of St Cuthbert from Chester-le-Street to Durham in 995. Refounded as a Benedictine monastery in 1083 by Bishop William de Saint-Calais. H. S. Offler, Durham Episcopal Charters, 1071–1152, Surtees Society 179 (1068); Liber Vitae Dunelmensis, ed. A. H. Thompson, Surtees Soc. 136 (1923).

> i, fol. 340c; Regesta regum Anglo-Normannorum III, No. 255; Clay, Early

Yorkshire Charters (1952), IX, No. 7; Ransford, Early Charters of Waltham Abbey (1989), No. 14; Regesta regum Anglo-Normannorum III, No. 256; Ransford, Early Charters of Waltham Abbey (1989), No. 11; Clay, Early Yorkshire Charters (1935), IV, No. 34; Major, Blyborough charters, No. 1; Regesta regum Anglo-Normannorum III, No. 166

[] Ecclesia Sancti Firmini De Crauelai

Monastery of St Firmin, Crawley, Bucks, founded before the reign of Edward the Confessor (1042–1066).

i, fol. 149a

[] Ecclesia Sancti Germani

Priory of St German, Cornwall; ancient foundation to which canons were introduced c.1050 by Bishop Leofric of Exeter; became an Augustinian house before 1184.

i, fol. 120c

[] Ecclesia Sancti Guthlaci

Collegiate church of St Guthlac in the castle at Hereford from the time of Edward the Confessor. Finaly became a priory of St Peter's, Gloucester, in 1143. General cartulary. Oxford, Balliol Collge, ms 271.

i, fol. 186b; i, fol. 182d; i, fol. 182d; i, fol. 182d; i, fol. 182d; i, fol. 182d; i, fol. 182d; i, fol. 182d; Regesta regum Anglo-Normannorum III, No. 398; Walker, Charters of the Earldom of Hereford (1964), No. 43; Regesta regum Anglo-Normannorum III, No. 396; Walker, Charters of the Earldom of Hereford (1964), No. 33; Walker, Charters of the Earldom of Hereford (1964), No. 63; Walker, Charters of the Earldom of Hereford (1964), No. 40

[] Ecclesia Sancti Johannis De Beuerlaco

Pre-Conquester minster church at Beverley, founded by St John of Beverley, archbishop of York 705–18. House of secular canons by the eleventh century.

i, fol. 304a; i, fol. 304a; i, fol. 304a; i, fol. 304a; i, fol. 304a; Dugdale, Monasticon Anglicanum, III, pp. 548–50, No. V; Dugdale, Monasticon Anglicanum, III, p. 547, No. III; Regesta regum Anglo-Normannorum III, No. 101; Regesta regum Anglo-Normannorum III, No. 100; Regesta regum Anglo-Normannorum III, No. 99; Regesta regum Anglo-Normannorum III, No. 102; i, fol. 304b; i, fol. 304b; i, fol. 304b; i, fol. 304b; i, fol. 304b; i, fol. 304b; i, fol. 304b; i, fol. 304b; i, fol. 304b; i, fol. 304b; i, fol. 304b; i, fol. 304b; i, fol. 304b; i, fol. 304b; i, fol. 304b; i, fol. 304a; i, fol. 304a; i, fol. 304a; i, fol. 304a; i, fol. 304a; i, fol. 304a; i, fol. 304a; i, fol. 304a; i, fol. 304b; i, fol. 304a; i, fol. 304a; i, fol. 304a; i, fol. 304b; i, fol. 304b; i, fol. 304b; i, fol. 304b; i, fol. 304a

[] Ecclesia Sancti Martini De Douere

St Martin's, Dover. Secular canons in 1086, Augustinian canons after 1131.

i, fol. 013a; i, fol. 002b; i, fol. 002b; i, fol. 002b; i, fol. 002b; i, fol. 001c; i, fol. 002b; i, fol. 002b; i, fol. 002b; i, fol. 002b; i, fol. 002b; i, fol. 002b; i, fol. 002b; i, fol. 002b; i, fol. 002b; i, fol. 002b

[] Ecclesia Sancti Martini Londonie

Church of St Martin le Grand, founded by Engelric, predecessor of Count Eustache.

Regesta regum Anglo-Normannorum III, No. 534; Regesta regum Anglo-Normannorum III, No. 524; Regesta regum Anglo-Normannorum III, No. 533;

Regesta regum Anglo-Normannorum III, No. 553; Regesta regum Anglo-Normannorum III, No. 545; Regesta regum Anglo-Normannorum III, No. 546; Regesta regum Anglo-Normannorum III, No. 535; Regesta regum Anglo-Normannorum III, No. 528; i, fol. 137b; Regesta regum Anglo-Normannorum III, No. 530; Regesta regum Anglo-Normannorum III, No. 559; Regesta regum Anglo-Normannorum III, No. 556; Regesta regum Anglo-Normannorum III, No. 531; Regesta regum Anglo-Normannorum III, No. 544; Regesta regum Anglo-Normannorum III, No. 537; Regesta regum Anglo-Normannorum III, No. 548; Regesta regum Anglo-Normannorum III, No. 543; Regesta regum Anglo-Normannorum III, No. 523; Regesta regum Anglo-Normannorum III, No. 522; Regesta regum Anglo-Normannorum III, No. 521; Regesta regum Anglo-Normannorum III, No. 527; Regesta regum Anglo-Normannorum III, No. 525; Regesta regum Anglo-Normannorum III, No. 540; Regesta regum Anglo-Normannorum III, No. 538; Regesta regum Anglo-Normannorum III, No. 846; Regesta regum Anglo-Normannorum III, No. 845; Regesta regum Anglo-Normannorum III, No. 526; Regesta regum Anglo-Normannorum III, No. 550; Gervers, Cartulary of Knights St John Essex (1982), No. 4; Gervers, Cartulary of Knights St John Essex (1982), No. 5; Regesta regum Anglo-Normannorum III, No. 541; Regesta regum Anglo-Normannorum III, No. 542; Regesta regum Anglo-Normannorum III, No. 551; Regesta regum Anglo-Normannorum III, No. 547; ii, fol. 020b; ii, fol. 020b; ii, fol. 014a; Regesta regum Anglo-Normannorum III, No. 558; Regesta regum Anglo-Normannorum III, No. 532; Regesta regum Anglo-Normannorum III, No. 539; ii, fol. 032a; ii, fol. 029a; ii, fol. 029a

[] Ecclesia Sancti Michaelis
Church of St Michael, Shrewsbury, mentioned in Domesday Book. Possibly founded by Earl Roger of Shrewsbury; VCH Shrops i, 291; Mon. Ang. vi, 1426, 1464.

i, fol. 252d; i, fol. 252d

[] Ecclesia Sancti Michaelis De Monte
St Michael's Mount, Cornwall, became a priory of Mont-Saint-Michel under Abbot Bernard (1131–49); originally granted to the abbey by Robert of Mortain (d. 1094). The Cartulary of St Michael's Mount, ed. Peter L. Hull, Devon and Cornwall Record Society, N.S. 5 (1962 for 1958)

i, fol. 100d; i, fol. 120d

[] Ecclesia Sancti Michaelis De Norwic
Church of St Michael of Norwich.

ii, fol. 201b; ii, fol. 201b; ii, fol. 201b

[] Ecclesia Sancti Neoti
St Neot's, Cornwall.

i, fol. 121b

[] Ecclesia Sancti Neoti
Priory of St Neot, Huntingdonshire; founded c.974, its monks were replaced by monks of Bec when Richard de Clare gave the church to Bec c.1081–2. BL Cotton Faust. A iv, general cartualry.

Dugdale, Monasticon Anglicanum, III, p. 473, No. XIII; Dugdale, Monasticon Anglicanum, III, p. 474, No. XVI; Dugdale, Monasticon Anglicanum, III, p. 473, No. VIII; Regesta regum Anglo-Normannorum III, No. 778; Regesta regum Anglo-Normannorum III, No. 777; i, fol. 216b; Dugdale, Monasticon Anglicanum, III, p. 474, No. XVII; Pipe Roll 31 Henry I, 048–hn; Pipe Roll 31 Henry I, 048–hn; Pipe Roll 31 Henry I, 048–hn; Pipe Roll 8 Henry II, 08–nh; Pipe Roll 9 Henry II, 19–bubd; Pipe Roll 5 Henry II, 18–bubd; Dugdale, Monasticon Anglicanum, III, p. 473, No. X; Dugdale, Monasticon Anglicanum, III, p. 473, No. IX; Dugdale, Monasticon Anglicanum, III, p. 473, No. XII; Dugdale, Monasticon Anglicanum, III, p. 473, No. XI; Dugdale, Monasticon Anglicanum, III, pp. 472–73, No. VII; Dugdale, Monasticon Anglicanum, III, p. 473, No. XIV; i, fol. 207b

[] Ecclesia Sancti Nicolai

Saint Nicholas in the Castle, Carisbrook. Given to Quarr Abbey when that was founded.

i, fol. 52c; i, fol. 52c

[] Ecclesia Sancti Pancratii De Lewes

St Pancras, Lewes, Sussex, founded by William I de Warenne and his wife Gundreda as the first Cluniac house in England in 1076. The Chartulary of the Priory of St. Pancras of Lewes, ed. L. F. Salzman, 2 vols, Sussex Record Society 38, 40 (1933–5); W. Budgen and L F. Salzmann, The chartulary of Lewes Priory. The portions relating to counties other than Sussex, Sussex Record Society, Additional Volume, 1943; The Norfolk Portion of the Chartulary of the priory of St Pancras of Lewes, ed. J. H. Bullock, Nordfolk Record Society 12, 1939. F. Liebermann, 'The annals of Lewes priory', EHR xvii (1902).

Clay, Early Yorkshire Charters (1949), VIII, No. 8; Clay, Early Yorkshire Charters (1955), XI, No. 294; i, fol. 21a; Stenton, English Feudalism, App., No. 45; Round, Ancient Charters (1888), No. 31; Dugdale, Monasticon Anglicanum, III, pp. 345–46, No. I; Scott, Charters of Monks Horton Priory, ArCant, 10, No. X; Regesta regum Anglo-Normannorum III, No. 447; Round, Ancient Charters (1888), No. 29; Regesta regum Anglo-Normannorum III, No. 449; Regesta regum Anglo-Normannorum III, No. 446; Regesta regum Anglo-Normannorum III, No. 448; Clay, Early Yorkshire Charters (1949), VIII, No. 48; Regesta regum Anglo-Normannorum III, No. 444; i, fol. 26a; Douglas, Social Structure of Med. E. Anglia (1927), No. 22; Pipe Roll 31 Henry I, 070–ss; Scott, Charters of Monks Horton Priory, ArCant, 10, No. III; Pipe Roll 31 Henry I, 070–ss; Clay, Early Yorkshire Charters (1949), VIII, No. 34; Dugdale, Monasticon Anglicanum, IV, pp. 13–14, No. V; Pipe Roll 6 Henry II, 05–nfsf; Pipe Roll 11 Henry II, 109–kn; Clay, Early Yorkshire Charters (1949), VIII, No. 37; Scott, Charters of Monks Horton Priory, ArCant, 10, No. VII; Stenton, English Feudalism, App., No. 9; Pipe Roll 31 Henry I, 072–ss; Pipe Roll 31 Henry I, 072–ss; Dugdale, Monasticon Anglicanum, IV, p. 14, No. VII; Clay, Early Yorkshire Charters (1949), VIII, No. 33; Dugdale, Monasticon Anglicanum, IV, p. 14, No. VIII; Clay, Early Yorkshire Charters (1949), VIII, No. 38; Round, Ancient Charters (1888), No. 41; Stenton, English Feudalism, App., No. 20; Dugdale, Monasticon Anglicanum, IV, p. 13, No. IV; Greenway, Charters of the Honour of Mowbray (1972), No. 3; Clay, Early Yorkshire Charters (1949), VIII, No. 4; Greenway, Charters of the Honour of Mowbray (1972), No. 2; Round, Ancient Charters (1888), No. 5; Round, Ancient Charters (1888), No. 9; Clay, Early Yorkshire Charters (1949), VIII, No. 110; Clay, Early Yorkshire Charters (1949), VIII, No. 49; Clay, Early Yorkshire Charters (1949), VIII, No. 36; Round, Ancient Charters (1888), No. 4; Clay, Early Yorkshire Charters (1949), VIII, No. 32; Clay, Early Yorkshire Charters (1949), VIII, No. 9; Clay, Early Yorkshire Charters (1949), VIII, No. 7; Clay, Early Yorkshire

Charters (1949), VIII, No. 40; Dugdale, Monasticon Anglicanum, IV, pp. 14–15, No. IX; Clay, Early Yorkshire Charters (1949), VIII, No. 53; Clay, Early Yorkshire Charters (1949), VIII, No. 35; Clay, Early Yorkshire Charters (1949), VIII, No. 39; Clay, Early Yorkshire Charters (1949), VIII, No. 41; Clay, Early Yorkshire Charters (1949), VIII, No. 42; Clay, Early Yorkshire Charters (1949), VIII, No. 14; Clay, Early Yorkshire Charters (1949), VIII, No. 52; Clay, Early Yorkshire Charters (1955), XI, No. 295; Clay, Early Yorkshire Charters (1949), VIII, No. 16; Regesta regum Anglo-Normannorum III, No. 445; i, fol. 26b

[] Ecclesia Sancti Pauli De Bedeford

College of secular canons at Bedford, recorded in Domesday Book. In 1166 the canons adopted a rule and the church was refounded, by Simon de Beauchamp, as Newnham priory.

Pipe Roll 12 Henry II, 012–bubd; Regesta regum Anglo-Normannorum III, No. 81; i, fol. 211a

[] Ecclesia Sancti Pauli Londoniensis

Cathedral church of St Paul's, London. M. Gibbs, Early Charters of the Cathedral Church of St Paul, London, Camden Third Series lviii (London, 1939).

Gibbs, Early Charters of St Pauls (1939), No. 2; Gibbs, Early Charters of St Pauls (1939), No. 48; Gibbs, Early Charters of St Pauls (1939), No. 33; Gibbs, Early Charters of St Pauls (1939), No. 13; Gibbs, Early Charters of St Pauls (1939), No. 35; i, fol. 136b; i, fol. 136b; i, fol. 136b; i, fol. 136b; i, fol. 136b; i, fol. 30d; i, fol. 128a; i, fol. 127d; i, fol. 127d; Gibbs, Early Charters of St Pauls (1939), No. 32; i, fol. 128a; Gibbs, Early Charters of St Pauls (1939), No. 24; i, fol. 127d; i, fol. 128a; i, fol. 128a; i, fol. 128a; i, fol. 128a; i, fol. 128a; i, fol. 128a; i, fol. 128b; i, fol. 128a; i, fol. 211a; i, fol. 34a; Gibbs, Early Charters of St Pauls (1939), No. 62; Gibbs, Early Charters of St Pauls (1939), No. 44; Gibbs, Early Charters of St Pauls (1939), No. 29; Gibbs, Early Charters of St Pauls (1939), No. 56; Gibbs, Early Charters of St Pauls (1939), No, 59; Gibbs, Early Charters of St Pauls (1939), No. 25; ii, fol. 012b; ii, fol. 012b; ii, fol. 012b; Gibbs, Early Charters of St Pauls (1939), No. 66; Gibbs, Early Charters of St Pauls (1939), No. 27; Gibbs, Early Charters of St Pauls (1939), No. 156; Gibbs, Early Charters of St Pauls (1939), No. 163; Gibbs, Early Charters of St Pauls (1939), No. 19; Gibbs, Early Charters of St Pauls (1939), No. 21; Gibbs, Early Charters of St Pauls (1939), No. 43; Gibbs, Early Charters of St Pauls (1939), No. 48; Gibbs, Early Charters of St Pauls (1939), No. 26; Gibbs, Early Charters of St Pauls (1939), No. 8; Gibbs, Early Charters of St Pauls (1939), No. 47; Gibbs, Early Charters of St Pauls (1939), No. 91; Gibbs, Early Charters of St Pauls (1939), No. 47; Gibbs, Early Charters of St Pauls (1939), No. 47; Gibbs, Early Charters of St Pauls (1939), No. 67; Gibbs, Early Charters of St Pauls (1939), No. 47; Gibbs, Early Charters of St Pauls (1939), No. 92; Gibbs, Early Charters of St Pauls (1939), No. 16; Gibbs, Early Charters of St Pauls (1939), No. 9; Regesta regum Anglo-Normannorum III, No. 563; Regesta regum Anglo-Normannorum III, No. 564; Regesta regum Anglo-Normannorum III, No. 565; Gibbs, Early Charters of St Pauls (1939), No. 39; Gibbs, Early Charters of St Pauls (1939), No. 28; i, fol. 211a; i, fol. 136b; Gibbs, Early Charters of St Pauls (1939), No. 11; ii, fol. 013a; ii, fol. 013b; ii, fol. 013b; ii, fol. 013b; ii, fol. 013a; ii, fol. 013b; ii, fol. 013a; ii, fol. 013a; ii, fol. 013a; ii, fol. 013a

[] Ecclesia Sancti Petri Eboracensis

Pre-Conquest minster church in York.

i, fol. 283a; i, fol. 298c; i, fol. 303d; i, fol. 298b; i, fol. 283a; i, fol. 298b; i, fol. 302c; i, fol. 302c; i, fol. 302d; i, fol. 302d; i, fol. 302d; i, fol. 302d; Regesta regum Anglo-Normannorum III, No. 984; i, fol. 298b; Regesta regum Anglo-Normannorum III, No. 981; Clay, Early Yorkshire Charters (1936), V, No. 333; Clay, Early Yorkshire Charters (1955), XI, No. 101; Dugdale, Monasticon Anglicanum, III, pp. 548–50, No. V; Dugdale, Monasticon Anglicanum, III, p. 547, No. III; Greenway, Charters of the Honour of Mowbray (1972), No. 325; Clay, Early Yorkshire Charters (1936), V, No. 133; Clay, Early Yorkshire Charters (1955), XI, No. 30; Clay, Early Yorkshire Charters (1955), XI, No. 26; i, fol. 303d; i, fol. 303d; i, fol. 303d; i, fol. 303d; i, fol. 303d; Clay, Early Yorkshire Charters (1949), VIII, No. 99; Clay, Early Yorkshire Charters (1955), X, No. 67; Dugdale, Monasticon Anglicanum, III, p. 501, No. XIV; Clay, Early Yorkshire Charters (1936), V, No. 129; i, fol. 303a; Clay, Early Yorkshire Charters (1939), VI, No. 133; Greenway, Charters of the Honour of Mowbray (1972), No. 7; i, fol. 303b; i, fol. 303b; i, fol. 303a; i, fol. 298c; i, fol. 303b; i, fol. 303b; i, fol. 303b; i, fol. 303b; i, fol. 303b; i, fol. 303b; i, fol. 303b; i, fol. 303b; i, fol. 303b; i, fol. 303b; i, fol. 303a; i, fol. 298c; i, fol. 303a; i, fol. 303a; i, fol. 303b; i, fol. 303b; i, fol. 303c; i, fol. 303a; i, fol. 303a; i, fol. 303b; i, fol. 303c; i, fol. 303a; i, fol. 303a; i, fol. 303a; i, fol. 303b; i, fol. 298c; i, fol. 303a; i, fol. 303a; Regesta regum Anglo-Normannorum III, No. 978; i, fol. 303b

[] Ecclesia Sancti Petroc
St Petroc, Cornwall.

i, fol. 120d; i, fol. 120d; i, fol. 120d; i, fol. 117d; i, fol. 117d; i, fol. 121a; i, fol. 121a; i, fol. 121a

[] Ecclesia Sancti Pierani
St Piran's, Cornwall.

i, fol. 121b

[] Ecclesia Sancti Probi
St Probus, Cornwall.

i, fol. 121b

[] Ecclesia Sancti Stefani De Lancaueton
St Stephen's, Launceston, Cornwall. The secular canons were disbanded and a new Augustinian priory established by William Warelwast bishop of Exeter and Stephen of Mortain in 1126–7. The Cartulary of Launceston Priory (Lambeth Palace MS.719): A Calendar, ed. Peter L. Hull, Devon and Cornwall Record Society, N.S., 30 (Exeter, 1987)

i, fol. 120d; i, fol. 120b; i, fol. 120b; i, fol. 120b; Hull, Cartulary of Launceston Priory (1987), No. 7; Bearman, Charters of the Redvers Family (1994), App. II No. 11; Regesta regum Anglo-Normannorum III, No. 435; Hull, Cartulary of Launceston Priory (1987), No. 12; Hull, Cartulary of Launceston Priory (1987), No. 13; Hull, Cartulary of Launceston Priory (1987), No. 5; Hull, Cartulary of Launceston Priory (1987), No. 3; Hull, Cartulary of Launceston Priory (1987), No. 14

[] Ecclesia Saresberiensis
Cathedral church of Salisbury. William Henry Rich-Jones, The Register of St. Osmund, 2 vols, Rolls Series (London, 1883–84); idem and William Dunn Macray, Sarum Charters and Documents, Rolls Series (London, 1891).

Pipe Roll 2 Henry II, 56–hm; Pipe Roll 3 Henry II, 071–ws; Pipe Roll 9 Henry II, 57–hm; Pipe Roll 2 Henry II, 19–ws; Pipe Roll 6 Henry II, 17d–wl; Pipe Roll 6 Henry II, 17c–wl; Pipe Roll 7 Henry II, 59–hm; Pipe Roll 4 Henry II, 151–ws; Pipe Roll 7 Henry II, 08–wl; Pipe Roll 11 Henry II, 041a–hm; Pipe Roll 8 Henry

II, 12a–wl; Pipe Roll 9 Henry II, 46b–wl; Pipe Roll 7 Henry II, 51a–bk; Pipe
Roll 6 Henry II, 17b–wl; Pipe Roll 6 Henry II, 17a–wl; Pipe Roll 4 Henry II,
174a–hm; Pipe Roll 5 Henry II, 47a–hm; Pipe Roll 9 Henry II, 46a–wl; Pipe Roll
4 Henry II, 174b–hm; Pipe Roll 12 Henry II, 101b–hm; Pipe Roll 12 Henry II,
072b–wl; Pipe Roll 12 Henry II, 072a–wl; Pipe Roll 11 Henry II, 078; Pipe Roll
11 Henry II, 057–wl; Pipe Roll 11 Henry II, 056–wl; Pipe Roll 11 Henry II,
041b–hm; Pipe Roll 10 Henry II, 43–bk; Pipe Roll 10 Henry II, 14–wl; Pipe Roll
12 Henry II, 129–ws; Pipe Roll 8 Henry II, 12b–wl; Pipe Roll 5 Henry II,
47b–hm; Pipe Roll 8 Henry II, 37a–hm; Pipe Roll 7 Henry II, 09–wl; Pipe Roll 4
Henry II, 116–wl; Pipe Roll 8 Henry II, 30–wi; Pipe Roll 8 Henry II, 37b–hm;
Pipe Roll 6 Henry II, 22–ws; Pipe Roll 5 Henry II, 38–bkws; Pipe Roll 5 Henry
II, 39–wl; Regesta regum Anglo-Normannorum III, No. 785; Pipe Roll 10
Henry II, 26a–hm; Pipe Roll 10 Henry II, 27a–hm; Pipe Roll 10 Henry II,
26b–hm; Pipe Roll 10 Henry II, 27b–hm; Pipe Roll 3 Henry II, 079–wl; Pipe
Roll 3 Henry II, 106b–hm; Pipe Roll 3 Henry II, 106a–hm; Pipe Roll 6 Henry II,
50–hm; Pipe Roll 2 Henry II, 58–wl; Pipe Roll 6 Henry II, 49–hm; Pipe Roll 3
Henry II, 106c–hm; Regesta regum Anglo-Normannorum III, No. 790; Regesta
regum Anglo-Normannorum III, No. 788; Regesta regum Anglo-Normannorum
III, No. 789; Pipe Roll 31 Henry I, 013–dswl; i, fol. 77a; Regesta regum
Anglo-Normannorum III, No. 787; Regesta regum Anglo-Normannorum III,
No. 791

[] Ecclesia Wintoniensis
Cathedral priory of St Peter and St Swithin, known as Old Minster; founded in the
seventh century. A. W. Goodman, *Chartulary of Winchester Cathedral*
(Winchester, 1927); BL Add. 15350; Add. 29436.

i, fol. 41a; i, fol. 65c; Regesta regum Anglo-Normannorum III, No. 957; i, fol.
43a; i, fol. 43a; i, fol. 43a; i, fol. 43a; i, fol. 43c; i, fol. 50b; i, fol. 41d

[] Faber Regis
Unnamed king's smith.

i, fol. 36b

[] Filius Almari
English Domesday tenant of Count Alan in Norfolk. The association of his land in
Mileham and Stanfield with Stigand and the fact that part of them were held by
Bishop William of Thetford, successor of Bishop Aelmer of Elmham, brother of
Stigand, indicates that he was the son of Bishop Aelmer and nephew of Stigand of
Canterbury. Aelmer succeeded his brother as bishop of Elmham in 1047 and held
the office until his deposition in April 1070. Domesday records that he had a wife
before he became bishop (Norfolk 10.28).

ii, fol. 144b; ii, fol. 144b

[] Gifart
Domesday tenant of Robert fitz Corbucion.

ii, fol. 260a; ii, fol. 260a; ii, fol. 258b

[] Louel
Norman, tenant of Ralph Bainard in Domesday Norfolk.

i, fol. 16d; i, fol. 17a; ii, fol. 251b; ii, fol. 251b; ii, fol. 251a

[] Malus Vicinus
Occurs Domesday Suffolk as a tenant of Richard de Clare. His successor William
Mauvoisin was a benefactor of Stoke-by-Clare priory c.1130/50.

ii, fol. 447b

537

[] Miles Ricoardi

Unnamed knight of Ricoard de Torcy. One of the few sub-tenants to occur in Domesday Book.

i, fol. 26b

[] Miscellaneous Burgesses

i, fol. 189a; ii, fol. 118b; i, fol. 184a; i, fol. 280a; ii, fol. 103b; Pipe Roll 2 Henry II, 22–bubd; Pipe Roll 4 Henry II, 139–bubd; Pipe Roll 12 Henry II, 015–bd; Pipe Roll 12 Henry II, 097–dssm; Pipe Roll 11 Henry II, 065–dssm; Pipe Roll 31 Henry I, 142–cl; Pipe Roll 2 Henry II, 15a–cm; Pipe Roll 2 Henry II, 15b–cm; Pipe Roll 2 Henry II, 15c–cm; Pipe Roll 3 Henry II, 096a–cm; Pipe Roll 3 Henry II, 096b–cm; Pipe Roll 4 Henry II, 180–kn; Pipe Roll 3 Henry II, 102–kn; ii, fol. 107a; Pipe Roll 31 Henry I, 065–kn; Pipe Roll 31 Henry I, 065–kn; Pipe Roll 31 Henry I, 132a–dm; Pipe Roll 31 Henry I, 130–dm; Pipe Roll 31 Henry I, 026–ynb; Pipe Roll 31 Henry I, 077–gl; Pipe Roll 31 Henry I, 077–gl; Pipe Roll 12 Henry II, 080–gl; Pipe Roll 11 Henry II, 014–gl; Pipe Roll 31 Henry I, 114–ln; Pipe Roll 31 Henry I, 114–ln; Pipe Roll 7 Henry II, 07–nfsf; pipePipe Roll 4 Henry II, 177–nb; Pipe Roll 11 Henry II, 064–dssm; Pipe Roll 12 Henry II, 097–dssm; Pipe Roll 2 Henry II, 67–kn; Pipe Roll 31 Henry I, 016–ds; Pipe Roll 6 Henry II, 51–dv; Pipe Roll 31 Henry I, 114–ln; Pipe Roll 31 Henry I, 114–ln; ii, fol. 118a; Pipe Roll 6 Henry II, 09–ox; Pipe Roll 6 Henry II, 30–hf; Pipe Roll 31 Henry I, 016–ds; Pipe Roll 31 Henry I, 132b–dm; Pipe Roll 31 Henry I, 063–ht; Pipe Roll 31 Henry I, 063–ht; Pipe Roll 31 Henry I, 095–nf; Pipe Roll 31 Henry I, 095–nf; Pipe Roll 31 Henry I, 006–ox; Clay, Early Yorkshire Charters (1935), IV, No. 50; Pipe Roll 31 Henry I, 016–ds; Pipe Roll 31 Henry I, 075–st; Pipe Roll 31 Henry I, 075–st; Pipe Roll 31 Henry I, 095–nf; Pipe Roll 31 Henry I, 095–nf; Pipe Roll 31 Henry I, 139b–bk; Pipe Roll 31 Henry I, 139c–bk; Pipe Roll 31 Henry I, 139a–bk; Pipe Roll 31 Henry I, 154–dv; pipe, 57, 129–nfsf; i, fol. 80c; i, fol. 143a; i, fol. 143c; i, fol. 218b; ii, fol. 107a; ii, fol. 114a; ii, fol. 114a; i, fol. 253a; i, fol. 166b; Pipe Roll 11 Henry II, 031–lomx; i, fol. 136c; i, fol. 186a

[] Miscellaneous Clerics

i, fol. 89b; i, fol. 97c; i, fol. 56d; i, fol. 283b; i, fol. 181c; i, fol. 181c; i, fol. 181d; i, fol. 302c; i, fol. 302b; i, fol. 302d; i, fol. 302d; i, fol. 302d; i, fol. 302d; i, fol. 57a; i, fol. 38a; i, fol. 187b; i, fol. 174d; i, fol. 182c; i, fol. 181c; i, fol. 012b; i, fol. 104b; i, fol. 247d; i, fol. 247d; ii, fol. 013b; i, fol. 65a; i, fol. 65d; i, fol. 65b; i, fol. 66a; i, fol. 142b; i, fol. 142b; i, fol. 24a; i, fol. 66a; i, fol. 38a; i, fol. 75d; i, fol. 86c; i, fol. 86d; i, fol. 89c; i, fol. 24a; i, fol. 16d; i, fol. 91c; i, fol. 75d; ii, fol. 133a; i, fol. 56d; i, fol. 66a; i, fol. 48b; i, fol. 130b; i, fol. 130d; i, fol. 127a; i, fol. 127a; i, fol. 129c; i, fol. 129d; i, fol. 130a; i, fol. 202b; i, fol. 129d; i, fol. 130a; i, fol. 189d; i, fol. 128d; i, fol. 17b

[] Miscellaneous Englishmen

i, fol. 68b; i, fol. 68b; i, fol. 68b; i, fol. 155b; i, fol. 371b; i, fol. 36a; i, fol. 69c; i, fol. 71d

[] Miscellaneous Freemen

ii, fol. 447a; i, fol. 174b; ii, fol. 101a; ii, fol. 184b; i, fol. 181c; i, fol. 40d; i, fol. 43d; ii, fol. 101a; ii, fol. 273a; ii, fol. 273a; ii, fol. 120a; ii, fol. 120a; ii, fol. 273a; ii, fol. 016b; i, fol. 249c; ii, fol. 170b; ii, fol. 101a; ii, fol. 447a; ii, fol. 447a; ii, fol. 447a; ii, fol. 447a; ii, fol. 447b; ii, fol. 283a; i, fol. 166b; ii, fol. 101b; ii, fol. 167a

[] Miscellaneous Frenchmen

ii, fol. 118a; i, fol. 23b; i, fol. 182b; i, fol. 182b; i, fol. 174c; i, fol. 003c; i, fol. 140c; i, fol. 70d; i, fol. 28d; i, fol. 130a; i, fol. 263c; ii, fol. 250a; ii, fol. 250a; i, fol. 175a; i, fol. 179c; i, fol. 69b; i, fol. 210a; i, fol. 23c; i, fol. 23c; i, fol. 215a; i, fol. 173a; i, fol. 173d; i, fol. 174c; i, fol. 247b; i, fol. 247b; i, fol. 247b; i, fol. 247b; i, fol. 247b; i, fol. 130d; i, fol. 23d; i, fol. 25b; i, fol. 234a; i, fol. 23d; i, fol. 52a; i, fol. 166d; i, fol. 175a; i, fol. 167b; i, fol. 233d; i, fol. 56b; ii, fol. 311a

[] Miscellaneous Knights

i, fol. 145b; i, fol. 147b; i, fol. 252b; Pipe Roll 12 Henry II, 104–hm; Pipe Roll 12 Henry II, 095–dv; Pipe Roll 31 Henry I, 009–ntdb; Pipe Roll 31 Henry I, 138–mb; Pipe Roll 12 Henry II, 098–dssm; i, fol. 198b; i, fol. 200d; i, fol. 196a; i, fol. 201b; i, fol. 195d; i, fol. 192c; i, fol. 152a; ii, fol. 439a; i, fol. 133d; i, fol. 111b; i, fol. 67a; i, fol. 72b; i, fol. 34c; i, fol. 71c; i, fol. 283a; i, fol. 198d; i, fol. 138d; i, fol. 113b; i, fol. 113b; i, fol. 29a; ii, fol. 023a; i, fol. 200d; i, fol. 140a; i, fol. 198d; i, fol. 138d; i, fol. 137b; i, fol. 134a; i, fol. 200a; i, fol. 198b; i, fol. 197d; i, fol. 198d; i, fol. 215b; i, fol. 283a; i, fol. 140a; ii, fol. 039b; ii, fol. 039b; i, fol. 28c; i, fol. 215b; i, fol. 283a; i, fol. 194a; i, fol. 283a; i, fol. 302b; i, fol. 344a; i, fol. 283a; i, fol. 89b; i, fol. 204d; i, fol. 205a; i, fol. 205c; i, fol. 205d; i, fol. 205d; i, fol. 206a; i, fol. 283a; i, fol. 194b; i, fol. 111b; i, fol. 312c; i, fol. 283a; i, fol. 012b; i, fol. 012a; i, fol. 127a; i, fol. 129b; i, fol. 127a; i, fol. 140c; i, fol. 28d; i, fol. 95d; i, fol. 89b; ii, fol. 099b; i, fol. 235c; i, fol. 195b; i, fol. 89b; i, fol. 312c; i, fol. 203d; i, fol. 182b; i, fol. 221d; i, fol. 221d; i, fol. 312c; ii, fol. 060a; i, fol. 326d; ii, fol. 086a; i, fol. 140c; ii, fol. 100b; ii, fol. 065b; i, fol. 111a; i, fol. 198c; i, fol. 58d; i, fol. 61a; i, fol. 61b; i, fol. 61c; i, fol. 61c; i, fol. 62c; i, fol. 32b; i, fol. 78a; i, fol. 198d; ii, fol. 087a; i, fol. 009d; i, fol. 109a; i, fol. 82d; i, fol. 63c; i, fol. 41c; i, fol. 44c; i, fol. 35c; ii, fol. 086a; ii, fol. 086b; ii, fol. 086b; i, fol. 128d; ii, fol. 035a; i, fol. 35a; ii, fol. 024a; i, fol. 67a; i, fol. 011a; ii, fol. 024a; i, fol. 129b; i, fol. 88c; i, fol. 211d; i, fol. 97b; ii, fol. 087a; i, fol. 29b; i, fol. 27b; i, fol. 62d; i, fol. 29b; i, fol. 29a; i, fol. 29a; i, fol. 28c; i, fol. 28d; i, fol. 66d; i, fol. 70b; i, fol. 67d; i, fol. 91b; i, fol. 65d; i, fol. 27b; Chibnall, English Lands of Abbey of Bec (1951), No. XXIV; i, fol. 67a; i, fol. 61a; i, fol. 95d; i, fol. 182c; i, fol. 220c; i, fol. 186b; i, fol. 182c; i, fol. 260b; i, fol. 182b; i, fol. 181d; i, fol. 182c; i, fol. 182d; i, fol. 253b; i, fol. 156d; i, fol. 253c; i, fol. 264b; i, fol. 221c; ii, fol. 072a; ii, fol. 055b; ii, fol. 059b

[] Miscellaneous Laywomen

ii, fol. 117a

[] Miscellaneous Men

i, fol. 194c; i, fol. 141d; i, fol. 150a; i, fol. 202a; i, fol. 200c; i, fol. 150a; i, fol. 150a; i, fol. 217c; ii, fol. 182a; i, fol. 331c; i, fol. 331c; i, fol. 247c; i, fol. 329a; i, fol. 361a; i, fol. 267a; i, fol. 153b; i, fol. 20a; i, fol. 141d; ii, fol. 187a; ii, fol. 010a

[] Miscellaneous Provosts

ii, fol. 120a; i, fol. 39c; i, fol. 142c; i, fol. 002c; ii, fol. 099b; i, fol. 49d; ii, fol. 003a

[] Miscellaneous Sokemen

i, fol. 197c; i, fol. 137a; ii, fol. 69a; i, fol. 285c; ii, fol. 088a; i, fol. 199d; i, fol. 194c; i, fol. 235b; i, fol. 141a; i, fol. 143c; i, fol. 285c; i, fol. 209d; i, fol. 303a; i, fol. 303a; i, fol. 303a; i, fol. 303a; i, fol. 303a; i, fol. 303a; i, fol. 303a; i, fol. 303a; ii, fol. 071a; i, fol. 287b; i, fol. 195a; i, fol. 197c; i, fol. 190a; i, fol. 214a; i, fol. 133a; i, fol. 309a; i, fol. 218a; i, fol. 211d; ii, fol. 033a; i, fol. 145c; i, fol. 137b; i, fol. 220c; i, fol. 292c; i, fol. 283d; i, fol. 285b; i, fol. 202b; ii, fol. 090a; i, fol. 232b; i, fol. 227c; ii, fol. 021b; i, fol. 210a; i, fol. 285c; i, fol. 220a; i, fol. 132d; King, Peterborough Descriptio Militum (1969), pp. 97–101; King, Peterborough Descriptio Militum (1969), pp. 97–101; King, Peterborough Descriptio Militum (1969), pp. 97–101; i, fol. 143b; i, fol. 139c; i, fol. 140a; i, fol. 138b; i, fol. 228d; i, fol. 228d; i, fol. 219c; i, fol. 133a; i, fol. 133a; i, fol. 133a; i, fol. 132d; i, fol. 143c; i, fol. 196c; i, fol. 139d; i, fol. 133a; i, fol. 139d; i, fol. 142c; i, fol. 133a; i, fol. 203c; i, fol. 013d; i, fol. 195b; i, fol. 194a; i, fol. 194a; i, fol. 191a; i, fol. 189d; i, fol. 193d; i, fol. 190a; i, fol. 286d; i, fol. 292c; i, fol. 220a; i, fol. 284a; ii, fol. 028b; ii, fol. 090a; i, fol. 195a; i, fol. 285a; i, fol. 228d; i, fol. 285a; i, fol. 197c; i, fol. 285c; ii, fol. 028b; i, fol. 210b; i, fol. 198b; ii, fol. 022a; i, fol. 197c; i, fol. 218d; ii, fol. 057b; ii, fol. 062a; ii, fol. 057b

[] Miscellaneous Thegns

i, fol. 77b; i, fol. 75c; i, fol. 003a; i, fol. 116a; i, fol. 330c; i, fol. 330d; Pipe Roll 31 Henry I, 129–dm; Pipe Roll 31 Henry I, 132–dm; i, fol. 292c; i, fol. 142b; i, fol. 207c; i, fol. 330c; i, fol. 250d; i, fol. 170c; i, fol. 49d; i, fol. 53d; i, fol. 98d; i, fol. 67c; i, fol. 67c; i, fol. 65b; i, fol. 89b; i, fol. 70b; i, fol. 224b; i, fol. 316b; i, fol. 302c; i, fol. 90d; i, fol. 371a; i, fol. 77a; i, fol. 84d; i, fol. 102b; i, fol. 102b; i, fol. 102b; i, fol. 102b; i, fol. 102b; i, fol. 102b; i, fol. 102b; i, fol. 102b; i, fol. 102b

[] Miscellaneous Vavassores

ii, fol. 446a; ii, fol. 446a; ii, fol. 446b; ii, fol. 447a; ii, fol. 446b; ii, fol. 446a; ii, fol. 446b; ii, fol. 446b; ii, fol. 446b; ii, fol. 446a; ii, fol. 446a; ii, fol. 446a; ii, fol. 446a; ii, fol. 446a

[] Miscellaneous Women Clerics

i, fol. 91c; ii, fol. 264b

[] Nepos Episcopi Hermani

An Englishman, nephew of Bishop Herman of Ramsey and Sherborne 1045–78; became a 'miles' (knight or thegn) at the king's command.

i, fol. 66a

[] Neptis Episcopi

Niece of Geoffrey bishop of Coutances and his tenant in Domesday Devon. Possibly same as the wife of Ingelger.

i, fol. 103b

[] Presbiter Drogonis

Priest of Drogo de Beuvrière, mentioned in Domesday Yorkshire.

i, fol. 324b; i, fol. 324b; i, fol. 324b

[] Tosard

Norman, Domesday tenant of William de Warenne. Ancestor of the Tusard family. He was apparently dead by the time his grant, as Tosard, to Lewes was confirmed by William II de Warenne (c.1101–18); this text does not bear the interpretation put upon it that Tosard became a monk of Lewes; cf. VCH Sussex vii, 53). An early charter for Castle Acre by Hugh de Wanchy was attested by Tosard, and Robert and Rainald sons of W. Tosard. He is probably the same as this W. Tosard and probably distinct from the William Tosard became a monk of Saint-Martin-de-Sées before 1100, when he gave the abbey the church of Saint-Nicholas-des-Bois, Orne (Arch. Orne H938, fol. 120). Several generations of Tosard's descendants are found int he castle Acre cartulary (BL Harley 2110, fols 9–10).

> Clay, Early Yorkshire Charters (1949), VIII, No. 14; Dugdale, Monasticon Anglicanum, IV, pp. 49–50, No. II; Dugdale, Monasticon Anglicanum, IV, pp. 49–50, No. II; i, fol. 26a

[] Trauers

Norman, occurs Domesday Hampshire. Travers (traversus) is doubtless a byname; as such it was not uncommon. Given this man's appearance in Hampshire, closely associated with the men of William fitz Osbern, the best documentary comparison is probably provided by Cart. Préaux (Arch. Eure, H7111, no. 315) in which Claricia filia Radulfi Travers made a grant, attested by William fitz Herbrand. Hugh Travers was given land at Littleton, Worcestershire, by Abbot Walter of Evesham (d. 1104) after 1086 (BL Cotton Vesp. E xxiv, fol. 11v).

> i, fol. 52d

[] Uxor Prepositi

Occurs Domesday Wiltshire.

> i, fol. 66a; i, fol. 66a

BIBLIOGRAPHY AND ABBREVIATIONS

The Bibliography begins with a number of essential references works which have been extensively used but to which no specific reference is made in the Prosopography. All matter cited in the Prosopography, whether primary or secondary, then follows in a single alphabetical list.

The Prosopography is based upon a number of 'foundation texts' (see p. 121 above), identified here by an asterisk *.

The principal system of reference is by place; e.g. one should look under **'Caen'** for the full reference to Musset, *Actes Caen . . .*, or to Walmsley, *'Charters and Customals'*. In the same way, any secondary abbreviation will be subordinate to the main place reference; hence, **'Feudal Book'** will be found under **'Bury St Edmunds'**. Monographs are listed under the author's surname; so **'Stenton**, English Feudalism'. All such key-words, including abbreviations such as **'PR'**, are given below in **bold** type.

G. R. C. Davis, *Medieval Cartularies of Great Britain: A Short Catalogue* (London, 1958)

H. Stein, *Bibliographie générale des cartulaires français*, Paris 1907

Pierre Chaplais, *Diplomatic Documents preserved in the Public Record Office*, I: *1101–1272* (London, 1963)

A Descriptive Catalogue of Ancient Deeds in the Public Record Office (HMSO), The Deputy Keeper of the Records, 6 vols (1890–1915)

Property and privilege in medieval and early modern England and Wales: Cartularies and other Registers Series 1: Cartularies from the British Library, London (Reading: Research Publications, 1990)

David Knowles and R. Neville Hadcock, *Medieval Religious Houses England and Wales* (1971)

Alison Binns, *Dedications of Monastic Houses in England and Wales, 1066–1216* (Woodbridge, 1989)

Abingdon D.C. Douglas, 'Some early surveys from the abbey of Abingdon', *EHR* 44 (1929), 618–25*

C. F. Slade and Gabrielle Lambrick, *Two cartularies of Abingdon Abbey*, Oxford Historical Society n.s. 32–33 (Oxford, 1990–92)

Abingdon *Milites Chronicon Monasterii de Abingdon*, ed. J. Stevenson, 2 vols, Rolls Series, London, 1858*

Almenesches L. Musset, 'Les premiers temps de l'abbaye d'Almenèches des origines au XIIe siècle' in *L'abbaye d'Almenèches-Argentan et Sainte Opportune. Sa vie et son culte*, ed. Dom Y. Chaussy (Paris, 1970)

Alta Ripa L. B. L., 'Charters relating to the family of De Alta Ripa, and Nunnery of Gokewell, Co. Lincoln', *Collectanea Topographica et Genealogica*, 4 (1837), 241–42*

Anc. Chh. J. H. Round, *Ancient Charters, Royal and Private, prior to A.D. 1200* (Pipe Roll Society, 10, 1888)*

Anc. Ev. *Anciens évêchés de Bretagne,* Geslin de Bourgogne et A. de Barthélemy, 6 vols (Saint-Brieuc and Paris, 1855–79)

ANS *Anglo-Norman Studies* (Proceedings of the Battle Conference)

Athelney E. H. Bates, *Two Cartularies of the Benedictine Abbeys of Muchelney and Athelney in the County of Somerset* (Somerset Record Society, 14, 1899)

Angers/Anjou *Cartulaire de Saint-Laud d'Angers,* ed. A. Planchenault, Angers 1903, Documents historiques sur l'Anjou t. iv

Premier et Second livres des Cartulaires de l'abbaye Saint-Serge et Saint-Bach à Angers, ed. Y. Chauvin, 2 vols, Angers, 1997

Cartularium Beatae Mariae Caritatis Andegauensis, (Cart. Ronceray) ed. P. Marchegay, Archives d'Anjou t. 3, Angers, 1854

Cartulaire de l'abbaye de Saint-Aubin d'Angers, ed. B. de Broussillon, Angers 1896 (Doc. hist. sur l'Anjou, t. 1–3)

Chroniques des comtes d'Anjou, ed. Marchegay et Salmon, Paris 1856–71

Chroniques des comtes d'Anjou et des seigneurs d'Amboise, ed. L. Halphen et R. Poupardin, Paris, 1913

Cartulaire noir de la Cathedrale d'Angers, ed. Urseau, Angers 1908 (Doc. hist. sur l'Anjou t. v [indiqué 'Cartulaire noir de Saint-Maurice'])

Chartes de Saint-Julien de Tours, ed. abbé Denis, 1913

Obituaire de la cathédrale d'Angers, reconstitué et publié par Urseau, Angers, 1930

Cartularium Sanctae Mariae de Rota, Andegavensis diocensis, D.A. Sigoigne, with monastic tables by D. de Farcy, 1904

Arch. dépt (or **Arch.**) Archives départementales

Arras B.-M. Tock ed., *Les chartes des évêques d'Arras (1093–1203)* (Paris, 1991)

Bacqueville-en-Caux l'abbé Sauvage, *Les chartes de fondation de prieuré de Bacqueville-en-Caux*, Rouen, 1882

Bacton Barbara Dodwell, 'Some charters relating to the Honour of Bacton', in *A Medieval Miscellany for Doris Mary Stenton*, edd. Patricia M. Barnes and C. F. Slade, Pipe Roll Society N.S. 36 for 1960 (London, 1962), pp. 147–65*

Bates, David Bates ed., *Regesta Regis Willelmi Primi* (Oxford, 1998)

Bath Frances M. R. Ramsey, *English Episcopal Acta X: Bath and Wells 1061–1205* (Oxford, 1995)

Two Chartularies of the Priory of St Peter at Bath, ed. W. Hunt, Somerset Record Society 7 (London, 1893)*

Battle [Alfred Walter Francis Fuller], *Charters of Battle Abbey in the Fuller Collection in the University of London Library* (London, 1979)

The Chronicle of Battle Abbey, ed. E. Searle (Oxford, 1980)

Bayeux *Antiquus cartularius ecclesiae Baiocensis (Livre Noir)*, ed. V. Bourrienne, 2 vols (Rouen, 1902–3)

E. Anquetil, *Le Livre Rouge de l'évêché de Bayeux*, 2 vols Bayeux 1908–11

Beauchamp Emma Mason, *The Beauchamp Cartulary Charters 1100–1268*, Pipe Roll Society N.S. 43 for 1971–73 (London, 1980)*

Beaumont-le-Roger *Cartulaire de Sainte-Trinité de Beaumont-le-Roger*, ed. E. Deville, Paris, 1912

Bec André Porée, *Histoire de l'abbaye du Bec*, (Evreux 1901, rpt. Brussels, 1980)

Marjorie Chibnall, *Select Documents of the English Lands of the Abbey of Bec* (London, 1951)*

Bellême Gérard Louise, La seigneurie de Bellême X–XII siècles, (Le Pays Bas-Normand 83 Année, nos. 199 and 200 1990, nos. 201–202, 1991)

Kathleen Thompson, Family and influence to the south of Normandy in the eleventh century: the lordship of Bellême, in: *Journal of Medieval History* 11 (1985) pp. 215–226

Belvoir G., 'Grant of the church of Tallington, Co. Linc. to the Priory of Belvoir, by William de Albineio Brito', *Collectanea Topographica et Genealogica*, 1 (1834), 32–33*

J. H. Round, 'Fragment of a Belvoir Cartulary', *H. M. C. Rutland*, IV (1905), 173; also cf. pp. 105–71

Bermondsey *Excerpta a Chronicis de Bermondsey*, in *Monasticon Anglicanum* iv, 95–7*

Berry *Essai de reconstruction du cartulaire A de l'abbaye de Saint-Sulpice de Bourges*, ed. L. Buhot de Kersenis, Mém. soc. des antiquaires de Centre t. xxv, Bourges, 1912

Fragments du cartulaire de la Chapelle-Aude, A. M. Chazaut, Moulins 1860, Publication de la soc.d'emulation du Bourbonnais

Nouveaux extraits du cartulaire de la Chapelle-Aude, ed. P. Gautier, Bull. soc. d'emul. de Bourbonnais t. xxi

G. Devailly, *Le Berry du Xe siècle au milieu du XIIIe* (Paris/La Haye, 1973)

Bib. mun. Bibliothèque municipale

B.I.H.R. *Bulletin of the Institute of Historical Research*

BL British Library, London

BL Chh. Warner, George F. and Henry J. Ellis, *Facsimiles of Royal and Other Charters in the British Museum, I: William I – Richard I* (London, 1903)

Blyth *Blyth Priory Cartulary*, ed. R.M. Timson, Thoroton Rec. Soc. ser. vol. 27, 1973*

Blyborough Kathleen Major, 'Blyborough charters', in *A Medieval Miscellany for Doris Mary Stenton*, edd. Patricia M. Barnes and C. F. Slade, Pipe Roll Society n.s. 36 for 1960 (London, 1962), pp. 203–19*

Blythburgh Christopher Harper-Bill, *Blythburgh Priory Cartulary*, Suffolk Charters 2–3 (Woodbridge, 1980–81)

BN Bibliothèque Nationale, Paris

Boarstall H. E. Salter and A. H. Cooke, *The Boarstall Cartulary*, Oxford Rec. Soc. 88 (1930)

Bodl. Bodleian Library, Oxford

Boroughs Ballard, Adolphus, *British Borough Charters, 1042–1216* (Cambridge, 1913)

Boxgrove L. Fleming, *The Cartulary of Boxgrove Priory* (Sussex Record Society, 59, 1960)

Bracton's Notebook *Bracton's Notebook*, ed. W.F. Maitland (London, 1887)

Brassart, Douai F. Brassart, *Histoire du château et de la châtellenie de Douai depuis le X siècle jusqu'en 1798*, 3 vols, 1877–87

Brecon Banks, R. W., 'Cartularium prioratus S. Johannis Evangelistae de Brecon', *Archaeologia Cambrensis*, 4th S., 13 (1882), 275–308; 14 (1883), 18–49, 137–68, 221–36, 274–311

Bridlington William T. Lancaster, *Abstract of Charters of Bridlington Priory* (London [privately], 1912)

Brinkburn W. Page, *The Chartulary of Brinkburn Priory* (Surtees Society, 90, 1892)

Bruton anon., *Two Cartularies of the Augustinian Priory of Bruton and the Cluniac Priory of Montacute* (Somerset Record Society, 8, 1894)

Buckland F. W. Weaver, *A Cartulary of Buckland Priory* (Somerset Record Society, 25, 1909)

Burton G. Wrottesley, 'The Burton Chartulary', William Salt Arch. Soc. Collections for a History of Staffordshire v, pt. 1 (1894)

Charters of Burton Abbey, ed. P.H. Sawyer, Royal Historical Society (London, 1979)

Bury St Edmund's Thomas Arnold, *Memorials of St. Edmund's Abbey,* 3 vols, Rolls Series 96 (London, 1890–96)

H. W. C. Davis, 'The Liberties of Bury St Edmunds', *E.H.R.,* 24 (1909), 417–31

G., 'Grant of lands at Pridington, in Hawkedon, Suffolk, from Richard Fitz Gilbert, Earl of Clare, to the Abbey of St. Edmund', *Collectanea Topographica et Genealogica,* 1 (1834), 388–89

Feudal Book, *Feudal Book of Abbot Baldwin,* in David C. Douglas, *Feudal Documents from the Abbey of Bury St. Edmunds* (British Academy, London, 1932)*

Feudal Documents, David C. Douglas, *Feudal Documents from the Abbey of Bury St. Edmunds* (British Academy, London, 1932)*

Kalendar, R. H. C. Davis, *The Kalendar of Abbot Samson of Bury St Edmunds and Related Documents* (Royal Historical Society, 1954)

Caen E. Deville, *Analyse d'un ancien cartulaire de l'abbaye de Saint-Etienne de Caen,* Evreux, 1905

L. Musset, *Les Actes de Guillaume le Conquérant et de la reine Mathilde pour les abbayes caennaises,* Caen, 1967

John Walmsley, ed. *Charters and Custumals of the Abbey of Holy Trinity, Caen Part 2 The French Estates* (Records of Social and Economic History n.s. 22, Oxford, 1994)

Cambrai Ch. de Smedt, ed. *Gesta pontificum cameracensium, Gestes des ev. de c. de 1092 à 1138* (Soc. de l'Hist. de France 79, 1880)

Chronicon cameracense et atrebatense, sive historia utriusque ecclesiæ . . . conscripta a Balderico Noviomensi, PL cxlix

idem, *Ex historia Cameracensi,* ibid

Cambridgeshire G. Fowler, 'An early Cambridgeshire feodary', *EHR* xlvi (1932), 442–3* (the so-called 'Braybrooke Feodary)

Canonsleigh Vera C. M. London, *The Cartulary of Canonsleigh Abbey. Harleian MS. no. 3660: A Calendar,* Devon & Cornwall Record Society new ser., vol. 8 (Torquay, 1965 for 1962)

Canterbury C. R. Cheney, *English Episcopal Acta II: Canterbury 1162–1190* and *III: Canterbury 1193–1205* (Oxford, 1986; repr. 1991)

Charles Hardwick, *Historia Monasterii Sancti Augustini Cantuariensis by Thomas of Elmham,* Rolls Ser. (London, 1858)

Audrey M. Woodcock, *Cartulary of the Priory of St Gregory's Canterbury,* Camden Society, 3rd Series, 88 (1956)*

Irene Josephine Churchill, *Table of Canterbury Archbishopric Charters*, Camden Miscellany, v. 15 [no. 3] (London, 1929)

G. J. Turner and H. E. Salter, *The Register of St. Augustine's Abbey Canterbury commonly called the Black Book*, 2 vols (London, 1915–24)

Carisbrooke *Cartulary of Carisbrooke Priory,* ed. Dom S. F. Hockey, Isle of Wight Record Society 2, 1981

Carmen *The Carmen de Hastingi Proelio of Guy, bishop of Amiens*, ed. Catherine Morton and Hope Muntz (Oxford, 1972)

Cart. Antiqu. Lionel Landon and J. Conway Davies, *The Cartae Antiquae Rolls*, 2 vols, Pipe Roll Society 55, N.S. 17 (1939), 71 = N.S. 33(1957)

CDF J. H. Round ed., *Calendar of Documents preserved in France, illustrative of the history of Great Britain and Ireland*, vol. I (Public Record Office, 1899)

Cerne B. F. Lock, 'The Cartulary of Cerne Abbey', Proc. Dorset Nat. Hist. & Antiq. Field Club, xxviii (1907), 65–95; xxix (1908), 195–223

Chanteux H. Chanteux, *Recueil des actes de'Henry I Beauclerc*, 3 vols, thèse de l'Ecole des Chartes, 1932

Charroux *Chartes et documents pour servir à l'histoire de l'abbaye de Charroux*, ed. P. de Monsabert (Archives historiques du Poitou, t. 39)

Charité-sur-Loire R. de Lespinasse. *Cartulaire du prieuré de la Charité-sur-Loire, ordre du Cluny*, Nevers/Paris 1887 (Soc. nivernaise des Lettres, Sciences et Arts)

Chartes normandes *Recueil des facsimilés de chartes normandes*, ed. J. J. Vernier, SHN 1919

Chartres *Cartulaire de Saint-Père de Chartres*, ed. B. Guérard, Paris, 1840

Archives d'Eure-et-Loir. Collection de cartulaires chartrains t. 11 (fasc. 1). Cartulaire de la leproserie du Grand-Beaulieu de Chartres et du prieuré de Notre-Dame de la Bourdinière, ed. R. Merlet et M. Jusselin, Chartres 1909; t.1 *Cartulaire de Saint-Jean-en-Vallée* [often called livre rouge of Grand-Beaulieu], ed. R. Merlet

R. Merlet et abbé Clerval, *Un manuscrit chartrain du XIe siècle. Fulbert évêque de Chartres martyrologe nécrologe*, 1893 (Soc. Arch. Eure-et-Loir)

Chertsey anon., *Chertsey Abbey Cartularies*, vols 1–2, Surrey Record Society 12 (1915–63)

Chester Geoffrey Barraclough, 'Some charters of the Earls of Chester', in *A Medieval Miscellany for Doris Mary Stenton*, edd. Patricia M. Barnes and C. F. Slade, Pipe Roll Society n.s. 36 for 1960 (London, 1962), pp. 25–43* (**Chester 1**)

G. Barraclough, *Facsimiles of Early Cheshire Charters*, Record Society of Lancashire and Cheshire ([Preston], 1957)

G. Barraclough, *The Charters of the Anglo-Norman Earls of Chester, c. 1071–1237*, Record Society of Lancashire and Cheshire vol. 126 ([Chester], 1988)* (**Chester 2**)

James Tait, *The Chartulary or Register of the Abbey of St. Werburgh, Chester*, Chetham Society 79, 82 (Manchester, 1920–23)

A. T. Thacker and Geoffrey Barraclough, *The Earldom of Chester and its charters*, Journal of the Chester Archaeological Society. [Special issue] 71 (Chester 1991)

Chichester anon., *Ancient Charters of the Dean and Chapter of Chichester, 689–1674*, West Sussex County Record Office (Chichester, 1972)

Walter Divie Peckham, *The Chartulary of the High Church of Chichester*, Sussex Rec. Soc., 46 ([Lewes], 1946)

Chicksand, G. H. Fowler, 'Early charters of the priory of Chicksand', *Bedfordshire Historical Record Society*, 1 (1913), 101–28

Chocques *Histoire de l'abbaye de Chocques, ordre de Saint Augustin, au diocèse de Saint-Omer*, par M. l'Abbé Robert, *Mémoires de la société academique des antiquaires de la Morinie* xv (1876), 335–568

Cirencester Charles Derek Ross and M. Devine, *The Cartulary of Cirencester Abbey Gloucestershire*, 3 vols (London, 1964; Oxford, 1977)

Clerkenwell W. O. Hassall, *Cartulary of St. Mary Clerkenwell*, Camden 3rd Ser., 71 (1949)

Cluny *Recueil des chartes de l'abbaye de Cluny*, 6 vols, Paris, 1876–93, A. Bernard et A. Bruel

G. F. Duckett, *Charters and Records illustrative of the English Foundations of the Ancient Abbey of Cluni*, 2 vols (London, 1888)

Cockersand, *The Chartulary of Cockersand Abbey*, 3 vols in 7 parts, Chetham Society, NS 38–40, 43, 56–57, 64 (1898–1909)

Colchester S. A. Moore, *Cartularium Monasterii S. Johannis Baptistae de Colecestriae*, 2 vols, Roxburghe Club (1897)

J. H. Round, 'The early charters of St. John's Abbey Colchester', *English Historical Review*, 16 (1901), 721–30

Coll. et Top. *Collectanea Topographica et Genealogia*, John Gough Nicholl, 8 vols, 1834–43

Colne J. L. Fisher, *Cartularium Prioratus de Colne* (Essex Archaeological Society, Occassional Publications, 1, 1946)*

Comp. Peer. *The Complete Peerage* by G.E.C., revised edn, V. Gibbs, H. A. Doubleday, Lord Howard de Walden, G. H. White and R. S. Lea, London, 1910–59

Conques G. Desjardins, *Cartulaire de l'abbaye de Conques-en-Rouergue (801–1225)*, Paris, 1879

Liber miraculorum sancte Fidis, ed. A. Bouillet, Paris, 1897

Coventry M. J. Franklin, *English Episcopal Acta 14: Coventry and Lichfield 1072–1159* (Oxford, 1997)

Creon, E. M. Poynton, 'The Fee of Creon', *Genealogist* n.s. 18*

Crouch, Beaumont Twins David Crouch, *The Beaumont Twins: the roots and branches of power in the twelfth century* (Cambridge, 1986)

Curia Regis Rolls, i–xv (1922–72)

Dalton, P. Dalton, *Conquest, Anarchy and Lordship. Yorkshire, 1066–1154* (Cambridge, 1994)

Danelaw Chh. F. M. Stenton, *Documents illustrative of the Social and Economic History of the Danelaw, from various Collections*, British Academy. Records of the Social and Economic History of England and Wales, 5 (London, 1920)*

Dauzat A. Dauzat et Ch. Rostaing, *Dictionnaire étymologique des noms de lieux en France*, 2nd edn, Paris, 1989

Daventry M. J. Franklin, *The Cartulary of Daventry Priory*, The Publications of the Northamptonshire Record Society 35 (Northampton, 1988)*

DB *Domesday Book, seu Liber Censualis Willelmi Primi Regis Angliae*, ed. Abraham Farley, 2 vols Record Commission (London, 1783)*; Farley's edition was reprinted with an English translation in 40 volumes, Gen. Ed. John Morris (Philimore, Chichester, 1974–1986)

Domesday Book, seu Liber Censualis Willelmi Primi Regis Angliae, Additamenta [Exon Domesday], Record Commission (London, 1816), contains **Tax Returns** and **Exon**

Great Domesday: facsimile, ed. R. W. H. Erskine, Alecto Historical Editions (London, 1986)

Domesday Names: An Index of Personal and Place Names in Domesday Book, compiled by K. S. B. Keats-Rohan and David E. Thornton (Woodbridge, 1997)

Delisle, Rec. L. Delisle and E. Berger, *Recueil des actes de Henri II, roi d'Angleterre et duc de Normandie*, 3 vols (Paris, 1894–27)

Dom. Mon. D. C. Douglas ed., *The Domesday Monachorum of Christ Church, Canterbury* (London, 1944)*

Droitwich, J. H. Round, *'The Worcestershire Survey'*, Feudal England, rptd. 1964, 146

Du Boulay, Lordship. . .Canterbury F. R. H. Du Boulay, *The Lordship of Canterbury* (London, 1966)

Du Chesne André Du Chesne, *Histoire généalogique des maisons de Guines, d'Ardre, de Gand et de Coucy* (Paris, 1631)

idem, *Histoire généalogique de la maison de Béthune* (Paris, 1639)

Dunstable G. Herbert Fowler, *A Digest of the Charters preserved in the Cartulary of the Priory of Dunstable*, Befordshire Record Society, 10 (1926)

Durham *Liber Vitae Dunelmensis*, ed. A. H. Thompson, Surtees Soc. 136 (1923)

H. S. Offler, *Durham Episcopal Charters*, 1071–1152, Surtees Society 179 (1068)

W. Greenwell, *Feodarium Prioratus Dunelmensis*, Surtees Soc., 58

Simeon of Durham, *Opera Omnia*, ed. T. Arnold, 2 vols Rolls Series, (London 1882, 1885)

Eadmer, *Historia Novorum in Anglia*, ed. M. Rule, Rolls Series (London, 1884)

idem, *The Life of St Anselm, Archbishop of Canterbury*, ed. Sir Richard Southern (1962, rpt Oxford, 1972)

Early Bucks. Charters G. H. Fowler and J. G. Jenkins, *Early Buckinghamshire Charters*, Records Branch of the Buckinghamshire Archaeological Society 3 (Bedford, 1939)

East Anglia, D. C. Douglas, *Social Structures of Medieval East Anglia* (1927)*

EEA *English Episcopal Acta* (published by OUP for the British Academy since 1980): See under name of diocese

Eng. Hist. Doc. D. C. Douglas, and George Greenaway, *English Historical Documents, 1042–1189* (London, 1961)

EHR *English Historical Review*

English, Holderness Barbara English, *The Lords of Holderness 1086–1260* (Oxford, 1979)

Essex C. Hart, *The Early Charters of Essex: The Norman Period*, Dept. Eng. Local Hist., Occas. Papers, 11 (Leicester, 1957)

Evesham *Chronicon Abbatiae de Evesham*, ed. W. D. Macray, Rolls Series, London, 1863

Excerpta A. Ballard, *An Eleventh-Century Inquisition of St Augustine's, Canter-*

bury, Records of the Social and Economic History of England and Wales vol. IV, part II (British Academy, Oxford, 1920)*

Exeter Frank Barlow, ed. *English Episcopal Acta XI/XII: Exeter 1046–1257* (1996)

[T.] P[hillips], 'List of charters in the cartulary of St. Nicholas, at Exeter', *Collectanea Topographica et Genealogica*, 1 (1834), 60–65, 184–89, 250–54, 374–88

Exon *see* **DB**

EYC W. Farrer (vols i–iii) and C. Clay (vols iv–xii), *Early Yorkshire Charters*, vols i–ii (Edinburgh, 1914–16), vols iii–xii published by the Yorkshire Record Society (Rec. Ser. Ext. Ser., 1935–65)

Eye Vivien Brown, *Eye Priory Cartulary and Charters*, Suffolk Charters 12–13 (Woodbridge, 1992–94)*

Eynsham H. E. Salter, *Eynsham cartulary*, 2 vols, Oxford Historical Society, 49 and 51 (1907–08)*

Family Trees K. S. B. Keats-Rohan ed., *Family Trees and the Roots of Politics; The Prosopography of Britain and France from the tenth to the Twelfth Century* (Woodbridge, 1997)

Farrer, Itinerary, W. Farrer, 'An outline itinerary of Henry I', *EHR* xxxiv (1919), 303–579

Fauroux Marie Fauroux ed., *Recueil des actes des ducs de Normandie (911–1066)*, Société des Antiquaires de Normandie t. 36, Caen, 1961

FEA *John Le Neve, Fasti Ecclesiæ Anglicanæ 1066–1300*, new edn Diana Greenaway, Institute of Historical Research, London, *Vol. I, St Paul's, London* (1968); *II, Monastic Cathedrals (Northern and Southern Provinces* (1971); *III, Lincoln* (1977); *IV, Salisbury* (1991); *V, Chichester* (1996)

Fees *Book of Fees, commonly called the Testa de Nevill*, 3 vols (Public Record Office, 1921–1931)

Flanders *Actes des comtes de Flandre, 1071–1128*, ed. Fernand Vercauteren (Brussels, 1938)

Fontenay *Cartulaire de l'abbaye de Fontenay le Marmion*, ed. G. Saige, Monaco, 1885

L. Musset, 'Actes inédits du XIIe siècle. IV Deux nouvelles chartes normandes de l'abbaye de Bourgueil. V. Autour des origines de Saint-Étienne de Fontenay', *Bulletin de la Sociéte archéologique de Normandie*, 57 (1961–2) 5–41

Fountains William T. Lancaster, *Abstracts of the Charters and Other Documents contained in the Chartulary of the Cistercian Abbey of Fountains in the West Riding of the County of York*, 2 vols (Leeds, 1915)

Fougères *Documents inédits sur l'histoire de Bretagne. Chartes du prieuré de la Sainte-Trinité Fougères*, A. La Borderie and Delabigne Villeneuve, Bull. arch. de l'assoc. bretonne, 1851, 178–99, 236–50

France *Catalogue des Actes d'Henri Ier, roi de France*, ed. F. Soehnée (Paris, 1907)

Recueil des Actes de Philippe I, roi de France, ed. M. Prou (Paris, 1908)

Furness Atkinson, J. C, *The Coucher Book of Furness Abbey*, 3 vols, Chetham Soc., NS, 9, 11, 14 (1886–88); J. Brownbill, *The Coucher Book of Furness. Volume II*, 3 vols, Chetham, 74, 76, 78 (1915–19)

Gaimar *Lestoire des Engleis*, ed. Alexander Bell, Anglo-Norman Texts Society (Oxford, 1960)

Lestorie des Engles solum la translacion Maistre Geffrei Gaimar, ed. Thomas Duffus Hardy and Charles Trice Martin, 2 vols, Rolls Series (London, 1888)

Gall. Christ. *Gallia Christiana*, vol. xi (Paris, 1759)

GASA *Gesta Abbatum Monasterii Sancti Albani a Thoma Walsingham . . . compilata*, ed. H. T. Riley, 3 vols, Rolls Ser., London, 1867–9

Gilbertine B. Golding, *Gilbert of Sempringham and the Gilbertine Order* (Oxford, 1995)

The Book of St Gilbert, ed. and trans. R. Foreville and G. Keir, Oxford, 1987

F. M. Stenton, *Transcripts of Charters relating to the Gilbertine Houses Sixle, Ormsby, Catley, Cullington and Alvingham*, Lincoln Record Society, 18 (Horncastle, 1922)

see also **Sempringham**

Glamorgan George T. Clark, *Cartae et alia munimenta quae ad Dominium de Galmorgancia pertinent*, rev. by Godfrey L. Clark, 6 vols (Cardiff, 1910)

Glastonbury *The Great Chartulary of Glastonbury*, ed. Dom Aelred Watkin, Somerset Record Society lix, lxiii–iv, 1947–56*

F. W. Weaver, *A Feodary of Glastonbury Abbey*, Somerset Rec. Soc., 26 (1910)

Gloucester *Historia et cartularium monasterii sancti Petri Gloucestriae*, ed. W. H. Hart, 3 vols, Rolls Series, London 1863–7

Robert B. Patterson, *Earldom of Gloucester Charters: The Charters and Scribes of the Earls and Countesses of Gloucester to A.D. 1217* (Oxford, 1973)

David Walker, 'Some charters relating to St. Peter's Abbey, Gloucester', in *A Medieval Miscellany for Doris Mary Stenton*, edd. Patricia M. Barnes and C. F. Slade, Pipe Roll Society n.s. 36 for 1960 (London, 1962), pp. 247–68*

Gloucestershire A. S. Ellis, 'Landholders of Domesday Gloucestershire', *Transactions Bristol and Gloucestershire Archaeolgical Society* 4 (1879–80)*, also printed privately as *Some Account of the Landholders of Gloucestershire Named in Domesday Book* (1880)

Godstow Godstow *The English Register of Godstow Nunnery*, ed. A. Clark, 3 vols, Early English Texts Society, Original Series, cxxix, cxxx, cxlii, 1905–11

Gorram G. C. G., 'Some additional particulars and charters relating to the Anglo-Breton family De Gorram', *Collectanea Topographica et Genealogica*, 6 (1840), 284–89; 8 (1843), 81–116

Goring Thomas Robert Gamber-Parry, *A Collection of Charters relating to Goring, Streatley and the Neighbourhood, 1181–1546, preserved in the Bodleian Library*, 2 vols, Oxf. Rec. Soc. Ser., 13–14 (Oxford, 1931–32)

Green, Aristocracy, Judith A. Green, *The Aristocracy of Norman England* (Cambridge, 1997)

Green, Government Judith A. Green, *The Government of England under Henry I* (Cambridge, 1986)

Green, Sheriffs, Judith A. Green, *English sheriffs to 1154* (London, 1990)

Grestain D. Bates and V. Gazeau, 'L'abbaye de Grestain et la famille d'Herluin de Conteville', *Annales de Normandie* 40 (1990)

Guillotel, Actes Hubert Guillotel, *Les actes des ducs de Bretagne (944–1148)*, Thèse pour le Doctorat en Droit de l'Université de Droit, d'Economie et de Sciences Sociales de Paris (July, 1973)

Guisborough W. Brown, *Cartularium Prioratus de Gyseburne*, Surtees Soicety, 86 (1889), 99 (1894 for 1891)

Hampshire Harry William Gidden, *The Charters of the Borough of Southamp-*

ton, Publications of the Southampton Record Society [4] (Southampton, 1909–10)

Katharine A. Hanna, *The Cartularies of Southwick Priory*, Hampshire Record Series 9–10 ([Winchester], 1988–89)

Norah Dermott Harding, *Bristol Charters, 1155–1373*, Bristol record soc. 1 (Bristol, 1930)

H. Ellis, 'Original documents relating to Bristol and the neighbourhood', *Journal British Arch. Assoc.*, 31 (1875), 289–305

E. O. Blake, *The Cartulary of the Priory of St Denys near Southampton*, 2 vols, Southampton Record Society 24–25 (1981)

see also **Winchester**

Harrold G. Herbert Fowler, *Records of Harrold Priory*, Befordshire Historical Record Society 17 (1935)

C. R. Cheney, *'Harrold Priory: A Twelfth Century Dispute' and Other Articles*, Beds. Hist Rec. Soc., 32 (1952 for 1951)

Haskins, NI C. H. Haskins, *Norman Institutions* (Harvard U. P., Cambridge, U.S.A., 1918)

Hastings College M. Gardiner, 'Some lost Anglo-Saxon charters and the endowment of Hastings College', Sussex Arch. Coll. 127 (1989)

for the Domesday prebends *see Chartulary of the High Church of Chichester* (as above), no. 945, pp. 299–302

Hatton. . .Seals L. C. Loyd, and D. M. Stenton, *Sir Christopher Hatton's Book of Seals* (Oxford, 1950)

Haughmond Una Rees, *The Cartulary of Haughmond Abbey*, Transactions of the Shropshire Archaeological Society (Cardiff, 1985)

Heads D. Knowles and C. N. L. Brooke, *Heads of Religious Houses* (Cambridge, 1976),

Healaugh Park J. S. Purvis, *The Cartulary of the Priory of Healaugh Park*, Yorkshire Record Society 92 (1937)

Hereford V. H. Galbraith and J. Tait, *Herefordshire Domesday, circa 1160–1170*, Pipe Roll Soc. 63 (n.s. 25, London, 1950

Julia Barrow, *English Episcopal Acta VII: Hereford 1079–1234* (Oxford, 1993)

Willam W. Capes, *Registrum Thome de Charlton Episcopi Herefordensis A.D. MCCCXXVII – MCCCXLIV,* Cant and York Soc., 14, 1913

Bannister, A. T., 'A lost Cartulary of Hereford Cathedral', *Trans. Woolhope Club*, 1914–17 (Hereford, 1918), pp. 268–77

David Walker,, 'Charters of the Earldom of Hereford', in *Camden Miscellany*, 4th Series, I (London, 1964), pp. 1–75

Hesdin *Cartulaire-chronique du prieuré de Saint-Georges de Hesdin*, ed. R. Fossier, ed. CNRS, Paris 1988

Hist. Coll. Staffs. William Salt Society, Collections for a History of Staffordshire

HKF W. Farrer, *Honors and Knights' Fees*, 3 vols (Manchester, 1923–5)

Hospitallers Michael Gervers, *The Cartulary of the Knights of St. John of Jerusalem in England : secunda camera, Essex*, 2 vols Records of Social and Economic History. New series 6, 23 (Oxford; New York, 1982–96)*

M. Gervers, *The Hospitaller Cartulary in the British Library (Cotton MS Nero E VI) : a study of the manuscript and its composition with a critical edition of two fragments of earlier cartularies for Essex*, Studies and Texts: Pontifical Institute of Mediaeval Studies 50 (Toronto, 1981)

Robert Gladstone, 'Early charters of the Knights Hospitallers, relating to Much Wollton, near Liverpool', *Trans. Hist Soc. Lancs and Cheshire*, NS, 18 (1903), 173–96

Hugh Candidus *The Chronicle of Hugh Candidus, a monk of Peterborough*, ed. W. T. Mellows (Oxford, 1949)

Huntingdon W. M. Noble, 'A Cartulary of the priory of St Mary of Huntingdon', *Trans. Cambs. and Hunts. Arch Soc.*, 4 (1930), 89–280

Hyde E. Edwards, *Liber Monasterii de Hyda*, Rolls Series, London, 1856

Simon Keynes, ed. *The 'Liber Vitae' of the New Minster and Hyde Abbey*, Winchester, English Manuscripts in Facsimile 26, Copenhagen, 1996

ICC/IE *Inquisitio comitatus Cantabrigiensis. . .subjicitur Inquisitio Eliensis*, ed. N. E. S. A. Hamilton, London, 1876*

Ipswich L. B. L., 'Grant of Sprouton, Co. Suffolk, by Rodbert de Blancheville to the Canons of Ipswich', *Collectanea Topographica et Genealogica*, 4 (1837), 242–43

Jumièges *Chartes de l'abbaye de Jumièges*, ed. J.-J. Vernier, 2 vols Soc. Hist. Norm., 1916

Keats-Rohan K. S. B. Keats-Rohan, 'The devolution of the Honor of Wallingford 1066–1154', *Oxoniensia*, liv (1989), 311–18

———— 'The making of Henry of Oxford: Englishmen in a Norman World', ibid., 287–310

———— 'William the Conqueror and the Breton contingent in the non-Norman Conquest 1066–1086', *Anglo-Norman Studies*, (*Proceedings of the Battle Conference*) xiii (1991), 157–72

———— 'Le problème de la suzeraineté et la lutte pour le pouvoir: la rivalité bretonne et l'état Anglo-normand 1066–1154', *Mémoires de la Société d'Histoire et d'Archéologie de Bretagne*, lxviii (1991), 45–69

———— 'The Bretons and Normans of England 1066–1154: the family, the fief, and the feudal monarchy', *Nottingham Mediaeval Studies* 36 (1992), 42–78

———— 'Two studies in North French Prosopography 1) Ivo fitz Fulcoin, the Counts of Maine, the lords of Bellême and the foundation of L'Abbayette c.996 2) Wigan the Marshal, *alias* Guigan Algason and Other Bretons in Orderic Vitalis's *Ecclesiastical History*', *Journal of Medieval History*, 20 (1994), 3–37

———— 'The prosopography of post-Conquest England: four case studies', *Medieval Prosopography* 14.1 (1993), 1–52

———— 'Robert of Torigny's Genealogies Revisited', *Nottingham Med. Stud.* 37 (1993), 21–7

———— 'The Continental Origins of English Landholders 1066–1220 Project', *Medieval Prosopography* 14.2 (1993), 21–33

———— 'Roger de Montbegon and his family', *Transactions of the Historical Society of Lancashire and Cheshire*, 144 (1994), 181–5

———— 'Les Bretons et la politique de la colonisation d'Angleterre (c.1042–1135), MSHAB, 73 (1996) 181–215

———— 'Domesday Book and the Malets: Patrimony and the private histories of public lives', *Nottingham Medieval Studies* xli (1997) 13–56 (which contains an elaboration of '*Antecessor noster*: The Parentage of Countess Lucy Made Plain', *Prosopon*, 2, May, 1995)

Kendale, *Records relating to the Barony of Kendale*, ed. J. F. Curwen, Cumb. and Westm. Antiq. and Arch Soc., Rec. Ser., 4–6

Kirkstall William T. Lancaster, and W. P. Baildon, *The Coucher Book of . . . Kirkstall*, Thoresby Soc., 8 (1904)

Kirkstead Kirkstead B., W. H. B., 'The Kirkstead Chartulary', *The Genealogist*, NS, 17 (1900), 161–62; 19 or 18 (1901 or 02), 89–92

La Borderie, Rec. *Recueil d'actes inédits des ducs et princes de Bretagne xi–xiii siècles*, A. de la Borderie, Bull. mém. soc. arch. d'Ille-et-Vilaine, xvii, 1885

Lambert of Ardres Lambert of Ardres, *Historia comitum Ghisnensium*, in *MGH SS* xxiv, pp. 550–642, and ed. De Godefroy de Menilglaize, Paris (1855)

Lancashire W. Farrer, *The Lancashire Pipe Rolls and the Early Lancashire Charters 1130–1216* (Liverpool, 1902)

Launceston *The Cartulary of Launceston Priory (Lambeth Palace MS.719): A Calendar*, ed. Peter L. Hull, Devon and Cornwall Record Society, N.S., 30 (Exeter, 1987)*

Lechaudé-d'Anisy, Abbayes Lechaudé-d'Anisy, *Les anciennes abbayes de Normandie* (SAN, Mémoires, vols Vll, V111)

Leicestershire, J. H. Round, 'The Leicestershire Survey', *Feudal England*, rptd. 1964, 161–5*

Le Maho J. Le Maho, 'L'apparition des seigneuries châtelaines dans le Grand-Caux à l'époque ducale, *Archéologie Médiévale* vi (1976)

Le Melletier J. Le Melletier, *De la Manche vers l'Angleterre au temps de la Conquête, Cahier de L'Odae*, no. 3, n.d

Le Prevost, Eure *Mémoires et Notes de M. Auguste Le Prevost pour servir a l'histoire du département de l'Eure*, 3 vols (Evreux, 1862–1869)

Lessay *L'ancienne abbaye de Saint-Trinité de Lessay*, G. Rabillon du Lattay, Mortain n.d

Lewes *The Chartulary of the Priory of St. Pancras of Lewes*, ed. L. F. Salzman, 2 vols, Sussex Record Society 38, 40 (1933–5)

W. Budgen and L. F. Salzmann, *The chartulary of Lewes Priory. The portions relating to counties other than Sussex*, Sussex Record Society, Additional Volume, 1943

The Norfolk Portion of the Chartulary of the priory of St Pancras of Lewes, ed. J. H. Bullock, Nordfolk Record Society 12, 1939

J. H. Round, 'Some early grants to Lewes Priory', *Sussex Arch. Collections*, 40 (1896), 58–78

Lewis, 'Jurors', C. P. Lewis, 'The Domesday Jurors', *Haskins Society Journal* v (1995)

Lib. Bernewelle J. W. Clark, *Liber Memorandum . . . de Bernewelle* (Cambridge, 1897)

Lib. Eliensis E. O. Blake, *Liber Eliensis*, Camden 3rd Ser., 92 (London, 1962)

Little Malvern G. S. S., 'Charters relating to the gift of a virgate of land in Knightwick, Co. Worcester, to the Priory of Little Malvern, by Simon de Mans, temp. Hen. I', *Collectanea Topographica et Genealogica*, 4 (1837), 238–40

Lincoln *David M. Smith, English Episcopal Acta I: Lincoln 1067–1185* (London, 1980)

The Registrum Antiquissimum *of the Cathedral Church of Lincoln*, ed. C. W. Foster and K. Major, 9 vols, Lincoln Record Society, 1931–68

————, *The Royal Charters of the City of Lincoln, Henry II to William III* (Cambridge, 1911)

Lincolnshire *Lincolnshire Domesday and Lindsey Survey*, ed. C. W. Foster and T. Longley (Lincoln Record Society 19, 1924, rpt. 1976)

Lincolnshire Claims, *Domesday Book*, ed. Farley, i, fols 375–7

Lindsey Lindsey Survey, printed in Appendix II above *

Lisieux R. N. Sauvage, 'Fragment d'un cartulaire de Saint-Pierre-de-Lisieux', Études Lexoviennes 3 (1928), 327–57

Llandaff David Crouch ed., *Llandaff Episcopal Acta 1140–1287*, South wales record Society, 1989

Llan Dâv J. G. Evans ed, *The Text of the Book of Llan Dâv reproduced from the Gwysaney Manuscript* (Old Welsh Texts iv, Oxford, 1893, reprinted Aberystwyth, 1980)

Loders L. Guilloreau, *Cartulaire de Loders* (Evreux, 1908)

London, Aldgate, G. A. J. Hodgett, *The Cartulary of Holy Trinity Aldgate*, London Record Society, 8 (1871)

St Bartholmew's Nellie J. M. Kerling, *Cartulary of St Bartholomew's Hospital*

St Martin le Grand, A. J. Kempe, *Historical Notices of . . . St. Martin le Grand of London* (London, 1825)

St Paul's, London Marion Gibbs, *Early Charters of the Cathedral Church of St. Paul, London*, Camden Soc., 3rd Ser., 58 (London, 1939)*

Westminster Abbey E. Mason, Jennifer Bray and Desmond J. Murphy, *Westminster Abbey Charters 1066–c.1214*, London Record Society publications 25 (London, 1988)*

Longueville *Chartes du Prieuré de Longueville*, P. Le Cacheux, SHN 1934

Louviers *Cartulaire de Louviers*, T. Bonnin, 5 vols, Louviers 1870–83

Loyd L. C. Loyd, *The Origins of Some Anglo-Norman Families*, Harleian Society Publications vol. 103 (Leeds, 1951, rpt. Baltimore, 1992)

Luffield G. R. Elvey, *Luffield Priory Charters*, 2 vols, Publications of the Northamptonshire Record Society 22 (Oxford, 1968), 26 (1975)*

Le Mans/Maine *Actus pontificum Cenomannis in urbe degentium*, ed. Busson et Ledru, Le Mans 1902 (Arch. hist. du Maine t. 2)

Cartulaire d'Assé-le-Riboul, d'Azé et du Genéteil, ed. B. de Broussillon, du Brossay and Ledru Arch. hist. du Maine, t. 3, Le Mans 1902

Cartulaire de Saint-Michel-de-l'Abbayette, ed. B. de Broussillom, Paris, 1894

Cartulaire de Saint-Pierre-de-la-Cour, Le Mans 1907, Archives historiques du Maine t. iv

Cartulaire de Saint-Pierre-de-la-Couture, ed. Bénédictines de Solesmes, Le Mans, 1881

Cartulaire de Saint-Victeur au Mans, ed. B. de Broussillon, Paris, 1895

Cartulaire de Saint-Vincent au Mans, ed. Menjot d'Elbenne, Mamers, 1886–1913

Liber controversiarum Sancti Vincentii Cenomannensis, ou Second Cartualire de l'abbaye de Saint-Vincent du Mans, ed. A. Chédeville (Paris, 1968)

Cartulaire de l'abbaye de Saint-Calais, L. Froger (Mamers-Le Mans, 1888)

'Catalogue des actes des évêques du Mans jusqu'à la fin du xiii', L. Célier, *Revue historique et archéologique du Maine* t. 63–5 (1908–9)

Liber Albus capituli Cenomannensis, ed. Lottin (Le Mans, 1869)

Necrologie-Obituaire de la Cathédrale du Mans, G. Bossu et A. Ledru, Archives historiques du Maine 7, Le Mans 1906

L. Guilloreau, 'L'obituaire de Saint-Vincent du Mans', *Revue Mabillon,* 34, 1913, 113–127, 35, 1913, 242–58

P. L. Piolin, *Histoire d l'église du Mans,* 6 vols Paris 1851–63

A. Angot, *Dictionnaire historique, topographique et bibliographique de la Mayenne,* 4 vols 1900–02, reprinted Mayenne 1975–6

Bertrand de Broussillon, 'La maison de Laval', Bull. Comm. Hist. et Arch. de Mayenne, vol. 8 (Le Mans, 1893), pp. 62–106, vol. 9 (1894), pp. 198–244

Géographie ancienne du diocèse du Mans, Paris, 1845

Maintenon Moutié and de Dion, *Cartulaire de Saint-Thomas d'Epernon et de Notre-Dame de Maintenon,* Rambouillet, 1878

Malmsbury J. S. Brewer and C. T. Martin, *Registrum Malmesberiens. The Register of Malmesbury Abbey,* 2 vols, Rolls Ser. (London, 1879–80)

Marcigny *Cartulaire de Marcigny-sur-Loire,* ed. J. Richard, Dijon, 1957

Marmoutier *Cartulaire manceau de Marmoutier,* ed. E. Laurain, Laval 1911

Cartulaire de Marmoutiers pour le Perche, ed. abbé Barret, Mortagne 1894 (Doc. sur la Province du Perche, 3 ser. t.ii)

Cartulaire blésois de Marmoutier, ed. Métais, Chartres et Blois, 1891

Cartulaire dunois de Marmoutier, ed. Mabille, Châteaudun, 1874

Cartulaire vendômois de Marmoutier, ed. Trémault, Vendôme, 1893

Marrig T. S., 'Ground plan and charters of St. Andrews's Priory in the parish of Marrigg, North Riding, Co. Ebor.', *Collectanea Topographica et Genealogica,* 5 (1838), 100–124, 221–59

Mason J. F. A. Mason, 'The Officers and Clerks of the Norman Earls of Shropshire', *Transactions of the Shropshire Arachaeological Society* lvii, 1957–60

idem 'Barons and their officials in the later eleventh century', *ANS* 13

Merton A. Heales, *The records of Merton Priory in the County of Surrey* (London, 1898)

Meulan *Recueil des chartes de Saint-Nicaise de Meulan,* E. Houth, Pontoise 1924

E. Houth, *Les comtes de Meulan, ixe–xiiie siècle,* Mém. soc. hist. et arch. de Pontoise, du Val d'Oise, et du Vexin, t. 70, 1981

Miræus et Foppens Miræus et Foppens ed., *Opera diplomatica et historica,* 4 vols (Louvain and Brussels, 1723–48)

Missenden *Cartulary of Missenden Abbey,* ed. J. G. Jenkins, part I 1938, II 1946, III 1962, Bucks. Rec. Soc.*

Mon. Ang. *Monasticon Anglicanum,* ed. W. Dugdale, rev. ed. by J. Caley, H. Ellis and B. Bandinel, 6 vols in 8° (London, 1817–30; repr. 1846)*

Monasticon *ut supra*

Mon. Exon. *Monasticon Diocesis Exoniensis,* ed. G. Oliver (Exeter, 1846)

Monk Bretton J. W. Walker, *Abstracts of the Chartularies of the Priory of Monk Bretton,* Yorkshire Archaeological Society Record Series, 66 (1924)

Monks Horton James R. Scott, 'Charters of Monks Horton Priory', *Archaeologia Cantiana,* 10 (1876), 269–81*

Mons *La chronique de Gislebert de Mons,* éd. Léon Vanderkindere, Brussels 1904

Montacute anon., *Two Cartularies of the Augustinian Priory of Bruton and the Cluniac Priory of Montacute* (Somerset Record Society, 8, 1894)

Mont-Morel *Cartulaire de l'abbaye de Mont-Morel (Cartulaire du Manche)*, M. Dubosc, Saint-Lô 1878

Montivilliers, Bouvris J-M. Bouvris, 'La renaissance de l'abbaye de Montivilliers et son dévelopement jusqu'à la fin du XIe siècle', in *L'Abbaye de Montivilliers à travers les âges. Actes du colloque organisé à Montivilliers le 8 mars 1986*; Recueil de l'Association des Amis du Vieux Havre, no. 48 (1988)

Morice, Preuves I, Dom Hyacinthe Morice, *Mémoires pour servir de preuves à l'histoire ecclésiastique et civile de Bretagne*, 3 vols (Paris, 1742–6), vol. 1

Mowbray Diana E Greenway, *Charters of the Honour of Mowbray, 1107–1191*, Records of social and economic history. New series 1 (OUP at London, 1972)*

MSHAB *Mémoires de la Société d'Histoire et d'Archéologie de Bretagne*

Muchelney E. H. Bates, *Two Cartularies of the Benedictine Abbeys of Muchelney and Athelney in the County of Somerset* (Somerset Record Society, 14, 1899)

Neath A. G. Foster, 'Two deeds relating to Neath abbey', *South Wales and Monmouth Record Society*, Publications no. 2 (1950), 201–06

Neustria Pia *Neustria Pia*, ed. A. du Monstier (Rouen, 1663)

Newnham J. Godber, *The Cartulary of Newnham Priory*, Bedfordshire Historical Record Society 43 (1964)

Newington Longueville H. E. Salter, *Newington Longeville Charters*, Oxford Rec. Soc., 3 (1921), 11–12, 30 etc.

Northants Chh. F. M. Stenton, *Facsimiles of Early Charters from Northamptonshire Collections*, Northants Rec. Soc. (1930)

Northants Survey, printed in Appendix I above

Northumberland Families W. Percy Hedley, *Northumberland Families*, 2 vols (Newcastle-upon-Tyne, 1968–70)

Norwich C. Harper-Bill, *English Episcopal Acta VI: Norwich 1070–1214* (Oxford, 1990)

Charters of Norwich Cathedral Priory, Pipe Roll Society, 1974, NS, 40 for 1965–66

n.s. New Series

Obituaires A. Molinier, *Obituaires de la province de Sens, t. 1, Diocèse de Paris et de Sens*, Paris, 1902, 2 vols in 4°; t. 2, *Diocèse de Chartres*, Paris, 1906

A Vidier et L Mirot, *Obituaires de la province de Sens, t. 3, Diocèses d'Orléans, Auxerre, Nevers, Paris*, 1909, 1 vol. in 4°

Old Warden G. H. Fowler, ed. *The Cartulary of Old Warden Abbey*, Beds. Hist Rec. Soc., 13 (1930)

Ord. Vit. *The Ecclesiastical History of Orderic Vitalis*, ed. M. Chibnall, 6 vols (Oxford, 1969–80)

Orderic Vitalis, ed. Le Prévost, vol. v, pp. 182ff, *Rotulus primus monasterii S. Ebrulfi (saec. xi exeunte)*

Ormerod G. Ormerod, *History of the County Palatine and City of Chester*, 2nd edn, revised T. Helsby, 3 vols (LOndon, 1882)

Oseney H. E. Salter, *The Oseney Cartulary*, 6 vols, Oxford Historical Society (1929–36)*

Otterton L. Guilloreau, 'Chartes d'Otterton', *Revue Mabillon*, 5 (1909–10), 169–206

Oxford H. E. Salter, *Facsimiles of Early Charters in Oxford Muniment Rooms* (Oxford, 1929)

H. E. Salter, *A Cartulary of the Hospital of St. John the Baptist*, 3 vols Oxford Hist Soc., 66, 68–69 (Oxford, 1914–16)

S. R. Wigram, *Cartulary of the Monastery of St Frideswide at Oxford*, 2 vols, Oxford Historical Society 28 (1895), 31 (1896)

Paris *Cartulaire général de Paris I, 528–1180* , R. de Lasteyrie du Saillant (Hist. gén. de Paris), Paris, 1887

Recueil des chartes et documents de Saint-Martin-des-Champs, J. Depoin, 5 vols (Archives de la France monastique 13, 16, 18, 20, 21) Paris, 1912–21

Recueil des chartes de Saint-Germain-des-Près, des origines du début au XIIIe siècle, ed. R. Poupardin vol. i (558–1182), Paris, 1909

Percy Cart. T. Martin, *The Percy Chartulary*, Surtees Soc., 117 (1911)

Péronne *Charters of Saint-Fursif of Péronne,* ed. W. M. Newman and M. A. Rouse, Med. Acad. Amer. 1977

Peterborough Edmund King, *Peterborough Abbey 1086–1310, A study in the land market,* Cambridge, 1973

E. King, 'The Peterborough "Descriptio Militum" (Henry I)', EHR 84 (1969), 84–101*

Picardy J. Lestocquoy, *Histoire de la Picardie*, Paris, 1962

Robert Fossier, *La terre et les hommes en Picardie jusqu'à la fin du XIIIe siècle* (Amiens, 1987)

Placita *Placita Anglo-Normannica,* ed. M. M. Bigelow (Boston, U.S.A., 1879)

Pont-Audemer Alfred Canel, *Conférence sur l'histoire de la ville de Pont-Audemer,* Rouen, 1973

idem, *Essai historique, archéolgique et statistique sur l'arrondissement de Pont-Audemer,* Eure, 2 vols, Paris, 1833

idem, *Histoire de la ville de Pont-Audemer,* 2 vols 1885

Ponthieu *Recueil des Actes des Comtes de Ponthieu,* ed. C. Brunel, 1930

Pontoise *Cartulaire de l'abbaye de Saint-Martin de Pontoise publié d'après des documents inédits (1032–1199),* J. Depoin, Pontoise, 1895–1901

Pontefract R. Holmes, *The Chartulary of St John of Pontefract*, 2 vols, Yorkshire Archaeological Society Record Series, 25 (1899), 30 (1902)

PR *Pipe Roll* (published by the *Pipe Roll Society,* 1887–)

Pytchley Book of Fees *Henry of Pytchley's Book of Fees,* ed. W. T. Mellows, Northants Rec. Soc. ii, 1927

Quarr *The Charters of Quarr Abbey*, ed. Dom S.F. Hockey, Isle of Wight Record Society 3, 1991

Quimperlé *Cartulaire de l'Abbaye de Sainte-Croix de Quimperlé* (2nd edn L. Maître and Paul de Berthou, Rennes-Paris

Ramsey *Cartularium monasterii de Rameseia,* ed. W. H. Hart and P. A. Lyons, 3 vols, Rolls Series, 1884–93*

Chronicon abbatiae Rameseiensis, ed. W. D. Macray, Rolls Series, London 1886

RBE *Red Book of the Exchequer,* ed. H. Hall, 3 vols, Rolls Series, 1896; text of *Cartae Baronum* i, 186–445*

Reading B. R. Kemp, *Reading Abbey Cartularies: British Library manuscripts, Egerton 3031, Harley 1708 and Cotton Vespasian E XXV,* Camden Society vols 31, 33 (London, 1986–87)

Rec. Hist. Fr. *Recueil des Historiens des Gaules et de la France* (Dom Bouquet), 24 vols, 1738–1904

Redon *Cartulaire de l'abbaye de Redon*, ed. Aurélien de Courson (Paris, 1863)

Redvers Robert Bearman, *Charters of the Redvers Family and the Earldom of Devon, 1090–1217*, Devon and Cornwall Record Society. New series 37 (Exeter, 1994)*

Rennes *Cartulaire de l'abbaye de Saint-Georges de Rennes*, ed. P. de la Bigne Villenueve, extr. du Bull. et Mém. Soc. Arch. d'Ille-et-Vilaine, Rennes, 1876

Cartulaire de l'abbaye de Saint-Sulpice-la-Fôret, ed. P. Anger, Bull. et Mém soc. archéologique du dépt d'Ille-et-Vilaine, années 1905–10

Richmond *Registrum Honoris de Richmond*, ed. R. Gale (London, 1722)

Rievaulx Atkinson, J. C, *Cartularium Abbathiae de Rievalle*, Surtees Soc., 83 (Durham, 1889)

Robert of Torigny, *Chronique de Robert de Torigni suivie de divers opuscules historiques de cet auteur*, ed. L. Delisle, 2 vols (SHN, 1872, 1873)

for idem, *Interpolations, see under* William of Jumièges

Ronton George Wrottesley, 'The Ronton Chartulary', Wm Salt Arch. Soc., Collections for a History of Staffordshire, 4 (1883), 264–95]

Rot. de Dom. *Rotuli de Dominabus*, ed. J. H. Round (Pipe Roll Society, London 1913)

Rot. Tur. Lond. Hardy, Thomas Duffus, *Rotuli chartarum in turri Londinensi asservati, 1199–1216*, HMSO (London, 1837)

Roumare 'Norman and Wessex charters of the Roumare family', in *A Medieval Miscellany for Doris Mary Stenton*, edd. Patricia M. Barnes and C. F. Slade, Pipe Roll Society N.S. 36 for 1960 (London, 1962), pp. 77–88*

Rouen *Chartularium Monasterii Sanctæ Trinitatis de Monte Rothomagi*, ed. A. Deville, in *Cartulaire de Saint Bertin*, ed. B. Guérard (Paris, 1841), pp. 402–487

Pouillés de la Provence du Rouen, ed. A. Longnon, 1903 (Rec. Hist. Fr.)

Le Cacheux M. J., *Histoire de l'abbaye de Saint-Amand de Rouen* (Caen, 1937)

Le Cacheux, P., 'Une charte de Jumieges concernant l'epreuve par le fer chaud' (*SHN, Mélanges*, vol. Xl (1927), pp. 203–2T7)

Round J. H. Round, *Feudal England*, 1895, reset 1964

———— *The King's Serjeants and Officers of State*, 1911

———— *Peerage and Family History* (Westminster, 1901)

———— •A charter of William, Earl of Essex', *English Historical Review*, 6 (1891), 364–67

———— 'A Bachepuz charter', *The Ancestor. [An Illustrated] Quarterly Review of County and Family History, Heraldry and Antiquities*, 12 (1905), 152–55

———— 'A Woodham Ferrers charter', *Trans. Essex Arch Soc.*, NS, 10 (1909), 303–06

RRAN *Regesta Regum Anglo-Normannorum*, i, ed. H.W.C. Davis, ii, ed. C. Johnson and H. A. Cronne, iii, ed. H. A. Cronne and R. H. C. Davis (Oxford, 1913–1968)*

Rufford C. J. Holdsworth, *Rufford Charters*, 3 vols, Thoroton Soc. Rec. Ser., 29–30, 34 (1972–80)*

Runcorn James Tait, 'The Foundation Charter of Runcorn (later Norton) Priory', *Chetham Miscellanies*, N.S., 7 (1939)*

St Albans Matthew Paris, *Gesta abbatum monasterii Sancti Albani*, ed. H. T. Riley, 3 vols, Rolls Series (London, 1867–9)

St Bees J. Wilson, *The Register of the Priory of St Bees*, Surtees Society 126 (1915)

St Benet, Holme *Cartulary of St Benet of Holme*, ed. J. R. West, 2 vols, *Norwich Record Society* ii and iii, 1932

Saint-Benoît-sur-Loire *Recueil des chartes de l'abbaye de Saint-Benoît-sur-Loire* ed. M. Prou and A. Vidier, 2 vols 1900–32, Doc. Soc. hist. arch. du Gâtinais, nos. 5–6

Saint-Florent *Chartes normandes de l'abbaye de Saint-Florent Saumur de 710–1200*, ed. P. Marchegay, Mém. soc. des antiqu. de Normandie, 1880, pp. 663–711

Chartes mancelles de l'abbaye Saint-Florent, ed. P. Marchegay, Revue historique et archéologique du Maine t. iii, 1878

Chartes poitevins de Saint-Florent, ed. P. Marchegay, Poitiers 1873, Arch hist. de Poitou t. 2

Saint-Gabriel L. Musset, 'Actes Inédits du xie Siècle, I: Les plus anciennes Chartes du Prieuré de Saint-Gabriel (Calvados)', *Bulletin de la Société des Antiquaires de Normandie* 52 (1952–54)

Saint-Leu d'Esserent *Cartulaire du prieuré de Saint-Leu d'Esserent*, ed. E. Muller (Pontoise, 1901)

St Michael's Mount *The Cartulary of St Michael's Mount*, ed. Peter L. Hull, Devon and Cornwall Record Society, n.s. 5 (1962 for 1958)

Saint-Nicaise de Reims Jeannine Cossé-Durlin, *Cartulaire de Saint-Nicaise de Reims (XIIIe siècle)*, Paris, 1991

Saint-Pierre de Gand *Chartes et documents de l'abbaye de Saint-Pierre de Mont-Blandin à Gand*, A. van Lokeren, Gand, 1868

Les annales de Saint-Pierre de Gand et de Saint-Amand, P. Grierson, 1937

Saint-Pierre-sur-Dives *Les Diplomes de Henri Ier, roi d'Angleterre, pour l'abbaye de Saint-Pierre sur Dive*, ed. R. N. Sauvage (SHN, Mélanges, vol. XII, 1933)

Saint-Sauveur-le-Vicomte L. Delisle, *Histoire du château et des sires de Saint-Sauveur-le-Vicomte, suivi de pièces justificatives* (Valognes, 1867)

Saint-Sever L. Musset, 'Les origines et le patrimonie de l'abbaye de Saint-Sever', in *La Normandie bénédictine au temps du Guillaume le Conquérant*, J. Daoust (Lille, 1967), pp. 357–367

Saint-Victeur-en-Caux *Recueil des chartes de Saint-Victeur-en-Caux*, ed. Ch. de Robillard de Beaurepaire, Mél. soc. hist. Normandie, 5me ser. 1898, 333–453

Saint-Wandrille *Etudes critiques sur l'abbaye de Saint-Wandrille; pt.II Recueil des actes et des chartes*, F. Lot, Bib. Ecole. Hautes Etudes 204, Paris, 1913

Saint-Ymer *Cartulaire de Saint-Ymer-en-Auge et de Briquebec*, ed. C. Bréard, SHN 1908

Savigny *Rouleaux des morts du IXe au XVe siècle*, ed. L. Delisle, Paris, 1864

J. Van Moolerbroeke, *Vital l'Ermite predicateur . . . fondateur de l'abbaye normande de Savigny* (includes no. of charters), Revue Avranchin, Mar. 1991, 109 Année, t. lxviii, no. 346

D. Pichot, 'Cartulaires manceaux de Savigny', *Revue Avranchin* 1976

'Catalogue des chartes mancelles de . . . Savigny conservées aux Archives

Nationales', par Mme. Guilbaud, *Annales de Bretagne* (1962) 267–97 (1963) 389–400

R. de Martonne, 'Les seigneurs de Mayenne et le cartulaire de Savigny', *Bull. soc. hist. et arch. de la Mayenne* 1880, 118–39

Salisbury William Henry Rich-Jones, *The Register of St. Osmund*, 2 vols, Rolls Series (London, 1883–84)

William Henry Rich-Jones and William Dunn Macray, *Sarum Charters and Documents*, Rolls Series (London, 1891)

Sallay J. McNulty, *The Cartulary of the Cistercian Abbey of Sallay in Craven*, 2 vols, Yorks. Arch. Soc Rec. Ser., 87 (1933), 90 (1934)

Sanders I. J. Sanders, *English Baronies. A Study of Their Origin and Descent 1086–1327* (Oxford, 1960)

Sandford Agnes M. Leys, *The Sandford Cartulary*, 2 vols, Oxfords. Rec. Soc., 19 (1937), 22 (1941)

Scotland *Early Scottish Charters prior to A.D. 1153*, collected with notes and an index by Sir Archibald Campbell Lawrie (1905)

G. W. S. Barrow, *Regesta Regum Scottorum 1: The acts of Malcolm IV, king of Scots, 1153-1165* (Edinburgh, 1960)

Selborne W. Dunn Macray, *Calendar of Charters and Documents relating to Selborne and its Priory, preserved in the Muniment Room of Magdalen College, Oxford*, 2 vols, Hampshire Rec Soc., 2nd Ser. (London, 1891–94)

Selby J. T. Fowler, *The Coucher Book of Selby*, 2 vols, Yorkshire Archaeological Society Record Series, 10 (1891), 13 (1893)

Sele *The Chartulary of the Priory of St Peter at Sele*, ed. L. F. Salzmann (Cambridge, 1923)

Sempringham E. M. Poynton, 'Charters relating to the Priory of Sempringham', *The Genealogist*, NS, 15 (1898–99), 158–61, 221–27; 16 (1899–1900), 30–5, 76–83, 153–57, 223–28; 17 (1900), 29–35, 164–68– 232–39

SHN *Société de l'Histoire de Normandie*

Shrewsbury Una Rees, *The Cartulary of Shrewsbury Abbey*, 2 vols (Aberystwyth, 1975)*

Sibton Philippa Brown, *Sibton Abbey Cartularies and Charters*, Suffolk Charters 7–10 (Woodbridge, 1985–88)*

Simeon of Durham *see* **Durham**

Staffordshire R. W. Eyton and G. Wrottesley, 'The Staffordshire Cartulary', *Collections for History of Staffordshire* ii pt 1 and iii pt 1 (1881–2)

G. Wrottesley and R. W. Eyton, 'The Liber Niger scaccarii, Staffordscira, or feodary of A.D. 1166, with notes added . . .', *Collections for a History of Staffordshire* i (1880), 145–240

Stanley H. Ellis, 'History of the Cistercian abbey of Stanley in Wiltshire, with texts of a Calendar of the Muniments and of some unpublished charters of the abbey, preserved in the British Museum', *Wilts. Arch. and Nat. Hist Mag.*, 15 (1875), 239–307

Stenton, Feudalism F. M. Stenton, *The First Century of English Feudalism 1066–1166 being The Ford Lectures delivered in the University of Oxford in Hilary Term 1929* (Oxford 1932): Appendix, pp. 257–88

Stogursey T. D. Tremlett and Noel Blakiston, *Stogursey Charters: Charters and Other Documents relating to the Property of the Alien Priory of Stogursey,*

Somerset, now belonging to Eton College, Somerset Rec. Soc., 61 (1949 for 1946)*

Stoke-by-Clare C. Harper-Bill and R. Mortimer, *Stoke by Clare Priory Cartulary: BL Cotton Appx. XXI*, Suffolk Charters 4–6 (Woodbridge, 1982–84)*

Stone George Wrottesley, 'The Stone Chartulary', Wm Salt Arch. Soc., *Collections for a History of Staffordshire*, vi pt 1 (1885), 1–28

Tavistock H. P. R. Finberg, 'Some early Tavistock Charters', *English Historical Review*, 62 (1947), 352–77*

Tax Returns *see under* **DB**

TEAS *Transactions of the Essex Archaeological Society*

Tewkesbury J. H. Round, 'The spurious Tewksbury Charter', *The Genealogist*, NS, 8 (1891), 204–10 cf. Kirk

J. H. Round, 'Last Words on the Tewksbury Charter', *The Genealogist*, NS, 9 (1892), 55–56

Textus Roffensis Thomas Hearne, *Textus Roffensis*, 2 vols (Oxford, 1720)

Peter H. Sawyer, *Textus Roffensis: Rochester Cathedral Library Manuscript A.3.5*, 2 vols, Early English MSS in Facsimile, 7, 9 (Copenhagen, London, 1957–62)

Thame H. E. Salter, *The Thame Cartulary*, 2 vols, Oxfords. Rec. Soc., 25–26 (1947–48)

Temple Marquis d'Albon, *Cartulaire général de l'ordre du Temple 1119–50*, Paris, 1914

Thorney, Liber Vitae 'The *Liber Vitae* of Thorney Abbey', in *Words, Names and History. Selected Writings of Cecily Clark*, ed. P. Jackson (Woodbridge, 1995, 301–347

Thoroton, R. Thoroton, *The Antiquities of Nottinghamshire*, ed and enlarged by J. Thoresby, 3 vols (London, 1797), i, 77

Thurgarton Trevor Foulds, *The Thurgarton Cartulary* (Stamford, 1994)*

Tiron *Cartulaire . . .Saint-Trinité de Tiron*, ed. L. Merlet, Chartres 1883 (Soc. arch. d'Eure et Loir)

Totnes H. R. Watkin, *The History of Totnes Priory and Medieval Town*, 2 vols (Torquay, 1917)

Tréport *Cartulaire de l'abbaye de Saint-Michel-du-Tréport*, ed. P. Laffleur de Kermingant, Paris, 1880

Histoire de l'abbaye de Saint-Michel de Tréport, R. B. Coquelin and C. Lormier, Soc. Hist. Norm., Rouen, 1879

Troarn R. N. Sauvage, *L'abbaye de Saint-Martin de Troarn* (Caen, 1911)

Tutbury Avrom Saltman, *Cartulary of Tutbury Priory*, (HMSO and Staffordshire Record Society, 1962)

Van Caeneghem R. C. Van Caeneghem, *English lawsuits from William I to Richard 1*, 2 vols, Selden Society 106–7 (1990–91)

idem, *Royal writs in England from the Conquest to Glanville*, Selden Society 77 (London, 1959)

VCH *The Victoria County History*, 1933–

Walden H. Collar, 'The Book of the Foundation of Walden Abbey', *Essex Review* 45 (1936), 73–236; 46 (1937), 12–234; 47 (1938), 36–220

Wales J. Conway Davies, *Episcopal Acts and Cognate Documents relating to Welsh Dioceses, 1066–1272*, 2 vols (Cardiff, 1948)

Waltham Rosalind Ransford, *The Early Charters of the Augustinian Canons of Waltham Abbey, Essex, 1062–1230* (Woodbridge, 1989)*

Walmsley *see under* **Caen**

Warlop E. Warlop, *The Flemish Nobility Before 1300*, 4 vols (Kortrijk, 1975–6)

Whalley *The Coucher Book of Whalley Abbey*, ed. W. A. Hulton, 4 vols, Chetham, 10–11, 16, 20 (1847–49)

Whitby Atkinson, J. C., *Cartularium de Whiteby*, 2 vols, Surtees Society 69 (1879), 72 (1881)

Wightman, Lacy Family W. E. Wightman, *The Lacy Family in England and Normandy 1066–1194* (Oxford, 1966)

William of Jumièges *The* Gesta Normannorum Ducum *of William of Jumièges, Orderic Vitalis, and Robert of Torigny*, ed. E. M. C. van Houts (2 vols, Oxford 1992–5)

William of Malmesbury William of Malmesbury, *De Gestis Pontificum Anglorum*, ed. N. E. S. A. Hamilton (RS, 1870)

—— *Gesta Regum Anglorum*, ed. W. Stubbs, 2 vols (RS, 1887, 1889)

—— *Historia Novella*, ed. K. R. Potter (Edinburgh, 1955)

William of Poitiers Raymonde Foreville, ed., *Guillaume de Poitiers, Histoire de Guillaume le Conquérant,* Paris 1952 (Les classiques de l'histoire de France au Moyen Age)

Williams, English Ann Williams, *The English and the Norman Conquest* (Woodbridge, 1995)

—— 'Vice-comital family', A. Williams, 'A vice-comital family in pre-Conquest Warwickshire', Anglo-Norman Studies xi, 279–95

Wilton *Registrum Wiltunense*, ed. R. C. Hoare et al. (London, 1827)

Winchcombe D. Royce, *Landboc sive Registrum Monasterii Beatiae Mariae Virginis et Sanctoi Cenhelmi de Winchelcumba*, 2 vols (Exeter, 1892–93)

J. Prynne, *Cartularium monasterii de Winchcombe* ([Middle Hill], 1854)

Winchester M. J. Franklin, *English Episcopal Acta VIII: Winchester 1070–1204* (Oxford, 1993)

Chartulary of Winchester Cathedral, ed. A. W. Goodman (Winchester, 1927)

M. Biddle, *Winchester in the Middle Ages* (includes Winchester Surveys)

Worcester R. R. Darlington, *The Cartulary of Worcester Cathedral Priory (Register I)*, Pipe Roll Soc., NS 38 (London, 1962–63)*

William Hale Hale, *Registrum sive Liber Irrotularius et Consuetudinarius Prioratus Beateae Mariae Wigorniensis*, Camden Soc., Old Ser., 91 (1865)

Thomas Hearne, *Hemingi Chartularium Ecclesiae Wigorniensis*, 2 vols (Oxford, 1723)

Worcester Fragment J. H. Round, 'The Worcestershire Survey', *Feudal England*, rptd. 1964, Fragment of a Survey, 146–7*

Wulfric of Haselbury John of Ford, *The Life of Wulfric of Haselbury*, ed. Maurice Bell, Somerset Record Society 47 (1933)

York Janet E. Burton, *English Episcopal Acta V: York 1070–1154* (Oxford, 1988)

Janet E. Burton, *The Cartulary of the Treasurer of York Minster and Related Documents* (York, 1978)